Canadian ORGANIZATIONAL BEHAVIOUR 9

STEVEN L. McSHANE
THE UNIVERSITY OF WESTERN AUSTRALIA

SANDRA L. STEEN
UNIVERSITY OF REGINA

KEVIN TASA
YORK UNIVERSITY

Mc Graw Hill Education | McGraw-Hill Ryerson

McGraw-Hill Ryerson

Canadian Organizational Behaviour
Ninth edition

ISBN-13: 978-1-25-903053-6
ISBN-10: 1-25-903053-9

9 10 11 12 WEB 20 19 18 17

Printed and bound in Canada.

Director of Product Management: Rhondda McNabb
Group Product Manager: Kim Brewster
Marketing Manager: Cathie Lefebvre
Product Developer: Tracey Haggert
Photo/Permissions Research: Monika Schurmann
Senior Product Team Associate: Stephanie Giles
Supervising Editor: Joanne Limebeer
Copy Editor: Evan Turner, Row House Publishing Services
Production Coordinator: Scott Morrison
Manufacturing Production Coordinator: Emily Hickey
Cover Design: Michelle Losier
Cover Image: Richard Du Toit/Getty Images
Interior Design: Michelle Losier
Page Layout: Laserwords Private Limited
Printer: Webcom

Library and Archives Canada Cataloguing in Publication

McShane, Steven L. (Steven Lattimore), author
Canadian organizational behaviour / Steven L. McShane, University of Western Australia, Sandra L. Steen, University of Regina, Kevin Tasa, York University.–Ninth edition.

Includes bibliographical references and index.
ISBN 978-1-25-903053-6 (bound)

1. Organizational behavior–Canada–Textbooks. 2. Organizational behavior–Canada–Case studies. 3. Teams in the workplace–Textbooks. 4. Corporate culture–Textbooks. I. Steen, Sandra (Sandra L.), author II. Tasa, Kevin, 1967-, author III. Title.
HD58.7.M33 2014 658.300971 C2014-903308-7

Dedicated with love and devotion to Donna, and to our wonderful daughters, Bryton and Madison—S.L.M.

For Aaron, Matt, and Jess—S.L.S.

Dedicated to Ena and Vidya. Thanks—K.T.

About the Authors

STEVEN L. MCSHANE Steven L. McShane is Winthrop Professor of Management at The University of Western Australia (UWA) Business School, and has received awards as the best teacher in the university and in the MBA program. Steve has been an active instructor in executive programs in Australia and Asia. He is also a popular visiting speaker at numerous universities, having given dozens of invited talks and seminars over the past few years to faculty and students in Canada, China, Malaysia, India, the United States, and other countries.

Steve earned his Ph.D. from Michigan State University, where he specialized in organizational behaviour and labour relations. He also holds a Master of Industrial Relations from the University of Toronto, and an undergraduate degree from Queen's University in Canada. Steve is a past President of the Administrative Sciences Association of Canada and served as Director of Graduate Programs in Simon Fraser University's business faculty.

Along with co-authoring *Canadian Organizational Behaviour,* Ninth Edition, Steve is lead co-author of Organizational Behavior, Seventh Edition (2015) and *M: Organizational Behavior, Third Edition* (2016) in the United States, and *Organisational Behaviour: Asia Pacific* Fourth Edition (2013) in that region. He is also co-author of editions or translations of his organizational behaviour book in China, India, Quebec, Taiwan, and Brazil. Steve has published several dozen articles and conference papers on workplace values, training transfer, organizational learning, exit-voice-loyalty, employee socialization, wrongful dismissal, media bias in business magazines, and other diverse topics.

Steve enjoys spending his leisure time swimming, body board surfing, canoeing, skiing, and travelling with his wife and two daughters.

SANDRA L. STEEN Sandra L. Steen teaches in the Paul J. Hill School of Business and the Kenneth Levene Graduate School of Business at the University of Regina. Sandra also leads executive education and professional development sessions with the Centre for Management Development, Faculty of Business Administration. Sandra has an integrated education and background in both organizational behaviour and human resource management. She received her MBA from the University of Regina and has more than 25 years of leading, managing, teaching, and consulting across a wide range of organizations in the private, public, and not-for-profit sectors. Sandra teaches in the undergraduate, MBA, International MBA, and Executive MBA programs at the University of Regina. In addition to *Canadian Organizational Behaviour,* Ninth Edition, Sandra is co-author with Professors Raymond Noe (Ohio State University), John R. Hollenbeck (Michigan State University), Barry Gerhart (University of Wisconsin-Madison), and Patrick Wright (Cornell University) of *Human Resource Management,* Third Canadian Edition (2013).

Sandra is a Certified Human Resources Professional (CHRP) and a member of the Saskatchewan Association of Human Resource Professionals. Sandra has received recognition for her teaching accomplishments including "Inspiring Teacher Award–Business Administration." In her leisure time, Sandra enjoys time at the lake with husband and Aaron, and their children, Matt and Jess.

KEVIN TASA Dr. Kevin Tasa is an Associate Professor of Organizational Behaviour at the Schulich School of Business, York University. Prior to joining Schulich he was an Associate Professor, and Director of the MBA program, at the DeGroote School of Business, McMaster University. He was awarded the Basu Teaching Award by the MBA student association at McMaster and has also been nominated for the Sidney Schulich MBA Award for Teaching Excellence at Schulich. He is an editorial board member of the *Journal of Organizational Behavior* and teaches courses in Managerial Negotiation and Organizational Behaviour at the masters and doctoral levels. With Roy Lewicki, Bruce Barry, and David Saunders, he co-authored *Essentials of Negotiation,* one of the most widely used negotiation textbooks in Canadian business schools.

Kevin received his doctorate in Organizational Behaviour from the Rotman School of Management at the University of Toronto. He also holds an MSc in Health Administration from the University of Toronto and a BComm from the University of Saskatchewan. His research has been published in top-tier journals such as *Academy of Management Journal, Journal of Applied Psychology, Organizational Behavior and Human Decision Processes* and *Journal of Organizational Behavior.* Currently, his research focuses on team dynamics, such as boundary spanning and decision making under stress, as well as the situational and psychological determinants of unethical behaviour in negotiation.

Finally, Kevin frequently teaches seminars on negotiation skills and conflict management, serving as a faculty member with institutions such as the Physician Management Institute of the Canadian Medical Association, the Schulich Executive Education Centre, Linamar Corporation, the University of Alberta Executive Education, and the Hamilton Health Science Centre.

Brief Contents

PART ONE

Introduction

Chapter 1 Introduction to the Field of Organizational Behaviour 1

PART TWO

Individual Behaviour and Processes

Chapter 2 Individual Behaviour, Personality, and Values 26

Chapter 3 Perceiving Ourselves and Others in Organizations 56

Chapter 4 Workplace Emotions, Attitudes, and Stress 81

Chapter 5 Foundations of Employee Motivation 109

Chapter 6 Applied Performance Practices 138

Chapter 7 Decision Making and Creativity 162

PART THREE

Team Processes

Chapter 8 Team Dynamics 189

Chapter 9 Communicating in Organizations 218

Chapter 10 Power and Influence in the Workplace 244

Chapter 11 Conflict and Negotiation in the Workplace 269

Chapter 12 Leadership in Organizational Settings 297

PART FOUR

Organizational Processes

Chapter 13 Designing Organizational Structures 321

Chapter 14 Organizational Culture 347

Chapter 15 Organizational Change 372

Additional Cases CA-1

Appendix A Theory Building and Systematic Research Methods A-1

Appendix B Scoring Keys for Self-Assessment Exercises B-1

Glossary GL-1

Endnotes EN-1

Name and Organization Index NI-1

Subject Index SI-1

Contents

Preface xiii
Acknowledgments xxiii

PART ONE

Introduction

CHAPTER 1

Introduction to the Field of Organizational Behaviour 1

LEARNING OBJECTIVES 1

Welcome to the Field of Organizational Behaviour! 2
The Field of Organizational Behaviour 2
- Historical Foundations of Organizational Behaviour 3
- Why Study Organizational Behaviour? 3

Perspectives of Organizational Effectiveness 5
- Open Systems Perspective 5

Global Connections 1.1: Zara's Open Systems Thinking for Fast Fashion 7
- Organizational Learning Perspective 8
- High-Performance Work Practices (HPWP) Perspective 10
- Stakeholder Perspective 11
- Connecting the Dots: An Integrative Model of Organizational Behaviour 13

Contemporary Challenges for Organizations 15
- Globalization 15
- Increasing Workforce Diversity 15
- Emerging Employment Relationships 17

Anchors of Organizational Behaviour Knowledge 19
- The Systematic Research Anchor 19

Debating Point: Is There Enough Evidence to Support Evidence-Based Management? 20
- The Multidisciplinary Anchor 20
- The Contingency Anchor 21
- The Multiple Levels of Analysis Anchor 21

The Journey Begins 21
Chapter Summary 22
Key Terms 22
Critical-Thinking Questions 23
Case Study Ancol Ltd. 23
Web Exercise Diagnosing Organizational Stakeholders 24
Self-Assessment It All Makes Sense? 24
Self-Assessments for Chapter 1 25

PART TWO

Individual Behaviour and Processes

CHAPTER 2

Individual Behaviour, Personality, and Values 26

LEARNING OBJECTIVES 26

MARS Model of Individual Behaviour and Performance 27
- Employee Motivation 28
- Ability 28

Global Connections 2.1: Applying MARS at Iceland Foods 29
- Role Perceptions 30
- Situational Factors 30

Types of Individual Behaviour 31
- Task Performance 31
- Organizational Citizenship 31
- Counterproductive Work Behaviours 32
- Joining and Staying with the Organization 32
- Maintaining Work Attendence 33

Personality in Organizations 33
- Personality Determinants: Nature versus Nurture 34
- Five-Factor Model of Personality 34
- Jungian Personality Theory and the Myers-Briggs Type Indicator 36
- Personality Testing in Organizations 38

Values in the Workplace 38

Debating Point: Should Companies Use Personality Tests to Select Job Applicants? 39
- Types of Values 40
- Values and Individual Behaviour 41
- Values Congruence 41

Ethical Values and Behaviour 43
- Three Ethical Principles 43
- Moral Intensity, Moral Sensitivity, and Situational Influences 43
- Supporting Ethical Behaviour 45

Values Across Cultures 46
- Individualism and Collectivism 46
- Power Distance 47

Global Connections 2.2: Working with High Power Distance in China 48
- Uncertainty Avoidance 48

Achievement-Nurturing Orientation 48
Caveats About Cross-Cultural Knowledge 49
Diversity of Canadian Cultural Values 49
Chapter Summary 50
Key Terms 51
Critical-Thinking Questions 51
Case Study Ethics Dilemma Vignettes 52
Class Exercise Test Your Knowledge of Personality 53
Self-Assessment Are You Introverted or Extraverted? 54
Self-Assessments for Chapter 2 55

CHAPTER 3

Perceiving Ourselves and Others in Organizations 56

LEARNING OBJECTIVES 56
Self-Concept: How We Perceive Ourselves 57
Self-Concept Complexity, Consistency, and Clarity 57
Self-Enhancement 59
Self-Verification 59
Self-Evaluation 60
The Social Self 61
Self-Concept and Organizational Behaviour 62
Perceiving the World Around Us 62
Perceptual Organization and Interpretation 64
Specific Perceptual Processes and Problems 65
Stereotyping in Organizations 65
Attribution Theory 68
Self-Fulfilling Prophecy 69
Other Perceptual Effects 71
Improving Perceptions 72
Awareness of Perceptual Biases 72
Improving Self-Awareness 72
Debating Point: Do We Need Diversity Training Programs? 73
Meaningful Interaction 74
Global Connections 3.1: Experiencing Meaningful Interaction on the Frontline 75
Global Mindset: Developing Perceptions Across Borders 75
Developing a Global Mindset 76
Chapter Summary 77
Key Terms 78
Critical-Thinking Questions 78
Case Study Hy Dairies Ltd. 79
Web Exercise Diversity & Stereotyping on Display in Corporate Websites 79
Self-Assessment How Much Does Work Define Your Self-Concept? 80
Self-Assessments for Chapter 3 80

CHAPTER 4

Workplace Emotions, Attitudes, and Stress 81

LEARNING OBJECTIVES 81
Emotions in the Workplace 82
Types of Emotions 83
Emotions, Attitudes, and Behaviour 83
How Emotions Influence Attitudes and Behaviour 85
Generating Postive Emotions at Work 85
Cognitive Dissonance 86
Debating Point: Is Having Fun at Work Really a Good Idea? 87
Emotions and Personality 87
Managing Emotions at Work 88
Emotional Display Norms Across Cultures 88
Emotional Dissonance 89
Emotional Intelligence 89
Emotional Intelligence Outcomes and Training 91
Job Satisfaction 91
Job Satisfaction and Work Behaviour 92
Job Satisfaction and Performance 93
Job Satisfaction and Customer Satisfaction 94
Job Satisfaction and Business Ethics 95
Organizational Commitment 95
Consequences of Affective and Continuance Commitment 96
Building Organizational Commitment 97
Work-Related Stress 98
General Adaptation Syndrome 98
Consequences of Distress 99
Stressors: The Causes of Stress 99
Harassment and Incivility 99
Work Overload 100
Global Connections 4.1: Working to Death in China 100
Low Task Control 101
Individual Differences in Stress 101
Managing Work-Related Stress 101
Remove the Stressor 102
Withdraw From the Stressor 102
Change Stress Perceptions 102
Control Stress Consequences 103
Receive Social Support 103
Chapter Summary 104
Key Terms 104
Critical-Thinking Questions 104
Case Study Rough Seas on the LINK650 105
Team Exercise Ranking Jobs on Their Emotional Labour 106

Self-Assessment Are You in Touch with Your Emotions? 107
Self-Assessments for Chapter 4 108

CHAPTER 5
Foundations of Employee Motivation 109
LEARNING OBJECTIVES 109
Employee Engagement 110
Employee Drives and Needs 111
Individual Differences in Needs 112
Needs and Drives Theories 113
Maslow's Needs Hierarchy Theory 113
McClelland's Learned Needs Theory 114
Four-Drive Theory 116
Expectancy Theory of Motivation 119
Expectancy Theory in Practice 120
Organizational Behaviour Modification and Social Cognitive Theory 121
Organizational Behaviour Modification 121
Global Connections 5.1: Reinforcing Work Behaviour Through Gamification 123
Social Cognitive Theory 124
Goal Setting and Feedback 124
Balanced Scorecard 125
Characteristics of Effective Feedback 126
Sources of Feedback 127
Evaluating Goal Setting and Feedback 128
Organizational Justice 128
Debating Point: Does Equity Motivate More Than Equality? 129
Equity Theory 129
Procedural Justice 132
Chapter Summary 133
Key Terms 134
Critical-Thinking Questions 134
Case Study Predicting Harry's Work Effort 134
Class Exercise Needs Priority Exercise 135
Self-Assessment Needs-Strength Questionnaire 136
Self-Assessments for Chapter 5 137

CHAPTER 6
Applied Performance Practices 138
LEARNING OBJECTIVES 138
The Meaning of Money in the Workplace 139
Financial Reward Practices 140
Membership- and Seniority-Based Rewards 140
Job Status–Based Rewards 140
Competency-Based Rewards 141
Performance-Based Rewards 142
Improving Reward Effectiveness 144
Debating Point: Is it Time to Ditch the Performance Review? 145
Job Design Practices 146
Global Connections 6.1: When Rewards Go Wrong 147
Job Design and Work Efficiency 147
Job Design and Work Motivation 149
Job Design Practices that Motivate 151
Empowerment Practices 153
Supporting Empowerment 153
Self-Leadership Practices 154
Self-Leadership Strategies 154
Effectiveness of Self-Leadership 156
Personal and Situational Predictors of Self-Leadership 156
Chapter Summary 156
Key Terms 157
Critical-Thinking Questions 157
Case Study YakkaTech Ltd. 158
Team Exercise Is Student Work Enriched? 159
Self-Assessment What is Your Attitude Towards Money? 160
Self-Assessments for Chapter 6 161

CHAPTER 7
Decision Making and Creativity 162
LEARNING OBJECTIVES 162
Rational Choice Paradigm of Decision Making 163
Rational Choice Decision-Making Process 164
Problems with the Rational Choice Paradigm 165
Identifying Problems and Opportunities 165
Problems with Problem Identification 165
Identifying Problems and Opportunities More Effectively 166
Global Connections 7.1: Famous Missed Opportunities 167
Searching for, Evaluating, and Choosing Alternatives 168
Problems with Goals 168
Problems with Information Processing 168
Problems with Maximization 170
Evaluating Opportunities 170
The Role of Emotions and Intuition 171
Emotions and Making Choices 171
Intuition and Making Choices 172
Making Choices More Effectively 172
Implementing Decisions 173
Evaluating Decision Outcomes 173
Escalation of Commitment 173
Evaluating Decision Outcomes More Effectively 175
Creativity 175
The Creative Process 175
Characteristics of Creative People 177
Organizational Conditions Supporting Creativity 178
Activities that Encourage Creativity 179

Employee Involvement in Decision Making 179
Debating Point: Should Organizations Practise Democracy? 180
Global Connections 7.2: Brasilata, the Ideas Company 181
Benefits of Employee Involvement 181
Contingencies of Employee Involvement 182
Chapter Summary 183
Key Terms 183
Critical-Thinking Questions 183
Case Study Employee Involvement Cases 184
Team Exercise Where in the World Are We? 186
Self-Assessment Do You Have a Creative Personality? 188
Self-Assessments for Chapter 7 188

PART THREE

Team Processes

CHAPTER 8

Team Dynamics 189
LEARNING OBJECTIVES 189
Teams and Informal Groups 190
Global Connections 8.1: Team Motivation at Pixar 192
Informal Groups 192
Advantages and Disadvantages of Teams 193
The Challenges of Teams 193
A Model of Team Effectiveness 194
Organizational and Team Environment 194
Team Design Elements 195
Task Characteristics 195
Team Size 197
Team Composition 197
Team States 199
Team Norms 199
Team Cohesion 200
Team Efficacy 202
Team Trust 203
Team Processes 204
Internal Team Processes 204
External Team Processes 204
Team Development 205
Self-Directed Teams 207
Success Factors for Self-Directed Teams 208
Virtual Teams 208
Debating Point: Are Virtual Teams More Trouble than They're Worth? 209
Success Factors for Virtual Teams 210
Team Decision Making 210
Constraints on Team Decision Making 211
Improving Creative Decision Making in Teams 211
Chapter Summary 213
Key Terms 214
Critical Thinking Questions 214
Case Study ArbreCorp Ltée 214
Team Exercise Team Tower Power 215
Self-Assessment What Team Roles Do You Prefer? 216
Self-Assessments for Chapter 8 217

CHAPTER 9

Communicating in Organizations 218
LEARNING OBJECTIVES 218
The Importance of Communication 219
A Model of Communication 220
Influences on Effective Encoding and Decoding 221
Communication Channels 221
Internet-Based Communication 222
Problems with E-Mail 223
Workplace Communication Through Social Media 224
Nonverbal Communication 225
Choosing the Best Communication Channel 228
Social Acceptance 228
Media Richness 228
Communication Channels and Persuasion 230
Communication Barriers (Noise) 230
Information Overload 231
Cross-Cultural and Gender Communication 232
Nonverbal Differences Across Cultures 232
Global Connections 9.1: Politely Waiting for Some Silence 233
Gender Differences in Communication 233
Improving Interpersonal Communication 234
Getting Your Message Across 234
Active Listening 234
Improving Communication Throughout the Hierarchy 235
Workspace Design 236
Internet-Based Organizational Communication 236
Direct Communication with Top Management 237
Communicating through the Grapevine 237
Grapevine Characteristics 237
Debating Point: Should Management Use the Grapevine to Communicate to Employees? 238
Grapevine Benefits and Limitations 238
Chapter Summary 239
Key Terms 240
Critical Thinking Questions 240
Case Study Communicating with the Millennials 240
Team Exercise Active Listening Exercise 241
Self-Assessment Are You an Active Listener? 242
Self-Assessments for Chapter 9 243

CHAPTER 10

Power and Influence in the Workplace 244

LEARNING OBJECTIVES 244

The Meaning of Power 245
Sources of Power in Organizations 247
Legitimate Power 247
Reward Power 249
Coercive Power 249
Expert Power 249
Referent Power 250
Contingencies of Power 251
Substitutability 251
Centrality 251
Visibility 251
Debating Point: How Much Power Do CEOs Really Possess? 252
Discretion 253
The Power of Social Networks 253
Social Capital and Sources of Power 253
Gaining Power from Social Networks 255
Consequences of Power 256
Influencing Others 257
Global Connections 10.1: The Art and Science of Managing Your Boss 258
Types of Influence Tactics 258
Consequences and Contingencies of Influence Tactics 261
Organizational Politics 262
Minimizing Organizational Politics 263
Chapter Summary 264
Key Terms 265
Critical Thinking Questions 265
Case Study Resonus Corporation 266
Team Exercise Deciphering the Network 266
Self-Assessment How Do You Influence Coworkers and Other Peers? 267
Self-Assessments for Chapter 10 268

CHAPTER 11

Conflict and Negotiation in the Workplace 269

LEARNING OBJECTIVES 269

The Meaning and Consequences of Conflict 270
Is Conflict Good or Bad? 270
Global Connections 11.1: High Cost of On-Board Conflicts 271
The Emerging View: Task and Relationship Conflict 272
Conflict Process Model 274
Structural Sources of Conflict in Organizations 274
Incompatible Goals 275
Differentiation 275
Interdependence 276
Scarce Resources 276
Ambiguous Rules 276
Communication Problems 276
Interpersonal Conflict Handling Styles 277
Choosing the Best Conflict Handling Style 278
Cultural and Gender Differences in Conflict Handling Styles 279
Structural Approaches to Conflict Management 280
Emphasizing Superordinate Goals 280
Reducing Differentiation 280
Improving Communication and Mutual Understanding 281
Reducing Interdependence 282
Increasing Resources 282
Clarifying Rules and Procedures 282
Third-Party Conflict Resolution 282
Choosing the Best Third-Party Intervention Strategy 283
Resolving Conflict through Negotiation 284
Distributive versus Integrative Negotiations 285
Preparing to Negotiate 285
Debating Point: Is Creating Value Such a Good Negotiation Strategy? 286
Distributive Strategies That Work 286
Integrative Strategies That Work 287
Expert versus Average Negotiators 289
Chapter Summary 290
Key Terms 291
Critical Thinking Questions 291
Case Study Car Wars At Wolfsburg 291
Class Exercise The Contingencies of Conflict Handling 292
Self-Assessment What Is Your Preferred Conflict Handling Style? 295
Self-Assessments for Chapter 11 296

CHAPTER 12

Leadership in Organizational Settings 297

LEARNING OBJECTIVES 297

What is Leadership? 298
Shared Leadership 298
Transformational Leadership Perspective 299
Develop and Communicate a Strategic Vision 300
Global Connections 12.1: Leading the Vision of Vancouver as a Liveable City 301

Model the Vision 302
Encourage Experimentation 302
Build Commitment Toward the Vision 302
Transformational Leadership and Charisma 303
Evaluating the Transformational Leadership Perspective 303
Managerial Leadership Perspective 304
Task-Oriented and People-Oriented Leadership 305
Servant Leadership 306
Leadership Theories 306
Path-Goal Leadership Theory 306
Other Managerial Leadership Theories 309
Leadership Substitutes 311
Implicit Leadership Perspective 311
Prototypes of Effective Leaders 311
The Romance of Leadership 311
Personal Attributes Perspective of Leadership 312
Authentic Leadership 314
Debating Point: Should Leaders *Really* be Authentic all the Time? 315
Leadership Attributes Perspective Limitations and Practical Implications 315
Cross-Cultural and Gender Issues in Leadership 316
Gender and Leadership 316
Chapter Summary 317
Key Terms 318
Critical-Thinking Questions 318
Case Study A Window on Life 318
Team Exercise Leadership Diagnostic Analysis 319
Self-Assessment Do Leaders Make a Difference? 320
Self-Assessments for Chapter 12 320

PART FOUR

Organizational Processes

CHAPTER 13

Designing Organizational Structures 321
LEARNING OBJECTIVES 321
Division of Labour and Coordination 322
Division of Labour 322
Coordinating Work Activities 323
Elements of Organizational Structure 325
Span of Control 325
Debating Point: Should Organizations Cut Back Middle Management? 328
Centralization and Decentralization 328
Global Connections 13.1: Svenska Handelsbanken's Decentralized Structure 329
Formalization 329
Mechanistic Versus Organic Structures 330
Forms of Departmentalization 331
Simple Structure 331
Functional Structure 331
Divisional Structure 333
Team-Based Structure 335
Matrix Structure 336
Network Structure 338
Contingencies of Organizational Design 340
External Environment 340
Organizational Size 341
Technology 341
Organizational Strategy 342
Chapter Summary 342
Key Terms 343
Critical Thinking Questions 343
Case Study Merritt's Bakery 344
Team Exercise The Club Ed Exercise 345
Self-Assessment Which Organizational Structure Do You Prefer? 345
Self-Assessments for Chapter 13 346

CHAPTER 14

Organizational Culture 347
LEARNING OBJECTIVES 347
Elements of Organizational Culture 348
Content of Organizational Culture 350
Organizational Subcultures 351
Deciphering Organizational Culture through Artifacts 351
Organizational Stories and Legends 352
Organizational Language 352
Rituals and Ceremonies 352
Physical Structures and Symbols 352
Is Organizational Culture Important? 353
Contingencies of Organizational Culture and Effectiveness 354
Debating Point: Is Corporate Culture an Overused Phrase? 356
Organizational Culture and Business Ethics 357
Merging Organizational Cultures 357
Bicultural Audit 358
Strategies for Merging Different Organizational Cultures 358
Changing and Strengthening Organizational Culture 359
Actions of Founders and Leaders 359
Align Artifacts with the Desired Culture 360
Introduce Culturally Consistent Rewards and Recognition 361
Support Workforce Stability and Communication 361
Use Attraction, Selection, and Socialization for Cultural "Fit" 361

Global Connections 14.1: Ensuring the Cultural Shoe Fits at Zappos 362
Organizational Socialization 362
Organizational Socialization as a Learning and Adjustment Process 363
Organizational Socialization and Psychological Contracts 363
Stages of Organizational Socialization 364
Improving the Socialization Process 365
Chapter Summary 366
Key Terms 367
Critical-Thinking Questions 367
Case Study Hillton's Transformation 368
Team Exercise Organizational Culture Metaphors 369
Self-Assessment Which Corporate Culture Do You Prefer? 370
Self-Assessments for Chapter 14 371

CHAPTER 15

Organizational Change 372

LEARNING OBJECTIVES 372

Lewin's Force Field Analysis Model 373
Understanding Resistance to Change 374
Why Employees Resist Change 376
Unfreezing, Changing, and Refreezing 378
Creating an Urgency for Change 378
Reducing the Restraining Forces 379
Global Connections 15.1: Communicate, Involve, or Change Your People 382
Refreezing the Desired Conditions 382
Leadership, Coalitions, and Pilot Projects 383
Transformational Leadership and Change 383
Coalitions, Social Networks, and Change 383
Pilot Projects and Diffusion of Change 384
Four Approaches to Organizational Change 386
Action Research Approach 386
Debating Point: What's the Best Speed for Organizational Change? 387
Appreciative Inquiry Approach 388
Large Group Intervention Approach 390
Parallel Learning Structures Approach 391
Cross-Cultural and Ethical Issues in Organizational Change 391
Organizational Behaviour: The Journey Continues 392
Chapter Summary 392
Key Terms 393
Critical-Thinking Questions 393
Case Study TransAct Insurance Corporation 394
Team Exercise Strategic Change Incidents 395
Self-Assessment Are You Tolerant of Change? 396
Self-Assessments for Chapter 15 396

Additional Cases

Case 1: A Mir Kiss? CA-1
Case 2: Arctic Mining Consultants CA-2
Case 3: Barrie Super Subs CA-3
Case 4: Fran Hayden Joins Dairy Engineering CA-4
Case 5: Going to the X-Stream CA-6
Case 6: Keeping Suzanne Chalmers CA-8
Case 7: Northwest Canadian Forest Products Limited (Revised) CA-9
Case 8: The Regency Grand Hotel CA-11
Case 9: Simmons Laboratories CA-12
Case 10: Star Enterprises—Rita's Issues at Work CA-15
Case 11: Tamarack Industries CA-16
Case 12: The Outstanding Faculty Award CA-17

Appendix A

Theory Building and Systematic Research Methods A-1

Appendix B

Scoring Keys for Self-Assessment Exercises B-1

Glossary GL-1

Endnotes EN-1

Name and Organization Index NI-1

Subject Index SI-1

Preface

Welcome to the evolving world of organizational behaviour! Knowledge is replacing infrastructure. Social media and virtual teams are transforming the way employees work together. Values and self-leadership are replacing command-and-control management. Knowledge is replacing infrastructure. Companies are looking for employees with emotional intelligence and effective team behaviours, not just technical smarts.

Canadian Organizational Behaviour, Ninth Edition, is written in the context of these emerging workplace realities. This edition explains how emotions produce employee motivation, attitudes, and decisions; how social networks shape power and communication; how self-concept influences individual outcomes, team cohesion, leadership, and behaviour; and how adopting a global mindset has become an important characteristic of employees in this increasingly interconnected world. This book also presents the reality that organizational behaviour is not just for managers; it is relevant and valuable to anyone who works in and around organizations.

Canadian and Global Focus

Canadian Organizational Behaviour, Ninth Edition, is written by Canadians for Canadians. It includes several Canadian cases, is anchored by Canadian and global scholarship, and is filled with Canadian examples of organizational behaviour in practice.

For example, you will read about how Shopify, the Ottawa-based ecommerce web platform company, motivates employees through job enrichment; how critical decision-making errors occurred before and after the railway disaster at Lac Megantic, Quebec; how Vancity Savings Credit Union carefully hires job applicants whose personal values are aligned with the financial institution's values; how Tim Hortons' chairman and former CEO Paul House keeps his perceptions in focus by visiting the restaurants and working beside frontline employees; and how G Adventures in Toronto maintains a strong organizational culture.

Along with its Canadian focus, *Canadian Organizational Behaviour,* Ninth Edition, recognizes that we live in a world of increasing globalization. This emerging reality is discussed in the first chapter; several global and cross-cultural issues are also covered throughout the book. Every chapter includes global examples that illustrate OB concepts. Some of these appear in *Global Connections* features, but most are embedded in the text or found in captioned photos. For example, you will read how Tencent founder and CEO "Pony" Ma Huateng relies on transformational leadership rather than charisma to lead China's social media revolution; how the MARS model of individual behaviour helps Iceland Foods Group in the United Kingdom create a high-performing workforce; how Brasilata in Sao Paulo, Brazil, succeeds through employee involvement and creativity; how the CEO of Alcoa Russia fended off corruption by emphasizing the company's values; and how DHL Express in Africa succeeds through high employee engagement.

Global Connections 2.2:

WORKING WITH HIGH POWER DISTANCE IN CHINA[97]

As the only Westerner in a 50-employee start-up winery in China, Emilie Bourgois soon noticed that Chinese managers seem to use their power more directly than do European, Canadian, or American bosses. "I was surprised to see that taking the initiative most of the time was seen as rude and as a failure to respect the executives' authority," says Bourgois, a public relations professional from Bordeaux, France. "At work, everyone had to perform well in their own tasks, but permission was required for anything other than what was expected."

This high power distance was also apparent in how Chinese managers interacted with staff. "Western-style bosses tend to develop a closer relationship with employees," Bourgois suggests. "The hierarchy is much more clearly divided in Chinese-dominant companies than it is in foreign ones."

Bourgois worked well with her colleagues at the Chinese winery, but she acknowledges that "beyond that, there is still an important cultural gap." She is now employed in the Beijing office of executive recruitment firm Antal International, where cultural differences seem to be less pronounced because the company has team building events to improve bonding and mutual understanding.

Emilie Bourgois

Emilie Bourgois, second from right with coworkers at Antal International in Beijing, discovered in an earlier job that Chinese-dominant companies have higher power distance compared to most Western firms.

Courtesy of Vancity

Vancouver City Savings Credit Union (Vancity) is one of Canada's truly values-driven organizations. And to sustain its focus on values, Vancity aims to "screen for skills and hire for fit." Specifically, it carefully selects job applicants whose personal values are aligned with the financial institution's values. "I can tell if someone is just quoting off a Vancity website," says operations vice-president Ellen Pekeles about job applicants who claim to hold Vancity's values. "But when they really talk about it [Vancity's values], and you can see they care . . . you can't fake that." Vancity also gives new hires a five-day orientation that outlines the company's values. At the end of that program, new hires are offered a severance package if they feel their personal values are misaligned with Vancity's values.[73]

Linking Theory with Reality

Every chapter of *Canadian Organizational Behaviour*, Ninth Edition, is filled with examples to make OB knowledge more meaningful and reflect the relevance and excitement of this field. These stories about real people and organizations translate academic theories into relevant knowledge and real-life application. For example, we describe how Toronto Western Hospital applied appreciative inquiry to form a future vision of the organization and develop a positive leadership program; how Deloitte Touche Tohmatsu motivates its employees in Australia through innovative game-based positive reinforcement; and how Vancouver-based HootSuite Media thrives on a culture of collaboration and creativity through hackathons, monthly parliaments, and a Canadiana-themed team-oriented work environment.

These real-life stories appear in many forms. Every chapter of *Canadian Organizational Behaviour*, Ninth Edition, is filled with captioned photos and in-text anecdotes about work life. Lengthier examples are distinguished in a feature we call Global Connections, which "connect" OB concepts with real organizational incidents and situations.

Case studies in each chapter as well as video case studies associated with this book connect OB concepts to emerging workplace realities. These stories provide representation across Canada and around the planet. They also cover a wide range of industries–from software to government, and from small businesses to the largest global organizations.

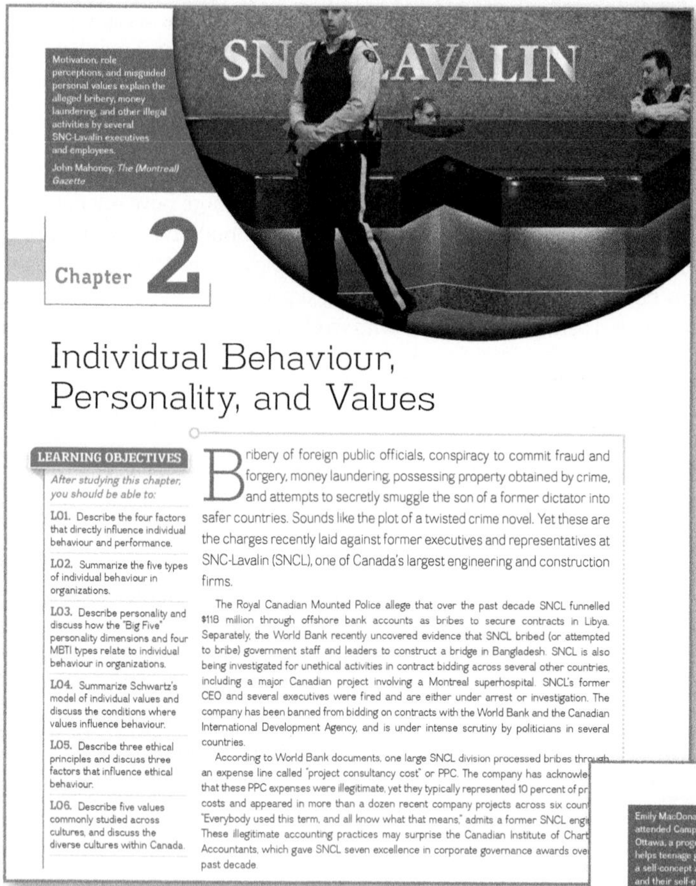

Motivation, role perceptions, and misguided personal values explain the alleged bribery, money laundering, and other illegal activities by several SNC-Lavalin executives and employees.

John Mahoney, *The (Montreal) Gazette*

Chapter 2

Individual Behaviour, Personality, and Values

LEARNING OBJECTIVES

After studying this chapter, you should be able to:

LO1. Describe the four factors that directly influence individual behaviour and performance.

LO2. Summarize the five types of individual behaviour in organizations.

LO3. Describe personality and discuss how the "Big Five" personality dimensions and four MBTI types relate to individual behaviour in organizations.

LO4. Summarize Schwartz's model of individual values and discuss the conditions where values influence behaviour.

LO5. Describe three ethical principles and discuss three factors that influence ethical behaviour.

LO6. Describe five values commonly studied across cultures, and discuss the diverse cultures within Canada.

Bribery of foreign public officials, conspiracy to commit fraud and forgery, money laundering, possessing property obtained by crime, and attempts to secretly smuggle the son of a former dictator into safer countries. Sounds like the plot of a twisted crime novel. Yet these are the charges recently laid against former executives and representatives at SNC-Lavalin (SNCL), one of Canada's largest engineering and construction firms.

The Royal Canadian Mounted Police allege that over the past decade SNCL funnelled $118 million through offshore bank accounts as bribes to secure contracts in Libya. Separately, the World Bank recently uncovered evidence that SNCL bribed (or attempted to bribe) government staff and leaders to construct a bridge in Bangladesh. SNCL is also being investigated for unethical activities in contract bidding across several other countries, including a major Canadian project involving a Montreal superhospital. SNCL's former CEO and several executives were fired and are either under arrest or investigation. The company has been banned from bidding on contracts with the World Bank and the Canadian International Development Agency, and is under intense scrutiny by politicians in several countries.

According to World Bank documents, one large SNCL division processed bribes through an expense line called "project consultancy cost" or PPC. The company has acknowle that these PPC expenses were illegitimate, yet they typically represented 10 percent of pr costs and appeared in more than a dozen recent company projects across six coun "Everybody used this term, and all know what that means," admits a former SNCL engi These illegitimate accounting practices may surprise the Canadian Institute of Chart Accountants, which gave SNCL seven excellence in corporate governance awards ove past decade.

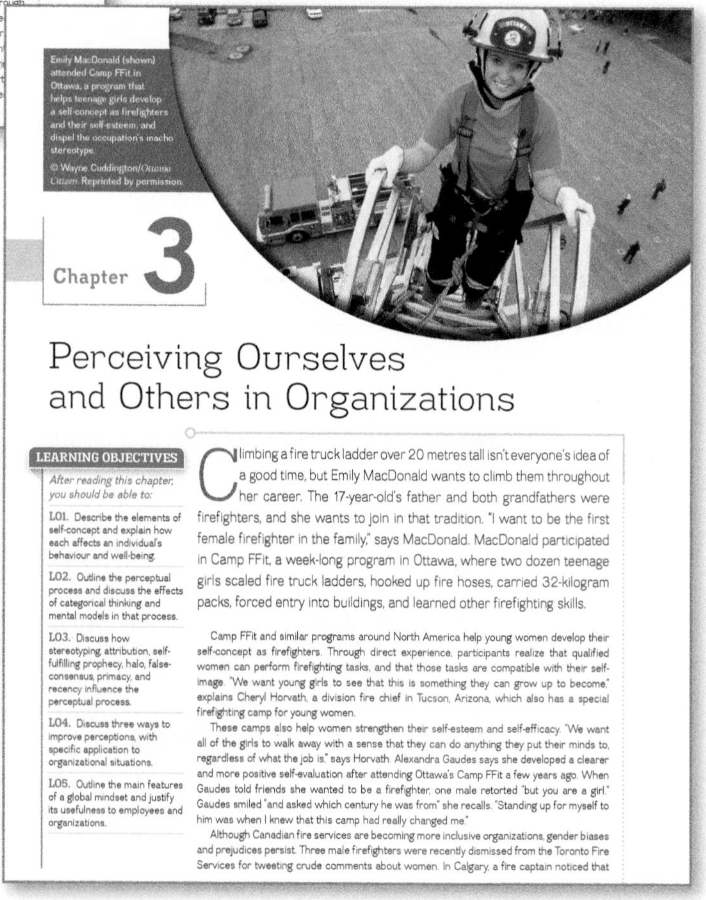

Emily MacDonald (shown) attended Camp FFit in Ottawa, a program that helps teenage girls develop a self-concept as firefighters and their self-esteem, and dispel the occupation's macho stereotype.

© Wayne Cuddington/*Ottawa Citizen*. Reprinted by permission.

Chapter 3

Perceiving Ourselves and Others in Organizations

LEARNING OBJECTIVES

After reading this chapter, you should be able to:

LO1. Describe the elements of self-concept and explain how each affects an individual's behaviour and well-being.

LO2. Outline the perceptual process and discuss the effects of categorical thinking and mental models in that process.

LO3. Discuss how stereotyping, attribution, self-fulfilling prophecy, halo, false-consensus, primacy, and recency influence the perceptual process.

LO4. Discuss three ways to improve perceptions, with specific application to organizational situations.

LO5. Outline the main features of a global mindset and justify its usefulness to employees and organizations.

Climbing a fire truck ladder over 20 metres tall isn't everyone's idea of a good time, but Emily MacDonald wants to climb them throughout her career. The 17-year-old's father and both grandfathers were firefighters, and she wants to join in that tradition. "I want to be the first female firefighter in the family," says MacDonald. MacDonald participated in Camp FFit, a week-long program in Ottawa, where two dozen teenage girls scaled fire truck ladders, hooked up fire hoses, carried 32-kilogram packs, forced entry into buildings, and learned other firefighting skills.

Camp FFit and similar programs around North America help young women develop their self-concept as firefighters. Through direct experience, participants realize that qualified women can perform firefighting tasks, and that those tasks are compatible with their self-image. "We want young girls to see that this is something they can grow up to become," explains Cheryl Horvath, a division fire chief in Tucson, Arizona, which also has a special firefighting camp for young women.

These camps also help women strengthen their self-esteem and self-efficacy. "We want all of the girls to walk away with a sense that they can do anything they put their minds to, regardless of what the job is," says Horvath. Alexandra Gaudes says she developed a clearer and more positive self-evaluation after attending Ottawa's Camp FFit a few years ago. When Gaudes told friends she wanted to be a firefighter, one male retorted "but you are a girl." Gaudes smiled "and asked which century he was from" she recalls. "Standing up for myself to him was when I knew that this camp had really changed me."

Although Canadian fire services are becoming more inclusive organizations, gender biases and prejudices persist. Three male firefighters were recently dismissed from the Toronto Fire Services for tweeting crude comments about women. In Calgary, a fire captain noticed that

Contemporary Theory Foundation

Canadian Organizational Behaviour, Ninth Edition, has a solid foundation of contemporary and classic research and writing. You can see this in the references. Each chapter is based on dozens of articles, books, and other sources. The most recent literature receives thorough coverage, resulting in what we believe is the most up-to-date organizational behaviour textbook available. The topics in this book reflect our strong belief that organizational behaviour is multi-disciplinary, not aligned mainly with one social science field. This book's references also reveal that we reach out to marketing, information management, human resource management, and other business disciplines for new ideas. Our approach is also to focus information that readers value, namely OB knowledge and practices. Consequently, with a few classic exceptions, we avoid writing a "who's-who" book; most scholars are named in the references, not in the main text.

EXHIBIT 1.4

An Integrating Model of Organizational Behaviour

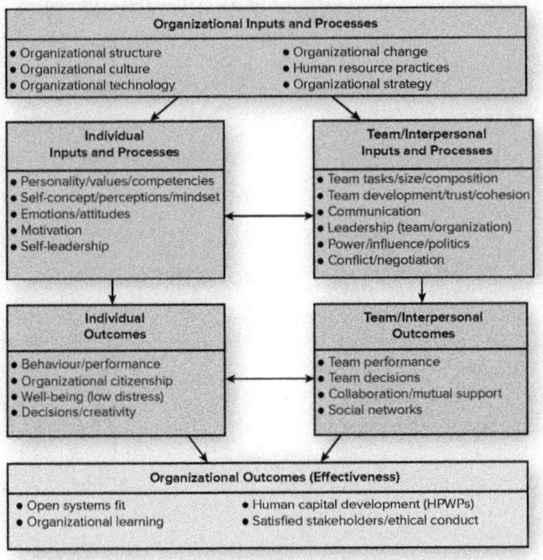

EXHIBIT 10.3

Centrality in Social Networks

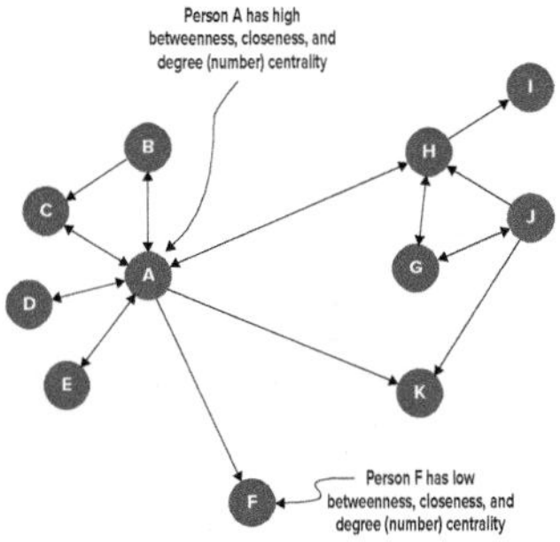

One of the driving forces for writing *Canadian Organizational Behaviour* was to provide a more responsive conduit for emerging OB knowledge to reach students, practitioners, and fellow scholars. To its credit, this is apparently the first major OB book to discuss the full self-concept model (not just core self-evaluation), workplace emotions, social identity theory, global mindset, four-drive theory, specific elements of social networks, appreciative inquiry, affective events theory (but without the jargon), somatic marker theory (also without the jargon), virtual teams, mindfulness in ethical behaviour, Schwartz's values model, employee engagement, learning orientation, workaholism, and several other groundbreaking topics. This edition continues this leadership by introducing the latest knowledge on predictors of moral sensitivity, applying social networks for viral change, distinguishing the two main types of matrix organizational structure, the degrees of virtuality (ranging from in-situ to virtual teams), task interdependence as a contingency in the team cohesion-performance relationship, communicator characteristics that influence coding and decoding, and the social and information processing characteristics of job design.

Organizational Behaviour Knowledge for Everyone

Another distinctive feature of *Canadian Organizational Behaviour*, Ninth Edition is that it is written for everyone in organizations, not just managers. The philosophy of this book is that everyone who works in and around organizations needs to understand and make use of organizational behaviour knowledge. People throughout the organization–systems analysts, production employees, accounting professionals, and others–are taking on more responsibilities as companies remove layers of management and give the rest of us more autonomy and accountability for our work outcomes. This book helps everyone to make sense of organizational behaviour, and provides the conceptual tools to work more effectively in the workplace.

Debating Point:

SHOULD COMPANIES USE PERSONALITY TESTS TO SELECT JOB APPLICANTS?

Personality theory has made significant strides over the past two decades, particularly in demonstrating that specific traits are associated with specific workplace behaviours and outcomes. Various studies have reported that specific Big Five dimensions predict overall job performance, organizational citizenship, leadership, counterproductive work behaviours, training performance, team performance, and a host of other important outcomes. These findings cast a strong vote in favour of personality testing in the workplace.

A few prominent personality experts urge caution, however.[55] They point out that although traits are associated with workplace behaviour to some extent, there are better predictors of work performance, such as work samples and past performance. Furthermore, selection procedures typically assume that more of a personality trait is better, whereas several (although not all) studies indicate that the best candidates might be closer to the middle than the extremes of the range.[56] For instance, job performance apparently increases with conscientiousness, yet employees with high conscientiousness might be so thorough that they become perfectionists, which can stifle rather than enhance job performance.[57] A third concern is that, depending on how the selection decision applies the test results, personality instruments may unfairly discriminate against specific groups of people.[58]

A fourth worry is that most personality tests are self-reported scales, so applicants might try to fake their answers. Worse, the test scores might not represent the individual's personality or anything else meaningful because test takers often don't know what personality traits the company is looking for. Studies show that candidates who try to fake "good" personality scores change the selection results. Supporters of personality testing offer the counterargument that few job applicants try to fake their scores.[59] One major study recently found that most personality dimensions are estimated better by observers than by self-ratings, but few companies rely on ratings from other people.[60]

Finally, personality testing might not convey a favourable image of the company. Amtrak's use of personality testing at Metrolink resulted in conflict with the railway worker unions. The British operations of PricewaterhouseCoopers (PwC) discovered that its personality test discouraged female applicants from applying because of concerns that the test was too impersonal and could be faked. "Our personality test was seen to alienate women and so we had to respond to that," says PwC's head of diversity.[61]

Active Learning and Critical Thinking Support

We teach organizational behaviour, so we understand how important it is to use a textbook that offers deep support for active learning and critical thinking. Business school accreditation associations also emphasize the importance of the learning experience, which further reinforces our attention on classroom activities. *Canadian Organizational Behaviour*, Ninth Edition includes more than two dozen case studies in various forms and levels of complexity. It offers four dozen self-assessments, most of which have been empirically tested and validated. This book is also a rich resource for in-class activities, some of which are not available in other organizational behaviour books, such as the Employee Involvement Cases, Deciphering the (Social) Network, Ethics Dilemma Vignettes, and the Club Ed exercise.

Key Terms

ability, p. 28
achievement-nurturing orientation, p. 48
collectivism, p. 46
conscientiousness, p. 35
counterproductive work behaviours (CWBs) p. 32
extraversion, p. 35
five-factor model (FFM), p. 34
individualism, p. 46
mindfulness, p. 44
moral intensity, p. 43
moral sensitivity, p. 44
motivation, p. 28
Myers-Briggs Type Indicator (MBTI), p. 36
neuroticism, p. 35
organizational citizenship behaviours (OCBs) p. 31
personality, p. 34
power distance, p. 47
presenteeism, p. 33
role perceptions, p. 30
uncertainty avoidance, p. 48

Critical-Thinking Questions

1. A provincial government department has high levels of absenteeism among the office staff. The head of office administration argues that employees are misusing the organization's sick leave benefits. However, some of the mostly female staff members have explained that family responsibilities interfere with work. Using the MARS model, as well as your knowledge of absenteeism behaviour, discuss some of the possible reasons for absenteeism here and how it might be reduced.
2. It has been said that all employees are motivated. Do you agree with this statement?
3. Studies report that heredity has a strong influence on an individual's personality. What are the implications of this in organizational settings?
4. All candidates applying for a management trainee position are given a personality test that measures the five dimensions in the five-factor model. Which personality traits would you consider to be the most important for this type of job? Explain your answer.
5. Compare and contrast personality with personal values, and identify values categories in Schwartz's values circumplex that likely relate to one or more personality dimensions in the five-factor personality model.
6. This chapter discussed values congruence mostly in the context of an employee's personal values versus the organization's values. But values congruence also relates to the juxtaposition of other pairs of value systems. Explain how values congruence is relevant with respect to organizational versus professional values (i.e., values of a professional occupation, such as physician, accountant, pharmacist).
7. "All decisions are ethical decisions." Comment on this statement, particularly by referring to the concepts of moral intensity and moral sensitivity.
8. The organization that you have been working in for five years is now suffering from a global recession and it changes the compensation structure. Discuss the role of moral intensity, moral sensitivity and situational influences in this context.
9. People in a particular South American country have high power distance and high collectivism. What does this mean, and what are the implications of this information when you (a senior executive) visit employees working for your company in that country?

Changes to the Ninth Edition

Canadian Organizational Behaviour, Ninth Edition has benefited since the previous edition by reviews from dozens of organizational behaviour instructors and researchers in Canada and several other countries. As a result, there are numerous improvements throughout the book. Chapter 8 (teams) and Chapter 12 (leadership) have been significantly revised, and almost every other chapter has noticeable updates and revisions. This edition introduces "Debating Point," a valuable feature in every chapter that helps students think critically about seemingly obvious ideas. Along with dozens of conceptual improvements, this edition has substantially revised the examples. All chapter-opening case studies are new or revised. Most captioned photos and Global Connections features are new or updated. We have also added more than 100 new in-text examples. Many of the OB-by-the-Numbers features have been updated or changed. Here are the main conceptual improvements in *Canadian Organizational Behaviour,* Ninth Edition:

- *Chapter 1: Introduction to the Field of Organizational Behaviour*–This edition introduces an integrated model of organization behaviour to help students see the relationship among the main concepts throughout this book. The opening chapter also updates and revises content on why study OB, the organizational learning perspective, and emerging employment relationships.
- *Chapter 2: Individual Behaviour, Personality, and Values*–This edition updates several topics in this chapter, including new information about organizational citizenship behaviours, elements of task performance, the importance of role clarity, the influence of values on individual behaviour, predictors of moral sensitivity, and strategies to support ethical behaviour.
- *Chapter 3: Perceiving Ourselves and Others in Organizations*–This book was apparently the first to discuss the full model of self-concept and its relevance to organizational behaviour. This edition further refines this important topic, including a new exhibit that illustrates the full set of self-concept characteristics and processes. Other improvements to this chapter are found in the topics on perceptual organization and interpretation, attribution rules, fundamental attribution error, and improving perceptions through meaningful interaction.
- *Chapter 4: Workplace Emotions, Attitudes, and Stress*–This was the first OB book to discuss theories of emotion (i.e. affective events theory, somatic marker hypothesis, affect infusion model) and to integrate those concepts with attitudes, motivation, decision making, and other topics. This edition continues this tradition by updating information on types of emotions, the relationship between emotions and attitudes, and emotional dissonance. The topics of cognitive dissonance and emotional intelligence outcomes and training have also been updated.
- *Chapter 5: Foundations of Employee Motivation*–This chapter revises the key elements of goal setting by introducing the SMARTER model. It also updates and rewrites content on employee drives, Maslow's needs hierarchy, and four-drive theory.
- *Chapter 6: Applied Performance Practices*–This edition is apparently the first OB book to introduce social and information processing as two important job characteristics that are overlooked in the traditional model. This edition also updates discussion of the meaning of money.
- *Chapter 7: Decision Making and Creativity*–This edition has minor changes to a few decision making topics, including the rational choice paradigm, evaluating options, and the role of emotions in decision making and choice.
- *Chapter 8: Team Dynamics*–This edition includes substantial changes to the topic of team dynamics. The team effectiveness model has been revised in order to differentiate between team states and team processes. And several new and important topics that predict team performance are introduced, including boundary spanning, teamwork behaviour, and taskwork behaviour. This edition also introduces the punctuated equilibrium model of team development and the topic of transactive memory systems.

- *Chapter 9: Communicating in Organizations*–This edition further updates the topic of communication, and the title is changed to reflect this specific focus. This edition updates the topics of speech patterns in communication, influences on encoding and decoding of messages, recent developments in social media, cross-cultural communication and changes to workplace design.
- *Chapter 10: Power and Influence in the Workplace*–You will find several new developments in this chapter. Building on recent additions to the topic of social networks, the chapter now includes more discussion on the power of visibility within social networks and the links between social networks and personal power. This edition also revises and updates writing on the meaning of coercive power and recent research on the topic bullying in the workplace. The section on organizational politics has also been updated, with more examples and insight into new research on the topic.
- *Chapter 11: Conflict and Negotiation in the Workplace*–The most noticeable change in this chapter is that the negotiation section has been completely rewritten and updated. It is now organized around the topics of distributive and integrative negotiations. New information is provided on how to prepare for a negotiation, how to set limits, and distributive and integrative negotiation strategies that actually work. A new section on the distinction between mediation and arbitration is also added. The chapter concludes with a summary of the behavioral differences between expert negotiators and average negotiators.
- *Chapter 12: Leadership in Organizational Settings*–This chapter has been completely reorganized and substantially rewritten. Transformational leadership is widely considered the core perspective on this subject, so we now begin the chapter with the transformational leadership perspective (after the chapter introduction, which also describes shared leadership). The transformational leadership perspective also now includes "encourage experimentation" as one of its four elements. The second perspective, managerial leadership, is described and contrasted with transformational leadership. The managerial leadership perspective incorporates earlier behavioural leadership concepts, contemporary contingency leadership theories, and servant leadership. The other two leadership perspectives – implicit leadership and leadership attributes – have minor updates from the previous edition.
- *Chapter 13: Designing Organizational Structures*–This chapter revises and updates the matrix structure topic, including the two main forms of this structure (divisional-based and project-based), and specific problems with matrix structures. The topic of coordinating work activities has also been updated.
- *Chapter 14: Organizational Culture*–The section on changing and strengthening organizational culture has been revised, particularly with the addition of supporting workforce stability and communication. The issue of espoused versus enacted values is more clearly highlighted, and the topics of organizational culture effectiveness contingencies and socialization agents have been revised.
- *Chapter 15: Organizational Change*–This edition is apparently the first OB book to discuss social networks and viral change as an organizational change initiative. We also significantly revise and update the discussion on why employees resist change (such as negative valence of change). Parts of the section on resistance to change have also been rewritten.

Supporting the OB Learning Experience

The changes described above refer only to the text material. *Canadian Organizational Behaviour,* Ninth Edition also has improved technology supplements, cases, team exercises, and self-assessments.

Case Study: ETHICS DILEMMA VIGNETTES

Purpose This exercise is designed to make you aware of the ethical dilemmas people face in various business situations, as well as the competing principles and values that operate in these situations.

Instructions (Small Class) The instructor will form teams of four or five students. Team members will read each case below and discuss the extent to which the company's action in each case was ethical. Teams should be prepared to justify their evaluation using ethics principles and the perceived moral intensity of each incident.

subsequent sales of the high-margin ink cartridges required for each printer. One global printer manufacturer now designs its printers so that they work only with ink cartridges made in the same region. Ink cartridges purchased in Canada will not work with the same printer model sold in Europe, for example. This "region coding" of ink cartridges does not improve performance. Rather, it prevents consumers and grey marketers from buying the product at a lower price in another region. The company says this policy allows it to maintain stable prices within a region rather than continually changing prices due to currency fluctuations.

CHAPTER CASES AND ADDITIONAL CASES

Every chapter includes at least one short case that challenges students to diagnose issues and apply ideas from that chapter. One dozen additional cases appear at the end of the book.

Additional Cases

- Case 1 A MIR KISS?
- Case 2 ARCTIC MINING CONSULTANTS
- Case 3 BARRIE SUPER SUBS
- Case 4 FRAN HAYDEN JOINS DAIRY ENGINEERING
- Case 5 GOING TO THE X-STREAM
- Case 6 KEEPING SUZANNE CHALMERS
- Case 7 NORTHWEST CANADIAN FOREST PRODUCTS LIMITED (REVISED)
- Case 8 THE REGENCY GRAND HOTEL
- Case 9 SIMMONS LABORATORIES
- Case 10 STAR ENTERPRISES—RITA'S ISSUES AT WORK
- Case 11 TAMARACK INDUSTRIES
- Case 12 THE OUTSTANDING FACULTY AWARD

Case 5 GOING TO THE X-STREAM

Roy Smollan, Auckland University of Technology, New Zealand

Gil Reihana was the chief executive officer of X-Stream, a company he launched in Auckland, New Zealand, six years ago at the age of 25, after graduating with a bachelor's degree in information technology and management. He had inherited $300,000 and had persuaded various family members to invest additional money. X-Stream assembled personal computers for the New Zealand and Australian markets and sold them through a number of chain stores and independent retailers. The company had soon established a reputation for quality hardware, customized products, excellent delivery times and after-sales service. Six months ago it had started a software division, specializing in webpage design and consulting on various applications for the development of electronic their own way. In the beginning, he had met with each staff member in January to discuss with them how happy they were in their jobs, what their ambitions were, and what plans they would like to make for the coming year in terms of their own professional development. As the company had grown this had become more difficult and he had left each member of his senior management team to do this with their own staff, but did not monitor whether they were doing it or how well it worked. Now he tried to keep in touch with staff by having lunch with them in the cafeteria occasionally.

Denise Commins (affectionately known to all staff as Dot Com) was the chief financial officer. She and Gil could not be more different. Denise was quiet, methodical, and very

Several cases are new to this book, many of which are written by Canadian instructors. Others are classics that have withstood the test of time.

TEAM EXERCISES AND SELF-ASSESSMENTS

Experiential exercises and self-assessments represent an important part of the active learning process. *Canadian Organizational Behaviour,* Ninth Edition, facilitates that process by offering a team/class exercise in every chapter. Self-assessments personalize the meaning of several organizational behaviour concepts, and this edition features one self-assessments per chapter in the text with additional self-scoring, interactive self-assessments with detailed feedback found on *Connect.* To ensure that students make full use of these excellent resources, we have included an icon indicating where the text content corresponds to one of the chapter's self-assessments and directing students to *Connect,* and there is a convenient table at the end of the chapter containing a brief description of the self-assessments and whether they are in-text or on Connect.

Class Exercise: TEST YOUR KNOWLEDGE OF PERSONALITY

Purpose This exercise is designed to help you think about and understand the effects of the Big Five personality dimensions on individual preferences and outcomes.

Instructions (Large Class) Below are several questions relating to the Big Five personality dimensions and various preferences or outcomes. Answer each of these questions relying on your personal experience or best guess. Later, the instructor will show you the answers based on scholarly results. You will *not* be graded on this exercise. Instead, it illustrates the many ways that personality influences human behaviour and preferences.

Instructions (Small Class)

1. The instructor will organize students into teams. Members of each team work together to answer each of the questions below relating to the Big Five personality dimensions and various preferences or outcomes.
2. The instructor will reveal the answers based on scholarly results. (*Note:* The instructor might create a competition to see which team has the most answers correct.)

Personality and Preferences Questions You have been asked to select job applicants for a nine-month over-winter assignment working in an Antarctic research station with a dozen other people. Assuming that all candidates have equal skills, experience, and health, identify which level of each personality dimension would be best for people working in these remote, confined, and isolated conditions.

Self-Assessment: ARE YOU INTROVERTED OR EXTRAVERTED?

Purpose This self-assessment is designed to help you estimate the extent to which you are introverted or extraverted.

Instructions The statements in the scale below refer to personal characteristics that might or might not be characteristic of you. Mark the box indicating the extent to which the statement accurately or inaccurately describes you. Then use the scoring key in Appendix B at the end of this book to calculate your results. This exercise should be completed alone so that you can assess yourself honestly without concerns of social comparison. Class discussion will focus on the meaning and implications of extraversion and introversion in organizations.

IPIP Introversion-Extraversion Scale

How accurately does each of the statements listed below describe you?	Very accurate description of me	Moderately accurate	Neither accurate nor inaccurate	Moderately inaccurate	Very inaccurate description of me
1. I feel comfortable around people.	○	○	○	○	○
2. I make friends easily.	○	○	○	○	○
3. I keep in the background.	○	○	○	○	○
4. I don't talk a lot.	○	○	○	○	○
5. I would describe my experiences as somewhat dull.	○	○	○	○	○
6. I know how to captivate people.	○	○	○	○	○
7. I don't like to draw attention to myself.	○	○	○	○	○
8. I am the life of the party.	○	○	○	○	○
9. I am skilled in handling social situations.	○	○	○	○	○
10. I have little to say.	○	○	○	○	○

Source: Adapted from instruments described and/or presented in L. R. Goldberg, J. A. Johnson, H. W. Eber, R. Hogan, M. C. Ashton, C. R. Cloninger, and H. C. Gough, "The International Personality Item Pool and the Future of Public-Domain Personality Measures," *Journal of Research in Personality* 40 (2006), pp. 84–96.

INDEXES, MARGIN NOTES, AND GLOSSARY

While minimizing unnecessary jargon, *Canadian Organizational Behaviour* assists the learning process by highlighting key terms in bold and providing brief definitions in the margin. These definitions are also presented in an alphabetical glossary at the end of the text. We have also developed comprehensive indexes of the content, names, and organizations described in this book. Also look for the Learning Objectives presented at the beginning of each chapter, and then linked to chapter content by numbered icons. An excellent study tool!

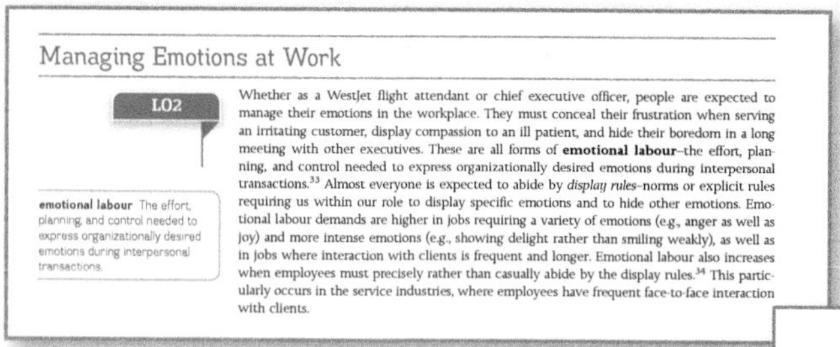

Managing Emotions at Work

LO2

Whether as a WestJet flight attendant or chief executive officer, people are expected to manage their emotions in the workplace. They must conceal their frustration when serving an irritating customer, display compassion to an ill patient, and hide their boredom in a long meeting with other executives. These are all forms of **emotional labour**–the effort, planning, and control needed to express organizationally desired emotions during interpersonal transactions.[33] Almost everyone is expected to abide by *display rules*–norms or explicit rules requiring us within our role to display specific emotions and to hide other emotions. Emotional labour demands are higher in jobs requiring a variety of emotions (e.g., anger as well as joy) and more intense emotions (e.g., showing delight rather than smiling weakly), as well as in jobs where interaction with clients is frequent and longer. Emotional labour also increases when employees must precisely rather than casually abide by the display rules.[34] This particularly occurs in the service industries, where employees have frequent face-to-face interaction with clients.

emotional labour The effort, planning, and control needed to express organizationally desired emotions during interpersonal transactions.

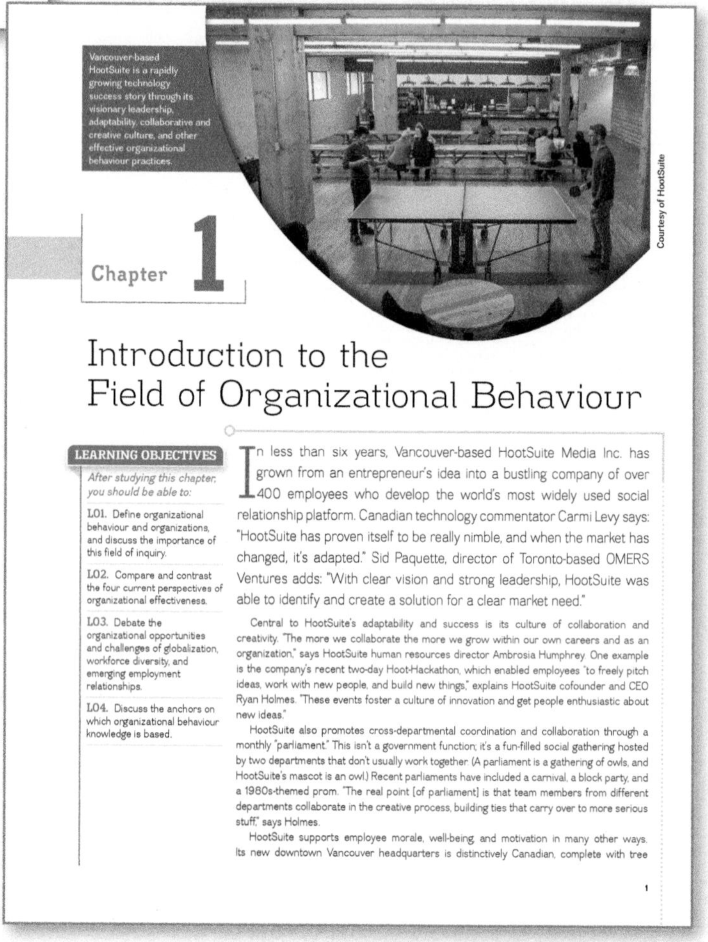

Introduction to the Field of Organizational Behaviour

LEARNING OBJECTIVES

After studying this chapter, you should be able to:

LO1. Define organizational behaviour and organizations, and discuss the importance of this field of inquiry.

LO2. Compare and contrast the four current perspectives of organizational effectiveness.

LO3. Debate the organizational opportunities and challenges of globalization, workforce diversity, and emerging employment relationships.

LO4. Discuss the anchors on which organizational behaviour knowledge is based.

In less than six years, Vancouver-based HootSuite Media Inc. has grown from an entrepreneur's idea into a bustling company of over 400 employees who develop the world's most widely used social relationship platform. Canadian technology commentator Carmi Levy says: "HootSuite has proven itself to be really nimble, and when the market has changed, it's adapted." Sid Paquette, director of Toronto-based OMERS Ventures adds: "With clear vision and strong leadership, HootSuite was able to identify and create a solution for a clear market need."

Central to HootSuite's adaptability and success is its culture of collaboration and creativity. "The more we collaborate the more we grow within our own careers and as an organization," says HootSuite human resources director Ambrosia Humphrey. One example is the company's recent two-day Hoot-Hackathon, which enabled employees "to freely pitch ideas, work with new people, and build new things," explains HootSuite cofounder and CEO Ryan Holmes. "These events foster a culture of innovation and get people enthusiastic about new ideas."

HootSuite also promotes cross-departmental coordination and collaboration through a monthly "parliament." This isn't a government function; it's a fun-filled social gathering hosted by two departments that don't usually work together. (A parliament is a gathering of owls, and HootSuite's mascot is an owl.) Recent parliaments have included a carnival, a block party, and a 1960s-themed prom. "The real point [of parliament] is that team members from different departments collaborate in the creative process, building ties that carry over to more serious stuff," says Holmes.

HootSuite supports employee morale, well-being and motivation in many other ways. Its new downtown Vancouver headquarters is distinctively Canadian, complete with tree

1

Teaching and Learning Tools

Available with Canadian Organizational Behaviour, Ninth Edition, is a comprehensive package of supplementary materials designed to enhance teaching and learning. The student content is authored by Claude Dupuis, Athabasca University. The instructor content is authored by Sandra Steen, University of Regina.

McGraw-Hill Connect™ is a web-based assignment and assessment platform that gives students the means to better connect with their coursework, with their instructors, and with the important concepts that they will need to know for success now and in the future.

With Connect, instructors can deliver assignments, quizzes and tests online. Instructors can edit existing questions and author entirely new problems. Track individual student performance–by question, assignment or in relation to the class overall–with detailed grade reports. Integrate grade reports easily with Learning Management Systems (LMS).

By choosing Connect, instructors are providing their students with a powerful tool for improving academic performance and truly mastering course material. Connect allows students to practice important skills at their own pace and on their own schedule. Importantly, students' assessment results and instructors' feedback are all saved online-so students can continually review their progress and plot their course to success.

Connect also provides 24/7 online access to an eBook-an online edition of the text-to aid them in successfully completing their work, wherever and whenever they choose.

Key Features

Simple Assignment Management With Connect, creating assignments is easier than ever, so you can spend more time teaching and less time managing.

- Create and deliver assignments easily with selectable end-of-chapter questions and testbank material to assign online.
- Streamline lesson planning, student progress reporting, and assignment grading to make classroom management more efficient than ever.
- Go paperless with the eBook and online submission and grading of student assignments.

Smart Grading When it comes to studying, time is precious. Connect helps students learn more efficiently by providing feedback and practice material when they need it, where they need it.

- Automatically score assignments, giving students immediate feedback on their work and side-by-side comparisons with correct answers.
- Access and review each response; manually change grades or leave comments for students to review.
- Reinforce classroom concepts with practice tests and instant quizzes.

Instructor Library The Connect Instructor Library is your course creation hub. It provides all the critical resources you'll need to build your course, just how you want to teach it.

- Assign eBook readings and draw from a rich collection of textbook-specific assignments.
- Access instructor resources, including ready-made PowerPoint presentations and media to use in your lectures.
- View assignments and resources created for past sections.
- Post your own resources for students to use.

eBook Connect reinvents the textbook learning experience for the modern student. Every Connect subject area is seamlessly integrated with Connect eBooks, which are designed to keep students focused on the concepts key to their success.

- Provide students with a Connect eBook, allowing for anytime, anywhere access to the textbook.
- Merge media, animation and assessments with the text's narrative to engage students and improve learning and retention.
- Pinpoint and connect key concepts in a snap using the powerful eBook search engine.
- Manage notes, highlights and bookmarks in one place for simple, comprehensive review.

LEARNSMART®

No two students are alike. Why should their learning paths be? LearnSmart uses revolutionary adaptive technology to build a learning experience unique to each student's individual needs. It starts by identifying the topics a student knows and does not know. As the student progresses, LearnSmart adapts and adjusts the content based on his or her individual strengths, weaknesses and confidence, ensuring that every minute spent studying with LearnSmart is the most efficient and productive study time possible. Authored by Sandra Steen, University of Regina.

SMARTBOOK™

As the first and only adaptive reading experience, SmartBook is changing the way students read and learn. SmartBook creates a personalized reading experience by highlighting the most important concepts a student needs to learn at that moment in time. As a student engages with SmartBook, the reading experience continuously adapts by highlighting content based on what each student knows and doesn't know. This ensures that he or she is focused on the content needed to close specific knowledge gaps, while it simultaneously promotes long-term learning.

INSTRUCTOR RESOURCES

McShane Connect is a one-stop shop for instructor resources, including:

Instructor's Manual: Written by the text authors, the Instructor's Manual accurately represents the text's content and supports instructors' needs. Each chapter includes the learning objectives, glossary of key terms, a chapter synopsis, complete lecture outline with thumbnail images of corresponding PowerPoint® slides, and solutions to the end-of-chapter discussion questions. It also includes teaching notes for the chapter case(s), team exercises, and self-assessments. Many chapters include supplemental lecture notes and suggested videos. The Instructor's Manual also includes teaching notes for the end-of-text cases.

Computerized Test Bank: Written by the McShane student Connect author, Claude Dupuis from Athabasca University, this flexible and easy to use electronic testing program allows instructors to create tests from book specific items. The Test Bank contains a broad selection of multiple choice, true/false, and essay questions and instructors may add their own questions as well. Each question identifies the relevant page reference and difficulty level. Multiple versions of the test can be created and printed.

PowerPoint® Presentations: Written by the text authors, these robust presentations offer high quality visuals to bring key OB concepts to life.

Video Program: The accompanying video program is available to instructors through video streaming in Connect or on DVD. Teaching notes can be found in the Instructor's Resource section in Connect.

Management Asset Gallery-for Instructors and Students: Management Asset Gallery is a one-stop-shop for a wealth of McGraw-Hill management assets, making it easier for instructors to locate specific materials to enhance their courses, and for students (Student Asset Gallery) to supplement their knowledge. The Instructor Asset Gallery includes non-text-specific management resources (Self-Assessments, Test Your Knowledge exercises, videos*, Manager's HotSeat, and additional group and individual exercises) along with supporting PowerPoint® and Instructor Manual materials.

The Manager's HotSeat: A resource within the Management Asset Gallery, the Manager's HotSeat allows students to watch over 14 real managers apply their years of experience to confront daily issues such as ethics, diversity, teamwork, and the virtual workplace. Students are prompted for their feedback throughout each scenario and then submit a report critiquing the manager's choices, while defending their own. The Manager's HotSeat is ideal for group or classroom discussions.

connect INSIGHT

NEW to the ninth edition of McShane! Visualized data tailored to your needs as an instructor makes it possible to quickly confirm early signals of success, or identify early warning signs regarding student performance or concept mastery–even while on the go.

*The 'Management in the Movies' videos are not licensed for distribution outside of the USA, however adopting instructors are able to access the Instructor Notes.

Acknowledgements

Organizational behaviour is a fascinating subject. It is also incredibly relevant and valuable, which becomes apparent while developing a world-class book such as *Canadian Organizational Behaviour, Ninth Edition.* Throughout this project, we witnessed the power of teamwork, the excitement of creative thinking, and the motivational force of the vision that we collectively held as our aspiration. The tight coordination and innovative synergy was evident throughout this venture. Our teamwork is even more amazing when you consider that most of us in this project are scattered throughout Canada, and the lead co-author (Steve) spends most of his time on the other side of the planet!

Group Product Manager Kim Brewster led the development of *Canadian Organizational Behaviour* with unwavering enthusiasm and foresight. Product Developer Tracey Haggert orchestrated the daily process with superhuman skill and determination, which is particularly important given the magnitude of this revision, the multiple authors, the pressing deadlines, and the 24-hour time zones in which we operated. Photo researcher and permissions editor Monika Schurmann efficiently and persistently tracked down the images that we sought out. Michelle Losier created a refreshing book design that elegantly incorporated the writing, exhibits, examples, photos, and many other resources that we pack into this volume. We also extend our thanks to Evan Turner for superb copy editing, and Supervising Editor Joanne Limebeer for leading the production process like a precision timepiece. Thanks to you all. This has been a truly wonderful journey!

Several dozen instructors around the world reviewed parts or all of *Canadian Organizational Behaviour,* Ninth Edition, or related editions in the United States, Asia Pacific region, and elsewhere since the previous Canadian edition. Their compliments were energizing, and their suggestions significantly improved the final product. The following people from Canadian colleges and universities provided the most recent feedback for improvements specifically for *Canadian Organizational Behaviour,* Ninth Edition:

Stan Arnold	*Humber College*
Gordon Barnard	*Durham College*
Anna Bortolon	*Conestoga College*
Julie Bulmash	*George Brown College*
Kerry Couet	*Grant MacEwan University*
Claude Dupuis	*Athabasca University*
Patricia Fitzgerald	*St Mary's University*
Thomas Foard	*University of Guelph*
Allan Fraser	*Cape Breton University*
Carolyn Gaunt	*Cambrian College*
Simon Gortana	*Seneca College of Applied Arts and Technology*
Maurice Grzeda	*Laurentian University*
Iren Heder	*University of Victoria*
Mike Kelly	*Nova Scotia Community College*
Lesley McCannell	*Kwantlen Polytechnic University*
David Richards	*Lakehead University*
Kirsten Robertson	*Simon Fraser University*
Peter Seidl	*British Columbia Institute of Technology*
Halinka Szwender	*Camosun College*
Hayfaa Tlaiss	*University of New Brunswick*
Diane White	*Seneca College*
Yanelia Yabar	*Red Deer College*

We would also like to extend thanks to the exceptional efforts of Claude Dupuis, Athabasca University, who championed and wrote Connect, and revised the test bank. His enthusiasm and expertise in organizational behaviour teaching really glows in his work on this project.

Steve would like to thank Kevin Tasa for joining as a co-author of *Canadian Organizational Behaviour*. His scholarly expertise and practical orientation are a unique combination that contribute significantly to this book. Steve also thanks Sandra Steen for her contribution to this and previous editions, and for her exceptional work on the instructor side of Connect as well as for authoring LearnSmart. The students who attend Steve's courses in organizational behaviour and leadership effectiveness deserve special recognition for sharing their real-life experiences and providing valuable ongoing feedback on the book and class activities. But more than anyone else, Steve is forever indebted to his wife Donna McClement and to their wonderful daughters, Bryton and Madison. Their love and support give special meaning to Steve's life.

Vancouver-based HootSuite is a rapidly growing technology success story through its visionary leadership, adaptability, collaborative and creative culture, and other effective organizational behaviour practices.

Courtesy of HootSuite

Chapter 1

Introduction to the Field of Organizational Behaviour

LEARNING OBJECTIVES

After reading this chapter, you should be able to:

LO1. Define organizational behaviour and organizations, and discuss the importance of this field of inquiry.

LO2. Compare and contrast the four current perspectives of organizational effectiveness.

LO3. Debate the organizational opportunities and challenges of globalization, workforce diversity, and emerging employment relationships.

LO4. Discuss the anchors on which organizational behaviour knowledge is based.

In less than six years, Vancouver-based HootSuite Media Inc. has grown from an entrepreneur's idea into a bustling company of over 400 employees who develop the world's most widely used social relationship platform. Canadian technology commentator Carmi Levy says: "HootSuite has proven itself to be really nimble, and when the market has changed, it's adapted." Sid Paquette, director of Toronto-based OMERS Ventures adds: "With clear vision and strong leadership, HootSuite was able to identify and create a solution for a clear market need."

Central to HootSuite's adaptability and success is its culture of collaboration and creativity. "The more we collaborate the more we grow within our own careers and as an organization," says HootSuite human resources director Ambrosia Humphrey. One example is the company's recent two-day Hoot-Hackathon, which enabled employees "to freely pitch ideas, work with new people, and build new things," explains HootSuite cofounder and CEO Ryan Holmes. "These events foster a culture of innovation and get people enthusiastic about new ideas."

HootSuite also promotes cross-departmental coordination and collaboration through a monthly "parliament." This isn't a government function; it's a fun-filled social gathering hosted by two departments that don't usually work together. (A parliament is a gathering of owls, and HootSuite's mascot is an owl.) Recent parliaments have included a carnival, a block party, and a 1980s-themed prom. "The real point [of parliament] is that team members from different departments collaborate in the creative process, building ties that carry over to more serious stuff," says Holmes.

HootSuite supports employee morale, well-being, and motivation in many other ways. Its new downtown Vancouver headquarters is distinctively Canadian, complete with tree stump chairs, meeting room tents, and a cabin with cots where employees can take a nap. Employees also enjoy an exercise room, games area, and a generously outfitted kitchen (with free coffee and beer on tap). HootSuite has avoided the dreaded annual performance reviews. Instead, it relies on developmental coaching, recognition, and meaningful work to motivate and train staff. "No one is cracking a whip at HootSuite, because they don't have to," observes Paul Donnelly, one of HootSuite's first employees. "Everyone has the same goal of building something incredible, and they are self-motivated to do so."[1]

Welcome to the Field of Organizational Behaviour!

Visionary leadership. Collaboration and creativity. Pleasant, team-oriented facilities. Meaningful work. Developmental coaching. These are just a few of the organizational behaviour topics and practices that HootSuite Media Inc. has relied on to achieve its success. In every sector of the economy, organizations need to employ skilled and motivated people who can be creative, work in teams, and maintain a healthy lifestyle. They need leaders with foresight and vision, who support innovative work practices, and make decisions that consider the interests of multiple stakeholders. In other words, the best companies succeed through the concepts and practices that we discuss in this organizational behaviour book.

Our purpose is to help you understand what goes on in organizations, including the thoughts and behaviour of employees and teams. We examine the factors that make companies effective, improve employee well-being, and drive successful collaboration among coworkers. We look at organizations from numerous and diverse perspectives, from the deepest foundations of employee thoughts and behaviour (personality, self-concept, commitment, etc.) to the complex interplay between the organization's structure and culture and its external environment. Along this journey, we emphasize why things happen and what you can do to predict and manage organizational events.

We begin this chapter by introducing you to the field of organizational behaviour and why it is important to your career and to organizations. Next, this chapter describes the "ultimate dependent variable" in organizational behaviour by presenting the four main perspectives of organizational effectiveness. We then introduce an integrating model of organizational behaviour to help guide you through the topics in this book. This is followed by an overview of three challenges facing organizations: globalization, increasing workforce diversity, and emerging employment relationships. We complete this opening chapter by describing four anchors that guide the development of organizational behaviour knowledge.

The Field of Organizational Behaviour

LO1

organizational behaviour (OB) The study of what people think, feel, and do in and around organizations.

organizations Groups of people who work interdependently toward some purpose.

Organizational behaviour (OB) is the study of what people think, feel, and do in and around organizations. It looks at employee behaviour, decisions, perceptions, and emotional responses. It examines how individuals and teams in organizations relate to each other and to their counterparts in other organizations. OB also encompasses the study of how organizations interact with their external environments, particularly in the context of employee behaviour and decisions. OB researchers systematically study these topics at multiple levels of analysis, namely, the individual, team (including interpersonal), and organization.[2]

The definition of organizational behaviour begs the question: What are organizations? **Organizations** are groups of people who work interdependently toward some purpose.[3] Notice that organizations are not buildings or government-registered entities. In fact, many organizations exist without either physical walls or government documentation to confer their legal status. Organizations have existed for as long as people have worked together. Massive temples dating back to 3500 BCE were constructed through the organized actions of multitudes of people. Craftspeople and merchants in ancient Rome formed guilds, complete with elected managers. More than 1,000 years ago, Chinese factories were producing 125,000 tons of iron each year. Closer to home, the Hudson's Bay Company holds the distinction of being North America's oldest commercial enterprise. Founded in 1670, the Winnipeg-based company was granted exclusive control over one-quarter of North America for almost 200 years.[4]

Throughout history, these and other organizations have consisted of people who communicate, coordinate, and collaborate with each other to achieve common objectives. One key feature of organizations is that they are collective entities. They consist of human beings (typically, but not necessarily, employees), and these people interact with each other in an *organized* way. This organized relationship requires some minimal level of communication, coordination, and collaboration to achieve organizational objectives. As such, all organizational members have degrees of interdependence with each other; they accomplish goals by sharing materials, information, or expertise with co workers.

A second key feature of organizations is that their members have a collective sense of purpose. This collective purpose isn't always well defined or agreed on. Although most companies have vision and mission statements, these documents are sometimes out of date or don't describe what employees and leaders try to achieve in reality. Still, imagine an organization without a collective sense of purpose. It would be a collection of people without direction or unifying force. So, whether it's developing leading-edge Internet products at HootSuite or designing better aircraft at Bombardier Inc., people working in organizations do have some sense of collective purpose. As Steve Jobs, the late cofounder of Apple Inc. and Pixar Animation Studios, once said: "A company is one of humanity's most amazing inventions. It's totally abstract. Sure, you have to build something with bricks and mortar to put the people in, but basically a company is this abstract construct we've invented, and it's incredibly powerful."[5]

HISTORICAL FOUNDATIONS OF ORGANIZATIONAL BEHAVIOUR

Organizational behaviour emerged as a distinct field around the early 1940s, but organizations have been studied by experts in other fields for many centuries. The Greek philosopher Plato wrote about the essence of leadership. Around the same time, the Chinese philosopher Confucius extolled the virtues of ethics and leadership. In 1776, Adam Smith discussed the benefits of job specialization and division of labour. One hundred years later, German sociologist Max Weber wrote about rational organizations, the work ethic, and charismatic leadership. Soon after, industrial engineer Frederick Winslow Taylor proposed systematic ways to organize work processes and motivate employees through goal setting and rewards.[6]

In the early 1900s, before he became Canada's longest serving prime minister, William Lyon Mackenzie King was a pioneering consultant who wrote about the need for more worker involvement and organizational reward systems. In the 1930s, Harvard professor Elton Mayo and his colleagues countered prevailing OB practices that focused on changes to working conditions and job duties, by establishing the "human relations" school of management. Their theories emphasized the study of employee attitudes and informal group dynamics in the workplace. Also during that time, Mary Parker Follett offered new ways of thinking about constructive conflict, team dynamics, power, and leadership. Chester Barnard, another OB pioneer and respected executive, wrote insightful views regarding organizational communication, coordination, leadership and authority, organizations as open systems, and team dynamics.[7] This brief historical tour indicates that OB has been around for a long time; it just wasn't organized into a unified discipline until around World War II.

WHY STUDY ORGANIZATIONAL BEHAVIOUR?

Organizational behaviour instructors face a challenge: Students who have not yet begun their careers tend to value courses related to specific jobs, such as accounting and marketing.[8] However, OB doesn't have a specific career path—there is no "vice president of OB"—so students sometimes have difficulty recognizing the future value that OB knowledge can offer.

Elton Mayo (left), Fritz Roethlisberger (right), and others at Harvard University reported that employee attitudes, formal team dynamics, informal groups, and supervisor leadership style influenced employee performance and well-being. This countered the dominant view, which attempted to improve work efficiency by changing working conditions and job duties. Mayo's human relations approach laid the foundation for the field of organizational behaviour as we know it today.[11]

HBS Archives Photograph Collection: Faculty and Staff. Baker Library Historical Collections. Harvard Business School.

Meanwhile, students with several years of work experience identify OB as one of the most important courses. Why? Because they have learned through experience that OB *does make a difference* to one's career success. OB helps us to make sense of and predict the world in which we live.[9] We use OB theories to question our personal beliefs and assumptions and to adopt more evidence-based models of workplace behaviour.

But probably the greatest value of OB knowledge is that it helps us to get things done in the workplace.[10] By definition, organizations are people who work together to accomplish things, so we need a toolkit of knowledge and skills to work successfully with others. Building a high-performance team, motivating co workers, handling workplace conflicts, influencing your boss, and changing employee behaviour are just a few of the areas of knowledge and skills offered in organizational behaviour. No matter what career path you choose, you'll find that OB concepts play an important role in performing your job and working more effectively within organizations.

McGraw Hill Education connect

Is OB just common sense? See page **24** or visit **connect.mcgrawhill.com** to assess the extent to which your personal theories about what goes on in organizations are consistent with current organizational behaviour evidence.

Organizational Behaviour is for Everyone A common misunderstanding is that organizational behaviour is for managers. Although this knowledge is critical for effective management, this book pioneered the broader view that OB is valuable for everyone who works in and around organizations. Whether you are a software engineer, customer service representative, foreign exchange analyst, or chief executive officer, you need to understand and apply the many organizational behaviour topics that are discussed in this book. Most organizations will probably always have managers, and this book recognizes the relevance of OB knowledge in these vital roles. But all employees need OB knowledge as the work environment increasingly expects us to be self-motivated and to work effectively with coworkers without management intervention. In the words of one forward-thinking OB writer more than four decades ago: Everyone is a manager.[12]

OB and the Bottom Line Up to this point, our answer to the question "Why study OB?" has focused on how organizational behaviour knowledge benefits you as an individual. However, OB knowledge is just as important for the organization's financial health. HootSuite illustrates this point: its success has been driven by visionary leadership, teamwork, a creative culture, and many other organizational behaviour practices.

Numerous studies have reported that OB practices are powerful predictors of the organization's survival and success.[13] One investigation found that hospitals with higher levels of specific OB activities (e.g., training, staff involvement, reward and recognition) have lower patient mortality rates. Another study found that companies receiving "the best place to work" awards have significantly higher financial and long-term stock market performance. Companies with higher levels of employee engagement have significantly higher sales and profitability (see Chapter 5).

The bottom-line value of organizational behaviour is also supported by Canadian and international research into the best predictors of investment portfolio performance. These investigations suggest that specific OB characteristics (leadership, employee attitudes, performance-based rewards, employee development, work-life balance, and so on) are important "positive screens" for selecting companies with the highest and most consistent long-term investment gains. For example, a leading Canadian investment analyst recently identified the top five factors to consider when deciding whether to invest in a company. First on his list is whether the company's "management team has great prior experience and a vested interest in their company."[14]

Perspectives of Organizational Effectiveness

LO2

Almost all organizational behaviour theories have the implicit or explicit objective of making organizations more effective.[15] In fact, **organizational effectiveness** is considered the "ultimate dependent variable" in organizational behaviour.[16] This means that organizational effectiveness is the outcome that most OB theories are ultimately trying to achieve. Many theories use different labels–organizational performance, success, goodness, health, competitiveness, excellence–but they are basically presenting models and recommendations that help organizations to be more effective.

organizational effectiveness A broad concept represented by several perspectives, including the organization's fit with the external environment, internal subsystems configuration for high performance, emphasis on organizational learning, and ability to satisfy the needs of key stakeholders.

Many years ago, OB experts thought the best indicator of a company's effectiveness is how well it achieved its stated objectives. According to this definition, Loblaw Companies Limited would be an effective organization if it meets or exceeds its annual sales and profit targets. Today, we know this isn't necessarily so. Any leadership team could set corporate goals that are easy to achieve, yet would put the organization out of business. These goals could also be left in the dust by competitors' more aggressive objectives.

Worse still, some goals might aim the organization in the wrong direction. Consider the following situation at a Canadian airline several years ago: The board gave the new CEO a mandate to reduce costs and dramatically improve profitability. The CEO accomplished these organizational goals by reducing the training budget and cancelling the purchase of new aircraft. Within a few years (after the CEO had taken a job elsewhere), the company was burdened by higher maintenance costs to keep the old planes flying safely and was losing customers to airlines with better-trained staff and more modern fleets. The airline never recovered and was eventually acquired by Air Canada. The CEO achieved the stated goals, but the company was ineffective in the long run.

This book takes the view that the best yardstick of organizational effectiveness is a composite of four perspectives: open systems, organizational learning, high-performance work practices, and stakeholders.[17] Organizations are effective when they have a good fit with their external environment, are learning organizations, have efficient and adaptive internal subsystems (i.e., high-performance work practices), and satisfy the needs of key stakeholders. Let's examine each of these perspectives in more detail.

open systems A perspective which holds that organizations depend on the external environment for resources, affect that environment through their output, and consist of internal subsystems that transform inputs to outputs.

OPEN SYSTEMS PERSPECTIVE

The **open systems** perspective of organizational effectiveness is one of the earliest and well entrenched ways of thinking about organizations.[18] Indeed, the other major organizational effectiveness perspectives might be considered detailed extensions of the open systems model. This perspective views organizations as complex organisms that "live" within an external environment, rather like the illustration in Exhibit 1.1. The word *open* describes this permeable relationship, whereas *closed systems* operate without dependence on or interaction with an external environment.

As open systems, organizations depend on the external environment for resources, including raw materials, job applicants, financial resources, information, and equipment. The external environment also consists of rules and expectations, such as laws and cultural norms, that place demands on how organizations should operate. Some environmental resources (e.g., raw materials) are transformed into outputs that are exported to the external environment, whereas other resources (e.g., job applicants, equipment) become subsystems in the transformation process.

Inside the organization are numerous subsystems, such as departments, teams, informal groups, work processes, technological configurations, and other elements. Many of these subsystems are also systems with their own subsystems.[19] For example, the Canadian Tire store in Belleville, Ontario, is a subsystem of the Canadian Tire chain, but the Belleville store is also a system with its own subsystems of departments, teams, and work processes. An organization's subsystems are dependent on each other as they transform inputs into outputs. Some outputs (e.g., products, services, community support) may be valued by the external environment, whereas other outputs (e.g., employee layoffs, pollution) are undesirable by-products that may have adverse effects on the environment and the organization's relationship with that environment. Throughout this process, organizations receive feedback from the external environment regarding the value of their outputs and the availability of future inputs.

Organization-Environment Fit According to the open systems perspective, organizations are effective when they maintain a good "fit" with their external environment.[20] Good fit exists when the organization's inputs, processes, and outputs are aligned with the needs and expectations of the external environment. There are three ways that companies maintain a good environmental fit. The most common strategy to fit with the external environment is to change the company's products and services as well as how those outputs are produced. Zara, the world's largest fashion retailer, relies on continuous adaptation to maintain a good fit with its highly volatile external environment. As Global Connections 1.1 describes, the Spanish company receives continuous feedback from each of its 6,000 stores, and then uses that feedback along with ongoing creativity to rapidly design, manufacture, and deliver new styles. In contrast, fashion retailers with a poor environmental fit are overstocked with products that few people want to buy and respond slowly to changing preferences.

EXHIBIT 1.1

Open Systems Perspective of Organizations

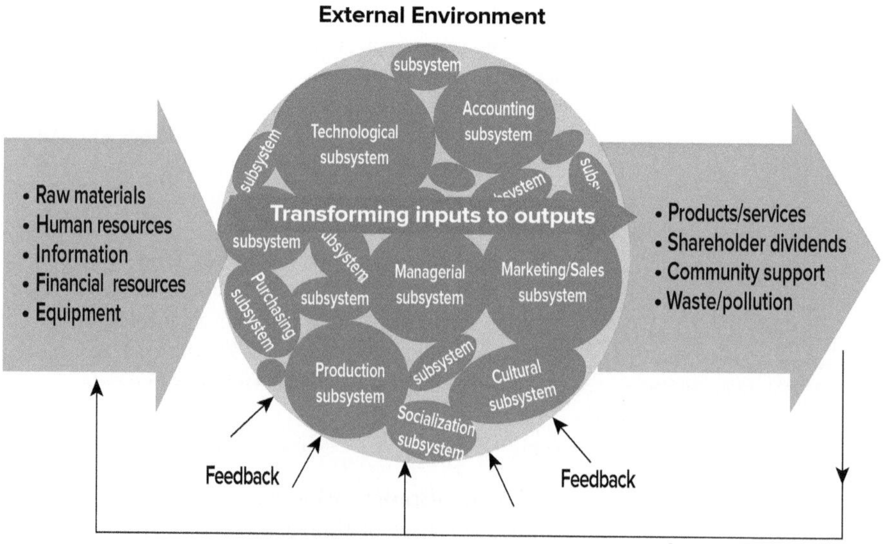

Global Connections 1.1:

ZARA'S OPEN SYSTEMS THINKING FOR FAST FASHION

As the world's largest clothing retailer, Zara thrives in one of the world's most volatile industries. What's their secret to success? The Spanish company has a business model that applies open systems thinking.

In the fashion industry, customer preferences change quickly and have limited predictability. Zara maintains a close fit with that turbulent environment by experimenting with numerous new styles, receiving almost immediate and continuous feedback about which ones are most popular, learning what minor adjustments would make the styles more appealing, and quickly producing and delivering new or revised styles to better fit current demand. In fact, Zara practically invented the notion of "fast fashion," whereby the company responds quickly to customer preferences and fashion trends. This contrasts with most other retailers, who produce a limited variety of styles, produce only two or three batches of new designs each year, and require up to six months for those designs to show up in stores.

The nucleus of this open systems process is an aircraft hangar-sized room at Zara's headquarters in A Coruña, Spain (shown in this photo). In the centre of the room is a long line of facing desks where regional managers from two dozen countries are in daily contact with each of the company's 6,000 stores in 86 countries. Equally important, sales staff are trained to ask customers about why they bought a garment or how a garment could be designed more to their liking. These customer comments are then quickly reported back to headquarters. On both sides of the room are designers and other staff who use this continuous store feedback to revise existing styles as well as spark ideas for new designs.

Suppose several regional managers receive reports that the new line of women's white jackets is selling slowly; however, customers have told sales staff they would buy that style of jacket in a cream-colour with silkier fabric. Designers receive this information and quickly get to work designing a cream-coloured jacket with the preferred material. Some regional differences exist, of course, but Zara reports that most of its products are in demand globally. Zara also produces limited stock of a large variety of designs. This allows the company to sample a wider array of market preferences while minimizing the problem of having too much inventory. In fact, knowing that Zara's products are constantly changing attracts customers back to the stores more often.

Rapid and rich feedback from stores is vital, but Zara also thrives on its quick response to that feedback. Most fashion retailers rely on independent manufacturers in distant countries who require several months lead time to produce a garment. Zara uses these low-cost manufacturers to some extent, but half of its garments are made "in proximity" from nearby Spanish companies as well as in Portugal, Morocco, and Turkey. Nearby manufacturing costs more, but often takes less than three weeks for a new design from these nearby sites to arrive in the stores, which receive new stock twice each week.[21]

Zara, the Spanish fashion retail giant, relies on an open systems perspective to achieve success in one of the world's most volatile industries.

A second way that organizations maintain a good fit is actively managing their external environment. Many firms manage their environment through marketing, which attempts to increase demand for their products or services. Others gain exclusive rights to particular resources (e.g., exclusive rights to sell a known brand) or restrict competitor access to valued resources. Still others lobby for legislation that strengthens their position in the marketplace or try to delay legislation that would disrupt their business activities.

The third way organizations maintain a healthy fit is to change their business or market location. In other words, if the external environment is too challenging, organizations move to a new environment that can sustain them. For example, IBM exited the computer products industry when senior executives (correctly) predicted that selling computers would be less prosperous than the rapidly growing technology services business.

Internal Subsystems Effectiveness According to the open systems perspective, an organization's effectiveness isn't just its fit with the external environment. Effectiveness is also how well the company internally transforms inputs into outputs. The most common

organizational efficiency The amount of outputs relative to inputs in the organization's transformation process.

indicator of this internal transformation process is **organizational efficiency** (also called *productivity*), which is the ratio of inputs to outputs.[22] Companies that produce more goods or services with less labour, materials, and energy are more efficient. At the same time, organizations need transformation processes that are *adaptive* and *innovative*. [23] Adaptivity makes the organization's transformation process more responsive to changing conditions and customer needs. Innovation enables the company to design work processes that are superior to what competitors can offer. Zara (described in Global Connections 1.1) has a highly adaptive transformation process because it is able to continuously revise styles in line with customer preferences. At the same time, Zara is highly efficient because new fashion ideas become products on store racks within a few weeks (whereas most fashion companies require several months).

An important feature of effective organizations is that their internal subsystems coordinate well with each other.[24] This coordination becomes a significant challenge as companies grow because they develop increasingly complex subsystems. This complexity increases the risk that information will get lost, ideas and resources are hoarded, messages are misinterpreted, and rewards are distributed unfairly. Subsystems are also interconnected, so small changes to work practice in one subsystem may ripple through the organization and undermine the effectiveness of other subsystems. Consequently, organizations need to maintain an efficient and adaptable transformation process through work procedures, informal communication, and other coordinating mechanisms (see Chapter 13).

ORGANIZATIONAL LEARNING PERSPECTIVE

The open systems perspective has traditionally focused on physical resources that enter the organization and are processed into physical goods (outputs). This was representative of the industrial economy, but at HootSuite and many other companies knowledge is by far the most important input. Even in companies that produce physical products, knowledge is a key ingredient to success.[25] The **organizational learning** perspective takes the view that effective organizations find ways to acquire, share, use, and store knowledge. These processes build the organization's stock of knowledge, known as its **intellectual capital.**

organizational learning A perspective which holds that organizational effectiveness depends on the organization's capacity to acquire, share, use, and store valuable knowledge.

intellectual capital A company's stock of knowledge, including human capital, structural capital, and relationship capital.

Intellectual capital exists in three forms: human capital, structural capital, and relationship capital.[26] **Human capital** refers to the knowledge, skills, and abilities that employees carry around in their heads. Human capital is a competitive advantage because it is valuable, rare, difficult to imitate, and nonsubstitutable.[27] Specifically, human capital is valuable because employees are essential for the organization's survival and success. It is also rare and difficult to imitate, meaning that talented people are difficult to find and it is costly and challenging for competitors to duplicate another firm's human capital. Finally, human capital is nonsubstitutable because it cannot be easily replaced by technology.

human capital The stock of knowledge, skills, and abilities among employees that provide economic value to the organization.

In spite of its competitive advantage, human capital is a huge risk for most organizations. Employees remove valuable knowledge when they leave, which makes the company less effective.[28] "Ninety-five percent of my assets drive out the gate every evening," says Jim Goodnight, CEO of statistical software developer SAS Institute, Inc. "As such, it's my job to maintain a work environment that keeps those people coming back every morning. The creativity they bring to SAS is a competitive advantage for us."[29]

Fortunately, even if every employee left the organization, some intellectual capital remains as structural capital. **Structural capital** includes the knowledge captured and retained in an organization's systems and structures, such as the documentation of work procedures and the physical layout of the production line.[30] Structural capital also includes the organization's finished products because knowledge can be extracted by taking them apart to discover how they work and are constructed (i.e., reverse engineering). The third form of intellectual capital is **relationship capital,** which is the value derived from an organization's relationships with customers, suppliers, and others who provide added mutual value for the organization. It includes the organization's goodwill, brand image, and combination of relationships that organizational members have with people outside the organization.[31]

structural capital Knowledge embedded in an organization's systems and structures.

relationship capital The value derived from an organization's relationships with customers, suppliers, and others.

An organization's intellectual capital develops and is maintained through the four organizational learning processes shown in Exhibit 1.2: acquiring, sharing, using, and storing knowledge.[32]

EXHIBIT 1.2

Four Organizational Learning Processes

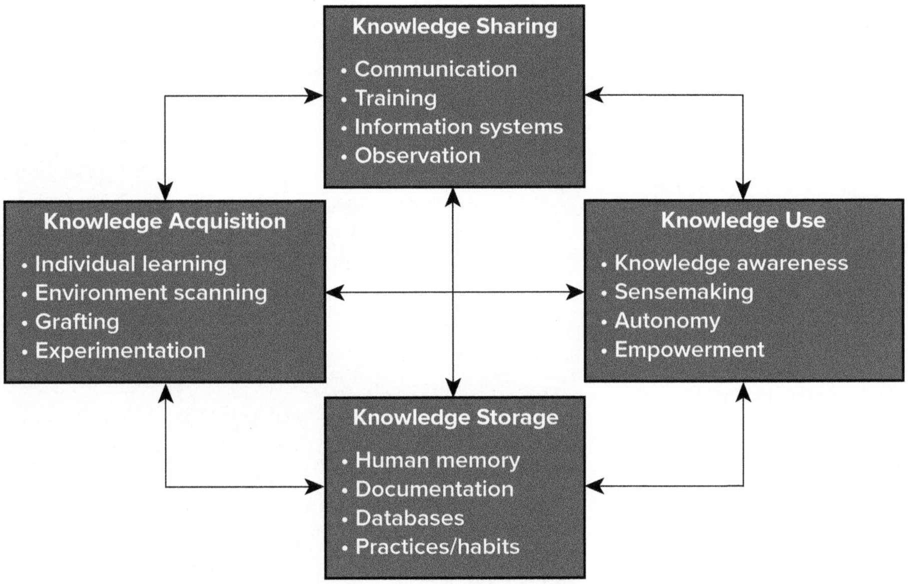

Knowledge Acquisition Knowledge acquisition includes extracting information and ideas from the external environment as well as through insight. HootSuite, the social media technology company described in the opening case study, achieves this by actively recruiting talented people and buying entire companies (called *grafting*). It also acquires knowledge through experimentation–generating new ideas and products through creative discovery and testing. A third knowledge acquisition strategy is environmental scanning, such as actively monitoring customer trends and competitor activities. A fourth strategy is individual learning, such as when employees acquire formal training from sources outside the organization.

Knowledge Sharing Knowledge sharing refers to distributing knowledge throughout the organization. This mainly occurs through communication with and learning from co-workers (training, observation, etc.). Research suggests that companies encourage informal communication through their organizational structure, physical work space, corporate culture, and social activities.[33] The opening case study described several of these practices at HootSuite. Company intranets and digital information repositories also support knowledge sharing.

Knowledge Use The competitive advantage of knowledge ultimately comes from using it in ways that add value to the organization and its stakeholders. To do this, employees must be aware that the knowledge exists, be able to locate it, and have enough freedom to apply it. This requires a culture that encourages experimentation and open communications, and recognizes that mistakes are part of that process.

Knowledge Storage and Organizational Memory Knowledge storage is the process of holding knowledge for later retrieval. Stored knowledge, often called *organizational memory*, includes knowledge that employees recall as well as knowledge embedded in the organization's systems and structures.[34] One way of retaining the organization's memory is motivating employees to remain with the company. HootSuite and other progressive businesses achieve this by introducing more appealing work practices, such as developmental coaching, pleasant work environments, and jobs that offer more autonomy. A second organizational memory strategy is to systematically transfer knowledge to other employees. This occurs when newcomers apprentice with skilled employees, thereby acquiring knowledge that is not documented. A third strategy is to document knowledge that was previously hidden in the minds of individual employees. For instance, Reliance Industries, India's largest

Courtesy of the Duha Group.

Winnipeg-based Duha Group is a role model for organizational learning. The global colour marketing and manufacturing firm practises knowledge acquisition by learning from other companies, encouraging staff to discover better production methods, and enabling customers to communicate directly with the Duha Group's 700 employees worldwide using social network technologies. In fact, the recent shift to communicating through social media has dramatically improved "how the information was getting from the customer to the people who needed it, and then back to the customer," says Global Operations Excellence Coordinator Rick Duha. Social network technology also supports knowledge sharing within the company, as does formal in-house training, employee-led lunch-and-learn sessions, and informal mentoring.[35]

business enterprise, encourages employees to write about their successes and failures through a special intranet knowledge portal. One of these reports alone provided information that later prevented a costly plant shutdown.[36]

One last point about the organizational learning perspective: effective organizations not only learn; they also unlearn routines and patterns of behaviour that are no longer appropriate.[37] Unlearning removes knowledge that no longer adds value and, in fact, may undermine the organization's effectiveness. Some forms of unlearning involve replacing dysfunctional policies, procedures, and routines. Other forms of unlearning erase attitudes, beliefs, and assumptions. BlackBerry (formerly Research in Motion) held strong beliefs and assumptions about phones with physical keypads, which resulted in their slow response to smartphones and tablets with touchscreen technology. Organizational unlearning is particularly important for organizational change, which we discuss in Chapter 15.

HIGH-PERFORMANCE WORK PRACTICES (HPWP) PERSPECTIVE

The open systems perspective states that successful companies are efficient and adaptive at transforming inputs into outputs. However, the open systems perspective does not offer guidance about specific subsystem characteristics or organizational practices that make the transformation process more effective. Consequently, an entire field of research has blossomed around the objective of determining specific "bundles" of **high-performance work practices (HPWP)** that better enable companies to transform inputs into outputs through human capital.[38]

high-performance work practices (HPWP) A perspective which holds that effective organizations incorporate several workplace practices that leverage the potential of human capital.

The HPWP perspective is founded on the belief that human capital–the knowledge, skills, and abilities that employees possess–is an important source of competitive advantage for organizations.[39] This is similar to the organizational learning perspective, except the HPWP perspective tries to figure out specific ways to generate the most value from this human capital. Researchers have investigated numerous potential high-performance work practices, but we will focus on the four discussed in most studies: employee involvement, job autonomy, competency development, and rewards for performance and competency development.[40] Each of these four work practices individually improves organizational effectiveness, but studies suggest that they have a stronger effect when bundled together.[41]

The first two factors–involving employees in decision making and giving them more autonomy over their work activities–tend to strengthen employee motivation as well as improve decisions, organizational responsiveness, and commitment to change. In high-performance workplaces, employee involvement and job autonomy often take the form of self-directed teams (see Chapter 8). The third factor, employee competency development, refers to recruiting, selecting, and training so employees are equipped with the relevant skills, knowledge, and other personal characteristics. The fourth high-performance work practice involves linking performance and skill development to various forms of financial and nonfinancial rewards valued by employees.

HPWP practices improve an organization's effectiveness in at least three ways.[42] First, as we mentioned earlier, these activities develop employee skills and knowledge (human capital), which improves work performance. Second, companies with superior human capital tend to adapt better to rapidly changing environments. Employees with a deep and broad skill set can perform diverse tasks and have more confidence to handle unfamiliar situations. A third explanation is that HPWP practices strengthen employee motivation and positive attitudes toward the employer. HPWPs represent the company's investment in its workforce, which motivates employees to reciprocate through greater effort in their jobs and assistance to co workers.

The HPWP perspective is still developing, but it already reveals important information about specific organizational practices that improve the input-output transformation process. Still, this perspective has been criticized for focusing on shareholder and customer needs at the expense of employee well-being.[43] This concern illustrates that the HPWP perspective offers an incomplete picture of organizational effectiveness. The remaining gaps are mostly filled by the stakeholder perspective of organizational effectiveness.

STAKEHOLDER PERSPECTIVE

stakeholders Individuals, groups, and other entities that affect, or are affected by, the organization's objectives and actions.

The three organizational effectiveness perspectives described so far mainly pay attention to processes and resources, yet they only minimally acknowledge the importance of relations with **stakeholders**. Stakeholders include anyone with a stake in the company–employees, shareholders, suppliers, labour unions, government, communities, consumer and environmental interest groups, and so on (see Exhibit 1.3).[44] The stakeholder perspective personalizes the open systems perspective; it identifies specific people and social entities in the external environment as well as within the organization (the internal environment). It is also consistent with the reality that stakeholder relations are dynamic; they can be negotiated and managed, not just taken as a fixed condition.[45] Organizations are more effective when they consider the needs and expectations of any individual group, or other entity that affects, or is affected by, the organization's objectives and actions. In other words, the stakeholder perspective requires organizational leaders and employees to understand, manage, and satisfy the interests of their stakeholders.[46]

Understanding, managing, and satisfying the interests of stakeholders is more challenging than it sounds because stakeholders have conflicting interests and organizations don't have the resources to satisfy every stakeholder to the fullest. Therefore, organizational leaders need to decide which groups receive higher and lower priority and resources.[47] There is some evidence that corporate leaders rely on their personal values to prioritize stakeholders. Another factor is how much power each stakeholder has over the organization. This makes sense when one considers that the most powerful stakeholders present the greatest threat and opportunity to the company's survival. Even so, organizations cannot ignore less powerful stakeholders because they may be important in the longer term. Also, ignoring less powerful stakeholders might violate the norms and standards of society, which would undermine relations with communities, government, and other powerful stakeholders.

values Relatively stable, evaluative beliefs that guide a person's preferences for outcomes or courses of action in a variety of situations.

Values, Ethics, and Corporate Social Responsibility This brings us to one of the key strengths of the stakeholder perspective, namely, that it incorporates values, ethics, and corporate social responsibility into the organizational effectiveness equation.[48] The stakeholder perspective states that to manage the interests of diverse stakeholders, leaders ultimately need to rely on their personal and organizational values for guidance. **Values** are

EXHIBIT 1.3

Organizational Stakeholders

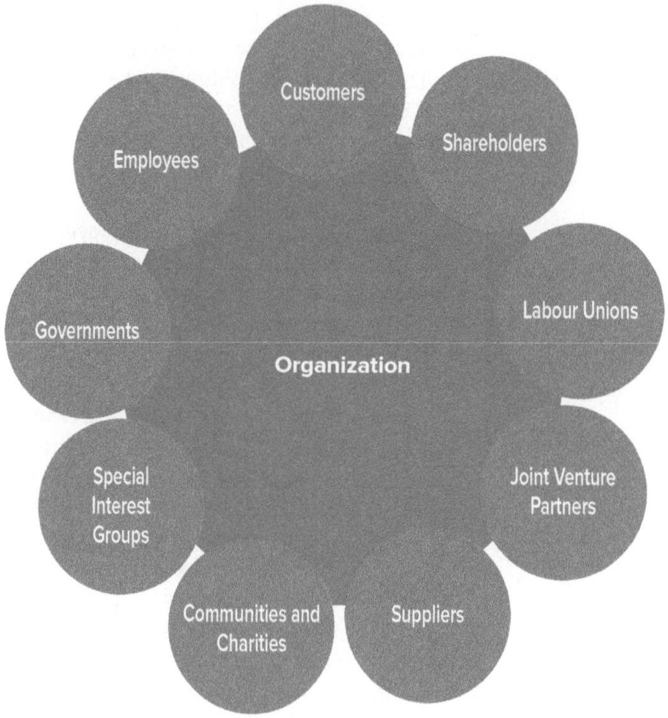

Note: This exhibit does not show the complete set of possible stakeholders.

relatively stable, evaluative beliefs that guide our preferences for outcomes or courses of action in a variety of situations.[49] Values help us to know what is right or wrong, or good or bad, in the world. Chapter 2 explains how values anchor our thoughts and to some extent motivate our actions. Although values exist within individuals, groups of people often hold similar values, so we tend to ascribe these *shared values* to the team, department, organization, profession, or entire society. For example, Chapter 14 discusses the importance and dynamics of organizational culture, which includes shared values across the company or within subgroups.

Many companies have adopted the values-driven organization model, whereby employee decisions and behaviour are guided by the company's espoused values rather than by expensive and often demoralizing command-and-control management (i.e., top-down decisions with close supervision of employees).[50] Vancity Savings, Canada's largest cooperative financial institution and the country's top ranked corporate citizen, has a clear set of dominant values that guide employee decisions and behaviour. "Our values shape everything we do at Vancity," says Vancity's website. "You'll see our values reflected in the outstanding service we deliver, in our innovative approach to investing and in the deeper level of accountability we maintain to our members and the greater community."[51]

As we see in the Vancity example, the stakeholder perspective's focus on values also brings ethics and corporate social responsibility into the organizational effectiveness equation. In fact, the stakeholder perspective emerged out of earlier writing on ethics and corporate social responsibility. **Ethics** refers to the study of moral principles or values that determine whether actions are right or wrong and outcomes are good or bad. We rely on our ethical values to determine "the right thing to do." Ethical behaviour is driven by the moral principles we use to make decisions. These moral principles represent fundamental values. According to one global survey, almost 80 percent of MBA students believe a well-run company operates according to its values and code of ethics.[52] Chapter 2 provides more detail about ethical principles and related influences on moral reasoning.

ethics The study of moral principles or values that determine whether actions are right or wrong and outcomes are good or bad.

corporate social responsibility (CSR) Organizational activities intended to benefit society and the environment beyond the firm's immediate financial interests or legal obligations.

Corporate social responsibility (CSR) consists of organizational activities intended to benefit society and the environment beyond the firm's immediate financial interests or legal obligations.[53] It is the view that companies have a contract with society, in which they must serve stakeholders beyond shareholders and customers. In some situations, the interests of the firm's shareholders should be secondary to those of other stakeholders.[54] As part of CSR, many

Courtesy of MTN.

MTN Group is the largest mobile (cell) telecommunications company in Africa and a leader in corporate social responsibility (CSR). Through its award-winning "21 Days of Y'ello Care" program, most of the company's 34,000 employees volunteer for specific CSR events held over three weeks each year. This photo shows a recent CSR initiative: painting schools and hospitals throughout the 21 African and Middle Eastern countries where MTN does business. Y'ello Care themes in other years included fighting against malaria, planting trees, reducing traffic accidents, and supporting orphanages.[55]

companies have adopted the triple-bottom-line philosophy: They try to support or "earn positive returns" in the economic, social, and environmental spheres of sustainability. Firms that adopt the triple bottom line aim to survive and be profitable in the marketplace (economic), but they also intend to maintain or improve conditions for society (social) as well as the physical environment.[56] Companies are particularly eager to become "greener," that is, minimizing any negative effect they have on the physical environment. This activity ranges from reducing and recycling waste in the production process to using goats to mow the lawn (which is one of the many environmental initiatives at Google).

Not everyone agrees that organizations need to cater to a wide variety of stakeholders. Many years ago, economist Milton Friedman pronounced that "there is one and only one social responsibility of business—to use its resources and engage in activities designed to increase its profits."[57] Friedman is highly respected for developing economic theory, but few writers take this extreme view today. Some argue that companies need to give shareholders first priority, but the effect of CSR on shareholders and company success is more complex than this simple advice. Indeed, 93 percent of Canadians believe that CSR should be as important to companies as profit and shareholder value; 78 percent of Canadians say they would leave their current job if they found a more environmentally friendly employer.[58] The emerging evidence is that companies with a positive CSR reputation tend to have better financial performance, more loyal employees (stronger organizational identification), and better relations with customers, job applicants, and other stakeholders.[59]

CONNECTING THE DOTS: AN INTEGRATIVE MODEL OF ORGANIZATIONAL BEHAVIOUR

Open systems, organizational learning, high-performance work practices, and stakeholders represent the four perspectives of organizational effectiveness. This is the ultimate dependent variable in organizational behaviour, so all other OB variables have a direct or indirect effect on overall effectiveness. This relationship between organizational effectiveness and other OB variables is shown in Exhibit 1.4. This diagram is an integrating roadmap for the field of organizational behaviour, and for the structure of this book. You might think of it as a meta-model, because Exhibit 1.4 highlights many concepts, each of which has its own explanatory models. For instance, you will learn about models of employee motivation in Chapter 5 and models of leadership in Chapter 12. Exhibit 1.4 gives you a bird's-eye view of the book and its various topics, to see how they fit together.

EXHIBIT 1.4

An Integrating Model of Organizational Behaviour

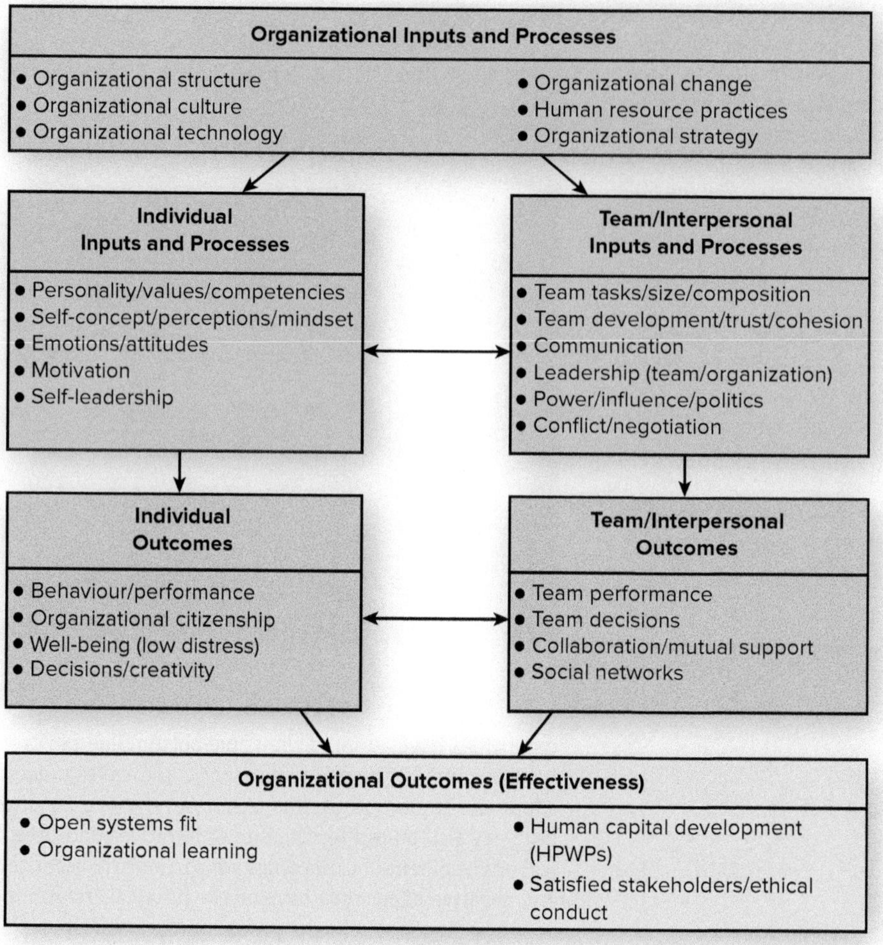

As Exhibit 1.4 illustrates, individual inputs and processes influence individual outcomes, which in turn have a direct effect on the organization's effectiveness. For example, how well organizations transform inputs to outputs and satisfy key stakeholders is dependent on how well employees perform their jobs and make logical and creative decisions. Individual inputs, processes, and outcomes are identified in the two left-side boxes of our integrating OB model and are the centre of attention in Part 2 of this book. After introducing a model of individual behaviour and results, we will learn about personality and values–two of the most important individual characteristics–and later examine various individual processes, such as self-concept, perceptions, emotions, attitudes, motivation, and self-leadership.

Part 3 of this book directs our attention to team and interpersonal inputs, processes, and outcomes. These topics are found in the two boxes on the right side of Exhibit 1.4. The chapter on team dynamics (Chapter 8) offers an integrative model for that specific topic, which shows how team inputs (i.e., team composition, size, and other team characteristics) influence team processes (team development, cohesion, and others), which then affect team performance and other outcomes. Later chapters in Part 3 examine specific interpersonal and team processes listed in Exhibit 1.4, including communication, power and influence, conflict, and leadership.

Notice in Exhibit 1.4 that team processes and outcomes affect individual processes and outcomes. For instance, an employee's personal well-being is partly affected by the mutual support he or she receives from team members and other coworkers. The opposite is also true; individual processes affect team and interpersonal dynamics in organizations. For example, we will learn that self-concept among individual team members influences the team's cohesion.

The top area of Exhibit 1.4 highlights the macro-level influence of organizational inputs and processes on both teams and individuals. These organizational-level variables are mainly discussed in Part 4, including organizational structure, organizational culture, and organizational change. However, we will also refer to human resource practices, information systems, and additional organization-level variables throughout this book where they have a known effect on individual, interpersonal, and team dynamics.

Contemporary Challenges for Organizations

LO3

A message threaded throughout the previous section on organizational effectiveness is that organizations are deeply affected by the external environment. Consequently, they need to maintain a good organization-environment fit by anticipating and adjusting to changes in society. The external environment is continuously changing, but some changes over the past decade and in the decade to come are more profound than others. These changes require corporate leaders and all other employees to make personal and organizational adjustments. In this section, we highlight three of the major challenges facing organizations: globalization, increasing workforce diversity, and emerging employment relationships.

GLOBALIZATION

Maja Baiocco was delighted when her employer, PricewaterhouseCoopers LLP, sent her on a two-year international assignment in Zurich. Baiocco, an asset management auditor in the accounting firm's Toronto office, welcomed the opportunity to gain global experience and boost her career. "This company (PwC) is global and opportunities are global, and I know that international experiences are important to expand my experience and open new opportunities for advancement," she says.[60] Maja Baiocco is developing her career in a world of increasing globalization. **Globalization** refers to economic, social, and cultural connectivity with people in other parts of the world. Organizations globalize when they actively participate in other countries and cultures. Although businesses have traded goods across borders for centuries, the degree of globalization today is unprecedented because information technology and transportation systems allow a much more intense level of connectivity and interdependence around the planet.[61]

globalization Economic, social, and cultural connectivity with people in other parts of the world.

Globalization offers numerous benefits to organizations in terms of larger markets, lower costs, and greater access to knowledge and innovation. At the same time, there is considerable debate about whether globalization benefits developing nations, and whether it is primarily responsible for increasing work intensification, as well as reducing job security and work-life balance in developed countries.[62]

Globalization is now well entrenched, so the most important issue in organizational behaviour is how corporate leaders and employees alike can lead and work effectively in this emerging reality[63] Throughout this book, we will refer to the effects of globalization on teamwork, diversity, cultural values, organizational structure, leadership, and other themes. Each topic highlights that globalization has brought more complexity to the workplace, but also more opportunities and potential benefits for individuals and organizations. Globalization requires additional knowledge and skills that we will also discuss in this book, such as emotional intelligence, a global mindset, nonverbal communication, and conflict handling.

INCREASING WORKFORCE DIVERSITY

In most Japanese corporations, the board of directors consists exclusively of older generation Japanese males. If the group has any diversity, it is whether the board member has an engineering or non-engineering education. Hitachi Chairman Takashi Kawamura recognized that this lack of diversity limited the conglomerate's potential. "Governance handled by Japanese men with homogenous thinking is no good," says Kawamura. "To be global is to bring diversity into the company's governance." Hitachi is in the process of diversifying its board, which now includes three foreign executives, including one female executive.[64]

Hitachi Chairman Takashi Kawamura is increasing the **surface-level diversity** of the conglomerate's board of directors. Surface-level diversity refers to the observable demographic and other overt differences among members of a group, such as their race, ethnicity, gender, age, and physical capabilities.[65] Surface-level diversity is increasing in many other parts of the world due to more open and less discriminatory immigration policies. For instance,

surface-level diversity The observable demographic or physiological differences in people, such as their race, ethnicity, gender, age, and physical disabilities.

Patty Baxter (centre) discovered that advertising sales at Metro Guide Publishing in Halifax, Nova Scotia, were falling, partly because her young sales staff (all under 35 years old) were communicating with clients almost completely by text message and email. Older salespeople produced more advertising sales because they were constantly talking with clients on the phone. Baxter solved the problem by retaining consultant Mary Jane Copps to coach the younger employees on using the phone for effective sales. Copps explains that younger employees are missing out on the power of voice conversation. "To build and expand relationships with our customers, potential customers, family and friends . . . we need to pick up the phone."[66]

Photo by Dean Casavechia

19 percent of Canadians belong to a "visible minority" group, up from 16 percent in 2006, 13 percent in 2001, and just 5 percent in 1981.[67]

deep-level diversity
Differences in the psychological characteristics of employees, including personalities, beliefs, values, and attitudes.

Diversity also includes differences in the psychological characteristics of employees, including personalities, beliefs, values, and attitudes. We can't directly see this **deep-level diversity,** but it is evident in a person's decisions, statements, and actions. A popular example is the apparent deep-level diversity across generations.[68] The Canadian workforce is currently almost equally divided into three working-age generations: 39 percent Baby Boomers (born from 1946 and 1964), 29 percent Generation X (born from 1965 to 1980), and 30 percent Millennials (also called Generation Y, born after 1980).[69]

Wild claims have been made about how much employees differ across these three groups, but more systematic research indicates that generational deep-level diversity is more subtle. In fact, some differences are due to age, not cohort (i.e., Boomers had many of the same attitudes as Millennials when they were that age).[70] One recent investigation of 23,000 Canadian undergraduate college and university students reported that, compared with the other groups, Millennials expect more rapid career advancement regarding promotions and pay increases.[71] These observations are consistent with other studies, which have found that Millennials are more self-confident, are more self-focused, and have less work centrality (i.e., work is less of a central life interest) when compared to Baby Boomers. Generation X employees typically average somewhere between these two cohorts.[72]

Consequences of Diversity Diversity presents both opportunities and challenges in organizations.[73] Diversity is an advantage because it provides a broader range of knowledge. Furthermore, teams with some forms of diversity (particularly occupational diversity) make better decisions on complex problems than do teams whose members have similar backgrounds. There is also some evidence that diversity award-winning companies have higher financial returns, at least in the short run.[74] This is consistent with anecdotal evidence from many corporate leaders, namely that having a diverse workforce improves customer service and creativity. "If you want to serve a diverse client base, you have to have a diverse workforce," says an executive at Royal Bank of Canada's wealth management group. "If you don't do diversity well, they (high net-worth clients) won't give you their money."[75]

Is workforce diversity a sound business proposition? Yes, but research indicates that the reasons are not clear-cut because most forms of diversity have both challenges and benefits.[76] Teams with diverse employees usually take longer to perform effectively because they experience numerous communication problems and create "faultlines" in informal group dynamics. Diversity is also a source of conflict, which can reduce information sharing and morale. But even with these challenges, companies need to make diversity a priority because surface-level diversity is a moral and legal imperative. Ethically, companies that offer an inclusive workplace are, in essence, making fair and just decisions regarding employment and the allocation of rewards. Fairness is a well-known predictor of employee loyalty and satisfaction.

EMERGING EMPLOYMENT RELATIONSHIPS

Combine globalization with increasing workforce diversity, then add in recent developments in information technology. The resulting concoction has created incredible changes in employment relationships. A few decades ago, most (although not all) employees in Canada and similar cultures would finish their workday after eight or nine hours and could separate their personal time from the workday. There were no smartphones or Internet connections to keep them tethered to work on a 24/7 schedule. Even business travel was more of an exception due to its high cost. Most competitors were located in the same country, so they had similar work practices and labour costs. Today, work hours are longer (although arguably less than 100 years ago), employees experience more work-related stress, and there is growing evidence that family and personal relations are suffering.

work–life balance The degree to which a person minimizes conflict between work and nonwork demands.

Little wonder that one of the most important employment issues over the past decade has been **work-life balance.** Work-life balance occurs when people are able to minimize conflict between their work and nonwork demands.[77] Most employees lack this balance because they spend too many hours each week performing or thinking about their job, whether at the workplace, at home, or on vacation. This focus on work leaves too little time to fulfil nonwork needs and obligations. Our discussion of work-related stress (Chapter 4) will examine work-life balance issues in more detail.

virtual work Work performed away from the traditional physical workplace by using information technology.

Another employment relationship trend is **virtual work,** whereby employees use information technology to perform their jobs away from the traditional physical workplace.[78] Some virtual work occurs when employees are connected to the office while travelling or at clients' offices. However, the most common form involves working at home rather than commuting to the office (called *telecommuting* or *teleworking*). A recent large-scale global survey revealed that only 8 percent of Canadian employees who have online access to their workplace actually telecommute on a frequent basis, compared to 17 percent of employees globally. Even if

OB by the NUMBERS

Global Work–Life Balance Index[79]

Based on interviews with more than 16,000 business respondents from the Regus global contacts database. This exhibit shows the Regus work–life balance index for each country listed, as well as globally (includes several countries not shown here). A higher score indicates that employees in that country experience better work–life balance. The index is standardized to 100 as the average country score in the first survey (in 2010).

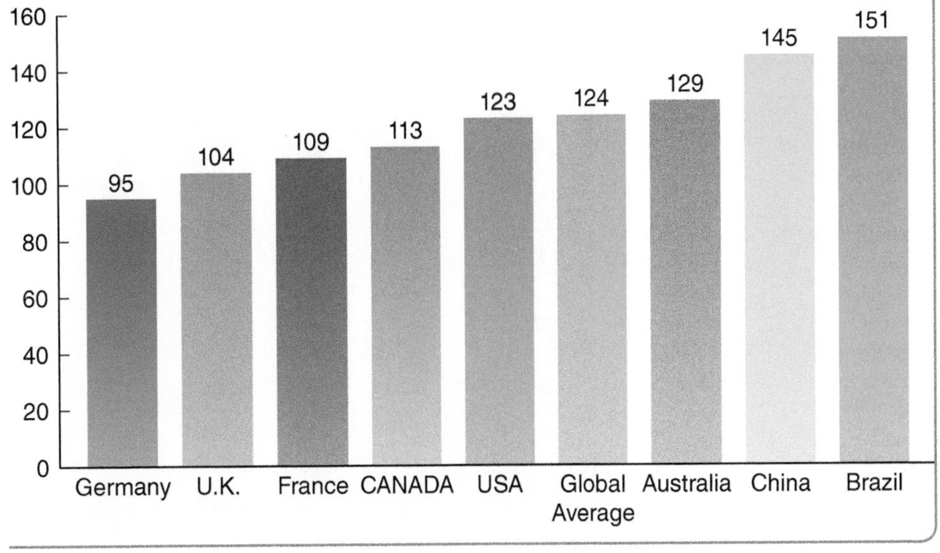

their employer gave them the opportunity, only 21 percent of Canadians say they would be very likely to telecommute, whereas 34 percent of employees globally would telecommute if given the opportunity. A recent survey of 500 business owners across Canada found that only 23 percent (most of them larger companies) offer telecommuting to any of their employees.[80]

connect

Are you a good telecommuter? Visit **connect.mcgrawhill.com** to assess how well you might adjust to telecommuting.

These recent surveys reveal that many Canadian employers have doubts about the benefits of virtual work. The evidence suggests that telecommuting offers many benefits for the organization and its employees, but it also presents several challenges. One of the most consistent observations is that telework is ranked as one of the most popular perks. It attracts job applicants, particularly the educated, tech-savvy younger generation. Telework also improves work-life balance for most people, mainly because they don't need to spend time commuting to another location. A study of 25,000 IBM employees found that female telecommuters with children were able to work 40 hours per week, whereas non-telecommuters could only manage 30 hours before feeling work-life balance tension.[81]

Telework can also improve employee productivity because employees experience less stress and tend to allocate some former commuting time to work activity. Another benefit is that employees remain productive when the weather or natural disasters block access to the office. For instance, when floods limited access to downtown Calgary, Telus Corp. employees in that city remained productive by working from home.

Telework also has environmental and financial benefits. Cisco Systems employees worldwide who telework avoid almost 50,000 metric tonnes of greenhouse gas emission. Telus expects telework to reap significant cost reductions in real estate costs because it has been able to reduce its office space by 25 percent in recent years. Telework also reduces employee costs. One Telus employee in Delta, B.C., recently estimated that she saves $650 each month in travel costs by working from home most days.[82]

Telecommuting also presents several challenges that may offset its benefits in some situations.[84] There is fairly consistent evidence that employees who telecommute most of the time experience more social isolation and less cohesion with their coworkers. To minimize these

A few years ago, Chris Keehn commuted for three hours, round trip, between his home and office at Deloitte LLC in downtown Chicago. Most days, his young daughter would be asleep when he left in the morning and when he returned home at night. The senior tax accountant solved this problem by becoming a teleworker four days each week. Working from home gives Keehn more time to take his daughter to school and attend her evening basketball games. Keehn even found that he communicates more often with his team. "I actually talk to them more now," he explains. "On the day I go into the office, I make sure I touch base with everyone."[83]

©ktadeo/Flickr.com

problems, many companies require employees to work at the office at least once or twice each week. Another issue is that some employees who cannot telework (as well as some who choose not to) feel that teleworking is unfair to them (i.e., teleworkers have more freedom and benefits). At the same time, at least one study reports that teleworkers also feel an unfair disadvantage, believing that employees on company premises receive more support and promotional opportunities. For this reason, virtual work arrangements are also more successful in organizations that evaluate employees by their performance outcomes rather than "face time" (i.e., face-to-face with the boss and coworkers).[85] Telecommuting's main benefit is work-life balance, but some studies have found that family relations suffer rather than improve if employees lack sufficient space and resources for a home office. Finally, telework is better suited to people who are self-motivated, organized, can work effectively with broadband and other technology, and have sufficient fulfillment of social needs elsewhere in their life.

Anchors of Organizational Behaviour Knowledge

LO4

Globalization, increasing workforce diversity, and emerging employment relationships are just a few of the trends that challenge organizations and make the field of organizational behaviour more relevant than ever before. To understand these and other topics, the field of organizational behaviour relies on a set of basic beliefs or knowledge structures (see Exhibit 1.5). These conceptual anchors represent the principles on which OB knowledge is developed and refined.[86]

THE SYSTEMATIC RESEARCH ANCHOR

A key feature of OB knowledge is that it should be based on systematic research, which typically involves forming research questions, systematically collecting data, and testing hypotheses against those data.[87] Appendix A at the end of this book provides a brief overview of these research methods. Systematic research investigation produces **evidence-based management,** which involves making decisions and taking actions based on this research evidence. It makes perfect sense, doesn't it, that management practice should be founded on the best available systematic knowledge? Yet many of us who study organizations using systematic methods are amazed at how often corporate leaders embrace fads, consulting models, and their own pet beliefs without bothering to find out if they actually work![88]

evidence-based management
The practice of making decisions and taking actions based on research evidence.

Corporate leaders and other decision makers have difficulty applying evidence-based management for a number of reasons. One reason is that they are bombarded with so many ideas from newspapers, books, consultant reports, and other sources that it is a challenge to figure out which ones are based on good evidence. Another problem is that good OB research is necessarily generic; it is rarely described in the context of a specific problem in a specific organization. Managers therefore have the difficult task of figuring out which theories are relevant to their unique situation.

EXHIBIT 1.5

Anchors of Organizational Behaviour Knowledge

Systematic research anchor	Study organizations using systematic research methods
Multidisciplinary anchor	Import knowledge from other disciplines, not just create its own knowledge
Contingency anchor	Recognize that the effectiveness of an action may depend on the situation
Multiple levels of analysis anchor	Understand OB events from three levels of analysis: individual, team, organization

Debating Point:
IS THERE ENOUGH EVIDENCE TO SUPPORT EVIDENCE-BASED MANAGEMENT?

One of the core anchors of organizational behaviour is that knowledge must be built on a solid foundation of scientifically-based research. This evidence-based management (EBM) approach particularly embraces scientific methods—relevant measures, appropriate sampling, systematic experimental design, and the like—because they produce more valid theories to guide management decisions. Scholars also advise that managers need to become more aware of these well-studied cause–effect principles, and to use diagnostic tools (such as surveys and checklists) to effectively apply those principles in the workplace. Invariably, supporters of the evidence-based management movement contrast this systematic approach with reliance on management fads, hyped consulting, and untested personal mental models.

It seems obvious that we should rely on good evidence rather than bad evidence (or no evidence at all) to make good decisions in the workplace. Yet, there is another side to this debate.[89] The question isn't whether good evidence is valuable; it is about the meaning of "good evidence." One concern is that scholars might be advocating an interpretation of good evidence that is far too narrow. They typically limit evidence to empirical research and consider qualitative information as "anecdotal." Albert Einstein tried to avoid this questionable view by keeping the following message framed on his wall: "Not everything that can be counted counts, and not everything that counts can be counted."

Another concern is that managers don't view organizational research as particularly relevant to the issues they face.[90] This partly occurs because reviewers usually set high standards for studies with uncontaminated, quantifiable measures in environments that control for other factors. But managers do not operate in these pristine conditions. Their world is much more complex with more obscure indicators of key variables. One indicator of this research–practice gap is that most organizational studies are correlational surveys whereas managers typically require knowledge of behavioural interventions. Only about 2 percent of organizational studies are real-world interventions.[91]

A third critique of the EBM movement is that the systematic elements of organizational research studies (e.g., sample size, measurement reliability, advanced data analysis methods) sometimes mask other potentially serious faults. Cross-cultural studies, for instance, often use college student samples to represent an entire culture. Lab studies with students assume they replicate workplace conditions without considering substantial differences in skills and team dynamics between the two settings. Indeed, some meta-analyzes report substantially different results of studies using students versus employees. Finally, even if the published research is valid, it is usually biased because studies with nonsignificant results are much less likely to be published.

A third reason why organizational leaders accept fads and other knowledge that lacks sufficient evidence is that consultants and popular book writers are rewarded for marketing their concepts and theories, not for testing to see if they actually work. Indeed, some management concepts have become popular (some have even found their way into OB textbooks!) because of heavy marketing, not because of any evidence that they are valid. Finally, as we will learn in Chapter 3, people form perceptions and beliefs quickly and tend to ignore evidence that their beliefs are inaccurate.

OB experts have proposed a few simple suggestions to create a more evidence-based organization.[92] First, be skeptical of hype, which is apparent when so-called experts say the idea is "new," "revolutionary," and "proven." In reality, most management ideas are adaptations, evolutionary, and never proven (science can disprove, but never prove; it can only find evidence to support a practice). Second, the company should embrace collective expertise rather than rely on charismatic stars and management gurus. Third, stories provide useful illustrations and possibly preliminary evidence of a useful practice, but they should never become the main foundation to support management action. Instead, rely on more systematic investigation with a larger sample. Finally, take a critical and neutral approach to popular trends and ideologies. Executives tend to get caught up in what their counterparts at other companies are doing without determining the validity or relevance of those trendy practices to their organization.

THE MULTIDISCIPLINARY ANCHOR

Another organizational behaviour anchor is that the field should welcome theories and knowledge in other disciplines, not just from its own isolated research base. For instance, psychological research has aided our understanding of individual and interpersonal behaviour. Sociologists have contributed to our knowledge of team dynamics, organizational socialization, organizational power, and other aspects of the social system. OB knowledge has also benefited from knowledge in emerging fields such as communications, marketing, and information systems. This theory borrowing from other disciplines is inevitable. Organizations have central roles in society, so they are the subject of many social sciences. Furthermore, organizations consist of people who interact with each other, so there is an inherent intersection between OB and most disciplines that study human beings.

Borrowing theories from other disciplines has helped the field of OB to nurture a diversity of knowledge and perspectives about organizations, but there are a few concerns.[93] One issue is whether OB suffers from a "trade deficit"–importing far more knowledge from other disciplines than is exported to other disciplines. By relying on theories developed in other fields, OB knowledge necessarily lags rather than leads in knowledge production. In contrast, OB-bred theories allow researchers to concentrate on the quality and usefulness of the theory.

Finally, heavy reliance on theories borrowed from other disciplines may leave OB vulnerable to a lack of common identity. The field could potentially become a place for researchers who are raised in and mainly identify with the other disciplines (psychology, sociology, and so on) rather than with organizational behaviour. The lack of identification as an "OB scholar" might further challenge the field's ability to develop its own theory and may weaken its focus on practical relevance.

THE CONTINGENCY ANCHOR

People and their work environments are complex, and the field of organizational behaviour recognizes this by stating that a particular action may have different consequences in different situations. In other words, no single solution is best all of the time.[94] Of course, it would be so much simpler if we could rely on "one best way" theories, in which a particular concept or practice has the same results in every situation. OB experts do search for simpler theories, but they also remain skeptical about sure-fire recommendations; an exception is somewhere around the corner. Thus, when faced with a particular problem or opportunity, we need to understand and diagnose the situation and select the strategy most appropriate *under those conditions.*[95]

THE MULTIPLE LEVELS OF ANALYSIS ANCHOR

Earlier in this chapter, we introduced an integrating model of organizational behaviour (Exhibit 1.4). Within that model were three distinct groups of variables represented by different sections or parts of this book: individual-level, team-level (including interpersonal relations), and organizational-level variables. The field of OB recognizes that what goes on in organizations can be placed into these three levels of analysis. In fact, some of the advanced empirical research currently being conducted carefully identifies the appropriate level of analysis for each variable in the study and then measures them at that level of analysis. For example, team norms and cohesion are measured as a team variable, not as a characteristic of individuals within each team.

Although OB research and writing pegs each variable within one of these levels of analysis, most variables are understood best by thinking of them from all three levels of analysis.[96] For instance, communication is located in this book as a team (interpersonal) process, but it also includes individual and organizational processes. Therefore, you should try to think about each OB topic at the individual, team, and organizational levels, not just at one of these levels.

The Journey Begins

This chapter gives you some background about the field of organizational behaviour. But it's only the beginning of our journey. Throughout this book, we will challenge you to learn new ways of thinking about how people work in and around organizations. We begin this process in Chapter 2 by presenting a basic model of individual behaviour, then introducing over the next few chapters various stable and mercurial characteristics of individuals that relate to elements of the individual behaviour model. Next, this book moves to the team level of analysis. We examine a model of team effectiveness and specific features of high-performance teams. We also look at decision making and creativity, communication, power and influence, conflict, and leadership. Finally, we shift our focus to the organizational level of analysis, where the topics of organizational structure, organizational culture, and organizational change are examined in detail.

Chapter Summary

LO1 Define organizational behaviour and organizations, and discuss the importance of this field of inquiry.

Organizational behaviour is the study of what people think, feel, and do in and around organizations. Organizations are groups of people who work interdependently toward some purpose. OB theories help people to (a) make sense of the workplace, (b) question and rebuild their personal mental models, and (c) get things done in organizations. OB knowledge is for everyone, not just managers. OB knowledge is just as important for the organization's financial health.

LO2 Compare and contrast the four current perspectives of organizational effectiveness.

The open systems perspective views organizations as complex organisms that "live" within an external environment. They depend on the external environment for resources, then use organizational subsystems to transform those resources into outputs that are returned to the environment. Organizations receive feedback from the external environment to maintain a good "fit" with that environment. Fit occurs by adapting to the environment, managing the environment, or moving to another environment. According to the organizational learning perspective, organizational effectiveness depends on the organization's capacity to acquire, share, use, and store valuable knowledge. Intellectual capital consists of human capital, structural capital, and relationship capital. Knowledge is retained in the organizational memory; companies also selectively unlearn.

The high-performance work practices (HPWP) perspective identifies a bundle of systems and structures to leverage workforce potential. The most widely identified HPWPs are employee involvement, job autonomy, developing employee competencies, and performance/skill-based rewards. HPWPs improve organizational effectiveness by building human capital, increasing adaptability, and strengthening employee motivation and attitudes. The stakeholder perspective states that leaders manage the interests of diverse stakeholders by relying on their personal and organizational values for guidance. Ethics and corporate social responsibility (CSR) are natural variations of values-based organizations because they rely on values to guide the most appropriate decisions involving stakeholders. CSR consists of organizational activities intended to benefit society and the environment beyond the firm's immediate financial interests or legal obligations.

LO3 Debate the organizational opportunities and challenges of globalization, workforce diversity, and emerging employment relationships.

Globalization, which refers to various forms of connectivity with people in other parts of the world, has several economic and social benefits, but it may also be responsible for work intensification, and reduced job security and work-life balance. Workforce diversity is apparent at both the surface level (observable demographic and other overt differences in people) and deep level (differences in personalities, beliefs, values, and attitudes). There is some evidence of deep-level diversity across generational cohorts. Diversity may be a competitive advantage by improving decision making and team performance on complex tasks, yet it also brings numerous challenges such as dysfunctional team conflict and lower team performance. One emerging employment relationship trend is the call for more work-life balance (minimizing conflict between work and nonwork demands). Another employment trend is virtual work, particularly working from home (telework). Working from home potentially increases employee productivity and reduces employee stress, but it may also lead to social isolation, reduced promotion opportunities, and tension in family relations.

LO4 Discuss the anchors on which organizational behaviour knowledge is based.

The multidisciplinary anchor states that the field should develop from knowledge in other disciplines (e.g., psychology, sociology, economics), not just from its own isolated research base. The systematic research anchor states that OB knowledge should be based on systematic research, which is consistent with evidence-based management. The contingency anchor states that OB theories generally need to consider that there will be different consequences in different situations. The multiple levels of analysis anchor states that OB topics may be viewed from the individual, team, and organization levels of analysis.

Key Terms

corporate social responsibility (CSR), p. 12
deep-level diversity, p. 16
ethics, p. 12
evidence-based management, p. 19
globalization, p. 15
high-performance work practices (HPWP), p. 10
human capital, p. 8
intellectual capital, p. 8
open systems, p. 5
organizational behaviour (OB), p. 2
organizational effectiveness, p. 5
organizational efficiency, p. 8
organizational learning, p. 8
organizations, p. 2
relationship capital, p. 8
stakeholders, p. 11
structural capital, p. 8
surface-level diversity, p. 15
values, p. 12
virtual work, p. 17
work-life balance, p. 17

Critical-Thinking Questions

1. A friend suggests that organizational behaviour courses are useful only to people in management careers. Discuss the accuracy of your friend's statement.
2. A young college or university student from Canada is interested in doing international business across China, India, Brazil, and Russia. Discuss how the knowledge of OB can be useful to the student.
3. After hearing a seminar on organizational learning, a mining company executive argues that this perspective is relevant to software and other knowledge businesses, but it ignores the fact that mining companies cannot rely on knowledge alone to stay in business. They also need physical capital (such as extracting and ore-processing equipment) and land (where the minerals are located). In fact, these two may be more important than what employees carry around in their heads. Evaluate the mining executive's comments.
4. It is said that the CEO and other corporate leaders are keepers of the organization's memory. Please discuss this.
5. A common refrain among executives is "People are our most important asset." Relate this statement to any two of the four perspectives of organizational effectiveness presented in this chapter. Does this statement apply better to some perspectives than to others? Why or why not?
6. Corporate social responsibility is one of the hottest issues in corporate boardrooms these days, partly because it is becoming increasingly important to employees and other stakeholders. In your opinion, why have stakeholders given CSR more attention recently? Does abiding by CSR standards potentially cause companies to have conflicting objectives with specific stakeholders in some situations?
7. Look through the list of chapters in this textbook, and discuss how globalization could influence each organizational behaviour topic.
8. "Organizational theories should follow the contingency approach." Comment on the accuracy of this statement.
9. What does *evidence-based management* mean? Describe situations you have heard about in which companies have practiced evidence-based management, as well as situations in which companies have relied on fads that lacked sufficient evidence of their worth.

Case Study: ANCOL LTD.

By Steven L. McShane, University of Western Australia

Paul Simard was delighted when Ancol Ltd. offered him the job of manager at its Jonquiere, Quebec plant. Simard was happy enough managing a small metal stamping plant with another company, but the headhunter's invitation to apply for the plant manager job at one of Canada's leading metal fabrication companies was irresistible. Although the Jonquiere plant was the smallest of Ancol's 15 operations across Canada, the plant manager position was a valuable first step in a promising career.

One of Simard's first observations at Ancol's Jonquiere plant was that relations between employees and management were strained. Taking a page from a recent executive seminar that he attended on building trust in the workplace, Simard ordered the removal of all time clocks from the plant. Instead, the plant would assume that employees had put in their full shift. This symbolic gesture, he believed, would establish a new level of credibility and strengthen relations between management and employees at the site.

Initially, the 250 production employees at the Jonquiere plant appreciated their new freedom. They felt respected and saw this gesture as a sign of positive change from the new plant manager. Two months later, however, problems started to appear. A few people began showing up late, leaving early, or taking extended lunch breaks. Although this represented only about 5 percent of the employees, others found the situation unfair. Moreover, the increased absenteeism levels were beginning to have a noticeable effect on plant productivity. The problem had to be managed.

Simard asked supervisors to observe and record when the employees came or went and to discuss attendance problems with those abusing their privileges. But the supervisors had no previous experience with keeping attendance and many lacked the necessary interpersonal skills to discuss the matter with subordinates. Employees resented the reprimands, so relations with supervisors deteriorated. The additional responsibility of keeping track of attendance also made it difficult for supervisors to complete their other responsibilities. After just a few months, Ancol found it necessary to add another supervisor position and reduce the number of employees assigned to each supervisor.

But the problems did not end there. Without time clocks, the payroll department could not deduct pay for the amount of time that employees were late. Instead, a letter of reprimand was placed in the employee's personnel file. However, this required yet more time and additional skills from the supervisors. Employees did not want these letters to become a permanent record, so they filed grievances with their labour union. The number of grievances doubled over six months, which required even more time for both union officials and supervisors to handle these disputes.

Nine months after removing the time clocks, Paul Simard met with union officials, who agreed that it would be better to put the time clocks back in. Employee-management relations had deteriorated below the level when Simard had started. Supervisors were burnt out from overwork. Productivity had dropped due to poorer attendance records and increased administrative workloads.

A couple of months after the time clocks were put back in place, Simard attended an operations meeting at Ancol's headquarters in Toronto. During lunch, Simard described the time clock incident to Liam Jackson, Ancol's plant manager in Northern British Columbia. Jackson looked surprised, then chuckled. Jackson explained that the previous BC plant manager had done something like that with similar consequences six or seven years ago. The previous manager had left some time ago, but Jackson heard about the BC time clock from a supervisor during the manager's retirement party two months ago.

"I guess it's not quite like lightning striking the same place twice," said Simard to Jackson. "But it sure feels like it."

Discussion Questions

1. Discuss the consequences of the time clock removal on Ancol's effectiveness as an organization using any two of the perspectives of organizational effectiveness.
2. What changes should occur to minimize the likelihood of these problems in the future?

Web Exercise: DIAGNOSING ORGANIZATIONAL STAKEHOLDERS

Purpose This exercise is designed to help you understand how stakeholders influence organizations as part of the open systems anchor.

Materials Students need to select a company and, prior to class, retrieve and analyze publicly available information over the past year or two about that company. This may include annual reports, which are usually found on the websites of publicly traded companies. Where possible, students should also scan full-text newspaper and magazine databases for articles published over the previous year about the company.

Instructions The instructor may have students work alone or in groups for this activity. Students will select a company and investigate the relevance and influence of various stakeholder groups on the organization. Stakeholders can be identified from annual reports, newspaper articles, website statements, and other available sources. Stakeholders should be rank-ordered in terms of their perceived importance to the organization.

Students should be prepared to present or discuss their rank ordering of the organization's stakeholders, including evidence for this ordering.

Discussion Questions

1. What are the main reasons why certain stakeholders are more important than others for this organization?
2. On the basis of your knowledge of the organization's environmental situation, is this rank order of stakeholders in the organization's best interest, or should specific other stakeholders be given higher priority?
3. What societal groups, if any, are not mentioned as stakeholders by the organization? Does this lack of reference to these unmentioned groups make sense?

Self-Assessment: IT ALL MAKES SENSE?

Purpose This exercise is designed to help you assess the extent to which your personal theories about what goes on in organizations are consistent with current organizational behaviour evidence.

Instructions (Note: Your instructor might conduct this activity as a self-assessment or as a team activity.) Read each of the statements below and circle whether each statement is true or false, in your opinion. The class will consider the answers to each question and discuss the implications for studying organizational behaviour.

Due to the nature of this activity, the instructor will provide the answers to these questions. There is no scoring key in Appendix B.

1.	True	False	A happy worker is a productive worker.
2.	True	False	A decision maker's effectiveness increases with the number of choices or alternatives available to her/him.
3.	True	False	Organizations are more effective when they minimize conflict among employees.
4.	True	False	Employees have more power with many close friends than with many acquaintances.
5.	True	False	Companies are more successful when they have strong corporate cultures.
6.	True	False	Employees perform better without stress.
7.	True	False	The best way to change people and organizations is by pinpointing the source of their current problems.
8.	True	False	Female leaders involve employees in decisions to a greater degree than do male leaders.
9.	True	False	The best decisions are made without emotion.
10.	True	False	If employees feel they are paid unfairly, nothing other than changing their pay will reduce their feelings of injustice.

SELF-ASSESSMENTS FOR CHAPTER 1

SELF-ASSESSMENT NAME	DESCRIPTION	LOCATION
It all makes sense?	Helps you to assess the extent to which your personal theories about what goes on in organizations are consistent with current organizational behaviour evidence.	Page 24 connect
Are you a good telecommuter?	Estimates personal characteristics that relate to employee success at telecommuting, thereby providing a rough indication of how well you might adjust to telecommuting.	connect

Motivation, role perceptions, and misguided personal values explain the alleged bribery, money laundering, and other illegal activities by several SNC-Lavalin executives and employees.

John Mahoney, *The (Montreal) Gazette*

Chapter 2

Individual Behaviour, Personality, and Values

LEARNING OBJECTIVES

After reading this chapter, you should be able to:

LO1. Describe the four factors that directly influence individual behaviour and performance.

LO2. Summarize the five types of individual behaviour in organizations.

LO3. Describe personality and discuss how the "Big Five" personality dimensions and four MBTI types relate to individual behaviour in organizations.

LO4. Summarize Schwartz's model of individual values and discuss the conditions where values influence behaviour.

LO5. Describe three ethical principles and discuss three factors that influence ethical behaviour.

LO6. Describe five values commonly studied across cultures, and discuss the diverse cultures within Canada.

Bribery of foreign public officials, conspiracy to commit fraud and forgery, money laundering, possessing property obtained by crime, and attempts to secretly smuggle the son of a former dictator into safer countries. Sounds like the plot of a twisted crime novel. Yet these are the charges recently laid against former executives and representatives at SNC-Lavalin (SNCL), one of Canada's largest engineering and construction firms.

The Royal Canadian Mounted Police allege that over the past decade SNCL funnelled $118 million through offshore bank accounts as bribes to secure contracts in Libya. Separately, the World Bank recently uncovered evidence that SNCL bribed (or attempted to bribe) government staff and leaders to construct a bridge in Bangladesh. SNCL is also being investigated for unethical activities in contract bidding across several other countries, including a major Canadian project involving a Montreal superhospital. SNCL's former CEO and several executives were fired and are either under arrest or investigation. The company has been banned from bidding on contracts with the World Bank and the Canadian International Development Agency, and is under intense scrutiny by politicians in several countries.

According to World Bank documents, one large SNCL division processed bribes through an expense line called "project consultancy cost" or PCC. The company has acknowledged that these PCC expenses were illegitimate, yet they typically represented 10 percent of project costs and appeared in more than a dozen recent company projects across six countries. "Everybody used this term, and all know what that means," admits a former SNCL engineer. These illegitimate accounting practices may surprise the Canadian Institute of Chartered Accountants, which gave SNCL seven excellence in corporate governance awards over the past decade.

Why did SNCL engage in such blatant wrongdoing? One explanation is that its executives were highly motivated through bonuses and promotions associated with winning contracts. A few employees apparently also received bribery money. Another factor is that the company's recent CEOs either turned a blind eye to the wrongdoing or supported perceptions that this is how to win new business. As one former executive explained, SNCL had "a corporate culture where it was common practice to do all that was necessary, including the payment of 'commissions' and other benefits to obtain contracts."

A third explanation is that SNCL staff detached their behaviour from their personal values. They explained either that they were just doing their job or that their boss "ordered" them to perform these tasks. In fact, at least three executives facing RCMP charges have filed wrongful dismissal lawsuits against SNCL, claiming they were innocent pawns in the scandal. Even SNCL's board seems to have downplayed personal responsibility. When it received an anonymous letter describing the bribery funds, the board only "took note" of the allegations, pointing out that they have "received anonymous letters before that have no credibility." And when the extent of wrongdoing at SNCL eventually became public, the board chair said: "Clearly, our board of directors can't govern something that they don't know about, or prevent something they are not aware of."[1]

The extent of wrongdoing at SNC-Lavalin (SNCL) is rare in Canadian organizations, but this opening case study illustrates the dark side of several topics that we discuss in this chapter. First, it refers to some of the four direct drivers of individual behaviour and performance, such as the motivation to engage in wrongful activities and the role perceptions among some staff that this behaviour was normal practice to win contracts. The events at SNCL also tie in with the five types of individual behaviour that represent the individual-level dependent variables found in most organizational behaviour research. Later in this chapter we look at the two most stable characteristics of individuals, namely their personality and values. For example, we discuss how personal values influence behaviour, as well as the conditions where personal values become disconnected from behaviour (such as at SNCL). Finally, this chapter presents the topics of ethical and cross-cultural values. For instance, we explore the strategies recently introduced at SNCL to improve ethical conduct.

MARS Model of Individual Behaviour and Performance

LO1

For most of the past century, experts have investigated the direct predictors of individual behaviour and performance.[2] One of the earliest formulas was *performance = person × situation,* where *person* includes individual characteristics and *situation* represents external influences on the individual's behaviour. Another frequently mentioned formula is *performance = ability × motivation.*[3] Sometimes known as the "skill-and-will" model, this formula elaborates two specific characteristics within the person that influence individual performance. Ability, motivation, and situation are by far the most commonly mentioned direct predictors of individual behaviour and performance, but in the 1960s researchers identified a fourth key factor: role perceptions (the individual's expected role obligations).[4]

Exhibit 2.1 illustrates these four variables–motivation, ability, role perceptions, and situational factors–which are represented by the acronym *MARS.*[5] All four factors are critical influences on an individual's voluntary behaviour and performance; if any one of them is low in a given situation, the employee would perform the task poorly. For example, motivated salespeople with clear role perceptions and sufficient resources (situational factors) will not perform their jobs as well if they lack sales skills and related knowledge (ability). Motivation, ability, and role perceptions are clustered together in the model because they are located within the person. Situational factors are external to the individual but still affect his or her behaviour and performance.[6] The four MARS variables are the direct predictors of employee performance, customer service, coworker collegiality, ethical behaviour, and all other forms of voluntary behaviour in the workplace. Global Connections 2.1 explains how the MARS model

EXHIBIT 2.1

MARS Model of Individual Behaviour and Results

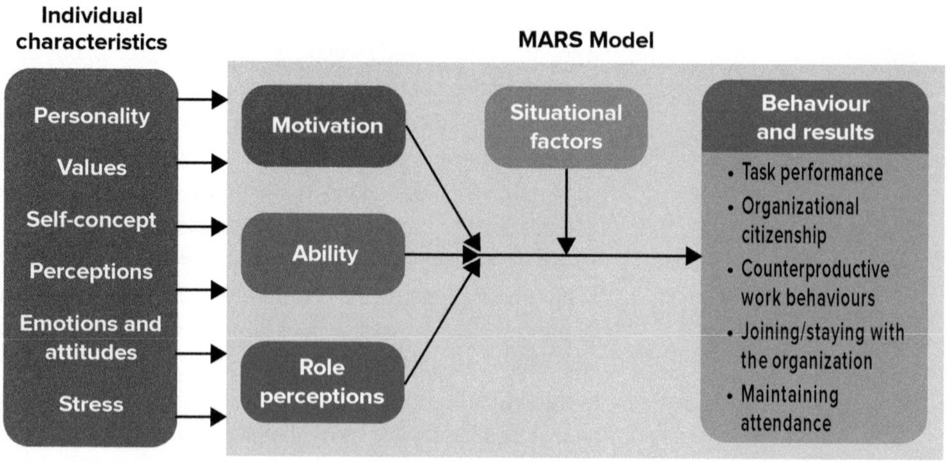

has driven the success of Iceland Foods in the United Kingdom. Let's look in more detail at each of the four factors in the MARS model.

EMPLOYEE MOTIVATION

motivation The forces within a person that affect his or her direction, intensity, and persistence of voluntary behaviour.

Motivation represents the forces within a person that affect his or her direction, intensity, and persistence of voluntary behaviour.[7] *Direction* refers to the path along which people steer their effort. People have choices about where they put their effort; they have a sense of what they are trying to achieve and at what level of quality, quantity, and so forth. In other words, motivation is goal-directed, not random. People are motivated to arrive at work on time, finish a project a few hours early, or aim for many other targets. The second element of motivation, called *intensity*, is the amount of effort allocated to the goal. Intensity is all about how much people push themselves to complete a task. For example, two employees might be motivated to finish their project a few hours early (direction), but only one of them puts forth enough effort (intensity) to achieve this goal.

Finally, motivation involves varying levels of *persistence;* that is, continuing the effort for a certain amount of time. Employees sustain their effort until they reach their goal or give up beforehand. To help remember these three elements of motivation, consider the metaphor of driving a car in which the thrust of the engine is your effort. Direction refers to where you steer the car, intensity is how much you put your foot down on the gas pedal, and persistence is for how long you drive towards your destination. Remember that motivation is a force that exists within individuals; it is not their actual behaviour. Thus, direction, intensity, and persistence are cognitive (thoughts) and emotional conditions that directly cause us to move.

ABILITY

ability The natural aptitudes and learned capabilities required to successfully complete a task.

Employee abilities also make a difference in behaviour and task performance. **Ability** includes both the natural aptitudes and the learned capabilities required to successfully complete a task. *Aptitudes* are the natural talents that help employees learn specific tasks more quickly and perform them better. There are many physical and mental aptitudes, and our ability to acquire skills is affected by these aptitudes. For example, finger dexterity is an aptitude by which individuals learn more quickly and potentially achieve higher performance at picking up and handling small objects with their fingers. Employees with high finger dexterity are not necessarily better than others at first; rather, their learning tends to be faster and performance potential tends to be higher. *Learned capabilities* are the skills and knowledge that you currently possess. These capabilities include the physical and mental skills and knowledge you have acquired. Learned capabilities tend to wane over time when not in use. Aptitudes and learned capabilities (skills and knowledge) are the main elements

Global Connections 2.1:

APPLYING MARS AT ICELAND FOODS

Pardon the pun, but Iceland Foods Group Limited has become one of the hottest food companies in the United Kingdom. The frozen foods retailer achieved record profits in each of the past seven years and has expanded to more than 800 stores with 23,000 (mostly part-time) employees. Iceland Foods is consistently ranked as one of the best large organizations to work for in the UK. Employee turnover (22 percent) is well below the industry average; 40 percent have been employed with Iceland Foods for more than five years.

The key drivers of Iceland Foods' success are the four variables depicted in the MARS model. The first of these is employee motivation. "A well-motivated staff is priceless," says Malcolm Walker, the company's founder and CEO. "That is our secret weapon. Our staff are on fire." Employees receive cash prizes, iPads, and other perks for going the extra mile, while those at the top-performing stores also share a bonus. Store managers with the best results are rewarded with free vacations and luxury cars.

Ability is a second element that contributes to employee performance. Almost all (94 percent) of Iceland Foods employees say they receive all the training they need to do their job well. Store employees attend numerous short training sessions focused on a single skill, while store managers go through a full management development program. The company also developed the Iceland Driver Academy program, where drivers for the company's new online shopping service learn to be "ambassadors for the service on our customers' doorsteps."

Third, the company ensures that employees have clear role perceptions. In fact, in the latest staff survey 98 percent of them said they are clear about what is expected of them in their jobs. The company also develops role clarity through annual meetings of store managers, where Walker and his executive team highlight the company's vision and values. Finally, Iceland Foods gives employees sufficient resources to apply their motivation, ability, and role perceptions. For example, the company arranges for sufficient staff in the stores and equipment to perform daily tasks.[8]

Courtesy of Iceland Foods

Iceland Foods Group has become one of the most successful food retailers in the United Kingdom through the four variables in the MARS model.

of a broader concept called *competencies,* which are characteristics of a person that result in superior performance.[9] Some experts include personality and values as competencies, whereas others describe competencies as action-oriented results, such as serving customers and providing creative ideas.

The challenge is to match a person's abilities with the job's requirements because a good match tends to increase employee performance and well-being. One matching strategy is to select applicants who already demonstrate the required competencies. For example, companies ask applicants to perform work samples, provide references for checking their past performance, and complete various selection tests. A second strategy is to train employees who lack specific knowledge or skills needed for the job.[10] The third person-job matching strategy is to redesign the job so that employees are given tasks only within their current abilities. For example, a complex task might be simplified–some aspects of the work are transferred to others– so that a new employee performs only tasks that he or she is currently able to perform. As the employee becomes more competent at these tasks, other tasks are added back into the job.

OB by the NUMBERS

The Skills Gap and Responsibility for Training Employees?[11]

91% of Canadian employees polled believe the employer should pay for their training.

82% of Canadian executives polled say they are willing to provide technical training to new employees.

64% of Canadian executives polled say they are somewhat or very concerned about losing employees after they have received training from the company.

72% of Canadian executives polled say there is a gap between the skill level and experience that job applicants have, and what organizations in their industry are seeking.

55% of Canadian employees polled say that over the past year they extended their knowledge through education and training.

43% of Canadian executives polled believe employees should provide their own training to close the skills gap (43% said employers should provide training to close that skills gap).

role perceptions The degree to which a person understands the job duties assigned to or expected of him or her.

ROLE PERCEPTIONS

Motivation and ability are important influences on individual behaviour and performance, but employees also require accurate **role perceptions** to perform their jobs well. Role perceptions refer to how clearly people understand the job duties (roles) assigned to or expected of them. These perceptions range from role clarity to role ambiguity. A recent global survey suggests that most employees lack role clarity. Asked what would most improve their performance, employees identified "greater clarity about what the organization needs from me" as the first or second most important factor.[12]

Role clarity exists in three forms. First, employees have clear role perceptions when they understand the specific duties or consequences for which they are accountable. This may seem obvious, but employees are occasionally evaluated on job duties they were never told was within their zone of responsibility. Second, role clarity exists when employees understand the priority of their various tasks and performance expectations. This is illustrated in the classic dilemma of prioritizing quantity versus quality, such as how many customers to serve in an hour (quantity) versus how well the employee should serve each customer (quality). Role perception as prioritization also exists in the allocation of time and resources to various tasks, such as how much time you should coach employees each week versus meet with suppliers and clients. Third, role clarity is about understanding the preferred behaviours or procedures for accomplishing the assigned tasks. These are situations in which there are two or more ways to perform a task and the employee knows which approach is preferred by the company.

Role perceptions are important because they represent how well employees know where to direct their effort. Employees with role clarity perform work more accurately and efficiently whereas those with role ambiguity waste considerable time and energy by performing the wrong tasks or in the wrong way. Furthermore, role clarity is essential for coordination with coworkers and other stakeholders. For instance, performers at Canada's Cirque du Soleil depend on each other to perform precise behaviours at exact times, such as catching each other in midair. Role clarity ensures that these expectations are met and the performances are executed safely. Finally, role clarity motivates employees because they have a higher belief that their effort will produce the expected outcomes. In other words, people are more confident exerting the required effort when they know what is expected of them.

SITUATIONAL FACTORS

Individual behaviour and performance also depend on the situation.[13] This refers to conditions beyond the employee's immediate control that constrain or facilitate behaviour and performance.[14] For example, employees who are motivated, skilled, and know their role obligations will nevertheless perform poorly if they lack time, budget, physical work facilities, and other situational conditions. Situational factors also refer to environmental cues that guide employee behaviour.[15] Workplaces are safer, for example, when hazards are clearly identified. The hazard is a situational factor in employee safety, but so are the barriers and warning signs that cue employees to avoid that hazard.

EXHIBIT 2.2

Five Types of Individual Behaviour in the Workplace

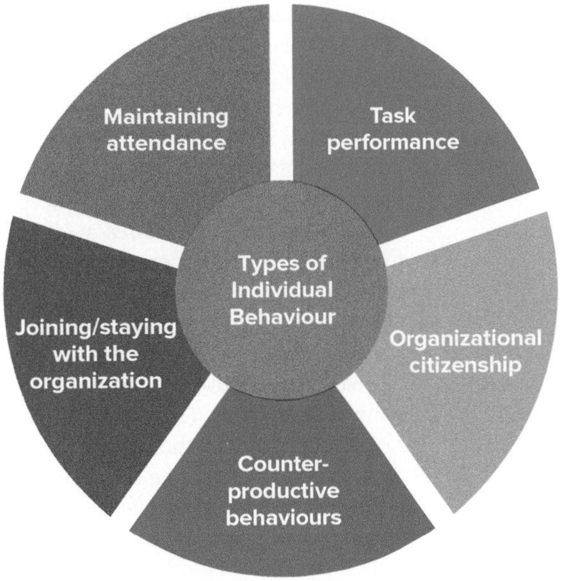

Types of Individual Behaviour

LO2

The four elements of the MARS model–motivation, ability, role perceptions, and situational factors–affect all voluntary workplace behaviours and performance. There are many varieties of individual behaviour, but most can be organized into the five categories described over the next few pages: task performance, organizational citizenship behaviours, counterproductive work behaviours, joining and staying with the organization, and maintaining work attendance (Exhibit 2.2).

TASK PERFORMANCE

Task performance refers to goal-directed behaviours under the individual's control that support organizational objectives.[16] Most jobs require incumbents to complete several tasks. For example, foreign exchange traders at RBC Capital Markets in Toronto and elsewhere must be able to identify and execute profitable trades, work cooperatively with clients and coworkers, assist in training new staff, and work on special telecommunications equipment without error. These tasks involve various degrees of working with people, data, things, and ideas.[17] Foreign exchange traders almost continuously work with data, such as performing technical analysis of trends; they coordinate and share information with coworkers and clients throughout the day (people); and they are frequently interpreting and synthesizing information from charts, news, and other sources (ideas). Foreign exchange traders spend little time interacting with things (e.g., manufacturing, designing, arranging) other than incidentally working with equipment.

When discussing task performance, we mainly think about performing the work efficiently and accurately. However, this *proficiency* is only one form of goal-directed behaviour to support organizational objectives. A second form of behaviour is *adaptability*, which refers to how well the employee responds to, copes with, and supports new circumstances and work patterns. A third form of task-related behaviour is *proactivity*, which refers to how well the employee anticipates environmental changes and initiates new work patterns that are aligned with those changes.[18]

organizational citizenship behaviours (OCBs) Various forms of cooperation and helpfulness to others that support the organization's social and psychological context.

ORGANIZATIONAL CITIZENSHIP

Employee behaviour extends beyond performing specific tasks. It also includes various forms of cooperation and helpfulness to others that support the organization's social and psychological context.[19] These activities are called **organizational citizenship behaviours (OCBs)**.

Some OCBs are directed toward individuals, such as assisting coworkers with their work problems, adjusting assigned work schedules to accommodate coworkers, showing genuine courtesy toward coworkers, and sharing work resources (supplies, technology, staff) with coworkers. Other OCBs represent cooperation and helpfulness toward the organization, such as supporting the company's public image, taking discretionary action to help the organization avoid potential problems, offering ideas beyond those required for their own job, attending voluntary functions that support the organization, and keeping up with new developments in the organization.[20]

Some experts define OCBs as discretionary behaviours (employees don't have to perform them) based on the notion that they are outside the employee's job duties. Yet contrary to this view, research has found that many employees believe it is part of their job to engage in some OCBs. Furthermore, companies sometimes (if not always) advise employees that helping coworkers, supporting the company's public image, and other OCBs are conditions of employment.[21] Indeed, there are many cases of employees losing their jobs because they failed to engage in some of these OCBs. Therefore, OCBs are best described as behaviours that support the organization's social and psychological context through cooperation and helpfulness to others. Some of these behaviours might be discretionary behaviours, but many are work requirements.

OCBs can have a significant effect on individual, team, and organizational effectiveness. Employees who engage in more individual-directed OCBs tend to have higher task performance because they receive more support from coworkers. OCBs also increase team performance where members depend on each other.[22] However, engaging in OCBs can also have negative consequences.[23] Employees who perform more OCBs tend to have higher work-family conflict. Also, performing OCBs takes time and energy away from performing tasks, so employees who give more attention to OCBs risk lower career success in companies that reward task performance.

COUNTERPRODUCTIVE WORK BEHAVIOURS

counterproductive work behaviours (CWBs) Voluntary behaviours that have the potential to directly or indirectly harm the organization.

Organizational behaviour is interested in all workplace behaviours, including dysfunctional activities collectively known as **counterproductive work behaviours (CWBs)**. CWBs are voluntary behaviours that have the potential to directly or indirectly harm the organization.[24] Some of the many types of CWBs include harassing coworkers, creating unnecessary conflict, deviating from preferred work methods (e.g., shortcuts that risk work quality), being untruthful, stealing, sabotaging work, avoiding work obligations (tardiness), and wasting resources. CWBs are not minor concerns; research suggests that they can substantially undermine the organization's effectiveness.

JOINING AND STAYING WITH THE ORGANIZATION

Organizations are people working together toward common goals, so hiring and retaining talent is another critical set of behaviours.[25] Although a weak economy has increased the pool of job applicants and reduced job turnover, employers still face challenges finding qualified

Courtesy of Brandt Industries Ltd.

Over the past forty years, the Brandt Group of Companies has grown from a small manufacturer with $1 million sales to become Saskatchewan's largest privately-held company with $1.2 billion sales and more than 1,800 employees. Brandt is also rated as one of Canada's 50 best managed firms and one of the country's fastest growing companies. What is the secret to this multi-industry conglomerate's success? "There are a lot of things that it takes to be a successful business, but first and foremost, it's the people part of the business that you have to get right," advises CEO Gavin Semple. "You have to find the right people, keep those people, and establish a culture that's conducive to people wanting to come to work and wanting to contribute."[26]

applicants for specific job groups. One recent report estimates that 68 percent of Canadian employers feel challenged by the skills shortage. This problem is acute in Lloydminster, Alberta and nearby communities, where unemployment is less than 3 percent. "The employees really hold the power," says the owner of a small marketing materials company in that area.[27]

Even when companies are able to hire qualified staff in the face of shortages, they need to ensure that these employees stay with the company. Companies with high turnover suffer because of the high cost of replacing people who leave. More important, as was mentioned in the previous chapter, much of an organization's intellectual capital is the knowledge carried around in employees' heads. When people leave, some of this vital knowledge is lost, often resulting in lower productivity, poorer customer service, and so forth.

MAINTAINING WORK ATTENDANCE

Along with attracting and retaining employees, organizations need everyone to show up for work at scheduled times. Statistics Canada reports that Canadian employees miss an average of almost 10 days of scheduled work each year, which is up from an average of 8.1 days lost a decade ago and is much higher than the average of 5 days absence in the United States and United Kingdom. However, Canadian absenteeism rates are modest compared to chronic absenteeism in some occupations and cultures. For instance, one study reported that more than 25 percent of primary and secondary school teachers in India, Uganda, and Indonesia are absent from work on any given work day. The study warned that this absenteeism rate undermines the quality of children's education to such an extent that it threatens the economic development of those countries.[28]

Why are employees absent or late for work?[29] Employees often point to situational factors, such as bad weather, transit strike, personal illness, and family demands (e.g., sick children). These are usually important factors, but some people still show up for work because of their strong motivation to attend, whereas others take sick leave at the slightest sign of bad weather or illness. Employees who experience job dissatisfaction, workplace incivility, or work-related stress are more likely to be absent or late for work because taking time off is a way of temporarily withdrawing from those difficult conditions. Absenteeism is also higher in organizations with generous sick leave because this benefit minimizes the financial loss of taking time away from work. Another factor in absenteeism is the person's values and personality. Finally, studies report that absenteeism is higher in teams with strong absence norms, meaning that team members tolerate and even expect coworkers to take time off.

presenteeism Attending scheduled work when one's capacity to perform is significantly diminished by illness or other factors.

Presenteeism Although organizational leaders worry about absenteeism, presenteeism may be more serious in some situations.[30] Presenteeism occurs when people attend work even though their capacity to work is significantly diminished by illness, fatigue, personal problems, or other factors. Employees who attend work when they are unwell or unfit may worsen their own condition and increase health and safety risks of coworkers. Also, these employees tend to be less productive and may reduce the productivity of coworkers.

There are many reasons why people show up for work when they shouldn't.[31] Presenteeism is more common among employees with low job security (such as new and temporary staff), who lack sick leave pay or similar financial buffers, and whose absence would immediately affect many people (i.e., high centrality). Company or team norms about absenteeism also account for presenteeism. Personality also plays a role; some people possess traits that motivate them to show up for work when others would gladly recover at home. Personality is a widely cited predictor of most forms of individual behaviour. It is also the most stable personal characteristic, so we introduce this topic next.

Personality in Organizations

LO3

While applying for several jobs in the Canadian publishing industry, Christina was surprised that three of the positions required applicants to complete a personality test. "One page is a list of characteristics–sentimental, adventurous, attractive, compelling, helpful, etc.–and you check off the ones that best describe what others expect of you," Christina recalls of one personality test. "The second page is the same list, but you check off the ones that you think truly describe you." Christina didn't hear back from the first company after completing its personality test, so for the second company she completed the personality test "according to a sales personality" because that job was in sales. When writing the personality test at the third firm, she answered questions the way she thought someone would if they were "a good person, but honest" about what they thought. None of the applications resulted in a job offer, leaving Christina wondering what personality profile these companies were seeking and whether her strategy of guessing the best answer on these personality tests was a good idea.[32]

personality The relatively enduring pattern of thoughts, emotions, and behaviours that characterize a person, along with the psychological processes behind those characteristics.

These companies were attempting to measure Christina's personality. **Personality** is the relatively enduring pattern of thoughts, emotions, and behaviours that characterize a person, along with the psychological processes behind those characteristics.[33] It is, in essence, the bundle of characteristics that make us similar to or different from other people. We estimate an individual's personality by what they say and do, and we infer the person's internal states–including thoughts and emotions–from these observable behaviours.

People typically exhibit a wide range of behaviours, yet within that variety are discernible patterns that we refer to as *personality traits*.[34] Traits are broad concepts that allow us to label and understand individual differences. For example, you probably have some friends who are more talkative than others. You might know some people who like to take risks and others who are risk-averse. Each trait implies that there is something within the person, rather than environmental influences alone, that predicts this behavioural tendency. In fact, studies report that an individual's personality traits measured in childhood predict various behaviours and outcomes in adulthood, including educational attainment, employment success, marital relationships, illegal activities, and health-risk behaviours.[35]

Although people have behavioural tendencies, they do not act the same way in all situations. Such consistency would be considered abnormal because it indicates a person's insensitivity to social norms, reward systems, and other external conditions.[36] People vary their behaviour to suit the situation, even if the behaviour is at odds with their personality. For example, talkative people remain relatively quiet in a library where "no talking" rules are explicit and strictly enforced. However, personality differences are still apparent in these situations because talkative people tend to do more talking in libraries relative to how much other people talk in libraries.

PERSONALITY DETERMINANTS: NATURE VERSUS NURTURE

Most experts now agree that personality is shaped by both nature and nurture, although the relative importance of each continues to be debated and studied. *Nature* refers to our genetic or hereditary origins–the genes that we inherit from our parents. Studies of identical twins, particularly those separated at birth, reveal that heredity has a very large effect on personality; up to 50 percent of variation in behaviour and 30 percent of temperament preferences can be attributed to a person's genetic characteristics.[37] In other words, genetic code not only determines our eye colour, skin tone, and physical shape; it also significantly affects our attitudes, decisions, and behaviour.

Our personality is also affected by *nurture*–our socialization, life experiences, and other forms of interaction with the environment. Personality develops and changes mainly when people are young; it stabilizes by about 30 years of age, although some experts say personality development continues to occur through to age 50.[38] The main explanation of why personality becomes more stable over time is that we form a clearer and more rigid self-concept as we get older. This increasing clarity of "who we are" serves as an anchor for our behaviour because the executive function–the part of the brain that manages goal-directed behaviour–tries to keep our behaviour consistent with our self-concept.[39] As self-concept becomes clearer and more stable with age, behaviour and personality therefore also become more stable and consistent. We discuss self-concept in more detail in Chapter 3. The main point here is that personality is not completely determined by heredity; life experiences, particularly early in life, also shape each individual's personality traits.

five-factor model (FFM) The five broad dimensions representing most personality traits: conscientiousness, emotional stability, openness to experience, agreeableness, and extraversion.

FIVE-FACTOR MODEL OF PERSONALITY

Hundreds of personality traits (sociable, depressed, cautious, talkative, and so forth) have been described over the years, so experts have tried to organize them into smaller clusters. The most researched and respected clustering of personality traits is the **five-factor model (FFM)**.[40] Several decades ago, personality experts identified more than 17,000 words that

EXHIBIT 2.3

Five-Factor Model Personality Dimensions

Personality dimension	People with higher scores on this dimension tend to be more:
Conscientiousness	Organized, dependable, goal-focused, thorough, disciplined, methodical, industrious
Agreeableness	Trusting, helpful, good-natured, considerate, tolerant, selfless, generous, flexible
Neuroticism	Anxious, insecure, self-conscious, depressed, temperamental
Openness to experience	Imaginative, creative, unconventional, curious, nonconforming, autonomous, perceptive
Extraversion	Outgoing, talkative, energetic, sociable, assertive

describe an individual's personality. These words were distilled down to five broad personality dimensions, each with a cluster of specific traits. Similar results were found in studies of different languages, suggesting that the five-factor model is fairly robust across cultures. These "Big Five" dimensions, represented by the handy acronym *CANOE*, are outlined in Exhibit 2.3 and described below:

conscientiousness A personality dimension describing people who are organized, dependable, goal-focused, thorough, disciplined, methodical, and industrious.

neuroticism A personality dimension describing people who tend to be anxious, insecure, self-conscious, depressed, and temperamental.

extraversion A personality dimension describing people who are outgoing, talkative, sociable, and assertive.

- *Conscientiousness.* **Conscientiousness** characterizes people who are organized, dependable, goal-focused, thorough, disciplined, methodical, and industrious. People with low conscientiousness tend to be careless, disorganized, and less thorough.
- *Agreeableness.* This dimension includes the traits of being trusting, helpful, good-natured, considerate, tolerant, selfless, generous, and flexible. People with low agreeableness tend to be uncooperative and intolerant of others' needs as well as more suspicious and self-focused.
- *Neuroticism.* **Neuroticism** characterizes people who tend to be anxious, insecure, self-conscious, depressed, and temperamental. In contrast, people with low neuroticism (high emotional stability) are poised, secure, and calm.
- *Openness to experience.* This dimension is the most complex and has the least agreement among scholars. It generally refers to the extent to which people are imaginative, creative, unconventional, curious, nonconforming, autonomous, and aesthetically perceptive. Those who score low on this dimension tend to be more resistant to change, less open to new ideas, and more conventional and fixed in their ways.
- *Extraversion.* **Extraversion** characterizes people who are outgoing, talkative, energetic, sociable, and assertive. The opposite is *introversion,* which characterizes those who are quiet, cautious, and less interactive with others. Extraverts get their energy from the outer world (people and things around them), whereas introverts get their energy from the internal world, such as personal reflection on concepts and ideas. Introverts do not necessarily lack social skills. Rather, they are more inclined to direct their interests to ideas than to social events. Introverts feel quite comfortable being alone, whereas extraverts do not.

connect

Are you introverted or extraverted? See page 54 or visit connect.mcgrawhill.com to assess your degree of introversion or extraversion.

The Big Five personality dimensions are associated with each of the five types of behaviour described earlier.[41] Agreeableness, conscientiousness, and emotional stability (low neuroticism) cluster around the broad characteristic of "getting along," which relates to many organizational citizenship behaviours. People with high agreeableness are more sensitive to others (more empathy, less conflict), those with high conscientiousness are more dependable, and those with high emotional stability are more upbeat. Some writers suggest that extraversion also relates to getting along because extraverts are more motivated to interact with others. Another broad characteristic, called "getting ahead" is associated with openness to experience, extraversion, conscientiousness, and emotional stability. Those with high openness to experience are more eager to try out new ideas, extraverts are more assertive, those with high conscientiousness are more goal-oriented, and those with high emotional stability are more confident in their ability to perform well. Most personality dimensions relate to both getting along and getting ahead because specific traits within those dimensions have different effects. For instance, conscientious includes the specific trait called dependability which motivates getting along, as well as the trait called goal-orientation which motivates getting ahead.

Personality traits are fairly good at predicting a number of workplace behaviours and outcomes, particularly when we strip away the effects of employee ability and other factors. Conscientiousness and emotional stability (low neuroticism) stand out as the best personality predictors of individual performance for most job groups.[42] Various studies have reported that conscientious employees set higher personal goals for themselves, are more motivated, and have higher performance expectations, compared to employees with low levels of conscientiousness. They also tend to have higher levels of organizational citizenship and work better in organizations that give employees more freedom than is found in traditional command-and-control workplaces. People with higher emotional stability have a more positive (can-do) belief system and are better at directing their energy toward the task at hand.[43]

The other three personality dimensions predict more specific types of employee behaviour and performance.[44] Extraversion is associated with performance in sales and management jobs, where employees must interact with and influence people. Agreeableness is associated with performance in jobs where employees are expected to be cooperative and helpful, such as working in teams, customer relations, and other conflict-handling situations. People high on the openness-to-experience personality dimension tend to be more creative and adaptable to change. Finally, personality influences well-being, including emotional reactions to situations and preferred coping mechanisms.[45] However, remember that the Big Five personality dimensions cluster several specific traits, and each trait's effect varies for different types of performance. Also, the relationship between a personality trait and performance is sometimes (or often) non-linear. People with very high or very low levels of agreeableness, for example, might be less effective than those with moderate agreeableness.[46]

connect

Are you a sensing or intuitive type? Visit **connect.mcgrawhill.com** to estimate your score on this Jungian personality type.

JUNGIAN PERSONALITY THEORY AND THE MYERS-BRIGGS TYPE INDICATOR

Myers-Briggs Type Indicator (MBTI) An instrument designed to measure the elements of Jungian personality theory, particularly preferences regarding perceiving and judging information.

The five-factor model of personality may have the most research support, but it is not the most popular in practice. That distinction goes to Jungian personality theory, which is measured through the **Myers-Briggs Type Indicator (MBTI)** (see Exhibit 2.4). Nearly a century ago, Swiss psychiatrist Carl Jung proposed that personality is primarily represented by the individual's preferences regarding perceiving and judging information.[47] Jung explained that perceiving, which involves how people prefer to gather information or perceive the world around them, occurs through two competing orientations: *sensing (S)* and *intuition (N)*. Sensing involves perceiving information directly through the five senses; it relies on an organized structure to acquire factual and preferably quantitative details. In contrast,

EXHIBIT 2.4

Jungian and Myers-Briggs Type Indicator Types[48]

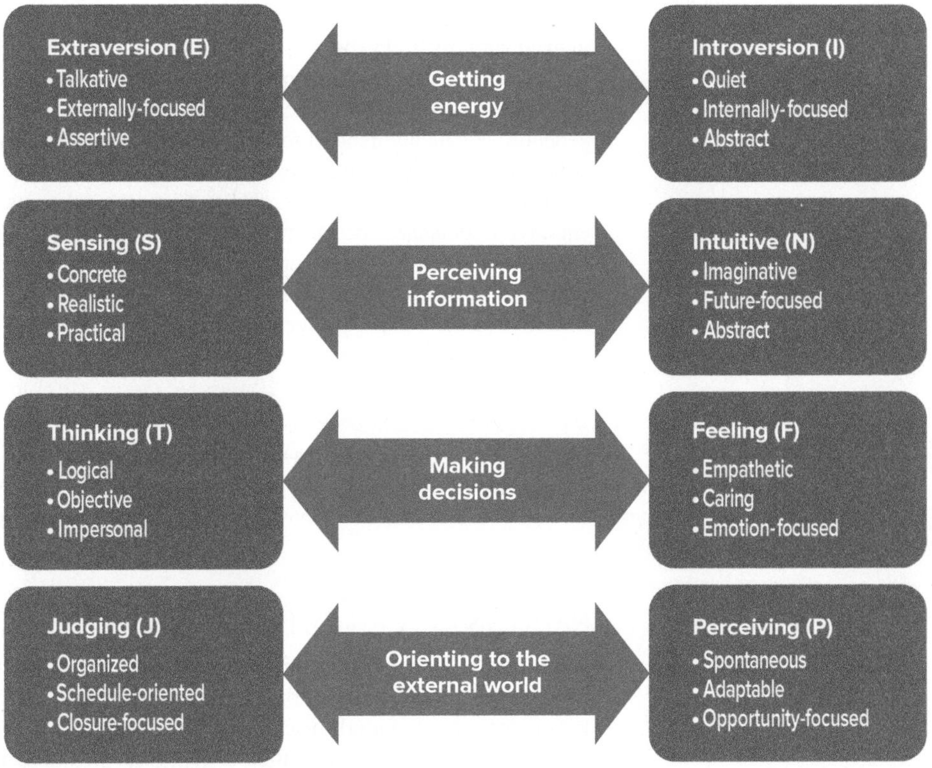

Source: Modified and reproduced by special permission of the Publisher, CPP, Inc., Mountain View, CA 994043 from *Introduction to Type and Careers* by Allen L. Hammer. Copyright 1993 by CPP, Inc. All rights reserved. Further reproduction is prohibited without the Publisher's written consent.

intuition relies more on insight and subjective experience to see relationships among variables. Sensing types focus on the here and now, whereas intuitive types focus more on future possibilities.

Jung also proposed that judging—how people process information or make decisions based on what they have perceived—consists of two competing processes: *thinking (T)* and *feeling (F)*. People with a thinking orientation rely on rational cause-effect logic and systematic data collection to make decisions. Those with a strong feeling orientation, on the other hand, rely on their emotional responses to the options presented, as well as to how those choices affect others. Jung noted that along with differing in the four core processes of sensing, intuition, thinking, and feeling, people also differ in their degrees of extraversion-introversion, which was introduced earlier as one of the Big Five personality traits.

Along with measuring the personality traits identified by Jung, the MBTI measures Jung's broader categories of *perceiving* and *judging*, which represents a person's attitude toward the external world. People with a perceiving orientation are open, curious, and flexible; prefer to adapt spontaneously to events as they unfold; and prefer to keep their options open. Judging types prefer order and structure and want to resolve problems quickly.

The MBTI is one of the most widely used personality tests in work settings as well as in career counselling and

© Glow Images/Alamy RF

More than 200 agencies of the U.S. federal government administer the Myers-Briggs Type Indicator (MBTI) to some or most of their employees. At least one-quarter of employees at the Environmental Protection Agency (EPA), from frontline staff to political leaders, know their MBTI type. EPA training coordinator Brian Twillman says work relationships are much better when people know their MBTI scores. "If we had not had the MBTI introduced into the agency as it's been, there would be a lot of blind spots within the agency with managers," claims Twillman, who says he is an INFP whereas the EPA is dominated by INTJ staff.[49]

executive coaching.[50] Even so, the MBTI and Jung's psychological types model have received uneven support.[51] On the one hand, MBTI seems to improve self-awareness for career development and mutual understanding. It also does a reasonably good job of representing Jung's psychological types. On the other hand, the MBTI poorly predicts job performance and is generally not recommended for employment selection or promotion decisions. For example, although one study found that intuitive types are more common in higher level than lower level management, other research has found no relationship between any MBTI types and effective leadership. One recent large-scale study also reported that the MBTI scores of team members are not useful for predicting the team's development. Finally, the MBTI overlaps with four of the five dimensions of the five-factor personality model, yet it does so less satisfactorily than existing Big Five personality measures.[52]

connect

Can you identify someone's personality from the words he or she uses when blogging? Visit **connect.mcgrawhill.com** to assess how well you decipher personality traits from blogging words.

PERSONALITY TESTING IN ORGANIZATIONS

Personality has gained considerable attention in OB research and in the workplace. The MBTI instrument is mostly used for team building and career development. The five-factor model is more commonly found in scholarly research, but it is increasingly used to assess job applicants. The applicant's personality is typically measured using a self-completed paper-and-pencil test. However, a few firms have discovered how to estimate an applicant's personality from their writing on blogs, Facebook pages, and other public sources. Extraversion, openness to experience, and agreeableness are usually the easiest traits to estimate from the content of online sources, whereas neuroticism is the most difficult.[53]

The use of personality testing is illustrated at Amtrak. Soon after Amtrak won the Metrolink commuter service contract in Southern California, it required train engineers and conductors to complete a Big Five personality inventory as a condition of future employment. A horrendous Metrolink accident claiming two dozen lives occurred two years before Amtrak took over because a train engineer ran a red light while distracted by text messaging.[54] As a result, Amtrak apparently prefers train crew members with a "focused introverted" personality, because employees with these traits are not distracted while operating the train or performing repetitive tasks.

Personality testing wasn't always this popular in organizations. Two decades ago, companies avoided personality tests due to concerns that they do not predict job-related behaviour and might unfairly discriminate against visible minorities and other identifiable groups. Personality testing slowly regained acceptance as studies reported that specific traits correlated with specific indicators of job performance (as we described earlier). Today, personality testing flourishes to such an extent in organizations that some experts warn we may have gone too far in our use of those tests.

connect

What are your dominant values? Visit **connect.mcgrawhill.com** to assess which of the 10 categories of values in Schwartz's circumplex model are most important to you.

Values in the Workplace

LO4

While growing up in Saskatchewan, Colleen Abdoulah developed strong personal values from her parents. In particular, she learned to value equality ("you're no better than anyone and they are no better than you"), having the courage to do the right thing, and forming relationships with people so they feel a sense of ownership. Abdoulah not only practises these values

Debating Point:
SHOULD COMPANIES USE PERSONALITY TESTS TO SELECT JOB APPLICANTS?

Personality theory has made significant strides over the past two decades, particularly in demonstrating that specific traits are associated with specific workplace behaviours and outcomes. Various studies have reported that specific Big Five dimensions predict overall job performance, organizational citizenship, leadership, counterproductive work behaviours, training performance, team performance, and a host of other important outcomes. These findings cast a strong vote in favour of personality testing in the workplace.

A few prominent personality experts urge caution, however.[55] They point out that although traits are associated with workplace behaviour to some extent, there are better predictors of work performance, such as work samples and past performance. Furthermore, selection procedures typically assume that more of a personality trait is better, whereas several (although not all) studies indicate that the best candidates might be closer to the middle than the extremes of the range.[56] For instance, job performance apparently increases with conscientiousness, yet employees with high conscientiousness might be so thorough that they become perfectionists, which can stifle rather than enhance job performance.[57] A third concern is that, depending on how the selection decision applies the test results, personality instruments may unfairly discriminate against specific groups of people.[58]

A fourth worry is that most personality tests are self-reported scales, so applicants might try to fake their answers. Worse, the test scores might not represent the individual's personality or anything else meaningful because test takers often don't know what personality traits the company is looking for. Studies show that candidates who try to fake "good" personality scores change the selection results. Supporters of personality testing offer the counterargument that few job applicants try to fake their scores.[59] One major study recently found that most personality dimensions are estimated better by observers than by self-ratings, but few companies rely on ratings from other people.[60]

Finally, personality testing might not convey a favourable image of the company. Amtrak's use of personality testing at Metrolink resulted in conflict with the railway worker unions. The British operations of PricewaterhouseCoopers (PwC) discovered that its personality test discouraged female applicants from applying because of concerns that the test was too impersonal and could be faked. "Our personality test was seen to alienate women and so we had to respond to that," says PwC's head of diversity.[61]

every day, she has instilled them at Wide Open West, the Denver-based Internet, cable, and phone provider where she served as CEO for several years and is now its chairwoman. "[Our employees] display the courage to do the right thing, serve each other and our customers with humility, and celebrate our learnings and success with grace," says Abdoulah. "Anyone can set values, but we have operationalized our values so that they affect everything we do every day."[62]

Colleen Abdoulah and other successful people often refer to their personal values and the critical events that formed those values earlier in life. *Values*, a concept that we introduced in Chapter 1, are stable, evaluative beliefs that guide our preferences for outcomes or courses of action in a variety of situations.[63] They are perceptions about what is good or bad, right or wrong. Values tell us what we "ought" to do. They serve as a moral compass that directs our motivation and, potentially, our decisions and actions.

People arrange values into a hierarchy of preferences, called a *value system*. Some individuals value new challenges more than they value conformity. Others value generosity more than frugality. Each person's unique value system is developed and reinforced through socialization from parents, religious institutions, friends, personal experiences, and the society in which he or she lives. As such, a person's hierarchy of values is stable and long-lasting. For example, one study found that value systems of a sample of adolescents were remarkably similar 20 years later when they were adults.[64]

Notice that our description of values has focused on individuals, whereas executives often describe values as though they belong to the organization. In reality, values exist only within individuals—we call them *personal values*. However, groups of people might hold the same or similar values, so we tend to ascribe these *shared values* to the team, department, organization, profession, or entire society. The values shared by people throughout an organization *(organizational values)* receive fuller discussion in Chapter 14 because they are a key part of corporate culture. The values shared across a society *(cultural values)* receive attention later in this chapter.

Values and personality traits are related to each other, but the two concepts differ in a few ways.[65] The most noticeable distinction is that values are evaluative–they tell us what we *ought* to do–whereas personality traits describe what we naturally *tend* to do. A second distinction is that personality traits have minimal conflict with each other (e.g., you can have high agreeableness and high introversion), whereas some values are opposed to other values. For example, someone who values excitement and challenge would have difficulty also valuing stability and moderation. Third, although personality and values are both partly determined by heredity, values are influenced more by socialization whereas personality traits are more innate.

TYPES OF VALUES

Values come in many forms, and experts on this topic have devoted considerable attention to organizing them into clusters. Several decades ago, social psychologist Milton Rokeach developed two lists of values, distinguishing means (instrumental values) from end goals (terminal values). Although Rokeach's lists are still mentioned in some organizational behaviour sources, they were replaced by another model almost two decades ago. The instrumental-terminal values distinction was neither accurate nor useful, and it overlooked values that are now included in the current dominant model.

Today, the dominant model of personal values is the one developed and tested by social psychologist Shalom Schwartz and his colleagues.[66] Schwartz's list of 57 values builds on Rokeach's earlier work but does not distinguish instrumental from terminal values. Instead, research has found that human values are organized into the circular model (circumplex) shown in Exhibit 2.5. This model clusters the 57 specific values into 10 broad values categories: universalism, benevolence, tradition, conformity, security, power, achievement, hedonism, stimulation, and self-direction. For example, conformity includes four specific values: politeness, honouring parents, self-discipline, and obedience.

These 10 broad values categories are further clustered into four quadrants. One quadrant, called *openness to change,* refers to the extent to which a person is motivated to pursue

EXHIBIT 2.5

Schwartz's Values Circumplex

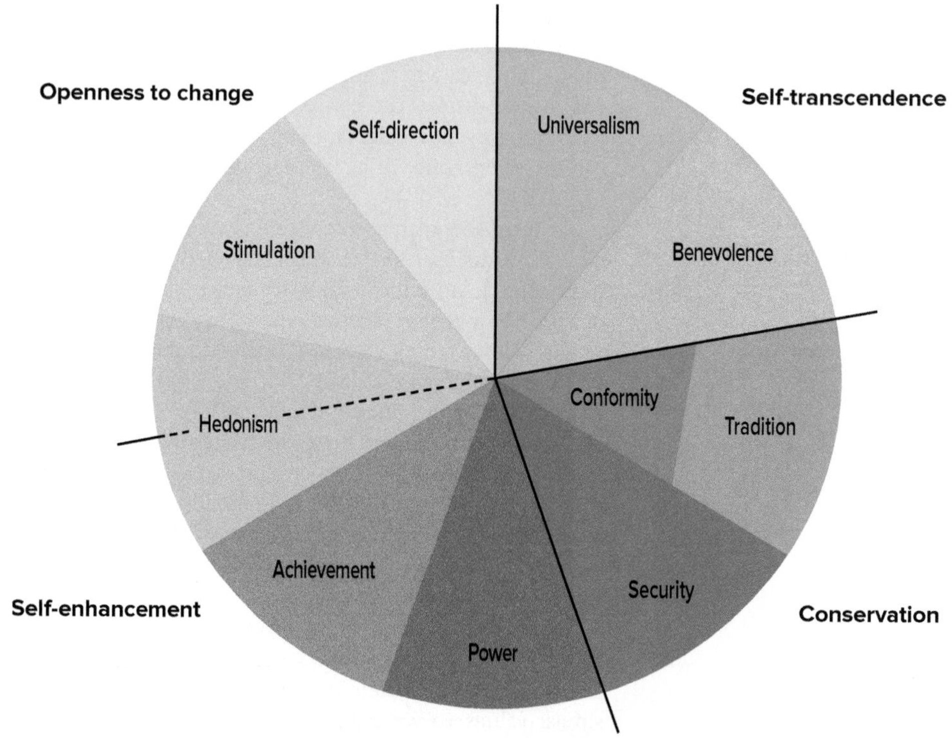

Sources: S. H. Schwartz, "Universals in the Content and Structure of Values: Theoretical Advances and Empirical Tests in 20 Countries," *Advances in Experimental Social Psychology*, 25 (1992), pp. 1-65; S. H. Schwartz and G. Sagie, "Value Consensus and Importance: A Cross-National Study," *Journal of Cross-Cultural Psychology*, 31 (July 2000), pp. 465-497.

innovative ways. This quadrant includes the value categories of self-direction (creativity, independent thought), stimulation (excitement and challenge), and hedonism (pursuit of pleasure, enjoyment, gratification of desires). The opposing quadrant is *conservation*, which is the extent to which a person is motivated to preserve the status quo. The conservation quadrant includes the value categories of conformity (adherence to social norms and expectations), security (safety and stability), and tradition (moderation and preservation of the status quo).

The third quadrant in Schwartz's circumplex model, called *self-enhancement*, refers to how much a person is motivated by self-interest. This quadrant includes the value categories of achievement (pursuit of personal success), power (dominance over others), and hedonism (a values category shared with openness to change). The opposite of self-enhancement is *self-transcendence*, which refers to motivation to promote the welfare of others and nature. Self-transcendence includes the value categories of benevolence (concern for others in one's life) and universalism (concern for the welfare of all people and nature).

VALUES AND INDIVIDUAL BEHAVIOUR

Personal values guide our decisions, behaviour, and performance to some extent. For instance, one recent study found that achievement values predict a student's performance in college courses, even after controlling for personality traits. Another study reported that achievement, benevolence, and self-direction values are associated with specific forms of organizational citizenship behaviour when working in student teams.[67]

Although people think they act consistently with their hierarchy of values, there is often a "disconnect" between personal values and individual behaviour.[68] One influence on the values-behaviour link is the situation. Work environments influence our behaviour, at least in the short term, so they necessarily encourage or discourage values-consistent behaviour. This sometimes occurs without our awareness, but more often we blame the situation for preventing us to apply our values. In the opening case study to this chapter, for example, several SNC-Lavalin employees blamed the situation for their unethical activities by claiming that their boss ordered or forced them to engage in this wrongdoing.

Another factor is that we are more likely to apply values when we actively think about them and understand their relevance to the situation. Some situations easily trigger awareness of our values. For example, you become aware that you value security when asked to perform a risky task. However, values are abstract concepts, so their relevance to specific situations is not obvious much of the time. We literally need to be reminded of our dominant personal values in these situations to ensure that we apply those values. Furthermore, we need to understand that the values we think about are relevant to the situation, such as making a decision or forming an attitude.[69]

The effect of values awareness on behaviour was apparent in the following study:[70] Students were given a math test and paid for each correct answer. One group submitted their results to the experimenter for scoring, so they couldn't lie about their results. A second group could lie because they scored the test themselves and told the experimenter their test score. A third group was similar to the second (they scored their own test), but that test included the following statement, and students were required to sign their name to that statement: "I understand that this short survey falls under (the university's) honour system." (The university had no such honour system.) The researchers estimated that some students cheated when they scored their own test without the "honour system" statement, whereas no one given the "honour system" form lied about their results. The message here is that people are more likely to apply their values (honesty, in this case) when explicitly reminded of those values and see their relevance to the situation.

VALUES CONGRUENCE

Values tell us what is right or wrong and what we ought to do. This evaluative characteristic affects how comfortable we are with specific organizations and individuals. The key concept here is *values congruence*, which refers to how similar a person's values hierarchy is to the values hierarchy of the organization, a coworker, or another source of comparison. *Person-organization values congruence* occurs when a person's values are similar to the

Courtesy of Vancity.

Vancouver City Savings Credit Union (Vancity) is one of Canada's truly values-driven organizations. And to sustain its focus on values, Vancity aims to "screen for skills and hire for fit." Specifically, it carefully selects job applicants whose personal values are aligned with the financial institution's values. "I can tell if someone is just quoting off a Vancity website," says operations vice-president Ellen Pekeles about job applicants who claim to hold Vancity's values. "But when they really talk about it [Vancity's values], and you can see they care . . . you can't fake that." Vancity also gives new hires a five-day orientation that outlines the company's values. At the end of that program, new hires are offered a severance package if they feel their personal values are misaligned with Vancity's values.[71]

organization's dominant values. This form of values congruence increases (to some extent) the chance that employees will make decisions and act in ways consistent with organizational expectations. It also leads to higher job satisfaction, loyalty, and organizational citizenship as well as lower stress and turnover.[72] "The most difficult but rewarding accomplishment in any career is 'living true' to your values and finding companies where you can contribute at the highest level while being your authentic self," says an executive in the pharmaceutical industry.[73]

Are organizations the most successful when every employee's personal values align with the company's values? Not at all! While a comfortable degree of values congruence is necessary for the reasons just noted, organizations also benefit from some level of incongruence. Employees with diverse values offer different perspectives, which potentially lead to better decision making. Also, too much congruence can create a "corporate cult" that potentially undermines creativity, organizational flexibility, and business ethics.

A second type of values congruence involves how consistent the values apparent in our actions (enacted values) are with what we say we believe in (espoused values). This *espoused-enacted value congruence* is especially important for people in leadership positions because any obvious gap between espoused and enacted values undermines their perceived integrity, a critical feature of effective leaders. One global survey reported that 55 percent of employees believe senior management behaves consistently with the company's core values.[74] Some companies try to maintain high levels of espoused-enacted values congruence by surveying subordinates and peers about whether the manager's decisions and actions are consistent with the company's espoused values.

A third category, *organization-community values congruence*, refers to the similarity of an organization's dominant values with the prevailing values of the community or society in which it conducts business.[75] Global organizations may experience higher employee turnover and difficult community relations if they try to impose their home country's values in other cultures where they do business. Thus, globalization calls for a delicate balancing act: Companies depend on shared values to maintain consistent standards and behaviours, yet they need to operate within the values of different cultures around the world.

Ethical Values and Behaviour

LO5

When 2,100 Canadians were asked to identify the most important attribute of a leader of this country, 48 percent chose honesty. The other attributes–intelligence, decisiveness, and compassion–were far less frequently mentioned. Similarly, employees typically choose honesty/ethics as the most important characteristic of effective corporate leaders.[76] *Ethics* refers to the study of moral principles or values that determine whether actions are right or wrong and outcomes are good or bad (see Chapter 1). People rely on their ethical values to determine "the right thing to do." The importance of ethical conduct is apparent in the opening case study to this chapter. The wrongdoing at SNC-Lavalin over the past decade inflicted considerable damage to the Canadian engineering and construction firm's reputation and its ability to secure new business. For example, most of the company's divisions have been banned for a decade from bidding on World Bank tenders.

THREE ETHICAL PRINCIPLES

To better understand business ethics, we need to consider three distinct types of ethical principles: utilitarianism, individual rights, and distributive justice.[77] While your personal values might sway you more towards one principle than the others, all three should be actively considered to put important ethical issues to the test.

- *Utilitarianism.* This principle advises us to seek the greatest good for the greatest number of people. In other words, we should choose the option that provides the highest degree of satisfaction to those affected. This is sometimes known as a *consequential principle* because it focuses on the consequences of our actions, not on how we achieve those consequences. One problem with utilitarianism is that it is almost impossible to evaluate the benefits or costs of many decisions, particularly when many stakeholders have wide-ranging needs and values. Another problem is that most of us are uncomfortable engaging in behaviours that seem, well, unethical to attain results that are ethical.
- *Individual rights.* This principle reflects the belief that everyone has entitlements that let her or him act in a certain way. Some of the most widely cited rights are freedom of movement, physical security, freedom of speech, fair trial, and freedom from torture. The individual-rights principle includes more than legal rights; it also includes human rights that everyone is granted as a moral norm of society. One problem with individual rights is that certain individual rights may conflict with others. The shareholders' right to be informed about corporate activities may ultimately conflict with an executive's right to privacy, for example.
- *Distributive justice.* This principle suggests that people who are similar to each other should receive similar benefits and burdens; those who are dissimilar should receive different benefits and burdens in proportion to their dissimilarity. For example, we expect that two employees who contribute equally in their work should receive similar rewards, whereas those who make a lesser contribution should receive less. A variation of the distributive justice principle says that inequalities are acceptable when they benefit the least well off in society. Thus, employees in risky jobs should be paid more if their work benefits others who are less well off. One problem with the distributive justice principle is that it is difficult to agree on who is "similar" and what factors are "relevant." We discuss distributive justice further in Chapter 5.

MORAL INTENSITY, MORAL SENSITIVITY, AND SITUATIONAL INFLUENCES

Along with ethical principles and their underlying values, three other factors influence ethical conduct in the workplace: the moral intensity of the issue, the individual's moral sensitivity, and situational influences.[78]

moral intensity The degree to which an issue demands the application of ethical principles.

Moral Intensity

Moral intensity is the degree to which an issue demands the application of ethical principles. Decisions with high moral intensity have more significant ethical

EXHIBIT 2.6 Factors Influencing Perceived Moral Intensity*

Moral intensity factor	Moral intensity question	Moral intensity is higher when:
Magnitude of consequences	How much harm or benefit will occur to others as a result of this action?	The harm or benefit is larger.
Social consensus	How many other people agree that this action is ethically good or bad?	Many people agree.
Probability of effect	(a) What is the chance that this action will actually occur? (b) What is the chance that this action will actually have good or bad consequences?	The probability is higher.
Temporal immediacy	How long after the action will the consequences occur?	The time delay is shorter.
Proximity	How socially, culturally, psychologically, and/or physically close to me are the people affected by this decision?	Those affected are close rather than distant.
Concentration of effect	(a) How many people are affected by this action? (b) Are the people affected by this action easily identifiable as a group?	Many people are affected. Those affected are easily identifiable as a group.

*These are factors people tend to think about when determining the moral intensity of an issue. Whether some of these questions should be relevant is itself an ethical question.

Sources: Based on information in T. J. Jones, "Ethical Decision Making by Individuals in Organizations: An Issue Contingent Model," *Academy of Management Review* 16 (1991), pp. 366-395; J. Tsalikis, B. Seaton, and P Shepherd, "Relative Importance Measurement of the Moral Intensity Dimensions," *Journal of Business Ethics* 80, no. 3 (2008), pp. 613-626.

outcomes, so the decision maker needs to more carefully apply ethical principles to resolve it. Several factors influence the moral intensity of an issue, including those listed in Exhibit 2.6. Keep in mind that this list represents the factors people tend to think about; some of them might not be considered morally acceptable when people are formally making ethical decisions.[79]

moral sensitivity A person's ability to recognize the presence of an ethical issue and determine its relative importance.

Moral Sensitivity **Moral sensitivity** (also called *ethical sensitivity*) is a characteristic of the person, namely his or her ability to detect a moral dilemma and estimate its relative importance. This awareness includes both cognitive (logical thinking) and emotional level awareness that something is or could become morally wrong.[80] People with high moral sensitivity can more quickly and accurately estimate the moral intensity of the issue. This awareness does not necessarily translate into more ethical behaviour; it just means they are more likely to know when unethical behaviour occurs. For instance, some observers suggest that SNC-Lavalin's board of directors lacked moral sensitivity because they underestimated the severity of the wrongdoing and did not proactively investigate the problems much sooner.[81]

Several factors predict and change a person's moral sensitivity.[82] Empathy is a key influence because it involves being sensitive to the needs of others and, consequently, makes us more aware of ethical dilemmas involving others. Women typically have higher moral sensitivity compared to men, possibly because women tend to have higher empathy. Another factor is expertise or knowledge of prescriptive norms and rules. For example, accountants would be more morally sensitive regarding the appropriateness of specific accounting procedures than would someone who is not trained in this profession. A third influence on moral sensitivity is direct experience with moral dilemmas. These experiences likely generate internal cues that trigger awareness of future ethical dilemmas with similar characteristics.

mindfulness A person's receptive and impartial attention to and awareness of the present situation as well as to one's own thoughts and emotions in that moment.

A final predictor of moral sensitivity is the person's **mindfulness**.[83] Mindfulness refers to a person's receptive and impartial attention to and awareness of the present situation as well as to one's own thoughts and emotions in that moment. Mindfulness increases moral sensitivity because it involves actively monitoring the environment as well as being sensitive to our responses to that environment. This vigilance requires effort as well as skill to receptively evaluate our thoughts and emotions.

Unfortunately, we have a natural tendency to minimize effort, which leads to less mindfulness. For instance, research indicates that we have lower moral sensitivity when observing an organization, team, or individual we believe has high ethical standards.[84] We assume the source is unlikely to engage in any misconduct, so we switch from mindfulness to automatic pilot. If unusual activity is detected, we are less likely to interpret that event as unethical. For instance, one of the most serious cases of accounting fraud in North America occurred because the company's chief financial officer was highly respected in the industry. He had recently been awarded the chief financial officer of the year award, so employees took longer to realize that he was engaging in fraudulent activities. Even though some of his practices seemed suspicious, accounting staff initially assumed the chief financial officer was introducing innovative–and legal–accounting procedures.[85]

Situational Influences A final reason why good people engage in unethical decisions and behaviour is the situation in which the conduct occurs. As an example, in the opening case study for this chapter, some SNC-Lavalin employees and managers explained that they engaged in illegal activities because their boss put pressure on them to do so. In one recent survey, one-third of Canadians strongly or somewhat agreed that "in my workplace, delivering results is more important than doing the right thing." Furthermore, 22 percent of Canadians polled agreed that "I feel that I have to compromise my own personal ethics or values to keep my job."[86] Company pressure and other situational factors do not justify unethical conduct. Rather, we need to be aware of these factors so that organizations can reduce their influence in the future.

SUPPORTING ETHICAL BEHAVIOUR

Most large and medium-size organizations in Canada and other developed countries apply one or more strategies to improve ethical conduct. One of the most basic steps in this direction is a code of ethical conduct–a statement about desired practices, rules of conduct, and philosophy about the organization's relationship to its stakeholders and the environment.[87] These codes are supposed to motivate and guide employee behaviour, signal the importance of ethical conduct, and build the firm's trustworthiness to stakeholders. However, critics suggest that they do little to reduce unethical conduct. This problem became apparent at SNC-Lavalin. SNCL's code of ethical conduct was so elegant that the Canadian Institute of

BUSHUKHIN VALERY/ITAR-TASS /Landov

When William O'Rourke became Alcoa Russia's first CEO, he knew that bribery was a serious problem in that country, so he made his position clear to staff: "We don't condone it. We don't participate in it. We are not going to do it. Period." This ethical mandate was soon tested when local police stopped delivery of an expensive furnace and warned that delivery would resume only after Alcoa paid $25,000 to a government official. "My bonus was based in large part on making the planned investments happen on time," says O'Rourke, adding that a few Alcoa executives in the United States implied that he should do whatever it takes to keep the work on schedule. "Nonetheless, I stood my ground." The new furnace arrived three days later without any bribery payment. More than 18 months passed before the bribery attempts stopped.[88]

Chartered Accountants praised it when recently awarding the Canadian engineering and construction firm an excellence in corporate governance award!

Another strategy is to carefully and frequently train employees in proper ethical conduct. SNCL has taken this route.[89] Compliance officers have been hired throughout the organization, and one of their main functions is to provide in-person training to more than 3,000 of SNCL's employees working in positions with a higher level of corruption risk. All employees complete an annual certification to ensure they recall the main features of the company's code of ethics and business conduct.

Anonymous reporting is an increasingly popular method of preventing or curtailing unethical conduct. SNCL has a telephone hotline and website operated by an independent organization, where employees can anonymously report suspicious behaviour. The company's chief compliance officer also serves as an ombudsperson, which includes confidentially investigating the anonymous information about corporate wrongdoing. Furthermore, due to the severity of SNCL's ethical challenges, the company introduced a three-month amnesty program, giving employees the opportunity to declare past wrongdoing without the threat of being fired or facing damage claims from the company. Almost three dozen employees came forward under that program. Finally, SNC-Lavalin has initiated a form of ethics audit, whereby an independent entity monitors and evaluates the company's ethics initiatives. The monitor reports to the World Bank, which may lead the World Bank to lift the ban against SNCL in less than the full decade.

Training, hotlines, audits, and related activities improve ethical conduct to some extent, but the most powerful foundation is a set of shared values that reinforces ethical conduct. "A good, ethical system requires more than just signposts pointing employees in the right direction," advises the Canadian Centre for Ethics and Corporate Policy. Instead, ethical conduct occurs through "a set of beliefs, values, norms and practices that comprise an ethical culture." As we describe in Chapter 14 (organizational culture), an ethical culture is supported by the conduct and vigilance of corporate leaders. By acting with the highest moral standards, leaders not only gain support and trust from followers; they role-model the ethical standards that employees are more likely to follow.[90]

Values Across Cultures

LO6

An Australian manager had an unusual experience soon after Infosys, the technology giant headquartered in India, acquired the Australian firm where the manager worked. The manager met with a project team from India, where he described the project and then suggested that the team share ideas about how to successfully complete the project. "They didn't know what he meant," says an Infosys executive familiar with the incident. "Then one of the people just said: 'We were wondering when you are going to tell us what the plan was.'"[91]

individualism A cross-cultural value describing the degree to which people in a culture emphasize independence and personal uniqueness.

This incident illustrates the fact that expectations and values differ around the world. The team from India assumed the manager would make the decisions without their involvement, whereas the Australian manager was more comfortable with an egalitarian relationship where everyone contributes to the project plan. Over the next few pages, we introduce five values that have cross-cultural significance: individualism, collectivism, power distance, uncertainty avoidance, and achievement-nurturing orientation. Exhibit 2.7 summarizes these values and lists countries that have high, medium, or low emphasis on these values.

connect

How much do you value individualism and collectivism? Visit connect.mcgrawhill.com to estimate your score on these two values, as well as learn about the topic of cross-cultural values.

collectivism A cross-cultural value describing the degree to which people in a culture emphasize duty to groups to which they belong, and to group harmony.

INDIVIDUALISM AND COLLECTIVISM

Two seemingly inseparable cross-cultural values are individualism and collectivism. **Individualism** is the extent to which we value independence and personal uniqueness. Highly individualist people value personal freedom, self-sufficiency, control over their own lives, and appreciation of the unique qualities that distinguish them from others. Canadians, Americans, Chileans, and South Africans generally exhibit high individualism, whereas Taiwan and Venezuela are countries with low individualism.[92] **Collectivism** is the extent to which we value our duty

EXHIBIT 2.7 Five Cross-Cultural Values

Value	Sample Countries	Representative Beliefs/Behaviours in "High" Cultures
Individualism	High: Canada, United States, Chile, South Africa Medium: Japan, Denmark Low: Taiwan, Venezuela	Defines self more by one's uniqueness; personal goals have priority; decisions have low consideration of effect on others; relationships are viewed as more instrumental and fluid.
Collectivism	High: Israel, Taiwan Medium: India, Denmark Low: Canada, United States, Germany, Japan	Defines self more by one's in-group membership; goals of self-sacrifice and harmony have priority; behaviour regulated by in-group norms; in-group memberships are viewed as stable with a strong differentiation with out-groups.
Power Distance	High: India, Malaysia Medium: Canada, United States, Japan Low: Denmark, Israel	Reluctant to disagree with or contradict the boss; managers are expected and preferred decision makers; perception of dependence (versus interdependence) with the boss.
Uncertainty Avoidance	High: Belgium, Greece Medium: Canada, United States, Norway Low: Denmark, Singapore	Prefer predictable situations; value stable employment, strict laws, and low conflict; dislike deviations from normal behaviour.
Achievement Orientation	High: Austria, Japan Medium: Canada, United States, Brazil Low: Sweden, Netherlands	Focus on outcomes (versus relationships); decisions based on contribution (equity versus equality); low empathy or showing emotions (versus strong empathy and caring)

Sources: Individualism and collectivism descriptions and results are from the meta-analysis reported in D. Oyserman, H. M. Coon, and M. Kemmelmeier, "Rethinking Individualism and Collectivism: Evaluation of Theoretical Assumptions and Meta-Analyses," *Psychological Bulletin,* 128 (2002), pp. 3-72. The other information is from G. Hofstede, *Culture's Consequences,* 2nd ed. (Thousand Oaks, CA: Sage, 2001).

to groups to which we belong and to group harmony. Highly collectivist people define themselves by their group memberships, emphasize their personal connection to others in their in-groups, and value the goals and well-being of people within those groups.[93] Low collectivism countries include Canada, Japan, and Germany, whereas Israelis and Taiwanese have relatively high collectivism.

Contrary to popular belief, individualism is not the opposite of collectivism. In fact, the two concepts are typically uncorrelated.[94] For example, cultures that highly value duty to one's group do not necessarily give a low priority to personal freedom and uniqueness. Generally, people across all cultures define themselves by both their uniqueness and their relationship to others. It is an inherent characteristic of everyone's self-concept, which we discuss in the next chapter. Some cultures clearly emphasize uniqueness or group obligations more than the other, but both have a place in a person's values and self-concept.

Also note that people in Japan have relatively low collectivism. This is contrary to many cross-cultural books, which claim that Japan is one of the most collectivist countries on the planet! There are several explanations for the historical misinterpretation, ranging from problems defining and measuring collectivism to erroneous reporting of early cross-cultural research. Whatever the reasons, studies consistently report that people in Japan tend to have relatively low collectivism and moderate individualism (as indicated in Exhibit 2.7).[95]

connect

What is your level of power distance? Visit **connect.mcgrawhill.com** to estimate your score on this cross-cultural value.

power distance A cross-cultural value describing the degree to which people in a culture accept unequal distribution of power in a society.

POWER DISTANCE

Power distance refers to the extent to which people accept unequal distribution of power in a society.[96] Those with high power distance accept and value unequal power. They value obedience to authority and are comfortable receiving commands from their superiors without

Global Connections 2.2:

WORKING WITH HIGH POWER DISTANCE IN CHINA[97]

As the only Westerner in a 50-employee start-up winery in China, Emilie Bourgois soon noticed that Chinese managers seem to use their power more directly than do European, Canadian, or American bosses. "I was surprised to see that taking the initiative most of the time was seen as rude and as a failure to respect the executives' authority," says Bourgois, a public relations professional from Bordeaux, France. "At work, everyone had to perform well in their own tasks, but permission was required for anything other than what was expected."

This high power distance was also apparent in how Chinese managers interacted with staff. "Western-style bosses tend to develop a closer relationship with employees," Bourgois suggests. "The hierarchy is much more clearly divided in Chinese-dominant companies than it is in foreign ones."

Bourgois worked well with her colleagues at the Chinese winery, but she acknowledges that "beyond that, there is still an important cultural gap." She is now employed in the Beijing office of executive recruitment firm Antal International, where cultural differences seem to be less pronounced because the company has team building events to improve bonding and mutual understanding.

Emilie Bourgois

Emilie Bourgois, second from right with coworkers at Antal International in Beijing, discovered in an earlier job that Chinese-dominant companies have higher power distance compared to most Western firms.

consultation or debate. They also prefer to resolve differences through formal procedures rather than directly. In contrast, people with low power distance expect relatively equal power sharing. They view the relationship with their boss as one of interdependence, not dependence; that is, they believe their boss is also dependent on them, so they expect power sharing and consultation before decisions affecting them are made. People in India and Malaysia tend to have high power distance, whereas people in Denmark and Israel generally have low power distance. Canadians collectively have medium-low power distance. Global Connections 2.2 illustrates high power distance in China, from the perspective of a Western (French national) employee.

UNCERTAINTY AVOIDANCE

uncertainty avoidance A cross-cultural value describing the degree to which people in a culture tolerate ambiguity (low uncertainty avoidance) or feel threatened by ambiguity and uncertainty (high uncertainty avoidance).

Uncertainty avoidance is the degree to which people tolerate ambiguity (low uncertainty avoidance) or feel threatened by ambiguity and uncertainty (high uncertainty avoidance). Employees with high uncertainty avoidance value structured situations in which rules of conduct and decision making are clearly documented. They usually prefer direct rather than indirect or ambiguous communications. Uncertainty avoidance tends to be high in Belgium and Greece and very high in Japan. It is generally low in Denmark and Singapore. Canadians collectively have medium-low uncertainty avoidance.

ACHIEVEMENT-NURTURING ORIENTATION

achievement-nurturing orientation A cross-cultural value describing the degree to which people in a culture emphasize competitive versus cooperative relations with other people.

Achievement-nurturing orientation reflects a competitive versus cooperative view of relations with other people.[98] People with a high achievement orientation value assertiveness, competitiveness, and materialism. They appreciate people who are tough, and they favour the acquisition of money and material goods. In contrast, people in nurturing-oriented cultures emphasize relationships and the well-being of others. They focus on human interaction and caring rather than competition and personal success. People in Sweden, Norway, and the Netherlands score very low on achievement orientation (i.e., they have a high nurturing orientation). In contrast, very high achievement orientation scores have been reported in Japan and Austria. Canada and the United States place a little above the middle of the range on achievement-nurturing orientation.

CAVEATS ABOUT CROSS-CULTURAL KNOWLEDGE

Cross-cultural organizational research has gained considerable attention over the past two decades, likely due to increased globalization and cultural diversity within organizations. Our knowledge of cross-cultural dynamics has blossomed, and many of these findings will be discussed throughout this book, particularly regarding leadership, conflict handling, and influence tactics. However, we also need to raise a few warning flags about cross-cultural knowledge. One problem is that too many studies have relied on small, convenient samples (such as students attending one university) to represent an entire culture.[99] The result is that many cross-cultural studies draw conclusions that might not generalize to the cultures they intended to represent.

A second problem is that cross-cultural studies often assume that each country has one culture.[100] In reality, many countries (including Canada) have become culturally diverse. As more countries embrace globalization and multiculturalism, it becomes even less appropriate to assume that an entire country has one unified culture.

A third concern is that cross-cultural research and writing continues to rely on a major study conducted almost four decades ago of 116,000 IBM employees across dozens of countries. That study helped to ignite subsequent cross-cultural research, but its findings are becoming out of date as values in some cultures have shifted over the years. For example, value systems seem to be converging across Asia as people in these countries interact more frequently with each other and adopt standardized business practices.[101] At least one recent review has recommended that future studies should no longer rely on the IBM study to benchmark values of a particular culture.[102]

DIVERSITY OF CANADIAN CULTURAL VALUES

You might think from reading some cross-cultural studies that Canada is a homogeneous country where people hold identical or very similar values. Of course, anyone who lives here knows otherwise. But even Canadians may be surprised at how much cultural diversity exists within this country, even when excluding the incredible variety of new Canadians who grew up elsewhere in the world.[103]

Consider Canada's historical diversity of two cultural clusters–Anglophones and Francophones. At one time, Francophones were more religious, traditional, and deferent to authority, compared with Anglophones. Now, the situation is almost reversed. Francophones have lower scores than Anglophones on respect for patriarchal authority (i.e.,the father should be the head of the household), and they tend to have more tolerant or morally permissive opinions regarding marriage, sexual activity, and nonmarried parenthood.[104] There is some evidence that Anglophone and Francophone values are converging, but these two sub-cultures within Canada are still easily identifiable as a form of deep level diversity.[105]

Canada's cultural diversity is further evident in the values of aboriginal (First Nations) people and their organizations.[106] Organizations with aboriginal founders and leaders tend to have a strong collectivist value, low power distance, low uncertainty avoidance, and a relatively nurturing rather than achievement orientation. These values are evident from consensus-oriented decision making (low power distance), focus more on the group than individuals (high collectivism), fewer rules and procedures (low uncertainty avoidance), and emphasis on the holistic well-being of employees and community (nurturing more than achievement orientation).

Canadian versus American Values Canadians increasingly shop at American stores and have close associations with friends and coworkers in the United States. Yet, the values held by people in these two countries are more divergent today than a few decades ago. "Canadians may like Americans, speak the same language, and consume more of their fast food and popular culture, but we embrace a different hierarchy of values," writes social policy researcher Michael Adams.[107] Another Canadian cultural expert is even more emphatic: the 49th parallel border is more than just an imaginary geographic division; it is a symbol of the widening ideological divide in North America.[108]

Canadians have significantly higher tolerance or moral permissiveness than do Americans. Canadians are also more willing to allow collective rights over individual rights and are less accepting of large wealth differences within society.[109] Another striking difference is that

Canadians question authority and value autonomy from these institutions, whereas Americans have a relatively high deference to authority. Canadians are much less likely to be associated with a religious institution and to believe that these institutions should influence public policy. They are also much more likely than Americans to believe that organizations work better without a single leader. Perhaps the most significant difference is in the value of patriarchal authority. In the early 1980s, more than 40 percent of Canadians and Americans believed that the father should be the master of the home. Today, only 18 percent of Canadians hold this view, compared to almost 50 percent of Americans.[110]

Although there is strong evidence that Canadian and American values differ, we also need to take into account diversity of values within each country. For instance, one major study reported that the United States and Canada seem to consist of four cultural groups: the Southern U.S., Northern U.S., Anglophone (English-speaking) Canada, and Francophone (French-speaking) Canada. The Southern U.S. is largely inhabited by people with the most conservative, hawkish, and deeply religious values of the four groups. Francophone Canadians, the second cluster, hold the most tolerant or morally permissive values. This leaves Anglophone Canadians and Americans residing in the northern states. Research suggests that these two groups have very similar cultural values.[111]

Chapter Summary

LO1 Describe the four factors that directly influence individual behaviour and performance.

Four variables–motivation, ability, role perceptions, and situational factors–which are represented by the acronym MARS, directly influence individual behaviour and performance. Motivation represents the forces within a person that affect his or her direction, intensity, and persistence of voluntary behaviour; ability includes both the natural aptitudes and the learned capabilities required to successfully complete a task; role perceptions are the extent to which people understand the job duties (roles) assigned to them or expected of them; situational factors include conditions beyond the employee's immediate control that constrain or facilitate behaviour and performance.

LO2 Summarize the five types of individual behaviour in organizations.

There are five main types of workplace behaviour. Task performance refers to goal-directed behaviours under the individual's control that support organizational objectives. Organizational citizenship behaviours consist of various forms of cooperation and helpfulness to others that support the organization's social and psychological context. Counterproductive work behaviours are voluntary behaviours that have the potential to directly or indirectly harm the organization. Joining and staying with the organization refers to agreeing to become an organizational member and remaining with the organization. Maintaining work attendance includes minimizing absenteeism when capable of working and avoiding scheduled work when not fit (i.e., low presenteeism).

LO3 Describe personality and discuss how the "Big Five" personality dimensions and four MBTI types relate to individual behaviour in organizations.

Personality is the relatively enduring pattern of thoughts, emotions, and behaviours that characterize a person, along with the psychological processes behind those characteristics. Personality traits are broad concepts about people that allow us to label and understand individual differences. Personality is developed through hereditary origins (nature) as well as socialization (nurture). The "Big Five" personality dimensions include conscientiousness, agreeableness, neuroticism, openness to experience, and extraversion. Conscientiousness and emotional stability (low neuroticism) predict individual performance in most job groups. Extraversion is associated with performance in sales and management jobs, whereas agreeableness is associated with performance in jobs requiring cooperation and openness to experience is associated with performance in creative jobs.

Based on Jungian personality theory, the Myers-Briggs Type Indicator (MBTI) identifies competing orientations for getting energy (extraversion vs. introversion), perceiving information (sensing vs. intuiting), processing information and making decisions (thinking vs. feeling), and orienting to the external world (judging vs. perceiving). The MBTI improves self-awareness for career development and mutual understanding but is more popular than valid.

LO4 Summarize Schwartz's model of individual values and discuss the conditions where values influence behaviour.

Values are stable, evaluative beliefs that guide our preferences for outcomes or courses of action in a variety of situations. Compared to personality traits, values are evaluative (rather than descriptive), more likely to conflict with each other, and are formed more from socialization than heredity. Schwartz's model organizes 57 values into a circumplex of ten dimensions along two bipolar dimensions: openness to change to conservation and self-enhancement to self-transcendence. Values influence behaviour when the situation facilitates that connection and when we actively think about them and understand their relevance to the situation. Values congruence refers to how similar a person's values hierarchy is to the values hierarchy of another source (organization, person, etc.).

LO5 Describe three ethical principles and discuss three factors that influence ethical behaviour.

Ethics refers to the study of moral principles or values that determine whether actions are right or wrong and outcomes are good or bad. Three ethical principles are utilitarianism, individual rights, and distributive justice. Ethical behaviour is influenced by the degree to which an issue demands the application of ethical principles (moral intensity), the individual's ability to recognize the presence and relative importance of an ethical issue (moral sensitivity), and situational forces. Ethical conduct at work is supported by codes of ethical conduct, mechanisms for communicating ethical violations, the organization's culture, and the leader's behaviour.

LO6 Review five values commonly studied across cultures and discuss the diverse cultures within Canada.

Five values commonly studied across cultures are individualism (valuing independence and personal uniqueness); collectivism (valuing duty to in-groups and to group harmony); power distance (valuing unequal distribution of power); uncertainty avoidance (tolerating or feeling threatened by ambiguity and uncertainty); and achievement-nurturing orientation (valuing competition vs. cooperation). Canada consists of several cultures in addition to those brought by new Canadians. Anglophones and Francophones differ in their values, although these values have almost reversed over the past several decades. Aboriginal values also differ from others in Canada. Canadians and Americans also have noticeably different values, although North America might be divided into four clusters that cross national boundaries.

Key Terms

ability, p. 28
achievement-nurturing orientation, p. 48
collectivism, p. 46
conscientiousness, p. 35
counterproductive work behaviours (CWBs) p. 32
extraversion, p. 35
five-factor model (FFM), p. 34
individualism, p. 46
mindfulness, p. 44
moral intensity, p. 43
moral sensitivity, p. 44
motivation, p. 28
Myers-Briggs Type Indicator (MBTI), p. 36
neuroticism, p. 35
organizational citizenship behaviours (OCBs) p. 31
personality, p. 34
power distance, p. 47
presenteeism, p. 33
role perceptions, p. 30
uncertainty avoidance, p. 48

Critical-Thinking Questions

1. A provincial government department has high levels of absenteeism among the office staff. The head of office administration argues that employees are misusing the organization's sick leave benefits. However, some of the mostly female staff members have explained that family responsibilities interfere with work. Using the MARS model, as well as your knowledge of absenteeism behaviour, discuss some of the possible reasons for absenteeism here and how it might be reduced.
2. It has been said that all employees are motivated. Do you agree with this statement?
3. Studies report that heredity has a strong influence on an individual's personality. What are the implications of this in organizational settings?
4. All candidates applying for a management trainee position are given a personality test that measures the five dimensions in the five-factor model. Which personality traits would you consider to be the most important for this type of job? Explain your answer.
5. Compare and contrast personality with personal values, and identify values categories in Schwartz's values circumplex that likely relate to one or more personality dimensions in the five-factor personality model.
6. This chapter discussed values congruence mostly in the context of an employee's personal values versus the organization's values. But values congruence also relates to the juxtaposition of other pairs of value systems. Explain how values congruence is relevant with respect to organizational versus professional values (i.e., values of a professional occupation, such as physician, accountant, pharmacist).
7. "All decisions are ethical decisions." Comment on this statement, particularly by referring to the concepts of moral intensity and moral sensitivity.
8. The organization that you have been working in for five years is now suffering from a global recession and it changes the compensation structure. Discuss the role of moral intensity, moral sensitivity and situational influences in this context.
9. People in a particular South American country have high power distance and high collectivism. What does this mean, and what are the implications of this information when you (a senior executive) visit employees working for your company in that country?

Case Study: ETHICS DILEMMA VIGNETTES

Purpose This exercise is designed to make you aware of the ethical dilemmas people face in various business situations, as well as the competing principles and values that operate in these situations.

Instructions (Small Class) The instructor will form teams of four or five students. Team members will read each case below and discuss the extent to which the company's action in each case was ethical. Teams should be prepared to justify their evaluation using ethics principles and the perceived moral intensity of each incident.

Instructions (Large Class) Working alone, read each case below and determine the extent to which the company's action in each case was ethical. The instructor will use a show of hands to determine the extent to which students believe the case represents an ethical dilemma (high or low moral intensity) and the extent to which the main people or company in each incident acted ethically.

CASE ONE

A large European bank requires all employees to open a bank account with that bank. The bank deposits employee paycheques to those accounts. The bank explains that this is a formal policy which all employees agree to at the time of hire. Furthermore, failure to have an account with the bank shows disloyalty, which could limit the employee's career advancement opportunities with the bank. Until recently, the bank has reluctantly agreed to deposit paycheques to accounts at other banks for a small percentage of employees. Now, bank executives want to reinforce the policy. They announced that employees have three months to open an account with the bank or face disciplinary action.

CASE TWO

A 16-year-old hired as an office administrator at a small import services company started posting her thoughts about the job on her Facebook site. After her first day, she wrote: "first day at work. omg!! So dull!!" Two days later, she complained "all i do is shred holepunch n scan paper!!! omg!" Two weeks later she added "im so totally bord!!!" These comments were intermixed with the other usual banter about her life. Her Facebook site did not mention the name of the company where she worked. Three weeks after being hired, the employee was called into the owner's office, where he fired her for the comments on Facebook, then had her escorted from the building. The owner argues that these comments put the company in a bad light, and her "display of disrespect and dissatisfaction undermined the relationship and made it untenable."

CASE THREE

Computer printer manufacturers usually sell printers at a low margin over cost and generate much more income from subsequent sales of the high-margin ink cartridges required for each printer. One global printer manufacturer now designs its printers so that they work only with ink cartridges made in the same region. Ink cartridges purchased in Canada will not work with the same printer model sold in Europe, for example. This "region coding" of ink cartridges does not improve performance. Rather, it prevents consumers and grey marketers from buying the product at a lower price in another region. The company says this policy allows it to maintain stable prices within a region rather than continually changing prices due to currency fluctuations.

CASE FOUR

Judy Price is a popular talk show radio personality and opinionated commentator on the morning phone-in show of a Toronto radio station. Ms. Price is married to John Tremble, a lawyer who was recently elected for the first time to the parliament of Ontario. He also became Minister of the Environment and Conservation in the newly formed government that defeated the previous government. The radio station's board of directors is very concerned that the station's perceived objectivity will be compromised if Ms. Price remains on air as a commentator and talk show host while her husband holds such a public position in the province. For example, the radio station manager believes that Ms. Price gave minimal attention to the Environment Ministry's slow response to a leakage of toxic chemicals a week ago at a large manufacturing company. Ms. Price denied that her views are biased and argued that the incident didn't merit as much attention as other issues that particular day. To ease the board's concerns, the station manager has transferred Ms. Price from a talk show host and commentator to the hourly news reporting position, where most script is edited by others. Although technically a lower position, Ms. Price's total salary package remains the same. Ms. Price is now seeking professional advice to determine whether the radio station's action represents a form of discrimination on the basis of marital status.

CASE FIVE

For the past few years, the design department of a small (40-employee) company has been using a particular software program, but the three employees who use the software have been complaining for more than a year that the software is out of date and is slowing down their performance. The department agreed to switch to a competing software program, costing several thousand dollars. However, the next version won't be released for six months and buying the current version will not allow much discount on the next version. The company has put in advance orders for the next version. Meanwhile, one employee was able to get a copy of the current version of the software from a friend in the industry. The company has allowed the three employees to use this current version of the software even though they did not pay for it.

Class Exercise: TEST YOUR KNOWLEDGE OF PERSONALITY

Purpose This exercise is designed to help you think about and understand the effects of the Big Five personality dimensions on individual preferences and outcomes.

Instructions (Large Class) Below are several questions relating to the Big Five personality dimensions and various preferences or outcomes. Answer each of these questions relying on your personal experience or best guess. Later, the instructor will show you the answers based on scholarly results. You will *not* be graded on this exercise. Instead, it illustrates the many ways that personality influences human behaviour and preferences.

Instructions (Small Class)

1. The instructor will organize students into teams. Members of each team work together to answer each of the questions below relating to the Big Five personality dimensions and various preferences or outcomes.
2. The instructor will reveal the answers based on scholarly results. (*Note:* The instructor might create a competition to see which team has the most answers correct.)

Personality and Preferences Questions

1. You have been asked to select job applicants for a nine-month over-winter assignment working in an Antarctic research station with a dozen other people. Assuming that all candidates have equal skills, experience, and health, identify which level of each personality dimension would be best for people working in these remote, confined, and isolated conditions.

Personality dimension	Low	Below average	Average	Above average	High
Conscientiousness	○	○	○	○	○
Agreeableness	○	○	○	○	○
Neuroticism	○	○	○	○	○
Openness to experience	○	○	○	○	○
Extraversion	○	○	○	○	○

2. Listed below are several jobs. Please check no more than two personality dimensions that you believe are positively associated with preferences for each occupation.

	Personality Dimension				
Job	Extraversion	Conscientiousness	Agreeableness	Neuroticism	Openness to experience
Budget analyst	○	○	○	○	○
Corporate executive	○	○	○	○	○
Engineer	○	○	○	○	○
Journalist	○	○	○	○	○
Life insurance agent	○	○	○	○	○
Nurse	○	○	○	○	○
Physician	○	○	○	○	○
Production supervisor	○	○	○	○	○
Public relations director	○	○	○	○	○
Research analyst	○	○	○	○	○
Schoolteacher	○	○	○	○	○
Sculptor	○	○	○	○	○

3. On which two personality dimensions should team members have the highest scores, on average, to produce the best team performance?

   ○ Conscientiousness
   ○ Agreeableness
   ○ Neuroticism
   ○ Openness to experience
   ○ Extraversion

4. Rank order (1 = highest, 5 = lowest) the Big Five personality dimensions in terms of how much you think they predict a person's degree of life satisfaction. (*Note:* Personality dimensions are ranked by their absolute effect, so ignore the negative or positive direction of association.)

   ___ Conscientiousness
   ___ Agreeableness
   ___ Neuroticism
   ___ Openness to experience
   ___ Extraversion

5. Which two Big Five personality dimensions are positively associated with enjoyment of workplace humour?

   ○ Conscientiousness
   ○ Agreeableness
   ○ Neuroticism
   ○ Openness to experience
   ○ Extraversion

Self-Assessment: ARE YOU INTROVERTED OR EXTRAVERTED?

Purpose This self-assessment is designed to help you estimate the extent to which you are introverted or extraverted.

Instructions The statements in the scale below refer to personal characteristics that might or might not be characteristic of you. Mark the box indicating the extent to which the statement accurately or inaccurately describes you. Then use the scoring key in Appendix B at the end of this book to calculate your results. This exercise should be completed alone so that you can assess yourself honestly without concerns of social comparison. Class discussion will focus on the meaning and implications of extraversion and introversion in organizations.

IPIP Introversion-Extraversion Scale

How accurately does each of the statements listed below describe you?	Very accurate description of me	Moderately accurate	Neither accurate nor inaccurate	Moderately inaccurate	Very inaccurate description of me
1. I feel comfortable around people.	○	○	○	○	○
2. I make friends easily.	○	○	○	○	○
3. I keep in the background.	○	○	○	○	○
4. I don't talk a lot.	○	○	○	○	○
5. I would describe my experiences as somewhat dull.	○	○	○	○	○
6. I know how to captivate people.	○	○	○	○	○
7. I don't like to draw attention to myself.	○	○	○	○	○
8. I am the life of the party.	○	○	○	○	○
9. I am skilled in handling social situations.	○	○	○	○	○
10. I have little to say.	○	○	○	○	○

Source: Adapted from instruments described and/or presented in L. R. Goldberg, J. A. Johnson, H. W. Eber, R. Hogan, M. C. Ashton, C. R. Cloninger, and H. C. Gough, "The International Personality Item Pool and the Future of Public-Domain Personality Measures," *Journal of Research in Personality* 40 (2006), pp. 84–96.

SELF-ASSESSMENTS FOR CHAPTER 2

SELF-ASSESSMENT NAME	DESCRIPTION	LOCATION
Are you introverted or extraverted?	Estimates the extent to which you have an introverted or extraverted personality.	Page 54 connect
Are you a sensing or intuitive type?	Estimates your score on this Jungian personality type (S/N).	connect
Can you identify personality traits from blogging words?	Assesses how well you can relate a sample of words used in blogs to their associated personality.	connect
What are your dominant values?	Assesses which of the 10 categories of values in Schwartz's circumplex model are most important to you.	connect
How much do you value individualism and collectivism?	Estimates your score on these two cross-cultural values.	connect
What is your level of power distance?	Estimates your score on this cross-cultural value.	connect

Emily MacDonald (shown) attended Camp FFit in Ottawa, a program that helps teenage girls develop a self-concept as firefighters, improve their self-esteem, and dispel the occupation's macho stereotype.

© Wayne Cuddington/*Ottawa Citizen*. Reprinted by permission.

Chapter 3

Perceiving Ourselves and Others in Organizations

LEARNING OBJECTIVES

After reading this chapter, you should be able to:

LO1. Describe the elements of self-concept and explain how each affects an individual's behaviour and well-being.

LO2. Outline the perceptual process and discuss the effects of categorical thinking and mental models in that process.

LO3. Discuss how stereotyping, attribution, self-fulfilling prophecy, halo, false-consensus, primacy, and recency influence the perceptual process.

LO4. Discuss three ways to improve perceptions, with specific application to organizational situations.

LO5. Outline the main features of a global mindset and justify its usefulness to employees and organizations.

Climbing a fire truck ladder over 20 metres tall isn't everyone's idea of a good time, but Emily MacDonald wants to climb them throughout her career. The 17-year-old's father and both grandfathers were firefighters, and she wants to join in that tradition. "I want to be the first female firefighter in the family," says MacDonald. MacDonald participated in Camp FFit, a week-long program in Ottawa, where two dozen teenage girls scaled fire truck ladders, hooked up fire hoses, carried 32-kilogram packs, forced entry into buildings, and learned other firefighting skills.

Camp FFit and similar programs around North America help young women develop their self-concept as firefighters. Through direct experience, participants realize that qualified women can perform firefighting tasks, and that those tasks are compatible with their self-image. "We want young girls to see that this is something they can grow up to become," explains Cheryl Horvath, a division fire chief in Tucson, Arizona, which also has a special firefighting camp for young women.

These camps also help women strengthen their self-esteem and self-efficacy. "We want all of the girls to walk away with a sense that they can do anything they put their minds to, regardless of what the job is," says Horvath. Alexandra Gaudes says she developed a clearer and more positive self-evaluation after attending Ottawa's Camp FFit a few years ago. When Gaudes told friends she wanted to be a firefighter, one male retorted "but you are a girl." Gaudes smiled "and asked which century he was from" she recalls. "Standing up for myself to him was when I knew that this camp had really changed me."

Although Canadian fire services are becoming more inclusive organizations, gender biases and prejudices persist. Three male firefighters were recently dismissed from the Toronto Fire Services for tweeting crude comments about women. In Calgary, a fire captain noticed that three female firefighters were employed at the station where he was temporarily assigned, so he asked a few male crew members: "How did you guys get stuck with so many (expletives) at your hall?" He repeated the obscenity against women when asked to clarify. Initially fired for the remark, the captain was soon reinstated with a brief demotion and suspension. However, all three female firefighters in that unit experienced such a backlash over the captain's discipline that one went on stress leave, another took unpaid leave, and the third requested permanent transfer to another type of work.[1]

Firefighting services across Canada and in most parts of the world face two challenges in attracting and keeping women in this occupation: (1) the self-concept women have about themselves as firefighters and (2) perceptions that others have about firefighters and of women in these roles. We discuss both of these related topics in this chapter. First, we examine how people perceive themselves–their self-concept–and how that self-perception affects their decisions and behaviour. Next, we focus on perceptions in organizational settings, beginning with how we select, organize, and interpret information. We also review several specific perceptual processes such as stereotyping, attribution, and self-fulfilling prophecy. We then identify potentially effective ways to improve perceptions. The final section of this chapter reviews the main elements of global mindset, a largely perceptual process valued in this increasingly globalized world.

connect

How much does work define your self-concept? See page 80 or visit connect.mcgrawhill.com to assess your level of work centrality.

Self-Concept: How We Perceive Ourselves

LO1

Why are there so few female firefighters in Canada and most other countries? As the opening case study to this chapter suggests, many women do not see themselves as firefighters and have doubts about doing that job. This self-concept incompatibility is further reinforced by gendered perceptions of firefighters held by family, friends, and the media. "We don't have a lot of parents telling their daughters 'hey honey, when you grow up, you can be a firefighter,'" admits Karen DuPont, Assistant Chief of the Houston Fire Department.[2]

self-concept An individual's self-beliefs and self-evaluations.

Self-concept refers to an individual's self-beliefs and self-evaluations.[3] It is the "Who am I?" and "How do I feel about myself?" that people ask themselves and that guide their decisions and actions. Whether contemplating a career as a firefighter or a financial analyst, we compare our images of that job with our current (perceived self) and desired (ideal self) images of ourselves. We also evaluate our current and desired competencies to determine whether there is a good fit with that job. Recent studies suggest that we have an individual self (our personal traits), relational self (interpersonal relations), and collective self (our membership in identifiable social groups).[4]

SELF-CONCEPT COMPLEXITY, CONSISTENCY, AND CLARITY

An individual's self-concept can be described by three characteristics: complexity, consistency, and clarity (see Exhibit 3.1). *Complexity* refers to the number of distinct and important roles or identities that people perceive about themselves.[5] Everyone has some degree of complexity because they see themselves in different roles at various times (student, friend, daughter, sports fan, etc.). But complexity isn't just the number of selves that define who we are; it is also the separation of those selves. A self-concept has low complexity when the individual's most important identities are highly interconnected, such as when they are all work-related (manager, engineer, family income-earner).

EXHIBIT 3.1

Self-Concept Characteristics and Processes

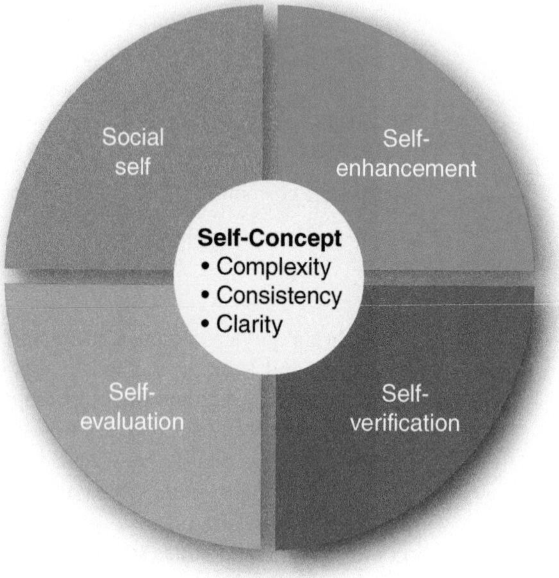

A second characteristic of an individual's self-concept is its internal *consistency*. High internal consistency exists when most of the individual's self-perceived roles require similar personality traits, values, and other attributes. Low consistency occurs when some self-perceptions require personal characteristics that conflict with characteristics required for other aspects of self. Low self-concept consistency would exist if you see yourself as a very exacting engineer, but also a cavalier and risk-oriented skier.

Clarity, the third characteristic of self-concept is the degree to which you have a clear, confidently defined, and stable self-concept.[6] Clarity occurs when we are confident about "who we are," can describe our important identities to others, and provide the same description of ourselves across time. Self-concept clarity increases with the person's age and the consistency of their multiple selves.[7]

Effects of Self-Concept Characteristics on Well-Being and Behaviour

Self-concept complexity, consistency, and clarity influence a person's well-being, behaviour, and performance. People tend to have better psychological well-being when they have multiple selves (complexity) that are well established (clarity) and are similar to each other and compatible with personal traits (consistency).[9] Self-concept complexity protects our self-esteem when some roles are threatened or damaged. A complex self is rather like a ship with several compartments that can be sealed off from each other. If one compartment is damaged, the other compartments (selves) remain intact so the ship remains afloat. In contrast, people with low complexity, including when their multiple selves are interconnected, suffer severe loss when they experience failure because these events affect a large part of themselves.

People also tend to have better well-being when their multiple selves are in harmony with each other and with the individual's personality and values (consistency).[10] Some self-concept diversity helps people to adapt, but too much variation causes internal tension and conflict. Finally, well-being tends to increase with self-concept clarity. People who are unsure of their self-views are more easily influenced by others, experience more stress when making decisions, and feel more threatened by social forces that undermine their self-confidence and self-esteem.[11]

Self-concept complexity, consistency, and clarity have more varied effects on behaviour and performance.[12] On the one hand, people who define themselves mainly by their work (i.e., low complexity) tend to have lower absenteeism and turnover. They also tend to have better performance due to more investment in skill development, longer hours, more concentration on work, and so forth. On the other hand, low complexity commonly results in higher stress and depression when the main self-aspect is damaged or threatened, which further undermines individual performance.

© Deborah Baic/*The Globe and Mail*/The Canadian Press

Hélène Joy appeared on several popular television programs, but the lack of job security as an actor motivated her to join her mother's real estate business. "It lasted a week," Joy recalls of her short-lived real estate career. "I realized that acting is what I do, and who I am." The experience helped Joy form a clearer self-concept, which provided a new determination to achieve her ideal self. "I guess I was never really committed till then, and once I did commit, I haven't stopped working." Today, Joy is a lead actor in the popular Canadian TV series *Murdoch Mysteries* and has received several awards for her acting talent.[8]

Self-concept clarity tends to improve performance and is considered vital for leadership roles.[13] Clarity also focuses personal energy so employees direct their effort more efficiently toward their career objectives. Another benefit of high self-concept clarity is that people feel less threatened by interpersonal conflict, so they use more constructive problem-solving behaviours to resolve the conflict. However, those with very high clarity may have role inflexibility such that they cannot adapt to changing job duties or environmental conditions.

In addition to the three self-concept characteristics, Exhibit 3.1 illustrates four processes that shape self-concept and motivate a person's decisions and behaviour. Let's look at each of these four "selves": self-enhancement, self-verification, self-evaluation, and social self (social identity).

SELF-ENHANCEMENT

self-enhancement A person's inherent motivation to have a positive self-concept (and to have others perceive him/her favourably), such as being competent, attractive, lucky, ethical, and important.

A century ago, educational philosopher John Dewey said that "the deepest urge in human nature is the desire to be important."[14] Dewey recognized that people are inherently motivated to perceive themselves (and to be perceived by others) as competent, attractive, lucky, ethical, and important.[15] This **self-enhancement** is observed in many ways. Individuals tend to rate themselves above average, believe that they have a better than average probability of success, and attribute their successes to personal motivation or ability while blaming the situation for their mistakes. People don't see themselves as above average in all circumstances. Instead, it is most apparent for things that are important to them and are relatively common or everyday rather than rare.[16]

Self-enhancement has both positive and negative consequences in organizational settings.[17] On the positive side, individuals tend to experience better mental and physical health and adjustment when they amplify their self-concept. Overconfidence also generates a "can-do" attitude (which we discuss later) that motivates persistence in difficult or risky tasks. On the negative side, self-enhancement causes people to overestimate future returns in investment decisions, use less conservative accounting practices, and take longer to recognize their mistakes. Some research also suggests that self-enhancement is a factor in high accident rates among novice drivers. Generally, though, successful companies strive to help employees feel valued and integral members of the organization.

SELF-VERIFICATION

self-verification A person's inherent motivation to confirm and maintain his/her existing self-concept.

Along with being motivated by self-enhancement, people try to confirm and maintain their existing self-concept.[19] This process, called **self-verification,** stabilizes an individual's

OB by the NUMBERS

Self-Enhancement Makes Most of Us Above Average![18]

- **94%** of professors at a large American university rated their teaching as above-average compared with others at their university.
- **90%** of Canadians recently rated themselves as healthy (yet 48% of Canadians lack sufficient physical activity and 54% fall short of healthy eating standards).
- **74%** of investment fund managers said they were above average at their jobs.
- **70%** of college students recently said they have above average academic ability (64% of college students in 1966 said they were above average).
- **69%** of U.S. federal government workers rated their performance above average compared to coworkers in their unit (only 1 percent rated their performance below average).
- **62%** of recent college students said they have above average leadership ability (only 41% of college students in 1966 claimed to be above average).
- **40%** of Swedish student drivers overestimated their driving competence (13% underestimated their driving competence).
- **37%** of consumers in a large U.S. survey panel overestimated their actual credit rating (only 4.6% underestimated their credit rating).

Note: Some studies cited above are not representative of the entire population. The survey of professor teaching ability is not recent.

self-view, which, in turn, provides an important anchor that guides his or her thoughts and actions. Employees actively communicate their self-concept so coworkers understand it and provide verifying feedback when observed. For example, you might let coworkers know that you are a very organized person; later, they point out situations where you have indeed been very organized. Unlike self-enhancement, self-verification includes seeking feedback that is not necessarily flattering (e.g., I'm a numbers person, not a people person). Social scientists continue to debate whether and under what conditions people prefer information that supports self-enhancement or self-verification.[20] In other words, do we prefer compliments rather than accurate critique about weaknesses that we readily acknowledge? The answer is likely an emotional tug-of-war; we enjoy compliments, but less so if they are significantly contrary to our self-view.

Self-verification has implications for organizational behaviour.[21] First, it affects the perceptual process because employees are more likely to remember information that is consistent with their self-concept and nonconsciously screen out information (particularly negative information) that seems inconsistent with it. Second, the clearer their self-concept, the less people will consciously accept feedback that contradicts that self-concept. Third, employees are motivated to interact with others who affirm their self-views, and this affects how well they get along with their boss and team members. For instance, new employees are more satisfied and perform better when the socialization process allows them to affirm their authentic self–they can demonstrate and receive support for "who they are"–rather than when the socialization process mainly steers them into the company's image of an ideal employee.[22]

connect

What is your level of general self-efficacy? Visit connect.mcgrawhill.com to assess yourself on this component of self-evaluation.

SELF-EVALUATION

Almost everyone strives to have a positive self-concept, but some people have a more positive evaluation of themselves than do others. This *self-evaluation* is mostly defined by three elements: self-esteem, self-efficacy, and locus of control.[23]

Self-Esteem *Self-esteem*–the extent to which people like, respect, and are satisfied with themselves–represents a global self-evaluation. Some experts also believe that self-esteem is a person's rating of his/her success at social inclusion. In other words, people have higher self-esteem when they believe they are connected to and accepted by others. People with high self-esteem are less influenced by others, tend to persist in spite of failure, and think more rationally. Role-specific self-esteem (e.g., a good student, a good driver, a good parent) predicts attitudes and behaviours about that role, whereas a person's overall self-esteem predicts much more general attitudes and behaviours (e.g., satisfaction with self).[24]

self-efficacy A person's belief that he or she has the ability, motivation, correct role perceptions, and favourable situation to complete a task successfully.

Self-Efficacy **Self-efficacy** refers to a person's belief that he or she can successfully complete a task.[25] Those with high self-efficacy have a "can do" attitude. They believe they possess the energy (motivation), ability, clear expectations (role perceptions), and resources (situational factors) to perform the task. In other words, self-efficacy is an individual's perception regarding the MARS model in a specific situation. Although originally defined in terms of specific tasks, self-efficacy is also a general trait related to self-concept.[26] General self-efficacy is a perception of one's competence to perform across a variety of situations. People with higher general self-efficacy have a more positive overall self-evaluation.

connect

Do you have an internal or external locus of control? Visit connect.mcgrawhill.com to estimate you locus of control focus.

locus of control A person's general belief about the amount of control he or she has over personal life events.

Locus of Control **Locus of control** is defined as a person's general beliefs about the amount of control he or she has over personal life events.[27] Individuals with more of an internal locus of control believe their personal characteristics (i.e., motivation and abilities) mainly influence life's outcomes. Those with more of an external locus of control believe events in their life are due mainly to fate, luck, or conditions in the external environment. Locus of control is a generalized belief, so people with an external locus can feel in control in familiar situations (such as performing common tasks). However, their underlying locus of control would be apparent in new situations in which control over events is uncertain.

People with a more internal locus of control have a more positive self-evaluation. They also tend to perform better in most employment situations, are more successful in their careers, earn more money, and are better suited for leadership positions. Internals are also more satisfied with their jobs, cope better in stressful situations, and are more motivated by performance-based reward systems.[28] One worrisome observation is that over the past four decades, there has been a shift away from an internal to a more external locus of control among young people.[29]

THE SOCIAL SELF

Everyone has a self-concept that includes at least a few identities (manager, parent, golfer, etc.) and each identity is defined by a set of attributes. These attributes highlight both the person's uniqueness (personal identity) or association with others (social identity).[30] *Personal identity* (also known as internal self-concept) consists of attributes that make us unique and distinct from people in the social groups to which we have a connection. For instance, an unusual achievement that distinguishes you from other people typically becomes a personal identity characteristic. Personal identity refers to something about you as an individual without reference to a larger group.

At the same time, human beings are social animals; they have an inherent drive to be associated with others and to be recognized as part of social communities. This drive to belong is reflected in self-concept by the fact that all individuals define themselves to some degree by their relationships.[31] *Social identity* (also called external self-concept) is the central theme of **social identity theory**, which says that people define themselves by the groups to which they belong or have an emotional attachment. For instance, someone might have a social identity as a Canadian, a Université Laval alumnus, and an employee at Desjardins Group (see Exhibit 3.2).

social identity theory A theory stating that people define themselves by the groups to which they belong or have an emotional attachment.

Social identity is a complex combination of many memberships arranged in a hierarchy of importance. One factor determining importance is how easily you are identified as a member of the reference group, such as by your gender, age, and ethnicity. A second factor is your minority status in a group. It is difficult to ignore your gender in a class where most other

EXHIBIT 3.2

Social Identity Theory Example

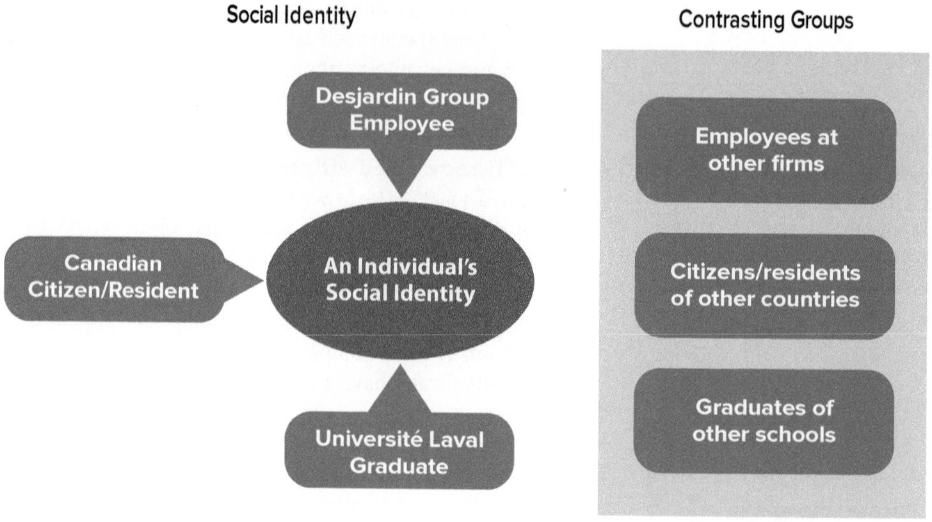

students are the opposite gender, for example. In that context, gender tends to become a stronger defining feature of your social identity than it is in social settings where there are many people of the same gender.

The group's status is another important social identity factor because association with the group makes us feel better about ourselves (i.e., self-enhancement). Medical doctors usually define themselves by their profession because of its high status. Some people describe themselves by where they work ("I work at Google") because their employer has a good reputation. Others never mention where they work because their employer is noted for poor relations with employees or has a poor reputation in the community.[32]

Everyone tries to balance his or her personal and social identities, but the priority for uniqueness (personal identities) versus relatedness (social identities) differs from one person to the next. People whose self-concepts are heavily defined by social rather than personal identities are more motivated to abide by team norms and more easily influenced by peer pressure. Those who place more emphasis on personal identities, on the other hand, speak out more frequently against the majority and are less motivated to follow the team's wishes. Furthermore, expressing disagreement with others is a sign of distinctiveness and can help employees form a clearer self-concept, particularly when that disagreement is based on differences in personal values.[33]

SELF-CONCEPT AND ORGANIZATIONAL BEHAVIOUR

Self-concept has become a hot topic in the social sciences and is starting to bloom in organizational behaviour research.[34] As we noted throughout this section, self-concept is a factor in perceptual and decision processes and biases, employee motivation, team dynamics, leadership development, employee stress, and several other OB topics. So, we will discuss self-concept throughout this book, including later parts of this chapter.

Perceiving the World Around Us

LO2

perception The process of receiving information about and making sense of the world around us.

Although we spend considerable time perceiving ourselves, most of our perceptual energy is directed toward the outer world. Whether as a structural engineer, forensic accountant, or senior executive, we need to make sense of the world around us, including the conditions that challenge the accuracy of those perceptions. **Perception** is the process of receiving information about and making sense of the world around us. It entails determining which information to notice, how to categorize this information, and how to interpret it within the framework of our existing knowledge.

This perceptual process generally follows the steps shown in Exhibit 3.3. Perception begins when environmental stimuli are received through our senses. Most stimuli that bombard our senses are screened out; the rest are organized and interpreted. The process of attending to

EXHIBIT 3.3

Model of the Perceptual Process

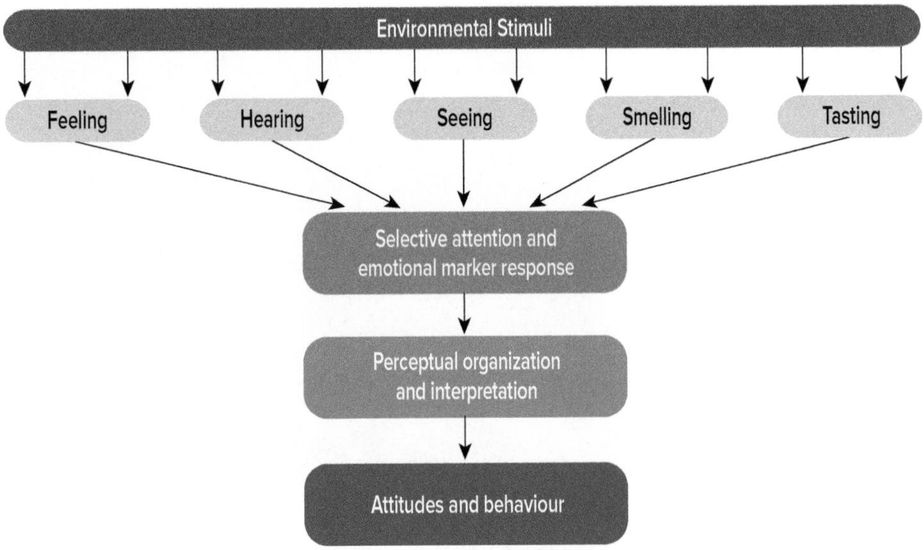

selective attention The process of attending to some information received by our senses and ignoring other information.

some information received by our senses and ignoring other information is called **selective attention**. Selective attention is influenced by characteristics of the person or object being perceived, particularly size, intensity, motion, repetition, and novelty. For example, a small, flashing red light on a nurses' work station console is immediately noticed because it is bright (intensity), flashing (motion), a rare event (novelty), and has symbolic meaning that a patient's vital signs are failing. Notice that selective attention is also influenced by the context in which the target is perceived. The selective attention process is triggered by things or people who might be out of context, such as someone with a foreign accent in a setting where most people have a local accent.

Characteristics of the perceiver also influence selection attention, usually without the perceiver's awareness.[35] When information is received through the senses, our brain quickly and nonconsciously assesses whether it is relevant or irrelevant to us and then attaches emotional markers (worry, happiness, boredom) to the retained information.[36] Emotional markers help us to store information in memory; those emotions are later reproduced when recalling the perceived information. The selective attention process is far from perfect, however. The Greek philosopher Plato acknowledged this imperfection long ago when he wrote that we see reality only as shadows reflecting against the rough wall of a cave.[37]

One selective attention bias is the effect of our assumptions and expectations about future events. You are more likely to notice a particular coworker's e-mail among the daily bombardment of messages when you expect to receive that e-mail (even more so if it is a valuable message). Unfortunately, expectations and assumptions also cause us to screen out potentially important information. In one study, students were asked to watch a 30-second video clip in which several people passed around two basketballs. Students who were instructed just to watch the video clip easily noticed someone dressed in a gorilla suit walking among the players for nine seconds and stopping to thump his/her chest. But only half of the students who were asked to count the number of times one basketball was passed around noticed the intruding gorilla.[38]

confirmation bias The process of screening out information that is contrary to our values and assumptions and to more readily accept confirming information.

Another selective attention problem, called **confirmation bias**, is the nonconscious tendency for people to screen out information that is contrary to their decisions, beliefs, values, and assumptions, whereas confirming information is more readily accepted through the perceptual process.[39] This bias includes overweighting positive information, perceiving only positive information, and restricting cognitive attention to a favoured hypothesis. When we make important decisions, such as investing in a costly project, for example, we tend to pay attention to information that is consistent with the success of that decision and to ignore contrary or seemingly irrelevant information. In an exercise where student pilots became unsure of their location, they tried to find their true location by relying on less reliable information that was consistent with their assumptions than on more accurate information that was contrary to those assumptions. This faulty selective attention also occurs when police detectives and other forensic experts form theories too early in the investigation.[40]

"It is a capital mistake to theorize before you have all the evidence," warned the mythical detective Sherlock Holmes in *A Study in Scarlet*. "It biases the judgment." Law enforcement agencies try to follow this advice, but "tunnel vision" misperceptions still occur. For instance, Ottawa police eventually dropped charges against two young men accused of drawing anti-Jewish images on a warplane outside the Canadian War Museum. Surveillance cameras showed the men at the scene around 4 a.m., but the two (who had no history of vandalism or anti-Jewish activity) had apparently just stopped to take the photos (which they later supplied to police) on their way home from work. The offending graffiti was already there. "The police have made up their mind . . . no matter how much evidence you present to demonstrate your innocence," suggests their lawyer.[41]

Design Pics Inc./Alamy

connect

How much perceptual structure do you need? Visit **connect.mcgrawhill.com** to assess yourself on this aspect of social perception.

PERCEPTUAL ORGANIZATION AND INTERPRETATION

categorical thinking Organizing people and objects into preconceived categories that are stored in our long-term memory.

People make sense of information even before they become aware of it. This sense making partly includes **categorical thinking**—the mostly nonconscious process of organizing people and objects into preconceived categories that are stored in our long-term memory.[42] Categorical thinking relies on a variety of automatic perceptual grouping principles. Things are often grouped together based on their similarity or proximity to others. If you notice that a group of similar-looking people includes several professors, for instance, you will likely assume that the others in that group are also professors. Another form of perceptual grouping is based on the need for cognitive closure, such as filling in missing information about what happened at a meeting that you didn't attend (e.g., who was there, where it was held). A third form of grouping occurs when we think we see trends in otherwise ambiguous information. Several studies have found that people have a natural tendency to see patterns that really are random events, such as presumed winning streaks among sports stars or in gambling.[43]

The process of "making sense" of the world around us also involves interpreting incoming information, not just organizing it. This happens as quickly as selecting and organizing because the previously mentioned emotional markers are tagged to incoming stimuli, which are essentially quick judgments about whether that information is good or bad for us. How much time does it take to make these quick judgments? Recent studies estimate that we make reliable judgments about another individual's trustworthiness based on viewing a facial image for as little as 50 milliseconds (1/20th of a second) In fact, whether we see a face for a minute or for just 200 milliseconds, our opinion of whether we like or trust that person is about the same.[44] Collectively, these studies reveal that selective attention, perceptual organization, and interpretation operate very quickly and to a large extent without our awareness.

mental models Knowledge structures that we develop to describe, explain, and predict the world around us.

Mental Models To achieve our goals with some degree of predictability and sanity, we need road maps of the environments in which we live. These road maps, called **mental models**, are knowledge structures that we develop to describe, explain, and predict the world around us.[45] They consist of visual or relational images in our mind, such as what the classroom looks like or what happens when we submit an assignment late. Mental models partly rely on the process of perceptual grouping to make sense of things; they fill in the missing pieces, including the causal connection among events. For example, you have a mental model about attending a class lecture or seminar, including assumptions or expectations about where the instructor and students arrange themselves in the room, how they ask and answer questions, and so forth. In other words, we create a mental image of a class in progress.

Mental models play an important role in sense making, yet they also make it difficult to see the world in different ways. For example, accounting professionals tend to see corporate problems from an accounting perspective, whereas marketing professionals see the same problems from a marketing perspective. Mental models also block our recognition of new opportunities. How do we change mental models? That's a tough challenge. After all, we developed these knowledge structures from several years of experience and reinforcement. The most important way to minimize the perceptual problems with mental models is to be aware of and frequently question them. We need to ask ourselves about the assumptions we make. Working with people from diverse backgrounds is another way to break out of existing mental models. Colleagues from different cultures and areas of expertise tend to have different mental models, so working with them makes our own assumptions more obvious.

Specific Perceptual Processes and Problems

LO3

Embedded within the general perceptual process are specific sub-processes and associated biases and other errors. We will examine several of these perceptual processes and biases as well as their implications for organizational behaviour, beginning with the most widely known one: stereotyping.

STEREOTYPING IN ORGANIZATIONS

One reason why few women become firefighters is that they, along with family and friends, usually depict firefighters as rugged, risk-oriented, physically strong, and male. Although this image has kernels of truth–firefighting requires above average physical strength and has above average risk–several important features of the occupation are seldom mentioned, such as helping others, teamwork, and safety consciousness. In other words, people have a stereotype of firefighters that is neither accurate nor desirable for most women.

stereotyping The process of assigning traits to people based on their membership in a social category.

Stereotyping is the perceptual process in which we assign characteristics to an identifiable group and then automatically transfer those features to anyone we believe is a member of that group.[46] The assigned characteristics tend to be difficult to observe, such as personality traits and abilities, but they can also include physical characteristics and a host of other qualities. For instance, people in most parts of the world stereotype professors and scientists in general as intelligent, absent-minded, and socially inept.[47] Stereotypes are formed to some extent from personal experience, but they are mainly provided to us through media images (e.g., movie characters) and other cultural prototypes. Consequently, stereotypes are shared beliefs across an entire society and sometimes across several cultures, rather than beliefs that differ from one person to the next.

Stereotyping involves assigning a group's perceived attributes to individuals known or believed to be members of that group. Everyone identified as a member of the stereotyped group is assumed to possess these characteristics. If we learn that someone is a professor, for example, we implicitly assume the person is probably also intelligent, absent-minded, and socially inept. Historically, stereotypes were defined as exaggerations or falsehoods. This is often true, but some stereotypes have kernels of truth. Some features of the stereotype are more common among people in the group than in other groups. Still, stereotypes embellish or distort the kernels of truth and include other features that are false.

Why People Stereotype People engage in stereotyping because, as a form of categorical thinking, it is a natural and mostly nonconscious "energy-saving" process that simplifies

Jason Blumer defies anyone's stereotype of an accountant. The president (he prefers Chief Innovation Officer) of a boutique CPA firm in Greenville, South Carolina, usually wears jeans, T-shirts, and flip-flops around the office. He writes a popular blog, is a Twitter maniac, Skypes with clients, and hams it up with distorted photos on his iPad. "There is a new day dawning, and this country better realize we CPAs are now cool, Mac-loving, flip-flop wearing, global-serving, math-hating innovators," says Blumer about his stereotype-busting ways.[48]

our understanding of the world. It is easier to remember features of a stereotype than the constellation of characteristics unique to everyone we meet.[49] A second reason is that we have an innate need to understand and anticipate how others will behave. We don't have much information when first meeting someone, so we rely heavily on stereotypes to fill in the missing pieces. The higher the perceiver's need for cognitive closure, the higher the reliance on stereotypes.

A third explanation for stereotyping is that it is motivated by the observer's own self-enhancement and social identity. Earlier in this chapter we explained that people define themselves by the groups to which they belong or have an emotional attachment. They are also motivated to maintain a positive self-concept. This combination of social identity and self-enhancement leads to the process of categorization, homogenization, and differentiation:[50]

- *Categorization.* Social identity is a comparative process, and the comparison begins by categorizing people into distinct groups. By viewing someone (including yourself) as a Nova Scotian, for example, you remove that person's individuality and, instead, see him or her as a prototypical representative of the group called Nova Scotians. This categorization then allows you to distinguish Nova Scotians from people who live in, say, Ontario or Alberta.
- *Homogenization.* To simplify the comparison process, we tend to think that people within each group are very similar to each other. For instance, we think Nova Scotians collectively have similar attitudes and characteristics, whereas Ontarians collectively have their own set of characteristics. Of course, every individual is unique, but we tend to lose sight of this fact when thinking about our social identity and how we compare to people in other social groups.
- *Differentiation.* Along with categorizing and homogenizing people, we tend to assign more favourable characteristics to people in our groups than to people in other groups.[51] This differentiation is motivated by self-enhancement because being in a "better" group produces higher self-esteem. Differentiation is often subtle, but it can escalate into a "good guy-bad guy" contrast when groups engage in overt conflict with each

Radius Images/Alamy

Women represent more than one-third of the workforce and upwards of 20 percent of middle managers in many countries, yet they comprise less than 10 percent of corporate board members worldwide. Some say the problem is mainly systemic discrimination, such as nonconsciously relying on a male prototype of the ideal board member when selecting candidates for this role. Others suggest the lack of women in the boardroom is due to more explicit prejudice. Female corporate board members are rarest (1% or less) in four Middle East countries and Japan; they have the highest percentage of board seats in Norway (40.1%), Sweden (27.3%), and Finland (24.5%). Only about 10 percent of boardroom seats in Canada are held by women.[52]

other. In other words, when out-group members threaten our self-concept, we are particularly motivated (often without our awareness) to assign negative stereotypes to them. Some research suggests that men have stronger differentiation biases than do women, but we all differentiate to some extent.

Problems with Stereotyping Everyone engages in stereotyping, but this process distorts perceptions in various ways. One distortion is that stereotypes do not accurately describe every person in a social category. Consider how accountants are typically stereotyped in films and literature. Although sometimes depicted as loyal and conscientious, accountants are usually shown as boring, monotonous, cautious, unromantic, obtuse, antisocial, shy, dysfunctional, devious, calculating, and malicious.[53] The traditional accountant stereotype perhaps fits the description of a few accountants, but it is certainly not characteristic of all—or even most—people in this profession. Even so, once we categorize someone as an accountant, the stereotypic features of accountants (boring, antisocial, etc.) are transferred to that person, even though we have not attempted to verify those characteristics in that person.

Another problem with stereotyping is that it lays the foundation for discriminatory attitudes and behaviour. Most of this perceptual bias occurs as *unintentional (systemic) discrimination,* whereby decision makers rely on stereotypes to establish notions of the "ideal" person in specific roles. A person who doesn't fit the ideal tends to receive a less favourable evaluation. The more serious form of stereotype bias is *intentional discrimination* or *prejudice,* in which people hold unfounded negative attitudes toward people belonging to a particular stereotyped group.[54] Although it would be nice to believe that overt prejudice is disappearing, it still exists. One such incident was described in this chapter's opening case study about the Calgary fire department captain who demonstrated a strong negative attitude toward female firefighters. These prejudices were based on his perceptions of women and stereotypes and prototypes of the ideal firefighter.

Prejudicial discrimination has also been reported in employment selection decisions. A French study of 2,300 help-wanted ads found that job applicants with French-sounding names were much more likely to get job interviews than were applicants with North African or sub-Saharan African names, even though employers received identical résumés for both names! Furthermore, when applicants personally visited human resource staff, those with foreign names were often told the job had been filled, whereas few of the applicants with French names received this message (even when visiting afterwards).[55]

If stereotyping is such a problem, shouldn't we try to avoid this process altogether? Unfortunately, it's not that simple. Most experts agree that categorical thinking (including stereotyping) is an automatic and nonconscious process. Specialized training programs can minimize stereotype activation to some extent, but for the most part the process is hardwired in our brain cells.[56] Also remember that stereotyping helps us in several valuable (although fallible) ways described earlier: minimizing mental effort, filling in missing information, and supporting our social identity. The good news is that while it is very difficult to prevent the *activation* of stereotypes, we can minimize the *application* of stereotypic information. In other words, although we automatically categorize people and assign stereotypic traits to them, we can consciously minimize the extent that we rely on that stereotypic information. Later in this chapter, we identify ways to minimize stereotyping and other perceptual biases.

ATTRIBUTION THEORY

attribution process The perceptual process of deciding whether an observed behaviour or event is caused largely by internal or external factors.

Another widely-discussed perceptual phenomenon in organizational settings is the **attribution process**.[57] Attribution involves forming beliefs about the causes of behaviour or events. The most popular version of attribution theory is that we perceive whether an observed behaviour or event is caused mainly by characteristics of the person (internal factors) or by the environment (external factors). Internal factors include the person's ability or motivation, whereas external factors include resources, coworker support, or luck. If someone doesn't show up for an important meeting, for instance, we infer either internal attributions (the coworker is forgetful, lacks motivation, etc.) or external attributions (traffic, a family emergency, or other circumstances prevented the coworker from attending).

People rely on the three attribution rules–consistency, distinctiveness, consensus–to decide whether someone's behaviour and performance are mainly caused by their personal characteristics or environmental influences (see Exhibit 3.4).[58] To illustrate how these three attribution rules operate, imagine a situation where an employee is making poor-quality products on a

EXHIBIT 3.4

Attribution Theory Rules

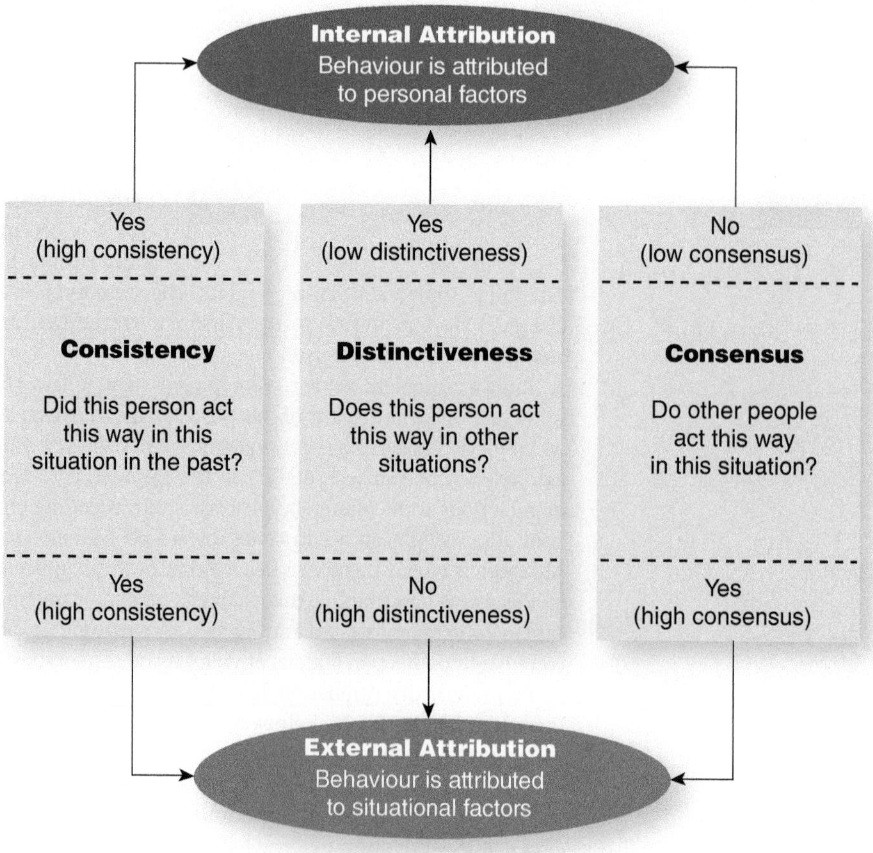

particular machine. We would probably conclude that the employee lacks skill or motivation (an internal attribution) if the employee consistently makes poor-quality products on this machine (high consistency), the employee makes poor-quality products on other machines (low distinctiveness), and other employees make good-quality products on this machine (low consensus).

In contrast, we would decide that there is something wrong with the machine (an external attribution) if the employee consistently makes poor-quality products on this machine (high consistency), the employee makes good-quality products on other machines (high distinctiveness), and other employees make poor-quality products on this machine (high consensus). Notice that consistency is high for both internal and external attributions. This occurs because low consistency (the person's output quality on this machine is sometimes good and sometimes poor) weakens our confidence about whether the source of the problem is the person or the machine.

The attribution process is important because understanding cause-effect relationships enables us to work effectively with others and to assign praise or blame to them.[59] Suppose a coworker didn't complete his or her task on a team project. You would approach this situation differently if you believe the coworker was lazy or lacked sufficient skill (an internal attribution) than if you believed the poor performance was due to lack of time or resources available to the coworker (an external attribution). Similarly, our respect for leaders depends on whether we believe their actions are due to personal characteristics or the situation. We also react differently to attributions of our own behaviour and performance. For instance, students who make internal attributions about their poor grades are more likely to drop out of their programs than if they make external attributions about those grades.[60]

Attribution Errors We are strongly motivated to assign internal or external attributions to someone's behaviour, but this perceptual process is also susceptible to errors. One such error is **self-serving bias**–the tendency to attribute our failures to external causes (such as bad luck) more than internal causes (e.g., inefficiency), while successes are due more to internal than external factors.[61] Simply put, we take credit for our successes and blame others or the situation for our mistakes. In annual reports, for example, executives mainly refer to their personal qualities as reasons for the company's successes and to external factors as reasons for the company's failures. Similarly, entrepreneurs in one recent study overwhelmingly cited situational causes for their business failure (funding, economy) whereas they understated personal causes such as lack of vision and social skills.[62]

self-serving bias The tendency to attribute our favourable outcomes to internal factors and our failures to external factors.

Why do people engage in self-serving bias? Fictional New York crime investigator Philo Vance gave us the answer nearly a century ago when he quipped: "Bad luck is merely a defensive and self-consoling synonym for inefficiency."[63] In other words, self-serving bias is associated with the self-enhancement process described earlier in this chapter. By pointing to external causes of their own failures (e.g., bad luck) and internal causes of their successes, people generate a more positive (and self-consoling) self-concept.

Another widely studied attribution error is **fundamental attribution error** (also called *correspondence bias*), which is the tendency to overemphasize internal causes of another person's behaviour and to discount or ignore external causes of their behaviour.[64] According to this perceptual error, we are more likely to think a coworker arrives late for work because they aren't motivated than because of environmental constraints (such as traffic congestion). The explanation for fundamental attribution error is that observers can't easily see the external factors that constrain another person's behaviour. Also, people like to think that human beings (not the situation) are the prime sources of their behaviour. However, fundamental attribution error might not be as common or severe as was previously thought. There is evidence that people from Asian countries are less likely to engage in this bias because those cultures emphasize the context of behaviour more than do Western cultures.[65] But a recent review of past studies suggests that fundamental attribution error isn't very noticeable in any society.[66]

fundamental attribution error The tendency to see the person rather than the situation as the main cause of that person's behaviour.

SELF-FULFILLING PROPHECY

Self-fulfilling prophecy occurs when our expectations about another person cause that person to act in a way that is consistent with those expectations. In other words, our perceptions can influence reality. Exhibit 3.5 illustrates the four steps in the self-fulfilling-prophecy

self-fulfilling prophecy The perceptual process in which our expectations about another person cause that person to act more consistently with those expectations.

EXHIBIT 3.5

The Self-Fulfilling-Prophecy Cycle

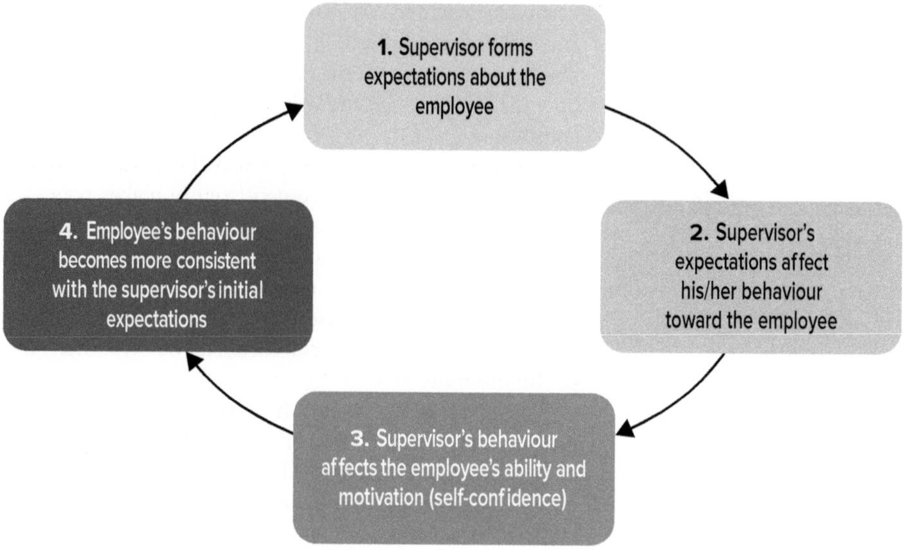

process using the example of a supervisor and a subordinate.[67] The process begins when the supervisor forms expectations about the employee's future behaviour and performance. These expectations are sometimes inaccurate because first impressions are usually formed from limited information. The supervisor's expectations influence his or her behaviour toward employees. In particular, high-expectancy employees (those expected to do well) receive more emotional support through nonverbal cues (e.g., more smiling and eye contact), more frequent and valuable feedback and reinforcement, more challenging goals, better training, and more opportunities to demonstrate good performance.

The third step in self-fulfilling prophecy includes two effects of the supervisor's behaviour on the employee. First, through better training and more practice opportunities, a high-expectancy employee learns more skills and knowledge than a low-expectancy employee. Second, the employee becomes more self-confident, which results in higher motivation and willingness to set more challenging goals.[68] In the final step, high-expectancy employees have higher motivation and better skills, resulting in better performance, while the opposite is true of low-expectancy employees.

Self-fulfilling prophecy has been observed in many contexts. One of the most famous studies occurred in the Israeli Defence Force. Four combat command course instructors were told that one-third of the incoming trainees had high command potential, one-third had normal potential, and the rest had unknown potential. The trainees had been randomly placed into these categories by the researchers, but the instructors were led to believe that the information they received was accurate. Consistent with self-fulfilling prophecy, high-expectancy soldiers performed significantly better by the end of the course than did trainees in the other groups. They also had more favourable attitudes toward the course and the instructor's leadership effectiveness. Other studies have reported that the initial expectations managers and teachers have of their employees and students tend to influence the self-perceptions (particularly self-efficacy) of those followers and can lead to higher or lower performance.[69]

Contingencies of Self-Fulfilling Prophecy The self-fulfilling prophecy effect is stronger in some situations than in others. It has a stronger effect at the beginning of a relationship, such as when employees are first hired. It is also stronger when several people (rather than just one person) hold the same expectations of the individual. In other words, we might be able to ignore one person's doubts about our potential but not the collective doubts of several people. The self-fulfilling-prophecy effect is also stronger among people with a history of low achievement. These people tend to have lower self-esteem, so they are more easily influenced by others' opinions of them.[70]

The main lesson from the self-fulfilling-prophecy literature is that leaders need to develop and maintain a positive, yet realistic, expectation toward all employees. This recommendation

positive organizational behaviour A perspective of organizational behaviour that focuses on building positive qualities and traits within individuals or institutions as opposed to focusing on what is wrong with them.

is consistent with the emerging philosophy of **positive organizational behaviour**, which suggests that focusing on the positive rather than negative aspects of life will improve organizational success and individual well-being. Communicating hope and optimism is so important that it is identified as one of the critical success factors for physicians and surgeons. Training programs that make leaders aware of the power of positive expectations seem to have minimal effect, however. Instead, generating positive expectations and hope depend on a corporate culture of support and learning. Hiring supervisors who are inherently optimistic toward their staff is another way of increasing the incidence of positive self-fulfilling prophecies.

OTHER PERCEPTUAL EFFECTS

Self-fulfilling prophecy, attribution, and stereotyping are among the most common perceptual processes and biases in organizational settings, but there are many others. Four additional biases that have received attention in organizational settings are briefly described below.

halo effect A perceptual error whereby our general impression of a person, usually based on one prominent characteristic, colours our perception of other characteristics of that person.

Halo Effect The **halo effect** occurs when our general impression of a person, usually based on one prominent characteristic, distorts our perception of other characteristics of that person.[71] If a supervisor who values punctuality notices that an employee is sometimes late for work, the supervisor might form a negative image of the employee and evaluate that person's other traits unfavourably as well. The halo effect is most likely to occur when concrete information about the perceived target is missing or we are not sufficiently motivated to search for it. Instead, we use our general impression of the person to fill in the missing information.

false-consensus effect A perceptual error in which we overestimate the extent to which others have beliefs and characteristics similar to our own.

False-Consensus Effect The **false-consensus effect** (also called *similar-to-me effect*) occurs when people overestimate the extent to which others have similar beliefs or behaviours to our own.[72] Employees who are thinking of quitting their jobs overestimate the percentage of coworkers who are also thinking about quitting, for example. There are several explanations for false-consensus effect. One is that we are comforted by the belief that others are similar to us, particularly regarding less acceptable or divisive behaviour. Put differently, we perceive "everyone does it" to reinforce our self-concept regarding behaviours that do not have a positive image (quitting our job, parking illegally, etc.). A second explanation is that we interact more with people who have similar views and behaviours, which causes us to overestimate how common those views/behaviours are in the entire organization or society. Third, as noted earlier in this chapter, we are more likely to remember information that is consistent with our own views and selectively screen out communication that is contrary to our beliefs. Finally, our social identity process homogenizes people within groups, so we tend to think that everyone in that group has similar opinions and behaviour, including the false-consensus topic.

primacy effect A perceptual error in which we quickly form an opinion of people based on the first information we receive about them.

Primacy Effect The **primacy effect** is our tendency to quickly form an opinion of people on the basis of the first information we receive about them.[73] It is the notion that first impressions are lasting impressions. This rapid perceptual organization and interpretation occurs because we need to make sense of the world around us. The problem is that first impressions—particularly negative first impressions—are difficult to change. After categorizing someone, we tend to select subsequent information that supports our first impression and screen out information that opposes that impression.

recency effect A perceptual error in which the most recent information dominates our perception of others.

Recency Effect The **recency effect** occurs when the most recent information dominates our perceptions.[74] This perceptual bias is most common when people (especially those with limited experience) are making an evaluation involving complex information. For instance, auditors must digest large volumes of information in their judgments about financial documents, and the most recent information received prior to the decision tends to get weighted more heavily than information received at the beginning of the audit. Similarly, when supervisors evaluate the performance of employees over the previous year, the most recent performance information dominates the evaluation because it is the most easily recalled.

Improving Perceptions

LO4

We can't bypass the perceptual process, but we should try to minimize perceptual biases and distortions. Three potentially effective ways to improve perceptions include awareness of perceptual biases, self-awareness, and meaningful interaction.

AWARENESS OF PERCEPTUAL BIASES

One of the most obvious and widely practised ways to reduce perceptual biases comes from being aware that they exist. For example, diversity awareness training tries to minimize discrimination by making people aware of systemic discrimination as well as prejudices that occur through stereotyping. This training also attempts to dispel myths about people from various cultural and demographic groups. Awareness of perceptual biases can reduce these biases to some extent by making people more mindful of their thoughts and actions. However, awareness training has only a limited effect.[75] One problem is that teaching people to reject incorrect stereotypes has the unintended effect of reinforcing rather than reducing reliance on those stereotypes. Another problem is that diversity training is ineffective for people with deeply held prejudices against those groups.

Self-fulfilling-prophecy awareness training has also failed to live up to expectations.[76] This training approach informs managers about the existence of the self-fulfilling prophecy effect and encourages them to engage in more positive rather than negative self-fulfilling prophecies. Unfortunately, research has found that managers continue to engage in negative self-fulfilling prophecies after they complete the training program.

IMPROVING SELF-AWARENESS

A more successful way to minimize perceptual biases is by increasing self-awareness.[77] We need to become more aware of our beliefs, values, and attitudes and, from that insight, gain a better understanding of biases in our own decisions and behaviour. This self-awareness tends to reduce perceptual biases by making people more open-minded and nonjudgmental toward others. Self-awareness is equally important in other ways. The emerging concept of authentic leadership emphasizes self-awareness as the first step in a person's ability to effectively lead others (see Chapter 12). Essentially, we need to understand our own values, strengths, and biases as a foundation for building a vision and leading others toward that vision.[78]

But how do we become more self-aware? One approach is to complete formal tests that indicate any implicit biases we might have towards others. The Implicit Association Test (IAT) apparently reveals biases. Although the accuracy of the IAT is being hotly debated by scholars, it attempts to detect subtle racial, age, and gender bias by associating positive and negative words with specific demographic groups.[79] Many people are much more cautious about their stereotypes and prejudices after discovering that their test results show a personal bias against older people or individuals from different ethnic backgrounds.[80]

Debating Point:

DO WE NEED DIVERSITY TRAINING PROGRAMS?[81]

In most large corporations, diversity training programs are well-entrenched bastions in the battle against workplace discrimination. In most programs, participants are reminded to respect cultural and gender differences. They also learn common assumptions and biases that people make about other demographic groups. When companies lose discrimination cases, one of their first requirements is to introduce diversity training.

In spite of the good intentions, several sources argue that diversity training might not be very useful. One concern is that most sessions are mandatory, so employees aren't really committed to their content. Furthermore, biases and prejudices are deeply anchored, so a half-day lecture and group chat on diversity won't change employee perceptions and behaviour. Even if these programs motivate employees to be more tolerant of others and to avoid stereotypes, these good intentions evaporate quickly in companies that lack a corporate culture that embraces diversity.

It gets worse. One major review reported that the presence of diversity training increased the percentage of white women in management, but it decreased by the same degree the percentage of African American and other non-white women in management. There is some concern that discussing demographic and cultural differences increases rather than decreases stereotyping. For instance, students in one study showed more bias against the elderly after watching a video encouraging them to be less biased against older people! Diversity training programs might also produce ill-feelings among participants. One program for incoming students at the University of Delaware was cancelled after white students complained it made them feel racist and gay students felt pressured to reveal their sexual orientation.

Johari Window A model of mutual understanding that encourages disclosure and feedback to increase our own open area and reduce the blind, hidden, and unknown areas.

Another way to reduce perceptual biases through increased self-awareness is by applying the **Johari Window**.[82] Developed by Joseph Luft and Harry Ingram (hence the name "Johari"), this model of self-awareness and mutual understanding divides information about you into four "windows"–open, blind, hidden, and unknown–based on whether your own values, beliefs, and experiences are known to you and to others (see Exhibit 3.6). The *open area* includes information about you that is known both to you and to others. The *blind area* refers to information that is known to others but not to you. For example, your colleagues might notice that you are self-conscious and awkward when meeting the company chief executive, but you are unaware of this fact. Information known to you but unknown to others is found in the *hidden area*. Finally, the *unknown area* includes your values, beliefs, and experiences that aren't known to you or others.

EXHIBIT 3.6

Johari Window Model of Self-Awareness and Mutual Understanding

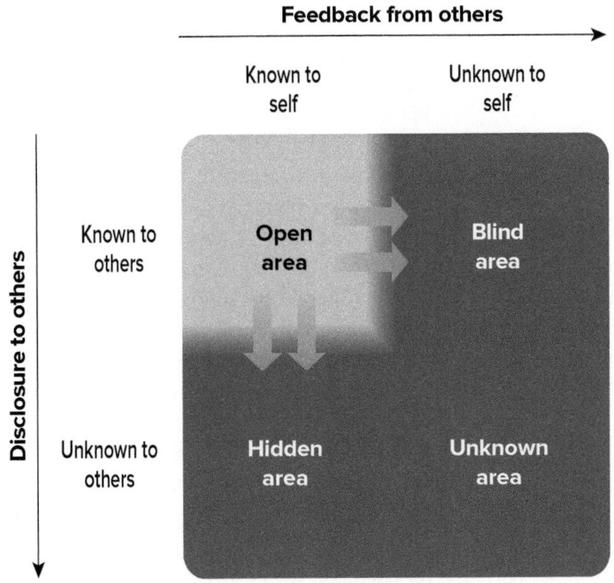

Source: Based on J. Luft, Of Human Interaction (Palo Alto, CA: National Press Books, 1969).

The main objective of the Johari Window is to increase the size of the open area so that both you and colleagues are aware of your perceptual limitations. This objective is partly accomplished by reducing the hidden area through *disclosure*–informing others of your beliefs, feelings, and experiences that may influence the work relationship. The open area also increases through *feedback* from others about your behaviour. Feedback reduces your blind area because, according to recent studies, people near you are good sources of information about many (but not all) of your traits and behaviours.[83] Finally, the combination of disclosure and feedback occasionally produces revelations about you in the unknown area.

connect

How well do you understand the other person's perspective? Visit connect.mcgrawhill.com to estimate your cognitive empathy.

connect

How well do you experience the emotions that others are experiencing? Visit connect.mcgrawhill.com to estimate your emotional empathy.

MEANINGFUL INTERACTION

The Johari Window relies on direct conversations about ourselves and others, whereas meaningful interaction is a more indirect, yet potentially powerful, approach to improving self-awareness and mutual understanding.[84] Meaningful interaction is any activity in which people engage in valued (meaningful, not trivial) activities. The activities might be work-related, such as when senior executives work alongside frontline staff. Or the activities might occur outside the workplace, such as when sales staff from several countries participate in outdoor challenges.

contact hypothesis A theory stating that the more we interact with someone, the less prejudiced or perceptually biased we will be against that person.

Meaningful interaction is founded on the **contact hypothesis**, which states that, under certain conditions, people who interact with each other will be less perceptually biased because they have a more personal understanding of the other person and their group.[85] Simply spending time with members of other groups can improve this understanding to some extent. However, meaningful interaction is strongest when people work closely and frequently with each other on a shared goal that requires mutual cooperation and reliance. Furthermore, everyone should have equal status in that context, should be engaged in a meaningful task, and should have positive experiences with each other in those interactions.

Global Connections 3.1 describes several examples of meaningful interaction where executives work beside frontline staff or frontline staff work with employees in other parts of the organization. However, meaningful interaction events sometimes occur naturally. As an example, several years ago executives at Daishowa-Marubeni's Peace River Pulp Division in Alberta were working through difficult discussions with environmentalists. During those meetings, the river threatened to flood, so everyone got involved sandbagging the dyke. One Peace River Pulp executive vividly recalls the occasion, because he was sandbagging alongside one of the most active environmental critics. "We both looked at one another and I think we both realized we had more in common than we may have thought," he says.[86]

empathy A person's understanding of and sensitivity to the feelings, thoughts, and situations of others.

Meaningful interaction reduces dependence on stereotypes because we gain better knowledge about individuals and experience their unique attributes in action. Meaningful interaction also potentially improves empathy toward others. **Empathy** refers to understanding and being sensitive to the feelings, thoughts, and situations of others.[88] People empathize when they visualize themselves in the other person's place as if they are the other person. This perceptual experience is both cognitive and emotional, meaning that empathy is about understanding as well as feeling what the other person feels in that context. Empathizing with others improves our sensitivity to the external causes of another person's performance and behaviour, thereby reducing fundamental attribution error. A supervisor who imagines what it's like to be a single mother, for example, would become more sensitive to the external causes of lateness and other events among such employees. However, trying to empathize with others without spending time with them might actually increase rather than reduce stereotyping and other perceptual biases.[89]

Global Connections 3.1:

EXPERIENCING MEANINGFUL INTERACTION ON THE FRONTLINE[87]

Tim Hortons is Canada's largest food service chain, a business that would overwhelm many executives with its complex logistics, evolving strategy, and ongoing demands to grow shareholder value. Yet company chairman and former CEO Paul House still manages to find time to regularly visit stores and occasionally work beside frontline employees. "The lifeblood of this business is in the stores," says House. "You can't run a business from the corner office. You have to be out to understand what's going on."

Paul House and many other executives realize that working in frontline jobs gives them a reality check about the business and its employees. "I think it's a great experience. . . to never lose contact or touch with the people who get the job done," says Calgary Transit director Doug Morgan, who worked five shifts beside frontline staff without being recognized, as part of the *Undercover Boss* reality television series. Orkin Canada president Gary Muldoon, who also served as an undercover boss, agrees. "I got a better appreciation for the stresses our people are under every day."

Some companies have extended this frontline experience to other headquarters staff. At Singapore grocery chain FairPrice, all senior staff work in a store two days each year, usually stocking shelves, cashiering, or rounding up trolleys. FairPrice CEO Sean Kian Peng calls the initiative "management by attachment" because the experience helps executives empathize better with frontline staff.

Denver-based telecommunication company WideOpenWest (WOW) applies a similar practice. Its professional and management staff are asked to work one day every few months at either the company's call centre or with installers at customers' homes. Colleen Abdoulah, the Canadian-born chairwoman and former CEO of WOW, assists installers by fetching ladders from the van and drilling holes where instructed. She says the experience is always valuable, even though her technical skills aren't always up to standard. "The couple whose home we were in were relieved to find out I was the CEO of WOW and not a regular installer," admits Abdoulah about a recent installation job.

John Rennison/*The Hamilton Spectator*

Tim Hortons chairman Paul House (centre) and other executives keep their perceptions in focus by regularly visiting and working alongside frontline staff.

Global Mindset: Developing Perceptions Across Borders

LO5

Rakuten Inc. is Japan's most popular e-commerce website and one of the ten largest internet companies in the world. The Tokyo-based firm is rapidly expanding beyond Japanese borders, which demands a more global focus. "In the online business, which easily crosses national boundaries, domestic companies are not our sole rivals," explains Rakuten CEO Hiroshi Mikitani. Therefore, Mikitani recently made English the company's official in-house language. Even more important, Rakuten is seeking out job applicants with international experience and a mindset to match. "Since we declared our intention to make English our official language, we've had more applicants that clearly have a global mindset," says Mikitani.[90]

global mindset An individual's ability to perceive, appreciate, and empathize with people from other cultures, and to process complex cross-cultural information.

Global mindset has become an important attribute of job applicants at Rakuten and other companies with international operations. A **global mindset** refers to an individual's ability to perceive, know about, and process information across cultures. It includes (a) an awareness of, openness to, and respect for other views and practices in the world, (b) the capacity to empathize and act effectively across cultures, (c) ability to process complex information about novel environments, and (d) the ability to comprehend and reconcile intercultural matters with multiple levels of thinking.[91]

Let's look at each of these features. First, global mindset occurs as people develop more of a global than local/parochial frame of reference about their business and its environment.

Employing people with a global mindset is so important at Keppel Offshore & Marine that it is one of the Singapore-based offshore rig designer and builder's core values. Keppel supports global mindset development by encouraging professional and management staff to visit one of the company's 30 operations worldwide, attend debriefing sessions where coworkers have returned from those international tours, and accept assignments at one of Keppel's other operations. "I think that overseas exposure can help to develop a person professionally and personally," says a Keppel executive.[92]

© Munshi Ahmed/Bloomberg/Getty Images.

They also have more knowledge and appreciation of many cultures and do not judge the competence of others by their national or ethnic origins. Second, global mindset includes understanding the mental models held by colleagues from other cultures as well as their emotional experiences in a given situation. Furthermore, this empathy translates into effective use of words and behaviours that are compatible with the local culture. Third, people with a strong global mindset are able to process and analyze large volumes of information in new and diverse situations. Finally, global mindset involves the capacity to quickly develop useful mental models of situations, particularly at both a local and global level of analysis.

As you can imagine, employees who develop a global mindset offer tremendous value to organizations.[93] They develop better relationships across cultures by understanding and showing respect to distant colleagues and partners. They can sift through huge volumes of ambiguous and novel information transmitted in multinational relationships. They have a capacity to form networks and exchange resources more rapidly across borders. They also develop greater sensitivity and respond more quickly to emerging global opportunities.

DEVELOPING A GLOBAL MINDSET

Developing a global mindset involves improving one's perceptions, so the practices described earlier on awareness, self-awareness, and meaningful interaction are relevant. As with most perceptual capabilities, a global mindset begins with self-awareness—understanding one's own beliefs, values, and attitudes. Through self-awareness, people are more open-minded and nonjudgmental when receiving and processing complex information for decision making. In addition, companies develop a global mindset by giving employees opportunities to compare their own mental models with those of coworkers or partners from other regions of the world. For example, employees might participate in online forums about how well the product's design or marketing strategy is received in Canada versus India or Chile. When companies engage in regular discussions about global competitors, suppliers, and other stakeholders, they eventually move the employee's sphere of awareness more toward that global level.

A global mindset develops through better knowledge of people and cultures. Some of that knowledge is acquired through formal programs, such as diversity training, but deeper absorption results from immersion in those cultures. Just as executives need to experience frontline jobs to better understand their customers and employees, employees also need to have meaningful interaction with colleagues from other cultures in those settings. The more people embed themselves in the local environment (such as following local practices, eating local food, and using the local language), the more they tend to understand the perspectives and attitudes of their colleagues in those cultures.

Developing a Global Mindset Through Immersion Ernst & Young, IBM, Procter & Gamble, and a few other organizations have introduced special programs to accelerate global mindset development by sending teams of employees on social responsibility missions in developing countries for one or two months. "We need people with a global mindset, and what better way to develop a global mindset, and what more realistic way, than for somebody to have an immersion experience with just enough safety net," says an Ernst & Young senior executive.[94]

IBM's Corporate Service Corps program is a case in point. Each year about 500 IBMers from dozens of countries are organized into small teams and dispatched to developing countries. For one month, these diverse teams assist local people on an economic or social development project. "These people actually go out and work in emerging markets, to work in NGOs (nongovernment organizations), to work in these other kinds of environments, so they can get a perspective and learn . . . how to think about problems from another perspective, from another point of view," explains an IBM executive.[95]

Chapter Summary

LO1 Describe the elements of self-concept and explain how each affects an individual's behaviour and well-being.

Self-concept includes an individual's self-beliefs and self-evaluations. It has three structural characteristics–complexity, consistency, and clarity–all of which influence employee well-being, behaviour, and performance. People are inherently motivated to promote and protect their self-concept (self-enhancement) and to verify and maintain their existing self-concept (self-verification). Self-evaluation consists of self-esteem, self-efficacy, and locus of control. Self-concept also consists of both personality identity and social identity. Social identity theory explains how people define themselves in terms of the groups to which they belong or have an emotional attachment.

LO2 Outline the perceptual process and discuss the effects of categorical thinking and mental models in that process.

Perception involves selecting, organizing, and interpreting information to make sense of the world around us. Perceptual organization applies categorical thinking–the mostly nonconscious process of organizing people and objects into preconceived categories that are stored in our long-term memory. Mental models–knowledge structures that we develop to describe, explain, and predict the world around us–also help us make sense of incoming stimuli.

LO3 Discuss how stereotyping, attribution, self-fulfilling prophecy, halo, false-consensus, primacy, and recency effects influence the perceptual process.

Stereotyping occurs when people assign traits to others based on their membership in a social category. This assignment economizes mental effort, fills in missing information, and enhances our self-concept, but it also lays the foundation for prejudice and systemic discrimination. The attribution process involves deciding whether an observed behaviour or event is caused mainly by the person (internal factors) or the environment (external factors). Attributions are decided by perceptions of the consistency, distinctiveness, and consensus of the behaviour. This process is subject to self-serving bias and fundamental attribution error. A self-fulfilling prophecy occurs when our expectations about another person cause that person to act in a way that is consistent with those expectations. This effect is stronger when employees first join the work unit, when several people hold these expectations, and when the employee has a history of low achievement. Four other perceptual errors commonly noted in organizations are the halo effect, false-consensus effect, primacy effect, and recency effect.

LO4 Discuss three ways to improve perceptions, with specific applications to organizational situations.

One way to minimize perceptual biases is to become more aware of their existence. Awareness of these biases makes people more mindful of their thoughts and actions, but this training sometimes reinforces rather than reduces reliance on stereotypes and tends to be ineffective for people with deeply held prejudices. A second strategy is to become more aware of biases in our own decisions and behaviour. Self- awareness increases through formal tests such as the IAT and by applying the Johari Window, which is a process in which others provide feedback to you about your behaviour, and you offer disclosure to them about yourself. The third strategy is meaningful interaction, which applies the contact hypothesis that people who interact will be less prejudiced or perceptually biased toward one another. Meaningful interaction is strongest when people work closely and frequently with relatively equal status on a shared meaningful task that requires cooperation and reliance on one another. Meaningful interaction helps improve empathy, which is a person's understanding and sensitivity to the feelings, thoughts, and situations of others.

LO5 Outline the main features of a global mindset and justify its usefulness to employees and organizations.

A global mindset refers to an individual's ability to perceive, know about, and process information across cultures. This includes (1) an awareness of, openness to, and respect for other views and practices in the world; (2) the capacity to empathize and act effectively across cultures; (3) an ability to process complex information about novel environments; and (4) the ability to comprehend and reconcile intercultural matters with multiple levels of thinking. A global mindset enables people to develop better cross-cultural relationships, to digest huge volumes of cross-cultural information, and to identify and respond more quickly to emerging global opportunities. Employees develop a global mindset through self-awareness, opportunities to compare their own mental models with people from other cultures, formal cross-cultural training, and immersion in other cultures.

Key Terms

attribution process, p. 68
categorical thinking, p. 64
confirmation bias, p. 63
contact hypothesis, p. 74
empathy, p. 74
false-consensus effect, p. 71
fundamental attribution error, p. 69
global mindset, p. 75
halo effect, p. 71
Johari Window, p. 73
locus of control, p. 61
mental models, p. 65
perception, p. 63
positive organizational behaviour, p. 71
primacy effect, p. 72
recency effect, p. 72
selective attention, p. 63
self-concept, p. 57
self-efficacy, p. 61
self-enhancement, p. 59
self-fulfilling prophecy, p. 69
self-serving bias, p. 69
self-verification, p. 59
social identity theory, p. 61
stereotyping, p. 65

Critical-Thinking Questions

1. You are manager of a district that has just hired several recent university and college graduates. Most of these people are starting their first full-time job, although most or all have held part-time and summer positions in the past. They have general knowledge of their particular skill area (accounting, engineering, marketing, etc.) but know relatively little about specific business practices and developments. Explain how you would nurture the self-concepts of these new hires to strengthen their performance and maintain their psychological well-being. Also explain how you might reconcile the tendency for self-enhancement while preventing the new employees from forming a negative self-evaluation.
2. Do you define yourself in terms of the school you attend? Why or why not? What are the implications of your answer for your university or college?
3. Imagine a situation of conflict between you and your boss. Discuss how understanding the elements of self-concept, its complexity, consistency, and clarity may be useful in such situations.
4. Several years ago, senior executives at Canadian energy company CanOil wanted to acquire an exploration company (HBOG) that was owned by an American energy company, AmOil. Rather than face a hostile takeover and unfavourable tax implications, CanOil's two top executives met with the CEO of AmOil to discuss a friendly exchange of stock to carry out the transaction. AmOil's chief executive was previously unaware of CanOil's plans, and as the meeting began, the AmOil executive warned that he was there merely to listen. The CanOil executives were confident that AmOil wanted to sell HBOG because energy legislation at the time made HBOG a poor investment for AmOil. AmOil's CEO remained silent for most of the meeting, which CanOil executives interpreted as an implied agreement to proceed to buy AmOil stock on the market. But when CanOil launched the stock purchase a month later, AmOil's CEO was both surprised and outraged. He thought he had given the CanOil executives the cold shoulder, remaining silent to show his disinterest in the deal. The misunderstanding nearly bankrupted CanOil because AmOil reacted by protecting its stock. What perceptual problem(s) likely occurred that led to this misunderstanding?
5. What mental models do you have about attending a lecture in the program you are attending? Are these mental models helpful? Could any of these mental models hold you back from achieving the full benefit of the lecture?
6. During a diversity management session, a manager suggests that stereotypes are a necessary part of working with others. "I have to make assumptions about what's in the other person's head, and stereotypes help me do that," she explains. "It's better to rely on stereotypes than to enter a working relationship with someone from another culture without any idea of what they believe in!" Discuss the merits of and problems with the manager's statement.
7. Describe how a manager or coach could use the process of self-fulfilling prophecy to enhance an individual's performance.
8. Self-awareness is increasingly recognized as an important ingredient for effective leadership. Suppose that you are responsible for creating a leadership development program in a government organization. What activities or processes would you introduce to help participants in this program to constructively develop a better self-awareness of their personality, values, and personal biases?
9. Almost everyone in a college or university business program has developed some degree of global mindset. What events or activities in your life have helped to nurture the global mindset you have developed so far? What actions can you take now, while still attending school, to further develop your global mindset?

Case Study: HY DAIRIES LTD.

Syd Gilman read the latest sales figures with a great deal of satisfaction. The vice-president of marketing at Hy Dairies, Ltd., a large Canadian milk products manufacturer, was pleased to see that the marketing campaign to improve sagging sales of Hy's gourmet ice cream brand was working. Sales volume and market share of the product had increased significantly over the past two quarters compared with the previous year.

The improved sales of Hy's gourmet ice cream could be credited to Rochelle Beauport, who was assigned to the gourmet ice cream brand last year. Beauport had joined Hy less than two years ago as an assistant brand manager after leaving a similar job at a food products firm. She was one of the few nonwhite women in marketing management at Hy Dairies and had a promising career with the company. Gilman was pleased with Beauport's work and tried to let her know this in the annual performance reviews. He now had an excellent opportunity to reward her by offering the recently vacated position of market research coordinator. Although technically only a lateral transfer with a modest salary increase, the marketing research coordinator job would give Beauport broader experience in some high-profile work, which would enhance her career with Hy Dairies. Few people were aware that Gilman's own career had been boosted by working as marketing research coordinator at Hy several years before.

Rochelle Beauport had also seen the latest sales figures on Hy's gourmet ice cream and was expecting Gilman's call to meet with her that morning. Gilman began the conversation by briefly mentioning the favourable sales figures, and then explained that he wanted Beauport to take the marketing research coordinator job. Beauport was shocked by the news. She enjoyed brand management and particularly the challenge involved with controlling a product that directly affected the company's profitability. Marketing research coordinator was a technical support position–a "backroom" job–far removed from the company's bottom-line activities. Marketing research was not the route to top management in most organizations, Beauport thought. She had been sidelined.

After a long silence, Beauport managed a weak "Thank you, Mr. Gilman." She was too bewildered to protest. She wanted to collect her thoughts and reflect on what she had done wrong. Also, she did not know her boss well enough to be openly critical.

Gilman recognized Beauport's surprise, which he naturally assumed was her positive response to hearing of this wonderful career opportunity. He, too, had been delighted several years earlier about his temporary transfer to marketing research to round out his marketing experience. "This move will be good for both you and Hy Dairies," said Gilman as he escorted Beauport from his office.

Beauport was preoccupied with several tasks that afternoon, but was able to consider the day's events that evening. She was one of the top women and few minorities in brand management at Hy Dairies and feared that she was being sidelined because the company didn't want women or nonwhite people in top management. Her previous employer had made it quite clear that women "couldn't take the heat" in marketing management and tended to place women in technical support positions after a brief term in lower brand management jobs. Obviously Syd Gilman and Hy Dairies were following the same game plan. Gilman's comments that the coordinator job would be good for her was just a nice way of saying that Beauport couldn't go any further in brand management at Hy Dairies.

Beauport now faced the difficult decision of whether to confront Gilman and try to change Hy Dairies' sexist and possibly racist practices or to leave the company.

Discussion Questions

1. Apply your knowledge of stereotyping and social identity theory to explain what went wrong here.
2. What other perceptual error is apparent in this case study?
3. What can organizations do to minimize misperceptions in these types of situations?

Web Exercise: DIVERSITY & STEREOTYPING ON DISPLAY IN CORPORATE WEBSITES

Purpose This exercise is designed to help you diagnose evidence of diversity and stereotyping in corporate websites.

Materials Students need to complete their research for this activity prior to class, including selecting one or more large or medium-sized public or private organizations and retrieving sample images of people from the organization's website.

Instructions The instructor may have students work alone or in groups for this activity. Students will select one or more medium-large sized public or private organizations. Students will closely examine images in the selected company's website in terms of how women, visible minorities, people with disabilities, Aboriginal peoples, and older employees and clients are portrayed. Specifically, students should be prepared to discuss and provide details in class regarding:

1. The percentage of images showing (i.e., visual representations of) women, visible minorities, people with disabilities, Aboriginal peoples, and older employees and clients. Students should also be sensitive to the size and placement of these images in the website or documents therein.
2. The roles in which women, visible minorities, people with disabilities, Aboriginal peoples, and older employees and clients are depicted. For example, are women shown more in traditional or non-traditional occupations and roles in these websites?
3. Pick one or more of the best examples of diversity on display and one stereotypic image you can find from the website to show in class, either in printed form, or as a web link that can be displayed in class.

Self-Assessment: HOW MUCH DOES WORK DEFINE YOUR SELF-CONCEPT?

Work is an important part of our lives, but some people view it as secondary to other life interests whereas others view work as central to their identity as individuals. The following scale estimates the extent to which you view work as a central or not-so-central life interest. Read each of the statements below and decide how accurate each one is in describing your focus in life. Then use the scoring key in Appendix B at the end of this book to calculate your results. Remember that there are no right or wrong answers to these questions. Also, this self-assessment should be completed alone so that you can rate yourself honestly without concerns of social comparison. Class discussion will focus on the meaning of this scale and its relevance to self-concept and perceptions.

Work Centrality Scale

Please indicate the extent to which you agree or disagree with each statement below in describing your focus in life.	Strongly Disagree	Moderately Disagree	Slightly Disagree	Slightly Agree	Moderately Agree	Strongly Agree
1. The most important things that happen in life involve work.	○	○	○	○	○	○
2. Work is something people should get involved in most of the time.	○	○	○	○	○	○
3. Work should be only a small part of one's life.	○	○	○	○	○	○
4. Work should be considered central to life.	○	○	○	○	○	○
5. In my view, an individual's personal life goals should be work-oriented.	○	○	○	○	○	○
6. Life is worth living only when people get absorbed in work.	○	○	○	○	○	○

Source: R. N. Kanungo, Work Alienation: an Integrative Approach (New York: Praeger, 1982).

SELF-ASSESSMENTS FOR CHAPTER 3

SELF-ASSESSMENT NAME	DESCRIPTION	LOCATION
How much does work define your self-concept?	Estimates the extent to which you view work as a central or not-so-central life interest.	Page 80 connect
What is your locus of control?	Estimates the extent to which you have an internal or external locus-of-control.	connect
How much general self-efficacy do you have?	Estimates your general self-efficacy (a component of self-evaluation); that is, your general belief that you have the ability, motivation, and resources to complete tasks successfully in a broad range of situations.	connect
How much perceptual structure do you need?	Estimates your personal need for perceptual structure; that is how much you need to be aware of events around you.	connect
Assessing your perspective taking (cognitive empathy)	Estimates of a form of empathy; specifically how well you cognitively understand another person's situational and individual circumstances.	connect
Assessing your emotional empathy	Estimates of a form of empathy; specifically how well you are able to experience the emotions or feelings of another person.	connect

WestJet Airlines generates plenty of positive emotions among employees and guests, which translates into happy guests and greater financial success than most other airlines.

Stuart Gradon, *Calgary Herald*/CP Images

Chapter 4

Workplace Emotions, Attitudes, and Stress

LEARNING OBJECTIVES

After reading this chapter, you should be able to:

LO1. Explain how emotions and cognition (conscious reasoning) influence attitudes and behaviour.

LO2. Discuss the dynamics of emotional labour and the role of emotional intelligence in the workplace.

LO3. Summarize the consequences of job dissatisfaction as well as strategies to increase organizational (affective) commitment.

LO4. Describe the stress experience and review three major stressors.

LO5. Identify five ways to manage workplace stress.

WestJet passengers travelling to Calgary from Hamilton and Toronto one November day were asked to scan their boarding pass at a large, Christmas gift box-like machine located at their respective gates. Someone dressed as Santa Claus (but in WestJet blue rather than red) then appeared on the box's large screen, jovially asking by name what each surprised passenger would like for Christmas. The chat with Santa raised holiday spirits, but the real delight occurred several hours later on arrival at Calgary Airport's luggage carousel number eight. Christmas lights and decorations came alive and fake snow fell as the conveyor started up. Then, instead of passenger luggage (which arrived later), the conveyor transported scarves, toys, smartphones, and other gifts, each carefully wrapped with the names of the passengers who had wished for them. WestJet employees had recorded the Christmas wishes and scurried around Calgary to find and wrap each gift.

The WestJet Miracle Christmas event symbolizes the airline's focus on positive emotions and attitudes. "That's what WestJet is all about," explains WestJet vice-president Richard Bartrem. "We like to share that fun, friendly, and caring spirit." Approximately 175 employees were directly involved, but WestJet CEO Gregg Saretsky reports that the event and its subsequent YouTube video had a powerful effect on all WestJet employees (called WestJetters). "[We have] almost 10,000 WestJetters, who are saying they have never felt more proud than to see the reflection of our culture in that video."

Since its founding two decades ago, WestJet has grown around the belief that happy employees provide better customer service, which results in a more successful airline. "If you take care of your people then the rest takes care of itself," says Saretsky. Even with the recent growing pains as it expanded into multiple bases (Toronto, Calgary, etc.), WestJet has been rated as Canada's most attractive employer and the best value airline in the world.

The company's fun attitude is evident from the humour of flight crews on many flights, particularly to vacation destinations. But with diverse clientele, WestJetters also rely on their emotional intelligence to know the merriment should be toned down when the plane mainly carries weary business travellers. "What we say to WestJetters who are working those flights is 'Read your audience.' If it's a 7 a.m. flight from Toronto to Montreal—it's probably not a good time to crack jokes and sing songs," says Saretsky. "But if it's a flight to Florida or Las Vegas and that's the mood on the plane, 'Bring it on.'"[1]

In less than two decades, WestJet Airlines Ltd. has grown to become one of the top-rated and most successful airlines in the world. CEO Gregg Saretsky reminds people that the company's success isn't due to just low fares and careful cost controls. Dozens of discount airlines have failed in Canada because they forgot the critical ingredient of having enthusiastic, energized, and loyal staff. In other words, WestJet and other organizations must pay attention to the themes discussed in this chapter: employee emotions, attitudes, and well-being.

This chapter begins by describing emotions and explaining how they influence attitudes and behaviour. Next, we consider the dynamics of emotional labour, followed by the popular topic of emotional intelligence. The specific work attitudes of job satisfaction and organizational commitment are then discussed, including their association with various employee behaviours and work performance. The final section looks at work-related stress, including the stress experience, three prominent stressors, individual differences in stress, and ways to combat excessive stress.

Emotions in the Workplace

LO1

Emotions influence almost everything we do in the workplace. This is a strong statement, and one that you would rarely find a dozen years ago among organizational behaviour experts. Most OB theories still assume that a person's thoughts and actions are governed primarily or exclusively by logical thinking (called *cognition*).[2] Yet ground-breaking neuroscience discoveries have revealed that our perceptions, attitudes, decisions, and behaviour are influenced by emotions as well as cognitions.[3] In fact, emotions may have a greater influence because they often occur before cognitive processes and, consequently, influence the latter. By ignoring emotionality, many theories have overlooked a large piece of the puzzle about human behaviour in the workplace.

"Biosensors. The whole company knows instantly when I'm displeased."

Emotions are physiological, behavioural, and psychological episodes experienced towards an object, person, or event that create a state of readiness.[4] These "episodes" are very brief events that typically subside or occur in waves lasting from milliseconds to a few minutes. Emotions are directed towards someone or something. For example, we experience joy, fear, anger, and other emotional episodes towards tasks, customers, or a software program we are using. This differs from *moods*, which are not directed towards anything in particular and tend to be longer-term emotional states.[5]

Emotions are experiences. They represent changes in our physiological state (e.g., blood pressure, heart rate), psychological state (e.g., thought process), and behaviour (e.g., facial expression).[6] Most of these emotional reactions are subtle; they occur without our awareness. This is an important point because the topic of emotions often conjures up images of people "getting emotional." In reality, most emotions are fleeting, low intensity events that influence our

emotions Physiological, behavioural, and psychological episodes experienced towards an object, person, or event that create a state of readiness.

behaviour without conscious awareness.[7] Finally, emotions put us in a state of readiness. When we get worried, for example, our heart rate and blood pressure increase to make our body better prepared to engage in fight or flight. Strong emotions trigger our conscious awareness of a threat or opportunity in the external environment.

TYPES OF EMOTIONS

People experience many emotions and various combinations of emotions, but all of them have two common features, illustrated in Exhibit 4.1.[8] One feature is that all emotions have an associated valence (called *core affect*) signalling that the perceived object or event should be approached or avoided. In other words, all emotions evaluate environmental conditions as good or bad, helpful or harmful, positive or negative, and so forth. Furthermore, negative emotions tend to generate stronger levels of activation than do positive emotions.[9] Fear and anger, for instance, are more intense experiences than are joy and delight, so they have a stronger effect on our actions. This valence asymmetry likely occurs because negative emotions protect us from harm and are therefore more critical for our survival.

The second feature is that emotions vary in their level of activation. By definition, emotions put us in a state of readiness and, as we discuss in the next chapter, are the primary source of individual motivation. Some emotional experiences, such as when we are suddenly surprised, are strong enough to consciously motivate us to act without careful thought. Most emotional experiences are more subtle, but even they activate enough to make us more aware of our environment.

EMOTIONS, ATTITUDES, AND BEHAVIOUR

attitudes The cluster of beliefs, assessed feelings, and behavioural intentions towards a person, object, or event (called an *attitude object*).

To understand how emotions influence our thoughts and behaviour in the workplace, we first need to know about attitudes. **Attitudes** represent the cluster of beliefs, assessed feelings, and behavioural intentions towards a person, object, or event (called an *attitude object*).[10] Attitudes are *judgments*, whereas emotions are *experiences*. In other words, attitudes involve evaluations of an attitude object, whereas emotions operate as events, usually without our awareness. Attitudes might also operate nonconsciously, but we are usually aware of and consciously think about those evaluations. Another distinction is that we experience most emotions very briefly, whereas our attitude towards someone or something is more stable over time.[11]

EXHIBIT 4.1

Circumplex Model of Emotions

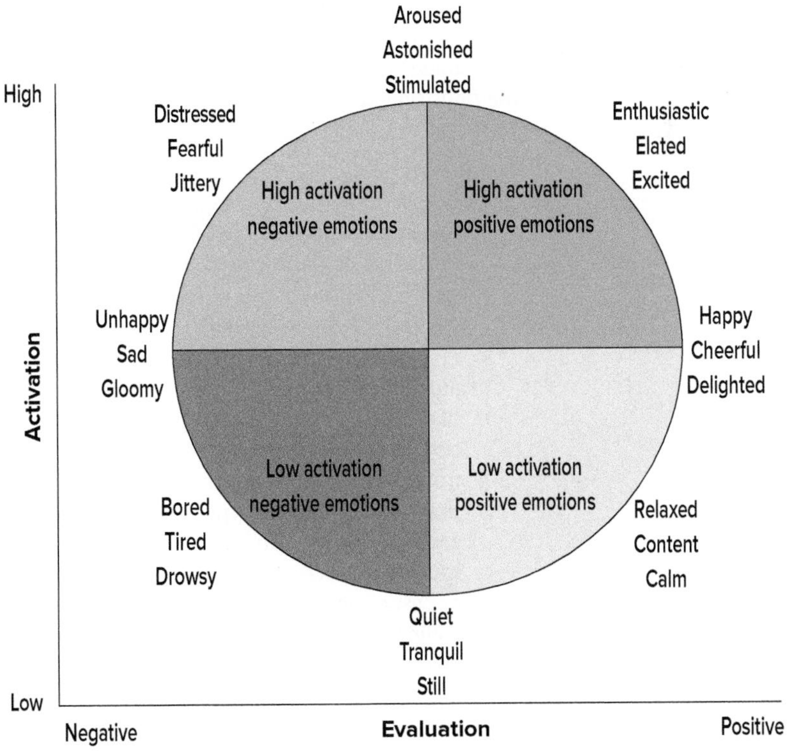

Sources: Adapted from: J. A. Russell, "Core Affect and the Psychological Construction of Emotion." *Psychological Review* 110, no. 1 (2003): 145–172; M. Yik, J.A. Russell, and J.H. Steiger. "A 12-Point Circumplex Structure of Core Affect." *Emotion* 11, no. 4 (2011): 705–31.

EXHIBIT 4.2

Model of Emotions, Attitudes, and Behaviour

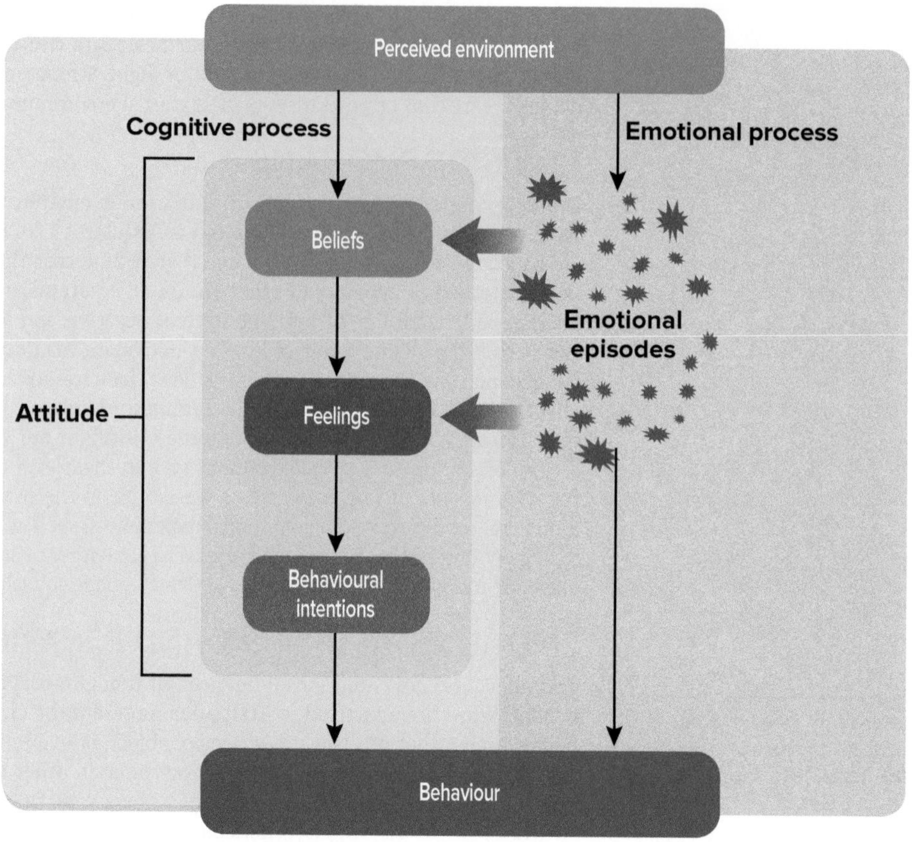

Until recently, experts believed that attitudes could be understood just by the three cognitive components illustrated on the left side of Exhibit 4.2: beliefs, feelings, and behavioural intentions. Now evidence suggests that a parallel emotional process is also at work, shown on the right side of the exhibit.[12] Using attitude towards mergers as an example, let's look more closely at this model, beginning with the traditional cognitive perspective of attitudes.

- *Beliefs.* These are your established perceptions about the attitude object–what you believe to be true. For example, you might believe that mergers reduce job security for employees in the merged firms, or that mergers increase the company's competitiveness in this era of globalization. These beliefs are perceived facts that you acquire from experience and other forms of learning. Each of these beliefs also has a valence; that is, we have a positive or negative feeling about each belief (e.g., better job security is good).
- *Feelings.* Feelings represent your conscious positive or negative evaluations of the attitude object. Some people think mergers are good; others think they are bad. Your like or dislike of mergers represents your assessed feelings. According to the traditional cognitive perspective of attitudes (left side of the model), feelings are calculated from your beliefs about mergers and the associated feelings about those beliefs. If you believe that mergers typically have negative consequences such as layoffs and organizational politics, you will form negative feelings towards mergers in general or about a specific planned merger in your organization. However, recent evidence suggests the opposite can also occur; your feelings about something can cause you to change your feelings about specific beliefs regarding that target.[13] For example, you might normally enjoy the challenge of hard work, but if you dislike your boss and he/she has high performance expectations, then you develop negative feelings about hard work.
- *Behavioural intentions.* Intentions represent your motivation to engage in a particular behaviour regarding the attitude object.[14] Upon hearing that the company will merge with another organization, you might become motivated to look for a job elsewhere or possibly to complain to management about the merger decision. Your feelings towards mergers motivate your behavioural intentions, and which actions you choose depends on your past experience, personality, and social norms of appropriate behaviour.

Several contingencies weaken the beliefs-feelings-intentions-behaviour relationship. First, people with the same beliefs might form quite different feelings towards the attitude object because they have different valences for those beliefs. Two employees might hold the common belief that their boss pushes employee performance, yet they form different feelings towards their boss because but one dislikes being pushed to perform better whereas the other employee appreciates this style of leadership.

Second, people with the same feelings towards the attitude object might develop different behavioural intentions. Suppose that two employees equally dislike their boss. One employee complains to the union or upper management while the other employee looks for a job elsewhere. They respond differently because of their unique experiences, personal values, self-concept, and so forth. Later in this chapter we describe the four main responses to dissatisfaction and other negative attitudes. Third, people with the same behavioural intention might behave differently. For example, two people might intend to quit because they dislike their boss, but only one does so because the other employee could not find better job opportunities.

HOW EMOTIONS INFLUENCE ATTITUDES AND BEHAVIOUR

The cognitive model has dominated attitude research for decades, yet we now know that emotions also have a central role in forming and changing employee attitudes.[15] The right side of Exhibit 4.2 illustrates this process, which (like the cognitive process) also begins with perceptions of the world around us. Our brain tags incoming sensory information with emotional markers based on a quick and imprecise evaluation of whether that information supports or threatens our innate drives. These markers are not calculated feelings; they are automatic and nonconscious emotional responses based on very thin slices of sensory information.[16] The experienced emotions then influence our feelings about the attitude object. For example, WestJet employees experienced positive emotions from the Christmas Miracle event, which has enhanced their positive attitude towards the company.

To explain this process in more detail, consider your attitude towards mergers. You might experience worry, nervousness, or relief upon learning that your company intends to merge with a competitor. The fuzzy dots on the right side of Exhibit 4.2 illustrate the numerous emotional episodes you experience upon hearing the merger announcement, subsequently thinking about the merger, discussing the merger with coworkers, and so on. These emotions are transmitted to the reasoning process, where they are logically analyzed along with other information about the attitude object.[17] Thus, while you are consciously evaluating whether the merger is good or bad, your emotions are already sending core affect (good-bad) signals, which then sways your conscious evaluation. In fact, we often deliberately "listen in" on our emotions to help us consciously decide whether to support or oppose something.[18]

The influence of both cognitive reasoning and emotions on attitudes is most apparent when they disagree with each other. People occasionally experience this mental tug-of-war, sensing that something isn't right even though they can't think of any logical reason to be concerned. This conflicting experience indicates that the person's logical analysis of the situation (left side of Exhibit 4.2) can't identify reasons to support the emotional reaction (right side of Exhibit 4.2).[19] Should we pay attention to our emotional response or our logical analysis? This question is not easy to answer, but some studies indicate that while executives tend to make quick decisions based on their gut feelings (emotional response), the best decisions tend to occur when executives spend time logically evaluating the situation.[20] Thus, we should pay attention to both the cognitive and emotional sides of the attitude model, and hope they agree with each other most of the time!

GENERATING POSITIVE EMOTIONS AT WORK

Some companies seem to be well aware of the dual cognitive-emotional attitude process because they try to inject more positive experiences in the workplace.[21] At Toronto advertising firm Grip Ltd., employees collaborate in funky spaces that resemble a fast-food restaurant, a sauna, and a hot tub (complete with beer-filled cooler). ClearlyContacts employees in Vancouver participate in several fun events each year, including Halloween costume contests, harbour boat cruises, and the annual summer BBQ. Employees at Razer's offices in Singapore zoom around on scooters and pit their gaming skills against each other on the state-of-the-art online gaming console. "Sometimes I can't believe that I have been here for seven months

Corus Entertainment employees enjoy interesting work creating television and radio programs, but the company's recently-built Toronto headquarters has measurably increased morale by putting more fun into the workplace. One popular feature is the lakeside sandy beach with cottage-like Muskoka chairs. Another is a slide that transports people down three storeys (shown here). "It's a little break from our days," says Corus employee Jaimie Galloro. Even after being in the building for three years, Galloro says "the novelty has not worn off."[22]

Photo by Adrian Abdool

already," admits one employee at the gaming peripherals company. "I guess you don't feel the time passing when you are having so much fun."[23]

Some critics might argue that the organization's main focus should be to create positive emotions through the job itself as well as natural everyday occurrences such as polite customers and supportive coworkers. Still, most people perform work that produces some negative emotions, and research has found that humour and fun at work–whether natural or contrived–can potentially offset some of the negative experiences.[24] Overall, corporate leaders need to keep in mind that emotions shape employee attitudes and, as we will discuss later, attitudes influence various forms of work-related behaviour.

One last comment about Exhibit 4.2: Notice the arrow from the emotional episodes to behaviour. It indicates that emotions directly (without conscious thinking) influence a person's behaviour. This occurs when we jump suddenly if someone sneaks up on us. It also occurs in everyday situations because even low-intensity emotions automatically change our facial expressions. These actions are not carefully thought out. They are automatic emotional responses that are learned or hardwired by heredity for particular situations.[25]

COGNITIVE DISSONANCE

Imagine that you have just signed a contract for new electronic whiteboards to be installed throughout the company's meeting rooms. The deal was expensive but, after consulting several staff, you felt that the technology would be valuable in this electronic age. Yet, you felt a twinge of regret soon after signing the contract. This emotional experience is **cognitive dissonance,** which occurs when people perceive that their beliefs, feelings, and behaviour are incongruent with each other.[26] This inconsistency generates emotions (such as feeling hypocritical) that motivate the person to create more consistency by changing one or more of these elements.

cognitive dissonance An emotional experience caused by a perception that our beliefs, feelings, and behaviour are incongruent with each other.

Why did you experience cognitive dissonance after purchasing the electronic whiteboards? Perhaps you remembered that some staff wanted flexibility, whereas the whiteboards require special markers and computer software. Or maybe you had a fleeting realization that buying electronic whiteboards costing several times more than traditional whiteboards is inconsistent

Debating Point:
IS HAVING FUN AT WORK REALLY A GOOD IDEA?

"Fun at work" has become such a hot business fad that companies without a "Fun" committee are considered insensitive task masters. Having fun at work can improve employee attitudes in many situations, but are special fun events really necessary or beneficial?

Some critics vote "No"! They argue that contrived fun events at work can backfire.[27] Some types of fun aren't fun at all to some people. In fact, most employees might be offended by the silliness of some activities contrived by management or a few staff. Others resent having fun forced on them. One expert recently warned: "Once the idea of fun is formally institutionalized from above, it can lead to employees becoming resentful. They feel patronized and condescended, and it breeds anger and frustration."

The meaning and value of fun at work might also vary across generations; what works for Millennials could backfire for Baby Boomers, and vice versa. Another concern is that fun-focused companies might take their eye off the bottom line. "At the end of the day, you have to make money to stay here," says Mike Pitcher, CEO of LeasePlan USA (which does have a "fun" committee). "If work was [all] fun, they'd call it fun."[28]

with your personal values (and company culture) of thrift and value. Whatever the reason, the dissonance occurs because your attitude (being cost conscious is good) is inconsistent with your behaviour (buying expensive whiteboards). Like most other people, you like to think of yourself–and be viewed by others–as rational and logical. You experience dissonance because this purchase decision is contrary to your attitudes about being frugal and maximizing value.

How do we reduce cognitive dissonance?[29] Reversing the behaviour might work, but few behaviours can be undone. In any event, dissonance still exists because others know about the behaviour and that you performed it voluntarily. It would be too expensive to remove the electronic whiteboards after they have been installed and, in any event, coworkers already know that you made this purchase and did so willingly.

More often, people reduce cognitive dissonance by changing their beliefs and feelings. One dissonance-reducing strategy is to develop more favourable attitudes towards specific features of the decision, such as forming a more positive opinion about the whiteboards' capacity to store whatever is written on them. People are also motivated to discover positive features of the decision they didn't notice earlier (e.g., the boards can change handwriting into typed text) and to discover subsequent problems with the alternatives they didn't choose (e.g., few traditional boards can be used as projection screens). A third strategy is more indirect; rather than try to overlook the high price of the electronic whiteboards, you reduce dissonance by emphasizing how your other decisions have been frugal. This framing compensates for your expensive whiteboard fling and thereby maintains your self-concept as a thrifty decision maker. Each of these mental acrobatics maintains some degree of consistency between the person's behaviour (buying expensive whiteboards) and attitudes (being thrifty, appreciating good value).

EMOTIONS AND PERSONALITY

Our coverage of the dynamics of workplace emotions wouldn't be complete unless we mention that emotions are also partly determined by an individual's personality, not just workplace experiences.[30] Some people experience positive emotions as a natural trait. People with more positive emotions typically have higher emotional stability and are extraverted (see Chapter 2). Those who experience more negative emotions tend to have higher neuroticism (lower emotional stability) and are introverted. Positive and negative emotional traits affect a person's attendance, turnover, and long-term work attitudes.[31] While positive and negative personality traits have some effect, other research concludes that the actual situation in which people work has a noticeably stronger influence on their attitudes and behaviour.[32]

connect

What is your emotional personality? Visit **connect.mcgrawhill.com** to assess your emotional trait tendencies.

Managing Emotions at Work

LO2

emotional labour The effort, planning, and control needed to express organizationally desired emotions during interpersonal transactions.

Whether as a WestJet flight attendant or chief executive officer, people are expected to manage their emotions in the workplace. They must conceal their frustration when serving an irritating customer, display compassion to an ill patient, and hide their boredom in a long meeting with other executives. These are all forms of **emotional labour**–the effort, planning, and control needed to express organizationally desired emotions during interpersonal transactions.[33] Almost everyone is expected to abide by *display rules*–norms or explicit rules requiring us within our role to display specific emotions and to hide other emotions. Emotional labour demands are higher in jobs requiring a variety of emotions (e.g., anger as well as joy) and more intense emotions (e.g., showing delight rather than smiling weakly), as well as in jobs where interaction with clients is frequent and longer. Emotional labour also increases when employees must precisely rather than casually abide by the display rules.[34] This particularly occurs in the service industries, where employees have frequent face-to-face interaction with clients.

EMOTIONAL DISPLAY NORMS ACROSS CULTURES

Not long ago, *L'Express* published a special series of articles about living in Canada, including information about Canadian politics, geography, business opportunities, male-female relationships, immigration procedures, and culture. The Paris-based magazine also warned that French citizens might experience some culture shock when moving to Canada. One article noted that French managers might find Canadians somewhat more abrupt and less apologetic in their correspondence. Another article commented that Canadian waiters provide "hyper-friendly, always smiling" service, which can seem a bit too insincere to many Europeans. "It's fun, it's nice, but for us it could be a bit hypocritical," explains Laurence Pivot, who edited the special edition of *L'Express*. "It's too much. It's too friendly."[35]

The French magazine's advice highlights the fact that norms about displaying or hiding your true emotions vary considerably across cultures.[36] One major study points to Ethiopia, Japan, and Austria (among others) as cultures that discourage emotional expression. Instead, people are expected to be subdued, have relatively monotonic voice intonation, and avoid

Russian culture isn't known for friendly customer service. Yet Aeroflot's service ratings are now the highest among East European airlines and exceed those of several North American airlines. The Russian firm accomplished this by training flight attendants to show positive emotions through polite communication as well as smiling and other nonverbal behaviour (shown here). An Aeroflot instructor gently reminds recruits that they must not provide "the silent service of Soviet times. You need to talk to [the passenger]. And you need to smile and smile and smile." The program also encourages trainees to develop a positive attitude through deep acting. This involves "teaching people to be happy, to enjoy what they are doing and to have a positive outlook," explains one Aeroflot trainee.[37]

© James HILL/CONTACT Press Images

physical movement and touching that display emotions. In contrast, cultures such as Kuwait, Egypt, Spain, and Russia allow or encourage more vivid display of emotions and expect people to act more consistently with their true emotions. In these cultures, people are expected to more honestly reveal their thoughts and feelings, be dramatic in their conversational tones, and be animated in their use of nonverbal behaviours. For example, 81 percent of Ethiopians and 74 percent of Japanese agreed that it is considered unprofessional to express emotions overtly in their culture, whereas 43 percent of Americans, 33 percent of Italians, and only 19 percent of Spaniards, Cubans, and Egyptians agreed with this statement.[38]

EMOTIONAL DISSONANCE

emotional dissonance The psychological tension experienced when the emotions people are required to display are quite different from the emotions they actually experience at that moment.

Most jobs expect employees to engage in some level of emotional labour, such as displaying courtesy to unruly passengers or maintaining civility to coworkers. Often, employees are supposed to show emotions that are quite different from the emotions they actually experience at that moment. This incongruence produces an emotional tension called **emotional dissonance.** Employees often handle these discrepancies by engaging in *surface acting;* they pretend that they feel the expected emotion even though they actually experience a different emotion.

One problem with surface acting is that it can lead to higher stress and burnout.[39] By definition, emotional labour requires effort and attention, which consume personal energy. Emotional labour also potentially requires people to act contrary to their self-view, which can lead to psychological separation from self. These problems are greater when employees need to frequently display emotions that oppose their genuine emotions. A second problem with surface acting is that pretending to feel particular emotions can be challenging. A genuine emotion automatically activates a complex set of facial muscles and body positions, all of which are difficult to replicate when pretending to have these emotions. Meanwhile, our true emotions tend to reveal themselves as subtle gestures, usually without our awareness. More often than not, observers see when we are faking and sense that we feel a different emotion.[40]

Employees can somewhat reduce psychological damage caused by surface acting by viewing their act as a natural part of their role. Flight attendants can remain pleasant to unruly passengers more easily when they define themselves by their customer service skill. By adopting this view, their faking is not deprivation of personal self-worth. Instead, it is demonstration of their skill and professionalism. The dissonant interactions are accomplishments rather than dreaded chores.[41] Another strategy is to engage in *deep acting* rather than surface acting.[42] Deep acting involves visualizing reality differently, which then produces emotions more consistent with the required emotions. Faced with an angry passenger, a flight attendant might replace hostile emotions with compassion by viewing the passenger's behaviour as a sign of his or her discomfort or anxiety. Deep acting requires considerable emotional intelligence, which we discuss next.

connect

Are you in touch with your emotions? Visit **connect.mcgrawhill.com** to assess how well you know your emotional intelligence.

Emotional Intelligence

emotional intelligence (EI) A set of abilities to perceive and express emotion, assimilate emotion in thought, understand and reason with emotion, and regulate emotion in oneself and others.

The University of South Florida (USF) College of Medicine discovered from surveys that its graduates required emotional intelligence training to perform their jobs better. "We've created a lot of doctors that are like House," says USF's medical college Dean, referring to the fictional TV physician with the caustic interpersonal style. Now, some USF students are assigned to one of America's top hospitals, where they develop their ability to understand and manage emotions through coaching and role modelling by hospital staff. "You have to have an emotionally intelligent, collaborative, interdisciplinary team practicing if you want young trainees to adopt that as their model," explains the hospital CEO.[43]

USF's College of Medicine and many other organizations increasingly recognize that **emotional intelligence (EI)** improves performance in many types of jobs. In the opening

EXHIBIT 4.3

Dimensions of Emotional Intelligence

Abilities		Yourself	Others
	Recognition of Emotions	Awareness of our own emotions	Awareness of others' emotions
	Regulation of Emotions	Management of our own emotions	Management of others' emotions

Sources: D. Goleman, "An EI-Based Theory of Performance," in *The Emotionally Intelligent Workplace*, ed. C. Cherniss and D. Goleman (San Francisco: Jossey-Bass, 2001), p. 28; Jordan, Peter J., and Sandra A. Lawrence. "Emotional intelligence in teams: Development and initial validation of the short version of the Workgroup Emotional Intelligence Profile (WEIP-S)," *Journal of Management & Organization* 15 (2009): 452–469.

case study, for example, WestJet CEO Gregg Saretsky pointed out that WestJetters need to be aware of passenger moods and emotions to determine how much humour to convey during the flight. This emotional intelligence also applies to individual interactions, such as showing calm and polite concern to an irate passenger. Emotional intelligence includes a set of *abilities* to recognize and regulate their own emotions as well as the emotions of other people. This definition refers to the four main dimensions shown in Exhibit 4.3.[44]

- *Awareness of our own emotions.* This is the ability to perceive and understand the meaning of your own emotions. You are more sensitive to subtle emotional responses to events and understand their message. Self-aware people are better able to eavesdrop on their emotional responses to specific situations and to use this awareness as conscious information.[45]
- *Management of our own emotions.* Emotional intelligence includes the ability to manage your own emotions, something that we all do to some extent. We keep disruptive impulses in check. We try not to feel angry or frustrated when events go against us. We try to feel and express joy and happiness towards others when the occasion calls for these emotional displays. We try to create a second wind of motivation later in the workday. Notice that management of your own emotions goes beyond displaying behaviours that represent desired emotions in a particular situation. It includes generating or suppressing emotions. In other words, the deep acting described earlier requires high levels of the self-regulation component of emotional intelligence.
- *Awareness of others' emotions.* This dimension refers to the ability to perceive and understand the emotions of other people. To a large extent, awareness of other people's emotions is represented by *empathy*–having an understanding of and sensitivity to the feelings, thoughts, and situations of others (see Chapter 3). This ability includes understanding the other person's situation, experiencing his or her emotions, and knowing his or her needs even though unstated. Awareness of others' emotions extends beyond empathy. It also includes being organizationally aware, such as sensing office politics and understanding social networks.
- *Management of others' emotions.* This dimension of EI involves managing other people's emotions. This includes consoling people who feel sad, emotionally inspiring your team members to complete a class project on time, getting strangers to feel comfortable working with you, and managing dysfunctional emotions among staff who experience conflict with customers or other employees.

These four dimensions of emotional intelligence form a hierarchy.[46] Awareness of your own emotions is lowest because you need awareness to engage in the higher levels of emotional intelligence. You can't manage your own emotions if you don't know what they are (i.e., low self-awareness). Managing other people's emotions is the highest level of EI because this ability requires awareness of your own and others' emotions. To diffuse an angry conflict between two employees, for example, you need to understand the emotions they are experiencing and manage your emotions (and display of emotions). To manage your own emotions, you also need to be aware of your current emotions.

EMOTIONAL INTELLIGENCE OUTCOMES AND TRAINING

Does emotional intelligence make a difference in employee performance and well-being? A few OB experts question the usefulness of the emotional intelligence concept, claiming that there is a lack of agreement on its definition and that existing concepts such as personality and general intelligence can be used instead.[47] However, a consensus is slowly emerging around the meaning of EI, and there is considerable research suggesting that this concept does help us to understand what goes on in social relations.

Most jobs involve social interaction with coworkers or external stakeholders, so employees need emotional intelligence to work effectively.[48] Research suggests that people with high EI are better at interpersonal relations, perform better in jobs requiring emotional labour, are superior leaders, make better decisions involving social exchanges, are more successful in many aspects of job interviews, and are better at knowledge sharing. For example, leaders need substantial emotional intelligence because their work involves regulating their own emotions as part of emotional labour (e.g., showing patience to employees even when they might feel frustrated) as well as regulating the emotions of others (e.g., helping staff members feel optimism for the future even though they just lost an important contract). However, emotional intelligence does not improve some forms of performance, such as tasks that require minimal social interaction.[49]

Given the potential value of emotional intelligence, it's not surprising that some organizations try to measure this ability in job applicants. For instance, EI is one factor considered for entry into the elite para-rescue jumper training program in the United States Air Force (USAF), which costs $250,000 per graduate and has an 80 percent failure rate. USAF research has found that trainees with high scores on several emotional intelligence dimensions are more than twice as likely to complete the para-rescue jumper program.[50]

Several studies have found that companies can also increase employees' emotional intelligence through training programs designed for that purpose.[51] For instance, staff members at a Netherlands residence for people with intellectual disabilities completed an EI training program where they learned about the concept, reviewed feedback on their initial EI test scores, applied EI dimensions to case studies, developed two personal goals to improve their EI profile, and later received professional feedback based on videos showing them meeting with difficult clients. Generally, employees improve their emotional intelligence through awareness of the concept, self-awareness of their EI scores, and coaching and other forms of feedback. Emotional intelligence also increases with age; it is part of the process called maturity.

So far, this chapter has introduced the model of emotions and attitudes, as well as emotional intelligence as the means by which we manage emotions in the workplace. The next two sections look at two specific attitudes: job satisfaction and organizational commitment. These two attitudes are so important in our understanding of workplace behaviour that some experts suggest the two combined should be called "overall job attitude."[52]

Job Satisfaction

LO3

job satisfaction A person's evaluation of his or her job and work context.

Probably the most studied attitude in organizational behaviour is **job satisfaction,** a person's evaluation of his or her job and work context.[53] It is an *appraisal* of the perceived job characteristics, work environment, and emotional experiences at work. Satisfied employees have a favourable evaluation of their jobs, based on their observations and emotional experiences. Job satisfaction is best viewed as a collection of attitudes about different aspects of the job and work context. You might like your coworkers but be less satisfied with your workload, for instance.

How satisfied are employees at work? The answer depends on the person, the workplace, and the country. Global surveys, such as the one shown in Exhibit 4.4, indicate with some consistency that job satisfaction tends to be highest in the Nordic countries (such as Norway

EXHIBIT 4.4

Job Satisfaction in Selected Countries[54]

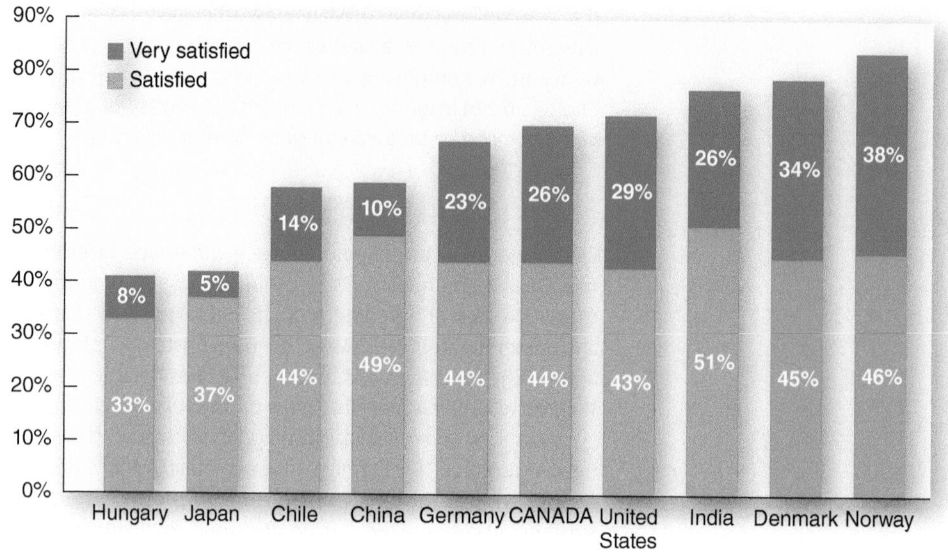

Note: Percentage of employees in each country who said they are, in general, satisfied or very satisfied working for their current employer.

Data based on: Randstad, Women in Leadership: Still a Tough Battle, *Randstad Workmonitor*, Global Press Report, Wave 1, 2013, Randstad Holdings nv (Amsterdam: March 2013). Survey data were collected from a minimum of 400 interviews per country of adults working 24 hours or more per week. Respondents were asked: "How satisfied are you in general working for your current employer?"

and Denmark) and India, and above average in Canada and the United States. The lowest levels of overall job satisfaction are usually recorded in Hungary and several Asian countries (e.g., Japan, Mainland China).[55]

Can we conclude from these surveys that most employees in Norway, Denmark, and India are happy at work? Possibly, but their overall job satisfaction probably isn't as high as these statistics suggest. One problem is that surveys often use a single direct question, such as: "How satisfied are you with your job?" Many dissatisfied employees are reluctant to reveal their feelings in a direct question because this is tantamount to admitting that they made a poor job choice and are not enjoying life. This inflated result is evident by the fact that employees tend to report much less satisfaction with specific aspects of their work. For instance, 82 percent of Canadian federal government employees agree that they like their job overall, yet only 64 percent would recommend their department or agency as a great place to work.[56] Furthermore, studies report that many employees plan to look for work within the next year or would leave their current employer if the right opportunity came along.[57]

A second problem is that cultural values make it difficult to compare job satisfaction across countries. People in China and Japan tend to subdue their emotions in public, and there is evidence that they also avoid extreme survey ratings such as "very satisfied." A third problem is that job satisfaction changes with economic conditions. Employees with the highest job satisfaction in current surveys tend to be in countries where the economies are chugging along quite well.[58]

JOB SATISFACTION AND WORK BEHAVIOUR

Brad Bird pays a lot of attention to job satisfaction. "In my experience, the thing that has the most significant impact on a budget–but never shows up in a budget–is morale," advises Bird, who has directed several award-winning animation and live-action films at Pixar Animation Studios and Walt Disney Studios. "If you have low morale, for every dollar you spend, you get 25 cents of value. If you have high morale, for every dollar your spend, you get about $3 dollars of value."[59]

Brad Bird's opinion about the importance of job satisfaction is consistent with the actions of leaders in many companies. Employers monitor job satisfaction and related employee attitudes,

exit-voice-loyalty-neglect (EVLN) model The four ways, as indicated in the name, that employees respond to job dissatisfaction.

and actively compete to win best-workplace awards. In some firms, executive bonuses depend partly on employee satisfaction ratings. The reason for this attention is simple: Job satisfaction affects many of the individual behaviours introduced in Chapter 2 (task performance, organizational citizenship, quitting, absenteeism, etc.).[60] A useful template for organizing and understanding the consequences of job dissatisfaction is the **exit-voice-loyalty-neglect (EVLN) model.** As the name suggests, the EVLN model identifies four ways that employees respond to dissatisfaction:[61]

- *Exit.* Exit includes leaving the organization, transferring to another work unit, or at least trying to get away from the dissatisfying situation. The traditional theory is that job dissatisfaction builds over time and is eventually strong enough to motivate employees to search for better work opportunities elsewhere. This is likely true to some extent, but the most recent opinion is that specific "shock events" quickly energize employees to think about and engage in exit behaviour. For example, the emotional reaction you experience to an unfair management decision or a conflict episode with a coworker motivates you to look at job ads and speak to friends about job opportunities where they work. This begins the process of re-aligning your self-concept more with another company than with your current employer.[62]
- *Voice.* Voice is any attempt to change, rather than escape from, the dissatisfying situation. Voice can be a constructive response, such as recommending ways for management to improve the situation, or it can be more confrontational, such as filing formal grievances or forming a coalition to oppose a decision.[63] In the extreme, some employees might engage in counterproductive behaviours to get attention and force changes in the organization.
- *Loyalty.* In the original version of this model, loyalty was not an outcome of dissatisfaction. Rather, it determined whether people chose exit or voice (i.e., high loyalty resulted in voice; low loyalty produced exit).[64] More recent writers describe loyalty as an outcome, but in various and somewhat unclear ways. Generally, they suggest that "loyalists" are employees who respond to dissatisfaction by patiently waiting—some say they "suffer in silence"—for the problem to work itself out or be resolved by others.[65]
- *Neglect.* Neglect includes reducing work effort, paying less attention to quality, and increasing absenteeism and lateness. It is generally considered a passive activity that has negative consequences for the organization.

Which of the four EVLN alternatives do employees use? It depends on the person and situation.[66] The individual's personality, values, and self-concept are important factors. For example, people with a high-conscientiousness personality are less likely to engage in neglect and more likely to engage in voice. Past experience also influences which EVLN action is applied. Employees who were unsuccessful with voice in the past are more likely to engage in exit or neglect when experiencing job dissatisfaction in the future. Another factor is loyalty, as it was originally intended in the EVLN model. Specifically, employees are more likely to quit when they have low loyalty to the company, and they are more likely to engage in voice when they have high loyalty. Finally, the response to dissatisfaction depends on the situation. Employees are less likely to use the exit option when there are few alternative job prospects, for example. Dissatisfied employees are more likely to use voice than the other options when they are aware that other employees are dependent on them.[67]

JOB SATISFACTION AND PERFORMANCE

Is a happy worker a more productive worker? Most corporate leaders likely think so. Yet, for most of the past century, organizational behaviour scholars have challenged this "happy worker" hypothesis, concluding that job satisfaction minimally affects job performance. Now OB experts are concluding that maybe the popular saying is correct after all; there is a *moderately* positive relationship between job satisfaction and performance. In other words, workers tend to be more productive to *some extent* when they have more positive attitudes towards their job and workplace.[68]

Founded just two decades ago, Admiral Group has grown rapidly to 6,500 employees, 13 brands, and 3.5 million customers in the United Kingdom and other countries. The highly successful Welsh insurance firm also stands out as the second best large company to work for in the United Kingdom and the only one to be on the list every year (14 years). "We know that our people spend a lot of time in work and we want to make sure that they enjoy this time," says Admiral CEO Henry Engelhardt. Although job satisfaction is important for its own sake, Admiral believes that morale also contributes to job performance. "We have a simple philosophy at Admiral: if people like what they do, they'll do it better," says Engelhardt.[69]

© Northcliffe Media Wales

Why is job satisfaction associated with performance relationship only to some extent? One reason is that general attitudes (such as job satisfaction) don't predict specific behaviours very well. As the EVLN model explained, reduced performance (a form of neglect) is only one of four possible responses to dissatisfaction. A second reason is that some employees are tethered to technology or coworkers so much that they have little control over their performance. An assembly line worker, for instance, installs a fixed number of windshields each hour with about the same quality of installation whether he or she is happy or unhappy with work. A third consideration is that job performance might cause job satisfaction, rather than vice versa.[70] Higher performers receive more rewards (including recognition) and, consequently, are more satisfied than low-performing employees who receive fewer rewards. The connection between job satisfaction and performance isn't stronger because many organizations do not reward good performance very well.

JOB SATISFACTION AND CUSTOMER SATISFACTION

Fifteen years ago, DaVita Inc. rebounded from near-bankruptcy with a new name and a more successful way to operate a business. The Denver-based provider of kidney care and dialysis services developed an employee-first culture, in which employees are supported as valued teammates. The theory is that happier employees will provide better service to the company's clients across its 2,000 clinics. "The attitude that teammates bring into that clinic affects patients' quality of care and their quality of life," explains a DaVita executive. This view is echoed by Container Store chairman and CEO Kip Tindell. "We really believe that if you put the employees first, they really and truly will take better care of the customer than anybody else," says Tindell.[71]

service profit chain model
A theory explaining how employees' job satisfaction influences company profitability indirectly through service quality, customer loyalty, and related factors.

DaVita and the Container Store are applying the **service profit chain model,** which proposes that job satisfaction has a positive effect on customer service, which flows on to shareholder financial returns. Exhibit 4.5 diagrams this process. Specifically, workplace practices affect job satisfaction, which influences employee retention, motivation, and behaviour. These employee outcomes affect service quality, which then influence customer satisfaction and perceptions of value, customer referrals, and ultimately the company's profitability and growth. The service profit chain model has considerable research support. However, the

EXHIBIT 4.5

Service Profit Chain Model

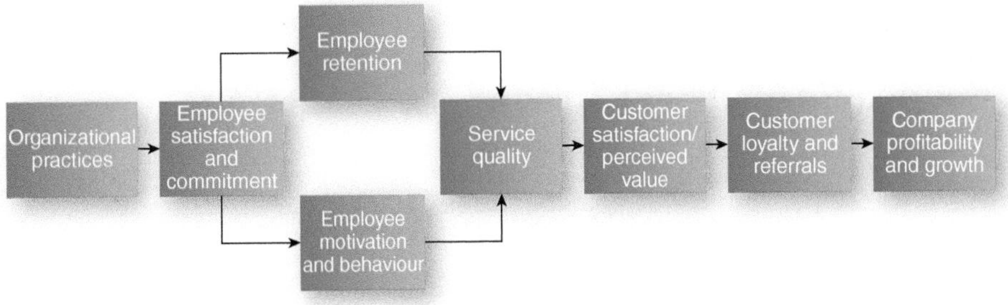

This model is based on: J. I. Heskett, W. E. Sasser, and L. A. Schlesinger, *The Service Profit Chain* (New York: Free Press) 1997; A. J. Rucci, S. P. Kirn, and R. T. Quinn, "The Employee-Customer-Profit Chain At Sears," *Harvard Business Review* 76 (1998): 83-97; S. P. Brown and S. K. Lam, "A Meta-Analysis of Relationships Linking Employee Satisfaction to Customer Responses," *Journal of Retailing* 84, no. 3 (2008): 243-255.

benefits of job satisfaction do take considerable time to flow through to the organization's bottom line.[72]

Behind the service profit chain model are two key explanations why satisfied employees tend to produce happier and more loyal customers.[73] One explanation is that employees are usually in a more positive mood when they feel satisfied with their jobs and working conditions. Employees in a good mood more naturally and frequently display friendliness and positive emotions. When employees have good feelings, their behaviour "rubs off" on most (but not all) customers, so customers feel happier and consequently form a positive evaluation of the service experience (i.e., higher service quality). The effect is also mutual; happy customers make employees happier, which can lead to a virtuous cycle of positive emotions in the service experience.

The second explanation is that satisfied employees are less likely to quit their jobs, so they have better knowledge and skills to serve clients. Lower turnover also enables customers to have the same employees serve them, so there is more consistent service. Some evidence indicates that customers build their loyalty to specific employees, not to the organization, so keeping employee turnover low tends to build customer loyalty.

JOB SATISFACTION AND BUSINESS ETHICS

Before leaving the topic of job satisfaction, we should mention that job satisfaction is also an ethical issue that influences the organization's reputation in the community. People spend a large portion of their time working in organizations, and many societies now expect companies to provide work environments that are safe and enjoyable. Indeed, employees in several countries closely monitor ratings of the best companies to work for, an indication that employee satisfaction is a virtue worth considerable goodwill to employers. This virtue is apparent when an organization has low job satisfaction. The company tries to hide this fact, and when morale problems become public, corporate leaders are usually quick to improve the situation.

connect

How committed are you to your school? Visit **connect.mcgrawhill.com** to assess your affective organizational commitment to your school.

Organizational Commitment

Organizational commitment represents the other half (with job satisfaction) of what some experts call "overall job attitude." **Affective organizational commitment** is the employee's emotional attachment to, involvement in, and identification with an organization. Affective

OB by the NUMBERS

Affective Commitment Around the Planet[74]

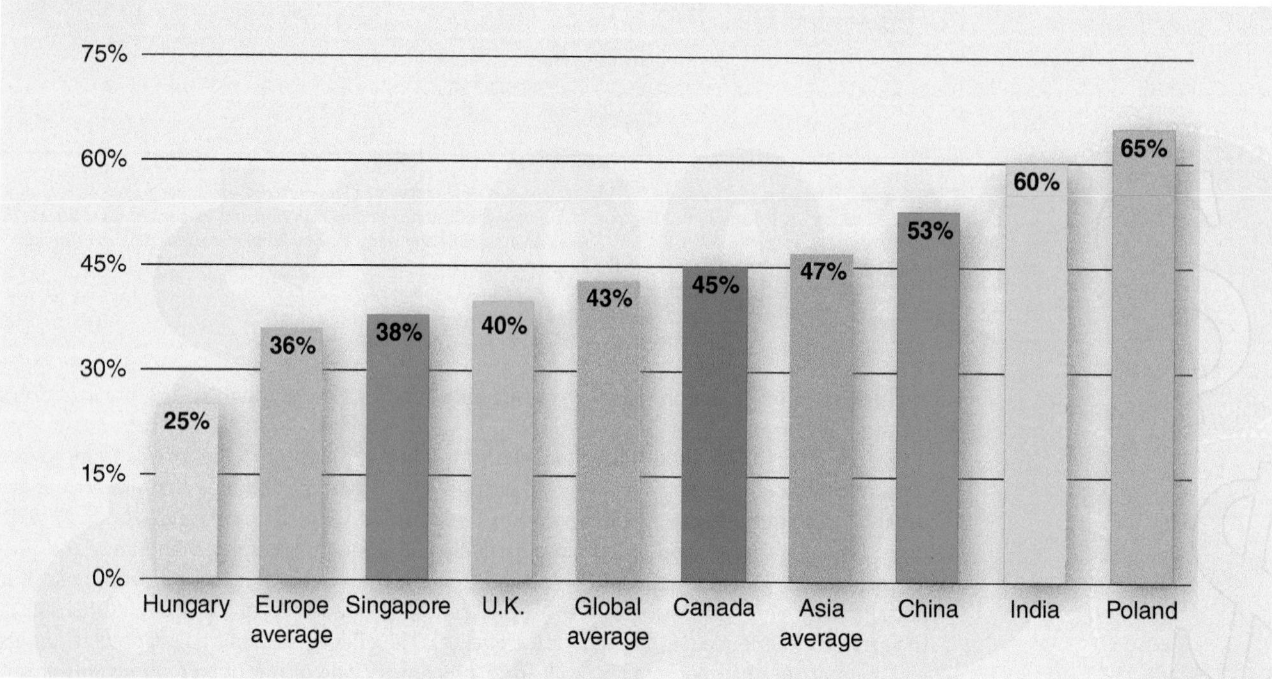

Note: Percentage of employees surveyed in selected countries who say they feel "totally committed" to their employer. More than 134,000 people in 29 countries were surveyed for Kelly Services.

Data provided in several country-specific news releases from Kelly Services. For a white paper summary of the survey, see: Kelly Services, "Employee Loyalty Rises During Global Economic Recession, Kelly International Workforce Survey Finds," Kelly Services (Troy, MI: 8 March 2010).

affective organizational commitment An individual's emotional attachment to, involvement in, and identification with an organization.

continuance commitment An individual's calculative attachment to an organization.

commitment is a psychological bond whereby one chooses to be dedicated to and responsible for the organization.[75] The pride that WestJetters feel towards their employer indicates their affective commitment because they feel an emotional bond to WestJet and identify with its values and reputation.

Affective commitment is often distinguished from **continuance commitment,** which is a calculative attachment to the organization. This calculation takes two forms.[76] One form occurs where an employee has no alternative employment opportunities (e.g., "I dislike working here but there are no other jobs available.") This condition exists where unemployment is high, employees lack sufficient skills to be attractive to other employers, or the employee's skills are so specialized that there is limited demand for them nearby. The other form of continuance commitment occurs when leaving the company would be a significant financial sacrifice (e.g., "I hate this place but can't afford to quit!"). This perceived sacrifice condition occurs when the company offers high pay, benefits, and other forms of economic exchange in the employment relationship, or where quitting forfeits a large deferred financial bonus.

CONSEQUENCES OF AFFECTIVE AND CONTINUANCE COMMITMENT

Affective commitment can be a significant competitive advantage.[77] Employees with a strong psychological bond to the organization are less likely to quit their jobs and be absent from work. They also have higher work motivation and organizational citizenship, as well as somewhat higher job performance. Organizational commitment also improves customer satisfaction because long-tenure employees have better knowledge of work practices and because clients like to do business with the same employees. One warning is that employees with very high loyalty tend to have high conformity, which results in lower creativity. There are also cases of dedicated employees who violated laws to defend the organization. However, most companies suffer from too little rather than too much employee loyalty.

In contrast to the benefits of affective commitment, employees with high levels of continuance commitment tend to have *lower* performance and are *less* likely to engage in organizational citizenship behaviours. Furthermore, unionized employees with high continuance commitment are more likely to use formal grievances, whereas employees with high affective commitment engage in more cooperative problem solving when employee-employer relations sour.[78] Although some level of financial connection may be necessary, employers should not rely on continuance commitment instead of affective commitment. Employers still need to win employees' hearts (affective commitment) beyond tying them financially to the organization (continuance commitment).

BUILDING ORGANIZATIONAL COMMITMENT

There are almost as many ways to build affective commitment as there are topics in this textbook, but here are the most frequently mentioned strategies in the literature:

Justice and Support Affective commitment is higher in organizations that fulfill their obligations to employees and abide by humanitarian values, such as fairness, courtesy, forgiveness, and moral integrity. These values relate to the concept of organizational justice, which we discuss in the next chapter. Similarly, organizations that support employee well-being tend to cultivate higher levels of loyalty in return.[79]

Shared Values The definition of affective commitment refers to a person's identification with the organization, and that identification is highest when employees believe their values are congruent with the organization's dominant values. Also, employees experience more comfort and predictability when they agree with the values underlying corporate decisions. This comfort increases their motivation to stay with the organization.[80]

trust Positive expectations one person has towards another person in situations involving risk.

Trust **Trust** refers to positive expectations one person has towards another person in situations involving risk.[81] Trust means putting faith in the other person or group. It is also a reciprocal activity: To receive trust, you must demonstrate trust. Employees identify with and feel obliged to work for an organization only when they trust its leaders. This explains why layoffs are one of the greatest blows to affective commitment; by reducing job security, companies reduce the trust employees have in their employer and the employment relationship.[82]

Organizational Comprehension Organizational comprehension refers to how well employees understand the organization, including its strategic direction, social dynamics, and physical layout.[83] This awareness is a necessary prerequisite to affective commitment because it is difficult to identify with or feel loyal to something that you don't know very well. Furthermore, lack of information produces uncertainty, and the resulting stress can distance employees from that source of uncertainty (i.e., the organization). The practical implication here is to ensure that employees develop a reasonably clear and complete mental model of the organization. This occurs by giving staff information and opportunities to keep up to date about organizational events, interact with coworkers, discover what goes on in different parts of the organization, and learn about the organization's history and future plans.[84]

Employee Involvement Employee involvement increases affective commitment by strengthening the employee's psychological ownership and social identity with the organization.[85] Employees feel that they are part of the organization when they participate in decisions that guide the organization's future (see Chapter 7). Employee involvement also builds loyalty because giving this power is a demonstration of the company's trust in its employees.

Organizational commitment and job satisfaction represent two of the most often studied and discussed attitudes in the workplace. Each is linked to emotional episodes and cognitive judgments about the workplace and relationship with the company. Emotions also play an important role in another concept that is on everyone's mind these days: stress. The final section of this chapter provides an overview of work-related stress and how it can be managed.

Work-Related Stress

LO4

stress An adaptive response to a situation that is perceived as challenging or threatening to the person's well-being.

When asked if they often feel stressed, most employees these days say "Yes"! Not only do most people understand the concept; they claim to have plenty of personal experience with it. **Stress** is most often described as an adaptive response to a situation that is perceived as challenging or threatening to the person's well-being.[86] It is a physiological and psychological condition that prepares us to adapt to hostile or noxious environmental conditions. Our heart rate increases, muscles tighten, breathing speeds up, and perspiration increases. Our body also moves more blood to the brain, releases adrenaline and other hormones, fuels the system by releasing more glucose and fatty acids, activates systems that sharpen our senses, and conserves resources by shutting down our immune system. One school of thought suggests that stress is a negative evaluation of the external environment. However, critics of this "cognitive appraisal" perspective point out that stress is more accurately described as an emotional experience, which may occur before or after a conscious evaluation of the situation.[87]

Whether stress is a complex emotion or a cognitive evaluation of the environment, it has become a pervasive experience in the daily lives of most people. One large survey recently reported that 72 percent of adult Canadians believe they experience excessive stress. In another recent study, 48 percent of Canadian small business owners say that within the past year they have suffered from work-related stress to such a degree that it affected other aspects of their lives.[88]

Stress is typically described as a negative experience. This is known as *distress*–the degree of physiological, psychological, and behavioural deviation from healthy functioning. However, some level of stress–called *eustress*–is a necessary part of life because it activates and motivates people to achieve goals, change their environments, and succeed in life's challenges. For example, more than two-thirds of 42,000 American employees polled report that on-the-job stress either energizes them or has no effect.[89] Our focus is on the causes and management of distress, because it has become a chronic problem in many societies.

GENERAL ADAPTATION SYNDROME

general adaptation syndrome A model of the stress experience, consisting of three stages: alarm reaction, resistance, and exhaustion.

The word *stress* was first used more than 500 years ago to describe the human response to harsh environmental conditions. However, it wasn't until the 1930s that Canadian researcher Hans Selye (often described as the father of stress research) first documented the stress experience, called the **general adaptation syndrome.** Selye determined (initially by studying rats) that people have a fairly consistent and automatic physiological response to stressful situations, which helps them to cope with environmental demands.[90]

The general adaptation syndrome consists of the three stages shown in Exhibit 4.6. The *alarm reaction* stage occurs when a threat or challenge activates the physiological stress responses that were noted above. The individual's energy level and coping effectiveness decrease in response to the initial shock. The second stage, *resistance*, activates various biochemical, psychological, and behavioural mechanisms that give the individual more energy and engage coping mechanisms to overcome or remove the source of stress. To focus energy on the source of the stress, the body reduces resources to the immune system during this stage. This explains why people are more likely to catch a cold or some other illness when they experience prolonged stress. People have a limited resistance capacity, and if the source of stress persists, the individual will eventually move into the third stage, *exhaustion*. Most of us are able to remove the source of stress or remove ourselves from that source before becoming too exhausted. However, people who frequently reach exhaustion have increased risk of long-term physiological and psychological damage.[91]

connect

How stressed are you? Visit **connect.mcgrawhill.com** to assess your perceived general level of stress.

EXHIBIT 4.6

General Adaptation Syndrome

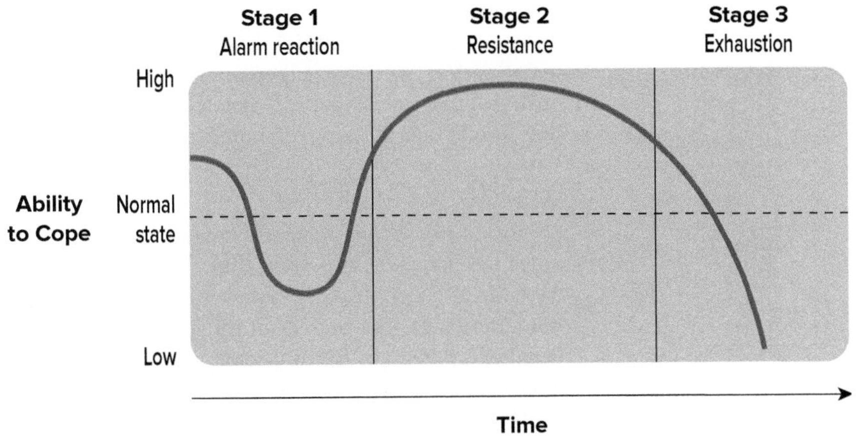

Source: Adapted from H. Selye, *The Stress of Life* (New York: McGraw-Hill, 1956).

CONSEQUENCES OF DISTRESS

Stress takes its toll on the human body.[92] Many people experience tension headaches, muscle pain, and related problems mainly due to muscle contractions from the stress response. Studies have found that high stress levels also contribute to cardiovascular disease, including heart attacks and strokes, and may be associated with some forms of cancer. Stress also produces various psychological consequences, such as job dissatisfaction, moodiness, depression, and lower organizational commitment. Furthermore, various behavioural outcomes have been linked to high or persistent stress, including lower job performance, poor decision making, and increased workplace accidents and aggressive behaviour. Most people react to stress through "fight or flight," so increased absenteeism is another outcome because it is a form of flight.[93]

A particular stress consequence, called *job burnout,* occurs when people experience emotional exhaustion, cynicism, and reduced feelings of personal accomplishment.[94] *Emotional exhaustion,* the first stage, is characterized by a lack of energy, tiredness, and a feeling that one's emotional resources are depleted. This is followed by *cynicism* (also called *depersonalization*), which is an indifferent attitude towards work, emotional detachment from clients, a cynical view of the organization, and a tendency to strictly follow rules and regulations rather than adapt to the needs of others. The final stage of burnout, called *reduced personal accomplishment,* entails feelings of diminished confidence in one's ability to perform the job well. In such situations, employees develop a sense of learned helplessness as they no longer believe that their efforts make a difference.

STRESSORS: THE CAUSES OF STRESS

stressors Environmental conditions that place a physical or emotional demand on the person.

Before identifying ways to manage work-related stress, we must first understand its causes, known as stressors. **Stressors** include any environmental conditions that place a physical or emotional demand on a person.[95] There are numerous stressors in the workplace and in life in general. In this section, we'll highlight three of the most common work-related stressors: harassment and incivility, workload, and lack of task control.

HARASSMENT AND INCIVILITY

psychological harassment Repeated and hostile or unwanted conduct, verbal comments, actions, or gestures that affect an employee's dignity or psychological or physical integrity and that result in a harmful work environment for the employee.

One of the fastest-growing sources of workplace stress is **psychological harassment.** Psychological harassment includes repeated hostile or unwanted conduct, verbal comments, actions, and gestures that undermine an employee's dignity or psychological or physical integrity. This covers a broad landscape of behaviours, from threats and bullying to subtle yet persistent forms of incivility.[96]

Some form or degree of psychological harassment exists in almost every workplace. One recent global survey of 16,517 employees reported that 83 percent of Europeans, 65 percent of employees in North and South America, and 55 percent of people in Asia have been physically or emotionally bullied. More than two-thirds of teachers in the UK say they have experienced or witnessed workplace bullying within the past 12 months. The government of Quebec, which passed the first workplace anti-harassment legislation in North America, received more than 2,500 harassment complaints in the first year alone! Labour bureaus in Japan received more than 32,000 harassment complaints in a recent year, a fivefold increase from six years earlier.[97]

Sexual harassment is a type of harassment in which a person's employment or job performance is conditional and depends on unwanted sexual relations (called *quid pro quo* harassment) and/or the person experiences sexual conduct from others (such as posting pornographic material) that unreasonably interferes with work performance or creates an intimidating, hostile, or offensive working environment (called *hostile work environment* harassment).[98]

WORK OVERLOAD

"We just keep rushing along in a confused state of never having time to do the things that seem to be pressing upon us." Sound familiar? Most Canadians probably had this thought over the past year. But although this comment comes from Canada, it wasn't written in the past year or even in the past decade. It came from an article called "Let's Slow Down!" in a Royal Bank of Canada newsletter in 1949![99] The fact is, people have been struggling for more than a half-century with the pace of life, including the challenges of performing too many tasks and working too many hours.

Unfortunately, work overload has worsened over the past few decades. In 1991, approximately 30 percent of Canadians estimated that they work an average of 45 hours or more per week. Ten years later (2001), that figure had jumped to more than 45 percent. In the most recent poll (2011), 60 percent of Canadians reported working an average of 45 hours or more each week.[100] Global Connections 4.1 describes how overwork has also become a serious matter in China.

Why do employees work such long hours? One explanation is the combined effects of technology and globalization. People increasingly work with coworkers in distant time zones,

Global Connections 4.1:

WORKING TO DEATH IN CHINA[101]

Wang Jijiang has been working non-stop for 36 hours, and the marathon is taking its toll. "My brain doesn't seem to be working," says the 25-year-old media planner in Shanghai. "I don't have time to take a nap. Actually, I don't even have the energy to think if I'm tired or not." Wang does not receive overtime pay, yet most months she has to work 10 or 12 hours to complete her tasks. The workday extends well past midnight during the company's busy year-end period.

Stress seems to be on the rise in China due to increasing workloads and hours of work. More than 30 percent of employees in one recent poll said they worked more than 10 hours every day over the previous six months. Another survey reported that 70 percent of white-collar workers in downtown Beijing show signs of overwork. A global survey recently reported that employees in China are much more likely than employees in any other country to think their time at work (away from personal life) has increased over the past two years.

Jose Luis Pelaez Inc/Getty Images

Stress seems to be on the rise in China due to increasing workloads and hours of work.

Overwork and its consequences have been well known for several decades in Japan, where the word *karoshi* means "death from overwork." In China, working to death (called *guolaosi*) also seems to be a serious concern. Although difficult to calculate, one prominent newspaper estimates that *guolaosi* claims the lives of 600,000 people in China each year. For example, an engineer at Foxconn's Shenzhen factory died suddenly after working nonstop for 34 hours during a month of extended night shifts. A dozen other employees at the factory took their own lives around that time, many apparently due to overwork and the impersonal conditions. An employee at Web game operator 17173.com in Fuzhou City died of viral myocarditis due to overwork. A junior auditor in the Shanghai office of PricewaterhouseCoopers (PwC) died of cerebral meningitis, which many believe was caused by overwork. PwC says the employee was on sick leave at the time of her death, but her microblog included many messages posted from work after midnight complaining of her ailment and overwork (including "overtime again" and "I'd die for sleep").

"Those accounting firms used to be my ideal work destinations and I had dreamed of working there since I was a fresh student in university," says Kong Ranran, an accounting student at Peking University in Beijing. However, Kong's opinion changed after a recent three-month internship at PricewaterhouseCoopers. "I saw the tough situation behind the halo and it was definitely not appealing," she says. "The work hours are endless and it is impossible to squeeze any time for leisure or anything else." Kong now prefers a government job where she thinks there is some work–life balance.

and their constantly-on communications habits make it difficult to separate work from personal life. A second factor is that many people are caught up in consumerism; they want to buy more goods and services, and doing so requires more income through longer work hours. A third reason, called the "ideal worker norm," is that professionals expect themselves and others to work longer work hours. For many, toiling away far beyond the normal workweek is a badge of honour, a symbol of their superhuman capacity to perform above others.[102]

LOW TASK CONTROL

One of the most important findings emerging from stress research is that employees are more stressed when they lack control over how and when they perform their tasks as well as lack control over the pace of work activity. Work is potentially more stressful when it is paced by a machine, involves monitoring equipment, or the work schedule is controlled by someone else. Low task control is a stressor because employees face high workloads without the ability to adjust the pace of the load to their own energy, attention span, and other resources. Furthermore, the degree to which low task control is a stressor increases with the burden of responsibility the employee must carry.[103] Assembly-line workers have low task control, but their stress can be fairly low if their level of responsibility is also low. In contrast, sports coaches are under immense pressure to win games (high responsibility), yet they have little control over what happens on the playing field (low task control).

connect

Are you a workaholic? Visit connect.mcgrawhill.com to assess yourself on this stress-related personal characteristic.

INDIVIDUAL DIFFERENCES IN STRESS

People experience different stress levels when exposed to the same stressor. One factor is the employee's physical health. Regular exercise and a healthy lifestyle produce a larger store of energy to cope with stress. A second individual difference is the coping strategy employees use to ward off a particular stressor.[104] People sometimes figure out ways to remove the stressor or to minimize its presence. Seeking support from others, reframing the stressor in a more positive light, blaming others for the stressor, and denying the stressor's existence are some other coping mechanisms. Some coping strategies work better for some stressors and some are better across all stressors.[105] Thus, someone who uses a less effective coping mechanism in a particular situation would experience more stress in response to that situation. People have a tendency to rely on one or two coping strategies, and those who rely on generally poor coping strategies (such as denying the stressor exists) are going to experience more stress.

Personality is the third and possibly the most important reason why people experience different levels of stress when faced with the same stressor.[106] Individuals with low neuroticism (high emotional stability) usually experience lower stress levels because, by definition, they are less prone to anxiety, depression, and other negative emotions. Extraverts also tend to experience lower stress than do introverts, likely because extraversion includes a degree of positive thinking and extraverts interact with others, which helps buffer the effect of stressors. People with a positive self-concept–high self-esteem, self-efficacy, and internal locus of control (see Chapter 3)–feel more confident and in control when faced with a stressor. In other words, they tend to have a stronger sense of optimism.[107]

While positive self-concept protects us from stress, workaholism attracts more stressors and weakens the capacity to cope with them. The classic **workaholic** (also called *work addict*) is highly involved in work, feels compelled or driven to work because of inner pressures, and has a low enjoyment of work. Workaholics are compulsive and preoccupied with work, often to the exclusion and detriment of personal health, intimate relationships, and family.[108]

workaholic A person who is highly involved in work, feels compelled to work, and has a low enjoyment of work.

Managing Work-Related Stress

LO5

Many people deny the existence of their stress until it has more serious outcomes. This avoidance strategy creates a vicious cycle because the failure to cope with stress becomes another stressor on top of the one that created the stress in the first place. To prevent this vicious cycle, employers and employees need to apply one or more of the stress management strategies described below: remove the stressor, withdraw from the stressor, change stress perceptions, control stress consequences, and receive social support.[109]

REMOVE THE STRESSOR

There are many ways to remove the stressor, but some of the more common actions involve assigning employees to jobs that match their skills and preferences, reducing excessive workplace noise, having a complaint system and taking corrective action against harassment, and giving employees more control over the work process. Another important way that companies can remove stressors is by facilitating better work–life balance. Work–life balance initiatives minimize conflict between the employee's work and nonwork demands. Five of the most common work–life balance initiatives are flexible and limited work time, job sharing, telecommuting, personal leave, and child care support.[110]

- *Flexible and limited work time.* An important way to improve work–life balance is limiting the number of hours that employees are expected to work and giving them flexibility in scheduling those hours. For example, San Jorge Children's Hospital offers a unique form of work flexibility that has dramatically reduced turnover and stress. The Puerto Rican medical centre introduced a "ten month work program" in which employees can take summer months off to care for their children while out of school.[111]
- *Job sharing.* Job sharing splits a career position between two people so they experience less time-based stress between work and family. They typically work different parts of the week, with some overlapping work time in the weekly schedule to coordinate activities. This strategy gives employees the ability to work part-time in jobs that are naturally designed for full-time responsibilities.
- *Telecommuting.* Telecommuting (also called *teleworking*) involves working from home or a site close to home rather than commuting a longer distance to the office every day (see Chapter 1). By reducing or eliminating commuting time, employees can more easily fulfill family obligations, such as temporarily leaving the home office to pick up the kids from school. Consequently, telecommuters tend to experience better work–life balance.[112] However, teleworking may increase stress for those who crave social interaction and who lack the space and privacy necessary to work at home.
- *Personal leave.* Employers with strong work–life values offer extended maternity, paternity, and personal leave for employees to care for a new family or take advantage of a personal experience. Most countries provide 12 to 16 weeks of paid leave, with some offering one year or more of fully or partially paid maternity leave.[113]
- *Child care support.* Many large and medium-sized employers provide on-site or subsidized child care facilities. Child care support reduces stress because employees are less rushed to drop off children and less worried during the day about how well their children are doing.[114]

WITHDRAW FROM THE STRESSOR

Removing the stressor may be the ideal solution, but it is often not feasible. An alternative strategy is to permanently or temporarily remove employees from the stressor. Permanent withdrawal occurs when employees are transferred to jobs that are more compatible with their abilities and values. Temporarily withdrawing from stressors is the most frequent way that employees manage stress. Vacations and holidays are important opportunities for employees to recover from stress and re-energize for future challenges. A small number of companies offer paid or unpaid sabbaticals.[115] Many firms also provide innovative ways for employees to withdraw from stressful work throughout the day, such as games rooms, ice cream cart breaks, nap rooms, and cafeterias that include live piano recitals.

CHANGE STRESS PERCEPTIONS

Earlier, we said that individuals experience different stress levels because they have different degrees of positive self-evaluation and optimism. Consequently, another way to manage stress is to help employees improve their self-concept so job challenges are not perceived as threatening. Personal goal setting and self-reinforcement can also reduce the stress that people

© Photo by Jake Brennan

Writing software code can be taxing work, but employees at Vigilant Global have ways to temporarily withdraw from these stressors. The Montreal firm that designs software solutions for the finance industry has a games room where employees play table tennis or foosball (shown in this photo), enjoy electronic games, or relax with an ebook. And for the ultimate withdrawal from stressors, Vigilant Global has a dedicated Zen room with massage chairs and spa-like background music.[116]

experience when they enter new work settings. Research also suggests that some (but not all) forms of humour can improve optimism and create positive emotions by taking some psychological weight off the situation.[117]

CONTROL STRESS CONSEQUENCES

Regular exercise and maintaining a healthy lifestyle is an effective stress management strategy because it controls stress consequences. Research indicates that physical exercise reduces the physiological consequences of stress by helping employees moderate their breathing and heart rate, muscle tension, and stomach acidity.[118] Many companies offer Pilates, yoga, and other exercise and meditation classes during the workday. Research indicates that various forms of meditation reduce anxiety, reduce blood pressure and muscle tension, and moderate breathing and heart rate.[119] Wellness programs can also help control the consequences of stress. These programs inform employees about better nutrition and fitness, regular sleep, and other good health habits. Many large employers offer *employee assistance programs (EAPs)*—counselling services that help employees resolve marital, financial, or work-related troubles, but some counselling also varies with the industry.

connect

How do you cope with stressful situations? Visit **connect.mcgrawhill.com** to identify the type of coping strategy you prefer to use in stressful situations.

RECEIVE SOCIAL SUPPORT

Social support occurs when coworkers, supervisors, family members, friends, and others provide emotional and/or informational support to buffer an individual's stress experience. For instance, one recent study found that employees whose managers are good at empathizing experienced fewer stress symptoms than did employees whose managers were less empathetic. Social support potentially (but not always) improves the person's optimism and self-confidence because support makes people feel valued and worthy. Social support also provides information to help the person interpret, comprehend, and possibly remove the stressor. For instance, to reduce a new employee's stress, coworkers could describe ways to handle difficult customers. Seeking social support is called a "tend and befriend" response to stress, and research suggests that women often follow this route rather than the "fight-or-flight" response mentioned earlier.[120]

Chapter Summary

LO1 Explain how emotions and cognition (conscious reasoning) influence attitudes and behaviour.

Emotions are physiological, behavioural, and psychological episodes experienced towards an object, person, or event that create a state of readiness. Emotions differ from attitudes, which represent a cluster of beliefs, feelings, and behavioural intentions towards a person, object, or event. Beliefs are a person's established perceptions about the attitude object. Feelings are positive or negative evaluations of the attitude object. Behavioural intentions represent a motivation to engage in a particular behaviour towards the target.

Attitudes have traditionally been described as a purely rational process in which beliefs predict feelings, which predict behavioural intentions, which predict behaviour. We now know that emotions have an influence on behaviour that is equal to or greater than that of cognition. This dual process is apparent when we internally experience a conflict between what logically seems good or bad and what we emotionally feel is good or bad in a situation. Emotions also affect behaviour directly. Behaviour sometimes influences our subsequent attitudes through cognitive dissonance.

LO2 Discuss the dynamics of emotional labour and the role of emotional intelligence in the workplace.

Emotional labour consists of the effort, planning, and control needed to express organizationally desired emotions during interpersonal transactions. It is more common in jobs requiring a variety of emotions and more intense emotions, as well as in jobs where interaction with clients is frequent and has a long duration. Cultures also differ on the norms of displaying or concealing a person's true emotions. Emotional dissonance is the psychological tension experienced when the emotions people are required to display are quite different from the emotions they actually experience at that moment. Deep acting can minimize this dissonance, as can the practice of hiring people with a natural tendency to display desired emotions.

Emotional intelligence is the ability to perceive and express emotion, assimilate emotion in thought, understand and reason with emotion, and regulate emotion in oneself and others. This concept includes four components arranged in a hierarchy: self-awareness, self-management, awareness of others' emotions, and management of others' emotions. Emotional intelligence can be learned to some extent, particularly through personal coaching.

LO3 Summarize the consequences of job dissatisfaction, as well as strategies to increase organizational (affective) commitment.

Job satisfaction represents a person's evaluation of his or her job and work context. Four types of job dissatisfaction consequences are quitting or otherwise getting away from the dissatisfying situation (exit), attempting to change the dissatisfying situation (voice), patiently waiting for the problem to sort itself out (loyalty), and reducing work effort and performance (neglect). Job satisfaction has a moderate relationship with job performance and with customer satisfaction. Affective organizational commitment (loyalty) is the employee's emotional attachment to, identification with, and involvement in a particular organization. This contrasts with continuance commitment, which is a calculative bond with the organization. Companies build loyalty through justice and support, shared values, trust, organizational comprehension, and employee involvement.

LO4 Describe the stress experience and review three major stressors.

Stress is an adaptive response to a situation that is perceived as challenging or threatening to a person's well-being. The stress experience, called the general adaptation syndrome, involves moving through three stages: alarm, resistance, and exhaustion. Stressors are the causes of stress and include any environmental conditions that place a physical or emotional demand on a person. Three stressors that have received considerable attention are harassment and incivility, work overload, and low task control.

LO5 Identify five ways to manage workplace stress.

Many interventions are available to manage work-related stress, including removing the stressor, withdrawing from the stressor, changing stress perceptions, controlling stress consequences, and receiving social support.

Key Terms

affective organizational commitment, p. 97
attitudes, p. 84
cognitive dissonance, p. 87
continuance commitment, p. 97
emotional dissonance, p. 90
emotional intelligence (EI), p. 90
emotional labour, p. 89
emotions, p. 84
exit-voice-loyalty-neglect (EVLN) model, p. 94
general adaptation syndrome, p. 99
job satisfaction, p. 92
psychological harassment, p. 100
service profit chain model, p. 95
stress, p. 99
stressors, p. 100
trust, p. 98
workaholic, p. 102

Critical-Thinking Questions

1. Studies suggest that university and college instructors are frequently required to engage in emotional labour. Identify the situations in which emotional labour is required for this job. In your opinion, is emotional labour more troublesome for college instructors or for call centre staff working at an emergency service?

2. "Emotional intelligence is more important than cognitive intelligence in influencing an individual's success." Do you agree or disagree with this statement? Support your perspective.
3. Recall a traumatic national or global event, such as the train derailment that took many lives in Lac-Mégantic, Quebec, or the fire that destroyed homes in Slave Lake, Alberta. Based on what you have learned in this chapter, discuss what has happened to you in terms of your cognitive reasoning, your emotional reactions, and your ability to logically deal with these stressful situations.
4. It has almost become a mandatory practice for companies to ensure that employees have fun at work. Many workplaces now have fully-stocked lounges, games rooms, funky painted walls, and regular social events. A few even have a slide to travel down to the next floor. However, some experts warn that imposing fun at work can have negative consequences. "Once the idea of fun is formally institutionalized from above, it can lead to employees becoming resentful," warns one critic. "They feel patronized and condescended, and it breeds anger and frustration." Apply the attitude model to explain how fun activities might improve customer satisfaction, as well as how they might result in poorer customer satisfaction.
5. Job satisfaction leads to increased job performance. This statement has supplanted earlier thought on how job performance doesn't necessarily depend on job satisfaction. What has caused the shift in thought over the years, and do you agree with this assessment?
6. In this chapter, we highlighted work-related stressors such as harassment and incivility, workload, and lack of task control. Of course, there are many nonwork-related stressors that increasingly come into the discussion. Please discuss these and discuss their impact on the work environment.
7. Two college graduates recently joined the same major newspaper as journalists. Both work long hours and have tight deadlines for completing their stories. They are under constant pressure to scout out new leads and be the first to report new controversies. One journalist is increasingly fatigued and despondent and has taken several days of sick leave. The other is getting the work done and seems to enjoy the challenges. Use your knowledge of stress to explain why these two journalists are reacting differently to their jobs.
8. A senior official of a labour union stated: "All stress management does is help people cope with poor management. [Employers] should really be into stress reduction." Discuss the accuracy of this statement.

Case Study: ROUGH SEAS ON THE LINK650

Professor Suzanne Baxter was preparing for her first class of the semester when Shaun O'Neill knocked lightly on the open door and announced himself: "Hi, Professor, I don't suppose you remember me?" Professor Baxter had large classes, but she did remember that Shaun was a student in her organizational behaviour class a few years ago. Shaun had decided to work in the oil industry for a couple of years before returning to school to complete his diploma.

"Welcome back!" Baxter said as she beckoned him into the office. "I heard you were working on an oil rig in the United Kingdom. How was it?"

"Well, Professor," Shaun began, "I had worked two summers in the Texan oil fields and my family's from Ireland, so I hoped to get a job on the LINK650. It's that new WestOil drilling rig that arrived with so much fanfare in the North Sea fields a few years ago. The LINK650 was built by LINK, Inc. in Texas. A standard practice in this industry is for the rig manufacturer to manage its day-to-day operations, so employees on the LINK650 are managed completely by LINK managers with no involvement from WestOil. We all know that drilling rig jobs are dangerous, but they pay well and offer generous time off. A local newspaper there said that nearly one thousand people lined up to complete job applications for the 50 nontechnical positions. I was lucky enough to get one of those jobs.

"Everyone hired on the LINK650 was enthusiastic and proud. We were one of the chosen few and were really pumped up about working on a new rig that had received so much media attention. I was quite impressed with the recruiters–so were several other hires–because they really seemed to be concerned about our welfare out on the platform. I later discovered that the recruiters came from a consulting firm that specializes in hiring people. Come to think of it, we didn't meet a single LINK manager during that process. Maybe things would have been different if some of those LINK supervisors had interviewed us.

"Working on LINK650 was a real shock, even though most of us had some experience working in the oil fields. I'd say that none of the 50 nontechnical people hired was quite prepared for the brutal jobs on the oil rig. We did the dirtiest jobs in the biting cold winds of the North Sea. Still, during the first few months most of us wanted to show the company that we were dedicated to getting the job done. A couple of the new hires quit within a few weeks, but most of the people hired with me really got along well–you know, just like the ideas you mentioned in class. We formed a special bond that helped us through the bad weather and gruelling work.

"The LINK650 supervisors were another matter. They were mean taskmasters who had worked for many years on oil rigs in the Gulf of Mexico or North Sea. They seemed to relish the idea of treating their employees the same way they had been treated before becoming managers. We put up with their abuse for the first few months, but things got worse when the LINK650 was shut down twice to correct mechanical problems. These setbacks embarrassed LINK's management and they put more pressure on the supervisors to get us back on schedule.

"The supervisors started to ignore equipment problems and pushed us to get jobs done more quickly without regard to safety procedures. They routinely shouted obscenities at employees in front of others. A couple of my workmates were fired and a couple of others quit their jobs. I almost lost my job one day just because my boss thought I was deliberately working slowly. He didn't realize–or care–that the fittings I was connecting were damaged. Several people started finding ways to avoid the supervisors and get as little work done as possible. Many of my coworkers developed back problems. We jokingly called it the 'rigger's backache' because some employees faked their ailment to leave the rig with paid sick leave.

"Along with having lousy supervisors, we were always kept in the dark about the problems on the rig. Supervisors said that they didn't know anything, which was partly true, but they said we shouldn't be so interested in things that didn't concern us. But the rig's problems, as well as its future contract work, were a major concern to crew members who weren't ready to quit. Their job security depended on the rig's production levels and whether WestOil would sign contracts to drill new holes. Given the rig's problems, most of us were concerned that we would be laid off at any time.

"Everything came to a head when Bob MacKenzie was killed because someone secured a hoist improperly. Not sure if it was mentioned in the papers here, but it was big news around this time last year. A government inquiry concluded that the person responsible wasn't properly trained and that employees were being pushed to finish jobs without safety precautions. Anyway, while the inquiry was going on, several employees decided to unionize the rig. It wasn't long before most employees on LINK650 had signed union cards. That really shocked LINK's management and the entire oil industry because it was, I think, just the second time that a rig had ever been unionized there.

"Since then, management has been doing everything in its power to get rid of the union. It sent a 'safety officer' to the rig, although we eventually realized that he was a consultant the company hired to undermine union support. Several managers were sent to special seminars on how to manage a unionized workforce, although one of the topics was how to break the union.

"So you see, Professor, I joined LINK as an enthusiastic employee and quit last month with no desire to lift a finger for them. It really bothers me, because I was always told to do your best, no matter how tough the situation. It's been quite an experience."

Discussion Questions

1. Identify the various ways that employees expressed their job dissatisfaction on the LINK650.
2. Shaun O'Neill's commitment to the LINK organization dwindled over his two years of employment. Discuss the factors that affected his organizational commitment.

Team Exercise: RANKING JOBS ON THEIR EMOTIONAL LABOUR

Purpose This exercise is designed to help you understand the jobs in which people tend to experience higher or lower degrees of emotional labour.

Instructions

Step 1: Individually rank-order the extent that the jobs listed below require emotional labour. In other words, assign a "1" to the job you believe requires the most effort, planning, and control to express organizationally desired emotions during interpersonal transactions. Assign a "10" to the job you believe requires the least amount of emotional labour. Mark your rankings in column 1.

Step 2: The instructor will form teams of four or five members and each team will rank-order the items on the basis of consensus (not simply averaging the individual rankings). These results are placed in column 2.

Step 3: The instructor will provide expert ranking information. This information should be written in column 3. Then students calculate the differences in columns 4 and 5.

Step 4: The class will compare the results and discuss the features of jobs with high emotional labour.

Occupational Emotional Labour Scoring Sheet

Occupation	(1) Individual ranking	(2) Team ranking	(3) Expert ranking	(4) Absolute difference of 1 and 3	(5) Absolute difference of 2 and 3
Bartender					
Cashier					
Dental hygienist					
Insurance adjuster					
Lawyer					
Librarian					
Postal clerk					
Registered nurse					
Social worker					
Television announcer					
			TOTAL		
				Your score	Team score

(The lower the score, the better.)

Self-Assessment: ARE YOU IN TOUCH WITH YOUR EMOTIONS?

Purpose: This self-assessment is designed to help you understand the meaning and dimensions of emotional intelligence and to estimate your perceptions of your emotional intelligence.

Overview Emotional intelligence has become an important concept and ability in the workplace. It is a skill that people develop throughout their lives to help them interact better with others, make better decisions, and manage the attitudes and behaviour of other people. Although emotional intelligence is best measured as an ability test, this scale offers you an opportunity to estimate your perceptions and self-awareness of this ability in yourself.

Instructions Read each of the statements below and select the response that best describes you. Then use the scoring key in Appendix B of this book to calculate your results. This self-assessment is completed alone so that students rate themselves honestly without concerns of social comparison. However, class discussion will focus on the meaning and dimensions of emotional intelligence, its application in the workplace, and the best ways to measure emotional intelligence.

Emotional Intelligence Self-Assessment

To what extent do you agree or disagree with each of these statements?	Strongly Agree	Moderately Agree	Slightly Agree	Slightly Disagree	Moderately Disagree	Strongly Disagree
1. I tend to describe my emotions accurately.	○	○	○	○	○	○
2. I show respect for others' opinions, even when I think those opinions are wrong.	○	○	○	○	○	○
3. I know how others are feeling, even when they try to hide their feelings.	○	○	○	○	○	○
4. I am good at getting people enthusiastic and motivated.	○	○	○	○	○	○
5. When I get worried or angry, I have difficulty suppressing those emotions such that others do not notice them.	○	○	○	○	○	○
6. I have a talent for gauging from their body language a person's true feelings.	○	○	○	○	○	○
7. I usually know when I am feeling frustrated.	○	○	○	○	○	○
8. I tend to have difficulty getting people in the right emotional frame of mind.	○	○	○	○	○	○
9. I am very much aware of my own emotions.	○	○	○	○	○	○
10. I am able to understand all sides of a disagreement before forming an opinion.	○	○	○	○	○	○
11. I can easily cheer people up when they are feeling discouraged or sad.	○	○	○	○	○	○
12. I am sometimes unaware when I get emotional about an issue.	○	○	○	○	○	○
13. I can tell when others do not mean what they say.	○	○	○	○	○	○
14. I am good at controlling my own emotions when the situation requires such control.	○	○	○	○	○	○
15. I sometimes don't realize how others are feeling about an issue.	○	○	○	○	○	○
16. I have a talent for getting others to share my keenness for an idea.	○	○	○	○	○	○

Sources: Copyright © 2011 Steven L McShane. This self-assessment was inspired by similar instruments, particularly: N. S. Schutte, et al, "Development and validation of a measure of emotional intelligence," *Personality and Individual Differences* 25, no. 2 (1998): 167-177; C-S Wong and K. S. Law, "The effects of leader and follower emotional intelligence on performance and attitude: An exploratory study," *Leadership Quarterly* 13 (2002): 243-274; P. J. Jordan, and S. A. Lawrence, "Emotional intelligence in teams: Development and initial validation of the short version of the Workgroup Emotional Intelligence Profile (WEIP-S)," *Journal of Management & Organization* 15 (2009): 452-469.

SELF-ASSESSMENTS FOR CHAPTER 4

SELF-ASSESSMENT NAME	DESCRIPTION	LOCATION
Are you in touch with your emotions?	Estimates your emotional trait tendencies.	Page 107 connect
What is your emotional personality?	Assesses self-perceptions of your emotional intelligence on the four dimensions.	connect
How committed are you to your school?	Estimates your affective organizational commitment to your school.	connect
How stressed are you?	Estimates your perceived general level of stress.	connect
Are you a workaholic?	Estimates the degree to which you have this stress-related personal characteristic.	connect
How do you cope with stressful situations?	Identifies the type of coping strategy you prefer to use in stressful situations.	connect

By providing training, flexible work, peer recognition, autonomy, and open communication, Telus Corp. now has one of the most engaged workforces among companies worldwide of similar size and workforce mix.

Courtesy of Telus.

Chapter 5

Foundations of Employee Motivation

LEARNING OBJECTIVES

After reading this chapter, you should be able to:

LO1. Define employee engagement.

LO2. Explain the role of human drives and emotions in employee motivation and behaviour.

LO3. Summarize Maslow's needs hierarchy, McClelland's learned needs theory, and four-drive theory, and discuss their implications for motivating employees.

LO4. Discuss the expectancy theory model, including its practical implications.

LO5. Outline organizational behaviour modification (OB Mod) and social cognitive theory, and explain their relevance to employee motivation.

LO6. Describe the characteristics of effective goal setting and feedback.

LO7. Summarize equity theory and describe ways to improve procedural justice.

A few years ago, about half of Telus Corp. employees were highly or moderately engaged in their work. That's about average for a large Canadian organization, and fairly good considering that Telus had rocky employee relations less than a decade ago. But Telus executives knew that employee motivation had to be much higher for the Vancouver-based telecommunications giant to become a truly world-class organization. Today, employee engagement at Telus has risen to 83 percent, the highest score of any organization in the world with similar size and workforce mix (based on a major consulting firm's data from thousands of companies in dozens of countries).

"[Telus] has developed an internal culture that is highly motivated, highly learned, highly collaborative, and highly engaged," says Dan Pontefract, Telus Corp.'s senior director of learning and collaboration. Pontefract explains that engaged employees "want to go the extra mile, are willing to stay, and will recommend their place of employment and its products and services to others."

One key driver of employee engagement at Telus is extensive training and career development. "This continuing investment in our employees is one of the reasons we are getting such fantastic results at the engagement level," says Telus CEO Darren Entwistle. Employee engagement has been further bolstered by the company's strong "customer first" mandate, as well by its growing social responsibility reputation to serve local communities ("we give where we live"). Telus employees are also motivated through various forms of reward and recognition, including Bravo, a peer recognition program in which coworkers send congratulatory notes and award points to their peers.

Telus also boosted employee engagement by giving employees more flexibility and autonomy to perform their work. Telus is a pioneer in telecommuting, and aims to have up to 70 percent of its staff working from home or elsewhere. It also empowers employees to decide how to organize their workday and how to best serve customers. And rather than banning Facebook, Twitter, and other social media, Telus actively embraces these technologies to improve communication and collaboration with senior management and other employees.

"I'm able to pick up my work and go directly to the customers," says Telus service technician Sukh Toor (shown in photo). "It's great for me personally, because I have a lot more ownership of the customer relationship. Having the ability to work where and when makes the most sense [and it] also makes me a lot more effective."[1]

Telus Corp. has developed a highly engaged workforce by investing in training, offering more flexible work, empowering staff with greater autonomy, and creating a motivational peer recognition system. It has also generated a clear customer-focused organizational mandate and encouraged (rather than banned) social media to open lines of communication with each other and senior management. These practices generate high levels of employee motivation. *Motivation* (see Chapter 2) refers to the forces within a person that affect the direction, intensity, and persistence of voluntary behaviour.[2] Motivated employees are willing to exert a particular level of effort (intensity), for a certain amount of time (persistence), towards a particular goal (direction). Motivation is one of the four essential drivers of individual behaviour and performance.

This chapter introduces the core theories of employee motivation. We begin by discussing employee engagement, an increasingly popular concept associated with motivation. Next, we explain how drives and emotions are the prime movers of employee motivation. Three theories that focus on drives and needs–Maslow's needs hierarchy, McClelland's learned needs theory, and four-drive theory–are introduced and evaluated. Next, we turn our attention to the popular rational decision model of employee motivation: expectancy theory. Organizational behaviour modification and social cognitive theory are then introduced, which relate to learning the expectancies that motivate employees through the expectancy theory model. Next, we look at goal setting and feedback, which are considered the most robust and useful motivational concepts and practices in organizations. This chapter closes with the topic of motivation through organizational justice, including the elements and dynamics of equity theory and procedural justice.

Employee Engagement

LO1

employee engagement
Individual's emotional and cognitive motivation, particularly a focused, intense, persistent, and purposive effort towards work-related goals.

When executives at Telus and other companies discuss employee motivation these days, they are just as likely to use the phrase **employee engagement.** Although its definition is still being debated,[3] we cautiously define employee engagement as an individual's emotional and cognitive (logical) motivation, particularly a focused, intense, persistent, and purposive effort towards work-related goals. It is typically described as an emotional involvement in, commitment to, and satisfaction with the work. Employee engagement also includes a high level of absorption in the work–the experience of focusing intensely on the task with limited awareness of events beyond that work. Finally, employee engagement is often described in terms of self-efficacy–the belief that you have the ability, role clarity, and resources to get the job done (see Chapter 3).

Employee engagement is on the minds of many business leaders these days because it seems to be a strong predictor of employee and work unit performance. A major report for the British government concluded that employee engagement is so important to the country's international competitiveness that government should urgently raise awareness of and support for employee engagement practices throughout all sectors of the economy.[4] Standard Chartered Bank found that branches with higher employee engagement provide significantly higher customer service quality, have 46 percent lower employee turnover, and produce 16 percent higher profit margin growth than branches with lower employee engagement.

DHL Express, Sub-Saharan Africa

Employee engagement is a foundation of business success at DHL Express, the global courier division of Germany's Deutsche Post. "Motivated and engaged employees are crucial to the success of any business and, at DHL, they form the cornerstone of our service," explains a DHL Express executive in Africa. DHL builds employee engagement by setting clear goals and regularly letting employees know that they are valued. Another influence on employee engagement is the company's award-winning Certified International Specialist (CIS) program. This program not only teaches employees about international shipping and DHL's business strategy, it also explains how each employee has an important role in this complex business. "CIS is not a traditional training platform," says DHL CEO Ken Allen. "It was designed first and foremost as an engagement tool."[5]

It isn't always clear from these studies whether employee engagement makes companies more successful, or whether the company's success makes employees more engaged. For example, Telus executives acknowledge that the company's success seems to have a positive effect on employee motivation. However, these interventions suggest that employee engagement causes the company outcomes more than vice versa.

The challenge facing organizational leaders is that most employees aren't very engaged.[6] The numbers vary, but one recent large-scale survey estimates that only 16 percent of employees in Canada are engaged, 70 percent are not engaged, and 14 percent are actively disengaged. Actively disengaged employees tend to be disruptive at work, not just disconnected from work. Canada's scores are lower than for employees in the United States, Brazil, Panama, Australia, and a few other countries. The lowest levels of employee engagement (and highest levels of employee disengagement) are in South and East Asia, the Middle East, and Africa.

This leads to the question: What are the drivers of employee engagement? Goal setting, employee involvement, organizational justice, organizational comprehension (knowing what's going on in the company), employee development opportunities, sufficient resources, and an appealing company vision are some of the more commonly mentioned influences.[7] In other words, building an engaged workforce calls on most topics in this book, such as the MARS model (Chapter 2), building affective commitment (Chapter 4), motivation practices (Chapter 5), organizational-level communication (Chapter 9), and leadership (Chapter 12).

Employee Drives and Needs

LO2

To figure out how to nurture a more engaged and motivated workforce, we first need to understand the motivational "forces" or prime movers of employee behaviour.[8] Our starting point is **drives** (also called *primary needs*), which we define as hardwired characteristics of the brain that attempt to keep us in balance by correcting deficiencies. Drives accomplish this task by producing emotions that energize us to act on our environment.[9] Drives are receiving increasing attention because recent neuroscience (brain) research has highlighted the central

drives Hardwired characteristics of the brain that correct deficiencies or maintain an internal equilibrium by producing emotions to energize individuals.

role of emotions in human decisions and behaviour. There is no agreed upon list of human drives, but research has consistently identified several, such as the drive for social interaction, for competence or status, to comprehend what's going on around us, and to defend ourselves against physiological and psychological harm.[10]

Drives are innate and universal, which means that everyone has them and they exist from birth. Furthermore, drives are the "prime movers" of behaviour because they generate emotions, which put people in a state of readiness to act on their environment. Emotions play a central role in motivation.[11] In fact, both words *(emotion* and *motivation)* originate from the same Latin word, *movere,* which means "to move."

needs Goal-directed forces that people experience.

Exhibit 5.1 illustrates how drives and emotions translate into felt **needs** and behaviour. Drives, and the emotions produced by these drives, produce human needs. We define needs as goal-directed forces that people experience. They are the motivational forces of emotions channelled towards particular goals to correct deficiencies or imbalances. As one leading neuroscientist explains: "drives express themselves directly in background emotions and we eventually become aware of their existence by means of background feelings."[12] In other words, needs are the emotions that we become aware of.

Consider the following example: You arrive at work to discover a stranger sitting at your desk. Seeing this situation produces emotions (worry, curiosity) that motivate you to act. These emotions are generated from drives, such as the drive to defend and drive to comprehend. When strong enough, these emotions motivate you to do something about this situation, such as finding out who that person is and possibly seeking reassurance from coworkers that your job is still safe. In this case, you have a need to make sense (comprehend) what is going on, to feel secure, and possibly to correct a sense of personal violation. Notice that your emotional reactions to seeing the stranger sitting at your desk represent the forces that move you, but you channel those emotions towards specific goals.

INDIVIDUAL DIFFERENCES IN NEEDS

Everyone has the same drives; they are hardwired in us through evolution. However, people develop different intensities of needs in a particular situation. Exhibit 5.1 explains why this difference occurs. The left side of the model shows that the individual's self-concept (as well as personality and values), social norms, and past experience amplify or suppress drive-based emotions, thereby resulting in stronger or weaker needs.[13] People who define themselves as very sociable typically experience a stronger need for social interaction if alone for a while, whereas people who view themselves as less sociable would experience a less intense need to be with others over that time. These individual differences also explain why needs can be "learned" to some extent. Socialization and reinforcement may cause people to alter their self-concept somewhat, resulting in a stronger or weaker need for social interaction, achievement, and so on. We will discuss learned needs later in this chapter.

Self-concept, social norms, and past experience also regulate a person's motivated decisions and behaviour, as the right side of Exhibit 5.1 illustrates. Consider the earlier example of the stranger sitting at your desk. You probably wouldn't walk up to the person and demand that he or she leave; such blunt behaviour is contrary to social norms in most cultures. Employees who view themselves as forthright might approach the stranger directly, whereas those who have a different self-concept or have had negative experiences with direct confrontation are

EXHIBIT 5.1

Drives, Needs, and Behaviour

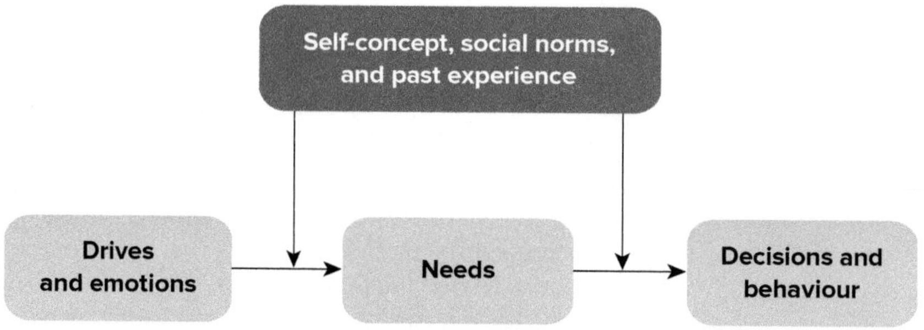

more likely to first gather information from coworkers before approaching the intruder. In short, your drives (drive to comprehend, to defend, to bond, etc.) and resulting emotions energize you to act, and your self-concept, social norms, and past experience direct that energy into goal-directed behaviour.

Exhibit 5.1 provides a useful template for understanding how drives and emotions are the prime sources of employee motivation and how individual characteristics (self-concept, experience, values) influence goal-directed behaviour. You will see pieces of this theory when we discuss four-drive theory, expectancy theory, equity theory, and other concepts in this chapter. The remainder of this section describes theories that try to explain the dynamics of drives and needs.

connect

To what extent do you value motivating jobs? Visit connect.mcgrawhill.com to assess your growth need strength (self-actualization).

Needs and Drives Theories

MASLOW'S NEEDS HIERARCHY THEORY

LO3

Maslow's needs hierarchy theory A motivation theory of needs arranged in a hierarchy, whereby people are motivated to fulfill a higher need as a lower one becomes gratified.

By far, the most widely known theory of human motivation is **Maslow's needs hierarchy theory** (see Exhibit 5.2). Developed by psychologist Abraham Maslow in the 1940s, the model condenses and integrates the long list of drives and needs that had been previously studied into a hierarchy of five basic categories (from lowest to highest):[14] *physiological* (need for food, air, water, shelter, etc.), *safety* (need for security and stability), *belongingness/love* (need for interaction with and affection from others), *esteem* (need for self-esteem and social esteem/status), and *self-actualization* (need for self-fulfillment, realization of one's potential). Along with these five categories, Maslow identified the desire to know and the desire for aesthetic beauty as two innate drives that do not fit within the hierarchy.

Maslow suggested that we are motivated simultaneously by several primary needs (drives), but the strongest source of motivation is the lowest unsatisfied need at the time. As the person satisfies a lower-level need, the next higher need in the hierarchy becomes the primary motivator and remains so even if never satisfied. The exception to this need fulfilment process is self-actualization; as people experience self-actualization, they desire more rather than less

EXHIBIT 5.2

Maslow's Needs Hierarchy

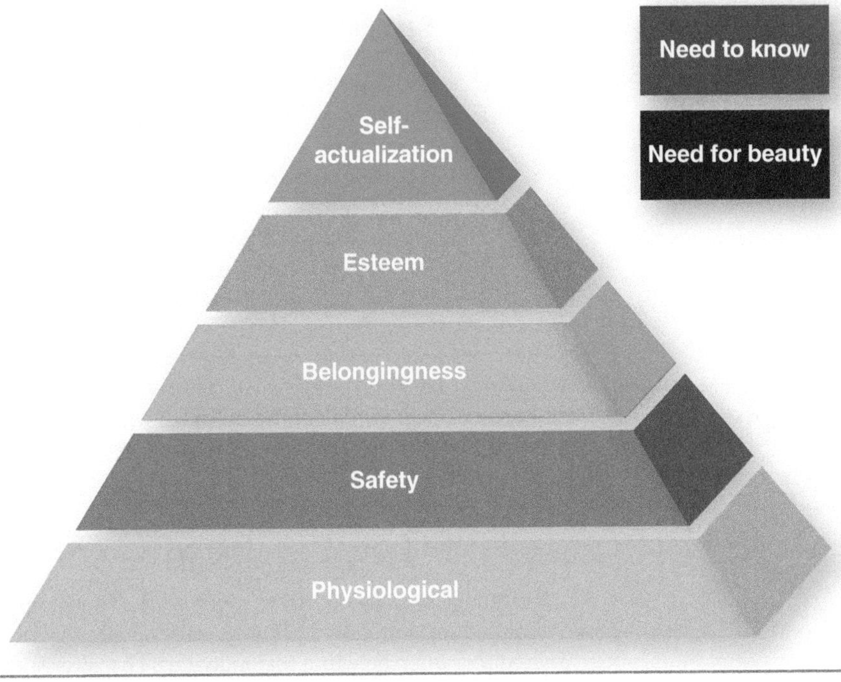

Source: Based on information in A. H. Maslow, "A Theory of Human Motivation," *Psychological Review* 50 (1943), pp. 370-396.

of this need. Thus, while the bottom four groups are *deficiency needs* because they become activated when unfulfilled, self-actualization is known as a *growth need* because it continues to develop even when fulfilled.

Limitations of Needs Hierarchy Models In spite of its popularity, Maslow's needs hierarchy theory has been dismissed by most motivation experts.[15] Other needs hierarchy models have also failed to adequately depict human motivation. Studies have concluded that people do not progress through the hierarchy as Maslow's theory predicts. Some people fulfill their esteem needs before their safety needs, for example. Furthermore, Maslow's theory suggested that a person's needs are fulfilled for a long time, whereas evidence indicates that need fulfillment tends to occur more briefly.

However, the main problem with Maslow's and other needs hierarchy models is that people don't fit into a one-size-fits-all needs hierarchy. Instead, these hierarchies vary from one person to the next. Some place social status at the top of their personal hierarchy; others view personal development and growth above social relations or status. Employee needs are strongly influenced by self-concept, personal values, and personality.[16] People have different hierarchies of values (their values system–see Chapter 2), so they also have parallel differences in their needs hierarchies. If your most important values lean towards stimulation and self-direction, you probably pay more attention to self-actualization needs. If power and achievement are at the top of your value system, status needs will likely be at the top of your needs hierarchy. A person's values hierarchy can change over time, so his or her needs hierarchy also changes over time.[17]

Maslow's Contribution to Motivation Although needs hierarchy theory has failed the reality test, Maslow deserves credit for bringing a more holistic, humanistic, and positive approach to the study of human motivation.[18]

- *Holistic perspective.* Maslow explained that the various needs should be studied together (holistically) because human behaviour is typically initiated by more than one need at the same time. Previously, motivation experts had splintered needs or drives into dozens of categories, each studied in isolation.[19]
- *Humanistic perspective.* Maslow introduced the then-novel idea that higher-order needs are influenced by personal and social influences, not just instincts.[20] In other words, he was among the first to recognize that human thoughts (including self-concept, social norms, past experience) play a role in motivation. Earlier motivation experts had focused almost entirely on human instincts without considering that motivation could be shaped by human thought.
- *Positive perspective.* Maslow popularized the concept of *self-actualization,* suggesting that people are naturally motivated to reach their potential and that organizations and societies need to be structured to help people continue and develop this motivation.[21] This positive view of motivation contrasted with the dominant position that needs become activated by deficiencies such as hunger. Indeed, Maslow is considered a pioneer in *positive organizational behaviour.* Positive OB says that focusing on the positive rather than negative aspects of life will improve organizational success and individual well-being (see Chapter 3). In other words, this approach advocates building positive qualities and perspectives within individuals or institutions as opposed to focusing on their failures and weaknesses.[22]

connect

How strong are your need for achievement and need for affiliation? See page 136 or visit connect.mcgrawhill.com to estimate your need strength for these two needs.

McCLELLAND'S LEARNED NEEDS THEORY

The general motivation model shown earlier in this chapter illustrated that needs are shaped, amplified, or suppressed through self-concept, social norms, and past experience. Maslow noted this when he wrote that individual characteristics influence the strength of higher-order needs, such as the need to belong. Psychologist David McClelland further investigated the

Heineken USA had been losing market share, but incoming CEO Dolf van den Brink (left in photo) soon discovered one major reason: Heineken's staff needed more achievement motivation. To encourage more risk-oriented, entrepreneurial thinking, van den Brink developed more achievement values, such as 'Hunt as a pack' and 'Do what it takes to win, but be responsible.' The company then held a pirate-themed event to introduce and celebrate these values. "We need to be a nimble, humble, agile and an entrepreneurial company again," explains van den Brink. "To have a challenger mindset, we needed to unleash everyone's inner pirate," says Maggie Timoney, a Heineken USA executive who was previously head of Heineken Canada.[23]

© Julie Brown Photography

idea that need strength can be altered through social influences. In particular, he recognized that a person's needs can be strengthened or weakened through reinforcement, learning, and social conditions. McClelland examined three "learned" needs: achievement, power, and affiliation.[24]

need for achievement (nAch)
A learned need in which people want to accomplish reasonably challenging goals and desire unambiguous feedback and recognition for their success.

Need for Achievement People with a strong **need for achievement (nAch)** want to accomplish reasonably challenging goals through their own effort. They prefer working alone rather than in teams, and they choose tasks with a moderate degree of risk (i.e., neither too easy nor impossible to complete). High-nAch people also desire unambiguous feedback and recognition for their success. Money is a weak motivator, except when it provides feedback and recognition.[25] In contrast, employees with a low nAch perform their work better when money is used as an incentive. Successful entrepreneurs tend to have a high nAch, possibly because they establish challenging goals for themselves and thrive on competition.[26]

need for affiliation (nAff)
A learned need in which people seek approval from others, conform to their wishes and expectations, and avoid conflict and confrontation.

Need for Affiliation **Need for affiliation (nAff)** refers to a desire to seek approval from others, conform to their wishes and expectations, and avoid conflict and confrontation. People with a strong nAff try to project a favourable image of themselves. They tend to actively support others and try to smooth out workplace conflicts. High nAff employees generally work well in coordinating roles to mediate conflicts and in sales positions where the main task is cultivating long-term relations. However, they tend to be less effective at allocating scarce resources and making other decisions that potentially generate conflict. People in decision-making positions must have a relatively low need for affiliation so their choices and actions are not biased by a personal need for approval.[27]

need for power (nPow)
A learned need in which people want to control their environment, including people and material resources, to benefit either themselves (personalized power) or others (socialized power).

Need for Power People with a high **need for power (nPow)** want to exercise control over others and are concerned about maintaining their leadership position. They frequently rely on persuasive communication, make more suggestions in meetings, and tend to publicly evaluate situations more frequently. McClelland pointed out that there are two types of nPow. Individuals who enjoy their power for its own sake, use it to advance personal interests, and wear their power as a status symbol have *personalized power*. Others mainly have a high need for *socialized power* because they desire power as a means to help others.[28] McClelland argues that effective leaders should have a high need for socialized rather than personalized power. They must have a high degree of altruism and social responsibility and be concerned about the consequences of their own actions on others.

Learning Needs McClelland believed that needs can be learned (more accurately, strengthened or weakened), and the training programs he developed supported that proposition. In his achievement motivation program, trainees wrote achievement-oriented stories and practised achievement-oriented behaviours in business games. They also completed a detailed achievement plan for the next two years and formed a reference group with other trainees to maintain their new-found achievement motivation.[29] Participants attending these achievement motivation programs subsequently started more new businesses, had greater community involvement, invested more in expanding their businesses, and employed twice as many people compared with a matched sample of non-participants. These training programs increased achievement motivation by altering participant self-concept and reinforced achievement experiences. When writing an achievement plan, for example, participants were encouraged (and supported by other participants) to experience the anticipated thrill of succeeding.

FOUR-DRIVE THEORY

One of the central messages of this chapter is that emotions are at the core of employee motivation. Social scientists increasingly agree that human beings have several hardwired drives, including social interaction, learning, and getting ahead. These drives generate emotions, which represent the prime movers or sources of individual effort. Most organizational behaviour theories of motivation focus on the cognitive aspects of human motivation; **four-drive theory** is one of the few to recognize the central role of human emotions in the motivation process.[30]

four-drive theory A motivation theory based on the innate drives to acquire, bond, learn, and defend that incorporates both emotions and rationality.

According to four-drive theory, everyone has the drive to acquire, to bond, to comprehend, and to defend. These drives are innate and universal, meaning that they are hardwired in our brains and are found in all human beings. They are also independent of each other. There is no hierarchy of drives, so one drive is neither dependent on nor inherently inferior or superior to another drive. Four-drive theory also states that these four drives are a complete set–there are no fundamental drives excluded from the model. Another key feature is that three of the four drives are proactive–we regularly try to fulfill them. Only the drive to defend is reactive–it is triggered by threat. Thus, any notion of fulfilling drives is temporary, at best.

Four-drive theory identified the four drives based on their considerable discussion in earlier research (which we noted earlier in this chapter). These drives are:

- *Drive to acquire.* This is the drive to seek, take, control, and retain objects and personal experiences. The drive to acquire extends beyond basic food and water; it includes enhancing one's self-concept through relative status and recognition in society.[31] Thus, it is the foundation of competition and the basis of our need for esteem. Four-drive theory states that the drive to acquire is insatiable because the purpose of human motivation is to achieve a higher position than others, not just to fulfill one's physiological needs.
- *Drive to bond.* This is the drive to form social relationships and develop mutual caring commitments with others. It explains why people form social identities by aligning their self-concept with various social groups (see Chapter 3). It may also explain why people who lack social contact are more prone to serious health problems.[32] The drive to bond motivates people to cooperate and, consequently, is a fundamental ingredient in the success of organizations and the development of societies.
- *Drive to comprehend.* This is the drive to satisfy our curiosity, to know and understand ourselves and the environment around us.[33] When observing something that

is inconsistent with or beyond our current knowledge, we experience a tension that motivates us to close that information gap. In fact, studies have revealed that people who are removed from any novel information will crave even boring information; in one classic Canadian experiment, participants deprived of information eventually craved month-old stock reports![34] The drive to comprehend is related to the higher-order needs of growth and self-actualization described earlier.

- *Drive to defend.* This is the drive to protect ourselves physically and socially. Probably the first drive to develop, it creates a "fight-or-flight" response in the face of personal danger. The drive to defend goes beyond protecting our physical self. It includes defending our relationships, our acquisitions, and our belief systems.

How Drives Influence Motivation and Behaviour Four-drive theory is derived from recent neuroscience research regarding the emotional marker process and how emotions are channelled into decisions and behaviour.[35] As we described in previous chapters, our perceptions of the world around us are quickly and nonconsciously tagged with emotional markers. According to four-drive theory, the four drives determine which emotions are tagged to incoming stimuli. When these emotions are strong enough, they demand our attention and motivate us to act on this observation.

Most of the time, we aren't aware of our emotional experiences because they are subtle and fleeting. However, emotions do become conscious experiences when they are sufficiently strong or when they significantly conflict with each other. Under these circumstances, we become aware of these emotions and our mental skill (social norms, past experience, and personal values) direct the motivational force of our emotions to decisions and behaviour that seem to reduce that tension (see Exhibit 5.3). In other words, our mental skill set chooses courses of action that are acceptable to society, consistent with our own moral compass, and have a high probability of achieving the goal of fulfilling those felt needs.[36] This is the process described at the beginning of this chapter: drives produce emotions, various personal characteristics (self-concept, social norms, experience) interpret these emotions into goal-directed needs, and those personal characteristics also direct those needs into decisions and behaviour.

Evaluating Four-Drive Theory Although four-drive theory was introduced recently, it is based on a deep research foundation dating back more than three decades. The drives have been identified from psychological and anthropological studies. Furthermore, Shalom Schwartz recently reported that four-drive theory maps well onto the ten dimensions in his

EXHIBIT 5.3

Four-Drive Theory of Motivation

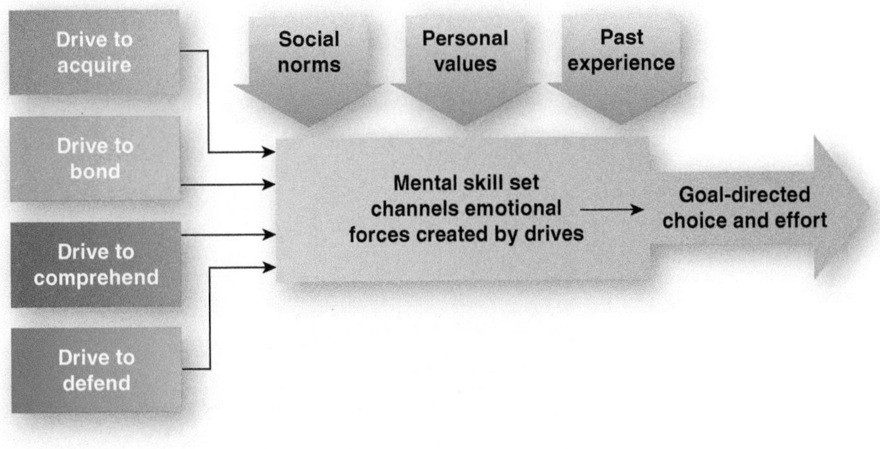

Source: Based on information in P. R. Lawrence and N. Nohria, *Driven: How Human Nature Shapes Our Choices* (San Francisco: Jossey-Bass, 2002).

circumplex model of personal values (see Chapter 2).[37] The translation of drives into goal-directed behaviour originates from considerable research on emotions and neural processes. The theory explains why needs vary from one person to the next, but avoids the assumption that everyone has the same needs hierarchy. Notice, too, that four-drive theory satisfies two of Maslow's criteria for any motivation theory: it is holistic (it relates to all drives, not just one or two) and humanistic (it acknowledges the role of human thought and social influences, not just instinct). Four-drive theory also provides a much clearer understanding of the role of emotional intelligence in employee motivation and behaviour. Employees with high emotional intelligence are more sensitive to emotions generated by the four drives, are better able to avoid impulsive behaviour from those drives, and can judge the best way to act to fulfill those drive demands in a social context.

Even with its well-researched foundation, four-drive theory is far from complete. Most experts would argue that one or two other drives exist that should be included. Furthermore, social norms, personal values, and past experience probably don't represent the full set of individual characteristics that translate emotions into goal-directed effort. For example, personality and self-concept probably also moderate the effect of drives and needs on decisions and behaviour.

Practical Implications of Four-Drive Theory The central advice from four-drive theory is that organizations should ensure that jobs and workplaces provide a balanced opportunity to fulfill the four drives.[38] There are really two recommendations here. The first is that the best workplaces for employee motivation and well-being offer conditions that help employees fulfill all four drives. Employees continually seek fulfillment of their innate drives, so successful companies provide sufficient rewards, learning opportunities, social interaction, and so forth, for all employees.

The second recommendation is that fulfillment of the four drives must be kept in balance; that is, organizations should avoid too much or too little opportunity to fulfill each drive. The reason for this advice is that the four drives counterbalance each other. The drive to bond counterbalances the drive to acquire; the drive to defend counterbalances the drive to comprehend. An organization that fuels the drive to acquire without the drive to bond may eventually suffer from organizational politics and dysfunctional conflict. Change and novelty in the workplace will aid the drive to comprehend, but too much of it will trigger the drive

Canadians continuously strive to fulfill the four drives identified in four-drive theory. A recent poll of more than 7,000 Canadian employees and job seekers reported that being recognized for doing good work and getting respect from colleagues top our list of everyday needs. "People want to feel valued and they stay where they feel valued," says Carolyn Clark, Senior Vice President, Human Resources, Americas for FRHI Hotels & Resorts (the parent company for Fairmont Hotels & Resorts) in Toronto. "Everything you do in the business must make [employees] feel like heroes and heroines and you must acknowledge the huge contribution they make," suggests an executive Intercontinental Hotels Group. "Everyone says they do this, but very few companies do."[39]

Courtesy of Fairmont Hotels and Resorts.

to defend to such an extent that employees become territorial and resistant to change. Thus, the workplace should offer enough opportunity to keep all four drives in balance. These recommendations help explain why Telus Corp., described at the beginning of this chapter, has a highly motivated workforce.

Expectancy Theory of Motivation

LO4

expectancy theory A motivation theory based on the idea that work effort is directed towards behaviours that people believe will lead to desired outcomes.

The theories described so far mainly explain what motivates us. They help us to understand the internal origins of employee motivation. But these drives and needs theories don't tell us what we are motivated to do. Four-drive theory recognizes that social norms, personal values, and past experience direct our effort, but it doesn't offer any more detail about what actions people follow when they are motivated.

Expectancy theory, on the other hand, predicts an individual's chosen direction, level, and persistence of effort through logical analysis of what actions would most likely satisfy the underlying needs. Essentially, the theory states that work effort is directed towards behaviours that people believe will most likely produce the desired outcomes. This is, essentially, a basic economic model of deciding which choice offers the highest expected payoff (called *subjective expected utility,* which we discuss in Chapter 7).[40] As illustrated in Exhibit 5.4, an individual's effort level depends on three factors: effort-to-performance (E-to-P) expectancy, performance-to-outcome (P-to-O) expectancy, and outcome valences. Employee motivation is influenced by all three components of the expectancy theory model. If any component weakens, motivation weakens.

- *E-to-P expectancy.* This is the individual's perception that his or her effort will result in a particular level of performance. In some situations, employees may believe that they can unquestionably accomplish the task (a probability of 1.0). In other situations, they expect that even their highest level of effort will not result in the desired performance level (a probability of 0.0). In most cases, the E-to-P expectancy falls somewhere between these two extremes.
- *P-to-O expectancy.* This is the perceived probability that a specific behaviour or performance level will lead to a particular outcome. In extreme cases, employees may believe that accomplishing a particular task (performance) will definitely result in a particular outcome (a probability of 1.0), or they may believe that successful performance will have no effect on this outcome (a probability of 0.0). More often, the P-to-O expectancy falls somewhere between these two extremes.
- *Outcome valences.* A *valence* is the anticipated satisfaction or dissatisfaction that an individual feels towards an outcome. It ranges from negative to positive. (The actual range

EXHIBIT 5.4

Expectancy Theory of Motivation

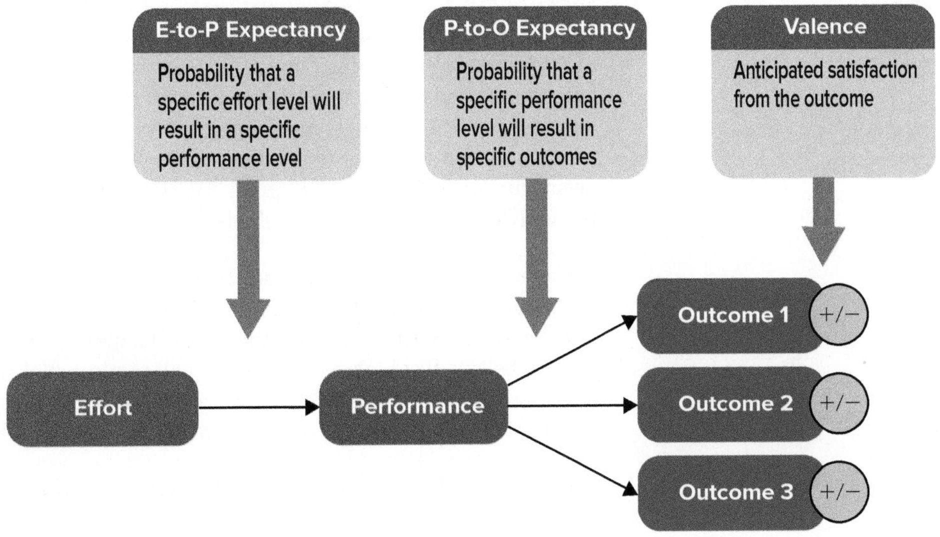

EXHIBIT 5.5 Practical Applications of Expectancy Theory

Expectancy theory component	Objective	Applications
E → P expectancies	To increase the employee's belief s/he is capable of performing the job successfully	• Select people with the required skills and knowledge. • Provide required training and clarify job requirements. • Provide sufficient time and resources. • Assign simpler or fewer tasks until employees can master them. • Provide examples of similar employees who have successfully performed the task. • Provide coaching to employees who lack self-confidence.
P → O expectancies	To increase the employee's belief that his/her good performance will result in certain (valued) outcomes	• Measure job performance accurately. • Clearly explain the outcomes that will result from successful performance. • Describe how the employee's rewards were based on past performance. • Provide examples of other employees whose good performance has resulted in higher rewards.
Outcome valences	To increase the employee's expected value of outcomes resulting from desired performance	• Distribute rewards that employees value. • Individualize rewards. • Minimize the presence of countervalent outcomes.

doesn't matter; it may be from −1 to +1 or from −100 to +100.) An outcome valence represents a person's anticipated satisfaction with the outcome.[41] Outcomes have a positive valence when they are consistent with our values and satisfy our needs; they have a negative valence when they oppose our values and inhibit need fulfillment.

EXPECTANCY THEORY IN PRACTICE

One of the appealing characteristics of expectancy theory is that it provides clear guidelines for increasing employee motivation.[42] Several practical applications of expectancy theory are listed in Exhibit 5.5 and described below.

Increasing E-to-P Expectancies E-to-P expectancies are influenced by the individual's belief that he or she can successfully complete the task. Some companies increase this can-do attitude by assuring employees that they have the necessary competencies, clear role perceptions, and necessary resources to reach the desired levels of performance. An important part of this process involves matching employee competencies to job requirements and clearly communicating the tasks required for the job. Similarly, E-to-P expectancies are learned, so behaviour modelling and supportive feedback (positive reinforcement) typically strengthen the individual's belief that he or she is able to perform the task.

Increasing P-to-O Expectancies The most obvious ways to improve P-to-O expectancies are to measure employee performance accurately and distribute more valued rewards to those with higher job performance. P-to-O expectancies are perceptions, so employees also need to believe that higher performance will result in higher rewards. Furthermore, they need to know how that connection occurs, so leaders should use examples, anecdotes, and public ceremonies to illustrate when behaviour has been rewarded.

Increasing Outcome Valences One size does not fit all when motivating and rewarding people. Organizational leaders need to find ways to individualize rewards or, where standard rewards are necessary, to identify rewards that do not have a negative valence for some staff. Consider the following Canadian story: Top-performing employees in one organization were rewarded with a one-week Caribbean cruise with the company's executive team. Many were likely delighted, but at least one top performer was aghast at the thought of going on a cruise with senior management. "I don't like schmoozing, I don't like feeling trapped. Why couldn't they just give me the money?" she complained. The employee went on the cruise, but spent most of her time working in her stateroom.[43]

One other observation about increasing outcome valences is to watch out for countervalent outcomes that offset outcomes with positive valences. For example, several employees in one work unit were individually motivated to perform well because this achievement gave them a feeling of accomplishment and rewarded them with higher pay. But their performance was considerably lower when they worked together with others because peer pressure discouraged performance above a fairly low standard. In this situation, the positive valence outcomes (feeling of accomplishment, higher pay) were offset by the negative valence outcome of peer pressure.

Overall, expectancy theory is a useful model that explains how people rationally figure out the best direction, intensity, and persistence of effort. It has been tested in a variety of situations and predicts employee motivation in different cultures.[44] However, critics have a number of concerns with how the theory has been tested. Another concern is that expectancy theory ignores the central role of emotion in employee effort and behaviour. The valence element of expectancy theory captures some of this emotional process, but only peripherally.[45] Finally, expectancy theory outlines how expectancies (probability of outcomes) affect motivation, but it doesn't explain how employees develop these expectancies. Two theories that provide this explanation are organizational behaviour modification and social cognitive theory, which we describe next.

Organizational Behaviour Modification and Social Cognitive Theory

LO5

Expectancy theory states that motivation is determined by employee beliefs about expected performance and outcomes. But how do employees learn these expectancy beliefs? How do they learn, for example, that some work activities are more likely to produce a pay increase or promotion whereas other activities have little effect? The answer to this question directs us to two theories: organizational behaviour modification (OB Mod) and social cognitive theory. These theories explain how people *learn* what to expect from their actions. Consequently, OB Mod and social cognitive theory are also theories of motivation because, as expectancy theory explains, the learned expectancies affect the person's direction, intensity, and persistence of effort.

ORGANIZATIONAL BEHAVIOUR MODIFICATION

For most of the first half of the 1900s, the dominant paradigm about managing individual behaviour was *behaviourism*, which argues that a good theory should rely exclusively on behaviour and the environment and ignore nonobservable cognitions and emotions.[46] Although behaviourists don't deny the existence of human thoughts and attitudes, they view them as unobservable and, therefore, irrelevant to scientific study. A variation of this paradigm, called **organizational behaviour modification (OB Mod),** eventually entered organizational studies of motivation and learning.[47]

organizational behaviour modification (OB Mod) A theory that explains employee behaviour in terms of the antecedent conditions and consequences of that behaviour.

A-B-Cs of OB Mod The core elements of OB Mod are depicted in the A-B-C model shown in Exhibit 5.6. Essentially, OB Mod attempts to change behaviour (B) by managing its antecedents (A) and consequences (C).[48] *Consequences* are events following a particular behaviour that influence its future occurrence, such as new information you receive from an incoming text message on your smartphone, or congratulatory notes from coworkers for helping them complete a difficult task. Consequences also include no outcome at all, such as when no one says anything about how well you have been serving customers.

Antecedents are events preceding the behaviour, informing employees that a particular action will produce specific consequences. An antecedent may be a sound from your smartphone signalling that a text message has arrived, or it might be your supervisor's request to complete a specific task by tomorrow. Notice that antecedents do not cause behaviour. The sound from your smartphone doesn't cause us to open the text message. Rather, the sound (antecedent) is a

EXHIBIT 5.6

A-B-Cs of Organizational Behaviour Modification

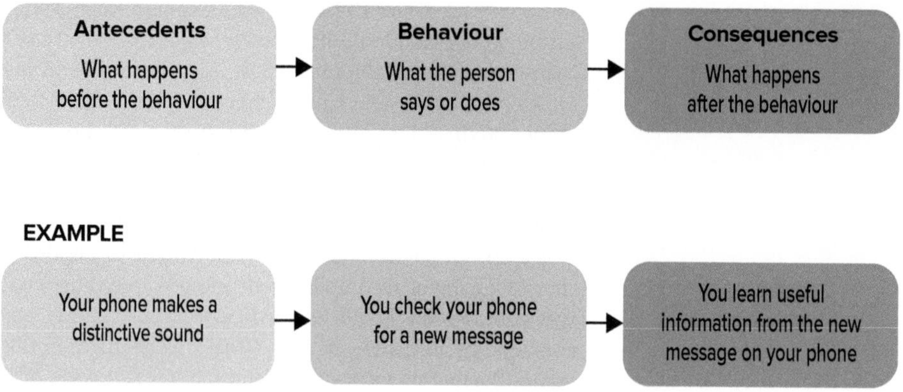

Sources: Adapted from T. K. Connellan, *How to Improve Human Performance* (New York: Harper & Row, 1978), p. 50; F. Luthans and R. Kreitner, *Organizational Behaviour Modification and Beyond* (Glenview, IL: Scott, Foresman, 1985), pp. 85-88.

cue signalling that if you check your phone messages (behaviour), you will find a new message with potentially useful information (consequence).

OB Mod identifies four types of consequences (called the *contingencies of reinforcement*).[49] *Positive reinforcement* occurs when the introduction of a consequence increases or maintains the frequency or future probability of a specific behaviour. An example of this is receiving praise after completing a project. *Punishment* occurs when a consequence decreases the frequency or future probability of a specific behaviour occurring. Most of us would consider being demoted or being criticized by our coworkers as forms of punishment. A third type of consequence is *extinction.* Extinction occurs when the target behaviour decreases because no consequence follows it. For instance, research suggests that performance tends to decline when managers stop congratulating employees for their good work.[50]

The fourth consequence in OB Mod, called *negative reinforcement,* is often confused with punishment. It's actually the opposite; it occurs when the removal or avoidance of a consequence increases or maintains the frequency or future probability of a specific behaviour. For example, managers apply negative reinforcement when they *stop* criticizing employees whose substandard performance has improved.

Which of these four consequences works best? In most situations, positive reinforcement should follow desired behaviours and extinction (do nothing) should follow undesirable behaviours. This approach is preferred because punishment and negative reinforcement generate negative emotions and attitudes towards the punisher (e.g., supervisor) and organization. However, some form of punishment (dismissal, suspension, demotion, etc.) may be necessary for extreme behaviours, such as deliberately hurting a coworker or stealing inventory. Indeed, research suggests that, under certain conditions, punishment maintains a sense of fairness.[51]

Along with the four consequences, OB Mod considers the frequency and timing of these reinforcers (called the *schedules of reinforcement*).[52] The most effective reinforcement schedule for learning new tasks is *continuous reinforcement*–providing positive reinforcement after every occurrence of the desired behaviour. The best schedule for motivating employees is a *variable ratio schedule* in which employee behaviour is reinforced after a variable number of times. Salespeople experience variable ratio reinforcement because they make a successful sale (the reinforcer) after a varying number of client calls. The variable ratio schedule makes behaviour highly resistant to extinction because the reinforcer is never expected at a particular time or after a fixed number of accomplishments.

Evaluating OB Mod Everyone uses organizational behaviour modification principles in one form or another to motivate others. We thank people for a job well done, are silent when displeased, and sometimes try to punish those who go against our wishes. OB Mod also occurs in various formal programs to reduce absenteeism, improve task performance and organizational citizenship behaviour, encourage safe work behaviours, and have a healthier lifestyle. Employees at Calgary-based International Fitness Holdings reinforce coworker behaviour by posting positive comments on a public Facebook-like "team wall" and giving points to the favoured recipient. Each employee gets 300 points annually to distribute to peers, which can be traded in for paid time off, gas coupons, and other rewards.

Global Connections 5.1:

REINFORCING WORK BEHAVIOUR THROUGH GAMIFICATION

When James Sanders meets a client, he uses his phone to report the client's name, where they met, and the topic discussed. The information is recorded at Deloitte Touche Tohmatsu's website in Melbourne, Australia, where Sanders works. This information is available to others at the professional services firm, which avoids the problem of duplicate visits. Deloitte employees are also motivated to document and share this information because of Deloitte's process of game-based positive reinforcement (gamification).

Deloitte employees earn virtual "badges" for recording their client meetings. The company also awards badges for blogging about new ideas on the social network site, for completing online training sessions, and for a host of other desired behaviours. Employees with the most badges are ranked on leaderboards in various categories. Employees can also display their badges on LinkedIn and other public social network sites.

Ford of Canada successfully applied gamification to reinforce certification training among its dealership employees. The company motivated participants to "gear up" by learning new content and then testing themselves on that content at a specially-designed website. Dealership employees earned badges displayed on a virtual Ford car or in a virtual trophy case as they progressed through the training modules. The system also generated healthy competition using leaderboards that posted the names of employees who earned the most points.

Deloitte introduced a similar game-based system to motivate online learning at its leadership academy. In addition to Ford of Canada's activities, Deloitte had unexpected reinforcers in the form of surprise secret badges. These unique badges rewarded special behaviours, such as having everyone in the department complete a particular learning module the same week.

Gamification seems to have a powerful effect on employee motivation and behaviour. Ford of Canada's learning game resulted in a huge increase in online learning among dealership employees. Deloitte found that the number of learners returning to the leadership academy each week increased by 37 percent, they spend more time at the learning site, and they complete more learning modules.

Frank Farrall, Deloitte Digital lead partner, says that badges and leaderboards provide strong reinforcement, particularly for more competitive staff. "It's meant to incentivize you from a peer-comparison point," he says. "Any time you put a leaderboard up, the increase in activity is dramatic and noticeable." More generally, he suggests that game-based positive reinforcement taps into everyone's natural motivation to engage in the reinforced behaviour. "If you can gamify the process, you are rewarding the behaviour and it's like a dopamine release in the brain," Farrall explains. "Humans like a game."[53]

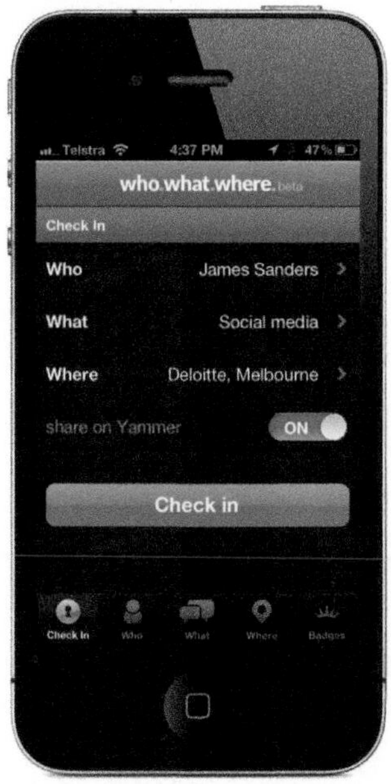

Courtesy of Deloitte

Toronto-based Cineplex Inc. also has a peer-to-peer recognition program (called Encore), as well as several awards to reinforce employee experimentation with new ideas. "There's a speed that exists within the organization and a pace that is probably not found in a lot of other companies," explains a Cineplex executive. "If we have a new idea that we find is working at one theatre, we will implement those changes in the other theatres as quickly as possible."[54] Global Connections 5.1 describes an innovative and increasingly popular behaviour modification strategy that relies on "gamification"–reinforcing behaviour through online games in which employees earn "badges" and compete for top positions on leaderboards.

In spite of its widespread use, organizational behaviour modification has a number of limitations. One limitation is "reward inflation," in which the reinforcer is eventually considered an entitlement. For this reason, most OB Mod programs must run infrequently and for a short duration. Another concern is that the variable ratio schedule of reinforcement tends to create a lottery-style reward system, which might be viewed as too erratic for formal rewards and is unpopular to people who dislike gambling. Probably the most significant problem is OB Mod's radical view that behaviour is learned only through personal interaction with the environment.[55] This view is no longer accepted; instead, experts recognize that people also learn and are motivated by observing others and inferring possible consequences of their actions. This learning process is explained by social cognitive theory.

SOCIAL COGNITIVE THEORY

social cognitive theory A theory that explains how learning and motivation occur by observing and modelling others as well as by anticipating the consequences of our behaviour.

Social cognitive theory states that much learning occurs by observing and modelling others as well as by anticipating the consequences of our behaviour.[56] Although observation and modelling (imitation) have been studied for many years as sources of motivation and learning, Canadian-born social scientist Albert Bandura reframed these ideas within a cognitive (internal thoughts) perspective as an alternative to the behaviourist approach. There are several pieces to social cognitive theory, but the three most relevant to employee motivation are learning behaviour consequences, behaviour modelling, and self-regulation.

Learning Behaviour Consequences People learn the consequences of behaviour by observing or hearing about what happened to other people, not just by directly experiencing the consequences [57] Hearing that a coworker was fired for being rude to a client increases your perception that rude behaviour will result in being fired. In the language of expectancy theory, learning behaviour consequences changes a person's perceived P-to-O probability. Furthermore, people logically anticipate consequences in related situations. For instance, the story about the fired employee might also strengthen your P-to-O expectancy that being rude towards coworkers and suppliers (not just clients) will get you fired.

Behaviour Modelling Along with observing others, people learn by imitating and practising their behaviours.[58] Direct sensory experience helps to acquire tacit knowledge and skills, such as the subtle person-machine interaction while driving a vehicle. Behaviour modelling also increases self-efficacy (see Chapter 3), because people gain more self-confidence after observing others and performing the task successfully themselves. Self-efficacy particularly improves when observers identify with the model, such as someone who is similar in age, experience, gender, and related features.

self-reinforcement Reinforcement that occurs when an employee has control over a reinforcer but doesn't 'take' it until completing a self-set goal.

Self-Regulation An important feature of social cognitive theory is that human beings set goals and engage in other forms of intentional, purposive action. They establish their own short and long-term objectives, choose their own standards of achievement, work out a plan of action, consider back-up alternatives, and have the forethought to anticipate the consequences of their goal-directed behaviour. Furthermore, people self-regulate by engaging in **self-reinforcement;** they reward and punish themselves for exceeding or falling short of their self-set standards of excellence.[59] For example, you might have a goal of completing the rest of this chapter, after which you reward yourself by having a snack. Raiding the refrigerator is a form of self-induced positive reinforcement for completing this reading assignment.

OB Mod and social cognitive theory explain how people learn probabilities of success (E-to-P expectancies) as well as probabilities of various outcomes (P-to-O expectancies). As such, these theories explain motivation through their relationship with expectancy theory of motivation, described earlier. Elements of these theories also help us to understand other motivation processes. For instance, self-regulation is the cornerstone of motivation through goal setting and feedback, which we discuss next.

Goal Setting and Feedback

LO6

The City of Toronto's Customer Service Call Centre is a busy place. The centre handles 27,000 calls per month or about 1,200 calls per day.[60] That works out to an average of 35 calls per customer services representative. Toronto's Revenue Services department, which is responsible for the call centre, knows that productivity could be better. It estimates that 40 percent of incoming calls are answered within five minutes, whereas other call centres have much faster response times. Another concern is that 30 percent of callers hang up before the call is handled by someone at the contact centre. The City of Toronto has set a goal of immediately reducing that abandonment rate to 20 percent and to 16 percent within the next two years. City of Toronto call centre staff aren't just aware of these goals; they probably also receive some form of visual feedback at their worksite. Contact centres often have large electronic screens showing statistics for these key performance indicators.

goal setting The process of motivating employees and clarifying their role perceptions by establishing performance objectives.

Customer contact centres partly motivate employees through **goal setting,** which is the process of motivating employees and clarifying their role perceptions by establishing performance objectives. Goal setting potentially improves employee performance in two ways: (1) by amplifying the intensity and persistence of effort and (2) by giving employees clearer role perceptions so their effort is channelled towards behaviours that will improve work performance. Goal setting is more complex than simply telling someone to "do your best." It requires several specific characteristics.[61] One popular acronym–SMARTER–captures these characteristics fairly well.[62]

connect

What is your goal orientation? Visit **connect.mcgrawhill.com** to assess whether you have more of a learning or avoidance goal orientation.

- *Specific.* Employees put more effort into a task when they work towards goals that state what needs to be accomplished, how it should be accomplished, and where, when, and with whom it should be accomplished. Specific goals clarify performance expectations, so employees can direct their effort more efficiently and reliably.
- *Measurable.* Setting goals doesn't have much value if you don't know whether they have been achieved. That's why goals need to be measurable. This measurement ideally includes how much (quantity), how well (quality), and at what cost the goal was achieved. Measurement can be a problem however, because people tend to focus only on goals that are easily measured.[63]
- *Achievable.* Ideally, goals should be challenging without being so difficult that employees lose their motivation to achieve them.[64] This idea reflects the E-to-P expectancy described earlier in this chapter. The lower the E-to-P expectancy that the goal can been accomplished, the less committed (motivated) the employee is to the goal.
- *Relevant.* Goals need to be relevant to the individual's job and within his or her control. For example, a goal to reduce waste materials would have little value if employees don't have much control over waste in the production process.
- *Time-framed.* Goals need a due date. They should specify when the objective should be completed or when it will be assessed for comparison against a standard.
- *Exciting.* Goals tend to be more effective when employees are committed to them, not just compliant. Challenging goals tend to be more exciting for most (but not all) employees because they are more likely to fulfill a person's achievement or growth needs when the goal is achieved. Goal commitment also increases when employees are involved in goal setting.[65]
- *Reviewed.* The motivational value of goal setting depends on employees receiving feedback about reaching those goals.[66] Measurement (listed above) is part of that feedback, but so is the process of reviewing goal progress (during) and accomplishment (after). Reviewing goal progress and accomplishment helps employees to redirect their effort. It is also a potential source of recognition that fulfills growth needs.

BALANCED SCORECARD

balanced scorecard (BSC)
A goal-setting and reward system that translates the organization's vision and mission into specific, measurable performance goals related to financial, customer, internal, and learning/growth (i.e., human capital) processes.

One organization-wide approach to goal setting is the **balanced scorecard (BSC),** which attempts to represent objectives across various stakeholders and processes. The balanced scorecard translates the organization's vision and mission into specific, measurable key performance indicators (KPIs) related to financial, customer, internal, and learning/growth (i.e., human capital) processes. These goals cascade down to departments and to employees within those departments. For example, an airline might include on-time performance as one of its customer process goals and number of hours of safety training per employee as a learning and growth process goal. These specific goals are linked to various work units and employees. BSC goals are often weighted and scored to create a composite measure of goal achievement across the organization each year.

Balanced scorecards have been introduced in a variety of organizations across Canada, such as the Canadian Tourism Commission (CTC), Edmonton/Villeneuve Airports, Royal Canadian Mounted Police, and several public health agencies and centres across

Canada.[67] The balanced scorecard at the CTC–the Canadian government's agency responsible for marketing Canada abroad–includes a set of financial and non-financial measures organized around five themes: shareholder/stakeholder, customer, budget/finance, internal operations, and workforce. Some of CTC's highest priority BSC indicators recently have been attributable tourism export revenue; partner contributions; and employee engagement.

In spite of their popularity, BSCs present a number of challenges. As with most goal setting and feedback systems, the quality of the process is only as good as the goals established and the feedback available. Some companies choose goals that are easily measured rather than valuable. Others go to great lengths to measure internal processes, but these measures create a paperwork bureaucracy that raises overhead costs and employee resentment for diverting resources from the company's main functions. One report from the Royal Canadian Mounted Police (RCMP), which has a highly-regarded BSC, warned that people get caught up on the measures whereas they need discipline to focus on achieving BSC goals. The RCMP report also noted that BSC systems suffer when they become overburdened with too many indicators and when those indicators don't resonate with employees.[68]

CHARACTERISTICS OF EFFECTIVE FEEDBACK

Feedback–information that lets us know whether we have achieved the goal or are properly directing our effort towards it–is a critical partner in goal setting. Along with clarifying role perceptions and improving employee skills and knowledge, feedback motivates when it is constructive and when employees have strong self-efficacy.[69] Effective feedback has many of the same characteristics as effective goal setting. It should be *specific* and *relevant*, that is, the information should refer to specific metrics (e.g., sales increased by 5 percent last month) and to the individual's behaviour or outcomes within his or her control. Feedback should also be *timely;* the information should be available soon after the behaviour or results occur so that employees see a clear association between their actions and the consequences. Effective feedback is also *credible*. Employees are more likely to accept feedback from trustworthy and believable sources.

The final characteristic of effective feedback is that it should be *sufficiently frequent*. How frequent is "sufficiently"? The answer depends on at least two things. One consideration is the employee's knowledge and experience with the task. Feedback is a form of reinforcement, so

Until recently, A&W Canada kitchen staff didn't get much feedback from customers. Only one percent of customers completed comment cards, and that feedback wasn't timely. Now, A&W Canada customers provide direct feedback in a few seconds using iPad-equipped kiosks near the exit. The cumulative ratings are updated instantly on screens in the kitchen area. Up to one-third of customers have used the feedback kiosks at the company's six test sites in Ottawa. "It's very motivational," says Nancy Wuttunee, A&W Canada's senior director of operational excellence. "You may not be perfect all the time, but it encourages you to improve all the time." Employees agree, saying they watch the feedback screens "all the time" and enjoy receiving the feedback.[70]

Chris Mikula/*Ottawa Citizen*. Reprinted by permission.

employees working on new tasks should receive more frequent feedback because they require more behaviour guidance and reinforcement. Employees who perform repetitive or familiar tasks can receive less frequent feedback. The second factor is how long it takes to complete the task (i.e., its cycle time). Feedback is necessarily less frequent in jobs with a long cycle time (e.g., executives and scientists) than in jobs with a short cycle time (e.g., grocery store cashiers).

Feedback Through Strengths-Based Coaching Forty years ago, Peter Drucker argued that leaders are more effective when they focus on strengths rather than weaknesses. "The effective executive builds on strengths–their own strengths, the strengths of superiors, colleagues, subordinates; and on the strength of the situation," wrote the late management guru.[71] Rox Ltd. is one of many organizations to apply this strengths-based perspective to employee feedback. "It's important to reward and encourage strengths. Instead of looking at weakness, look at areas for development," says Kyron Keogh, co founder of the award-winning luxury retail jewellery chain headquartered in Glasgow, Scotland. "It's vital to ensure that staff stay motivated and upbeat in a sales environment."[72]

strengths-based coaching A positive organizational behaviour approach to coaching and feedback that focuses on building and leveraging the employee's strengths rather than trying to correct his or her weaknesses.

This positive approach to feedback is the essence of **strengths-based coaching** (also known as *appreciative coaching*)–maximizing employees' potential by focusing on their strengths rather than weaknesses.[73] In strengths-based coaching, employees describe areas of work where they excel or demonstrate potential. The coach guides this discussion by asking exploratory questions that guide employees to discover ways of leveraging this strength. Situational barriers are identified as well as strategies to overcome those barriers to leveraging the employee's potential.

Strengths-based coaching can potentially motivate employees because they inherently seek feedback about their strengths, not their flaws. Thus, strengths-based feedback is consistent with the process of self-enhancement (see Chapter 3). Strengths-based coaching also makes sense because personality becomes quite stable by the time an individual reaches early career, which limits the flexibility of the person's interests, preferences, and competencies.[74] In spite of these research observations, most companies focus goal setting and feedback on tasks that employees are performing poorly. After the initial polite compliments, many coaching or performance feedback sessions analyze the employee's weaknesses, including determining what went wrong and what the employee needs to do to improve. These inquisitions sometimes produce so much negative feedback that employees become defensive; they can also undermine self-efficacy, thereby making the employee's performance worse rather than better. By focusing on weaknesses, companies fail to realize the full potential of the employee's strengths.[75]

SOURCES OF FEEDBACK

Feedback can originate from nonsocial or social sources. Nonsocial sources provide feedback without someone communicating that information. Corporate intranets allow many executives to receive feedback instantaneously on their computer, usually in the form of graphic output on an executive dashboard. Employees at contact centres view electronic displays showing how many callers are waiting and the average time they have been waiting. Nova Chemicals operators in Alberta receive feedback from a computer screen that monitors in real time the plant's operational capacity, depicted as a gently flowing green line, and actual production output, shown as a red squiggly line. Soon after Nova installed the feedback system, employees engaged in friendly bouts of rivalry to determine who could keep the actual production output as close as possible to the plant's maximum capacity.[76]

multisource (360-degree) feedback Information about an employee's performance collected from a full circle of people, including subordinates, peers, supervisors, and customers.

Multisource (360-Degree) Feedback **Multisource (360-degree) feedback** is a social form of feedback that has been widely used in organizations. As the name implies, multisource feedback is information about an employee's performance collected from a full circle of people, including subordinates, peers, supervisors, and customers. Multisource feedback tends to provide more complete and accurate information than feedback from a supervisor alone. It is particularly useful when the supervisor is unable to observe the employee's behaviour or performance throughout the year. Lower-level employees also feel a greater sense of fairness and open communication when they are able to provide upward feedback about their boss's performance.[77]

However, multisource feedback also creates challenges. Having several people review so many other people can be expensive and time-consuming. With multiple opinions, the 360-degree process can also produce ambiguous and conflicting feedback, so employees may require guidance to interpret the results. A third concern is that peers may provide inflated rather than accurate feedback to avoid conflicts during the forthcoming year. A final concern is that employees experience a stronger emotional reaction when they receive critical feedback from many people rather than from just one person (such as the boss). "Initially you do take it personally," admits a manager at software maker Autodesk. "[360-degree feedback] is meant to be constructive, but you have to internally battle that."[78]

Choosing Feedback Sources With so many sources of feedback—multisource feedback, executive dashboards, customer surveys, equipment gauges, nonverbal communication from your boss—which one works best under which conditions? The preferred feedback source depends on the purpose of the information. To learn about their progress towards goal accomplishment, employees usually prefer nonsocial feedback sources, such as computer printouts or feedback directly from the job. This is because information from nonsocial sources is considered more accurate than information from social sources. Negative feedback from nonsocial sources is also less damaging to self-esteem. In contrast, social sources tend to delay negative information, leave some of it out, and distort the bad news in a positive way.[79] When employees want to improve their self-image, they seek out positive feedback from social sources. It feels better to have coworkers say that you are performing the job well than to discover this from a computer screen.

EVALUATING GOAL SETTING AND FEEDBACK

Goal setting represents one of the "tried-and-true" theories in organizational behaviour, so much so that it is rated by experts as one of the top OB theories in terms of validity and usefulness.[80] In partnership with goal setting, feedback also has an excellent reputation for improving employee motivation and performance. At the same time, putting goal setting into practice can create problems.[81] One concern is that goal setting tends to focus employees on a narrow subset of measurable performance indicators while ignoring aspects of job performance that are difficult to measure. The saying, "What gets measured, gets done" applies here.

A second problem is that when goal achievement is tied to financial rewards, many employees are motivated to set easy goals (while making the boss think they are difficult) so that they have a higher probability of receiving the bonus or pay increase. As a former CEO at Ford once quipped: "At Ford, we hire very smart people. They quickly learn how to make relatively easy goals look difficult!"[82] A third problem is that setting performance goals is effective in established jobs but seems to interfere with the learning process in new, complex jobs. Therefore, goal setting is less useful—and may be dysfunctional—where an intense learning process is occurring.

Organizational Justice

LO7

When Robert Meggy first introduced a profit sharing plan at Great Little Box Company, he felt that the size of profit sharing bonus should correspond to the person's position and seniority in the organization. "It used to be a program based on seniority and a number of other variables but there were a number of complaints about that," recalls the CEO of the Vancouver-based corrugated box and point-of-purchase display manufacturer. "Now that it's equal across the board, we don't have that problem." In other words, employees felt that the original bonus distribution system lacked fairness, a condition that Meggy considers vital to a successful company. "I certainly believe in fair pay," says Meggy. "You don't have to be the best paying but you do have to be fair."[83]

Most organizational leaders know that treating employees fairly is both morally correct and good for employee motivation, loyalty, and well-being. Yet feelings of injustice are regular occurrences in the workplace. To minimize these incidents, we need to first understand that there are two forms of organizational justice: distributive justice and procedural justice.[84] **Distributive justice** refers to perceived fairness in the outcomes we receive compared to our contributions and the outcomes and contributions of others. **Procedural justice,** on the other hand, refers to fairness of the procedures used to decide the distribution of resources.

distributive justice Perceived fairness in the individual's ratio of outcomes to contributions relative to a comparison of other's ratio of outcomes to contributions.

procedural justice Perceived fairness of the procedures used to decide the distribution of resources.

Debating Point:

DOES EQUITY MOTIVATE MORE THAN EQUALITY?[85]

It seems obvious that employees with higher performance, skills, or other contributions to the organization should receive more generous pay and other rewards. Increasing the pay differential (wage dispersion) between high and low contributors should boost employee motivation to achieve a higher standard of performance. It should also increase company performance by motivating the top performers to stay and the bottom performers to leave. A large wage dispersion is also consistent with justice and fairness. Differentiating rewards based on employee performance, skills, and other forms of contribution is consistent with the principle of meritocracy. It is also consistent with the ethical principle of justice, which states that those who contribute more should receive more in return (Chapter 2). Furthermore, performance-based pay is one of the pillars of high performance work practices (see Chapter 1).

But workplaces that have large wage dispersions might not be receiving the performance dividends they expect. Several (but not all) studies have found that sports teams with relatively small pay differences among team members perform better than sport teams with relatively high pay differences. Teams that pay huge salaries or bonuses to stars do not score more points or win more games. Also, turnover among players and managers tends to increase with the size of the wage dispersion. One recent study extended these observations to all industries. Companies that have a higher dispersion of wage increases (larger increases to higher-paid staff) perform worse than companies with an equal dispersion of wage increases. Another study reported that information technology companies with larger salary differences among top management teams had worse shareholder returns and market-to-book value compared to IT companies with less pay inequality.

Why would larger pay ranges undermine rather than enhance employee and organizational performance? One reason is that pay differences produce status differences, which can undermine cooperation among employees. A second reason is that large pay differences might increase (rather than decrease) feelings of injustice. Most people think they are above average, so large pay differences clearly place many employees below their self-evaluations. Also, employees tend to underestimate the contribution of higher-paid coworkers and assume those higher-paid coworkers also receive other rewards (such as preferential treatment). In short, lower-paid employees often believe higher-paid employees are overpaid, which reduces the lower-paid workers' motivation and performance.

EQUITY THEORY

At its most basic level, the employment relationship is about employees exchanging their time, skills, and behaviour for pay, fulfilling work, skill development opportunities, and so forth. What is considered "fair" in this exchange relationship varies with each person and situation. An *equality principle* operates when we believe that everyone in the group should receive the same outcomes, such as when everyone gets subsidized meals in the company cafeteria. The *need principle* is applied when we believe that those with the greatest need should receive more outcomes than others with less need. The *equity principle* infers that people should be paid in proportion to their contribution. The equity principle is the most common distributive justice rule in organizational settings, so let's look at it in more detail.

equity theory A theory explaining how people develop perceptions of fairness in the distribution and exchange of resources.

Feelings of equity are explained by **equity theory,** which says that employees determine feelings of equity by comparing their own outcome/input ratio to the outcome/input ratio of some other person.[86] As Exhibit 5.7 illustrates, the *outcome/input ratio* is the value of the outcomes you receive divided by the value of the inputs you provide in the exchange relationship. Inputs include such things as skill, effort, reputation, performance, experience, and hours worked. Outcomes are what employees receive from the organization, such as pay, promotions, recognition, interesting jobs, and opportunities to improve one's skills and knowledge.

Equity theory states that we compare our outcome/input ratio with that of a comparison other.[87] The comparison other might be another person or group of people in other jobs (e.g., comparing your pay with the CEO's pay) or another organization. Some research suggests that employees frequently collect information on several referents to form a "generalized" comparison other.[88] For the most part, however, the comparison other varies from one person to the next and is not easily identifiable.

The comparison of our own outcome/input ratio with the ratio of someone else results in perceptions of equity, underreward in equity, or overreward inequity. In the equity condition, people believe that their outcome/input ratio is similar to the ratio of the comparison other. In the underreward inequity situation, people believe their outcome/input ratio is lower than

EXHIBIT 5.7

Equity Theory Model

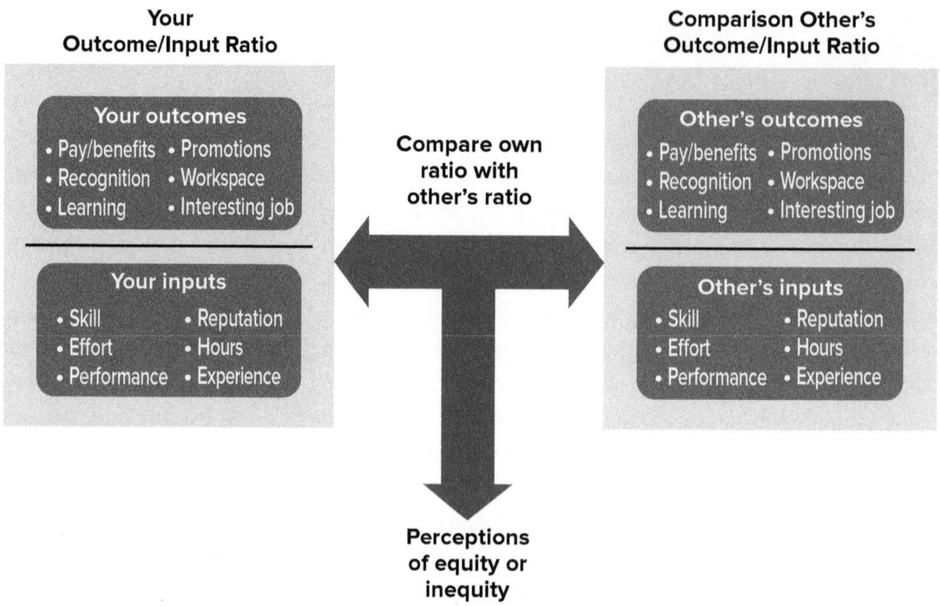

the comparison other's ratio. In the overreward inequity condition, people believe their ratio of outcomes/inputs is higher than the comparison other's ratio.

Inequity and Employee Motivation How do perceptions of equity or inequity affect employee motivation? The answer is illustrated in Exhibit 5.8. When people believe they are under- or overrewarded, they experience negative emotions (called inequity tension). As we have pointed out throughout this chapter, emotions are the engines of motivation. In the case of inequity, people are motivated to reduce the emotional tension. Most people have a strong emotional response when they believe a situation is unfair, and this emotion nags them until they take steps to correct the perceived inequity.

There are several ways to try to reduce the inequity tension.[89] Let's consider each of these in the context of underreward inequity. One action is to reduce our inputs so the outcome/input ratio is similar to the higher-paid coworker. Some employees do this by working more slowly, offering fewer suggestions, and engaging in less organizational citizenship behaviour. A second action is to increase our outcomes. Some people who think they are underpaid ask for a pay raise. Others make unauthorized use of company resources. A third behavioural response is to increase the comparison other's inputs. You might subtly ask the better-paid coworker to do a larger share of the work, for instance. A fourth action is to reduce the comparison with other's outcomes. This might occur by ensuring that the coworker gets less desirable jobs or working conditions. Another action, although uncommon, is to ask the company to reduce the coworker's pay so it is the same as yours.

A fifth action is perceptual rather than behavioural. It involves changing our beliefs about the situation. For example you might believe that the coworker really is doing more

EXHIBIT 5.8

Motivational Effects of Inequity Perceptions

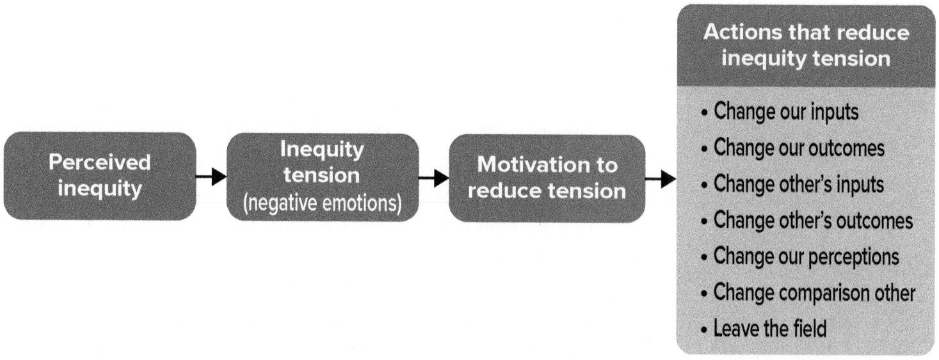

Foxconn received unwanted attention a few years ago for poor working conditions at its plants throughout China. Now, some employees are complaining that the Taiwan-based company has unfair pay practices. Foxconn pays lower wages to employees at its factory in Henan province and other provinces with high unemployment. But the company temporarily transfers many of these lower-paid workers to higher-wage plants, such as Shenzhen near Hong Kong, for training or to assist with higher workloads at those sites. The low-wage employees from Henan soon discover how much more their Shenzhen coworkers earn, which creates feelings of inequity. "It feels like Henan workers are second-class citizens at Foxconn," complains an Henan employee who was temporarily transferred to the higher-wage Shenzhen factory.[90]

© YM YIK/epa/Corbis

(e.g., working longer hours) for that higher pay. Alternatively, we might change our perceptions of the value of some outcomes. For example, you might initially feel it is unfair that a coworker gets more work-related travel than you do, but later you conclude that this travel is more inconvenient than desirable. A sixth action to reduce the inequity tension is to change the comparison other. Rather than compare yourself with the higher-paid coworker, you might increasingly compare yourself with a friend or neighbour who works in a similar job. Finally, if the inequity tension is strong enough and can't be reduced through other actions, you might leave the field. This occurs by moving to another department, joining another company, or keeping away from the work site where the overpaid coworker is located.

People who feel overreward inequity would reverse these actions. Some overrewarded employees reduce their feelings of inequity by working harder; others encourage the underrewarded coworker to work at a more leisurely pace. A common reaction, however, is that the overrewarded employee changes his or her perceptions to justify the more favourable outcomes, such as believing the assigned work is more difficult or his or her skills are more valuable than the lower-paid coworker. As the late author Pierre Burton once said: "I was underpaid for the first half of my life. I don't mind being overpaid for the second half."[91]

connect

How sensitive are you to inequities? Visit **connect.mcgrawhill.com** to assess your degree of equity sensitivity.

Individual Differences: Equity Sensitivity People vary in their *equity sensitivity*, that is, how strongly they feel about outcome/input ratios with others.[92] At one end of the equity sensitivity continuum are people who are tolerant of situations where they are underrewarded. They might still prefer equal outcome/input ratios, but they don't mind if others receive more than they do for the same inputs. In the middle are people who fit the standard equity theory model; they want their outcome/input ratio to be equal to the outcome/input ratio of the comparison other. At the other end of the equity sensitivity continuum are people who feel more comfortable when they receive proportionately more

OB by the NUMBERS

Not Paid What They're Worth[93]

77% of Canadian female executives polled say they have to work longer hours and harder than a male counterpart to attain executive positions.

46% of Canadians polled believe they are paid less than they deserve.

43% of Americans polled say they are underpaid for the work they do.

5% of Canadians polled believe they are paid more than they deserve.

4% of Americans polled say they are overpaid for the work they do

than others. They might accept having the same outcome/input ratio as others, but they would prefer receiving more than others performing the same work.

Evaluating Equity Theory Equity theory is widely studied and quite successful at predicting various situations involving feelings of workplace injustice.[94] However, equity theory isn't so easy to put into practice because it doesn't identify the comparison other and doesn't indicate which inputs or outcomes are most valuable to each employee. The best solution here is for leaders to know their employees well enough to minimize the risk of inequity feelings. Open communication is also a key, enabling employees to let decision makers know when they feel decisions are unfair. A second problem is that equity theory accounts for only some of our feelings of fairness or justice in the workplace. Experts now say that procedural justice is at least as important as distributive justice.

PROCEDURAL JUSTICE

At the beginning of this section we noted that fairness comes in two forms: distributive and procedural. *Procedural justice* refers to fairness of the procedures used to decide the distribution of resources. In other words, people evaluate fairness of the distribution of resources (distributive justice) as well as fairness of the conditions determining that distribution and its possible alteration (procedural justice).

There are several ways to improve procedural justice.[95] A good way to start is by giving employees 'voice' in the process; encourage them to present their facts and perspectives on the issue. Voice also provides a "value-expressive" function; employees tend to feel better after having an opportunity to speak their mind. Procedural justice is also higher when the decision maker is perceived as unbiased, relies on complete and accurate information, applies existing policies consistently, and has listened to all sides of the dispute. If employees still feel unfairness in the allocation of resources, their feelings tend to weaken if the company has a way of appealing the decision to a higher authority.

Finally, people usually feel less injustice when they are given a full explanation of the decision and their concerns are treated with respect. If employees believe a decision is unfair, refusing to explain how the decision was made could fuel their feelings of inequity. For instance, one Canadian study found that nonwhite nurses who experienced racism tended to file grievances only after experiencing disrespectful treatment in their attempt to resolve the racist situation. Another study reported that employees with repetitive strain injuries were more likely to file workers' compensation claims after experiencing disrespectful behaviour from management. A third recent study noted that employees have stronger feelings of injustice when the manager has a reputation of treating people unfairly most of the time.[96]

Consequences of Procedural Injustice Procedural justice has a strong influence on a person's emotions and motivation. Employees tend to experience anger towards the source of the injustice, which generates various response behaviours that scholars categorize as either withdrawal or aggression.[97] Notice how these response behaviours are similar to the fight-or-flight responses described earlier in the chapter regarding situations that activate our drive to defend. Research suggests that being treated unfairly threatens our self-concept and social status, particularly when others see that we have been unjustly treated. Employees retaliate to restore their self-esteem and reinstate their status and power in the relationship with the perpetrator of the injustice. Employees also engage in these counterproductive behaviours to educate the decision maker, thereby trying to minimize the likelihood of future injustices.[98]

Chapter Summary

LO1

Define employee engagement.

Employee engagement is defined as an individual's emotional and cognitive (rational) motivation, particularly a focused, intense, persistent, and purposive effort towards work-related goals. It is emotional involvement in, commitment to, and satisfaction with the work, as well as a high level of absorption in the work and sense of self-efficacy about performing the work.

LO2

Explain the role of human drives and emotions in employee motivation and behaviour.

Motivation consists of the forces within a person that affect his or her direction, intensity, and persistence of voluntary behaviour in the workplace. Drives (also called primary needs) are neural states that energize individuals to correct deficiencies or maintain an internal equilibrium. They are the "prime movers" of behaviour, activating emotions that put us in a state of readiness to act. Needs–goal-directed forces that people experience–are shaped by the individual's self-concept (including personality and values), social norms, and past experience.

LO3

Summarize Maslow's needs hierarchy, McClelland's learned needs theory, and four-drive theory and discuss their implications for motivating employees.

Maslow's needs hierarchy groups needs into a hierarchy of five levels and states that the lowest needs are initially most important but higher needs become more important as the lower ones are satisfied. Although very popular, the theory lacks research support because it wrongly assumes that everyone has the same hierarchy. The emerging evidence suggests that needs hierarchies vary from one person to the next according to their personal values.

McClelland's learned needs theory argues that needs can be strengthened through learning. The three needs studied in this respect have been need for achievement, need for power, and need for affiliation. Four-drive theory states that everyone has four innate drives–the drives to acquire, bond, comprehend, and defend. These drives activate emotions that people regulate through a skill set that considers social norms, past experience, and personal values. The main recommendation from four-drive theory is to ensure that individual jobs and workplaces provide a balanced opportunity to fulfill the four drives.

LO4

Discuss the expectancy theory model, including its practical implications.

Expectancy theory states that work effort is determined by the perception that effort will result in a particular level of performance (E-to-P expectancy), the perception that a specific behaviour or performance level will lead to specific outcomes (P-to-O expectancy), and the valences that the person feels for those outcomes. The E-to-P expectancy increases by improving the employee's ability and confidence to perform the job. The P-to-O expectancy increases by measuring performance accurately, distributing higher rewards to better performers, and showing employees that rewards are performance-based. Outcome valences increase by finding out what employees want and using these resources as rewards.

LO5

Outline organizational behaviour modification (OB Mod) and social cognitive theory and explain their relevance to employee motivation.

Organizational behaviour modification takes the behaviourist view that the environment teaches people to alter their behaviour so they maximize positive consequences and minimize adverse consequences. Antecedents are environmental stimuli that provoke (not necessarily cause) behaviour. Consequences are events following behaviour that influence its future occurrence. Consequences include positive reinforcement, punishment, negative reinforcement, and extinction. The schedules of reinforcement also influence behaviour.

Social cognitive theory states that much learning and motivation occurs by observing and modelling others as well as by anticipating the consequences of our behaviour. It suggests that people typically infer (rather than only directly experience) cause-effect relationships, anticipate the consequences of their actions, develop self-efficacy in performing behaviour, exercise personal control over their behaviour, and reflect on their direct experiences. The theory emphasizes self-regulation of individual behaviour, including self-reinforcement, which is the tendency of people to reward and punish themselves as a consequence of their actions.

LO6

Describe the characteristics of effective goal setting and feedback.

Goal setting is the process of motivating employees and clarifying their role perceptions by establishing performance objectives. Goals are more effective when they are SMARTER (specific, measurable, achievable, relevant, time-framed, exciting, and reviewed). Effective feedback is specific, relevant, timely, credible, and sufficiently frequent. Strengths-based coaching (also known as *appreciative coaching*) maximizing employee potential by focusing on their strengths rather than weaknesses. Employees usually prefer nonsocial feedback sources to learn about their progress towards goal accomplishment.

LO7

Summarize equity theory and describe ways to improve procedural justice.

Organizational justice consists of distributive justice (perceived fairness in the outcomes we receive relative to our contributions and the outcomes and contributions of others) and procedural justice (fairness of the procedures used to decide the distribution of resources). Equity theory has four elements: outcome/input ratio, comparison other, equity evaluation, and consequences of inequity. The theory also explains what people are motivated to do when they feel inequitably treated. Companies need to consider not only equity of the distribution of resources but also fairness in the process of making resource allocation decisions.

Key Terms

balanced scorecard (BSC), p. 125
distributive justice, p. 128
drives, p. 112
employee engagement, p. 110
equity theory, p. 129
expectancy theory, p. 119
four-drive theory, p. 116
goal setting, p. 124
Maslow's needs hierarchy theory, p. 113
multisource (360-degree) feedback, p. 127
need for achievement (nAch), p. 115
need for affiliation (nAff), p. 115
need for power (nPow), p. 116
needs, p. 112
organizational behaviour modification (OB Mod), p. 121
procedural justice, p. 128
self-reinforcement, p. 124
social cognitive theory, p. 124
strengths-based coaching, p. 127

Critical-Thinking Questions

1. Four-drive theory is conceptually different from Maslow's needs hierarchy in several ways. Describe these differences. At the same time, needs are based on drives, so the four drives should parallel the seven needs that Maslow identified (five in the hierarchy and two additional needs). Map Maslow's needs onto the four drives in four-drive theory.
2. Learned needs theory states that needs can be strengthened or weakened. How might a company strengthen the achievement needs of its management team?
3. Two friends who have just completed an organizational behaviour course at another college inform you that employees must fulfill their need for self-esteem and social esteem before they can reach their full potential through self-actualization. What theory are these friends referring to? How does their statement differ from what you learned about that theory in this chapter?
4. You just closed a deal with an organizational client and this helps you in achieving your target that was set for you by the unit. Use expectancy theory to discuss how the events that will follow may increase your motivation and engagement.
5. Describe a situation in which you used organizational behaviour modification to motivate someone's behaviour. What specifically did you do? What was the result?
6. Using your knowledge of the characteristics of effective goals, establish two meaningful goals related to your performance in this class.
7. Most people think they are "worth more" than they are paid. Furthermore, most employees seem to feel that they exhibit better leadership skills and interpersonal skills than others. Please comment on this human tendency.
8. A large organization has hired you as a consultant to identify day-to-day activities for middle managers to minimize distributive and procedural injustice. The company explains that employees have complained about distributive injustice because they have different opinions about what is fair (equity, equality, need) and what outcomes and inputs have the greatest value. They also experience procedural injustice due to misperceptions and differing expectations. Given these ambiguities, what would you recommend to middle managers?

Case Study: PREDICTING HARRY'S WORK EFFORT

By Robert J. Oppenheimer, Concordia University

Purpose This exercise is designed to help you to understand expectancy theory and how its elements affect a person's level of effort towards job performance.

Instructions This exercise may be completed either individually or in small teams of 4 or 5 people. When the individuals (or teams) have completed the exercise, the results will be discussed and compared with others in the class.

Read the following interview case. Then calculate whether Harry will engage in high or "just acceptable" performance effort under the conditions described. Valence scores range from −1.0 to +1.0. All expectancies are probabilities ranging from 0 (no chance) to 1.0 (definitely will occur). The effort level scores are calculated by multiplying each valence by the appropriate P-to-O expectancy, summing these results, then multiplying the sum by the E-to-P expectancy.

INTERVIEW WITH HARRY

Interviewer: Hi, Harry. I have been asked to talk to you about your job. Do you mind if I ask you a few questions?

Harry: No, not at all.

Interviewer: Thanks, Harry. What are the things that you would anticipate getting satisfaction from as a result of your job?

Harry: What do you mean?

Interviewer: Well, what is important to you with regard to your job here?

Harry: I guess most important is job security. As a matter of fact, I can't think of anything that is more important to me.

I think getting a raise would be nice, and a promotion would be even better.

Interviewer: Anything else that you think would be nice to get, or for that matter, that you would want to avoid?

Harry: I certainly would not want my buddies to make fun of me. We're pretty friendly, and this is really important to me.

Interviewer: Anything else?

Harry: No, not really. That seems to be it.

Interviewer: How satisfied do you think you would be with each of these?

Harry: What do you mean?

Interviewer: Well, assume that something that you would really like has a value of +1.0 and something you would really not like, that is you would want to avoid, has a value of −1.0, and something you are indifferent about has a value of 0.

Harry: OK. Getting a raise would have a value of .5; a promotion is more important, so I'd say .7; and having my buddies make fun of me, .9.

Interviewer: But, I thought you didn't want your buddies to make fun of you.

Harry: I don't.

Interviewer: But you gave it a value of .9.

Harry: Oh, I guess it should be −.9.

Interviewer: Ok, I just want to be sure I understand what you're saying. Harry, what do you think the chances are of these things happening?

Harry: That depends.

Interviewer: On what?

Harry: On whether my performance is high or just acceptable.

Interviewer: What if it is high?

Harry: I figure I stand about a 50–50 chance of getting a raise and/or a promotion, but I also think that there is a 90 percent chance that my buddies will make fun of me.

Interviewer: What about job security?

Harry: I am certain my job is secure here, whether my performance is high or just acceptable. I can't remember the last guy who was doing his job and got fired. But if my performance is just acceptable, my chances of a raise or promotion are about 10 percent. However, then the guys will not make fun of me. That I am certain about.

Interviewer: What is the likelihood of your performance level being high?

Harry: That depends. If I work very hard and put out a high degree of effort, I'd say that my chance of my performance being high is about 90 percent. But if I put out a low level of effort, you know—if I just take it easy—then I figure that the chances of my doing an acceptable job is about 80 percent.

Interviewer: Well, which would you do: put out a low level or a high level of effort?

Harry: With all the questions you asked me, you should be able to tell me.

Interviewer: You may be right!

Harry: Yeah? That's nice. Hey, if you don't have any other questions, I'd like to join the guys for coffee.

Interviewer: OK, thanks for your time.

Harry: You're welcome.

Discussion Question

1. Use the expectancy theory model to predict Harry's motivation to achieve high or "just acceptable" performance in his job. Identify and discuss the factors that influence this motivation.

Class Exercise: NEEDS PRIORITY EXERCISE

Purpose This class exercise is designed to help you understand employee needs in the workplace.

Instructions (Small Class) *Step 1:* The table below lists in alphabetical order 16 characteristics of the job or work environment. Working alone, use the far-left column to rank-order the importance of these characteristics to you personally. Write in "1" beside the most important characteristic, "2" for the second most important, and so on through to "16" for the least important characteristic on this list.

Step 2: Identify any three (3) of these work attributes that you believe have the largest score differences between Generation Y (Millennial) male and female postsecondary students across Canada (i.e., those born in 1980 or after). Indicate which gender you think identifies that attribute as more important.

Step 3: Students are assigned to teams, where they compare each other's rank-order results as well as perceived gender differences in needs. Note reasons for the largest variations in rankings and be prepared to discuss these reasons with the entire class. Students should pay close attention to different needs, self-concepts, and various forms of diversity (ethnicity, profession, age, etc.) within your class to identify possible explanations for any variation of results across students.

Step 4: The instructor will provide results of a recent large-scale survey of Canadian Generation-Y/Millennial postsecondary students (i.e., born in 1980 or after). When these results are presented, identify the reasons for any noticeable differences in the class. Relate the differences to your understanding of the emerging view of employee needs and drives in work settings. For gender differences, discuss reasons why men and women might differ on these work-related attributes.

Instructions (Large Class) *Step 1* and *Step 2*: Same as above.

Step 3: The instructor will ask students, by a show of hands (or use of classroom technology), to identify their top-ranked attributes as well as the attributes believed to have the greatest gender differences among Gen-Y Canadians.

Step 4: Same as above.

Personal Ranking of Work-Related Attributes

Attributes of Work (Listed Alphabetically)	Your Ranking (1 = most important)
Challenging work	
Commitment to social responsibility	
Good health and benefits plan	
Good initial salary level	
Good people to report to	
Good people to work with	
Good training opportunities/developing new skills	
Good variety of work	
Job security	
Opportunities for advancement in position	
Opportunities to have a personal impact	
Opportunities to have a social impact	
Opportunity to travel	
Organization is a leader in its field	
Strong commitment to employee diversity	
Work–life balance	

Self-Assessment: NEEDS-STRENGTH QUESTIONNAIRE

Although everyone has the same innate drives, secondary or learned needs vary from one person to the next in the same situation. This self-assessment estimates the strength you feel on specific needs. Read each of the statements below and check the response that you believe best reflects your position regarding each statement. Then use the scoring key in Appendix B at the end of the book to calculate your results. To receive a meaningful estimate of your need strength, you need to answer each item honestly and with reflection on your personal experiences. Class discussion will focus on the meaning of the needs measured in this self-assessment as well as their relevance in the workplace.

Personal Needs Questionnaire

How accurately do each of the following statements describe you?	Very accurate description of me	Moderately accurate	Neither accurate nor inaccurate	Moderately inaccurate	Very inaccurate description of me
1. I would rather be myself than be well thought of.	○	○	○	○	○
2. I'm the type of person who never gives up.	○	○	○	○	○
3. When the opportunity occurs, I want to be in charge.	○	○	○	○	○
4. I try not to say things that others don't like to hear.	○	○	○	○	○
5. I find it difficult to talk about my ideas if they are contrary to group opinion.	○	○	○	○	○
6. I tend to take control of things.	○	○	○	○	○
7. I am not highly motivated to succeed.	○	○	○	○	○
8. I usually disagree with others only if I know my friends will back me up.	○	○	○	○	○
9. I try to be the very best at what I do.	○	○	○	○	○
10. I seldom make excuses or apologize for my behaviour.	○	○	○	○	○
11. If anyone criticizes me, I can take it.	○	○	○	○	○
12. I try to outdo others.	○	○	○	○	○
13. I seldom change my opinion when people disagree with me.	○	○	○	○	○
14. I try to achieve more than what others have accomplished.	○	○	○	○	○
15. To get along and be liked, I tend to be what people expect me to be.	○	○	○	○	○

Sources: Adapted from instruments described and/or presented in L. R. Goldberg, J. A. Johnson, H. W. Eber, R. Hogan, M. C. Ashton, C. R. Cloninger, and H. C. Gough, "The International Personality Item Pool and the Future of Public-Domain Personality Measures," *Journal of Research in Personality* 40 (2006), pp. 84–96; H. J. Martin, "A Revised Measure of Approval Motivation and Its Relationship to Social Desirability," *Journal of Personality Assessment* 48 (1984), pp. 508–519.

SELF-ASSESSMENTS FOR CHAPTER 5

SELF-ASSESSMENT NAME	DESCRIPTION	LOCATION
To what extent do you value motivating jobs?	Assesses the value you place on a job that is motivating.	Page 136 connect
How strong are your need for achievement and need for affiliation?	Assesses your need for achievement versus affiliation.	connect
What is your goal orientation?	Estimates whether you have more of a learning or avoidance goal orientation.	connect
How sensitive are you to inequities?	Estimates your degree of equity sensitivity.	connect
Needs-Strength Questionnaire	Estimates the strength you feel on specific learned needs.	connect

Shopify has a highly motivated workforce, driven by enriched jobs and rewards aligned with the company's success.

Courtesy of Shopify. Photo by Ben Courtice.

Chapter 6

Applied Performance Practices

LEARNING OBJECTIVES

After reading this chapter, you should be able to:

LO1. Discuss the meaning of money and identify several individual, team, and organizational-level performance-based rewards.

LO2. Describe five ways to improve reward effectiveness.

LO3. List the advantages and disadvantages of job specialization.

LO4. Diagram the job characteristics model and describe three ways to improve employee motivation through job design.

LO5. Define empowerment and identify strategies that support empowerment.

LO6. Describe the five elements of self-leadership and identify specific personal and work environment influences on self-leadership.

Shopify has become one of the world's most popular ecommerce platforms. Initially designed for small businesses, it is also the online retail centre for some of the world's best-known brands (e.g., Google, Budweiser, Gatorade, Wikipedia, Pixar, Tesla Motors). Shopify Inc., the Ottawa-based company that developed its namesake ecommerce service, is Canada's first $1-billion Internet start-up since the dot-com crash more than a dozen years ago. In fact, it is one of only 39 tech companies in North America with such a lofty valuation.

What's the secret to Shopify's success? The main competitive advantage in any technology company is a skilled, highly motivated workforce. Shopify is particularly renowned for motivating employees through enriched jobs. "Shopify allows you to work on exciting, challenging projects with some amazingly talented people," says user interface designer Ryan Langlois. Developer Matt Helm agrees. "You get to work on some really interesting projects, with new technologies that you don't get to work with anywhere else." Office admin staffer Laura Larcher also appreciates the meaningful work: "It's very rare that you can come in to a workspace where you can do what you love and feel inspired at the same time without any boundaries," she says.

Along with the variety and significance of their work, Shopify employees are motivated by the high degree of job autonomy. "I have a lot of freedom here," says Tariq Zaid, Shopify's Director of Strategic Initiatives. "I can be very creative, and people only embrace that." Employee freedom extends beyond the job itself to the work area. The company provides an annual allowance so employees have funds to personalize their workspace as they please.

Shopify offers a variety of rewards to further motivate employees. Everyone gets free meals at the office, $250 annually for health-related gear or activities, company-wide trips, and a two-hour housecleaning service every two weeks. Shopify distributes a large monthly bonus which is determined by how helpful employees have been to coworkers, customers, and other stakeholders. Specifically, Shopify scans its online communication platform, called Unicorn, where employees chat about their projects, triumphs, and tribulations. The posts and discussions reveal which employees have made the greatest contribution to others. Employees are also connected to Shopify's success through a generous share ownership plan. In fact, employees own one-fifth of the company. "This is a place where we really encourage people to act like owners," says Shopify's chief platform officer, Harley Finkelstein.[1]

Shopify's incredible success is attributed to a talented group of people who are highly motivated to keep the technology company at the front of the ecommerce revolution. This motivation is supported by enriched jobs, performance-based rewards, and an empowering work environment. All three topics are discussed in this chapter, along with self-leadership, which is also apparent among Shopify's employees.

The chapter begins by examining the meaning of money. This is followed by an overview of financial reward practices, including the different types of rewards and how to implement rewards effectively. Next, we look at the dynamics of job design, including specific job design strategies for motivating employees. We then consider the elements of empowerment, as well as conditions that support empowerment. The final part of the chapter explains how employees manage their own performance through self-leadership.

connect

What is your attitude towards money? See page **160** or visit **connect.mcgrawhill.com** to assess how much you budget, respect, and worry about money.

The Meaning of Money in the Workplace

LO1

Rewarding people with money is one of the oldest and certainly the most widespread applied performance practices. At the most basic level, money and other financial rewards represent a form of exchange; employees provide their labour, skill, and knowledge in return for money and benefits from the organization. From this perspective, money and related rewards align employee goals with organizational goals. This concept of economic exchange can be found across cultures. The word for *pay* in Malaysian and Slovak means "to replace a loss"; in Hebrew and Swedish it means "making equal."[2]

However, money is much more than an object of compensation for an employee's contribution to organizational objectives. Money relates to our needs, our emotions, and our self-concept. It is a symbol of achievement and status, a motivator, a source of enhanced or reduced anxiety, and an influence on our propensity to make ethical or risky decisions.[3] According to one source, "Money is probably the most emotionally meaningful object in contemporary life: only food and sex are its close competitors as common carriers of such strong and diverse feelings, significance, and strivings."[4]

The meaning of money varies considerably from one person to the next.[5] Studies report that money is viewed as a symbol of status and prestige, as a source of security, as a source of evil, or as a source of anxiety or feelings of inadequacy. It is considered a taboo topic in many social settings. Recent studies also examine money as both a "tool" (i.e., money is valued because it is an instrument for acquiring other things of value) and as a "drug" (i.e., money is an object of addictive value in itself).

One large-scale study revealed that money generates a variety of emotions, most of which are negative, such as anxiety, depression, anger, and helplessness.[6] A widely studied model of money attitudes suggests that people have a strong "money ethic" when they believe that money is not evil; that it is a symbol of achievement, respect, and power; and that it should be budgeted carefully. These attitudes towards money influence an individual's ethical conduct, organizational citizenship, and many other behaviours and attitudes.[7]

The meaning of money seems to differ between men and women.[8] One recent study reported that men tend to view money as a symbol of power and status, whereas women are more likely to view its value in terms of things for which it can be exchanged. An earlier study revealed that in almost all 43 countries studied men attach more importance or value to money than do women. The meaning of money also seems to vary across cultures.[9] People in countries with high power distance (such as China and Japan) tend to have a high respect and priority for money, whereas people in countries with a strong egalitarian culture (such as Denmark, Austria, and Israel) are discouraged from openly talking about money or displaying their personal wealth. One study suggests that Swiss culture values saving money whereas Italian culture places more value on spending it.

The motivational effect of money is much greater than was previously believed, and this effect is due more to its symbolic value than to what it can buy.[10] Philosopher John Stuart Mill made this observation 150 years ago when he wrote: "The love of money is not only one of the strongest moving forces of human life, but money is, in many cases, desired in and for itself."[11] People who earn higher pay tend to have higher job performance because the higher paycheque enhances their self-concept evaluation. Others have noted that the symbolic value of money depends on how it is distributed in the organization and how many people receive that financial reward.

Overall, current organizational behaviour knowledge indicates that money is much more than a means of exchange between employer and employee. It fulfills a variety of needs, influences emotions, and shapes or represents a person's self-concept. These findings are important to remember when the employer is distributing financial rewards in the workplace. Over the next few pages, we look at various reward practices and how to improve the implementation of performance-based rewards.

Financial Reward Practices

Financial rewards come in many forms, which can be organized into the four specific objectives identified in Exhibit 6.1: membership and seniority, job status, competencies, and performance.

MEMBERSHIP- AND SENIORITY-BASED REWARDS

Membership-based and seniority-based rewards (sometimes called "pay for pulse") represent the largest part of most paycheques. Some employee benefits, such as the free meals and housekeeping services provided for employees at Shopify, are provided equally to everyone, whereas others increase with seniority. For example, employees with 10 or more years of service at the Paul Sherrer Institut near Zurich, Switzerland, receive an annual loyalty bonus equal to a half month's salary; those with 20 or more years of service at the natural and engineering sciences research centre receive a bonus equal to a full month's salary.[12]

These membership- and seniority-based rewards potentially attract job applicants (particularly those who desire predictable income) and reduce turnover. However, they do not directly motivate job performance; on the contrary, they discourage poor performers from seeking work better suited to their abilities. Instead, the good performers are lured to better-paying jobs. Some of these rewards are also "golden handcuffs"–they discourage employees from quitting because of deferred bonuses or generous benefits that are not available elsewhere. However golden handcuffs potentially weaken job performance because they generate continuance rather than affective commitment (see Chapter 4).

JOB STATUS–BASED REWARDS

Almost every organization rewards employees to some extent on the basis of the status or worth of the jobs they occupy. In some parts of the world, companies measure job worth through **job evaluation.** Most job evaluation methods give higher value to jobs that require more skill and effort, have more responsibility, and have more difficult working conditions.[13] The higher worth assigned to a job, the higher the minimum and maximum pay for people in that job. Along with receiving higher pay, employees with more valued jobs sometimes receive larger offices, company-paid vehicles, and other perks.

job evaluation Systematically rating the worth of jobs within an organization by measuring their required skill, effort, responsibility, and working conditions.

EXHIBIT 6.1 **Reward Objectives, Advantages, and Disadvantages**

Reward objective	Sample rewards	Advantages	Disadvantages
Membership/ seniority	• Fixed pay • Most employee benefits • Paid time off	• May attract applicants • Minimizes stress of insecurity • Reduces turnover	• Doesn't directly motivate performance • May discourage poor performers from leaving • "Golden handcuffs" may undermine performance
Job status	• Promotion-based pay increase • Status-based benefits	• Tries to maintain internal equity • Minimizes pay discrimination • Motivates employees to compete for promotions	• Encourages hierarchy, which may increase costs and reduce responsiveness • Reinforces status differences • Motivates job competition and exaggerated job worth
Competencies	• Pay increase based on competency • Skill-based pay	• Improves workforce flexibility • Tends to improve quality • Motivates career development	• Relies on subjective measurement of competencies • Skill-based pay plans are expensive
Task performance	• Commissions • Merit pay • Gainsharing • Profit sharing • Share Options	• Motivates task performance • Attracts performance-oriented applicants • Organizational rewards create an ownership culture • Pay variability may avoid layoffs during downturns	• May weaken job content motivation • May distance reward giver from receiver • May discourage creativity • Tends to address symptoms, not underlying causes of behaviour

Job status-based rewards try to improve feelings of fairness, such as that people in higher-valued jobs should get higher pay. These rewards also motivate employees to compete for promotions. However, at a time when companies are trying to be more cost-efficient and responsive to the external environment, job status-based rewards potentially do the opposite by encouraging a bureaucratic hierarchy. These rewards also reinforce a status mentality, whereas Generation-X and Generation-Y employees expect a more egalitarian workplace. Furthermore, status-based pay potentially motivates employees to compete with each other for higher-status jobs and to raise the value of their own jobs by exaggerating job duties and hoarding resources.[14]

COMPETENCY-BASED REWARDS

Over the past two decades, many companies have shifted reward priorities from job status to skills, knowledge, and other competencies that lead to superior performance. The most common practices identify a list of competencies relevant across all job groups as well as competencies specific to each broad job group. Employees progress through the pay range within that job group based on how well they demonstrate each of those competencies.[15] *Skill-based pay* plans are a more specific variation of competency-based rewards in which people receive higher pay based on their mastery of measurable skills.[16] High Liner Foods, the Nova Scotia-based frozen seafood company, assigns pay rates to employees based on the number and difficulty of skills they have mastered. "We're setting our sites up for a skill-based pay system, so as employees learn and demonstrate certain skills, they move into a different pay bracket," explains Art Christianson, senior vice president of High Liner's U.S. plant operations.

Competency-based rewards motivate employees to learn new skills.[17] This tends to support a more flexible workforce, increase employee creativity, and allow employees to be more adaptive to new practices in a dynamic environment. Product or service quality also tends to improve because employees with multiple skills are more likely to understand the work process and know how to improve it. However, competency-based pay plans have not always worked out as well as promised by their advocates. They are often over-designed, making it difficult to communicate these plans to employees. Competency definitions tend to be abstract, which raises questions about fairness when employers are relying on these definitions to award pay increases. Skill-based pay systems measure specific skills, so they are usually more objective. However, they are expensive because employees spend more time learning new tasks.[18]

PERFORMANCE-BASED REWARDS

Performance-based rewards have existed since Babylonian days 4,000 years ago, but their popularity has increased dramatically over the past few decades. Here is an overview of some of the most popular individual, team, and organizational performance-based rewards.

Individual Rewards Many employees receive individual bonuses or other rewards for accomplishing a specific task or exceeding annual performance goals. As was described in the opening case study to this chapter, the Ottawa-based ecommerce technology company

OB by the NUMBERS

Global Variations in Performance-based Pay[19]

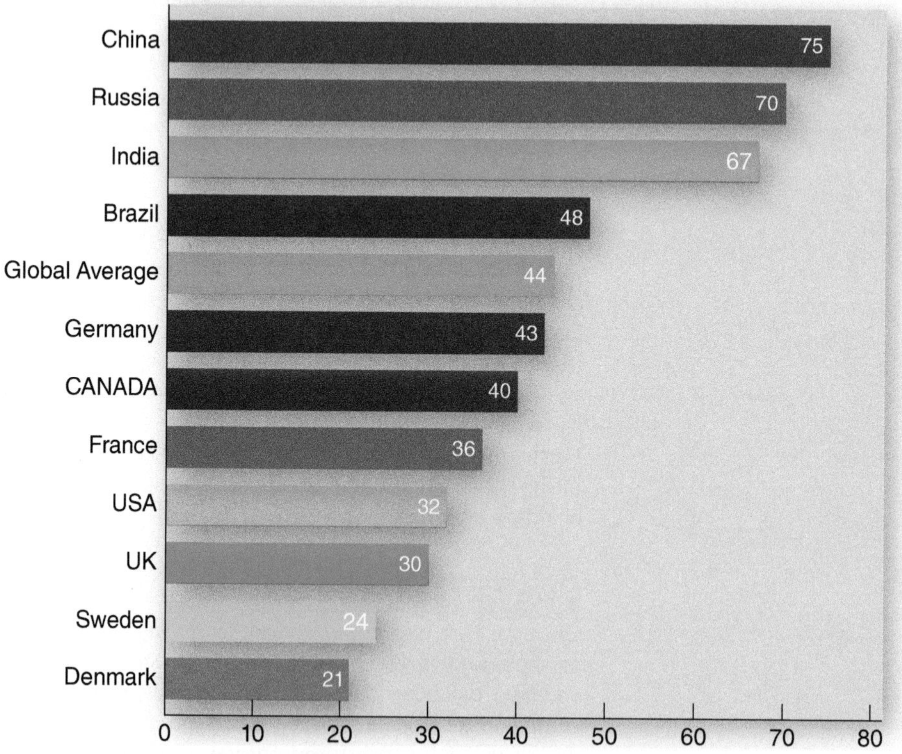

Percentage of employees surveyed in selected countries who say their pay is "variable, such that a portion is dependent upon your individual performance/productivity targets." Data were collected in 2013 from more than 120,000 people in 31 countries for Kelly Services. The global average includes respondents from all 31 countries, not just those shown in this chart.

Shopify offers employees monthly bonuses based on how much they have helped coworkers, customers, or other stakeholders. Housekeeping staff in many hotels are paid a piece rate—a specific amount earned for each room cleaned. Other hotels pay an hourly rate plus a per-room bonus. Real estate agents and other salespeople typically earn *commissions*, in which their pay depends on the sales volume they generate.

Team Rewards Organizations have shifted their focus from individuals to teams over the past two decades, and accompanying this transition has been the introduction of more team-based rewards. Nucor Inc., the American steelmaker that employs 2,500 people in Canada, relies heavily on team-based rewards. The steelmaker's employees earn bonuses which can exceed half their total pay based on how much steel is produced by the team. This team-based bonus system also includes penalties. If employees catch a bad batch of steel before it leaves the mini-mill, they lose their bonus for that shipment. But if a bad batch makes its way to the customer, the team loses three times its usual bonus.[20]

gainsharing plan A team-based reward that calculates bonuses from the work unit's cost savings and productivity improvement.

Another form of team-based performance reward, called a **gainsharing plan,** calculates bonuses from the work unit's cost savings and productivity improvement. Whole Foods Market uses gainsharing to motivate cost savings in its grocery stores. The food retailer assigns a monthly payroll budget to teams operating various departments within a store. If payroll money is unspent at the end of the month, the surplus is divided among members of that Whole Foods Market team.[21] Several American hospitals have cautiously introduced a form of gainsharing whereby physicians and other medical staff in a medical unit (cardiology, orthopaedics, etc.) are collectively rewarded for cost reductions in surgery and patient care. These cost reductions mainly occur through negotiating better prices of materials.[22] Gainsharing plans tend to improve team dynamics, knowledge sharing, and pay satisfaction. They also create a reasonably strong link between effort and performance because much of the cost reduction and labour efficiency is within the team's control.[23]

Organizational Rewards Along with individual and team-based rewards, many firms rely on organizational-level rewards to motivate employees. Texas-based Hilcorp Energy Company launched Double Drive, a program that rewards every employee with a new car or $50,000 equivalent cash if they met three targets in five years: doubling the company's value, its oil field production rate, and its net oil and gas reserves. The company achieved these targets. Hilcorp's current companywide incentive is $100,000 to every employee if the company doubles these three results again over the next five years. Another unique organizational reward is the "growth-sharing" plan negotiated by the British Columbia government with most of its employees. Government employees receive a small negotiated pay increase, but a larger increase will occur if the province's economic growth exceeds the rate projected by an independent panel.[24]

employee share ownership plans (ESOPs) A reward system that encourages employees to buy company shares.

Shopify aligns employee behaviour with the company's success through an **employee share ownership plan (ESOP).** Most ESOPs encourage employees to buy company shares, usually at a discounted price. Some companies are owned entirely by employees, such as the Great Western Brewing Company in Saskatchewan. Whether fully or partly owned by employees, the financial reward of ESOPs occurs in the form of dividends and market appreciation of the shares.

share options A reward system that gives employees the right to purchase company shares at a future date at a predetermined price.

While ESOPs involve purchasing company shares, **share options** give employees the right to purchase company shares at a predetermined price up to a fixed expiration date. For example, an employer might offer employees the right to purchase 100 shares at $50 at any time between two and six years from now. If the share price is, say, $60 two years later, employees could earn $10 from these options, or they could wait up to six years for the share price to rise further. If the share price never rises above $50 during that time, they are "out of the money" and employees would just let the options expire. The intention of share options is to motivate employees to make the company more profitable, thereby raising the company's share price and enabling them to reap the value above the exercise price of the share options.

profit-sharing plan A reward system that pays bonuses to employees on the basis of the previous year's level of corporate profits.

Another type of organizational-level reward is the **profit-sharing plan,** in which employees receive a percentage of the previous year's company profits. An interesting application of this reward occurs at Svenska Handelsbanken AB. In years when the Swedish bank is more profitable than the average of competing banks, it transfers one-third of the difference in profits to an employee fund. Every employee receives one share in the fund for each year of service, which can be cashed out at 60 years of age (even if they continue working for the bank beyond that age).[25]

Courtesy of Lee Valley Tools Ltd.

Lee Valley Tools, the iconic Ottawa-based manufacturer and retailer of quality woodworking and gardening tools, has a profit-sharing plan that aligns employee behaviour with the company's success. Lee Valley distributes 25 percent of its annual profits to its 850 employees, with the CEO receiving the same amount of profit-sharing bonus as the lowest-paid employee. Only employees with less than two years' service receive a smaller payout. "You get tremendous loyalty from employees if they enjoy their work and they are participating in the income," says Lee Valley Tools' founder and chairman Leonard Lee. "Our staff know that if they save a box, it saves us a dollar. And they'll get 25 cents out of that dollar."[26]

Evaluating Organizational-Level Rewards How effective are organizational-level rewards? Research indicates that ESOPs and share options tend to create an ownership culture in which employees feel aligned with the organization's success.[27] Profit sharing tends to create less of an ownership culture, but it has the advantage of automatically adjusting employee compensation with the firm's prosperity, thereby reducing the need for layoffs or negotiated pay reductions during recessions.

The main problem with ESOPs, share options, and profit sharing is that employees often perceive a weak connection between individual effort and corporate profits or the value of company shares. Even in small firms, the company's share price or profitability is influenced by economic conditions, competition, and other factors beyond the employee's immediate control. This low individual performance-to-outcome expectancy suppresses the incentive's motivational effect. Another concern is that some companies (more in the United States than in Canada) use ESOPs as a replacement for employee pension plans. This is a risky strategy because these pension plans lack diversification. If the company goes bankrupt, employees lose both their jobs and a large portion of their retirement nest egg.[28]

Improving Reward Effectiveness

LO2

Performance-based rewards have come under attack over the years for discouraging creativity, distancing management from employees, distracting employees from the meaningfulness of the work itself, and being quick fixes that ignore the true causes of poor performance. Recent studies have even found that very large rewards (relative to the usual income) can result in lower, rather than higher, performance.[29] While these issues have kernels of truth under specific circumstances, they do not necessarily mean that we should abandon performance-based pay. On the contrary, top-performing companies are more likely to have performance-based (or competency-based) rewards, which is consistent with evidence that these rewards are one of the high-performance work practices (see Chapter 1).[30] Reward systems do motivate most employees, but only under the right conditions. Here are some of the more important strategies for improving reward effectiveness.

Link Rewards to Performance Organizational behaviour modification theory and expectancy theory (Chapter 5) both recommend that employees with better performance should be rewarded more than those with poorer performance. Unfortunately, this simple principle seems to be unusually difficult to apply. Few employees see a relationship between job performance and the amount of pay they and coworkers receive. One recent global survey reported that only 42 percent of employees globally say they think there is a clear link between their job performance and pay. Only 25 percent of Swedish employees, 27 percent of Canadian employees, and 36 percent of American employees see a pay-performance link.[31]

How can companies improve the pay-performance linkage? Inconsistencies and bias can be minimized through gainsharing, ESOPs, and other plans that use objective performance measures. Where subjective measures of performance are necessary, companies should rely on multiple sources of information. Companies also need to apply rewards soon after the performance occurs, and in a large-enough dose (such as a bonus rather than a pay increase), so that employees experience positive emotions when they receive the reward.[32]

Ensure That Rewards Are Relevant Companies need to align rewards with performance within the employee's control. The more employees see a "line of sight" between their daily actions and the reward, the more they are motivated to improve performance. BHP Billiton applies this principle by rewarding bonuses to top executives based on the company's overall performance, whereas front-line mining staff earn bonuses based on the production

Debating Point:

IS IT TIME TO DITCH THE PERFORMANCE REVIEW?

More than 90 percent of Fortune 500 companies use performance reviews to link rewards to the performance of some or most employees. Advocates argue that these evaluations provide critical documentation, communication, and decisions necessary to reward contributors and remove those who fail to reach the minimum standard. Indeed, it can be difficult to fire poor performers in some jurisdictions unless the company has systematically documented the employee's shortcomings. Evaluations provide clear feedback about job performance, so employees know where they stand and are motivated to improve. Performance reviews have their faults, but supporters say these problems can be overcome by using objective information (such as goal setting and 360-degree feedback) rather than subjective ratings, being supportive and constructive throughout the review, and providing informal performance feedback throughout the year.

Several experts—and most employees—disagree.[33] In spite of mountains of advice over the years on how to improve performance reviews, this activity seems to inflict more damage than deliver benefits. Apple Inc. trashed its formal performance evaluation process a decade ago. Zappos and dozens of other companies have since followed Apple's lead. Most companies that ditched their performance reviews never brought them back again.

According to various polls and studies, performance reviews are stressful, morale sapping, and dysfunctional events that typically descend into political arenas and paperwork bureaucracies. Even when managers actively coach employees throughout the year, the annual appraisal meeting places them in the awkward and incompatible role as an all-powerful and all-knowing evaluator. Another issue is that rating employees, even on several factors, grossly distorts the complexity of performance in most jobs. A single score on customer service, for instance, would hide variations in knowledge, empathy, efficiency, and other elements of service. "Who am I to tell somebody they're a three out of five?" asks Don Quist, CEO of the Hood Group. Quist is so opposed to performance reviews that employees at the Edmonton, Alberta, engineering firm were issued badges with a big "X" through the phrase "Employee Evaluation."[34]

Many perceptual biases—halo, recency, primacy, stereotyping, fundamental attribution error—are common in performance reviews and difficult to remove through training. Seemingly objective practices such as goal setting and 360-degree feedback are fraught with bias and subjectivity. Various studies have also found that managers across the organization use different criteria to rate employee performance. One study discovered that management's evaluations of 5,000 customer service employees were unrelated to ratings that customers gave those employees. "The managers might as well have been rating the employees' shoe sizes, for all the customers cared," quipped one investigator.[35]

Is there an alternative to the performance evaluation? One repeated suggestion is to conduct "performance previews" or "feedforward" events that focus on future goals and advice. Instead of a postmortem dissection of the employee's failings, managers use past performance as a foundation for development.[36] Also, substantial rewards should never be based on performance reviews or similar forms of evaluation. Instead, they should be linked to measurable team and organizational levels outcomes and judiciously to individual indicators (sales, project completion, etc.), where appropriate.

output, safety performance, and other local indicators. Reward systems also need to correct for situational factors. Salespeople in one region may have higher sales because the economy is stronger there than elsewhere, so sales bonuses need to be adjusted for such economic factors.

Use Team Rewards for Interdependent Jobs Team rewards are better than individual rewards when employees work in highly interdependent jobs because it is difficult to measure individual performance in these situations. Nucor Corp. relies on team-based bonuses for this reason; producing steel is a team effort, so employees earn bonuses based on team performance. Team rewards also encourage co operation, which is more important when work is highly interdependent. A third benefit of team rewards is that they tend to support employee preferences for team-based work. One concern, however, is that employees (particularly the most productive employees) in Canada and many other low-collectivism cultures prefer rewards based on their individual performance rather than team performance.[37]

Ensure That Rewards Are Valued It seems obvious that rewards work best when they are valued. Yet companies sometimes make false assumptions about what employees want, with unfortunate consequences. For instance, a manager at one Canadian firm honoured an employee's 25th year of service by buying her a box of Timbits to be shared with other staff. The employee was insulted. She privately complained later to coworkers that she would rather receive nothing than "a piddling box of doughnuts."[38] The solution, of course, is to ask employees what they value. Campbell Soup did this several years ago at its Canadian distribution centres. Executives thought the employees would ask for more money in a special team reward program. Instead, distribution staff said the most valued reward was a leather jacket with the Campbell Soup logo on the back. The leather jackets cost much less, yet were worth much more than the financial bonus the company had intended to distribute.[39]

Watch Out for Unintended Consequences Performance-based reward systems sometimes have an unexpected–and undesirable–effect on employee behaviours.[40] Consider the pizza company that decided to reward its drivers for on-time delivery. The plan got more hot pizzas to customers on time, but it also increased the accident rates of the company's drivers because the incentive motivated them to drive recklessly.[41] Global Connections 6.1 describes a few other examples in which reward systems had unintended consequences. The solution here is to carefully think through the consequences of rewards and, where possible, test incentives in a pilot project before applying them across the organization.

Financial rewards come in many forms and, as was mentioned at the outset of this section, influence employees in complex ways. But money isn't the only thing that motivates people to join an organization and perform effectively. One survey reported that 58 percent of the 7,000 Canadians polled are prepared to accept a lesser role or lower wage to perform work that is more meaningful to them or their organization. "The reward of doing a job well is in having done the job. The money is a by-product," says Richard Currie, who built Loblaws into one of the top ten mass retailing companies in the world and is currently Chancellor of the University of New Brunswick.[46] In other words, companies motivate employees mainly by designing interesting and challenging jobs, which is the topic we discuss next.

Job Design Practices

LO3

How do you build a better job? That question has challenged organizational behaviour experts as well as psychologists, engineers, and economists for a few centuries. Some jobs have very few tasks and usually require very little skill. Other jobs are immensely complex and require years of experience and learning to master them. From one extreme to the other, jobs have different effects on work efficiency and employee motivation. The challenge, at least from the organization's perspective, is to find the right combination so that work is performed efficiently but employees are engaged and satisfied.[47] This objective requires careful **job design**–the process of assigning tasks to a job, including the interdependency of those tasks with other jobs. A *job* is a set of tasks performed by one person. To understand this issue more fully, let's begin by describing early job design efforts aimed at increasing work efficiency through job specialization.

job design The process of assigning tasks to a job, including the interdependency of those tasks with other jobs.

Global Connections 6.1:

WHEN REWARDS GO WRONG

There is an old saying that "what gets rewarded gets done." But what companies reward isn't always what they had intended their employees to do. Here are a few dramatic examples of how performance-based rewards produce unintended consequences:

- Until a few years ago, most public transit bus drivers in Santiago, Chile, were paid by the number of fare-paying passengers. This incentive system motivated drivers to begin their route on time, take shorter breaks, and drive efficiently, but it also had horrendous unintended consequences. To take on more passengers, bus drivers aggressively raced with competing busses to the next passenger waiting area, sometimes cutting off each other and risking the safety of people in nearby vehicles. Drivers reduced time at each stop by speeding off before passengers were safely on board. They also left the bus doors open, resulting in many passenger injuries and fatalities during the journey. Some drivers drove past waiting areas if there was only one person waiting. Studies reported that Santiago's transit busses caused one fatal accident every three days, and that drivers paid per-passenger caused twice as many traffic accidents as drivers paid per hour. Santiago now pays drivers partly by the distance travelled. Unfortunately, drivers are no longer motivated to ensure that passengers pay the fare (about one-third are freeloaders) and they sometimes skip passenger stops altogether when they are behind schedule.[42]
- A commercial laundry plant recently introduced an attendance reward in which employees with perfect monthly attendance (no unexcused absences and no lateness more than 5 minutes) had their named entered in a draw for a $75 gift card. Employees with perfect attendance records over six months had a chance to receive a further $100 gift card. The attendance reward had the opposite effect than expected. Employees who were previously tardy reduced their lateness by only a couple of minutes, so they were just within the allowable 5 minutes. Those with previously excellent records had higher tardiness and absenteeism and 6 percent lower productivity when the program was active. These workers were demotivated by the attendance award, apparently upset that the company didn't recognize their earlier good performance and was now unfairly rewarding those who are still tardy (but within the 5-minute limit). Another effect was that after employees became ineligible for the monthly reward (they were late or absent once), their tardiness record shot up and productivity dropped. A third effect of the reward was that more employees called in sick, which enabled them to remain eligible for the monthly award.[43]
- Several years ago, a food processing plant discovered that insect parts were somehow getting into the frozen peas during processing. To solve this serious problem, management decided to reward employees for any insect parts they found in the peas. The incentive worked! Employees found hundreds of insect parts that they dutifully turned in for the bonus. The problem was that many of these insect pieces came from the employees' backyards, not from the production line.[44]
- Integrated steel companies often rewarded managers for increased labour efficiency. The lower the labour-hours required to produce a ton of steel, the larger the manager's bonus. Unfortunately, steel firms usually didn't count the work of outside contractors in the formula, so the reward system motivated managers to hire expensive contractors in the production process. By employing more contractors, the managers received a healthy bonus even though the true cost of production increased, not decreased.[45]

© Ximena Salazar Aravena

When transit bus drivers in Santiago, Chile, were paid per passenger, they engaged in dangerous driving to transport as many passengers as possible.

JOB DESIGN AND WORK EFFICIENCY

Li Mei's first job at a toy factory in China's Pearl River Delta involved using four pens to paint the eyes on dolls. The 18-year-old was given exactly 7.2 seconds to paint each doll–about 4,000 every day. Eventually, the paint fumes made Li Mei too faint to work, so she was moved to another department that stamped out plastic doll parts. Again, the work was repetitive: open the machine, insert the plastic, press the machine, remove the plastic. Li Mei repeated this cycle 3,000 times each day. After several months of this work, Li Mei was exhausted and disillusioned. "I'm tired to death and I don't earn much," she says despondently. "It makes everything meaningless."[48]

job specialization The result of division of labour in which work is subdivided into separate jobs assigned to different people.

Li Mei performs jobs with a high degree of **job specialization.** Job specialization occurs when the work required to make a toy–or any other product or service–is subdivided into separate jobs assigned to different people. Each resulting job includes a narrow subset of tasks, usually completed in a short cycle time. *Cycle time* is the time required to complete the task before starting over with another item or client. Li Mei had an average cycle time of 7.2 seconds, which means she repeats the same set of tasks hundreds of times each hour.

Why would companies divide work into such tiny bits? The simple answer is that job specialization potentially improves work efficiency. One reason for this higher efficiency is that employees have less variety of tasks to juggle (such as painting dolls versus operating a doll parts machine), so there is less time lost changing over to a different type of activity. Even when people can change tasks quickly, their mental attention lingers on the previous type of work, which slows down performance on the new task.[49] A second reason for increased work efficiency is that employees can become proficient more quickly in specialized jobs. There are fewer physical and mental skills to learn and therefore less time to train and develop people for high performance. A third reason is that shorter work cycles give employees more frequent practice with the task, so jobs are mastered more quickly. A fourth reason why specialization tends to increase work efficiency is that employees with specific aptitudes or skills can be matched more precisely to the jobs for which they are best suited.[50]

The benefits of job specialization were noted more than 2,300 years ago by the Chinese philosopher Mencius and Greek philosopher Plato. Scottish economist Adam Smith wrote 250 years ago about the advantages of job specialization. Smith described a small factory where 10 pin makers collectively produced as many as 48,000 pins per day because they performed specialized tasks. One person straightened the metal, another cut it, another sharpened one end of the cut piece, yet another added a white tip to the other end, and so forth. In contrast, Smith explained that if these 10 people worked alone producing complete pins, they would collectively manufacture no more than 200 pins per day.[51]

scientific management The practice of systematically partitioning work into its smallest elements and standardizing tasks to achieve maximum efficiency.

Scientific Management One of the strongest advocates of job specialization was Frederick Winslow Taylor, an American industrial engineer who introduced the principles of **scientific management** in the early 1900s.[52] Scientific management consists of a toolkit of activities. Some of these interventions–employee selection, training, goal setting, and work

The Arsenal of Venice introduced job specialization 200 years before economist Adam Smith famously praised this form of job design. Founded in 1104 CE, the state-owned shipbuilder eventually employed up to 4,000 people in specialized jobs (carpenters, iron workers, warehouse supervisors, etc.) to build ships and accessories (e.g., ropes). In 1570, the Arsenal had become so efficient through specialization that it built 100 ships in two months. The organization even had an assembly line along the waterway where workers apportioned food, ammunition, and other supplies from specially designed warehouses to the completed vessels.[53]

incentives—are common today but were rare until Taylor popularized them. However, scientific management is mainly associated with high levels of job specialization and standardization of tasks to achieve maximum efficiency.

According to Taylor, the most effective companies have detailed procedures and work practices developed by engineers, enforced by supervisors, and executed by employees. Even the supervisor's tasks should be divided: One person manages operational efficiency, another manages inspection, and another is the disciplinarian. Taylor and other industrial engineers demonstrated that scientific management significantly improves work efficiency. No doubt, some of the increased productivity can be credited to the training, goal setting, and work incentives, but job specialization quickly became popular in its own right.

Problems with Job Specialization Frederick Winslow Taylor and his contemporaries focused on how job specialization reduces labour "waste" by improving the mechanical efficiency of work (i.e., matching skills, faster learning, less switchover time). Yet they didn't seem to notice how this extreme job specialization adversely affects employee attitudes and motivation. Some jobs—such as painting eyes on dolls—are so specialized that they soon become tedious, trivial, and socially isolating. Employee turnover and absenteeism tend to be higher in specialized jobs with very short cycle times. Companies sometimes have to pay higher wages to attract job applicants to this dissatisfying, narrowly defined work.[54]

Job specialization affects output quality, but in two opposing ways. Job incumbents of specialized jobs potentially produce higher quality results because, as we mentioned earlier, they master their work faster than do employees in jobs with many and varied tasks. This higher proficiency explains why specialist lawyers tend to provide better quality service than do generalist lawyers.[55] But many jobs (such as Li Mei's position in the toy factory) are specialized to the point that they are highly repetitive and tedious. In these repetitive jobs, the positive effect of higher proficiency is easily offset by the negative effect of lower attentiveness and motivation caused by the tedious work patterns.

Job specialization also undermines work quality by disassociating job incumbents from the overall product or service. By performing a small part of the overall work, employees have difficulty striving for better quality or even noticing flaws with that overall output. As one observer of an automobile assembly line reports: "Often [employees] did not know how their jobs related to the total picture. Not knowing, there was no incentive to strive for quality—what did quality even mean as it related to a bracket whose function you did not understand?"[56]

Job Design and Work Motivation

LO4

motivator-hygiene theory Herzberg's theory stating that employees are primarily motivated by growth and esteem needs, not by lower-level needs.

job characteristics model A job design model that relates the motivational properties of jobs to specific personal and organizational consequences of those properties.

Frederick Winslow Taylor may have overlooked the motivational effect of job characteristics, but it is now the central focus of many job design initiatives. Organizational behaviour scholar Frederick Herzberg is credited with shifting the spotlight in the 1950s when he introduced **motivator-hygiene theory.**[57] Motivator-hygiene theory proposes that employees experience job satisfaction when they fulfill growth and esteem needs (called *motivators*) and they experience dissatisfaction when they have poor working conditions, job security, and other factors categorized as lower-order needs (called *hygienes*). Herzberg argued that only characteristics of the job itself motivate employees, whereas the hygiene factors merely prevent dissatisfaction. It might seem obvious to us today that the job itself is a source of motivation, but the concept was radical when Herzberg proposed the idea.

Motivator-hygiene theory has been soundly rejected by research studies, but Herzberg's ideas generated new thinking about the motivational potential of the job itself.[58] Out of subsequent research emerged the **job characteristics model,** shown in Exhibit 6.2. The job characteristics model identifies five core job dimensions that produce three psychological states. Employees who experience these psychological states tend to have higher levels of internal work motivation (motivation from the work itself), job satisfaction (particularly satisfaction with the work itself), and work effectiveness.[59]

EXHIBIT 6.2

The Job Characteristics Model

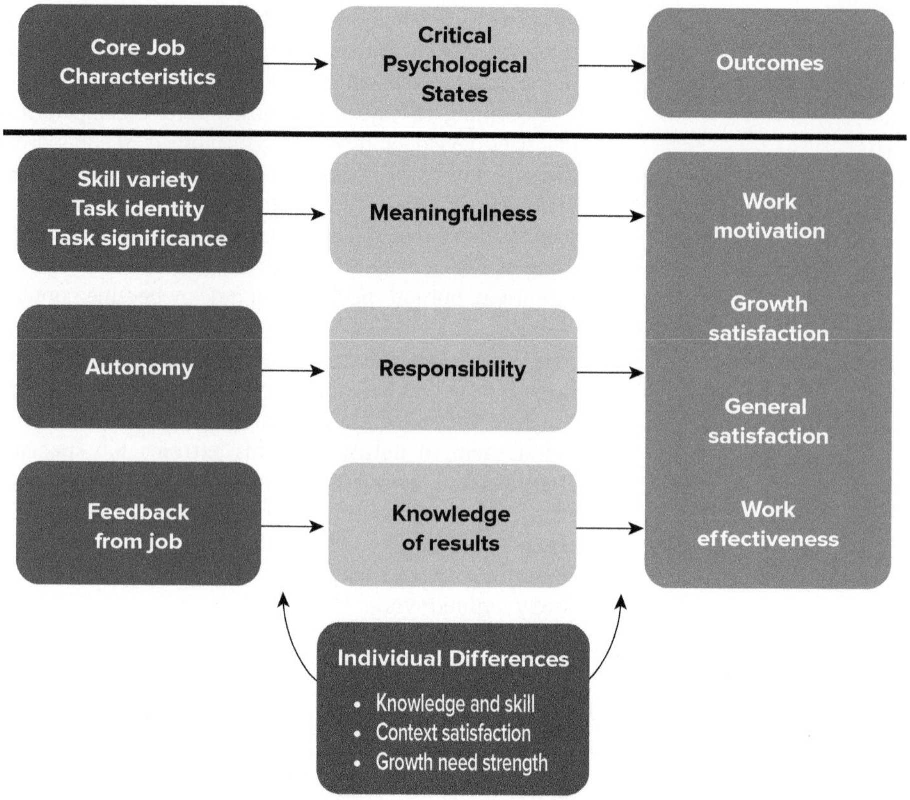

Source: J. R. Hackman and G. Oldham, *Work Redesign* (Reading, MA: Addison-Wesley, 1980), p. 90. Used with permission.

Core Job Characteristics The job characteristics model identifies five core job characteristics. Under the right conditions, employees are more motivated and satisfied when jobs have higher levels of these characteristics:

- *Skill variety.* **Skill variety** refers to the use of different skills and talents to complete a variety of work activities. For example, sales clerks who normally only serve customers might be assigned the additional duties of stocking inventory and changing storefront displays.
- *Task identity.* **Task identity** is the degree to which a job requires completion of a whole or identifiable piece of work, such as assembling an entire broadband modem rather than just soldering in the circuitry.
- *Task significance.* **Task significance** is the degree to which the job affects the organization and/or larger society. It is an observable characteristic of the job (you can see how it benefits others) as well as a perceptual awareness.
- *Autonomy.* Jobs with high levels of **autonomy** provide freedom, independence, and discretion in scheduling the work and determining the procedures to be used to complete the work. In autonomous jobs, employees make their own decisions rather than rely on detailed instructions from supervisors or procedure manuals. Autonomy is considered the core motivational element of job design.[60] As we learned in Chapter 4, autonomy is also an important mechanism to reduce stress in some situations.
- *Job feedback.* Job feedback is the degree to which employees can tell how well they are doing from direct sensory information from the job itself. Airline pilots can tell how well they land their aircraft, and road crews can see how well they have prepared the roadbed and laid the asphalt.

skill variety The extent to which employees must use different skills and talents to perform tasks within their jobs.

task identity The degree to which a job requires completion of a whole or an identifiable piece of work.

task significance The degree to which a job has a substantial impact on the organization and/or larger society.

autonomy The degree to which a job gives employees the freedom, independence, and discretion to schedule their work and determine the procedures used in completing it.

Critical Psychological States The five core job characteristics affect employee motivation and satisfaction through three critical psychological states, shown in Exhibit 6.2. Skill variety, task identity, and task significance directly contribute to the job's *experienced meaningfulness*—the belief that one's work is worthwhile or important. Autonomy directly contributes to feelings of *experienced responsibility*—a sense of being personally accountable for the work outcomes. The third critical psychological state is *knowledge of results*—an awareness of the work outcomes based on information from the job itself.

Individual Differences Job design doesn't increase work motivation for everyone in every situation. Employees must have the required skills and knowledge to master the more challenging work. Otherwise, job design tends to increase stress and reduce job performance. The original model also states that employees will be motivated by the five core job characteristics only when they are satisfied with their work context (e.g., working conditions, job security) and have a high *growth need strength.* Growth need strength refers to an individual's need for personal growth and development, such as work that offers challenge, cognitive stimulation, learning, and independent thought and action.[61] However, research findings have been mixed, suggesting that employees might be motivated by job design no matter how they feel about their job context or how high or low they score on growth needs.[62]

Social and Information Processing Job Characteristics The job characteristics model overlooks two clusters of job features: social characteristics and information processing demands.[63] One *social characteristic* is the extent to which the job requires employees to interact with other people (coworkers, clients, government representatives, etc.). This required social interaction is associated with emotional labour, discussed in Chapter 4, as well as with *task interdependence,* which we discuss in Chapter 8 as an element of team dynamics. A second social characteristic of the job is feedback from others. Earlier, we said that feedback from the job itself is motivational. Social forms of feedback, such as from clients and coworkers, is also important, particularly for rapid learning and when the feedback is positive (see Chapter 5).

The other cluster of job characteristics missing from the earlier model relates to the information processing demands of the work.[64] One information processing demand is how predictable the job duties are from one day to the next (called *task variability*). Employees in jobs with high task variability have nonroutine work patterns; they would perform different types of tasks on one day than another day, and not necessarily know what tasks will be required next. The second information processing demand, called *task analyzability,* refers to how much the job can be performed using known procedures and rules. Jobs with high task analyzability have a ready-made "cookbook" to guide job incumbents through most decisions and actions, whereas jobs with low task analyzability require employee creativity and judgment to determine the best course of action. Task variability and task analyzability are important job characteristics to consider when designing organizational structures, so we discuss both of them further in Chapter 13.

JOB DESIGN PRACTICES THAT MOTIVATE

Three main strategies can increase the motivational potential of jobs: job rotation, job enlargement, and job enrichment.

Job Rotation Bang & Olufsen has always had fairly complex jobs at its manufacturing plants. When the Danish government established guidelines for employers to reduce monotonous and repetitive work, however, the Danish audio and multimedia company took further steps by training employees on all assembly stations and rotating them through different jobs every three or four hours.[65] Bang & Olufsen executives have introduced the practice of moving employees from one job to another for the purpose of improving the motivational and physiological conditions of the work.

Frederick Florin/AFP/Getty Images

EYE Lighting International staff do kaizen events and other forms of quality improvement. But to make their daily routines more engaging, the American subsidiary of Iwasaki Electric of Japan practises job rotation. "Every employee on the factory floor changes positions at least once a day," says EYE Lighting president Tom Salpietra. "The employees love it because they don't get bored in their daily job. Ergonomically, it's good for them because they're not doing the same repetitive task day-in and day-out when they come here." Salpietra adds that job rotation "allows us a tremendous amount of flexibility" when assigning work. By performing a variety of jobs, employees also develop a better picture of the production process and ways to improve product quality.[66]

EXHIBIT 6.3

Job Enlargement of Video Journalists

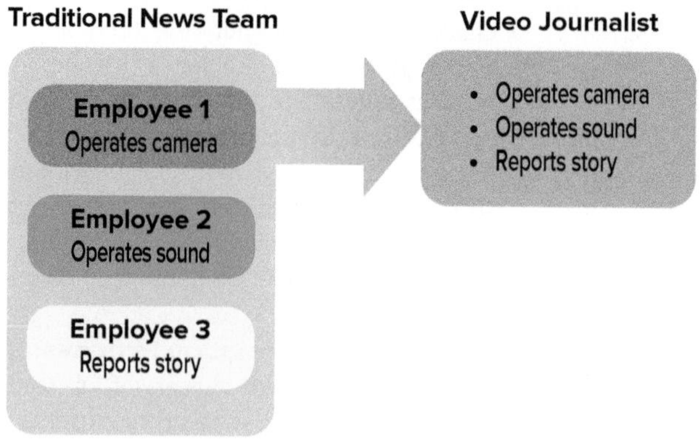

There are three potential benefits of job rotation. First, it minimizes health risks from repetitive strain and heavy lifting because employees use different muscles and physical positions in the various jobs. Second, it supports multi-skilling (employees learn several jobs), which increases workforce flexibility in staffing the production process and in finding replacements for employees on vacation. A third benefit of job rotation is that it potentially reduces the boredom of highly repetitive jobs. Organizational behaviour experts continue to debate whether job rotation really is a form of job redesign because the jobs remain the same; they are still highly specialized. However, job rotation does increase variety throughout the workday, which explains why anecdotal evidence suggests it has some positive effects on employee attitudes.

job enlargement The practice of adding more tasks to an existing job.

Job Enlargement **Job enlargement** adds tasks to an existing job. This might involve combining two or more complete jobs into one or just adding one or two more tasks to an existing job. Either way, skill variety increases because there are more tasks to perform. Video journalist is an example of an enlarged job. As Exhibit 6.3 illustrates, a traditional news team consists of a camera operator, a sound and lighting specialist, and the journalist who writes and presents or narrates the story. One video journalist performs all of these tasks.

Job enlargement significantly improves work efficiency and flexibility. However, research suggests that simply giving employees more tasks won't affect motivation, performance, or job satisfaction. These benefits result only when skill variety is combined with more autonomy and job knowledge.[67] In other words, employees are motivated when they perform a variety of tasks *and* have the freedom and knowledge to structure their work to achieve the highest satisfaction and performance. These job characteristics are at the heart of job enrichment.

job enrichment The practice of giving employees more responsibility for scheduling, coordinating, and planning their own work.

Job Enrichment **Job enrichment** occurs when employees are given more responsibility for scheduling, co ordinating, and planning their own work.[68] For example, customer service employees at American Express go "off-script," meaning that they use their own discretion regarding how long they should spend with a client and what to say to them.[69] Previously, employees had to follow strict statements and take a fixed time for specific types of customer issues. Generally, people in enriched jobs experience higher job satisfaction and work motivation, along with lower absenteeism and turnover. Productivity is also higher when task identity and job feedback are improved. Product and service quality tend to improve because job enrichment increases the jobholder's felt responsibility and sense of ownership over the product or service.[70]

One way to increase job enrichment is by combining highly interdependent tasks into one job. This *natural grouping* approach is reflected in the video journalist job. Along with being an enlarged job, video journalism is an example of job enrichment because it naturally groups tasks together to complete an entire product (i.e., a news story). By forming natural work units, jobholders have stronger feelings of responsibility for an identifiable body of work. They feel a sense of ownership and, therefore, tend to increase job quality. Forming natural work units increases task identity and task significance because employees perform a complete product or service and can more readily see how their work affects others.

A second job enrichment strategy, called *establishing client relationships,* involves putting employees in direct contact with their clients rather than using the supervisor as a go-between. By being directly responsible for specific clients, employees have more information and can make decisions affecting those clients.[71] Establishing client relationships also increases task significance because employees see a line-of-sight connection between their work and consequences for customers.

Forming natural task groups and establishing client relationships are common ways to enrich jobs, but the heart of the job enrichment philosophy is to give employees more autonomy over their work. This basic idea is at the core of one of the most widely mentioned–and often misunderstood–practices, known as empowerment.

Empowerment Practices

LO5

empowerment A psychological concept in which people experience more self-determination, meaning, competence, and impact regarding their role in the organization.

When companies design enriched jobs, employees who perform those jobs typically say they feel "empowered." In fact, empowerment is a well-known outcome of job enrichment, but it is also due to other work conditions as well as employee characteristics. **Empowerment** is a psychological experience represented by four dimensions: self-determination, meaning, competence, and impact of the individual's role in the organization.[72]

- *Self-determination.* Empowered employees feel that they have freedom, independence, and discretion over their work activities.
- *Meaning.* Employees who feel empowered care about their work and believe that what they do is important.
- *Competence.* Empowered people are confident about their ability to perform the work well and have a capacity to grow with new challenges.
- *Impact.* Empowered employees view themselves as active participants in the organization; that is, their decisions and actions have an influence on the company's success.

SUPPORTING EMPOWERMENT

Chances are that you have heard leaders say they are "empowering" the workforce. Yet empowerment is a state of mind, so what these executives really mean is that they are changing the work environment to support the feeling of empowerment.[73] Numerous individual, job design, and organizational or work-context factors support empowerment.[74] At the individual level, employees must possess the necessary competencies to be able to perform the work as well as handle the additional decision-making requirements.

Job characteristics clearly influence the degree to which people feel empowered.[75] Employees are much more likely to experience self-determination when working in jobs with a high degree of autonomy and minimal bureaucratic control. They experience more meaningfulness when working in jobs with high levels of task identity and task significance. They experience more self-confidence when working in jobs that allow them to receive feedback about their performance and accomplishments.

Several organizational and work-context factors also influence empowerment. Employees experience more empowerment in organizations where they are given the necessary training and tools to perform their jobs, and where corporate leaders demonstrate their trust in employees. Empowerment also requires a learning orientation culture. In other words, empowerment flourishes in organizations that appreciate the value of employee learning and that accept reasonable mistakes as a natural part of the learning process.

With the right individuals, job characteristics, and organizational environment, empowerment can substantially improve motivation and performance. For instance, a study of bank employees concluded that empowerment improved customer service and tended to reduce conflict between employees and their supervisors. A study of nurses reported that empowerment is associated with higher trust in management, which ultimately influences job satisfaction, belief and acceptance of organizational goals and values, and effective organizational commitment. Empowerment also tends to increase personal initiative because employees identify with and assume more psychological ownership of their work.[76]

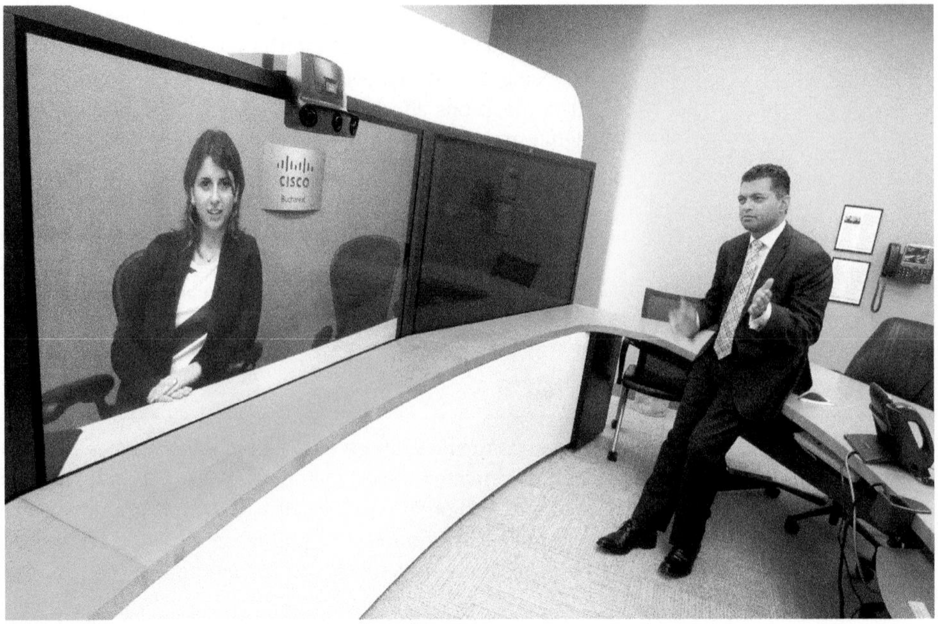

Peter Power/*The Globe and Mail*/CP Images

Cisco Canada nurtures a culture of trust by giving its employees plenty of flexibility in how, where, and when they do their work. In fact, job descriptions are deliberately vague at the global technology company so employees have autonomy to accomplish their tasks. "We're not overly structured and processed," explains David Clarkson, Cisco Canada's director of human resources. "If you tell people where they need to go, they can fill in the blanks." Cisco believes that employees feel empowered when the company demonstrates trust in them and provides the training and tools needed to accomplish their work. "It gives them a sense of empowerment," says Willa Black, Cisco Canada's VP of corporate affairs.[77]

Self-Leadership Practices

LO6

What is the most important characteristic that companies look for in their employees? Leadership potential, ability to work in a team, and good communication skills are important, but the top of the list in a survey of 800 British employers is self-motivation. Frode Gronvold can identify with these survey results. The chairman of Linstow Management Centre, which develops and manages major shopping centres in Latvia and Estonia, seeks out people who demonstrate self-leadership. "I really appreciate when I have colleagues who take initiative," says Gronvold. "I like people with a creative state of mind, who at the same time are autonomous, self-driven, self-motivated, with the ability to cooperate and get the best out of each other. These are the main skills that I am looking for in my employees."[78]

self-leadership The process of influencing oneself to establish the self-direction and self-motivation needed to perform a task.

Frode Gronvold looks for people who engage in **self-leadership.** They establish the self-direction and self-motivation needed to perform a task without their managers generating that motivation or initiative.[79] Self-leadership includes a toolkit of behavioural activities borrowed from social cognitive theory and goal setting (see Chapter 5). It also includes constructive thought processes that have been extensively studied in sports psychology. Overall, self-leadership suggests that individuals mostly regulate their own actions through these behavioural and cognitive (thought) activities.

connect

How well do you practise self-leadership? Visit **connect.mcgrawhill.com** to estimate how much you engage in several self-leadership activities.

SELF-LEADERSHIP STRATEGIES

Although self-leadership consists of several processes, the five main activities are identified in Exhibit 6.4. These elements, which generally follow each other in a sequence, are personal goal setting, constructive thought patterns, designing natural rewards, self-monitoring, and self-reinforcement.[80]

Personal Goal Setting The first step in self-leadership is to set goals for your own work effort. In self-leadership, these goals are self-determined, rather than being assigned by or jointly decided with a supervisor. Research suggests that employees are more focused

EXHIBIT 6.4

Elements of Self-Leadership

and perform better when they set their own goals, particularly in combination with other self-leadership practices.[81] Personal goal setting also requires a high degree of self-awareness, because people need to understand their current behaviour and performance before establishing meaningful goals for personal development.

Constructive Thought Patterns Before beginning a task and while performing it, employees should engage in positive (constructive) thoughts about that work and its accomplishment. In particular, employees are more motivated and better prepared to accomplish a task after they have engaged in positive self-talk and mental imagery.

self-talk The process of talking to ourselves about our own thoughts or actions.

- *Positive Self-Talk.* Do you ever talk to yourself? Most of us do, according to a major study of Canadian college students.[82] **Self-talk** refers to any situation in which we talk to ourselves about our own thoughts or actions. The problem is that most self-talk is negative; we criticize much more than encourage or congratulate ourselves. Negative self-talk undermines our confidence and potential to perform a particular task. In contrast, positive self-talk creates a "can-do" belief and thereby increases motivation by raising our self-efficacy and reducing anxiety about challenging tasks.[83] We often hear that professional athletes "psyche" themselves up before an important event. They tell themselves that they can achieve their goal and that they have practised enough to reach that goal. They are motivating themselves through self-talk.
- *Mental Imagery.* You've probably heard the phrase "I'll cross that bridge when I come to it!" Self-leadership takes the opposite view. It suggests that we need to mentally practise a task and imagine successfully performing it beforehand. This process, known as **mental imagery,** has two parts. One part involves mentally practising the task, anticipating obstacles to goal accomplishment, and working out solutions to those obstacles before they occur. By mentally walking through the activities required to accomplish the task, we begin to see problems that may occur. We can then imagine what responses would be best for each contingency.[84]

mental imagery The process of mentally practising a task and visualizing its successful completion.

While one part of mental imagery helps us to anticipate things that could go wrong, the other part involves visualizing successful completion of the task. You might imagine the experience of completing the task and the positive results that follow, such as being promoted, receiving a prestigious award, or taking time off work. This visualization increases goal commitment and motivates people to complete the task effectively. This is the strategy that Tony Wang applies to motivate himself. "Since I am in sales, I think about the reward I get for closing new business–the commission check–and the things it will allow me to do that I really enjoy," explains the sales employee. "Or I think about the feeling I get when I am successful at something and how it makes me feel good, and use that to get me going."[85]

Designing Natural Rewards Self-leadership recognizes that employees actively craft their jobs. To varying degrees, they can alter tasks and work relationships to make the work more motivating.[86] One way to build natural rewards into the job is to alter the way a task is accomplished. People often have enough discretion in their jobs to make slight changes to suit their needs and preferences.

Self-Monitoring Self-monitoring is the process of keeping track at regular intervals of one's progress towards a goal by using naturally occurring feedback. Some people can receive feedback from the job itself, such as members of a lawn maintenance crew who can see how they are improving the appearance of their client's property. But many of us are unable to observe our work output so readily. Instead, many people need to design feedback systems. Salespeople might arrange to receive monthly reports on sales levels in their territory. Production staff might have gauges or computer feedback systems installed so they can see how many errors are made on the production line. Research suggests that people who have control over the timing of performance feedback perform their tasks better than do those with feedback assigned by others.[87]

Self-Reinforcement Self-leadership includes engaging in *self-reinforcement,* which is part of social cognitive theory described in Chapter 5. Self-reinforcement occurs whenever an employee has control over a reinforcer but doesn't "take" the reinforcer until completing a self-set goal.[88] A common example is taking a break after reaching a predetermined stage of your work. The work break is a self-induced form of positive reinforcement. Self-reinforcement also occurs when you decide to do a more enjoyable task after completing a task that you dislike. For example, after slogging through a difficult report, you might decide to spend time doing a more pleasant task, such as catching up on industry news by scanning websites.

EFFECTIVENESS OF SELF-LEADERSHIP

Self-leadership is shaping up to be a valuable applied performance practice in organizational settings. A respectable body of research shows consistent support for most elements of self-leadership. Self-set goals and self-monitoring increased the frequency of wearing safety equipment among employees in a mining operation. Airline employees who received constructive thought training experienced better mental performance, enthusiasm, and job satisfaction than coworkers who did not receive this training. Mental imagery helped supervisors and process engineers in a pulp-and-paper mill to transfer what they learned in an interpersonal communication skills class back to the job.[89] Studies also indicate that constructive thought processes improve individual performance in cycling, hockey goaltending, ice skating, soccer, and other sports. Indeed, studies show that almost all Olympic athletes rely on mental rehearsal and positive self-talk to achieve their performance goals.[90]

connect

Do you have a proactive personality? Visit **connect.mcgrawhill.com** to assess the extent to which taking personal initiative is part of your disposition.

PERSONAL AND SITUATIONAL PREDICTORS OF SELF-LEADERSHIP

Some research suggests that self-leadership behaviours are more frequently found in people with higher levels of conscientiousness and extroversion. Some writers also suggest that people with a positive self-concept evaluation (i.e., self-esteem, self-efficacy, and internal locus of control) are more likely to apply self-leadership strategies.[91]

The work environment also seems to influence the extent to which employees engage in self-leadership. Specifically, employees require some degree of autonomy to engage in some or most aspects of self-leadership. They probably also feel more confident with self-leadership when their boss is empowering rather than controlling and where there is a high degree of trust between them. Employees are also more likely to engage in self-monitoring in companies that emphasize continuous measurement of performance.[92] Overall, self-leadership promises to be an important concept and practice for improving employee motivation and performance.

Chapter Summary

LO1 Discuss the meaning of money and identify several individual, team, and organizational-level performance-based rewards.

Money (and other financial rewards) is a fundamental part of the employment relationship, but it also relates to our needs, our emotions, and our self-concept. It is viewed as a symbol of status and prestige, as a source of security, as a source of evil, or as a source of anxiety or feelings of inadequacy.

Organizations reward employees for their membership and seniority, job status, competencies, and performance. Membership-based rewards may attract job applicants and seniority-based rewards reduce turnover, but these reward objectives tend to discourage turnover among those with the lowest performance. Rewards based on job status try to maintain internal equity and motivate employees to compete for promotions. However, they tend to encourage a bureaucratic hierarchy, support status differences, and motivate employees to compete and hoard resources. Competency-based rewards are becoming increasingly popular because they encourage employees to develop their skills. However, they tend to be subjectively measured and can result in higher costs as employees spend more time learning new skills.

Awards and bonuses, commissions, and other individual performance-based rewards have existed for centuries and are widely used. Many companies are shifting to team-based rewards such as gainsharing plans and to organizational rewards such as employee share ownership plans (ESOPs), share options, and profit sharing. ESOPs and share options create an ownership culture, but employees often perceive a weak connection between individual performance and the organizational reward.

LO2 Describe five ways to improve reward effectiveness.
Financial rewards have a number of limitations, but reward effectiveness can be improved in several ways. Organizational leaders should ensure that rewards are linked to work performance, rewards are aligned with performance within the employee's control, team rewards are used where jobs are interdependent, rewards are valued by employees, and rewards have no unintended consequences.

LO3 List the advantages and disadvantages of job specialization.
Job design is the process of assigning tasks to a job, including the interdependency of those tasks with other jobs. Job specialization subdivides work into separate jobs for different people. This increases work efficiency because employees master the tasks quickly, spend less time changing tasks, require less training, and can be matched more closely with the jobs best suited to their skills. However, job specialization may reduce work motivation, create mental health problems, lower product or service quality, and increase costs through discontentment, absenteeism, and turnover.

LO4 Diagram the job characteristics model and describe three ways to improve employee motivation through job design.
The job characteristics model is a template for job redesign that specifies core job dimensions, psychological states, and individual differences. The five core job dimensions are skill variety, task identity, task significance, autonomy, and job feedback. Jobs also vary in their required social interaction (task interdependence) and information processing characteristics (task variability and analyzability). Contemporary job design strategies try to motivate employees through job rotation, job enlargement, and job enrichment. Organizations introduce job rotation to reduce job boredom, develop a more flexible workforce, and reduce the incidence of repetitive strain injuries. Job enlargement involves increasing the number of tasks within the job. Two ways to enrich jobs are clustering tasks into natural groups and establishing client relationships.

LO5 Define empowerment and identify strategies that support empowerment.
Empowerment is a psychological concept represented by four dimensions: self-determination, meaning, competence, and impact regarding the individual's role in the organization. Individual characteristics seem to have a minor influence on empowerment. Job design is a major influence, particularly autonomy, task identity, task significance, and job feedback. Empowerment is also supported at the organizational level through a learning orientation culture, sufficient information and resources, and corporate leaders who trust employees.

LO6 Describe the five elements of self-leadership and identify specific personal and work environment influences on self-leadership.
Self-leadership is the process of influencing oneself to establish the self-direction and self-motivation needed to perform a task. This includes personal goal setting, constructive thought patterns, designing natural rewards, self-monitoring, and self-reinforcement. Constructive thought patterns include self-talk and mental imagery. Self-talk occurs in any situation in which a person talks to himself or herself about his or her own thoughts or actions. Mental imagery involves mentally practising a task and imagining successfully performing it beforehand. People with higher levels of conscientiousness, extroversion, and a positive self-concept are more likely to apply self-leadership strategies. It also increases in workplaces that support empowerment and have high trust between employees and management.

Key Terms

autonomy, p. 150
employee share ownership plans (ESOPs), p. 143
empowerment, p. 153
gainsharing plans, p. 143
job characteristics model, p. 149
job design, p. 146
job enlargement, p. 152
job enrichment, p. 152
job evaluation, p. 140
job specialization, p. 148
mental imagery, p. 155
motivator-hygiene theory, p. 149
profit-sharing plans, p. 143
scientific management, p. 149
self-leadership, p. 154
self-talk, p. 155
share options, p. 143
skill variety, p. 150
task identity, p. 150
task significance, p. 150

Critical-Thinking Questions

1. As a consultant, you have been asked to recommend either a gainsharing plan or a profit-sharing plan for employees who work in the four regional distribution and warehousing facilities of a large retail organization. Which reward system would you recommend? Explain your answer.
2. Which of the performance reward practices–individual, team or organizational–would work better in improving organizational goals. Please comment with reference to an organization of your choice.
3. Kelowna Tire Corporation redesigned its production facilities around a team-based system. However, the company

president believes that employees will not be motivated unless they receive incentives based on their individual performance. Give three explanations why Kelowna Tire should introduce team-based rather than individual rewards in this setting.

4. What can organizations do to increase the effectiveness of financial rewards?
5. Most of us have watched pizzas being made while waiting in a pizzeria. What level of job specialization do you usually notice in these operations? Why does this high or low level of specialization exist? If some pizzerias have different levels of specialization than others, identify the contingencies that might explain these differences.
6. Can a manager or supervisor "empower" an employee? Discuss fully.
7. Describe a time when you practised self-leadership to successfully perform a task. With reference to each step in the self-leadership process, describe what you did to achieve this success.
8. Can self-leadership replace formal leadership in an organizational setting?

Case Study: YAKKATECH LTD.

By Steven L. McShane, The University of Western Australia

YakkaTech Ltd. is an information technology services firm employing 1,500 people across Canada. YakkaTech has a consulting division, which mainly installs and upgrades enterprise software systems and related hardware on the client's site. YakkaTech also has a customer service division, which consists of four customer contact centres serving clients within each region.

Each customer contact centre consists of a half-dozen departments representing functional specializations (computer systems, intranet infrastructure, storage systems, enterprise software systems, customer billing, etc.). These centres typically have more than two dozen employees in each department. When a client submits a problem to the centre using the online form, the message or call is directed to the department where the issue best applies. The query is given a "ticket" number and is assigned to the next available employee in that department. Individual employees are solely responsible for the tickets assigned to them. The employee investigates and corrects the issue, and the ticket is "closed" when the client agrees that the problem has been resolved.

If the client experiences the same problem again, even a few days later, a new ticket is issued and sent to whichever employee is available to receive the ticket. A client's problems are almost always handled by different employees each time, even when the issue is sent to the same department. Furthermore, when a customer centre department is heavily backlogged, clients are redirected to the same department at another regional centre where their problem can be addressed more quickly.

At one time, YakkaTech operated more than a dozen small customer contact centres in each city because client problems had to be diagnosed and resolved on-site. Today, employees can investigate most software and hardware system faults from the centre through remote monitoring systems, rather than personally visit the client. Consequently, eight years ago, YakkaTech amalgamated its customer service operations into four large regional centres. Customer service staff work entirely within the centre. When a client visit is required, the ticket is transferred to an individual or team in the consulting business, who then visits the client.

YakkaTech's customer service business has nearly doubled over the past five years, but with this growth has come increasing customer complaints regarding poor quality service. Many say that employees seem indifferent to the client's problems. Others have commented on the slow response to their problems where the issue requires involvement of more than one department. Several clients have also complained that they are continually educating YakkaTech's customer service employees about details of their unique IT systems infrastructure.

Another concern is that until 18 months ago, YakkaTech's voluntary employee turnover rates in the contact centres had risen above the industry average. This increased labour costs due to the cost of recruiting new technical staff as well as lower productivity of new employees. According to results of an employee survey two years ago (as well as informal comments since then), many employees felt that their work is monotonous. Some also said that they felt disconnected from the consequences of their work. A few also complained about ongoing conflicts with people in other departments and the stress of serving dissatisfied clients.

Eighteen months ago, YakkaTech's executive team decided to raise pay rates for its customer service staff to become among the highest in the industry. The assumption was that the high pay rates would improve morale and reduce turnover, thereby reducing hiring costs and improving productivity. In addition, YakkaTech introduced a vested profit-sharing plan, in which employees received the profit-sharing bonus only if they remained with the company for two years after the bonus was awarded. Employees who quit or were fired for just cause before the vesting period forfeited the bonus.

Employee turnover rates dropped dramatically, so the executive team concluded that customer service quality and productivity would improve. Instead, customer complaints and productivity remain below expectations and, in some cases, have worsened. Experienced employees continue to complain about the work. There are a few disturbing incidents where employees are careless at solving client problems or do not bother to forward tickets that should have been assigned to another department. Employee referrals (where staff recommend friends to join the company) have become rare events, whereas at one time they represented a significant source of qualified job applicants. Furthermore, a few executives have recently overheard employees say that they would like to work elsewhere but can't afford to leave YakkaTech.

Discussion Questions

1. What symptom(s) in this case suggest that something has gone wrong?
2. What are the main causes of these symptoms?
3. What actions should YakkaTech executives take to correct these problems?

Team Exercise: IS STUDENT WORK ENRICHED?

Purpose This exercise is designed to help you learn how to measure the motivational potential of jobs and evaluate the extent that jobs should be further enriched.

Instructions (Small Class) Being a student is like a job in several ways. You have tasks to perform, and someone (such as your instructor) oversees your work. Although few people want to be students most of their lives (the pay rate is too low!), it may be interesting to determine how enriched your job is as a student.

1. Students are placed into teams (preferably four or five people).
2. Working alone, each student completes both sets of measures in this exercise. Then, using the guidelines below, they individually calculate the score for the five core job characteristics as well as the overall motivating-potential score for the job.
3. Members of each team compare their individual results. The group should identify differences of opinion for each core job characteristic. They should also note which core job characteristics have the lowest scores and recommend how these scores could be increased.
4. The entire class will then meet to discuss the results of the exercise. The instructor may ask some teams to present their comparisons and recommendations for a particular core job characteristic.

Instructions (Large Class)

1. Working alone, each student completes both sets of measures in this exercise. Then, using the guidelines below, each student individually calculates the score for the five core job characteristics as well as the overall motivating-potential score for the job.
2. Using a show of hands or classroom technology, students indicate their results for each core job characteristic. The instructor will ask for results for several ranges across the scales. Alternatively, students can complete this activity prior to class and submit their results through online classroom technology. Later, the instructor will provide feedback to the class showing the collective results (i.e., distribution of results across the range of scores).
3. Where possible, the instructor might ask students with very high or very low results to discuss their views with the class.

Job Diagnostic Survey

Circle the number on the right that best describes student work.	Very little			Moderately			Very much
1. To what extent does student work permit you to decide on your own how to go about doing the work?	1	2	3	4	5	6	7
2. To what extent does student work involve doing a whole or identifiable piece of work, rather than a small portion of the overall work process?	1	2	3	4	5	6	7
3. To what extent does student work require you to do many different things, using a variety of your skills and talents?	1	2	3	4	5	6	7
4. To what extent are the results of your work as a student likely to significantly affect the lives and well-being of other people (e.g., within your school, your family, society)?	1	2	3	4	5	6	7
5. To what extent does working on student activities provide information about your performance?	1	2	3	4	5	6	7

Circle the number on the right that best describes student work.	Very inaccurate			Uncertain			Very accurate
6. Being a student requires me to use a number of complex and high-level skills.	1	2	3	4	5	6	7
7. Student work is arranged so that I do *not* have the chance to do an entire piece of work from beginning to end.	7	6	5	4	3	2	1
8. Doing the work required of students provides many chances for me to figure out how well I am doing.	1	2	3	4	5	6	7
9. The work students must do is quite simple and repetitive.	7	6	5	4	3	2	1
10. The work of a student is the type where a lot of other people can be affected by how well the work gets done.	1	2	3	4	5	6	7
11. Student work denies me any chance to use my personal initiative or judgment in carrying out the work.	7	6	5	4	3	2	1
12. Student work provides me the chance to completely finish the pieces of work I begin.	1	2	3	4	5	6	7
13. Doing student work by itself provides very few clues about whether I am performing well.	7	6	5	4	3	2	1
14. As a student, I have considerable opportunity for independence and freedom in how I do the work.	1	2	3	4	5	6	7
15. The work I perform as a student is *not* very significant or important in the broader scheme of things.	7	6	5	4	3	2	1

Source: Adapted from the Job Diagnostic Survey, developed by J. R. Hackman and G. R. Oldham. The authors have released any copyright ownership of this scale [see J. R. Hackman and G. Oldham, *Work Redesign* (Reading, MA: Addison-Wesley, 1980), p. 275].

Calculating The Motivating-Potential Score			
Scoring Core Job Characteristics: Use the following set of calculations to estimate the motivating-potential score for the job of being a student. Use your answers from the Job Diagnostic Survey that you completed above.			
Skill variety (SV)	$\frac{\text{Question } 3 + 6 + 9}{3} =$ ________	Autonomy	$\frac{\text{Question } 1 + 11 + 14}{3} =$ ________
Task identity (TI)	$\frac{\text{Question } 2 + 7 + 12}{3} =$ ________	Job feedback	$\frac{\text{Question } 5 + 8 + 13}{3} =$ ________
Task significance (TS)	$\frac{\text{Question } 4 + 10 + 15}{3} =$ ________		

Calculating Motivating-Potential Score (MPS): Use the following formula and the results above to calculate the motivating-potential score. Notice that skill variety, task identity, and task significance are averaged before being multiplied by the score for autonomy and job feedback.	
$\left(\frac{SV+TI+TS}{3}\right) \times \text{Autonomy} \times \text{Job Feedback}$	
$\left(\frac{\_\_\_\_ + \_\_\_\_ + \_\_\_\_}{3}\right) + \_\_\_\_ + \_\_\_\_ = \_\_\_\_$	

Self-Assessment: WHAT IS YOUR ATTITUDE TOWARDS MONEY?

Purpose This exercise is designed to help you understand the types of attitudes towards money and assess your attitude towards money.

Instructions Read each of the statements below and circle the response that you believe best reflects your position regarding each statement. Then use the scoring key in Appendix B at the end of the book to calculate your results. This exercise should be completed alone so that you can assess yourself honestly without concerns of social comparison. Class discussion will focus on the meaning of money, including the dimensions measured here and other aspects of money that may have an influence on behaviour in the workplace.

Money Attitude Scale

To what extent do you agree or disagree that . . .	Strongly agree	Agree	Neutral	Disagree	Strongly disagree
1. I sometimes purchase things because I know they will impress other people.	5	4	3	2	1
2. I regularly put money aside for the future.	5	4	3	2	1
3. I tend to get worried about decisions involving money.	5	4	3	2	1
4. I believe that financial wealth is one of the most important signs of a person's success.	5	4	3	2	1
5. I keep a close watch on how much money I have.	5	4	3	2	1
6. I feel nervous when I don't have enough money.	5	4	3	2	1
7. I tend to show more respect to people who are wealthier than I am.	5	4	3	2	1
8. I follow a careful financial budget.	5	4	3	2	1
9. I worry about being financially secure.	5	4	3	2	1
10. I sometimes boast about my financial wealth or how much money I make.	5	4	3	2	1
11. I keep track of my investments and financial wealth.	5	4	3	2	1
12. I usually say "I can't afford it," even when I can afford something.	5	4	3	2	1

Sources: Adapted from J. A. Roberts and C. J. Sepulveda, "Demographics and Money Attitudes: A Test of Yamauchi and Templer's (1982) Money Attitude Scale in Mexico," *Personality and Individual Differences*, 27 (July 1999), pp. 19-35; K. Yamauchi and D. Templer, "The Development of a Money Attitudes Scale," *Journal of Personality Assessment*, 46 (1982), pp. 522-528.

SELF-ASSESSMENTS FOR CHAPTER 6

SELF-ASSESSMENT NAME	DESCRIPTION	LOCATION
What is your attitude towards money?	Assesses how much you budget, respect, and worry about money.	Page 160 connect
Are you empowered as a student?	Assesses your level of empowerment overall and on each of its four dimensions.	connect
How well do you practise self-leadership?	Estimates how much you engage in several self-leadership activities.	connect
Do you have a proactive personality?	Assesses the extent to which your disposition includes the tendency to take personal initiative.	connect

The Canadian Press/Paul Chiasson

As the Lac-Mégantic train disaster illustrated, decisions can sometimes have disastrous consequences.

Chapter 7

Decision Making and Creativity

LEARNING OBJECTIVES

After reading this chapter, you should be able to:

LO1. Describe the rational choice paradigm of decision making.

LO2. Explain why people differ from the rational choice paradigm when identifying problems/opportunities, evaluating/choosing alternatives, and evaluating decision outcomes.

LO3. Discuss the roles of emotions and intuition in decision making.

LO4. Describe employee characteristics, workplace conditions, and specific activities that support creativity.

LO5. Describe the benefits of employee involvement and identify four contingencies that affect the optimal level of employee involvement.

On July 6, 2013 the fourth deadliest rail accident in Canadian history occurred in Lac-Mégantic, Quebec. At 1:15 a.m. a locomotive and 72 rail cars, owned by U.S.-based Montreal, Maine and Atlantic Railway (MMA), derailed and killed 47 people. The explosion and fire destroyed 30 buildings in the downtown area.

According to the investigation by the Transportation Safety Board of Canada (TSB), a series of poor decisions through the night led to the ghastly accident. MMA's operating manual included a procedure allowing engineers to leave a running locomotive with 8.1 million litres of explosive crude oil parked on the main line, unattended, with an unlocked locomotive cab. Each manual brake takes 2–3 minutes to set and, in this case, the engineer only activated 10 of the 72 brakes. In 2009, the National Transportation Safety Board of the United States noted that the cars on this train have a high incidence of tank failures during accidents, citing their inadequate design as a factor.

The TSB's investigation also revealed several other questionable choices. MMA's rail traffic controller had been warned that the train was having technical difficulties while it was still in Nantes on the evening of Friday July 5, 2013. And, freight trains operated by MMA were allowed by regulators in Canada and the United States to have single person train operation (SPTO). MMA had previously negotiated with the Canadian regulator to have the government allow MMA to have SPTO as a cost-cutting measure.

On July 5, the freight train departed from a CPR yard in Côte Saint-Luc, passed through Farnham and stopped at the designated crew change point in Nantes at approximately 23:00. The engineer left the train unattended with one locomotive running, which helped power the compressor that activated the vacuum brakes of the train. At 23:50 Nantes Fire Department and a police officer from Sûreté du Québec's Lac-Mégantic detachment responded to a 9-1-1 call made by a citizen who reported a fire on the first locomotive. Protocol required them to shut down the locomotive to restrict the fire. Once the fire was extinguished they notified the

MMA's rail traffic controller in Farnham. By 00:13, two MMA track maintenance employees confirmed to the police officer and the rail traffic controller that the train was safe. In the end, when the locomotive was shut down, the compressor powering the vacuum brakes was disabled, allowing the train to roll downhill from Nantes to Lac-Mégantic—leading to catastrophic results.[1]

The Lac-Mégantic disaster reveals the complexities, ambiguities, and importance of decision making in organizations. All businesses, governments, and not-for-profit agencies depend on employees to foresee and correctly identify problems, to survey alternative responses and pick the best one based on a variety of stakeholder interests, and to execute those decisions effectively. Decision making is such a vital function for an organization's health that it might be equated with the importance of breathing to a human being. Indeed, great leaders typically resuscitate organizations by encouraging and teaching employees at all levels to make decisions more efficiently and effectively.

This chapter examines decision making from three perspectives or paradigms. We begin with the rational choice paradigm, which has historically (but misguidedly) been viewed as the ideal way to make decisions. Next, we review the rational choice elements from the "imperfect rationality" paradigm–a set of theories that identify human limitations in the quest for perfectly rational decision making. This chapter then examines the dual rational-emotional paradigm, which recognizes that emotions play a central role (both good and bad) in the decision-making process. The latter part of this chapter focuses on two topics that intertwine with decision making: creativity and employee involvement.

Rational Choice Paradigm of Decision Making

LO1

decision making The conscious process of making choices among alternatives with the intention of moving towards some desired state of affairs.

rational choice paradigm The view in decision making that people should—and typically do—use logic and all available information to choose the alternative with the highest value.

subjective expected utility The probability (expectancy) of satisfaction (utility) resulting from choosing a specific alternative in a decision.

Decision making is the process of making choices among alternatives with the intention of moving towards some desired state of affairs.[2] This is vital to an organization's health, rather like breathing is to a human being. Indeed, leaders increasingly view themselves as physicians who resuscitate organizations by encouraging and teaching employees at all levels to make decisions more quickly, effectively, and creatively. All businesses, governments, and not-for-profit agencies depend on employees to foresee and correctly identify problems, to survey alternatives and pick the best one based on a variety of stakeholder interests, and to execute those decisions effectively.

How should people make decisions in organizations? Most business leaders would likely answer this question by saying that effective decision making involves identifying, selecting, and applying the best possible alternative. In other words, the best decisions use pure logic and all available information to choose the alternative with the highest value–such as highest expected profitability, customer satisfaction, employee well-being, or some combination of these outcomes. These decisions sometimes involve complex calculations of data to produce a formula that points to the best choice.

In its extreme form, this calculative view of decision making represents the **rational choice paradigm,** which has dominated decision-making philosophy in Western societies for most of written history.[3] It was established 2,500 years ago when Plato and his contemporaries in ancient Greece raised logical debate and reasoning to a fine art. About 400 years ago, Descartes and other European philosophers emphasized that the ability to make logical decisions is one of the most important accomplishments of human beings. In the 1700s, Scottish philosophers refined the notion that the best choice is the one that offers the greatest satisfaction or "utility."

The rational choice paradigm selects the choice with the highest utility through the calculation of **subjective expected utility (SEU).**[4] Subjective expected utility is the probability (expectancy) of satisfaction (utility) for each alternative. SEU is the foundation of several organizational behaviour theories, including the attitude model in Chapter 4 and expectancy theory of motivation in Chapter 5.

To understand SEU, consider this example: Suppose that you need to select one supplier from among many that offer a particular raw material for your company. Rationally, you would choose the supplier that will produce highest overall satisfaction ("utility") for your company. That expected satisfaction depends on the expected satisfaction (utility) of each outcome as well as the probability ("expected" in subjective expected utility) that each supplier will provide that outcome. One outcome might be the timely delivery of raw materials. You might estimate that one supplier will consistently deliver the product on time whereas other suppliers have lower probabilities of timely delivery. Another outcome might be the quality of raw materials. Again, you discover that suppliers differ in their likelihood of providing consistently high quality materials. Multiply the utility of each outcome together with the probability of that outcome occurring, then add those results across all outcomes to figure out which supplier has the highest overall subjective expected utility. The key point from this example is that all decisions rely to some degree on (a) the expected value of the outcomes (utility) and (b) the probability of those good or bad outcomes occurring (expectancy).

RATIONAL CHOICE DECISION-MAKING PROCESS

Along with its reliance on subjective expected utility, the rational choice paradigm assumes that decision makers follow the systematic process illustrated in Exhibit 7.1.[5] The first step is to identify the problem or recognize an opportunity. A *problem* is a deviation between the current and the desired situation–the gap between "what is" and "what ought to be." This deviation is a symptom of more fundamental causes that need to be corrected.[6] The "ought to be" refers to goals, and these goals later help to evaluate the selected choice. For instance, if the goal is to answer incoming client calls within 30 seconds, the problem is the gap between that goal and the actual time the call centre takes to answer most client calls. An *opportunity* is a deviation between current expectations and a potentially better situation that was not previously expected. In other words, decision makers realize that some decisions may produce results beyond current goals or expectations.

The second step involves choosing the best decision process. This step is really a meta-decision–deciding how to decide–because it refers to choosing among the different approaches and processes to make the decision.[7] One meta-decision is whether to solve the problem alone or involve others in the process. Later in this chapter, we'll examine the contingencies of employee involvement in the decision. Another meta-decision is whether to assume the decision is programmed or nonprogrammed. *Programmed decisions* follow standard operating procedures; they have been resolved in the past, so the optimal solution has already been identified and documented. In contrast, *nonprogrammed decisions* require all steps in the decision model because the problems are new, complex, or ill-defined.

EXHIBIT 7.1

Rational Choice Decision-Making Process

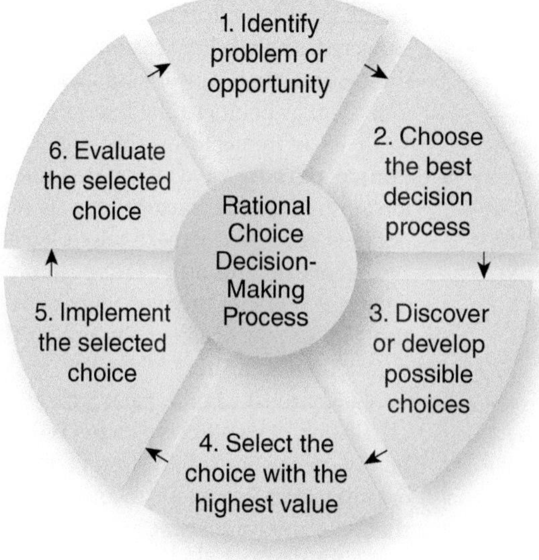

The third step in the rational choice decision-making process is to identify and/or develop a list of possible choices. This usually begins by searching for ready-made solutions, such as practices that have worked well on similar problems. If an acceptable solution cannot be found, then decision makers need to design a custom-made solution or modify an existing one. The fourth step is to select the choice with the highest SEU. This calls for all possible information about all possible alternatives and their outcomes, but the rational choice paradigm assumes this can be accomplished with ease.

The fifth step in the rational choice decision-making process is to implement the selected alternative. Rational choice experts have little to say about this step because they assume implementation occurs without any problems. This is followed by the sixth step, evaluating whether the gap has narrowed between "what is" and "what ought to be." Ideally, this information should come from systematic benchmarks so that relevant feedback is objective and easily observed.

PROBLEMS WITH THE RATIONAL CHOICE PARADIGM

The rational choice paradigm seems so logical, yet it is impossible to apply in reality because people are not and cannot be perfectly rational.[8] Instead, we need to examine theories that explain why people engage in imperfect rationality. Over the next several pages, we re-examine each step in the rational choice decision-making process, but with more detail about what really happens from the lens of "imperfect rationality."

Identifying Problems and Opportunities

LO2

When Albert Einstein was asked how he would save the world in one hour, he replied that the first 55 minutes should be spent defining the problem and the last 5 minutes solving it.[9] Einstein's point is that problem identification is not just the first step in decision making; it is arguably the most important step. But problems and opportunities are not clearly labelled objects that appear on our desks. Instead, they are conclusions that we form from ambiguous and conflicting information.[10]

PROBLEMS WITH PROBLEM IDENTIFICATION

The problem identification stage is, itself, filled with problems. Below are five of the most widely recognized concerns.[11]

© The Canadian Press/Winston Neutel/AP Images

A light rain had just begun when the 5:30pm GO Transit train left downtown Toronto, Canada, for its outer suburbs destination. Within the next 15 minutes, the rain became torrential and the nearby river flooded the train tracks ahead. The driver stopped in time, but the water rose so quickly that it surrounded the train before the driver could reverse. Passengers scrambled to the upper level of the double-decker train and were stranded for up to 7 hours. GO Transit officials later explained that it is difficult to define the situation as a flooding problem. "We knew there was a thunderstorm warning coming, but that's not unusual," said a GO Transit official later. A senior executive added that a general advisory about possible flooding in low-lying areas wouldn't have changed their plans: "Life is never as black and white as that," he said. "Our challenge is managing grey."[12]

Stakeholder Framing Employees, suppliers, customers, and other stakeholders present (or hide) information in ways that makes the decision maker see the situation as a problem, opportunity, or steady sailing. Employees point to external factors rather than their own faults as the cause of production delays. Suppliers market their new products as unique opportunities and competitor products as problems to be avoided. Stakeholders also offer a concise statement of the situation as a problem or otherwise in the hope the decision maker will accept their verdict without further analysis. Decision makers fall prey to these constructed realities because they have a need to simplify the daily bombardment of complex and often ambiguous information.

Decisive Leadership Various studies have found that executives are evaluated by their decisiveness, including how quickly they determine that the situation is a problem, opportunity, or nothing worth their attention.[13] Consequently, many leaders announce problems or opportunities before having a chance to logically assess the situation. The result is often a misguided effort to solve an ill-defined problem by wasting funds on a poorly identified opportunity.

Solution-Focused Problems When decision makers do recognize that the situation requires a decision, they sometimes describe the problem as a veiled solution.[14] For instance, someone might say: "The problem is that we need more control over our suppliers." This isn't a description of the problem; it is a rephrased statement of a solution to a problem that has not been adequately diagnosed. Decision makers engage in solution-focused problem identification because it provides comforting closure to the otherwise ambiguous and uncertain nature of problems. People with a strong need for cognitive closure (those who feel uncomfortable with ambiguity) are particularly prone to solution-focused problems. Some decision makers take this solution focus a step further by seeing all problems as solutions that have worked well for them in the past, even though they were applied under different circumstances.

Perceptual Defence People sometimes fail to become aware of problems because they block out bad news as a coping mechanism. Their brain refuses to see information that threatens their self-concept. The tendency to engage in perceptual defence varies from one decision maker to the next. Studies also report that perceptual defence is more common when decision makers have limited options to solve the problem.[15]

Mental Models Decision makers are victims of their own problem framing due to existing mental models. Mental models are visual or relational images in our mind of the external world; they fill in information that we don't immediately see, which helps us understand and navigate in our surrounding environment (see Chapter 3). Many mental images are also prototypes—they represent models of how things should be. Unfortunately, these mental models can blind us from seeing unique problems or opportunities because they produce a negative evaluation of things that are dissimilar to the mental model. If an idea doesn't fit the existing mental model of how things should work, then it is quickly dismissed as unworkable or undesirable. Connections 7.1 describes several examples where mental models caused missed opportunities.

IDENTIFYING PROBLEMS AND OPPORTUNITIES MORE EFFECTIVELY

Recognizing problems and opportunities will always be a challenge, but one way to improve the process is by becoming aware of the five problem identification biases described above. For example, by recognizing that mental models restrict a person's perspective of the world, decision makers are more motivated to consider other perspectives of reality. Along with increasing their awareness of problem identification flaws, leaders require considerable willpower to resist the temptation of looking decisive when a more thoughtful examination of the situation should occur.

A third way to improve problem identification is for leaders to create a norm of "divine discontent." They are never satisfied with the status quo, and this aversion to complacency creates a mindset that more actively searches for problems and opportunities.[16] Finally, employees can minimize problem identification errors by discussing the situation with colleagues. It is

Global Connections 7.1:

FAMOUS MISSED OPPORTUNITIES

Mental models create road maps that guide our decisions. Unfortunately, these maps also potentially block our ability to see emerging problems and opportunities. Here are a few famous examples:

- In the mid-1990s, two Stanford PhD students decided to sell their new search engine software for $1 million so they could concentrate on completing their education. Executives at Excite, Inc., a popular search engine company at that time, weren't interested because they were focused on building a media company. "If our search is only just good enough, then that's okay with us," Excite's CEO apparently said, even after the students reduced the price to $750,000. Executives at Yahoo! and Infoseek also decided not to buy the search engine. After these rejections, the two students, Larry Page and Sergey Brin, decided to form their own company—called Google—to realize the potential of their new invention. Several years later, Excite cofounder Joe Kraus acknowledged the decision error: "Let me just say that we were wrong," said Kraus about passing up the opportunity to own the core technology that made Google famous. "I'll be the first to stand up and say 'whoops.'"[17]
- One of the most famous commercials in history—the Apple Macintosh "1984" ad—almost never got aired because the computer maker's external board members thought it was the worst commercial they had ever seen. They complained that the commercial mentioned the product and company only in the last few seconds. The company asked the creative agency that produced the commercials to sell the two Superbowl time slots where they would have been shown, but the agency's CEO claimed that he could not find a buyer for the 60-second slot. The single 60-second ad shown during the Superbowl became one of the top news stories over the next week and has since been rated as the best commercial in history. Apple's board members subsequently apologized for their misjudgment of the "1984" commercial and applauded the Macintosh team for a successful launch.[18]
- Even though Harry Potter books were becoming the world's best sellers, Hollywood filmmakers were reluctant to produce film versions unless the Hogwarts School of Witchcraft was set in the United States or, at least, that Harry was an American at the British academy. Some filmmakers even insisted that all the main characters had to be Americans for the films to have any degree of success. Fortunately, after considerable persuasion, Hollywood decision makers reluctantly agreed to keep the location and characters all British.[19]
- Have you ever taken a "selfie" with a Kodak? Probably not. The Eastman Kodak Company, commonly known as Kodak, became so famous for its photographic film products that it held a dominant 89 percent market share in the United States in 1976. The company's ubiquity was such that its tagline "Kodak moment" was a way to describe a personal event that demanded to be recorded forever. But by the 1990s Kodak was struggling financially, and in January 2011 the company filed for bankruptcy. Although Kodak developed a digital camera in 1975, the first of its kind, the product was dropped for fear it would threaten Kodak's photographic film business. Kodak only started producing digital cameras in the 1990s. Yet despite new digital cameras from Sony hitting the market in 2001, and consumers starting to shift to the new technology, management at Kodak invested in aggressive marketing, still believing that photographic film was its main breadwinner.[20]

AP Photo/Ben Margot/CP Images

Preconceived mental models of business success prevented Yahoo! executives from recognizing the potential of Google's search engine.

much easier to discover blind spots in problem identification when listening to how others perceive the situation. Opportunities also become apparent when outsiders explore this information from their different mental models.

Searching for, Evaluating, and Choosing Alternatives

According to the rational choice paradigm of decision making, people rely on logic to evaluate and choose alternatives. This paradigm assumes that decision makers have well-articulated and agreed-on organizational goals, that they efficiently and simultaneously process facts about all alternatives and the consequences of those alternatives, and that they choose the alternative with the highest payoff.

bounded rationality The view that people are bounded in their decision-making capabilities, including access to limited information, limited information processing, and tendency towards satisficing rather than maximizing when making choices.

Nobel Prize-winning organizational scholar Herbert Simon questioned these assumptions a half century ago. He argued that people engage in **bounded rationality** because they process limited and imperfect information and rarely select the best choice.[21] Simon and other OB experts demonstrated that how people evaluate and choose alternatives differs from the rational choice paradigm in several ways, as illustrated in Exhibit 7.2. These differences are so significant that many economists are now shifting from rational choice to bounded rationality assumptions in their theories. Let's look at these differences in terms of goals, information processing, and maximization.

PROBLEMS WITH GOALS

The rational choice paradigm assumes that organizational goals are clear and agreed-on. In fact, these conditions are necessary to identify "what ought to be" and, therefore, provide a standard against which each alternative is evaluated. Unfortunately, organizational goals are often ambiguous or in conflict with each other.

PROBLEMS WITH INFORMATION PROCESSING

The rational choice paradigm also makes several assumptions about the human capacity to process information. It assumes that decision makers can process information about all alternatives and their consequences, whereas this is not possible in reality. Instead, people evaluate only a few alternatives and only some of the main outcomes of those alternatives.[22] For example, there may be dozens of computer brands to choose from and dozens of features to consider, yet people typically evaluate only a few brands and a few features.

EXHIBIT 7.2

Rational Choice Assumptions versus Organizational Behaviour Findings about Choosing Alternatives

Rational Choice Paradigm Assumptions	Observations from Organizational Behaviour
Goals are clear, compatible, and agreed upon	Goals are ambiguous, in conflict, and lack full support
Decision makers can calculate all alternatives and their outcomes	Decision makers have limited information processing abilities
Decision makers evaluate all alternatives simultaneously	Decision makers evaluate alternatives sequentially
Decision makers use absolute standards to evaluate alternatives	Decision makers evaluate alternatives against an implicit favourite
Decision makers use factual information to choose alternatives	Decision makers process perceptually distorted information
Decision makers choose the alternative with the highest payoff	Decision makers choose the alternative that is good enough (satisficing)

A related problem is that decision makers typically evaluate alternatives sequentially rather than all at the same time. This sequential evaluation occurs partly because all alternatives are not usually available to the decision maker at the same time.[23] Consequently, as a new alternative comes along, it is immediately compared to an **implicit favourite**–an alternative that the decision maker prefers and that is used as a comparison with other choices. When choosing a new computer system, for example, people typically have an implicit favourite brand or model in their heads that they use to compare with the others. This sequential process of comparing alternatives with an implicit favourite occurs even when decision makers aren't consciously aware that they are doing this.[24]

implicit favourite A preferred alternative that the decision maker uses repeatedly as a comparison with other choices.

Although the implicit favourite comparison process seems to be hardwired in human decision making (i.e., we naturally compare things), it often undermines effective decision making because people distort information to favour their implicit favourite over the alternative choices. They tend to ignore problems with the implicit favourite and advantages of the alternative. Decision makers also overweight factors on which the implicit favourite is better and underweight areas in which the alternative is superior.[25]

Biased Decision Heuristics Subjective expected utility is the cornerstone of rational choice decision making, yet psychologists Amos Tversky and Daniel Kahneman discovered that human beings have built-in *decision heuristics* that automatically distort either the probability of outcomes or the value (utility) of those outcomes. Three of the most widely studied heuristic biases are anchoring and adjustment, availability, and representativeness:[26]

- *Anchoring and adjustment heuristic*. The **anchoring and adjustment heuristic** states that we are influenced by an initial anchor point and do not sufficiently move away from that point as new information is provided.[27] The anchor point might be an initial offer price, initial opinion of someone, or initial estimated probability that something will occur. This bias affects the value we assign to choices and their outcomes. For example, suppose you ask someone whether the population of Chile is above or below 50 million, then you ask that person to estimate Chile's population. Next, you ask a second person whether the population of Chile is above or below 10 million, then you ask him or her to estimate that country's actual population. If these two people don't actually know Chile's population, chances are that the first person will give a much higher population estimate than will the second person. The initial anchor point (50 million vs. 10 million) biases their estimate.

anchoring and adjustment heuristic A natural tendency for people to be influenced by an initial anchor point such that they do not sufficiently move away from that point as new information is provided.

- *Availability heuristic*. The **availability heuristic** is the tendency to estimate the probability of something occurring by how easily we can recall those events. Unfortunately, how easily we recall something is due to more than just its frequency (probability).[28] For instance, we easily remember emotional events (such as earthquakes and shark attacks), so we overestimate how often these traumatic events occur. We also have an easier time recalling recent events. If the media report several incidents of air pollution, we likely give more pessimistic estimates of air quality generally than if there have been no recent reports.

availability heuristic A natural tendency to assign higher probabilities to objects or events that are easier to recall from memory, even though ease of recall is also affected by nonprobability factors (e.g., emotional response, recent events).

- *Representativeness heuristic*. The **representativeness heuristic** states that we pay more attention to whether something resembles (is representative of) something else than on more precise statistics about its probability.[29] Suppose that one-fifth of the students in your class are in engineering and the others are business majors. Statistically, there is a 20 percent chance that any individual in that class is an engineering student. Yet, if one student looks and acts like a stereotype of an engineer, we tend to believe the person is an engineer even though there is much stronger and more reliable statistical evidence that he/she is a business major. Another form of the representativeness heuristic, known as the *clustering illusion*, is the tendency to see patterns from a small sample of events when those events are, in fact, random. For example, most players and coaches believe that players are more likely to have a successful shot on the net when their previous two or three shots have been successful. The representativeness heuristic is at work here because players and coaches believe these sequences are causally connected (representative) when, in reality, they are more likely random events.

representativeness heuristic A natural tendency to evaluate probabilities of events or objects by the degree to which they resemble (are representative of) other events or objects rather than on objective probability information.

PROBLEMS WITH MAXIMIZATION

satisficing Selecting an alternative that is satisfactory or "good enough," rather than the alternative with the highest value (maximization).

One of the main assumptions of the rational choice paradigm is that people want to–and are able to–choose the alternative with the highest payoff (i.e., the highest "utility" in subjective expected utility). Yet rather than aiming for maximization, people engage in **satisficing**–they choose an alternative that is satisfactory or "good enough."[30] People satisfice when they select the first alternative that exceeds a standard of acceptance for their needs and preferences. Satisficing partly occurs because alternatives present themselves over time, not all at once. Consider the process of hiring new employees. It is impossible to choose the best possible job candidate because people apply over a period of time and the best candidate might not apply until next month, after earlier candidates have found other jobs. Consequently, as we mentioned earlier, decision makers rely on sequential evaluation of new alternatives against an implicit favourite. This necessarily calls for a satisficing decision rule–choose the first alternative that is "good enough."

A second reason why people engage in satisficing rather than maximization is that they lack the capacity and motivation to process the huge volume of information required to identify the best choice. Studies report that people like to have choices, but making decisions when there are many alternatives can be cognitively and emotionally draining. Consequently, when exposed to many alternatives, decision makers become cognitive misers by engaging in satisficing.[31] They also respond to many choices by discarding many of them using easily identifiable factors (i.e., colour, size) and by evaluating alternatives using only a handful of criteria.

When presented with a large number of choices, people often choose a decision strategy that is even less cognitively challenging than satisficing; they don't make any decision at all! One study reported that many employees put off registering for the company's pension plan when they face dozens of investment options, even though signing up would give them tax benefits, company contributions to that plan, and long-term financial security. The company pension plan registration rate increases dramatically when employees are given only two or three initial investment options, such as a growth fund, balanced fund, and capital stable investment. The dozens of other investment choices are then presented after the employee has signed up.[32]

EVALUATING OPPORTUNITIES

Opportunities are just as important as problems, but what happens when an opportunity is "discovered" is quite different from the process of problem solving. Decision makers do not evaluate several alternatives when they find an opportunity; after all, the opportunity *is* the solution, so why look for others! An opportunity is usually experienced as an exciting and rare revelation, so decision makers tend to have an emotional attachment to the opportunity. Unfortunately, this emotional preference motivates decision makers to apply the opportunity and short-circuit any detailed evaluation of it.[33]

People avoid making choices in decisions that have too many alternatives. In one study, grocery store customers saw one of two jam-tasting booths. Thirty percent of consumers who visited the booth displaying 6 types of jam purchased one of those products. In contrast, only three percent of customers who saw the booth displaying 24 types of jam made a purchase. The larger number of choices discouraged them from making any decision. Other studies of decisions about chocolates, term essays, and pension plan investment options revealed similar results.[34]

© mrPliskin/iStock

The Role of Emotions and Intuition

LO3

EMOTIONS AND MAKING CHOICES

Herbert Simon and many other experts have found that people do not evaluate alternatives nearly as well as is assumed by the rational choice paradigm. However, they neglected to mention another glaring weakness with rational choice: It completely ignores the effect of emotions in human decision making. Just as both the rational and emotional brain centres alert us to problems, they also influence our choice of alternatives.[35] Emotions affect the evaluation of alternatives in three ways.

Emotions Form Early Preferences The emotional marker process described in previous chapters (Chapters 3 through 5) shapes our preferences for each alternative before we consciously evaluate those alternatives. Our brain very quickly attaches specific emotions to information about each alternative, and our preferred alternative is strongly influenced by those initial emotional markers.[36] Of course, logical analysis also influences which alternative we choose, but it requires strong logical evidence to change our initial preferences (initial emotional markers). Yet even logical analysis depends on emotions to sway our decision. Specifically, neuroscientific evidence says that information produced from logical analysis is tagged with emotional markers that then motivate us to choose or avoid a particular alternative. Ultimately, emotions, not rational logic, energize us to make the preferred choice. In fact, people with damaged emotional brain centres have difficulty making choices.

connect

What is your preferred decision-making style? Visit connect.mcgrawhill.com to assess your preference for logical or intuitive decision making.

Emotions Change the Decision Evaluation Process Moods and specific emotions influence the *process* of evaluating alternatives.[37] For instance, we pay more attention to details when in a negative mood, possibly because a negative mood signals that there is something wrong that requires attention. When in a positive mood, on the other hand, we pay less attention to details and rely on a more programmed decision routine. This phenomenon explains why executive teams in successful companies are often less vigilant about competitors and other environmental threats.[38] Research also suggests that decision makers rely on stereotypes and other shortcuts to speed up the choice process when they experience anger. Anger also makes them more optimistic about the success of risky alternatives, whereas the emotion of fear tends to make them less optimistic. Overall, emotions shape *how* we evaluate information, not just which choice we select.

Emotions Serve as Information When We Evaluate Alternatives The third way that emotions influence the evaluation of alternatives is through a process called "emotions as information." Marketing experts have found that we listen in on our emotions to gain guidance when making choices.[39] This process is similar to having a temporary improvement in emotional intelligence. Most emotional experiences remain below the level of conscious awareness, but people actively try to be more sensitive to these subtle emotions when making a decision.

When buying a new car, for example, you not only logically evaluate each vehicle's features; you also try to gauge your emotions when visualizing what it would be like to own each of the cars on your list of choices. Even if you have solid information about the quality of each vehicle on key features (purchase price, fuel efficiency, maintenance costs, resale value, etc.), you are swayed by your emotional reaction and actively try to sense that emotional response when thinking about it. Some people pay more attention to these gut feelings, and personality tests such as the Myers-Briggs Type Indicator (see Chapter 2) identify individuals who listen in on their emotions more than others.[40] But everyone consciously pays attention to their emotions to some degree when choosing alternatives. This phenomenon ties directly into our next topic, intuition.

INTUITION AND MAKING CHOICES

intuition The ability to know when a problem or opportunity exists and to select the best course of action without conscious reasoning.

Do you have a gut instinct–a feeling inside–when something isn't quite right? Or perhaps a different emotional experience occurs when you sense an opportunity in front of your eyes? These emotional experiences potentially (but not necessarily) indicate your **intuition**–the ability to know when a problem or opportunity exists and to select the best course of action without conscious reasoning.[41] Intuition is both an emotional experience and a rapid nonconscious analytic process. As mentioned in the previous section, the gut feelings we experience are emotional signals that have enough intensity to make us consciously aware of them. These signals warn us of impending danger or motivate us to take advantage of an opportunity. Some intuition also directs us to preferred choices relative to other alternatives in the situation.

All gut feelings are emotional signals, but not all emotional signals are intuition. The main distinction is that intuition involves rapidly comparing our observations with deeply held patterns learned through experience.[42] These "templates of the mind" represent tacit knowledge that has been implicitly acquired over time. They are mental models that help us to understand whether the current situation is good or bad, depending on how well that situation fits our mental model. When a template fits or doesn't fit the current situation, emotions are produced that motivate us to act. Studies have found that chess masters experience emotional signals when they see an opportunity through quick observation of a chessboard. They can't immediately analyze why this opportunity exists, but can do so when given time to think about the situation. Their intuition signals the opportunity long before this rational analysis takes place.

As mentioned, some emotional signals are not intuition, so gut feelings shouldn't always guide our decisions. The problem is that emotional responses are not always based on well-grounded mental models. Instead, we sometimes compare the current situation to more remote templates, which may or may not be relevant. A new employee might feel confident about relations with a supplier, whereas an experienced employee senses potential problems. The difference is that the new employee relies on templates from other experiences or industries that might not work well in this situation. Thus, the extent to which our gut feelings in a situation represent intuition depends on our level of experience in that situation.

So far, we have described intuition as an emotional experience (gut feeling) and a process in which we compare the current situation with well-established templates of the mind. Intuition also relies on *action scripts*–programmed decision routines that speed up our response to pattern matches or mismatches.[43] Action scripts effectively shorten the decision-making process by jumping from problem identification to selection of a solution. In other words, action scripting is a form of programmed decision making. Action scripts are generic, so we need to consciously adapt them to the specific situation.

MAKING CHOICES MORE EFFECTIVELY

It is very difficult to get around the human limitations of making choices, but a few strategies help to minimize these concerns. One important discovery is that decisions tend to have a higher failure rate when leaders are decisive rather than contemplative about the available options. Of course, decisions can also be ineffective when leaders take too long to make a choice, but research indicates that a lack of logical evaluation of alternatives is a greater concern. By systematically assessing alternatives against relevant factors, decision makers minimize the implicit favourite and satisficing problems that occur when they rely on general subjective judgments. This recommendation does not suggest that we ignore intuition; rather, it suggests that we use it in combination with careful analysis of relevant information.[44]

A second piece of advice is to remember that decisions are influenced by both rational and emotional processes. With this point in mind, some decision makers deliberately revisit important issues later so that they look at the information in different moods and have allowed their initial emotions to subside. For example, if you sense that your team is feeling somewhat too self-confident when making an important competitive decision, you might decide to have the team members revisit the decision a few days later when they are thinking more critically.

scenario planning A systematic process of thinking about alternative futures and what the organization should do to anticipate and react to those environments.

Another strategy is **scenario planning,** which is a disciplined method for imagining possible futures.[45] It typically involves thinking about what would happen if a significant environmental condition changed and what the organization should do to anticipate and react to such an outcome. Scenario planning is a useful vehicle for choosing the best solutions under possible scenarios long before they occur, because alternative courses of action are evaluated without the pressure and emotions that occur during real emergencies.

Kjetil Odin Johnsen, CEO at Whatif AS

Scenario planning helps decision makers figure out the best solutions to crises before they occur. Dreyer Kompetense, a Norwegian company, has created "What If," a board game that applies scenario planning to shipping, IT security, and other industries. Participants first review several dozen scenarios and choose an event with the greatest risk. For example, one scenario in the shipping exercise is a situation where a fire knocks out all engines, resulting in a collision with another vessel. The team then identifies actions to prepare their company or ship for these high-risk scenarios.[46]

Implementing Decisions

Implementing decisions is often skipped over in most writing about the decision-making process. Yet leading business writers emphasize that execution–translating decisions into action–is one of the most important and challenging tasks in the decision-making process.[47] For instance, when Bill Utt became CEO of KBR, a Fortune 300 engineering firm, he and his executive team fairly quickly made three strategic decisions that would improve the company's future prospects. Implementing those decisions, however, took much longer. "I expected that it would take two years to complete the three challenges," says Utt. "One thing I have learned over my career is that it is easy to develop a strategy and to find the organization's deficiencies; however, the hard part is in the implementation and having the focus, determination and stamina to see these successfully through."[48] Implementing decisions is mainly about organizational change, which we discuss in Chapter 15, but also relates to leadership (Chapter 12) and several other topics throughout this book.

Evaluating Decision Outcomes

Contrary to the rational choice paradigm, decision makers aren't completely honest with themselves when evaluating the effectiveness of their decisions. One problem is *confirmation bias* (also known as *post-decisional justification* in the context of decision evaluation), which is the "unwitting selectivity in the acquisition and use of evidence."[49] When evaluating decisions, people with confirmation bias ignore or downplay the negative features of the selected alternative and overemphasize its positive features. Confirmation bias gives people an excessively optimistic evaluation of their decisions, but only until they receive very clear and undeniable information to the contrary. Unfortunately, it also inflates the decision maker's initial evaluation of the decision, so reality often comes as a painful shock when objective feedback is finally received.

escalation of commitment The tendency to repeat an apparently bad decision or allocate more resources to a failing course of action.

ESCALATION OF COMMITMENT

Another reason why decision makers don't evaluate their decisions very well is due to **escalation of commitment**–the tendency to repeat an apparently bad decision or allocate more resources to a failing course of action.[50] There are plenty of examples of this decision-making problem. For example, the British Columbia Ferry Services ordered the design and construction of three catamaran-style ferries for its route between the city of Vancouver and Vancouver Island. These "PacifiCats" were supposed to travel faster than conventional ferries and cost $210 million "right down to the toilet paper." Not only did costs balloon to nearly $500 million, the ferries were almost unusable due to their damaging wake, maintenance problems, poor manoeuvrability, and high fuel costs. The three ferries were eventually auctioned off for $20 million.

Why are decision makers led deeper and deeper into failing projects? Several explanations have been identified and discussed over the years, but the four main influences are self-justification effect, self-enhancement effect, prospect theory effect, and sunk costs effect.

Self-Justification Effect People engage in behaviours that convey a positive public image of themselves. In decision making, this self-justification typically involves appearing to be rational and competent. People are therefore motivated to demonstrate that their decisions will be successful, and this includes continuing to support those decisions even when there is evidence that they are not having the desired outcomes. In contrast, pulling the plug symbolizes the project's failure and the decision maker's incompetence. This self-justification effect is particularly evident when decision makers are personally identified with the project, have staked their reputations to some extent on the project's success, and have low self-esteem.[51]

Self-Enhancement Effect People have a natural tendency to feel good about themselves–to feel luckier, more competent, and more successful than average–regarding things that are important to them (see Chapter 3).[52] This self-enhancement supports a positive self-concept, but it also increases the risk of escalation of commitment. When presented with evidence that a project is in trouble, the self-enhancement process biases our interpretation of the information as a temporary aberration from an otherwise positive trend line. And when we eventually realize that the project isn't going as well as planned, we continue to invest in the project because our probability of rescuing the project is above average. Self-justification and self-enhancement often occur together, but they are different mechanisms. Self-justification is a deliberate attempt to maintain a favourable public image, whereas self-enhancement operates mostly nonconsciously, distorting information so we do not recognize the problem sooner and biasing our probabilities of success so we continue to invest in the losing project.[53]

prospect theory effect A natural tendency to feel more dissatisfaction from losing a particular amount than satisfaction from gaining an equal amount.

Prospect Theory Effect **Prospect theory effect** is the tendency to experience stronger negative emotions when losing something of value than the positive emotions when gaining something of equal value. This prospect theory effect motivates us to avoid losses, which typically occurs by taking the risk of investing more in that losing project. Stopping a project is a certain loss, which is more painful to most people than the uncertainty of success associated with continuing to fund the project. Given the choice, decision makers choose escalation of commitment, which is the less painful option at the time.[54] An example can be found in the 2013 Oscar-nominated movie *Captain Phillips,* based on the true story of a hijacked freighter sailing off the coast of Africa. In the movie, Captain Phillips, played by Tom Hanks, is held hostage by Somali pirates on a small emergency vessel. With the U.S. military closing in, Captain Phillips tries to convince the leader of the Somali group that giving up is the best option. The Somali leader's response: "I've come too far." Here, the sure loss of giving up was less appealing than the risky option of holding out longer and seeing what might happen. In the end, all but one of the Somali pirates were shot and killed, and the remaining survivor was sentenced to 30 years in prison.

Sunk Costs Effect Another disincentive to axing a failing project is sunk costs–the value of resources already invested in the decision.[55] Rational choice theory states that investing resources should be determined by expected future gains and risk, not the size of earlier resources invested in the project. Yet people inherently feel motivated to invest more resources in projects that have high sunk costs. A variation of sunk costs is time investment. Time is a resource, so the more time decision makers have devoted to a project, the more motivated they are to continuing investing in that project. Finally, sunk costs can take the form of closing costs, that is, the financial or nonfinancial penalties associated with shutting down a project. As with other forms of sunk costs, the higher the closing costs, the more motivated decision makers are to engage in escalation of commitment.

Escalation of commitment is usually framed as poor decision making, but some experts argue that throwing more money into a failing project is sometimes a logical attempt to further understand an ambiguous situation. This strategy is essentially a variation of testing unknown waters. By adding more resources, the decision maker gains new information about the effectiveness of these funds, which provides more feedback about the project's future success. This strategy is particularly common where the project has high closing costs.[56]

EVALUATING DECISION OUTCOMES MORE EFFECTIVELY

One of the most effective ways to minimize escalation of commitment and confirmation bias is to ensure that the people who made the original decision are not the same people who later evaluate that decision. This separation of roles minimizes the self-justification effect because the person responsible for evaluating the decision is not connected to the original decision. However, the second person might continue to escalate the project if he or she empathizes with the decision maker, has a similar mindset, or has similar attributes such as age. A second strategy is to publicly establish a preset level at which the decision is abandoned or re-evaluated. This is similar to a stop-loss order in the stock market, whereby the stock is sold if it falls below a certain price. The problem with this solution is that conditions are often so complex that it is difficult to identify an appropriate point to abandon a project.[57]

A third strategy is to find a source of systematic and clear feedback.[58] At some point, even the strongest escalation and confirmation bias effects deflate when the evidence highlights the project's failings. A fourth strategy to improve the decision evaluation process is to involve several people in the evaluation. Coworkers continuously monitor each other and might notice problems sooner than someone working alone on the project.

Creativity

LO4

creativity The development of original ideas that make a socially recognized contribution.

The entire decision-making process described over the preceding pages depends on **creativity**—the development of original ideas that make a socially recognized contribution.[59] Creativity is at work when imagining opportunities, such as how a company's expertise might be redirected to untapped markets. Creativity is present when developing alternatives, such as figuring out new places to look for existing solutions or working out the design of a custom-made solution. Creativity also helps us choose alternatives because we need to visualize the future in different ways and to figure out how each choice might be useful or a liability in those scenarios. In short, creativity is an essential component of decision making as well as a powerful resource for corporate competitive advantage and individual career development.

The value of creativity in decision making is evident at Google, the Internet search engine company. Google's creative culture includes a natural practice of experimenting with ideas and seeking out different uses of technology. Perhaps most famous is the company's policy of giving engineers 20 percent of their time to develop projects of their choosing. "Almost everything that is interesting which Google does started out as a 20 percent time idea," explains a Google executive. Google News and the photos linked to Google Maps were two projects developed from the 20 percent time rule.[60]

connect

How well do you engage in divergent thinking? Visit **connect.mcgrawhill.com** to assess your creative bench strength.

"It's a new financial world and this bank needs to think outside the box, so, anybody got any ideas . . . any ideas at all?"

Credit: *US Banker*, 2010. Reprinted with permission of Kevin Pope.

THE CREATIVE PROCESS

How does creativity occur? That question has puzzled experts for hundreds of years and has been the fascination of Einstein, Poincaré, and many other scientists who have reflected on the creativity that contributed to their own important discoveries. More than a century ago, German physicist Hermann von Helmholtz gave a public talk in which he described the process that led to his innovations (energy physics, instruments for examining eyes, and many others). A few decades later, London School of Economics professor Graham Wallas built on Helmholtz's ideas to construct the four-stage model shown in Exhibit 7.3.[61] This model remains the most reputable and influential nearly a century later.

EXHIBIT 7.3

The Creative Process Model

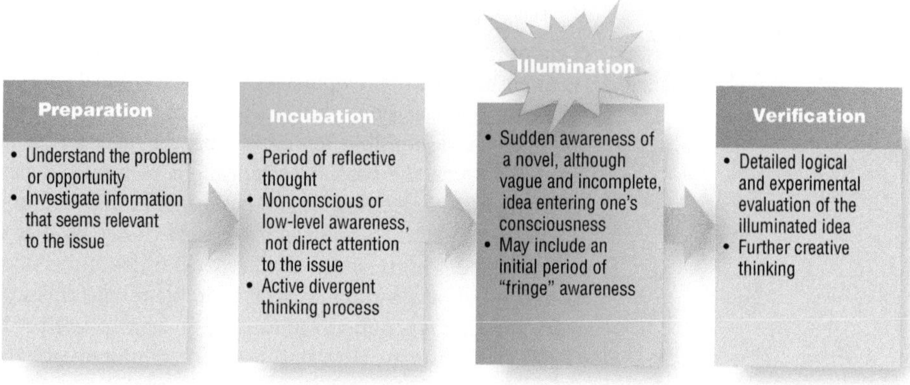

Source: Based on G. Wallas, *The Art of Thought* (London: Jonathan Cape, 1926, Chap. 4).

The first stage is *preparation*–the process of investigating the problem or opportunity in many ways. Preparation involves developing a clear understanding of what you are trying to achieve through a novel solution and then actively studying information seemingly related to the topic. It is a process of developing knowledge and possibly skills about the issue or object of attention. The second stage, called *incubation,* is the period of reflective thought. We put the problem aside, but our mind is still working on it in the background.[62] The important condition here is to maintain a low-level awareness by frequently revisiting the problem. Incubation does not mean that you forget about the problem or issue.

divergent thinking Reframing a problem in a unique way and generating different approaches to the issue.

Incubation assists **divergent thinking**–reframing the problem in a unique way and generating different approaches to the issue. This contrasts with *convergent thinking*–calculating the conventionally accepted "right answer" to a logical problem. Divergent thinking breaks us away from existing mental models so that we can apply concepts or processes from completely different areas of life. The discovery of Velcro is a case in point. In the 1940s, Swiss engineer Georges de Mestral had just returned home from a walk with his dog through the countryside when he noticed that his clothing and the dog's fur were covered in burrs. While struggling to remove the barbed seeds, de Mestral engaged in divergent thinking by recognizing that the adhesion used by burrs could be used to attach other things together. It took another dozen years of hard work, but de Mestral eventually perfected the hook-and-loop fastener, which he trademarked as Velcro.[63]

Illumination (also called insight), the third stage of creativity, refers to the experience of suddenly becoming aware of a unique idea.[64] Wallas and others also suggest that this stage begins with a "fringe" awareness before the idea fully enters our consciousness. Illumination is often visually depicted as a light bulb, but a better image would be a flash of light or perhaps a briefly flickering candle–these bits of inspiration are fleeting and can be quickly lost if not documented. For this reason, many creative people keep a journal or notebook nearby so that they can jot down their ideas before they disappear. Also, flickering ideas don't keep a particular schedule; they might come to you at any time of day or night.

Illumination presents ideas that are usually vague, roughly drawn, and untested. Verification, therefore, provides the essential final stage of creativity, whereby we flesh out the illuminated ideas and subject them to detailed logical evaluation and experimentation. This stage often calls for further creativity as the ideas evolve into finished products or services. Thus, although *verification* is labelled the final stage of creativity, it is really the beginning of a long process of creative decision making towards development of an innovative product or service.

connect

Do you have a creative personality? See page 188 or visit connect.mcgrawhill.com to assess the extent to which you have a disposition for creative thinking.

EXHIBIT 7.4

Characteristics of Creative People

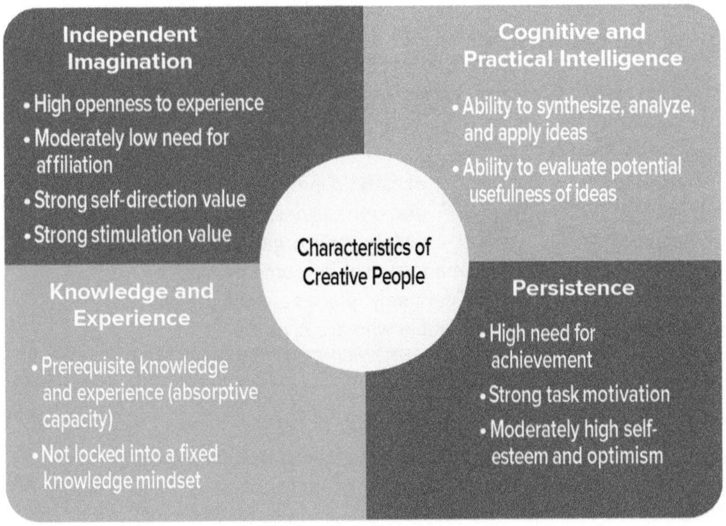

CHARACTERISTICS OF CREATIVE PEOPLE

Everyone is creative, but some people have a higher potential for creativity. Four of the main characteristics that give individuals more creative potential are intelligence, persistence, knowledge and experience, and a cluster of personality traits and values representing independent imagination (see Exhibit 7.4).

- *Cognitive and practical intelligence.* Creative people have above-average intelligence to synthesize information, analyze ideas, and apply their ideas.[65] Like the fictional sleuth Sherlock Holmes, creative people recognize the significance of small bits of information and are able to connect them in ways that few others can imagine. They also have *practical intelligence*–the capacity to evaluate the potential usefulness of their ideas.
- *Persistence.* Creative people have persistence, which includes a higher need for achievement, a strong motivation from the task itself, and a moderate or high degree of self-esteem. Persistence is vital because people need this motivation to continue working on and investing in a project in spite of failures and advice from others to quit. In fact, people have a general tendency to dismiss or criticize creative ideas, so creative people need persistence to withstand these negative social forces.[66]
- *Knowledge and experience.* Creative people require a foundation of knowledge and experience to discover or acquire new knowledge.[67] However, this expertise is a double-edged sword. As people acquire knowledge and experience about a specific topic, their mental models tend to become more rigid. They are less adaptable to new information or rules about that knowledge domain. Some writers suggest that expertise also increases "mindless behaviour" because expertise reduces the tendency to question why things happen.[68] To overcome the limitations of expertise, some corporate leaders like to hire people from other industries and areas of expertise. For instance, when Geoffrey Ballard, founder of Ballard Power Systems, hired a chemist to develop a better battery, the chemist protested that he didn't know anything about batteries. Ballard replied: "That's fine. I don't want someone who knows batteries. They know what won't work."[69]
- *Independent imagination.* Creative people possess a cluster of personality traits and values that support an independent imagination: high openness to experience, moderately low need for affiliation, and strong values around self-direction and stimulation.[70] Openness to experience is a Big Five personality dimension representing the extent to which a person is imaginative, curious, sensitive, open-minded, and original (see Chapter 2). Creative people have a moderately low need for affiliation so they are less embarrassed when making mistakes. Self-direction includes the values of creativity and independent thought; stimulation includes the values of excitement and challenge. Together, these values form openness to change–representing the motivation to pursue innovative ways (see Chapter 2).

OB by the NUMBERS

The Creativity Advantage[71]

53% of Canadian federal government employees mostly or strongly agree that innovation is valued in their work unit.

66% of 1,461 American managers and consultants polled believe their organization's management "to some degree" or "definitely" places a premium on people who are creative.

60% of 600 senior global HR leaders polled identify creativity as one of the most important leadership qualities over the next five years (top choice, followed by integrity).

57% of 1,966 American employees say that innovation/creativity/out-of-the-box thinking will prove to be the most useful over the next year.

41% of 251,507 U.S. Federal Government employees surveyed agree or strongly agree that creativity and innovation are rewarded in their organization.

ORGANIZATIONAL CONDITIONS SUPPORTING CREATIVITY

Intelligence, persistence, expertise, and independent imagination represent a person's creative potential, but the extent to which these characteristics produce more creative output depends on how well the work environment supports the creative process.[72] Several job and workplace characteristics have been identified in the literature, and different combinations of situations can equally support creativity; there isn't one best work environment.[73]

One of the most important conditions that supports creative practice is that the organization has a *learning orientation;* that is, leaders recognize that employees make reasonable mistakes as part of the creative process. "Creativity comes from failure," Samsung Electronics CEO and vice chairman Yun Jong-yong advises employees. "We should reform our corporate culture to forgive failure if workers did their best."[74] Motivation from the job itself is another important condition for creativity.[75] Employees tend to be more creative when they believe their work benefits the organization and/or larger society (i.e., task significance) and when they have the freedom to pursue novel ideas without bureaucratic delays (i.e., autonomy). Creativity is about changing things, and change is possible only when employees have the authority to experiment. More generally, jobs encourage creativity when they are challenging and aligned with the employee's competencies.

Along with supporting a learning orientation and intrinsically motivating jobs, companies foster creativity through open communication and sufficient resources. They also provide a comfortable degree of job security, which explains why creativity suffers during times of downsizing and corporate restructuring.[76] Some companies also support creativity by designing nontraditional workspaces, such as unique building design or unconventional office areas.[77] Google is one example. The Internet innovator has funky offices in several countries that include hammocks, gondola and hive-shaped privacy spaces, slides, and brightly painted walls.

To some degree, creativity also improves with support from leaders and coworkers. One study reported that effective product champions provide enthusiastic support for new ideas. Other studies suggest that coworker support can improve creativity in some situations whereas competition among coworkers improves creativity in other situations.[78] Similarly, it isn't clear how much pressure should be exerted on employees to produce creative ideas. Extreme time pressures are well-known creativity inhibitors, but lack of pressure doesn't seem to produce the highest creativity either.

© Rob Newell Photography

When it comes to creative thinking, Alex Beim sees the light. The founder and chief creative technologist of Tangible Interaction Design in Vancouver, Canada, designed the digital graffiti walls at a Chanel outlet in New York City and Converse Shoes in Amsterdam, as well as the colour-changing illuminated lightweight orbs (called zygotes) at the Vancouver Olympics. "I get ideas all the time for designs I want to create," says Beim, who now employs a team of people. "I love researching the idea, seeing it come to life and watching the happiness it brings to people."[79]

ACTIVITIES THAT ENCOURAGE CREATIVITY

Hiring people with strong creative potential and providing a work environment that supports creativity are two cornerstones of a creative workplace. The third cornerstone consists of various activities that help employees think more creatively. One set of activities involves redefining the problem. Employees might be encouraged to revisit old projects that have been set aside. After a few months of neglect, these projects might be seen in new ways.[80] Another strategy involves asking people unfamiliar with the issue (preferably with different expertise) to explore the problem with you. You would state the objectives and give some facts and then let the other person ask questions to further understand the situation. By verbalizing the problem, listening to questions, and hearing what others think, you are more likely to form new perspectives on the issue.[81]

A second set of creativity activities, known as *associative play*, attempts to bring out creativity by literally engaging in playful activities.[82] For example, British media giant OMD sends employees to two-day retreats in the countryside, where they play grapefruit croquet, chant like medieval monks, and pretend to be dog collars. "Being creative is a bit like an emotion; we need to be stimulated," explains Harriet Frost, one of OMD's specialists in building creativity. "The same is true for our imagination and its ability to come up with new ideas. You can't just sit in a room and devise hundreds of ideas."[83] Another associative play activity, called *morphological analysis*, involves listing different dimensions of a system and the elements of each dimension and then looking at each combination. This encourages people to carefully examine combinations that initially seem nonsensical.

A third set of activities that promote creative thinking falls under the category of *cross-pollination*.[84] Cross-pollination occurs when people from different areas of the organization exchange ideas or when new people are brought into an existing team. Mother, the London-based creative agency, has unusual policies and working conditions that apply this creative process. The company's 100 or so employees perform their daily work around one monster-size table–a 2.5-metre-wide reinforced-concrete slab that extends 91 metres like a skateboard ramp around the entire floor. Every three weeks, employees are asked to relocate their laptop, portable telephone, and trolley to another area around the table. Why the musical-chairs exercise? "It encourages cross-pollination of ideas," explains Stef Calcraft, one of Mother's founding partners. "You have people working on the same problem from different perspectives. It makes problem-solving much more organic."[85]

Cross-pollination highlights the fact that creativity rarely occurs alone. Some creative people may be individualistic, but most creative ideas are generated through teams and informal social interaction. "This whole thing about the solitary tortured artist is nonsense I think," says John Collee, the screenwriter who penned such films as Happy Feet and Master and Commander. "All the great creative people I know have become great precisely because they know how to get along with people and swim around in the communal unconscious."[86] This notion of improving creativity through social interaction leads us to the final section of this chapter: employee involvement in decision making.

Employee Involvement in Decision Making

LO5

Nishith Desai Associates (NDA) isn't your typical law firm. About 60 percent of decisions at the 100-member Mumbai, India-based organization occur through consensus. Another 25 percent are reached through majority vote of the partners, and the remainder are determined by the executive committee or the CEO. The law firm also has representative committees. The compensation committee, for example, consists of staff voted into the position and who have three or more years of professional experience. Overall, NDA strives to become a democratic organization by relying on various levels and forms of employee involvement in decision making.[87]

employee involvement The degree to which employees influence how their work is organized and carried out.

Employee involvement (also called *participative management*) refers to the degree to which employees influence how their work is organized and carried out.[88] Employee involvement has become a natural process in every organization, but the level of involvement varies with the situation. In some organizations, such as NDA, almost everyone has a high degree of involvement in some corporate-wide decisions during a given year, whereas other organizations might give employees only low levels of involvement.[89]

Debating Point:

SHOULD ORGANIZATIONS PRACTISE DEMOCRACY?

Most organizational experts recommend some degree of employee involvement, but a few go further by proposing that organizations should operate like democracies rather than hierarchical fiefdoms. Organizational democracy consists of the highest form of involvement, whereby employees have real institutionalized control—either directly or through representation—over organizational decisions. In addition, no one in a democratic enterprise holds higher authority except where such power is explicitly granted by the others (such as through employee election of the company's leaders). Democracy also gives all organizational members protection against arbitrary or unjust decisions (such as protection against being fired without cause).[90]

Some readers might think workplace democracy as an extreme way to run an organization, but advocates point out that it is the principle on which many societies have operated for centuries and most others aspire. Democratic governance has been established in several high-profile and successful companies, such as Semco SA and W. L. Gore & Associates, as well as many employee-owned firms and worker cooperatives. Legislation in several countries (particularly in continental Europe) requires companies to give employees control over some organizational decisions through works councils or board membership.[91]

Advocates point out that as a form of participation, workplace democracy can improve the quality of organizational decisions and employee commitment to those decisions. Indeed, democracy inherently advocates shared leadership (where everyone should be a leader in various ways), which is increasingly recommended for improved decision making and organizational effectiveness. Democratic enterprises might also be more flexible and innovative. Rather than obediently follow management's standard operating procedures, employees in democratic organizations have the opportunity—and likely to expectation—to adapt and experiment with new work practices as circumstances change. This form of organization also encourages more organizational learning.[92]

A final argument is that the democratic enterprise is ethically superior to the traditional hierarchical organization.[93] It respects individual rights and dignity, more fully satisfies the standards of ethical conduct, and is more likely than traditional management to adopt the multiple stakeholder approach expected by society. Indeed, some European governments have debated the notion that organizational democracy is a potentially effective way to minimize corporate wrongdoing because it actively monitors top decision makers and continually holds them accountable for their actions.

The democratic enterprise model has a number of vocal advocates, but few practitioners. There is somewhat more employee involvement today than a few decades ago, but still far from the democratic ideal. Most firms operate with the traditional model that management retains control and employees have few rights. There may be reasons for this intransigence. One argument against organizational democracy is that employees have a contractual rather than ownership relationship with the organization. Legally (and possibly morally) they have no right to assume citizenship rights or control over the business. A second consideration is that employees might emphasize their own interests to the detriment of other stakeholders. In contrast, traditional organizations give management an explicit obligation to serve multiple stakeholders to ensure the organization's survival and success.

Another concern is that workplace democracy might dilute accountability. Although moderate levels of employee involvement can improve decision-making quality and commitment, there is a real risk that no one will take responsibility for decisions when everyone has a say in them. In addition, democracy often results in slower decision making, which could lead to a lethargic corporate response to changes in the external environment. Finally, the democratic enterprise model presumes that employees want to control their organizations, but some research suggests that employees prefer a more moderate level of workplace involvement. For this reason (and others noted above), employee-owned companies often maintain a more traditional hierarchical worker–management relationship.[94]

A low level of involvement occurs where employees are individually asked for specific information but the problem is not described to them. Somewhat higher involvement occurs where employees the problem is described and employees are asked individually or collectively for information relating to that problem. Moving further up the involvement scale, the problem is described to employees, who are collectively given responsibility for developing recommendations. However, the decision maker is not bound to accept those recommendations. At the highest level of involvement, the entire decision-making process is handed over to employees. They identify the problem, discover alternative solutions, choose the best alternative, and implement that choice. The original decision maker serves only as a facilitator to guide the team's decision process and keep everyone on track.

Global Connections 7.2:

BRASILATA, THE IDEAS COMPANY

Steel can manufacturing may be a mature industry, but the folks at Brasilata don't see it that way. The Brazilian company relies on employee involvement to fuel its extraordinary productivity and innovation. It has won top industry and supplier awards almost every year, including the coveted Sherwin-Williams "Best Packaging Supplier" award. It has also been ranked among the 20 most innovative companies in Brazil as well as one of the best places to work in that country.

At the heart of Brasilata's business model is the Simplification Project (*Projeto Simplificação*), which encourages all 900 employees across the company's four production facilities to think up as many suggestions as possible. "The Simplification Project is like panning for ideas (incremental innovations), thereby stimulating the internal innovative environment and entrepreneurial spirit," explains Brasilata CEO, Antonio Carlos Álvares Teixeira, who is also a business professor.

Ideas are so important that Brasilata employees are called "inventors" and everyone signs an "innovation contract" that reinforces their commitment to continuous improvement. After a slow start two decades ago (with only one idea per person each year), the company now receives more than 200,000 ideas each year —an average of more than 220 ideas per employee. Brasilata holds a party every six months, in which all employees invited to celebrate teams and individuals with the best ideas. Employees are also rewarded with bonuses representing 15 percent of net annual profits.

Some employee suggestions have sown the seeds of innovative products, such as an award-winning paint can that withstands heavy impact when dropped. Other ideas have dramatically improved productivity, some of which made jobs redundant. But employees aren't worried about losing their jobs because Brasilata has been able to maintain a no-layoff policy even during the worst downturns.[95]

Courtesy of Brasilata SA Embalagens Metalicas.

Brasilata has become one of the most innovative and productive manufacturing businesses in Brazil by involving employees in company decisions.

BENEFITS OF EMPLOYEE INVOLVEMENT

For the past half century, organizational behaviour experts have advised that employee involvement potentially improves decision-making quality and commitment.[96] However, a recent global suggests that this message hasn't been received by business leaders. Only 39 percent of employees believe senior leaders in their organization do a good job of involving employees in decisions that affect them and only 38 percent agree that their company acts on those suggestions effectively. Employees believe that their company falls short even on low level involvement: 42 percent say their organization does a good job of soliciting employees' opinions or suggestions.[97] As Global Connections 7.2 describes, involving employees in company decisions can result in considerable benefits for both the company and employees.

Employee involvement improves decision making in several ways. To begin with, it improves the identification of problems and opportunities. Employees are, in many respects, the sensors of the organization's environment. When the organization's activities misalign with customer expectations, employees are usually the first to know. Employee involvement provides a conduit for organizational leaders to be alerted to such problems.[98] Employee involvement can also potentially improve the number and quality of solutions generated. In a well-managed meeting, team members create synergy by pooling their knowledge to form new alternatives. In other words, several people working together can potentially generate more and better solutions than the same people working alone.

A third benefit of employee involvement is that, under specific conditions, it improves the evaluation of alternatives. Numerous studies on participative decision making, constructive conflict, and team dynamics have found that involvement brings out more diverse perspectives, tests ideas, and provides more valuable knowledge, all of which help the decision maker to select the best alternative.[99] A mathematical theorem introduced in 1785 by the Marquis de Condorcet states that the alternative selected by the team's majority is more likely to be correct than is the alternative selected by any team member individually.[100]

Along with improving decision quality, involvement tends to strengthen employee commitment to the decision. Rather than viewing themselves as agents of someone else's decision, those who participate in a decision feel personally responsible for its success. Involvement also has positive effects on employee motivation, satisfaction, and turnover. It also increases skill variety, feelings of autonomy, and task identity, all of which increase job enrichment and potentially employee motivation. Participation is also a critical practice in organizational change because employees are more motivated to implement the decision and less likely to resist changes resulting from the decision.[101]

CONTINGENCIES OF EMPLOYEE INVOLVEMENT

If employee involvement is so wonderful, why don't leaders leave all decisions to employees? The answer is that the optimal level of employee involvement depends on the situation. The employee involvement model shown in Exhibit 7.5 lists four contingencies: decision structure, source of decision knowledge, decision commitment, and risk of conflict in the decision process.[102]

- *Decision structure.* At the beginning of this chapter, we learned that some decisions are programmed, whereas others are nonprogrammed. Programmed decisions are less likely to need employee involvement because the solutions are already worked out from past incidents. In other words, the benefits of employee involvement increase with the novelty and complexity of the problem or opportunity.
- *Source of decision knowledge.* Subordinates should be involved in some level of decision making when the leader lacks sufficient knowledge and subordinates have additional information to improve decision quality. In many cases, employees are closer to customers and production activities, so they often know where the company can save money, improve product or service quality, and realize opportunities. This is particularly true for complex decisions where employees are more likely to possess relevant information.
- *Decision commitment.* Participation tends to improve employee commitment to the decision. If employees are unlikely to accept a decision made without their involvement, some level of participation is usually necessary.
- *Risk of conflict.* Two types of conflict undermine the benefits of employee involvement. First, if employee goals and norms conflict with the organization's goals, only a low level of employee involvement is advisable. Second, the degree of involvement depends on whether employees will agree on the preferred solution. If conflict is likely to occur, high involvement (i.e., employees make the decision alone) would be difficult to achieve.

Employee involvement is an important component of the decision-making process. To make the best decisions, we need to involve people who have the most valuable information and who will increase commitment to implement the decision. Employee involvement is a formative stage of team dynamics, so it carries many of the benefits and challenges of working in teams. The next chapter provides a closer look at team dynamics, including processes for making decisions in teams.

EXHIBIT 7.5

Model of Employee Involvement in Decision Making

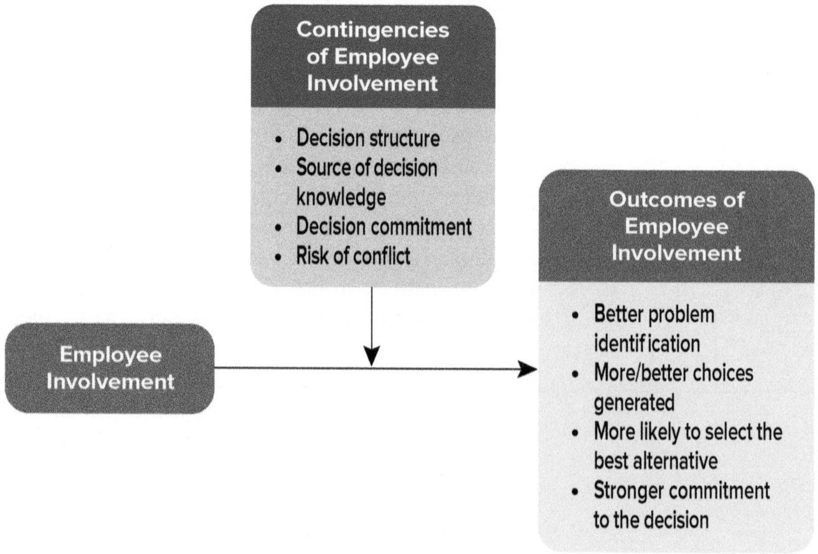

Chapter Summary

LO1 Describe the rational choice paradigm in decision making.

Decision making is a conscious process of making choices among one or more alternatives with the intention of moving towards some desired state of affairs. The rational choice paradigm relies on subjective expected utility to identify the best choice. It also follows the logical process of identifying problems and opportunities, choosing the best decision style, developing alternative solutions, choosing the best solution, implementing the selected alternative, and evaluating decision outcomes.

LO2 Explain why people differ from the rational choice paradigm when identifying problems/opportunities, evaluating/choosing alternatives, and evaluating decision outcomes.

Stakeholder framing, perceptual defence, mental models, decisive leadership, and solution-oriented focus affect our ability to objectively identify problems and opportunities. We can minimize these challenges by being aware of the human limitations and discussing the situation with colleagues.

Evaluating and choosing alternatives is often challenging because organizational goals are ambiguous or in conflict, human information processing is incomplete and subjective, and people tend to satisfice rather than maximize. Decision makers also short-circuit the evaluation process when faced with an opportunity rather than a problem. People generally make better choices by systematically evaluating alternatives. Scenario planning can help to make future decisions without the pressure and emotions that occur during real emergencies.

Confirmation bias and escalation of commitment make it difficult to accurately evaluate decision outcomes. Escalation is mainly caused by the self-justification effect, self-enhancement effect, the prospect theory effect, and sunk costs effect. These problems are minimized by separating decision choosers from decision evaluators, establishing a preset level at which the decision is abandoned or re-evaluated, relying on more systematic and clear feedback about the project's success, and involving several people in decision making.

LO3 Discuss the roles of emotions and intuition in decision making.

Emotions shape our preferences for alternatives and the process we follow to evaluate alternatives. We also listen in to our emotions for guidance when making decisions. This latter activity relates to intuition–the ability to know when a problem or opportunity exists and to select the best course of action without conscious reasoning. Intuition is both an emotional experience and a rapid unconscious analytic process that involves both pattern matching and action scripts.

LO4 Describe employee characteristics, workplace conditions, and specific activities that support creativity.

Creativity is the development of original ideas that make a socially recognized contribution. The four creativity stages are preparation, incubation, insight, and verification. Incubation assists divergent thinking, which involves reframing the problem in a unique way and generating different approaches to the issue.

Four of the main features of creative people are intelligence, persistence, expertise, and independent imagination. Creativity is also strengthened for everyone when the work environment supports a learning orientation, the job has high intrinsic motivation, the organization provides a reasonable level of job security, and project leaders provide appropriate goals, time pressure, and resources. Three types of activities that encourage creativity are redefining the problem, associative play, and cross-pollination.

LO5 Describe the benefits of employee involvement and identify four contingencies that affect the optimal level of employee involvement.

Employee involvement refers to the degree that employees influence how their work is organized and carried out. The level of participation may range from an employee providing specific information to management without knowing the problem or issue, to complete involvement in all phases of the decision process. Employee involvement may lead to higher decision quality and commitment, but several contingencies need to be considered, including the decision structure, source of decision knowledge, decision commitment, and risk of conflict.

Key Terms

anchoring and adjustment heuristic, p. 169
availability heuristic, p. 169
bounded rationality, p. 168
creativity, p. 175
decision making, p. 163
divergent thinking, p. 176
employee involvement, p. 179
escalation of commitment, p. 173
implicit favourite, p. 169
intuition, p. 172
prospect theory effect, p. 174
rational choice paradigm, p. 163
representativeness heuristic, p. 169
satisficing, p. 170
scenario planning, p. 172
subjective expected utility, p. 163

Critical-Thinking Questions

1. A management consultant is hired by a manufacturing firm to determine the best site for its next production facility. The consultant has had several meetings with the company's senior executives regarding the factors to consider when making the recommendation. Discuss the decision-making problems that might prevent the consultant from choosing the best site location.

2. You have been asked to personally recommend a new travel agency to handle all airfare, accommodation, and related travel needs for your organization of 500 staff. One of your colleagues, who is responsible for the company's economic planning, suggests that the best travel agent could be selected mathematically by inputting the relevant factors for each agency and the weight (importance) of each factor. What decision-making approach is your colleague recommending? Is this recommendation a good idea in this situation? Why or why not?
3. Intuition is both an emotional experience and an unconscious analytic process. One problem, however, is that not all emotions signalling that there is a problem or opportunity represent intuition. Explain how we would know if our "gut feelings" are intuition or not, and if not intuition, suggest what might be causing them.
4. A developer received financial backing for a new business financial centre along a derelict section of the waterfront, a few miles from the current downtown area of a large European city. The idea was to build several high-rise structures, attract large tenants to those sites, and have the city extend transportation systems out to the new centre. Over the next decade, the developer believed that others would build in the area, thereby attracting the regional or national offices of many financial institutions. Interest from potential tenants was much lower than initially predicted and the city did not build transportation systems as quickly as expected. Still, the builder proceeded with the original plans. Only after financial support was curtailed did the developer reconsider the project. Using your knowledge of escalation of commitment, discuss three possible reasons why the developer was motivated to continue with the project.
5. Ancient Book Company has a problem with new book projects. Even when others are aware that a book is far behind schedule and may engender little public interest, sponsoring editors are reluctant to terminate contracts with authors whom they have signed. The result is that editors invest more time with these projects than on more fruitful projects. As a form of escalation of commitment, describe two methods that Ancient Book Company can use to minimize this problem.
6. A fresh graduate is offered a job by an employer she admires even before she could start the job search. The student thinks it is an opportunity and jumps to it. Do you think there is an effect of emotions in her decision making?
7. Think of a time when you experienced the creative process. Maybe you woke up with a brilliant (but usually sketchy and incomplete) idea, or you solved a baffling problem while doing something else. Describe this incident to your class and explain how the experience followed the creative process.
8. Two characteristics of creative people are that they have relevant experience and are persistent in their quest. Does this mean that people with the most experience and the highest need for achievement are the most creative? Explain your answer.
9. Employee involvement applies just as well to the classroom as to the office or factory floor. Explain how student involvement in classroom decisions typically made by the instructor alone might improve decision quality. What potential problems may occur in this process?

Case Study: EMPLOYEE INVOLVEMENT CASES

SCENARIO 1: THE PRODUCTIVITY DIVIDEND DECISION

As head of the transmission/distribution group (TD group) in the city's water agency (a government corporation), you have been asked to reduce costs over the next year by a minimum of three percent without undermining service. Your department employs about 300 people, who are responsible for constructing and maintaining water lines throughout the city. Although you have an engineering background, the work is complex and involves several professions and trades. Even the TD group's first line supervisors (one or two levels below you in the hierarchy) are not fully knowledgeable of all aspects of the business.

You believe that most employees support or at least accept the city's recent mandate to reduce costs (called the "productivity dividend initiative"). The city leaders have stated that this initiative will not result in any layoffs this year. However, the labor union representing most nonmanagement staff in the water agency (including most of your employees) is concerned that the productivity dividend initiative will reduce employment numbers over time and increase employee workloads. Although the TD group is a separate department within the city water agency, it affects most other work units in the agency. It is possible, for example, that ideas that reduce costs in the TD group might increase costs elsewhere. The TD group employees may be unaware of or care about these repercussions because there is limited interaction with or social bonding with employees in the departments.

SCENARIO 2: THE SUGAR SUBSTITUTE RESEARCH DECISION

You are the head of research and development (R&D) for a major beer company. While working on a new beer product, one of the scientists in your unit seems to have tentatively identified a new chemical compound that has few calories but tastes closer to sugar than current sugar substitutes. The company has no foreseeable need for this product, but it could be patented and licensed to manufacturers in the food industry.

The sugar-substitute discovery is in its preliminary stages and would require considerable time and resources before it would be commercially viable. This means that it would necessarily take some resources away from other projects in the lab. The sugar-substitute project is beyond your technical expertise, but some of the R&D lab researchers are familiar with that field of chemistry. As with most forms of research, it is difficult to determine the amount of research required to further identify and perfect the sugar substitute. You do not know how much demand is expected for this product. Your department has a decision process for funding projects that are behind schedule. However, there are no rules or precedents about funding projects that would be licensed but not used by the organization.

The company's R&D budget is limited, and other scientists in your work group have recently complained that they require more resources and financial support to get their projects completed. Some of these R&D projects hold promise for future beer sales. You believe that most researchers in the R&D unit are committed to ensuring that the company's interests are achieved.

SCENARIO 3: COAST GUARD CUTTER DECISION

You are the captain of a 72-metre Coast Guard cutter, with a crew of 16, including officers. Your mission is general at-sea search and rescue. At 2:00 am this morning, while en route to your home port after a routine 28-day patrol, you received word from the nearest Coast Guard station that a small plane had crashed 100 kilometres offshore. You obtained all the available information concerning the location of the crash, informed your crew of the mission, and set a new course at maximum speed for the scene to commence a search for survivors and wreckage.

You have now been searching for 20 hours. Your search operation has been increasingly impaired by rough seas, and there is evidence of a severe storm building. The atmospherics associated with the deteriorating weather have made communications with the Coast Guard station impossible. A decision must be made shortly about whether to abandon the search and place your vessel on a course that would ride out the storm (thereby protecting the vessel and your crew, but relegating any possible survivors to almost certain death from exposure) or to continue a potentially futile search and the risks it would entail.

Before losing communications, you received an update weather advisory concerning the severity and duration of the storm. Although your crew members are extremely conscientious about their responsibility, you believe that they would be divided on the decision of leaving or staying.

SCENARIO 4: THE SOCIAL MEDIA POLICY DECISION

The industry initiatives agency is a group of 120 professionals responsible for marketing the state as a good place for companies to operate their business or open new operations. Although you report to the head of the state's employment and commerce department, your agency is semi-autonomous in its policies and practices from the parent department. One of your highest priorities is to recruit and retain young, well-educated, high-potential employees for this growing agency. During a recent recruiting drive at universities and polytechnics, some potential applicants candidly stated that the state government seems out of touch with the younger generation, particularly their use of technology. A few observed that your agency's website doesn't provide much recruitment information, and they couldn't find the department's Facebook or Twitter sites.

These comments led to you think about having a social media policy in the industry initiatives agency, particularly whether or to what degree the agency should allow or possibly even encourage its staff to have work-related Facebook sites, personal blogs, and Twitter sites, and to participate in those sites during work hours. You personally know very little about emerging social media, although many of your direct reports (functional managers and team leaders) have varying degrees of knowledge about them. A few even have their own personal Facebook sites and one manager has her own blog on travel. Some direct reports are strongly opposed to social media in the workplace, whereas others are likely very supportive. However, you believe that all of their views are in the agency's best interests.

This social media policy decision would be within your mandate; unlike most governments, neither the state government nor the employment and commerce department has such a policy or restrictions on any policy that is designed by your agency. However, a few specific government departments prohibit Facebook and texting activity during work and, due to concerns about breaches of confidentiality and employer reputation, do not allow employees to mention work-related matters in any social media. Your decision is to develop a policy specifying whether and, if so, to what degree agency staff should be allowed or encouraged to engage in social network site activity during work hours.

Discussion Questions (for all four scenarios)

1. To what extent should your subordinates be involved in this decision? Select one of the following levels of involvement:
    - *Decide alone.* Use your personal knowledge and insight to complete the entire decision process without conferring with anyone else.
    - *Receive information from individuals.* Ask specific individuals for information. They do not make recommendations and might not even know what the problem is about.
    - *Consult with individuals.* Describe the problem to selected individuals and seek both their information and recommendations. The final decision is made by you, which may or may not take the advice from others into account.
    - *Consult with the team.* You bring together a team of people (all department staff or a representation of them if the department is large), who are told about the problem and provide their ideas and recommendations. You make the final decision, which may or may not reflect the team's information.
    - *Facilitate the team's decision.* The entire decision-making process is handed over to a team or committee of subordinates. You serve only as a facilitator to guide the decision process and keep everyone on track. The team identifies the problem, discovers alternative solutions,

chooses the best alternative, and implements their choice.

2. What factors led you to choose this level of employee involvement rather than the others?
3. What problems might occur if less or more involvement occurred in this case (where possible)?

Sources: The Productivity Dividend Decision and The Social Media Policy Decision: © 2013 Steven L. McShane. The Sugar Substitute Research Decision: © 2002 Steven L. McShane. The Coast guard cutter case is adapted from V. H. Vroom and A. G. Jago, *The New Leadership: Managing Participation in Organizations* (Englewood Cliffs, NJ: Prentice Hall, 1988), © 1987 V. H. Vroom and A. G. Jago. Used with permission of the authors.

Team Exercise: WHERE IN THE WORLD ARE WE?

Purpose This exercise is designed to help you understand the potential advantages of involving others in decisions rather than making decisions alone.

Materials Students require an unmarked copy of the map of Canada with grid marks (Exhibit 1). Students are not allowed to look at any other maps or use any other materials. The instructor will provide a list of communities located somewhere on Exhibit 1. The instructor will also provide copies of the answer sheet after students have individually and in teams estimated the locations of communities.

Instructions

- *Step 1:* Using the table below, write down the list of communities identified by your instructor. Then, working alone, estimate the location on Exhibit 1 of these communities, all of which are in Canada. For example, mark a small "1" on Exhibit 1 on the spot where you believe the first community is located. Mark a small "2" where you think the second community is located, and so on. Please be sure to number each location clearly and with numbers small enough to fit within one grid space.
- *Step 2:* The instructor will organize students into approximately equal-sized teams (typically five or six people per team). Working with your team members, reach a consensus on the location of each community listed in the table. The instructor might provide teams with a separate copy of this map, or each member can identify the team's numbers using a different coloured pen on their individual maps. The team's decision for each location should occur by consensus, not voting or averaging.
- *Step 3:* The instructor will provide or display an answer sheet, showing the correct locations of the communities. Using this answer sheet, students will count the minimum number of grid squares between the location they individually marked and the true location of each community. Write the number of grid squares in the second column of the table, then add up the total. Next, count the minimum number of grid squares between the location the team marked and the true location of each community. Write the number of grid squares in the third column of the table, then add up the total.
- *Step 4:* The instructor will ask for information about the totals and the class will discuss the implication of these results for employee involvement and decision making.

List of Selected Communities in Canada

Number	Community	Individual distance in grid units from the true location	Team distance in grid units from the true location
1.			
2.			
3.			
4.			
5.			
6.			
7.			
8.			
		Total:	Total:

EXHIBIT 1

Map of Canada

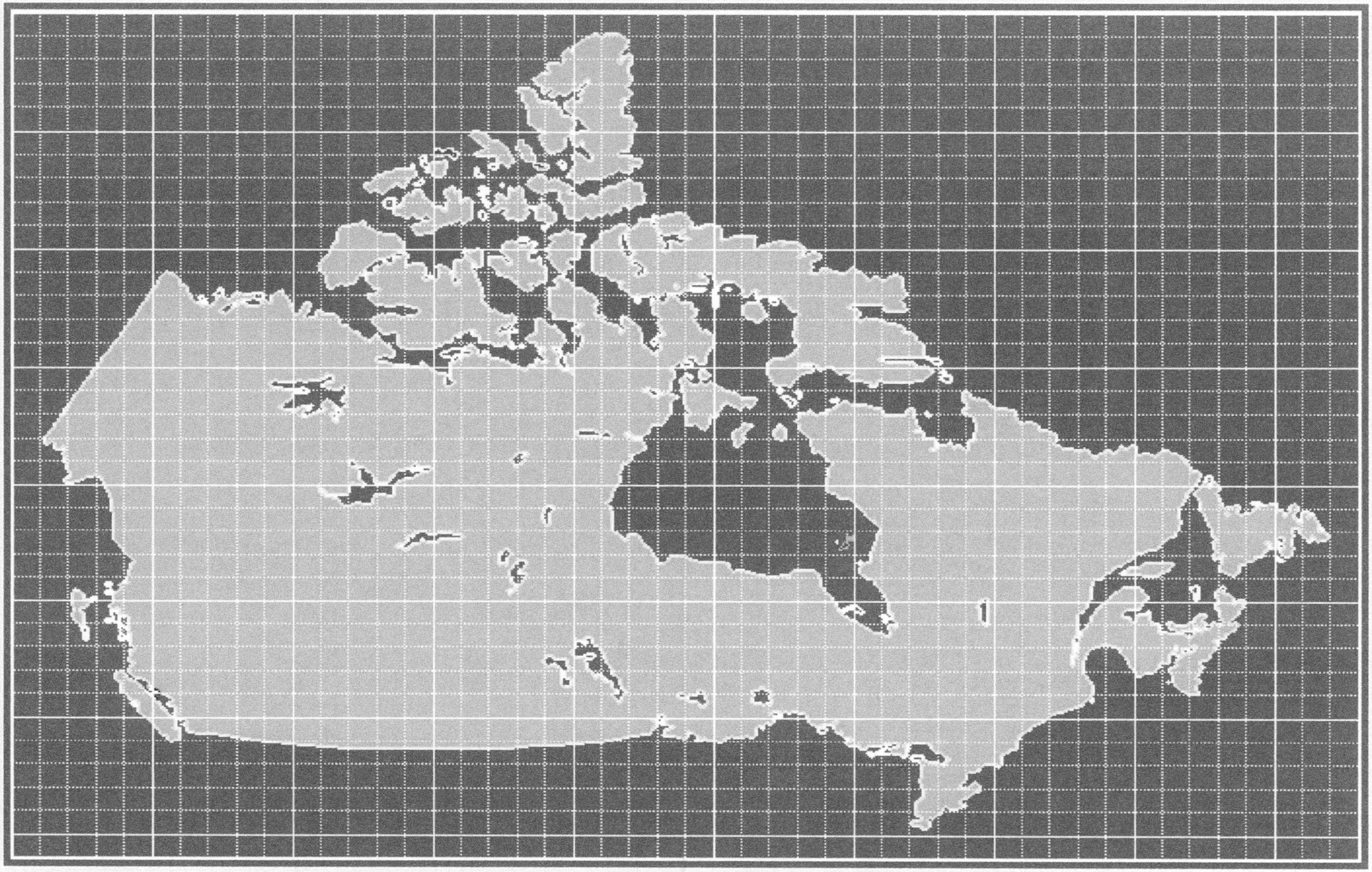

Self-Assessment: DO YOU HAVE A CREATIVE PERSONALITY?

Purpose This self-assessment is designed to help you measure the extent to which you have a creative personality.

Instructions Listed below is an adjective checklist with 30 words that may or may not describe you. Put a mark in the box beside each word that you think accurately describes you. Please do not mark the boxes for words that do not describe you. When finished, you can score the test using the scoring key in Appendix B at the end of the book. This exercise should be completed alone so that you can assess yourself without concerns of social comparison. Class discussion will focus on how this scale might be applied in organizations and on the limitations of measuring creativity in work settings.

Adjective Checklist

Affected	☐	Honest	☐	Reflective	☐
Capable	☐	Humorous	☐	Resourceful	☐
Cautious	☐	Individualistic	☐	Self-confident	☐
Clever	☐	Informal	☐	Sexy	☐
Commonplace	☐	Insightful	☐	Sincere	☐
Confident	☐	Intelligent	☐	Snobbish	☐
Conservative	☐	Inventive	☐	Submissive	☐
Conventional	☐	Mannerly	☐	Suspicious	☐
Dissatisfied	☐	Narrow interests	☐	Unconventional	☐
Egotistical	☐	Original	☐	Wide interests	☐

Source: Adapted from and based on information in H. G. Gough and A. B. Heilbrun, Jr., *The Adjective Check List Manual* (Palo Alto, CA: Consulting Psychologists Press, 1965).

SELF-ASSESSMENTS FOR CHAPTER 7

SELF-ASSESSMENT NAME	DESCRIPTION	LOCATION
Do you have a creative personality?	Estimates the extent to which you have a creative personality.	Page 188 connect
What is your preferred decision-making style?	Assesses your preference for logical or intuitive decision making.	connect
How well do you engage in divergent thinking?	Assesses your creative bench strength.	connect

When designing a team, it is best to decide on the team's strategy before selecting team members. It certainly helps when trying to win Olympic gold.

UPI/Molly Riley/LANDOV

Chapter 8

Team Dynamics

LEARNING OBJECTIVES

After reading this chapter, you should be able to:

LO1. Explain why employees join informal groups and discuss the benefits and limitations of teams.

LO2. Outline the team effectiveness model and discuss how task characteristics, team size, and team composition influence team effectiveness.

LO3. Discuss how shared perceptions among team members, called team states, emerge and influence team effectiveness.

LO4. Discuss how team processes, such as taskwork, teamwork, team boundary spanning, and team development determine team effectiveness.

LO5. Discuss the characteristics and factors required for success of self-directed teams and virtual teams.

LO6. Identify four constraints on team decision making and discuss the advantages and disadvantages of four structures aimed at improving team decision making.

To many Canadians, the gold medal performances of both the women's and men's hockey teams at the Vancouver Olympics were a source of immense national pride. And those lofty expectations placed great pressure on Team Canada executives to once again create winning teams for the 2014 Sochi Olympics in Russia. We now know both teams went on to repeat as gold medalists. However, the case of the men's team shows how challenging it can be to create a team built to succeed.

The main questions surrounding the team and its prospects for victory focused not only on who made the team, but also on which players were left out. Steve Yzerman, Team Canada's executive director was forced to make those decisions. Three notable members of the 2010 gold-winning team were left off of the 2014 team, along with a number of the NHL's highest goal-scorers at the time.

Two years before the Olympics, Team Canada executives decided that a new strategy was called for; specifically, they felt that with the larger ice surfaces found in international games, to win in Sochi they would have to adopt a defence-first strategy. This decision was a major factor in determining who should be on the team and who should be left off. Even the coaching staff was chosen based on their experience coaching defence-oriented teams. The choice of players seemed to follow naturally from this defensive system. "This team was built for possession and defence. The players were likely selected so that they would be most effective in the hands of the NHL's finest defensive minds."

Did the team selection process match the strategy? The team conceded only three goals throughout the tournament, never trailed in any of their games, and even though they scored half as many goals as in 2010 they won every game. Jonathan Toews, who played on the team said, "It's an amazing feeling to be part of a team like that, whether your role is big or small [. . .] we're just an amazing team to watch, the way we worked together, and we were just all over them. It was fun to be a part of."[1]

The Team Canada story shows that team composition is not merely a matter of choosing the best performers; there must be a match between the team's task and the members of the team. And as the complexity of the modern organization has increased, so has awareness that major projects require teams of people working together to accomplish goals. This trend towards teamwork is, in fact, increasingly common in many industries. More than half of North American organizations polled in one survey use teams to a high or very high extent to conduct day-to-day business. By comparison, only 50 percent of executives a decade ago said their work was done in teams. Two decades ago, only 20 percent of those executives said they worked in teams.[2] Teamwork has also become more important in scientific research. A study of almost 20 million research publications reported that the percentage of journal articles written by teams rather than individuals has increased substantially over the past five decades. Team-based articles also had a much higher number of subsequent citations, suggesting that journal articles written by teams are superior to articles written by individuals.[3]

Why are teams becoming so important, and how can organizations strengthen their potential for organizational effectiveness? We find the answers to these and other questions in this chapter on team dynamics. This chapter begins by defining *teams* and examining the reasons why organizations rely on teams and why people join informal groups in organizational settings. A large segment of this chapter examines a model of team effectiveness, which includes team and organizational environment, team design, team processes, and shared perceptions among team members—called team states. We then turn our attention to two specific types of teams: self-directed teams and virtual teams. The final section of this chapter looks at the challenges and strategies for making better decisions in teams.

Teams and Informal Groups

LO1

teams Groups of two or more people who interact and influence each other, are mutually accountable for achieving common goals associated with organizational objectives, and perceive themselves as a social entity within an organization.

Teams are groups of two or more people who interact and influence each other, are mutually accountable for achieving common goals associated with organizational objectives, and perceive themselves as a social entity within an organization.[4] This definition has a few important components worth repeating. First, all teams exist to fulfill some purpose, such as repairing electric power lines, assembling a product, designing a new social welfare program, or making an important decision. Second, team members are held together by their interdependence and need for collaboration to achieve common goals. All teams require some form of communication so that members can coordinate and share common objectives. Third, team members influence each other, although some members may be more influential than others regarding the team's goals and activities. Finally, a team exists when its members perceive themselves to be a team.

Exhibit 8.1 briefly identifies various types of teams in organizations along with three distinguishing characteristics: permanence, skill differentiation, and authority differentiation.[5] Team permanence refers to how long that type of team usually exists. Although many employees work in teams that exist indefinitely (e.g., departmental teams), an emerging trend in organizations is the formation of teams that exist very briefly, sometimes only for one eight-hour shift.[6] For example, action teams often disband after a few days or weeks. The second distinguishing characteristic, skill differentiation, refers to the degree to which individuals bring diverse skills and knowledge to the team. Some advisory teams have high skill differentiation because companies attempt to include representatives from most occupational groups in the organization. In contrast, most functional departments consist of employees with very similar skills (e.g., sales department staff tend to have similar skills).

Authority differentiation, the third distinguishing characteristic of teams, refers to the degree that decision-making responsibility is distributed throughout the team (low differentiation) or is vested in one or a few members of the team. Departmental teams tend to have

EXHIBIT 8.1 Types of Teams in Organizations

Team type	Description	Permanence	Skill differentiation	Authority differentiation
Departmental teams	Teams that consist of employees who have similar or complementary skills and are located in the same unit of a functional structure; usually minimal task interdependence because each person works with employees in other departments.	High	Low to medium	High
Production/ service/ leadership teams	Typically multiskilled (employees have diverse competencies), team members collectively produce a common product/service or make ongoing decisions.	High	Medium to high	Medium
Self-directed teams	Similar to production/service teams except (1) they are organized around work processes that complete an entire piece of work requiring several interdependent tasks and (2) they have substantial autonomy over the execution of those tasks (i.e., they usually control inputs, flow, and outputs with little or no supervision).	High	Medium to high	Low
Task force (project) teams	Usually multiskilled, temporary teams whose assignment is to solve a problem, realize an opportunity, or design a product or service.	Low	Medium	Medium
Action teams	Similar to task forces, these highly skilled teams are formed for a short duration and given considerable autonomy to resolve an urgent problem or opportunity, such as solving an emergency or crisis.	Low	Medium	Low
Advisory teams	Teams that provide recommendations to decision makers; include committees, advisory councils, work councils, and review panels; may be temporary, but often permanent, some with frequent rotation of members.	Low to medium	Medium to high	Medium
Skunkworks	Multiskilled teams that are usually located away from the organization and are relatively free of its hierarchy; often initiated by an entrepreneurial team leader who borrows people and resources *(bootlegging)* to design a product or service.	Medium	Medium to high	Medium
Virtual teams	Teams whose members operate across space, time, and organizational boundaries and are linked through information technologies to achieve organizational tasks; may be a temporary task force or permanent service team.	Varies	Medium to high	Medium
Communities of practice	Teams (but often informal groups) bound together by shared expertise and passion for a particular activity or interest; main purpose is to share information; often rely on information technologies as the main source of interaction.	Medium	Low to medium	Low

Global Connections 8.1:

TEAM MOTIVATION AT PIXAR

Ten years after the enormous success of *Toy Story* and *Toy Story 2,* Pixar studios was planning another sequel. After investing millions of dollars and three years of work during 2009, *Toy Story 3* was a few months away from its scheduled release date. However, after watching the material that was ready, Pixar owner Steve Jobs and other Pixar team members were faced with a tough choice. Many felt the movie wasn't good enough—so what should they do?

With so much already invested, and sky-high expectations stemming from the success of the earlier films, even acknowledging that the final product wasn't good enough was hard. But what made the decision easier was a culture of open communication and sharing at Pixar. Jobs firmly believed that great ideas came not just from great minds, but from great teams. In terms of layout, the office was designed with a large atrium at its centre that ensured people from different teams crossed each other's paths frequently enough to greet each other and have some conversation. The culture was such that frank opinions and open conversation were encouraged. The result was a cross-pollination of ideas and an environment where people felt they could express their opinions. In the end, the team made the difficult decision to push back the film's release date. The remade version went on to make $200,000,000 at the box office—more than the combined earnings of *Toy Story* and *Toy Story 2*—and has a score of 99 percent on the film review aggregate website Rotten Tomatoes.[7]

AF archive/Alamy

high authority differentiation because they typically have a formal manager, whereas self-directed teams have low authority differentiation because the entire team makes key decisions. The team leader, if there is one, does not have final decision-making authority.

INFORMAL GROUPS

This chapter mostly focuses on formal teams, but employees also belong to informal groups. All teams are groups, but many groups do not satisfy our definition of teams. Groups include people assembled together, whether or not they have any interdependence or organizationally focused objective. The friends you meet for lunch are an *informal group,* but they wouldn't be called a team because they have little or no interdependence (each person could just as easily eat lunch alone) and no organizationally mandated purpose. Instead, they exist primarily for the benefit of their members. Although the terms are used interchangeably, *teams* has largely replaced *groups* in the language of business when referring to employees who work together to complete organizational tasks.[8]

Why do informal groups exist? One reason is that human beings are social animals. Our drive to bond is hardwired through evolutionary development, creating a need to belong to informal groups.[9] This is evident by the fact that people invest considerable time and effort forming and maintaining social relationships without any special circumstances or ulterior motives. A second reason why people join informal groups is provided by social identity theory, which states that individuals define themselves by their group affiliations (see Chapter 3). Thus, we join groups–particularly those that are viewed favourably by others and that have values similar to our own–because they shape and reinforce our self-concept.[10]

A third reason why informal groups exist is that they accomplish personal objectives that cannot be achieved by individuals working alone. For example, employees will sometimes congregate to oppose organizational changes because this collective effort has more power than individuals who try to bring about change alone. These informal groups, called coalitions, are discussed in Chapter 10. A fourth explanation for informal groups is that we are comforted by the mere presence of other people and are therefore motivated to be near them in stressful situations. When in danger, people congregate near each other even though doing so serves no protective purpose. Similarly, employees tend to mingle more often after hearing rumors that the company might be acquired by a competitor. As Chapter 4 explained, this social support minimizes stress by providing emotional and/or informational support to buffer the stress experience.[11]

Informal Groups and Organizational Outcomes Informal groups are not created to serve organizational objectives. Nevertheless, they have a profound influence on organizations and employees. Informal groups potentially minimize employee stress because, as mentioned above, group members provide emotional and informational social support. This stress-reducing capability of informal groups improves employee well-being, thereby improving organizational effectiveness. Informal groups are also the backbone of *social networks*, which are important sources of trust building, information sharing, power, influence, and employee well-being in the workplace.[12] Chapter 9 describes the growing significance of social networking sites similar to Facebook and LinkedIn to encourage the formation of informal groups and associated communication. Chapter 10 explains how social networks are a source of influence in organizational settings. Employees with strong informal networks tend to have more power and influence because they receive better information and preferential treatment from others and their talent is more visible to key decision makers.

Advantages and Disadvantages of Teams

Why do teams succeed at some organizations while so many others fail? The answer to this question has a long history.[13] Early research on British coal mining in the 1940s, the Japanese economic miracle of the 1970s, and a huge number of investigations since then have revealed that *under the right conditions*, teams make better decisions, develop better products and services, and create a more engaged workforce than do employees working alone.[14] Similarly, team members can quickly share information and coordinate tasks, whereas these processes are slower and prone to more errors in traditional departments led by supervisors. Teams typically provide superior customer service because they provide more breadth of knowledge and expertise to customers than individual "stars" can offer.

In many situations, people are potentially more motivated when working in teams than when working alone.[15] One reason for this motivation is that, as we mentioned a few paragraphs ago, employees have a drive to bond and are motivated to fulfill the goals of groups to which they belong. This motivation is stronger when the team is part of the employee's social identity.

Second, people are more motivated in teams because they are accountable to fellow team members, who monitor performance more closely than a traditional supervisor. This is particularly true where the team's performance depends on the worst performer, such as on an assembly line, where how fast the product is assembled depends on the speed of the slowest employee. Third, under some circumstances, performance improves when employees work near others because coworkers become benchmarks of comparison. Employees are also motivated to work harder because of apprehension that their performance will be compared to the performance of others.

THE CHALLENGES OF TEAMS

process losses Resources (including time and energy) expended towards team development and maintenance rather than the task.

In spite of their many benefits, teams are not always as effective as individuals working alone.[16] The main problem is that teams have additional costs called **process losses**–resources (including time and energy) expended towards team development and maintenance rather than the task.[17] Team members need time and effort to resolve their disagreements, develop mutual understanding of their goals, determine the best strategy for accomplishing those goals, negotiate their specific roles, and agree on informal rules of conduct. An employee working alone on a project does not have these disagreements, misunderstandings, divergent viewpoints, or coordination problems with himself or herself (at least, not nearly as much as with other people). Teams may be necessary when the work is so complex it requires knowledge and skills from several people. But for tasks that can be performed alone, process losses can make teams much less effective than a one-person project.

Process losses are amplified when more people are added or replace others on the team.[18] The new team members consume time and effort figuring out how to work well with other team members. Performance also suffers among current team members because they divert attention to accommodating and integrating the newcomer. Process losses increase even after new members are integrated because the larger team requires more coordination, more time for conflict resolution, and so forth. The software industry even has a name for the problems of adding people to a team: **Brooks's law** says that adding more people to a late software project only makes it later! Although these problems are well known, research has found that managers consistently underestimate the process losses caused by adding more people to an existing team.[19]

Brooks's law The principle that adding more people to a late software project only makes it later.

Social Loafing The process losses described above are mainly about coordination, but teams also suffer from motivational process losses. The best-known motivational process loss is **social loafing,** which occurs when people exert less effort (and usually perform at a lower level) in teams than working alone.[20] Social loafing is higher when individual performance is hidden or difficult to distinguish from the performance of others. Individual performance tends to be hidden in very large teams and where the team produces a single output, such as finding a single solution to a customer's problem. There is less social loafing when each team member's contribution is more noticeable; this can be achieved by reducing the size of the team, for example, or measuring each team member's performance. "When the group is smaller, there's nowhere to hide," explains Strategic Investments principal David Zebro. "You have to pull your weight."[21]

social loafing The problem that occurs when people exert less effort (and usually perform at a lower level) when working in teams than when working alone.

Social loafing is less prevalent when the task is interesting, because individuals are more motivated by the work itself to perform their duties.[22] For example, one recent study revealed that student apathy explains some of the social loafing that occurs in university student teams. Social loafing is also less common when the team's objective is important, possibly because individuals experience more pressure from coworkers to perform well. Finally, social loafing occurs less frequently among members who value team membership and believe in working towards the team's objectives.

In summary, teams can be very powerful forces for competitive advantage, or they can be much more trouble than they are worth. To understand when teams are better than individuals working alone, we need to more closely examine the conditions that make teams effective or ineffective. The next few sections of this chapter discuss the model of team effectiveness.

A Model of Team Effectiveness

LO2

Why are some teams effective while others fail? To answer this question, we first need to clarify the meaning of team effectiveness. A team is effective when it benefits the organization, its members, and survives long enough to accomplish its mandate.[23] First, most teams exist to serve some organizational purpose, so effectiveness is partly measured by the achievement of those objectives. Second, a team's effectiveness relies on the satisfaction and well-being of its members. People join groups to fulfill their personal needs, so effectiveness is partly measured by this need fulfillment. Finally, team effectiveness includes the team's ability to survive long enough to fulfill its purpose. Earlier, we pointed out that very short-lived teams are an emerging trend in organizations. Yet even these "flash teams" could fall apart literally (people refuse to join or stay with the team) or cognitively (members become cognitively and emotionally disengaged from the team).

Researchers have developed several models over the years to identify the features or conditions that make some teams more effective than others.[24] Exhibit 8.2 integrates the main components of these team effectiveness models. We will closely examine each component over the next several pages. This exhibit is a meta-model because each component (team composition, team cohesion, etc.) includes its own set of theories and models to explain how that component operates.

ORGANIZATIONAL AND TEAM ENVIRONMENT

The organizational and team environment represents all conditions beyond the team's boundaries that influence its effectiveness. The environment is typically viewed as a resource pool that either supports or inhibits the team's ability to function and achieve its objectives.[25]

EXHIBIT 8.2

Team Effectiveness Model

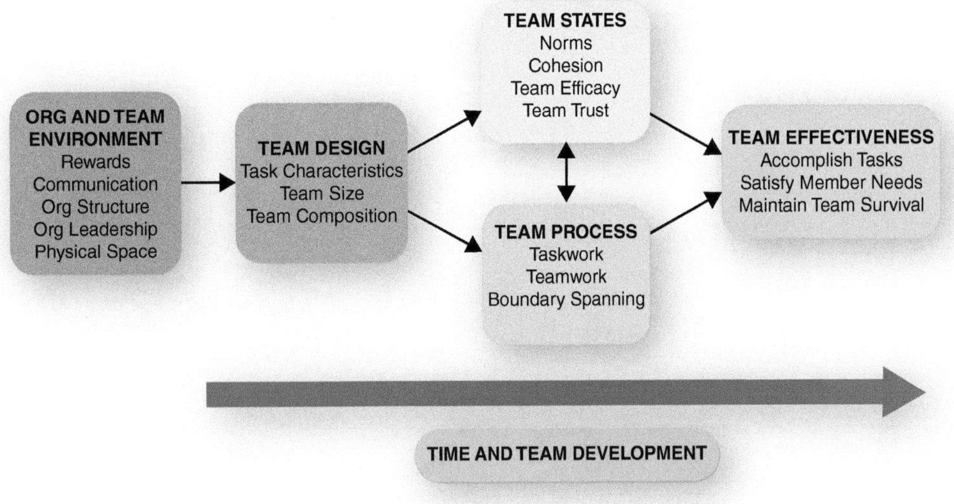

Team members tend to work together more effectively when they receive some team-based rewards, when the organization's leadership is supportive of team-oriented work structures (rather than "star" individuals), when the organization's structure assigns teams distinctive clusters of work activity, when information systems support team coordination, and when the physical layout of the team's workspace encourages frequent communication.[26]

Along with being a resource, the environment generates drivers for change within teams. External competition is an environmental condition that affects team dynamics, such as increasing motivation of team members to work together. Another environmental driver would be changing societal expectations, such as higher safety standards, which require teams to alter their norms of behaviour. These external forces for change, not only motivate teams to redesign themselves; these forces are also the focus of the team's attention. For instance, teams develop better ways of working together so they provide better customer service.

Team Design Elements

Even when it operates in a team-friendly environment, the team's effectiveness will fall short of its potential if the task characteristics, team size, team composition, and team roles are poorly designed.

TASK CHARACTERISTICS

One reason for the shift to teamwork is that making decisions and satisfying customers have become much more complex. Complex work requires skills and knowledge beyond the competencies of one person. Teams are particularly well suited for complex work that can be divided into more specialized roles, and where the people in those specialized roles require frequent coordination with each other.

Task complexity demands teamwork, but teams also work better when the work is well-structured rather than ambiguous. Assembling automobiles consists of well-structured tasks, whereas a team performing a new medical procedure would have novel and less-structured work activities. The main benefit of well-structured tasks is that it is easier to coordinate the work among several people. Yet compared to individuals working alone, teams are more likely to stumble when faced with ambiguous work activities. Performing a new medical procedure would lack the task structure of assembling cars dozens of times each day, for example. Fortunately, teams can perform ambiguous tasks reasonably well when they have well-structured roles. The medical team members have enough role clarity to generally know what to expect of each other–the surgeon, scrub technicians, operating room nurses, anesthesiologist, and others–and how to coordinate most work challenges even in these unique situations.[27]

Courtesy of PSA Peugeot Citroën

PSA Peugeot Citroën, Europe's second largest automaker, has set up an "obeya room" (Japanese for "big room") to speed up team decision making. The walls are plastered with graphs and notes so team members can visualize key issues. The obeya room creates a unique team environment that encourages face-to-face interaction to quickly solve critical, focused decisions. At one session, for example, managers figured out how to significantly reduce accidents among temporary workers. "The themes for projects in progress are displayed on the walls, with red when something is wrong," explains PSA Peugeot Citroën chairman Philippe Varin. "Everyone takes the same problem and tries to fix it."[28]

connect

What team roles do you prefer? See page **216** or visit **connect.mcgrawhill.com** to assess your role preferences in teams.

task interdependence The extent to which team members must share materials, information, or expertise in order to perform their jobs.

An important task-related influence on team effectiveness is **task interdependence**—the extent to which team members must share materials, information, or expertise to perform their jobs.[29] Apart from complete independence, there are three levels of task interdependence, as illustrated in Exhibit 8.3. The lowest level of interdependence, called *pooled interdependence,* occurs when an employee or work unit shares a common resource, such as machinery, administrative support, or a budget, with other employees or work units. This would occur in a team setting where each member works alone but shares raw materials or machinery to perform her or his otherwise independent tasks. Interdependence is higher under *sequential interdependence,* in which the output of one person becomes the direct input for another person or unit. Sequential interdependence occurs where team members are organized in an assembly line.

Reciprocal interdependence, in which work output is exchanged back and forth among individuals, produces the highest degree of interdependence. People who design a new product or service would typically have reciprocal interdependence because their design decisions affect others involved in the design process. Any decision made by the design engineers would influence the work of the manufacturing engineer and purchasing specialist, and vice versa. Employees with reciprocal interdependence should be organized into teams to facilitate coordination in their interwoven relationship.

As a rule, the higher the level of task interdependence, the greater the need to organize people into teams rather than have them work alone. A team structure improves interpersonal communication and thus results in better coordination. High task interdependence also motivates most people to be part of the team. However, the rule that a team should be formed when employees have high interdependence applies when team members have the same task goals, such as serving the same clients or collectively assembling the same product. When team members have different goals (such as serving different clients) but must depend on other team members to achieve those unique goals, teamwork might create excessive conflict. Under these circumstances, the company should try to reduce the level of interdependence or rely on supervision as a buffer or mediator among employees.

EXHIBIT 8.3

Levels of Task Interdependence

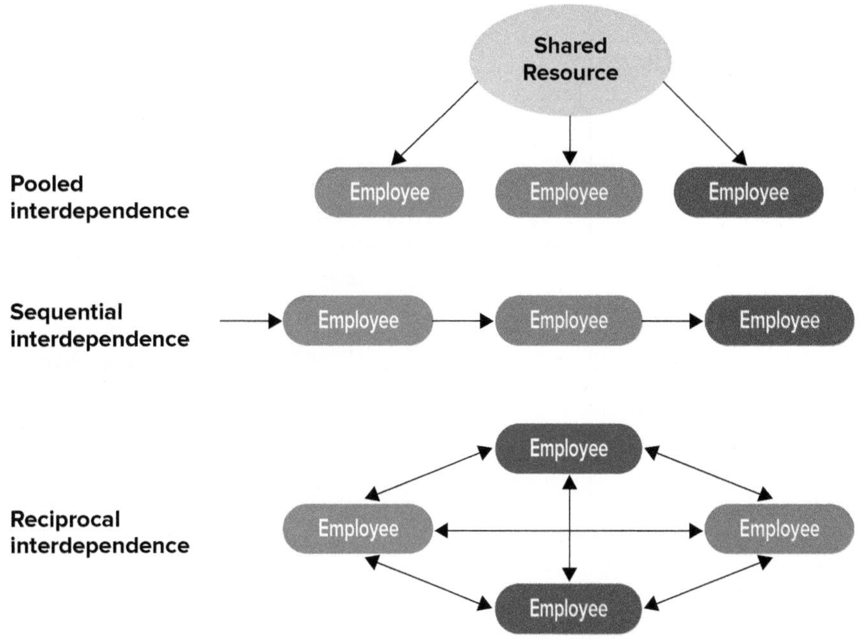

TEAM SIZE

What is the ideal size for a team? By now you probably understand that the answer to this question depends on the type of team we are talking about. The tasks performed by leadership teams and project teams tend to be complex and knowledge intensive, so increases in team size might capitalize on additional expertise or resources. On the other hand, production teams engage in work that is more routine and standardized, so additional members might add unnecessary coordination requirements.[30]

Generally, teams should be large enough to provide the necessary competencies and perspectives to perform the work, yet small enough to maintain efficient coordination and meaningful involvement of each member.[31] "You need to have a balance between having enough people to do all the things that need to be done, while keeping the team small enough so that it is cohesive and can make decisions effectively and speedily," says Broadcast Australia CEO Jim Hassell, who has also held executive roles at IBM and NBN Corp.[32] Small teams (say, less than a dozen members) operate effectively because they have less process loss. Members of smaller teams also tend to feel more engaged because they have more influence on the group's norms and goals and feel more responsible for the team's success and failure. Also, members of smaller teams get to know each other better, which improves mutual trust as well as perceived support, help, and assistance from those team members.[33]

Should companies have 100-person teams if the task is highly complex? The answer is that a group this large probably isn't a team, even if management calls it one. A team exists when its members interact and influence each other, are mutually accountable for achieving common goals associated with organizational objectives, and perceive themselves as a social entity within an organization. It is very difficult for everyone in a 100-person work unit to influence each other and experience enough cohesion to perceive themselves as team members. However, such complex tasks can usually be divided into smaller clusters of people.

TEAM COMPOSITION

In most workplaces, employees must have more than technical skills; they must also be able and willing to work in a team environment. Some companies go to great lengths to hire people who possess team competencies. The most frequently mentioned characteristics or behaviours of effective team members are depicted in the "Five C's" model illustrated in Exhibit 8.4: cooperating, coordinating, communicating, comforting, and conflict resolving. The first three competencies are mainly (but not entirely) task-related, while the last two primarily assist team maintenance:[34]

- *Cooperating*. Effective team members are willing and able to work together rather than alone. This includes sharing resources and being sufficiently adaptive or flexible to

EXHIBIT 8.4

Five C's of Team Member Competency

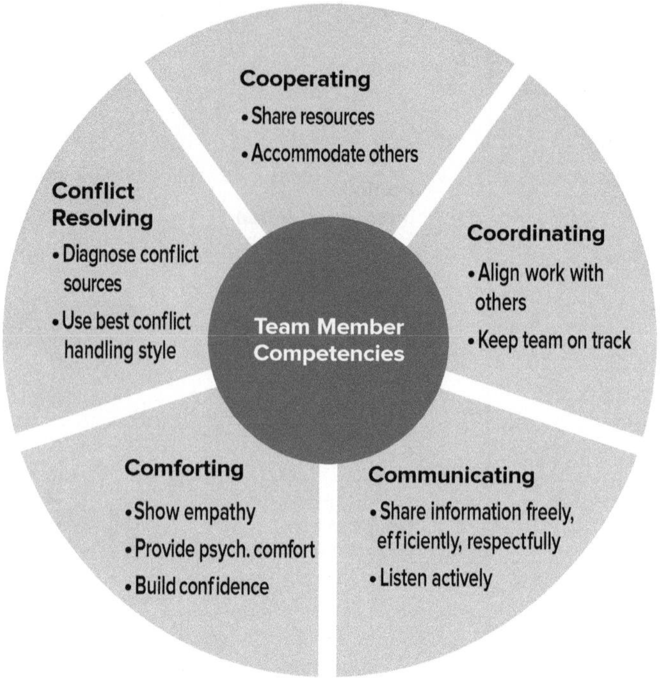

Sources: Based on information in V. Rousseau, C. Aubé, and A. Savoie, "Teamwork Behaviors: A Review and an Integration of Frameworks," *Small Group Research* 37, no. 5 (2006), pp. 540–570; M.L. Loughry, M.W. Ohland, and D. D. Moore, "Development of a Theory-Based Assessment of Team Member Effectiveness," *Educational and Psychological Measurement* 67, no. 3 (2007), pp. 505–524.

accommodate the needs and preferences of other team members, such as rescheduling use of machinery so that another team member with a tighter deadline can use it.

- *Coordinating.* Effective team members actively manage the team's work so that it is performed efficiently and harmoniously. For example, effective team members keep the team on track and help to integrate the work performed by different members. This typically requires that effective team members know the work of other team members, not just their own.
- *Communicating.* Effective team members transmit information freely (rather than hoarding), efficiently (using the best channel and language), and respectfully (minimizing arousal of negative emotions).[35] They also listen actively to coworkers.
- *Comforting.* Effective team members help coworkers to maintain a positive and healthy psychological state. They show empathy, provide psychological comfort, and build coworker feelings of confidence and self-worth.
- *Conflict resolving.* Conflict is inevitable in social settings, so effective team members have the skills and motivation to resolve dysfunctional disagreements among team members. This requires effective use of various conflict-handling styles as well as diagnostic skills to identify and resolve the structural sources of conflict.

Which employees tend to have these team competencies? Top of the list are those with high conscientiousness and extroversion personality traits, as well as with emotional intelligence. Furthermore, the old saying "One bad apple spoils the barrel" seems to apply to teams; one team member who lacks these teamwork competencies may undermine the dynamics of the entire team.[36]

Team Diversity Diversity, another important dimension of team composition, has both positive and negative effects on teams.[37] The main advantage of diverse teams is that they make better decisions than do homogeneous teams in some situations. One reason is that people from different backgrounds tend to see a problem or opportunity from different angles. Team members have different mental models, so they are more likely to identify viable solutions to difficult problems. A second reason is that diverse team members have a broader pool of technical competencies.

Along with potentially better decision making, diverse teams provide better representation of the team's constituents, such as other departments or clients from similarly diverse backgrounds. This representation not only brings different viewpoints to the decision; it also gives stakeholders a belief that they have a voice in that decision process. As we learned in Chapter 5, voice is an important ingredient in procedural justice, so constituents feel the decision is fairer when the decision-making team includes members with similar surface or deep-level diversity.

Against these advantages are a number of challenges created by team diversity. Employees with diverse backgrounds take longer to become a high-performing team. This partly occurs because bonding is slower among people who are different from each other, especially when teams have deep-level diversity (i.e., different beliefs and values). Diverse teams are susceptible to "fault lines"–hypothetical dividing lines that may split a team into subgroups along gender, ethnic, professional, or other dimensions.[38] These fault lines reduce team effectiveness by reducing the motivation to communicate and coordinate with team mates on the other side of the hypothetical divisions. In contrast, members of teams with minimal diversity experience higher satisfaction, less conflict, and better interpersonal relations. Consequently, homogeneous teams tend to be more effective on tasks requiring a high degree of cooperation and coordination, such as emergency response teams.

role A set of behaviours that people are expected to perform because they hold certain positions in a team and organization.

Team Roles An important part of the team process is forming and reinforcing team roles. A **role** is a set of behaviours that people are expected to perform because they hold certain positions in a team and organization.[39] In a team setting, some roles help the team achieve its goals; other roles maintain relationships within the team. Some team roles are formally assigned to specific people. For example, team leaders are usually expected to initiate discussion, ensure that everyone has an opportunity to present his or her views, and help the team reach agreement on the issues discussed.

Team members are assigned specific roles within their formal job responsibilities. Yet, team members also assume informal roles that suit their personality and values as well as the wishes of other team members. These informal roles, which are negotiated throughout the team development process, range from supporting others to initiating new ideas. Informal team roles are shared, but many are eventually associated with one or two people on the team.[40]

Transactive Memory A transactive memory system describes how task-relevant knowledge is distributed within a team and the collective awareness of who knows what. To illustrate, consider the example of a group of business students working on a sustainability case competition. A case competition requires a visually arresting slide deck, engaging speakers, and a well-rounded, thorough presentation. Having one person with sound sustainability knowledge is a must, but what about the rest of the team? One person could bring in knowledge of finance and quantitative ability, another could bring his/her marketing background to use the sustainability-centric recommendation as a branding tool, while another might possess knowledge of strategy and use that to tell the entire story in a meaningful way. Clearly defined and complementary strengths make for a much stronger team, but unless team members know who has what skill, those skills might get wasted and lead to process losses. Thus, the idea behind the transactive member concept is for teams to not only organize around complementary skills, but to devote time and energy towards understanding how those skills are distributed. This is important because research shows that teams with more well-developed transactive memory systems outperform teams with less well-developed systems.[41]

Team States

LO3

The third set of elements in the team effectiveness model, collectively known as *team states*, includes team norms, cohesion, team efficacy, and trust. These elements represent motivational or cognitive characteristics of the team that continuously evolve.

TEAM NORMS

norms The informal rules and shared expectations that groups establish to regulate the behaviour of their members.

Norms are the informal rules and shared expectations that groups establish to regulate the behaviour of their members. Norms apply only to behaviour, not to private thoughts or feelings. Furthermore, norms exist only for behaviours that are important to the team.[42] Norms are enforced in various ways. Coworkers grimace if we are late for a meeting, or they make sarcastic comments if we don't have our part of the project completed on time. Norms are also directly reinforced through praise from high-status members, more access to valued resources, or other rewards available to the team. But team members often conform to prevailing norms without direct reinforcement or punishment because they identify with the group and want to align their behaviour with the team's expectations. The more closely the person's social identity is connected to the group, the more the individual is motivated to avoid negative sanctions from that group.[43]

How Team Norms Develop Norms develop when teams form because people need to anticipate or predict how others will act. Even subtle events during the team's formation, such as how team members initially greet each other and where they sit in the first meetings, can initiate norms that are later difficult to change. Norms also form as team members discover behaviours that help them function more effectively (such as the need to respond quickly to e-mail).[44] In particular, a critical event in the team's history can trigger formation of a norm or sharpen a previously vague one. A third influence on team norms are the experiences and values that members bring to the team. If members of a new team value work-life balance, norms are likely to develop that discourage long hours and work overload.[45]

Preventing and Changing Dysfunctional Team Norms Team norms often become deeply anchored, so the best way to avoid norms that undermine organizational success or employee well-being is to establish desirable norms when the team is first formed. One way to do this is to clearly state desirable norms when the team is created. Another approach is to select people with appropriate values. If organizational leaders want their teams to have strong safety norms, they should hire people who already value safety and who clearly identify the importance of safety when the team is formed.

The suggestions so far refer to new teams, but how can organizational leaders maintain desirable norms in older teams? One solution comes from a recent study, namely that leaders often have the capacity to alter existing norms.[46] By speaking up or actively coaching the team, they can often subdue dysfunctional norms while developing useful norms. A second suggestion is to introduce team-based rewards that counter dysfunction norms. However, studies report that employees might continue to adhere to a dysfunctional team norm (such as limiting output) even though this behaviour reduces their paycheque. Finally, if dysfunctional norms are deeply ingrained and the previous solutions don't work, it may be necessary to disband the group and replace it with people having more favourable norms.

TEAM COHESION

team cohesion The degree of attraction people feel towards the team and their motivation to remain members.

Team cohesion refers to the degree of attraction people feel towards the team and their motivation to remain members. It is a characteristic of the team, including the extent to which its members are attracted to the team, are committed to the team's goals or tasks, and feel a collective sense of team pride.[47] Thus, team cohesion is an emotional experience, not just a calculation of whether to stay or leave the team. It exists when team members make the team part of their social identity. Team cohesion is associated with team development because team members develop a team identity as part of the team development process.

Influences on Team Cohesion Several factors influence team cohesion, but the six described here seem to be the most important: member similarity, team size, member interaction, difficult entry, team success, and external competition or challenges. For the most part, these factors reflect the individual's social identity with the group and beliefs about how team membership will fulfill personal needs.

- *Member similarity.* Social scientists have long known that people are attracted to others who are similar to them.[48] This similarity-attraction effect occurs because we assume that people who look like us and have similar backgrounds are more trustworthy and are more likely to accept us. We also expect to have fewer negative experiences, such as conflicts and violations of our expectations and beliefs. Thus, teams have higher cohesion or become cohesive more quickly when members are similar to each other. In contrast, it is more difficult and takes longer for teams with diverse members to become cohesive. This difficulty depends on the form of diversity, however. Teams consisting of people from different job groups seem to gel together just as well as teams of people from the same job.[49]

- *Team size.* Smaller teams tend to have more cohesion than larger teams because it is easier for a few people to agree on goals and coordinate work activities. However, small teams have less cohesion when they lack enough members to perform the required tasks.
- *Member interaction.* Teams tend to have more cohesion when team members interact with each other fairly regularly. This occurs when team members perform highly interdependent tasks and work in the same physical area.
- *Somewhat difficult entry.* Teams tend to have more cohesion when entry to the team is restricted. The more elite the team, the more prestige it confers on its members, and the more they tend to value their membership in the unit. At the same time, research suggests that severe initiations can weaken team cohesion because of the adverse effects of humiliation, even for those who successfully endure the initiation.[50]
- *Team success.* Team cohesion increases with the team's level of success because people are attracted to groups that fulfill their needs and goals.[51] Furthermore, individuals are more likely to attach their social identity to successful teams than to those with a string of failures.[52]
- *External competition and challenges.* Team cohesion tends to increase when members face external competition or a valued objective that is challenging. This might include a threat from an external competitor or friendly competition from other teams. Employees value their membership on the team because of its ability to overcome the threat or competition and as a form of social support. However, cohesion can dissipate when external threats are severe because these threats are stressful and cause teams to make less effective decisions.[53]

Consequences of Team Cohesion Teams with higher cohesion tend to perform better than those with low cohesion.[54] In fact, the team's existence depends on a minimal level of cohesion because it motivates team members to remain members and to help the team achieve its mutually-agreed objectives. Members of high-cohesion teams spend more time together, share information more frequently, and are more satisfied with each other. They provide each other with better social support in stressful situations and work to minimize dysfunctional conflict.[55] When conflict does arise, high-cohesion team members tend to resolve their differences swiftly and effectively.

However, at least two contingencies make the cohesion-performance relationship somewhat more complex. First, team cohesion has less effect on team performance when the team has low task interdependence.[56] High cohesion motivates employees to coordinate and cooperate with other team members. But people don't need to cooperate or coordinate as much when little of their work depends on other team members (low task interdependence), so the motivational effect of high cohesion is less relevant in teams with low interdependence.

Courtesy *Atlantic Business Magazine* and Lighthouse Media Group

A Lighthouse Built on High Cohesion

The staff at Lighthouse Media Group in Bridgewater, Nova Scotia, are a highly cohesive group that successfully keeps its much larger competitors off-guard. "Lighthouse staff members [have] kept us independent in the face of stiff competition and corporate takeovers," says Lighthouse president Lynn Hennigar. Its weekly newspaper, the *Bridgewater Bulletin,* has received more than 200 newspaper industry awards. Lighthouse's mostly female staff often demonstrate their cohesion when faced with new challenges. For instance, the team performed above any reasonable expectations when the press broke down, which threatened to delay getting the paper out on time. On another occasion, when putting together an interactive presentation promoting Nova Scotia tourism, Lighthouse staff displayed skills that Hennigar admits she didn't even know about. "Lighthouse succeeds because of its multi-talented, highly dedicated team of employees," says Hennigar. "It's a team that embraces change."[57]

EXHIBIT 8.5

Effect of Team Cohesion on Task Performance

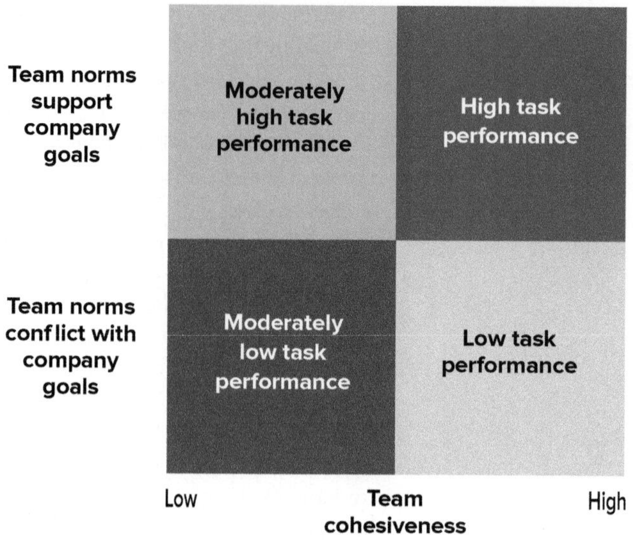

Second, the effect of cohesion on team performance depends on whether the team's norms are compatible with or opposed to the organizational objectives.[58] As Exhibit 8.5 illustrates, teams with high cohesion perform better when their norms are aligned with the organization's objectives, whereas higher cohesion can potentially reduce team performance when norms are counterproductive. This effect occurs because cohesion motivates employees to perform at a level more consistent with team norms. If a team's norm tolerates or encourages absenteeism, employees will be more motivated to take unjustified sick leave. If the team's norm discourages absenteeism, employees are more motivated to avoid taking sick leave.

One last comment about team cohesion and performance: Recall earlier in this section we said that team performance (success) increases cohesion, whereas we are now saying that team cohesion causes team performance. Both statements are correct, but there is some evidence that team performance has a stronger effect on cohesion than vice versa. In other words, a team's performance will likely affect its cohesion, whereas a team's cohesion has less of an effect on its performance.[59]

connect

Are you a team player? Visit **connect.mcgrawhill.com** to assess your preferences about teamwork.

team efficacy The collective belief among team members of the team's capability to successfully complete a task.

TEAM EFFICACY

Have you ever been in a team where everyone believed the team was highly likely to succeed? If so, you were in a team with high **team efficacy**, which is the shared perception among team members about the team's overall level of capability. A vast amount of research has shown that teams with high levels of efficacy outperform teams with low levels of efficacy, especially when task interdependence is high.[60] When a team has high efficacy, members are more likely to set ambitious goals, put forth greater effort, persist longer when faced with challenging obstacles, and view negative feedback as an opportunity rather than a challenge.

On the other hand, teams characterized by low team efficacy are more likely to experience apathy, uncertainty, and a lack of direction. Research has shown that the dysfunctional characteristics associated with low efficacy include heightened anxiety,[61] greater social loafing,[62] and less vigilance in decision-making processes.[63] Researchers have also found a link between team efficacy and the extent to which individual team members engage in the behaviours described in the team competency model presented earlier in the chapter. For example, in teams with high efficacy, individual team members are more likely to display coordination and cooperative type behaviours.[64]

EXHIBIT 8.6

Three Foundations of Trust in Teams

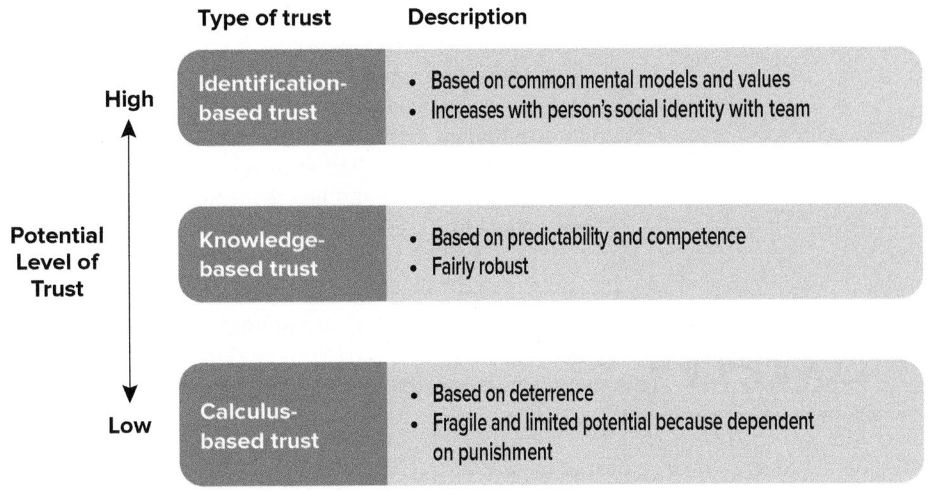

Considering how important team efficacy is to overall team performance, it is worthwhile to consider where this perception comes from and how it can be developed. In general, teams have higher levels of efficacy when individual team members are more confident about their own team-specific skills, when the team is composed of members who have knowledge about the team's task, and when team members show visible teamwork behaviours such as contributing to the task and managing relationship dynamics.[65] Having a leader who uses a more participative versus directly style can also increase team efficacy.[66]

TEAM TRUST

Any relationship–including the relationship among team members–depends on a certain degree of trust. *Trust* refers to positive expectations one person has towards another person in situations involving risk (see Chapter 4).[67] Trust is ultimately perceptual, in which we trust others based on our beliefs about their ability, integrity, and benevolence. It also has an emotional component, where you experience positive feelings towards those you trust.[68] Trust is built on three foundations: calculus, knowledge, and identification (see Exhibit 8.6).[69]

- *Calculus-based trust.* This foundation represents a logical calculation that other team members will act appropriately because they face sanctions if their actions violate reasonable expectations.[70] It offers the lowest potential trust and is easily broken by a violation of expectations. Some scholars suggest that calculus-based trust is not trust at all. Instead, it might be trust in the system rather than in the other person. In any event, calculus-based trust alone cannot sustain a team's relationship, because it relies on deterrence.
- *Knowledge-based trust.* This form of trust is based on the predictability of another team member's behaviour. This predictability refers only to "positive expectations" as the definition of trust states, because you would not trust someone who tends to engage in harmful or dysfunctional behaviour. Knowledge-based trust includes our confidence in the other person's ability or competence, such as the confidence that exists when we trust a physician.[71] Knowledge-based trust offers a higher potential level of trust and is more stable because it develops over time.
- *Identification-based trust.* This foundation is based on mutual understanding and an emotional bond among team members. It occurs when team members think, feel, and act like each other. High-performance teams exhibit this level of trust because they share the same values and mental models. Identification-based trust is potentially the strongest and most robust of all three types of trust. The individual's self-concept is based partly on membership in the team and he or she believes the members' values highly overlap, so any transgressions by other team members are quickly forgiven. People are more reluctant to acknowledge a violation of this high-level trust because it strikes at the heart of their self-concept.

Dynamics of Team Trust Employees typically join a team with a moderate or high level–not a low level–of trust in their new coworkers.[72] The main explanation for the initially high trust (called *swift trust*) in organizational settings is that people usually believe fellow team members are reasonably competent (knowledge-based trust) and they tend to develop some degree of social identity with the team (identification-based trust). Even when working with strangers, most of us display some level of trust, if only because it supports our self-concept of being a good person. However, trust is fragile in new relationships because it is based on assumptions rather than well-established experience. Consequently, studies report that trust tends to decrease rather than increase over time. This is unfortunate because employees become less forgiving and less cooperative towards others as their level of trust decreases, and this undermines team and organizational effectiveness.[73]

connect

How trusting are you? Visit **connect.mcgrawhill.com** to assess your trust propensity.

Team Processes

LO4

The next set of elements in the team effectiveness model, collectively known as *team processes*, refers to the interactions and activities that occur within a team as it works towards its goal. Traditionally, researchers have looked at the team's internal dynamics, such as task coordination and interpersonal relationships, to describe team process. However, there is growing recognition that team interactions with external parties also determine how well a team performs. For this reason we will describe both internal and external team processes. We will also describe the element of time, or in other words how teams develop.

INTERNAL TEAM PROCESSES

teamwork behaviour Activities that are devoted to enhancing the quality of the interactions, interdependencies, cooperation, and coordination of teams.

taskwork behaviour Efforts devoted to understanding the task requirements, discovering the "rules" by which the tasks are to be performed, establishing the patterns of interaction with equipment, exchanging task-related information, developing team solutions to problems, and so forth.

Internal team processes have historically been categorized as either *teamwork* or *taskwork*. **Teamwork behaviour** has been described as activities that are devoted to enhancing the quality of the interactions, interdependencies, cooperation, and coordination of teams.[74] During interactions between team members, teamwork behaviour takes the form of overt actions and verbal statements that contribute to the coordination demands of the team's task.[75] For example, a team member would be engaging in teamwork behaviour when they steer their fellow team members towards on-topic conversations, suggest setting time deadlines for completing tasks, or attempt to resolve a conflict within the group.

On the other hand, **taskwork behaviour** has been described as team members' efforts that are devoted to understanding the task requirements, discovering the "rules" by which the tasks are to be performed, establishing the patterns of interaction with equipment, exchanging task-related information, developing team solutions to problems, and so forth. Thus, taskwork represents the technical performance of the team's task, whereas teamwork behaviours are used to direct, align, and monitor taskwork.[76] To illustrate, the taskwork of a surgical team includes the tasks carried out to complete a surgical procedure, such as patient preparation, use of anesthesia, and suturing incisions. On the other hand, teamwork behaviours in a surgical team might include individual activities such as the identification of goals, suggestions for improving coordination, and efforts to resolve conflict, all of which help to ensure that the patient is effectively prepared for surgery, anesthesia is appropriately administered, and incisions are properly sutured. To perform well, a team needs to find excel at both types of internal process.

EXTERNAL TEAM PROCESSES

team boundary spanning Team actions that establish or enhance linkages and manage interactions with parties in the external environment.

Processes that occur between team members matter a great deal, but teams must also interact with people and groups who exist beyond the team's boundary. **Team boundary spanning** refers to team actions that establish or enhance linkages and manage interactions with parties in the external environment.[77] In their classic study of product development teams, Ancona and Caldwell (1992) classified external activities into different types and showed how these types impact overall team performance. They described the first type as *ambassador activities* because these activities encompassed such behaviours as protecting the team from outside pressure, persuading others to support the team, and lobbying for resources. The ambassador function tends to focus on the team's ability to mould and shape the beliefs of external constituents. Scholars often refer to ambassador activities as *vertical boundary spanning* because these activities frequently involve communicating with those higher in the organization's hierarchy, such as corporate or division managers.[78]

The second type of boundary activity was labelled *task coordination*. This type represents interactions aimed at coordinating technical or design issues, with examples including discussing design problems with others, obtaining feedback on the product design, and coordinating and negotiating with outsiders. In contrast to ambassador activities, task coordination activities show higher levels of communication laterally through the organization. Thus, they are often referred to as *horizontal boundary spanning*. As predictors of performance, ambassador and task coordinator activity were both positively related.[79] A third type of boundary spanning, called *scouting activity*, is described as a general scanning for ideas and information about the competition, the market, or the technology; thus, scouting activity is mostly directed at obtaining information from sources external to the organization. Although it would seem that scouting activity should be helpful, research has shown instead that prolonged scouting can actually harm team performance because it detracts from internal team processes.

TEAM DEVELOPMENT

Our model of team effectiveness also includes a longitudinal dimension, signifying that things like team processes and team states are not stable over time. For example, researchers have discovered that perceptions of team efficacy measured shortly after a team is created do correlate with team performance. However, team efficacy measured closer to the midpoint of a team's task is a much stronger predictor of team performance than efficacy measured earlier.[80] What is known about the changes teams experience over time? Team members must get to know and trust each other, understand and agree on their respective roles, discover appropriate and inappropriate behaviours, and learn how to coordinate with each other. The longer that team members work together, the better they develop common or complementary mental models, mutual understanding, and effective performance routines to complete the work.

Two popular models that capture team development activities are shown in Exhibit 8.5.[81] The first shows teams moving systematically from one stage to the next, while the dashed lines illustrate that teams might fall back to an earlier stage of development as new members join or other conditions disrupt the team's maturity. *Forming*, the first stage of team development, is a period of testing and orientation in which members learn about each other and evaluate the benefits and costs of continued membership. People tend to be polite, will defer to authority, and try to find out what is expected of them and how they will fit into the team. The *storming* stage is marked by interpersonal conflict as members become more proactive and compete for various team roles. Members try to establish norms of appropriate behaviour and performance standards.

During the *norming* stage, the team develops its first real sense of cohesion as roles are established and a consensus forms around group objectives and a common or complementary team-based mental model. By the *performing* stage, team members have learned to efficiently coordinate and resolve conflicts. In high-performance teams, members are highly cooperative, have a high level of trust in each other, are committed to group objectives, and identify with the team. Finally, the *adjourning* stage occurs when the team is about to disband. Team members shift their attention away from task orientation to a relationship focus.

The second model of team development focuses more directly on how teams pay attention to time and deadlines. This model, known as the *punctuated equilibrium model*, states that teams working under strict deadlines experience three important phases: the initial meeting, a midpoint transition, and the period close to the endpoint.[82] Each of these phases is connected by a period of inertia in which major changes to the team's task and direction are unlikely to occur. For example, a student team working on a project with a deadline would experience the first phase in their initial meetings. Here, they might agree on how to allocate workload and discuss overall goals for the project. After a period of inertia in which work progresses smoothly, the team experiences a spike in activity around the midpoint. If the team manages team process effectively at the midpoint they set themselves up for another period of relative inertia leading to a positive endpoint. However, without questioning their approach at this crucial phase they set themselves up for tension and conflict as work progresses to the endpoint. The most important practical lesson from these models of team development is that teams need to carefully attend to the issue of time pacing.[83]

EXHIBIT 8.7

Models of Team Development

The Five-Stage Model

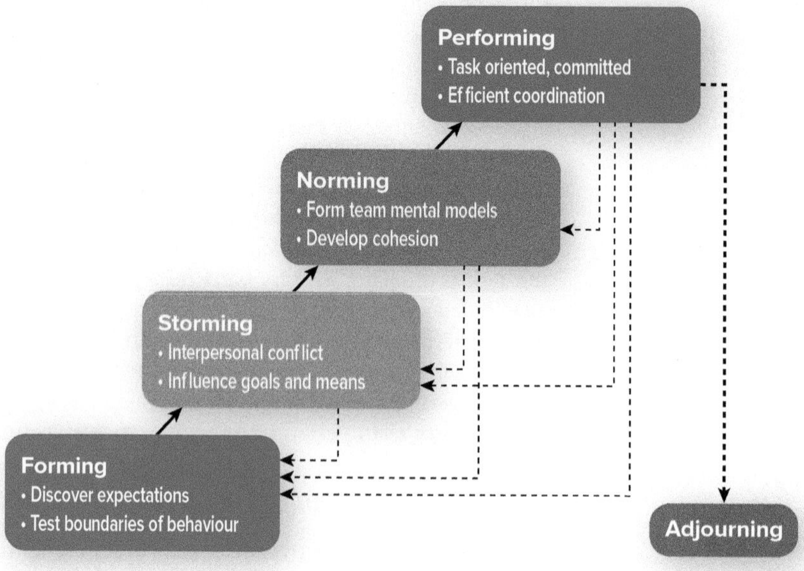

The Punctuated Equilibrium Model

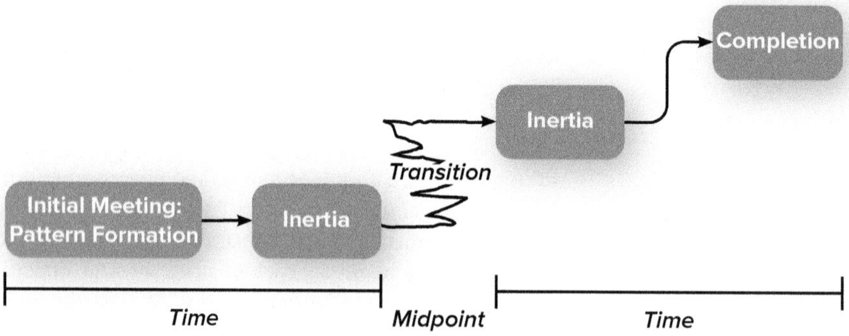

Developing Team Identities and Mental Models Although these models depict team development fairly well, they are not a perfect representation of the process. For instance, some teams remain in a particular stage longer than others and sometimes regress back to earlier stages of development. The models also mask two sets of processes that are the essence of team development: developing team identity and developing team mental models and coordinating routines.[84]

- *Developing team identity.* Team development is apparent when its members shift from viewing the team as something "out there" to something that is part of themselves. In other words, team development occurs when employees take ownership of the team's success and make the team part of their social identity.[85]
- *Developing team mental models and coordinating routines.* Team development includes developing habitual routines with team mates and forming shared or complementary mental models.[86] Team mental models are visual or relational mental images that are shared by team members, such as what good customer service looks like. A recent meta-analysis supports the view that teams are more effective when their members share common mental models of the work.[87]

team building A process that consists of formal activities intended to improve the development and functioning of a work team.

Accelerating Team Development through Team Building **Team building** consists of formal activities intended to improve the development and functioning of a work team.[88] To a large extent, team building attempts to speed up the team development process. This process may be applied to new teams, but it is more commonly introduced for existing teams that have regressed to earlier stages of team development due to membership turnover or loss of focus.

Some team-building interventions are task-focused. They clarify the team's performance goals, increase the team's motivation to accomplish these goals, and establish a mechanism for systematic feedback on the team's goal performance. A second type of team building tries to improve the team's problem-solving skills. A third category clarifies and reconstructs each member's perceptions of her or his role as well as the role expectations that member has of other team members. Role definition team building also helps the team to develop shared mental models–common internal representations of the external world, such as how to interact with clients, maintain machinery, and engage in meetings. Research studies indicate that team processes and performance depend on how well team members share common or complementary mental models about how they should work together.[89] A fourth–and likely the most common–type of team building is aimed at helping team members learn more about each other, build trust in each other, and develop ways to manage conflict within the team. Popular interventions such as wilderness team activities, paintball wars, and obstacle-course challenges are typically offered to build trust.

Do team building interventions improve team development and effectiveness? The most effective team building seems to be those in which employees receive training on specific team competencies, such as coordinating, conflict resolving, and communicating.[90] However, many team-building activities are less successful.[91] One problem is that team building interventions are used as general solutions to general team problems. A better approach is to begin with a sound diagnosis of the team's health and then select team-building interventions that address specific weaknesses.[92] Another problem is that team building is applied as a one-shot medical inoculation that every team should receive when it is formed. In truth, team building is an ongoing process, not a three-day jump start.[93] Finally, we must remember that team building occurs on the job, not just on an obstacle course or in a national park. Organizations should encourage team members to reflect on their work experiences and to experiment with just-in-time learning for team development.

The team effectiveness model is a useful template for understanding how teams work–and don't work–in organizations. With this knowledge in hand, let's briefly investigate two types of teams that have emerged over the past couple of decades to become important forms of team work in organizations: self-directed teams and virtual teams.[94]

self-directed teams Cross-functional work groups that are organized around work processes, complete an entire piece of work requiring several interdependent tasks, and have substantial autonomy over the execution of those tasks.

Self-Directed Teams

LO5

Self-directed teams (SDTs) are cross-functional groups organized around work processes, that complete an entire piece of work requiring several interdependent tasks, and that have substantial autonomy over the execution of those tasks.[95] This definition captures two distinct

Courtesy *Canadian Outback Adventures & Events,* www.canadianoutback.com

The Amazing Chase Team Building Challenge

One of the most popular team building activities offered by Calgary-based, Canadian Outback Adventures & Events is the "Amazing Chase." The Amazing Chase combines planning, strategy, communication, and teamwork in a race against the clock. Courses can be custom-designed, set up outdoors or even indoors with creative use of covered walkways and public transit. The overall goal is for teams to work together to navigate route markers, deal with road blocks and detours, and finish the race in the least amount of time. "One of my favourite things was the way that people were able to get creative and have some fun problem solving," says a Bentall Capital spokesperson. "For the teams themselves I think getting exposure to others in our department that they do not work with day-to-day was a key! It proved the old adage, "no one is good at everything, but everyone is good at something."[96]

OB by the NUMBERS

More Virtual Teams, More Virtual Challenges[97]

80% **managers** polled in large North American companies say that their firm's reliance on virtual teams will grow in importance over the next three years.

70% **North American chief information officers** polled who indicate that managing virtual teams is a very important globalization challenge (highest rated issue on the list).

58% **of managers** who say that it is somewhat or very important that all members of their department work from the same location.

features of SDTs. First, these teams complete an entire piece of work requiring several interdependent tasks. This type of work arrangement clusters the team members together while minimizing interdependence and interaction with employees outside the team. The result is a close-knit group of employees who depend on each other to accomplish their individual tasks. The second distinctive feature of SDTs is that they have substantial autonomy over the execution of their tasks. In particular, these teams plan, organize, and control work activities with little or no direct involvement of a higher-status supervisor.

Self-directed teams are found in several industries, ranging from petrochemical plants to aircraft parts manufacturing. Most of the top-rated manufacturing firms in North America apparently rely on SDTs.[98] Indeed, self-directed teams have become such a popular way to organize employees in manufacturing, services, and government work that many companies don't realize they have them. The popularity of SDTs is consistent with research indicating that they potentially increase both productivity and job satisfaction.[99] For instance, one study found that car dealership service shops that organize employees into SDTs are significantly more profitable than shops where employees work without a team structure. Another study reported that both short- and long-term measures of customer satisfaction increased after street cleaners in a German city were organized into SDTs.

SUCCESS FACTORS FOR SELF-DIRECTED TEAMS

The successful implementation of self-directed teams depends on several factors.[100] SDTs should be responsible for an entire work process, such as making an entire product or providing a service. This structure keeps each team sufficiently independent from other teams, yet it demands a relatively high degree of interdependence among employees within the team.[101] SDTs should also have sufficient autonomy to organize and coordinate their work. Autonomy allows them to respond more quickly and effectively to client and stakeholder demands. It also motivates team members through feelings of empowerment. Finally, SDTs are more successful when the work site and technology support coordination and communication among team members and increase job enrichment.[102] Too often, management calls a group of employees a "team," yet the work layout, assembly-line structure, and other technologies isolate the employees from each other.

Virtual Teams

virtual teams Teams whose members operate across space, time, and organizational boundaries and are linked through information technologies to achieve organizational tasks.

Virtual teams are teams whose members operate across space, time, and organizational boundaries and are linked through information technologies to achieve organizational tasks.[103] Virtual teams differ from traditional teams in two ways: (1) They are not usually co-located (do not work in the same physical area), and (2) due to their lack of co-location, members of virtual teams depend primarily on information technologies rather than face-to-face interaction to communicate and coordinate their work effort. Teams have degrees of *virtuality*. Team virtuality increases with the geographic dispersion of team members, percentage of members who work apart, and percentage of time that members work apart. For example, a team has low virtuality when all of its members live in the same city and only one or two members work from home each day. High virtuality exists when team members are spread around the world and only a couple of members have ever met in person.

Debating Point:

ARE VIRTUAL TEAMS MORE TROUBLE THAN THEY'RE WORTH?

Virtual teams were rare before the Internet was born. Today, they are almost as commonplace as face-to-face teams. Virtual teams are increasingly possible because more of us are employed in knowledge work rather than physical production. Furthermore, information technologies make it easier to communicate instantaneously with coworkers around the globe. To some extent, virtual teams have even become "cool." It is almost a badge of honour to say that you are a member of a far-flung team of people from several continents.

But whether they are stylish or commonplace, virtual teams seem to be increasingly necessary for an organization's competitive advantage. This chapter points out that we need virtual teams to effectively engage in organizational learning. Knowledge has become the currency of organizational success, and globalization has ensured that such knowledge is scattered around the world. In short, organizations are at a disadvantage unless they use lots of virtual teams.

How could anyone claim that virtual teams aren't worth the effort, particularly when organizational learning is one of the four pillars of organizational effectiveness (see Chapter 1)? Well, actually, there are a few arguments against them. For the most part, critics don't deny the potential value of sharing knowledge through virtual teams. Rather, they have added up the negative features and concluded that they outweigh the benefits. In fact, when chief information officers were asked to identify the top challenges of globalization, 70 percent listed managing virtual teams as the top concern.[104]

One persistent problem with virtual teams is that they lack the richness of face-to-face communication. We'll provide more detail about this important matter in Chapter 9, but no information technology to date equals the volume and variety of information transmitted among people located in the same room. This is one reason Toyota, PSA Peugeot Citroën, and other companies arrange for teams to meet in the same physical space. They can exchange information in larger volumes, much faster, and more accurately compared with the clumsy methods currently available to virtual teams. Multiperson video chat is getting closer to face-to-face, but it requires considerable bandwidth and still falls short on communication richness.

Another problem with virtual teams is that people trust others more easily when they are nearby.[105] Various studies have reported that virtual team members either have lower trust compared with co-located team members, or their trust is much more fragile. In fact, experts offer one main recommendation to increase trust among virtual team members—have them spend time together as co-located teams.

A third drawback with virtual teams is that the farther away people are located, the more they differ in experiences, beliefs, culture, and expectations. These differences can be advantageous for some decisions, of course, but they can also be a curse for team development and performance. "Everyone must have the same picture of what success looks like," advises Rick Maurer, a North American leadership consultant. "Without that laser-like focus, it is too easy for people in Bangalore to develop a different picture of success than the picture held by their colleagues in Brussels. Now multiply that by a couple more locations and you've got a mess."[106]

Here's one more reason why companies should think twice before relying on virtual teams: People seem to have less influence or control over distant than over co-located coworkers. A team member who stops by your cubicle to ask how your part of the report is coming along has much more effect than an impersonal—or even a flaming—e-mail from afar.

Perhaps that is why surveys reveal less satisfaction with virtual team members than co-located team members.[107] One study reported that distant colleagues received two to three times as many complaints as co-located colleagues about working half-heartedly (or not at all) on shared projects, falling behind on projects, not making deadlines, failing to warn about missing deadlines, making changes with- out warning, and providing misleading information. When asked how long it takes to resolve these problems, more than half of the respondents indicated a few days for co-located team members, whereas most estimated a few weeks or longer for distant team members.

Virtual teams have become commonplace in most organizations. Two-thirds of human resource managers estimate that reliance on virtual teams will grow rapidly over the next few years.[108] In global companies such as IBM, almost everyone in knowledge work is part of a virtual team. One reason virtual teams have become so widespread is that information technologies have made it easier than ever before to communicate and coordinate with people at a distance.[109] The shift from production-based to knowledge-based work is a second reason why virtual teamwork is feasible. It isn't yet possible to make a physical product when team members are located apart, but most of us are now in jobs that mainly process knowledge.

Information technologies and knowledge-based work make virtual teams *possible*, but organizational learning and globalization are two reasons why they are increasingly *necessary*.

In Chapter 1, we learned that organizational learning is one of four perspectives of organizational effectiveness. Virtual teams represent a natural part of the organizational learning process because they encourage employees to share and use knowledge where geography limits more direct forms of collaboration. Globalization makes virtual teams increasingly necessary because employees are spread around the planet rather than around one building or city. Thus, global businesses depend on virtual teamwork to leverage the potential of their employees.

SUCCESS FACTORS FOR VIRTUAL TEAMS

Virtual teams face all the challenges of traditional teams, as well as the issues arising from time and distance. These challenges increase with the team's virtuality, particularly when it exists for only a short time.[110] Fortunately, OB research has identified the following strategies to minimize most virtual team problems.[111] First, virtual team members require more than the team competencies described earlier in this chapter. They also require good communication technology skills, strong self-leadership skills to motivate and guide their behaviour without peers or bosses nearby, and higher emotional intelligence so that they can decipher the feelings of other team members from e-mail and other limited communication media.

Second, virtual teams should have a toolkit of communication channels (e-mail, virtual whiteboards, video conferencing, etc.) as well as the freedom to choose the channels that work best for them. This may sound obvious, but unfortunately senior management tends to impose technology on virtual teams, often based on advice from external consultants, and expects team members to use the same communication technology throughout their work. In contrast, research suggests that communication channels gain and lose importance over time, depending on the task and level of trust.

Third, virtual teams need plenty of structure. In one recent review of effective virtual teams, many of the principles for successful virtual teams related mostly to creating these structures, such as clear operational objectives, documented work processes, and agreed upon roles and responsibilities.[112] The final recommendation is that virtual-team members should meet face-to-face fairly early in the team development process. This idea may seem contradictory to the entire notion of virtual teams, but so far, no technology has replaced face-to-face interaction for high-level bonding and mutual understanding.[113]

Team Decision Making

LO6

Self-directed teams, virtual teams, and practically all other groups are expected to make decisions. Under certain conditions, teams are more effective than individuals at identifying problems, choosing alternatives, and evaluating their decisions. To leverage these benefits, however, we first need to understand the constraints on effective team decision making. Then, we look at specific team structures that try to overcome these constraints.

Dennis Hengeveld/CartoonStock

CONSTRAINTS ON TEAM DECISION MAKING

Anyone who has spent enough time in the workplace can recite several ways in which teams stumble in decision making. The four most common problems are time constraints, evaluation apprehension, pressure to conform, and overconfidence.

Time Constraints There's a saying that committees keep minutes and waste hours. This reflects the fact that teams take longer than individuals to make decisions.[114] Teams consume time organizing, coordinating, and maintaining relationships (i.e., process losses). Team members require time to build rapport, agree on rules and norms of behaviour in the decision process, and understand each other's ideas.

Another time-related constraint in most team structures is that only one person can speak at a time.[115] This problem, known as **production blocking,** undermines idea generation in a few ways. First, team members need to listen in on the conversation to find an opportune time to speak up, but this monitoring makes it difficult for them to concentrate on their own ideas. Second, ideas are fleeting, so the longer they wait to speak up, the more likely their flickering ideas will die out. Third, team members might remember their fleeting thoughts by concentrating on them, but this causes them to pay less attention to the conversation. By ignoring what others are saying, team members miss other potentially good ideas.

production blocking A time constraint in team decision making due to the procedural requirement that only one person may speak at a time.

Evaluation Apprehension Team members are often reluctant to mention ideas that seem silly because they believe (often correctly) that other team members are silently evaluating them.[116] This **evaluation apprehension** is based on the individual's desire to create a favourable self-presentation and need to protect self-esteem. It is most common when meetings are attended by people with different levels of status or expertise or when members formally evaluate each other's performance throughout the year (as in 360-degree feedback). Creative ideas often sound bizarre or illogical when first presented, so evaluation apprehension tends to discourage employees from mentioning them in front of coworkers.

evaluation apprehension A decision-making problem that occurs when individuals are reluctant to mention ideas that seem silly because they believe (often correctly) that other team members are silently evaluating them.

Pressure to Conform Team cohesion leads employees to conform to the team's norms. This control keeps the group organized around common goals, but it may also cause team members to suppress their dissenting opinions, particularly when a strong team norm is related to the issue. When someone does state a point of view that violates the majority opinion, other members might punish the violator or try to persuade him or her that the opinion is incorrect. Conformity can also be subtle. To some extent, we depend on the opinions that others hold to validate our own views. If coworkers don't agree with us, we begin to question our own opinions even without overt peer pressure.

Overconfidence (Inflated Team Efficacy) Earlier in the chapter we described team efficacy and stated that in most situations it is better for a team to have higher rather than low levels. Unfortunately, teams sometimes become overconfident and develop a false sense of invulnerability.[117] In other words, the team's efficacy far exceeds reality regarding its competencies and the favourableness of the situation. Overconfident teams are less vigilant when making decisions, partly because they have more positive than negative emotions and moods during these events. They also engage in less discussion (task conflict) and are less likely to seek out or accept information located outside the team, both of which undermine the quality of team decisions.

Why do teams become overconfident? The main reason is a team-level variation of self-enhancement (see Chapter 3), whereby team members have a natural motivation to believe the team's capabilities and situation are above average. This above-average effect is stronger in cohesive teams because self-enhancement is stronger for important characteristics. It is also stronger when the team has external threats or competition because these adversaries generate "us-them" differentiation. Team efficacy is further inflated by the mutually reinforcing beliefs of the team. We develop a clearly and higher opinion of the team when other team members echo that opinion.

IMPROVING CREATIVE DECISION MAKING IN TEAMS

Team decision making is fraught with problems, but several solutions also emerge from these bad-news studies. Team members need to be confident in their decision making but not so confident that they collectively feel invulnerable. This calls for team norms that encourage critical thinking as well as team membership with sufficient diversity. Checks and balances need to be in place to prevent one or two people from dominating the discussion. The team should also be large enough to possess the collective knowledge to resolve the problem yet small enough that the team doesn't consume too much time or restrict individual input.

Along with these general recommendations, OB studies have identified four team structures that encourage creativity in a team setting: brainstorming, brainwriting, electronic brainstorming, and nominal group technique. These four structures emphasize idea creation (the central focus of creativity), but some also include team selection of alternatives.

brainstorming A freewheeling, face-to-face meeting where team members aren't allowed to criticize but are encouraged to speak freely, generate as many ideas as possible, and build on the ideas of others.

Brainstorming

Brainstorming is a team event where participants try to think up as many ideas as possible. The process was introduced by advertising executive Alex Osborn in 1939 and has four simple rules to maximize the number and quality of ideas presented: (1) Speak freely–describe even the craziest ideas; (2) don't criticize others or their ideas; (3) provide as many ideas as possible–the quality of ideas increases with the quantity of ideas; and (4) build on the ideas that others have presented. These rules are supposed to encourage divergent thinking while minimizing evaluation apprehension and other team dynamics problems.[118]

Brainstorming became popular when it was introduced, until a business magazine article in the 1950s misrepresented and lampooned the process. Also, over the past few decades, numerous lab studies have concluded that brainstorming doesn't produce as many ideas as individuals working alone. Production blocking and evaluation apprehension are identified as the main culprits.[119] These findings are perplexing because some of the most successful creative agencies and design firms say that brainstorming is a helpful tool.[120] The leaders of these companies might be mistaken, but a more likely explanation is their advice that brainstorming takes considerable skill and experience with a trained facilitator in a collaborative learning orientation culture. These conditions are missing from most lab studies, which are short-term events with inexperienced undergraduate students who barely know each other. Also, brainstorming sessions are intended to produce creative ideas, whereas lab studies tend to measure the number of ideas.[121]

Brainstorming likely improves team creativity, but it does have limitations. First, even with people who are trained and experienced, brainstorming suffers from production blocking. Great ideas are forgotten while team members listen to each other's ideas, and sparks of insight are forfeited if team members do not listen to each other's ideas. A second problem, called fixation or conformity effect, is that hearing another person's ideas tends to restrict the variety of ideas that we subsequently think about. In brainstorming, participants are asked to openly describe their ideas, but the first few verbal descriptions might cause participants to limit their thinking to ideas similar to those first suggestions rather than other categories of ideas. However, neuroscience studies report that people think more creatively when exposed to moderately creative (but not wildly nonsensical) ideas generated by other people.[122]

brainwriting A variation of brainstorming whereby participants write (rather than speak about) and share their ideas.

Brainwriting

Brainwriting is a variation of brainstorming that minimizes the problem of production blocking by removing conversation during idea generation.[123] There are many forms of brainwriting, but they all have the common feature that individuals write down their ideas rather than verbally describe them. In one version, participants write their ideas on cards and place them in the centre of the table. At any time, participants can pick up one or more cards in the centre to spark their thinking or further build (piggyback) on those ideas. In another variation, each person writes one idea on a card, then passes the card to the person on their right. The receiving person writes a new idea on a second card, both cards are sent to the next person, and the process is repeated. The limited research on brainwriting suggests that it produces more and better quality ideas than brainstorming due to the lack of production blocking.

electronic brainstorming A form of brainstorming that relies on networked computers for submitting and sharing creative ideas.

Electronic Brainstorming

Electronic brainstorming is similar to brainwriting but uses computer technology rather than handwritten cards to document and share ideas. After receiving the question or issue, participants enter their ideas using special computer software. The ideas are distributed anonymously to other participants, who are encouraged to piggyback on those ideas. Team members eventually vote electronically on the ideas presented. Face-to-face discussion usually follows. Electronic brainstorming can be quite effective at generating creative ideas with minimal production blocking, evaluation apprehension, or conformity problems.[124] It can be superior to brainwriting because ideas are generated anonymously and they are viewed by other participants more easily. Despite these numerous advantages, electronic brainstorming tends to be too structured and technology-bound.

nominal group technique A variation of brainstorming consisting of three stages: participants (1) silently and independently document their ideas, (2) collectively describe these ideas to the other team members without critique, and then (3) silently and independently evaluate the ideas presented.

Nominal Group Technique **Nominal group technique** is another variation of brainwriting that adds a verbal element to the process.[125] The activity is called "nominal" because participants are a group in name only during two of the three steps. After the problem is described, team members silently and independently write down as many solutions as they can. In the second stage, participants describe their solutions to the other team members, usually in a round-robin format. As with brainstorming, there is no criticism or debate, although members are encouraged to ask for clarification of the ideas presented. In the third stage, participants silently and independently rank-order or vote on each proposed solution. Nominal group technique has been applied in numerous laboratory and real-world settings, such as identifying ways to improve tourism in various countries.[126] This method tends to generate a higher number of ideas and better-quality ideas than do traditional interacting and possibly brainstorming groups.[127] However, production blocking and evaluation apprehension still occur to some extent. Training improves this structured approach to team decision making.[128]

Chapter Summary

LO1 **Explain why employees join informal groups and discuss the benefits and limitations of teams.**

Teams are groups of two or more people who interact and influence each other, are mutually accountable for achieving common goals associated with organizational objectives, and perceive themselves as a social entity within an organization. All teams are groups, because they consist of people with a unifying relationship; not all groups are teams, because some groups do not exist to serve organizational objectives.

People join informal groups (and are motivated to be on formal teams) for four reasons: (1) They have an innate drive to bond, (2) group membership is an inherent ingredient in a person's self-concept, (3) some personal goals are accomplished better in groups, and (4) individuals are comforted in stressful situations by the mere presence of other people. Teams have become popular because they tend to make better decisions, support the knowledge management process, and provide superior customer service. Teams are not always as effective as individuals working alone. Process losses and social loafing drag down team performance.

LO2 **Outline the team effectiveness model and discuss how task characteristics, team size, and team composition influence team effectiveness.**

Team effectiveness includes the team's ability to achieve its objectives, fulfill the needs of its members, and maintain its survival. The model of team effectiveness considers the team and organizational environment, team design, and team processes. Three team design elements are task characteristics, team size, and team composition. Teams tend to be better suited for situations in which the work is complex yet tasks are well-structured and have high task interdependence. Teams should be large enough to perform the work yet small enough for efficient coordination and meaningful involvement. Effective teams are composed of people with the competencies and motivation to perform tasks in a team environment. Team member diversity has advantages and disadvantages for team performance.

LO3 **Discuss how shared perceptions among team members, called team states, emerge and influence team effectiveness.**

Team states represent motivational or cognitive characteristics of the team that continuously evolve and which tend to be shared between team members. Examples include team norms, cohesion, team efficacy, and trust. Each of these elements influences team performance, but can also be changed by feedback about team performance. For example, a team that receives negative performance feedback might experience a drop in both cohesion and team efficacy.

LO4 **Discuss how team processes, such as taskwork, teamwork, team boundary spanning, and team development determine team effectiveness.**

As teams work together they can focus on elements of the task (referred to as taskwork) or elements of the team's internal dynamics or relationships (called teamwork behaviour). Together, these processes determine how well the team manages its internal environment. On the other hand, teams also face opportunities to interact and build relationships with people or groups in the external environment. These processes are called boundary spanning. In addition, teams develop through the stages of forming, storming, norming, performing, and eventually adjourning. Within these stages are two distinct team development processes: developing team identity and developing team mental models and coordinating routines. Team development can be accelerated through team building–any formal activity intended to improve the development and functioning of a work team.

LO5 **Discuss the characteristics and factors required for the success of self-directed teams and virtual teams.**

Self-directed teams (SDTs) complete an entire piece of work requiring several interdependent tasks, and they have substantial autonomy over the execution of their tasks. Members of virtual teams operate across space, time, and organizational boundaries and are linked through information technologies to achieve organizational tasks. Virtual teams are more effective when the team members have certain competencies, the team has the freedom to choose the preferred communication channels, and the members meet face-to-face fairly early in the team development process.

LO6 **Identify four constraints on team decision making and discuss the advantages and disadvantages of four structures aimed at improving team decision making.**

Team decisions are impeded by time constraints, evaluation apprehension, conformity to peer pressure, and overconfidence. Four structures potentially improve decision making in team settings: brainstorming, brainwriting, electronic brainstorming, and nominal group technique.

Key Terms

brainstorming, p. 212
brainwriting, p. 212
Brooks's law, p. 194
electronic brainstorming, p. 212
evaluation apprehension, p. 211
nominal group technique, p. 213
norms, p. 199
process losses, p. 193
production blocking, p. 211
role, p. 199
self-directed teams (SDTs), p. 207
social loafing, p. 194
task interdependence, p. 196
taskwork behaviour, p. 204
team boundary spanning, p. 204
team building, p. 206
team cohesion, p. 200
team efficacy, p. 202
teams, p. 190
teamwork behaviour, p. 204
virtual teams, p. 208

Critical-Thinking Questions

1. Informal groups exist in almost every form of social organization. What types of informal groups exist in your classroom? Why are students motivated to belong to these informal groups?
2. The late management guru Peter Drucker once said: "The now-fashionable team in which everybody works with everybody on everything from the beginning rapidly is becoming a disappointment." Discuss three problems associated with teams.
3. You have been put in charge of a cross-functional task force that will develop enhanced Internet banking services for retail customers. The team includes representatives from marketing, information services, customer service, and accounting, all of whom will move to the same location at headquarters for three months. Describe the behaviours you might observe during each stage of the team's development.
4. You have just been transferred from the Montreal office to the Vancouver office of your company, a national sales organization of electrical products for developers and contractors. In Montreal, team members regularly called customers after a sale to ask whether the products arrived on time and whether they are satisfied. But when you moved to the Vancouver office, no one seemed to make these follow-up calls. A recently hired coworker explained that other coworkers discouraged her from making those calls. Later, another coworker suggested that your follow-up calls were making everyone else look lazy. Give three possible reasons why the norms in Vancouver might be different from those in the Montreal office, even though the customers, products, sales commissions, and other characteristics of the workplace are almost identical.
5. A software engineer in Canada needs to coordinate with four team members in geographically dispersed areas of the world. What team challenges might the team experience and how it will affect the team design elements?
6. You have been assigned to a class project with five other students, none of whom you have met before, and some of whom come from different countries. To what extent would team cohesion improve your team's performance on this project? What actions would you recommend to build team cohesion among student team members in this situation?

Suppose that you were put in charge of a virtual team whose members are located in different cities around the world. What tactics could you use to build and maintain team trust and performance, as well as minimize the decline in trust and performance that often occurs in teams?

You are responsible for convening a major event in which senior officials from several state governments will try to come to an agreement on environmental issues. It is well known that some officials posture so that they appear superior, whereas others are highly motivated to solve the environmental problems that cross adjacent states. What team decision-making problems are likely to be apparent in this government forum, and what actions can you take to minimize these problems?

The chief marketing officer of Sawgrass Widgets wants marketing and sales staff to identify new uses for its products. Which of the four team structures for creative decision making would you recommend? Describe and justify this process to Sawgrass's chief marketing officer.

Case Study: ARBRECORP LTÉE

Steven L. McShane, The University of Western Australia, and David Lebeter

ArbreCorp Ltée is a sawmill operation in Québec, Canada, that is owned by a major forest products company, but operates independently of the parent company. It was built 30 years ago, and completely updated with new machinery five years ago. ArbreCorp receives raw logs from the area for cutting and planing into building-grade lumber, mostly 2-by-4 and 2-by-6 pieces of standard lengths. Higher grade logs leave ArbreCorp's sawmill department in finished form and are sent directly to the packaging department. The remaining 40 percent of sawmill output are cuts from lower grade logs, requiring further work by the planing department.

ArbreCorp has one general manager, 16 supervisors and support staff, and 180 unionized employees. The unionized employees are paid an hourly rate specified in the collective agreement, whereas management and support staff are paid a monthly salary. The mill is divided into six operating departments: boom, sawmill, planer, packaging, shipping, and maintenance. The sawmill, boom, and packaging departments operate a morning shift starting at 6:00 a.m. and an afternoon shift starting at 2:00 p.m. Employees in these departments rotate shifts every two weeks. The planer and shipping departments operate only morning shifts. Maintenance employees work the night shift (starting at 10:00 p.m.).

Each department, except for packaging, has a supervisor on every work shift. The planer supervisor is responsible for the packaging department on the morning shift, and the sawmill supervisor is responsible for the packaging department on the afternoon shift. However, the packaging operation is housed in a separate building from the other departments, so supervisors seldom visit the packaging department. This is particularly true for the afternoon shift, because the sawmill supervisor is the furthest distance from the packaging building.

PACKAGING QUALITY

Ninety percent of ArbreCorp's product is sold on the international market through Boismarché Ltée, a large marketing agency. Boismarché represents all forest products mills owned by ArbreCorp's parent company as well as several other clients in the region. The market for building-grade lumber is very price competitive, because there are numerous mills selling a relatively undifferentiated product. However, some differentiation does occur in product packaging and presentation. Buyers will look closely at the packaging when deciding whether to buy from ArbreCorp or another mill.

To encourage its clients to package their products better, Boismarché sponsors a monthly package quality award. The marketing agency samples and rates its clients' packages daily, and the sawmill with the highest score at the end of the month is awarded a framed certificate of excellence. Package quality is a combination of how the lumber is piled (e.g., defects turned in), where the bands and dunnage are placed, how neatly the stencil and seal are applied, the stencil's accuracy, and how neatly and tightly the plastic wrap is attached.

ArbreCorp won Boismarché's packaging quality award several times over the past five years, and received high ratings in the months that it didn't win. However, the mill's ratings have started to decline over the past year or two, and several clients have complained about the appearance of the finished product. A few large customers switched to competitors' lumber, saying that the decision was based on the substandard appearance of ArbreCorp's packaging when it arrived in their lumberyard.

BOTTLENECK IN PACKAGING

The planing and sawmilling departments have significantly increased productivity over the past couple of years. The sawmill operation recently set a new productivity record on a single day. The planer operation has increased productivity to the point where last year it reduced operations to just one (rather than two) shifts per day. These productivity improvements are due to better operator training, fewer machine breakdowns, and better selection of raw logs. (Sawmill cuts from high-quality logs usually do not require planing work.)

Productivity levels in the boom, shipping, and maintenance departments have remained constant. However, the packaging department has recorded decreasing productivity over the past couple of years, with the result that a large backlog of finished product is typically stockpiled outside the packaging building. The morning shift of the packaging department is unable to keep up with the combined production of the sawmill and planer departments, so the unpackaged output is left for the afternoon shift. Unfortunately, the afternoon shift packages even less product than the morning shift, so the backlog continues to build. The backlog adds to ArbreCorp's inventory costs and increases the risk of damaged stock.

ArbreCorp has added Saturday overtime shifts as well as extra hours before and after the regular shifts for the packaging department employees to process this backlog. Last month, the packaging department employed 10 percent of the workforce but accounted for 85 percent of the overtime. This is frustrating to ArbreCorp's management, because time and motion studies recently confirmed that the packaging department is capable of processing all of the daily sawmill and planer production without overtime. With employees earning one and a half or two times their regular pay on overtime, ArbreCorp's cost competitiveness suffers.

Employees and supervisors at ArbreCorp are aware that people in the packaging department tend to extend lunch by 10 minutes and coffee breaks by 5 minutes. They also typically leave work a few minutes before the end of shift. This abuse has worsened recently, particularly on the afternoon shift. Employees who are temporarily assigned to the packaging department also seem to participate in this time loss pattern after a few days. Although they are punctual and productive in other departments, these temporary employees soon adopt the packaging crew's informal schedule when assigned to that department.

Discussion Questions

1. What symptom(s) in this case suggest that something has gone wrong?
2. What are the main causes of these symptoms?
3. What actions should executives take to correct these problems?

Team Exercise: TEAM TOWER POWER

Purpose This exercise is designed to help you understand team roles, team development, and other issues in the development and maintenance of effective teams.

Materials The instructor will provide enough LEGO® pieces or similar materials for each team to complete the assigned task. All teams should have identical (or very similar) amounts and types of pieces. The instructor will need a measuring tape and stopwatch. Students may use writing materials during the design stage (see Instructions). The instructor will distribute a "Team Objectives Sheet" and "Tower Specifications Effectiveness Sheet" to all teams.

Instructions The instructor will divide the class into teams. Depending on class size and space availability, teams may have between four and seven members, but all should be approximately equal size.

Each team has 20 minutes to design a tower that uses only the materials provided, is freestanding, and provides an optimal return on investment. Team members may wish to draw their tower on paper or a flip-chart to facilitate the tower's design. Teams are free to practise building their tower during this stage. Preferably, each team will have a secluded space so that the design can be created privately. During this stage, each team will complete the Team Objectives Sheet distributed by the instructor. This sheet requires the Tower Specifications Effectiveness Sheet, also distributed by the instructor.

Each team will show the instructor that it has completed its Team Objectives Sheet. Then, with all teams in the same room, the instructor will announce the start of the construction phase. The time allowed for construction will be closely monitored, and the instructor will occasionally call out the time elapsed (particularly if there is no clock in the room).

Each team will advise the instructor as soon as it has completed its tower. The team will write down the time elapsed, as determined by the instructor. The team also may be asked to assist the instructor by counting the number of blocks used and measuring the height of the tower. This information gets added to the Team Objectives Sheet. Then the team calculates its profit.

After presenting the results, the class will discuss the team dynamics elements that contribute to team effectiveness. Team members will discuss their strategy, division of labour (team roles), expertise within the team, and other elements of team dynamics.

Source: Several published and online sources describe variations of this exercise, but there is no known origin to this activity.

Self-Assessment: WHAT TEAM ROLES DO YOU PREFER?

Purpose This self-assessment is designed to help you identify your preferred roles in meetings and similar team activities.

Instructions Read each of the statements below and circle the response that you believe best reflects your position regarding each statement. Then use the scoring key in Appendix B at the end of the book to calculate your results for each team role. This exercise should be completed alone so that you can assess yourself honestly without concerns of social comparison. Class discussion will focus on the roles that people assume in team settings. This scale assesses only a few team roles.

Team Roles Preferences Scale

Circle the number that best reflects your position regarding each of these statements.	Does not describe me at all	Does not describe me very well	Describes me somewhat	Describes me well	Describes me very well
1. I usually take responsibility for getting the team to agree on what the meeting should accomplish.	1	2	3	4	5
2. I tend to summarize to other team members what the team has accomplished so far.	1	2	3	4	5
3. I'm usually the person who helps other team members overcome their disagreements.	1	2	3	4	5
4. I try to ensure that everyone gets heard on issues.	1	2	3	4	5
5. I'm usually the person who helps the team determine how to organize the discussion.	1	2	3	4	5
6. I praise other team members for their ideas more than do others in the meetings.	1	2	3	4	5
7. People tend to rely on me to keep track of what has been said in meetings.	1	2	3	4	5
8. The team typically counts on me to prevent debates from getting out of hand.	1	2	3	4	5
9. I tend to say things that make the group feel optimistic about its accomplishments.	1	2	3	4	5
10. Team members usually count on me to give everyone a chance to speak.	1	2	3	4	5
11. In most meetings, I am less likely than others to criticize the ideas of teammates.	1	2	3	4	5
12. I actively help teammates to resolve their differences in meetings.	1	2	3	4	5
13. I actively encourage quiet team members to describe their ideas about each issue.	1	2	3	4	5
14. People tend to rely on me to clarify the purpose of the meeting.	1	2	3	4	5
15. I like to be the person who takes notes or minutes of the meeting.	1	2	3	4	5

SELF-ASSESSMENTS FOR CHAPTER 8

SELF-ASSESSMENT NAME	DESCRIPTION	LOCATION
What team roles do you prefer?	Assesses the types of roles you prefer in team meetings and activities.	Page 216 connect
Are you a team player?	Estimates how much you enjoy working in teams.	connect
How trusting are you?	Assesses your general propensity to trust others.	connect

BC Hydro designs communication technology to enhance employee interaction.

John Lehmann/*The Globe and Mail*/CP Images

Chapter 9

Communicating in Organizations

LEARNING OBJECTIVES

After reading this chapter, you should be able to:

LO1. Explain why communication is important in organizations and discuss four influences on effective communication encoding and decoding.

LO2. Compare and contrast the advantages of and problems with electronic mail, other verbal communication media, and nonverbal communication.

LO3. Explain how social acceptance and media richness influence the preferred communication channel.

LO4. Discuss various barriers (noise) to effective communication, including cross-cultural and gender-based differences in communication.

LO5. Explain how to get your message across more effectively, and summarize the elements of active listening.

LO6. Summarize effective communication strategies in organizational hierarchies, and review the role and relevance of the organizational grapevine.

As Canada's third largest electrical utility, BC Hydro services over 94 percent of British Columbia's population using 30 hydroelectric facilities and three natural gas power plants. The number of employees, the expansive geographical area it covers, and the size of its operations posed a significant problem for BC Hydro with respect to the creating and sharing of ideas.

John Atwater, BC Hydro's Intranet Manager, described the communication problem as causing "a lot of unproductive knowledge" due to the fact that staff were duplicating each other's efforts because of the inefficient exchange of accurate and timely information. Recognizing that work is "inherently social," Atwater explains BC Hydro searched for a communication technology that would encourage broad collective knowledge, the distribution of documents, and notifications of events without time lags while supporting the human side of teamwork.

To promote effective communication, BC Hydro implemented an extranet site to help employees and experts to connect more seamlessly. The extranet platform facilitates the sharing of ideas, knowledge of new technologies, and best practices in real time on users' computers or mobile devices. Like Facebook, users have their own personal profile site where they can identify their interests, skills, and activities they are involved in, and easily upload material. The extranet supports team collaboration by allowing participants to log on to each other's site, post and watch how-to videos, tag items, leave comments and ask questions, and share information through discussion threads, links, news feeds, and resources. One manager describes the extranet as "vital" to the job because "our office spans the entire province" and "it takes everything that we had written down or in our heads and puts it into a visual, easy to manage platform."

Internal communication is a significant concern, particularly for large and complex organizations where everyone needs to be confident that they have access to the same timely, accurate information. As this BC Hydro example demonstrates, in today's business world, communication must integrate social networking, the exchange of current news and information, as well as offer the ability to reach across distances in prompt and accessible ways.[1]

When Facebook and other social media sites gained popularity, many businesses blocked employee access and banned their use, claiming they encouraged time wasting and were portals for distributing intellectual property. Now, many companies are adopting social media as a cornerstone of their communication strategy. They are discovering that these new channels offer significant potential for information sharing and social bonding, and that the workforce increasingly uses and expects their organizations to provide these communication channels. Even with these technological developments, we may still be at the beginning of this revolution. Each new method of social interaction creates fascinating changes in how people communicate with each other in the workplace.

communication The process by which information is transmitted and *understood* between two or more people.

Communication refers to the process by which information is transmitted and *understood* between two or more people. We emphasize the word "understood" because transmitting the sender's intended meaning is the essence of good communication. This chapter begins by discussing the importance of effective communication, outlining the communication process model, and discussing factors that improve communication coding and decoding. Next, we identify types of communication channels, including e-mail and social media sites, followed by factors to consider when choosing a communication medium. This chapter then identifies barriers to effective communication. The latter part of this chapter offers an overview of ways to communicate in organizational hierarchies and offers insight about the pervasive organizational grapevine.

The Importance of Communication

LO1

Effective communication is vital to all organizations, so much so that no company could exist without it. The reason? Recall from Chapter 1 that organizations are defined as groups of people who work interdependently towards some purpose. People work interdependently only when they can communicate with each other. Although organizations rely on a variety of coordinating mechanisms (which we discuss in Chapter 13), frequent, timely, and accurate communication remains the primary means through which employees and work units effectively synchronize their work.[2] Chester Barnard, a telecommunications CEO and a respected pioneer in organizational behaviour theory, made this observation back in 1938: "An organization comes into being when there are persons able to communicate with each other."[3]

In addition to coordination, communication plays a central role in organizational learning. It is the means through which knowledge enters the organization and is distributed to employees.[4] A third function of communication is decision making. Imagine the challenge of making a decision without any information about the decision context, the alternatives available, the likely outcomes of those options, or the extent to which the decision is achieving its objectives. All of these ingredients require communication from coworkers as well as from stakeholders in the external environment. For example, airline cockpit crews make much better decisions–and thereby cause far fewer accidents–when the captain encourages the crew to openly share information.[5]

A fourth function is to change behaviour.[6] When communicating to others, we are often trying to alter their beliefs and feelings and ultimately their behaviour. This influence process might be passive, such as merely describing the situation more clearly and fully, or it might be a deliberate attempt to change someone's thoughts and actions. We discuss the topic of persuasion later in this chapter, and further in Chapter 10.

Fifth, communication supports employee well-being.[7] Informationally, communication conveys knowledge that helps employees to better manage their work environment. For instance, research shows that new employees adjust much better to the organization when coworkers communicate subtle nuggets of wisdom, such as how to avoid office politics, complete work procedures correctly, find useful resources, handle difficult customers, and so on.[8] Emotionally, the communication experience itself is a soothing balm. Indeed, people are less susceptible to colds, cardiovascular disease, and other physical and mental illnesses when they have regular social interaction.[9] In essence, people have an inherent drive to bond, to validate their self-worth, and to maintain their social identity. Communication is the means through which these drives and needs are fulfilled.

Finally, consider the following question: Does the manner in which we speak influence our success? Research does, in fact, provide substantial support for the link between speech styles and subsequent status attainment. When we say speech styles, we mean things like hesitation (e.g., "well," "um"), hedges (e.g., "kinda," "sort of"), disclaimers (e.g., "This may be a bad idea, but . . ."), and formal addresses (e.g., "no sir"). People who speak assertively, by avoiding these tentative speech styles, are judged by observers as more likely to be promoted and supported by superiors. These effects also work in negotiation–people who use assertive speech are judged to be more competent and cooperative by negotiation counterparts.[10]

A Model of Communication

To understand the key interpersonal features of effective communication, let's examine the model presented in Exhibit 9.1, which provides a useful "conduit" metaphor for thinking about the communication process.[11] According to this model, communication flows through channels between the sender and receiver. The sender forms a message and encodes it into words, gestures, voice intonations, and other symbols or signs. Next, the encoded message is transmitted to the intended receiver through one or more communication channels (media). The receiver senses the incoming message and decodes it into something meaningful. Ideally, the decoded meaning is what the sender had intended.

In most situations, the sender looks for evidence that the other person received and understood the transmitted message. This feedback may be a formal acknowledgment, such as "Yes, I know what you mean," or indirect evidence from the receiver's subsequent actions. Notice that feedback repeats the communication process. Intended feedback is encoded, transmitted, received, and decoded from the receiver to the sender of the original message. This model recognizes that communication is not a free-flowing conduit. Rather, the transmission of meaning from one person to another is hampered by *noise*–the psychological, social, and structural barriers that distort and obscure the sender's intended message. If any part of the communication process is distorted or broken, the sender and receiver will not have a common understanding of the message.

EXHIBIT 9.1

The Communication Process Model

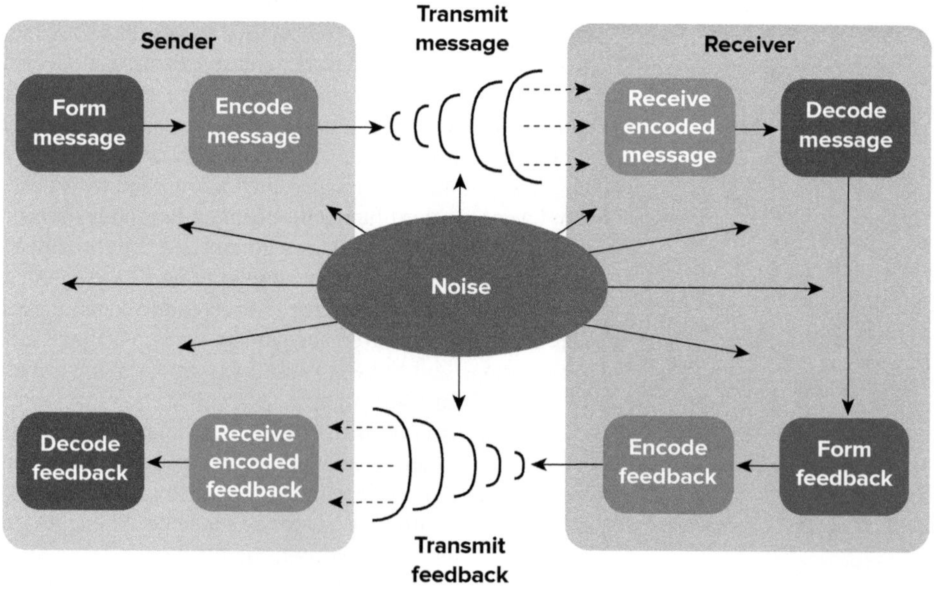

INFLUENCES ON EFFECTIVE ENCODING AND DECODING

According to the communication process model, effective communication depends on the ability of sender and receiver to efficiently and accurately encode and decode information. How well this encoding-decoding process works depends on whether the sender and receiver have similar codebooks, the sender's proficiency at encoding the message to the audience, the sender and receiver's motivation and ability to transmit messages through that particular communication channel, and their common mental models of the communication context.[12]

Similar Codebooks The sender and receiver rely on "codebooks," which are dictionaries of symbols, language, gestures, idioms, and other tools used to convey information. With similar codebooks, the communication participants are able to encode and decode more accurately because they assign the same or similar meaning to the transmitted symbols and signs. Communication efficiency also improves because there is less need for redundancy (repeating the message in different ways) and less need for confirmation feedback ("So, are you saying that. . . ?").

Message Encoding Proficiency Even with the same codebooks, some people are better than others at communicating the message because, through experience, they have learned which words and gestures transmit the message best to that audience. Suppose that you have spoken to several employee groups about the company's new product development plans. With each session, you learn which words, symbols, voice intonations, and other features transmit the message better than others. Through experience, you fine-tune the presentation so the audience receives your message more efficiently and effectively.

Communication Channel Motivation and Ability The encoding-decoding process depends on the sender's and receiver's motivation and ability to use the selected communication channel. Some people prefer face-to-face conversations, whereas others would rather prepare or receive written documentation. Some people are skilled at communicating through Twitter tweets, whereas others are more effective at writing detailed reports. So, even if both parties have the same codebooks and are skilled at using those codebooks for a particular message, message encoding and decoding can be hampered by a communication channel that the sender, receiver, or both dislike or lack proficiency.[13]

Shared Mental Models of the Communication Context Mental models are internal representations of the external world that allow us to visualize elements of a setting and relationships among those elements (see Chapter 3). A sender and receiver with shared mental models of the communication context have similar images and expectations regarding the location, time, layout, and other contextual features of the information. These shared mental models potentially increase the accuracy of the message content and reduce the need for communication about that context. Notice that shared mental models of the communication context differs from a shared codebook. Codebooks are symbols used to convey message content, whereas mental models are knowledge structures of the communication setting. For example, a Russian cosmonaut and Canadian astronaut might have shared mental models about the layout and features of the international space station (communication context), yet they experience poor communication because of language differences (i.e., different codebooks).

Communication Channels

LO2

A central feature of the communication model is the channel or medium through which information is transmitted. There are two main types of channels: verbal and nonverbal. Verbal communication uses words, so it includes spoken or written channels. Nonverbal communication is any part of communication that does not use words. Spoken and written communication are both verbal (i.e., they both use words), but they are quite different from each other and have different strengths and weaknesses in communication effectiveness, which we discuss later in this section. Also, written communication has traditionally been a much slower than spoken communication at transmitting messages, although electronic mail, Twitter "tweets," and other Internet-based communication channels have significantly improved written communication efficiency.

INTERNET-BASED COMMUNICATION

In the early 1960s, with funding from the U.S. Department of Defense, university researchers began discussing how to collaborate better by connecting their computers through a network. Their rough vision of connected computers became a reality in 1969 as the Advanced Research Projects Agency Network (ARPANET). ARPANET initially had only a dozen or so connections and was very slow and expensive by today's standards, but it marked the birth of the Internet. Two years later, a computer engineer developing ARPANET sent the first electronic mail (e-mail) message between different computers on a network. By 1973, most communication on ARPANET was through e-mail. ARPANET was mostly restricted to U.S. Defense-funded research centres, so in 1979 two graduate students at Duke University developed a public network system, called Usenet. Usenet allowed people to post information that could be retrieved by anyone else on the network, making it the first public computer-mediated social network.[14]

We have come a long way since the early days of ARPANET and Usenet. Texting, instant messaging, and social media didn't exist in organizations a dozen years ago, whereas they are now gaining popularity. However, e-mail remains the medium of choice in most workplaces (see Exhibit 9.2).[15] E-mail messages can be written, edited, and transmitted quickly. Information can be effortlessly appended and conveyed to many people. E-mail is also asynchronous (messages are sent and received at different times), so there is no need to coordinate a communication session. With advances in computer search technology, e-mail software has also become an efficient filing cabinet.[16]

E-mail tends to be the preferred medium for sending well-defined information for decision making. It is also central for coordinating work, although text messaging and Twitter tweets might overtake e-mail for this objective. When e-mail was introduced in the workplace more than two decades ago, it tended to increase the volume of communication and significantly altered the flow of that information within groups and throughout the organization.[17] Specifically, it reduced some face-to-face and telephone communication but increased communication with people further up the hierarchy. Some social and organizational status differences still exist with e-mail,[18] but they are somewhat less apparent than in face-to-face communication. By hiding age, race, and other features, e-mail reduces stereotype biases. However, it also tends to increase reliance on stereotypes when we are already aware of the other person's personal characteristics.[19]

EXHIBIT 9.2

The Changing World of Workplace Communication Technology

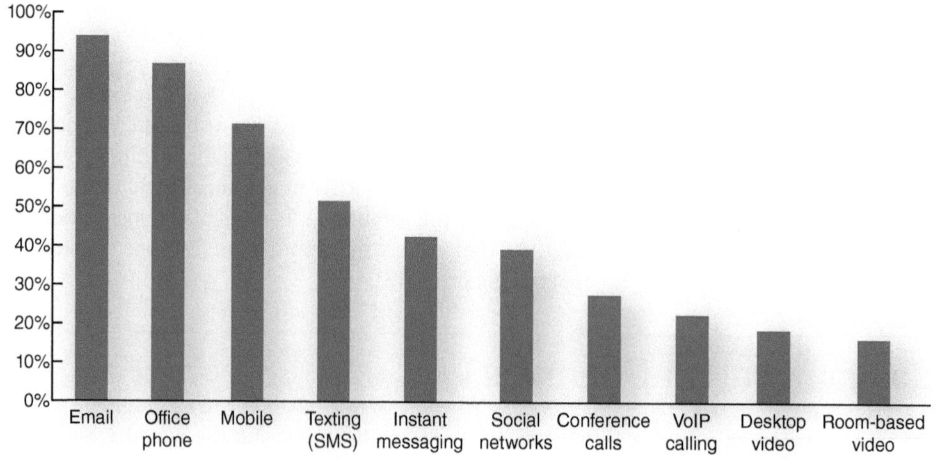

Percentage of 1,000 American technology-empowered workers who use various communications technologies in the workplace at least once per week. Based on survey results reported by: M. Wolf, A. Sinclair, A. Levie, et al. "How Real-Time Communications and Video Are Transforming the Workplace," San Jose, CA: Skype and Giga Omni Media, 2011.

PROBLEMS WITH E-MAIL

In spite of the wonders of e-mail, anyone who has used this communication medium knows that it has its limitations. Here are the top four complaints:

Poor Medium for Communicating Emotions People rely on facial expressions and other nonverbal cues to interpret the emotional meaning of words; e-mail lacks this parallel communication channel. Indeed, people consistently and significantly overestimate the degree to which they understand the emotional tone of e-mail messages.[20] Senders try to clarify the emotional tone of their messages by using expressive language ("Wonderful to hear from you!"), highlighting phrases in boldface or quotation marks, and inserting graphic faces (called emoticons or "smileys") representing the desired emotion. Recent studies suggest that writers are getting better at using these emotion markers. Still, they do not replace the full complexity of real facial expressions, voice intonation, and hand movements.[21]

Growing frustrations with the challenges of communicating in an era when employees are experiencing significant stress because of e-mail proliferation, and the resultant loss of productivity, has led some large corporations to adopt e-mail-free zones. Loblaws Co. Ltd., Intel, and PBD Worldwide Fulfilment Services (PBD) are some of the companies that have attempted to tackle e-mail overload in recent years. Liz Margles, vice-president of communications for food giant Loblaws, described her initial reaction to the company's No E-mail Wednesdays as shock and skepticism. However, she soon began to feel "unburdened." The positive effects of escaping from the barrage of e-mails included being able to engage conversations with her colleagues, as well as more deep thinking.[22] In 2007–2008, Intel implemented two pilot programs to try to reduce the noise and distractions associated with e-mails: Quiet Tuesdays and No E-mail Fridays. On Tuesday mornings, the participants of the Intel experiment placed their e-mails and phones off-line. According to Nathan Zeldes, Intel's former IT Principal Engineer and consultant on the projects, 45 percent of post-pilot survey respondents found Quiet Tuesdays to be effective and 71 percent recommended extending it.[23] On Fridays, participants were discouraged from e-mailing other members of their intra-group and instead seek out face-to-face communications. Zeldes explained that "the notion that talking to people results in 'longer and more personal dialogues' is not universally true—a short phone call can often resolve an issue that could degenerate into an endless ping-pong of e-mails."[24] Also in

tofumax/iStock/Thinkstock

Founded in 2007, the mandate of the Information Overload Research Group (IORG) is to understand the effects of information excess in society and to research solutions, including best practices and technologies. The IORG is a nonprofit organization made up of communications and information industry practitioners, academic researchers and consultants, dedicated to "reducing information pollution."[25]

2007, PBD, an Atlanta-based shipping company, instituted a policy of no exchanges of internal e-mails on Fridays and PBD continues to currently encourage this practice.[26] Scott Dockter, president and chief executive officer of PBD, states the No E-mail Friday philosophy has been "extremely successful and is a great reminder to all PBD employees that communication is more than just e-mail." He explains that the approach "stays relevant today due to the new youth in our workplace that aren't very familiar with communication outside of texting or e-mail."[27] Most organizations that have attempted to reduce e-mail dependency by implementing no e-mail periods point out that they adopted this practice to increase efficiency, foster better internal communications, and encourage employees to try to use alternate communications to facilitate connections.

Reduces Politeness and Respect E-mail messages are often less diplomatic than written letters. Indeed, the term "flaming" has entered our language to describe e-mail and other electronic messages that convey strong negative emotions to the receiver. People who receive e-mail are partly to blame because they tend to infer a more negative or neutral interpretation of the e-mail than was intended by the sender.[28] Even so, e-mail flame wars occur mostly because senders are more likely to send disparaging messages by e-mail than other communication channels. One reason is that individuals can post e-mail messages before their emotions subside, whereas the sender of a traditional memo or letter would have time for sober second thoughts. A second reason is that e-mail has low social presence (it is impersonal); people are more likely to communicate messages through impersonal channels that they would never say in face-to-face conversation. Fortunately, research has found that flaming decreases as teams move to later stages of development and when explicit norms and rules of communication are established.[29]

Poor Medium for Ambiguous, Complex, and Novel Situations E-mail is usually satisfactory for well-defined situations, such as giving basic instructions or presenting a meeting agenda, but it can be cumbersome and dysfunctional in ambiguous, complex, and novel situations. As we will describe later in this section, these circumstances require communication channels that transmit a larger volume of information with more rapid feedback. In other words, when the issue gets messy, stop e-mailing and start talking, preferably face-to-face.

Contributes to Information Overload E-mail contributes to information overload.[30] Approximately 20 trillion e-mails (excluding 70 trillion spam e-mails) are now transmitted annually around the world, up from just 1.1 trillion in 1998. The e-mail glut occurs because messages are created and copied to many people without much effort. The number of e-mail messages will probably decrease as people become more familiar with it; until then, e-mail volume continues to rise.

WORKPLACE COMMUNICATION THROUGH SOCIAL MEDIA

Although e-mail dominates most workplace communication, it may eventually be overtaken by emerging forms of social media. Social media are Internet or mobile-based channels that allow users to generate and interactively share information. The better-known social media include Facebook, LinkedIn, Twitter, Wikipedia, and Typepad (blogs), but there are many others.

Unlike traditional websites that merely "push" information from the creator to the audience, social media are more conversational and reciprocally interactive between sender and receiver, resulting in a sense of community.[31] Social media typically enable users to develop a public identity through the social media content. Social media are "social" because they encourage formation of communities through links, interactive conversations, and for some platforms such as wikis, common space for collaborative content development. The audience can become participants in the conversation by contributing feedback and by linking someone else's content to their own social media spaces.

One recent model suggests that social media serve several functions: presenting the individual's identity, enabling conversations, sharing information, sensing the presence of others in the virtual space, maintaining relationships, revealing reputation or status, and supporting communities (see Exhibit 9.3).[32] For instance, Facebook has a strong emphasis on maintaining relationships but relatively low emphasis on sharing information or forming

EXHIBIT 9.3

Functions of Communicating Through Social Media

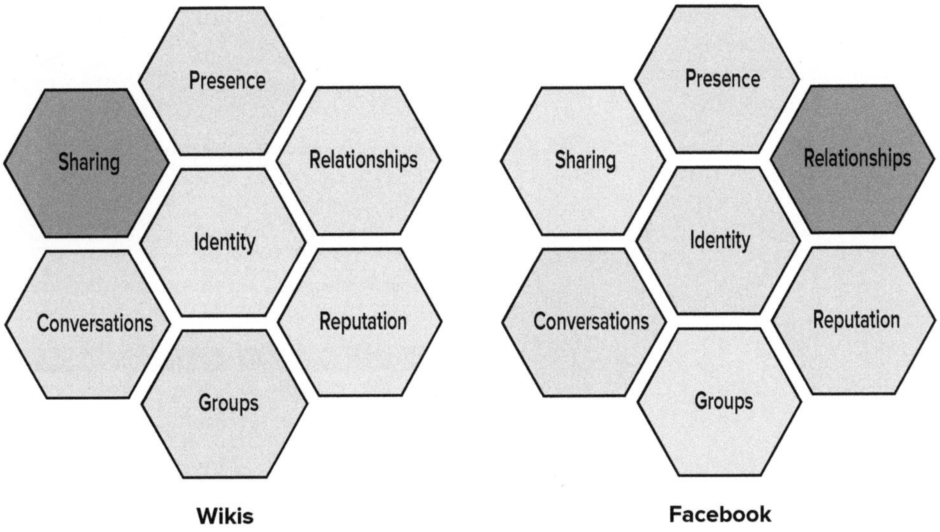

Source: Based on J. H. Kietzmann, K. Hermkens, I. P. McCarthy, and B. S. Silvestre, (2011). Social media? Get serious! Understanding the functional building blocks of social media. *Business Horizons*, Vol. 54, No. 3, pp. 241–51.

communities (groups). Wikis, on the other hand, focus on sharing information or forming communities but have much lower emphasis on presenting the user's identity or reputation.

A few studies conclude (with caution) that social media offer considerable versatility and potential in the workplace.[33] Even so, companies have been reluctant to introduce these communication tools, mainly because they lack knowledge, staff/resources, and technical support to put them into practice.[34] Indeed, a common practice is to simply ban employee access to social media (usually after discovering excess employee activity on Facebook) without thinking through the potential of this type of communication channel.

Many companies prefer their employees spend time interacting with colleagues and accessing corporate information instead of surfing personal social media sites. The benefits can include employees spending less time disengaging with the organization, while increasing their understanding and connection with the company and their colleagues. Servus Credit Union adopted elements of social media when it introduced a comprehensive employee portal called The Village. Servus Credit Union, a member-owned, community-based financial institution, has 100 locations in Alberta and is the third largest credit union in Canada. It recently launched an employee portal in order to amalgamate disparate information from various local branch portals and multiple websites. The portal incorporates social media features, such as, employee profiles where the employee can post their picture and bio, as well social media tools, such as "like" type features, where employees can rate their experience and feedback regarding the portal's search engine. The Village also includes a place where employees can post items for sale and photo galleries for social events. According to Habanero Consulting, the Canadian firm who created the portal, the "integration of social features better connects end-users with content."[35]

NONVERBAL COMMUNICATION

Nonverbal communication includes facial gestures, voice intonation, physical distance, and even silence. This communication channel is necessary where noise or physical distance prevents effective verbal exchanges and the need for immediate feedback precludes written communication. But even in quiet face-to-face meetings, most information is communicated nonverbally. Rather like a parallel conversation, nonverbal cues signal subtle information to both parties, such as reinforcing their interest in the verbal conversation or demonstrating their relative status in the relationship.[36]

Nonverbal communication differs from verbal (i.e., written and spoken) communication in a couple of ways. First, it is less rule-bound than verbal communication. We receive

Servus Credit Union introduced an employee portal called The Village to create a single source for information across the organization.

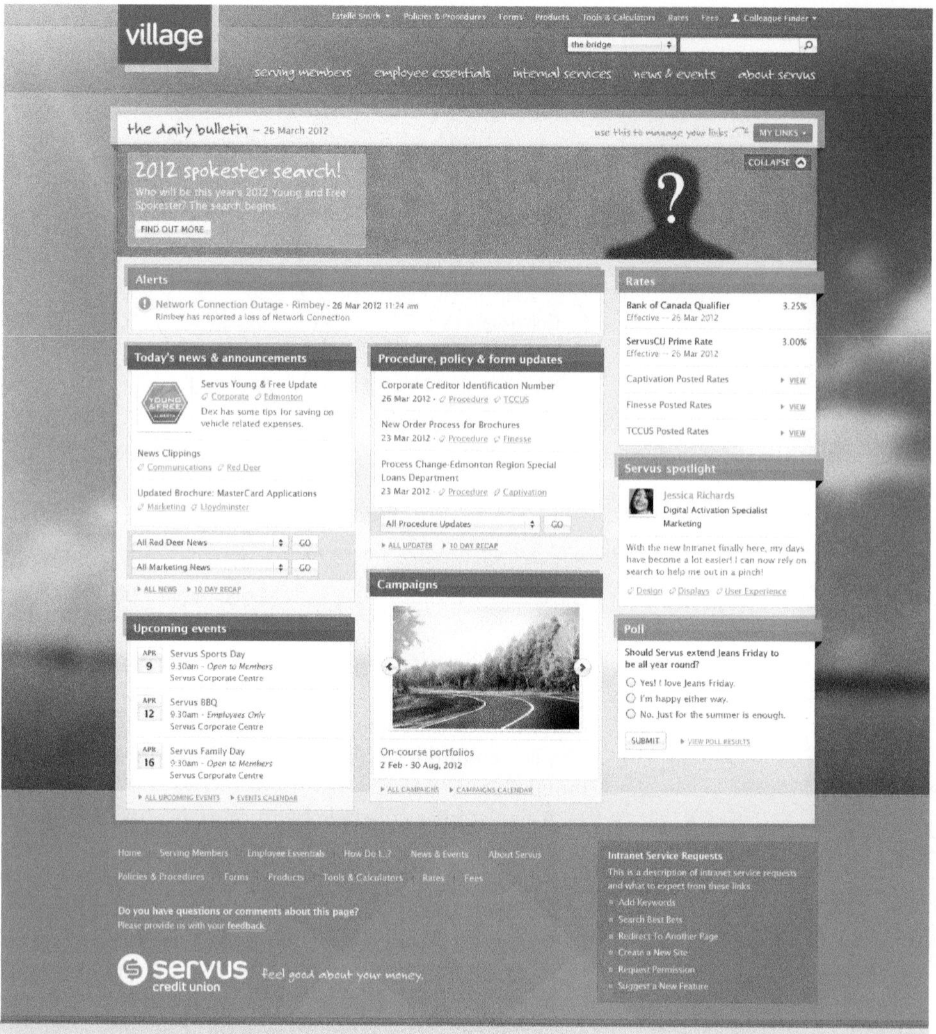

Courtesy of Servus Credit Union

considerable formal training on how to understand spoken words, but very little on how to understand the nonverbal signals that accompany those words. Consequently, nonverbal cues are generally more ambiguous and susceptible to misinterpretation. At the same time, many facial expressions (such as smiling) are hardwired and universal, thereby providing the only reliable means of communicating across cultures.

The other difference between verbal and nonverbal communication is that the former is typically conscious, whereas most nonverbal communication is automatic and nonconscious. We normally plan the words we say or write, but we rarely plan every blink, smile, or other gesture during a conversation. Indeed, as we just mentioned, many of these facial expressions communicate the same meaning across cultures because they are hardwired nonconscious responses to human emotions.[37] For example, pleasant emotions cause the brain centre to widen the mouth, whereas negative emotions produce constricted facial expressions (squinting eyes, pursed lips, etc.).

emotional contagion The nonconscious process of "catching" or sharing another person's emotions by mimicking that person's facial expressions and other nonverbal behaviour.

Emotional Contagion One of the most fascinating aspects of nonverbal communication is **emotional contagion,** which is the automatic process of "catching" or sharing another person's emotions by mimicking that person's facial expressions and other nonverbal behaviour. Technically, human beings have brain receptors that cause them to mirror what they observe. In other words, to some degree our brain causes us to act as though we are the person we are watching.[38]

Consider what happens when you see a coworker accidentally bang his or her head against a filing cabinet. Chances are, you wince and put your hand on your own head as if you had hit

OB by the NUMBERS

Top Ten Body Language Mistakes in Job Interviews[39]

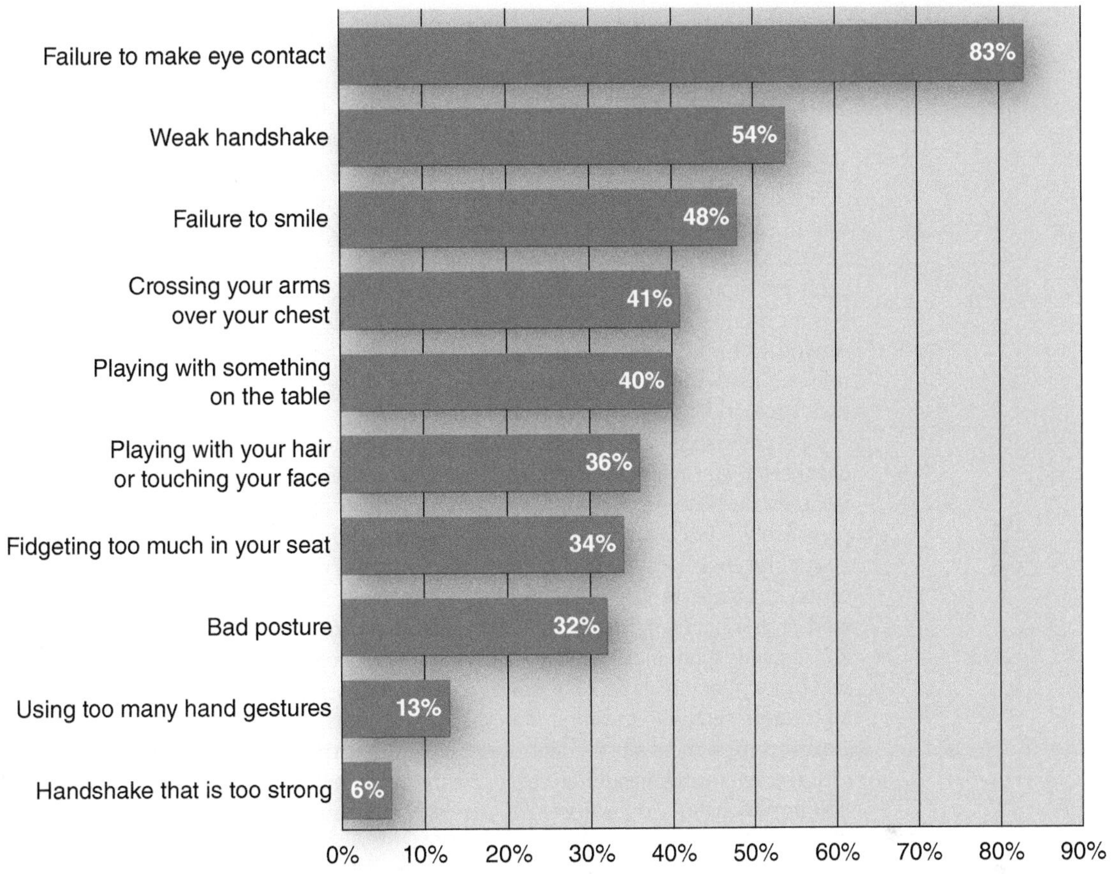

Percentage of employers surveyed in the United Kingdom who reported the biggest body language turnoffs in job interviews. Similar results were found in a U.S. survey one year earlier.

the cabinet. Similarly, while listening to someone describe a positive event, you tend to smile and exhibit other emotional displays of happiness. While some of our nonverbal communication is planned, emotional contagion represents nonconscious behaviour—we automatically mimic and synchronize our nonverbal behaviours with other people.[40]

Emotional contagion influences communication and social relationships in three ways.[41] First, mimicry provides continuous feedback, communicating that we understand and empathize with the sender. To consider the significance of this, imagine employees remaining expressionless after watching a coworker bang his or her head! The lack of parallel behaviour conveys a lack of understanding or caring. A second function is that mimicking the nonverbal behaviours of other people seems to be a way of receiving emotional meaning from those people. If a coworker is angry with a client, your tendency to frown and show anger while listening helps you to experience that emotion more fully. In other words, we receive meaning by expressing the sender's emotions as well as by listening to the sender's words.

The third function of emotional contagion is to fulfill the drive to bond that we mentioned earlier in this chapter and was introduced in Chapter 5. Bonding develops through each person's awareness of a collective sentiment. Through nonverbal expressions of emotional contagion, people see others share the same emotions that they feel. This strengthens relations among team members as well as between leaders and followers by providing evidence of their similarity.

Choosing the Best Communication Channel

LO3

Which communication channel is most appropriate in a particular situation? Two important sets of factors to consider are (a) social acceptance and (b) media richness.

SOCIAL ACCEPTANCE

Social acceptance refers to how well the communication medium is approved and supported by the organization, teams, and individuals involved in the exchange.[42] One factor in social acceptance is organizational, team, and cultural norms regarding the use of specific communication channels. Norms partly explain why face-to-face meetings are daily events among staff in some firms, whereas computer-based video conferencing (such as Skype) and Twitter tweets are the media of choice in other organizations. Studies report that national culture plays an important role in preferences for specific communication channels.[43] For instance, when communicating with people further up the hierarchy, Koreans are much less likely than Americans to use e-mail because this medium is less respectful of the superior's status. Other research has found that the preference for e-mail depends on the culture's emphasis on context, time, and space in social relationships.

A second social acceptance factor is individual preferences for specific communication channels.[44] You may have noticed that some coworkers ignore (or rarely check) voice mail, yet they quickly respond to text messages or Twitter tweets. These preferences are due to personality traits as well as previous experience and reinforcement with particular channels.

A third social acceptance factor is the symbolic meaning of a channel.[45] Some communication channels are viewed as impersonal whereas others are more personal; some are considered professional whereas others are casual; some are "cool" whereas others are old-fashioned. For instance, phone calls and other synchronous communication channels convey a greater sense of urgency than do text messages and other asynchronous channels. The importance of a channel's symbolic meaning is perhaps most apparent in stories about managers who use e-mails or text messages to inform employees that they are fired or laid off. These communication events make headlines because e-mail and text messages are considered inappropriate (too impersonal) for transmission of that particular information.[46]

MEDIA RICHNESS

media richness A medium's data-carrying capacity, that is, the volume and variety of information that can be transmitted during a specific time.

Along with social acceptance, people need to determine the best level of **media richness** for their message. Media richness refers to the medium's data-carrying capacity—the volume and variety of information that can be transmitted during a specific time.[47] Exhibit 9.4 illustrates various communication channels arranged in a hierarchy of richness, with face-to-face interaction at the top and lean data-only reports at the bottom. A communication channel has high richness when it is able to convey multiple cues (such as both verbal and nonverbal information), allows timely feedback from receiver to sender, allows the sender to customize the message to the receiver, and makes use of complex symbols (such as words and phrases with multiple meanings).

Face-to-face communication is at the top of media richness because it allows us to communicate both verbally and nonverbally at the same time, to receive feedback almost immediately from the receiver, to quickly adjust our message and style, and to use complex language such as metaphors and idioms (e.g., "spilling the beans").

According to media richness theory, rich media are better than lean media when the communication situation is nonroutine and ambiguous. In nonroutine situations (such as an unexpected and unusual emergency), the sender and receiver have little common experience, so they need to transmit a large volume of information with immediate feedback. Lean media work well in routine situations because the sender and receiver have common expectations through shared mental models. Ambiguous situations also require rich media because the parties must share large amounts of information with immediate feedback to resolve multiple and conflicting interpretations of their observations and experiences.[48] Choosing the wrong medium reduces communication effectiveness. When the situation is routine or clear, using a rich medium—such as holding a special meeting—would seem like a waste of time. On the other hand, if a unique and ambiguous issue is handled through e-mail or another lean medium, then issues take longer to resolve and misunderstandings are more likely to occur.

EXHIBIT 9.4

Media Richness Hierarchy

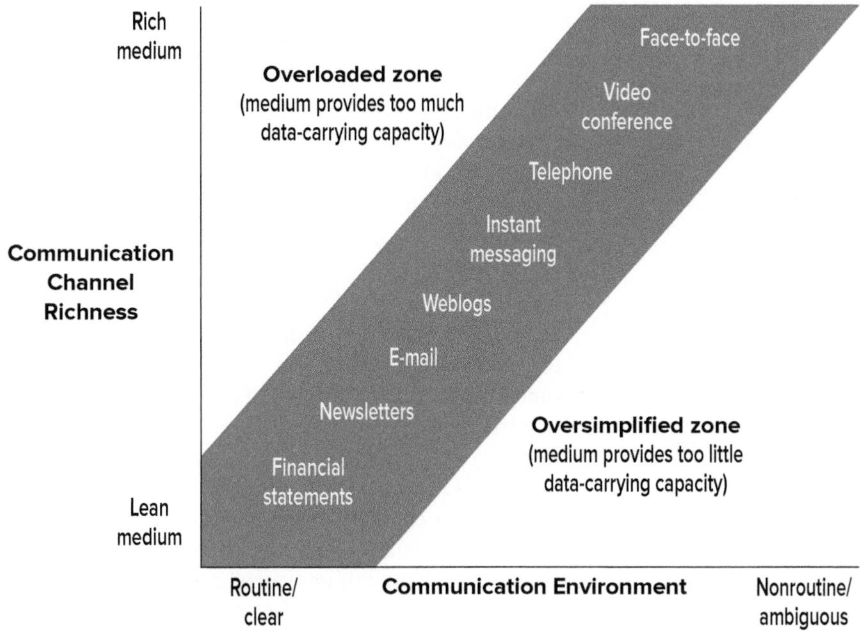

Source: Based on R. Lengel and R. Daft, "The Selection of Communication Media as an Executive Skill," *Academy of Management Executive* 2, no. 3 (August, 1988), p. 226; R. L. Daft and R. H. Lengel, "Information Richness: A New Approach to Managerial Behavior and Organization Design," *Research in Organizational Behavior,* 1984, p. 199.

Exceptions to Media Richness Theory Research generally supports media richness theory for traditional channels (face-to-face, written memos, etc.). However, the model doesn't fit reality nearly as well when electronic communication channels are studied.[49] Three factors seem to explain why electronic channels may have more media richness than the theory proposes:

- *Ability to multi-communicate.* It is usually difficult (as well as rude) to communicate face-to-face with someone while simultaneously transmitting messages to someone else using another medium. Most information technologies, on the other hand, require less social etiquette and attention, so employees can easily engage in two or more communication events at the same time. In other words, they can multi-communicate.[50] For example, people routinely scan Web pages while carrying on telephone conversations. Some write text messages to a client while simultaneously listening to a discussion at a large meeting. People multitask less efficiently than they think they do, but some are good enough that they likely exchange as much information through two or more lean electronic media as through one high media richness channel.
- *Communication proficiency.* Earlier in this chapter we explained that communication effectiveness is partially determined by the sender's competency and motivation with the communication channel. People with higher proficiency can "push" more information through the channel, thereby increasing the channel's information flow. Experienced smartphone users, for instance, can whip through messages in a flash, whereas new users struggle to type notes and organize incoming messages. In contrast, there is less variation in the ability to communicate through casual conversation and other natural channels because most of us develop good levels of proficiency throughout life and possibly through hardwired evolutionary development.[51]
- *Social presence effects.* Channels with high media richness tend to have more social presence, that is, the participants experience a stronger physical presence of each other.[52] However, high social presence also sensitizes both parties to their relative status and self-presentation, which can distort or divert attention away from the

message.[53] Face-to-face communication has very high media richness, yet its high social presence can disrupt the efficient flow of information through that medium. During a personal meeting with the company's CEO, for example, you might concentrate more on how you come across than on what the CEO is saying to you. In other words, the benefits of media richness channels may be offset by social presence distractions, whereas lean media have much less social presence to distract or distort the transmitted information.

COMMUNICATION CHANNELS AND PERSUASION

persuasion The use of facts, logical arguments, and emotional appeals to change another person's beliefs and attitudes, usually for the purpose of changing the person's behaviour.

Some communication channels are more effective than others for **persuasion;** that is, using facts, logical arguments, and emotional appeals to change another person's beliefs and attitudes, usually for the purpose of changing the person's behaviour. (For an expanded discussion of persuasion, see Chapter 10.) Studies support the long-held view that spoken communication, particularly face-to-face interaction, is more persuasive than e-mails, websites, and other forms of written communication. There are three main reasons for this persuasive effect.[54] First, spoken communication is typically accompanied by nonverbal communication. People are persuaded more when they receive both emotional and logical messages, and the combination of spoken with nonverbal communication provides this dual punch. A lengthy pause, raised voice tone, and (in face-to-face interaction) animated hand gestures can amplify the emotional tone of the message, thereby signalling the vitality of the issue.

A second reason why conversations are more persuasive is that spoken communication offers the sender high-quality immediate feedback whether the receiver understands and accepts the message (i.e., is being persuaded). This feedback allows the sender to adjust the content and emotional tone of the message more quickly than with written communication. A third reason is that people are persuaded more under conditions of high social presence than low social presence. The sender can more easily monitor the receiver's listening in face-to-face conversations (high social presence), so listeners are more motivated to pay attention and consider the sender's ideas. When people receive persuasion attempts through a website, e-mail, or other source of written communication, on the other hand, they experience a higher degree of anonymity and psychological distance from the persuader. These conditions reduce the motivation to think about and accept the persuasive message.

Although spoken communication tends to be more persuasive, written communication can also persuade others to some extent. Written messages have the advantage of presenting more technical detail than can occur through conversation. This factual information is valuable when the issue is important to the receiver. Also, people experience a moderate degree of social presence in written communication when they are exchanging messages with close associates, so messages from friends and coworkers can be persuasive.

Communication Barriers (NOISE)

LO4

In spite of the best intentions of sender and receiver to communicate, several barriers (called "noise" earlier in Exhibit 9.1) inhibit the effective exchange of information. As author George Bernard Shaw once wrote, "The greatest problem with communication is the illusion that it has been accomplished." One barrier is the imperfect perceptual process of both sender and receiver. As receivers, we don't listen as well as senders assume, and our needs and expectations influence what signals get noticed and ignored. We aren't any better as senders, either. Some studies suggest that we have difficulty stepping out of our own perspectives and stepping into the perspectives of others, so we overestimate how well other people understand the message we are communicating.[55]

Language issues can be huge sources of communication noise because sender and receiver might not have the same "codebook." They might not speak the same language, or might have different meanings for particular words and phrases. The English language (among others) also has built-in ambiguities that cause misunderstandings. Consider the question "Can you close the door?" You might assume the sender is asking whether shutting the door is permitted. However, the question might be asking whether you are physically able to shut the door or whether the door is designed such that it can be shut. In fact, this question might not be a question at all; the person could be politely *telling* you to shut the door.[56]

"That's my commendation for deciphering all the sales talk when we needed to upgrade the computer."

The ambiguity of language isn't always dysfunctional noise.[57] Corporate leaders sometimes purposively use obscure language to reflect the ambiguity of the topic or to avoid unwanted emotional responses produced from more specific words. They might use metaphors to represent an abstract vision of the company's future, or use obtuse phrases such as "rightsizing" and "restructuring" to obscure the underlying message that people would be fired or laid off. One study reported that people rely on more ambiguous language when communicating with people who have different values and beliefs. In these situations, ambiguity minimizes the risk of conflict.[58]

Jargon–specialized words and phrases for specific occupations or groups–is usually designed to improve communication efficiency. However, it is a source of communication noise when transmitted to people who do not possess the jargon codebook. Furthermore, people who use jargon excessively put themselves in an unflattering light. For example, former Home Depot and Chrysler CEO Robert Nardelli announced at one news conference: "I'm blessed to have individuals with me who can take areas of responsibility and do vertical dives to really get the granularity and make sure that we're coupling horizontally across those functions so that we have a pure line of sight towards the customer." Business journalists weren't impressed, even if they did figure out what Nardelli meant.[59]

Another source of noise in the communication process is the tendency to filter messages. Filtering may involve deleting or delaying negative information or using less harsh words so the message sounds more favourable.[60] Filtering is less likely to occur when corporate leaders create a "culture of candour." This culture develops when leaders themselves communicate truthfully, seek out diverse sources for information, and protect and reward those who speak openly and truthfully.[61]

INFORMATION OVERLOAD

Start with a daily avalanche of e-mail, then add in cell phone calls, text messages, PDF file downloads, Web pages, hard copy documents, some Twitter tweets, blogs, wikis, and other sources of incoming information. Together, you have created a perfect recipe for **information overload.**[62] As Exhibit 9.5 illustrates, information overload occurs whenever the job's information load exceeds the individual's capacity to get through it. Employees have a certain

> **information overload**
> A condition in which the volume of information received exceeds the person's capacity to process it.

EXHIBIT 9.5

Dynamics of Information Overload

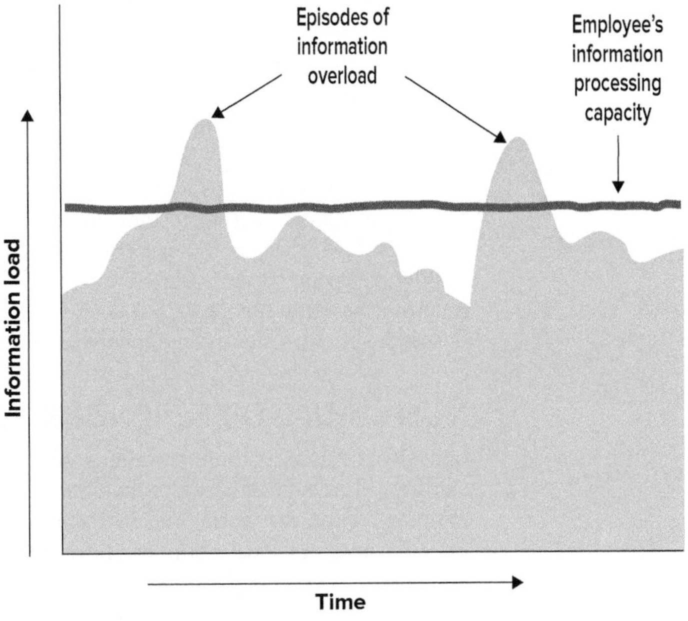

information processing capacity–the amount of information that they are able to process in a fixed unit of time. At the same time, jobs have a varying *information load*–the amount of information to be processed per unit of time. Information overload creates noise in the communication system because information gets overlooked or misinterpreted when people can't process it fast enough. The result is poorer quality decisions as well as higher stress.[63]

Information overload problems can be minimized by increasing our information processing capacity, reducing the job's information load, or through a combination of both. Studies suggest that employees often increase their information processing capacity by temporarily reading faster, scanning through documents more efficiently, and removing distractions that slow information processing speed. Time management also increases information processing capacity. When information overload is temporary, information processing capacity can increase by working longer hours. Information load can be reduced by buffering, omitting, and summarizing. Buffering involves having incoming communication filtered, usually by an assistant. Omitting occurs when we decide to overlook messages, such as using software rules to redirect e-mails from distribution lists to folders that we never look at. An example of summarizing would be where we read executive summaries rather than the full report.

Cross-Cultural and Gender Communication

Increasing globalization and cultural diversity have brought more cross-cultural communication issues.[64] Voice intonation is one form of cross-cultural communication barrier. How loudly, deeply, and quickly people speak varies across cultures, and these voice intonations send secondary messages that have different meaning in different cultures.

As mentioned earlier, language is an obvious cross-cultural communications challenge. Words are easily misunderstood in verbal communication, either because the receiver has a limited vocabulary or the sender's accent distorts the usual sound of some words. In one cross-cultural seminar, for example, participants at German electronics company Siemens were reminded that a French coworker might call an event a "catastrophe" as a casual exaggeration, whereas someone in Germany usually interprets this word literally as an earth-shaking event. Similarly, KPMG staff from the United Kingdom sometimes referred to another person's suggestions as "interesting." They had to clarify to their German colleagues that "interesting" might not be complimenting the idea.[65]

Communication includes silence, but its use and meaning varies from one culture to another.[66] One study estimated that silence and pauses represented 30 percent of conversation time between Japanese doctors and patients, compared to only 8 percent of the time between American doctors and patients. Why is there more silence in Japanese conversations? One reason is that interpersonal harmony and saving face are more important in Japanese culture, and silence is a way of disagreeing without upsetting that harmony or offending the other person.[67] In addition, silence symbolizes respect and indicates that the listener is thoughtfully contemplating what has just been said.[68] Empathy is very important in Japan, and this shared understanding is demonstrated without using words. In contrast, most people in the United States and many other cultures view silence as a *lack* of communication and often interpret long breaks as a sign of disagreement.

Conversational overlaps also send different messages in different cultures. Japanese people usually stop talking when they are interrupted, whereas talking over the other person's speech is more common in Brazil, France, and some other countries. The difference in communication behaviour is, again, due to interpretations. Talking while someone is speaking to you is considered quite rude in Japan, whereas Brazilians and French are more likely to interpret this as the person's interest and involvement in the conversation.

NONVERBAL DIFFERENCES ACROSS CULTURES

Nonverbal communication represents another potential area for misunderstanding across cultures. Many nonconscious or involuntary nonverbal cues (such as smiling) have the same meaning around the world, but deliberate gestures often have different interpretations. For example, most of us shake our head from side to side to say "No," but a variation of head shaking means "I understand" to many people in India. Filipinos raise their eyebrows to give an affirmative answer, yet Arabs interpret this expression (along with clicking one's tongue) as a negative response. Most Americans are taught to maintain eye contact with the speaker to

Global Connections 9.1:

POLITELY WAITING FOR SOME SILENCE[69]

Miho Aizu has attended many meetings where participants communicated in English. Until recently, the manager at Accenture in Japan thought she communicated well in those sessions. But in a recent training program conducted by the professional services firm, Aizu learned that Japanese cultural norms held back her involvement in cross-cultural business conversations. One such problem was that she tends to be too polite in waiting for others to finish talking. "I was told I needed to jump into discussions rather than wait until everyone had said what they wanted to say," says Aizu. Managers from North America, South America, the Middle East, and most of Europe seldom allow silence to occur, so Aizu and other Japanese participants are often left out of the conversation.

Dave and Les Jacobs/ Blend Images/Getty Images RF

Aizu also realized that her involvement is held back by the Japanese tendency to be overly self-conscious about imperfect language skills. "During the team discussions, there were many things I wanted to say, but I felt I had to brush up my English language and presentation skills," Aizu admits. In contrast, Accenture managers from many other non-English countries speak up in spite of their broken English.

In Japan, speaking well and waiting for others to finish are signs of respect and cultural refinement. But in meetings with managers across most other cultures, this lack of communication sends a different message. "There are many people who come to me and say they don't know what Japanese people are thinking," says Accenture Japan president Chikamoto Hodo. "Our people (at Accenture) are more talkative than most Japanese, but they still have a difficult time communicating with foreigners."

Accenture wants to develop leaders who can communicate effectively across its global operations, so it has developed special programs that coach its managers to engage in better conversations with colleagues and clients across cultures. While Accenture participants learn about Japanese communication practices, Aizu and other Accenture staff in Japan are coached to become more active communicators. "After various training programs, I am more able to say what I need to say, without worrying too much about the exact words," says Satoshi Tanaka, senior manager of human resources at Accenture Japan.

show interest and respect, whereas some First Nations peoples learn at an early age to show respect by looking down when an older or more senior person is talking to them.[70]

GENDER DIFFERENCES IN COMMUNICATION

Men and women have similar communication practices, but there are subtle distinctions that can occasionally lead to misunderstanding and conflict (see Exhibit 9.6).[71] One distinction is that men are more likely than women to view conversations as negotiations of relative status and power. They assert their power by directly giving advice to others (e.g., "You should do the following") and using combative language. There is also evidence that men dominate the talk time in conversations with women, as well as interrupt more and adjust their speaking style less than do women.

Men engage in more "report talk," in which the primary function of the conversation is impersonal and efficient information exchange. Women also do report talk, particularly when conversing with men, but conversations among women have a higher incidence of relationship building through "rapport talk." Women make more use of indirect requests ("Do you think you should. . . "), apologize more often, and seek advice from others more quickly than do men. Finally, research fairly consistently indicates that women are more sensitive than men to nonverbal cues in face-to-face meetings.[72] Together, these conditions can create communication conflicts. Women who describe problems get frustrated that men offer advice rather than rapport, whereas men become frustrated because they can't understand why women don't appreciate their advice.

Gender differences are also emerging in the use of social media to communicate.[73] Specifically, women are more likely to visit social networking sites like Facebook and Twitter, spend more time online, and clicked on more Web pages than their male counterparts. Women are also more active participants in photo sharing websites. Globally, women are outpacing men

EXHIBIT 9.6

Gender Differences in Communication

When Men Communicate	When Women Communicate
1. Report talk—giving advice, assert power	1. Rapport talk—relationship building
2. Give advice directly	2. Give advice indirectly
3. Dominant conversation style	3. Flexible conversation style
4. Apologize less often	4. Apologize more often
5. Less sensitive to nonverbal cues	5. More sensitive to nonverbal cues

in signing up for Twitter accounts and are more active Twitter users. Their reasons for using this communication channel also differ. Women tend to use Twitter as a conversational rather than functional medium. Overall women spend an average of 24.8 hours per month online, whereas men spend 22.9 hours per month online.

Improving Interpersonal Communication

LO5

Effective interpersonal communication depends on the sender's ability to get the message across and the receiver's performance as an active listener. In this section, we outline these two essential features of effective interpersonal communication.

GETTING YOUR MESSAGE ACROSS

This chapter began with the statement that effective communication occurs when the other person receives and understands the message. This is more difficult to accomplish than most people believe. To get your message across to the other person, you first need to empathize with the receiver, such as being sensitive to words that may be ambiguous or trigger the wrong emotional response. Second, be sure that you repeat the message, such as by rephrasing the key points a couple of times. Third, your message competes with other messages and noise, so find a time when the receiver is less likely to be distracted by these other matters. Finally, if you are communicating bad news or criticism, focus on the problem, not the person.

ACTIVE LISTENING

General Electric Company (GE) recently revised its famous leadership development program to become more aligned with the cultural diversity of its employees and emerging leaders. One discovery in past programs was that U.S. managers were good at talking, but didn't always give the same priority to active listening. GE "now majors people on listening," says Susan Peters, GE's chief learning officer. "It's something we have to really work on, to equal the playing field between our American leaders and our non-American leaders."[74]

Almost 2,000 years ago, the Greek philosopher Epictetus wrote: "Nature gave us one tongue, but two ears, so we may listen twice as much as we speak."[75] GE and other companies are increasingly applying this sage advice to leadership development. Active listening is a process of

EXHIBIT 9.7

Active Listening Process and Strategies

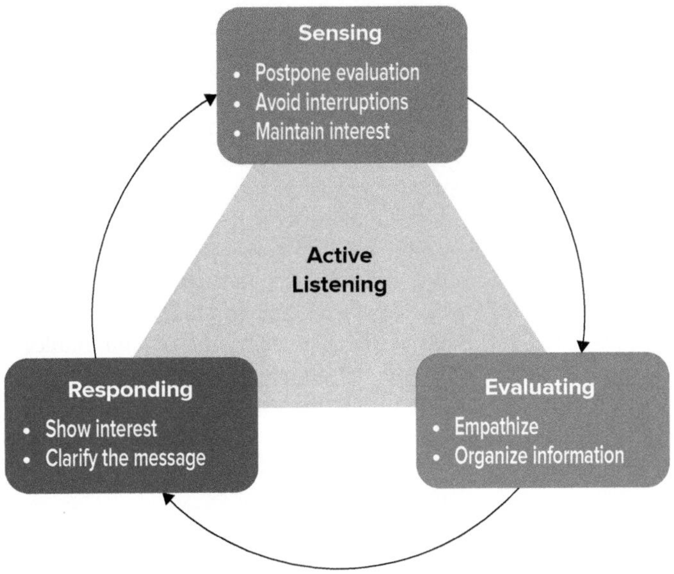

actively sensing the sender's signals, evaluating them accurately, and responding appropriately. These three components of listening–sensing, evaluating, and responding–reflect the listener's side of the communication model described at the beginning of this chapter. Listeners receive the sender's signals, decode them as intended, and provide appropriate and timely feedback to the sender (see Exhibit 9.7). Active listeners constantly cycle through sensing, evaluating, and responding during the conversation and engage in various activities to improve these processes.[76]

- *Sensing*. Sensing is the process of receiving signals from the sender and paying attention to them. Active listeners improve sensing in three ways. First, they postpone evaluation by not forming an opinion until the speaker has finished. Second, they avoid interrupting the speaker's conversation. Third, they remain motivated to listen to the speaker.
- *Evaluating*. This component of listening includes understanding the message meaning, evaluating the message, and remembering the message. To improve their evaluation of the conversation, active listeners empathize with the speaker–they try to understand and be sensitive to the speaker's feelings, thoughts, and situation. Evaluation also improves by organizing the speaker's ideas during the communication episode.
- *Responding*. This third component of listening involves providing feedback to the sender, which motivates and directs the speaker's communication. Active listeners accomplish this by maintaining sufficient eye contact and sending back channel signals (e.g., "I see"), both of which show interest. They also respond by clarifying the message–rephrasing the speaker's ideas at appropriate breaks ("So you're saying that . . . ?").

connect

Are you an active listener? See page 242 or visit **connect.mcgrawhill.com** to assess whether you are or not.

Improving Communication Throughout the Hierarchy

LO6

So far, we have focused on micro-level issues in the communication process, namely, sending and receiving information between two employees or the informal exchanges of information across several people. But in this era where knowledge is a competitive advantage, corporate leaders also need to maintain an open flow of communication up, down, and across the entire organization. In this section, we discuss three organization-wide communication strategies: workspace design, Web-based communication, and direct communication with top management.

WORKSPACE DESIGN

To improve information sharing and create a more sociable work environment, Intel has torn down the cubicle walls at its micro chip design centre near Portland, Oregon. "We realized that we were inefficient and not as collaborative as we would have liked," acknowledges Neil Tunmore, Intel's director of corporate services. The refurbished building includes more shared space where employees set up temporary work areas. There are also more meeting rooms where employees can collaborate in private.[77]

Intel and many other companies are improving communication by redesigning the workspace and employee territorial practices in that space.[78] The location and design of hallways, offices, cubicles, and communal areas (cafeterias, elevators) all shape whom we speak to as well as the frequency of that communication. Although these open space arrangements increase the amount of face-to-face communication, they also potentially produce more noise, distractions, and loss of privacy.[79] Others claim that open work spaces have minimal noise problems because employees tend to speak more softly and white noise technology blocks out most voices. Still, the challenge is to increase social interaction without these stressors.

Another workspace strategy is to cloister employees into team spaces, but also encourage sufficient interaction with people from other teams. Pixar Animation Studios constructed its campus in Emeryville, Calif. with these principles in mind. The buildings encourage communication among team members. At the same time, the campus encourages happenstance interactions with people on other teams. Pixar executives call this the "bathroom effect," because team members must leave their isolated pods to fetch their mail, have lunch, or visit the restroom.[80]

INTERNET-BASED ORGANIZATIONAL COMMUNICATION

For decades, employees received official company news through hard copy newsletters and magazines. Some firms still use these communication devices, but most have supplemented or replaced them completely with Web-based sources of information. The traditional company magazine is now typically published on Web pages or distributed in PDF format. The advantage of these *e-zines* is that company news can be prepared and distributed quickly.

wikis Collaborative web spaces where anyone in a group can write, edit, or remove material from the website.

Employees are increasingly skeptical of information that has been screened and packaged by management, so a few companies such as IBM are encouraging employees to post their own news on internal blogs and wikis. **Wikis** are collaborative Web spaces where anyone in a group can write, edit, or remove material from the website. Wikipedia, the popular online encyclopedia, is a massive public example of a wiki. IBM's WikiCentral now hosts more than 20,000 wiki projects involving 100,000 employees. The accuracy of wikis depends on the quality of participants, but IBM experts say that errors are quickly identified by IBM's online community. Another concern is that wikis have failed to gain employee support, likely because wiki involvement takes time and the company does not reward or recognize those who provide this time to wiki development.[81]

eBay Canada has an open concept office to encourage communication and camaraderie, but the noise can be distracting. "Our employees sometimes bid on items on eBay and when it gets down to the final seconds of an auction, tension mounts and the bidder often shouts out in excitement," says eBay Canada spokeswoman, Alexandra Brown. Fortunately, eBay staff found a solution that seems to work. When employees need quiet time they drape colourful bandanas across the top of their desks, on desk lamps, or around their heads, which communicates to others "QUIET PLEASE!" To reduce some of the distractions and stress associated with open-space offices, everyone also turns off the audio alert signal for incoming e-mail messages and uses wireless headsets rather than hands-free handsets. When employees need privacy to do undisturbed work, they can book and bring their laptops into meeting rooms that have Intranet and Internet access.[82]

Brad Swonetz/Redux Photos

Tony Hsieh likes to tweet. Even as CEO of Zappos, one of the world's largest online retailers, Hsieh discovered that tweeting is a powerful way to connect with his staff and the wider community. "What I found was that people really appreciated the openness and honesty (of tweets), and that led people to feel more of a personal connection with Zappos and me," Hsieh wrote in one of his Weblogs. Tweeting is so important at Zappos that new employees receive training on how to use the technology and are free to tweet to the public. But if tweeting the top boss seems too impersonal, Hsieh has the ultimate open-door policy. His desk is located in an open office setting in an area called "the jungle" (complete with fake vines hanging from the ceiling) where anyone can speak with him.[83]

DIRECT COMMUNICATION WITH TOP MANAGEMENT

Many believe that senior executives need to meet directly with employees and other stakeholders to improve morale as well as transmit and receive information more fully and meaningfully. Town hall meetings are mostly top-down communication, but the CEO's presentation is much more credible and personal than a video recording or written memo, and employees do have the opportunity to ask questions. Another strategy is for executives to hold roundtable forums to hear opinions from a representation of staff about various issues. At the departmental level, some companies hold daily or weekly "huddles"–brief stand-up meetings in which staff and their manager discuss goals and hear good news stories.

management by walking around (MBWA) A communication practice in which executives get out of their offices and learn from others in the organization through face-to-face dialogue.

A less formal approach to direct communication is **management by walking around (MBWA).** Coined by people at Hewlett-Packard four decades ago, this is essentially the practice in which senior executives get out of their offices and casually chat with employees on a daily or regular basis. Brian Scudamore, founder and CEO of 1-800-Got-Junk?, takes MBWA one step further. "I don't have my own office, and I very often move around to different departments for a day at a time," says Scudamore.[84]

These direct communication strategies potentially minimize filtering because executives listen directly to employees. They also help executives acquire a deeper meaning and quicker understanding of internal organizational problems. A third benefit of direct communication is that employees might have more empathy for decisions made further up the corporate hierarchy.

Communicating through the Grapevine

grapevine An unstructured and informal communication network founded on social relationships rather than organizational charts or job descriptions.

Organizational leaders may try their best to quickly communicate breaking news to employees through e-mails, Twitter tweets, and other direct formal channels, but employees still rely to some extent on the corporate **grapevine.** The grapevine is an unstructured and informal network founded on social relationships rather than organizational charts or job descriptions. What do employees think about the grapevine? Surveys of employees in two firms–one in Florida, the other in California–found that almost all employees use the grapevine, but very few of them prefer this source of information. The Californian survey also reported that only one-third of employees believe grapevine information is credible. In other words, employees turn to the grapevine when they have few other options.[85]

GRAPEVINE CHARACTERISTICS

Research conducted several decades ago reported that the grapevine transmits information very rapidly in all directions throughout the organization. The typical pattern is a cluster chain, whereby a few people actively transmit rumours to many others. The grapevine works through informal social networks, so it is more active where employees have similar backgrounds and are able to communicate easily. Many rumours seem to have at least a kernel of truth, possibly because they are transmitted through media-rich communication channels (e.g., face-to-face)

Debating Point:

SHOULD MANAGEMENT USE THE GRAPEVINE TO COMMUNICATE TO EMPLOYEES?

The grapevine has been the curse of management since modern-day organizations were invented. News flows with stealth-like efficiency below the surface, making it difficult to tell where information is travelling, what is being said to whom, or who is responsible for any misinformation. Although employees naturally flock to the grapevine for knowledge and social comfort in difficult times, its messages can be so distorted that they sometimes produce more stress than they alleviate. It is absurd to imagine management trying to systematically transmit important information—or any news whatsoever—through this uncontrollable, quirky communication channel.

But some communication experts are taking a second look at the grapevine, viewing it more as a resource than a nemesis. Their inspiration comes from marketing, where viral and word-of-mouth marketing have become hot topics.[86] Viral and word-of-mouth marketing occur when information seeded to a few people is transmitted to others based on patterns of friendship. In other words, information is passed along to others at the whim of those who first receive that information. Within organizations, this process is essentially the grapevine at work. Employees transmit information to other people within their sphere of everyday interaction.

The grapevine might seem to transmit information in strange and unreliable ways, but there are two contrary arguments. First, the grapevine channel is becoming more robust and reliable, thanks to social media and other emerging forms of electronic communication. These media have produced a stronger scaffolding than ever before, which potentially makes the grapevine more useful for transmitting information.

The second argument is that the grapevine tends to be more persuasive than traditional communication channels from management to employees. The grapevine is based on social net- works, which we discuss in the next chapter. Social networks are an important source of organizational power because they are built on trust, and trust increases acceptance of information sent through those networks. Consequently, the grapevine tends to be far more persuasive than other communication channels.

The power of the grapevine as a communication tool was recently illustrated when Novo Nordisk tried to change the image of its regulatory affairs staff.[87] The European pharmaceutical company made limited progress after a year of using traditional communication channels. "We had posters, meetings, competitions, and everything else you would expect," recalls communication adviser Jakob Wolter. "By the end of it, we'd achieved something—a general awareness among our people—but very little else."

So, Novo Nordisk took another route. During the half-yearly gathering of all employees, nine regulatory staff were given wax-sealed confidential envelopes that assigned them to one of three "secret societies." Between conference sessions, these employees met with the managing director, who assigned their manifesto, including a mandate and budget. They were also told to keep their mission secret, saying to inquisitive coworkers, "I can't tell you."

"The rumor mill started right there that day," says Wolter. "People were already wondering what on earth was going on." The societies were allowed to recruit more employees, which they did in subsequent months. Many employees throughout Novo Nordisk became intrigued, spreading their opinions and news to others. Meanwhile, empowered to improve their image and work processes, members of the three secret societies introduced several initiatives that brought about improvements.

and employees are motivated to communicate effectively. Nevertheless, the grapevine distorts information by deleting fine details and exaggerating key points of the story.[88]

Some of these characteristics might still be true, but the grapevine almost certainly has changed as e-mail, social networking sites, and Twitter tweets have replaced the traditional water cooler as sources of gossip. For example, several Facebook sites are unofficially themed around specific companies, allowing employees and customers to vent their complaints about the organization. Along with altering the speed and network of corporate grapevines, the Internet has expanded these networks around the globe, not just around the next cubicle.

GRAPEVINE BENEFITS AND LIMITATIONS

Should the grapevine be encouraged, tolerated, or quashed? The difficulty in answering this question is that the grapevine has both benefits and limitations.[89] One benefit, as was mentioned earlier, is that employees rely on the grapevine when information is not available through formal channels. It is also the main conduit through which organizational stories and other symbols of the organization's culture are communicated. A third benefit of the grapevine is that this social interaction relieves anxiety. This explains why rumour mills are most active during times of uncertainty.[90] Finally, the grapevine is associated with the drive to bond. Being a recipient of gossip is a sign of inclusion, according to evolutionary psychologists. Trying to quash the grapevine is, in some respects, an attempt to undermine the natural human drive for social interaction.[91]

While the grapevine offers these benefits, it is not a preferred communication medium. Grapevine information is sometimes so distorted that it escalates rather than reduces employee anxiety. Furthermore, employees develop more negative attitudes towards the organization when management is slower than the grapevine in communicating information. What should corporate leaders do with the grapevine? The best advice seem to be to listen to the grapevine as a signal of employee anxiety, then correct the cause of this anxiety. Some companies also listen to the grapevine and step in to correct blatant errors and fabrications. Most important, corporate leaders need to view the grapevine as a competitor, and meet this challenge by directly informing employees of news before it spreads throughout the grapevine.

Chapter Summary

LO1 Explain why communication is important in organizations and discuss four influences on effective communication encoding and decoding.

Communication refers to the process by which information is transmitted and *understood* between two or more people. Communication supports work coordination, organizational learning, decision making, changing others' behaviour, and employee well-being. The communication process involves forming, encoding, and transmitting the intended message to a receiver, who then decodes the message and provides feedback to the sender. Effective communication occurs when the sender's thoughts are transmitted to and understood by the intended receiver. The effectiveness of this process depends on whether the sender and receiver have similar codebooks, the sender's proficiency at encoding that message to the audience, the sender and receiver's motivation and ability to transmit messages through that particular communication channel, and their common mental models of the communication context.

LO2 Compare and contrast the advantages of and problems with electronic mail, other verbal communication media, and nonverbal communication.

The two main types of communication channels are verbal and nonverbal. Various forms of Internet-based communication are widely used in organizations, with e-mail the most popular. Although efficient and a useful filing cabinet, e-mail is relatively poor at communicating emotions; it tends to reduce politeness and respect; it is an inefficient medium for communicating in ambiguous, complex, and novel situations; and it contributes to information overload. An emerging set of communication channels is social media, which are Internet- or mobile-based channels that allow users to generate and interactively share information. Social media are more conversational and reciprocally interactive than traditional channels. They are "social" by encouraging collaboration and the formation of virtual communities. Nonverbal communication includes facial gestures, voice intonation, physical distance, and even silence. Unlike verbal communication, nonverbal communication is less rule-bound and is mostly automatic and nonconscious. Some nonverbal communication is automatic through a process called emotional contagion.

LO3 Explain how social acceptance and media richness influence the preferred communication channel.

The most appropriate communication medium partly depends on its social acceptance and media richness. Social acceptance refers to how well the communication medium is approved and supported by the organization, teams, and individuals. This contingency includes organization and team norms, individual preferences for specific communication channels, and the symbolic meaning of a channel. A communication medium should also be chosen for its data-carrying capacity (media richness). Nonroutine and ambiguous situations require rich media. However, technology-based lean media might be almost as effective as rich media for transferring information. This particularly occurs where users can multi-communicate and have high proficiency with that technology, and where social distractions of high media richness channels reduce the efficient processing of information through those channels. These contingencies are also considered when selecting the best channels for persuasion.

LO4 Discuss various barriers (noise) to effective communication, including cross-cultural and gender-based differences in communication.

Several barriers create noise in the communication process. People misinterpret messages because of misaligned codebooks due to different languages, jargon, and use of ambiguous phrases. Filtering messages and information overload are two other communication barriers. These problems are often amplified in cross-cultural settings where the above problems occur along with differences in meaning of nonverbal cues, silence, and conversational overlaps. There are also some communication differences between men and women, such as the tendency for men to exert status and engage in report talk in conversations, whereas women use more rapport talk and are more sensitive than are men to nonverbal cues.

LO5 Explain how to get your message across more effectively, and summarize the elements of active listening.

To get a message across, the sender must learn to empathize with the receiver, repeat the message, choose an appropriate time for the conversation, and be descriptive rather than evaluative. Listening includes sensing, evaluating, and responding. Active listeners support these processes by postponing evaluation, avoiding interruptions, maintaining interest, empathizing, organizing information, showing interest, and clarifying the message.

LO6 Summarize effective communication strategies in organizational hierarchies, and review the role and relevance of the organizational grapevine. Some companies try to encourage communication through workspace design, as well as through Internet-based communication channels. Some executives also meet directly with employees, such as through management by walking around (MBWA) and town-hall meetings, to facilitate communication across the organization.

In any organization, employees rely on the grapevine, particularly during times of uncertainty. The grapevine is an unstructured and informal network founded on social relationships rather than organizational charts or job descriptions. Although early research identified several unique features of the grapevine, some of these features may be changing as the Internet plays an increasing role in grapevine communication.

Key Terms

communication, p. 219
emotional contagion, p. 226
grapevine, p. 237
information overload, p. 231
management by walking around (MBWA), p. 237
media richness, p. 228
persuasion, p. 230
wikis, p. 236

Critical-Thinking Questions

1. You have been hired as a consultant to improve communication between engineering and marketing staff in a large high-technology company. Use the communication model and the four ways to improve that process to devise strategies to improve communication effectiveness among employees between these two work units.
2. "An organization comes into being when people can communicate with each other." Discuss the benefits and limitations of communicating with e-mails amongst team members.
3. Senior management at a consumer goods company wants you to investigate the feasibility of using a virtual reality platform (such as Second Life) for monthly online meetings involving its three-dozen sales managers located in several cities and countries. Use the social acceptance and media richness factors described in this chapter to identify information you need to consider when conducting this evaluation.
4. Wikis are collaborative websites where anyone in the group can post, edit, or delete any information. Where might this communication technology be most useful in organizations?
5. Under what conditions, if any, do you think it is appropriate to use e-mail to notify an employee that he or she has been laid off or fired? Why is e-mail usually considered an inappropriate channel to convey this information?
6. Suppose that you are part of a virtual team and must persuade other team members on an important matter (such as switching suppliers or altering the project deadline). Assuming that you cannot visit these people in person, what can you do to maximize your persuasiveness?
7. Explain why men and women are sometimes frustrated with each other's communication behaviours.
8. In your opinion, has the introduction of e-mail and other information technologies increased or decreased the amount of information flowing through the corporate grapevine? Explain your answer.

Case Study: COMMUNICATING WITH THE MILLENNIALS

By Steven L. McShane, The University of Western Australia

The Millennials (including Generation Y) have arrived in the workplace, and they are bringing new ways to communicate. Surveys report that cell phones (particularly smartphones) have become the medium of choice among Millennials. Almost all (97 percent) Millennials in the United States with cell phones send text messages, 84 percent access the Internet, and 73 percent send or receive e-mail using their cell phones. In contrast, among cell phone owners over 50 years old, less than two-thirds send text messages, only about one-third access the Internet, and only about one-third send or receive e-mails using their phones.

Millennial communication also relies much more on social media. Almost 90 percent of Millennials regularly visit Facebook, LinkedIn, or other social networking sites, whereas only about half of Americans over 50 visit these sites. Thirty percent of Millennials use Twitter, compared to less than 10 percent of people over 50 years old.

These statistics send a clear message: Millennials prefer different communication channels (cell phones, social media) and different communication styles (i.e., short, informal messages) than those dictated by most organizations. These gaps between corporate and personal communication preferences not only produce dysfunctional conflict and frustration; they also undermine the company's ability to attract future talent. "[Millennials] will judge companies on the social media practices and policies, which includes how companies utilize social media in their operations, their digital awareness, and any restrictions imposed on employees' access and usage of social media during work time," warns Barry Thomas, director of Cook Medical Asia-Pacific.

Most companies aren't hearing the message. They continue to block social networking, text messaging, and other channels preferred by Millennials. Some firms argue these practices are workplace intrusions that undermine productivity. Others justify blocking communication through these channels due to security risks.

Whether these arguments are valid remains uncertain, but a growing chorus of experts are advising that companies need to adapt to the communication styles of Millennials rather than reject them outright. Furthermore, companies need to make better use of the communication skills that Millennials bring to the workplace

"A new employee who comes in with the ability to manage a network of 1,000 Facebook friends every day. That's a fabulous skill in, let's say, a sales organization," says Ross Smith, Director of Test at Microsoft, Inc. The problem, he suggests, is that many companies don't know how to leverage that communication potential. "It's likely that the organization has no idea, particularly because the organization is generally going to be run by boomer, Gen X managers, who aren't savvy Facebook users. But the Gen Y or millennial employee coming in certainly knows how to do that."

Smith believes the solution is to give Millennials more freedom to try out new communication practices. "If the senior leaders or the organization can develop a culture of high trust, then the individual's going to be free to experiment and suggest new things and try new ways of doing things and uncover how Facebook skills map to a sales organization."

St. Luke's Medical Center in Boise, Idaho, is a case in point. Hospital leaders discovered that the younger medical staff were texting each other with medical orders and patient updates. Texting is one of the preferred communication methods among these physicians and nurses, and it is a much more efficient than the hospital's formal practice of phoning and paging people. But texting through public networks lacks security (it could be hacked by outsiders) and violates industry regulations. Another hospital would have banned the practice without further thought, but St. Luke's is instead contracted with an IT company to set up a secure texting system for the hospital.

"I've heard [officials of] other organizations say, 'We can't do that,'" says Jennifer Mensik, St. Luke's administrator of nursing and patient care services. "But when people are trying to do the best they can for the patient, they're going to try to find a workaround. That should be an alert to some of the older generation that this is a good idea. Let's not stop it. Let's figure out how we can do it legally and correctly."

Although companies need to adapt to Millennial communication preferences, the reverse is also true. Millennials need to spruce up their skills using older technologies. For instance, advertising sales at Metro Guide Publishing in Halifax, Nova Scotia, were down, and publisher Patty Baxter noticed that the office lacked the buzz of sales calls. The problem, she realized, was that most of Metro Guide's new generation of employees were e-mailing clients rather than selling advertising by telephone.

Baxter explains that e-mail doesn't work in business deals, where personal rapport and quick understanding of the client's needs are critical. "You're not selling if you're just asking a question and getting an answer back," she says. Baxter also suggests that phone calls tend to result in fewer communication errors, citing a recent incident in which a sales employee misinterpreted a client's e-mail about a possible advertising sale. Metro Guide sales staff now receive on-the-job coaching with phone-use consultant Mary Jane Copps, who observes that Millennial employees (as well as others) often suffer from phone phobia. "It's a lack of confidence that they'll be able to say the right words in the right order in the right amount of time," she explains.

Discussion Questions

1. Take a poll of your class (at least, the Gen-X and Gen-Y members). At school or work, how many regularly (e.g., daily or every few days) send or receive information (not entertainment) using (a) e-mail, (b) instant messages or Twitter tweets, (c) cell phone text messages, (d) reading/ writing blogs, (e) visiting/authoring social media sites (e.g., Facebook, Instagram), (f) watching/creating online videos (e.g., YouTube)?
2. Even within this generation, there are different preferences for communication media. After conducting the poll, ask students who don't regularly use one or more of these methods why they don't like that particular communication medium. Ask those who very often use these sources to give their point of view.
3. Companies have been slow and reluctant to adopt social media channels, cell phone text messaging, and similar forms of communication. If you were a senior manager, how would you introduce these communication technologies in the workplace to share information and knowledge more effectively?

Sources: Hughes, Mark. "Fishing for Reliable Staff in Gen Y Waters." *China Daily*, 12 October 2012; Putre, Laura. "A Clash of Ages." *Hospitals & Health Networks*, March 2013, 40-44; Hofschneider, Anita. "Bosses Say 'Pick up the Phone'." *Wall Street Journal*, 28 August 2013; Brenner, Joanna, and Aaron Smith. "72 percent of Online Adults Are Social Networking Site Users." In *Internet & American Life Project*. Washington, DC: Pew Research Center, 2013; Robison, Wesley. "How Microsoft Builds Trust in the Workplace." *psfk*, 27 September 2013; Duggan, Maeve. "Cell Phone Activities 2013." In *Internet & American Life Project*. Washington, DC: Pew Research Center, 2013.

Team Exercise: ACTIVE LISTENING EXERCISE

By Mary Gander, Winona State University

Purpose This exercise is designed to help you understand the dynamics of active listening in conversations and to develop active listening skills.

Instructions For each of the four vignettes presented here, student teams (or students working individually) will compose three statements that demonstrate active listening. Specifically, one statement will indicate that you show empathy for the situation; the second will ask for clarification and detail in a nonjudgmental way; and the third statement will provide nonevaluative feedback to the speaker. Here are details about each of these three types of responses:

- *Showing empathy: acknowledge feelings.* Sometimes it sounds like a speaker wants you to agree with him or her, but in reality the speaker mainly wants you to understand how he or she feels. "Acknowledging feelings" involves taking in the speaker's statements while looking at the "whole message" including body language, tone of voice, and level of arousal, and trying to determine what emotion the speaker is conveying. Then you let the speaker know that you realize what he or she is feeling by acknowledging it in a sentence.
- *Asking for clarification and detail while withholding your judgment and own opinions.* This conveys that you are trying to understand and not just trying to push your opinions onto the speaker. To formulate a relevant question in asking for more clarification, you will have to listen carefully to what the speaker says. Frame your question as someone trying to understand in more detail; often asking for a specific example is useful. This also helps the speaker evaluate his or her own opinions and perspective.
- *Providing nonevaluative feedback: feeding back the message you heard.* This will allow the speaker to determine if he or she conveyed the message to you and will help prevent troublesome miscommunication. It will also help the speaker become more aware of how he or she is coming across to another person (self-evaluation). Just think about what the speaker is conveying; paraphrase it in your own words, and say it back to the speaker (without judging the correctness or merit of what was said), asking him or her if that is what was meant.

After teams (or individual students) have prepared the three statements for each vignette, the instructor will ask them to present their statements and explain how these statements satisfy the active listening criteria.

VIGNETTE #1 A colleague stops by your desk and says, "I am tired of the lack of leadership around here. The boss is so wishy-washy, he can't get tough with some of the slackers around here. They just keep milking the company, living off the rest of us. Why doesn't management do something about these guys? And you are always so supportive of the boss; he's not as good as you make him out to be."

Develop three statements that respond to the speaker in this vignette by (a) showing empathy, (b) seeking clarification, and (c) providing nonevaluative feedback.

VIGNETTE #2 Your coworker stops by your cubicle; her voice and body language show stress, frustration, and even some fear. You know she has been working hard and has a strong need to get her work done on time and done well. You are trying to concentrate on some work and have had a number of interruptions already. She abruptly interrupts you and says, "This project is turning out to be a mess. Why can't the other three people on my team quit fighting with each other?"

Develop three statements that respond to the speaker in this vignette by (a) showing empathy, (b) seeking clarification, and (c) providing nonevaluative feedback.

VIGNETTE #3 One of your subordinates is working on an important project. He is an engineer who has good technical skills and knowledge and was selected for the project team because of that. He stops by your office and appears to be quite agitated: His voice is loud and strained, and his face has a look of bewilderment. He says, "I'm supposed to be working with four other people from four other departments on this new project, but they never listen to my ideas and seem to hardly know I'm at the meeting!"

Develop three statements that respond to the speaker in this vignette by (a) showing empathy, (b) seeking clarification, and (c) providing nonevaluative feedback.

VIGNETTE #4 Your subordinate comes into your office in a state of agitation, asking if she can talk to you. She is polite and sits down. She seems calm and does not have an angry look on her face. However, she says, "It seems like you consistently make up lousy schedules; you are unfair and unrealistic in the kinds of assignments you give certain people, me included. Everyone else is so intimidated they don't complain, but I think you need to know that this isn't right and it's got to change."

Develop three statements that respond to the speaker in this vignette by (a) showing empathy, (b) seeking clarification, and (c) providing nonevaluative feedback.

Self-Assessment: ARE YOU AN ACTIVE LISTENER?

Purpose This self-assessment is designed to help you estimate your strengths and weaknesses on various dimensions of active listening.

Instructions Think back to face-to-face conversations you have had with a coworker or client in the office, hallway, factory floor, or other setting. Indicate the extent that each item below describes your behaviour during those conversations. Answer each item as truthfully as possible so that you get an accurate estimate of where your active listening skills need improvement. Then use the scoring key in Appendix B to calculate your results for each scale. This exercise is completed alone so students assess themselves honestly without concerns of social comparison. However, class discussion will focus on the important elements of active listening.

Active Listening Skills Inventory

When listening to others in face-to-face, telephone, or similar conversations, how often do you do the following?	Never or Rarely	Seldom	Some-times	Often	Almost always
1. I keep an open mind when others describe their ideas.	○	○	○	○	○
2. I organize the speaker's ideas while s/he is talking to me.	○	○	○	○	○
3. I ask questions to show I understand and am focused on the speaker's message.	○	○	○	○	○
4. I interrupt before the speaker sufficiently presents his/her views.	○	○	○	○	○
5. While listening, I mentally sort out the speaker's ideas so s/he makes sense to me.	○	○	○	○	○
6. I use gestures and words (nodding, agreeing) to show I am listening.	○	○	○	○	○
7. I let my mind wander when listening to people.	○	○	○	○	○
8. I try to visualize and feel the speaker's experience while s/he is describing those events.	○	○	○	○	○
9. I summarize the speaker's ideas to confirm that I understand him/her correctly.	○	○	○	○	○
10. I focus on what the speaker is saying to me even when it doesn't sound interesting.	○	○	○	○	○
11. I see the topic from my perspective rather than from the speaker's perspective.	○	○	○	○	○
12. I show interest while listening to others.	○	○	○	○	○

SELF-ASSESSMENTS FOR CHAPTER 9

SELF-ASSESSMENT NAME	DESCRIPTION	LOCATION
Are you an active listener?	The assessment is designed to assess your strengths and weaknesses on various dimensions of active listening	Page 242 connect

At Toronto City Hall, councillors turned their backs on Mayor Rob Ford to protest his leadership.

Moe Doiron/*The Globe and Mail*/CP Images

Chapter 10

Power and Influence in the Workplace

LEARNING OBJECTIVES

After reading this chapter, you should be able to:

LO1. Describe the dependence model of power and describe the five sources of power in organizations.

LO2. Discuss the four contingencies of power.

LO3. Explain how people and work units gain power through social networks.

LO4. Describe eight types of influence tactics, three consequences of influencing others, and three contingencies to consider when choosing an influence tactic.

LO5. Identify the organizational conditions and personal characteristics that support organizational politics, as well as ways to minimize organizational politics.

In a landslide election, Rob Ford was elected as mayor with the highest voter turnout the City of Toronto had ever seen. The general public identified with Ford's ordinary citizen persona and his message to halt the gravy train of government expenditures. Toronto City Council consists of 45 members and each member, including the mayor, has only one vote. In order to succeed in having agenda items passed, the mayor needs the backing of at least 22 councillors. As mayor, Ford pulled together an executive committee of 12 like-minded, mostly male, conservative councillors to support his administration and platform. Ford used his power to appoint chairs of city committees to select individuals who would ensure that his agenda was endorsed. According to some members who later broke rank, Ford's executive team was expected to vote in solidarity and councillors who did not follow the mayor's direction were bullied or punished by having their projects thwarted.

In *Crazy Town*, her book about the Ford regime, Robyn Doolittle describes Ford's demand for loyalty and silencing of opposition: ". . . [I]t wasn't just executive committee members who felt the administration's muscle. The mayor's office frequently used aggressive tactics to bring centrist votes on side." Even media outlets critical of Ford were penalized and entirely cut off from city hall communications. For a time, Ford's persuasive hold over Council was successful and he faced minimal opposition. In the early years of his tenure as mayor, Ford's administration triumphantly secured the cancellation of a vehicle registration tax, stopped a public transit fare hike, and passed a balanced budget with no tax increases. However, as reports surfaced about Ford's highly questionable conduct and that he was the subject of a criminal investigation, Ford's power over his team and Council dissipated to the point that he became embattled with his own executive. Ultimately, Council voted to strip many of Ford's mayoral powers, including his capacity to appoint and dismiss the chairs of city committees, his ability to speak first and last in Council meetings, and his authority to specify key matters in the Council's agenda. They also reduced Ford's office budget. After Council passed a motion seeking that Ford step down as mayor, councillors protested against Ford by literally turning their backs and shunning him each time he stood to speak in chambers.[1]

As this opening story illustrates, power and influence are never far from the actions of leaders and followers. Some suggest that Ford abused his power by sidelining people and being aggressive towards others. This might seem to paint Toronto City Hall as an institution mired in organizational politics and vulnerable to abuse of power, but every organization faces similar challenges to some degree. The Ford story demonstrates the multiple facets of power, including how legitimate power can enact change when needed, the sway of referent power to garner greater power, and how visible displays of coercive power can control people and information as a source of power. Although this story illustrates the dark side of power and influence, these concepts are equally relevant to ethical conduct and organizational performance. In fact, some OB experts point out that power and influence are inherent in all organizations. They exist in every business and in every decision and action.

This chapter unfolds as follows: First, we define power and present a basic model depicting the dynamics of power in organizational settings. The chapter then discusses the five bases of power, as well as information as a power base. Next, we look at the contingencies necessary to translate those sources into meaningful power. Our attention then turns to social networks and how they provide power to members through social capital. The latter part of this chapter examines the various types of influence in organizational settings, as well as the contingencies of effective influence strategies. The final section of this chapter looks at situations in which influence becomes organizational politics, as well as ways of minimizing dysfunctional politics.

The Meaning of Power

LO1

power The capacity of a person, team, or organization to influence others.

Power is the capacity of a person, team, or organization to influence others.[2] There are a few important features of this definition. First, power is not the act of changing someone's attitudes or behaviour; it is only the *potential* to do so. People frequently have power they do not use; they might not even know they have power. Second, power is based on the target's *perception* that the power holder controls (i.e., possesses, has access to, or regulates) a valuable resource that can help them achieve their goals.[3] People might generate power by convincing others that they control something of value, whether or not they actually control that resource. This perception is also formed from the power holder's behaviour as someone who is not swayed by authority or norms. For instance, one recent study found that people are perceived as more powerful just by their behaviour, such as putting their feet on a table.[4] To illustrate, Bruno Iksil, the disgraced former star trader at JP Morgan's London office known for his aggressive trading style, apparently created an image of power by dressing more casually than other staff. However, power is not a personal feeling of power. You might feel powerful or think you have power over others, but this is not power unless others believe you have that capacity.

Third, power involves asymmetric (unequal) *dependence* of one party on another party.[5] This dependent relationship is illustrated in Exhibit 10.1. The line from Person B to the goal shows that he/she believes Person A controls a resource that can help or hinder Person A in achieving that goal. Person A—the power holder in this illustration—might have power over Person B by controlling a desired job assignment, useful information, rewards, or even the privilege of being associated with him or her! For example, if you believe a coworker has expertise (the resource) that would substantially help you to write a better report (your goal), then that coworker has some power over you because you value that expertise to achieve your goal. Whatever the resource is, Person B perceives a dependence on Person A (the power holder) to provide the resource so Person B can reach his/her goal.

Although dependence is a key element of power relationships, we use the phrase "asymmetric dependence" because the less powerful party still has some degree of power–called **countervailing power**–over the power holder. In Exhibit 10.1, Person A dominates the power relationship, but Person B has enough countervailing power to keep Person A in the exchange relationship and impact how the power is used. For example, although managers have power over subordinates in many ways (e.g., controlling job security, preferred work assignments), employees have countervailing power by possessing skills and knowledge to keep production humming and customers happy, something that management can't accomplish alone.

countervailing power The capacity of a person, team, or organization to keep a more powerful person or group in the exchange relationship.

Finally, the power relationship depends on some minimum level of trust. Trust indicates a level of expectation that the more powerful party will deliver the resource. For example, you trust your employer to give you a paycheque at the end of each pay period. Even those in extremely dependent situations will usually walk away from the relationship if they lack a minimum level of trust in the more powerful party.

Let's look at this power dependence model in the employee-manager relationship. You depend on your boss for supporting your continued employment, satisfactory work arrangements, and other valued resources. At the same time, your manager depends on you to complete required tasks and to work effectively with others in the completion of their work. Managers (and the companies they represent) typically have more power, whereas employees have weaker countervailing power. But sometimes employees do have the stronger power base in the relationship. Notice that the strength of your power in the employee-manager relationship doesn't depend on your actual control over valued resources; it depends on the perceptions that your boss and others have about this resource control. Finally, trust is an essential ingredient in this relationship. Even with strong power, the employee-manager relationship comes apart when one party no longer sufficiently trusts the other.

The dependence model reveals only the core features of power dynamics between people and work units in organizations. We also need to learn about the specific sources of power and contingencies that allow that power to be applied effectively as influence. As Exhibit 10.2 illustrates, power is derived from five sources: legitimate, reward, coercive, expert, and referent. The model also identifies four contingencies of power: the employee's or department's substitutability, centrality, discretion, and visibility. Over the next few pages, we will discuss each of these sources and contingencies of power in the context of organizations.

EXHIBIT 10.1

Dependence in the Power Relationship

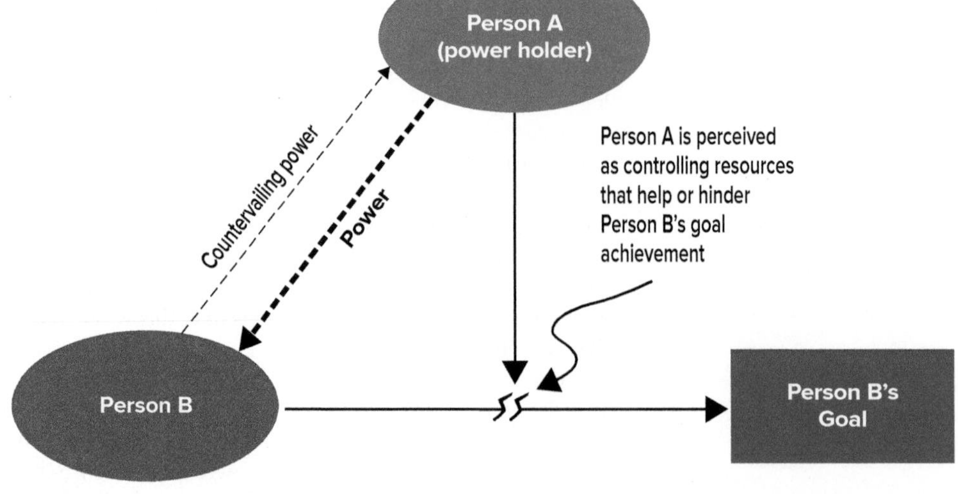

EXHIBIT 10.2

Sources and Contingencies of Power

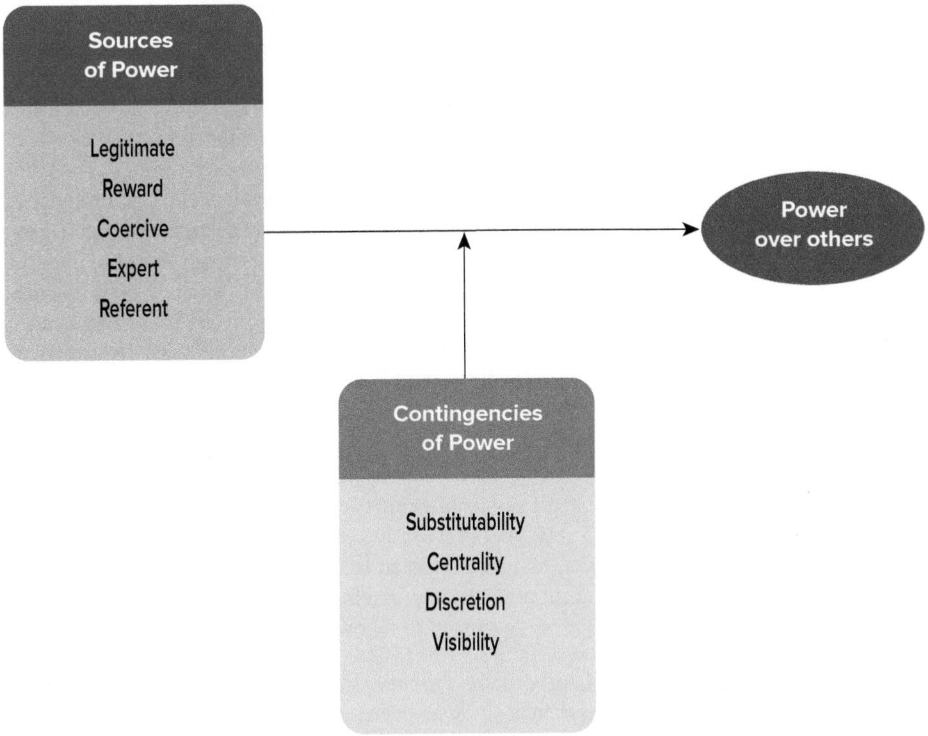

Sources of Power in Organizations

A half-century ago, social scientists John French and Bertrand Raven identified five sources of power found in organizations. Although variations of this list have been proposed over the years, the original list remains surprisingly intact.[6] Three sources of power–legitimate, reward, and coercive–originate mostly (but not completely) from the power holder's formal position or informal role. In other words, the person is granted these sources of power formally by the organization or informally by coworkers. Two other sources of power–expert and referent–originate mainly from the power holder's own characteristics; in other words, people carry these power bases around with them. However, even personal sources of power are not completely within the person because they depend on how others perceive them. Raven subsequently proposed information power as an addition source of power. We present information power as forms of legitimate and expert power rather than as a distinct power base.

LEGITIMATE POWER

legitimate power An agreement among organizational members that people in certain roles can request certain behaviours of others.

Legitimate power is an agreement among organizational members that people in certain roles can request a set of behaviours from others. This perceived right or obligation originates from formal job descriptions as well as informal rules of conduct. The most obvious example of legitimate power is a manager's right to tell employees what tasks to perform, who to work with, what office resources they can use, and so forth. Employees follow the boss's requests because there is mutual agreement that employees will follow a range of directives from people in these positions of authority. Employees defer to this authority whether or not they will be rewarded or punished for complying with those requests.

Notice that legitimate power has restrictions; it only gives the power holder the right to ask for a *range* of behaviours from others. This range–known as the "zone of indifference"–is the set of behaviours that individuals are willing to engage in at the other person's request.[7] Although most employees accept the boss's right to deny them access to Facebook during company time, some might draw the line when the boss asks them to work several hours beyond the regular workday. There are also occasions where employees actively oppose the boss's actions.

The size of the zone of indifference (and, consequently, the magnitude of legitimate power) increases with the level of trust in the power holder. Some values and personality traits also make people more obedient to authority. Those who value conformity and tradition and also have high power distance (i.e., they accept an unequal distribution of power) tend to have higher deference to authority. The organization's culture represents another influence on the willingness of employees to follow orders. A 3M scientist might continue to work on a project after being told by superiors to stop working on it because the 3M culture supports an entrepreneurial spirit, which includes ignoring your boss's authority from time to time.[8]

Managers are not the only people with legitimate power in organizations. Employees also have legitimate power over their bosses and coworkers through legal and administrative rights as well as informal norms.[9] For example, an organization might give employees the right to request information that is required for their job. Laws give employees the right to refuse work in unsafe conditions. More subtle forms of legitimate power also exist. Human beings have a **norm of reciprocity**–a feeling of obligation to help someone who has helped you.[10] If a coworker previously helped you handle a difficult client, that coworker has power because you feel an obligation to help the coworker on something of similar value in the future. The norm of reciprocity is a form of legitimate power because it is an informal rule of conduct that we are expected to follow.

norm of reciprocity A felt obligation and social expectation of helping or otherwise giving something of value to someone who has already helped or given something of value to you.

Legitimate Power Through Information Control A particularly potent form of legitimate power occurs where people have the right to control the information that others receive.[11] These information gatekeepers gain power in two ways. First, information is a resource, so those who need that information are dependent on the gatekeeper to provide that resource. For example, the maps department of a mining company has incredible power when other departments are dependent on the map department to deliver maps required for exploration projects.

Second, information gatekeepers gain power by selectively distributing information so those receiving the information perceive the situation differently.[12] Executives depend on middle managers and employees to provide an accurate picture of the company's operations. Yet, as we learned in the previous chapter on communication, information is often filtered as it flows up the

A French television program recently revealed how far people are willing to follow orders. As a variation of the 1960s experiments conducted by Stanley Milgram, 80 contestants administered electric shocks whenever a volunteer (an actor who didn't receive the shocks at all) answered a question incorrectly. Shocks increased in 20-volt increments, from 20 volts for the first mistake through to 460 volts. Contestants often hesitated after hearing the volunteer screaming for them to stop, yet continued the shocks after the host reminded them of their duty. Only 16 of the 80 contestants refused to administer the strongest shocks.[13]

© Yami 2

hierarchy. Middle managers and employees filter information so it puts them in a more positive light and to steer the executive team towards one decision rather than another. In other words, these information gatekeepers can potentially influence executive decisions by framing their reality through selective distribution of information.

REWARD POWER

Reward power is derived from the person's ability to control the allocation of rewards valued by others and to remove negative sanctions (i.e., negative reinforcement). Managers have formal authority that gives them power over the distribution of organizational rewards such as pay, promotions, time off, vacation schedules, and work assignments. Employees also have reward power over their bosses through their feedback and ratings in 360-degree feedback systems. These ratings affect supervisors' promotions and other rewards, so supervisors tend to behave differently towards employees after 360-degree feedback is introduced.

COERCIVE POWER

Coercive power is the ability to apply punishment. For many of us, the first thought is of a manager threatening an employee with dismissal. Yet, employees can also wield coercive power. Although the term "coercive" seems to imply penalizing duress, coercive power can materialize in both a direct or indirect form and, while perceived by the recipient as negative pressure, may not always be exercised with an adverse intent. Examples of direct and indirect forms of negative coercive power occur when employees are sarcastic towards coworkers or threaten to ostracize them if they fail to conform to team norms.[14] Some organizations rely on peer-based pressure to control coworker behaviour in a team setting. For example, Mount Sinai Hospital, an internationally recognized large, acute care hospital located in downtown Toronto, Ontario, uses a formal peer performance review for providing feedback to nursing leadership staff. All nursing leadership staff are required to complete an annual peer review and as part of the process must obtain two colleagues to serve as peer reviewers. While most peer review systems are confidential, Mount Sinai's peer performance review encourages verbal feedback in a face-to-face meeting. As such, we can see this process utilizes a systematic indirect form of coercive power applied by peers to influence work performance.

EXPERT POWER

For the most part, legitimate, reward, and coercive power originate from the position.[15] Expert power, on the other hand, originates mainly from within the power holder. It is an individual's or work unit's capacity to influence others by possessing knowledge or skills valued by others.

One important form of expert power is the perceived ability to manage uncertainties in the business environment. Organizations are more effective when they operate in predictable environments, so they value people who can cope with turbulence in the consumer trends, societal changes, unstable supply lines, and so forth. Expertise can help companies cope with uncertainty in three ways. These coping strategies are arranged in a hierarchy of importance, with prevention being the most powerful:[16]

- *Prevention.* The most effective strategy is to prevent environmental changes from occurring. For example, financial experts acquire power by preventing the organization from experiencing a cash shortage or defaulting on loans.
- *Forecasting.* The next best strategy is to predict environmental changes or variations. In this respect, trendspotters and other marketing specialists gain power by predicting changes in consumer preferences.
- *Absorption.* People and work units also gain power by absorbing or neutralizing the impact of environmental shifts as they occur. An example is the ability of maintenance crews to come to the rescue when machines break down.

Many people respond to expertise just as they respond to authority–hey mindlessly follow the guidance of these experts.[17] In one classic study, for example, a researcher posing as a hospital physician telephoned on-duty nurses to prescribe a specific dosage of medicine to a hospitalized patient. None of the nurses knew the person calling, and hospital policy forbade them from accepting treatment by telephone (i.e., they lacked legitimate power). Furthermore, the medication was unauthorized and the prescription was twice the maximum daily dose. Yet, almost all 22 nurses who received the telephone call followed the "doctor's" orders until stopped by researchers.[18]

This doctor-nurse study is a few decades old, but the power of expertise remains just as strong today, sometimes with tragic consequences. The Canadian justice system recently discovered that one of its "star" expert witnesses—a forensic child pathology expert—had provided inaccurate cause-of-death evaluations in at least 20 cases, a dozen of which resulted in wrongful or highly questionable criminal convictions. The pathologist's reputation as a renowned authority was the main reason why his often-weak evidence was accepted without question. "Experts in a courtroom—we give great deference to experts," admits a Canadian defence lawyer familiar with this situation.[19]

referent power The capacity to influence others on the basis of an identification with and respect for the power holder.

charisma A personal characteristic or special "gift" that serves as a form of interpersonal attraction and referent power over others.

REFERENT POWER

People have **referent power** when others identify with them, like them, or otherwise respect them. As with expert power, referent power originates within the power holder. It is largely a function of the person's interpersonal skills and tends to develop slowly. Referent power is also associated with **charisma.** Experts have difficulty agreeing on the meaning of charisma, but it is most often described as a form of interpersonal attraction whereby followers ascribe almost magical powers to the charismatic individual.[20] Some writers describe charisma is a special "gift" or trait within the charismatic person, while others say it is mainly in the eyes of the beholder. However, all agree that charisma produces a high degree of trust, respect, and devotion towards the charismatic individual.

Aspiring entrepreneurs often appear on the highly popular CBC show *Dragons' Den* specifically to pitch their ideas to Arlene Dickinson (right) because they want to tap into the marketing mogul's significant communications expertise. For example, after eleven weeks on the market, nutritionist and author Joey Shulman (left) already had sales for her low-calorie snack SkinnyChews of $152,000 at margins of 64 percent with minimal marketing. Shulman explains that she made a pitch on *Dragons' Den* not for the investment money, but because she needed marketing assistance to get "the word to the masses" about the product.[21] She agreed to Dickinson's deal of $375,000 for a 25 percent stake plus $375,000 worth of media placement. Although other Dragon investors put forth more generous bids, with David Chilton of *The Wealthy Barber* fame offering Shulman exactly what she asked for, partnering with Dickinson made sense to Shulman because of the marketing maven's expertise. Dickinson, a self-made multi-millionaire and marketing pioneer, is owner of Venture Communications, a creative marketing powerhouse recognized as one of the 50 Best Managed Companies in Canada. Dickinson recently launched a social media website, YouInc.com, for entrepreneurs seeking to launch a business. Dickinson's website provides tips and professional advice from experts who participate in entrepreneur-created clusters called flash groups.

Contingencies of Power

LO2

Let's say that you have expert power because of your ability to forecast and possibly even prevent dramatic changes in the organization's environment. Does this expertise mean that you are influential? Not necessarily. As was illustrated earlier in Exhibit 10.2, sources of power generate power only under certain conditions. Four important contingencies of that effect to what degree power can be invoked or used are substitutability, centrality, visibility, and discretion.[22]

SUBSTITUTABILITY

substitutability A contingency of power pertaining to the availability of alternatives.

Substitutability refers to the availability of alternatives. Power is strongest when someone has a monopoly over a valued resource. Conversely, power decreases as the number of alternative sources of the critical resource increases. If you–and no one else–has expertise across the organization on an important issue, you would be more powerful than if several people in your company possess this valued knowledge. Conversely, power decreases as the number of alternative sources of the critical resource increases. Substitutability refers not only to other sources that offer the resource, but also to substitutions of the resource itself. For instance, labour unions are weakened when companies introduce technologies that replace the need for their union members. Technology is a substitute for employees and, consequently, reduces union power.

Nonsubstitutability is strengthened by controlling access to the resource. Professions and labour unions gain power by controlling knowledge, tasks, or labour to perform important activities. For instance, the medical profession is powerful because it controls who can perform specific medical procedures. Labour unions that dominate an industry effectively control access to labour needed to perform key jobs. Employees become nonsubstitutable when they possess knowledge (such as operating equipment or serving clients) that is not documented or readily available to others. Nonsubstitutability also occurs when people differentiate their resource from the alternatives. Some people claim that consultants use this tactic. They take skills and knowledge that many other consulting firms can provide and wrap them into a package (with the latest buzz words, of course) so that it looks like a service that no one else can offer.

CENTRALITY

centrality A contingency of power pertaining to the degree and nature of interdependence between the power holder and others.

Centrality refers to the power holder's importance based on the degree and nature of interdependence with others.[23] Centrality increases with the number of people dependent on you as well as how quickly and severely they are affected by that dependence. Think about your own centrality for a moment: If you decided not to show up for work or school tomorrow, how many people would have difficulty performing their jobs because of your absence? How soon after they arrive at work would these coworkers notice that you are missing and would have to adjust their tasks and work schedule as a result? If you have high centrality, most people in the organization would be adversely affected by your absence, and they would be affected quickly.

The extent to which centrality leverages power is apparent in well-timed labour union strikes, such as the New York City transit strike during the busy Christmas shopping season a few years ago. The illegal three-day work stoppage clogged roads and caused half of city workers to miss or arrive very late for work. "[The Metropolitan Transit Authority] told us we got no power, but we got power," said one striking transit worker. "We got the power to stop the city."[24] This example reveals that various contingencies of power can work in tandem to concentrate power. In this situation, we see that since New Yorkers rely on public transit more than some urban dwellers, substitutability and centrality converge to enhance power for the union.

VISIBILITY

Lucy Shadbolt and her team members work from home and other remote locations for most of her workweek. While the manager of British Gas New Energy enjoys this freedom, she also knows that working remotely can be a career liability due to the lack of visibility. "When I go into the office, where we hot-desk, I have to make an effort to position myself near my boss," says Shadbolt. "You need to consciously build relationships when you don't have those water-cooler moments naturally occurring."[25]

Lucy Shadbolt recognizes that power does not flow to unknown people in the organization. Instead, employees gain power when their talents remain in the forefront of the minds of their boss, coworkers, and others. In other words, power increases with your visibility. One way to increase visibility is to take people-oriented jobs and work on projects that require frequent interaction with senior executives. "You can take visibility in steps," advises an executive at a pharmaceutical firm. "You can start by making yourself visible in a small group, such as a staff meeting. Then when you're comfortable with that, seek out larger arenas."[26]

Debating Point:

HOW MUCH POWER DO CEOS REALLY POSSESS?

It seems reasonable to assume that chief executive officers wield enormous power. They have legitimate power by virtue of their position at the top of the organizational hierarchy. They also have tremendous reward and coercive power because they direct budgets and other resources towards or away from various individuals and work units. Refusing to go along with the CEO's wishes can be an unfortunate career decision. Some CEOs also gain referent power because their lofty position creates an aura of reverence. Even in this era of equality and low power distance, most employees further down the organization are in awe when the top executive visits.

CEO power is equally apparent through various contingencies. Top executives are almost always visible; some amplify that visibility when they become synonymous with the company's brand.[27] CEOs also have high centrality. Few strategic decisions are put into motion unless the top dog is on board. CEOs are supposed to have replacements-in-waiting (to make them substitutable), yet more than a few don't take enough time to mentor an heir-apparent. Some CEOs create an image of being too unique to be replicated.

These points make it evident that CEOs have considerable power . . . except that many CEOs and a few experts don't agree.[28] New CEOs quickly discover that they no longer have expertise over a specific area of the company or subject matter. Instead, they oversee the entire organization and its vast external environment—a domain so broad that CEOs necessarily become jacks-of-all-trades and masters-of-none. Consequently, more than any other position, the CEO depends on the expertise of others to get things done. CEOs don't even have much knowledge about what goes on in the organization. Reliable sources of information become more guarded when communicating to the top dog; employees further down the hierarchy carefully filter information so the CEO hears more of the good and less of the bad news.

The biggest Achilles heel for CEO power is that their discretion is much more restricted than most people realize. To begin with, CEOs are rarely at the top of the power pyramid. Instead, they report to the company board, which can reject their proposals and fire them for acting contrary to the board's wishes. The board's power over the CEO is particularly strong when the company has one or two dominant shareholders. But CEOs have been fired by the board even when the company's ownership is dispersed and the CEO is the company's founder! At one time, some CEOs had more power by serving as the board's chair and personally selecting board members. Today, corporate governance rules and laws have curtailed this practice, resulting in more power for the board and less power for the CEO.[29]

The CEO's discretion is also held in check by the power of various groups within the organization. One such group is the CEO's own executive team. These executives constantly monitor their boss, because their careers and reputation are affected by his or her actions, and some of them are eager to fill the top job themselves.[30] Similarly, the actions of hospital CEOs are restricted to some extent by the interests and preferences of physicians associated with the hospital.

One cross-cultural study found that the CEO's discretion is limited in countries where laws offer greater rights to many stakeholders (rather than just shareholders) and give employees more protection from dismissal and other company actions. The study also reported that the CEO's discretion is limited in cultures with high uncertainty avoidance, because these social values require executives to take measured rather than bold steps towards change.[31]

You might think that CEOs have one remaining form of discretion: They can still overrule their vice presidents. Technically they can, but one group of experts points out that doing so has nasty repercussions. It triggers resentment and sends morale into a tailspin. Worse, this action motivates direct reports to seek out the CEO's involvement much earlier, which overwhelms the CEO's schedule and leaves less time for other priorities. A related observation is that CEOs are the official voice of the organization, so they have much less discretion about what they can say in public or in private conversations.

Finally, though it seems safe to claim that CEOs have high centrality, a few executives see their situation differently. "I am the least important person in this building," claims Mike Brown, CEO of Provena United Samaritans Medical Center in Illinois. "This place would run without me for weeks, but the most important groups here are the people taking care of the patients."[32]

Employees also gain visibility by being, quite literally, visible. Some people (such as Lucy Shadbolt) strategically locate themselves in more visible work areas, such as those closest to the boss or where other employees frequently pass by. People often use public symbols as subtle (and not-so-subtle) cues to make their power sources known to others. Many professionals display their educational diplomas and awards on office walls to remind visitors of their expertise. Medical professionals wear white coats with a stethoscope around their neck to symbolize their legitimate and expert power in hospital settings. Other people play the game of "face time"–spending more time at work and showing that they are working productively.

DISCRETION

The freedom to exercise judgment–to make decisions without referring to a specific rule or receiving permission from someone else–is another important contingency of power in organizations.[33] Consider the plight of first-line supervisors. It may seem they have legitimate, reward, and coercive power over employees, but this power is often curtailed by specific rules.[34] Take for example the Tim Hortons' employee whose employment was terminated by "three managers" after offering a single 16-cent Timbit to a baby because of the store's policy prohibiting giving away free food.[35] Head officer later reinstated the employee. This example illustrates the various power dynamics of discretion. We see that the store managers punished an employee for exercising her discretion in good faith, but contrary of company policy; whereas head office exercised its discretion to overrule the authority of the managers.

Research indicates that managerial discretion varies considerably across industries, and that managers with an internal locus of control are viewed as more powerful because they don't act like they lack discretion in their job.[36]

In summary, power decreases with more substitutability alternatives and power increases with higher levels of the contingency factors of centrality, discretion, and visibility.

connect

Do you have a guanxi *orientation?* Visit **connect.mcgrawhill.com** to assess how well you nurture interpersonal connections.

The Power of Social Networks

LO3

"It's not what you know, but who you know that counts!" This often-heard statement reflects the idea that employees get ahead not just by developing their competencies, but by locating themselves within **social networks**–social structures of individuals or social units (e.g., departments, organizations) that are connected to each other through one or more forms of interdependence.[37] Some networks are held together due to common interests, such as when employees who exercise over their lunch hours spend more time together. Other networks form around common status, expertise, kinship, or physical proximity. For instance, employees are more likely to form networks with coworkers who have common educational backgrounds and occupational interests.[38]

social networks Social structures of individuals or social units that are connected to each other through one or more forms of interdependence.

Social networks exist everywhere because people have a drive to bond. However, there are cultural differences in the norms of active network involvement. Several writers suggest that social networking is more of a central life activity in Asian cultures that emphasize *guanxi*, a Chinese term referring to an individual's network of social connections. *Guanxi* is an expressive activity because being part of a close-knit network of family and friends reinforces one's self-concept. *Guanxi* is also an instrumental activity because it is a strategy for receiving favours and opportunities from others. People across all cultures rely on social networks for both expressive and instrumental purposes, but these activities seem to be somewhat more explicit in Confucian cultures.[39]

social capital The knowledge and other resources available to people or social units (teams, organizations) from a durable network that connects them to others.

SOCIAL CAPITAL AND SOURCES OF POWER

Social networks generate power through **social capital**–the goodwill and resulting resources shared among members in a social network.[40] Social networks produce trust, support, sympathy, forgiveness, and similar forms of goodwill among network members, and this goodwill motivates and enables network members to share resources with each other.[41]

Social networks offer a variety of resources, each of which potentially enhances the power of its members. Probably the best-known resource is information from other network members, which improves the individual's expert power.[42] The goodwill of social capital opens communication pipelines among those within the network. Network members receive valuable knowledge more easily and more quickly from fellow network members than do people outside that network.[43] With better information access and timeliness, members have more power because their expertise is a scarce resource; it is not widely available to people outside the network.

Increased visibility is a second contributor to a person's power through social networks. When asked to recommend someone for valued positions, other network members more readily think of you than people outside the network. Similarly, they are more likely to mention your name when asked to identify people with expertise in your areas of knowledge. A third resource from social networks is increased referent power. People tend to gain referent power through networking because members of the network identify with or at least have greater trust in each other. Referent power is also apparent by the fact that reciprocity increases among network members as they become more embedded in the network.[44]

Networks can also help with salary negotiations. In one study, a group of researchers examined data from over 3000 salary negotiations in a high-tech company over a 10-year period. As expected, they found that job applicants who were racial minorities negotiated lower salaries than those who were majority members. However, they found that this effect was dramatically reduced when they controlled for the number of social ties a person had. In this case, a social tie refers to whether someone knows an existing employee of the company. The implication, then, is that networking has the potential to benefit everyone, but especially those who are visible minorities.[45]

A common misperception is that social networks are free spirits that cannot be orchestrated by corporate leaders. In reality, company structures and practices can shape these networks to some extent.[46] But even if organizational leaders don't try to manage social networks, they need to be aware of them. Indeed, people gain power in organizations by knowing what the social networks around them look like.[47] "You look at an org chart within a company and you see the distribution of power that should be," says a senior marketing executive at Thomson Reuters. "You look at the dynamics in the social networks [to] see the distribution of power that is. It reflects where information is flowing–who is really driving things."[48]

Operations staff at a global oil and gas company were not using the best available production methods because they didn't share best practices with their peers in other countries or with the company's technical experts (see left diagram above). Instead, employees shared information mainly with local coworkers and technical staff who they already knew well. The company's solution was to transfer some field staff to teams in other regions. These transfers eventually formed and strengthened network relationships across borders (see right diagram), which dramatically improved knowledge sharing and social capital. Within a year, productivity increased by 10 percent and costs due to poor quality fell by two-thirds.[49]

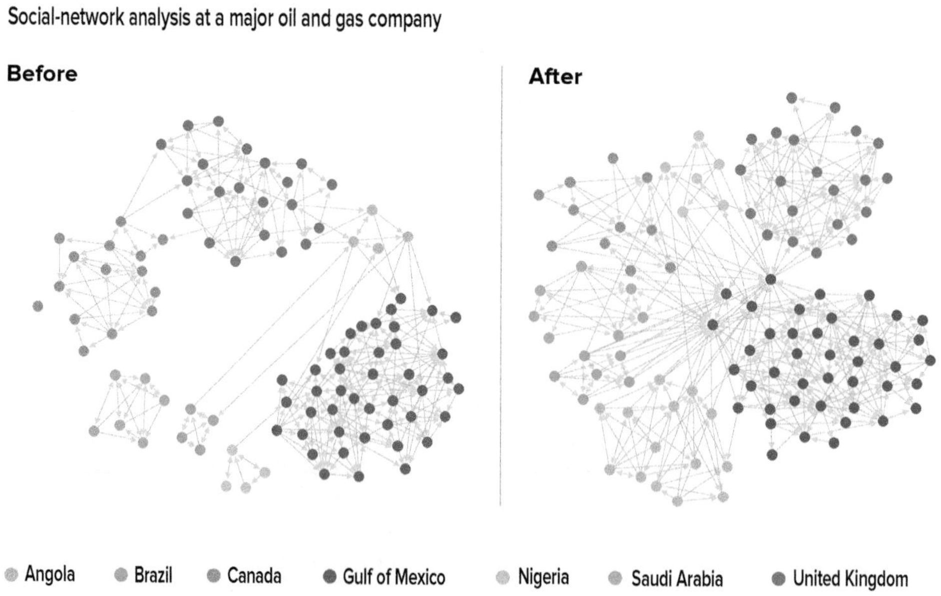

Source: Exhibit from "Organizing for an emerging world," July 2012, *McKinsey Quarterly,* www.mckinsey.com/insights/mckinsey_quarterly. McKinsey & Company. Reprinted by permission.

GAINING POWER THROUGH SOCIAL NETWORKS

How do individuals (and teams and organizations) gain the most social capital from social networks? To answer this question, we need to consider the number, depth, variety, and centrality of connections that people have in their networks.

Strong Ties, Weak Ties, Many Ties The volume of information, favours, and other social capital that people receive from networks usually increases with the number of people connected to you. Some people have an amazing capacity to maintain their connectivity with many people, and emerging communication technologies (Twitter, Facebook, LinkedIn, etc.) have further amplified this capacity to maintain these numerous connections.[50] At the same time, the more people you know, the less time and energy you have to form "strong ties." Strong ties are close-knit relationships, which are evident from how often we interact with people, how much we share resources with them, and whether we have multiple or single-purpose relationships with them (e.g., friend, coworker, sports partner). The main advantages of having strong ties are that they offer resources more quickly and sometimes more plentifully than are available in weak ties (i.e., acquaintances).

Some minimal connection strength is necessary to remain in any social network, but strong connections aren't necessarily the most valuable ties. Instead, having weak ties (i.e., being merely acquaintances) with people from diverse networks can be more valuable than having strong ties (i.e., having close friendships) with people in similar networks.[51] Why is this so? Close ties– our close-knit circle of friends– tend to be similar to us, and similar people tend to have the same information and connections that we already have.[52] Weak ties, on the other hand, are acquaintances who are usually different from us and therefore offer resources we do not possess. Furthermore, by serving as a "bridge" across several unrelated networks, we receive unique resources from each network rather than more of the same resources. In addition, sometimes rules and regulations preclude individuals gaining an advantage from close social connections, e.g., several Canadian jurisdictions allow employers to have anti-nepotism policies prohibiting employment of family members.

The strength of weak ties is most apparent in job hunting and career development.[53] People with diverse networks tend to be more successful job seekers because they have a wider net to catch new job opportunities. In contrast, people who belong to similar overlapping networks tend to receive fewer leads, many of which they already knew about. As careers require more movement across many organizations and industries, you need to establish connections with people across a diverse range of industries, professions, and other spheres of life.

Social Network Centrality Earlier in this chapter, we explained that centrality is an important contingency of power. This contingency also applies to social networks.[54] The more central a person (or team or organization) is located in the network, the more social capital and therefore more power he/she acquires. Centrality is your importance in that network. Three factors determine your centrality in a social network. One factor is your "betweenness," which literally refers to how much you are located between others in the network. In Exhibit 10.3, Person A has high betweenness centrality because he/she is a gatekeeper who controls the flow of information to and from many other people in the network. Person G has less betweenness, whereas Person F and several other network members in the diagram have no betweenness. The more betweenness you have, the more you control the distribution of information and other resources to people on either side of you.

A second factor in centrality is the number or percentage of connections you have to others in the network (called "degree centrality"). Recall that the more people connected to you, the more resources (information, favours, etc.) will be available. The number of connections also increases centrality because you are more visible to other members of the network. Although being a member of a network gives you access to resources in that network, having a direct connection to people makes that resource sharing more fluid.

A third factor in centrality is the "closeness" of the relationship with others in the network. High closeness occurs when a member has shorter, more direct, and efficient paths or connections with others in the network. For example, Person A has fairly high closeness centrality because he/she has direct paths to most of the network, and many of these paths are short (implying efficient and high quality communication links). Your centrality increases with the closeness with others because they are affected more quickly and significantly by you.

EXHIBIT 10.3

Centrality in Social Networks

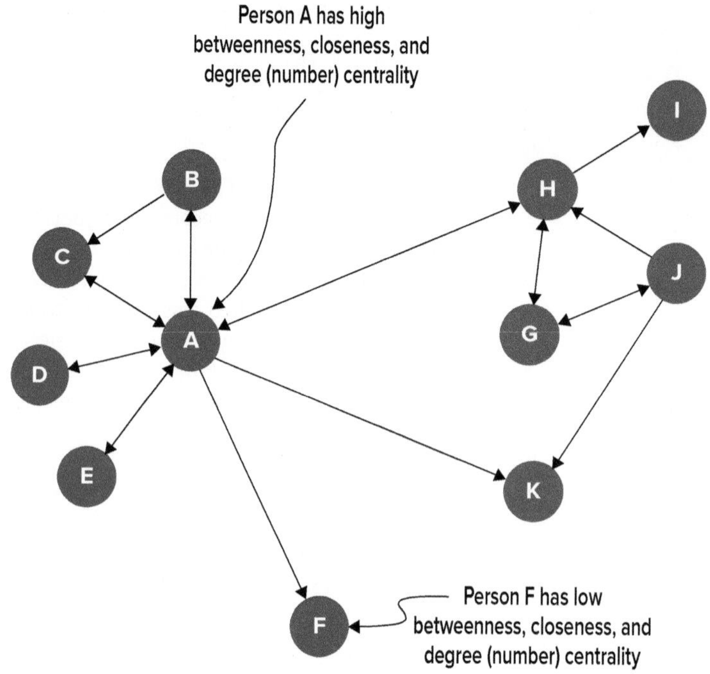

structural hole An area between two or more dense social network areas that lacks network ties.

One last observation is that Exhibit 10.3 illustrates two clusters of people in the network. The gap between these two clusters is called a **structural hole.**[55] Notice that Person A provides the main bridge across this structural hole (connecting to H and K in the other cluster). This bridging role gives Person A additional power in the network. By bridging this gap, Person A becomes a broker–someone who connects two independent networks and controls information flow between them. Research shows that the more brokering relationships you have, the more likely you are to get early promotions and higher pay.

The Dark Side of Social Networks Social networks are natural elements of all organizations, yet they can create a formidable barrier to those who are not actively connected to it.[56] Women are often excluded from informal management networks because they do not participate in golf games and other male-dominated social events. Nina Smith, who leads Sage Software's Business Management Division, has had several conversations with female executives about these power dynamics. "I'm still trying to knock down the Boys Club and I still have women at Sage coming to me and saying, 'Nina, that's the boys' network and I can't get in."[57] Several years ago, executives at Deloitte Touche Tohmatsu discovered that inaccessibility to powerful social networks partly explained why many junior female employees left the accounting and consulting firm before reaching partnership level. The global accounting and consulting firm now relies on mentoring, formal women's network groups, and measurement of career progress to ensure that female staff members have the same career development opportunities as their male colleagues.[58] Empirical research confirms that the effect of social networks can constrain the opportunities and advancement of women to corporate board memberships.[59]

Consequences of Power

How does power affect the power holder? The answer depends to some extent on the type of power.[60] When people feel empowered (high self-determination, meaning, competence, and impact), they believe they have power over themselves and freedom from being influenced by others. Empowerment tends to increase motivation, job satisfaction, organizational commitment, and job performance. However, this feeling of being in control and free from others' authority also increases automatic rather than mindful thinking. In particular, people who feel powerful usually are more likely to rely on stereotypes, have difficulty empathizing, and generally have less accurate perceptions compared with people with less power.[61]

The other type of power is one in which an individual has power over others, such as the legitimate, reward, and coercive power that managers have over employees in the workplace. This type of power produces a sense of duty or responsibility for the people over whom you have power. Consequently, people who have power over others tend to be more mindful of their actions and engage in less stereotyping.

connect

How do you influence coworkers and other peers? See page 267 or visit **connect.mcgrawhill.com** to discover the types of influence you might employ and your preference for various tactics.

Influencing Others

LO4

influence Any behaviour that attempts to alter someone's attitudes or behaviour.

So far, this chapter has focused on the sources and contingencies of power as well as power derived from social networks. But power is only the *capacity* to influence others. It represents the potential to change someone's attitudes and behaviour. **Influence,** on the other hand, refers to any behaviour that attempts to alter someone's attitudes or behaviour.[62] Influence is power in motion. It applies one or more sources of power to get people to alter their beliefs, feelings, and activities. Consequently, our interest in the remainder of this chapter is on how people use power to influence others.

Influence tactics are woven throughout the social fabric of all organizations. This is because influence is an essential process through which people coordinate their efforts and act in concert to achieve organizational objectives. Indeed, influence is central to the definition of leadership. Influence operates down, across, and up the corporate hierarchy. Executives ensure that subordinates complete required tasks. Employees influence coworkers to help them with their job assignments. And as Global Connections 10.1 describes, upward influence tactics–better known as managing your boss–are important for your personal career success and achievement of the organization's objectives.

EXHIBIT 10.4 Types of Influence Tactics in Organizations

Influence Tactic	Description
Silent authority	Influencing behaviour through legitimate power without explicitly referring to that power base
Assertiveness	Actively applying legitimate and coercive power by applying pressure or threats
Information control	Explicitly manipulating someone else's access to information for the purpose of changing their attitudes and/or behaviour
Coalition formation	Forming a group that attempts to influence others by pooling the resources and power of its members
Upward appeal	Gaining support from one or more people with higher authority or expertise
Persuasion	Using logical arguments, factual evidence, and emotional appeals to convince people of the value of a request
Impression management (including ingratiation)	Actively shaping through self-presentation and other means the perceptions and attitudes that others have of us, which includes ingratiation (refers to the influencer's attempt to be more liked by the targeted person or group)
Exchange	Promising benefits or resources in exchange for the target person's compliance

Global Connections 10.1:

THE ART AND SCIENCE OF MANAGING YOUR BOSS[63]

Iain McMath doesn't like to have an avalanche of information hinder his executive decision process. "I do things based on intuition, so when I meet with my financial director I only need a one-page summary," says the managing director of services firm Sodexo Motivation Solutions Ltd. in Surrey, England. Unfortunately, the financial director didn't initially figure out McMath's preferences. "She . . . . was coming to the meetings with a file of 600 pages," McMath recalls. "I would then get frustrated because she gave me too much information, and she would get frustrated because she thought I didn't understand the importance of the data."

McMath's financial director eventually adjusted her behaviour to fit her boss's preferences. This alignment not only reduced conflict and frustration; it helped the financial director to manager her boss by creating a more favourable impression. Managing your boss is the process of improving the relationship with your manager for the benefit of each other and the organization. It includes developing bases of power that enable you to influence the manager to achieve organizational objectives. Most executives say it is a key factor in everyone's career success. "It is crucial to understand how to manage your manager," says Tracey Andrews, manager of learning and development at British department store chain John Lewis. "Start by getting to know how your manager thinks and works and what his/her priorities are."

Along with aligning your behaviour with the manager's preferred style, managing your boss involves becoming a valuable resource by making your manager's job easier. This begins by performing your own job well. "Managing your manager is all about going that extra step," advises Chris Barber, who leads a team of 12 people as director of a photography studio in Warwickshire, UK. "It doesn't mean manipulating people . . . it's about doing your job well and helping your manager to get the best results."

Managing your boss also requires some impression management. For example, you need to "be a 'problem solver' rather than a 'problem pyromaniac'," says John Shetcliffe, Managing Director, John Shetcliffe Marketing in Hertfordshire, England. Problem pyromaniacs turn everything into problems for the boss to fix, whereas problem solvers offer the boss solutions when problems arise. Shetcliffe recommends a related impression management strategy for managing your boss: "Don't supply just bad news; announce good news too. Otherwise, little by little you become the bad news!"

monkeybusinessimages/iStock/Thinkstock

Managing your boss is an important form of influence in organizations. "It is crucial to understand how to manage your manager," says an executive at British department store chain John Lewis.

TYPES OF INFLUENCE TACTICS

Organizational behaviour researchers have devoted considerable attention to the various types of influence tactics found in organizational settings. They do not agree on a definitive list, but the most commonly discussed influence tactics are identified in Exhibit 10.4 and described over the next few pages.[64] The first five are known as "hard" influence tactics because they force behaviour change through position power (legitimate, reward, and coercion). The latter three–persuasion, impression management, and exchange–are called "soft" tactics because they rely more on personal sources of power (referent, expert) and appeal to the target person's attitudes and needs.

Silent Authority The silent application of authority occurs where someone complies with a request because of the requester's legitimate power as well as the target person's role expectations.[65] This deference occurs when you comply with your boss's request to complete a particular task. If the task is within your job scope and your boss has the right to make this request, then this influence strategy operates without negotiation, threats, persuasion, or other tactics. Silent authority is the most common form of influence in high power distance cultures.[66]

Assertiveness Assertiveness might be called "vocal authority" because it involves actively applying legitimate and coercive power to influence others. This includes persistently reminding the target of his or her obligations, frequently checking the target's work, confronting the target, and using threats of sanctions to force compliance.

Information Control Earlier in this chapter we explained that people with centrality in social networks have the power to control information. This power translates into influence when the power holder selectively distributes information such that it reframes the situation and causes others to change their attitudes and/or behaviour. Controlling information might include withholding information that is more critical or favourable, or by distributing information to some people but not to others. According to one major survey, almost half of employees believe coworkers keep others in the dark about work issues if it helps their own cause. Another study found that CEOs influence their board of directors by selectively feeding and withholding information.[68]

OB by the NUMBERS

Bullying Bosses By the Numbers[67]

64% of 16,517 workers polled worldwide say they have been bullied at work.

57% of 800 Canadian human resource professionals polled believe that managers bullying/intimidating employees is a significant problem in today's workplace.

36% of British employees polled say they had broken down in tears from cruel taunts from bosses.

25% of 900 American pharmacists surveyed say that management has used intimidation to get them to achieve performance targets.

24% of 5,600 American employees say they have been yelled at by their boss in front of coworkers.

Coalition Formation When people lack sufficient power alone to influence others in the organization, they might form a **coalition** of people who support the proposed change. A coalition is influential in three ways.[69] First, it pools the power and resources of many people, so the coalition potentially has more influence than any number of people operating alone. Second, the coalition's mere existence can be a source of power by symbolizing the legitimacy of the issue. In other words, a coalition creates a sense that the issue deserves attention because it has broad support. Third, coalitions tap into the power of the social identity process introduced in Chapter 3. A coalition is an informal group that advocates a new set of norms and behaviours. If the coalition has a broad-based membership (i.e., its members come from various parts of the organization), then other employees are more likely to identify with that group and, consequently, accept the ideas the coalition is proposing.

coalition A group that attempts to influence people outside the group by pooling the resources and power of its members.

Upward Appeal **Upward appeal** involves calling upon higher authority or expertise, or symbolically relying on these sources to support the influencer's position. It occurs when someone says "The boss likely agrees with me on this matter; let's find out!" Upward appeal also occurs when relying on the authority of the firm's policies or values. By reminding others that your request is consistent with the organization's overarching goals, you are implying support from senior executives without formally involving them.

upward appeal A type of influence in which someone with higher authority or expertise is called on in reality or symbolically to support the influencer's position.

Persuasion *Persuasion*, which we discussed in Chapter 9, is one of the most effective influence strategies for career success. The ability to present facts, logical arguments, and emotional appeals to change another person's attitudes and behaviour is not just an acceptable way to influence others; in many societies, it is a noble art and a quality of effective leaders. The effectiveness of persuasion as an influence tactic depends on characteristics of the persuader, message content, communication medium, and the audience being persuaded (see Exhibit 10.5).[70] People are more persuasive when listeners believe they have expertise and credibility, such as when the persuader does not seem to profit from the persuasion attempt and states a few points against the position.

The message is more important than the messenger when the issue is important to the audience. Persuasive message content acknowledges several points of view so the audience does not feel cornered by the speaker. The message should also be limited to a few strong arguments, which are repeated a few times, but not too frequently. The message should use emotional appeals (such as graphically showing the unfortunate consequences of a bad decision), but only in combination with logical arguments and specific recommendations to overcome the threat. Finally, message content is more persuasive when the audience is warned

EXHIBIT 10.5 **Elements of Persuasion**

Persuasion Element	Characteristics of Effective Persuasion
Persuader characteristics	Expertise Credibility No apparent profit motive Appears somewhat neutral (acknowledges benefits of the opposing view)
Message content	Multiple viewpoints (not exclusively supporting the supported option) Limited to a few strong arguments (not many arguments) Repeat arguments, but not excessively Use emotional appeals in combination with logical arguments Offers specific solutions to overcome the stated problems Inoculation effect—audience warned of counterarguments that opposition will present
Communication medium	Media-rich channels are usually more persuasive
Audience characteristics	Persuasion is LESS effective when the audience: • has higher self-esteem • has higher intelligence • has a self-concept tied to an opposing position

inoculation effect A persuasive communication strategy of warning listeners that others will try to influence them in the future and that they should be wary about the opponent's arguments.

impression management Actively shaping through self-presentation and other means the perceptions and attitudes that others have of us.

about opposing arguments. This **inoculation effect** causes listeners to generate counterarguments to the anticipated persuasion attempts, which makes the opponent's subsequent persuasion attempts less effective.[71]

Two other considerations when persuading people are the medium of communication and characteristics of the audience. Generally, persuasion works best in face-to-face conversations and through other media-rich communication channels. The personal nature of face-to-face communication increases the persuader's credibility, and the richness of this channel provides faster feedback that the influence strategy is working. With respect to audience characteristics, it is more difficult to persuade people who have high self-esteem and intelligence, as well as a self-concept that is strongly tied to the opposing viewpoint.[72]

Impression Management (including Ingratiation) Silent authority, assertiveness, information control, coalitions, and upward appeals are somewhat (or very!) forceful ways to influence other people. In contrast, a very "soft" influence tactic is **impression management**–actively shaping the perceptions and attitudes that others have of us.[73] Impression management mostly occurs through self-presentation. We craft our public images to create various forms, such as being important, vulnerable, threatening, or pleasant. For the most part, employees routinely engage in pleasant impression management behaviours to satisfy the basic norms of social behaviour, such as the way they dress and how they behave towards colleagues and customers.

"Our task is to find out what management thinks we should be doing, and then to make management think we're doing it."

Credit: Copyright © Ted Goff.

Impression management is a common strategy for people trying to get ahead in the workplace. In fact, career professionals encourage people to develop a personal "brand"; that is, to form and display an (accurate) impression of your distinctive competitive advantage.[74] Furthermore, people who master the art of personal branding rely on impression management through distinctive personal characteristics such as black shirts, tinted hair, or unique signatures. "In today's economy, your personal brand is being judged every day," says Coca-Cola Co. senior vice president Jerry Wilson. "Either position yourself, or others will position you."[75]

One sub-category of impression management is *ingratiation*, which is any attempt to increase liking by, or perceived similarity to, some targeted person.[76] Ingratiation comes in several flavours. Employees might flatter their boss in front of others, demonstrate that they have similar attitudes as their boss (e.g., agreeing with the boss's proposal), and ask their boss for advice. Ingratiation is one of the more effective influence tactics at boosting a person's career success (i.e., performance appraisal feedback, salaries, and promotions).[77] However, people who engage in high levels of ingratiation are less (not more) influential and less likely to get promoted.[78] Why the opposite effect? Those who engage in too much ingratiation are viewed as insincere and self-serving. The terms "apple polishing" and "brown-nosing" are applied to those who ingratiate to excess or in ways that suggest selfish motives for the ingratiation.

Exchange Exchange activities involve the promise of benefits or resources in exchange for the target person's compliance with your request. Negotiation is an integral part of exchange influence activities. For instance, you might negotiate your boss for a day off in return for working a less desirable shift at a future date. Exchange also includes applying the norm of reciprocity that we described earlier, such as reminding the target of past benefits or favours with the expectation that the target will now make up for that debt. Earlier in this chapter we explained how people gain power through social networks. They also use norms of reciprocity to influence others in the network. Active networkers build up "exchange credits" by helping colleagues in the short-term for reciprocal benefits in the long term.

CONSEQUENCES AND CONTINGENCIES OF INFLUENCE TACTICS

Faced with a variety of influence strategies, you are probably asking: Which ones are best? The best way to answer this question is to describe how people react when others try to influence them: resistance, compliance, or commitment (see Exhibit 10.6).[79] *Resistance* occurs when people or work units oppose the behaviour desired by the influencer. At the extreme, they refuse to engage in the behaviour. However, there are degrees of resistance, such as when people perform the required duties yet demonstrate their continued opposition by performing the tasks poorly or continuing to complain about the imposed work. *Compliance* occurs when

EXHIBIT 10.6

Consequences of Hard and Soft Influence Tactics

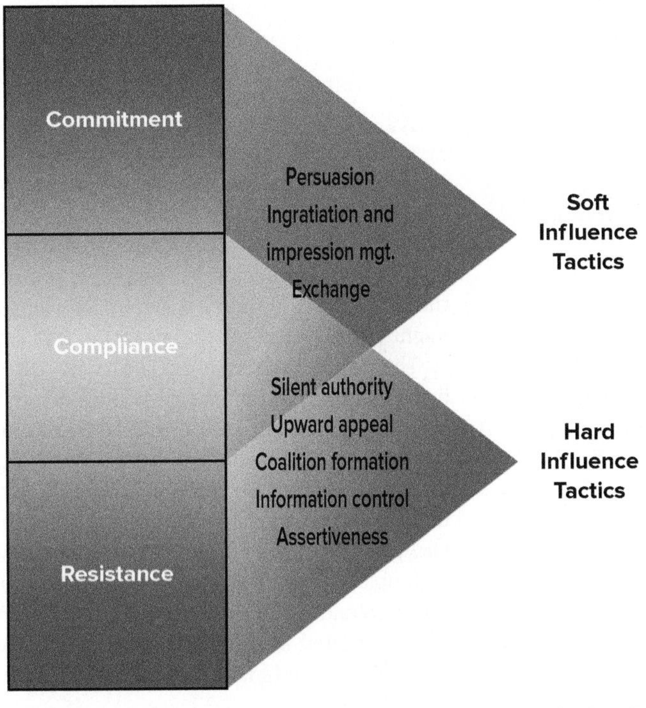

people are motivated to implement the influencer's request for purely instrumental reasons. Without external sources to prompt the desired behaviour, compliance would not occur. Furthermore, compliance usually involves engaging in the behaviour with no more effort than is required. *Commitment* is the strongest outcome of influence, whereby people identify with the influencer's request and are highly motivated to implement it even when extrinsic sources of motivation are not present.

Generally, people react more favourably to "soft" tactics than to "hard" tactics. Soft influence tactics rely on personal sources of power (expert and referent power), which tend to build commitment to the influencer's request. In contrast, hard tactics rely on position power (legitimate, reward, and coercion), so they tend to produce compliance or, worse, resistance. Hard tactics also tend to undermine trust, which can hurt future relationships.

Apart from the general preference for soft rather than hard tactics, the most appropriate influence strategy depends on a few contingencies. One obvious contingency is which sources of power are strongest. Those with expertise tend to have more influence using persuasion, whereas those with a strong legitimate power base are usually more successful applying silent authority.[80] A second contingency is whether the person being influenced is higher, lower, or at the same level in the organization. As an example, employees may face adverse career consequences by being too assertive with their boss. Meanwhile, supervisors who engage in ingratiation and impression management tend to lose the respect of their staff.

Finally, the most appropriate influence tactic depends on personal, organizational, and cultural values.[81] People with a strong power orientation might feel more comfortable using assertiveness, whereas those who value conformity might feel more comfortable with upward appeals. At an organizational level, firms with a competitive culture might foment more use of information control and coalition formation, whereas companies with a learning orientation would likely encourage more influence through persuasion. The preferred influence tactics also vary across societal cultures. Research indicates that ingratiation is much more common among managers in Canada than in Hong Kong, possibly because this tactic disrupts the more distant roles that managers and employees expect in high power distance cultures.

connect

How politically charged is your school? Visit **connect.mcgrawhill.com** to assess the level of organizational politics, and to assist your learning about this topic and influence tactics.

Organizational Politics

LO5

You might have noticed that organizational politics has not been mentioned yet, even though some of the practices or examples described over the past few pages are usually considered political tactics. The phrase was carefully avoided because, for the most part, organizational politics is in the eye of the beholder. You might perceive a coworker's attempt to influence the boss as acceptable behaviour for the good of the organization, whereas someone else might perceive the coworker's tactic as brazen organizational politics.

organizational politics
Behaviours that others perceive as self-serving tactics at the expense of other people and possibly the organization.

This perceptual issue explains why OB experts increasingly discuss influence tactics as behaviours and organizational politics as perceptions.[82] The influence tactics described earlier are perceived as **organizational politics** when they seem to be self-serving behaviours at the expense of others and possibly contrary to the interests of the entire organization. Of course, some tactics are so blatantly selfish and counterproductive that almost everyone correctly sees them as organizational politics. In other situations, however, a person's behaviour might be viewed as political or in the organization's best interest, depending on your point of view.

Employees who experience organizational politics have lower job satisfaction, organizational commitment, organizational citizenship, and task performance, as well as higher levels of work-related stress and motivation to leave the organization. "A politically charged work environment can hinder productivity, erode trust, and lead to morale and retention issues," says

Ciaran Griffin/Photodisc/Thinkstock

The vacation roster is a scarce resource, and resource scarcity brings out the worst office politics. One recent poll reported that 13 percent of British employees refused to tell others when they would take their vacations, so coworkers wouldn't book the same dates. Another seven percent said they protected their vacation plans by lying to coworkers about those plans. Five percent were even more Machiavellian; they strategically booked vacation dates that scuttled the preferred holiday times of a disliked coworker. "I know this is true," says an employee from Newport, Wales, who was not part of the survey. "I had a colleague who knew my holiday habits and would go in on January 2nd and book every week that he knew I habitually had for holidays because he knew my wife's holidays were fixed and could not be changed. He didn't really need those days; he did it out of spite."[83]

Renan Silva, a corporate project management office specialist at Serasa Experian, a credit bureau in São Paulo, Brazil.[84] And because political tactics serve individuals rather than organizations, they potentially divert resources away from the organization's effective functioning and potentially threaten its survival.

MINIMIZING ORGANIZATIONAL POLITICS

Researchers have identified several conditions that support organizational politics, so we can identify corresponding strategies to keep political activities to a minimum.[85] First, organizational politics is triggered by scarce resources in the workplace. When budgets are slashed, people rely on political tactics to safeguard their resources and maintain the status quo. Although not easy to maintain or add resources, sometimes this action may be less costly than the consequences of organizational politics.

Second, organizational politics is suppressed when resource allocation decisions are clear and simplified. Political tactics are fuelled by ambiguous, complex, or nonexistent formal rules because those tactics help people get what they want when decisions lack structural guidelines. Third, organizational change tends to bring out more organizational politics, mainly because change creates ambiguity and threatens he employee's power and other valued resources.[86] Consequently, leaders need to apply the organizational change strategies that we describe in Chapter 15, particularly through communication, learning, and involvement. Research has found that employees who are kept informed of what is going on in the organization and who are involved in organizational decisions are less likely to observe organizational politics.

Finally, political behaviour is more common in work units and organizations where it is tolerated and reinforced. Some companies seem to nurture self-serving behaviour through reward systems and by demonstrating it in the behaviours of organizational leaders. To minimize political norms, the organization needs to diagnose and alter systems and role modeling that support self-serving behaviour. They should support organizational values that oppose political tactics, such as altruism and customer focus. One of the most important strategies is for leaders to become role models of organizational citizenship rather than symbols of successful organizational politicians.

connect

How Machiavellian are you? Visit **connect.mcgrawhill.com** to assess how much you value the political tactics emphasized by Machiavelli.

Machiavellian values The belief that deceit is a natural and acceptable way to influence others and that getting more than one deserves is acceptable.

Personal Characteristics Several personal characteristics affect a person's motivation to engage in self-serving behaviour.[87] This includes a strong need for personal as opposed to socialized power. Those with a need for personal power seek power for its own sake and try to acquire more power. Some individuals have strong **Machiavellian values.** Machiavellianism is named after Niccolò Machiavelli, the 16th-century Italian philosopher who wrote *The Prince,* a famous treatise about political behaviour. People with high Machiavellian values are comfortable with getting more than they deserve, and they believe that deceit is a natural and acceptable way to achieve this goal. They seldom trust coworkers and tend to use cruder influence tactics, such as bypassing one's boss or being assertive, to get their own way.[88]

Chapter Summary

LO1 Describe the dependence model of power and describe the five sources of power in organizations.

Power is the capacity to influence others. It exists when one party perceives that he or she is dependent on the other for something of value. However, the dependent person must also have countervailing power–some power over the dominant party–to maintain the relationship and the parties must have some level of trust.

There are five power bases. Legitimate power is an agreement among organizational members that people in certain roles can request certain behaviours of others. This power has restrictions represented by the target person's zone of indifference. It also includes the norm of reciprocity (a feeling of obligation to help someone who has helped you) as well as control over the flow of information to others. Reward power is derived from the ability to control the allocation of rewards valued by others and to remove negative sanctions. Coercive power is the ability to apply punishment. Expert power is the capacity to influence others by possessing knowledge or skills that they value. An important form of expert power is the (perceived) ability to manage uncertainties in the business environment. People have referent power when others identify with them, like them, or otherwise respect them.

LO2 Discuss the four contingencies of power.

Four contingencies determine whether these power bases translate into real power. Individuals and work units are more powerful when they are non-substitutable, that is, there is a lack of alternatives. Employees, work units, and organizations reduce substitutability by controlling tasks, knowledge, and labour, and by differentiating themselves from competitors. A second contingency is centrality. People have more power when they have high centrality, that is, the number of people affected is large and people are quickly affected by their actions. The third contingency, visibility, refers to the idea that power increases to the extent that a person's or work unit's competencies are known to others. Discretion, the fourth contingency of power, refers to the freedom to exercise judgment. Power increases when people have freedom to use their power.

LO3 Explain how people and work units gain power through social networks.

Social networks are social structures of individuals or social units (e.g., departments, organizations) that are connected to each other through one or more forms of interdependence. People receive power in social networks through social capital, which is the goodwill and resulting resources shared among members in a social network. Three main resources from social networks are information, visibility, and referent power.

Employees gain social capital through their relationship in the social network. Social capital tends to increase with the number of network ties. Strong ties (close-knit relationships) can also increase social capital because these connections offer more resources and offer them more quickly. However, having weak ties with people from diverse networks can be more valuable than having strong ties with people in similar networks. Weak ties provide more resources that we do not already possess. Another influence on social capital is the person's centrality in the network. Network centrality is determined in several ways, including the extent to which you are located between others in the network (betweenness), how many direct ties you have (degree), and the closeness of these ties. People also gain power by bridging structural holes– linking two or more clusters of people in a network.

LO4 Describe eight types of influence tactics, three consequences of influencing others, and three contingencies to consider when choosing an influence tactic.

Influence refers to any behaviour that attempts to alter someone's attitudes or behaviour. The most widely studied influence tactics are silent authority, assertiveness, information control, coalition formation, upward appeal, impression management, persuasion, and exchange. "Soft" influence tactics such as friendly persuasion and subtle ingratiation are more acceptable than "hard" tactics such as upward appeal and assertiveness. However, the most appropriate influence tactic also depends on the influencer's power base; whether the person being influenced is higher, lower, or at the same level in the organization; and personal, organizational, and cultural values regarding influence behaviour.

LO5 **Identify the organizational conditions and personal characteristics that support organizational politics, as well as ways to minimize organizational politics.**

Organizational politics refers to influence tactics that others perceive to be self-serving behaviours at the expense of others and sometimes contrary to the interests of the organization. It is more common when ambiguous decisions allocate scarce resources and when the organization tolerates or rewards political behaviour. Individuals with a high need for personal power and strong Machiavellian values have a higher propensity to use political tactics. Organizational politics can be minimized by providing clear rules for resource allocation, establishing a free flow of information, using education and involvement during organizational change, supporting team norms and a corporate culture that discourage dysfunctional politics, and having leaders who role model organizational citizenship rather than political savvy.

Key Terms

centrality, p. 251
charisma, p. 250
coalition, p. 259
countervailing power, p. 246
impression management, p. 260
influence, p. 257
inoculation effect, p. 260
legitimate power, p. 247
Machiavellian values, p. 264
norm of reciprocity, p. 248
organizational politics, p. 262
power, p. 245
referent power, p. 250
social capital, p. 253
social networks, p. 253
structural hole, p. 256
substitutability, p. 251
upward appeal, p. 259

Critical-Thinking Questions

1. What role does countervailing power play in the power relationship? Give an example of your own encounter with countervailing power at school or work.
2. Until recently, a mining company's data resided in the department that was responsible for that information. Property data were on the computers in land administration, hydrocarbon data were in the well administration group, maps were found in the map department, and so on. The executive team concluded that this arrangement was dysfunctional, so the CEO announced that all information would be placed on a central server system so it is widely accessible. If someone needs a colour map, for example, he or she can retrieve it from the central server without going through the map department. Rather than welcome the change, employees in several departments complained, offering several arguments why other groups should not have direct access to their data files. Some departments tried to opt out of the centralized server system. Using the model of sources and contingencies of power, explain why some groups opposed the central server model of data access.
3. You have just been hired as a brand manager of toothpaste for a large consumer products company. Your job mainly involves encouraging the advertising and production groups to promote and manufacture your product more effectively. These departments aren't under your direct authority, although company procedures indicate that they must complete certain tasks requested by brand managers. Describe the sources of power you can use to ensure that the advertising and production departments will help you make and sell toothpaste more effectively.
4. How does social networking increase a person's power? What social networking strategies could you initiate now to potentially enhance your future career success?
5. List the eight influence tactics described in this chapter in terms of how they are used by students to influence their university teachers. Which influence tactic is applied most often? Which is applied least often, in your opinion? To what extent is each influence tactic considered legitimate behaviour or organizational politics?
6. Consider a situation when there is a single female member in a team of six and she is generally excluded from informal gatherings of the team. What kind of influence tactics can she use to make up for this limitation?
7. In the mid-1990s, the CEO of Apple Computer invited the late Steve Jobs (who was not associated with the company at the time) to serve as a special adviser and raise morale among Apple employees and customers. While doing this, Jobs spent more time advising the CEO on how to cut costs, redraw the organization chart, and hire new people. Before long, most of the top people at Apple were Jobs' colleagues, who began to systematically evaluate and weed out teams of Apple employees. While publicly supporting Apple's CEO, Jobs privately criticized him and, in a show of non-confidence, sold 1.5 million shares of Apple stock he had received. This action caught the attention of Apple's board of directors, who soon after decided to replace the CEO with Steve Jobs. The CEO claimed Jobs was a conniving back-stabber who used political tactics to get his way. Others suggest that Apple would be out of business today if he hadn't taken over the company. In your opinion, were Steve Jobs' actions examples of organizational politics? Justify your answer.
8. This book frequently emphasizes that successful companies engage in organizational learning. How do political tactics interfere with organizational learning objectives?

Case Study: RESONUS CORPORATION

By Steven L. McShane, The University of Western Australia. Based on an earlier case written by John A. Seeger.

Frank Choy is normally a quiet person, but his patience has already worn thin by interdepartmental battles. Choy joined Resonus Corporation, a hearing aid designer and manufacturer, eight months ago as director of engineering. Production of the latest product has been delayed by two months and Choy's engineering services department (ESD)–which prepares final manufacturing specifications–is taking the heat as the main culprit for these delays. Similar delays have been occurring at Resonus for the past few years. The previous engineering director was fired after 18 montvhs; the director before him quit after about the same amount of time.

Bill Hunt, CEO of Resonus for the past 15 years, responded to these problems by urging everyone to remain civil. "I'm sure we can resolve these differences if we just learn to get along better," he said whenever a dispute broke out. Hunt disliked firing anyone, but felt the previous engineering director was too confrontational. "I spent too much time smoothing out arguments when he was here," Hunt thought to himself soon after Choy was hired. "Frank (Choy), on the other hand, seems to fit into our culture of collegiality."

Hunt was groomed by the company's founder and took great pride in preserving the organization's family spirit. He also discouraged bureaucracy, believing that Resonus operated best through informal relationships among its managers. Most Resonus executives were similarly informal, except Jacqui Blanc, the production director, who insisted on strict guidelines. Hunt tolerated Blanc's formal style because soon after joining Resonus five years ago, she discovered and cleaned up fraudulent activity involving two production managers and a few suppliers.

The organizational chart shows that Frank Choy oversees two departments: ESD and research. In reality, "Doc" Kalandry, the research director, informally reports directly to the CEO (Hunt) and has never considered the director of engineering as his boss. Hunt actively supports this informal reporting relationship because of Doc's special status in the organization. "Doc Kalandry is a living genius," Hunt told Choy soon after he joined the firm. "With Doc at the helm of research, this company will continue to lead the field in innovation." Hunt's first job at Resonus was in the research group and Choy suspected that Hunt still favoured that group.

Everyone at Resonus seems to love Doc's successful products, his quirky style, and his over-the-top enthusiasm, but some of Choy's ESD staff are also privately concerned. Says one engineer: "Doc is like a happy puppy when he gets a new product idea. He delights in the discovery, but also won't let go of it. He also gets Hunt too enthusiastic. But Doc's too optimistic; we've had hundreds of production change orders already this year. If I were in Frank's shoes, I'd put my foot down on all this new development."

Soon after joining Resonus, Choy realized that ESD employees get most of the blame and little of the credit for their work. When production staff find a design fault, they directly contact the research design engineer who developed the technology rather than the ESD group who prepare the specifications. Research engineers willingly work with production because they don't want to let go of their project. "The designers seem to feel they're losing something when one of us (ESD) tries to help," Choy explains.

Meanwhile, production supervisors regularly critique ESD staff whereas they tend to accept explanations from the higher-status research department engineers. "Production routinely complains about every little specification error, many of which are due to design changes made by the research group," says one frustrated ESD technician. "Many of us have more than 15 years' experience in this work. We shouldn't have to prove our ability all the time, but we spend as much time defending ourselves as we do getting the job done."

Choy's latest troubles occurred when Doc excitedly told Hunt (Resonus' CEO) about new nano-processor technology that he wanted to install in the forthcoming high-end hearing aid product. As with most of Doc's previous last-minute revisions, Hunt endorsed this change and asked Choy and Blanc (the production director) to show their commitment, even though production was scheduled to begin in less than three weeks. Choy wanted to protest, knowing that his department would have to tackle unexpected incompatibility design errors. Instead, he quietly agreed to Hunt's request to avoid acting like his predecessor and facing similar consequences (getting fired). Blanc curtly stated that her group was ready if Choy's ESD unit could get accurate production specifications ready on time and if the sales director would stop making wild delivery promises to customers.

When Doc's revised design specs arrived more than a week later, Choy's group discovered numerous incompatibilities that had to be corrected. Even though several ESD staff were assigned to 12-hour days on the revisions, the final production specifications weren't ready until a couple of days after the deadline. Production returned these specs two days later, noting a few elements that required revision because they were too costly or difficult to manufacture in their current form. By that time, the production director had to give priority to other jobs and move the new hearing aid product further down the queue. This meant that manufacturing of the new product was delayed by at least two months. The sales director was furious and implied that Frank Choy's incompetence was to blame for this catastrophe.

Discussion Questions

1. What sources and contingencies of power existed among the executives and departments at Resonus?
2. What influence tactics were evident in this case study? Would you define any of these influence activities as organizational politics? Why or why not?
3. Suppose you are a consultant invited to propose a solution to the problems facing this organization's product delays. What would you recommend, particularly regarding power dynamics among the executives and departments?

Team Exercise: DECIPHERING THE NETWORK

Purpose This exercise is designed to help students interpret social network maps, including their implications for organizational effectiveness.

Materials The instructor will distribute several social network diagrams to each student.

Instructions (Smaller classes) The instructor will organize students into teams (typically 4 to 7 people, depending on class size). Teams will examine each social network diagram to answer the following questions:

1. What aspects of this diagram suggest that the network is not operating as effectively as possible?
2. Which people in this network seem to be most powerful? Least powerful? What information or features of the diagram lead you to this conclusion?
3. If you were responsible for this group of people, how would you change this situation to improve their effectiveness?

After teams have diagnosed each social network map, the class will debrief by hearing each team's assessments and recommendations.

Instructions (Larger classes) This activity is also possible in large classes by projecting each social network diagram on a screen and giving students a minute or two to examine the diagram. The instructor can then ask specific questions to the class, such as pointing to a specific individual in the network and asking whether he/she has high or low power, what level of centrality is apparent, and whether the individual's connections are mainly strong or weak ties. The instructor might also ask which quadrant on the map indicates the most concern and then allow individual students to provide their explanation why.

Self-Assessment: HOW DO YOU INFLUENCE COWORKERS AND OTHER PEERS?

Purpose This exercise is designed to help you understand different forms of influence when working with coworkers (i.e., people at the same organizational level), as well as estimate your preference for each influence tactic in this context.

Instructions Think about the occasions when a coworker disagreed with you, opposed your preference, or were reluctant to actively support your point of view about something at work. These conflicts might have been about company policy, assignment of job duties, distribution of resources, or any other matter. What did you do to try to get the coworker to support your preference?

The statements below describe ways that people try to influence coworkers. Thinking about your own behaviour **over the past six (6) months,** relatively how often did you engage in each of these behaviours to influence coworkers (i.e., people at a similar level in the organization)?* Circle the most accurate number for each statement. When done, use the scoring key in Appendix B to calculate your results. This exercise is completed alone so students assess themselves honestly without concerns of social comparison. However, class discussion will focus on the types of influence in organizations and which influence tactics are most and least successful or popular when influencing coworkers.

*NOTE: If you have not been in the workforce recently, complete this instrument thinking about influencing another student instead of a coworker.

Coworker Influence Scale

Over the past six months, how often did you use the following tactics to influence coworkers?	Rarely/ Never	Seldom	Sometimes	Often	Almost always
1. Gave the coworker logical reasons why the matter should be decided in my favour.	1	2	3	4	5
2. Made my authority or expertise regarding the issue known without being obvious about it.	1	2	3	4	5
3. Tried to negotiate a solution, where I would offer something in return for the coworker's support.	1	2	3	4	5
4. Demanded that the matter should be resolved in my favour.	1	2	3	4	5
5. Avoided showing the coworker information that opposed my preference.	1	2	3	4	5
6. Enlisted the support of other employees so the coworker would see that I have the more popular preference.	1	2	3	4	5
7. Claimed or demonstrated that my preference has management support.	1	2	3	4	5
8. Said something positive about the coworker, hoping this would increase his/her support for my views.	1	2	3	4	5
9. Tried to convince the coworker using factual information and logic.	1	2	3	4	5
10. Subtly let the coworker know about my expertise on the matter.	1	2	3	4	5
11. Offered to support or assist the coworker on something if he/she would agree with me on this matter.	1	2	3	4	5
12. Showed impatience or frustration with the coworker's opposition to my preference.	1	2	3	4	5

(Continued)

Continued

Over the past six months, how often did you use the following tactics to influence coworkers?	Rarely/ Never	Seldom	Sometimes	Often	Almost always
13. Presented information in a way that looked better for my preference.	1	2	3	4	5
14. Claimed that other staff support my position on this matter.	1	2	3	4	5
15. Suggested or threatened to have the issue resolved by higher management.	1	2	3	4	5
16. Became friendlier towards the coworker, hoping this would create a more favourable opinion of my viewpoint.	1	2	3	4	5
17. Helped the coworker to see the benefits of my preference and/or the negative outcomes of other choices.	1	2	3	4	5
18. Quietly or indirectly showed the coworker my authority, expertise, or right to have this matter decided in my favour.	1	2	3	4	5
19. Mentioned that I had helped to coworker in the past, hoping that he/she would reciprocate by supporting me now.	1	2	3	4	5
20. Let the coworker know that I might be disagreeable or uncooperative in future if he/she did not support me now.	1	2	3	4	5
21. Framed and selected information that mainly agreed with (rather than opposed) my preference.	1	2	3	4	5
22. Made sure that at least a few other people were on my side of this issue.	1	2	3	4	5
23. Pointed out that my view was consistent with the company's values or policies.	1	2	3	4	5
24. Showed more respect towards the coworker, hoping this would encourage him/her to support me.	1	2	3	4	5

SELF-ASSESSMENTS FOR CHAPTER 10

SELF-ASSESSMENT NAME	DESCRIPTION	LOCATION
How do you influence coworkers and other peers?	Assesses the types of influence you might employ and your preference for various tactics.	Page 267 connect
Do you have a *guanxi* orientation?	Estimates the degree to which you display traditional *guanxi* values.	connect
How politically charged is your school?	Assesses the level of organizational politics at your school.	connect
How Machiavellian are you?	Assesses how much you value the political tactics emphasized by Machiavelli.	connect

L'Oréal Canada employees (from left) Ashley Bancroft, Christian Bouchard, and Wendy Stewart say the company's Valorizing Intergenerational Differences training has helped them to leverage the company's creative potential by minimizing dysfunctional conflict and improving relations with coworkers.

Chapter 11

Conflict and Negotiation in the Workplace

LEARNING OBJECTIVES

After reading this chapter, you should be able to:

LO1. Define conflict and debate its positive and negative consequences in the workplace.

LO2. Distinguish task from relationship conflict and describe three strategies to minimize relationship conflict during task conflict episodes.

LO3. Diagram the conflict process model and describe six structural sources of conflict in organizations.

LO4. Outline the five conflict handling styles and discuss the circumstances in which each would be most appropriate.

LO5. Apply the six structural approaches to conflict management and describe the three types of third-party dispute resolution.

LO6. Describe distributive and integrative negotiations and outline strategies skilled negotiators use to claim value and create value.

L'Oréal Canada boasts a diverse workforce. Its 1,200 employees represent 61 nationalities, 42 percent are women, and employees are spread across the three main generations: baby boomers (25%), Gen-X (33%), and Gen-Y (42%). These different forms of diversity have been immensely beneficial to the company and society. "From diversity stems stimulating, rich debates that propel our teams to think forward and encourage innovation," says Marie-Josée Lamothe, L'Oréal Canada's chief marketing officer and chief communications officer.

But rich debates can easily deteriorate into dysfunctional battles when participants fail to keep their differences in perspective. L'Oréal Canada's executives anticipated this risk several years ago as its workforce demography began shifting to a balance across the three generations. (Gen-Y is now its largest cohort.) These generations differed in their needs and expectations, which might lead to dysfunctional intergenerational conflict. "We realized we could be faced with an interesting problem," recalls Marjolaine Rompré, L'Oréal Canada's director of learning and development. "We called it Generation Shock."

Rather than have that generation shock turn into dysfunctional conflict, L'Oréal Canada introduced a full-day seminar, called Valorizing Intergenerational Differences, which aims to help employees across all generations understand and value each other's perceptions, values, and expectations. In one part of the program, for example, employees sit together in their generational cohorts and ask questions to employees in the other cohorts. "Each group is interested and surprised to see what's important to the other group," says Rompré.

Participants say the program leverages the company's creative potential by minimizing dysfunctional conflict and improving relations with coworkers. "The Valorizing Intergenerational Differences training really helped me to understand where people from each generation are coming from," says key account manager Ashley Bancroft, shown left in this photo with national accounts directors Christian Bouchard and Wendy Stewart. It has also helped L'Oréal Canada to become one of the best places to work for in Canada, including one of the country's best diversity employers.[1]

L'Oréal Canada has prospered through diversity, but it has also proactively addressed the potential downside of dysfunctional conflict by introducing a training program to improve mutual understanding. This chapter investigates the dynamics of conflict in organizational settings. It begins by defining conflict and discussing the age-old question: Is conflict good or bad? Next, we look at the conflict process and examine in detail the main factors that cause or amplify conflict. The five styles of handling conflict are then described, including important contingencies of conflict handling as well as gender and cross-cultural differences. Next, we look at the role of managers and others in third-party conflict resolution. The final section of this chapter reviews key issues in negotiating conflict resolution.

The Meaning and Consequences of Conflict

LO1

conflict The process in which one party perceives that its interests are being opposed or negatively affected by another party.

One of the facts of life is that organizations are continuously adapting to their external environment and introducing better ways to transform resources into outputs (see Chapter 1). There is no clear road map on how companies should change, and employees and other stakeholders rarely agree completely on the direction or form of these adjustments. Employees have divergent personal and work goals, which lead them to prefer different directions the organization should take.

These differences in goals and viewpoints, along with a few other key factors described in this chapter, lead to conflict. **Conflict** is a process in which one party perceives that its interests are being opposed or negatively affected by another party.[2] It may occur when one party obstructs another's goals in some way, or just from one party's perception that the other party is going to do so. Conflict is ultimately based on perceptions; it exists whenever one party *believes* that another might obstruct its efforts, whether the other party actually intends to do so.

IS CONFLICT GOOD OR BAD?

One of the oldest debates in organizational behaviour is whether conflict is good or bad–or, more recently, what forms of conflict are good or bad–for organizations.[3] The dominant view over most of this time has been that conflict is dysfunctional.[4] At the turn of the previous century, European administrative theorists Henri Fayol and Max Weber emphasized that organizations work best through harmonious relations. Elton Mayo, who founded Harvard University's human relations school and is considered one of the founders of organizational behaviour, was convinced that employee-management conflict undermines organizational effectiveness. These and other critics warn that even moderately low levels of disagreement tatter the fabric of workplace relations and sap energy away from productive activities. Disagreement with one's supervisor, for example, wastes productive time, violates the hierarchy of command, and questions the efficient assignment of authority (where managers made the decisions and employees followed them).

Although the "conflict-is-bad" perspective is now considered too simplistic, it can indeed have negative consequences under some circumstances (see Exhibit 11.1).[5] Conflict has been criticized for consuming otherwise productive time. For instance, almost one-third of the 5,000 employees recently surveyed across nine countries reported that they are frequently or always dealing with workplace conflict. More than half of the employees in Germany complained that conflict was consuming their workday.[6]

Conflict can undermine job performance in other ways.[7] Conflict is often stressful, which consumes personal energy and distracts employees from their work. Conflict discourages people engaged in the dispute from sharing resources and coordinating with each other. It can reduce job satisfaction, resulting in higher turnover and lower customer service. Conflict fuels organizational politics, such as motivating employees to find ways to undermine the credibility of their opponents. Decision making suffers because people are less motivated to communicate valuable information. Ironically, with less communication, the feuding parties are

Global Connections 11.1:

HIGH COST OF ON-BOARD CONFLICTS

Airline customers suffer enough when experiencing or observing on-board conflicts with other passengers. But these are usually minor inconveniences compared to situations when flight crew members can't get along with each other. Consider the following recent events.

An American Airlines flight recently returned to the gate almost as soon as it began to taxi towards its takeoff area because, in the airline's words, "there was a disagreement between two flight attendants." One flight attendant was using her cell phone during the pre-departure preparations for the New York to Washington commuter flight. Her activities apparently prompted the other flight attendant to use the intercom and announce that everyone needed to turn off their phones and electronic devices, "including the other flight attendant." That comment led to a scuffle between the two crew members, which was serious enough that the pilots decided to cancel the flight. Passengers had to wait four hours for a new crew to arrive.

Exactly one week later, a United Airlines flight bound for Chicago returned to Raleigh/Durham shortly after takeoff because of conflict between two flight attendants. The cause of the tiff seemed almost trivial. "One flight attendant had crossed their leg and accidentally brushed the other person," explained a spokesperson at Raleigh/Durham International Airport after the flight had returned. Although apparently unintentional, the other flight attendant interpreted the incident as provocation because relations between the two were already fragile. "It appears there was a disagreement before that, that became elevated," the spokesperson said. Passengers had to wait three hours for an alternative flight. United Airlines faced the costs of an abandoned flight, compensation for travellers with missed connections, possibly overtime for the replacement crew, and loss of customer service reputation.

Pilots probably also have disagreements, but few are noticed and fewer still lead to flight delays. But cockpit conflict may have indirectly contributed to the cancellation of a recent Qantas flight from Dallas to Sydney, Australia. The flight operations managers decided to cancel the flight because thunderstorms delayed the departure and the pilots were already close to exceeding their maximum work hours. However, the captain and second officer were later suspended when the managers learned the pilots had an argument while preparing for departure regarding takeoff calculations to enter into the computer system. The airline had to fly in replacement pilots, resulting in an 18-hour delay.[8]

Izabela Habur/E+/Getty Images

Conflict among airline crew members can be costly for airlines and ruin their customer service reputation.

more likely to escalate their disagreement because each side relies increasingly on distorted perceptions and stereotypes of the other party. Finally, conflict among team members may undermine team cohesion and performance. As Connection 11.1 describes, airlines and customers alike suffer when flight crew members don't get along.

Benefits of Conflict In the 1920s, when most organizational scholars viewed conflict as inherently dysfunctional, educational philosopher and psychologist John Dewey praised its benefits: "Conflict is the gadfly of thought. It stirs us to observation and memory. It instigates to invention. It shocks us out of sheeplike passivity, and sets us at noting and contriving."[9] Three years later, political science and management theorist Mary Parker Follett similarly remarked that the "friction" of conflict should be put to use rather than treated as an unwanted consequence of differences.[10]

But it wasn't until the 1970s that conflict management experts began to embrace the "optimal conflict" perspective.[11] According to this view, organizations are most effective when

EXHIBIT 11.1: Consequences of Workplace Conflict

Negative Consequences	Positive Consequences
Uses otherwise productive time Less information sharing Higher stress, dissatisfaction, and turnover Increases organizational politics Wastes resources Weakens team cohesion (conflict among team members)	Better decision making —tests logic of arguments —questions assumptions More responsive to changing environment Stronger team cohesion (conflict between the team and outside opponents)

employees experience some level of conflict, but become less effective with high levels of conflict.[12] What are the benefits of conflict? As Dewey stated, conflict energizes people to debate issues and evaluate alternates more thoroughly. They probe and test each other's way of thinking to better understand the underlying issues that need to be addressed. This discussion and debate tests the logic of arguments and encourages participants to re-examine their basic assumptions about the problem and its possible solution. It prevents individuals and teams from making inferior decisions and potentially helps them to develop more sound and creative solutions.[13]

A second potential benefit is that moderate levels of conflict prevent organizations from becoming nonresponsive to their external environment. As mentioned, differences of opinion encourage employees to engage in active thinking, and this often involves ongoing questioning and vigilance about how the organization can be more closely aligned with its customers, suppliers, and other stakeholders.[14] A third benefit of conflict occurs when team members have a dispute or competition with external sources. This form of conflict represents an external challenge which, as was noted in the team dynamics chapter (Chapter 8), potentially increases cohesion within the team. People are more motivated to work together when faced with an external threat, such as conflict with people outside the team.

The Emerging View: Task and Relationship Conflict

LO2

task conflict A type of conflict in which people focus their discussion around the issue while showing respect for people with other points of view.

relationship conflict A type of conflict in which people focus on characteristics of other individuals, rather than on the issues, as the source of conflict.

Although many writers still refer to the "optimal conflict" perspective, an emerging school of thought is that there are two types of conflict with opposing consequences: task conflict and relationship conflict.[15] **Task conflict** (also called *constructive conflict*) occurs when people focus their discussion around the issue (i.e., the "task") while showing respect for people with other points of view. This type of conflict debates the merits and limitations of different positions so ideas and recommendations can be clarified, redesigned, and tested for logical soundness. By keeping the debate focused on the issue, participants calmly re-examine their assumptions and beliefs without having hostile emotions triggered by their drive to defend their self-concept. Research indicates that task conflict tends to produce the beneficial outcomes that we described earlier, particularly better decision making.[16] At the same time, there is likely an upper limit to the intensity of any disagreement, above which it would be difficult to remain constructive.

In contrast to task conflict, **relationship conflict** focuses on interpersonal differences between or among the adversaries. The parties refer to "personality clashes" and other interpersonal incompatibilities rather than legitimate differences of opinion regarding tasks or decisions. Relationship conflict involves one party questioning or critiquing personal characteristics of the other person. As such, it attempts (or is perceived to attempt) to undermine another person's competence. These personal attacks threaten self-esteem and oppose self-enhancement and self-verification processes (see Chapter 3). Consequently, they usually trigger defense mechanisms and a competitive orientation between the parties. Relationship conflict also reduces mutual trust because it emphasizes interpersonal differences that shred identification with the other person.[17] Relationship conflict escalates more easily than task conflict because the adversaries become less motivated to communicate and share information, making it more difficult for them to discover common ground and ultimately resolve the conflict. Instead, they rely more on distorted perceptions and stereotypes which, as we noted earlier, tends to further escalate the conflict.

Separating Task from Relationship Conflict If there are two types of conflict, then the obvious advice is to encourage task conflict and minimize relationship conflict. This recommendation sounds good in theory, but separating these two types of conflict isn't easy. Research indicates that we experience some degree of relationship conflict whenever we are engaged in constructive debate.[18] No matter how diplomatically someone questions our ideas and actions, they potentially trigger our drive to defend our ideas, our sense of competence, and our public image. The stronger the level of debate and the more the issue is tied to our self-concept, the higher the chance that the task conflict will evolve into (or mix with) relationship conflict.

Fortunately, three strategies or conditions potentially minimize the level of relationship conflict during task conflict episodes.[19]

- *Emotional intelligence and emotional stability.* Relationship conflict is less likely to occur, or is less likely to escalate, when team members have high levels of emotional intelligence and its associated personality characteristic: emotional stability.[20] Employees with higher emotional intelligence and stability are better able to regulate their emotions during debate, which reduces the risk of escalating perceptions of interpersonal hostility. They are also more likely to view a coworker's emotional reaction as valuable information about that person's needs and expectations, rather than as a personal attack.
- *Cohesive team.* Relationship conflict is suppressed when the conflict occurs within a highly cohesive team. The longer people work together, get to know each other, and develop mutual trust, the more latitude they give to each other to show emotions without being personally offended. This might explain why task conflict is more effective in top management teams than in teams of more junior staff.[21] Strong cohesion also allows each person to know about and anticipate the behaviours and emotions of their teammates. Another benefit is that cohesion produces a stronger social identity with the group, so team members are motivated to avoid escalating relationship conflict during otherwise emotionally turbulent discussions.
- *Supportive team norms.* Various team norms can hold relationship conflict at bay during task-focused debate. When team norms encourage openness, for instance, team members learn to appreciate honest dialogue without personally reacting to any emotional display during the

Marcus Clackson/E+/Getty Images

Intel is famous for encouraging lively debates among its employees. Intel cofounder Andy Grove introduced and embedded this culture of constructive confrontation long ago to help the computer chip designer make better decisions. But he also recognized the fine line between task and relationship conflict. "Constructive confrontation does not mean being loud, unpleasant or rude, and it is not designed to affix blame," warns Grove. "The essence of it is to attack a problem by speaking up in a businesslike way."[22]

disagreements.[23] Other norms might discourage team members from displaying negative emotions towards coworkers. Team norms also encourage tactics that diffuse relationship conflict when it first appears. For instance, research has found that teams with low relationship conflict use humour to maintain positive group emotions, which offsets negative feelings team members might develop towards some coworkers during debate.

Conflict Process Model

LO3

Now that we have outlined the history and current knowledge about conflict and its outcomes, let's look at the model of the conflict process, shown in Exhibit 11.2.[24] This model begins with the sources of conflict, which we will describe in the next section. At some point, the sources of conflict lead one or both parties to perceive that conflict exists. They become aware that one party's statements and actions are incompatible with their own goals. These perceptions usually interact with emotions experienced about the conflict.[25] Conflict perceptions and emotions manifest themselves in conflict–the decisions and behaviours of one party towards the other. These *conflict episodes* may range from subtle nonverbal behaviours to warlike aggression. Particularly when people experience high levels of conflict-generated emotions, they have difficulty finding the words and expressions that communicate effectively without further irritating the relationship.[26] Conflict is also manifested by the style each side uses to resolve the conflict. Some people tend to avoid the conflict whereas others try to defeat those with opposing views.

Exhibit 11.2 shows arrows looping back from manifest conflict to conflict perceptions and emotions. These arrows illustrate that the conflict process is really a series of episodes that potentially cycle into conflict escalation.[27] It doesn't take much to start this conflict cycle–just an inappropriate comment, a misunderstanding, or action that lacks diplomacy. These behaviours cause the other party to perceive that conflict exists. Even if the first party did not intend to demonstrate conflict, the second party's response may create that perception.

Structural Sources of Conflict in Organizations

The conflict model starts with the sources of conflict, so we need to understand these sources to effectively diagnose conflict episodes and subsequently resolve the conflict or occasionally to generate conflict where it is lacking. The six main conditions that cause conflict in organizational settings are incompatible goals, differentiation, interdependence, scarce resources, ambiguous rules, and communication problems.

EXHIBIT 11.2

Model of the Conflict Process

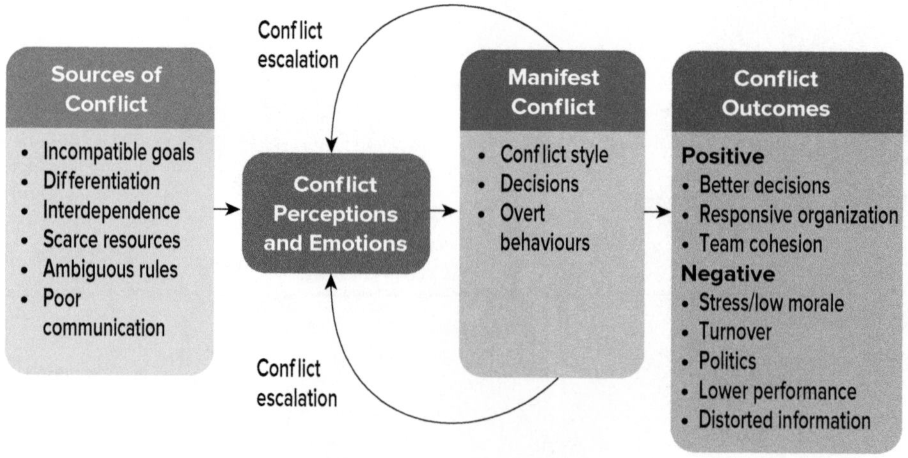

OB by the NUMBERS

Do Intergenerational Differences Increase or Decrease Productivity?[30]

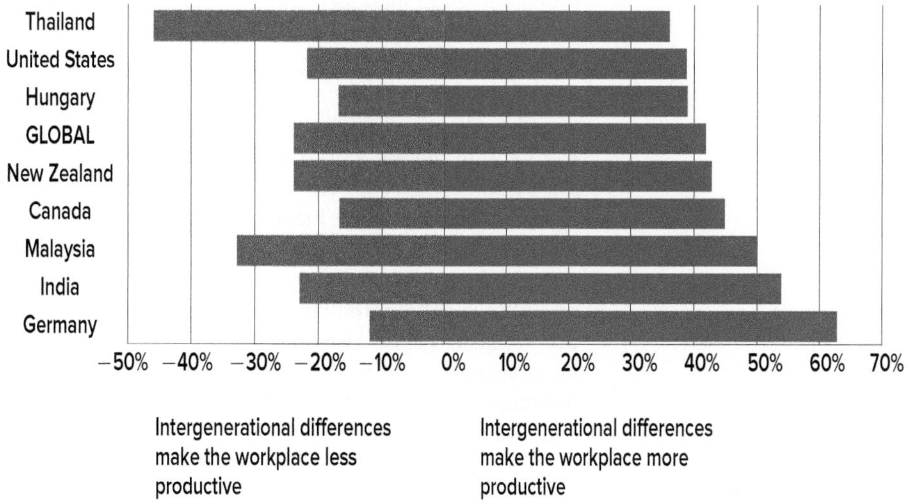

Percentage of employees by country who believe that intergenerational (Baby boomers, Gen X, and Gen Y) differences have a positive or negative effect on workplace productivity. Percentages do not add up to 100 percent because some respondents reported that generational differences have no effect on productivity. Based on a survey of 100,000 employees in 33 countries.

INCOMPATIBLE GOALS

Goal incompatibility occurs when the goals of one person or department seem to interfere with another person's or department's goals.[28] For example, the production department strives for cost efficiency by scheduling long production runs whereas the sales team emphasizes customer service by delivering the client's product as quickly as possible. If the company runs out of a particular product, the production team would prefer to have clients wait until the next production run. This infuriates sales representatives who would rather change production quickly to satisfy consumer demand.

DIFFERENTIATION

Another source of conflict is *differentiation*–differences among people and work units regarding their training, values, beliefs, and experiences. Differentiation differs from goal incompatibility; two people or departments may agree on a common goal (serving customers better) but have different beliefs about how to achieve that goal (e.g., standardize employee behaviour versus give employees autonomy in customer interactions). Consider the opening story to this chapter. Intergenerational conflicts occur because younger and older employees have different needs, different expectations, and different workplace practices, which sometimes produce conflicting preferences and actions. Recent studies suggest that these intergenerational differences occur because people develop social identities around technological developments and other pivotal social events that are unique to their era.[29]

Differentiation also produces the classic tension between employees from two companies brought together through a merger.[31] Even when people form both companies want the integrated organization to succeed, they fight over the "right way" to do things because of their unique experiences in the separate companies. This form of conflict emerged when CenturyLink recently acquired Qwest, creating the third largest telecommunications company in the United States. The two companies were headquartered in different parts of the country. "Their languages were different, their food was different, answers were different. We talked fast and interrupted, and they talked slow and were polite," recalls a senior Qwest executive. "If we said up, they said down. If we said yes, they said no. If we said go, they said stop." The result was "unnecessary misunderstandings" as executives tried to integrate the two companies.[32]

INTERDEPENDENCE

Conflict tends to increase with the level of task interdependence. Task interdependence refers to the extent to which employees must share materials, information, or expertise to perform their jobs (see Chapter 8). This interdependence includes sharing common resources, exchanging work or clients back and forth, and receiving outcomes (such as rewards) that are partly determined by the performance of others.[33] Higher interdependence increases the risk of conflict because there is a greater chance that each side will disrupt or interfere with the other side's goals.[34]

Other than complete independence, employees tend to have the lowest risk of conflict when working with others in a pooled interdependence relationship. Pooled interdependence occurs where individuals operate independently except for reliance on a common resource or authority. The potential for conflict is higher in sequential interdependence work relationships, such as an assembly line. The highest risk of conflict tends to occur in reciprocal interdependence situations. With reciprocal interdependence, employees have high mutual dependence on each other and, consequently, have a higher probability of interfering with each other's work and personal goals.

SCARCE RESOURCES

Resource scarcity generates conflict because each person or unit requiring the same resource necessarily undermines others who also need that resource to fulfill their goals. Most labour strikes, for instance, occur because there aren't enough financial and other resources for employees and company owners to each receive the outcomes they seek, such as higher pay (employees) and higher investment returns (shareholders). Budget deliberations within organizations also produce conflict because there aren't enough funds to satisfy the goals of each work unit. The more resources one group receives, the fewer resources a stakeholder will receive. Fortunately, these interests aren't perfectly opposing in complex negotiations, but limited resources are typically a major source of friction.

AMBIGUOUS RULES

Ambiguous–or nonexistent–rules breed conflict. This occurs because uncertainty increases the risk that one party intends to interfere with the other party's goals. Ambiguity also encourages political tactics and, in some cases, employees enter a free-for-all battle to win decisions in their favour. This explains why conflict is more common during mergers and acquisitions. Employees from both companies have conflicting practices and values, and few rules have developed to minimize the maneuvering for power and resources.[35] When clear rules exist, on the other hand, employees know what to expect from each other and have agreed to abide by those rules.

COMMUNICATION PROBLEMS

Conflict often occurs due to the lack of opportunity, ability, or motivation to communicate effectively. Let's look at each of these causes. First, when two parties lack the opportunity to communicate, they tend to rely more on stereotypes to understand the other party in the conflict. Unfortunately, stereotypes are sufficiently subjective that emotions can negatively distort the meaning of an opponent's actions, thereby escalating perceptions of conflict. Second, some people lack the necessary skills to communicate in a diplomatic, nonconfrontational manner. When one party communicates its disagreement arrogantly, opponents are more likely to heighten their perception of the conflict. This may lead the other party to reciprocate with a similar response, which further escalates the conflict.[36]

A third problem is that relationship conflict is uncomfortable, so people are less motivated to communicate with others in a disagreement. Unfortunately, less communication can further escalate the conflict because each side has less accurate information about the other side's intentions. To fill in the missing pieces, they rely on distorted images and stereotypes of the other party. Perceptions are further distorted because people in conflict situations tend to engage in more differentiation with those who are different from them (see Chapter 3). This differentiation creates a more positive self-concept and a more negative image of the opponent. We begin to see competitors less favourably so our self-concept remains positive during these uncertain times.[37]

Interpersonal Conflict Handling Styles

LO4

The six structural conditions described in the previous section lead to conflict perceptions and emotions which, in turn, motivate people to take some sort of action to address the conflict. Along with her pioneering view that some conflict is beneficial, Mary Parker Follett suggested there are different conflict handling styles. Conflict management experts subsequently expanded and refined this taxonomy of conflict handling styles, with most of them adapting variations of the five-category model shown in Exhibit 11.3 and described below. This model recognizes that how people approach a conflict situation depends on the relative importance they place on maximizing outcomes for themselves and maximizing outcomes for the other party.[38]

connect

What is your preferred conflict handling style? See page 295 or visit connect.mcgrawhill.com to assess your preferred way of handling conflict, and to assist your learning about this topic.

EXHIBIT 11.3

Interpersonal Conflict Handling Styles

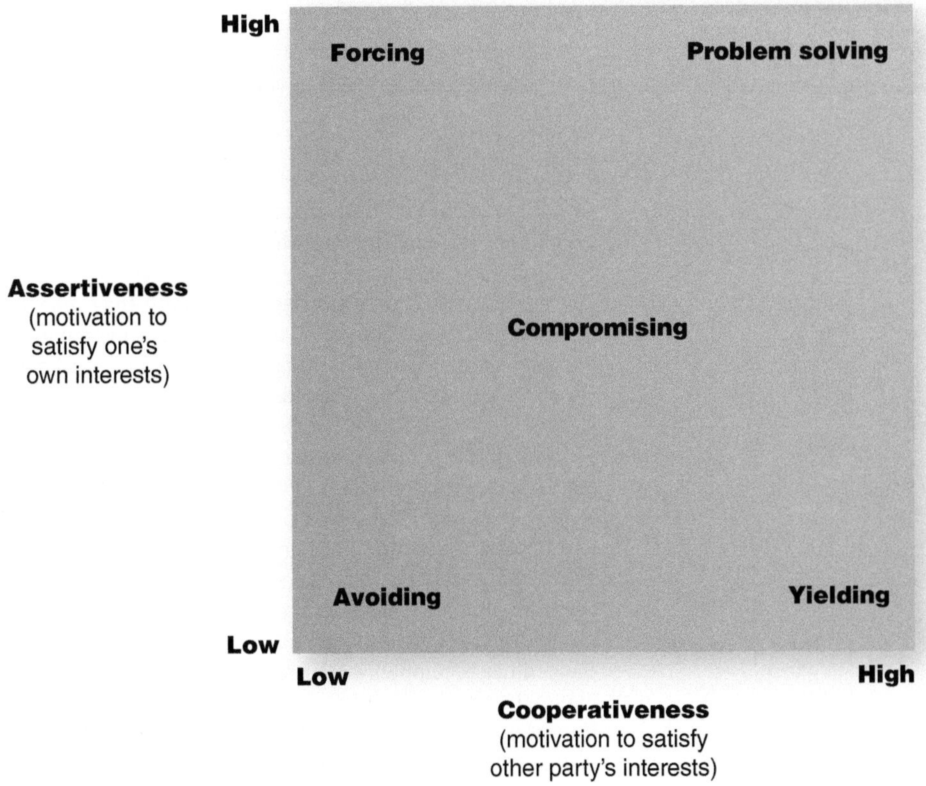

Source: C. K. W. de Dreu, A. Evers, B. Beersma, E. S. Kluwer, and A. Nauta, "A Theory-based Measure of Conflict Management Strategies in the Workplace," *Journal of Organizational Behavior,* 22 (2001), pp. 645-68. For other variations of this model, see: T. L. Ruble and K. Thomas, "Support For a Two-Dimensional Model of Conflict Behavior," *Organizational Behavior and Human Performance,* 16 (1976), p. 145. R. R. Blake, H. A. Shepard, and J. S. Mouton. *Managing Intergroup Conflict in Industry.* Houston: Gulf Publishing, 1964; M. A. Rahim, "Toward a theory of managing organizational conflict." *International Journal of Conflict Management* 13, no. 3 (2002): 206-235.

win–win orientation The belief that conflicting parties will find a mutually beneficial solution to their disagreement.

win–lose orientation The belief that conflicting parties are drawing from a fixed pie, so the more one party receives, the less the other party will receive.

- *Problem solving.* Problem solving tries to find a solution that is beneficial for both parties. This is known as the **win-win orientation** because people using this style believe the resources at stake are expandable rather than fixed if the parties work together to find a creative solution. Information sharing is an important feature of this style because both parties collaborate to identify common ground and potential solutions that satisfy everyone involved.
- *Forcing.* Forcing tries to win the conflict at the other's expense. People who use this style typically have a **win-lose orientation**–they believe the parties are drawing from a fixed pie, so the more one party receives, the less the other party will receive. Consequently, this style relies on some of the "hard" influence tactics described in Chapter 10, particularly assertiveness, to get one's own way.
- *Avoiding.* Avoiding tries to smooth over or evade conflict situations altogether. A common avoidance strategy is to minimize interaction with certain coworkers. For instance, 67 percent of employees in one large global survey said they go out of their way to avoid seeing coworkers with whom they have a disagreement. A smaller number (14 percent) have missed a day of work to avoid workplace conflict.[39] A second avoidance strategy is to steer clear of the sensitive topic when interacting with the other person in the conflict. These examples indicate that avoidance does not necessarily mean that we have a low concern for both one's own and the other party's interest. Instead, we might be very concerned about the issue but believe that avoidance is the best solution, at least for the short term.[40]
- *Yielding.* Yielding involves giving in completely to the other side's wishes, or at least cooperating with little or no attention to your own interests. This style involves making unilateral concessions and unconditional promises, as well as offering help with no expectation of reciprocal help.
- *Compromising.* Compromising involves looking for a position in which your losses are offset by equally valued gains. It involves matching the other party's concessions, making conditional promises or threats, and actively searching for a middle ground between the interests of the two parties.

CHOOSING THE BEST CONFLICT HANDLING STYLE

Chances are that you have a preferred conflict handling style. You might typically engage in avoiding or yielding because disagreement makes you feel uncomfortable and is contrary to your self-view as someone who likes to get along with everyone. Or perhaps you prefer the compromising and forcing strategies because they reflect your strong need for achievement and to control your environment. People usually gravitate towards one or two conflict handling styles that match their personality, personal and cultural values, and past experience.[41] However, the best style depends on the situation, so we need to understand and develop the capacity to use each style for the appropriate occasions.[42]

Exhibit 11.4 summarizes the main contingencies, as well as problems with using each conflict handling style. Problem solving has long been identified as the preferred conflict handling style where possible because dialogue and clever thinking helps people to break out of the limited boundaries of their opposing alternatives to find an integrated solution where both gain value. In addition, the problem solving style tends to improve long-term relationships, reduce stress, and minimize emotional defensiveness and other indications of relationship conflict.[43]

However, problem solving assumes there are opportunities for mutual gains, such as when the conflict is complex with multiple elements. If the conflict is simple and perfectly opposing (each party wants more of a single fixed pie), then this style will waste time and increase frustration. The problem solving approach also takes more time and requires a fairly high degree of trust, because there is a risk that the other party will take advantage of the information you have openly shared. As one study recently found, the problem solving style is more stressful when people experience strong feelings of conflict, likely because these negative emotions undermine trust in the other party.[44]

The conflict avoidance style is often ineffective because it doesn't resolve the conflict and may increase the other party's frustration. However, avoiding may be the best strategy where conflict has become emotionally charged or where conflict resolution would cost more than the benefits it would provide.[45] The forcing style is usually inappropriate because

EXHIBIT 11.4 Conflict Handling Style Contingencies and Problems

Conflict Handling Style	Preferred Style When. . .	Problems with this Style
Problem solving	• Interests are not perfectly opposing (i.e., not pure win–lose) • Parties have trust, openness, and time to share information • The issues are complex	• Sharing information that the other party might use to their advantage
Forcing	• You have a deep conviction about your position (e.g., believe other person's behaviour is unethical) • Dispute requires a quick solution • The other party would take advantage of more cooperative strategies	• Highest risk of relationship conflict • May damage long-term relations, reducing future problem solving
Avoiding	• Conflict has become too emotionally charged • Cost of trying to resolve the conflict outweighs the benefits	• Doesn't usually resolve the conflict • May increase other party's frustration
Yielding	• Other party has substantially more power • Issue is much less important to you than to the other party • The value and logic of your position isn't as clear	• Increases other party's expectations in future conflict episodes
Compromising	• Parties have equal power • Time pressure to resolve the conflict • Parties lack trust/openness for problem solving	• Sub-optimal solution where mutual gains are possible

it commonly generates relationship conflict more quickly or intensely than other conflict handling styles. However, forcing may be necessary where you know you are correct (e.g., the other party's position is unethical or based on obviously flawed logic), the dispute requires a quick solution, or the other party would take advantage of a more cooperative conflict handling style.

The yielding style may be appropriate when the other party has substantially more power, the issue is not as important to you as to the other party, and you aren't confident that your position has the best value or logical consistency.[46] On the other hand, yielding behaviours may give the other side unrealistically high expectations, thereby motivating them to seek more from you in the future. In the long run, yielding may produce more conflict than resolution. "Raised voices, red faces, and table thumping is a far less dysfunctional way of challenging each other than withdrawal, passivity, and sullen acceptance," argues one conflict management consultant. "It doesn't mean that people agree with you: they just take their misgivings underground and spread them throughout the organization, which has a corrosive effect."[47]

The compromising style may be best when there is little hope for mutual gain through problem solving, both parties have equal power, and both are under time pressure to settle their differences. However, we rarely know whether the parties have perfectly opposing interest, making compromise more appropriate than problem solving. Therefore, entering a conflict with the compromising style may cause the parties to overlook better solutions because they have not attempted to share enough information and creatively look for win-win alternatives.

CULTURAL AND GENDER DIFFERENCES IN CONFLICT HANDLING STYLES

Cultural differences are more than just a source of conflict. They also influence the preferred conflict handling style.[48] Some research suggests that people from collectivist cultures–where group goals are valued more than individual goals–are motivated to maintain harmonious relations and, consequently, are more likely than those from low collectivism cultures to manage disagreements through avoidance or problem solving. However, this view may be somewhat simplistic. Collectivism motivates harmony within the group but not necessarily with people outside the group. Indeed, research indicates that managers in some collectivist cultures are more likely to publicly shame those whose actions oppose their own.[49] Cultural values and norms influence the conflict handling style used most often in a society, but they also represent an important contingency when outsiders choose the preferred conflict handling approach. For example, people who frequently use the conflict avoidance style might have more problems in cultures where the forcing style is common.

According to some writers, men and women tend to rely on different conflict handling styles.[50] They suggest that, compared to men, women pay more attention to the relationship between the parties. Consequently, women tend to adopt a compromising or occasionally problem solving style in business settings and are more willing to compromise to protect the relationship. Compared to men, they are also slightly more likely to use the avoiding style. Men tend to be more competitive and take a short-term orientation to the relationship. In low collectivism cultures, men are more likely than women to use the forcing approach to conflict handling. We must be cautious about these observations, however, because differences between men and women on preferred conflict handling styles are fairly small.

Structural Approaches to Conflict Management

LO5

Conflict handling styles describe how we approach the other party in a conflict situation. But conflict management also involves altering the underlying structural causes of potential conflict. The main structural approaches are emphasizing superordinate goals, reducing differentiation, improving communication and understanding, reducing task interdependence, increasing resources, and clarifying rules and procedures.

EMPHASIZING SUPERORDINATE GOALS

superordinate goals Goals that the conflicting parties value and whose attainment requires the joint resources and effort of those parties.

One of the oldest recommendations for resolving conflict is to refocus the parties' attention around superordinate goals and away from the conflicting subordinate goals.[51] **Superordinate goals** are goals that the conflicting employees or departments value and whose attainment requires the joint resources and effort of those parties.[52] These goals are called superordinate because they are higher-order aspirations such as the organization's strategic objectives rather than objectives specific to the individual or work unit. Research indicates that the most effective executive teams frame their decisions as superordinate goals that rise above each executive's departmental or divisional goals. Similarly, one recent study reported that leaders reduce conflict through an inspirational vision that unifies employees and makes them less preoccupied with their subordinate goal differences.[53]

Suppose that marketing staff want a new product released quickly, whereas engineers want more time to test and add new features. Leaders can potentially reduce this interdepartmental conflict by reminding both groups of the company's mission to serve customers, or by pointing out that competitors currently threaten the company's leadership in the industry. By increasing commitment to corporate-wide goals (customer focus, competitiveness), engineering and marketing employees pay less attention to their competing departmental-level goals, which reduces their perceived conflict with coworkers. Superordinate goals also potentially reduce the problem of differentiation because they establish feelings of a shared social identity (work for the same company).[54]

REDUCING DIFFERENTIATION

Another way to minimize dysfunctional conflict is to reduce the differences that generate conflict. As people develop common experiences and beliefs, they become more motivated to coordinate activities and resolve their disputes through constructive discussion.[55] SAP, the German enterprise software company, applied this approach when it recently acquired Business Objects, a French company with a strong American presence. Immediately after

Sherman Hines/Alamy

Strained relations between Canadian National Railways (CN) and the Canadian Wheat Board (CWB) recently changed to cooperation when Claude Mongeau became CN's chief executive. Mongeau implemented a plan where the two companies share information so CN can provide hopper cars to grain elevators when they are needed. This information exchange alone dramatically gave each party a better understanding of the other's situation. But CN and CWB also tackled their longstanding conflicts by having executives and staff talk to each other more often about their needs and perceptions. "Under Claude, CN has quickly moved to a more collaborative model," says CWB chief operating officer Ward Weisensel. "That's not to say we agree on every issue, but with Claude we are able to discuss and explore and both parties are better able to understand each other."[56]

the merger, SAP began intermingling people from the two organizations. Several senior SAP executives transferred to Business Objects, and all of the acquired company's executives are on SAP's shared services team. "We also encourage cross-border, cross-functional teamwork on projects such as major product releases," says Business Objects CEO John Schwarz. "In this way team members come to depend on each other."[57] Essentially, SAP provided opportunities for managers and technical employees in the acquired firm to develop common experiences with their SAP counterparts by moving staff across the two companies or having them work together on joint projects.

IMPROVING COMMUNICATION AND MUTUAL UNDERSTANDING

A third way to resolve dysfunctional conflict is to give the conflicting parties more opportunities to communicate and understand each other. This recommendation applies two principles and practices introduced in Chapter 3: the Johari Window model and meaningful interaction. Although both were previously described as ways to improve self-awareness, they are equally valuable to improve other-awareness.

In the Johari Window process, individuals disclose more about themselves so others have a better understanding of the underlying causes of their behaviour. L'Oréal Canada's intergenerational seminar, described in the opening case study for this chapter, applied a variation of the Johari Window. The cosmetic company's program includes an activity in which each generational cohort answers questions from the other cohorts about what is important to them (such as security, performance, and collaboration). A variation of Johari Window also occurs in "lunch and learn" sessions, where employees in one functional area describe work and its challenges to coworkers in other areas. Houston-based Brookstone Construction introduced these information meetings which helped to reduce frustrations between its field and office staff.[58]

Meaningful interaction potentially improves mutual understanding through the contact hypothesis, which says that we develop a more person-specific and accurate understanding of others by interacting with and working closely with them.[59] For example, more than 18,000 employees and managers at the various companies of System Capital Management recently participated in the "Let's Make Ukraine Clean" campaign. In addition to improving the environment—each person picked up an average of about 100 kg (200 lbs.) of garbage—this volunteering opportunity improved relations among management and employees at the Ukraine's leading financial and industrial group.[60]

Although communication and mutual understanding can work well, there are two important warnings. First, these interventions should be applied only where differentiation is sufficiently low or *after* differentiation has been reduced. If perceived differentiation remains high, attempts to manage conflict through dialogue might escalate rather than reduce relationship conflict. The reason is that when forced to interact with people who we believe are quite different and in conflict with us, we tend to select information that reinforces that view.[61] The second warning is that people in collectivist and high power distance cultures are less comfortable with the practice of resolving differences through direct and open communication.[62] Remember, people in collectivist cultures refer an avoidance conflict handling style because it is the most consistent with harmony and face saving. Direct communication is a high-risk strategy because it easily threatens the need to save face and maintain harmony.

REDUCING INTERDEPENDENCE

Conflict occurs where people are dependent on each other, so another way to reduce dysfunctional conflict is to minimize the level of interdependence between the parties. Three ways to reduce interdependence among employees and work units are to create buffers, use integrators, and combine jobs.

- *Create buffers.* A buffer is any mechanism that loosens the coupling between two or more people or work units. This decoupling reduces the potential for conflict because the buffer reduces the effect of one party on the other. Building up inventories between people in an assembly line would be a buffer, for example, because each employee is less dependent in the short term on the previous person along that line.
- *Use integrators.* Integrators are employees who coordinate the activities of work units towards the completion of a common task. For example, an individual might be responsible for coordinating the efforts of the research, production, advertising, and marketing departments in launching a new product line. In some respects, integrators are human buffers; they reduce the frequency of direct interaction among work units that have diverse goals and perspectives. Integrators rarely have direct authority over the departments they integrate, so they must rely on referent power and persuasion to manage conflict and accomplish the work.
- *Combine jobs.* Combining jobs is both a form of job enrichment and a way to reduce task interdependence. Consider a toaster assembly system where one person inserts the heating element, another adds the sides, and so on. By combining these tasks so that each person assembles an entire toaster, the employees now have a pooled rather than sequential form of task interdependence and the likelihood of dysfunctional conflict is reduced.

INCREASING RESOURCES

An obvious way to reduce conflict caused by resource scarcity is to increase the amount of resources available. Corporate decision makers might quickly dismiss this solution because of the costs involved. However, they need to carefully compare these costs with the costs of dysfunctional conflict arising out of resource scarcity.

CLARIFYING RULES AND PROCEDURES

Conflicts that arise from ambiguous rules can be minimized by establishing rules and procedures. If two departments are fighting over the use of a new laboratory, a schedule might be established which allocates the lab exclusively to each team at certain times of the day or week.

Third-Party Conflict Resolution

third-party conflict resolution
Any attempt by a relatively neutral person to help conflicting parties resolve their differences.

Most of this chapter has focused on people directly involved in a conflict, yet many disputes among employees and departments are resolved with the assistance of a manager. **Third-party conflict resolution** is any attempt by a relatively neutral person to help the parties resolve their differences. There are three main third-party dispute resolution activities: arbitration, inquisition, and mediation. These interventions can be classified by their level of control over the process and control over the decision (see Exhibit 11.5).[63]

- *Arbitration.* Arbitrators have high control over the final decision, but low control over the process. Executives engage in this strategy by following previously agreed rules of due process, listening to arguments from the disputing employees, and making a

EXHIBIT 11.5

Types of Third-Party Intervention

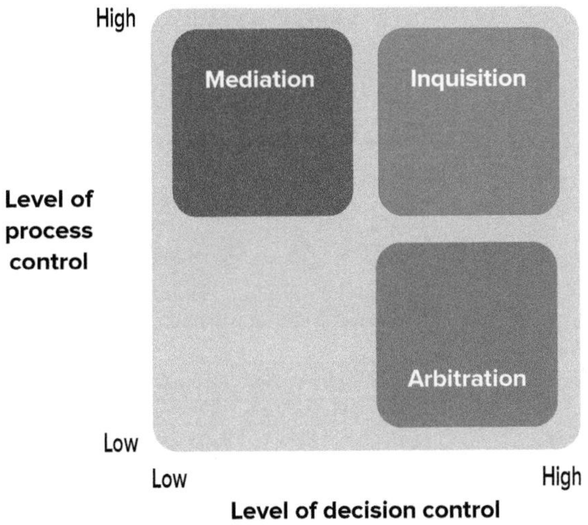

binding decision. Arbitration is applied as the final stage of grievances by unionized employees in many countries, but it is also becoming more common in nonunion conflicts.

- *Inquisition.* Inquisitors control all discussion about the conflict. Like arbitrators, they have high decision control because they choose the form of conflict resolution. However, they also have high process control because they choose which information to examine and how to examine it, and they generally decide how the conflict resolution process will be handled.
- *Mediation.* Mediators have high control over the intervention process. In fact, their main purpose is to manage the process and context of interaction between the disputing parties. However, the parties make the final decision about how to resolve their differences. Thus, mediators have little or no control over the conflict resolution decision.[64] Some mediation can involve a mediator with expert knowledge who shares information and opinion regarding industry standards and potential outcomes. Many organizations, such as Shell Canada, TD Canada Trust, and Royal Bank of Canada, have internal ombudspersons to investigate and mediate employment conflicts.
- *Mediation-arbitration.* Often referred to as "med-arb," this is an alternate hybrid dispute resolution process. While it promotes an opportunity for the parties to first attempt mediation, with the selected arbitrator facilitating negotiations, it also allows the arbitrator to shift into an adjudicative mode in order to make a determination based on the parties' arguments. The downside of this process is that while parties control the flow of information for negotiation purposes, deciding what they choose to reveal in mediation, parties may during the arbitration feel compelled to answer corollary questions that arise from the previously disclosed information. A positive aspect of med-arb is that parties enter the process with certainty that the dispute will be resolved either as a settlement in the mediation stage or as part of the binding decision made by the arbitrator. Most collective agreement contracts include a provision that the labour dispute between management and employee will be subject to med-arb.

CHOOSING THE BEST THIRD-PARTY INTERVENTION STRATEGY

Team leaders, executives, and coworkers regularly intervene in workplace disputes. Sometimes they adopt a mediator role; other times they serve as arbitrators. Occasionally, they begin with one approach then switch to another. However, research suggests that people in positions of authority (e.g., managers) usually adopt an inquisitional approach whereby they dominate the intervention process as well as make a binding decision.[65]

Managers tend to rely on the inquisition approach because it is consistent with the decision-oriented nature of managerial jobs, gives them control over the conflict process and

outcome, and tends to resolve disputes efficiently. However, inquisition is usually the least effective third-party conflict resolution method in organizational settings.[66] One problem is that leaders who take an inquisitional role tend to collect limited information about the problem, so their imposed decision may produce an ineffective solution to the conflict. Another problem is that employees often view inquisitional procedures and outcomes as unfair because they have little control over this approach. In particular, the inquisitional approach potentially violates several practices required to support procedural justice (see Chapter 5). As a result of these types of concerns, organizations have begun to appreciate the need for managers to receive negotiation and mediation training to help hone effective workplace conflict management skills.

Which third-party intervention is most appropriate in organizations? The answer partly depends on the situation, such as the type of dispute, the relationship between the manager and employees, and cultural values such as power distance.[67] Also, any third-party approach has more favourable results when it applies the procedural justice practices described in Chapter 5.[68] But generally speaking, for everyday disagreements between two employees, the mediation approach is usually best because it is less formal and gives employees more responsibility for resolving their own disputes. Having a neutral third party helps establish an appropriate context for conflict resolution. Although not as efficient as other strategies, mediation potentially offers the highest level of employee satisfaction with the conflict process and outcomes.[69] When employees cannot resolve their differences through mediation, arbitration seems to work best because the predetermined rules of evidence and other processes create a higher sense of procedural fairness.[70] Arbitration is also preferred where the organization's goals should take priority over individual goals.

negotiation Decision-making situations in which two or more interdependent parties attempt to reach agreement.

Resolving Conflict Through Negotiation

LO6

It is often said that people negotiate all the time. We negotiate things like the coordination of tasks on team projects, who will do the dishes, what movie we will see, and how to resolve a disagreement following an argument. As you can see, negotiation is not an obscure practice reserved for labour and management heads when hammering out a collective agreement. **Negotiation** refers to decision-making situations in which two or more interdependent parties attempt to reach agreement. We negotiate whenever we cannot achieve our objectives single-handedly.[71] Negotiation skills are essential because they help us meet our goals, reduce conflict, and build collaborative relationships.[72] Before we describe the strategies and tactics used by successful negotiators, it is necessary to understand the distinction between distributive and integrative negotiations.

DISTRIBUTIVE VERSUS INTEGRATIVE NEGOTIATIONS

Negotiation situations vary according to the interdependence of people's goals and the structure of the situation in which they are going to negotiate. When the goals of two or more people run in completely opposed directions, this is also known as a zero-sum or **distributive situation**. In distributive situations negotiators are motivated to win the competition, beat the other party, or gain the largest piece of the fixed resource that they can. To achieve these objectives, negotiators usually employ win-lose strategies and tactics. This approach to negotiation–called distributive bargaining–accepts the fact that there can only be one winner given the situation and pursues a course of action to be that winner. The purpose of the negotiation is to *claim value*–that is, to do whatever is necessary to claim the reward, gain the lion's share, or gain the largest piece possible.[73] An example of this type of negotiation is purchasing a used car when the only negotiable issue is price or buying a used refrigerator at a yard sale.

distributive situation When the goals of two or more people are zero-sum so that one can gain only at the other's expense.

In contrast, when parties' goals are linked so that one person's goal achievement helps others to achieve their goals, it is a mutual-gain situation, also known as a non-zero-sum or **integrative situation**, where there is a positive correlation between the goal attainments of both parties. If one person is a great music composer and the other is a great writer of lyrics, they can create a wonderful musical hit together. The music and words may be good separately, but fantastic together. To the degree that one person achieves his or her goal, the other's goals are not necessarily blocked, and may in fact be significantly enhanced. The distinction between distributive and integrative negotiations is important because the structure of the interdependence shapes the strategies and tactics a negotiator should employ.

integrative situation When parties' goals are linked, but not zero-sum, so that one person's goal achievement does not block the goal achievement of another.

PREPARING TO NEGOTIATE

Experienced negotiators often point to preparation as one of the most important factors contributing to positive outcomes. Although few people would disagree with the benefits of preparation, most have no idea what it is they should do to prepare. Regardless of the type of negotiation situation, all negotiators should consider their goals, the best alternative to a negotiated agreement (BATNA), and their limits.

Prepare and Set Goals

Always ask yourself what it is you hope to accomplish before beginning a negotiation. But don't just focus on quantitative indicators, such as the starting salary for a new job. Ask yourself about your overall interests, or the reasons underlying the positions you might take. For example, is salary the only thing that matters when you are starting a new job? Probably not. Looking more broadly at the situation might show that you want to work in a place that allows you to use the skills you have been trained on, to work on tasks that are interesting, or to live close to family if that is important to you. These kinds of things tap into your interests. By considering all these issues in advance, you minimize the likelihood that you will narrowly focus on just one issue in the negotiation; especially when the addition of other issue could have turned a distributive negotiation into an integrative one.

Know Your BATNA

To determine whether the opponent's offers are favourable, negotiators need to understand what outcome they might achieve through some other means (such as negotiating with someone else). This comparison is called the **best alternative to a negotiated agreement (BATNA)**. BATNA estimates your power in the negotiation because it represents the estimated cost of walking away from the relationship. If others are willing to negotiate with you for the product or service you need, then you have a high BATNA and considerable power in the negotiation because it would not cost you much to walk away from the current negotiation. Classic advice for people buying a new home is to "fall in low with two houses, not just one." Seriously considering a second house means you are less likely to overpay for the one that is your most preferred option. A common problem in negotiations, however, is that people tend to overestimate their BATNA; they wrongly believe there are plenty of other ways to achieve their objective rather than through this negotiation or underestimate other parties' BATNA.

best alternative to a negotiated settlement (BATNA) The best outcome you might achieve through some other course of action if you abandon the current negotiation.

Know Your Limits

In addition to goals and BATNA, you should also consider the point at which you are indifferent to a negotiated outcome. This point, sometimes called a *resistance*

Debating Point:

IS CREATING VALUE SUCH A GOOD NEGOTIATION STRATEGY?[74]

One of the bedrock principles of conflict management and negotiation is that the parties need to adopt a problem-solving approach. In negotiation, this win–win perspective is called *creating value:* discovering ways to achieve mutually satisfactory outcomes for both parties. Creating value is important for several reasons. First, creating value produces more trust. Some experts suggest that trust is vital in negotiations, because it enables each side to move forward with concessions and points of agreement.

Second, creating value involves sharing information, including a better understanding of each other's needs, so the parties can reach an optimal solution. This solution needs to determine the relative value that each side assigns to aspects of the issues or items negotiated. By identifying which items are more important to one party than the other, the resources can be divided up in a way that gains the most value for both sides.

Experts agree with these and other benefits of creating value, but some also warn that this scholarly picture isn't always as rosy in real life. The most potent problem with creating value is that it requires the parties to share information. This sharing is fine if you know the other party will reveal any mutual gains and discoveries from the information-sharing process, but this revelation doesn't always occur. Instead, Side B might discover something of value that could give it more of what it wants while making Side A think it has gained, at great loss to Side B.

Consider the following true example: Back in the days of the Model-T, the supplier of the car's door handles asked Ford for a 5 percent increase. Ford initially balked, but then agreed to the higher price if the supplier would reconfigure the bolt holes in the lids of the wooden crates used to deliver the door handles. The supplier was both perplexed and delighted; it didn't cost anything to make the change, but what was the value to Ford? Back then, Model-T floorboards were made of wood, and Ford staff figured out how to modify the supplier's crate lids as floorboards.

In this incident, Ford might have told the curious supplier why it was willing to pay this higher price, but this doesn't always occur. Sometimes, one side falsely believes the other side is making a significant sacrifice when, in fact, that other side has received considerable gains. If these gains had been revealed, the first party might have asked for even more!

Another concern is that it is sometimes difficult for each party to distinguish creating value from yielding—that is, giving the other party what they want. In an attempt to show collaboration, you give one concession here, another there, and so forth. Eventually, your position lacks negotiation options, because most of the concession space has been given away, while the other party has given very little. Creating value is an inherent tension with gaining value, because you must always keep your own interests equal to or greater than the interests of the other party.

point, helps you decide whether or not you should call off a negotiation. If you are a seller, your resistance point is the least you will minimally accept. If you are the buyer, your resistance point is the most you are willing to pay for an item. The reason you should think about this in advance is that too many people, especially those who don't even consider the limits, shift the way they view their bottom line in the face of a competitive offer from a counterpart. It is best to avoid this unless the evidence you receive clearly indicates that your limits may be unreasonable.

DISTRIBUTIVE STRATEGIES THAT WORK

To succeed in a distributive negotiation it is helpful to understand the concept of the bargaining zone, which is defined as the space between each party's resistance point.[75] Exhibit 11.6 displays one possible bargaining zone situation for a purely win-lose situation. As this model illustrates, the parties typically establish three main negotiating points. The *initial offer point* is the opening offer to the other party, the *target point* is the realistic goal or expectation for a final agreement, and the *resistance point* was defined above. It is important to remember that if the resistance points of the two parties overlap, as they do in Exhibit 11.6, then any deal that falls within the bargaining zone is a good deal because each side has done better than their resistance point. Therefore, they are both better off.

Most people, however, would prefer to reach a deal closer to their target point than their resistance point–and this is what we mean when we say that each side will try to claim as much value as possible. In a purely distributive situation, there are a few strategies that are known to lead to more value claiming.

Manage First Offers and Concessions Do you prefer to make the first offer in a negotiation or wait to hear what the other side offers first? Most people say they prefer to

EXHIBIT 11.6

Bargaining Zone Model of Negotiations

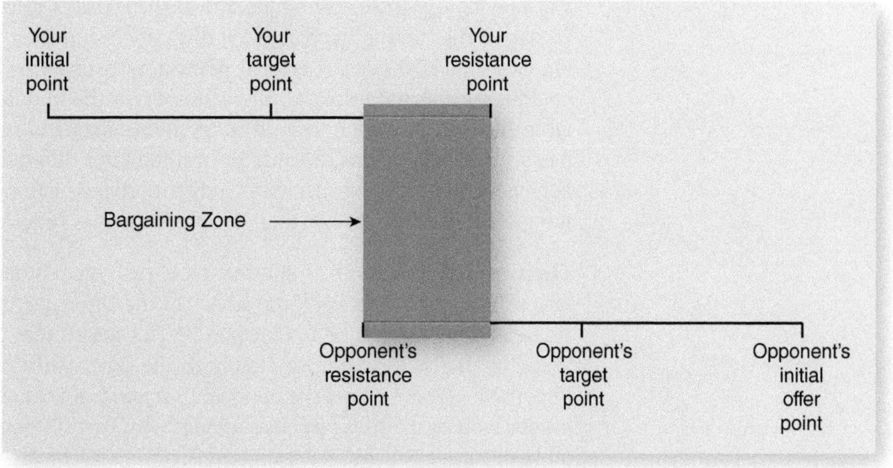

wait (about 80 percent in our experience), and are surprised to learn that if you are prepared and have a realistic sense about the structure of the bargaining zone, it is best to make the opening offer. The reason stems from research on the concept of anchoring and adjustment. First offers set "anchors," which tend to be highly influential in determining subsequent offer and concession-making behaviour. As we explained in Chapter 7, people tend to adjust their expectations around the initial point (or anchor), so if your initial request is high, opponents might move more quickly towards their resistance point along the bargaining zone.[76] It may even cause opponents to lower their resistance point.

After the first offer, negotiators need to make concessions.[77] Concessions serve at least three important purposes: (1) they enable the parties to move towards the area of potential agreement, (2) they symbolize each party's motivation to bargain in good faith, and (3) they tell the other party of the relative importance of the negotiation items. However, concessions need to be clearly labelled as such and should be accompanied by an expectation that the other party will reciprocate. They should also be offered in installments because people experience more positive emotions from receiving a few smaller concessions than from one large concession.[78] Generally, the best strategy is to be moderately tough and to concede just enough to communicate sincerity and commitment to resolve the conflict.[79]

Manage Time Negotiators make more concessions as the deadline gets closer.[80] This can be a liability if you are under time pressure, or it can be an advantage if the other party alone is under time pressure. Negotiators with more power in the relationship sometimes apply time pressure through an "exploding offer" whereby they give their opponent a very short time to accept their offer.[81] These time-limited offers are frequently found in consumer sales ("on sale today only!") and in some job offers. They produce time pressure, which can motivate the other party to accept the offer and forfeit the opportunity to explore their BATNA. Another time factor is that the more time someone has invested in the negotiation, the more committed they become to ensuring an agreement is reached. This commitment increases the tendency to make additional concessions not originally planned so that the negotiations do not fail.

INTEGRATIVE STRATEGIES THAT WORK

Many negotiation situations are not zero-sum, winner-take-all problems. In fact, most situations that appear distributive on the surface can be turned into an integrative situation by adding one or more issues to the mix. This is comforting for people who do not enjoy the competitive nature of distributive negotiations. The hallmark of success in an integrative situation is the reconciling of differences that exist between parties. These differences can include things like variation in preferences across the issues, difference in risk perceptions, and differences in time pressure. Value gets created when the parties agree to deals in which they exchange high priority issues for low priority issues, and vice-versa. For example, when a manager is trying to hire a new employee they might discover that the most important issues to the job candidate, in order of importance, are salary, start date, and coverage of moving expenses. If the manager is in a rush and needs someone to start right away, they might value start date over both salary and moving expenses. Therefore, a deal that creates value is one where the employee agrees to start earlier and in exchange for this concession they get a slight bump in salary (or moving expenses coverage). A critical point here is that this situation is not zero-sum. Both sides could treat it as such, split all the issues down the middle, and thus leave value sitting on the table. Instead, they are better off to try and understand the interests underlying their counterpart's positions and create value by searching for differences. As this example also shows, the behaviours that lead to success in a distributive situation often lead to suboptimal deals in an integrative situation. What then, are the strategies required to create value?

Gather Information Information is the corner stone of effective value creation.[82] Therefore, skilled negotiators heed the advice of the late management guru Stephen Covey: "Seek first to understand, then to be understood."[83] This means that we should present our case only after spending more time listening closely to the other party and asking for details. It is particularly important to look beyond the opponent's stated justifications to the unstated motivation for their claims. Probing questions (such as asking "why") and listening intently can reveal better solutions for both parties. Nonverbal communication can also convey important information about the other party's priorities. Negotiating in teams can also aid the information gathering process because some team members will hear information that others have ignored. Gleaning insight about the other party's interest can facilitate more creative problem solving and help you reframe the issues.

Discover Priorities Through Offers and Concessions Some types of offers and concessions are better than others at creating value. The key objective is to discover and signal which issues are more and less important to each side. Suppose that you have been asked to "second" (temporarily transfer) some of your best staff to projects in another division, whereas you need these people on site for other assignments and to coach junior staff. Through problem solving negotiation, you discover that the other division doesn't need those staff at their site; rather the division head mainly needs some guarantee that these people will be available. The result is that your division keeps the staff (important to you) while the other division has some guarantee these people will be available at specific times for their projects (important to them).

One way to figure out the relative importance of the issues to each party is to make multi-issue offers rather than discussing one issue at a time.[84] You might offer a client a specific price, delivery date, and guarantee period, for example. The other party's counteroffer to multiple items signals which are more and which are less important to them. Your subsequent concessions similarly signal how important each issue is to your group.

Build the Relationship Trust is critical for the problem solving style of conflict handling as well as in the value creation objective of negotiations.[85] How do you build trust in negotiations? One approach is to discover common backgrounds and interests, such as places you have lived, favourite hobbies and sports teams, and so forth. If there are substantial differences between the parties (age, gender, etc.), consider having team members that more closely match the backgrounds of the other party. First impressions are also important. Recall from earlier chapters in this book that people attach emotions to incoming stimuli in a fraction of a second. Therefore, you need to be sensitive to your nonverbal cues, appearance, and initial statements.

Signalling that we are trustworthy also helps strengthen the relationship. We can do this by demonstrating that we are reliable and will keep our promises as well as by identifying shared goals and values. Trustworthiness also increases by developing a shared understanding of the negotiation process, including its norms and expectations about speed and timing.[86] Finally, relationship building demands emotional intelligence.[87] This includes managing the emotions you display to the other party, particularly avoiding an image of superiority, aggressiveness,

or insensitivity. Emotional intelligence also involves managing the other party's emotions. We can use well-placed flattery, humour, and other methods to keep everyone in good mood and to break unnecessary tension.[88]

EXPERT VERSUS AVERAGE NEGOTIATORS

Are there certain behaviours that expert negotiators exhibit differently than other people? In a classic study conducted in the U.K., researchers selected a group of more than 50 expert negotiators and compared them to a similar-sized group of "average" negotiators. After watching both groups while they negotiated actual deals, it was clear that experts do in fact behave differently from average negotiators. A surprise finding was that experts do not actually spend more time preparing than most other people; instead, they differed substantially on *how they planned* and *what they planned for*. Expert negotiators spent a great deal more energy considering the things we mentioned earlier: goals, their BATNA, and their resistance point. Naïve negotiators rarely did so, and even if they did, the level of detail for each element was cursory at best.[89]

The researchers also examined differences between the two groups in terms of the face-to-face interactions while negotiating. These differences are summarized in Exhibit 11.7. What are the things experts do *less?* First, expert negotiators tend to use fewer irritators, which are words or phrases that have no persuasive value and tend to irritate one's counterpart. One of the most frequently used irritators is the phrase "generous offer" to describe one's proposal. Second, expert negotiators make fewer counterproposals than average negotiators–instead, they spent more time clarifying and understanding a proposal before putting another offer on the table. Third, an expert is less likely to get into a defend-and-attack spiral, whereby both sides use heated or emotional-laden comments in a back-and-forth manner. An average negotiator is over three times more likely to engage in such behaviour. And finally, experts spend much more face-to-face time ensuring that they understand their counterpart's perspective. In doing so, they will use phrases such as, "So do I understand. . ." and "If I understand you correctly. . .". These behaviours send a signal to a counterpart that they are being understood and listened to, both of which increase trust.

There are also behaviours that experts tend to exhibit *more* than average negotiators. The researchers discovered that experts ask more than twice as many questions. This makes sense because information gathering is central to value creation, and there is plenty of research supporting the argument that naïve negotiators tend to approach most negotiations with a distributive mentality (even when the situation is integrative). Expert negotiators were also

EXHIBIT 11.7: Differences Between Expert and Average Negotiators

Face-to-Face Behaviours	Expert Negotiators	Average Negotiators
Use of irritators "This is a generous offer. . ." "We're willing to be reasonable. . ."	2.3 per hour	10.8 per hour
Use of counterproposals	1.7 per hour	3.1 per hour
Defend/attack spirals "You can't blame us. . ." "It's not our fault. . ."	1.9% of comments	6.3% of comments
Testing understanding and summarizing "So do I understand. . ." "If I understand you correctly. . ."	17.2% of all behaviours	8.3% of all behaviours
Asking questions	21.3% of all behaviours	9.6% of all behaviours
Giving information about internal thoughts (feelings, concerns)	12.1 % of all behaviours	7.8% of all behaviours
Number of reasons to support an argument	1.8 on average	3.0 on average

more likely to use communication patterns in which they gave clues about how they were thinking about alternatives. For example, a skilled negotiator might say something like, "I'm uncertain how to react to what you've just said. I have some concerns about the meaning of two aspects of the offer. Can you help me resolve this?"

Finally, imagine a situation where your counterpart has made a claim or an offer and you intend to respond with reasons against their argument. How many reasons should you cite? Most people think that more is better here–and that is consistent with the trend between experts and average negotiators. In fact, experts tend to focus on only one or two counterarguments rather than presenting a laundry list. They do so because the greater the number of reasons, the more likely their overall argument will be diluted. So, keep it short, focused, and simple. You'll be more effective that way.

Chapter Summary

LO1 Define conflict and debate its positive and negative consequences in the workplace.

Conflict is the process in which one party perceives that its interests are being opposed or negatively affected by another party. The earliest view of conflict was that it was dysfunctional for organizations. Even today, we recognize that conflict sometimes or to some degree consumes productive time, increases stress and job dissatisfaction, discourages coordination and resource sharing, undermines customer service, fuels organizational politics, and undermines team cohesion. But conflict can also be beneficial. It is known to motivate more active thinking about problems and possible solutions, encourage more active monitoring of the organization in its environment, and improve team cohesion (where the conflict source is external).

LO2 Distinguish task from relationship conflict and describe three strategies to minimize relationship conflict during task conflict episodes.

Task conflict occurs when people focus their discussion around the issue while showing respect for people with other points of view. Relationship conflict exists when people view each other, rather than the issue, as the source of conflict. It is apparent when people attack each other's credibility and display aggression towards the other party. It is difficult to separate task from relationship conflict. However, three strategies or conditions that minimize relationship conflict during constructive debate are: (1) emotional intelligence of the participants, (2) team cohesion, and (3) supportive team norms.

LO3 Diagram the conflict process model and describe six structural sources of conflict in organizations.

The conflict process model begins with the five structural sources of conflict: incompatible goals, differentiation (different values and beliefs), interdependence, scarce resources, ambiguous rules, and communication problems. These sources lead one or more parties to perceive a conflict and to experience conflict emotions. This, in turn, produces manifest conflict, such as behaviours towards the other side. The conflict process often escalates through a series of episodes.

LO4 Outline the five conflict handling styles and discuss the circumstances in which each would be most appropriate.

There are five known conflict handling styles: problem solving, forcing, avoiding, yielding, and compromising. People who use problem solving have a win-win orientation. Others, particularly forcing, assume a win-lose orientation. In general, people gravitate towards one or two preferred conflict handling styles that match their personality, personal and cultural values, and past experience.

The best style depends on the situation. Problem solving is best when interests are not perfectly opposing, the parties trust each other, and the issues are complex. Forcing works best when you strongly believe in your position, the dispute requires quick action, and the other party would take advantage of a cooperative style. Avoid is preferred when the conflict has become emotional or the cost of resolution is higher than its benefits. Yielding works well when the other party has substantially more power, the issue is less important to you, and you are not confident in the logical soundness of your position. Compromising is preferred when the parties have equal power, they are under time pressure, and they lack trust.

LO5 Apply the six structural approaches to conflict management and describe the three types of third-party dispute resolution.

Structural approaches to conflict management include emphasizing superordinate goals, reducing differentiation, improving communication and understanding, reducing interdependence, increasing resources, and clarifying rules and procedures.

Third-party conflict resolution is any attempt by a relatively neutral person to help the parties resolve their differences. The three main forms of third-party dispute resolution are mediation, arbitration, and inquisition. Managers tend to use an inquisition approach, although mediation and arbitration are more appropriate, depending on the situation.

LO6 Describe distributive and integrative negotiations and outline strategies skilled negotiators use to claim value and create value.

Negotiation refers to decision-making situations in which two or more interdependent parties attempt to reach agreement. When negotiator goals run in opposite directions they find themselves in a distributive situation, and when their goals are not fully incompatible they are in an integrative situation. Effective distributive strategies include making ambitious opening offers and managing the concession-making process. In an integrative situation, value can be created by gathering information, sharing information, asking questions to understand a counterpart's perspective, and building the relationship.

Key Terms

best alternative to a negotiated agreement (BATNA), p. 285
conflict, p. 270
distributive situation, p. 285
integrative situation, p. 285
negotiation, p. 284
relationship conflict, p. 272
superordinate goals, p. 280
task conflict, p. 272
third-party conflict resolution, p. 282
win-lose orientation, p. 278
win-win orientation, p. 278

Critical-Thinking Questions

1. Distinguish task conflict from relationship conflict and explain how to apply the former with minimal levels of the latter.
2. The CEO of Creative Toys, Inc. read about cooperation in Japanese companies and vowed to bring this same philosophy to his company. His goal is to avoid all conflict, so that employees will work cooperatively and be happier at Creative Toys. Discuss the merits and limitations of the CEO's policy.
3. Conflict among managers emerged soon after a French company acquired a Swedish firm. The Swedes perceived the French management as hierarchical and arrogant, whereas the French thought the Swedes were naive, cautious, and lacking an achievement orientation. Identify the source(s) of conflict that best explain this conflict, and describe ways to reduce dysfunctional conflict in this situation.
4. You have just been transferred from one unit of the organization to another unit. On the last day of work in the first unit, your current manager calls your new manager informing her that you are a tough candidate and that you possess an attitude. The would-be manager calls you providing you with the information and expresses apprehension. How would you resolve this conflict?
5. You are a special assistant to the commander-in-chief of a peacekeeping mission to a war-torn part of the world. The unit consists of a few thousand peacekeeping troops from the Canada, France, India, and four other countries. The troops will work together for approximately one year. What strategies would you recommend to improve mutual understanding and minimize conflict among these troops?
6. The chief operating officer (COO) has noticed that production employees in the company's Mexican manufacturing operations are unhappy with some of the production engineering decisions made by engineers in the company's headquarters in Toronto. At the same time, the engineers complain that production employees aren't applying their engineering specifications correctly and don't understand why those specifications were put in place. The COO believes that the best way to resolve this conflict is to have a frank and open discussion between some of the engineers and employees representing the Mexican production crew. This open dialogue approach worked well recently among managers in the company's Toronto headquarters, so it should work equally well between the engineers and production staff. Based on your knowledge of communication and mutual understanding as a way to resolve conflict, discuss the COO's proposal.
7. Describe the inquisitional approach to resolve disputes between employees or work units. Discuss its appropriateness in organizational settings, including the suitability of its use with a multigenerational workforce.
8. Jane has just been appointed as purchasing manager of Tacoma Technologies, Inc. The previous purchasing manager, who recently retired, was known for his "winner-take-all" approach to suppliers. He continually fought for more discounts and was skeptical about any special deals that suppliers would propose. A few suppliers refused to do business with Tacoma Technologies, but senior management was confident that the former purchasing manager's approach minimized the company's costs. Jane wants to try a more collaborative approach for working with suppliers. Will her approach work? How should she adopt a more collaborative approach in future negotiations with suppliers?
9. You are a new program manager with responsibility for significant funding and external relations, and because of downsizing issues in your area, you have lost two valuable employees (actually 1.5, because the second person is on half time now; she used to be your manager and was the one you trained under). You have been in the new job approximately two weeks; however, you have been in the unit for more than a year and have seen how systems are managed from your manager's perspective. You now have her job. Out of the blue, a senior person (not in your area) comes to you and says he is taking most of your space (when the company had to let the 1.5 people go). He doesn't ask your permission, nor does he seem the least bit concerned with what your response. What do you do?

Case Study: CAR WARS AT WOLFSBURG

By Steven L. McShane, The University of Western Australia

Over the past 15 years, Volkswagen Group (VW) acquired several fiefdoms–Audi, Lamborghini, Bentley, Bugatti, Skoda, SEAT–that jealously guarded their brand and continuously rebelled against sharing knowledge. One member of VW's supervisory board (German equivalent of a board of directors) commented that managing the company is "like trying to ride a chariot with four or five horses, each of which pulls in a different direction."

Then Porsche AG entered the fray. The luxury sports car company, which relies on VW for some of its production work, began acquiring stock in VW and eventually achieved a controlling interest. Porsche CEO Wendelin Wiedeking was aware of VW's internal rivalries. "If you mix the Porsche guys with the Audi guys and the VW guys you will have trouble," says Wiedeking. "Each is proud to belong to his own company."

Yet Wiedeking stirred up a different type of conflict as Porsche tightened its grip over VW's supervisory board. Through an unswerving drive for efficient production and astute marketing, Wiedeking and his executive team transformed Porsche into the world's most profitable and prestigious car company. Wiedeking wanted to apply those practices at VW by closing down inefficient operations and money-losing car lines.

"Wiedeking is a Porsche CEO from another corporate culture," says German auto analyst Christoph Stuermer. "He's out to maximize profits by cutting costs. And he snubbed everyone, telling off VW management, interfering with their way of doing business." Ferdinand Dudenhoeffer, director of the Germany's Center of Automotive Research (CAR), agrees. "Porsche is very successful in being lean and profitable. It's not going to be harmonious."

Particularly offended by Wiedeking's plans was VW chairman Ferdinand Piëch, who had a different vision of Europe's largest automaker. Piëch, whose grandfather developed the VW Beetle, placed more emphasis on spectacular engineering than exceptional profits. For example, he supported the money-losing Bugatti brand, which VW acquired several years ago when Piëch was CEO. More recently, Piëch championed the Phaeton, VW's luxury car that broke new ground in innovation (it boasts 100 patents) but has not been a commercial success.

Wiedeking, on the other hand, believed that VW could be more profitable if it stopped producing the Phaeton and Bugatti. "Piëch sees his vision endangered by Wiedeking," says Dudenhoeffer. "Wiedeking said that there are no holy cows at VW, no more Phaetons, no more Bugattis." These ideas made Piëch's blood boil. "Anyone who says that VW should pull the Phaeton doesn't understand the world," grumbled Piëch, explaining that luxury cars represent the only segment with double-digit growth.

There is an unusual twist in the conflict involving Piëch, Wiedeking, and Porsche. Piëch is a member of the Porsche family. He is a cousin of Porsche chairman Wolfgang Porsche and owns a 10 percent share of the Porsche company. Piëch began his career at Porsche and became its chief engineer before moving to Audi and later VW. Furthermore, in what many consider a blatant conflict of interest, Piëch supported Porsche's initial investment in VW. But when Piëch's and Wiedeking's plans ended up on a collision course, that initial friendly investment in the partnership turned into all-out corporate war. "There was always a cease-fire between Piëch and the Porsches, but now it's war," claims auto analyst Ferdinand Dudenhoeffer. "This is like 'Dallas' and 'Dynasty' in Wolfsburg (city where VW has its headquarters). No company in the world is so self-absorbed with its problems."

Postscript Ironically, Porsche CEO Wendelin Wiedeking's plans backfired. Porsche had borrowed heavily to acquire its controlling interest in VW while maintaining its own business operations. Some estimate that Porsche had loans of more than US$14 billion. Furthermore, VW shares increased substantially during the takeover process, so Porsche owed massive taxes for the increased "paper profits" of the shares it owned. The timing couldn't have been worse. The great financial crisis hit the world, which cut Porsche sales and dried up funds, making it difficult for Porsche to pay interest on its loans and to renew loans that were coming due. In effect, it was on the brink of bankruptcy. In addition, a unique law allowed one German state (Lower Saxony), which had a 20 percent ownership in VW, to veto any important decisions in the company, including Porsche's control of VW.

Ultimately, Porsche agreed to give up its controlling interest in VW. Instead, it sold some of its business to VW and the Qatar government and, ultimately, agreed to be acquired by VW (rather than vice versa). Wiedeking lost his job as Porsche CEO, whereas Ferdinand Piëch (as chairman of VW's supervisory board) would effectively be head of both automakers. Complicated legal and financial matters delayed the complete acquisition, but VW recently completed its takeover of Porsche.

Discussion Questions

1. Identify and discuss the sources of conflict between Porsche and Volkswagen executives.
2. Describe the conflict handling styles used by Wendelin Wiedeking and Ferdinand Piëch. Were they appropriate in this situation?

The facts of this case were pieced together by Steven L. McShane from the following sources: M. Landler, "Twist in the Intrigue at VW May Help Chief Keep His Job," *New York Times*, 21 April 2006, 5; R. Hutton, "Porsche Ready to Swallow VW," *Autocar*, 7 November 2007; "German Carmaker Family Feud Plays out in VW Boardroom," *Deutsche Welle*, 18 September 2008; D. Hawranek, "Clans, Executives Sharpen Knives Backstage at Porsche and VW," *Spiegel Online*, 11 March 2008; N. D. Schwartz, "Porsche Takes a Controlling Interest in VW," *New York Times*, 17 September 2008; D. Hawranek, "German Carmaker Narrowly Averts Bankruptcy." *Spiegel Online*, 25 May 2009; C. Dougherty, "Porsche Chief Pays Full Price for his Overreach." *International Herald Tribune*, 24 July, 2009, 1; Bryant, Adam. "VW-Porsche merger ends years of wrangles." Financial Times (London), 5 July, 2012.

Class Exercise: THE CONTINGENCIES OF CONFLICT HANDLING

By Gerard A. Callanan and David F. Perri, West Chester University of Pennsylvania

Purpose This exercise is designed to help you understand the contingencies of applying conflict handling styles in organizational settings.

Instructions

Step 1: Participants will read each of the five scenarios presented below and select the most appropriate response from among the five alternatives. Each scenario has a correct response for that situation.

Step 2 (Optional): The instructor may ask each student to complete the Conflict Handling Scale handling self-assessment or a similar instrument. This instrument will provide an estimate of your preferred conflict handling style.

Step 3: As a class, participants give their feedback on the responses to each of the scenarios, with the instructor guiding discussion on the contextual factors embodied in each scenario.

For each scenario, the class should identify the response selected by the majority. In addition, participants will discuss how they decided on the choices they made and the contextual factors they took into account in making their selections.

Step 4: Students will compare their responses to the five scenarios with their results from the conflict handling self-assessment. Discussion will focus on the extent to which each person's preferred conflict handling style influenced their alternatives in this activity, and the implications of this style preference for managing conflict in organizations.

Scenario #1

Setting You are a manager of a division in the accounting department of a large Canadian bank. Nine exempt-level analysts and six nonexempt clerical staff report to you. Recently, one of your analysts, Jane Wilson, has sought the bank's approval for tuition reimbursement for the cost of an evening MBA program specializing in organizational behaviour. The bank normally encourages employees to seek advanced degrees on a part-time basis. Indeed, through your encouragement, nearly all of the members of your staff are pursuing additional schoolwork. You consult the bank's policy manual and discover that two approvals are necessary for reimbursement–yours and that of the manager of training and development, Kathy Gordon. Further, the manual states that approval for reimbursement will only be granted if the coursework is "reasonably job related." Based on your review of the matter, you decide to approve Jane's request for reimbursement. However, Kathy Gordon rejects it outright by claiming that coursework in organizational behaviour is not related to an accounting analyst position. She states that the bank will only reimburse the analyst for a degree in either accounting or finance. In your opinion, however, the interpersonal skills and insights to be gained from a degree in organizational behaviour are job related and can also benefit the employee in future assignments. The analyst job requires interaction with a variety of individuals at different levels in the organization, and it is important that interpersonal and communication skills be strong.

After further discussion it becomes clear that you and Kathy Gordon have opposite views on the matter. Since both of you are at the same organization level and have equal status, it appears that you are at an impasse. Although the goal of reimbursement is important, you are faced with other pressing demands on your time. In addition, the conflict has diverted the attention of your work group away from its primary responsibilities. Because the school term is about to begin, it is essential that you and Kathy Gordon reach a timely agreement to enable Jane to pursue her coursework.

Action Alternative	Ranking (1st & 2nd)
1. You go along with Kathy Gordon's view and advise Jane Wilson to select either accounting or finance as a major for her MBA.	______
2. You decide to withdraw from the situation completely, and tell Jane to work it out with Kathy Gordon on her own.	______
3. You decide to take the matter to those in higher management levels and argue forcefully for your point of view. You do everything in your power to ensure that a decision will be made in your favour.	______
4. You decide to meet Kathy Gordon halfway in order to reach an agreement. You advise Jane to pursue her MBA in accounting or finance, but also recommend she minor in organizational behaviour by taking electives in that field.	______
5. You decide to work more closely with Kathy Gordon by attempting to get a clear as well as flexible policy written that reflects both of your views. Of course, this will require a significant amount of your time.	______

Action Alternatives for Scenario #1 Please indicate your first (1) and second (2) choices from among the following alternatives by writing the appropriate number in the space provided.

Scenario #2

Setting You are the vice president of a relatively large division (80 employees) in a medium-sized consumer products company. Due to the recent turnover of minority staff, your division has fallen behind in meeting the company's goal for Equal Employment Opportunity (EEO) hiring. Because of a scarcity of qualified minority candidates, it appears that you may fall further behind in achieving stated EEO goals.

Although you are aware of the problem, you believe that the low level of minority hiring is due to increased attrition in minority staff as well as the lack of viable replacement candidates. However, the EEO officer believes that your hiring criteria are too stringent, resulting in the rejection of minority candidates with the basic qualifications to do the job. You support the goals and principles of EEO; however, you are concerned that the hiring of less-qualified candidates will weaken the performance of your division. The EEO officer believes that your failure to hire minority employees is damaging to the company in the short term because corporate goals will not be met, and in the long term because it will restrict the pool of minority candidates available for upward mobility. Both of you regard your concerns as important. Further, you recognize that both of you have the company's best interests in mind and that you have a mutual interest in resolving the conflict.

Action Alternatives for Scenario #2 Please indicate your first (1) and second (2) choices from among the following alternatives by writing the appropriate number in the space provided.

Scenario #3

Setting You are the manager in charge of the financial reporting section of a large insurance company. It is the responsibility of your group to make periodic written and oral reports to senior management regarding the company's financial

Action Alternative	Ranking (1st & 2nd)
1. You conclude that the whole problem is too complex an issue for you to handle right now. You put it on the "back burner" and decide to reconsider the problem at a later date.	______
2. You believe that your view outweighs the perspective of the EEO officer. You decide to argue your position more vigorously and hope that your stance will sway the EEO officer to agree with your view.	______
3. You decide to accept the EEO officer's view. You agree to use less stringent selection criteria and thereby hire more minority employees.	______
4. You give in to the EEO officer somewhat by agreeing to relax your standards a little bit. This would allow slightly more minority hiring (but not enough to satisfy the EEO goal) and could cause a small reduction in the overall performance of your division.	______
5. You try and reach a consensus that addresses each of your concerns. You agree to work harder at hiring more minority applicants and request that the EEO officer agree to help find the most qualified minority candidates available.	______

performance. The company's senior management has come to rely on your quick and accurate dissemination of financial data as a way to make vital decisions in a timely fashion. This has given you a relatively high degree of organizational influence. You rely on various operating departments to supply you with financial information according to a pre-established reporting schedule.

In two days, you must make your quarterly presentation to the company's Board of Directors. However, the Claims Department has failed to supply you with several key pieces of information that are critical to your presentation. You check the reporting schedule and realize that you should have had the information two days ago. When you call Bill Jones, the Claims Department manager, he informs you that he cannot possibly have the data to you within the next two days. He states that other pressing work has a higher priority. Although you explain the critical need for this data, he is unwilling to change his position. You believe that your presentation is vital to the company's welfare and explain this to Bill Jones. Although Bill has less status than you, he has been known to take advantage of individuals who are unwilling or unable to push their point of view. With your presentation less than two days away, it is critical that you receive information from the Claims Department within the next 24 hours.

Action Alternatives for Scenario #3 Please indicate your first (1) and second (2) choices from among the following alternatives by writing the appropriate number in the space provided.

Action Alternative	Ranking (1st & 2nd)
1. Accept the explanation from Bill Jones and try to get by without the figures by using your best judgment as to what they would be.	______
2. Tell Bill Jones that unless you have the data from his department on your desk by tomorrow morning, you will be forced to go over his head to compel him to give you the numbers.	______
3. Meet Bill Jones halfway by agreeing to receive part of the needed figures and using your own judgment on the others.	______
4. Try to get your presentation postponed until a later date, if possible.	______
5. Forget about the short-term need for information and try to achieve a longer term solution, such as adjusting the reporting schedule to better accommodate your mutual needs.	______

Scenario #4

Setting You are the production manager of a medium-sized building products company. You control a production line that runs on a three-shift basis. Recently, Ted Smith, the materials handling manager, requested you to accept a different packaging of the raw materials for the production process than what has been customary. He states that new machinery he has installed makes it much easier to provide the material in 45-kilogram sacks instead of the 22-kilogram bags that you currently receive. Ted further explains that the provision of the material in the 22-kilogram bags would put an immense strain on his operation, and he therefore has a critical need for you to accept the change. You know that accepting materials in the new packaging will cause some minor disruption in your production process, but should not cause long-term problems for any of the three shifts. However, you are a little annoyed by the proposed change because Ted did not consult with you before he installed the new equipment. In the past, you and he have been open in your communication. You do not think that this failure to consult you represents a change in your relationship.

Because you work closely with Ted, it is essential that you maintain the harmonious and stable working relationship that you have built over the past few years. In addition, you may need some help from him in the future, since you already know that your operation will have special material requirements in about two months. You also know that Ted has influence at higher levels of the organization.

Action Alternatives for Scenario #4 Please indicate your first (1) and second (2) choices from among the following alternatives by writing the appropriate number in the space provided.

Action Alternative	Ranking (1st & 2nd)
1. Agree to accept the raw material in the different format.	________
2. Refuse to accept the material in the new format because it would cause a disruption in your operation.	________
3. Propose a solution where you accept material in the new format during the first shift, but not during the second and third.	________
4. Tell Ted Smith that you do not wish to deal with the issue at this time, but that you will consider his request and get back to him at a later date.	________
5. You decide to tell Ted Smith of your concern regarding his failure to consult with you before installing new equipment. You inform him that you wish to find longer term solutions to the conflict between you.	________

Scenario #5

Setting You are employed as supervisor of the compensation and benefits section in the human resources department of a medium-sized pharmaceutical company. Your staff of three clerks is responsible for maintaining contacts with the various benefits providers and answering related questions from the company's employees. Your section shares support staff, word processing, and copier resources with the training and development section of the department. Recently, a disagreement has arisen between you and Beth Hanson, the training and development supervisor, over when the support staff should take their lunches. Beth would like the support staff to take their lunches an hour later to coincide with the time most of her people go to lunch. You know that the support staff does not want to change their lunch times. Further, the current time is more convenient for your staff.

At this time, you are hard-pressed to deal with the situation. You have an important meeting with the provider of dental insurance in two days. It is critical that you are well prepared for this meeting, and these other tasks are a distraction.

Action Alternatives for Scenario #5 Please indicate your first (1) and second (2) choices from among the following alternatives by writing the appropriate number in the space provided.

Action Alternative	Ranking (1st & 2nd)
1. Take some time over the next day and propose a solution whereby the support staff takes their lunch at the earlier time three days a week and at the later time two days a week.	________
2. Tell Beth Hanson you will deal with the matter in a few days, after you have addressed the more pressing issues.	________
3. Let Beth Hanson have her way by agreeing to a later lunch hour for the support staff.	________
4. Flat out tell Beth Hanson that you will not agree to a change in the support staff's lunchtime.	________
5. Devote more time to the issue. Attempt to achieve a broad-based consensus with Beth Hanson that meets her needs as well as yours and those of the support staff.	________

Source: G. A. Callanan and D. F. Perri, "Teaching Conflict Management Using a Scenario-Based Approach," *Journal of Education for Business,* 81 (Jan/Feb 2006), pp. 131–139.

Self-Assessment: WHAT IS YOUR PREFERRED CONFLICT HANDLING STYLE?

Purpose This self-assessment is designed to help you to identify your preferred conflict handling style.

Instructions Read each of the statements below and select the response that best indicates how often you handled conflict in the way described in that statement. Then use the scoring key in Appendix B to calculate your results for each conflict handling style. This exercise is completed alone so students assess themselves honestly without concerns of social comparison. However, class discussion will focus on the different conflict handling styles and the situations in which each is most appropriate.

Conflict Handling Style Scale

Over the past SIX (6) MONTHS, how often did you do the following to handle conflicts?	Never/rarely	Seldom	Sometimes	Often	Almost always
1. I went along with the other party's wishes rather than my own.	○	○	○	○	○
2. I compromised by accepting a middle ground solution.	○	○	○	○	○
3. I tried to creatively find the best solution for everyone.	○	○	○	○	○
4. I avoided differences of opinion as much as possible.	○	○	○	○	○
5. I pushed my own ideas and preferences.	○	○	○	○	○
6. I tried to make the dispute seem less important.	○	○	○	○	○
7. I accommodated the other party's wishes.	○	○	○	○	○
8. I did my best to get what I wanted.	○	○	○	○	○
9. I tried to figure out how to satisfy both my interests and the other party's.	○	○	○	○	○
10. I made sure that both sides gave in a little.	○	○	○	○	○
11. I worked towards a 50–50 compromise.	○	○	○	○	○
12. I fought for my own position.	○	○	○	○	○
13. I searched for a solution that satisfied both parties.	○	○	○	○	○
14. I delayed or avoided solving the disagreement.	○	○	○	○	○
15. I held my position.	○	○	○	○	○
16. I let the other side have its way.	○	○	○	○	○
17. I tried to settle the conflict with a half-way compromise.	○	○	○	○	○
18. I tried to find a solution that benefited both sides.	○	○	○	○	○
19. I avoided communicating with the people I had the conflict.	○	○	○	○	○
20. I gave the other party what they wanted.	○	○	○	○	○

Sources: This scale was created by Steven L McShane based on information or previous instruments in: R. R. Blake, H. A. Shepard, and J. S. Mouton, Managing Intergroup Conflict in Industry (Houston: Gulf Publishing, 1964); K. W. Thomas, "Conflict and Negotiation Processes in Organizations." In *Handbook of Industrial and Organizational Psychology*, edited by M. D. Dunnette and L. M. Hough, 651-718. 2nd ed. (Palo Alto, CA: Consulting Psychologists Press, 1992); C. K. W. de Dreu, A. Evers, B. Beersma, E. S. Kluwer, and A. Nauta, "A Theory-based Measure of Conflict Management Strategies in the Workplace," *Journal of Organizational Behavior*, 22 (2001), pp. 645-68; M. A. Rahim, *Managing Conflict in Organizations*. 4th ed. (New Brunswick, NJ: Transaction Publishers, 2011).

SELF-ASSESSMENTS FOR CHAPTER 11

SELF-ASSESSMENT NAME	DESCRIPTION	LOCATION
What is your preferred conflict handling style?	The assessment helps you see what approach you tend to take when dealing with conflict.	Page 295 connect

Norsat CEO Amiee Chan has revived and transformed the Vancouver-based technology company through her customer-centric vision and engaging stories about the company's success.

Mark van Manen/*The Province*

Chapter **12**

Leadership in Organizational Settings

LEARNING OBJECTIVES

After reading this chapter, you should be able to:

LO1. Define leadership and shared leadership.

LO2. Describe the four elements of transformational leadership and explain why they are important for organizational change.

LO3. Compare managerial leadership with transformational leadership, and describe the features of task-oriented, people-oriented, and servant leadership.

LO4. Discuss the elements of path-goal theory, Fiedler's contingency model, and leadership substitutes.

LO5. Describe the two components of the implicit leadership perspective.

LO6. Identify eight personal attributes associated with effective leaders and describe authentic leadership.

LO7. Discuss cultural and gender similarities and differences in leadership.

Amiee Chan faced a monumental leadership challenge when she was appointed CEO of Norsat International Inc. At the time (2006), the Richmond, B.C.-based provider of satellite ground stations and related technologies for remote and challenging environments was in financial difficulty due to reliance on one customer, the U.S. military. "We were financially in very deep trouble. We didn't have a lot of customer diversity," Chan recalls. "At one point, I had to sell my car to ensure we made payroll." Chan and her executive team stabilized Norsat's cash flow, refocused sales around achievable contracts, and began diversifying the business. Today, Norsat is profitable, has tripled its revenue, and sells to dozens of militaries and private sector companies in 87 countries.

Norsat's recovery and transformation has been guided by Chan's strong customer-focused vision and leadership to "communicate the vision to staff and get them excited about the changes." Chan explains that "strong customer support has been absolutely essential to our success and we frequently hear that our commitment to excellent service is a key differentiator for our customers." Chan also decentralized the approval process so the management team feels more empowered to achieve the vision.

Chan frequently communicates her customer-focused vision through appealing stories. She recounts how Norsat's support team was able to remotely reconfigure satellite ground systems in Haiti to support earthquake recovery operations in that country. In another incident, Norsat employees demonstrated creative thinking and hard work to arrange a high-definition broadcast in Tonga, even though that country did not have the capacity for such a transmission. In a third recent example, Norsat staff set up a satellite communications system in Afghanistan on short notice. That top-secret project enabled transmission of U.S. President Obama's surprise visit to that country.

Chan acknowledges that being a female leader in a male-dominated industry has its challenges. Some leaders in Asia even mistake her as a junior manager rather than the CEO. "Occasionally I'll go to a foreign country with a male colleague," says Chan. "They'll always assume I'm the procurement manager and the guy is the CEO."

Chan takes these incidents in stride, recognizing that leadership stereotypes will "melt away" over time. "People make assumptions because women are still underrepresented in the boardroom," Chan explains. "I know that these attitudes and stereotypes will only change over time as more women take on positions of power."[1]

Norsat's survival and transformation illustrates how leaders such as Amiee Chan can make a difference in an organization's survival and success. This opening case study also highlights specific aspects of leadership, such as the leader's vision, communication, and persistence. Leadership is one of the most researched and discussed topics in the field of organizational behaviour.[2] Google returns a whopping 306 million web pages where "leadership" is mentioned. Google Scholar lists 216,000 journal articles and books with "leader" or "leadership" in the title. Amazon lists more than 27,000 books in the English language with "leadership" in the title. From 2000 to 2009, the U.S. Library of Congress catalogue added 7,336 books or documents with the words "leader" or "leadership" in the citation, compared with 3,054 items added in the 1990s and only 146 items with these words (many of which were newspaper names) added during the first decade of the 1900s.

The topic of leadership captivates us because we are awed by individuals who influence and motivate a group of people beyond expectations. This chapter explores leadership from four perspectives: transformational, managerial, implicit, and personal attributes.[3] Although some of these perspectives are currently more popular than others, each helps us to more fully understand the complex issue of leadership. The final section of this chapter looks at cross-cultural and gender issues in organizational leadership. But first, we learn about the meaning of leadership as well as shared leadership.

What is Leadership?

LO1

Several years ago, 54 leadership experts from 38 countries reached a consensus that **leadership** is about influencing, motivating, and enabling others to contribute towards the effectiveness and success of the organizations of which they are members.[4] This definition has two key components. First, leaders motivate others through persuasion and other influence tactics. They use their communication skills, rewards, and other resources to energize the collective towards the achievement of challenging objectives. Second, leaders are enablers. They arrange the work environment–such as allocating resources, altering work relationships, and buffering from outside interferences–so employees can achieve organizational objectives more easily.

leadership Influencing, motivating, and enabling others to contribute towards the effectiveness and success of the organizations of which they are members.

SHARED LEADERSHIP

As part of its employee engagement initiative, Rolls-Royce Engine Services in Oakland, California involved employees directly with clients, encouraged weekly huddles for information sharing, and accepted employee requests for less micromanagement. Employees at the aircraft engine repair facility not only experienced higher levels of engagement and empowerment, they also accepted more leadership responsibilities. "I saw people around me, all front-line employees, who were leaders," says a machine programmer at the Rolls-Royce Oakland plant. "They weren't actually leading the company, but they were people you would listen to and follow. We didn't have titles, but people had respect for what we did."[5]

Rolls-Royce Engine Services has moved towards greater **shared leadership** by encouraging and enabling employees throughout the organization to informally assume leadership responsibilities in various ways and at various times.[6] Shared leadership is based on the idea that leadership is a role, not a position. It doesn't belong to just one individual in the work unit. Instead, employees lead each other as the occasion arises. Shared leadership exists when

shared leadership The view that leadership is a role, not a position assigned to one person; consequently, people within the team and organization lead each other.

Fernando Morales/*The Globe and Mail*/CP Images

At EllisDon, leaders aren't just people in management jobs. The Mississauga-based construction giant believes that leadership extends to every employee in the organization. "Everyone is a leader, everyone is accountable to each other, and everyone is involved in the success of the company as whole," explains EllisDon CEO Geoff Smith (shown here). "It's a leadership philosophy throughout our company." EllisDon supports this shared leadership approach by setting outcome goals and then giving employees a high degree of autonomy to achieve them. "My leadership mantra is to get out of the way," says Smith. "Get good people, give them the authority, give them the support, and then get out of their way. So, you create leaders around you."[7]

employees champion the introduction of new technologies and products.[8] It also exists when employees engage in organizational citizenship behaviours that improve the performance and well-being of coworkers and the overall team.

Shared leadership typically supplements formal leadership; that is, employees lead along with the formal manager, rather than as a replacement for that manager. However, W. L. Gore & Associates, Semco SA, Valve Corporation, and a few other unique companies rely almost completely on shared leadership because they don't have any formal managers on the organizational chart.[9] In fact, when Gore employees are asked in annual surveys "Are you a leader?" more than 50 percent of them answer "Yes."

The idea of shared leadership is quickly gaining popularity in the business community. Sergio Marchionne, the Canadian-Italian CEO of Fiat and Chrysler, says: "We've abandoned the Great Man model of leadership that long characterized Fiat and have created a culture where everyone is expected to lead."[10] The notion that everyone takes on an informal leadership role has a long history. John Gardner, the former White House cabinet member who introduced Medicare, wrote more than two decades ago that the "vitality" of large organizations depends on shared leadership.[11] He argued that organizations depend on employees across all levels of the organization seeking out opportunities and solutions rather than relying on formal leaders to do so. Gardner observed, for example, that successful teams consist of individuals other than the formal leader who take responsibility for healing rifts when conflicts arise, and for building confidence in others when events have turned for the worse.

Shared leadership flourishes in organizations where the formal leaders are willing to delegate power and encourage employees to take initiative and risks without fear of failure (i.e., a learning orientation culture). Shared leadership also calls for a collaborative rather than internally competitive culture because employees take on shared leadership roles when coworkers support them for their initiative. Furthermore, shared leadership lacks formal authority, so it operates best when employees learn to influence others through their enthusiasm, logical analysis, and involvement of coworkers in their idea or vision.

Transformational Leadership Perspective

LO2

Leadership research can be roughly organized into the four perspectives mentioned earlier: transformational, managerial, implicit, and personal attributes. By far the most popular leadership perspective today—and arguably the most important in the domain of leadership—is transformational leadership. **Transformational leadership** views leaders as change agents. They

transformational leadership A leadership perspective that explains how leaders change teams or organizations by creating, communicating, and modelling a vision for the organization or work unit and inspiring employees to strive for that vision.

create, communicate, and model a shared vision for the team or organization. They encourage experimentation so employees find a better path to the future. Through these and other activities, transformational leaders also build commitment in followers to strive for that vision. There are several models of transformational leadership, but four elements that are common throughout most of them and represent the core concepts of this leadership perspective are: develop and communicate a strategic vision, model the vision, encourage experimentation, and build commitment to the vision (see Exhibit 12.1).[12]

DEVELOP AND COMMUNICATE A STRATEGIC VISION

The heart of transformational leadership is a strategic *vision*.[13] A vision is a positive representation of a future state that energizes and unifies employees.[14] Sometimes this vision is created by the leader; at other times, it is formed by employees or other stakeholders and then adopted and championed by the formal leader. The opening case study to this chapter described how Amiee Chan has led Norsat's success through a customer-centric vision. William Rogers, CEO of British radio station group UKRD, emphasizes that one of the key features of successful leaders is their "clarity of vision, so people can say: 'I know where we're going, what this journey is about, what our noble cause is.' For us, it's not just running a radio group and commercial success–it's about changing people's lives, impacting on communities."[15] Connections 12.1 describes one of Canada's greatest civic examples of visionary leadership, namely how former mayor Art Phillips and his associates transformed Vancouver into one of the world's most liveable cities.

An effective strategic vision has several identifiable features.[16] It refers to an idealized future with a higher purpose. This purpose is associated with personal values that directly or indirectly fulfill the needs of multiple stakeholders. A values-based vision is also meaningful and appealing to employees, which energizes them to strive for that ideal. A vision needs to energize employees because it is usually a distant goal that is both challenging and abstract. A vision is challenging because it requires substantial transformation, such as new work practices and belief systems.

A strategic vision is necessarily abstract for two reasons. One reason is that it hasn't yet been experienced (at least, not in this company or industry), so it isn't possible to detail what the vision looks like. The other reason is that an abstract description enables the vision to remain stable over time, yet is sufficiently flexible to accommodate operational adjustments in a shifting external environment. For example, Norsat's customer-centric vision does not refer to specific goals such as expanding the product range or using specific communications

EXHIBIT 12.1

Elements of Transformational Leadership

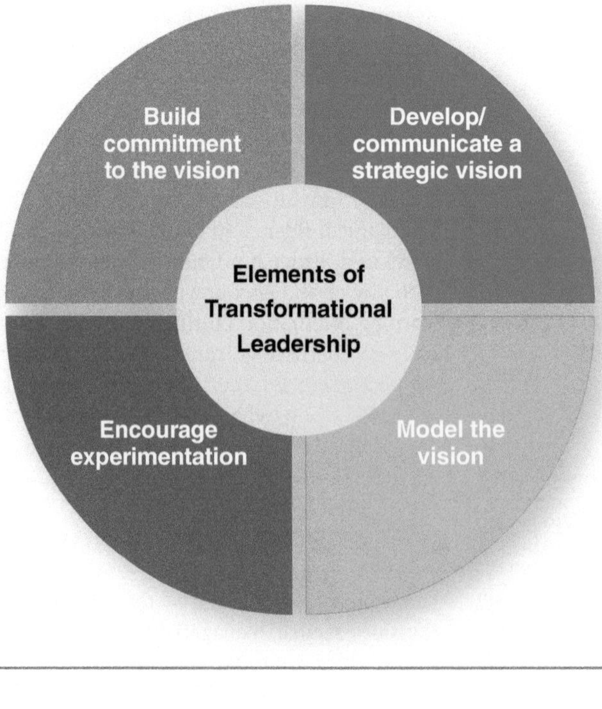

Global Connections 12.1:

LEADING THE VISION OF VANCOUVER AS A LIVEABLE CITY[17]

Vancouver is recognized as one of the world's most liveable cities. This accolade is due in large part to the leadership vision of the late Art Phillips, along with UBC professor Walter Hardwick and their civic party (TEAM) in the early 1970s. "The improvements in quality of life, living downtown, waterfront walks, and protecting neighbourhoods are all the results of Art Phillips' leadership," says former British Columbia premier Gordon Campbell. Current B.C. premier Christy Clark applauds Phillips as "a transformational leader who helped make one of Canada's great cities the envy of the world."

In the late 1960s, Phillips had established himself as one of Canada's most successful investment analysts. However, his attention turned to Vancouver politics when city planners attempted with little public consultation to build a freeway through the downtown, uproot Chinatown, allow a high-rise hotel near Stanley Park, sell land to suppress current property taxes (rather than to invest for future generations), and develop the downtown as an American-style concrete jungle. "He felt Vancouver was at a crucial turning point, headed in the wrong direction," recalls Carole Taylor, Phillips' wife and a distinguished journalist and politician. "Art could see what had to be done to create the future."

"Instead of being dead at night, we wanted the downtown core to be more European, a place to live and enjoy," said Phillips two decades later about this vision of Vancouver's future. "It was all about doing things differently. It was about bringing people in, not throwing them out, and making the city a place to enjoy, where people wanted to live." With this vision in mind, Phillips and Hardwick were elected to city council in the late 1960s. Their civic party won a landslide victory in the next election, which installed Phillips as mayor.

Along with redirecting Vancouver development towards a more liveable urban environment, Phillips is credited with introducing city government processes that support public input and active leadership of urban design. "He established institutions and ways of doing things that no one's ever altered. All succeeding mayors have built on what Art did," says urban affairs analyst Gordon Price, who served six terms as a Vancouver city councillor. "It was a brilliant moment in time."

George Diack/Vancouver Sun

In the 1970s, the late Art Phillips and his associates had an appealing vision of Vancouver's future that is largely responsible for its status today as one of the world's most liveable cities.

protocols. Instead, it describes the broader noble cause of reaching for the continuous ideal of serving customers better.

Another feature of an effective vision is that it is unifying. It is a superordinate objective that bonds employees together and aligns their personal values with the organization's values. In fact, a successful vision is really a shared vision, because employees collectively define themselves by this future state as part of their identification with the organization.

Communicate the Vision A strategic vision's effectiveness depends on how leaders convey it to followers and other stakeholders.[18] Words shape how we view the world, so successful transformational leaders carefully choose phrases that "frame" the vision and evoke desired images of the ideal future. For example, leaders at DaVita refer to the company as a village and employees (called teammates) are citizens of that village who "cross the bridge," meaning that they make a commitment to the community. "The words we use, while simple in nature, are packed with meaning," explains an executive at the largest dialysis treatment group in the United States.[19] Leaders also communicate the vision with sincerity and a level of passion that reflects their personal belief in the vision, and optimism that it can be reached. In other words, leaders communicate the vision nonverbally as well as verbally.

A third way leaders communicate the vision is through symbols, metaphors, stories, and other vehicles that transcend plain language.[20] These tools often borrow images of other experiences, thereby creating richer meaning of the not-yet-experienced vision. Borrowing from existing experiences also generates desired emotions, which motivates people to pursue the vision. When George Cohen, the ebullient CEO of McDonald's Canada, faced the difficult challenge of opening McDonalds restaurants in Moscow, he frequently reminded his team members that they were establishing "hamburger diplomacy." And in the mid-1800s, when ocean transportation was treacherous, Samuel Cunard emphasized that he was creating an "ocean railway." At the time, railroads provided one of the safest forms of transportation, and Cunard's metaphor reinforced the notion to employees and passengers alike that Cunard Steamship Lines, which at the time was based in Halifax, Nova Scotia, would provide equally safe transportation across the Atlantic Ocean.[21]

connect

What are your transformational leadership tendencies? Visit **connect.mcgrawhill.com** to estimate your transformational leadership score.

MODEL THE VISION

Transformational leaders not only talk about a vision; they enact it. They "walk the talk" by stepping outside the executive suite and doing things that symbolize the vision.[22] Leaders model the vision through significant events such as visiting customers, moving their offices closer to (or further from) employees, and holding ceremonies to symbolize significant change. However, they also enact the vision by ensuring that the more mundane daily activities–meeting agendas, dress codes, executive schedules–are consistent with the vision and its underlying values.

Modelling the vision is important because it legitimizes and demonstrates what the vision looks like in practice. Modelling is also important because it builds employee trust in the leader. The greater the consistency between the leader's words and actions, the more employees will believe in and be willing to follow the leader. In fact, one survey reported that leading by example is the most important characteristic of a leader.[23] "We hold our leaders to an even higher standard than our employees," says Nathan Bigler, human resource director at Eastern Idaho Regional Medical Center. "Leaders have to consistently walk the talk."[24]

ENCOURAGE EXPERIMENTATION

Transformational leadership is about change, and central to any change is discovering new behaviours and practices that are better aligned with the desired vision. Thus, effective transformational leaders encourage employees to question current practices and to experiment with new ways that are potentially more consistent with the visionary future state.[25] In other words, transformational leaders support a learning orientation (see Chapter 7). They encourage employees to continuously question the way things are currently done, actively experiment with new ideas and practices, and view reasonable mistakes as a natural part of the learning process.[26]

BUILD COMMITMENT TOWARDS THE VISION

Transforming a vision into reality requires employee commitment, and transformational leaders build this commitment in several ways.[27] Their words, symbols, and stories, such as Norsat CEO Amiee Chan's use of exceptional customer service stories to communicate her customer-centric vision of the company, build a contagious enthusiasm that energizes people to adopt the vision as their own. Leaders demonstrate a "can do" attitude by enacting and behaving consistently with their vision. This persistence and consistency reflect an image of honesty, trust, and integrity. By encouraging experimentation, leaders involve employees in the

Tencent founder and CEO "Pony" Ma Huateng has led China's social media revolution, yet he is described more as a humble college grad than an overconfident charismatic leader. "Ma always smiles, but more like a shy fresh graduate, rather than a sophisticated and charismatic leader," says one of China's major newspapers. Starting with a basic instant messaging service, Ma expanded the company into microblogging (Tencent Weibo), social networking (Qzone), online games, and online payments (TenPay). It recently launched a walkie-talkie style text/voice messaging system (WeChat), which already has 300 million users worldwide. Rather than relying on "the gift" of charisma, Ma has built Tencent through transformational leadership behaviours, including his vision of continuous innovation, encouragement of experimentation, and modelling that innovative spirit.[28]

change process so it is a collective activity. Leaders also build commitment through rewards, recognition, and celebrations as they pass milestones along the road to the desired vision.

TRANSFORMATIONAL LEADERSHIP AND CHARISMA

Some experts believe that charisma is an element of transformational leadership. They describe charismatic leadership either as an essential ingredient of transformational leadership or as transformational leadership in its highest form of excellence.[29] However, the emerging view, which this book adopts, is that charisma is distinct from transformational leadership. As noted in Chapter 10, *charisma* is a personal trait or relational quality that provides referent power over followers. Transformational leadership, in contrast, is a set of behaviours that engage followers towards a better future.[30]

Transformational leadership motivates followers through behaviours that persuade and earn trust, whereas charismatic leadership motivates followers directly through the leader's inherent referent power. For instance, communicating an inspiring vision is a transformational leadership behaviour that motivates followers to strive for that vision. This motivational effect exists separately from the leader's charismatic appeal. If the leader is highly charismatic, however, his or her charisma will amplify follower motivation.

Being charismatic is not inherently good or bad, but several research studies have concluded that charismatic leaders can produce negative consequences.[31] One concern with charismatic leadership is that it tends to produce dependent followers. Transformational leadership has the opposite effect–it builds follower empowerment, which tends to reduce dependence on the leader.

Another concern is that leaders who possess the gift of charisma may become intoxicated by this power, which leads to a greater focus on self-interest than on the common good. "Charisma becomes the undoing of leaders," warned Peter Drucker many years ago. "It makes them inflexible, convinced of their own infallibility, unable to change."[32] The late management guru witnessed the destructive effects of charismatic political leaders in Europe a century ago and foresaw that this personal or relational characteristic would create similar problems for organizations. The main point here is that transformational leaders are not necessarily charismatic, and charismatic leaders are not necessarily transformational.

EVALUATING THE TRANSFORMATIONAL LEADERSHIP PERSPECTIVE

Transformational leaders do make a difference.[33] Subordinates are more satisfied and have higher affective organizational commitment under transformational leaders. They also perform their jobs better, engage in more organizational citizenship behaviours, and make better or more creative decisions. One study of Canadian bank branches reported that organizational commitment and financial performance increased where the branch manager completed a transformational leadership training program.[34]

Transformational leadership is currently the most popular leadership perspective, but it faces a number of challenges.[35] One problem is that some models engage in circular logic. They define and measure transformational leadership by its effects on employees (e.g., inspire employees), then (not surprisingly) report that this leadership is effective because it inspires employees. Instead, transformational leadership needs to be defined purely as a set of behaviours that people use to lead others through the change process. A second concern is that some transformational leadership theories combine leader behaviours with the leader's personal characteristics of leaders. For instance, transformational leaders are described as visionary, imaginative, sensitive, and thoughtful, yet these personal characteristics are really predictors of transformational leadership behaviours.

A third concern is that transformational leadership is usually described as a universal concept, that is, it is good in all situations. Only a few studies have investigated whether this form of leadership is more valuable in some situations than others.[36] For instance, transformational leadership is probably more appropriate when organizations need to continuously adapt to a rapidly changing external environment than when the environment is stable. Preliminary evidence suggests that the transformational leadership perspective is relevant across cultures. However, there may be specific elements of transformational leadership, such as the way visions are communicated and modelled, that are more appropriate in North America than in other cultures.

Managerial Leadership Perspective

LO3

managerial leadership A leadership perspective stating that effective leaders help employees improve their performance and well-being towards current objectives and practices.

Leaders don't spend all (or even most) of their time transforming the organization or work unit. They also engage in **managerial leadership**—daily activities that support and guide the performance and well-being of individual employees and the work unit towards current objectives and practices. Leadership experts recognize that leading (transformational leadership) differs from managing (managerial leadership).[37] Although the distinction between these two perspectives remains somewhat fuzzy, each cluster has a reasonably clear set of activities and a strong research foundation.

One distinction between these two perspectives is that managerial leadership assumes the organization's (or department's) objectives are stable and aligned with the external environment.[38] It focuses on continuously developing or maintaining the effectiveness of employees and work units towards those established objectives and practices. In contrast, transformational leadership assumes the organization's current direction is misaligned and therefore needs to change towards a better future. This distinction is captured in the often-cited statement: "Managers are people who do things right and leaders are people who do the right thing."[39] Managers (more correctly, managerial leadership behaviours) "do things right" by enabling employees to perform established goals more effectively. Leaders (more correctly, transformational leadership behaviours) "do the right thing" by redirecting the organization towards a path that is better aligned with the external environment.

A second distinction is that managerial leadership is more micro-focused and concrete, because it relates to the specific performance and well-being objectives of individual employees and the immediate work unit. Transformational leadership is more macro-focused and abstract. It is directed towards an abstract strategic vision for an entire organization, department, or team.

Although transformational and managerial leadership are discussed as two leadership perspectives, they are better described as *interdependent* perspectives.[40] In other words, transformational leadership and managerial leadership depend on each other. Transformational leadership identifies, communicates, and builds commitment to a better future for the collective. But these transformational leadership behaviours are not enough for organizational success. That success also requires managerial leadership to translate the abstract vision into more specific operational behaviours and practices, and to continuously improve employee performance and well-being in the pursuit of that future ideal.

Managerial leadership also depends on transformational leadership to set the right direction. Otherwise, managers produce operational excellence towards long-range goals that are misaligned with the organization's long-term survival and for which employees lack commitment. For instance, the leaders at Dell Inc. relied on managerial excellence to produce low-cost computers, yet the company subsequently suffered because the external environment shifted towards higher-priced innovation products.[41] In other words, successful managerial leadership (operational efficiency with reasonably happy employees) was not enough to make Dell successful. It also needed transformational leadership to develop a vision that aligned the company's products more closely with the marketplace and inspired employees to work towards that vision.

© Graham Flack

T.G.I. Friday's UK business is thriving, thanks to the vision and managerial skill of CEO Karen Forrester. Forrester saw huge potential for the Texas-based company's UK operations, which were suffering from neglect. Her vision was to "bring the magic back" so customers could expect a consistently enjoyable restaurant experience based on authentic service. But Forrester complements this transformational leadership with managerial leadership behaviour. She weeded out staff who lacked commitment to revive the restaurant. She invested heavily in training so staff would serve customers better and more confidently. Forrester was recently named most people-focused CEO in the UK because she also demonstrates supportive leadership through her empathy, respect, and enthusiasm. "Without a doubt this industry is all about people," says Forrester. "If your people are looked after and they're happy, then your guests will be happy."[42]

An important message here is that managerial and transformational leadership are not embodied in different people or positions in the organization. As you might expect, senior executive positions require more transformational leadership behaviour than do management positions further down the hierarchy, likely because transformational leadership requires more discretion to enable macro-level change. However, every manager needs to apply both transformational and managerial behaviours to varying degrees. Indeed, frontline employees who engage in shared leadership may be managerial (helping coworkers through a difficult project) or transformational (championing a more customer-friendly culture in the work unit).

TASK-ORIENTED AND PEOPLE-ORIENTED LEADERSHIP

Managerial leadership research began in the 1940s and 1950s, when research teams at several universities launched an intensive research investigation to answer the question "What behaviours make leaders effective?" They studied first-line supervisors by asking subordinates to rate their bosses on many behaviours. These independent research teams essentially produced the same two clusters of leadership behaviour from literally thousands of items (Exhibit 12.2).[43]

One cluster, called *task-oriented leadership,* includes behaviours that define and structure work roles. Task-oriented leaders assign employees to specific tasks, set goals and deadlines, clarify work duties and procedures, define work procedures, and plan work activities. The other cluster represents *people-oriented leadership.* This cluster includes behaviours such as listening to employees for their opinions and ideas, creating a pleasant physical work environment, showing interest in staff, complimenting and recognizing employees for their effort, and showing consideration of employee needs.

These early studies tried to find out whether effective managers are more task-oriented or more people-oriented. This proved to be a difficult question to answer because each style has its advantages and disadvantages. In fact, recent evidence suggests that effective leaders rely on both styles, but in different ways.[44] When leaders apply high levels of people-oriented leadership behaviour, their employees tend to have more positive attitudes as well as lower absenteeism, grievances, and turnover. For instance, one recent study reported that followers have fewer stress symptoms when leaders show empathy towards employees.[45] When leaders have more task-oriented leadership, their employees tend to have higher job performance. Not surprisingly, employees generally prefer people-oriented bosses and they form negative attitudes towards bosses who are mostly task-oriented. However, task-oriented leadership is also appreciated to some degree. For example, university students value task-oriented instructors because they want clear objectives and well-prepared lectures that abide by the unit's objectives.[46]

EXHIBIT 12.2 Task- and People-Oriented Leadership Styles

Leaders are task-oriented when they. . .	Leaders are people-oriented when they. . .
Assign work and clarify responsibilities	Show interest in others as people
Set goals and deadlines	Listen to employees
Evaluate and provide feedback on work quality	Make the workplace more pleasant
Establish well-defined best work procedures	Show appreciation to employees for their performance contribution
Plan future work activities	Are considerate of employee needs

SERVANT LEADERSHIP

servant leadership The view that leaders serve followers, rather than vice versa; leaders help employees fulfill their needs and are coaches, stewards, and facilitators of employee development.

Servant leadership is an extension or variation of the people-oriented leadership because it defines leadership as serving others. In particular, servant leaders assist others in their need fulfillment, personal development, and growth.[47] Servant leaders ask, "How can I help you?" rather than expect employees to serve them. Servant leaders have been described as selfless, egalitarian, humble, nurturing, empathetic, and ethical coaches. The main objective of servant leadership is to help other stakeholders to fulfill their needs and potential, particularly "to become healthier, wiser, freer, more autonomous, more likely themselves to become servants."[48]

Servant leadership research suffers from ambiguous and conflicting definitions, but writers agree on a few features.[49] First, servant leaders have a natural desire or "calling" to serve others. This natural desire is a deep commitment to the growth of others for that purpose alone. It goes beyond the leader's role obligation to help others and is not merely an instrument to achieve company objectives. Second, servant leaders maintain a relationship with others that is humble, egalitarian, and accepting. Servant leaders do not view leadership as a position of power. Rather, they serve without drawing attention to themselves, without evoking superior status, and without being judgmental about others or defensive of criticisms received. Third, servant leaders anchor their decisions and actions in ethical principles and practices. They display sensitivity to and enactment of moral values and are not swayed by social pressures or expectations to deviate from those values. In this respect, servant leadership relies heavily on the idea of authentic leadership that we discuss later in this chapter.

Servant leadership was introduced four decades ago and has since had a steady following, particularly among practitioners and religious leaders. Scholarly interest in this topic has bloomed within the past few years, but the concept still faces a number of conceptual hurdles. Although servant leadership writers generally agree on the three features we described above, many have included other characteristics that lack agreement and might confound the concept with its predictors and outcomes. Still, the notion of leader as servant has considerable currency and for many centuries has been embedded in the principles of major religions. One recent study also found that companies have higher performance (return on assets) when their chief executive officer exhibits servant leadership behaviours.[50]

Leadership Theories

LO4

PATH-GOAL LEADERSHIP THEORY

The servant leadership model implies that leaders should be servants in all circumstances. However, the broader literature on task-oriented and people-oriented leadership has concluded that the best style is contingent on the situation.[51] This "it depends" view is more consistent with the contingency anchor of organizational behaviour discussed in Chapter 1. In other words, the most appropriate leadership style depends on the characteristics of the employees, work setting, the leader-follower relationship, and other factors.

Path-goal leadership theory is the dominant model that applies this contingency approach to managerial leadership. The main premise of path-goal theory is that effective

Colin Mcconnell/GetStock.com

Kevin Junor demonstrated exceptional leadership as a Canadian Forces officer and more recently as deputy superintendent of the Maplehurst Correctional Complex in Milton, Ontario. "Kevin is a blessed leader in every sense of the word," says former Canadian Forces Chief of the Defence Staff, General Rick Hillier. Junor suggests that his leadership philosophy is to serve others, rather than to have them serve him. "Now that I'm in a position of privilege, my role is to be a 'servant leader,' a servant for the person at the bottom," says Junor. He explains that "I'm not just leading my (management) team, I'm leading the inmates." Junor has received several awards, including the Order of Military Merit and the Harry Jerome Award, but he responds to these honours in classic servant leader style. "I see myself as a simple guy," he says. "So the fact the community looked at me like that, it was a very humbling experience."[52]

leaders choose one or more leadership styles to influence employee expectations (their preferred path) regarding achievement of desired results (their work-related goals), as well as their perceived satisfaction with those results (outcome valences). In other words, path-goal recognizes that leadership is an important influence in the expectancy theory of motivation (Chapter 5) and its underlying formula, subjective expected utility (Chapter 7).[53] Leaders clarify the link between employee behaviours and outcomes, influence the value of those outcomes, provide a work environment to facilitate goal accomplishment, and so forth.[54]

connect

What is your preferred managerial leadership style? Visit **connect.mcgrawhill.com** to assess your tendency to use one of three leadership styles.

path-goal leadership theory
A leadership theory stating that effective leaders choose the most appropriate leadership style(s), depending on the employee and situation, to influence employee expectations about desired results and their positive outcomes.

Path-Goal Leadership Styles Exhibit 12.3 presents the path-goal theory of leadership. This model specifically highlights four leadership styles and several contingency factors leading to three indicators of leader effectiveness. The four leadership styles are:[55]

- *Directive.* Directive leadership is the same as task-oriented leadership, described earlier. This leadership style consists of clarifying behaviours that provide a psychological structure for subordinates. This includes clarifying performance goals, the means to reach those goals, and the standards against which performance will be judged. It also includes judicious use of rewards and disciplinary actions.
- *Supportive.* Supportive leadership is the same as people-oriented leadership, described earlier. This style provides psychological support for subordinates. The leader is friendly and approachable; makes the work more pleasant; treats employees with equal respect; and shows concern for the status, needs, and well-being of employees.
- *Participative.* Participative leadership behaviours encourage and facilitate subordinate involvement in decisions beyond their normal work activities. The leader consults with employees, asks for their suggestions, and takes these ideas into serious consideration before making a decision. Participative leadership relates to involving employees in decisions (see Chapter 7).

EXHIBIT 12.3

Path-Goal Leadership Theory

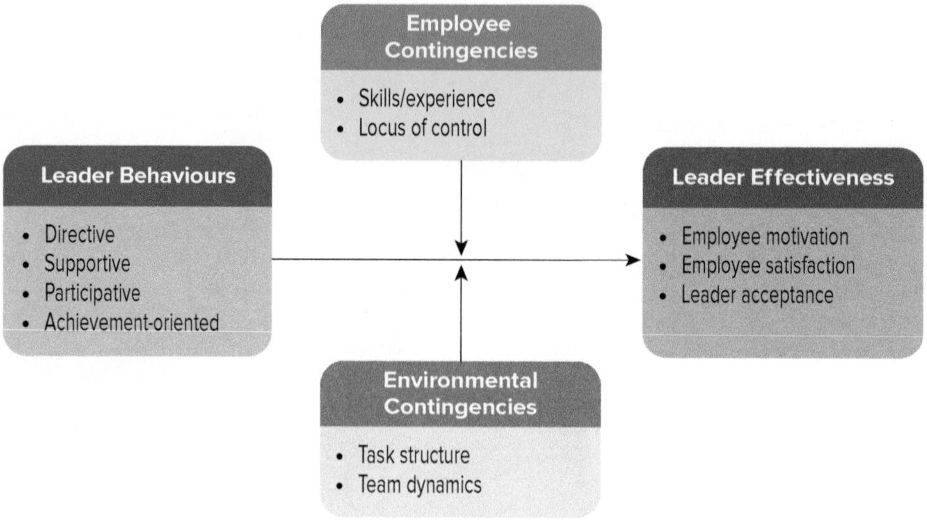

- *Achievement-oriented.* This leadership style emphasizes behaviours that encourage employees to reach their peak performance. The leader sets challenging goals, expects employees to perform at their highest level, continuously seeks improvement in employee performance, and shows a high degree of confidence that employees will assume responsibility and accomplish challenging goals. Achievement-oriented leadership applies goal-setting theory as well as positive expectations in self-fulfilling prophecy.

The path-goal model contends that effective leaders are capable of selecting the most appropriate behavioural style (or styles) for each situation. Also, leaders often use two or more styles at the same time, if these styles are appropriate for the circumstances.

Contingencies of Path-Goal Theory As a contingency theory, path-goal theory states that each of the four leadership styles will be effective in some situations but not in others. The path-goal leadership model specifies two sets of situational variables that moderate the relationship between a leader's style and effectiveness: (1) employee characteristics and (2) characteristics of the employee's work environment. Several contingencies have already been studied within the path-goal framework, and the model is open for more variables in the future.[56] However, only four contingencies are reviewed here.

- *Skill and experience.* A combination of directive and supportive leadership is best for employees who are (or perceive themselves to be) inexperienced and unskilled.[57] Directive leadership gives subordinates information about how to accomplish the task, whereas supportive leadership helps them cope with the uncertainties of unfamiliar work situations. Directive leadership is detrimental when employees are skilled and experienced because it introduces too much supervisory control.
- *Locus of control.* People with an internal locus of control believe that they have control over their work environment (see Chapter 3). Consequently, these employees prefer participative and achievement-oriented leadership styles and may become frustrated with a directive style. In contrast, people with an external locus of control believe that their performance is due more to luck and fate, so they tend to be more satisfied with directive and supportive leadership.
- *Task structure.* Leaders should adopt the directive style when the task is nonroutine, because this style minimizes role ambiguity that tends to occur in complex work situations (particularly for inexperienced employees).[58] The directive style is ineffective when employees have routine and simple tasks because the manager's guidance serves no purpose and may be viewed as unnecessarily close control. Employees in highly routine and simple jobs may require supportive leadership to help them cope with the tedious nature of the work and lack of control over the pace of work. Participative leadership is preferred for employees performing nonroutine tasks because the lack

of rules and procedures gives them more discretion to achieve challenging goals. The participative style is ineffective for employees in routine tasks because they lack discretion over their work.

- *Team dynamics.* Cohesive teams with performance-oriented norms act as a substitute for most leader interventions. High team cohesion substitutes for supportive leadership, whereas performance-oriented team norms substitute for directive and possibly achievement-oriented leadership. Thus, when team cohesion is low, leaders should use the supportive style. Leaders should apply a directive style to counteract team norms that oppose the team's formal objectives. For example, the team leader may need to exert authority if team members have developed a norm to "take it easy" rather than get a project completed on time.

Evaluating Path-Goal Theory Path-goal theory has received more research support than other managerial leadership models. In fact, one study reported that path-goal theory explained more about effective leadership than did the transformational leadership model.[59] This stronger effect is likely because most managers spend more of their time engaging in managerial rather than transformational leadership.[60]

Support for the path-goal model is far from ideal, however. A few contingencies (e.g., task structure) have limited research support. Other contingencies and leadership styles in the path-goal leadership model haven't been investigated at all.[61] Another concern is that as path-goal theory expands, the model may become too complex for practical use. Few people would be able to remember all the contingencies and the appropriate leadership styles for those contingencies.

Another limitation of path-goal theory is its assumption that effective leaders can adapt their behaviours and styles to the immediate situation. In reality, leaders typically have a preferred style. It takes considerable effort for leaders to choose and enact different styles to match the situation. In spite of these limitations, path-goal theory remains a relatively robust theory of managerial leadership.

OTHER MANAGERIAL LEADERSHIP THEORIES

Several other managerial leadership theories have developed over the years. Some overlap with the path-goal model's leadership styles, but most use simpler and more abstract contingencies. We will briefly mention only two here because of their popularity and historical significance to the field.

situational leadership theory A commercially popular but poorly supported leadership model stating that effective leaders vary their style (telling, selling, participating, delegating) with the motivation and ability of followers.

Situational Leadership Theory One of the most popular managerial leadership theories among practitioners is the **situational leadership theory (SLT),** developed by Paul Hersey and Ken Blanchard.[62] SLT suggests that effective leaders vary their style with the ability and motivation (or commitment) of followers. The most recent version uses four labels to describe followers, such as "enthusiastic beginner" (low ability, high motivation) and "disillusioned learner" (moderate ability and low motivation).

The situational leadership model also identifies four leadership styles–telling, selling, participating, and delegating–that Hersey and Blanchard distinguish by the amount of task-oriented and people-oriented behaviour provided. For example, "telling" has high task behaviour and low supportive behaviour. The situational leadership model has four quadrants, with each quadrant showing the leadership style that is most appropriate under different circumstances.

In spite of its popularity, several studies and at least three reviews have concluded that the situational leadership model lacks empirical support.[63] Only one part of the model apparently works, namely, that leaders should use "telling" (i.e., task-oriented style) when employees lack motivation and ability. This relationship is also documented in path-goal theory. The model's elegant simplicity is attractive and entertaining, but most parts don't represent reality very well.

Fiedler's contingency model A leadership model stating that leader effectiveness depends on whether the person's natural leadership style is appropriately matched to the situation (the level of situational control).

Fiedler's Contingency Model **Fiedler's contingency model,** developed by Fred Fiedler and his associates, is the earliest managerial leadership theory that adopted the contingency approach.[64] According to this model, leader effectiveness depends on whether the person's natural leadership style is appropriately matched to the situation. The theory examines two leadership styles that essentially correspond to the previously described people-oriented and task-oriented styles. Unfortunately, Fiedler's model relies on a questionnaire that does not measure either leadership style very well.

OB by the NUMBERS

How Satisfied are Employees with their Management's Leadership Style?[65]

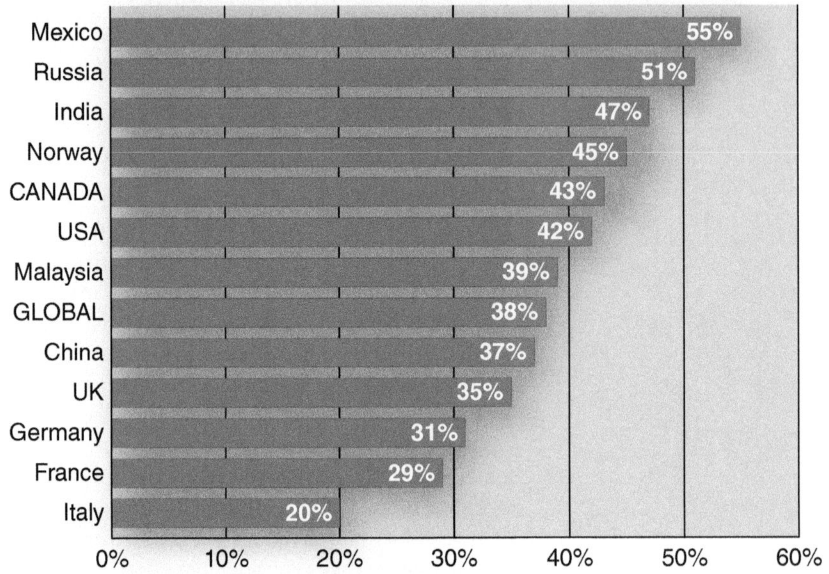

Percentage of employees surveyed in selected countries who indicate that they are satisfied with their management's leadership style. Data were collected for Kelly Services in 2012 from more than 168,000 people in 30 countries. The global average includes respondents from all 30 countries, not just those shown in this chart.

Fiedler's model suggests that the best leadership style depends on the level of *situational control*, that is, the degree of power and influence that the leader possesses in a particular situation. Situational control is affected by three factors in the following order of importance: leader-member relations, task structure, and position power.[66] *Leader-member relations* refers to how much employees trust and respect the leader and are willing to follow his or her guidance. *Task structure* refers to the clarity or ambiguity of operating procedures. *Position power* is the extent to which the leader possesses legitimate, reward, and coercive power over subordinates. These three contingencies form the eight possible combinations of *situation favourableness* from the leader's viewpoint. Good leader-member relations, high task structure, and strong position power create the most favourable situation for the leader because he or she has the most power and influence under these conditions.

Fiedler's theory lacks research support, mainly due to flaws with its leadership-style scale, its limited focus on only two leadership styles, and its creation of a single contingency variable (leader-member relations) based on an unexplainable arrangement of three situational factors in a hierarchy.[67] However, Fiedler's model makes two lasting contributions to leadership knowledge. One contribution is that it recognizes the importance of the leader's power in determining the best leadership style. Leader power is not explicit in other managerial leadership models.

Second, contrary to the assumptions of most leadership theories, Fiedler argues that leaders might not be able to change their style easily to fit the situation. Instead, they tend to rely mainly on one style that is most consistent with their personality and values. Leaders with high agreeableness personality and benevolence values tend to prefer supportive leadership, for example, whereas leaders with high conscientiousness personality and achievement values feel more comfortable with the directive style of leadership.[68] More recent scholars have also proposed that leadership styles are "hardwired" more than most contingency leadership theories assume.[69] Leaders might be able to alter their style temporarily, but they tend to rely mainly on one style that is most consistent with their personality and values.

LEADERSHIP SUBSTITUTES

leadership substitutes A theory identifying conditions that either limit a leader's ability to influence subordinates or make a particular leadership style unnecessary.

So far, we have looked at managerial leadership theories that recommend using different leadership styles in various situations. But one theory, called **leadership substitutes,** identifies conditions that either limit the leader's ability to influence subordinates or make a particular leadership style unnecessary. The literature identifies several conditions that possibly substitute for task-oriented or people-oriented leadership. Task-oriented leadership might be less important when performance-based reward systems keep employees directed towards organizational goals. Similarly, increasing employee skill and experience might reduce the need for task-oriented leadership. This proposition is consistent with path-goal leadership theory, which states that directive leadership is unnecessary–and may be detrimental–when employees are skilled or experienced.[70]

Some research suggests that effective leaders help team members learn to lead themselves through leadership substitutes; in other words, coworkers substitute for leadership in high-involvement team structures.[71] Coworkers instruct new employees, thereby providing directive leadership. They also provide social support, which reduces stress among fellow employees. Teams with norms that support organizational goals may substitute for achievement-oriented leadership, because employees encourage (or pressure) coworkers to stretch their performance levels.[72]

The leadership substitutes model has intuitive appeal, but the evidence so far is mixed. Some studies show that a few substitutes do replace the need for task- or people-oriented leadership, but others do not. The difficulties of statistically testing for leadership substitutes may account for some problems, but a few writers contend that the limited support is evidence that leadership plays a critical role regardless of the situation.[73] At this point, we can conclude that leadership substitutes might reduce the need for leaders, but they do not completely replace leaders in these situations.

connect

Do leaders make a difference? See page 320 or visit connect.mcgrawhill.com to assess your beliefs about the influence of leaders.

Implicit Leadership Perspective

LO5

The transformational and managerial leadership perspectives make the basic assumption that leaders "make a difference." Certainly, there is evidence that leaders do influence the performance of their departments and organizations. However, leadership also involves followers' perceptions about the characteristics and attributions of people in formal leadership positions. This perceptual perspective of leadership, called **implicit leadership theory,** has two components: leader prototypes and the romance or attribution of leadership.[74]

implicit leadership theory A theory stating that people evaluate a leader's effectiveness in terms of how well that person fits preconceived beliefs about the features and behaviours of effective leaders (leadership prototypes) and that people tend to inflate the influence of leaders on organizational events.

PROTOTYPES OF EFFECTIVE LEADERS

One aspect of implicit leadership theory states that everyone has *leadership prototypes*–preconceived beliefs about the features and behaviours of effective leaders.[75] These prototypes, which develop through socialization within the family and society, shape the follower's expectations and acceptance of others as leaders, and this in turn affects the willingness to remain as a follower. Leadership prototypes not only support a person's role as leader; they also influence our perception of the leader's effectiveness. In other words, people are more likely to believe a leader is effective when he or she looks like and acts consistently with their prototype of a leader.[76]

Why does this prototype comparison process occur? People want to trust their leader before they are willing to serve as followers, yet the leader's actual effectiveness usually isn't known for several months or possibly years. The prototype comparison process is a quick (although faulty) way of estimating the leader's effectiveness.

THE ROMANCE OF LEADERSHIP

Along with relying on implicit prototypes of effective leaders, followers tend to distort their perception of the leader's influence that leaders have on the organization's success.

Courtesy of Semco SA

As the CEO of a successful company (Semco SA) and the author of best-selling business books, Ricardo Semler is a giant among corporate leaders in South America. Yet he warns of the "romance of leadership" problems that can occur when employees are blinded by charismatic leadership. "People will naturally create and nurture a charismatic figure. The charismatic figure, on the other hand, feeds this," Semler explains. "The people at Semco don't look and act like me. They are not yes-men by any means. . . . [Yet] they credit me with successes that are not my own, and they don't debit me my mistakes."[77]

This "romance of leadership" effect exists because people in most cultures want to believe that leaders make a difference.

There are two basic reasons why people inflate their perceptions of the leader's influence over the environment.[78] First, leadership is a useful way for us to simplify life events. It is easier to explain organizational successes and failures in terms of the leader's ability than by analyzing a complex array of other forces. Second, there is a strong tendency in Canada and other Western cultures to believe that life events are generated more from people than from uncontrollable natural forces.[79] This illusion of control is satisfied by believing that events result from the rational actions of leaders. In other words, employees feel better believing that leaders make a difference, so they actively look for evidence that this is so.

One way that followers support their perceptions that leaders make a difference is through fundamental attribution error (see Chapter 3). Research has found that (at least in Western cultures) leaders are given credit or blame for the company's success or failure because employees do not readily see the external forces that also influence these events. Leaders reinforce this belief by taking credit for organizational successes.[80]

The implicit leadership perspective provides valuable advice to improve leadership acceptance. It highlights the fact that leadership is a perception of followers as much as the actual behaviours and formal roles of people calling themselves leaders. Potential leaders must be sensitive to this fact, understand what followers expect, and act accordingly. Individuals who do not naturally fit leadership prototypes need to provide more direct evidence of their effectiveness as leaders.

Personal Attributes Perspective of Leadership

LO6

Since the beginning of recorded civilization, people have been interested in the personal characteristics that distinguish great leaders from the rest of us.[81] One ground-breaking review in the late 1940s concluded that no consistent list of leadership traits could be distilled from previous research. This conclusion was revised a decade later, suggesting that a few traits are associated with effective leaders.[82] These nonsignificant findings caused many scholars to give up their search for the personal characteristics of effective leaders.

Over the past two decades, leadership experts have returned to the notion that effective leaders possess specific personal attributes.[83] Most scholarly studies long ago were apparently plagued by methodological problems, lack of theoretical foundation, and inconsistent definitions of leadership. The emerging research has largely addressed these problems, with the result that several attributes are consistently identified with effective leadership or leader emergence. The main leadership attributes are listed in Exhibit 12.4 and described below:[84]

- *Personality*. Most of the Big Five personality dimensions (see Chapter 2) are associated with effective leadership to some extent, but the strongest predictors are high levels of extroversion (outgoing, talkative, sociable, and assertive) and conscientiousness (careful, dependable, and self-disciplined). With high extroversion, effective leaders are comfortable having an influential role in social settings. With higher conscientiousness, effective leaders set higher goals for themselves (and others), are organized, and have a strong sense of duty to fulfill work obligations.

EXHIBIT 12.4 Attributes of Effective Leaders

Leadership attribute	Description
Personality	Effective leaders have higher levels of extroversion (outgoing, talkative, sociable, and assertive) and conscientiousness (careful, dependable, and self-disciplined).
Self-concept	Effective leaders have strong self-beliefs and a positive self-evaluation about their own leadership skills and ability to achieve objectives.
Leadership motivation	Effective leaders have a need for socialized power (not personalized power) to accomplish team or organizational goals.
Drive	Effective leaders have an inner motivation to pursue goals.
Integrity	Effective leaders have strong moral principles, which are demonstrated through truthfulness and consistency of words with deeds.
Knowledge of the business	Effective leaders have tacit and explicit knowledge about the company's environment, enabling them to make more intuitive decisions.
Cognitive and practical intelligence	Effective leaders have above-average cognitive ability to process information (cognitive intelligence) and ability to solve real-world problems by adapting to, shaping, or selecting appropriate environments (practical intelligence).
Emotional intelligence	Effective leaders have the ability to recognize and regulate their own emotions and the emotions of others.

- *Self-concept.* Successful leaders have a complex, internally consistent, and clear self-concept as a leader (see Chapter 3). This "leader identity" also includes a positive self-evaluation, including high self-esteem, self-efficacy, and internal locus of control.[85] While many people in leadership positions default to daily managerial leadership and define themselves as managers, effective leaders view themselves as both transformational and managerial, and are confident with both of these self-views.[86]
- *Leadership motivation.* Effective leaders don't just see themselves as leaders. They are also motivated to lead others. They have a strong need for *socialized power,* meaning that they want power to lead others in accomplishing organizational objectives and similar good deeds. This contrasts with a need for *personalized power,* which is the desire to have power for personal gain or for the thrill one might experience from wielding power over others (see Chapter 5).[87] Leadership motivation is also necessary because, even in collegial firms, leaders are in contests for positions further up the hierarchy. Effective leaders thrive rather than wither in the face of this competition.[88]
- *Drive.* Related to their high conscientiousness and positive self-concept, successful leaders have a moderately high need for achievement (see Chapter 5). This drive represents the inner motivation that leaders possess to pursue their goals and encourage others to move forward with theirs. Drive inspires inquisitiveness, an action orientation, and measured boldness to take the organization or team into uncharted waters.
- *Integrity.* Integrity involves having strong moral principles, which supports the tendency to be truthful and to be consistent in words and deeds. Leaders have a high moral capacity to judge dilemmas using sound values and to act accordingly. Notice that integrity is ultimately based on the leader's values, which provide an anchor for consistency. Several large-scale studies have reported that integrity and honesty are the most important characteristics of effective leaders.[89] Unfortunately, surveys also report that employees don't believe their leaders have integrity and, consequently, don't trust those leaders.

- *Knowledge of the business.* Effective leaders possess tacit and explicit knowledge of the business environment in which they operate, including subtle indications of emerging trends. Knowledge of the business also includes a good understanding of how their organization works effectively.
- *Cognitive and practical intelligence.* Leaders have above-average cognitive ability to process enormous amounts of information. Leaders aren't necessarily geniuses; rather, they have a superior ability to analyze a variety of complex alternatives and opportunities. Furthermore, leaders have practical intelligence. This means that they can think through the relevance and application of ideas in real-world settings. Practical intelligence is particularly evident where problems are poorly defined, information is missing, and more than one solution may be plausible.[90]
- *Emotional intelligence.* Effective leaders have a high level of emotional intelligence.[91] They are able to recognize and regulate emotions in themselves and in other people (see Chapter 4).

AUTHENTIC LEADERSHIP

authentic leadership The view that effective leaders need to be aware of, feel comfortable with, and act consistently with their values, personality, and self-concept.

A few paragraphs ago, we said that successful leaders have a complex, internally consistent, and clear self-concept as a leader, and that they have a strong positive self-evaluation. These characteristics lay the foundation for **authentic leadership,** which refers to how well leaders are aware of, feel comfortable with, and act consistently with their self-concept.[92] Authenticity is mainly about knowing yourself and being yourself (see Exhibit 12.5). Leaders learn more about their personality, values, thoughts, and habits by reflecting on various situations and personal experiences. They also improve this self-awareness by receiving feedback from trusted people inside and outside the organization. Both self-reflection and receptivity to feedback require high levels of emotional intelligence.

As people learn more about themselves, they gain a greater understanding of their inner purpose which, in turn, generates a long-term passion for achieving something worthwhile for the organization or society. Some leadership experts suggest that this inner purpose emerges from a life story, typically a transformative event or experience earlier in life that provides guidance for their later career and energy.[93] Norsat CEO Amiee Chan refers to one such transformative incident several years ago as a co-op engineering student. She was given the tedious task of replacing one circuit in each of 400 orange boxes. "When my supervisor noticed I was getting bored, he began describing the purpose of the device, which was a rescue beacon," she recalls. The supervisor then told Chan how one of those beacons recently saved lives on a family-owned fishing vessel off the Alaska coast. A sudden storm capsized the boat, but search and rescue teams were able to save the family within a few hours because of the rescue beacon. "This [story] forever stamped into my mind the value of what we do here, and I'm just as passionate about developing communications technology today as I was back then," says Chan.[94]

Authentic leadership is more than self-awareness; it also involves behaving in ways that are consistent with that self-concept rather than pretending to be someone else. To be themselves, great leaders regulate their decisions and behaviour in several ways. First, they develop their own style and, where appropriate, move into positions where that style is most effective. Although effective leaders adapt their behaviour to the situation to some extent, they invariably understand and rely on decision methods and interpersonal styles that feel most comfortable to them.

EXHIBIT 12.5

Authentic Leadership

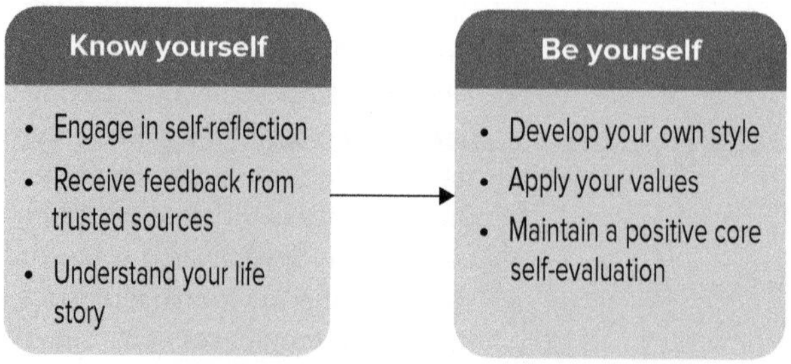

Debating Point:

SHOULD LEADERS *REALLY* BE AUTHENTIC ALL THE TIME?

According to popular business books and several scholarly articles, authentic leadership is one of the core attributes of effective leaders. Authentic leaders know themselves and act in accordance with that self-concept. They live their personal values and find a leadership style that best matches their personality. Furthermore, authentic leaders have a sense of purpose, often developed through a crisis or similar "crucible" event in their lives.

It makes sense that leaders should be authentic. After all, as singer Lisa Minnelli has often said: "I would rather be a first-rate version of myself than a second-rate version of anybody else."[95] In other words, leaders are better at acting out their natural beliefs and tendencies than by acting like someone else. Furthermore, authenticity results in consistency, which is a foundation of trust. So, by being authentic, leaders are more likely to be trusted by followers.[96]

But should leaders always be themselves and act consistently with their beliefs and personality? Not necessarily, according to a few experts. The concept of authentic leadership seems to be at odds with well-established research that people are evaluated as more effective leaders when they have a high rather than low self-monitoring personality.[97]

High "self-monitors" quickly understand their social environment and easily adapt their behaviour to that environment. In other words, high self-monitors change their behaviour to suit what others expect from them. In contrast, low self-monitors behave consistently with their personality and self-concept. They do not change their beliefs, style, or behaviours across social contexts. On the contrary, they feel much more content with high congruence between who they are and what they do, even when their natural style does not fit the situation.

Employees prefer an adaptive (i.e., high self-monitoring) leader because they have preconceived prototypes of how leaders should act (implicit leadership theory, which we discussed earlier in this chapter).[98] Authentic leaders are more likely to violate those prototypical expectations and, consequently, be viewed as less leader-like. The message from this is that leadership is a role that its incumbents are required to perform rather than to completely "act naturally." Ironically, while applauding the virtues of authentic leadership, leadership guru Warren Bennis acknowledged that "leadership is a performance art." His point was that leaders are best when they act naturally in that role, but the reality of any performance is that people can never be fully themselves.[99]

Furthermore, while being yourself is authentic, it may convey the image of being inflexible and insensitive.[100] This problem was apparent to a management professor and consultant when recently working with a client. The executive's staff followed a work process that was comfortable to the executive but not to many of her employees. When asked to consider adopting a process that was easier for her staff, the executive replied: "Look. This is just how I work." The executive was authentic, but the inflexibility undermined employee performance and morale.[101]

Second, effective leaders continually think about and consistently apply their stable hierarchy of personal values to those decisions and behaviours. Leaders face many pressures and temptations, such as achieving short term stock price targets at the cost of long term profitability. Experts note that authentic leaders demonstrate self-discipline by remaining anchored to their values. Third, leaders maintain consistency around their self-concept by having a strong, positive core self-evaluation. They have high self-esteem and self-efficacy as well as an internal locus of control (Chapter 3).

LEADERSHIP ATTRIBUTES, PERSPECTIVE LIMITATIONS, AND PRACTICAL IMPLICATIONS

Personality, experience, self-concept, and other personal characteristics potentially contribute to a leader's effectiveness. Still, the leadership attributes perspective has a few limitations.[102] First, it assumes that all effective leaders have the same personal characteristics that are equally important in all situations. This is probably a false assumption; leadership is far too complex to have a universal list of traits that apply to every condition. Some attributes might not be important all the time. Second, alternative combinations of attributes may be equally successful; two people with different sets of personal characteristics might be equally good leaders. Third, the attribute perspective views leadership as something within a person, yet experts emphasize that leadership is relational. People are effective leaders because of their favourable relationships with followers, so effective leaders cannot be identified without considering the quality of these relationships.[103]

Also remember from our discussion earlier in this chapter that, in the short term, followers tend to define others as effective or ineffective leaders based on their personal characteristics rather than whether the leader actually makes a difference to the organization's success. People who exhibit self-confidence, extroversion, and other traits are called leaders because they fit the widely-held prototype of an effective leader. Alternatively, if someone is successful, observers might assign several nonobservable personal characteristics to them, such as intelligence, confidence, and drive. In short, the link between personal characteristics and effective leadership is muddied by several perceptual distortions.

One important final point: The attribute perspective of leadership does not necessarily imply that leadership is a talent acquired at birth rather than developed throughout life. On the contrary, attributes indicate only leadership *potential*, not leadership performance. People with these characteristics become effective leaders only after they have developed and mastered the necessary leadership behaviours. People with somewhat lower leadership attributes may become very effective leaders because they have worked harder to apply their lower potential more fully.

Cross-Cultural and Gender Issues in Leadership

LO7

Along with the four perspectives of leadership presented throughout this chapter, cultural values and practices affect what leaders do. Culture shapes the leader's values and norms, which influence his or her decisions and actions. Cultural values also shape the expectations that followers have of their leaders. An executive who acts inconsistently with cultural expectations is more likely to be perceived as an ineffective leader. Furthermore, leaders who deviate from those values may experience various forms of influence to get them to conform to the leadership norms and expectations of the society. In other words, implicit leadership theory, described in the previous section of this chapter, explains differences in leadership practices across cultures.

Over the past several years, 150 researchers from dozens of countries have worked together on Project GLOBE (Global Leadership and Organizational Behaviour Effectiveness) to identify the effects of cultural values on leadership.[104] The project organized countries into 10 regional clusters, of which the United States, Great Britain, and similar countries are grouped into the "Anglo" cluster. The results of this massive investigation suggest that some features of leadership are universal and some differ across cultures. Specifically, the GLOBE project reports that "charismatic visionary" is a universally recognized concept and that middle managers around the world believe that it is characteristic of effective leaders. *Charismatic visionary* represents a cluster of concepts including visionary, inspirational, performance orientation, integrity, and decisiveness.[105]

In contrast, participative leadership is perceived as characteristic of effective leadership in low power distance cultures but less so in high power distance cultures. For instance, one study reported that Mexican employees expect managers to make decisions affecting their work. Mexico is a high power distance culture, so followers expect leaders to apply their authority rather than delegate their power most of the time.[106] In summary, there are similarities and differences in the concept and preferred practice of leadership across cultures.

GENDER AND LEADERSHIP

Studies in field settings have generally found that male and female leaders do not differ in their levels of task-oriented or people-oriented leadership. The main explanation is that real-world jobs require similar behaviour from male and female job incumbents.[107] However, women do adopt a participative leadership style more readily than their male counterparts. One possible reason is that, compared to boys, girls are often raised to be more egalitarian and less status-oriented, which is consistent with being participative. There is also some evidence that women have somewhat better interpersonal skills than men, and this translates into their relatively greater use of the participative leadership style. A third explanation is that subordinates, on the basis of their own gender stereotypes, expect female leaders to be more participative, so female leaders comply with follower expectations to some extent.

Surveys report that women are rated higher than men on the emerging leadership qualities of coaching, teamwork, and empowering employees.[108] Yet research also suggests that women are evaluated negatively when they try to apply the full range of leadership styles, particularly more directive and autocratic approaches. Thus, ironically, women may be well suited to contemporary leadership roles, yet they often continue to face limitations of leadership through the gender stereotypes and prototypes of leaders that are held by followers.[109] Overall, both male and female leaders must be sensitive to the fact that followers have expectations about how leaders should act, and negative evaluations may go to leaders who deviate from those expectations.

Chapter Summary

LO1 Define leadership and shared leadership.

Leadership is defined as the ability to influence, motivate, and enable others to contribute towards the effectiveness and success of the organizations of which they are members. Leaders use influence to motivate followers and arrange the work environment so they do the job more effectively. Shared leadership views leadership as a role rather than a formal position, so employees throughout the organization act informally as leaders as the occasion arises. These situations include serving as champions for specific ideas or changes as well as filling leadership roles where it is needed.

LO2 Describe the four elements of transformational leadership and explain why they are important for organizational change.

Transformational leadership begins with a strategic vision, which is a positive representation of a future state that energizes and unifies employees. A vision is values-based, a distant goal, abstract, and meaningful to employees. Transformational leaders effectively communicate the vision by framing it around values, showing sincerity and passion towards the vision, and using symbols, metaphors, and other vehicles that create richer meaning to the vision. Transformational leaders model the vision (walk the talk) and encourage employees to experiment with new behaviours and practices that are potentially more consistent with the visionary future state. They also build employee commitment to the vision through the above activities as well as by celebrating milestones to the vision. Some transformational leadership theories view charismatic leadership as an essential ingredient of transformational leadership. However, this view is inconsistent with the meaning of charisma and at odds with research on the dynamics and outcomes of charisma in leader-follower relationships.

LO3 Compare managerial leadership with transformational leadership, and describe the features of task-oriented, people-oriented, and servant leadership.

Managerial leadership includes the daily activities that support and guide the performance and well-being of individual employees and the work unit towards current objectives and practices. Transformational and managerial leadership are dependent on each other, but differ in their assumptions of stability versus change and their micro versus macro focus.

Task-oriented behaviours include assigning employees to specific tasks, clarifying their work duties and procedures, ensuring they follow company rules, and pushing them to reach their performance capacity. People-oriented behaviours include showing mutual trust and respect for subordinates, demonstrating a genuine concern for their needs, and having a desire to look out for their welfare.

Servant leadership defines leadership as serving others towards their need fulfillment and personal development and growth. Servant leaders have a natural desire or "calling" to serve others. They maintain a relationship with others that is humble, egalitarian, and accepting. Servant leaders also anchor their decisions and actions in ethical principles and practices.

LO4 Discuss the elements of path-goal theory, Fiedler's contingency model, and leadership substitutes.

Path-goal theory of leadership takes the view that effective managerial leadership involves diagnosing the situation and using the most appropriate style for the situation. The core model identifies four leadership styles–directive, supportive, participative, and achievement-oriented–and several contingencies relating to the characteristics of the employee and of the situation.

Two other contingency leadership theories include the situational leadership theory and Fiedler's contingency theory. Research support is quite weak for both theories. However, a lasting element of Fiedler's theory is the idea that leaders have natural styles and, consequently, companies need to change the leaders' environments to suit their style. Leadership substitutes theory identifies contingencies that either limit the leader's ability to influence subordinates or make a particular leadership style unnecessary.

LO5 Describe the two components of the implicit leadership perspective.

According to the implicit leadership perspective, people have leadership prototypes, which they use to evaluate the leader's effectiveness. Furthermore, people form a romance of leadership; they want to believe that leaders make a difference, so they engage in fundamental attribution error and other perceptual distortions to support this belief in the leader's impact.

LO6 Identify eight personal attributes associated with effective leaders and describe authentic leadership.

The attribute perspective identifies the characteristics of effective leaders. Recent writing suggests that leaders have specific personality characteristics, positive self-concept, drive, integrity, leadership motivation, knowledge of the business, cognitive and practical intelligence, and emotional intelligence. Authentic leadership refers to how well leaders are aware of, feel comfortable with, and act consistently with their self-concept. This concept consists mainly of two parts: self-awareness and engaging in behaviour that is consistent with one's self-concept.

LO7 Discuss cultural and gender similarities and differences in leadership.

Cultural values also influence the leader's personal values, which in turn influence his or her leadership practices. Women generally do not differ from men in the degree of people-oriented or task-oriented leadership. However, female leaders more often adopt a participative style. Research also suggests that people evaluate female leaders on the basis of gender stereotypes, which may result in higher or lower ratings.

than one was used) appropriate in this situation. The team should list these contingency factors clearly and, where possible, connect them to the contingencies described in path-goal theory. (Note: the team might identify path-goal leadership contingencies that are not described in the book. These, too, should be noted and discussed.)

Step 3: After the teams have diagnosed the incidents, each team will describe to the entire class the most interesting incidents as well as its diagnosis of that incident. Other teams will critique the diagnosis. Any leadership contingencies not mentioned in the textbook should also be presented and discussed.

Self-Assessment: DO LEADERS MAKE A DIFFERENCE?

Purpose This assessment is designed to help you to assess your beliefs about the influence of leaders.

Instructions Read each of the statements below and circle the response that best indicates your personal belief about that statement. Then use the scoring key in Appendix B to calculate the results for each leadership dimension. After completing this assessment, be prepared to discuss in class the relevance and level of implicit leadership theory.

Romance of Leadership Scale

To what extent do you agree or disagree that. . .	Strongly Agree	Agree	Neutral	Disagree	Strongly Disagree
1. Even in an economic recession, a good leader can prevent a company from doing poorly.	○	○	○	○	○
2. The quality of leadership is the single most important influence on how well the organization functions.	○	○	○	○	○
3. The CEO and executive team have relatively little effect on the company's success or failure.	○	○	○	○	○
4. Sooner or later, bad leadership at the top will result in declining organizational performance.	○	○	○	○	○
5. The effect of a company's leaders on organizational performance is fairly weak.	○	○	○	○	○
6. A company is only as good or as bad as its leaders.	○	○	○	○	○
7. Even the best leaders can't help an organization very much when the economy is bad or competition is tough.	○	○	○	○	○
8. It is impossible for an organization to do well when its leaders are average.	○	○	○	○	○
9. Compared with the economy, competition, and other external forces, leaders have only a small influence on a firm's performance.	○	○	○	○	○
10. The company's top executives have the power to make or break the organization.	○	○	○	○	○

Source: This instrument is adapted and condensed from B. Schyns, J. R. Meindl, and M. A. Croon. "The Romance of Leadership Scale: Cross-cultural Testing and Refinement." *Leadership* 3, no. 1 (2007): 29-46.

SELF-ASSESSMENTS FOR CHAPTER 12

SELF-ASSESSMENT NAME	DESCRIPTION	LOCATION
What are your transformational leadership tendencies?	Assesses your beliefs about the influence of leaders.	Page 320 connect
Do leaders make a difference?	Estimates your level of transformational leadership and its specific elements.	connect
What is your preferred managerial leadership style?	Assesses your tendency to use one of three managerial leadership styles.	connect

Valve Corporation has a flat, organic organizational structure to leverage the creative and entrepreneurial potential of its 300 employees.

Chapter 13

Designing Organizational Structures

LEARNING OBJECTIVES

After reading this chapter, you should be able to:

LO1. Describe three types of coordination in organizational structures.

LO2. Discuss the role and effects of span of control, centralization, and formalization, and relate these elements to organic and mechanistic organizational structures.

LO3. Identify and evaluate six types of departmentalization.

LO4. Explain how the external environment, organizational size, technology, and strategy are relevant when designing an organizational structure.

Valve Corporation's organizational structure literally operates on wheels. Employees at the Bellevue, Washington, software and entertainment company have no bosses or departments to determine their job duties or location. Instead, they figure out where their talents are best needed and move their desks (which have wheels) to that team. "Think of those wheels as a symbolic reminder that you should always be considering where you could move yourself to be more valuable," says Valve's quirky handbook. "There is no organizational structure keeping you from being in close proximity to the people who you'd help or be helped by most."

Valve's employees organize themselves into self-directed teams. "People commit to projects, and projects are self-organizing," explains Michael Abrash, a game programmer and technical writer who recently joined Valve. Each team agrees on its goals, deadlines, work rules, task assignments, and other issues. Each team has a lead member to coordinate the team, but he or she is not a traditional manager. Project roles are determined through mutual agreement; pay is calculated from peer evaluations of each employee's contribution to Valve.

Another indication of Valve's flat organizational structure is that employees make corporate-level decisions through consensus. "Everyone is constantly making big decisions for the company, and deciding where we'll go and what products we should build and so forth," says Greg Coomer, one of Valve's earliest employees. Cofounder Gabe Newell is technically Valve's CEO, but he avoids being viewed as the top dog. "Of all the people at this company who aren't your boss, Gabe is the MOST not your boss, if you get what we're saying," employees are advised in the handbook.

Contrary to what you might think, Valve isn't a start-up with a handful of people. It's a multibillion dollar company employing more than 300 engineers, artists, and other professionals. Yet for almost two decades, Valve's seemingly chaotic structure has suppressed bureaucracy and empowered employees to discover and produce innovative products. "Hierarchy is great for maintaining predictability and repeatability," says Valve's employee handbook. "But when you're an entertainment company that's spent the last decade going out of its way to recruit the most intelligent, innovative, talented people on Earth, telling them to sit at a desk and do what they're told obliterates 99 percent of their value."[1]

organizational structure The division of labour as well as the patterns of coordination, communication, workflow, and formal power that direct organizational activities.

Valve Corporation's organizational structure is different from most companies, but this design seems to serve the game maker and entertainment firm's strategic objectives. **Organizational structure** refers to the division of labour as well as the patterns of coordination, communication, workflow, and formal power that direct organizational activities. It formally dictates what activities receive the most attention as well as financial, power, and information resources. At Valve, for example, power and resources flow mainly to teams, who have almost complete autonomy over their work objectives and work processes.

Although the topic of organizational structure typically conjures up images of an organizational chart, this diagram is only part of the puzzle. Organizational structure includes these reporting relationships, but it also relates to job design, information flow, work standards and rules, team dynamics, and power relationships. As such, the organization's structure is an important instrument in an executive's toolkit for organizational change because it establishes new communication patterns and aligns employee behaviour with the corporate vision.[2]

For example, the Toronto Transit Commission's customer service advisory panel identified creation of a chief customer service officer position as the top priority for improving the organization's troubled customer service reputation. The TTC followed this advice, which immediately gave customer service a much higher priority in the organization. The chief customer officer reports directly to the CEO and, as a member of the executive team, makes other top TTC executives continuously aware of customers in corporate decisions.[3]

This chapter begins by introducing the two fundamental processes in organizational structure: division of labour and coordination. This is followed by a detailed investigation of the four main elements of organizational structure: span of control, centralization, formalization, and departmentalization. The latter part of this chapter examines the contingencies of organizational design, including external environment, organizational size, technology, and strategy.

Division of Labour and Coordination

LO1

All organizational structures include two fundamental requirements: the division of labour into distinct tasks and the coordination of that labour so employees are able to accomplish common goals.[4] Organizations are groups of people who work interdependently towards some purpose. To efficiently accomplish their goals, these groups typically divide the work into manageable chunks, particularly when there are many different tasks to perform. They also introduce various coordinating mechanisms to ensure that everyone is working effectively towards the same objectives.

DIVISION OF LABOUR

Division of labour refers to the subdivision of work into separate jobs assigned to different people. Subdivided work leads to job specialization, because each job now includes a narrow subset of the tasks necessary to complete the product or service. Although Valve Corporation's leaders don't do the organizing, employees self-organize into project teams, and members of each team agree to the tasks they should perform. Valve encourages staff to become multiskilled, but most people gravitate towards one area of expertise or another. As companies get larger, this horizontal division of labour is usually accompanied by vertical division of labour: Some people are assigned the task of supervising employees, others are responsible for managing those supervisors, and so on. Valve has been able to avoid (or limit) this vertical division of labour by relying on employees to manage themselves and each other. But even Valve has team leaders who coordinate the work as well as marketing and strategy leaders who guide and support employee decisions on these matters.

Why do companies divide the work into several jobs? As we described in Chapter 6, job specialization increases work efficiency.[5] Job incumbents can master their tasks quickly because work cycles are shorter. Less time is wasted changing from one task to another. Training costs are reduced because employees require fewer physical and mental skills to accomplish the assigned work. Finally, job specialization makes it easier to match people with specific aptitudes or skills to the jobs for which they are best suited. Although one person working alone might be able to design a new online game, doing so would take much longer than having the work divided among several people with the required diversity of skills. Some employees are talented at thinking up innovative storylines, whereas others are better at preparing online drawings or working through financial costs.

COORDINATING WORK ACTIVITIES

When people divide work among themselves, they require coordinating mechanisms to ensure that everyone works in concert. Coordination is so closely connected to division of labour that the optimal level of specialization is limited by the feasibility of coordinating the work. In other words, an organization's ability to divide work among people depends on how well those people can coordinate with each other. Otherwise, individual effort is wasted due to misalignment, duplication, and mistiming of tasks. Coordination also tends to become more expensive and difficult as the division of labour increases. Therefore, companies specialize jobs only to the point where it isn't too costly or challenging to coordinate the people in those jobs.[6]

Every organization–from the two-person corner convenience store to the largest corporate entity–uses one or more of the following coordinating mechanisms:[7] informal communication, formal hierarchy, and standardization (see Exhibit 13.1). These forms of coordination align the work of staff within the same department as well as across work units. These coordinating mechanisms are also critical when several organizations work together, such as in joint ventures and humanitarian aid programs.[8]

Coordination Through Informal Communication All organizations rely on informal communication as a coordinating mechanism. This process includes sharing information on mutual tasks as well as forming common mental models so that employees synchronize work activities using the same mental road map.[9] Informal communication is vital in nonroutine and ambiguous situations because employees need to exchange a large volume of

EXHIBIT 13.1 Coordinating Mechanisms in Organizations

Form of coordination	Description	Subtypes/strategies
Informal communication	Sharing information on mutual tasks; forming common mental models to synchronize work activities	Direct communication Liaison roles Integrator roles Temporary teams
Formal hierarchy	Assigning legitimate power to individuals, who then use this power to direct work processes and allocate resources	Direct supervision Formal communication channels
Standardization	Creating routine patterns of behaviour or output	Standardized skills Standardized processes Standardized output

Sources: Based on information in J. Galbraith, *Designing Complex Organizations* (Reading, MA: Addison-Wesley, 1973), pp. 8-19; H. Mintzberg, *The Structuring of Organizations* (Englewood Cliffs, NJ: Prentice Hall, 1979), Chap. 1; D. A. Nadler and M. L. Tushman, *Competing by Design: The Power of Organizational Architecture* (New York: Oxford University Press, 1997), Chap. 6.

information through face-to-face communication and other media-rich channels. Valve Corporation relies heavily on informal communication as a coordinating mechanism. Employees organize themselves into teams and physically move close to each other to communicate directly and often on projects that typically enter uncharted territory.

Although coordination through informal communication is easiest in small firms, information technologies have further enabled this coordinating mechanism in large organizations.[10] Companies employing thousands of people also support informal communication by keeping each production site small. Magna International, the Canadian global auto-parts manufacturer, keeps its plants to a maximum size of around 200 employees. Magna's leaders believe that employees have difficulty remembering each other's names in plants that are any larger, a situation that makes informal communication more difficult as a coordinating mechanism.[11]

Larger organizations also encourage coordination through informal communication by assigning *liaison roles* to employees, who are expected to communicate and share information with coworkers in other work units. Where coordination is required among several work units, companies create *integrator roles.* These people are responsible for coordinating a work process by encouraging employees in each work unit to share information and informally coordinate work activities. Integrators do not have authority over the people involved in that process, so they must rely on persuasion and commitment. Brand managers for luxury perfumes have integrator roles because they ensure that the work of fragrance developers, bottle designers, advertising creatives, production, and other groups are aligned with the brand's image and meaning.[12]

Another way that larger organizations encourage coordination through informal communication is by organizing employees from several departments into temporary teams. Temporary cross-functional teams give employees more authority and opportunity to coordinate through informal communication. This process is now common in vehicle design. As the design engineer begins work on product specifications, team members from manufacturing, engineering, marketing, purchasing, and other departments are able to provide immediate feedback as well as begin their contribution to the process. Without the informal coordination available through teams, the preliminary car design would pass from one department to the next—a much slower process.[13]

Coordination Through Formal Hierarchy Informal communication is the most flexible form of coordination, but it can become chaotic as the number of employees increases. Consequently, as organizations grow, they rely increasingly on a second coordinating mechanism: formal hierarchy.[14] Hierarchy assigns legitimate power to individuals, who then use this power to direct work processes and allocate resources. In other words, work is coordinated through direct supervision—the chain of command. For instance, Canadian Tire stores have managers and assistant managers who are responsible for ensuring that employees are properly trained, perform their respective tasks, and coordinate effectively with other staff.

A century ago, management scholars applauded the formal hierarchy as the best coordinating mechanism for large organizations. They argued that organizations are most effective when managers exercise their authority and employees receive orders from only one supervisor. The chain of command—in which information flows across work units only through supervisors and managers—was viewed as the backbone of organizational strength.

Although still important, formal hierarchy is much less popular today. One problem, which Valve's cofounders have tried to avoid, is that hierarchical organizations are not as

OB by the NUMBERS

Coordination Through Micromanagement[15]

37% of 524 American employees surveyed say they occasionally or frequently feel micromanaged by their boss.

31% of 97,000 employees surveyed in 30 countries describe their company's leadership as oppressive or authoritative.

25% of 500 American employees surveyed say they work for a "micromanager."

18% of 300 Canadian human resource managers say that micromanaging employees has the most negative effect on employee morale (second only to lack of open, honest communication).

9% of 11,045 American employees surveyed identify micromanagement as the most significant barrier to their productivity.

agile for coordination in complex and novel situations. Communicating through the chain of command is rarely as fast or accurate as direct communication between employees. Another concern with formal hierarchy is that managers are able to closely supervise only a limited number of employees. As the business grows, the number of supervisors and layers of management must increase, resulting in a costly bureaucracy. A third problem is that today's workforce demands more autonomy over work and more involvement in company decisions. Formal hierarchy coordination processes tend to limit employee autonomy and involvement.

Coordination Through Standardization Standardization, the third means of coordination, involves creating routine patterns of behaviour or output. This coordinating mechanism takes three distinct forms:

- *Standardized processes.* Quality and consistency of a product or service can often be improved by standardizing work activities through job descriptions and procedures.[16] For example, flow charts represent a standardized process coordinating mechanism. This coordinating mechanism works best when the task is routine (such as mass production) or simple (such as stocking shelves), but it is less effective in nonroutine and complex work such as product design (which Valve employees do).
- *Standardized outputs.* This form of standardization involves ensuring that individuals and work units have clearly defined goals and output measures (e.g., customer satisfaction, production efficiency). For instance, to coordinate the work of salespeople, companies assign sales targets rather than specific behaviours.
- *Standardized skills.* When work activities are too complex to standardize through processes or goals, companies often coordinate work effort by extensively training employees or hiring people who have learned precise role behaviours from educational programs. Valve Corporation relies on coordination through standardized skills. It carefully hires people for their skills in software engineering, animation, and related fields, so they can perform tasks without job descriptions or precise guidelines. Training is also a form of standardization through skills. Many companies have in-house training programs where employees learn how to perform tasks consistent with company expectations.

Division of labour and coordination of work represent the two fundamental ingredients of all organizations. But how work is divided, which coordinating mechanisms are emphasized, who makes decisions, and other issues are related to the four elements of organizational structure that we discuss over the next two sections of this chapter.

Elements of Organizational Structure

LO2

Organizational structure has four elements that apply to every organization. This section introduces three of them: span of control, centralization, and formalization. The fourth element–departmentalization–is presented in the next section.

connect

Which organizational structure do you prefer? See page 345 or visit connect.mcgrawhill.com to identify the organizational structure that best fits your needs and expectations.

SPAN OF CONTROL

Chief executive officers of large corporations are probably much busier today managing their direct reports than they were two or three decades ago. In the 1980s, CEOs of the largest companies had an average of only about five people (typically vice-presidents) reported directly to them. By the end of the 1990s, this span of control increased to an average of 6.5 direct reports. Today, CEOs of the largest North American firms have an average of ten direct reports, double the number a few decades earlier. This increase reflects the fact that most large companies are far more complex today. They operate in many markets, have more variety of products, and employ people with a broader array of technical specialties. Each type of variation demands top level attention, so CEOs have been forced to manage a wider span of control–directly oversee more vice-presidents–than ever before.[17]

span of control The number of people directly reporting to the next level in the hierarchy

Span of control (also called *span of management*) refers to the number of people directly reporting to the next level in the hierarchy. A narrow span of control exists when very few people report directly to a manager, whereas a wide span exists when a manager has many direct reports.[18] A century ago, French engineer and management scholar Henri Fayol strongly recommended a relatively narrow span of control, typically no more than 20 employees per supervisor and six supervisors per manager. Fayol championed formal hierarchy as the primary coordinating mechanism, so he believed that supervisors should closely monitor and coach employees. His views were similar to those of Napoleon, who declared that senior military leaders should have no more than five officers directly reporting to them. These prescriptions were based on the belief that managers simply could not monitor and control any more subordinates closely enough. [19]

Today, we know better. The best-performing manufacturing plants currently have an average of 38 production employees per supervisor (see Exhibit 13.2).[20] What's the secret here? Did Fayol, Napoleon, and others miscalculate the optimal span of control? The answer is that those sympathetic to hierarchical control believed that employees should perform the physical tasks, whereas supervisors and other management personnel should make the decisions and monitor employees to make sure they performed their tasks. In contrast, the best-performing manufacturing operations today rely on self-directed teams, so direct supervision (formal hierarchy) is supplemented with other coordinating mechanisms. Self-directed teams coordinate mainly through informal communication and various forms of standardization (i.e., training and processes), so formal hierarchy plays more of a supporting role.

Many firms that employ doctors, lawyers, and other professionals also have a wider span of control because these staff members coordinate their work mainly through standardized skills. For example, more than two dozen people report directly to Cindy Zollinger, cofounder and president of litigation-consulting firm Cornerstone Research. Zollinger explains that this large

EXHIBIT 13.2

Recommended, Actual, and Enforced Spans of Control[21]

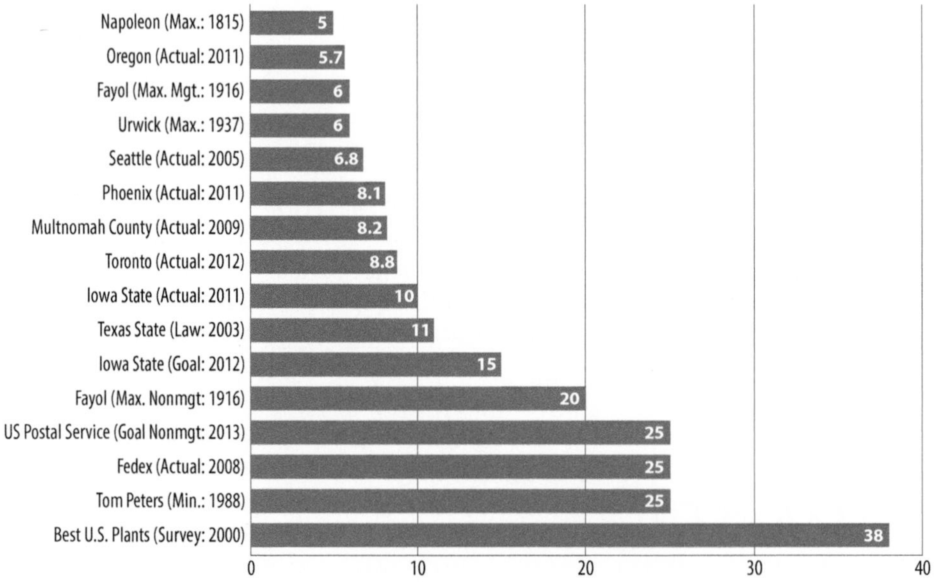

Note: Figures represent the average number of direct reports per manager. "Max." figures represent the maximum spans of control recommended by Napoleon Bonaparte, Henri Fayol, and Lindall Urwick. "Min." figure represents the minimum span of control recommended by Tom Peters. "Goal" figures represent span of control targets that the U.S. Postal Service and State of Iowa are trying to achieve. (USPS currently exceeds its goal.) The State of Texas figure represents the span of control mandated by law. The Best U.S. Plants figure is the average span of control in American manufacturing facilities identified by *Industry Week* magazine as the most effective. "Actual" figures are spans of control in the cities of Toronto, Phoenix, Seattle, and Portland (Multnomah County), the U.S. states of Oregon and Iowa, and Fedex Corporation in the years indicated. The City of Toronto excludes firefighters and Parks, which have unusually high spans of control. When these units are included, Toronto's span of control is 16.29.

number of direct reports is possible because she leads professional staff who don't require close supervision. "They largely run themselves," Zollinger explains. "I help them in dealing with obstacles they face, or in making the most of opportunities that they find."[22]

A second factor influencing the best span of control is whether employees perform routine tasks. A wider span of control is possible when employees perform routine jobs, because they require less direction or advice from supervisors. A narrow span of control is necessary when employees perform novel or complex tasks, because these employees tend to require more supervisory decisions and coaching. This principle is illustrated in a survey of property and casualty insurers. The average span of control in commercial-policy processing departments is around 15 employees per supervisor, whereas the span of control is 6.1 in claims service and 5.5 in commercial underwriting. Staff members in the latter two departments perform more technical work, so they have more novel and complex tasks, which requires more supervisor involvement. Commercial-policy processing, on the other hand, is like production work. Tasks are routine and have few exceptions, so managers have less coordinating with each employee.[23]

A third influence on span of control is the degree of interdependence among employees within the department or team.[24] Generally, a narrow span of control is necessary where employees perform highly interdependent work with others. More supervision is required for highly interdependent jobs because employees tend to experience more conflict with each other, which requires more of a manager's time to resolve. Also, employees are less clear on their personal work performance in highly interdependent tasks, so supervisors spend more time providing coaching and feedback.

Tall versus Flat Structures Span of control is interconnected with organizational size (number of employees) and the number of layers in the organizational hierarchy. Consider two companies with the same number of employees. If Company A has a wider span of control (more direct reports per manager) than Company B, then Company A necessarily has fewer layers of management (i.e., a flatter structure). The reason for this relationship is that a company with a wider span of control has more employees per supervisor, more supervisors for each middle manager, and so on. This larger number of direct reports, compared to a company with a narrower span of control, is possible only by removing layers of management.

The interconnection of span of control, organizational size (number of employees), and number of management layers has important implications for companies. Organizations employ more people as they grow, which means they must widen the span of control, build a taller hierarchy, or both. Most companies end up building taller structures because they rely on direct supervision to some extent as a coordinating mechanism and there are limits to how many people each manager can coordinate.

Unfortunately, building a taller hierarchy (more layers of management) creates problems. One concern is that executives in tall structures tend to receive lower-quality and less timely information. People tend to filter, distort, and simplify information before it is passed to higher levels in the hierarchy because they are motivated to frame the information in a positive light or to summarize it more efficiently. In contrast, information receives less manipulation in flat hierarchies, and is often received much more quickly than in tall hierarchies. "Any new idea condemned to struggle upward through multiple levels of rigidly hierarchical, risk averse management is an idea that won't see daylight . . . until it's too late," warns Sergio Marchionne, the Canadian-Italian CEO of both Fiat and Chrysler Corp.[25]

A second problem is that taller structures have higher overhead costs. With more managers per employee, tall hierarchies necessarily have more people administering the company, thereby reducing the percentage of staff who are actually making the product or providing the service. A third issue with tall hierarchies is that employees usually feel less empowered and engaged in their work. Hierarchies are power structures, so more levels of hierarchy tend to draw away power from people at the bottom of that hierarchy. Indeed, the size of the hierarchy itself tends to focus power around managers rather than employees.[26]

These problems have prompted companies to remove one or more levels in the organizational hierarchy.[27] KenGen had more than 15 layers of hierarchy a few years ago. Today, the 1,500 employees at Kenya's leading electricity generation company are organized in a hierarchy with only six layers. Sandvik also recently "delayered" its hierarchy. "We had as much as 13 layers in the Company between me as CEO and the most junior worker in the Company," says Olof Faxander, CEO of the Swedish manufacturer of tools and equipment for

Debating Point:

SHOULD ORGANIZATIONS CUT BACK MIDDLE MANAGEMENT?

Business leaders face the ongoing challenge of preventing their organization from ballooning into a fat bureaucracy with too many layers of middle managers. Indeed, it has become a mantra for incoming CEOs to gallantly state they will "delayer" or "flatten" the corporate hierarchy, usually as part of a larger mandate to "empower" the workforce.

As we describe in this chapter, there are several valid arguments for minimizing the corporate hierarchy, particularly by cutting back middle management. As companies employ more managers, they increase overhead costs and have a lower percentage of people actually generating revenue by making products or providing services. A taller hierarchy also undermines effective communication between front line staff—who receive valuable knowledge about the external environment—and the top executive team. Middle managers have a tendency to distort, simplify, and filter information as it passes from them to higher authorities in the company. A third reason for cutting back middle management is that they absorb organizational power. As companies add more layers, they remove more power that might have been assigned directly to front-line employees. In other words, tall hierarchies potentially undermine employee empowerment.

These concerns seem logical, but slashing the hierarchy can have several unexpected consequences that outweigh any benefits. In fact, a growing chorus of management experts warn about several negative long-term consequences of cutting out too much middle management.[28]

Critics of delayering point out that all companies need managers to translate corporate strategy into coherent daily operations. "Middle managers are the link between your mission and execution," advises a senior hospital executive. "They turn our strategy into action and get everyone on the same page."[29] Furthermore, managers are needed to make quick decisions, coach employees, and help resolve conflicts. These valuable functions are underserved when the span of control becomes too wide.

Delayering increases the number of direct reports per manager and thus significantly increases management workload and corresponding levels of stress. Managers partly reduce the workload by learning to give subordinates more autonomy rather than micromanaging them. However, this role adjustment itself is stressful (same responsibility, but less authority or control). Companies often increase the span of control beyond the point at which many managers are capable of coaching or leading their direct reports.

A third concern is that delayering results in fewer managerial jobs, so companies have less manoeuvrability to develop managerial skills. Promotions are also riskier because they involve a larger jump in responsibility in flatter, compared to taller, hierarchies. Furthermore, having fewer promotion opportunities means that managers experience more career plateauing, which reduces their motivation and loyalty. Chopping back managerial career structures also sends a signal that managers are no longer valued. "Delayering has had an adverse effect on morale, productivity and performance," argues a senior government executive. "Disenfranchising middle management creates negative perceptions and lower commitment to the organization with consequent reluctance to accept responsibility."[30]

mining and other industries. "We've flattened that [so we] only have up to seven layers in the Company."[31] At the same time, critics warn that cutting back middle management may do more harm than good.

CENTRALIZATION AND DECENTRALIZATION

centralization The degree to which formal decision-making authority is held by a small group of people, typically those at the top of the organizational hierarchy.

Centralization means that formal decision-making authority is held by a small group of people, typically those at the top of the organizational hierarchy. Most organizations begin with centralized structures, as the founder makes most of the decisions and tries to direct the business towards his or her vision. As organizations grow, however, they diversify and their environments become more complex. Senior executives aren't able to process all the decisions that significantly influence the business. Consequently, larger organizations typically *decentralize;* that is, they disperse decision authority and power throughout the organization. Global Connections 13.1 describes why Svenska Handelsbanken AB has a more decentralized organizational structure than is typically found in the banking industry.

The optimal level of centralization or decentralization depends on several contingencies that we will examine later in this chapter. However, different degrees of decentralization can occur simultaneously in different parts of an organization. For instance, 7-Eleven centralizes decisions about information technology and supplier purchasing to improve buying power,

Global Connections 13.1:

SVENSKA HANDELSBANKEN'S DECENTRALIZED STRUCTURE[32]

One of Europe's most successful banks doesn't believe in budgets or centralized financial targets. Instead, Sweden's Svenska Handelsbanken AB has a highly decentralized organizational structure. Branch managers and staff have considerable autonomy to run the local branches as their own businesses. Branches decide which customer types to focus their services, how much to lend, and how much to charge. Branches even have discretion about how to advertise products, how much to pay for property leases, and how many staff to hire.

© Telegraph & Argus

"The head office is there to support the branches. We don't tell them what to do," emphasizes Anders Bouvin, Handelsbanken's chief executive in the United Kingdom. "We don't offer any targets or budgeting . . . We have no volume goals, no profit goals, no timetable." Handelsbanken takes this unique approach to banking based on its experience that branch managers can make better decisions than the folks in head office. "The culture of our company is based on entrusting employees and allowing those who are closest to the customer and who know the customer best to take decisions," says Bouvin.

Bouvin points out that Handelsbanken's decentralized structure is also consistent with how human beings should be treated. "We are different, even in Sweden," Bouvin says. "This boils down to a fundamental humanist view. We believe that if you put trust in people, people will respond in a positive way and take responsibility and deliver results that they would not have achieved in a command and control environment."

Svenska Handelsbanken supports better customer service and higher empowerment by giving its branch managers and staff considerable autonomy to run the local branches.

increase cost efficiencies, and minimize complexity across the organization. Yet it decentralizes local inventory decisions to store managers because they have the best information about their customers and can respond quickly to local market needs. "We could never predict a busload of football players on a Friday night, but the store manager can," explains a 7-Eleven executive.[33]

FORMALIZATION

formalization The degree to which organizations standardize behaviour through rules, procedures, formal training, and related mechanisms.

Formalization is the degree to which organizations standardize behaviour through rules, procedures, formal training, and related mechanisms.[34] In other words, companies become more formalized as they increasingly rely on various forms of standardization to coordinate work. McDonald's Restaurants and most other efficient fast-food chains typically have a high degree of formalization because they rely on standardization of work processes as a coordinating mechanism. Employees have precisely defined roles, right down to how much mustard should be dispensed, how many pickles should be applied, and how long each hamburger should be cooked.

Older companies tend to become more formalized because work activities become routinized, making them easier to document into standardized practices. Larger companies also tend to have more formalization because direct supervision and informal communication among employees do not operate as easily when large numbers of people are involved. External influences, such as government safety legislation and strict accounting rules, also encourage formalization.

Formalization may increase efficiency and compliance, but it can also create problems.[35] Rules and procedures reduce organizational flexibility, so employees follow prescribed behaviours even when the situation clearly calls for a customized response. High levels of formalization tend to undermine organizational learning and creativity. Some work rules become so convoluted that organizational efficiency would decline if they were actually followed as prescribed. Formalization is also a source of job dissatisfaction and work stress. Finally, rules and procedures have been known to take on a life of their own in some organizations. They become the focus of attention rather than the organization's ultimate objectives of producing a product or service and serving its dominant stakeholders.

connect

Does your job require a mechanistic or organic structure? Visit **connect.mcgrawhill.com** to estimate whether the type of work you perform is better suited to one or the other of these organizational structures.

MECHANISTIC VERSUS ORGANIC STRUCTURES

mechanistic structure An organizational structure with a narrow span of control and a high degree of formalization and centralization.

organic structure An organizational structure with a wide span of control, little formalization, and decentralized decision making.

We discussed span of control, centralization, and formalization together because they cluster around two broader organizational forms: mechanistic and organic structures (see Exhibit 13.3).[36] A **mechanistic structure** is characterized by a narrow span of control and high degree of formalization and centralization. Mechanistic structures have many rules and procedures, limited decision making at lower levels, tall hierarchies of people in specialized roles, and vertical rather than horizontal communication flows. Tasks are rigidly defined and are altered only when sanctioned by higher authorities.

Companies with an **organic structure** have the opposite characteristics. They operate with a wide span of control, decentralized decision making, and little formalization. Tasks are fluid, adjusting to new situations and organizational needs. Valve Corporation, which was described at the beginning of this chapter, has a highly organic structure. With at most two layers (some claim it has one layer, and therefore no hierarchy), Valve's span of control is about as wide as a company can get. Decision making is decentralized down to teams and individuals. "Three people at the company can ship anything," says Greg Coomer, one of Valve's earliest employees. He explains that any employee alone can launch a product without permission, but the company encourages at least three people because "the work gets better if you just check with a couple of people before you decide to push a button."[37] Valve also has minimal formalization. The company doesn't have job descriptions and seems to have few lists of procedures for hiring, buying, or other activities.

As a general rule, mechanistic structures operate better in stable environments because they rely on efficiency and routine behaviours. Organic structures work better in rapidly changing (i.e., dynamic) environments because they are more flexible and responsive to the changes. Organic structures are also more compatible with organizational learning and high-performance workplaces because they emphasize information sharing and an empowered workforce rather than hierarchy and status.[38] However, the effectiveness of organic structures

EXHIBIT 13.3

Contrasting Mechanistic and Organic Organizational Structures

Mechanistic Structure	***Organic Structure***
• Narrow span of control • High centralization • High formalization	• Wide span of control • High decentralization • Low formalization

depends on how well employees have developed their roles and expertise.[39] Without these conditions, employees are unable to coordinate effectively with each other, resulting in errors and gross inefficiencies.

Forms of Departmentalization

LO3

Span of control, centralization, and formalization are important elements of organizational structure, but most people think about organizational charts when the discussion of organizational structure arises. The organizational chart represents the fourth element in the structuring of organizations, called *departmentalization.* Departmentalization specifies how employees and their activities are grouped together. It is a fundamental strategy for coordinating organizational activities because it influences organizational behaviour in the following ways:[40]

1. Departmentalization establishes the chain of command–the system of common supervision among positions and units within the organization. It frames the membership of formal work teams and typically determines which positions and units must share resources. Thus, departmentalization establishes interdependencies among employees and subunits.
2. Departmentalization focuses people around common mental models or ways of thinking, such as serving clients, developing products, or supporting a particular skill set. This focus is typically anchored around the common budgets and measures of performance assigned to employees within each departmental unit.
3. Departmentalization encourages specific people and work units to coordinate through informal communication. With common supervision and resources, members within each configuration typically work near each other, so they can use frequent and informal interaction to get the work done.

There are almost as many organizational charts as there are businesses, but the six most common pure types of departmentalization are simple, functional, divisional, team-based, matrix, and network.

SIMPLE STRUCTURE

Most companies begin with a *simple structure.*[41] They employ only a few people and typically offer only one distinct product or service. There is minimal hierarchy–usually just employees reporting to the owners. Employees perform broadly defined roles because there are insufficient economies of scale to assign them to specialized jobs. The simple structure is highly flexible and minimizes the walls that form between employees in other structures. However, the simple structure usually depends on the owner's direct supervision to coordinate work activities, so it is very difficult to operate as the company grows and becomes more complex.

FUNCTIONAL STRUCTURE

functional structure An organizational structure in which employees are organized around specific knowledge or other resources.

As organizations grow, they typically shift from a simple structure to a functional structure. Even after they adopt more complex organizational structures (which we discuss later), they will have a functional structure at some level of the hierarchy. A **functional structure** organizes employees around specific knowledge or other resources (see Exhibit 13.4). Employees with marketing expertise are grouped into a marketing unit, those with production skills are located in manufacturing, engineers are found in product development, and so on. Organizations with functional structures are typically centralized to coordinate their activities effectively.

Evaluating the Functional Structure The functional structure creates specialized pools of talent that typically serve everyone in the organization. This provides more economies of scale than are possible if functional specialists are spread over different parts of the organization. It increases employee identity with the specialization or profession. Direct

Courtesy of Chapman's Ice Cream

Chapman's Ice Cream Limited had a classic simple organizational structure when David and Penny Chapman started their business back in 1973. The couple and four employees performed all the work in a century-old creamery in Markdale, Ontario. "We did everything," recalls company president Penny Chapman (centre in photo). "We made the mixes, built the packages, we worked in cold storage . . . David went out on the road to do sales." Chapman's grew quickly by offering unique ice cream flavours. The work was eventually divided into more specialized tasks and a functional structure emerged around production, marketing, research, distribution, and other departments. Today, Chapman's is Canada's largest independent ice cream manufacturer, employing 500 people and producing more than 100 products on 16 production lines.[42]

supervision is easier in functional structures because managers oversee people with common issues and expertise.[43]

The functional structure also has limitations.[44] Grouping employees around their skills tends to focus attention on those skills and related professional needs rather than on the company's product, service, or client needs. Unless people are transferred from one function to the next, they might not develop a broader understanding of the business. Compared with other structures, the functional structure usually produces higher dysfunctional conflict and poorer coordination in serving clients or developing products. These problems occur because employees need to work with coworkers in other departments to complete organizational tasks, yet they have different subgoals and mental models of ideal work. Together, these problems require substantial formal controls and coordination when people are organized around functions.

EXHIBIT 13.4

A Functional Organizational Structure

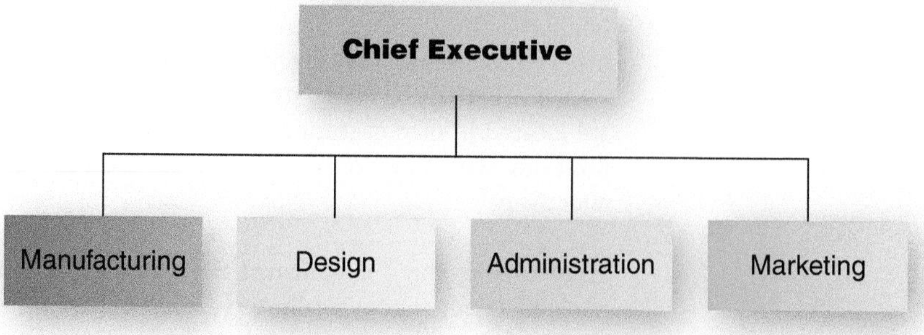

divisional structure An organizational structure in which employees are organized around geographic areas, outputs (products or services), or clients.

DIVISIONAL STRUCTURE

The **divisional structure** (sometimes called the *multidivisional* or *M-form* structure) groups employees around geographic areas, outputs (products or services), or clients. Exhibit 13.5 illustrates these three variations of divisional structure.[45] The *geographic divisional structure* organizes employees around distinct regions of the country or world. Exhibit 13.5 (*a*) illustrates a geographic divisional structure adopted by Canada's Barrick Gold Corporation, the world's largest gold-mining company. The *product/service divisional structure* organizes employees around distinct outputs. Exhibit 13.5 (*b*) illustrates a simplified version of this type of structure at Philips. The Dutch electronics company divides its workforce mainly into three divisions: health care products, lighting products, and consumer products. (Philips also has a fourth organizational group consisting of the research and design functions.) The *client divisional structure* organizes employees around specific customer groups. Exhibit 13.5 (*c*) illustrates a customer-focused divisional structure similar to one adopted by the Bank of Montreal.[46]

Which form of divisional structure should large organizations adopt? The answer depends mainly on the primary source of environmental diversity or uncertainty.[47] Suppose an organization has one type of product sold to people across the country. If customers have different needs across regions, or if provincial governments impose different regulations on the product, then a geographic structure would be best to be more vigilant of this diversity. On the other hand, if the company sells several types of products across the country and customer preferences and government regulations are similar everywhere, then a product structure would likely work best.

Coca-Cola, Nestlé, and many other food and beverage companies are organized mainly around geographic regions because consumer tastes and preferred marketing strategies vary considerably around the world. Even though McDonald's makes the same Big Mac throughout

EXHIBIT 13.5

Three Types of Divisional Structure

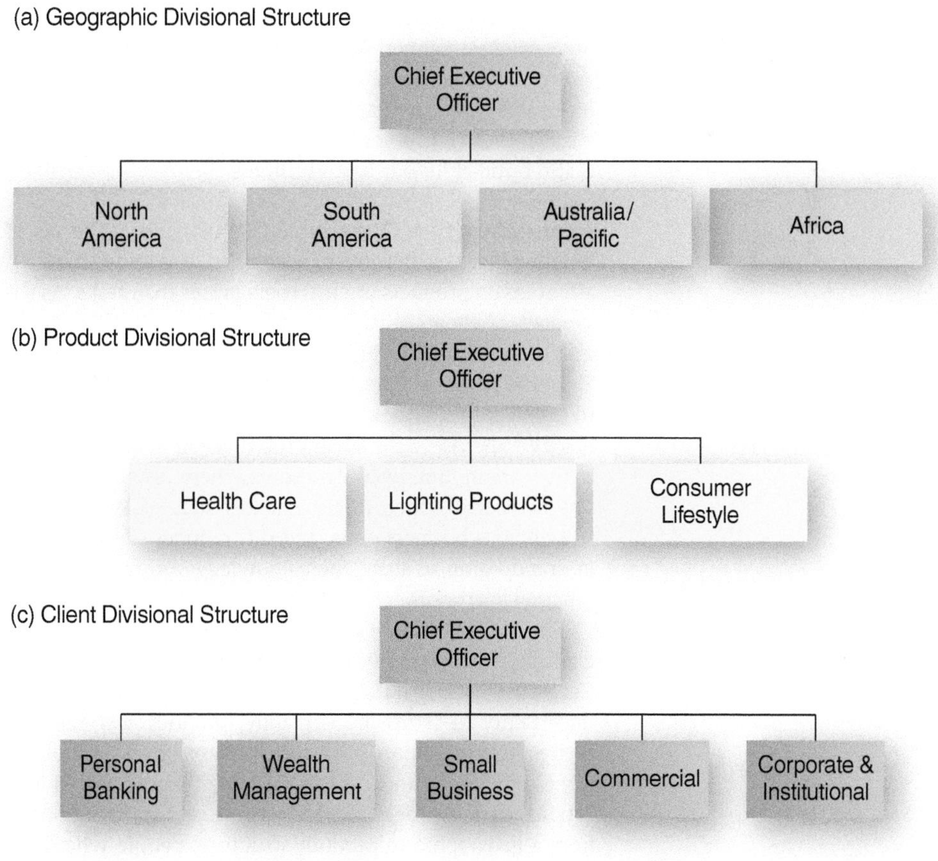

Note: Diagram (a) shows a global geographic divisional structure similar to Barrick Gold Corp.; diagram (b) is similar to the product divisions at Philips; diagram (c) is similar to the customer-focused structure at the Bank of Montreal.

the world, the company has more fish products in Hong Kong and more vegetarian products in India, in line with traditional diets in those countries. Philips, on the other hand, is organized around products because consumer preferences around the world are similar within each product group. Hospitals from Geneva, Switzerland, to Santiago, Chile, buy similar medical equipment from Philips, whereas the manufacturing and marketing of these products are quite different from Philips' consumer electronics business.

Many companies are moving away from structures that organize people around geographic clusters.[48] One reason is that clients can purchase products online and communicate with businesses from almost anywhere in the world, so local representation is becoming less important. Reduced geographic variation is another reason for the shift away from geographic structures; freer trade has reduced government intervention, and consumer preferences for many products and services are becoming more similar (converging) around the world. The third reason is that large companies increasingly have global business customers who demand one global point of purchase, not one in every country or region.

Globally Integrated Enterprise The shift away from geographic and towards product or client-based divisional structures reflects the trend towards the **globally integrated enterprise (GIE)**.[49] As the label implies, a globally integrated enterprise connects work processes around the world, rather than replicating them within each country or region. This type of organization typically organizes people around product or client divisions. Even functional units–production, marketing, design, human resources, and so on–serve the company worldwide rather than within specific geographic clusters. These functions are sensitive to cultural and market differences and have local representation to support that sensitivity. However, local representatives are associates of a global function rather than a local subsidiary copied across several regions. Indeed, a GIE is marked by a dramatic increase in virtual teamwork, because employees are assigned global projects and ongoing responsibilities for work units that transcend geographic boundaries.

globally integrated enterprise An organizational structure in which work processes and executive functions are distributed around the world through global centres, rather than developed in a home country and replicated in satellite countries or regions.

At the core of the GIE model is the notion that companies should move their operations to where the people with the best skill set and cost efficiencies are located. IBM senior executive Michael Cannon-Brookes describes the GIE structure using IBM's business in Japan as an example: "Under our GIE model, we now have the HR for IBM Japan done in Manila, accounts receivable done in Shanghai, the accounting done in Kuala Lumpur, procurement in Shenzhen, and the customer service help desk is in Brisbane. That is true global integration, and it is also optimal for our Japan business."[50]

Evaluating the Divisional Structure The divisional organizational structure is a building-block structure; it accommodates growth relatively easily and focuses employee attention on products or customers rather than tasks. As the company develops new products, services, or clients, it can sprout new divisions. This structure also directs employee attention to customers and products, rather than to their own specialized knowledge.[51]

These advantages are offset by a number of limitations. First, the divisional structure tends to duplicate resources, such as production equipment and engineering or information technology expertise. Also, unless the division is quite large, resources are not used as efficiently as they are in functional structures where resources are pooled across the entire organization. The divisional structure also creates silos of knowledge. Expertise is spread across several autonomous business units, and this reduces the ability and perhaps motivation of the people in one division to share their knowledge with counterparts in other divisions. In contrast, a functional structure groups experts together, thereby supporting knowledge sharing.

Finally, the preferred divisional structure depends on the company's primary source of environmental diversity or uncertainty. This principle seems to be applied easily enough at Coca-Cola, McDonald's, and Philips, but many global organizations experience diversity and uncertainty in terms of geography, product, *and* clients. Consequently, some organizations revise their structures back and forth or create complex structures that attempt to give all three dimensions equal status. This waffling generates further complications, because organizational structure decisions shift power and status among executives. If the company switches from a geographic to product structure, people who lead the geographic fiefdoms suddenly get demoted under the product chiefs. In short, leaders of global organizations struggle to find the best divisional structure, often resulting in the departure of some executives and frustration among those who remain.

TEAM-BASED STRUCTURE

We began this chapter describing Valve Corporation, the games software and entertainment company with an unusual organizational structure. Valve's structure is decidedly flat (minimal hierarchy), but it is perhaps best described as a completely team-based structure. A **team-based structure** is built around self-directed teams that complete an entire piece of work, such as manufacturing a product or developing an electronic game. This type of structure is usually organic. There is a wide span of control because teams operate with minimal supervision. In extreme situations such as at Valve, there is no formal leader, just someone selected by other team members to help coordinate the work and liaise with top management.

team-based structure An organizational structure built around self-directed teams that complete an entire piece of work.

Team structures are highly decentralized because almost all day-to-day decisions are made by team members rather than someone further up the organizational hierarchy. Many team-based structures also have low formalization because teams are given relatively few rules about how to organize their work. Instead, executives assign quality and quantity output targets and often productivity improvement goals to each team. Teams are then encouraged to use available resources and their own initiative to achieve those objectives.

Team-based structures are usually found within the manufacturing or service operations of larger divisional structures. Several GE Aircraft Engines plants are organized as team-based structures, but these plants operate within GE's larger divisional structure. However, a small number of firms apply the team-based structure from top to bottom, including W. L. Gore & Associates, Semco SA, and Valve Corporation, where almost all associates work in teams.

Evaluating the Team-Based Structure The team-based structure has gained popularity because it tends to be flexible and responsive in turbulent environments.[52] It tends to reduce costs because teams have less reliance on formal hierarchy (direct supervision). A cross-functional team structure improves communication and cooperation across traditional boundaries. With greater autonomy, this structure also allows quicker and more informed decision making.[53] For this reason, some hospitals have shifted from functional departments to cross-functional teams. Teams composed of nurses, radiologists, anaesthetists, a pharmacology representative, possibly social workers, a rehabilitation therapist, and other specialists communicate and coordinate more efficiently, thereby reducing delays and errors.[54]

TAXI has produced some of Canada's most memorable ads, such as Canadian Tire's "ice truck" commercial and the cute critters that populate the Telus ads and website. The Toronto-based creative agency fuels this creative energy through a team-based structure. "We believe a small team of bright people, about as many as can fit into a cab, should drive every piece of business," says TAXI's website. TAXI's team-based structure contrasts with the rigid functional structures found at many creative agencies. "[Other advertising firms] operated on a 19th-century model of many secular departments trying to integrate everything ad hoc," explains TAXI cofounder Paul Lavoie. "We needed a flexible infrastructure, able to move with the pace of change."[55]

Caia Images/Glow

Contrasted with these benefits, the team-based structure can be costly to maintain due to the need for ongoing interpersonal skills training. Teamwork potentially takes more time to coordinate than formal hierarchy during the early stages of team development. Employees may experience more stress due to increased ambiguity in their roles. Team leaders also experience more stress due to increased conflict, loss of functional power, and unclear career progression ladders. In addition, team structures suffer from duplication of resources and potential competition (and lack of resource sharing) across teams.[56]

MATRIX STRUCTURE

ABB Group, one of the world's largest power and automation technologies engineering firms, has five product divisions, such as power products and process automation. It employs more than 140,000 people across 100 countries, so the global giant also has eight regional groups (North America, IMEA, and so forth). What organizational structure would work best for ABB? For example, should the head of power products in North America report to the worldwide head of power products in Zurich, Switzerland, or to the head of North American operations?

For ABB, the answer is to have the regional product leaders report to both the regional chiefs and the product chiefs back at global headquarters. In other words, ABB has a **matrix structure**, which overlays two structures (in this case, a geographic divisional and product structure) to leverage the benefits of both.[57] Exhibit 13.6 shows a geographic-product matrix structure, which is a simplified version of ABB's structure. The dots represent the individuals who have two bosses. For example, the head of power products in North America reports to both the worldwide head of the product group as well as to the head of North American operations.

matrix structure An organizational structure that overlays two structures (such as a geographic divisional and a product structure) in order to leverage the benefits of both.

A common mistaken belief is that everyone in this type of matrix organizational structure reports to two bosses. In reality, only managers at one level in the organization (typically country-specific product managers) report to two bosses in this type of matrix design. For example, the manager responsible for power products in North America reports to both the worldwide head of the product group as well as to the head of North American operations. However, employees below that country product leader report to only a manager in North America.

The geographic-product matrix structure is likely the most common matrix design among global companies. For instance, Nestlé, Procter & Gamble, and Shell have variations of this

EXHIBIT 13.6

Matrix Organizational Structure Similar to ABB Group

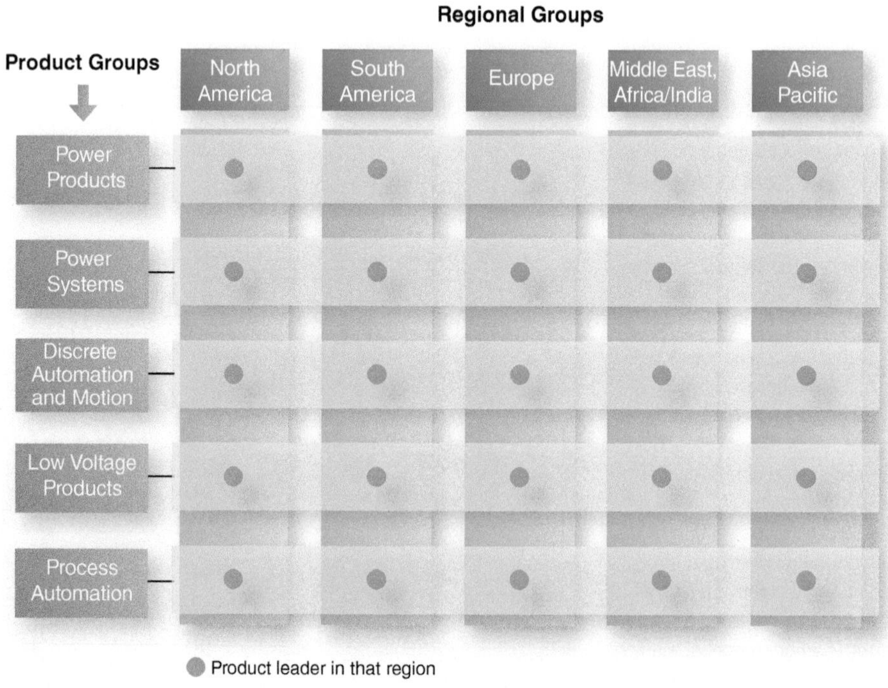

Note: This diagram is for illustrative purposes only. ABB's structure has eight regional groups rather than the five shown here. It also has four non-matrixed functional groups reporting directly to the CEO. Also, this diagram assumes ABB has a pure matrix structure, where both product and regional chiefs have equal power, whereas either the regional or product groups might have more direct line authority.

matrix structure because these firms recognize that regional groups and products/services groups are equally important. Other variations of matrix structures also exist in global businesses, however. Macquarie Group overlays client groups (such as securities, investment funds, and currencies/commodities) with four functional groups (risk management, legal/governance, financial management, and corporate operations).[58]

Global organizations tend to have complex designs that combine different types of structures, so a "pure" matrix design is relatively uncommon. A pure matrix gives equal power to leaders of both groups (regions and products, for example), whereas in reality companies often give more power to one set of groups while the other set of groups has "dotted line" or advisory authority. So, although ABB's head of power products has two bosses, one of them might have more final say or line authority than the other. Some companies also deviate from the pure matrix structure by applying it only to some regions. One such example is Cummins Inc., which is mainly organized around product divisions but has a matrix structure in China, India, and Russia. These markets are large, high potential, and potentially less visible to headquarters, so the country leaders are given as much authority as the product leaders within those regions. "I think in China there's still enough lack of transparency, there's still enough uniqueness to the market that having some kind of coordination across business units gets the greatest synergies," explains Michael Barbalas, China president of Goodrich Corporation.[59]

So far, we have described matrix structures for global or otherwise large and complex organizations. Another type of matrix structure overlays functional units with project teams and exists in small or large companies.[60] Bioware adopted this project-functional matrix structure soon after the Edmonton-based electronic games company was born a decade ago. Most Bioware employees have two managers. One manager leads the specific project where employees are assigned, such as *Star Wars, Baldur's Gate,* and *Dragon Age;* the other manager is head of the employee's functional specialization, such as art, programming, audio, quality assurance, and design.[61] Employees are assigned permanently to their functional unit but physically work with the temporary project team. When the project nears completion, the functional boss reassigns employees in his or her functional specialization to another project.

Evaluating the Matrix Structure The functional-project matrix structure usually makes very good use of resources and expertise, making it ideal for project-based organizations with fluctuating workloads. When properly managed, it improves communication efficiency, project flexibility, and innovation, compared to purely functional or divisional designs. It focuses employees on serving clients or creating products yet keeps people organized around their specialization, so knowledge sharing improves and human resources are used more efficiently. Matrix structures for global organizations (e.g., geographic-product structure) are also a logical choice when, as in the case of ABB Group, two different dimensions (regions and products) are equally important. Structures determine executive power and what should receive priority; the matrix structure works best when the business environment is complex and two different dimensions deserve equal attention and integration. Executives who have worked in a global matrix also say they have more freedom, likely because their two bosses are more advisory and less command and control.[62]

In spite of these advantages, the matrix structure has several well-known problems.[63] One concern is that it increases conflict among managers who equally share power. Employees working at the matrix level have two bosses and, consequently, two sets of priorities that aren't always aligned with each other. Project leaders might squabble with functional leaders regarding the assignment of specific employees to projects as well as regarding the employee's technical competence. However, successful companies manage this conflict by developing and promoting leaders who can work effectively in matrix structures. "Of course there's potential for friction," says Chandrasekhar Sripada, HR head at IBM India. "In fact, one of the prerequisites to attaining a leadership position at IBM is the ability to function in a matrix structure."[64]

Ambiguous accountability is another challenge with matrix structures. In a functional or divisional structure, one manager is responsible for everything, even the most unexpected issues. But in a matrix structure, the unusual problems don't get resolved because neither manager takes ownership of them.[65] Due to this ambiguous accountability, matrix structures have been blamed for corporate ethical misconduct, such as embezzlement at Hana Financial Group in Korea and massive bribes at Siemens AG in Germany. Oracle president Mark Hurd warned of this problem a few years ago when he was CEO of Hewlett-Packard: "The more

Hana Financial Group reorganized around a matrix structure that overlaps its client businesses (retail banking, brokerage, insurance) with product groups (money management, investments, bonds, etc.). The Korean bank says the new structure has noticeably improved collaboration across businesses and produced better financial results. However, Korea's financial supervisory service (FSS) claims Hana's matrix structure is also partly responsible for widespread embezzlement of gift certificates for tourists at about 60 bank branches. "In a matrix structure, marketing, performance reviews, and the power to make decisions on personnel lies with the head of the business unit, while internal control and risk management are the responsibility of the affiliated company's CEO," explains a high-ranking FSS official. "This can lead to a blind spot in management."[66]

© Seokyong Lee/Lee/Bloomberg/Getty Images

accountable I can make you, the easier it is for you to show you're a great performer," says Hurd. "The more I use a matrix, the easier I make it to blame someone else."[67] The combination of dysfunctional conflict and ambiguous accountability in matrix structures also explains why some employees experience more stress and some managers are less satisfied with their work arrangements.

NETWORK STRUCTURE

BMW AG and Daimler AG aren't eager to let you know this, but some of their vehicles designed and constructed with Germanic precision are neither designed nor constructed by them or in Germany. Much of BMW's X3, for example, was designed by Magna Steyr in Austria. The Canadian-based company also manufactured the vehicle in Austria, until BMW transferred this work to its manufacturing plant in the United States. The contract manufacturer also builds Daimler's off-road G-class Mercedes. Both BMW and Daimler Benz are hub organizations that own and market their respective brands, whereas Magna and other suppliers are spokes around the hub that provide production, engineering, and other services that get the auto firms' luxury products to customers.[68]

network structure An alliance of several organizations for the purpose of creating a product or serving a client.

BMW, Daimler, and many other organizations are moving towards a **network structure** as they design and build a product or serve a client through an alliance of several organizations.[69] As Exhibit 13.7 illustrates, this collaborative structure typically consists of several satellite organizations bee-hived around a hub or core firm. The core firm orchestrates the network process and provides one or two other core competencies, such as marketing or product development. In our example, BMW or Mercedes is the hub that provides marketing and management, whereas other firms perform many other functions. The core firm might be the main contact with customers, but most of the product or service delivery and support activities are farmed out to satellite organizations located anywhere in the world. Extranets (Web-based networks with partners) and other technologies ensure that information flows easily and openly between the core firm and its array of satellites.[70]

One of the main forces pushing towards a network structure is the recognition that an organization has only a few *core competencies.* A core competency is a knowledge base that

EXHIBIT 13.7

A Network Organizational Structure

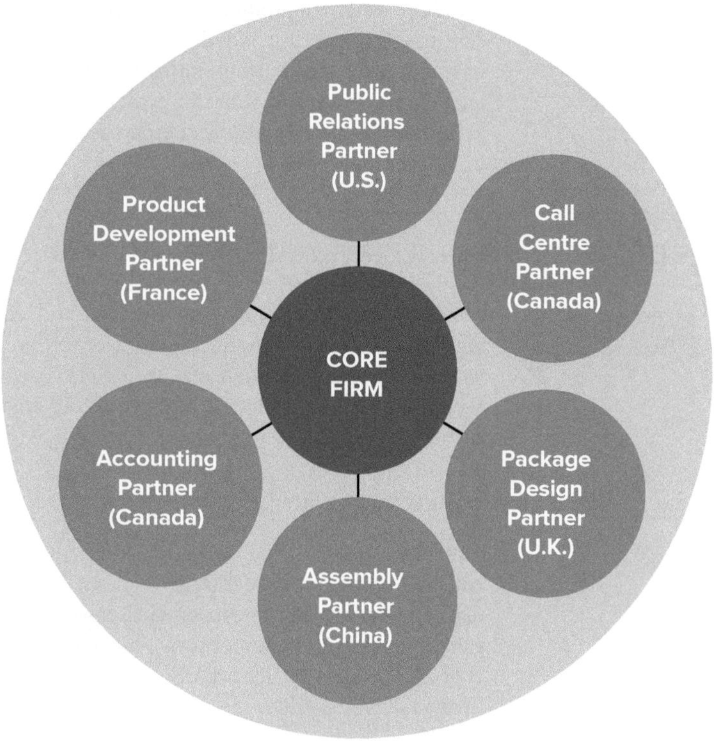

resides throughout the organization and provides a strategic advantage. As companies discover their core competency, they outsource noncritical tasks to other organizations that have a core competency at performing those tasks. For instance, BMW decided long ago that facilities management is not one of its core competencies, so it outsourced this function from its British engine plant to Dalkia, which specializes in facility maintenance and energy management.[71]

Companies are also more likely to form network structures when technology is changing quickly and production processes are complex or varied.[72] Many firms cannot keep up with the hyperfast changes in information technology, so they have outsourced their entire information system departments to IBM, HP Enterprise Business, and other firms that specialize in information system services. Similarly, many high-technology firms form networks with Toronto-based Celestica and other electronic equipment manufacturers that have expertise in diverse production processes.

Evaluating the Network Structure Organizational behaviour theorists have long argued that executives should think of their companies from the metaphor of plasma-like organisms rather than rigid machines.[73] Network structures come close to the organism metaphor because they offer the flexibility to realign their structure with changing environmental requirements. If customers demand a new product or service, the core firm forms new alliances with other firms offering the appropriate resources. For example, by working with Magna International, BMW was probably able to develop and launch the X3 vehicle much sooner than would have been the case if it had performed these tasks on its own. When BMW needs a different type of manufacturing, it isn't saddled with nonessential facilities and resources. Network structures also offer efficiencies because the core firm becomes globally competitive as it shops worldwide for subcontractors with the best people and the best technology at the best price. Indeed, the pressures of global competition have made network structures more vital, and computer-based information technology has made them possible.[74]

A potential disadvantage of network structures is that they expose the core firm to market forces. Other companies may bid up the price for subcontractors, whereas the short-term cost would be lower if the company hired its own employees to perform the same function. Another problem is that information technology makes worldwide communication much easier, but it will never replace the degree of control organizations have when manufacturing, marketing, and other functions are in-house. The core firm can use arm's-length incentives and contract provisions to maintain the subcontractor's quality, but these actions are relatively crude compared with maintaining the quality of work performed by in-house employees.

Contingencies of Organizational Design

LO4

Most organizational behaviour theories and concepts have contingencies: Ideas that work well in one situation might not work as well in another situation. This contingency approach is certainly relevant when choosing the most appropriate organizational structure.[75] In this section, we introduce four contingencies of organizational design: external environment, size, technology, and strategy.

EXTERNAL ENVIRONMENT

The best structure for an organization depends on its external environment. The external environment includes anything outside the organization, including most stakeholders (e.g., clients, suppliers, government), resources (e.g., raw materials, human resources, information, finances), and competitors. Four characteristics of external environments influence the type of organizational structure best suited to a particular situation: dynamism, complexity, diversity, and hostility.[76]

Dynamic versus Stable Environments Dynamic environments have a high rate of change, leading to novel situations and a lack of identifiable patterns. Organic structures in which employees are experienced and coordinate well in teamwork are better suited to dynamic environments so the organization can adapt more quickly to changes.[77] In contrast, stable environments are characterized by regular cycles of activity and steady changes in supply and demand for inputs and outputs. Events are more predictable, enabling the firm to apply rules and procedures. Mechanistic structures are more efficient when the environment is predictable, so they tend to be more profitable than organic structures under these conditions.

Complex versus Simple Environments Complex environments have many elements, whereas simple environments have few things to monitor. As an example, a major university library operates in a more complex environment than a small-town public library. The university library's clients require several types of services–book borrowing, online full-text databases, research centres, course reserve collections, and so on. A small-town public library has fewer of these demands placed on it. The more complex the environment, the more decentralized the organization should become. Decentralization is a logical choice for complex environments because decisions are pushed down to people and subunits with the necessary information to make informed choices.

Diverse versus Integrated Environments Organizations located in diverse environments have a greater variety of products or services, clients, and regions. In contrast, an integrated environment has only one client, product, and geographic area. The more diversified the environment, the more the firm needs to use a divisional structure aligned with that diversity. If it sells a single product around the world, a geographic divisional structure would align best with the firm's geographic diversity, for example. Diverse environments also call for decentralization. By pushing decision making further down the hierarchy, the company can adapt better and more quickly to diverse clients, government requirements, and other circumstances related to that diversity.

Hostile versus Munificent Environments Firms located in a hostile environment face resource scarcity and more competition in the marketplace. Hostile environments are typically dynamic ones because they reduce the predictability of access to resources and demand for outputs. Organic structures tend to be best in hostile environments. However,

Samsonite, the Swiss-based luggage company, recently abandoned its centralized organizational structure by delegating more power to country managers. The reason? "We've learned that all of our customers are more different than similar," explains Samsonite chief financial officer Kyle Gendreau. Luggage preferences vary across regions, so marketing and distribution decisions previously made at Samsonite's head office are now made by country and regional managers. This decentralization improves Samsonite's competitiveness by aligning marketing strategy and product offerings more closely with customer expectations. "Letting people be entrepreneurial on the ground drives growth," says Gendreau. "It's really paying off for us."[78]

© Reuters/Tyrone Siu/Landov

when the environment is extremely hostile–such as a severe shortage of supplies or tumbling market share–organizations tend to temporarily centralize so that decisions can be made more quickly and executives feel more comfortable being in control.[79] Ironically, centralization may result in lower-quality decisions during organizational crises, because top management has less information, particularly when the environment is complex.

ORGANIZATIONAL SIZE

Larger organizations have different structures than do smaller organizations, for good reason.[80] As the number of employees increases, job specialization increases due to a greater division of labour. The greater division of labour requires more elaborate coordinating mechanisms. Thus, larger firms make greater use of standardization (particularly work processes and outcomes) to coordinate work activities. These coordinating mechanisms create an administrative hierarchy and greater formalization. Historically, larger organizations make less use of informal communication as a coordinating mechanism. However, emerging information technologies and increased emphasis on empowerment have caused informal communication to regain its importance in large firms.[81]

Larger organizations also tend to be more decentralized than are smaller organizations. Executives have neither sufficient time nor expertise to process all the decisions that significantly influence the business as it grows. Therefore, decision-making authority is pushed down to lower levels, where employees are able to make decisions on issues within their narrower range of responsibility.

TECHNOLOGY

Technology is another factor to consider when designing the best organizational structure for the situation.[82] *Technology* refers to the mechanisms or processes an organization relies on to make its products or services. In other words, technology isn't just the equipment used to make something; it also includes how the production process is physically arranged and how the production work is divided among employees. The two main technological contingencies are variability and analyzability, both of which we described as job characteristics in Chapter 6.

Variability refers to the number of exceptions to standard procedure that tend to occur. In work processes with low variability, jobs are routine and follow standard operating procedures. *Analyzability* refers to the predictability or difficulty of the required work. The less analyzable the work, the more it requires experts with sufficient discretion to address the work challenges.

An organic, rather than a mechanistic, structure should be introduced where employees perform tasks with high variability and low analyzability, such as in a research setting. The reason is that employees face unique situations with little opportunity for repetition. In contrast, a mechanistic structure is preferred where the technology has low variability and high analyzability, such as an assembly line. The work is routine and highly predictable, an ideal situation for a mechanistic structure to operate efficiently.

ORGANIZATIONAL STRATEGY

organizational strategy The way the organization positions itself in its setting in relation to its stakeholders, given the organization's resources, capabilities, and mission.

Organizational strategy refers to the way the organization positions itself in its setting in relation to its stakeholders, given the organization's resources, capabilities, and mission.[83] In other words, strategy represents the decisions and actions applied to achieve the organization's goals. Although size, technology, and environment influence the optimal organizational structure, these contingencies do not necessarily determine structure. Instead, corporate leaders formulate and implement strategies that shape both the characteristics of these contingencies as well as the organization's resulting structure.

This concept is summed up with the simple phrase "structure follows strategy."[84] Organizational leaders decide how large to grow and which technologies to use. They take steps to define and manipulate their environments, rather than let the organization's fate be entirely determined by external influences. Furthermore, organizational structures don't evolve as a natural response to environmental conditions; they result from conscious human decisions. Thus, organizational strategy influences both the contingencies of structure and the structure itself.

If a company's strategy is to compete through innovation, a more organic structure would be preferred because it is easier for employees to share knowledge and be creative. If a company chooses a low-cost strategy, a mechanistic structure is preferred because it maximizes production and service efficiency.[85] Overall, it is now apparent that organizational structure is influenced by size, technology, and environment, but the organization's strategy may reshape these elements and loosen their connection to organizational structure.

Chapter Summary

LO1 Describe three types of coordination in organizational structures.

Organizational structure is the division of labour, as well as the patterns of coordination, communication, workflow, and formal power that direct organizational activities. All organizational structures divide labour into distinct tasks and coordinate that labour to accomplish common goals. The primary means of coordination are informal communication, formal hierarchy, and standardization.

LO2 Discuss the role and effects of span of control, centralization, and formalization, and relate these elements to organic and mechanistic organizational structures.

The four basic elements of organizational structure are span of control, centralization, formalization, and departmentalization. The optimal span of control—the number of people directly reporting to the next level in the hierarchy—depends on what coordinating mechanisms are present other than formal hierarchy, whether employees perform routine tasks, and how much interdependence there is among employees within the department.

Centralization occurs when formal decision authority is held by a small group of people, typically senior executives. Many companies decentralize as they become larger and more complex, but some sections of the company may remain centralized while other sections decentralize. Formalization is the degree to which organizations standardize behaviour through rules, procedures, formal training, and related mechanisms. Companies become more formalized as they get older and larger. Formalization tends to reduce organizational flexibility, organizational learning, creativity, and job satisfaction.

Span of control, centralization, and formalization cluster into mechanistic and organic structures. Mechanistic structures are characterized by a narrow span of control and a high degree of formalization and centralization. Companies with an organic structure have the opposite characteristics.

LO3 Identify and evaluate six types of departmentalization.

Departmentalization specifies how employees and their activities are grouped together. It establishes the chain of command, focuses people around common mental models, and encourages coordination through informal communication among people and subunits. A simple structure employs few people, has minimal hierarchy, and typically offers one distinct product or service. A functional structure organizes employees around specific knowledge or other resources. This structure fosters greater specialization and improves direct supervision, but it weakens the focus on serving clients or developing products.

A divisional structure groups employees around geographic areas, clients, or outputs. This structure accommodates growth and focuses employee attention on products or customers rather than tasks. However, this structure also duplicates resources and creates silos of knowledge. Team-based structures are very flat, with low formalization, and organize self-directed teams around work processes rather than functional specialties. The matrix structure combines two structures to leverage the benefits of both types. However, this approach requires more coordination than functional or pure divisional structures, may dilute accountability, and increases conflict. A network structure is an alliance of several organizations for the purpose of creating a product or serving a client.

LO4 **Explain how the external environment, organizational size, technology, and strategy are relevant when designing an organizational structure.**

The best organizational structure depends on whether the environment is dynamic or stable, complex or simple, diverse or integrated, and hostile or munificent. Another contingency is the organization's size. Larger organizations need to become more decentralized and more formalized. The work unit's technology—including variability of work and analyzability of problems—influences whether it should adopt an organic or mechanistic structure. The above-stated contingencies influence but do not necessarily determine structure. Instead, corporate leaders formulate and implement strategies that shape both the characteristics of these contingencies and the organization's resulting structure.

Key Terms

centralization, p. 328
divisional structure, p. 333
formalization, p. 329
functional structure, p. 331
globally integrated enterprise, p. 334
matrix structure, p. 335
mechanistic structure, p. 330
network structure, p. 338
organic structure, p. 330
organizational strategy, p. 342
organizational structure, p. 322
span of control, p. 326
team-based structure, p. 335

Critical-Thinking Questions

1. Valve Corporation's organizational structure was described at the beginning of this chapter. What coordinating mechanism is likely most common in this organization? Describe the extent and form in which the other two types of coordination might be apparent at Valve.
2. Think about the business school or other educational group where you are currently attending classes. What is the dominant coordinating mechanism used to guide or control the instructor? Why is this coordinating mechanism used the most here?
3. Administrative theorists concluded many decades ago that the most effective organizations have a narrow span of control. Yet today's top-performing manufacturing firms have a wide span of control. Why is this possible? Under what circumstances, if any, should manufacturing firms have a narrow span of control?
4. Leaders of large organizations struggle to identify the best level and types of centralization and decentralization. What should companies consider when determining the degree of decentralization?
5. Diversified Technologies Ltd. (DTL) makes four types of products, with each type to be sold to different types of clients. For example, one product is sold exclusively to automobile repair shops, whereas another is used mainly in hospitals. Expectations within each client group are surprisingly similar throughout the world. The company has separate marketing, product design, and manufacturing facilities in Asia, North America, Europe, and South America because, until recently, each jurisdiction had unique regulations governing the production and sales of these products. However, several governments have begun the process of deregulating the products that DTL designs and manufactures, and trade agreements have opened several markets to foreign-made products. Which form of departmentalization might be best for DTL if deregulation and trade agreements occur?
6. Mechanistic and organic structures are two organizational forms. How do the three types of coordination mechanisms operate through these forms?
7. From an employee perspective, what are the advantages and disadvantages of working in a matrix structure?
8. Suppose you have been hired as a consultant to diagnose the environmental characteristics of your college or university. How would you describe the school's external environment? Is the school's existing structure appropriate for this environment?

Case Study: MERRITT'S BAKERY

In 1979, Larry and Bobbie Merritt bought The Cake Box, a small business located in a tiny 42-square metre store in Tulsa, Oklahoma. The couple were the only employees. "I would make cakes and (wife) Bobbie would come in and decorate them," Larry recalls. Bobbie Merritt was already skilled in decorating cakes, whereas baking was a new occupation for Larry Merritt, who previously worked as a discount store manager. So, Larry spent hours pouring over baking books in the local library and testing recipes through trial-and-error experimentation. "I threw away a lot of ingredients that first year," he recalls.

Sales were initially slow. Then, a doughnut shop around the corner was put up for sale and its owner made it possible for the Merritts to buy that business. They moved to the larger location and changed the company's name to Merritt's Bakery to reflect the broader variety of products sold. The Merritts hired their first two employees, who performed front store sales and service. Over the next decade, Merritt's Bakery's physical space doubled and its revenues increased 13-fold. The company employed 20 people by the time it made its next move.

In 1993, Merritt's Bakery moved to a 557-square metre location across the street. The business became so popular that customers were lining up down the street to buy its fresh-baked goods. "That looks like success to a lot of people, but that was failure," says Bobbie Merritt. The problem was that the couple didn't want to delegate production to employees, but they couldn't produce their baked goods or decorate their carefully crafted cakes fast enough to keep up with demand. "We felt like failures because we had to work those 20 hours (per day)," she reflects.

At some point, the Merritts realized that they had to become business owners and managers rather than bakers. They devised a plan to grow the business and drew up an organizational structure that formalized roles and responsibilities. When a second Merritt's Bakery store opened across town in 2001, each store was assigned a manager, a person in charge of baking production, another in charge of cake decorating and pastries, and someone responsible for sales. A third store opened a few years later. Larry worked on maintaining quality by training bakery staff at each store. "Because it is so difficult to find qualified bakers nowadays, I want to spend more time teaching and developing our products," he said at the time.

Christian Merritt, one of Larry and Bobbie's sons, joined the business in 2000 and now runs the business. An engineer by training with experience in the telecommunications industry, Christian soon developed flow charts that describe precise procedures for most work activities, ranging from simple store-front tasks (cashiering) to unusual events such as a power outage. These documents standardized work activities to maintain quality with less reliance on direct supervision. Christian also introduced computer systems to pool information across stores about how much inventory exists, which products are selling quickly, and how much demand exists for Merritt's famous custom cakes. The information improved decision making about production, staffing, and purchasing without having to directly contact or manage each store as closely.

In late 2007, Merritt's Bakery's opened a dedicated production centre near the original store and moved all production staff into the building, affectionately called "the Fort." The centralized production facility reduced costs by removing duplication of staff and equipment, provided more consistent quality, and allowed the stores to have more front store space for customers.

Merritt's Bakery also refined its training programs, from the initial orientation session to a series for modules on specific skills. For example, front store staff complete a series of clinics that add up to 20 hours of training. The company also introduced special selection processes so people with the right personality and skills are hired into these jobs. Employees at Merritt's production facility receive decorator training through a graduated program over a longer time. One or two managers at the production site closely coach up to five new hires.

Today, Merritt's Bakery employs more than 80 people, including production managers, store managers, and a marketing director. Two-thirds of the business is in the creation of cakes for birthdays, weddings, and other events, but the company also has three busy and popular stores across Tulsa. "We're just now getting the pieces in place to start to treat Merritt's Bakery like a business, with a lot of parts that we manage from a distance," says Christian Merritt. "We're present but detached; we have our hands in a lot of things, but it's in managing stores instead of operating them."

Discussion Questions

1. How have the division and coordination of labour evolved at Merritt's Bakery from its beginnings to today?
2. Describe how span of control, centralization, and formalization have changed at Merritt's Bakery over the years? Is the company's organizational structure today more mechanistic or organic? Are these three organizational structure elements well-suited to the company in their current form? Why or why not?
3. What form of departmentalization currently exists at Merritt's Bakery? Would you recommend this form of departmentalization to this company? Why or why not?

Sources: S. Cherry, "Not Without Its Merritt's," *Tulsa World*, 13 April 2001, p. 19; D. Blossom, "Bakery Has Recipe for Success," *Tulsa World*, 28 October 2002, p. A7; M. Reynolds, "A Difficult Choice Pays Off for Merritt's Bakery," *Modern Baking*, March 2010, p. 39; "Flour Power," *Tulsa People*, May 2011. Information was also collected from the company's website: http://www.merrittsbakery.com.

Team Exercise: THE CLUB ED EXERCISE

Cheryl Harvey and Kim Morouney, Wilfred Laurier University

Purpose This exercise is designed to help you understand the issues to consider when designing organizations at various stages of growth.

Materials Each student team should have enough overhead transparencies or flip chart sheets to display several organizational charts.

Instructions Each team discusses the scenario presented. The first scenario is presented below. The instructor will facilitate discussion and notify teams when to begin the next step. The exercise and debriefing require approximately 90 minutes, although fewer scenarios can reduce the time somewhat.

- *Step 1:* Students are placed in teams (typically four or five people).
- *Step 2:* After reading Scenario #1 presented below, each team will design an organizational chart (departmentalization) that is most appropriate for this situation. Students should be able to describe the type of structure drawn and explain why it is appropriate. The structure should be drawn on a flip chart or using a software program for others to see during later class discussion. The instructor will set a fixed time (e.g., 15 minutes) to complete this task.

  Scenario #1 Determined never to shovel snow again, you are establishing a new resort business on a small Caribbean island. The resort is under construction and is scheduled to open one year from now. You decide it is time to draw up an organizational chart for this new venture, called Club Ed.
- *Step 3:* At the end of the time allowed, the instructor will present Scenario #2 and each team will be asked to draw another organizational chart to suit that situation. Again, students should be able to describe the type of structure drawn and explain why it is appropriate.
- *Step 4:* At the end of the time allowed, the instructor will present Scenario #3 and each team will be asked to draw another organizational chart to suit that situation.
- *Step 5:* Depending on the time available, the instructor might present a fourth scenario. The class will gather to present their designs for each scenario. During each presentation, teams should describe the type of structure drawn and explain why it is appropriate.

Source: Adapted from C. Harvey and K. Morouney, *Journal of Management Education* 22 (June 1998), pp. 425–429. Used with permission of the authors.

Self-Assessment: WHICH ORGANIZATIONAL STRUCTURE DO YOU PREFER?

Purpose This exercise is designed to help you understand how an organization's structure influences the personal needs and values of people working in that structure.

Instructions Personal values influence how comfortable you are working in different organizational structures. You might prefer an organization with clearly defined rules or no rules at all. You might prefer a firm where almost any employee can make important decisions or one where important decisions are screened by senior executives. Read each statement below and indicate the extent to which you would like to work in an organization with that characteristic. When finished, use the scoring key in Appendix B at the end of the book to calculate your results. This self-assessment should be completed alone so that you can assess yourself honestly without concerns of social comparison. Class discussion will focus on the elements of organizational design and their relationship to personal needs and values.

Organizational Structure Preference Scale

I would like to work in an organization where . . .	Not at all	A little	Somewhat	Very much	Score
1. A person's career ladder has several steps towards higher status and responsibility.	○	○	○	○	____
2. Employees perform their work with few rules to limit their discretion.	○	○	○	○	____
3. Responsibility is pushed down to employees who perform the work.	○	○	○	○	____
4. Supervisors have few employees, so they work closely with each person.	○	○	○	○	____
5. Senior executives make most decisions to ensure that the company is consistent in its actions.	○	○	○	○	____
6. Jobs are clearly defined so that there is no confusion over who is responsible for various tasks.	○	○	○	○	____
7. Employees have their say on issues, but senior executives make most of the decisions.	○	○	○	○	____
8. Job descriptions are broadly stated or nonexistent.	○	○	○	○	____
9. Everyone's work is tightly synchronized around top-management operating plans.	○	○	○	○	____
10. Most work is performed in teams without close supervision.	○	○	○	○	____
11. Work gets done through informal discussion with coworkers rather than through formal rules.	○	○	○	○	____
12. Supervisors have so many employees that they can't watch anyone very closely.	○	○	○	○	____
13. Everyone has clearly understood goals, expectations, and job duties.	○	○	○	○	____
14. Senior executives assign overall goals, but leave daily decisions to front line teams.	○	○	○	○	____
15. Even in a large company, the CEO is only three or four levels above the lowest position.	○	○	○	○	____

SELF-ASSESSMENTS FOR CHAPTER 13

SELF-ASSESSMENT NAME	DESCRIPTION	LOCATION
Which organizational structure do you prefer?	Identifies which of four organizational structures best fits your needs and expectations.	Page 345 connect
Does your job require a mechanistic or organic structure?	Estimates whether the type of work you perform is better suited to a mechanistic or organic organizational structure.	connect

Toronto-based G Adventures has become one of the world's most successful adventure travel companies by maintaining a strong organizational culture aligned with its external environment.

Courtesy of G Adventures

Chapter 14

Organizational Culture

LEARNING OBJECTIVES

After reading this chapter, you should be able to:

LO1. Describe the elements of organizational culture and discuss the importance of organizational subcultures.

LO2. List four categories of artifacts through which corporate culture is deciphered.

LO3. Discuss the importance of organizational culture and the conditions under which organizational culture strength improves organizational performance.

LO4. Compare and contrast four strategies for merging organizational cultures.

LO5. Describe five strategies for changing and strengthening an organization's culture, including the application of attraction-selection-attrition theory.

LO6. Describe the organizational socialization process and identify strategies to improve that process.

G Adventures has become one of the world's most successful adventure travel companies. One of the main reasons for this success is the Toronto-based firm's strong culture aligned with its external environment. "I've been on a soapbox for 15 of our 20 years telling our staff that our culture is our brand," says founder Bruce Poon Tip. "You have to believe that if you get your people and culture right, everything will fall into place."

Poon Tip learned several years ago that a strong and aligned corporate culture requires active leadership. As G Adventures grew, product quality and tour operator behaviour became increasingly varied from the values that had guided the company's growth and good reputation. To fix this problem, Poon Tip began a culture-building process by surveying G Adventures staff about what the company meant to them. From that feedback emerged a precise statement of the firm's five core values: we love changing people's lives, do the right thing, lead with service, create happiness and community, and embrace the bizarre.

Poon Tip formed two special work units—G Force (originally called the Culture Club) and Talent Agency—as formal structures to support the organization's culture. G Force has the mandate of communicating and celebrating G Adventures' culture. "[G Force] is a group whose job is to promote our culture all day, every day," says Poon Tip. It is also responsible for coordinating culture-oriented ceremonies and rituals, such as Haircuts and Hotdog Days, the Three Peak Challenge, and all other corporate events. The company's more than two-dozen offices worldwide have G Force representatives (called True Believers) to help spread the culture out from head office.

The Talent Agency is responsible for ensuring that job applicants are a good fit with the G Adventures culture. After applicants have been short-listed by senior staff, they participate in the company's quirky G-Factor Interview conducted by a random selection of a few frontline staff and a member of the Talent Agency. Applicants answer five unusual questions randomly chosen from the spin of a prize wheel. The interviews determine whether an applicant's values are compatible with the company's values. Even applicants with exceptional technical skills and experience won't get hired if they fail the G-Factor Interview. "[The G-Factor interviewers] have the final say on whether we can go ahead and recruit that person," Bruce Poon Tip explains.[1]

organizational culture The values and assumptions shared within an organization.

G Adventures has a strong organizational culture and applies several strategies we will describe in this chapter to maintain and sustain that culture throughout its meteoric growth. **Organizational culture** consists of the values and assumptions shared within an organization.[2] It defines what is important and unimportant in the company and, consequently, directs everyone in the organization towards the "right way" of doing things. You might think of organizational culture as the company's DNA—invisible to the naked eye, yet a powerful template that shapes what happens in the workplace.

This chapter begins by identifying the elements of organizational culture and then describing how culture is deciphered through artifacts. This is followed by a discussion of the relationship between organizational culture and performance, including the effects of cultural strength, fit, and adaptability. We then turn our attention to the challenges of and solutions to merging organizational cultures. The latter part of this chapter examines ways to change and strengthen organizational culture, including a closer look at the related topic of organizational socialization.

Elements of Organizational Culture

LO1

Organizational culture consists of shared values and assumptions. Exhibit 14.1 illustrates how these shared values and assumptions relate to each other and are associated with artifacts, which are discussed later in this chapter. *Values* are stable, evaluative beliefs that guide our preferences for outcomes or courses of action in a variety of situations (see Chapters 1 and 2).[3] They are conscious perceptions about what is good or bad, right or wrong. In the context of organizational culture, values are discussed as *shared values,* which are values that people within the organization or work unit have in common and place near the top of their hierarchy of values.[4] For example, G Adventures founder Bruce Poon Tip says the adventure travel company's employees embrace five shared values: change people's lives, do the right thing, lead with service, create happiness and community, and embrace the bizarre.

Organizational culture also consists of *shared assumptions*—a deeper element that some experts believe is the essence of corporate culture. Shared assumptions are nonconscious, taken-for-granted perceptions or ideal prototypes of behaviour that are considered the correct way to think and act towards problems and opportunities. Shared assumptions are so deeply ingrained that you probably wouldn't discover them by surveying employees. Only by observing employees, analyzing their decisions, and debriefing them on their actions would these assumptions rise to the surface.

Leaders frequently refer to their organization's shared values. PCL, the Edmonton-based construction company, lists five core values: honesty, integrity, respect, dynamic culture, and passion. Facebook, the social networking company, lists its core values as focus on impact, move fast, be bold, be open, and build social value. "There is a really great culture of empowerment here," says a Facebook employee. "We want people to take risks and be bold and really strive to make a huge impact, because that is what the company is trying to do."[5]

Espoused versus Enacted Values Do these values really represent the cultural content of PCL and Facebook? Probably, because their cultures are well known and deeply entrenched through various artifacts. However, the values statements of many organizations do not necessarily reflect the values that are widely shared and practised in the organization. This distinction occurs because corporate leaders typically describe *espoused values*—the values that they want others to believe guide the organization's decisions and actions.[6] Espoused values are usually socially desirable, so they present a positive public image. Even if top management acts consistently with the espoused values, lower-level employees might not do so.

EXHIBIT 14.1

Organizational Culture Assumptions, Values, and Artifacts

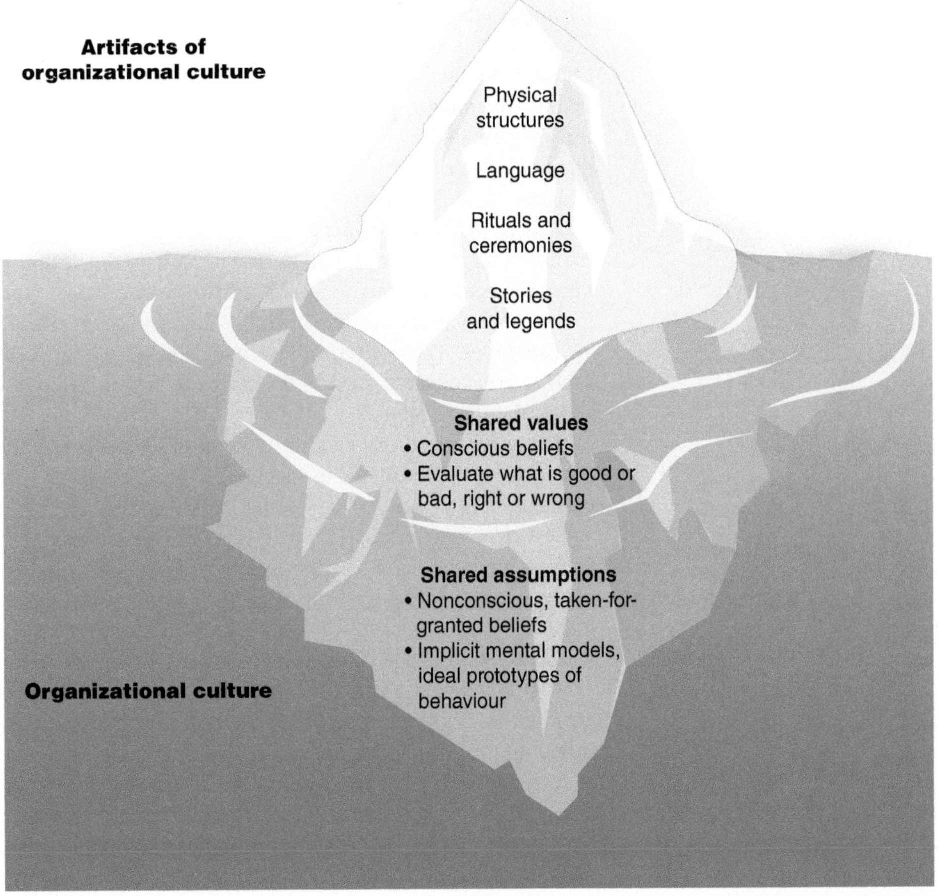

Employees bring diverse personal values to the organization, some of which might conflict with the organization's espoused values.

BP is a case in point.[7] The British energy giant lists responsibility as one of its core values, which means that "we aim for no accidents, no harm to people and no damage to the environment." Yet BP was at the centre of the Gulf of Mexico oil spill, now considered the worst environmental disaster in recent history. A few months before the spill occurred, the U.S. government penalized BP with the largest health and safety fine in history for failing to sufficiently improve safety at its Texas City refinery. Four years earlier, 15 employees died in an explosion at that refinery. A U.S. government report on that explosion concluded that BP "did not provide effective safety culture leadership." A few years earlier, officials in Norway and Alaska also reported problems with BP's "safety culture." In short, the energy company says it values responsibility, but the evidence suggests that this is only an espoused value.

The main point here is that an organization's culture is not defined by its espoused values. Instead, corporate culture consists of shared *enacted values*—the values that most leaders and employees truly rely on to guide their decisions and behaviour. These "values-in-use" are apparent by watching executives and other employees in action, including their decisions, where they focus their attention and resources, how they behave towards stakeholders, and the outcomes of those decisions and behaviour.

connect

What corporate culture do you prefer? See page 370 or visit **connect.mcgrawhill.com** to identify the corporate culture that fits most closely with your personal values.

CONTENT OF ORGANIZATIONAL CULTURE

Organizations differ in their cultural content, that is, the relative ordering of shared values.[8] G Adventures emphasizes "create happiness and community," whereas Netflix seems to prioritize individual performance with undertones of internal competitiveness. For instance, the online streaming media provider points out that "We're a team, not a family," that "Netflix leaders hire, develop, and cut smartly," and that "adequate performance gets a generous severance package."[9]

How many corporate cultures are there? Several models and measures classify organizational culture into a handful of easy-to-remember categories. One of these, shown in Exhibit 14.2, identifies seven corporate cultures. Another popular model identifies four organizational cultures organized in a two-by-two table representing internal versus external focus and flexibility versus control. Other models organize cultures around a circle with 8 or 12 categories. These circumplex models suggest that some cultures are opposite to others, such as an avoidance culture versus a self-actualization culture, or a power culture versus a collegial culture.[10]

These organizational culture models and surveys are popular with corporate leaders faced with the messy business of diagnosing their company's culture and identifying what kind of culture they want to develop. Unfortunately, they oversimplify the diversity of cultural values in organizations. The fact is, there are dozens of individual values, and many more combinations of values, so the number of organizational cultures that these models describe likely falls considerably short of the full set. A second concern is that organizational culture includes shared assumptions, not just shared values. Most organizational culture measures ignore assumptions because they represent a more subterranean aspect of culture.

A third concern is that many organizational culture models and measures incorrectly assume that organizations have a fairly clear, unified culture that is easily decipherable.[11] This "integration" perspective, as it is called, further assumes that when an organization's culture changes, it shifts from one unified condition to a new unified condition with only temporary ambiguity or weakness during the transition. These assumptions are probably incorrect or, at best, oversimplified. An organization's culture is usually quite blurry, so much so that it cannot be estimated through employee surveys alone. As we discuss next, organizations consist of diverse subcultures because employees across the organization have different clusters of experiences and backgrounds that have shaped their values and priorities.

Even these subcultural clusters can be ill-defined because values and assumptions ultimately vary from one employee to the next. As long as employees differ, an organization's

EXHIBIT 14.2 Organizational Culture Profile Dimensions and Characteristics

Organizational culture dimension	Characteristics of the dimension
Innovation	Experimenting, opportunity seeking, risk taking, few rules, low cautiousness
Stability	Predictability, security, rule-oriented
Respect for people	Fairness, tolerance
Outcome orientation	Action-oriented, high expectations, results-oriented
Attention to detail	Precise, analytic
Team orientation	Collaboration, people-oriented
Aggressiveness	Competitive, low emphasis on social responsibility

Source: Based on information in C. A. O'Reilly III, J. Chatman, and D. F. Caldwell, "People and Organizational Culture: A Profile Comparison Approach to Assessing Person-Organization Fit," *Academy of Management Journal* 34, no. 3 (1991), pp. 487–518.

culture will have noticeable variability. Thus, many of the popular organizational culture models and measures oversimplify the variety of organizational cultures and falsely presume that organizations can easily be identified within these categories.

ORGANIZATIONAL SUBCULTURES

When discussing organizational culture, we are really referring to the *dominant culture*, that is, the values and assumptions shared most consistently and widely by the organization's members. The dominant culture is usually supported by senior management, but not always. Cultural values and assumptions can also persist in spite of senior management's desire for another culture. Furthermore, organizations are composed of *subcultures* located throughout their various divisions, geographic regions, and occupational groups.[12] Some subcultures enhance the dominant culture by espousing parallel assumptions and values. Others differ from but do not conflict with the dominant culture. Still others are called *countercultures* because they embrace values or assumptions that directly oppose the organization's dominant culture. It is also possible that some organizations (including some universities, according to one study) consist of subcultures with no decipherable dominant culture at all.[13]

Subcultures, particularly countercultures, potentially create conflict and dissension among employees, but they also serve two important functions.[14] First, they maintain the organization's standards of performance and ethical behaviour. Employees who hold countercultural values are an important source of surveillance and critical review of the dominant order. They encourage constructive conflict and more creative thinking about how the organization should interact with its environment. Subcultures potentially support ethical conduct by preventing employees from blindly following one set of values. Subculture members continually question the "obvious" decisions and actions of the majority, thereby making everyone more mindful of the consequences of their actions.

The second function of subcultures is as spawning grounds for emerging values that keep the firm aligned with the evolving needs and expectations of customers, suppliers, communities, and other stakeholders. Companies eventually need to replace their dominant values with ones that are more appropriate for the changing environment. Those emerging cultural values and assumptions usually exist in subcultures long before they are ideal for the organization. If subcultures are suppressed, the organization may take longer to discover, develop, and adopt the emerging desired culture.

Deciphering Organizational Culture Through Artifacts

LO2

artifacts The observable symbols and signs of an organization's culture.

Shared values and assumptions are not easily measured through surveys and might not be accurately reflected in the organization's values statements. Instead, as Exhibit 14.1 illustrated earlier, an organization's culture needs to be deciphered through a detailed investigation of artifacts. **Artifacts** are the observable symbols and signs of an organization's culture, such as the way visitors are greeted, the organization's physical layout, and how employees are rewarded.[15] A few experts suggest that artifacts are the essence of organizational culture, whereas most others (including the authors of this book) view artifacts as symbols or indicators of culture. In other words, culture is cognitive (values and assumptions inside people's heads) whereas artifacts are observable manifestations of that culture. Either way, artifacts are important because they represent and reinforce an organization's culture.

Artifacts provide valuable evidence about a company's culture.[16] An organization's ambiguous (fragmented) culture is best understood by observing workplace behaviour, listening to everyday conversations among staff and with customers, studying written documents and e-mails, viewing physical structures and settings, and interviewing staff about corporate stories. In other words, to truly understand an organization's culture, we need to sample information from a variety of organizational artifacts.

The Mayo Clinic conducted such an assessment a few years ago. An anthropologist was hired to decipher the medical organization's culture at its headquarters in Minnesota and to identify ways of transferring that culture to its two newer sites in Florida and Arizona. For six weeks, the anthropologist shadowed employees, posed as a patient in waiting rooms, did countless interviews, and accompanied physicians on patient visits. The final report outlined Mayo's dominant culture and how its satellite operations varied from that culture.[17] Over the next few pages, we review four broad categories of artifacts: organizational stories and legends, organizational language, rituals and ceremonies, and physical structures and symbols.

ORGANIZATIONAL STORIES AND LEGENDS

Cirque du Soleil thrives on a culture of risk and creativity. This is apparent in stories about how the Montreal-based troupe that combines circus with theatre was started and survived during the lean years. One such story took place soon after it was formed. Cirque du Soleil was invited to perform at the Los Angeles Arts Festival, but they didn't have enough money to get back home and the festival could not provide funds in advance to cover Cirque du Soleil's costs. Cofounder Guy Laliberté took a gamble by literally emptying the troupe's bank account to transport the performers and equipment one way to California. "I bet everything on that one night [at the Los Angeles Arts Festival]," Laliberté recalls. "If we failed, there was no cash for gas to come home." Fortunately, the gamble paid off. Cirque du Soleil was a huge success, which led to more opportunities and successes in the years ahead.[18]

Stories such as Cirque du Soleil's risky business decision permeate strong organizational cultures. Some tales recount heroic deeds, whereas others ridicule past events that deviate from the firm's core values. Organizational stories and legends serve as powerful social prescriptions of the way things should (or should not) be done. They add human realism to corporate expectations, individual performance standards, and the criteria for getting fired. Stories also produce emotions in listeners, and these emotions tend to improve listeners' memory of the lesson within the story.[19] Stories have the greatest effect on communicating corporate culture when they describe real people, are assumed to be true, and are known by employees throughout the organization. Stories are also prescriptive–they advise people what to do or not to do.[20]

ORGANIZATIONAL LANGUAGE

The language of the workplace speaks volumes about the company's culture. How employees talk to each other, describe customers, express anger, and greet stakeholders are all verbal symbols of cultural values. The language of culture is apparent at The Container Store, where employees compliment each other about "being Gumby," meaning that they are being as flexible as the once-popular green toy to help a customer or another employee.[21] Language also highlights values held by organizational subcultures. Consultants working at Whirlpool kept hearing employees talk about the appliance company's "PowerPoint culture." This phrase, which names Microsoft's presentation software, implied that Whirlpool has a hierarchical culture in which communication is one-way (from executives to employees).[22]

© Brendan McDermid/Reuters/Corbis

At Goldman Sachs, "elephant trades" are apparently large investment transactions with huge profit potential, so the investment firm allegedly encourages its salespeople to go "elephant hunting" (seeking out these large trades from clients). The phrase is a cultural artifact, likely indicating that the company values profitability more than customer service or providing good value to clients. Former Goldman Sachs' manager Greg Smith reported that employees (particularly those in London) also routinely described their clients as muppets. "My muppet client didn't put me in comp on the trade we just printed," said one salesperson, meaning that the client was an idiot because he didn't compare prices, so the salesperson overcharged him. The "muppet" label seems to reveal a culture with a derogatory view of clients. "Being a muppet meant being an idiot, a fool, manipulated by someone else," Smith explains.[23]

RITUALS AND CEREMONIES

rituals The programmed routines of daily organizational life that dramatize the organization's culture.

ceremonies Planned displays of organizational culture, conducted specifically for the benefit of an audience.

Rituals are the programmed routines of daily organizational life that dramatize an organization's culture.[24] They include how visitors are greeted, how often senior executives visit subordinates, how people communicate with each other, how much time employees take for lunch, and so on. These rituals are repetitive, predictable, events that have symbolic meaning of underlying cultural values and assumptions. For instance, BMW's fast-paced culture is quite literally apparent in the way employees walk around the German automaker's offices. "When you move through the corridors and hallways of other companies' buildings, people kind of crawl, they walk slowly," observes a BMW executive. "But BMW people tend to move faster."[25] **Ceremonies** are more formal artifacts than rituals. Ceremonies are planned activities conducted specifically for the benefit of an audience. This would include publicly rewarding (or punishing) employees or celebrating the launch of a new product or newly won contract.

PHYSICAL STRUCTURES AND SYMBOLS

Winston Churchill once said: "We shape our buildings; thereafter, they shape us."[26] The former British prime minister was reminding us that buildings both reflect and influence an organization's culture. The size, shape, location, and age of buildings might suggest a company's emphasis on teamwork, environmental friendliness, hierarchy, or any other set of values.[27] Consider Mars, Inc., one of the world's largest food manufacturers (Uncle Ben's rice, M&M's candy, Pedigree pet food, etc.). The privately held company's low profile (some say secretive) culture is evident from its nondescript head offices in most countries. Mars head offices in Canada and the United Kingdom are buried in one of its manufacturing plants. Small signs indicate the company name and even less indication that the corporate chiefs are located there. Its global head office in Virginia could easily be mistaken for an upscale brick warehouse. There is no corporate identification at all, just a "private property" sign. Mars' head office is so low profile that locals call it the Kremlin. The chairman of Nestlé once thought he arrived at the wrong address when visiting his major competitor.[28]

Even if the building doesn't make much of a statement, there is a treasure trove of physical artifacts inside. Desks, chairs, office space, and wall hangings (or lack of them) are just a few of the items that might convey cultural meaning.[29] Consider the physical artifacts that you might notice when visiting the headquarters of Mother. Housed in a converted warehouse in an artsy district of London, the United Kingdom's largest independent creative agency has open space meeting areas separated only by dividers made of hanging strips of opaque plastic. The top floor of Mother's offices is one room dominated by a massive long rectangular concrete table around which dozens of staff work. Each of these physical artifacts alone might not say much, but put enough of them together and you can see how they symbolize Mother's edgy creative culture with a strong team orientation.[30]

Is Organizational Culture Important?

LO3

Does organizational culture improve organizational effectiveness? Launi Skinner thinks so. "You can have the best strategy in the world, but culture will kill strategy," warns the CEO of Vancouver-based First West Credit Union and former senior executive at Starbucks U.S. and 1-800-Got-Junk. Quicken Loans CEO Bill Emerson agrees. "The No. 1 thing is culture," he said recently when explaining why the Detroit-based finance company grew 133 percent the previous year. "It allows us to move very quickly and react very quickly in making business decisions." [31] Many writers of popular-press management books also assert that the most successful companies have strong cultures. In fact, one popular management book, *Built to Last*, suggests that successful companies are "cultlike" (although not actually cults, the authors are careful to point out.)[32]

So, are companies more effective when they have a strong culture? Yes, potentially, but research evidence indicates that it depends on a few conditions.[33] Before discussing these contingencies, let's examine the meaning of a "strong" organizational culture and its potential benefits. The strength of an organization's culture refers to how widely and deeply employees hold the company's dominant values and assumptions. In a strong organizational culture, most employees across all subunits understand and embrace the dominant values. These values

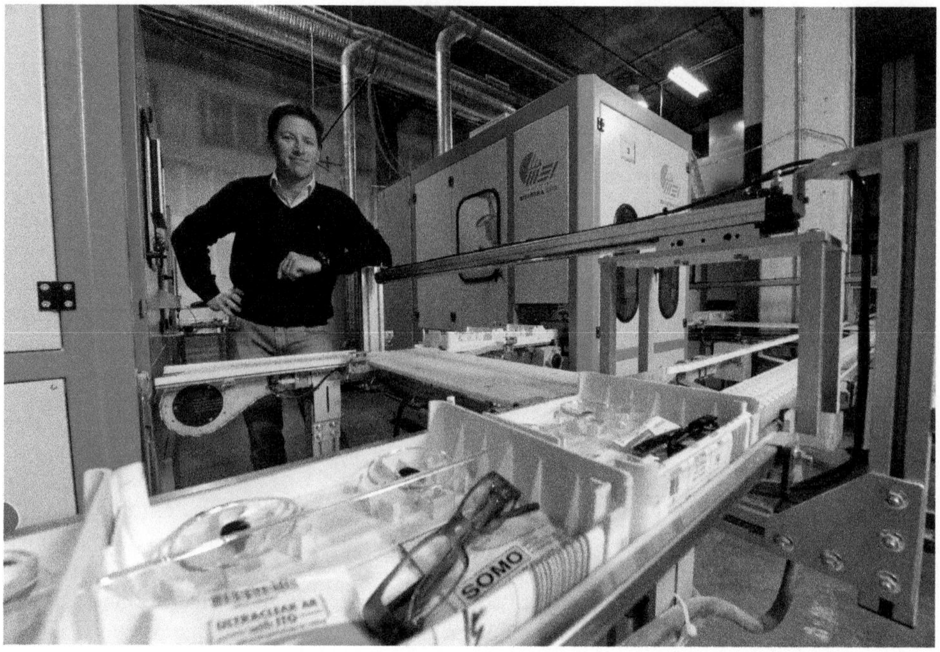

Glenn Baglo/*Vancouver Sun*

In less than a dozen years, Coastal.com and its subsidiaries (including Clearly Contacts) has become North America's largest online retailer of eyeglasses and contact lenses. According to founder and CEO Roger Hardy, corporate culture is the main reason for the Vancouver-based company's success. "Our corporate culture has allowed us to do that," says Hardy. "I think of it [the company's culture] as having been our competitive advantage for a long time." He adds that the company's culture was developed strategically, not haphazardly. "We defined our core values early on: hardworking, team work, bias to action, do more with less, always be innovating, agents of change."[34]

and assumptions are also institutionalized through well-established artifacts, which further entrench the culture. In addition, strong cultures tend to be long-lasting; some can be traced back to the values and assumptions established by the company's founder. In contrast, companies have weak cultures when the dominant values are held mainly by a few people at the top of the organization, are barely discernible from artifacts, and are in flux.

A few paragraphs ago we said that companies with stronger cultures are *potentially* more effective, and this occurs through the three important functions listed in Exhibit 14.3 and described below:

- *Control system.* Organizational culture is a deeply embedded form of social control that influences employee decisions and behaviour.[35] Culture is pervasive and operates nonconsciously. Think of it as an automatic pilot, nonconsciously directing employees so their behaviour is consistent with organizational expectations. For this reason, some writers describe organizational culture as a compass that points everyone in the same direction.
- *Social glue.* Organizational culture is the social glue that bonds people together and makes them feel part of the organizational experience.[36] Employees are motivated to internalize the organization's dominant culture because it fulfills their need for social identity. This social glue attracts new staff and retains top performers. It also becomes the common thread that holds employees together in global organizations. "The values of the company are really the bedrock–the glue which holds the firm together," says Nandan Nilekani, the head of the government of India's technology committee and former CEO of Infosys.[37]
- *Sense making.* Organizational culture helps employees to make sense of what goes on and why things happen in the company.[38] Corporate culture also makes it easier for them to understand what is expected of them. For instance, research has found that sales employees in companies with stronger organizational cultures have clearer role perceptions and less role-related stress.[39]

CONTINGENCIES OF ORGANIZATIONAL CULTURE AND EFFECTIVENESS

Studies have found only a moderately positive relationship between culture strength and organizational effectiveness. The reason for this weak link is that strong cultures improve organizational effectiveness only under specific conditions (see Exhibit 14.3). The three main contingencies

EXHIBIT 14.3

Potential Benefits and Contingencies of Culture Strength

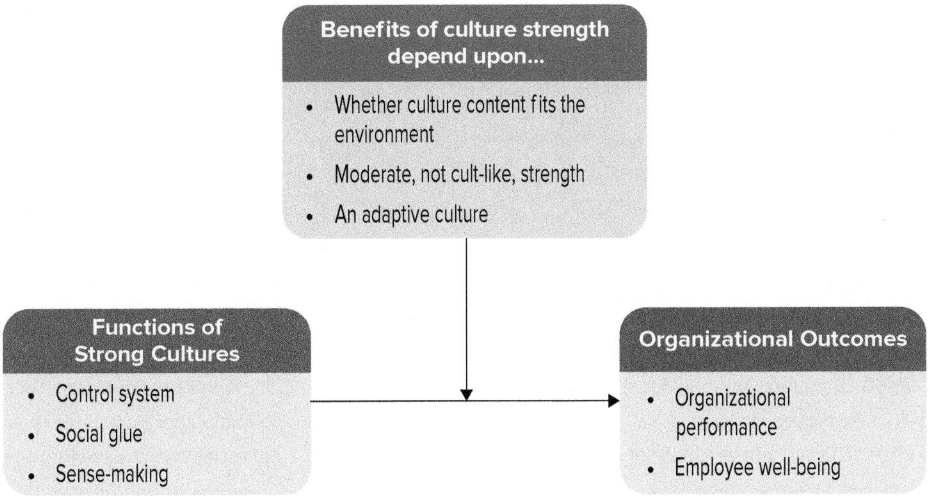

are: (1) whether the culture content is aligned with the environment, (2) whether the culture is moderately strong, not cult-like, and (3) whether the culture incorporates an adaptive culture.

Culture Content is Aligned with the External Environment The benefits of a strong culture depend on whether the culture content–its dominant values and assumptions–is aligned with the external environment. Companies require an employee-centric culture in environments where business success depends mainly on employee talent, whereas an efficiency-focused culture may be more critical for companies in environments with strong competition and standardized products. If the dominant values are congruent with the environment, then employees are more likely to engage in behaviours that improve the organization's interaction with that environment. But when the dominant values are misaligned with the environment, a strong culture encourages behaviours that can undermine the organization's connection with its stakeholders.

For example, Coles became a successful competitor in the Australian retail food industry after it was acquired by Wesfarmers, which injected a strong culture around performance and customer service. Wesfarmers is a highly successful Australian conglomerate, but it doesn't nurture the same culture in all of its businesses (food, hardware, clothing, office supplies, insurance, fertilizers, mining, and so on). Instead, Wesfarmers ensures each company maintains a strong culture around the values that matter most for that industry and its stakeholders. "It would be a huge mistake if we tried to impose one culture over all these businesses," explains Wesfarmers CEO Richard Goyder. "Bunnings (Australia's largest home improvement retailer) and Coles have to be customer-centric, whereas our coal business has to be absolutely focused on safety."[40]

Culture Strength is not the Level of a Cult A second contingency is the degree of culture strength. Various experts suggest that companies with very strong cultures (i.e., corporate "cults") may be less effective than companies with moderately strong cultures.[41] One reason why corporate cults may undermine organizational effectiveness is that they lock people into mental models, which can blind them to new opportunities and unique problems. The effect of these very strong cultures is that people overlook or incorrectly define subtle misalignments between the organization's activities and the changing environment.

The other reason why very strong cultures may be dysfunctional is that they suppress dissenting subcultures. The challenge for organizational leaders is to maintain not only a strong culture but one that allows subcultural diversity. Subcultures encourage task-oriented conflict, which improves creative thinking and offers some level of ethical vigilance over the dominant culture. In the long run, a subculture's nascent values could become important dominant values as the environment changes. Corporate cults suppress subcultures, thereby undermining these benefits.

adaptive culture An organizational culture in which employees are receptive to change, including the ongoing alignment of the organization to its environment and continuous improvement of internal processes.

Culture is an Adaptive Culture A third factor determining whether cultural strength improves organizational effectiveness is whether the culture content includes an **adaptive culture.**[42] An adaptive culture embraces change, creativity, open-mindedness, growth, and learning. Organizational leaders across many industries increasingly view an adaptive culture

Debating Point:

IS CORPORATE CULTURE AN OVERUSED PHRASE?

Corporate culture is probably one of the most frequently uttered phrases in organizations these days. That's quite an accomplishment for two words that were rarely paired together prior to 1982.[43] Executives say they have crafted the company's culture to attract top talent and better serve clients. Job applicants have made organizational culture one of the top factors in their decision whether to join the company. Journalists routinely blame corporate culture for business failures, deviant activities, and quirky employee conduct.

This chapter offers plenty of ammunition to defend the argument that organizational culture explains employee decisions and behaviour. A strong culture is a control system that directs employee decisions and behaviour. It is, after all, the "way we do things around here." The underlying assumptions of a company's culture further guide employee behaviour without conscious awareness. A strong culture also serves as the company's "social glue," which strengthens cohesion among employees. In other words, employees in strong cultures have similar beliefs and values which, in turn, increases their motivation to follow the corporate herd.

Organizational culture can be a useful concept to explain workplace activities, but some OB experts suggest that the phrase is overused. To begin with, corporate culture is usually presented as a singular thing within the company—one brand, one CEO, one culture. This presumption of a homogeneous culture—in which every employee understands and embraces the same few dominant values—just doesn't exist. Every organization has a fragmented culture to varying degrees. Furthermore, many employees engage in façades of conformity. They pretend to live the company's values but don't actually do so because they don't believe in them.[44] Fragmentation and façades suggest that culture is not a singular force field that manipulates people like mindless robots. Instead, employees ultimately make decisions based on a variety of influences, only one of which is the organization's enacted or espoused values and assumptions.

Another argument that corporate culture is overused to explain the workplace is that values don't drive behaviour as often as many people believe. Instead, employees turn to their values to guide behaviour only when they are reminded of their values or when the situation produces fairly obvious conflicting or questionable decisions.[45] Most of the time, frontline staff perform their jobs without much thought to their values. Their decisions are usually technical rather than values-based matters. As such, corporate culture has a fairly peripheral role in the workplace.

A third problem is that organizational culture is a blunt instrument for explaining workplace behaviour and for recommending how to change those behaviours. "Fix the culture" is almost meaningless because the problems prompting this advice could be due to any number of artifacts. Furthermore, some problems attributed to a poor corporate culture may be due to more mundane and precise dysfunctions—unintended consequences of poorly designed rewards, ineffective leadership, misaligned corporate strategy, biased information systems, and a host of other conditions. Rather than blame the company's culture, we should pay more attention to specific systems, structures, behaviours, and attitudes that explain what went wrong.

as an important ingredient for the organization's long-term success. "At the end of the day, you have to create a culture that not only accepts change but seeks out how to change," emphasizes Dan Akerson, who recently stepped down as CEO of General Motors. "It's critically important that we inculcate that into our culture."[46]

What does an adaptive culture look like? Employees who embrace an adaptive culture view the organization's survival and success in terms of ongoing adaptation to the external environment, which itself is continuously changing. They assume that their future depends on monitoring the external environment and serving stakeholders with the resources available. Thus, employees in adaptive cultures see things from an open-systems perspective and take responsibility for the organization's performance and alignment with the external environment.

In an adaptive culture, receptivity to change extends to internal processes and roles. Employees believe that satisfying stakeholder needs requires continuous improvement of internal work processes. They also recognize the importance of remaining flexible in their own work roles. The phrase "That's not my job" is found in nonadaptive cultures. Finally, an adaptive culture has a strong *learning orientation* because being receptive to change necessarily means that the company also supports action-oriented discovery. With a learning orientation, employees welcome new learning opportunities, actively experiment with new ideas and practices, view reasonable mistakes as a natural part of the learning process, and continuously question past practices (see Chapter 7).[47]

© Toby Melville/Reuters/Corbis

Barclays Bank PLC was found guilty of rigging interest rates (known as the Libor scandal), which caused the departure of the British bank's most senior executives. Incoming CEO Antony Jenkins (shown here) acted quickly to instil a new culture with higher ethical standards. In an e-mail to all 140,000 staff, Jenkins introduced the new values (respect, integrity, service, excellence, stewardship) and warned employees about not upholding Barclays' ethical culture. "There might be some who don't feel they can fully buy in to an approach which so squarely links performance to the upholding of our values," Jenkins wrote. "My message to those people is simple: Barclays is not the place for you. The rules have changed. You won't feel comfortable at Barclays and, to be frank, we won't feel comfortable with you as colleagues."[48]

ORGANIZATIONAL CULTURE AND BUSINESS ETHICS

An organization's culture influences the ethical conduct of its employees. This makes sense because good behaviour is driven by ethical values, and ethical values become embedded in an organization's dominant culture. Consider G Adventures, which was described at the beginning of this chapter. The Toronto-based adventure travel company has a strong culture that emphasizes "do the right thing." The deeply baked belief among staff is that travellers should enrich the communities they visit. This occurs by engaging with the local community and using local resources, rather than taking a trip to a distant land without contributing to that economy or getting very close to its people.

The opposite is equally true. There are numerous instances where an organization's culture has caused unethical conduct. For example, critics claim that News Corp's news tabloids have had a culture that rewards aggressive, partisan, and sensationalistic tactics. This culture may have uncovered news, but it allegedly also pushed some journalists and executives over the ethical line, including illegally hacking into the phones of celebrities, crime victims, and politicians. A British parliamentary committee (among others) concluded that News Corp's wrongdoing was caused by a wayward culture which "permeated from the top throughout the organization." As one journalist concluded: "Phone hacking is done by employees within the corporate culture of 'whatever it takes.'"[49] The point here is that culture and ethics go hand-in-hand. To create a more ethical organization, leaders need to work on the enacted culture that steers employee behaviour.

Merging Organizational Cultures

LO4

Top executives at EllisDon in Toronto couldn't believe their good fortune when Looby Construction indicated its interest in a takeover. Looby was a respected competitor, but EllisDon executives approached the potential acquisition cautiously. The two companies went through eight months of discussion before concluding that the acquisition made sense culturally as well as financially. "For us, the cultural fit is just as important or maybe more important than the financial side because if the culture doesn't fit, the financial side will never work," says EllisDon EO Geoff Smith. "To ensure this, we had to open up to them just as much as they had to open up to us." EllisDon vice-president Stephen Damp recalls how a deep level of compatible thinking resonated throughout those conversations. "You listen to how they [Looby executives and staff] approach their problems, their approach to their people, the market, the type of clients they like to work for," says Damp. "The whole time I was thinking: 'This is like having an internal conversation with Geoff [Smith].' Their culture is amazingly aligned with EllisDon."[50]

EllisDon executives are acutely aware that mergers and acquisitions often fail to add financial gains when the merging organizations have incompatible cultures.[51] Unless the acquired firm is left to operate independently, companies with clashing cultures tend to undermine employee performance and customer service. Several studies estimate that only between 30 percent and 50 percent of corporate acquisitions add value.[52]

BICULTURAL AUDIT

bicultural audit A process of diagnosing cultural relations between companies and determining the extent to which cultural clashes will likely occur.

Organizational leaders can minimize cultural collisions in corporate mergers and fulfill their duty of due diligence by conducting a bicultural audit.[53] A **bicultural audit** diagnoses cultural relations between the companies and determines the extent to which cultural clashes will likely occur. The bicultural audit process begins by identifying cultural differences between the merging companies. This might occur by surveying employees or, in the example of EllisDon and Looby Construction, through an extended series of meetings where executives and staff of both firms discuss how they think through important decisions in their business. From the survey data or meetings, the parties determine which differences between the two firms will result in conflict and which cultural values provide common ground on which to build a cultural foundation in the merged organization. The final stage involves identifying strategies and preparing action plans to bridge the two organizations' cultures.

STRATEGIES FOR MERGING DIFFERENT ORGANIZATIONAL CULTURES

In some cases, the bicultural audit results in a decision to end merger talks because the two cultures are too different to merge effectively. However, even with substantially different cultures, two companies may form a workable union if they apply the appropriate merger strategy. The four main strategies for merging different corporate cultures are assimilation, deculturation, integration, and separation (see Exhibit 14.4).[54]

Assimilation Assimilation occurs when employees at the acquired company willingly embrace the cultural values of the acquiring organization. Typically, this strategy works best when the acquired company has a weak, dysfunctional culture and the acquiring company's culture is strong and aligned with the external environment. The cultural assimilation strategy seldom produces cultural clashes because the acquiring firm's culture is highly respected and the acquired firm's culture is either weak or relatively similar to the other culture. A recent example of the assimilation strategy is the Southwest Airlines acquisition of AirTran Airways. The two firms already had similar cultures, but Southwest's legendary "Southwest way" culture also made the acquisition relatively free of culture clashes. "It's helpful that Southwest has a great cultural reputation," says a Southwest executive about the AirTran Airways acquisition.[55]

Deculturation Assimilation is rare. Employees usually resist organizational change, particularly when they are asked to throw away personal and cultural values. Under these conditions, some acquiring companies apply a *deculturation* strategy by imposing their culture and business practices on the acquired organization. The acquiring firm strips away artifacts and reward

EXHIBIT 14.4 Strategies for Merging Different Organizational Cultures

Merger strategy	Description	Works best when:
Assimilation	Acquired company embraces acquiring firm's culture.	Acquired firm has a weak culture.
Deculturation	Acquiring firm imposes its culture on unwilling acquired firm.	Rarely works—may be necessary only when acquired firm's culture doesn't work but employees don't realize it.
Integration	Merging companies combine the two or more cultures into a new composite culture.	Existing cultures can be improved.
Separation	Merging companies remain distinct entities with minimal exchange of culture or organizational practices.	Firms operate successfully in different businesses requiring different cultures.

Sources: Based on ideas in A. R. Malekzedeh and A. Nahavandi, "Making Mergers Work by Managing Cultures," *Journal of Business Strategy*, 11 (May-June 1990), pp. 55–57; K. W. Smith, "A Brand-New Culture for the Merged Firm," *Mergers and Acquisitions*, 35 (June 2000), pp. 45–50.

systems that support the old culture. People who cannot adopt the acquiring company's culture often lose their jobs. Deculturation may be necessary when the acquired firm's culture doesn't work, even when employees in the acquired company aren't convinced of this. However, this strategy is difficult to apply effectively because the acquired firm's employees resist the cultural intrusions from the buying firm, thereby delaying or undermining the merger process.

Integration A third strategy is to combine the two or more cultures into a new composite culture that preserves the best features of the previous cultures. Integration is slow and potentially risky because there are many forces preserving the existing cultures. Still, this strategy should be considered when the companies have relatively weak cultures or when their cultures include several overlapping values. Integration also works best when people realize that their company's existing culture is ineffective, which motivates them to adopt a new set of dominant values.

Separation A separation strategy occurs when the merging companies agree to remain distinct entities with minimal exchange of culture or organizational practices. This strategy is most appropriate when the two merging companies are in unrelated industries or operate in different countries, because the most appropriate cultural values tend to differ by industry and national culture. This strategy is also relevant advice for the corporate cultures of diversified conglomerates. Cultural separation is rare, however. Executives in acquiring firms usually have difficulty keeping their hands off the acquired firm. According to one estimate, only 15 percent of mergers leave the acquired company as a stand-alone unit.[55]

Changing and Strengthening Organizational Culture

LO5

Is it possible to change an organization's culture? Yes, but doing so isn't easy, the change rarely occurs quickly, and often the culture ends up changing (or replacing) corporate leaders. A few experts argue that an organization's culture "cannot be managed," so attempting to change the company's values and assumptions is a waste of time.[56] This may be an extreme view, but organizational culture experts generally agree that changing an organization's culture is a monumental challenge. At the same time, the external environment changes over time, so organizations need to shift their culture to maintain alignment with the emerging environment.

Over the next few pages, we will highlight five strategies that have had some success at altering corporate cultures. These strategies, illustrated in Exhibit 14.5, are not exhaustive, but each seems to work well under the right circumstances.

ACTIONS OF FOUNDERS AND LEADERS

An organization's culture begins with its founders and leaders.[57] You can see how leadership influences the organizational culture of G Adventures, which we described at the beginning of this chapter. Bruce Poon Tip pays close attention to the company's values, which reflect his personal values. "All companies, especially entrepreneurial companies, take the shape of the owner," says Poon Tip. For example, he points out that "we have a culture of winning and a culture of excellence that is driven by me."[58]

The importance of leadership on organizational culture relates to both transformational leadership and authentic leadership (see Chapter 12). In each of those models, leaders base their words and actions on personal values and those values potentially become a reflection of the organization's values. The company founder is arguably the most influential leader in an organization's culture because he or she forms the culture during its early stages.[59] The founder is often a visionary who provides a powerful role model for others to follow. The company's culture sometimes reflects the founder's personality, and this cultural imprint can remain with the organization for decades. The founder's activities are later retold as organizational stories to further reinforce the culture.

However, as Bruce Poon Tip discovered at G Adventures, an organization's culture can drift away from the founder's values, so leaders must continuously monitor and reinforce the desired values. This advice was recently echoed by Bill Emerson, CEO of Quicken Loans. "If you don't spend time to create a culture in your organization, one will create itself," warns Emerson. "And the one that creates itself is probably not going to be good."[60]

EXHIBIT 14.5

Strategies for Changing and Strengthening Organizational Culture

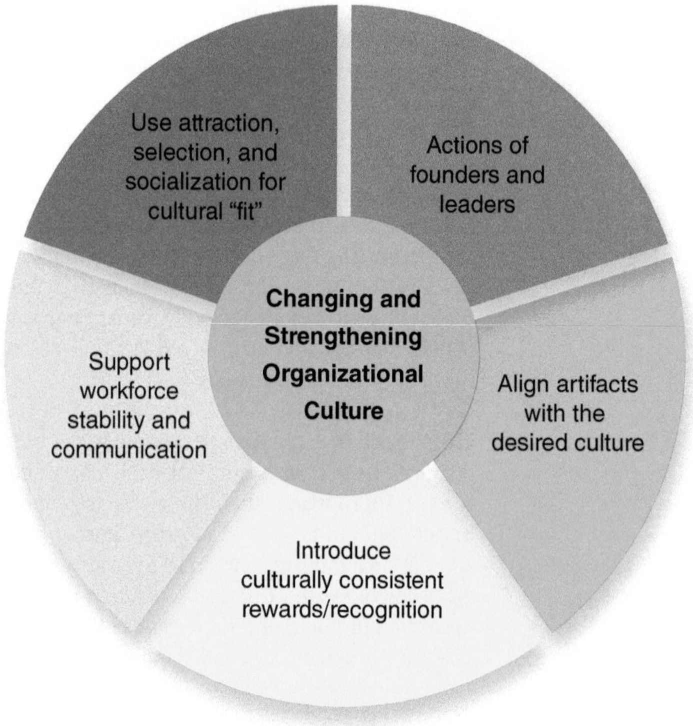

ALIGN ARTIFACTS WITH THE DESIRED CULTURE

Artifacts represent more than just the visible indicators of a company's culture. They are also mechanisms that keep the culture in place or shift the culture to a new set of values and assumptions. As we discuss in the next chapter on organizational change, systems and structures are powerful mechanisms to support the desired state of affairs. These systems and structures are artifacts, such as the workplace layout, reporting structure, office rituals, type of information distributed, and language that is reinforced or discouraged. Corporate cultures are also altered and strengthened through the artifacts of stories and behaviours. According to Max De Pree, former CEO of furniture manufacturer Herman Miller Inc., every organization needs "tribal storytellers" to keep the organization's history and culture alive.[61] Leaders play a role by creating memorable events that symbolize the cultural values they want to develop or maintain.

INTRODUCE CULTURALLY CONSISTENT REWARDS AND RECOGNITION

Reward systems and informal recognition practices are artifacts, but they deserve separate discussion because of their powerful effect on strengthening or reshaping an organization's culture.[62] For example, to change Home Depot's freewheeling culture, Robert Nardelli introduced precise measures of corporate performance and drilled managers with weekly performance objectives related to those metrics. A two-hour weekly conference call became a ritual in which Home Depot's top executives were held accountable for the previous week's goals. These actions reinforced a more disciplined (and centralized) performance-oriented culture.[63]

SUPPORT WORKFORCE STABILITY AND COMMUNICATION

An organization's culture is embedded in the minds of its employees. Organizational stories are rarely written down; rituals and ceremonies do not usually exist in procedure manuals; organizational metaphors are not found in corporate directories. Thus, a strong culture depends on a stable workforce. Workforce stability is also important because it takes time for employees to fully understand the organization's culture and how to enact it in their daily work lives. The organization's culture can literally disintegrate during periods of high turnover

@ National Post/Tim Fraser

Mike McDerment acknowledges that as a cofounder, he planted the seeds of Freshbooks' culture. But he believes the Toronto-based online accounting software developer has since been shaped by other staff. "I am not solely responsible for this," he says. "I'm just a cheerleader for our culture and a bit of a shepherd, but I'm not the only one." Freshbooks employees disagree. For example, Freshbooks product manager Melina Stathopolous says McDerment remains the main driver of the company's culture, including the belief that having a fun work environment translates into better customer service.[64]

and precipitous downsizing because the corporate memory leaves with these employees. Along with workforce stability, a strong organizational culture depends on a workplace where employees regularly communicate with each other. This ongoing communication enables employees to develop shared language, stories, and other artifacts.

Workforce stability and communication are key reasons why G Adventures has a strong culture. The adventure travel company maintains a low rate of employee turnover due to an award-winning supportive work environment. The company is famous for its quirky social events, in-house sports activities, and other forms of social bonding. Even the company's head office in Toronto is designed so employees can mingle with coworkers from other departments.

USE ATTRACTION, SELECTION, AND SOCIALIZATION FOR CULTURAL "FIT"

attraction-selection-attrition (ASA) theory A theory which states that organizations have a natural tendency to attract, select, and retain people with values and personality characteristics that are consistent with the organization's character, resulting in a more homogeneous organization and a stronger culture.

The opening case study to this chapter described how G Adventures maintains a strong culture by carefully selecting applicants whose values fit the company's culture. This process, along with weeding out people who don't fit the culture, is explained by **attraction-selection-attrition (ASA) theory**.[65] ASA theory states that organizations have a natural tendency to attract, select, and retain people with values and personality characteristics that are consistent with the organization's character, resulting in a more homogeneous organization and a stronger culture. Global Connections 14.1 describes how Zappos, the world's largest online shoe retailer, applies ASA theory to maintain a strong organizational culture.

- *Attraction.* Job applicants engage in self-selection by avoiding employment in companies whose values seem incompatible with their own values.[66] They look for subtle artifacts during interviews and through public information that communicates the company's culture. Some organizations often encourage this self-selection by actively describing their cultures. At the household products manufacturer Reckitt Benckiser, for instance, applicants can complete an online simulation that estimates their fit with the British company's hard-driving culture. Participants indicate how they would respond to a series of business scenarios. The exercise then calculates their cultural fit score and asks them to decide whether to continue pursuing employment with the company.[67]
- *Selection.* How well the person "fits" in with the company's culture is often a factor in deciding which job applicants to hire.[68] For example, every job applicant at G Adventures goes through a special G-Factor interview to determine cultural fit. A few employees are randomly selected to participate in each interview. Listening carefully

Global Connections 14.1:

ENSURING THE CULTURAL SHOE FITS AT ZAPPOS[69]

Tony Hsieh woke up one workday morning with a weird realization: he didn't want to go to work at the Internet advertising start-up company he cofounded. The company had expanded rapidly, and some of the new hires had transformed the friendly team-focused culture into a less desirable place. Hsieh and his cofounder sold that company to Microsoft, and Hsieh vowed to give organizational culture more attention at the next company he led.

That next start-up company, Zappos, has become the world's largest online shoe retailer and a poster child of the power of a strong organizational culture. Recruitment and selection are central to Zappos' cultural strength. "As long as we hire people whose personal values match our corporate values, you don't need to tell them how to behave," says Hsieh. "They can just be themselves." Zappos actively describes its culture in recruiting material, so job applicants quickly learn about the online retailer's core values such as "Deliver WOW through Service," "Embrace and Drive Change," and "Create Fun and A Little Weirdness."

Meanwhile, the company carefully selects applicants whose personal values are aligned with the company's values. The line manager looks for technical skills and experience, whereas the human resource department "does a separate set of interviews purely for culture fit," says Hsieh. Unusual methods are sometimes applied to estimate an applicant's cultural fit. For example, to determine an applicant's humility (one of Zappos' core values), staff ask the Zappos-hired driver how well he or she was treated by the applicant during the drive to the company's headquarters.

New recruits attend a four-week customer service program that also reinforces the company's values and employees' role as culture carriers. "We talk about it with our new hires, that every single one of us is responsible for our culture," says Zappos training manager Rachael Brown. Zappos also makes an unusual offer to the new recruits: it will pay $2,000 in addition to their regular pay to anyone who quits before the end of the training program. The incentive is intended to encourage new hires to leave the company if they believe their personal values don't fit Zappos' culture. (Less than 1 percent have accepted the offer.)

© Zappos.com

Online retailer Zappos relies on attraction, selection, and attrition practices to maintain a strong organizational culture.

to the applicant's responses to five unusual questions, they collectively decide whether the individual's personal values are sufficiently aligned with G Adventures' core values.

- *Attrition.* People are motivated to seek environments that are sufficiently congruent with their personal values and to leave environments that are a poor fit. This occurs because person–organization values congruence supports their social identity and minimizes internal role conflict. Even if employees aren't forced out, many quit when values incongruence is sufficiently high.[70] G Adventures, Zappos, Vancity, and a few other companies will even pay newcomers to quit within the first few weeks of employment if they think there is a cultural mismatch.

Organizational Socialization

LO6

Organizational socialization is another process that companies use to maintain a strong corporate culture and, more generally, help people to adjust to new employment. **Organizational socialization** is the process by which individuals learn the values, expected behaviours, and social knowledge necessary to assume their roles in the organization.[72] This process can potentially change employee values to become more aligned with the company's culture.

OB by the NUMBERS

Organizational Culture During the Hiring Process[71]

75% of 500 Canadian executives polled say cultural fit is more important than skills for selecting external candidates.

58% of 1,500 American job seekers polled wanted to know, during the hiring process, about the company's culture.

44% of Fortune 500 companies say they take steps to describe their corporate culture to job seekers.

51% of 2,303 American hiring managers surveyed say they search social network sites to determine if the job candidate is a good fit for the company's culture.

23% of 170,000 employees surveyed across 30 countries identified corporate culture as the top consideration when deciding to apply for a job.

However, changing an employee's personal values is much more difficult than is often assumed, because personal values are fairly stable beyond an individual's young adulthood. More likely, effective socialization gives newcomers a clearer understanding about the company's values and how they are translated into specific on-the-job behaviours.[73]

Along with supporting the organization's culture, socialization helps newcomers adjust to coworkers, work procedures, and other corporate realities. Research indicates that when employees are effectively socialized into the organization, they tend to perform better, have higher job satisfaction, and remain longer with the organization.[74]

ORGANIZATIONAL SOCIALIZATION AS A LEARNING AND ADJUSTMENT PROCESS

Organizational socialization is a process of both learning and adjustment. It is a learning process because newcomers try to make sense of the company's physical workplace, social dynamics, and strategic and cultural environment. They learn about the organization's performance expectations, power dynamics, corporate culture, company history, and jargon. They also need to form successful and satisfying relationships with other people from whom they can learn the ropes.[75] Thus, effective socialization enables new employees to form a cognitive map of the physical, social, and strategic and cultural dynamics of the organization without experiencing information overload.

organizational socialization The process by which individuals learn the values, expected behaviours, and social knowledge necessary to assume their roles in the organization.

Organizational socialization is also an adjustment process because individuals need to adapt to their new work environment. They develop new work roles that reconfigure their social identity, adopt new team norms, and practise new behaviours.[76] The adjustment process is fairly rapid for many people, usually occurring within a few months. However, newcomers with diverse work experience seem to adjust better than those with limited previous experience, possibly because they have a larger toolkit of knowledge and skills to make the adjustment possible.[77]

ORGANIZATIONAL SOCIALIZATION AND PSYCHOLOGICAL CONTRACTS

For 14 years, John Kolliopoulos was a loyal employee at Hudson's Bay Co. The information technology (IT) expert was proud to be employed at Canada's oldest company and he worked hard to perform his job. Then, one day, he and other IT department employees learned that management had outsourced the entire IT department. "All those feelings of loyalty went away when we were shown the door," recalls Kolliopoulos, who now works elsewhere in Toronto. "Now I no longer have any sense of faith or trust in any employer."[78]

John Kolliopoulos and his coworkers experienced the shock of having their psychological contract violated. The **psychological contract** refers to the individual's beliefs about the terms and conditions of a reciprocal exchange agreement between that person and another party (the employer in most work situations). The psychological contract is a perception formed during recruitment and throughout the organizational socialization process about what the employee is entitled to receive and is obliged to offer the employer in return.[79]

psychological contract The individual's beliefs about the terms and conditions of a reciprocal exchange agreement between that person and another party (typically an employer).

Job applicants form perceptions of what the company will offer them by way of career and learning opportunities, job resources, pay and benefits, quality of management, job security, and so forth. They also form perceptions about what the company expects from them, such as hours of work, continuous skill development, and demonstrated loyalty. For example, John Kolliopoulos believed that his psychological contract included long-term employment in return for hard work and loyalty to his employer. The psychological contract continues to develop and evolve after job applicants become employees, but they are also continuously testing the employer's fulfillment of that exchange relationship.

Types of Psychological Contracts Some psychological contracts are more transactional whereas others are more relational.[80] Transactional contracts are primarily short-term economic exchanges. Responsibilities are well defined around a fairly narrow set of obligations that do not change over the life of the contract. People hired in temporary positions and as consultants tend to have transactional contracts. To some extent, new employees also form transactional contracts until they develop a sense of continuity with the organization.

Relational contracts, on the other hand, are rather like marriages; they are long-term attachments that encompass a broad array of subjective mutual obligations. Employees with a relational psychological contract are more willing to contribute their time and effort without expecting the organization to pay back this debt in the short term. Relational contracts are also dynamic, meaning that the parties tolerate and expect that mutual obligations are not necessarily balanced in the short-run. Not surprisingly, organizational citizenship behaviours are more likely to prevail under relational than transactional contracts. Permanent employees are more likely to believe they have a relational contract.

STAGES OF ORGANIZATIONAL SOCIALIZATION

Organizational socialization is a continuous process, beginning long before the first day of employment and continuing throughout one's career within the company. However, it is most intense when people move across organizational boundaries, such as when they first join a company or get transferred to an international assignment. Each of these transitions is a process that can be divided into three stages. Our focus here is on the socialization of new employees, so the three stages are called pre-employment socialization, encounter, and role management (see Exhibit 14.6). These stages parallel the individual's transition from outsider to newcomer and then to insider.[81]

Stage 1: Pre-employment Socialization Think back to the months and weeks before you began working in a new job (or attending a new school). You actively searched for information about the company, formed expectations about working there, and felt some anticipation about fitting into that environment. The pre-employment socialization stage encompasses all the learning and adjustment that occurs before the first day of work. In fact, a large part of the socialization adjustment process occurs during this stage.[82]

The main problem with pre-employment socialization is that outsiders rely on indirect information about what it is like to work in the organization. This information is often distorted by inherent conflicts during the mating dance between employer and applicant.[83] One conflict occurs between the employer's need to attract qualified applicants and the applicant's need for complete information to make accurate employment decisions. Many firms use a "flypaper" approach by describing only positive aspects of the job and company, causing applicants to accept job offers from incomplete or false expectations. Another conflict that

EXHIBIT 14.6

Stages of Organizational Socialization

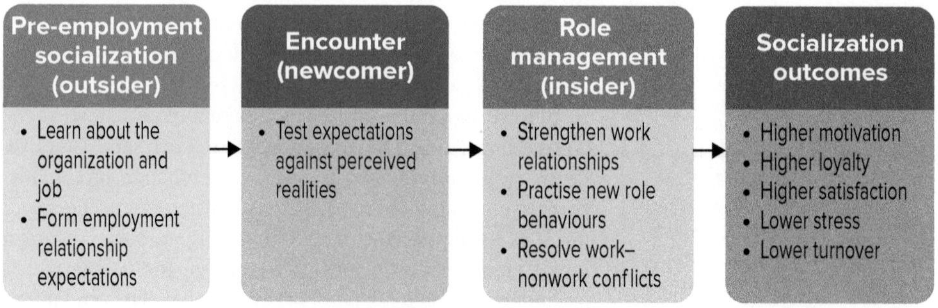

prevents accurate exchange of information occurs when applicants avoid asking important questions about the company because they want to convey a favourable image to their prospective employer. For instance, applicants usually don't like to ask about starting salaries and promotion opportunities because it makes them seem greedy or aggressive. Yet, unless the employer provides this information, applicants might fill in the missing details with false assumptions that produce an inaccurate psychological contract.

Two other types of conflict tend to distort pre-employment information for employers. Applicants engage in impression management when seeking employment, motivating them to hide negative information, act out of character, and occasionally embellish information about their past accomplishments. At the same time, employers are sometimes reluctant to ask certain questions or use potentially valuable selection devices because they might scare off applicants. Unfortunately, these exaggerated résumés and the hiring manager's reluctance to dig further during the interview cause employers to form inaccurate expectations about job candidates.

Stage 2: Encounter The first day on the job typically marks the beginning of the encounter stage of organizational socialization. This is the stage in which newcomers test how well their pre-employment expectations fit reality. Many companies fail the test, resulting in **reality shock**–the stress that results when employees perceive discrepancies between their pre-employment expectations and on-the-job reality.[84] Reality shock doesn't necessarily occur on the first day; it might develop over several weeks or even months as newcomers form a better understanding of their new work environment.

reality shock The stress that results when employees perceive discrepancies between their pre-employment expectations and on-the-job reality.

Reality shock is common in many organizations.[85] Unmet expectations sometimes occur because the employer is unable to live up to its promises, such as failing to provide challenging projects or the resources to get the work done. Reality shock also occurs because new hires develop distorted work expectations through the information exchange conflicts described above. Whatever the cause, reality shock impedes the socialization process because the newcomer's energy is directed towards managing the stress rather than learning and accepting organizational knowledge and roles.[86]

Stage 3: Role Management Role management, the third stage of organizational socialization, really begins during pre-employment socialization, but it is most active as employees make the transition from newcomers to insiders. They strengthen relationships with coworkers and supervisors, practise new role behaviours, and adopt attitudes and values consistent with their new positions and the organization. Role management also involves resolving the conflicts between work and nonwork activities, including resolving discrepancies between their personal values and those emphasized by the organizational culture.

IMPROVING THE SOCIALIZATION PROCESS

As we mentioned earlier, many companies overpromise to job applicants. They often exaggerate positive features of the job and neglect to mention the undesirable elements in the hope that the best applicants will get "stuck" on the organization. In contrast, a **realistic job preview (RJP)** offers a balance of positive and negative information about the job and work context.[87] This balanced description of the company and work helps job applicants to decide for themselves whether their skills, needs, and values are compatible with the job and organization.

realistic job preview (RJP) A method of improving organizational socialization in which job applicants are given a balance of positive and negative information about the job and work context.

RJPs scare away some applicants, but they also tend to reduce turnover and increase job performance.[88] This occurs because RJPs help applicants develop more accurate pre-employment expectations, which, in turn, minimize reality shock. RJPs represent a type of vaccination by preparing employees for the more challenging and troublesome aspects of work life. There is also some evidence that RJPs increase affective organizational commitment. This effect might occur because companies providing candid information are easier to trust. They also show respect for the psychological contract and concern for employee welfare.[89]

Socialization Agents Ask new employees what most helped them to adjust to their jobs and chances are they will mention helpful coworkers, bosses, or maybe even friends who work elsewhere in the organization. The fact is, socialization occurs mainly through these socialization agents.[91] Supervisors tend to provide technical information, performance

Facebook's global popularity has required the California social media company to expand its operation worldwide. To maintain its unique culture in these far-flung locations, Facebook dispatches a "landing team" of current employees to each new site. The main objective of the landing team is "a transfer of knowledge and of culture to make sure we're spreading our own unique Facebook culture in different offices around the world," says a landing team member who opened the office in Hyderabad, India. The landing team carefully selects applicants for their compatibility with that culture and coaches newcomers on the Facebook way of life.[90]

feedback, and information about job duties. They also improve the socialization process by giving newcomers reasonably challenging first assignments, buffering them from excessive demands, helping them form social ties with coworkers, and generating positive emotions around their new work experience.[92]

Coworkers are important socialization agents because they are easily accessible, can answer questions when problems arise, and serve as role models for appropriate behaviour. New employees tend to receive this information and support when coworkers welcome them into the work team. Coworkers also aid the socialization process by being flexible and tolerant in their interactions with new hires.

Coworkers play a more valuable role in newcomer socialization when companies help to strengthen social bonds with the new hires. For instance, on their first day of work at Adconion Media Group in Sydney, Australia, newcomers are asked to distribute a large bag of candy to coworkers as a way to make themselves known. At Clear Channel Communications Inc. in San Antonio, Texas, newcomers are paired with "peer coaches" before their first day of work, so they have someone to contact about their questions and guide them through the organizational entry process. Lupin Limited also has a popular buddy system for new hires. The buddy system not only improves socialization of newcomers at the Mumbai, India, pharmaceutical company; it has also become a valuable form of leadership development for the buddy coworker. "A happy by-product of the buddy program is the biggest supervisor training program the company has ever conducted in its history," says Divakar Kaza, Lupin's president of human resources.[93]

Chapter Summary

LO1 Describe the elements of organizational culture and discuss the importance of organizational subcultures.

Organizational culture consists of the values and assumptions shared within an organization. Shared assumptions are nonconscious, taken-for-granted perceptions or beliefs that have worked so well in the past that they are considered the correct way to think and act towards problems and opportunities. Values are stable, evaluative beliefs that guide our preferences for outcomes or courses of action in a variety of situations.

Organizations differ in their cultural content, that is, the relative ordering of values. There are several classifications of organizational culture, but they tend to oversimplify the wide variety of cultures and completely ignore the underlying assumptions of culture. Organizations have subcultures as well as the dominant culture. Subcultures maintain the organization's standards of performance and ethical behaviour. They are also the source of emerging values that replace misaligned core values.

LO2 **List four categories of artifacts through which corporate culture is deciphered.**

Artifacts are the observable symbols and signs of an organization's culture. Four broad categories of artifacts include organizational stories and legends, rituals and ceremonies, language, and physical structures and symbols. Understanding an organization's culture requires assessment of many artifacts because they are subtle and often ambiguous.

LO3 **Discuss the importance of organizational culture and the conditions under which organizational culture strength improves organizational performance.**

Organizational culture has three main functions: a form of social control, the "social glue" that bonds people together, and a way to help employees make sense of the workplace. Companies with strong cultures generally perform better than those with weak cultures, but only when the cultural content is appropriate for the organization's environment. Also, the culture should not be so strong that it drives out dissenting values, which may form emerging values for the future. Organizations should have adaptive cultures so that employees support ongoing change in the organization and their own roles.

LO4 **Compare and contrast five strategies for merging organizational cultures.**

Organizational culture clashes are common in mergers and acquisitions. This problem can be minimized by performing a bicultural audit to diagnose the compatibility of the organizational cultures. The four main strategies for merging different corporate cultures are integration, deculturation, assimilation, and separation.

LO5 **Describe five strategies for changing and strengthening an organization's culture, including the application of attraction-selection-attrition theory.**

An organization's culture begins with its founders and leaders, because they use personal values to transform the organization. The founder's activities are later retold as organizational stories. Companies also introduce artifacts as mechanisms to maintain or change the culture. A related strategy is to introduce rewards and recognition practices that are consistent with the desired cultural values. A fourth method to change and strengthen an organization's culture is to support workforce stability and communication. Stability is necessary because culture exists in employees. Communication activities improve sharing of the culture. Finally, companies strengthen and change their culture by attracting and selecting applicants with personal values that fit the company's culture, by encouraging those with misaligned values to leave the company, and by engaging in organizational socialization–the process by which individuals learn the values, expected behaviours, and social knowledge necessary to assume their roles in the organization.

LO6 **Describe the organizational socialization process and identify strategies to improve that process.**

Organizational socialization is the process by which individuals learn the values, expected behaviours, and social knowledge necessary to assume their roles in the organization. It is a process of both learning and adjustment. During this process, job applicants and newcomers develop and test their psychological contract–personal beliefs about the terms and conditions of a reciprocal exchange agreement between that person and another party (the employer).

Employees typically pass through three socialization stages: pre-employment, encounter, and role management. To manage the socialization process, organizations should introduce realistic job previews (RJPs) and recognize the value of socialization agents in the process. RJPs give job applicants a realistic balance of positive and negative information about the job and work context. Socialization agents provide information and social support during the socialization process.

Key Terms

adaptive culture, p. 355
artifacts, p. 351
attraction-selection-attrition (ASA) theory, p. 361
bicultural audit, p. 355
ceremonies, p. 352
organizational culture, p. 348
organizational socialization 363
psychological contract, p. 363
realistic job preview (RJP), p. 365
reality shock, p. 365
rituals, p. 352

Critical-Thinking Questions

1. Superb Consultants has submitted a proposal to analyze your organization's culture. The proposal states that Superb has developed a revolutionary new survey to tap the company's true culture. The survey takes just 10 minutes to complete, and the consultants say results can be based on a small sample of employees. Discuss the merits and limitations of this proposal.
2. Some people suggest that the most effective organizations have the strongest cultures. What do we mean by the "strength" of organizational culture, and what possible problems are there with a strong organizational culture?
3. The CEO of a manufacturing firm wants everyone to support the organization's dominant culture of lean efficiency and hard work. The CEO has introduced a new reward system to reinforce this culture and personally interviews all professional and managerial applicants to ensure that they bring similar values to the organization. Some employees who criticized these values had their careers sidelined until they left.

Two midlevel managers were fired for supporting contrary values, such as work-life balance. Based on your knowledge of organizational subcultures, what are the potential problems the CEO is creating?

4. Identify at least two artifacts you have observed in your department or school from each of the four broad categories: (a) organizational stories and legends, (b) rituals and ceremonies, (c) language, (d) physical structures and symbols.
5. "Organizations are more likely to succeed when they have an adaptive culture." What can an organization do to foster an adaptive culture?
6. Suppose you are asked by senior officers of a city government to identify ways to reinforce a new culture of teamwork and collaboration. The senior executive group clearly supports these values, but it wants everyone in the organization to embrace them. Identify four types of activities that would strengthen these cultural values.
7. Is it possible to have knowledge of what an organizational culture is before you become a part of the organization? How important is it for you to align yourself with your organizational culture?
8. Socialization is most intense when people pass through organizational boundaries. One example is your entry into the college or university that you are now attending. What learning and adjustment occurred as you moved from outsider to newcomer to insider as a student here?

Case Study: HILLTON'S TRANSFORMATION

Twenty years ago, Hillton was a small city (about 70,000 residents) that served as an outer suburb to a large Canadian metropolitan city. Hillton treated city employees like family and gave them a great deal of autonomy in their work. Everyone in the organization (including the two labour unions representing employees) implicitly agreed that the leaders and supervisors of the organization should rise through the ranks based on their experience. Few people were ever hired from the outside into middle or senior positions. The rule of employment at Hillton was to learn the job skills, maintain a reasonably good work record, and wait your turn for promotion.

As Hillton's population grew, so did the city's workforce to keep pace with the increasing demand for municipal services. This meant that employees were promoted fairly quickly and were almost assured lifetime employment. Until recently, Hillton had never laid off any employee. The organization's culture could be described as one of entitlement and comfort. Neither the elected city councillors nor the city manager bothered departmental managers about their work. There were few cost controls, because the rapid growth placed more emphasis on keeping up with the population expansion. The public became somewhat more critical of the city's poor service, including road construction at inconvenient times and the apparent lack of respect some employees showed towards taxpayers.

During these expansion years, Hillton put most of its money into "outside" (also called "hard") municipal services. These included road building, utility construction and maintenance, fire and police protection, recreational facilities, and land use control. This emphasis occurred because an expanding population demanded more of these services, and most of Hillton's senior people came from the outside services group. For example, Hillton's city manager for many years was a road development engineer. The "inside" workers (taxation, community services, etc.) tended to have less seniority, and their departments were given less priority.

As commuter and road systems developed, Hillton attracted more upwardly mobile professionals into the community. Some infrastructure demands continued, but now these suburban dwellers wanted more of the "soft" services, such as libraries, social activities, and community services. They also began complaining about the way the municipality was being run. By this time, the population had more than tripled, and it was increasingly apparent that the organization needed more corporate planning, information systems, organization development, and cost control systems. In various ways, residents voiced their concerns that the municipality was not providing the quality of management that they would expect from a city of its size.

A few years ago, a new mayor and council replaced most of the previous incumbents, mainly on the platform of improving the municipality's management structure. The new council gave the city manager, along with two other senior managers, an early retirement buyout package. Rather than promoting from the lower ranks, council decided to fill all three positions with qualified candidates from large municipal corporations in the region. The following year, several long-term managers left Hillton, and at least half of those positions were filled by people from outside the organization.

In less than two years, Hillton had eight senior or departmental managers hired from other municipalities who played a key role in changing the organization's value system. These eight managers became known (often with negative connotations) as the "professionals." They worked closely with one another to change the way middle- and lower-level managers had operated for many years. They brought in a new computer system and emphasized cost controls where managers previously had complete autonomy. Promotions were increasingly based more on merit than seniority.

The "professionals" frequently announced in meetings and newsletters that municipal employees must provide superlative customer service and that Hillton would become one of the most customer-friendly places for citizens and those who do business with the municipality. To this end, these managers were quick to support the public's increasing demand for more "soft" services, including expanded library services and recreational activities. And when population growth recently flattened out, the city manager and other professionals gained council support to lay off a few of the outside workers due to lack of demand for hard services.

One of the most significant changes was that the "outside" departments no longer held dominant positions in city management. Most of the "professional" managers had worked exclusively in administrative and related inside jobs. Two had Master of Business Administration degrees. This led to some tension between the professional managers and the older outside managers.

Even before the layoffs, managers of outside departments resisted the changes more than others. These managers complained that their employees with the highest seniority were turned down for promotions. They argued for more budget and warned that infrastructure problems would cause liability problems. Informally, these outside managers were supported by the labour union representing outside workers. The union leaders tried to bargain for more job guarantees, whereas the union representing inside workers focused more on improving wages and benefits. Leaders of the outside union made several statements in the local media that the city had "lost its heart" and that the public would suffer from the actions of the new professionals.

Discussion Questions

1. Contrast Hillton's earlier corporate culture with the emerging set of cultural values.
2. Considering the difficulty in changing organizational culture, why does Hillton's management seem to have been successful in this transformation?
3. Identify two other strategies that the city might consider to reinforce the new set of corporate values.

Team Exercise: ORGANIZATIONAL CULTURE METAPHORS

By David L. Luechauer, Butler University and Gary M. Shulman, Miami University

Purpose Both parts of this exercise are designed to help you understand, assess, and interpret organizational culture using metaphors.

PART A: ASSESSING YOUR SCHOOL'S CULTURE

Instructions A metaphor is a figure of speech that contains an implied comparison between a word or phrase that is ordinarily used for one thing but can be applied to another. Metaphors also carry a great deal of hidden meaning–they say a lot about what we think and feel about that object. Therefore, this activity asks you to use several metaphors to define the organizational culture of your university, college, or institute. (Alternatively, the instructor might ask students to assess another organization that most students know about.)

- *Step 1:* The class will be divided into teams of 4 to 6 members.
- *Step 2:* Each team will reach consensus on which words or phrases should be inserted in the blanks of the statements presented below. This information should be recorded on a flip chart or overhead acetate for class presentation. The instructor will provide 15 to 20 minutes for teams to determine which words best describe the college's culture.

  If our school was an animal, it would be a ___ because ___.

  If our school was a food, it would be ___ because ___.

  If our school was a place, it would be ___ because ___.

  If our school was a season, it would be ___ because ___.

  If our school was a TV show or movie, it would be ___ because ___.
- *Step 3:* The class will listen to each team present the metaphors that it believes symbolizes the school's culture. For example, a team that picks winter for a season might mean they are feeling cold or distant about the school and its people.
- *Step 4:* The class will discuss the discussion questions stated below.

DISCUSSION QUESTIONS FOR PART A

1. How easy was it for your group to reach consensus regarding these metaphors? What does that imply about the culture of your school?
2. How do you see these metaphors in action? In other words, what are some critical school behaviours or other artifacts that reveal the presence of your culture?
3. Think of another organization to which you belong (e.g., work, religious congregation). What is its dominant cultural values, how do you see them in action, and how do they affect the effectiveness of that organization?

PART B: ANALYZING AND INTERPRETING CULTURAL METAPHORS

Instructions Previously, you completed a metaphor exercise to describe the corporate culture of your school. That exercise gave you a taste of how to administer such a diagnostic tool and draw inferences from the results generated. This activity builds on that experience and is designed to help refine your ability to analyze such data and make suggestions for improvement. Five work teams (4 to 7 members/mixed gender in all groups) of an organization completed the metaphor exercise similar to the exercise in which you participated in class (see Part A above). Their responses are shown in the table below. Working in teams, analyze the information in this table and answer these questions:

DISCUSSION QUESTIONS FOR PART B

1. In your opinion, what are the dominant cultural values in this organization? Explain your answer.
2. What are the positive aspects of this type of culture?
3. What are the negative aspects of this type of culture?
4. What is this organization's main business, in your opinion? Explain your answer.
5. These groups all report to one manager. What advice would you give to that person about this unit?

Metaphor Results of Five Teams in an Organization

Team	Animal	Food	Place	TV Show	Season
1	Rabbit	Big Mac	Casino	*Parks & Recreation*	Spring
2	Horse	Taco	Racetrack	*Rookie Blue*	Spring
3	Elephant	Ribs	Circus	*Big Bang Theory*	Summer
4	Eagle	Big Mac	Las Vegas	*Dragons' Den*	Spring
5	Panther	Chinese	New York	*Criminal Minds*	Racing

Source: Adapted from D. L. Luechauer and G. M. Shulman, "Using A Metaphor Exercise To Explore The Principles Of Organizational Culture," *Journal of Management Education* 22 (December 1998), pp. 736–44. Used with permission of the authors.

Note: The television shows identified have been updated to reflect programs currently broadcast.

Self-Assessment: WHICH CORPORATE CULTURE DO YOU PREFER?

Purpose This self-assessment is designed to help you identify the corporate culture that fits most closely with your personal values.

Instructions Read each pair of statements in the Corporate Culture Preference Scale and circle the statement that describes the organization you would prefer to work in. Then use the scoring key in Appendix B at the end of the book to calculate your results for each subscale. The scale does not attempt to measure your preference for every corporate culture–just a few of the more common varieties. Also, keep in mind that none of these corporate cultures is inherently good or bad. The focus here is on how well you fit within each of them. This exercise should be completed alone so you can assess yourself honestly without concerns of social comparison. Class discussion will focus on the importance of matching job applicants to the organization's dominant values.

Corporate Culture Preference Scale

I would prefer to work in an organization:

1a.	Where employees work well together in teams.	*or*	1b.	That produces highly respected products or services.
2a.	Where top management maintains a sense of order in the workplace.	*or*	2b.	Where the organization listens to customers and responds quickly to their needs.
3a.	Where employees are treated fairly.	*or*	3b.	Where employees continuously search for ways to work more efficiently.
4a.	Where employees adapt quickly to new work requirements.	*or*	4b.	Where corporate leaders work hard to keep employees happy.
5a.	Where senior executives receive special benefits not available to other employees.	*or*	5b.	Where employees are proud when the organization achieves its performance goals.
6a.	Where employees who perform the best get paid the most.	*or*	6b.	Where senior executives are respected.
7a.	Where everyone gets her or his job done like clockwork.	*or*	7b.	That is on top of innovations in the industry.
8a.	Where employees receive assistance to overcome any personal problems.	*or*	8b.	Where employees abide by company rules.
9a.	That is always experimenting with new ideas in the marketplace.	*or*	9b.	That expects everyone to put in 110 percent for peak performance.
10a.	That quickly benefits from market opportunities.	*or*	10b.	Where employees are always kept informed about what's happening in the organization.
11a.	That can quickly respond to competitive threats.	*or*	11b.	Where most decisions are made by the top executives.
12a.	Where management keeps everything under control.	*or*	12b.	Where employees care for each other.

SELF-ASSESSMENTS FOR CHAPTER 14

SELF-ASSESSMENT NAME	DESCRIPTION	LOCATION
Which corporate culture do you prefer?	Identifies the corporate culture that fits most closely with your personal values and assumptions	Page 370 connect

Mitel Networks' chief marketing officer Martyn Etherington relied on communication, involvement, and organizational systems to change attitudes and behaviours in the telecommunication company's marketing group.

Jana Chytilova/*Ottawa Citizen*. Reprinted by permission.

Chapter 15

Organizational Change

LEARNING OBJECTIVES

After reading this chapter, you should be able to

LO1. Describe the elements of Lewin's force field analysis model.

LO2. Discuss the reasons why people resist organizational change and how change agents should view this resistance.

LO3. Outline six strategies for minimizing resistance to change, and debate ways to effectively create an urgency to change.

LO4. Discuss how leadership, coalitions, social networks, and pilot projects assist organizational change.

LO5. Describe and compare action research, appreciative inquiry, large group interventions, and parallel learning structures as formal approaches to organizational change.

LO6. Discuss two cross-cultural and three ethical issues in organizational change.

"There is a sea change happening within Mitel," proclaims chief marketing officer Martyn Etherington. The Kanata, Ontario, company that designs and sells communications systems for small businesses and (more recently) customer contact centres has embarked on a major transformation to keep ahead of new technologies (e.g., cloud services) and improve its competitive position. Mitel's board hired Richard McBee as CEO to lead the strategic change; Etherington was hired more recently to align Mitel's marketing people and activities with the new strategic direction.

During his first month on the job, Etherington and his senior marketing team interviewed Mitel sales staff across Canada, the U.S., and Europe. They also spoke with customers, channel partners, and industry experts to identify key marketing drivers and the associated metrics of what a "winner" marketing group at Mitel looks like. These ideals were then compared with the marketing group's current practices and outcomes to discover the gaps that required improvement. Based on this gap analysis, Etherington centralized decisions and reorganized the group around clients rather than products or specific projects. He also reduced the marketing group by 25 percent.

But most change in Mitel's marketing group involved altering employee mindsets and attitudes. One such change was to get staff thinking from the customer's perspective. "Our primary point of transformation was to shift our focus and actions from an "inside-out" [product-centric] perspective to an "outside-in" customer- and market-centric perspective," says Etherington. The other change was to focus attention on outcomes rather than activities. "Many marketing organizations are activity driven," Etherington warns. "They tend to operate with the intent of looking good by being busy, without necessarily focusing these activities on driving business outcomes."

Etherington acknowledges that some tensions developed during the change process. However, resistance was minimized through communication, involvement, and realignment of organizational systems and structures. Mitel's new structure around clients rather than products helped marketing staff to develop a client focus. New projects were supported only if they were justified against the new outcomes-based metrics, which reduced the activity-based mindset. Mitel's marketing staff were involved in the change process through the initial interviews and subsequent strategic review meetings. These review meetings also gave Etherington the opportunity to clarify the emerging customer-centric and outcomes-focused mindsets. "Like any process or cultural shift, the key to success lies in communication," he says.[1]

This opening case study about Mitel Networks illustrates many of the strategies and practices necessary to successfully change organizations. Martyn Etherington and his senior marketing team identified the need for change through systematic analysis of current practices against a "winner" ideal. Resistance to change occurred, but was mostly minimized through communication, involvement, and the realignment of organizational systems and structures. The transformational leadership of Martyn Etherington and Mitel CEO Richard McBee also played a critical role in the change process.

Although Mitel Networks' change process looks as though it proceeded smoothly, most organizational change is messy, requiring considerable leadership effort and vigilance. As we will describe throughout this chapter, the challenge of change is not so much in deciding which way to go; the challenge is in the execution of this strategy. When leaders discover the need for change and identify some ideas about the preferred route to a better future, the change process involves navigating around the numerous obstacles and gaining organization-wide support for that change.

This chapter unfolds as follows. We begin by introducing Lewin's model of change and its component parts. This discussion includes sources of resistance to change, ways to minimize this resistance, and ways to stabilize desired behaviours. Next, the chapter examines four approaches to organizational change–action research, appreciative inquiry, large group interventions, and parallel learning structures. The last section of this chapter considers both cross-cultural and ethical issues in organizational change.

Lewin's Force Field Analysis Model

LO1

"The velocity of change is so rapid, so quick, that if you don't accept the change and move with the change, you're going to be left behind."[2] This statement by BHP Billiton Chairman Jacques Nasser highlights one of the messages throughout this book: organizations operate as open systems that need to keep pace with ongoing changes in their external environment, such as consumer needs, global competition, technology, community expectations, government (de)regulation, and environmental standards. Successful organizations monitor their environments and take appropriate steps to maintain a compatible fit with new external conditions. Rather than resisting change, employees in successful companies embrace change as an integral part of organizational life. "I've always believed that when the rate of change inside an institution becomes slower than the rate of change outside, the end is in sight," says former General Electric CEO Jack Welch. "The only question is when."[3]

It is easy to see environmental forces pushing companies to change the way they operate. What is more difficult to see is the complex interplay of these forces on the internal dynamics of organizations. Social psychologist Kurt Lewin developed the force field analysis model to describe this process using the metaphor of a force field (see Exhibit 15.1).[4] Although it was developed more than 50 years ago, recent reviews affirm that Lewin's **force field analysis** model remains one of the most widely respected ways of viewing the change process.[5]

force field analysis Kurt Lewin's model of system-wide change that helps change agents diagnose the forces that drive and restrain proposed organizational change.

One side of the force field model represents the *driving forces* that push organizations towards a new state of affairs. These might include new competitors or technologies, evolving workforce expectations, or a host of other environmental changes. Corporate leaders also produce driving forces even when external forces for change aren't apparent. For instance, some experts call for "divine discontent" as a key feature of successful organizations, meaning

EXHIBIT 15.1

Lewin's Force Field Analysis Model

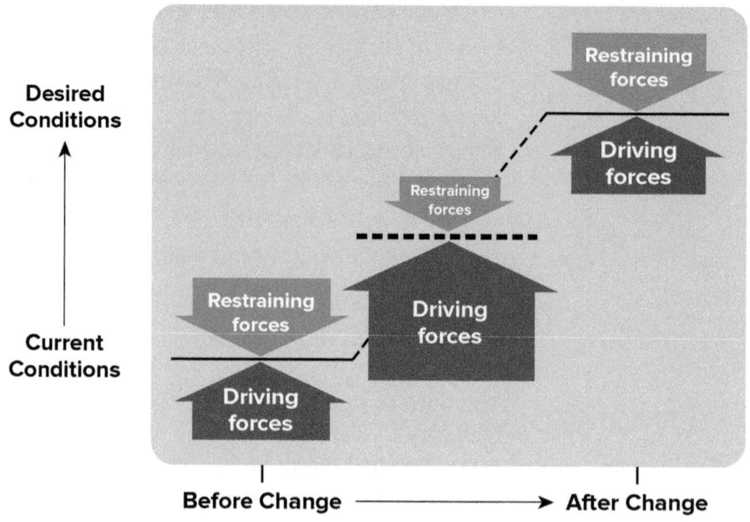

that leaders continually urge employees to strive for higher standards or better practices. Even when the company outshines the competition, employees believe they can do better. "We have a habit of divine discontent with our performance," says creative agency Ogilvy & Mather about its corporate culture. "It is an antidote to smugness."[6]

unfreezing The first part of the change process, in which the change agent produces disequilibrium between the driving and restraining forces.

refreezing The latter part of the change process, in which systems and structures are introduced that reinforce and maintain the desired behaviours.

The other side of Lewin's model represents the *restraining forces* that maintain the status quo. These restraining forces are commonly called "resistance to change" because they appear to block the change process. Stability occurs when the driving and restraining forces are roughly in equilibrium—that is, they are of approximately equal strength in opposite directions.

Lewin's force field model emphasizes that effective change occurs by **unfreezing** the current situation, moving to a desired condition, and then **refreezing** the system so it remains in the desired state. Unfreezing involves producing disequilibrium between the driving and restraining forces. As we will describe later, this may occur by increasing the driving forces, reducing the restraining forces, or having a combination of both. Refreezing occurs when the organization's systems and structures are aligned with the desired behaviours. They must support and reinforce the new role patterns and prevent the organization from slipping back into the old way of doing things. Over the next few pages, we use Lewin's model to understand why change is blocked and how the process can evolve more smoothly.

Understanding Resistance to Change

LO2

Robert Nardelli pushed hard to transform Home Depot from a loose configuration of fiefdoms to a more performance-oriented operation that delivered a consistent customer experience. Change did occur at the world's largest home improvement retailer, but at a price. Many talented managers and employees left the company, and some of those remaining continued to resent Nardelli's transformation. Disenchanted staff referred to the company as "Home Despot" because the changes took away their autonomy. Others named it "Home GEpot," a disparaging reference to the many former GE executives that Nardelli hired into top positions. After five years, the Home Depot board decided to replace Nardelli, partly because he made some unsuccessful strategic decisions and partly because some changes he introduced were unsuccessful.[7]

Robert Nardelli experienced considerable *resistance to change* at Home Depot. He has plenty of company. Only 42 percent of Canadian employees in one recent survey say that change is communicated well in their workplace. In another survey, 71 percent of Canadian human resource managers said employees resist changes put forward by management. This resistance is not short-lived. Twenty-one percent of 1,700 change agents surveyed across more than 40 countries acknowledged that employees still resisted a specific major change one or two years after it was implemented.[8]

Resistance to change takes many forms, ranging from overt work stoppages to subtle attempts to continue the old ways.[9] A study of Canadian bank employees reported that

OB by the NUMBERS

How Effectively Do Organizations Around the World Handle Change?[10]

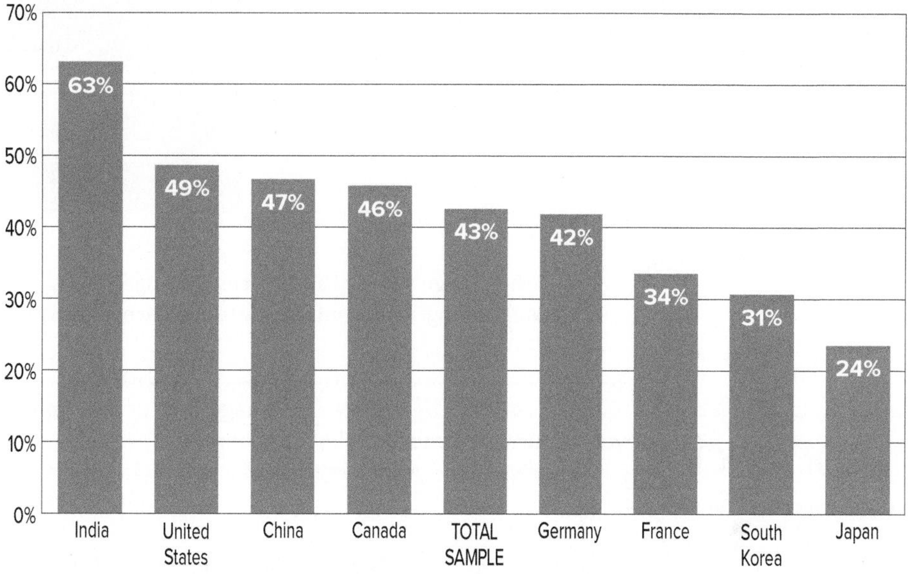

Percentage of employees, by selected countries, who agree or strongly agree that "change is handled effectively in my organization." Not all 28,810 employees across the 15 countries surveyed are shown here, but all are included in the "total sample" figure.

subtle resistance is much more common than overt resistance. Some employees in that study avoided the desired changes by moving into different jobs. Others continued to perform tasks the old way as long as management didn't notice. Even when employees complied with the planned changes, they showed resistance by performing the new task while letting customers know that they disapproved of these changes forced on them![11]

Most change agents are understandably frustrated by passive or active resistance to their planned change, but resistance is a common and natural human response. As Canadian-born economist John Kenneth Galbraith once quipped: "Faced with the choice between changing one's mind and proving that there is no need to do so, almost everyone gets busy on the proof."[12] Even when people support change, they typically assume that it is others–not themselves–who need to change.

Resistance is a form of conflict, but unfortunately change agents sometimes interpret that disagreement as relationship conflict (see Chapter 11). They describe the people who resist as unreasonable, dysfunctional, and irrational reactionaries to a desirable initiative. This perspective shapes the change agent's response to resistance, which tends to escalate the conflict, producing even stronger resistance to the change initiative. A more productive approach is to view resistance to change as task conflict. From the task conflict perspective, resistance is a signal that the change agent has not sufficiently prepared employees for change.[13] Employees might not feel a sufficiently strong urgency to change, or they might feel the change strategy is ill-conceived. Even if they recognize the need for change and agree with the strategy, employees might resist because they lack confidence to change or believe the change will make them worse off than the current situation. Resistance takes many forms, and change agents need to decipher those different types of resistance to understand their underlying causes.[14]

Resistance is also a form of voice, so discussion potentially improves procedural justice (see Chapter 5) as well as decision making (see Chapter 7). By redirecting initial forms of resistance into constructive conversations, change agents can increase employee perceptions and feelings of fairness. Furthermore, resistance is motivational; it potentially engages people to think

Three years after it merged with Continental Airlines, United Airlines has the lowest operational and customer service ranking among the largest 15 airlines in the United States. United executives say the poor results are partly due to the challenges of combining complex reservation and operational systems. But they also admit that the problems are also due to subtle forms of employee resistance to change. Some Continental employees have opposed United Airlines operational practices, while some United Airlines employees have failed to embrace Continental's customer service standards. "You know, the cultural change takes time," explains United Airlines CEO Jeffrey Smisek. "And people resist change. People are sort of set in their ways."[15]

© Michael Stravato/AP Images

about the change strategy and process. Change agents can harness that motivational force to ultimately strengthen commitment to the change initiative.

connect

Are you tolerant of change? See page 396 or visit **connect.mcgrawhill.com** to assess your natural tendency to tolerate change.

WHY EMPLOYEES RESIST CHANGE

Change management experts have developed a long list of reasons why people resist change.[16] Some people inherently oppose change because of their personality and values.[17] Aside from these dispositional factors, employees typically oppose organizational change because they lack sufficient motivation, ability, role clarity, or situational support to change their attitudes, decisions, and behaviour.[18] In other words, an employee's readiness for change depends on all four model elements of the MARS model. These MARS elements are the foundations of the six most commonly cited reasons why people resist change: (1) negative valence of change, (2) fear of the unknown, (3) not-invented-here syndrome, (4) breaking routines, (5) incongruent team dynamics, and (6) incongruent organizational systems and structures.

connect

Are you ready for change? Visit **connect.mcgrawhill.com** to identify conditions that are holding back your readiness for a specific change initiative.

Negative Valence of Change Employees tend to resist change when they believe the new work environment will have more negative than positive outcomes, particularly when the negative outcomes have a high probability of occurring and the positive outcomes have a low probability of occurring.[19] In other words, they apply (although imperfectly) the subjective expected utility formula (Chapter 7) to estimate whether the change will make them better or worse off. This cost-benefit analysis mainly considers personal outcomes. However, resistance also increases when employees believe the change will do more harm than good to the team and organization.[20]

Fear of the Unknown Organizational change usually has a degree of uncertainty, and employees tend to assume the worst when they are unsure whether the change will have good or bad outcomes. Uncertainty is also associated with lack of personal control, which is another source of negative emotions.[21] Consequently, the uncertainty inherent in most organizational change is usually considered less desirable than the relative certainty of the status quo. As such, it adds more negative valence to the cost-benefit calculation we described above.

Not-Invented-Here Syndrome Employees sometimes oppose or even discreetly undermine organizational change initiatives that originate elsewhere. This "not-invented-here"

Ray Davis, CEO of Umpqua Bank, warns that employees tend to revert to their past routines and habits unless the change is reinforced through systems and structures. "When you are leading for growth, you know you are going to disrupt comfortable routines and ask for new behaviour, new priorities, new skills," says Davis, whose Oregon-based bank is regarded as one of America's most innovative financial institutions. "Even when we want to change, and do change, we tend to relax and the rubber band snaps us back into our comfort zones."[22]

© John Lok/*The Seattle Times*

syndrome is most apparent among employees who are usually responsible for the knowledge or initiative, rather than the external sources.[23] For example, information technology staff are more likely to resist implementing new technology championed by marketing or finance employees. If the IT staff support the change, they are implicitly acknowledging another group's superior knowledge or initiative within IT's own area of expertise. To protect their self-worth, some employees deliberately inflate problems with changes that they did not initiate, just to "prove" that those ideas were not superior to their own. As one consultant warned: "Unless they're scared enough to listen, they'll never forgive you for being right and for knowing something they don't."[24]

An example of the not-invented-here syndrome occurred several years ago when Goldcorp CEO Rob McEwan decided to post the Canadian mining company's confidential geological data online and offer a handsome reward to anyone who could help find more gold on the property. The Goldcorp Challenge was a huge success, but the firm's geological staff complained just before the event was launched. "We have real concerns," they told McEwen. "You're going to ask the rest of the world to tell you where we're going to find gold in our mine, and we think they're going to think we're really dumb and that you don't have any confidence in us."[25]

Breaking Routines People typically resist initiatives that force them out of their comfort zones and require them to invest time and energy in learning new role patterns. Indeed, most employees in one survey admitted they don't follow through with organizational changes because they "like to keep things the way they are" or the changes seem to be too complicated or time wasting.[26]

Incongruent Team Dynamics Teams develop and enforce conformity to a set of norms that guide behaviour. However, conformity to existing team norms may discourage employees from accepting organizational change. For instance, organizational initiatives to improve customer service may be thwarted by team norms that discourage the extra effort expected to serve customers at this higher standard.

Incongruent Organizational Systems Rewards, information systems, patterns of authority, career paths, selection criteria, and other systems and structures are both friends and foes of organizational change. When properly aligned, they reinforce desired behaviours. When misaligned, they pull people back into their old attitudes and behaviour. Even enthusiastic employees lose momentum after failing to overcome the structural confines of the past.

Unfreezing, Changing, and Refreezing

LO3

According to Lewin's force field analysis model, effective change occurs by unfreezing the current situation, moving to a desired condition, and then refreezing the system so it remains in this desired state. Unfreezing occurs when the driving forces are stronger than the restraining forces. This happens by making the driving forces stronger, weakening or removing the restraining forces, or combining both.

The first option is to increase the driving forces, motivating employees to change through fear or threats (real or contrived). This strategy rarely works, however, because the action of increasing the driving forces alone is usually met with an equal and opposing increase in the restraining forces. A useful metaphor is pushing against the coils of a mattress. The harder corporate leaders push for change, the stronger the restraining forces push back. This antagonism threatens the change effort by producing tension and conflict within the organization.

The second option is to weaken or remove the restraining forces. The problem with this change strategy is that it provides no motivation for change. To some extent, weakening the restraining forces is like clearing a pathway for change. An unobstructed road makes it easier to travel to the destination but does not motivate anyone to go there. The preferred option, therefore, is to both increase the driving forces and reduce or remove the restraining forces. Increasing the driving forces creates an urgency for change, while reducing the restraining forces lessens motivation to oppose the change and removes obstacles such as lack of ability and situational constraints.

CREATING AN URGENCY FOR CHANGE

A few months after he became CEO of Nokia Corp, Canadian executive Stephen Elop sent employees a scorching email, warning them about the urgency for change. "I have learned that we are standing on a burning platform," wrote Elop. "And, we have more than one explosion–we have multiple points of scorching heat that are fuelling a blazing fire around us." Elop specifically described strong competition from Apple and Google, Nokia's tumbling brand preference, and its falling credit rating.[27]

Nokia has since sold its mobile phone division to Microsoft, where Elop is currently executive vice-president. But this incident illustrates Elop's strong belief that Nokia employees needed a stronger urgency for change.[28] Developing an urgency for change typically occurs by informing or reminding employees about competitors, changing consumer trends, impending government regulations, and other forms of turbulence in the external environment. These are the main driving forces in Lewin's model. They push people out of their comfort zones, energizing them to face the risks that change creates. In many organizations, however, leaders buffer employees from the external environment to such an extent that these driving forces are hardly felt by anyone below the top executive level. The result is that employees don't understand why they need to change and leaders are surprised when their change initiatives do not have much effect.

Customer-Driven Change Some companies fuel the urgency to change by putting employees in direct contact with customers. Dissatisfied customers represent a compelling driving force for change because the organization's survival typically depends on having customers who are satisfied with the product or service. Customers also provide a human element that further energizes employees to change current behaviour patterns.[29]

Executives at Shell Europe applied customer-driven change a few years ago. Many middle managers at the energy company seemed blissfully unaware that Shell wasn't achieving either its financial goals or its customer needs. To create an urgency for change, the European managers were loaded onto buses and taken out to talk with customers and employees who work with customers every day. "We called these 'bus rides.' The idea was to encourage people to think back from the customer's perspective rather than from the head office," explains Shell Europe's vice president of retailing. "The bus rides were difficult for a lot of people who, in their work history, had hardly ever had to talk to a customer and find out what was good and not so good about Shell from the customer's standpoint."[30]

Creating an Urgency for Change without External Forces Exposing employees to external forces can strengthen the urgency for change, but leaders often need to begin the change process before problems come knocking at the company's door. The challenge is

THE CANADIAN PRESS/Chris Young

Until recently, Canadian Pacific Railway Limited (CP) had the worst operational performance in North America. Yet one of the first things Hunter Harrison noticed when he became CEO was that few executives or employees were motivated to improve that dire situation. "It was a very permissive environment," he complained at the time. "Life was good, they propped their feet up." Not anymore. "We now have a leadership team that understands the urgency of making change and improving the culture of this organization," says Harrison (shown in this photo). CP executive vice-president and chief marketing officer Jane O'Hagan explains that Harrison's determination and speed of execution has been the key factor in the company's revival. "The arrival of Hunter has been a catalyst for change," she says. "Hunter certainly comes with a sense of urgency."[31]

greatest when companies are successful in their markets. Studies have found that when the organization is performing well, decision makers become less vigilant of external threats and are more resistant to change. "The biggest risk is that complacency can also come with that success," warns Richard Goyder, CEO of Wesfarmers, Australia's largest conglomerate. "That complacency may result in risk-aversion, or it may simply show up as a lack of urgency, as people take the foot off the accelerator and just assume that success will come as it always has."[32]

Creating an urgency for change when the organization is ahead of the competition requires a lot of persuasive influence that helps employees visualize future competitive threats and environmental shifts. "You want to create a burning platform for change even when there isn't a need for one," says Steve Bennett, former CEO of financial software company Intuit.[33] Experts warn, however, that employees may see the burning-platform strategy as manipulative—a view that produces cynicism about change and undermines trust in the change agent.[34] Fortunately, the urgency for change doesn't need to originate from problems or threats to the company; this motivation can also develop through a change champion's vision of a more appealing future. By creating a future vision of a better organization, leaders effectively make the current situation less appealing. When the vision connects to employee values and needs, it can be a motivating force for change even when external problems are insignificant.

REDUCING THE RESTRAINING FORCES

Earlier, we used the mattress metaphor to explain that increasing the driving forces alone will not bring about change because employees often push back harder to offset the opposing forces. Instead, change agents need to address each of the sources of resistance. Six of the main strategies are outlined in Exhibit 15.2. If feasible, communication, learning, employee involvement, and stress management should be attempted first.[35] However, negotiation and coercion are necessary for people who will clearly lose something from the change and in cases where the speed of change is critical.

Communication Communication is the highest priority and first strategy required for any organizational change. According to one recent survey, communication (together with involvement) is considered the top strategy for engaging employees in the change process.[36] Communication improves the change process in at least two ways.[37] One way is that communication is necessary to generate the urgency for change that we described previously. Leaders motivate employees to support the change by candidly telling them about the external threats and opportunities that make change so important. Whether through town hall meetings with

EXHIBIT 15.2 Strategies for Minimizing Resistance to Change

Strategy	Example	When Applied	Problems
Communication	Customer complaint letters are shown to employees.	When employees don't feel an urgency for change, don't know how the change will affect them, or resist change due to a fear of the unknown.	Time-consuming and potentially costly.
Learning	Employees learn how to work in teams as company adopts a team-based structure.	When employees need to break old routines and adopt new role patterns.	Time-consuming, potentially costly, and some employees might not be able to learn the new skills.
Employee involvement	Company forms a task force to recommend new customer service practices.	When the change effort needs more employee commitment, some employees need to protect their self-worth, and/or employee ideas would improve decisions about the change strategy.	Very time-consuming. Might lead to conflict and poor decisions if employees' interests are incompatible with organizational needs.
Stress management	Employees attend sessions to discuss their worries about the change.	When communication, training, and involvement do not sufficiently ease employee worries.	Time-consuming and potentially expensive. Some methods may not reduce stress for all employees.
Negotiation	Employees agree to replace strict job categories with multiskilling in return for increased job security.	When employees will clearly lose something of value from the change and would not otherwise support the new conditions. Also necessary when the company must change quickly.	May be expensive, particularly if other employees want to negotiate their support. Also tends to produce compliance but not commitment to the change.
Coercion	Company president tells managers to "get on board" the change or leave.	When other strategies are ineffective and the company needs to change quickly.	Can lead to more subtle forms of resistance, as well as long-term antagonism with the change agent.

Sources: Adapted from J. P. Kotter and L. A. Schlesinger, "Choosing Strategies for Change," *Harvard Business Review* 57 (1979), pp. 106–114; P. R. Lawrence, "How to Deal with Resistance to Change," *Harvard Business Review*, May–June 1954, pp. 49–57.

senior management or by directly meeting with disgruntled customers, employees become energized to change when they understand and visualize those external forces.

The second way that communication minimizes resistance to change is by illuminating the future and thereby reducing fear of the unknown. The more leaders communicate their vision, particularly details about that future and milestones already achieved towards that future, the more easily employees can understand their own roles in that future. "No. 1 is to always communicate, communicate, communicate," advises Randall Dearth, CEO of the purification technology company Calgon Carbon Corporation. "If you're bringing in change, you need to be able to make a very compelling case of what change looks like and why change is necessary."[38]

Learning Learning is an important process in most organizational change initiatives because employees need new knowledge and skills to fit the organization's evolving requirements. Learning not only helps employees perform better following the change; it also increases their readiness for change because they develop a stronger self-efficacy or confidence in their ability to function effectively following the change (called *change self-efficacy*). And when employees develop stronger change self-efficacy, they develop a stronger acceptance of and commitment to the change related to those acquired skills and knowledge.[39]

Employee Involvement Unless the change must occur quickly or employee interests are highly incompatible with the organization's needs, employee involvement is almost an essential part of the change process. In the chapter on decision making (Chapter 7), we described several potential benefits of employee involvement, all of which are relevant to organizational change. Employees who participate in decisions about a change tend to feel more personal responsibility for its successful implementation, rather than being disinterested agents of someone else's decisions.[40] This sense of ownership also minimizes the not-invented-here syndrome and fear of the unknown. Furthermore, the complexity of today's work environment demands that more people provide ideas regarding the best direction of the change effort. Employee involvement is such an important component of organizational change that special initiatives have been developed to allow participation in large groups. These change interventions are described later in the chapter.

Stress Management Organizational change is a stressful experience for many people because it threatens self-esteem and creates uncertainty about the future.[41] Communication, learning, and employee involvement can reduce some of the stressors.[42] However, research indicates that companies also need to introduce stress management practices to help employees cope with changes.[43] In particular, stress management minimizes resistance by removing some of the negative valence and fear of the unknown about the change process. Stress also saps energy, so minimizing stress potentially increases employee motivation to support the change process.

Negotiation As long as people resist change, organizational change strategies will require a variety of influence tactics. Negotiation is a form of influence that involves the promise of benefits or resources in exchange for the target person's compliance with the influencer's request. This strategy potentially gains support from those who would otherwise lose out from the change. However, this support is mostly compliance with, rather than commitment to, the change effort, so negotiation might not be effective in the long term.

Coercion If all else fails, leaders rely on coercion to change organizations. Coercion can include persistently reminding people of their obligations, frequently monitoring behaviour to ensure compliance, confronting people who do not change, and using threats of punishment (including dismissal) to force compliance. Replacing or threatening to replace staff who will not support the change is an extreme step, but it is fairly common in major organizational change. Global Connections 15.1 describes how Derrick Anderson relies on communication and involvement to bring about change at the London Borough of Lambeth. Still, the award-winning borough chief executive acknowledges that when these strategies don't work, you have to change the people.

For instance, when Martyn Etherington became chief marketing officer of Mitel Networks (described in the opening case study), some managers in that group were replaced with people whose values and skill set were more aligned with the changes that Etherington envisioned. Several years earlier, StandardAero CEO Bob Hamaberg threatened to fire senior managers who opposed his initiative to introduce lean management. "You must have senior management commitment," Hamaberg said bluntly at the time. "I had some obstacles. I removed the obstacles." Harsh words and actions, but due to this visionary transformation, StandardAero's Winnipeg business (where the company started) now employs almost 1,400 people and is a world leader in the aircraft engine repair and overhaul business.[44]

Firing people is the least desirable way to change organizations. However, dismissals and other forms of coercion are sometimes necessary when speed is essential and other tactics are ineffective. The above examples illustrate that it may be necessary to remove several members of an executive team who are unwilling or unable to change their existing mental models of the ideal organization. This is also a radical form of organizational "unlearning" (see Chapter 1) because when executives leave, they remove knowledge of the organization's past routines

Global Connections 15.1:

COMMUNICATE, INVOLVE, OR CHANGE YOUR PEOPLE[45]

Local councils throughout the United Kingdom have been under immense pressure as the British government cut their funding by 28 percent over the past five years and plans further budget reductions over the next few years. Councils have responded by slashing services and outsourcing business activities, but many of them faced stiff resistance from employees and citizens alike. The chief executive of one council lost her job after she failed to gain support for a plan to become a "virtual" government (where all council activities would be outsourced).

The Borough of Lambeth, Greater London's second largest council, survived this financial turmoil better than most through effective management of the change process and introduction of a "cooperative" model. This cooperative model devolves power and authority for specific services (such as playgrounds) to local citizen groups or to employees who form their own business-like trust. Lambeth chief executive Derrick Anderson (shown in photo) was recently named public leader of the year by *The Guardian* newspaper for deftly steering the borough through this minefield of change.

How has Anderson led the change process? The top priority, he says, is communication. "The most important principle of change is to communicate," Anderson advises. "I've put a lot of energy into talking to members and they will win the support of communities for this agenda." In addition, Anderson has been a strong advocate of involvement from elected councillors, employees, and citizens across the borough. For instance, more than 130 local and national organizations and 3,000 Lambeth residents have been consulted while Anderson's team have developed the cooperative council model.

But Anderson acknowledges that communication and involvement won't commit everyone to get on board. Resistance to change "can be a challenge," he says. For example, some borough managers try to avoid signing up their department for the cooperative model. "They will find a reason why their bit of the organization really ought to be left out of the conversation about cooperative working," Anderson complains.

Anderson emphasizes that he works hard to help employees adjust to the changes, but he also warns those who don't buy in to the council's agenda for change. "We will support staff to do their job. But if they don't want to do it, they're letting our residents down," Anderson advises. "I have a simple motto: If you can't change your people, you've got to change your people."

Derrick Anderson, chief executive of the Borough of Lambeth in London, UK, believes that communication and involvement improve the readiness for change for most staff, but for those who still resist, "you've got to change your people."

that have become dysfunctional.[46] Even so, coercion is a risky strategy because survivors (employees who do not leave) may have less trust in corporate leaders and engage in more political tactics to protect their own job security.

REFREEZING THE DESIRED CONDITIONS

Unfreezing and changing behaviour won't produce lasting change. People are creatures of habit, so they easily slip back into past patterns. Therefore, leaders need to refreeze the new behaviours by realigning organizational systems and team dynamics with the desired changes.[47] The desired patterns of behaviour can be "nailed down" by changing the physical structure and situational conditions. Organizational rewards are also powerful systems that refreeze behaviours.[48] If the change process is supposed to encourage efficiency, then rewards should be realigned to motivate and reinforce efficient behaviour. Information systems play a complementary role in the change process, particular as conduits for feedback.[49] Feedback mechanisms help employees learn how well they are moving towards the desired objectives, and they provide a permanent architecture to support the new behaviour patterns in the long term. The adage "What gets measured, gets done" applies here. Employees concentrate on the new priorities when they receive a continuous flow of feedback about how well they are achieving those goals.

Martyn Etherington made effective use of realigned systems and structures to support the changes that he championed at Mitel Networks. The opening case study to this chapter noted that he designed a new marketing group structure around clients so employees would be more client-centric rather than product-centric. He also introduced several outcome-based metrics, which realigned employee decisions and behaviours so they were more compatible with those metrics. Monthly review meetings were also focused around these metrics, so employees were more accountable for activities that actually drive business outcomes rather than just busy work activity.

Leadership, Coalitions, and Pilot Projects

LO4

Kurt Lewin's force field analysis model is a useful template to explain the dynamics of organizational change. But it overlooks four other ingredients in effective change processes: leadership, coalitions, social networks, and pilot projects.

TRANSFORMATIONAL LEADERSHIP AND CHANGE

The opening case study to this chapter described how Martyn Etherington transformed the marketing group at Mitel Networks so it was better aligned with the strategic changes ahead. Etherington, along with CEO Richard McBee and other executives, were transformational leaders in this change process. They developed a vision of Mitel's desired future state, communicated that vision in ways that were meaningful to others, made decisions and acted in ways that were consistent with that vision, and encouraged employees to experiment with ways to align work activities more closely with the vision.[50]

A key element of leading change is a strategic vision.[51] A leader's vision provides a sense of direction and establishes the critical success factors against which the real changes are evaluated. Furthermore, a vision provides an emotional foundation to the change because it links the individual's values and self-concept to the desired change.[52] A strategic vision also minimizes employee fear of the unknown and provides a better understanding of what behaviours employees must learn for the desired future.

COALITIONS, SOCIAL NETWORKS, AND CHANGE

One of the great truths of organizational change is that change agents cannot lead the initiative alone. They need the assistance of several people with a similar degree of commitment to the change.[53] Indeed, one recent study concluded that this group–often called a *guiding coalition*–appears to be the most important factor in the success of public sector organizational change programs.[54]

Membership in the guiding coalition extends beyond the executive team. Ideally, it includes a diagonal swath of employees representing different functions and most levels of the organization. The guiding coalition is sometimes formed from a special task force that initially investigates the opportunities for change. Members of the guiding coalition should also be influence leaders; that is, they should be highly respected by peers in their area of the organization. At the same time, one recent report on organizational change warned that it takes more than a few dedicated disciples to generate widespread change.[55] Guiding coalitions may be very important, but they alone do not generate commitment to change in the rest of the workforce.

Social Networks and Viral Change While a guiding coalition is a formally-structured group, change also occurs more informally through social networks. To some extent, coalition members support the change process by feeding in to these networks. But social networks play a role in organizational change whether or not the change process includes a formal coalition. Social networks are social structures of individuals or social units (e.g., departments, organizations) that are connected to each other through one or more forms of interdependence (see Chapter 10). They have an important role in communication and influence, both of which are key ingredients for organizational change.

AMV Photo/Digital Vision/Getty Images

Viral change is an unconventional, but increasingly respected, way to support the organizational change process. Based on the power and influence of social networks, viral change begins by gaining support from key influencers. As these people change their behaviour, others in the network eventually change their behaviour. This occurs partly because of the influencer's referent power and partly because social networks make it easier for coworkers to observe and mimic the influencer's changed behaviour. Although the viral change process is difficult to manage, Pfizer, Novo Nordisk, and a few other firms have been reasonably successful at using social networks to change employee attitudes and behaviour.[56]

The problem is that social networks are not easily controlled. Even so, some change agents have tapped into social networks to build a groundswell of support for a change initiative. This *viral change* process adopts principles found in word-of-mouth and viral marketing.[57] Viral and word-of-mouth marketing occur when information seeded to a few people is transmitted to others through their friendship connections. Within organizations, social networks represent the channels through which news and opinion about change initiatives are transmitted. Participants in that network have relatively high trust, so their information and views are more persuasive than when communication occurs through more formal channels of communication. Social networks also provide opportunities for behaviour observation–employees observe each other's behaviour and often adopt that behaviour themselves. So, when a change initiative causes change in the behaviour of some employees, the social network potentially spreads this behaviour change to others in that network.[58]

PILOT PROJECTS AND DIFFUSION OF CHANGE

Many companies introduce change through a pilot project. This cautious approach tests the effectiveness of the change as well as the strategies to gain employee support for the change without the enormous costs and risk of company-wide initiatives. Unlike centralized, system-wide changes, pilot projects are more flexible and less risky.[59] They also make it easier to select organizational groups that are most ready for change, thus increasing the pilot project's success.

Procter & Gamble (P&G) relied on a pilot project as a first step in shifting the consumer products company to "design thinking." Design thinking takes the view that new ideas emerge through discovery of the unknown rather than through structured surveys and other data collection methods that are framed from existing knowledge. This "abductive" approach is neither easy nor comfortable for most business people, which is the main reason why P&G began the change process through a pilot project at the company's global hair-care business in London, England. Participants in the program learned the meaning of design thinking and were coached in applying it to real world issues, such as how women actually use styling products. These participants not only learned about design thinking; they also developed skills to teach coworkers about this unique business decision-making approach. Eventually, more than 150 people across many areas of P&G's global business became trained facilitators,

EXHIBIT 15.3 Strategies for Diffusing Change from a Pilot Project

Motivation

- Widely communicate and celebrate the pilot project's success.
- Reward and recognize pilot project employees as well as those who work at transferring that change to other parts of the organization.
- Ensure that managers support and reinforce the desired behaviours related to the pilot project's success.
- Identify and address potential sources of resistance to change.

Ability

- Give employees the opportunity to interact with and learn from those in the pilot project.
- Reassign or temporarily second some pilot project employees to other work units, where they can coach and serve as role models.
- Give employees technical training to implement practices identified in the pilot project.

Role Perceptions

- Communicate and teach employees how the pilot project practices are relevant for their own functional areas.
- Ensure that the pilot project is described in a way that is neither too specific nor too general.

Situational Factors

- Give staff sufficient time and resources to learn and implement the pilot project practices in their work units.

developing the practice in everyday meetings. "These things are literally going on every day, and we don't even know where or when," says the P&G executive who initiated the change program.[60]

How do we diffuse the pilot project's change to other parts of the organization? Using the MARS model as a template (see Chapter 2), Exhibit 15.3 outlines several strategies to diffuse pilot projects. First, employees are more likely to adopt the practices of a pilot project when they are motivated to do so.[61] This occurs when they see that the pilot project is successful and people in the pilot project receive recognition and rewards for changing their previous work practices. Diffusion also occurs more successfully when managers support and reinforce the desired behaviours. More generally, change agents need to minimize the sources of resistance to change that we discussed earlier in this chapter.

Second, employees must have the ability–the required skills and knowledge–to adopt the practices introduced in the pilot project. According to innovation diffusion studies, people adopt ideas more readily when they have an opportunity to interact with and learn from others who have already applied the new practices.[62] For instance, Procter & Gamble's design thinking pilot project was diffused by having the original participants learn how to train coworkers and serve as role models and knowledge sources across the organization.

Third, pilot projects get diffused when employees have clear role perceptions–that is, when they understand how the practices in a pilot project apply to them even though they are in a completely different functional area. For instance, accounting department employees won't easily recognize how they can adopt quality improvement practices developed by employees in the production department. The challenge here is for change agents to provide guidance that is not too specific (not too narrowly defined around the pilot project environment) because it might not seem relevant to other areas of the organization. At the same time, the pilot project intervention should not be described too broadly or abstractly to other employees because this makes the information and role model too vague. Finally, employees require supportive situational factors, including the resources and time necessary to adopt the practices demonstrated in the pilot project.

Four Approaches to Organizational Change

LO5

So far, this chapter has examined the dynamics of change that occur every day in organizations. However, organizational change agents and consultants also apply various structured approaches to organizational change. This section introduces four of the leading approaches: action research, appreciative inquiry, large group interventions, and parallel learning structures.

action research A problem-focused change process that combines action orientation (changing attitudes and behaviour) and research orientation (testing theory through data collection and analysis).

ACTION RESEARCH APPROACH

Along with introducing the force field model, Kurt Lewin recommended an **action research** approach to the change process. The philosophy of action research is that meaningful change is a combination of action orientation (changing attitudes and behaviour) and research orientation (testing theory).[63] On one hand, the change process needs to be action-oriented because the ultimate goal is to change the workplace. An action orientation involves diagnosing current problems and applying interventions that resolve those problems. On the other hand, the change process is a research study because change agents apply a conceptual framework (such as team dynamics or organizational culture) to a real situation. As with any good research, the change process involves collecting data to diagnose problems more effectively and to systematically evaluate how well the theory works in practice.[64]

Within this dual framework of action and research, the action research approach adopts an open-systems view. It recognizes that organizations have many interdependent parts, so change agents need to anticipate both the intended and the unintended consequences of their interventions. Action research is also a highly participative process because open-systems change requires both the knowledge and the commitment of members within that system. Indeed, employees are essentially coresearchers as well as participants in the intervention. Overall, action research is a data-based, problem-oriented process that diagnoses the need for change, introduces the intervention, and then evaluates and stabilizes the desired changes. The main phases of action research are illustrated in Exhibit 15.4 and described here:[65]

- *Form client-consultant relationship.* Action research usually assumes that the change agent originates outside the system (such as a consultant), so the process begins by forming the client-consultant relationship. Consultants need to determine the client's readiness for change, including whether people are motivated to participate in the process, are open to meaningful change, and possess the abilities to complete the process.
- *Diagnose the need for change.* Action research is a problem-oriented activity that carefully diagnoses the problem through systematic analysis of the situation. Organizational diagnosis identifies the appropriate direction for the change effort by gathering and analyzing data about an ongoing system, such as through interviews and surveys of employees and other stakeholders. Organizational diagnosis also includes employee involvement in agreeing on the appropriate change method, the schedule for the actions involved, and the expected standards of successful change. Martyn Etherington applied this diagnostic process when leading change at Mitel Networks' marketing group. As the opening case study to this chapter described, Etherington gathered information from employees and other stakeholders to define the ideal "winner" state

EXHIBIT 15.4

The Action Research Process

Debating Point:

WHAT'S THE BEST SPEED FOR ORGANIZATIONAL CHANGE?

One of the great debates among organizational change experts is how quickly the change should occur. One view is that slow, incremental change is better because it gives employees more time to adjust to the new realities, to keep up with what needs to be learned, and to manage their stress in this process. Incremental change is also preferred because it gives change champions more time to change course if the current direction isn't working as hoped.

The value of incremental change was recently illustrated at Ergon Energy. Government legislation required companies to upgrade their record keeping system, but the Australian energy provider decided to make the changes incrementally because employees had already experienced constant change over the previous couple of years. "Even resilient staff such as those employed at Ergon Energy have a change tolerance level," explains Petá Sweeney, a consultant who worked with Ergon staff during this transition. "Consequently this led deliberately to discounting a revolutionary 'big bang' approach to record-keeping improvements." Sweeney reports that changing incrementally significantly improved employee engagement in the process. "Staff are more willing to participate in the change journey as well as offering suggestions for improvements. They do so knowing that changes will take place gradually and allow for time to fully bed down new practices and that effective enterprise wide changes require their help."[66]

In spite of these apparent virtues of incremental change, some experts claim that rapid change is usually much better. They do not claim that change needs to be radical or evenly rapid all of the time. Rather, they suggest that most change initiatives need to be, on average, much quicker than incremental. One argument is that companies operate in such a fast-paced environment that any speed less than "rapid" is risky; an incremental change initiative will put them further behind to the point that any change seems futile.

A second argument is that rapid change creates a collective sense of momentum, whereas inertia eventually catches up with incremental change.[67] In other words, employees feel the sense of progress when change occurs quickly. This forward movement generates its own energy that helps motivate employees towards the vision. Incremental change, by comparison, is sluggish and lethargic. A related argument is that any organizational change requires plenty of energy, particularly from the leaders who must continually communicate, role model, coach, and otherwise support and influence employees towards the new state of affairs.[68] This energy is finite, and it is more likely to run out when the change is spread over a long rather than a short period of time.

Third, incremental change doesn't necessarily give employees more time to adjust; instead, it typically gives them more time to dig in their heels! Rapid change, on the other hand, happens at such speed that employees don't have the opportunity to find ways to hold back, retrench, or even think about strategies to oppose the change effort. Finally, proponents of incremental change point to its benefits for minimizing stress, yet there is reason to believe that it often has the opposite effect. Changing slowly can feel like a slow train wreck—the more you see it coming, the more painful it feels. Quicker change, particularly when there are support systems to help employees through the process, may be less painful than changing incrementally.

for this group, its current situation, and the gap between them. He also uncovered key marketing drivers and established associated metrics, which made it easier to evaluate success of the change initiative.

- *Introduce intervention.* This stage in the action research model applies one or more actions to correct the problem. It may include any of the prescriptions mentioned in this book, such as building more effective teams, managing conflict, building a better organizational structure, or changing the corporate culture. An important issue is how quickly the changes should occur.[69] Some experts recommend *incremental change,* in which the organization fine-tunes the system and takes small steps towards a desired state. Others claim that *rapid change* is often required, in which the system is overhauled decisively and quickly.
- *Evaluate and stabilize change.* Action research recommends evaluating the effectiveness of the intervention against the standards established in the diagnostic stage. Unfortunately, even when these standards are clearly stated, the effectiveness of an intervention might not be apparent for several years or might be difficult to separate from

other factors. If the activity has the desired effect, the change agent and participants need to stabilize the new conditions. This refers to the refreezing process that was described earlier. Rewards, information systems, team norms, and other conditions are redesigned so they support the new values and behaviours.

The action research approach has dominated organizational change thinking since it was introduced in the 1940s. However, some experts are concerned that the problem-oriented nature of action research–in which something is wrong that must be fixed–focuses on the negative dynamics of the group or system rather than its positive opportunities and potential. This concern with action research has led to the development of a more positive approach to organizational change, called *appreciative inquiry*.[70]

APPRECIATIVE INQUIRY APPROACH

appreciative inquiry An organizational change strategy that directs the group's attention away from its own problems and focuses participants on the group's potential and positive elements.

Appreciative inquiry tries to break out of the problem-solving mentality of traditional change management practices by reframing relationships around the positive and the possible. It searches for organizational (or team) strengths and capabilities and then applies that knowledge for further success and well-being. Appreciative inquiry is therefore deeply grounded in the emerging philosophy of *positive organizational behaviour*, which suggests that focusing on the positive rather than the negative aspects of life will improve organizational success and individual well-being. In other words, this approach emphasizes building on strengths rather than trying to directly correct problems.[71]

Appreciative inquiry typically examines successful events, organizations, and work units. This focus becomes a form of behavioural modelling, but it also increases open dialogue by redirecting the group's attention away from its own problems. Appreciative inquiry is especially useful when participants are aware of their problems or already suffer from negativity in their relationships. The positive orientation of appreciative inquiry enables groups to overcome these negative tensions and build a more hopeful perspective of their future by focusing on what is possible.[72]

Appreciative inquiry's positive focus is illustrated by the intervention conducted a few years ago at Heidelberg USA. The American arm of the world's largest printing press manufacturer (Heidelberger Druckmaschinen AG) experienced morale-busting product setbacks as well as downsizing due to the economic recession. To rebuild employee morale and engagement, Heidelberg held a two-day appreciative inquiry summit involving one-third of its staff. Organized into diverse groups from across the organization, participants envisioned what Heidelberg would ideally look like in the future. From these sessions emerged a new vision and greater autonomy for employees to serve customers. "Appreciative inquiry can energize an organization even in tough times because it begins the conversation with possibilities instead of problems," says a senior executive at Heidelberg USA.[73]

Appreciative Inquiry Principles Appreciative inquiry embraces five key principles (see Exhibit 15.5).[74] One of these is the positive principle, which we describe above. A second principle, called the *constructionist principle*, takes the position that conversations don't describe reality; they shape that reality. In other words, how we come to understand something depends on the questions we ask and the language we use. Thus, appreciative inquiry requires sensitivity to and proactive management of the words and language used as well as the thoughts and feelings behind that communication. This relates to a third principle, called the *simultaneity principle*, which states that inquiry and change are simultaneous, not sequential. The moment we ask questions of others, we are changing those people. Furthermore, the questions we ask determine the information we receive, which in turn affects which change intervention we choose. The key learning point from this principle is to be mindful of effects that the inquiry has on the direction of the change process.

A fourth principle, called the *poetic principle*, states that organizations are open books, so we have choices in how they may be perceived, framed, and described. The poetic principle is reflected in the notion that a glass of water can be viewed as half full or half empty. Thus, appreciative inquiry actively frames reality in a way that provides constructive value for future development. The *anticipatory principle*, the fifth principle of appreciative inquiry, emphasizes the importance of a positive collective vision of the future state. People are motivated and guided by the vision they see and believe in for the future. Images that are mundane or

EXHIBIT 15.5 Five Principles of Appreciative Inquiry

Appreciative Inquiry Principle	Description
Positive principle	Focusing on positive events and potential produces more positive, effective, and enduring change.
Constructionist principle	How we perceive and understand the change process depends on the questions we ask and language we use throughout that process.
Simultaneity principle	Inquiry and change are simultaneous, not sequential.
Poetic principle	Organizations are open books, so we have choices in how they may be perceived, framed, and described.
Anticipatory principle	People are motivated and guided by the vision they see and believe in for the future.

Sources: Based on D. L. Cooperrider and D. K. Whitney, *Appreciative Inquiry: A Positive Revolution in Change.* (San Francisco: Berrett-Koehler, 2005), Chap. 7; D. K. Whitney and A. Trosten-Bloom. *The Power of Appreciative Inquiry: A Practical Guide to Positive Change.* 2nd ed. (San Francisco: Berrett-Koehler Publishers, 2010), Chap. 3.

disempowering will affect current effort and behaviour differently than will images that are inspiring and engaging. We noted the importance of visions earlier in this chapter (change agents) and in our discussion of transformational leadership (Chapter 12).

The Four-D Model of Appreciative Inquiry These five principles lay the foundation for appreciative inquiry's "Four-D" process. The model's name refers to its four stages, shown in Exhibit 15.6. Appreciative inquiry begins with *discovery*–identifying the positive elements of the observed events or organization.[75] This might involve documenting positive customer experiences elsewhere in the organization. Or it might include interviewing members of another organization to discover its fundamental strengths. As participants discuss their findings, they shift into the *dreaming* stage by envisioning what might be possible in an ideal organization. By pointing out a hypothetical ideal organization or situation, participants feel safer revealing their hopes and aspirations than they would if they were discussing their own organization or predicament.

As participants make their private thoughts public to the group, the process shifts into the third stage, called *designing*. Designing involves dialogue in which participants listen with selfless receptivity to each other's models and assumptions and eventually form a collective model for thinking within the team. In effect, they create a common image of what should be.

EXHIBIT 15.6

The Four-D Model of Appreciative Inquiry

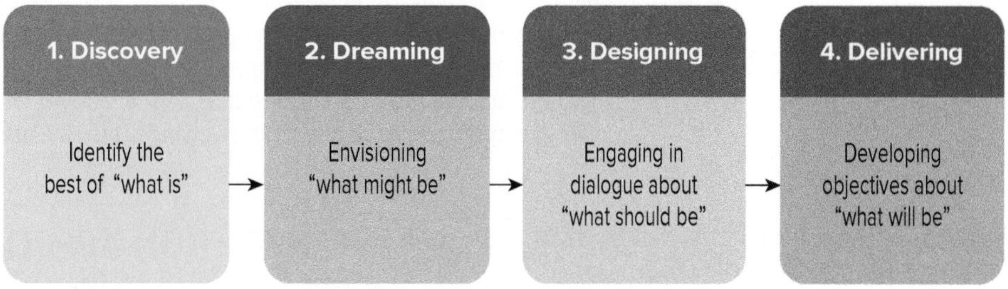

Sources: Based on F. J. Barrett and D. L. Cooperrider, "Generative Metaphor Intervention: A New Approach for Working with Systems Divided by Conflict and Caught in Defensive Perception," *Journal of Applied Behavioural Science* 26 (1990), p. 229; D. Whitney and C. Schau, "Appreciative Inquiry: An Innovative Process for Organization Change," *Employment Relations Today* 25 (Spring 1998), pp. 11–21; D. L. Cooperrider and D. K.Whitney, *Appreciative Inquiry: A Positive Revolution in Change,* (San Francisco: Berrett-Koehler, 2005), Chap. 3.

Toronto Western Hospital (TWH) held an appreciative inquiry (AI) retreat at which staff discussed the hospital's past successes and crafted a vision for its future. TWH's executive team felt the AI philosophy should guide daily leadership behaviour, so they developed and taught a positive leadership program, which has since been completed by almost 100 leaders at the hospital. Senior-vice president Kathy Sabo says the leadership program tries to "embed [AI] in our daily work differently than we do now—not just focused on a particular initiative but how do we enact it daily." The positive leadership program has apparently improved balanced scorecard results, patient satisfaction, and staff engagement. "We've seen really positive outcomes in how people apply the [AI] theory, how they behave as leaders, how that has impacted their staff," says Sabo.[76]

Charles Thatcher/The Image Bank/Getty Images

As this model takes shape, group members shift the focus back to their own situation. In the final stage of appreciative inquiry, called *delivering* (also known as *destiny*), participants establish specific objectives and direction for their own organization on the basis of their model of what will be.

Appreciative inquiry was introduced more than two decades ago, but it really gained popularity only within the past few years. Several success stories of organizational change from appreciative inquiry have emerged in a variety of organizational settings, including Canadian Tire, Toronto Western Hospital, British Broadcasting Corporation, Heidelberg USA, Castrol Marine, AVON Mexico, American Express, Green Mountain Coffee Roasters, and Hunter Douglas.[77]

Appreciative inquiry has much to offer, but it is not always the best approach to changing teams or organizations and, indeed, has not always been successful. This approach depends on participants' ability to let go of the problem-oriented approach, including the "blame game" of determining who may have been responsible for past failures. It also requires leaders who are willing to accept appreciative inquiry's less structured process.[78] Another concern is that research has not yet examined the contingencies of this approach.[79] In other words, we don't yet know under what conditions appreciative inquiry is a useful approach to organizational change and under what conditions it is less effective. Overall, appreciative inquiry can be an effective approach to organizational change, but we are still discovering its potential and limitations.

large group interventions
Highly participative events that view organizations as open systems (i.e., involve as many employees and other stakeholders as possible) and adopt a future and positive focus of change.

LARGE GROUP INTERVENTION APPROACH

Appreciative inquiry can occur in small teams, but it is often designed to involve a large number of people, such as the hundreds of employees who participated in the process at Heidelberg USA and Toronto Western Hospital. As such, appreciative inquiry is often identified as one of several large group organizational change interventions. **Large group interventions** adopt a "whole systems" perspective of the change process.[80] This means that they view organizations as open systems (see Chapter 1) and assume that change will be more successful when as many employees and other stakeholders as possible associated with the organizational system are included in the process.[81] Large group interventions are highly participative events because participants discuss their experiences, expectations, and ideas with others, typically in small groups within the large collective setting.

Similar to appreciative inquiry, large group interventions adopt a future-oriented positive focus rather than a past-oriented problem focus. *Future search conferences,* for instance, are large group interventions typically held over a few days in which participants identify emerging trends and develop strategies for the organization to realize potential under those future conditions. In addition to this strategy development, large group interventions generate a collective vision or sense-making about the organization and its future. This "meaning-making" process is important for the organization's evolving identity and how participants relate to that identity.

Large group interventions have occurred in a variety of companies and industries. Emerson & Cuming's chemical manufacturing facility in Canton, Massachusetts held a large group summit in which managers, supervisors, and production employees were organized into five stakeholder teams to identify initiatives that would improve the plant's safety, efficiency, and cooperation. Several Canadian school boards have conducted future search conferences, including the Ottawa-Carleton School Board, Toronto District School Board, and Lester B. Pearson School Board. The Canadian Nature Federation also held a future search event to assist their change process.[82]

Future search meetings and similar large group change events potentially minimize resistance to change and assist the quality of the change process, but they also have limitations.[83] One problem is that involving so many people invariably limits the opportunity to contribute and increases the risk that a few people will dominate the process. Another concern is that these events focus on finding common ground, and this may prevent the participants from discovering substantive differences that interfere with future progress. A third issue is that these events generate high expectations about an ideal future state that are difficult to satisfy in practice. Employees become even more cynical and resistant to change if they do not see meaningful decisions and actions resulting from these meetings.

PARALLEL LEARNING STRUCTURE APPROACH

parallel learning structure A highly participative arrangement composed of people from most levels of the organization who follow the action research model to produce meaningful organizational change.

Parallel learning structures are highly participative arrangements composed of people from most levels of the organization who follow the action research model to produce meaningful organizational change. They are social structures developed alongside the formal hierarchy with the purpose of increasing the organization's learning.[84] Ideally, participants in parallel learning structures are sufficiently free from the constraints of the larger organization that they can effectively solve organizational issues.

Royal Dutch/Shell relied on a parallel learning structure to introduce a more customer-focused organization.[85] Rather than try to change the entire organization at once, executives held weeklong "retail boot camps" with teams from six countries, consisting of frontline people (such as gas station managers, truck drivers, and marketing professionals). Participants learned about competitive trends in their regions and were taught powerful marketing tools to identify new opportunities. The teams then returned home to study their markets and develop proposals for improvement. Four months later, boot camp teams returned for a second workshop, at which each proposal was critiqued by Royal/Dutch Shell executives. Each team had 60 days to put its ideas into action; then the teams returned for a third workshop to analyze what worked and what didn't. This parallel learning process did much more than introduce new marketing ideas. It created enthusiasm in participants that spread contagiously to their coworkers, including managers above them, when they returned to their home countries.

Cross-Cultural and Ethical Issues in Organizational Change

LO6

Throughout this chapter, we have emphasized that change is an inevitable and often continuous phenomenon because organizations need to remain aligned with the dynamic external environment. Yet, we also need to be aware of cross-cultural and ethical issues with any change process. Many organizational change practices are built around Western cultural assumptions and values, which may differ from and sometimes conflict with assumptions and values in

© Bettman/Corbis

"Take away my people, but leave my factories, and soon grass will grow on the factory floors. Take away my factories, but leave my people, and soon we will have a new and better factory." —Attributed to Andrew Carnegie

other cultures.[86] One possible cross-cultural limitation is that Western organizational change models, such as Lewin's force field analysis, often assume that change has a beginning and an ending in a logical linear sequence (that is, a straight line from point A to point B). Yet change is viewed more as a cyclical phenomenon in some cultures, such as the earth's revolution around the sun or a pendulum swinging back and forth. Other cultures have more of an interconnected view of change, whereby one change leads to another (often unplanned) change, which leads to another change, and so on until the change objective is ultimately achieved in a more circuitous way.

Another cross-cultural issue with some organizational change interventions is the assumption that effective organizational change is necessarily punctuated by tension and overt conflict. Indeed, some change interventions encourage such conflict. But this direct confrontation view is incompatible with cultures that emphasize harmony and equilibrium. These cross-cultural differences suggest that a more contingency-oriented perspective is required for organizational change to work effectively in this era of globalization.

Some organizational change practices also face ethical issues.[87] One ethical concern is the risk of violating individual privacy rights. The action research model is built on the idea of collecting information from organizational members, yet this requires that employees provide personal information and reveal emotions they may not want to divulge.[88] A second ethical concern is that some change activities potentially increase management's power by inducing compliance and conformity in organizational members. For instance, action research is a system-wide activity that requires employee participation rather than allowing individuals to get involved voluntarily. A third concern is that some organizational change interventions undermine the individual's self-esteem. The unfreezing process requires that participants disconfirm their existing beliefs, sometimes including their own competence at certain tasks or interpersonal relations.

Organizational change is usually more difficult than it initially seems. Yet the dilemma is that most organizations operate in hyperfast environments that demand continuous and rapid adaptation. Organizations survive and gain competitive advantage by mastering the complex dynamics of moving people through the continuous process of change as quickly as the external environment is changing.

Organizational Behaviour: The Journey Continues

Nearly 100 years ago, industrialist Andrew Carnegie said: "Take away my people, but leave my factories, and soon grass will grow on the factory floors. Take away my factories, but leave my people, and soon we will have a new and better factory."[89] Carnegie's statement reflects the message woven throughout this textbook: Organizations are not buildings or machinery or financial assets; rather, they are the people in them. Organizations are human entities–full of life, sometimes fragile, and always exciting.

Chapter Summary

LO1 Describe the elements of Lewin's force field analysis model.

Lewin's force field analysis model states that all systems have driving and restraining forces. Change occurs through the process of unfreezing, changing, and refreezing. Unfreezing produces disequilibrium between the driving and restraining forces. Refreezing realigns the organization's systems and structures with the desired behaviours.

LO2 Discuss the reasons why people resist organizational change and how change agents should view this resistance.

Restraining forces are manifested as employee resistance to change. The main reasons why people resist change are the negative valence of change, fear of the unknown, not-invented-here syndrome, breaking routines, incongruent team dynamics, and incongruent organizational systems. Resistance to change should be viewed as a resource, not an inherent obstacle to change. Change agents need to view resistance as task conflict rather than relationship conflict. Resistance is a signal that the change agent has not sufficiently strengthened employee readiness for change. It is also seen as a form of voice, so discussion potentially improves procedural justice.

LO3 Outline six strategies for minimizing resistance to change, and debate ways to effectively create an urgency to change.

Organizational change requires employees to have an urgency for change. This typically occurs by informing them about driving forces in the external environment. Urgency to change also develops by putting employees in direct contact with customers. Leaders often need to create an urgency to change before the external pressures are felt, and this can occur through a vision of a more appealing future.

Resistance to change may be minimized by keeping employees informed about what to expect from the change effort (communicating); teaching employees valuable skills for the desired future (learning); involving them in the change process; helping employees cope with the stress of change; negotiating trade-offs with those who will clearly lose from the change effort; and using coercion (sparingly and as a last resort).

LO4 Discuss how leadership, coalitions, social networks, and pilot projects assist organizational change.

Every successful change also requires transformational leaders with a clear, well-articulated vision of the desired future state. They also need the assistance of several people (a guiding coalition) who are located throughout the organization. Change also occurs more informally through social networks. Viral change operates through social networks using influencers.

Many organizational change initiatives begin with a pilot project. The success of the pilot project is then diffused to other parts of the organization. This occurs by applying the MARS model, including motivating employees to adopt the pilot project's methods, training people to know how to adopt these practices, helping to clarify how the pilot can be applied to different areas, and providing time and resources to support this diffusion.

LO5 Describe and compare action research, appreciative inquiry, large group interventions, and parallel learning structures as formal approaches to organizational change.

Action research is a highly participative, open-systems approach to change management that combines an action-orientation (changing attitudes and behaviour) with research orientation (testing theory). It is a data-based, problem-oriented process that diagnoses the need for change, introduces the intervention, and then evaluates and stabilizes the desired changes.

Appreciative inquiry embraces the positive organizational behaviour philosophy by focusing participants on the positive and possible. Along with this positive principle, this approach to change applies the constructionist, simultaneity, poetic, and anticipatory principles. The four stages of appreciative inquiry include discovery, dreaming, designing, and delivering.

Large-group interventions are highly participative events that view organizations as open systems (i.e., involve as many employees and other stakeholders as possible), and adopt a future and positive focus of change. Parallel learning structures rely on social structures developed alongside the formal hierarchy with the purpose of increasing the organization's learning. They are highly participative arrangements, composed of people from most levels of the organization who follow the action research model to produce meaningful organizational change.

LO6 Discuss two cross-cultural and three ethical issues in organizational change.

One significant concern is that organizational change theories developed with a Western cultural orientation potentially conflict with cultural values in some other countries. Also, organizational change practices can raise one or more ethical concerns, including increasing management's power over employees, threatening individual privacy rights, and undermining individual self-esteem.

Key Terms

action research, p. 386
appreciative inquiry, p. 388
force field analysis, p. 373
large group interventions, p. 390
parallel learning structure, p. 391
refreezing, p. 374
unfreezing, p. 374

Critical-Thinking Questions

1. Chances are that the school you are attending is currently undergoing some sort of change to adapt more closely with its environment. Discuss the external forces that are driving the change. What internal drivers for change also exist?
2. Use Lewin's force field analysis to describe the dynamics of organizational change at Lambeth Council in London. Global Connections 15.1 about Lambeth council provides some information, but think about other forces for and against change beyond the information provided in this vignette.
3. Employee resistance is a symptom, not a problem, in the change process. What are some of the real problems that may cause employee resistance?
4. Senior management of a large multinational corporation is planning to restructure the organization. Currently, the organization is decentralized around geographic areas so that the executive responsible for each area has considerable autonomy over manufacturing and sales. The new structure will transfer power to the executives responsible for different

product groups; the executives responsible for each geographic area will no longer be responsible for manufacturing in their area but will retain control over sales activities. Describe two types of resistance senior management might encounter from this organizational change.

5. Discuss the role of reward systems in organizational change. Specifically, identify where reward systems relate to Lewin's force field model and where they undermine the organizational change process.
6. Web Circuits is a Malaysian-based custom manufacturer for high-technology companies. Senior management wants to introduce lean management practices to reduce production costs and remain competitive. A consultant has recommended that the company start with a pilot project in one department and, when successful, diffuse these practices to other areas of the organization. Discuss the advantages of this recommendation, and identify three ways (other than the pilot project's success) to make diffusion of the change effort more successful.
7. What is the role of formal and informal networks in organizations interested in undergoing change?
8. Suppose that you are vice president of branch services at the Kelowna Credit Union. You notice that several branches have consistently low customer service ratings even though there are no apparent differences in resources or staff characteristics. Describe an appreciative inquiry process in one of these branches that might help to overcome this problem.

Case Study: TRANSACT INSURANCE CORPORATION

TransAct Insurance Corporation (TIC) provides automobile insurance in parts of Canada that allow private insurers. Last year, a new CEO was hired by TIC's Board of Directors to improve the company's competitiveness and customer service. After spending several months assessing the situation, the new CEO introduced a strategic plan to improve TIC's competitive position. He also replaced three vice-presidents. Jim Leon was hired as vice-president of Claims, TIC's largest division with 1,500 employees, 50 claims centre managers, and 5 regional directors.

Jim immediately met with all claims managers and directors, and visited employees at TIC's 50 claims centres. As an outsider, this was a formidable task, but his strong interpersonal skills and uncanny ability to remember names and ideas helped him through the process. Through these visits and discussions, Jim discovered that the claims division had been managed in a relatively authoritarian, top-down manner. He could also see that morale was very low and employee-management relations were guarded. High workloads and isolation (adjusters work in tiny cubicles) were two other common complaints. Several managers acknowledged that the high turnover among claims adjusters was partly due to these conditions.

Following discussions with TIC's CEO, Jim decided to make morale and supervisory leadership his top priority. He initiated a divisional newsletter with a tear-off feedback form for employees to register their comments. He announced an open-door policy in which any Claims Division employee could speak to him directly and confidentially without going first to the immediate supervisor. Jim also fought organizational barriers to initiate a flex-time program so that employees could design work schedules around their needs. This program later became a model for other areas of TIC.

One of Jim's most pronounced symbols of change was the "Claims Management Credo" outlining the philosophy that every claims manager would follow. At his first meeting with the complete claims management team, Jim presented a list of what he thought were important philosophies and actions of effective managers. The management group was asked to select and prioritize items from this list. They were told that the resulting list would be the division's management philosophy and all managers would be held accountable for abiding by its principles. Most claims managers were uneasy about this process, but they also understood that the organization was under competitive pressure and that Jim was using this exercise to demonstrate his leadership.

The claims managers developed a list of 10 items, such as encouraging teamwork, fostering a trusting work environment, setting clear and reasonable goals, and so on. The list was circulated to senior management in the organization for their comment and approval, and sent back to all claims managers for their endorsement. Once this was done, a copy of the final document was sent to every claims division employee. Jim also announced plans to follow up with an annual survey to evaluate each claims manager's performance. This concerned the managers, but most of them believed that the credo exercise was a result of Jim's initial enthusiasm and that he would be too busy to introduce a survey after settling into the job.

One year after the credo had been distributed, Jim announced that the first annual survey would be conducted. All claims employees would complete the survey and return it confidentially to the human resources department where the survey results would be compiled for each claims centre manager. The survey asked the extent to which the manager had lived up to each of the 10 items in the credo. Each form also provided space for comments.

Claims centre managers were surprised that a survey would be conducted, but they were even more worried about Jim's statement that the results would be shared with employees. What "results" would employees see? Who would distribute these results? What happens if a manager gets poor ratings from his or her subordinates? "We'll work out the details later," said Jim in response to these questions. "Even if the survey results aren't great, the information will give us a good baseline for next year's survey."

The claims division survey had a high response rate. In some centres, every employee completed and returned a form. Each report showed the claim centre manager's average score for each of the 10 items as well as how many employees rated the manager at each level of the five-point scale. The reports also included every comment made by employees at that centre.

No one was prepared for the results of the first survey. Most managers received moderate or poor ratings on the 10 items. Very few managers averaged above 3.0 (out of a 5-point scale) on more than a couple of items. This suggested that, at best, employees were ambivalent about whether their claims centre manager had abided by the 10 management philosophy items. The comments were even more devastating than the ratings. Comments ranged from mildly disappointed to extremely critical of their claims manager. Employees also described their long-standing frustration with TIC, high workloads, and isolated working conditions. Several people bluntly stated that they were skeptical about the changes that Jim had promised. "We've heard the promises before, but now we've lost faith," wrote one claims adjuster.

The survey results were sent to each claims manager, the regional director, and employees at the claims centre. Jim instructed managers to discuss the survey data and comments with their regional manager and directly with employees. The claims centre managers were shocked to learn that the reports included individual comments. They had assumed the reports would exclude comments and only show averaged scores for all employees at the centre. Some managers went to their regional director, complaining that revealing the personal comments would ruin their careers. Many directors sympathized, but the results were already available to employees.

When Jim heard about these concerns, he agreed that the results were lower than expected and that the comments should not have been shown to employees. After discussing the situation with his directors, he decided that the discussion meetings between claims managers and their employees should proceed as planned. To delay or withdraw the reports would undermine the credibility and trust that Jim was trying to develop with employees. However, the regional director attended the meeting in each claims centre to minimize direct conflict between the claims centre manager and employees.

Although many of these meetings went smoothly, a few created harsh feelings between managers and their employees. Sources of some comments were easily identified by their content, and this created a few delicate moments in several sessions. A few months after these meetings, two claims centre managers quit and three others asked for transfers back to nonmanagement positions in TIC. Meanwhile, Jim wondered how to manage this process more effectively, particularly since employees expected another survey the following year.

Discussion Questions

1. What symptom(s) exist in this case to suggest that something has gone wrong?
2. What are the main causes of these symptoms?
3. What actions should the company take to correct these problems?

Team Exercise: STRATEGIC CHANGE INCIDENTS

Purpose This exercise is designed to help you identify strategies for facilitating organizational change in various situations.

Instructions

1. The instructor will place students into teams, and each team will be assigned one or both of the scenarios presented below.
2. Each team will diagnose the scenario to determine the most appropriate set of change management practices. Where appropriate, these practices should (a) create an urgency to change, (b) minimize resistance to change, and (c) refreeze the situation to support the change initiative. Each of these scenarios is based on real events.
2. Each team will present and defend its change management strategy. Class discussion regarding the appropriateness and feasibility of each strategy will occur after all teams assigned the same scenario have presented. The instructor will then describe what the organizations actually did in these situations.

Scenario 1: Greener Telco The chief executive officer of a large telephone company wants its executives to make the organization more environmentally friendly by encouraging employees to reduce waste in the workplace. Government and other stakeholders expect the company to take this action and be publicly successful. Consequently, the CEO wants to significantly reduce paper usage, garbage, and other waste throughout the company's many widespread offices. Unfortunately, a survey indicates that employees do not value environmental objectives and do not know how to "reduce, reuse, recycle." As the executive responsible for this change, you have been asked to develop a strategy that might bring about meaningful behavioural change towards this environmental goal. What would you do?

Scenario 2: Go Forward Airline A major airline had experienced a decade of rough turbulence, including two bouts of bankruptcy protection, 10 managing directors, and morale so low that employees had removed the company's logo from their uniforms because they were embarrassed to let others know where they worked. Service was terrible, and the airplanes rarely arrived or left the terminal on time. This was costing the airline significant amounts of money in passenger layovers. Managers were paralyzed by anxiety, and many had been with the firm so long that they didn't know how to set strategic goals that worked. One-fifth of all flights were losing money, and the company overall was near financial collapse (just three months to defaulting on payroll obligations). You and the recently hired CEO must get employees to quickly improve operational efficiency and customer service. What actions would you take to bring about these changes?

Self-Assessment: ARE YOU TOLERANT OF CHANGE?

Purpose This exercise is designed to help you understand how people differ in their tolerance of change.

Instructions Read each of the statements below and circle the response that best fits your personal belief. Then use the scoring key in Appendix B at the end of this book to calculate your results. This self-assessment should be completed alone so that you can rate yourself honestly without concerns of social comparison. Class discussion will focus on the meaning of the concept measured by this scale and its implications for managing change in organizational settings.

Tolerance of Change Scale

To what extent does each statement describe you? Indicate your level of agreement by marking the appropriate response on the right.	Strongly Agree	Moderately Agree	Slightly Agree	Neutral	Slightly Disagree	Moderately Disagree	Strongly Disagree
1. I generally prefer the unexpected to the predictable.	○	○	○	○	○	○	○
2. I am much more comfortable at events where I know most of the people there.	○	○	○	○	○	○	○
3. I don't consider new situations any more threatening than familiar situations.	○	○	○	○	○	○	○
4. I prefer solving problems that have only one "best" solution rather than many solutions.	○	○	○	○	○	○	○
5. I dislike ambiguous situations.	○	○	○	○	○	○	○
6. I avoid situations that are too complicated for me to easily understand.	○	○	○	○	○	○	○
7. I like situations that can be interpreted in more than one way.	○	○	○	○	○	○	○
8. I cope well with unexpected events.	○	○	○	○	○	○	○
9. Familiar situations are always preferable to me than unfamiliar situations.	○	○	○	○	○	○	○
10. I enjoy working in ambiguous situations.	○	○	○	○	○	○	○

Sources: Adapted from D. L. Mclain, "The Mstat-I: A New Measure of an Individual's Tolerance for Ambiguity," *Educational and Psychological Measurement* 53, no. 1 (1993): pp. 183–189; S. Budner, "Intolerance of Ambiguity as a Personality Variable," *Journal of Personality* 30 (1962): pp. 29–50.

SELF-ASSESSMENTS FOR CHAPTER 15

SELF-ASSESSMENT NAME	DESCRIPTION	LOCATION
Are you tolerant of change?	Assesses your natural tendency to tolerate change.	Page 396 connect
Are you ready for change?	Identifies conditions that are holding back your readiness for a specific change initiative.	connect

Additional Cases

Case 1 A MIR KISS?
Case 2 ARCTIC MINING CONSULTANTS
Case 3 BARRIE SUPER SUBS
Case 4 FRAN HAYDEN JOINS DAIRY ENGINEERING
Case 5 GOING TO THE X-STREAM
Case 6 KEEPING SUZANNE CHALMERS
Case 7 NORTHWEST CANADIAN FOREST PRODUCTS LIMITED (REVISED)
Case 8 THE REGENCY GRAND HOTEL
Case 9 SIMMONS LABORATORIES
Case 10 STAR ENTERPRISES—RITA'S ISSUES AT WORK
Case 11 TAMARACK INDUSTRIES
Case 12 THE OUTSTANDING FACULTY AWARD

Case 1 A MIR KISS?

By Steven L. McShane, The University of Western Australia

A team of psychologists at Moscow's Institute for Biomedical Problems (IBMP) wanted to learn more about the dynamics of long-term isolation in space. This knowledge would be applied to the International Space Station, a joint project of several countries that would send people into space for more than six months. It would eventually include a trip to Mars taking up to three years.

IBMP set up a replica of the Mir space station in Moscow. They then arranged for three international researchers from Japan, Canada, and Austria to spend 110 days isolated in a chamber the size of a train car. This chamber joined a smaller chamber where four Russian cosmonauts had already completed half of their 240 days of isolation. This was the first time an international crew was involved in the studies. None of the participants spoke English as their first language, yet they communicated throughout their stay in English at varying levels of proficiency.

Judith Lapierre, a French-Canadian, was the only female taking part in the experiment. Along with a PhD in public health and social medicine, Lapierre studied space sociology at the International Space University in France, and conducted isolation research in the Antarctic. This was her fourth trip to Russia, where she had learned the language. The mission was supposed to have a second female participant from the Japanese space program, but she was not selected by IBMP.

The Japanese and Austrian participants viewed the participation of a woman as a favourable factor, says Lapierre. For example, to make the surroundings more comfortable, they rearranged the furniture, hung posters on the wall, and put a tablecloth on the kitchen table. "We adapted our environment, whereas the Russians just viewed it as something to be endured," she explains. "We decorated for Christmas, because I'm the kind of person who likes to host people."

NEW YEAR'S EVE TURMOIL

Ironically, it was at one of those social events, the New Year's Eve party, when events took a turn for the worse. After drinking vodka (allowed by the Russian space agency), two of the Russian cosmonauts got into a fistfight that left blood splattered on the chamber walls. At one point, a colleague hid the knives in the station's kitchen because of fears that the two Russians were about to stab each other. The two cosmonauts, who generally did not get along, had to be restrained by other men. Soon after that brawl, the Russian commander grabbed Lapierre, dragged her out of view of the television monitoring cameras, and kissed her aggressively–twice. Lapierre fought him off, but the message didn't register. He tried to kiss her again the next morning.

The next day, the international crew complained to IBMP about the behaviour of the Russian cosmonauts. The Russian institute apparently took no action against any of the aggressors. Instead, the institute's psychologists replied that the incidents were part of the experiment. They wanted crew members to solve their personal problems with mature discussion, without asking for outside help. "You have to understand that Mir is an autonomous object, far away from anything," Vadim Gushin, the IBMP psychologist in charge of project, explained after the experiment had ended in March. "If the crew can't solve problems among themselves, they can't work together."

Following IBMP's response, the international crew wrote a scathing letter to the Russian institute and the space agencies involved in the experiment. "We had never expected such events to take place in a highly controlled scientific experiment where individuals go through a multistep selection process," they wrote. "If we had known . . . we would not have joined it as subjects." The letter also complained about IBMP's response to their concerns.

Informed of the New Year's Eve incident, the Japanese space program convened an emergency meeting on January 2nd to address the incidents. Soon after, the Japanese team member quit, apparently shocked by IBMP's inaction. He was replaced with a Russian researcher on the international team. Ten days after the fight–a little over a month after the international team began the mission–the doors between the Russian and international crew's chambers were barred at the request of the international research team. Lapierre later emphasized that this action was taken because of concerns about violence, not the incident involving her.

A STOLEN KISS OR SEXUAL HARASSMENT

By the end of the experiment in March, news of the fistfight between the cosmonauts and the commander's attempts to kiss Lapierre had reached the public. Russian scientists attempted to play down the kissing incident by saying that it was one fleeting kiss, a clash of cultures, and a female participant who was too emotional.

"In the West, some kinds of kissing are regarded as sexual harassment. In our culture it's nothing," said Russian scientist Vadim Gushin in one interview. In another interview, he explained: "The problem of sexual harassment is given a lot of attention in North America but less in Europe. In Russia it is even less of an issue, not because we are more or less moral than the rest of the world; we just have different priorities."

Judith Lapierre says the kissing incident was tolerable compared to this reaction from the Russian scientists who conducted the experiment. "They don't get it at all," she complains. "They don't think anything is wrong. I'm more frustrated than ever. The worst thing is that they don't realize it was wrong."

Norbert Kraft, the Austrian scientist on the international team, also disagreed with the Russian interpretation of events. "They're trying to protect themselves," he says. "They're trying to put the fault on others. But this is not a cultural issue. If a woman doesn't want to be kissed, it is not acceptable."

Sources: G. Sinclair Jr., "If You Scream in Space, Does Anyone Hear?" *Winnipeg Free* Press, May 5, 2000, p. A4; S. Martin, "Reining in the Space Cowboys," *The Globe & Mail,* April 19, 2000, p. R1; M. Gray, "A Space Dream Sours," *Maclean's,* April 17, 2000, p. 26; E. Niiler, "In Search of the Perfect Astronaut," *Boston Globe,* April 4, 2000, p. E4; J. Tracy, "110-Day Isolation Ends in Sullen . . . Isolation," *Moscow Times,* March 30, 2000, p. 1; M. Warren, "A Mir Kiss?" *Daily Telegraph* (London), March 30, 2000, p. 22; G. York, "Canadian's Harassment Complaint Scorned," *The Globe & Mail,* March 25, 2000, p. A2; S. Nolen, "Lust in Space," *The Globe & Mail,* March 24, 2000, p. A3.

Case 2 ARCTIC MINING CONSULTANTS

By Steven L. McShane, The University of Western Australia, and Tim Neale

Tom Parker enjoyed working outdoors. At various times in the past, he worked as a ranch hand, high steel rigger, headstone installer, prospector, and geological field technician. Now 43, Parker is a geological field technician and field coordinator with Arctic Mining Consultants. He has specialized knowledge and experience in all nontechnical aspects of mineral exploration, including claim staking, line cutting and grid installation, soil sampling, prospecting, and trenching. He is responsible for hiring, training, and supervising field assistants for all of Arctic Mining Consultants' programs. Field assistants are paid a fairly low daily wage (no matter how long they work, which may be up to 12 hours or more) and are provided meals and accommodation. Many of the programs are operated by a project manager who reports to Parker.

Parker sometimes acts as a project manager, as he did on a job that involved staking 15 claims near Eagle Lake, British Columbia. He selected John Talbot, Greg Boyce, and Brian Millar, all of whom had previously worked with Parker, as the field assistants. To stake a claim, the project team marks a line with flagging tape and blazes (ribbons, paint, or other trail markers) along the perimeter of the claim, cutting a claim post every 500 metres (called a "length"). The 15 claims would require almost 100 kilometres of line in total. Parker had budgeted seven days (plus mobilization and demobilization) to complete the job. This meant that each of the four stakers (Parker, Talbot, Boyce, and Millar) would have to complete more than seven lengths each day. The following is a chronology of the project.

DAY 1

The Arctic Mining Consultants' crew assembled in the morning and drove to Eagle Lake, from where they were flown by helicopter to the claim site. On arrival, they set up tents at the edge of the area to be staked, and agreed on a schedule for cooking duties. After supper, they pulled out the maps and discussed the job–how long it would take, the order in which the areas were to be staked, possible helicopter landing spots, and areas that might be more difficult to stake.

Parker pointed out that with only a week to complete the job, everyone would have to average seven and a half lengths per day. "I know that is a lot," he said, "but you've all staked claims before and I'm confident that each of you is capable of it. And it's only for a week. If we get the job done in time, there's a $300 bonus for each of you." Two hours later, Parker and his crew members had developed what seemed to be a workable plan.

DAY 2

Millar completed six lengths, Boyce six lengths, Talbot eight, and Parker eight. Parker was not pleased with Millar's or Boyce's production. However, he didn't make an issue of it, thinking that they would develop their "rhythm" quickly.

DAY 3

Millar completed five and a half lengths, Boyce four, and Talbot seven. Parker, who was nearly twice as old as the other three, completed eight lengths. He also had enough time remaining to walk over and check the quality of stakes that Millar and Boyce had completed, and then walk back to his own area for helicopter pickup back to the tent site.

That night Parker exploded with anger. "I thought I told you that I wanted seven and a half lengths a day!" he shouted at Boyce and Millar. Boyce said that he was slowed down by unusually thick underbrush in his assigned area. Millar said that he had done his best and would try to pick up the pace. Parker did not mention that he had inspected their work. He explained that as far as he was concerned, the field assistants were supposed to finish their assigned area for the day, no matter what.

Talbot, who was sharing a tent with Parker, talked to him later. "I think that you're being a bit hard on them, you know. I know that it has been more by luck than anything else that I've been able to do my quota. Yesterday I only had five lengths done after the first seven hours and there was only an hour before I was supposed to be picked up. Then I hit a patch of really open bush, and was able to do three lengths in 70 minutes. Why don't I take Millar's area tomorrow and he can have mine? Maybe that will help."

"Conditions are the same in all of the areas," replied Parker, rejecting Talbot's suggestion. "Millar just has to try harder."

DAY 4

Millar did seven lengths and Boyce completed six and a half. When they reported their production that evening, Parker grunted uncommunicatively. Parker and Talbot did eight lengths each.

DAY 5

Millar completed six lengths, Boyce six, Talbot seven and a half, and Parker eight. Once again Parker blew up, but he concentrated his diatribe on Millar. "Why don't you do what you say you are going to do? You know that you have to do seven and a half lengths a day. We went over that when we first got here, so why don't you do it? If you aren't willing to do the job then you never should have taken it in the first place!"

Millar replied by saying that he was doing his best, that he hadn't even stopped for lunch, and that he didn't know how he could possibly do any better. Parker launched into him again: "You have got to work harder! If you put enough effort into it, you will get the area done!"

Later Millar commented to Boyce, "I hate getting dumped on all the time! I'd quit if it didn't mean that I'd have to walk 80 kilometres to the highway. And besides, I need the bonus money. Why doesn't he pick on you? You don't get any more done than me; in fact, you usually get less. Maybe if you did a bit more he wouldn't be so bothered about me."

"I only work as hard as I have to," Boyce replied.

DAY 6

Millar raced through breakfast, was the first one to be dropped off by the helicopter, and arranged to be the last one picked up. That evening the production figures were Millar eight and a quarter lengths, Boyce seven, and Talbot and Parker eight each. Parker remained silent when the field assistants reported their performance for the day.

DAY 7

Millar was again the first out and last in. That night, he collapsed in an exhausted heap at the table, too tired to eat. After a few moments, he announced in an abject tone, "Six lengths. I worked like a dog all day and I only got a lousy six lengths!" Boyce completed five lengths, Talbot seven, and Parker seven and a quarter.

Parker was furious. "That means we have to do a total of 34 lengths tomorrow if we are to finish this job on time!" With his eyes directed at Millar, he added: "Why is it that you never finish the job? Don't you realize that you are part of a team, and that you are letting the rest of the team down? I've been checking your lines and you're doing too much blazing and wasting too much time making picture-perfect claim posts! If you worked smarter, you'd get a lot more done!"

DAY 8

Parker cooked breakfast in the dark. The helicopter drop-offs began as soon as morning light appeared on the horizon. Parker instructed each assistant to complete 8 lengths and, if they finished early, to help the others. Parker said that he would finish the other 10 lengths. Helicopter pickups were arranged for one hour before dark.

By noon, after working as hard as he could, Millar had only completed three lengths. "Why bother," he thought to himself, "I'll never be able to do another five lengths before the helicopter comes, and I'll catch the same amount of abuse from Parker for doing six lengths as for seven and a half." So he sat down and had lunch and a rest. "Boyce won't finish his eight lengths either, so even if I did finish mine, I still wouldn't get the bonus. At least I'll get one more day's pay this way."

That night, Parker was livid when Millar reported that he had completed five and a half lengths. Parker had done ten and a quarter lengths, and Talbot had completed eight. Boyce proudly announced that he finished seven and a half lengths, but sheepishly added that Talbot had helped him with some of it. All that remained were the two and a half lengths that Millar had not completed.

The job was finished the next morning and the crew demobilized. Millar has never worked for Arctic Mining Consultants again, despite being offered work several times by Parker. Boyce sometimes does staking for Arctic, and Talbot works full time with the company.

Case 3 BARRIE SUPER SUBS

By Steven L. McShane, The University of Western Australia (inspired by an earlier case by J. E. Dittrich and R. A. Zawacki)

Barrie Super Subs is one of the larger Super Subs restaurants, a chain of 300 restaurants across Canada. This outlet has a restaurant manager, an assistant manager, and several part-time team leaders. The restaurant manager rarely has time to serve customers, and frontline work by managers is discouraged by the head office. The assistant manager serves customers for a couple of hours during the busy lunchtime but otherwise assists the restaurant manager with purchasing, accounts, hiring, and other operations. Most team leaders are college students and serve customers alongside other employees, particularly from late afternoon to night closing. Most employees are also students who work part-time; a few are in high school. All regular staff earn minimum pay rates.

Barrie Super Subs has experienced below average profitability over the past 18 months, which has reduced the monthly bonus paid to the restaurant manager and assistant manager. This bonus is calculated by percentage of "wastage" (unsold, damaged, or unaccounted for food and drinks) relative to sales; the lower the percentage of wastage, the higher the bonus. Wastage occurs when employees drop or spill food, cut up more toppings than are sold, burn heated subs, prepare an order incorrectly, and eat or give away food without permission. When employees make mistakes, the expense is supposed to come out of their paycheque. Unauthorized eating and giving away food are grounds for immediate dismissal. However, team leaders are reluctant to report any accidental or deliberate wastage, even when confronted by the restaurant manager about the store's high wastage over the previous week and month. One team leader who reported several accidental wastage incidents eventually quit after being snubbed by coworkers who attended the same college classes.

Barrie Super Subs gives employees a food allowance if they work continuously for at least four and one-half hours. Staff complain that the allowance is meagre and that they are often ineligible for the food allowance because many shifts are only three or four hours. Employees who work these shorter shifts sometimes help themselves to food and drinks when the managers aren't around, claiming that their hard work justifies the free meal. Some also claim the food is a low company expense and makes up for their small paycheque, relative to what many of their friends earn elsewhere. Several (but not most) employees give some of their friends generous helpings as well as occasional free soft drinks and chips. Employees say handing out free food to friends makes them more popular with their peers.

Five months ago, the Barrie restaurant's wastage (mainly deliberate wastage) had risen to the point where the two managers no longer received a bonus. The restaurant manager reacted by giving the food allowance only to those who work for six or more hours in a single shift. This action excluded even more staff from receiving the food allowance, but it did not discourage employees from eating or giving away food. However, almost 20 percent of the experienced college staff left for other jobs over the following two months. Many of those who stayed discouraged friends from considering jobs at Super Subs. Morale declined, which dampened the fun atmosphere that had been experienced to some extent in past times. Relations between employees and managers soured further.

With relatively low unemployment, the restaurant manager found it difficult to hire replacements, particularly people with previous work experience of any kind. Temporary staff shortages required the two managers to spend more time working in food preparation and training the new staff. Their increased presence in the restaurant significantly reduced deliberate wastage, but accidental wastage increased somewhat as the greater number of inexperienced staff made more mistakes.

After three months, Barrie Super Subs' manager and assistant manager were confident that the situation had improved, so they spent less time training staff and serving customers. Indeed, they received a moderate bonus after the third month in the store. However, wastage increased again soon after the managers withdrew from daily operations. The experienced employees started eating more food, and the new staff soon joined this practice. Exasperated, the restaurant manager took bolder steps. He completely removed the food allowance and threatened to fire any employee caught consuming or giving away food.

Wastage dropped somewhat over the next month but is now creeping upward again.

Case 4 FRAN HAYDEN JOINS DAIRY ENGINEERING

By Glyn Jones, University of Waikato, New Zealand

BACKGROUND

Dairy Engineering (NZ) Ltd has its headquarters in Hamilton, New Zealand with manufacturing plants in South Auckland and Christchurch. The company manufactures equipment for the dairy industry. In its early years it focused on the domestic market but in the last five years has expanded into the export market. The company employs 450 people, which makes it a large company by New Zealand standards.

The case focuses on events in the Accounting Department at head office which is organized into two sections, Cost Accounting and Management Information Services (MIS). The Accounting Department is structured as is shown in the table below.

FRAN, THE NEW GRADUATE

Fran Hayden is in the final year of her Bachelor of Management Studies (BMS) degree at the University of Waikato where she has proved to be a high achiever. Fran was interested in a position with Dairy Engineering because of the opportunity to gain practical experience, the higher starting salary offered in industry, and that her boyfriend lived there.

Fran sent her curriculum vitae to the company and two weeks later she was invited to an interview with the Chief Accountant. She was surprised at the end of the interview to be offered the position of Assistant Cost Accountant. Fran said she would like to think it over. Two weeks later when she had still not replied she received a telephone call from Rob asking if she was going to take the position. Still not totally convinced, Fran decided however to accept the offer.

THE FIRST DAY AT WORK

Like many of her peers, Fran was glad to be leaving university after four years of study. She was looking forward to having money to spend as well as reducing her student debt. In order to "look the part" she had gone further into debt to buy new "corporate clothing." On reporting to the Accounting Department she got her first shock in the "real world." No one was expecting her! Even worse she found that that there was no vacancy for her in Cost Accounting! Instead, she had been assigned to MIS!

Fran was taken to MIS by one of her new colleagues, Mike, who introduced her to her colleagues, Tom and Adrian. They seemed to be a friendly bunch as apparently was her boss, Peter Bruton, who explained that her main duties were to assist with compiling information for the monthly Management Report known as "Big Brother."

After two weeks the time came for compiling "Big Brother." Fran found that her part was almost entirely clerical and consisted of photocopying, collating, binding, punching, and stamping the pages of the report. She then had to hand-deliver copies of the report to the senior manager at headquarters. After "Big Brother" was completed, Fran found again she had little to do. She began to wonder why MIS needed four people.

THE BIG OPPORTUNITY

One afternoon out of the blue the Chief Accountant called Fran to his office to tell her about an upcoming management workshop to be held in Auckland on Performance Measurement. Rob talked about the importance of staff development and that he would like to see one of his younger staff attending the workshop. He then asked Fran if she would be interested. She jumped at the opportunity. Unfortunately her boss was away on two weeks' leave at the time but Rob said he would talk with Peter.

Fran enjoyed the workshop, particularly rubbing shoulders with experienced managers, living in an Auckland hotel, and generally acting the management part. Even before returning to Hamilton, she wrote a detailed report on the workshop for the Chief Accountant.

On her return to Hamilton however she found all was far from well.

On Sunday evening, Fran was telephoned by her colleague Mike with some disturbing news. When Peter returned to work to find that Fran was in Auckland, he was furious, complaining that he had not been consulted and that his authority was being undermined.

Peter: "Fran is no longer employed in this section."

Fran returned to work full of trepidation only to find that the expected encounter with her boss did not take place because he was in Christchurch. She handed two copies of her report on the workshop to the Chief Accountant's secretary before taking the opportunity of her boss's absence to seek the advice of her colleagues:

Fran: "I am really worried. What do you think I should do?"

Adrian: "Stop worrying about it. He's just letting off steam. I have seen this all before. He'll get over it."

Fran: "Come on; get serious. He is my boss! He can make things very difficult for me."

Mike: "I think you should talk with Rob. After all, he's the one who suggested you go. It's not like it was your idea. He has to stick up for you."

Next day, Fran managed to get an appointment with the Chief Accountant. She started by saying that she found the workshop very useful. She then brought up her fears about Peter's displeasure with her attendance at the workshop to which the Chief Accountant responded:

Rob: "Well yes, he was a bit upset but don't worry, I will sort it out. The report was really good. By the way, I think you should treat it as confidential. Don't show it to anyone or discuss it with anyone. Is that ok? Don't worry about this. I assure you that I will sort it out."

Fran left the meeting feeling reassured but also a bit puzzled, wondering how Rob could have read her report in such a short time.

On Thursday, Peter returned to work and just before lunch called Fran into his office where he proceeded to attack her verbally, saying that she had "connived" behind his back to attend the workshop and that she had never asked for his permission. He said that he realized she was an intelligent "girl" but that she was "sneaky." He went on:

Peter: "You had better know which side your bread is buttered on–that for better or worse, you are in my section. No other section would want you."

He then called Mike in and told him:

Peter: "I don't want Fran wasting any more time–she is not to make any private calls from work."

Later in "confidence," he also told Janet, one of the administration clerks:

Peter: "Don't go talking with Fran–she has far too much work to catch up on."

Naturally Janet did tell Fran!

The following week, Vernon happened to pass Fran in the corridor and stopped to talk with her. Fran had met Vernon only briefly during her first week in the company and was surprised when he asked her why she looked so miserable. She explained and he said that they had better talk with the Chief Accountant and taking Fran with him, went to Rob's office. Vernon said that they needed a word and Fran listened as Vernon outlined the situation to Rob. Fran made it clear that if Peter continued to treat her this way, she would have to ask for a transfer. She also said that there was certainly not enough work in MIS to keep her occupied for more than a day or so each week.

The Chief Accountant listened and then asked her to give him a written report of what had happened since she had joined the company, including the latest incident with her boss. This, he said, would be brought up at the next senior management meeting. On the weekend Fran wrote the report which included a request for a transfer out of MIS on the basis of the lack of work and her boss's attitude towards her. On Monday morning she handed her report to the Chief Accountant's secretary.

Fran expected a reply but by early afternoon, had heard nothing. At the end of the day however, Peter called all his staff into his office. He was obviously in a good mood and told them that he had put his plan for revising "Big Brother" to the management meeting and had received an enthusiastic response. As he spoke, Fran noticed the colour draining out of Mike's face. On the way out, he told her that what Peter was describing was his revision plans, not his own. Mike resolved never to give his boss another one of his ideas telling Fran;

> **Mike:** "He just uses other people's brains–but that's the last time he uses mine."

Fran drove home from work feeling despondent. She wished she had never joined the company. Her job was boring, almost entirely clerical, and certainly did not require a degree. She was also taking the stresses home, resulting in quarrels with her boyfriend and flat mates.

Fran concluded that she had only two alternatives; a transfer or resignation. But to leave her job after less than five months would hardly impress any future employer. In desperation, she went to talk with Vernon who she thought would be sympathetic but received more unwelcome news; he told her about the outcome of the senior management meeting. Contrary to Fran's expectation, the Chief Accountant had not confronted Peter. In fact, it appeared he had been eclipsed by Peter's presentation for the revision of "Big Brother" and the Chief Accountant had not attempted to raise the issue.

Vernon was frank–she must either transfer or resign. Then, to Fran's surprise, he suggested she apply for a position in his section that would become vacant in three weeks' time. One of his assistant accountants was leaving to go overseas at short notice and he did not have a replacement. Vernon cautioned however that Fran's only chance was to apply directly to the Chief Accountant; that would force the issue. With a formal, written application before him, the Chief Accountant would have to make a decision. Just as certainly, Peter would resist the request. Later Fran drafted a letter to Rob requesting that she be transferred from MIS to the upcoming position in Cost Accounting.

THE CONFRONTATION

The next morning, Fran took her request to the Chief Accountant but after reading it he said:

> **Rob:** "You really needn't have done this, you know–I intended dealing with the situation."

Fran left Rob's office wondering what to believe. From her desk she watched as Peter made his way across to the Chief Accountant's office. The meeting was brief. Five minutes later, he left Rob's office and as he passed by, he said, in a loud voice;

> **Peter:** "Fran–you are finished in this company."

Fran saw her colleagues duck their heads down and pretend to be working. No one envied her position. She wondered how, in such a short time, she has ended up in such a situation.

Case 5 GOING TO THE X-STREAM

By Roy Smollan, Auckland University of Technology, New Zealand

Gil Reihana was the chief executive officer of X-Stream, a company he launched in Auckland, New Zealand, six years ago at the age of 25, after graduating with a bachelor's degree in information technology and management. He had inherited $300,000 and had persuaded various family members to invest additional money. X-Stream assembled personal computers for the New Zealand and Australian markets and sold them through a number of chain stores and independent retailers. The company had soon established a reputation for quality hardware, customized products, excellent delivery times and after-sales service. Six months ago it had started a software division, specializing in webpage design and consulting on various applications for the development of electronic business.

Gil was driven by a desire to succeed. He had started working part-time at an electronics retailer at age 16, and in his spare time took apart old computers in his garage to see how they were made. He was extroverted, energetic, and enthusiastic, often arriving at work before 5 a.m. and seldom leaving before 7 p.m. He felt that work should be challenging but fun too. He had initially picked a young senior management team that he thought shared his outlook. A casual, almost irreverent atmosphere developed. However, a poorly organized accounting department led to the demise of the first accountant after two years. Gil believed that major decisions should be made by consensus and that individuals should then be empowered to implement these decisions in their own way. In the beginning, he had met with each staff member in January to discuss with them how happy they were in their jobs, what their ambitions were, and what plans they would like to make for the coming year in terms of their own professional development. As the company had grown this had become more difficult and he had left each member of his senior management team to do this with their own staff, but did not monitor whether they were doing it or how well it worked. Now he tried to keep in touch with staff by having lunch with them in the cafeteria occasionally.

Denise Commins (affectionately known to all staff as Dot Com) was the chief financial officer. She and Gil could not be more different. Denise was quiet, methodical, and very patient. Her superb interpersonal skills complemented a highly analytical mind. At 55 she was considerably older than most of the employees and often showed a strong maternal side. Many of her team (and several from other departments as well) frequently consulted her on work issues and personal problems too. She enjoyed the informal relationships she had built up but found that the technical aspects of her role were becoming less rewarding.

Don Head, the marketing manager, was considered to be a rather ruthless operator, often undercutting the competition in terms of price, and, on more than one occasion, by circulating false rumours of defects in their products. He deemed himself "a ladies' man" and was known to flirt with a number of the staff. A case of sexual harassment had been dropped after a 22-year-old secretary had been paid a sizeable sum of money. Gil and the members of the senior management team had been furious but Don had denied any wrongdoing, claiming that she had "led him on." He had been at university with Gil and they spent many hours after work at a pub around the corner from the factory. With sales rising year after year, his marketing expertise and cunning were regarded as essential to the company's continuing growth. He had a department of eight whom he had carefully screened as ambitious self-starters. They were required to set and achieve their own targets, as long as they were "big hairy ambitious goals"; a phrase he had heard at a seminar.

Jason Palu, the production manager, was a softly spoken man who had started as a supervisor and who had quickly worked his way to the top position. He set extremely high standards for the production staff and was considered to be a perfectionist. He was highly regarded by his colleagues for his efficiency and reliability. There were very few occasions when an order could not be fulfilled on time and his goal was zero defects. He tended to be autocratic and some people complained that he never listened to them. He allocated work hours that did not suit people, and often insisted on overtime that was paid, but was usually at very short notice. When one production worker complained, Palu tersely remarked, "we have a job to do and we just have to get on with it. The company depends on us."

Heather Berkowitz was the chief webpage designer. She had blue hair, a ring through her nose, and dressed in a variety of exotic clothes that had been sourced from a number of second-hand stores. She seldom arrived at work much before 11 a.m. and often left before 4 p.m. She said she did her best work at home, often at night, so why should she "punch the clock like the drones on the assembly line"? Gil and others had often received emails from her that had been sent at all hours of the night. She had established a reputation as a top webpage designer, and although her physical appearance did not go down too well with some of the company's clients (or staff) the quality and quantity of her work was extremely high.

On Tuesdays at 9 a.m. the senior staff met to discuss weekly plans and any significant issues that had arisen. All employees were invited to the meeting, an opportunity that some took advantage of by attending. Gil trusted all staff to keep confidential matters within the company. He believed that if the organization shared information with employees they would be more likely to support management decisions. The meetings lacked formality and usually started with some jokes, usually at the expense of some members of staff. By and large the jokes were meant to be inoffensive, but were not always taken that way. Nicknames were often assigned to staff, mostly by Don Head, some quite derogatory. You were thought to be a "wet blanket" if you objected. Don seemed oblivious to the unflattering nickname he had been given, preferring to call himself Braveheart, sometimes even signing memos in this fashion.

Although employment agreements referred to a 40-hour week there was an expectation that staff would put in substantially more than that. Only the assembly line workers had to clock in and out, but this, Jason had explained, was due to the overtime that assembly staff were required to work to meet deadlines. The overtime pay was welcomed by some production staff and resented by some employees in other departments who believed they should be entitled to the same benefits.

Recently a conflict had arisen between Jason and Don. For some time, the company had been developing a top-of-the range laptop which was scheduled for launch in two weeks' time. Jason had been urging senior management to delay the introduction of the new X-MH until some hitches had been sorted out. A batch of chips acquired from abroad had contained some defective features. He wanted to postpone the new model until these problems had been completely sorted out, a process which he believed would take another month. Don found this to be unacceptable. A former All Blacks rugby team captain had been contracted to attend the launch and market the new model on a roadshow that would travel to New Zealand and Australia's main cities. He would not be available at the time Jason was prepared to release the X-MH. At a heated staff meeting, some of the senior staff backed Don, some agreed with Jason. Don had urged all of his department to attend the meeting, to present a united front and convey an image of power.

Heather Berkowitz had arrived halfway through the meeting and with a mouthful of muffin proclaimed that there was no rush to get out the "new toy." The company had plenty of other issues to which it could devote its energy. She said she had met the head of information technology of a chain of fast-food restaurants that wanted to revitalize its website. She maintained she needed three extra staff to get this up and running. She exited the meeting five minutes later. Don was fuming at the interruption and demanded that Gil should stick to the original launch date of the X-MH. Gil calmly replied that he understood Don's frustration, but that more consultation was necessary. He said that it would be discussed by the parties concerned during the week and a final decision would be made at the following Tuesday's staff meeting.

Don spent the rest of the day lobbying other members of the senior staff. He offered Dorothy the use of his beach cottage if she backed him and promised to support her on the acquisition of expensive new accounting software. She just laughed and said that she was convinced the senior management team would approve the new software. She also informed Don that a member of her staff had seen one of his sales representatives entering a strip joint the previous week at a time when the sales force had been engaged in a staff meeting.

Other problems had arisen in recent months. Ramesh Patel, the newly recruited head of e-business applications had, with help from a personal contact, developed a software programme that would help hotels and restaurants source products and services over the Internet. It was beginning to generate useful revenue. His contact had now billed X-Stream for $25,000 in consultancy fees and development costs. Ramesh claimed that his contact had owed him a favour and that no mention of money had ever been made. X-Stream had referred the matter to its legal counsel.

Les Kong, the research and development manager (hardware) had complained to Gil that he could no longer work under Jason Palu. While he considered him a very pleasant man, and a very capable production manager, he could no longer tolerate his strict control style. "You can't do creative work on command!" was his lament. He loved his job and had spent hours over several weekends developing and refining a new product.

There was considerable resentment from Jason and Don about the resources that had been invested in the software division, partly because they did not see the need for the company to diversify and partly because they claimed that money was being diverted from their departments to fund the new ventures. Ramesh claimed that "a good e-business starts at home—we should open up all our procurement via the Internet." His suggestion did not go down well with Jason and Don.

Gil had been pondering the structure of X-Stream for some time. The old functional structure no longer seemed appropriate. "Silo" mentality and departmental interests seemed to predominate and turf wars took place. The company had grown to 64 staff in New Zealand and eight in Australia. The ongoing development of new hardware and the introduction of the software side of the business had made management somewhat complicated. He missed the old days when he knew every member of staff. The informal decision making that was characteristic of the business might have to give way to more formal processes. Yet he did not want to lose the creativity that underpinned the company's success. Despite the open invitation to attend the management meetings, many staff complained that they never knew what was going on. He expected all senior managers to keep their departmental staff informed of developments. Some had done this admirably while others had virtually ignored his wishes.

A human resources manager, Alkina Bennelong, had been appointed a month previously and reported to Denise Commins. She had been reviewing the company's loosely worded job descriptions and person specifications, and the recruitment and selection systems, and had suggested more professional but more elaborate approaches. She had also suggested the introduction of a performance management system, including feedback from peers, direct reports, and outsiders, such as suppliers and customers. "Over my dead body!" was the retort of Don Head. "How can you allow subordinates to tell you how to do your job?" queried Jason Palu. "Can't see what the fuss is all about," said Heather Berkowitz. "Everybody keeps telling me what to do anyway, even though they don't understand the first thing about my job! But it doesn't worry me."

Case 6 KEEPING SUZANNE CHALMERS

By Steven L. McShane, The University of Western Australia

Thomas Chan hung up the telephone and sighed. The vice-president of software engineering at Advanced Photonics Inc. (API) had just spoken to Suzanne Chalmers, who called to arrange a meeting with Chan later that day. She didn't say what the meeting was about, but Chan almost instinctively knew that Suzanne was going to quit after working at API for the past four years. Chalmers is a software engineer in Internet Protocol (IP), the software that directs fibre-optic light through API's routers. It is very specialized work, and Suzanne is one of API's top talents in that area.

Thomas Chan had been through this before. A valued employee would arrange a private meeting. The meeting would begin with a few pleasantries, then the employee would announce that he or she wanted to quit. Some employees said they were leaving because of the long hours and stressful deadlines. They said they needed to decompress, get to know their kids again, or whatever. But that wasn't usually the real reason. Almost every organization in this industry was scrambling to keep up with technological advances and the competition. Employees would just leave one stressful job for another one.

Also, many of the people who left API joined a start-up company a few months later. These start-up firms can be pressure cookers where everyone works 16 hours each day and has to perform a variety of tasks. For example, engineers in these small firms might have to meet customers or work on venture capital proposals rather than focus on specialized tasks related to their knowledge. API now has over 6,000 employees, so it is easier to assign people to work that matches their technical competencies.

No, the problem isn't the stress or long hours, Chan thought. The problem is money—too much money. Most of the people who leave are millionaires. Suzanne Chalmers is one of them. Thanks to generous share options that have skyrocketed on the stock markets, many employees at API have more money than they can use. Most are under 40 years old, so it's too early for them to retire. But their financial independence gives them less reason to remain with API.

THE MEETING

The meeting with Suzanne Chalmers took place a few hours after the telephone call. It began like the others, with the initial pleasantries and brief discussion about progress on the latest fibre-optic router project. Then, Suzanne made her well-rehearsed statement: "Thomas, I've really enjoyed working here, but I'm going to leave Advanced Photonics." Suzanne took a breath, then looked at Chan. When he didn't reply after a few seconds, she continued: "I need to take time off. You know, get away to recharge my batteries. The project's nearly done and the team can complete it without me. Well, anyway, I'm thinking of leaving."

Chan spoke in a calm voice. He suggested that Suzanne should take an unpaid leave for two or maybe three months, complete with paid benefits, then return refreshed. Suzanne politely rejected that offer, saying that she needed to get away from work for a while. Thomas then asked Suzanne whether she was unhappy with her work environment—whether she was getting the latest computer technology to do her work and whether there were problems with coworkers. The workplace was fine, Suzanne replied. The job was getting a bit routine, but she had a comfortable workplace with excellent coworkers.

Chan then apologized for the cramped workspace, due mainly to the rapid increase in the number of people hired over the past year. He suggested that if Suzanne took a couple of months off, API would give her special treatment with a larger workspace with a better view of the park behind the campus-like building when she returned. She politely thanked Chan for that offer, but it wasn't what she needed. Besides, it wouldn't be fair to have a large workspace when other team members would be working in smaller quarters.

Chan was running out of tactics, so he tried his last hope: money. He asked whether Suzanne had higher offers. Suzanne replied that she regularly received calls from other companies, and some of them offered more money. Most were start-up firms that offered a lower salary but higher potential gains in share options. Chan knew from market surveys that Suzanne was already paid well in the industry. He also knew that API couldn't compete on share option potential. Employees working in start-up firms sometimes saw their shares increase by five or ten times their initial value, whereas shares at API and other large firms increased more slowly. However, Chan promised Suzanne that he would recommend that she receive a significant raise—maybe 25 percent more—and more share options. Chan added that Chalmers was one of API's most valuable employees and that the company would suffer if she left the firm.

The meeting ended with Chalmers promising to consider Chan's offer of higher pay and share options. Two days later, Chan received her resignation in writing. Five months later, Chan learned that after a few months travelling with her husband, Chalmers joined a start-up software firm in the area.

Case 7 NORTHWEST CANADIAN FOREST PRODUCTS LIMITED (REVISED)

By Peter Seidl, British Columbia Institute of Technology

Northwest Canadian Forest Products Limited owns and operates five sawmills in British Columbia and Alberta. These mills produce high-quality lumber for use in the manufacture of window frames, doors, and mouldings for markets in the United States and Japan in addition to lower-quality, commodity-type lumber used in the Canadian construction industry. (The firm's export markets tend to be more demanding and quality-conscious than its domestic markets, but are also more lucrative.) Currently, the president of the company is thinking about the long-term prospects of each of the mills and is paying particular attention to the Jackson Sawmill located in the small town of Jackson, BC.

This mill was originally built sixty years ago and was last upgraded twenty years ago. The president, June Batna, knows she will soon (in 2 to 3 years) have to decide whether or not to invest very substantial sums of money in new plant and equipment at the Jackson Sawmill. New investment is required in order to keep the mill up-to-date and competitive with similar mills throughout North America. However, the mill has consistently been the poorest performer (in terms of productivity and product quality) in the company over the past twenty years even though its equipment is of similar age, type, and quality as that found in the other mills.

The president would like to invest the money needed because the alternative to re-investing in Jackson would be to downsize the Jackson Sawmill by reducing production capacity and permanently laying off about half the 200-person workforce. The remaining part of the mill would serve the domestic market only. A new mill would then be built in Alberta in order to serve the more demanding, quality-conscious export markets. A new mill in Alberta would cost somewhat more than the anticipated investment required to modernize the Jackson Sawmill. However, Ms. Batna is willing to seriously consider implementing this alternative because she thinks that the labour relations climate in Alberta is much better than the one found at Jackson.

In fact, she attributes most, if not all, of the problems at Jackson to its poor labour-management relations. During the last round of collective bargaining, there was a strike at all four of the company's BC mills. The strike was, however, much more bitter at Jackson than elsewhere. Company buildings suffered minor damage during the strike at the hands of some striking employees. Since then, there have been two separate occasions when the entire workforce walked off the job for a day to protest the firings of two employees who were dismissed for insubordination.

The Jackson Sawmill has the worst safety record of all the company's mills. There is a joint labour-management health and safety committee (as required by law) but it is viewed as a waste of time by both sides. One management member of the safety committee, Des, the production manager and the second highest manager at the mill, has said: "The union guys start each safety committee meeting by complaining about safety but they just can't wait to complain about everything else they can possibly think of. Their whining and complaining is so predictable that I go to every safety meeting ready for a fight on workload and production issues as well as for a fight on safety. Of course, safety is everyone's responsibility but production issues are none of their business. Production is a management responsibility. Plans, budgets, and other management concerns are very definitely not part of the committee's job. Most of what's said at these meetings isn't worth listening to."

The union is also dissatisfied with the functioning of the safety committee. Ivan, the chief union steward who also serves on the committee, observes: "If the safety committee wasn't mandatory by law, management wouldn't even pretend to listen to us. We put forward our safety concerns but management says that we are mixing safety in with workload and production issues. They only want to talk about what they think are safety issues—like serious accidents. Thankfully, we don't have too many of those! But safety is more than just avoiding major accidents. We get far too many 'little accidents' and 'near-accidents' here. At least that's what management calls them. They just want us to work faster and faster. We complain and complain at the meetings but they just say 'that's a production issue and this is a safety committee.' They accuse us of trying to run the company when we ask for better equipment. They say we don't understand things like costs and limited budgets. We don't care about their budgets, we've got work issues to talk about and we'll keep speaking out for the crew no matter what. That's what the union is for."

Big Bad John, one of the mill's toughest and most experienced supervisors, describes his job as follows: "The job of supervisor is to keep a close watch on every move the crew makes. If I look away for a second, some guy is going to be doing something wrong - either with the equipment or with the logs. They're always making mistakes. Lots of mistakes! Some of these guys are just plain dumb. And lazy, too! Any chance they can get to steal some company time, they take. They start work late; they take long lunch breaks; they talk too much during their shifts. A minute here, a minute there–it all adds up. The younger guys are the worst. They always want to talk back to me, they can't follow my orders like most of the older guys can. Lousy attitude, that's what they've got."

Des, the production manager, has stated that "the mill has had a problem with worker motivation and attitude for as long as I can remember. But it's slowly getting worse as younger guys are being hired to replace the older, retiring guys. The new workers are better educated than the older ones and because of that they think they can treat their supervisors with disrespect. Don't get me wrong, we get the job done here but it takes a lot of effort on the part of the managers and, especially, the supervisors. The supervisors really earn their pay here. They watch the crew closely and have to put up with a lot of crap from them. Many of the grievances we have are a result of the discipline we have to hand out regarding horseplay, absenteeism, tardiness, careless workmanship, and not reaching production quotas. However, overall, the mill gets the product out the door, but only because we ensure that the crew works hard. Despite grumblings from the crew, we maintain a pretty good pace of work around here."

Vic, the youngest union steward, gives his view of labour–management relations: "The supervisors and the managers, they know it all. They think they're so smart. They treat the guys on the crew like children. Almost everyone on the crew has a high school education. Some even have college backgrounds. Most are raising families. We're not stupid! Sure, some guys come in late and miss a day of work now and then. Who can blame them? The pace of work is exhausting. How can you do a good job when you're tired and rushing all the time?" He adds: "Of course, we're not perfect. We make mistakes just like everyone else does. But nobody ever explains anything to the crew members. The supervisors just watch everyone like hawks and jump all over them, criticize them, and make them feel stupid when they use a piece of equipment the wrong way. We're always so rushed and busy here that the senior crew members don't have much time to explain things to the newer workers, the younger guys. The equipment could be in better shape. That would help."

Des, the production manager, has expressed his views on labour–management relations: "The union just doesn't understand–or even care about–the connection between the poor work ethic, the poor attitude on the part of the crew members here, and the mill's mediocre productivity and product quality. The union and the crew only take their very narrow 'employee-view' of how things are done around here. They don't understand the bigger picture. Well, it's very competitive out there. They don't understand what tight budgets, increasing costs, declining quality, missed production targets, and complaining customers mean to a business. They just sit back and complain about our management style. What they don't realize is that their attitude makes our management style necessary. Complaining is easy, no responsibility is needed. Managing, on the other hand, is challenging. And it's especially tough to control this particular crew. We've currently got 40 unresolved grievances–that's a lot of formal complaints for a mill of our size. Some of the union stewards actually go out among the crew and look for grievances just because they're mad they can't run the mill the way they want to. Sometimes I think the stewards want to create grievances where no real problems exist. They want to give us in management headaches."

Vic, a union steward, went on to say: "We've currently got 40 unresolved grievances at different stages of the grievance procedure–I don't have to tell you that's quite a lot for a mill of our size. Some crew members are really mad at management and file a lot of grievances. The grievances are mostly about challenging the discipline management hands out regarding horseplay, absenteeism, tardiness, careless workmanship, and not reaching production quotas. We–the shop stewards–try to calm them down but some guys are really angry about how they're treated. The stewards spend a lot of time trying to settle things outside the formal grievance process, but some of the crew really want the stewards to file grievances and some supervisors don't want to solve things informally. Things are pretty formal around here. It's all such a waste of time and energy. The pay is good but I wouldn't recommend this as a place to work to anyone unless they like being treated like a misbehaving child."

The president of the company has recently informed Digby, the mill's new general manager (he started last month), of the decision she will soon have to make regarding the mill's future. She told Digby that significant improvements in mill productivity and product quality are required if the mill is to receive a substantial investment in new plant and equipment. Without such improvements, the mill would be downsized and about half of the workforce would be permanently laid off. Half the supervisory and managerial personnel would also lose their jobs.

Digby has just telephoned Moe (the president of the local union who does not work at the mill but who is very familiar with developments at the mill) to tell him about the message from the company president. Upon hearing of the potential job losses, Moe was troubled and asked to meet with Digby to discuss the situation. However, Moe was also somewhat skeptical because the previous general manager once told him that some permanent layoffs would occur unless productivity was improved. No layoffs subsequently occurred. Therefore, Moe is uncertain if the company is serious about these potential future layoffs or merely bluffing in order to get the employees to work harder.

Case 8 THE REGENCY GRAND HOTEL

By Elizabeth Ho, Gucci Group, under the supervision of Steven L. McShane, The University of Western Australia

The Regency Grand Hotel is a five-star hotel in Bangkok, Thailand. The hotel was established fifteen years ago by a local consortium of investors and has been operated by a Thai general manager throughout this time. The hotel is one of Bangkok's most prestigious hotels and its 700 employees enjoy the prestige of being associated with the hotel. The hotel provides good welfare benefits, above-market-rate salary, and job security. In addition, a good year-end bonus amounting to four months' salary is rewarded to employees regardless of the hotel's overall performance during the year.

Recently, the Regency was sold to a large American hotel chain that was very keen to expand its operations into Thailand. When the acquisition was announced, the General Manager decided to take early retirement when the hotel changed ownership. The American hotel chain kept all of the Regency employees, although a few were transferred to other positions. John Becker, an American with 10 years of management experience with the hotel chain, was appointed as the new General Manager of the Regency Grand Hotel. Becker was selected as the new General Manager because of his previous successes in integrating newly acquired hotels in the United States. In most of the previous acquisitions, Becker took over operations with poor profitability and low morale.

Becker is a strong believer in empowerment. He expects employees to go beyond guidelines/standards to consider guest needs on a case-by-case basis. That is, employees must be guest-oriented at all times so as to provide excellent customer service. From his U.S. experience, Becker has found that empowerment increases employee motivation, performance, and job satisfaction, all of which contribute to the hotel's profitability and customer service ratings. Soon after becoming General Manager at The Regency Grand, Becker introduced the practice of empowerment so as to replicate the successes that he had achieved back home.

The Regency Grand hotel has been very profitable since it opened. The employees have always worked according to management's instructions. Their responsibility was to ensure that the instructions from their managers were carried out diligently and conscientiously. Innovation and creativity were discouraged under the previous management. Indeed, employees were punished for their mistakes and discouraged from trying out ideas that had not been approved by management. As a result, employees were afraid to be innovative and to take risks.

Becker met with the Regency's managers and department heads to explain that empowerment would be introduced in the hotel. He told them that employees must be empowered with decision-making authority so that they can use their initiative, creativity, and judgment to satisfy guest needs or handle problems effectively and efficiently. However, he stressed that the more complex issues and decisions were to be referred to superiors, who were to coach and assist rather than provide direct orders. Furthermore, Becker stressed that while mistakes were allowed, repetition of the same mistake more than twice could not tolerated. He advised his managers and department heads that they should not discuss or consult him on minor issues/problems and decisions. Nevertheless, he told them that they are to discuss important/major issues and decisions with him. He concluded the meeting by asking for feedback. Several managers and department heads told him that they liked the idea and would support it, while others simply nodded their heads. Becker was pleased with the response, and was eager to have his plan implemented.

In the past, the Regency had emphasized administrative control, resulting in many bureaucratic procedures throughout the organization. For example, the front counter employees needed to seek approval from their manager before they could upgrade guests to another category of room. The front counter manager would then have to write and submit a report to the General Manager justifying the upgrade. Soon after his meeting with managers, Becker reduced the number of bureaucratic rules at the Regency and allocated more decision-making authority to frontline employees. This action upset those who previously had decision-making power over these issues. As a result, several of these employees left the hotel.

Becker also began spending a large portion of his time observing and interacting with the employees at the front desk, lobby, restaurants, and various departments. This direct interaction with Becker helped many employees to understand what he wanted and expected of them. However, the employees had much difficulty trying to distinguish between a major and minor issue/decision. More often than not, supervisors would reverse employee decisions by stating that they were major issues requiring management approval. Employees who displayed initiative and made good decisions in satisfying the needs of the guests rarely received any positive feedback from their supervisors. Eventually, most of these employees lost confidence in making decisions, and reverted back to relying on their superiors for decision making.

Not long after the implementation of the practice of empowerment, Becker realized that his subordinates were consulting him more frequently than before. Most of them came to him to discuss or consult on minor issues. He had to spend most of his time attending to his subordinates. Soon he began to feel highly frustrated and exhausted, and very often would tell his secretary that "unless the hotel is on fire, don't let anyone disturb me."

Becker thought that the practice of empowerment would benefit the overall performance of the hotel. However, contrary to his expectation, the business and overall performance of the hotel began to deteriorate. There had been an increasing number of guest complaints. In the past, the hotel had minimal guest complaints. Now there were a significant number of formal written complaints every month. Many other guests voiced their dissatisfaction verbally to hotel employees.

The number of mistakes made by employees had been on an increase. Becker was very upset when he realized that two of the local newspapers and an overseas newspaper had published negative feedback on the hotel in terms of service standards. He was most distressed when an international travel magazine had voted the hotel as "one of Asia's nightmare hotels."

The stress levels of the employees were continuously mounting since the introduction of the practice of empowerment. Absenteeism due to illness was increasing at an alarming rate. In addition, the employee turnover rate had reached an all-time high. The good working relationships that were established under the old management had been severely strained. The employees were no longer united and supportive of each other. They were quick to "point fingers" at or to "back stab" one another when mistakes were made and when problems occurred.

Note: This case is based on true events, but the industry and names have been changed.

Case 9 SIMMONS LABORATORIES

Adapted by William Starbuck from a case written by Alex Bavelas

Brandon Newbridge was sitting alone in the conference room of the laboratory. The rest of the group had gone. One of the secretaries had stopped and talked for a while about her husband's coming enrollment in graduate school and had finally left. Brandon, alone in the laboratory, slid a little farther down in his chair, looking with satisfaction at the results of the first test run of the new photon unit.

He liked to stay after the others had gone. His appointment as project head was still new enough to give him a deep sense of pleasure. His eyes were on the graphs before him, but in his mind, he could hear Dr. William Goh, the project head, saying again, "There's one thing about this place you can bank on. The sky is the limit for anyone who can produce!" Newbridge felt again the tingle of happiness and embarrassment. Well, dammit, he said to himself, he had produced. He wasn't kidding anybody. He had come to the Simmons Laboratories two years ago. During a routine testing of some rejected Clanson components, he had stumbled on the idea of the photon correlator, and the rest just happened. Goh had been enthusiastic: A separate project had been set up for further research and development of the device, and he had gotten the job of running it. The whole sequence of events still seemed a little miraculous to Newbridge.

He shrugged out of the reverie and bent determinedly over the sheets when he heard someone come into the room behind him. He looked up expectantly; Goh often stayed late himself and now and then dropped in for a chat. This always made the day's end especially pleasant for Brandon. It wasn't Goh. The man who had come in was a stranger. He was tall and thin. He wore steel-rimmed glasses and had a very wide leather belt with a large brass buckle. Lucy remarked later that it was the kind of belt the Pilgrims must have worn.

The stranger smiled and introduced himself. "I'm Lester Zapf. Are you Brandon Newbridge?" Brandon said yes, and they shook hands. "Doctor Goh said I might find you in. We were talking about your work, and I'm very much interested in what you are doing." Brandon waved to a chair.

Zapf didn't seem to belong in any of the standard categories of visitors: customer, visiting fireman, shareholder. Brandon pointed to the sheets on the table. "These are the preliminary results of a test we're running. We have a new gadget by the tail and we're trying to understand it. It's not finished, but I can show you the section we're testing."

He stood up, but Zapf was deep in the graphs. After a moment, he looked up with an odd grin. "These look like plots of a Jennings surface. I've been playing around with some autocorrelation functions of surfaces–you know that stuff." Brandon, who had no idea what he was referring to, grinned back and nodded, and immediately felt uncomfortable. "Let me show you the monster," he said, and led the way to the workroom.

After Zapf left, Newbridge slowly put the graphs away, feeling vaguely annoyed. Then, as if he had made a decision, he quickly locked up and took the long way out so that he would pass Goh's office. But the office was locked. Newbridge wondered whether Goh and Zapf had left together.

The next morning, Newbridge dropped into Goh's office, mentioned that he had talked with Zapf, and asked who he was.

"Sit down for a minute," Goh said. "I want to talk to you about him. What do you think of him?" Newbridge replied truthfully that he thought Zapf was very bright and probably very competent. Goh looked pleased.

"We're taking him on," he said. "He's had a very good background in a number of laboratories, and he seems to have ideas about the problems we're tackling here." Newbridge nodded in agreement, instantly wishing that Zapf would not be placed with him.

"I don't know yet where he will finally land," Goh continued, "but he seems interested in what you are doing. I thought he might spend a little time with you by way of getting started." Newbridge nodded thoughtfully. "If his interest in your work continues, you can add him to your group."

"Well, he seemed to have some good ideas even without knowing exactly what we are doing," Newbridge answered. "I hope he stays; we'd be glad to have him."

Newbridge walked back to the lab with mixed feelings. He told himself that Zapf would be good for the group. He was no dunce; he'd produce. Newbridge thought again of Goh's promise when he had promoted him: "the man who produces gets ahead in this outfit." The words seemed to carry the overtones of a threat now.

That day Zapf didn't appear until mid-afternoon. He explained that he had had a long lunch with Goh, discussing his place in the lab. "Yes," said Newbridge, "I talked with Jerry this morning about it, and we both thought you might work with us for a while."

Zapf smiled in the same knowing way that he had smiled when he mentioned the Jennings surfaces. "I'd like to," he said.

Newbridge introduced Zapf to the other members of the lab. Zapf and Link, the group's mathematician, hit it off well and spent the rest of the afternoon discussing a method for analyzing patterns that Link had been worrying over the last month.

It was 6:30 when Newbridge finally left the lab that night. He had waited almost eagerly for the end of the day to come—when they would all be gone and he could sit in the quiet rooms, relax, and think it over. "Think what over?" he asked himself. He didn't know. Shortly after 5 p.m., they had almost all gone except Zapf, and what followed was almost a duel. Newbridge was annoyed that he was being cheated out of his quiet period and finally resentfully determined that Zapf should leave first.

Zapf was sitting at the conference table reading, and Newbridge was sitting at his desk in the little glass-enclosed cubby he used during the day when he needed to be undisturbed. Zapf had gotten the last year's progress reports out and was studying them carefully. The time dragged. Newbridge doodled on a pad, the tension growing inside him. What the hell did Zapf think he was going to find in the reports?

Newbridge finally gave up and they left the lab together. Zapf took several of the reports with him to study in the evening. Newbridge asked him if he thought the reports gave a clear picture of the lab's activities.

"They're excellent," Zapf answered with obvious sincerity. "They're not only good reports; what they report is damn good, too!" Newbridge was surprised at the relief he felt and grew almost jovial as he said good-night.

Driving home, Newbridge felt more optimistic about Zapf's presence in the lab. He had never fully understood the analysis that Link was attempting. If there was anything wrong with Link's approach, Zapf would probably spot it. "And if I'm any judge," he murmured, "he won't be especially diplomatic about it."

He described Zapf to his wife, who was amused by the broad leather belt and brass buckle.

"It's the kind of belt that Pilgrims must have worn," she laughed.

"I'm not worried about how he holds his pants up," he laughed with her. "I'm afraid that he's the kind that just has to make like a genius twice each day. And that can be pretty rough on the group."

Newbridge had been asleep for several hours when he was jerked awake by the telephone. He realized it had rung several times. He swung off the bed muttering about damn fools and telephones. It was Zapf. Without any excuses, apparently oblivious of the time, he plunged into an excited recital of how Link's patterning problem could be solved.

Newbridge covered the mouthpiece to answer his wife's stage-whispered "Who is it?" "It's the genius," replied Newbridge.

Zapf, completely ignoring the fact that it was 2:00 in the morning, went on in a very excited way to start in the middle of an explanation of a completely new approach to certain of the photon lab problems that he had stumbled on while analyzing past experiments. Newbridge managed to put some enthusiasm in his own voice and stood there, half-dazed and very uncomfortable, listening to Zapf talk endlessly about what he had discovered. It was probably not only a new approach but also an analysis that showed the inherent weakness of the previous experiment and how experimentation along that line would certainly have been inconclusive. The following day Newbridge spent the entire morning with Zapf and Link, the mathematician, the customary morning meeting of Brandon's group having been called off so that Zapf's work of the previous night could be gone over intensively. Zapf was very anxious that this be done, and Newbridge was not too unhappy to call the meeting off for reasons of his own.

For the next several days Zapf sat in the back office that had been turned over to him and did nothing but read the progress reports of the work that had been done in the last six months. Newbridge caught himself feeling apprehensive about the reaction that Zapf might have to some of his work. He was a little surprised at his own feelings. He had always been proud—although he had put on a convincingly modest face—of the way in which new ground in the study of photon-measuring devices had been broken in his group. Now he wasn't sure, and it seemed to him that Zapf might easily show that the line of research they had been following was unsound or even unimaginative.

The next morning (as was the custom) the members of the lab, including the secretaries, sat around a conference table. Brandon always prided himself on the fact that the work of the lab was guided and evaluated by the group as a whole, and he was fond of repeating that it was not a waste of time to include secretaries in such meetings. Often, what started out as a boring recital of fundamental assumptions to a naive listener, uncovered new ways of regarding these assumptions that would not have occurred to the researcher who had long ago accepted them as a necessary basis for his work.

These group meetings also served Brandon in another sense. He admitted to himself that he would have felt far less secure if he had had to direct the work out of his own mind, so to speak. With the group meeting as the principle of leadership, it was always possible to justify the exploration of blind alleys because of the general educative effect on the team. Zapf was there; Lucy and Martha were there; Link was sitting next to Zapf, their conversation concerning Link's mathematical study apparently continuing from yesterday. The other members, Bob Davenport, Georgia Thurlow, and Arthur Oliver, were waiting quietly.

Newbridge, for reasons that he didn't quite understand, proposed for discussion this morning a problem that all of them had spent a great deal of time on previously with the conclusion that a solution was impossible, that there was no feasible way of treating it in an experimental fashion. When Newbridge proposed the problem, Davenport remarked that there was hardly any use of going over it again, that he was satisfied that there was no way of approaching the problem with the equipment and the physical capacities of the lab.

This statement had the effect of a shot of adrenaline on Zapf. He said he would like to know what the problem was in detail and, walking to the blackboard, began setting down the "factors" as various members of the group began discussing the problem and simultaneously listing the reasons why it had been abandoned.

Very early in the description of the problem it was evident that Zapf was going to disagree about the impossibility of attacking it. The group realized this, and finally the descriptive materials and their recounting of the reasoning that had led to its abandonment dwindled away. Zapf began his statement, which, as it proceeded, might well have been prepared the previous night, although Newbridge knew this was impossible. He couldn't help being impressed with the organized and logical way that Zapf was presenting ideas that must have occurred to him only a few minutes before.

Zapf had some things to say, however, which left Newbridge with a mixture of annoyance, irritation, and at the same time, a rather smug feeling of superiority over Zapf in at least one area. Zapf held the opinion that the way that the problem had been analyzed was very typical of group thinking. With an air of sophistication that made it difficult for a listener to dissent, he proceeded to comment on the American emphasis on team ideas, satirically describing the ways in which they led to a "high level of mediocrity."

During this time, Newbridge observed that Link stared studiously at the floor, and he was very conscious of Georgia Thurlow and Bob Davenport's glances towards him at several points of Zapf's little speech. Inwardly, Newbridge couldn't help feeling that this was one point at least in which Zapf was off on the wrong foot. The whole lab, following Jerry's lead, talked if not practised the theory of small research teams as the basic organization for effective research. Zapf insisted that the problem could be approached and that he would like to study it for a while himself.

Newbridge ended the morning session by remarking that the meetings would continue and that the very fact that a supposedly insoluble experimental problem was now going to get another chance was another indication of the value of such meetings. Zapf immediately remarked that he was not at all averse to meetings to inform the group about the progress of its members. The point he wanted to make was that creative advances were seldom accomplished in such meetings, that they were made by an individual "living with" a problem closely and continuously, in a rather personal relationship to it.

Newbridge went on to say to Zapf that he was very glad that Zapf had raised these points and that he was sure the group would profit by re-examining the basis on which they had been operating. Newbridge agreed that individual effort was probably the basis for making major advances. He considered the group meetings useful primarily because they kept the group together and they helped the weaker members of the group keep up with the ones who were able to advance more easily and quickly in the analysis of problems.

It was clear as days went by and meetings continued that Zapf came to enjoy them because of the pattern that the meetings assumed. It became typical for Zapf to hold forth, and it was unquestionably clear that he was more brilliant, better prepared on the various subjects that were germane to the problem being studied, and more capable of going ahead than anyone there. Newbridge grew increasingly disturbed as he realized that his leadership of the group had been, in fact, taken over.

Whenever the subject of Zapf was mentioned in occasional meetings with Dr. Goh, Newbridge would comment only on the ability and obvious capacity for work that Zapf had. Somehow he never felt that he could mention his own discomforts, not only because they revealed a weakness on his part but also because it was quite clear that Goh himself was considerably impressed with Zapf's work and with the contacts he had outside the photon laboratory.

Newbridge now began to feel that perhaps the intellectual advantages that Zapf had brought to the group did not quite compensate for what he felt were evidences of a breakdown in the cooperative spirit he had seen in the group before Zapf's coming. More and more of the morning meetings were skipped. Zapf's opinion concerning the abilities of others of the group, except for Link, was obviously low. At times during morning meetings or in smaller discussions he had been on the point of rudeness, refusing to pursue an argument when he claimed it was based on another person's ignorance of the facts involved. His impatience of others led him to also make similar remarks to Dr. Goh. Newbridge inferred this from a conversation with Goh in which Goh asked whether Davenport and Oliver were going to be continued on; and his failure to mention Link, the mathematician, led Newbridge to feel that this was the result of private conversations between Zapf and Goh.

It was not difficult for Newbridge to make a quite convincing case on whether the brilliance of Zapf was sufficient recompense for the beginning of this breaking up of the group. He spoke privately with Davenport and Oliver, and it was quite clear that both of them were uncomfortable because of Zapf. Newbridge didn't press the discussion beyond the point of hearing them say that they did feel awkward, and that it was sometimes difficult to understand the arguments Zapf advanced, but often embarrassing to ask him to fill in the basis for his arguments. Newbridge did not interview Link in this manner.

About six months after Zapf's coming into the photon lab, a meeting was scheduled in which the sponsors of the research were coming to get some idea of the work and its progress. It was customary at these meetings for project heads to present the research being conducted in their groups. The members of each group were invited to other meetings that were held later in the day and open to all, but the special meetings were usually made up only of project heads, the head of the laboratory, and the sponsors.

As the time for the special meeting approached, it seemed to Newbridge that he must avoid the presentation at all cost. His reasons for this were that he could not trust himself to present the ideas and work that Zapf had advanced because of his apprehension about whether he could present them in sufficient detail and answer such questions about them as might be asked. On the other hand, he did not feel he could ignore these newer lines of work and present only the material that he had done or that had been started before Zapf's arrival. He felt also that it would not be beyond Zapf at all, in his blunt and undiplomatic way–if he were at the meeting, that is–to comment on his [Newbridge's] presentation and reveal Newbridge's inadequacy. It also seemed quite clear that it would not be easy to keep Zapf from attending the meeting, even though he was not on the administrative level of those invited.

Newbridge found an opportunity to speak to Goh and raised the question. He told Goh that, with the meetings coming up and with the interest in the work and with Zapf's contributions to the work, Zapf would probably like to come to the meetings; but there was a question of how the others in the group would feel if only Zapf were invited. Goh passed this over very lightly by saying that he didn't think the group would fail to understand Zapf's rather different position and that Zapf certainly should be invited. Newbridge immediately said he agreed: Zapf should present the work because much of it was work he had done, and this would be a nice way to recognize Zapf's contributions and to reward him, because he was eager to be recognized as a productive member of the lab. Goh agreed, and so the matter was decided.

Zapf's presentation was very successful and in some ways dominated the meeting. He attracted the interest and attention of many of those who had come, and a long discussion followed his presentation. Later in the evening–with the entire laboratory staff present–in the cocktail period before the dinner, a little circle of people formed about Zapf. One of them was Goh himself, and a lively discussion took place concerning the application of Zapf's theory. All of this disturbed Newbridge, and his reaction and behaviour were characteristic. He joined the circle, praised Zapf to Goh and to others, and remarked on the brilliance of the work.

Newbridge, without consulting anyone, began at this time to take some interest in the possibility of a job elsewhere. After a few weeks he found that a new laboratory of considerable size was being organized in a nearby city and that the kind of training he had would enable him to get a project-head job equivalent to the one he had at the lab with slightly more money.

He immediately accepted it and notified Goh by letter, which he mailed on a Friday night to Goh's home. The letter was quite brief, and Goh was stunned. The letter merely said that he had found a better position; that he didn't want to appear at the lab anymore for personal reasons; that he would be glad to come back at a later time to assist if there was any mix-up in the past work; that he felt sure Zapf could supply any leadership that the group required; and that his decision to leave so suddenly was based on personal problems–he hinted at problems of health in his family, his mother and father. All of this was fictitious, of course. Goh took it at face value but still felt that this was very strange behaviour and quite unaccountable, for he had always felt his relationship with Newbridge had been warm and that Newbridge was satisfied and, in fact, quite happy and productive.

Goh was considerably disturbed, because he had already decided to place Zapf in charge of another project that was going to be set up very soon. He had been wondering how to explain this to Newbridge, in view of the obvious help Newbridge was getting from Zapf and the high regard in which he held him. Goh had, indeed, considered the possibility that Newbridge could add to his staff another person with the kind of background and training that had been unique in Zapf and had proved so valuable.

Goh did not make any attempt to meet Newbridge. In a way, he felt aggrieved about the whole thing. Zapf, too, was surprised at the suddenness of Newbridge's departure. When Goh asked Zapf whether he preferred to stay with the photon group instead of the new project for the Air Force, he chose the Air Force project and went on to that job the following week. The photon lab was hard hit. The leadership of the lab was given to Link with the understanding that this would be temporary until someone could come in to take over.

Case 10 STAR ENTERPRISES—RITA'S ISSUES AT WORK[1]

By Nuzhat Lotia, University of Melbourne

Rita has been working for Star Enterprises for the last 13 years. Star Enterprises is a medium-sized auto-parts manufacturer and supplies parts to one of the largest car manufacturing companies in Australia. The company has 450 employees. Despite the recent financial crisis, Star Enterprises has not suffered great losses. This is due to their commitment to quality and reliability.

Rita started out on the factory floor when she began working for Star Enterprises as a 20-year-old. She has since worked her way through to her current position as the senior supervisor in the Quality Control Department. She has been working in this position for the last three years. She has moved up to more senior positions in the company because she is recognized as a hardworking and dedicated employee who takes great pride in the work that she does.

Rita is one of the most experienced workers in the section and the quality control manager relies heavily on her knowledge and experience. She knows almost everyone at the company and has developed good relations with her coworkers, who rely on her for support and expertise.

Recently, Rita has been very unhappy with the situation at work. It all started when her boss, Mr. Blake, the quality control manager, left for a senior position in Star Enterprises' sister company. After he left, Rita was asked by the general manager if she would consider working as the acting quality control manager until the position was filled. Rita was very happy to take up the opportunity. She had often taken on that position informally in the past when Mr. Blake had been away on leave or professional development. She had always felt that, being the most experienced person in the department, it was her responsibility to take on these additional duties while her boss was away. She felt a sense of pride in doing so.

When the offer of becoming the acting quality control manager was made to her six months ago, she was very excited and felt that the company had acknowledged her contribution, her experience, and her dedication to her work by giving her this responsibility. She was also quite happy to take on the position as it meant a pay rise as well, and she could do with the additional income as she had recently bought a house and was finding it difficult to manage with her current income.

Rita was really enjoying this added responsibility of managing the department. She had the opportunity to participate in senior management meetings and found that she was able to contribute to the discussions. The general manager was very supportive and would often drop by her office to make sure she was coping well with the work, and was always available for a chat if she needed help. While she had settled into this new role quite well, she was struggling with managing the budget and finances of the department. She had never dealt with departmental finances or managed budgets in her past roles, even when she was informally acting on the manager's behalf. She felt that she needed some formal training in the area to enable her to function well in this aspect of the job. She looked up some short courses being offered by professional development and training organizations and found one that she felt was perfect for her needs. The course was a bit expensive, but she felt that it would be very beneficial despite the cost.

The next day, she approached the general manager with a request for funding her to attend the 10-day training. While the general manager showed empathy for her situation, he said that he could not approve this expenditure as they had already advertised for the position and they would be hiring a manager soon, at which point she would go back to her senior supervisor role. He explained that he could not justify the expenditure on Rita's professional development.

Rita could not believe what she had just heard. She had been unaware that the manager position was being advertised. She was very upset and this was obvious from her face. She mumbled, "I understand," and quickly got up and left the general manager's office. The truth was that she did not understand; in fact, she felt betrayed. She had in her heart hoped that her acting role would eventually turn into a permanent position, as she felt that she had been doing her job really well except for the budgetary side of things, which she was quite willing to learn about.

After coming out of the general manager's office, she ran to her office, locked the door, and started crying. She felt very upset and angry. She felt that she had always given her best to the company, but had been let down. At that moment, she decided that if she was going to be treated so badly then she would have nothing to do with the company. She would quit tomorrow.

That evening at home, she realized that she could not make such a rash decision as she could not afford to lose the income. So, she thought to herself, *I will stay, but I will show them what they are losing out on.* She continued to work in the acting quality manager position, but no longer took any initiative and just went about the routine of the work. She avoided meeting with the general manager as well. Everyone in the department noticed this change in Rita, but could not figure out what had happened.

When the new manager, James Downer, joined and Rita returned to her senior supervisor position, she decided that she was not going to help him in any way. James was new to the industry. Before taking up this position, he had been working in quality control in a home appliances manufacturing company. While he had come highly recommended, he still had to learn a lot about auto manufacturing. He often approached Rita for advice. Rita would tell him what she knew and supported him initially, but then the resentment began to set in.

When James started making changes to the quality control systems that Rita had helped design and set up, the resentment grew but she bottled up her feelings. Rita would answer abruptly when James approached her for advice. She also started avoiding him. She would often walk away to the kitchen or to the printer when she saw him approaching her desk or would pick up the phone and start making a call. Every now and then, Rita would call in sick. She was once again beginning to consider quitting her job.

[1] Case study prepared by Nuzhat Lotia, Department of Management and Marketing, University of Melbourne. This case is not to be reproduced or distributed without permission.

Case 11 TAMARACK INDUSTRIES

By David J. Cherrington, Brigham Young University

Tamarack Industries manufactures motorboats primarily used for water skiing. Students are hired during summer months to fill in for permanent employees on vacation. In past years, students worked alongside permanent employees, but a few staff complained that the students were inexperienced, slow, and arrogant. In general, permanent staff disliked the students' behaviour, such as listening to music with earphones while working. This summer, the company reorganized all permanent employees into three production teams (they usually have four teams, but 25 percent are on holiday at any given time) and assigned the 16 summer students to their own team on the fourth production line.

The supervisor, Dan Jensen, decided to try a different strategy this summer and have all the college students work on the new line. He asked Mark Allen to supervise the new crew because Mark claimed that he knew everything about boats and could perform every job "with my eyes closed." Mark was happy to accept the new job and participated in selecting the student hires. Mark's crew was called "the Geek Team" because all the college students were savvy with computers, unlike most of the permanent employees.

Mark spent many hours training his student team to get the line running at full production. The college students learned quickly, and by the end of June their production rate was up to standard, with an error rate that was only slightly above normal. To simplify the learning process, Dan Jensen assigned the Geek Team long production runs that generally consisted of thirty to forty identical units. Thus the training period was shortened and errors were reduced. Shorter production runs were assigned to the experienced teams.

By the middle of July, a substantial rivalry had been created between the Geek Team and the older workers. At first, the rivalry was good-natured. But after a few weeks, the older workers became resentful of the remarks made by the college students. The Geek Team often met its production schedules with time to spare at the end of the day for goofing around. It wasn't uncommon for someone from the Geek Team to go to another line pretending to look for materials just to make demeaning comments. The experienced workers resented having to perform all the shorter production runs and began to retaliate with sabotage. They would sneak over during breaks and hide tools, dent materials, install something crooked, and in other small ways do something that would slow production for the Geek Team.

Dan felt good about his decision to form a separate crew of college students, but when he heard reports of sabotage and rivalry, he became very concerned. Because of complaints from the experienced workers, Dan equalized the production so that all of the crews had similar production runs. The rivalry, however, did not stop. The Geek Team continued to finish early and flaunt their performance in front of the other crews.

One day the Geek Team suspected that one of their assemblies was going to be sabotaged during the lunch break by one of the experienced crews. By skilful deception, they were able to substitute an assembly from the other experienced line for theirs. By the end of the lunch period, the Geek Team was laughing wildly because of their deception, while one experienced crew was very angry with the other one.

Dan Jensen decided that the situation had to be changed and announced that the job assignments between the different crews would be shuffled. The employees were told that when they appeared for work the next morning, the names of the workers assigned to each crew would be posted on the bulletin board. The announcement was not greeted with much enthusiasm, and Mark Allen decided to talk Dan out of his idea. Mark suspected that many of the college students would quit if their team was broken up.

Case 12 THE OUTSTANDING FACULTY AWARD

By David J. Cherrington, Brigham Young University; revised by Steven L. McShane, The University of Western Australia

I recently served on the Outstanding Faculty Award committee for the College of Business. This award is our college's highest honour for a faculty member, which is bestowed at a special reception ceremony. At the first meeting, our committee discussed the nomination process and decided to follow our traditional practice of inviting nominations from both the faculty and students. During the next month, we received six completed files with supporting documentation. Three of the nominations came from department chairs, two from faculty who recommended their colleagues, and one from a group of 16 graduate students.

At the second meeting, we agreed that we didn't know the six applicants well enough to make a decision that day, so we decided that we would read the applications on our own and rank them. There was no discussion about ranking criteria; I think we assumed that we shared a common definition of the word "outstanding."

During the third meeting, it quickly became apparent that each committee member had a different interpretation of what constitutes an "outstanding" faculty member. The discussion was polite, but we debated the extent to which this was an award for teaching, or research, or service to the college, or scholarly textbook writing, or consulting, or service to society, or some other factor. After three hours, we agreed on five criteria that we would apply to independently rate each candidate using a five-point scale.

When we reconvened the next day, our discussion was much more focused as we tried to achieve a consensus regarding how we judged each candidate on each criterion. After a lengthy discussion, we finally completed the task and averaged the ratings. The top three scores had an average rating (out of a maximum of 25) of 21, 19.5, and 18.75. I assumed the person with the highest total would receive the award. Instead, my colleagues began debating over the relevance of the five criteria that we had agreed on the previous day. Some committee members felt, in hindsight, that the criteria were incorrectly weighted or that other criteria should be considered.

Although they did not actually say this, I sensed that at least two colleagues on the committee wanted the criteria or weights changed because their preferred candidate didn't get the highest score using the existing formula. When we changed the weights in various ways, a different candidate among the top three received the top score. The remaining three candidates received lower ratings every time. Dr. H always received the lowest score, usually around 12 on the 25-point range.

After almost two hours of discussion, the Associate Dean turned to one committee member and said, "Dolan, I sure would like to see Dr. H in your department receive this honour. He retires next year and this would be a great honour for him and no one has received this honour in your department recently."

Dolan agreed, "Yes, this is Dr. H's last year with us and it would be a great way for him to go out. I'm sure he would feel very honoured by this award."

I sat there stunned at the suggestion while Dolan retold how Dr. H had been active in public service, his only real strength on our criteria. I was even more stunned when another committee member, who I think was keen to finish the meeting, said, "Well, I so move" and Dolan seconded it.

The Associate Dean, who was conducting the meeting, said, "Well, if the rest of you think this is a good idea, all in favour say aye." A few members said "Aye," and, without calling for nays, the Associate Dean quickly proceeded to explain what we needed to do to advertise the winner and arrange the ceremony.

During my conversations with other committee members over the next two weeks, I learned that everyone—including the two who said "Aye"—were as shocked as I was at our committee's decision. I thought we made a terrible decision, and I was embarrassed to be a member of the committee. A few weeks later, we were appropriately punished when Dr. H gave a 45-minute acceptance speech that started poorly and got worse.

Appendix A

Theory Building and Systematic Research Methods

Theory Building

theory A general set of propositions that describes interrelationships among several concepts.

People need to make sense of their world, so they form theories about the way the world operates. A **theory** is a general set of propositions that describes interrelationships among several concepts. We form theories for the purpose of predicting and explaining the world around us.[1] What does a good theory look like? First, it should be stated as clearly and simply as possible so that the concepts can be measured and there is no ambiguity regarding the theory's propositions. Second, the elements of the theory must be logically consistent with each other, because we cannot test anything that doesn't make sense. Third, a good theory provides value to society; it helps people understand their world better than they would without the theory.[2]

Theory building is a continuous process that typically includes the inductive and deductive stages shown in Exhibit A.1.[3] The inductive stage draws on personal experience to form a preliminary theory, whereas the deductive stage uses the scientific method to test the theory.

The inductive stage of theory building involves observing the world around us, identifying a pattern of relationships, and then forming a theory from these personal observations. For example, you might casually notice that new employees want their supervisor to give direction, whereas this leadership style irritates long-service employees. From these observations, you form a theory about the effectiveness of directive leadership. (See Chapter 12 for a discussion of this leadership style.)

Positivism versus Interpretivism

positivism A view held in quantitative research in which reality exists independent of the perceptions and interpretations of people.

Research requires an interpretation of reality, and researchers tend to perceive reality in one of two ways. A common view, called **positivism,** is that reality exists independent of the perceptions and interpretations of people. It is "out there" to be discovered and tested. Positivism is the foundation for most quantitative research (statistical analysis). It assumes that we

EXHIBIT A.1

Theory Building and Theory Testing

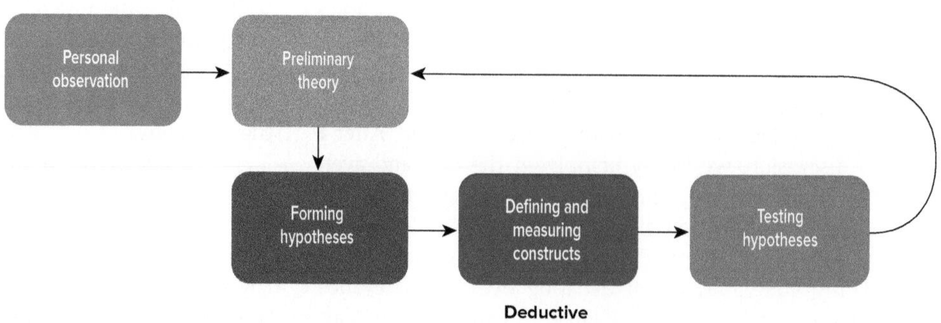

can measure variables and those variables have fixed relationships with other variables. For example, the positivist perspective says that we could study whether a supportive style of leadership reduces stress. If we find evidence that it does, then someone else studying leadership and stress would "discover" the same relationship.

interpretivism The view held in many qualitative studies that reality comes from shared meaning among people in a particular environment.

Interpretivism takes a different view of reality. It suggests that reality comes from shared meaning among people in a particular environment. For example, supportive leadership is a personal interpretation of reality, not something that can be measured across time and people. Interpretivists rely mainly on qualitative data, such as observation and nondirective interviews. They particularly listen to the language people use to understand the common meaning that people have towards various events or phenomena. For example, they might argue that you need to experience and observe supportive leadership to effectively study it. Moreover, you can't really predict relationships because the specific situation shapes reality.[4]

Most OB scholars identify themselves somewhere between the extreme views of positivism and interpretivism. Many believe that inductive research should begin with an interpretivist angle. We should consider a new topic with an open mind and search for shared meaning among people in the situation being studied. In other words, researchers should let the participants define reality rather than let the researcher's preconceived notions shape that reality. This process involves gathering qualitative information and letting this information shape their theory.[5] After the theory emerges, researchers shift to the positivist perspective by quantitatively testing relationships in that theory.

Theory Testing: The Deductive Process

hypotheses Statements making empirically testable declarations that certain variables and their corresponding measures are related in a specific way proposed by the theory.

Once a theory has been formed, we shift into the deductive stage of theory building. This process includes forming hypotheses, defining and measuring constructs, and testing hypotheses (see Exhibit A.1). **Hypotheses** make empirically testable declarations that certain variables and their corresponding measures are related in a specific way proposed by the theory. For instance, to find support for the directive leadership theory described earlier, we need to form and then test a specific hypothesis from that theory. One such hypothesis might be: "New employees are more satisfied with supervisors who exhibit a directive rather than nondirective leadership style." Hypotheses are indispensable tools of scientific research, because they provide the vital link between the theory and empirical verification.

DEFINING AND MEASURING CONSTRUCTS

Hypotheses are testable only if we can define and then form measurable indicators of the concepts stated in those hypotheses. Consider the hypothesis in the previous paragraph about new employees and directive leadership. To test this hypothesis, we first need to define the concepts, such as "new employees," "directive leadership," and "supervisor." These are known as **constructs,** because they are abstract ideas constructed by researchers that can be linked to observable information. Organizational behaviour researchers developed the construct called *directive leadership* to help them understand the different effects that leaders have on followers. We can't directly see, taste, or smell directive leadership; instead, we rely on indirect indicators of its existence, such as observing someone giving directions, maintaining clear performance standards, and ensuring that procedures and practices are followed.

constructs Abstract ideas constructed by researchers that can be linked to observable information.

As you can see, defining constructs well is very important because these definitions become the foundation for finding or developing acceptable measures of those constructs. We can't measure directive leadership if we have only a vague idea about what this concept means. The better the construct is defined, the better our chances of finding or developing a good measure of that construct. However, even with a good definition, constructs can be difficult to measure, because the empirical representation must capture several elements in the definition. A measure of directive leadership must be able to identify not only people who give directions, but also those who maintain performance standards and ensure that procedures are followed.

TESTING HYPOTHESES

The third step in the deductive process is to collect data for the empirical measures of the variables. Following our directive leadership example, we might conduct a formal survey in which new employees indicate the behaviour of their supervisors and their attitudes towards their supervisors. Alternatively, we might design an experiment in which people work with someone who applies either a directive or a nondirective leadership style. When the data have been collected, we can use various procedures to statistically test our hypotheses.

A major concern in theory building is that some researchers might inadvertently find support for their theory simply because they use the same information used to form the theory during the inductive stage. Consequently, the deductive stage must collect new data that are completely independent of the data used during the inductive stage. For instance, you might decide to test your theory of directive leadership by studying employees in another organization. Moreover, the inductive process may have relied mainly on personal observation, whereas the deductive process might use survey questionnaires. By studying different samples and using different measurement tools, we minimize the risk of conducting circular research.

Using the Scientific Method

scientific method A set of principles and procedures that help researchers to systematically understand previously unexplained events and conditions.

Earlier, we said that the deductive stage of theory building follows the scientific method. The **scientific method** is a systematic, controlled, empirical, and critical investigation of hypothetical propositions about the presumed relationships among natural phenomena.[6] There are several elements to this definition, so let's look at each one. First, scientific research is *systematic and controlled,* because researchers want to rule out all but one explanation for a set of interrelated events. To rule out alternative explanations, we need to control them in some way, such as by keeping them constant or removing them entirely from the environment.

Second, we say that scientific research is *empirical* because researchers need to use objective reality—or as close as we can get to it—to test a theory. They measure observable elements of the environment, such as what a person says or does, rather than relying on their own subjective opinion to draw conclusions. Moreover, scientific research analyzes these data using acceptable principles of mathematics and logic.

Third, scientific research involves *critical investigation.* This means that the study's hypotheses, data, methods, and results are openly described so that other experts in the field can properly evaluate the research. It also means that scholars are encouraged to critique and build on previous research. The scientific method encourages the refinement and eventually the replacement of a particular theory with one that better suits our understanding of the world.

Grounded Theory: An Alternative Approach

grounded theory A process of developing knowledge through the constant interplay of data collection, analysis, and theory development.

The scientific method dominates the quantitative approach to systematic research, but another approach, called **grounded theory,** dominates research using qualitative methods.[7] Grounded theory is a process of developing knowledge through the constant interplay of data collection, analysis, and theory development. It relies mainly on qualitative methods to form categories and variables, analyze relationships among these concepts, and form a model based on the observations and analysis. Grounded theory combines the inductive stages of theory development by cycling back and forth between data collection and analysis to converge on a robust explanatory model. This ongoing reciprocal process results in theory that is grounded in the data (thus, the name grounded theory).

Like the scientific method, grounded theory is a systematic and rigorous process of data collection and analysis. It requires specific steps and documentation, and adopts a positivist view by assuming that the results are generalizable to other settings. However, grounded theory also takes an interpretivist view by building categories and variables from the perceived realities of the subjects rather than from an assumed universal truth.[8] It also recognizes that personal biases are not easily removed from the research process.

Selected Issues in Organizational Behaviour Research

There are many issues to consider in theory building, particularly when we use the deductive process to test hypotheses. Some of the more important issues are sampling, causation, and ethical practices in organizational research.

SAMPLING IN ORGANIZATIONAL RESEARCH

representative sampling The process of sampling a population in such a way that one can extrapolate the results of that sample to the larger population.

When finding out why things happen in organizations, we typically gather information from a few sources and then draw conclusions about the larger population. If we survey several employees and determine that older employees are more loyal to their company, then we would like to generalize this statement to all older employees in our population, not just those whom we surveyed. Scientific inquiry generally requires that researchers engage in **representative sampling**–that is, sampling a population in such a way that we can extrapolate the results of the sample to the larger population.

One factor that influences representativeness is whether the sample is selected in an unbiased way from the larger population. Let's suppose that you want to study organizational commitment among employees in your organization. A casual procedure might result in sampling too few employees from the head office and too many located elsewhere in the country. If head office employees actually have higher loyalty than employees located elsewhere, the biased sampling would cause the results to underestimate the true level of loyalty among employees in the company. If you repeat the process again next year but somehow overweight employees from the head office, the results might wrongly suggest that employees have increased their organizational commitment over the past year. In reality, the only change may be the direction of sampling bias.

How do we minimize sampling bias? The answer is to randomly select the sample. A randomly drawn sample gives each member of the population an equal probability of being chosen, so there is less likelihood that a subgroup within that population will dominate the study's results.

The same principle applies to random assignment of subjects to groups in experimental designs. If we want to test the effects of a team development training program, we need to randomly place some employees in the training group and randomly place others in a group that does not receive training. Without this random selection, each group might have different types of employees, so we wouldn't know whether the training explains the differences between the two groups. Moreover, if employees respond differently to the training program, we couldn't be sure that the training program results are representative of the larger population. Of course, random sampling does not necessarily produce a perfectly representative sample, but we do know that it is the best approach to ensure unbiased selection.

The other factor that influences representativeness is sample size. Whenever we select a portion of the population, there will be some error in our estimate of the population values. The larger the sample, the less error will occur in our estimate. Let's suppose that you want to find out how employees in a 500-person firm feel about viewing social media (e.g., Facebook) at work. If you asked 400 of those employees, the information would provide a very good estimate of how the entire workforce in that organization feels. If you survey only 100 employees, the estimate might deviate more from the true population. If you ask only 10 people, the estimate could be quite different from what all 500 employees feel.

Notice that sample size goes hand in hand with random selection. You must have a sufficiently large sample size for the principle of randomization to work effectively. In our example of attitudes towards social media, we would do a poor job of random selection if our sample consisted of only 10 employees from the 500-person organization. The reason is that these 10 people probably wouldn't capture the diversity of employees throughout the organization. In fact, the more diverse the population, the larger the sample size should be, to provide adequate representation through random selection.

CAUSATION IN ORGANIZATIONAL RESEARCH

Theories present notions about relationships among constructs. Often, these propositions suggest a causal relationship, namely, that one variable has an effect on another variable. When discussing causation, we refer to variables as being independent or dependent. *Independent variables* are the presumed causes of *dependent variables*, which are the presumed effects. In our earlier example of directive leadership, the main independent variable (there might be others) would be the supervisor's directive or nondirective leadership style, because we presume that it causes the dependent variable (satisfaction with supervision).

In laboratory experiments (described later), the independent variable is always manipulated by the experimenter. In our research on directive leadership, we might have subjects (new employees) work with supervisors who exhibit directive or nondirective leadership behaviours. If subjects are more satisfied under the directive leaders, we would be able to infer an association between the independent and dependent variables.

Researchers must satisfy three conditions to provide sufficient evidence of causality between two variables.[9] The first condition of causality is that the variables are empirically associated with each other. An association exists whenever one measure of a variable changes systematically with a measure of another variable. This condition of causality is the easiest to satisfy, because there are several well-known statistical measures of association. A research study might find, for instance, that heterogeneous groups (in which members come from diverse backgrounds) produce more creative solutions to problems. This might be apparent because the measure of creativity (such as number of creative solutions produced within a fixed time) is higher for teams that have a high score on the measure of group heterogeneity. They are statistically associated or correlated with each other.

The second condition of causality is that the independent variable precedes the dependent variable in time. Sometimes, this condition is satisfied through simple logic. In our group heterogeneity example, it doesn't make sense to say that the number of creative solutions caused the group's heterogeneity, because the group's heterogeneity existed before the group produced the creative solutions. In other situations, however, the temporal relationship among variables is less clear. One example is the ongoing debate about job satisfaction and organizational commitment. Do companies develop more loyal employees by increasing their job satisfaction, or do changes in organizational loyalty cause changes in job satisfaction? Simple logic does not answer these questions; instead, researchers must use sophisticated longitudinal studies to build up evidence of a temporal relationship between these two variables.

The third requirement for evidence of a causal relationship is that the statistical association between two variables cannot be explained by a third variable. There are many associations that we quickly dismiss as being causally related. For example, there is a statistical association between the number of storks in an area and the birth rate in that area. We know that storks don't bring babies, so something else must cause the association between these two variables. The real explanation is that both storks and birth rates have a higher incidence in rural areas.

In other studies, the third variable effect is less apparent. Many years ago, before polio vaccines were available, a study in the United States reported a surprisingly strong association between consumption of a certain soft drink and the incidence of polio. Was polio caused by drinking this pop, or did people with polio have a unusual craving for this beverage? Neither. Both polio and consumption of the pop drink were caused by a third variable: climate. There was a higher incidence of polio in the summer months and in warmer climates, and people drink more liquids in these climates.[10] As you can see from this example, researchers have a difficult time supporting causal inferences, because third variable effects are sometimes difficult to detect.

ETHICS IN ORGANIZATIONAL RESEARCH

Organizational behaviour researchers need to abide by the ethical standards of the society in which the research is conducted. One of the most important ethical considerations is the individual subject's freedom to participate in the study. For example, it is inappropriate to force employees to fill out a questionnaire or attend an experimental intervention for research purposes only. Moreover, researchers have an obligation to tell potential subjects about any possible risks inherent in the study so that participants can make an informed choice about whether to be involved.

Finally, researchers must be careful to protect the privacy of those who participate in the study. This usually includes letting people know when they are being studied as well as guaranteeing that their individual information will remain confidential (unless publication of identities is otherwise granted). Researchers maintain anonymity through careful security of data. The research results usually aggregate data in numbers large enough that they do not reveal the opinions or characteristics of any specific individual. For example, we would report the average absenteeism of employees in a department rather than state the absence rates of each person. When researchers are sharing data with other researchers, it is usually necessary to specially code each case so that individual identities are not known.

Research Design Strategies

So far, we have described how to build a theory, including the specific elements of empirically testing the theory within the standards of scientific inquiry. But what are the different ways to design a research study so that we get the data necessary to achieve our research objectives? There are many strategies, but they mainly fall under three headings: laboratory experiments, field surveys, and observational research.

LABORATORY EXPERIMENTS

laboratory experiment Any research study in which independent variables and variables outside the researcher's main focus of inquiry can be controlled to some extent.

A **laboratory experiment** is any research study in which independent variables and variables outside the researcher's main focus of inquiry can be controlled to some extent. Laboratory experiments are usually located outside the everyday work environment, such as in a classroom, simulation lab, or any other artificial setting in which the researcher can manipulate the environment. Organizational behaviour researchers sometimes conduct experiments in the workplace (called *field experiments*) in which the independent variable is manipulated. However, researchers have less control over the effects of extraneous factors in field experiments than they have in laboratory situations.

Advantages of Laboratory Experiments There are many advantages of laboratory experiments. By definition, this research method offers a high degree of control over extraneous variables that would otherwise confound the relationships being studied. Suppose we wanted to test the effects of directive leadership on the satisfaction of new employees. One concern might be that employees are influenced by how much leadership is provided, not just the type of leadership style. An experimental design would allow us to control how often the supervisor exhibited this style so that this extraneous variable does not confound the results.

A second advantage of lab studies is that the independent and dependent variables can be developed more precisely than is possible in a field setting. For example, the researcher can ensure that supervisors in a lab study apply specific directive or nondirective behaviours, whereas real-life supervisors would use a more complex mixture of leadership behaviours. By using more precise measures, we are more certain that we are measuring the intended construct. Thus, if new employees are more satisfied with supervisors in the directive leadership condition, we are more confident that the independent variable was directive leadership rather than some other leadership style.

A third benefit of laboratory experiments is that the independent variable can be distributed more evenly among participants. In our directive leadership study, we can ensure that approximately half of the subjects have a directive supervisor, whereas the other half have a nondirective supervisor. In natural settings, we might have trouble finding people who have worked with a nondirective leader and, consequently, we couldn't determine the effects of this condition.

Disadvantages of Laboratory Experiments With these powerful advantages, you might wonder why laboratory experiments are the least appreciated form of organizational behaviour research.[11] One obvious limitation of this research method is that it lacks realism, and thus the results might be different in the real world. One argument is that laboratory experiment subjects are less involved than their counterparts in an actual work situation. This is sometimes true, although many lab studies have highly motivated participants. Another criticism is that the extraneous variables controlled in the lab setting might produce a different effect of the independent variable on the dependent variables. This might also be true, but remember that the experimental design controls variables in accordance with the theory and its hypotheses. Consequently, this concern is really a critique of the theory, not the lab study.

Finally, there is the well-known problem that participants are aware they are being studied and this causes them to act differently than they normally would. Some participants try to figure out how the researcher wants them to behave and then deliberately try to act that way. Other participants try to upset the experiment by doing just the opposite of what they believe the researcher expects. Still others might act unnaturally simply because they know they are being observed. Fortunately, experimenters are well aware of these potential problems and are usually (although not always) successful at disguising the study's true intent.

FIELD SURVEYS

field surveys Research design strategies that involve collecting and analyzing information in a natural environment, such as an office, a factory, or other existing location.

Field surveys collect and analyze information in a natural environment–an office, a factory, or some other existing location. The researcher takes a snapshot of reality and tries to determine whether elements of that situation (including the attitudes and behaviours of people in that situation) are associated with each other as hypothesized. Everyone does some sort of field research. You might think that people from some provinces are better drivers than others, so you "test" your theory by looking at the way people with out-of-province licence plates drive. Although your methods of data collection might not satisfy scientific standards, this is a form of field research because it takes information from a naturally occurring situation.

Advantages and Disadvantages of Field Surveys One advantage of field surveys is that the variables often have a more powerful effect than they would in a laboratory experiment. Consider the effect of peer pressure on the behaviour of members within the team. In a natural environment, team members would form very strong cohesive bonds over time, whereas a researcher would have difficulty replicating this level of cohesiveness and corresponding peer pressure in a lab setting.

Another advantage of field surveys is that the researcher can study many variables simultaneously, thereby permitting a fuller test of more complex theories. Ironically, this is also a disadvantage of field surveys because it is difficult for the researcher to contain his or her scientific inquiry. There is a tendency to shift from deductive hypothesis testing to more inductive exploratory browsing through the data. If these two activities become mixed together, the researcher can lose sight of the strict covenants of scientific inquiry.

The main weakness with field surveys is that it is very difficult to satisfy the conditions for causal conclusions. One reason is that the data are usually collected at one point in time, so the researcher must rely on logic to decide whether the independent variable really preceded the dependent variable. Contrast this with the lab study in which the researcher can usually be confident that the independent variable was applied before the dependent variable occurred. Increasingly, organizational behaviour studies use longitudinal research to provide a better indicator of temporal relations among variables, but this is still not as precise as the lab setting. Another reason why causal analysis is difficult in field surveys is that extraneous variables are not controlled as they are in lab studies. Without this control, there is a higher chance that a third variable might explain the relationship between the hypothesized independent and dependent variables.

OBSERVATIONAL RESEARCH

In their study of brainstorming and creativity, Robert Sutton and Andrew Hargadon observed 24 brainstorming sessions at IDEO, a product design firm in Palo Alto, California. They also attended a dozen "Monday morning meetings," conducted 60 semi-structured interviews with IDEO executives and designers, held hundreds of informal discussions with these people, and read through several dozen magazine articles about the company.[12]

Sutton and Hargadon's use of observational research and other qualitative methods was quite appropriate for their research objectives, which was to re-examine the effectiveness of brainstorming beyond the number of ideas generated. Observational research generates a wealth of descriptive accounts about the drama of human existence in organizations. It is a useful vehicle for learning about the complex dynamics of people and their activities, such as brainstorming. (Sutton and Hargadon's study is cited in Chapter 8 on team dynamics.)

Participant observation takes the observation method one step further by having the observer take part in the organization's activities. This experience gives the researcher a fuller understanding of the activities compared to just watching others participate in those activities.

In spite of its intuitive appeal, observational research has a number of weaknesses. The main problem is that the observer is subject to the perceptual screening and organizing biases that we discuss in Chapter 3 of this textbook. There is a tendency to overlook the routine aspects of organizational life, even though they may prove to be the most important data for research purposes. Instead, observers tend to focus on unusual information, such as activities that deviate from what the observer expects. Because observational research usually records only what the observer notices, valuable information is often lost.

Another concern with the observation method is that the researcher's presence and involvement may influence the people whom he or she is studying. This can be a problem in short-term observations, but in the long term people tend to return to their usual behaviour patterns. With ongoing observations, such as Sutton and Hargadon's study of brainstorming sessions at IDEO, employees eventually forget that they are being studied.

Finally, observation is usually a qualitative process, so it is more difficult to empirically test hypotheses with the data. Instead, observational research provides rich information for the inductive stages of theory building. It helps us to form ideas about the way things work in organizations. We begin to see relationships that lay the foundation for new perspectives and theory. We must not confuse this inductive process of theory building with the deductive process of theory testing.

Appendix **B**

Scoring Keys for Self-Assessment Exercises

The following pages provide scoring keys for self-assessments that are fully presented in this textbook. These self-assessments, as well as the self-assessments that are only summarized in this book, can also be scored automatically at McGraw-Hill CONNECT.

CHAPTER 2

SCORING KEY FOR THE INTROVERSION-EXTRAVERSION SCALE

Scoring Instructions: Use the table below to assign numbers to each box you checked. For example, if you checked "Moderately inaccurate" for statement #1 ("I feel comfortable around people."), you would assign a "1" to that statement. After assigning numbers for all 10 statements, add up the numbers to estimate your introversion-extraversion personality.

For statement items 1, 2, 6, 8, 9:	For statement items 3, 4, 5, 7, 10:
Very accurate description of me = 4	Very accurate description of me = 0
Moderately accurate = 3	Moderately accurate = 1
Neither accurate nor inaccurate = 2	Neither accurate nor inaccurate = 2
Moderately inaccurate = 1	Moderately inaccurate = 3
Very inaccurate description of me = 0	Very inaccurate description of me = 4

Interpreting Your Score: Extraversion characterizes people who are outgoing, talkative, sociable, and assertive. It includes several facets, such as friendliness, gregariousness, assertiveness, activity level, excitement-seeking, and cheerfulness. The opposite of extraversion is introversion, which refers to the personality characteristics of being quiet, shy, and cautious. Extraverts get their energy from the outer world (people and things around them), whereas introverts get their energy from the internal world, such as personal reflection on concepts and ideas. Introverts are more inclined to direct their interests to ideas rather than to social events.

This is the short version of the IPIP Introversion-Extraversion Scale, so it estimates overall introversion-extraversion but not specific facets within the personality dimension. Scores range from 0 to 40. Low scores indicate introversion; high scores indicate extraversion. The norms in the following table are estimated from results of early adults (under 30 years old) in Scotland and undergraduate psychology students in the United States. However, introversion-extraversion norms vary from one group to the next; the best norms are likely based on the entire class you are attending or with past students in this course.

IPIP Introversion-Extraversion Norm	
IPIP Introversion-Extraversion	**Interpretation**
35–40	High extraversion
28–34	Moderate extraversion
21–27	In-between extraversion and introversion
7–20	Moderate Introversion
0–6	High Introversion

CHAPTER 3
SCORING KEY FOR THE WORK CENTRALITY SCALE

Scoring Instructions: Use the table below to assign numbers to each box you checked. For example, if you checked "Moderately disagree" for statement #3 ("Work should be only a small part of one's life."), you would assign a "5" to that statement. After assigning numbers for all six statements, add up your scores to estimate your level of work centrality.

For statement items 1, 2, 4, 5, 6:	For statement item 3:
Strongly agree = 6	Strongly agree = 1
Moderately agree = 5	Moderately agree = 2
Slightly agree = 4	Slightly agree = 3
Slightly disagree = 3	Slightly disagree = 4
Moderately disagree = 2	Moderately disagree = 5
Strongly disagree = 1	Strongly disagree = 6

Interpreting Your Score: The work centrality scale measures the extent that work is an important part of the individual's self-concept. People with high work centrality define themselves mainly by their work roles and view nonwork roles as much less significant. Consequently, people with a high work centrality score likely have lower complexity in their self-concept. This can be a concern because if something goes wrong with their work role, their nonwork roles are not of sufficient value to maintain a positive self-evaluation. At the same time, work dominates our work lives, so those with very low scores would be more of the exception than the rule in most societies.

Scores range from 6 to 36 with higher scores indicating higher work centrality. The norms in the following table are based on a large sample of Canadian employees (average score was 20.7). However, work centrality norms vary from one group to the next. For example, the average score in a sample of Canadian nurses was around 17 (translated to the scale range used here).

Work Centrality Norms	
Work Centrality Score	**Interpretation**
29–36	High work centrality
24–28	Above average work centrality
18–23	Average work centrality
13–17	Below average work centrality
6–12	Low work centrality

CHAPTER 4
SCORING KEY FOR THE EMOTIONAL INTELLIGENCE SELF-ASSESSMENT

Scoring Instructions: Use the table below to assign numbers to each box you checked. Insert the number for each statement on the appropriate line below the table. For example, if you checked "Moderately disagree" for statement #1 ("I tend to describe my emotions accurately."), you would write a "2" on the line with "(1)" underneath it. After assigning numbers for all 16 statements, add up your scores to estimate your self-assessed emotional intelligence on the four dimensions and overall score.

For statement items 1, 2, 3, 4, 6, 7, 9, 10, 11, 13, 14, 16:	**For statement items 5, 8, 12, 15:**
Strongly agree = 6	Strongly agree = 1
Moderately agree = 5	Moderately agree = 2
Slightly agree = 4	Slightly agree = 3
Slightly disagree = 3	Slightly disagree = 4
Moderately disagree = 2	Moderately disagree = 5
Strongly disagree = 1	Strongly disagree = 6

Emotional Intelligence Dimension	**Calculation**	**Your Score**
Self-awareness of emotions	____ + ____ + ____ + ____ = (1) (7) (9) (12)	____________
Self-management of emotions	____ + ____ + ____ + ____ = (2) (5) (10) (14)	____________
Awareness of others' emotions	____ + ____ + ____ + ____ = (3) (6) (13) (15)	____________
Management of others' emotions	____ + ____ + ____ + ____ = (4) (8) (11) (16)	____________
Emotional intelligence total	Add up all dimension scores 5	____________

Interpreting Your Scores: This scale measures the four dimensions of emotional intelligence described in this book. The four dimensions are defined as follows:

- **Self-awareness of emotions:** This is the ability to perceive and understand the meaning of your own emotions.
- **Self-management of emotions:** This is the ability to manage your own emotions. It includes generating or suppressing emotions and displaying behaviours that represent desired emotions in a particular situation.
- **Awareness of others' emotions:** This is the ability to perceive and understand the emotions of other people, including the practices of empathy and awareness of social phenomena such as organizational politics.
- **Management of others' emotions:** This is the ability to manage other people's emotions. It includes generating or suppressing emotions in other people, such as reducing their sadness and increasing their motivation.

Scores on the four Emotional Intelligence Self-Assessment dimensions range from 4 to 20. The overall score ranges from 16 to 80. Norms vary from one group to the next. The following table shows norms from a sample of 75 MBA students in two countries (Australia and Singapore). For example, the top 10 percentile for Self-awareness of emotions is 19, indicating that 10 percent of people score 19 or 20 and 90 percent score below 19 on this dimension. Keep in mind that these scores represent self-perceptions. Evaluations from others (such as through 360-degree feedback) may provide a more accurate estimate of your emotional intelligence on some (not necessarily all) dimensions.

Emotional Intelligence Self-Assessment Norms

Percentile	Self-awareness of emotions	Self-management of emotions	Awareness of others' emotions	Management of others' emotions	TOTAL
Average score	16.3	14.9	14.3	14.6	60.2
Top 10 percentile	19	19	18	18	71
Top 25th percentile	18	17	16	17	64
Median (50th percentile)	16	15	15	15	60
Bottom 25th percentile	15	13	13	13	56
Bottom 10 percentile	14	11	11	10	51

CHAPTER 5
SCORING KEY FOR THE PERSONAL NEEDS QUESTIONNAIRE

Scoring Instructions: Use the table below to assign numbers to each box you checked. Insert the number for each statement on the appropriate line below the table. For example, if you checked "Moderately inaccurate" for statement #1 ("I would rather be myself than be well thought of."), you would write a "3" on the line with "(1)" underneath it. After assigning numbers for all 15 statements, add up your scores to estimate your results for the two learned needs measured by this scale.

For statement items 2, 3, 4, 5, 6, 8, 9, 12, 14, 15:	For statement items 1, 7, 10, 11, 13:
Very accurate description of me = 4	Very accurate description of me = 0
Moderately accurate = 3	Moderately accurate = 1
Neither accurate nor inaccurate = 2	Neither accurate nor inaccurate = 2
Moderately inaccurate =1	Moderately inaccurate = 3
Very inaccurate description of me = 0	Very inaccurate description of me = 4

Personal Needs Dimension	Calculation	Your Score
Need for achievement	____ + ____ + ____ + ____ + ____ + ____ + ____ = (2) (3) (6) (7) (9) (12) (14)	________
Need for social approval	____ + ____ + ____ + ____ + ____ + ____ + ____ + ____ = (1) (4) (5) (8) (10) (11) (13) (15)	________

Although everyone has the same innate drives, our secondary or learned needs vary based on our personality, values, and self-concept. This self-assessment provides an estimate of your need strength on two learned needs: need for achievement and need for social approval.

Interpreting Your Need for Achievement Score: This scale, formally called "achievement striving," estimates the extent to which you are motivated to take on and achieve challenging personal goals. This includes a desire to perform better than others and to reach one's potential. The scale ranges from 0 to 28. How high or low is your need for achievement? The ideal would be to compare your score with the collective results of other students in your class. Otherwise, the following table offers a rough set of norms with which you can compare your score on this scale.

Need for Achievement Norms	
Need for Achievement Score	**Interpretation**
24–28	High need for achievement
18–23	Above average need for achievement
12–17	Average need for achievement
6–11	Below average need for achievement
0–5	Low need for achievement

Interpreting Your Need for Social Approval Score: The need for social approval scale estimates the extent to which you are motivated to seek favourable evaluation from others. Founded on the drive to bond, the need for social approval is a secondary need, because people vary in this need based on their self-concept, values, personality, and possibly social norms. This scale ranges from 0 to 32. How high or low is your need for social approval? The ideal would be to compare your score with the collective results of other students in your class. Otherwise, the following table offers a rough set of norms on which you can compare your score on this scale.

Need for Social Approval Norms	
Need for Social Approval Score	**Interpretation**
28–32	High need for social approval
20–27	Above average need for social approval
12–19	Average need for social approval
6–11	Below average need for social approval
0–5	Low need for social approval

CHAPTER 6
SCORING KEY FOR THE MONEY ATTITUDE SCALE

Scoring Instructions: This instrument presents three dimensions using a smaller number of items from the original Money Attitude Scale. To calculate your score on each dimension, write the number that you circled in the scale to the corresponding item number in the scoring key below. For example, write the number you circled for the scale's first statement ("I sometimes purchase things . . .") on the line above "Item 1." Then add up the numbers for that dimension. The money attitude total score is calculated by adding up all scores and all dimensions.

Money Attitude Dimension	**Calculation**	**Your Score**
Money as power/prestige	___ + ___ + ___ + ___ = (1) (4) (7) (10)	________
Retention time	___ + ___ + ___ + ___ = (2) (5) (8) (11)	________
Money anxiety	___ + ___ + ___ + ___ = (3) (6) (9) (12)	________
Total score	Add up all dimension scores =	________

Interpreting Your Score: The three Money Attitude Scale dimensions measured here, as well as the total score, are defined as follows:

- **Money as power/prestige:** People with higher scores on this dimension tend to use money to influence and impress others.
- **Retention time:** People with higher scores on this dimension tend to be careful financial planners.
- **Money anxiety:** People with higher scores on this dimension tend to view money as a source of anxiety.
- **Money attitude total:** This is a general estimate of how much respect and attention you give to money.

Scores on the three Money Attitude Scale dimensions range from 4 to 20. The overall score ranges from 12 to 60. Norms vary from one group to the next. The following table shows how a sample of MBA students scored on the Money Attitude Scale. The table shows percentiles, that is, the percentage of people with the same or lower score. For example, the table indicates that a score of "13" on the retention scale is quite low because only 25 percent of students would have scored at this level or lower (75 percent scored higher). However, a score of

"12" on the prestige scale is quite high because 75 percent of students score at or below this number (only 25 percent scored higher).

Percentile (% with scores at or below this number)	Prestige Score	Retention Score	Anxiety Score	Total Score
Average score	9.89	14.98	12.78	37.64
Top 10 percentile	13	18	16	44
Top 25th percentile	12	17	15	41
Median (50th percentile)	10	15	13	38
Bottom 25th percentile	8	13	11	33
Bottom 10 percentile	7	11	8	29

CHAPTER 7
SCORING KEY FOR THE CREATIVE PERSONALITY SCALE

Scoring Instructions: Assign a positive point (+1) after each of the following words that you checked off in the self-assessment:

Capable _______	Informal _______	Resourceful _______
Clever _______	Insightful _______	Self-confident _______
Confident _______	Intelligent _______	Sexy _______
Egotistical _______	Inventive _______	Snobbish _______
Humorous _______	Original _______	Unconventional _______
Individualistic _______	Reflective _______	Wide interests _______

Assign a negative point (−1) after each of the following words that you checked off in the self-assessment:

Affected _______	Conventional _______	Narrow interests _______
Cautious _______	Dissatisfied _______	Sincere _______
Commonplace _______	Honest _______	Submissive _______
Conservative _______	Mannerly _______	Suspicious _______

Interpreting Your Score: This instrument estimates your creative potential as a personal characteristic. The scale recognizes that creative people are intelligent and persistent and possess an inventive thinking style. Creative personality varies somewhat from one occupational group to the next. The table below provides norms based on undergraduate and graduate university/college students.

Creative Personality Score	Interpretation
Above +9	You have a high creative personality.
+1 to +9	You have an average creative personality.
Below +1	You have a low creative personality.

CHAPTER 8
SCORING KEY FOR THE TEAM ROLES PREFERENCES SCALE

Scoring Instructions: Write the scores circled for each item on the appropriate line below (statement numbers are in parentheses), and add up each scale.

Team Roles Dimension	Calculation	Your Score
Encourager	____ + ____ + ____ = (6) (9) (11)	__________
Gatekeeper	____ + ____ + ____ = (4) (10) (13)	__________
Harmonizer	____ + ____ + ____ = (3) (8) (12)	__________
Initiator	____ + ____ + ____ = (1) (5) (14)	__________
Summarizer	____ + ____ + ____ = (2) (7) (15)	__________

Interpreting Your Score: The five team roles measured here are based on scholarship over the years. The following table defines these five roles and presents the range of scores for high, medium, and low levels of each role. These norms are based on results from a sample of MBA students.

Team Roles Preferences Definitions and Norms	
Team Role and Definition	**Interpretation**
Encourager: People who score high on this dimension have a strong tendency to praise and support the ideas of other team members, thereby showing warmth and solidarity to the group.	High: 12 and above Medium: 9 to 11 Low: 8 and below
Gatekeeper: People who score high on this dimension have a strong tendency to encourage all team members to participate in the discussion.	High: 12 and above Medium: 9 to 11 Low: 8 and below
Harmonizer: People who score high on this dimension have a strong tendency to mediate intragroup conflicts and reduce tension.	High: 11 and above Medium: 9 to 10 Low: 8 and below
Initiator: People who score high on this dimension have a strong tendency to identify goals for the meeting, including ways to work on those goals.	High: 12 and above Medium: 9 to 11 Low: 8 and below
Summarizer: People who score high on this dimension have a strong tendency to keep track of what was said in the meeting (i.e., act as the team's memory).	High: 10 and above Medium: 8 to 9 Low: 7 and below

CHAPTER 9

SCORING KEY FOR THE ACTIVE LISTENING SKILLS INVENTORY

Scoring Instructions: Use the first table below to score the response you marked for each statement. Then, in the second table on the next page, write that score on the line corresponding to the statement number (statement numbers are in parentheses) and add up each subscale. For example, if you checked "Seldom" for statement #1 ("I keep an open mind . . ."), you would write a "2" on the line with "(1)" underneath it. Calculate the overall Active Listening Inventory score by summing all subscales.

For statement items 4, 7, 11:	For statement items 1, 2, 3, 5, 6, 8, 9, 10, 12:
Rarely/never = 5	Rarely/never = 1
Seldom = 4	Seldom = 2
Sometimes = 3	Sometimes = 3
Often = 2	Often = 4
Almost always = 1	Almost always = 5

Active Listening Dimension	Calculation	Your Score
Sensing	___ + ___ + ___ + ___ = (1) (4) (7) (10)	________
Evaluating	___ + ___ + ___ + ___ = (2) (5) (8) (11)	________
Responding	___ + ___ + ___ + ___ = (3) (6) (9) (12)	________
Active listening total	Add up all dimension scores =	________

Interpreting Your Score: The three active listening dimensions are defined below.

- **Sensing:** Sensing is the process of receiving signals from the sender and paying attention to them. Active listeners improve sensing in three ways. They postpone evaluation by not forming an opinion until the speaker has finished, avoid interrupting the speaker's conversation, and remain motivated to listen to the speaker.
- **Evaluating:** This dimension of active listening includes understanding the message meaning, evaluating the message, and remembering the message. To improve their evaluation of the conversation, active listeners empathize with the speaker–they try to understand and be sensitive to the speaker's feelings, thoughts, and situation. Evaluation also improves by organizing the speaker's ideas during the communication episode.
- **Responding:** Responding, the third dimension of active listening, is feedback to the sender, which motivates and directs the speaker's communication. Active listeners show interest through nonverbal cues (eye contact, nodding, symbiotic facial expression) and by sending back channel signals (e.g., "I see"). They also clarify the message, such as by summarizing or rephrasing the speaker's ideas at appropriate breaks ("So you're saying that . . . ?").

Scores on the three Active Listening dimensions range from 4 to 20. The overall score ranges from 12 to 60. Norms vary from one group to the next. The following table shows norms from a sample of 70 MBA students in two countries (Australia and Singapore). For example, the top 10 percentile for Sensing is 17, indicating that 10 percent of people score 17 or above and 90 percent score below 17 on this dimension. Keep in mind that these scores represent self-perceptions. Evaluations from others (such as through 360-degree feedback) may provide a more accurate estimate of your active listening on one or more dimensions, particularly the responding dimension which is visible to others.

Active Listening Norms

Percentile (% with scores at or below this number)	Sensing Score	Evaluating Score	Responding Score	Total Score
Average score	14.5	14.4	16.7	45.6
Top 10 percentile	17	17	19	53
Top 25th percentile	15	16	18	48
Median (50th percentile)	15	14	17	45
Bottom 25th percentile	13	13	16	43
Bottom 10 percentile	11	12	14	39

CHAPTER 10
SCORING KEY FOR THE COWORKER INFLUENCE SCALE

Scoring Instructions: To calculate your scores on the Coworker Influence Scale, write the number circled for each statement on the appropriate line below (statement numbers are in parentheses), and add up each scale.

Team Roles Dimension	Calculation	Your Score
Persuasion	___ + ___ + ___ = (1) (9) (17)	________
Silent authority	___ + ___ + ___ = (2) (10) (18)	________
Exchange	___ + ___ + ___ = (3) (11) (19)	________
Assertiveness	___ + ___ + ___ = (4) (12) (20)	________
Information control	___ + ___ + ___ = (5) (13) (21)	________
Coalition formation	___ + ___ + ___ = (6) (14) (22)	________
Upward appeal	___ + ___ + ___ = (7) (15) (23)	________
Ingratiation	___ + ___ + ___ = (8) (16) (24)	________

Interpreting Your Score: Influence refers to any behaviour that attempts to alter someone's attitudes or behaviour. There are several types of influence, including the eight measured by this instrument. This instrument assesses your preference for using each type of influence on coworkers and other people at a similar level as your position in the organization.

- **Persuasion:** Persuasion refers to using logical and emotional appeals to change others' attitudes. This is one of the most widely used influence strategies towards others in any position (e.g., coworkers, bosses, subordinates).
- **Silent authority:** The silent application of authority occurs when someone complies with a request because the target person is aware of the requester's legitimate or expert power. This influence tactic is very subtle, such as making the target person aware of the status or expertise of the person making the request.
- **Exchange:** Exchange involves the promise of benefits or resources in exchange for the target person's compliance with your request. This tactic also includes reminding the target of past benefits or favours with the expectation that the target will now make up for that debt. Negotiation is also part of the exchange strategy.
- **Assertiveness:** Assertiveness involves actively applying legitimate and coercive power to influence others. This tactic includes demanding that the other person comply with your wishes, showing frustration or impatience with the other person, and using threats of sanctions to force compliance.
- **Information control:** Information control involves explicitly manipulating others' access to information for the purpose of changing their attitudes and/or behaviour. It includes screening out information that might oppose your preference and embellishing or highlighting information that supports your position. According to one survey, more than half of employees believe their coworkers engage in this tactic.
- **Coalition formation:** Coalition formation occurs when a group of people with common interests band together to influence others. It also exists as a perception, such as when you convince someone else that several people are on your side and support your position.
- **Upward appeal:** Upward appeal occurs when you rely on support from people higher up the organizational hierarchy. This support may be real (senior management shows support) or logically argued (you explain how your position is consistent with company policy).
- **Ingratiation:** Ingratiation is a special case of impression management in which you attempt to increase the perception of liking or similarity to another person in the hope that they will become more supportive of your ideas. Flattering the coworker, becoming friendlier with the coworker, helping the coworker (with expectation of reciprocity), showing support for the coworker's ideas, and asking for the coworker's advice are all examples of ingratiation.

Scores on the eight Coworker Influence Scale dimensions range from 3 to 15. Higher scores indicate that the person has a higher preference for and use of that particular tactic. Norms vary from one group to the next. The following table shows norms from a sample of 70 MBA students in two countries (Australia and Singapore). For example, the top 10 percentile for Assertiveness is 9, indicating that 10 percent of people score 9 or above and 90 percent score below 9 on this dimension. Keep in mind that these scores represent self-perceptions. Evaluations from others (such as through 360-degree feedback) may provide a more accurate estimate of your preferred influence tactics.

Coworker Influence Scale Norms

Percentile	Persuasion	Silent authority	Exchange	Assertiveness
Average score	12.6	10.0	7.3	5.4
Top 10 percentile	15	13	10	9
Top 25th percentile	14	12	9	6
Median (50th percentile)	13	10	8	5
Bottom 25th percentile	12	9	6	4
Bottom 10 percentile	10	7	4	3

Coworker Influence Scale Norms (cont'd)				
Percentile	**Information control**	**Coalition formation**	**Upward appeal**	**Ingratiation**
Average score	6.8	7.4	8.1	8.9
Top 10 percentile	10	10	11	13
Top 25th percentile	9	9	10	12
Median (50th percentile)	7	8	8	10
Bottom 25th percentile	5	6	6	7
Bottom 10 percentile	4	4	5	4

CHAPTER 11
SCORING KEY FOR THE CONFLICT HANDLING SCALE

Scoring Instructions: To estimate your preferred conflict handling styles, use the first table below to score the response you marked for each statement. Then, in the second table below, write that score on the line corresponding to the statement number (statement numbers are in parentheses) and add up each subscale. For example, if you checked "Seldom" for statement #1 ("I went along with the other . . ."), you would write a "2" on the line with "(1)" underneath it.

For ALL statement items:
Rarely/never = 1
Seldom = 2
Sometimes = 3
Often = 4
Almost always = 5

Conflict Handling Dimension	**Calculation**	**Your Score**
Problem solving	___ + ___ + ___ + ___ = (3) (9) (13) (18)	________
Forcing	___ + ___ + ___ + ___ = (5) (8) (12) (15)	________
Avoiding	___ + ___ + ___ + ___ = (4) (6) (14) (19)	________
Yielding	___ + ___ + ___ + ___ = (1) (7) (16) (20)	________
Compromising	___ + ___ + ___ + ___ = (2) (10) (11) (17)	________

Interpreting Your Score: This instrument measures your preference for and use of the five conflict handling dimensions:

- **Problem solving:** Problem solving tries to find a mutually beneficial solution for both parties. Information sharing is an important feature of this style because both parties need to identify common ground and potential solutions that satisfy both (or all) of them.
- **Forcing:** Forcing tries to win the conflict at the other's expense. It includes "hard" influence tactics, particularly assertiveness, to get one's own way.
- **Avoiding:** Avoiding tries to smooth over or avoid conflict situations altogether. It represents a low concern for both self and the other party. In other words, avoiders try to suppress thinking about the conflict.
- **Yielding:** Yielding involves giving in completely to the other side's wishes, or at least cooperating with little or no attention to your own interests. This style involves making unilateral concessions, unconditional promises, and offering help with no expectation of reciprocal help.
- **Compromising:** Compromising involves looking for a position in which your losses are offset by equally valued gains. It involves matching the other party's concessions, making conditional promises or threats, and actively searching for a middle ground between the interests of the two parties.

Scores on the five Conflict Handling Scale dimensions range from 4 to 20. Higher scores indicate that the person has a higher preference for and use of that particular conflict handling style. Norms vary from one group to the next. The following table shows norms from a sample of 70 MBA students in two countries (Australia and Singapore). For example, the top 10 percentile for Yielding is 14, indicating that 10 percent of people score 14 or above and 90 percent score below 14 on this dimension. Keep in mind that these scores represent self-perceptions. Evaluations from others (such as through 360-degree feedback) may provide a more accurate estimate of your preferred conflict handling style.

Conflict Handling Scale Norms

Percentile	Problem solving	Forcing	Avoiding	Yielding	Compromising
Average score	15.9	13.5	10.2	11.0	13.8
Top 10 percentile	19	17	14	14	17
Top 25th percentile	17	15	12	12	16
Median (50th percentile)	16	13	10	11	14
Bottom 25th percentile	15	12	8	10	12
Bottom 10 percentile	13	10	6	8	10

CHAPTER 12
SCORING KEY FOR THE ROMANCE OF LEADERSHIP SCALE

Scoring Instructions: Use the table below to score the response you marked for each statement. Then, add up the scores to calculate your Romance of Leadership score. For example, if you marked "Disagree" for statement #1 ("Even in an economic . . ."), you would write a "2" on the line with "(1)" underneath it.

For statement items 3, 5, 7, 9:	**For statement items 1, 2, 4, 6, 8, 10:**
Strongly disagree = 5	Strongly disagree = 1
Disagree = 4	Disagree = 2
Neutral = 3	Neutral = 3
Agree = 2	Agree = 4
Strongly agree = 1	Strongly agree = 5

Total Score: ____ + ____ + ____ + ____ + ____ + ____ + ____ + ____ + ____ + ____ = ____
(1) (2) (3) (4) (5) (6) (7) (8) (9) (10)

Interpreting Your Score: Romance of leadership is a phenomenon in which followers (and possibly other stakeholders) want to believe that leaders make a difference in the organization's success. People with a high romance of leadership score attribute the causes of organizational events much more to its leaders and much less to the economy, competition, and other factors beyond the leader's short-term control. This ranges from 10 to 50, with higher scores indicating that the person has a higher romance of leadership. The following norms are derived from a large sample of European employees with an average age in the mid 30s and work experience averaging about 15 years. However, these norms should be viewed with caution because the romance of leadership scale is a recent development and norms for any instrument can vary from one group to the next.

Romance of Leadership Norms	
Romance of Leadership Score	**Interpretation**
38–50	Above average romance of leadership
27–37	Average romance of leadership
10–26	Below average romance of leadership

CHAPTER 13
SCORING KEY FOR ORGANIZATIONAL STRUCTURE PREFERENCE SCALE

Scoring Instructions: Use the table below to assign numbers to each response you marked. Insert the number for each statement on the appropriate line below the table. For example, if you checked "Not at all" for item #1 ("A person's career ladder . . ."), you would write a "0" on the line with "(1)" underneath it. After assigning numbers for all 15 statements, add up the scores to estimate your degree of preference for a tall hierarchy, formalization, and centralization. Then calculate the overall score by summing all scales.

For statement items 2, 3, 8, 10, 11, 12, 14, 15	**For statement items 1, 4, 5, 6, 7, 9, 13**
Not at all = 3	Not at all = 0
A little = 2	A little = 1
Somewhat = 1	Somewhat = 2
Very much = 0	Very much = 3

Conflict Handling Dimension	Calculation	Your Score
Tall Hierarchy (H)	___ + ___ + ___ + ___ + ___ = (1) (4) (10) (12) (15)	______ (H)
Formalization (F)	___ + ___ + ___ + ___ + ___ = (2) (6) (8) (11) (13)	______ (F)
Centralization (C)	___ + ___ + ___ + ___ + ___ = (3) (5) (7) (9) (14)	______ (C)
Total score (Mechanistic)	Add up all dimension scores (H + F + C) =	______ (Total)

Interpreting Your Score: The three organizational structure dimensions and the overall score are defined below, along with the range of scores for high, medium, and low levels of each dimension based on a sample of MBA students:

Organizational Structure Preference Subscale Definitions and Norms	
Organizational Structure Preference Subscale Definition	**Interpretation**
Tall hierarchy: People with high scores on this dimension prefer to work in organizations with several levels of hierarchy and a narrow span of control (few employees per supervisor).	High: 11 to 15 Medium: 6 to 10 Low: Below 6
Formalization: People with high scores on this dimension prefer to work in organizations where jobs are clearly defined with limited discretion.	High: 12 to 15 Medium: 9 to 11 Low: Below 9
Centralization: People with high scores on this dimension prefer to work in organizations where decision making occurs mainly among top management rather than spread out to lower level staff.	High: 10 to 15 Medium: 7 to 9 Low: Below 7
Total Score (Mechanistic): People with high scores on this dimension prefer to work in mechanistic organizations, whereas those with low scores prefer to work in organic organizational structures. Mechanistic structures are characterized by a narrow span of control and high degree of formalization and centralization. Organic structures have a wide span of control, little formalization, and decentralized decision making.	High: 30 to 45 Medium: 22 to 29 Low: Below 22

CHAPTER 14
SCORING KEY FOR THE CORPORATE CULTURE PREFERENCE SCALE

Scoring Instructions: On each line below, write in a "1" if you circled the statement and a "0" if you did not. Then add up the scores for each subscale.

Control culture	___ +	___ +	___ +	___ +	___ +	___ =	______
	(2a)	(5a)	(6b)	(8b)	(11b)	(12a)	
Performance culture	___ +	___ +	___ +	___ +	___ +	___ =	______
	(1b)	(3b)	(5b)	(6a)	(7a)	(9b)	
Relationship culture	___ +	___ +	___ +	___ +	___ +	___ =	______
	(1a)	(3a)	(4b)	(8a)	(10b)	(12b)	
Responsive culture	___ +	___ +	___ +	___ +	___ +	___ =	______
	(2b)	(4a)	(7b)	(9a)	(10a)	(11a)	

Interpreting Your Score: These corporate cultures may be found in many organizations, but they represent only four of many possible organizational cultures. Also, keep in mind none of these cultures is inherently good or bad. Each is effective in different situations. The four corporate cultures are defined below, along with the range of scores for high, medium, and low levels of each dimension based on a sample of MBA students:

Corporate Culture Preference Subscale Definitions and Norms	
Corporate Culture Dimension and Definition	**Score Interpretation**
Control culture: This culture values the role of senior executives to lead the organization. Its goal is to keep everyone aligned and under control.	High: 3 to 6 Medium: 1 to 2 Low: 0
Performance culture: This culture values individual and organizational performance and strives for effectiveness and efficiency.	High: 5 to 6 Medium: 3 to 4 Low: 0 to 2
Relationship culture: This culture values nurturing and well-being. It considers open communication, fairness, teamwork, and sharing a vital part of organizational life.	High: 6 Medium: 4 to 5 Low: 0 to 3
Responsive culture: This culture values its ability to keep in tune with the external environment, including being competitive and realizing new opportunities.	High: 6 Medium: 4 to 5 Low: 0 to 3

CHAPTER 15
SCORING KEY FOR THE TOLERANCE OF CHANGE SCALE

Scoring Instructions: Use the table below to assign numbers to each box you checked. For example, if you checked "Moderately disagree" for statement #1 ("I generally prefer the unexpected . . ."), you would write a "2" beside that statement. After assigning numbers for all 10 statements, add up your scores to estimate your tolerance for change.

For statement items 1, 3, 7, 8, 10:	**For statement items 2, 4, 5, 6, 9 :**
Strongly agree = 7	Strongly agree = 1
Moderately agree = 6	Moderately agree = 2
Slightly agree = 5	Slightly agree = 3
Neutral = 4	Neutral = 4
Slightly disagree = 3	Slightly disagree = 5
Moderately disagree = 2	Moderately disagree = 6
Strongly disagree = 1	Strongly disagree = 7

Interpreting Your Score: This instrument is formally known as the "tolerance of ambiguity" scale. The original scale, developed 50 years ago, has since been revised and adapted. The instrument presented here is an adaptation of these revised instruments. People with a high tolerance of ambiguity are comfortable with uncertainty and new situations. These are characteristics of the hyperfast changes occurring in many organizations today. This instrument ranges from 10 to 70, with higher scores indicating a higher tolerance for change (i.e., higher tolerance for ambiguity). The table below indicates the range of scores for high, medium, and low tolerance for change. These norms are estimates from recent studies using some or all of these items.

Tolerance for Change Score	Interpretation
50–70	You seem to have a high tolerance for change.
30–49	You seem to have a moderate level of tolerance for change.
10–29	You seem to have a low degree of tolerance for change. Instead, you prefer stable work environments.

Glossary

The number following each definition indicates the chapter in which the term receives the fullest description.

A

ability The natural aptitudes and learned capabilities required to successfully complete a task. (2)

achievement-nurturing orientation A cross-cultural value describing the degree to which people in a culture emphasize competitive versus cooperative relations with other people. (2)

action research A problem-focused change process that combines action orientation (changing attitudes and behaviour) and research orientation (testing theory through data collection and analysis). (15)

adaptive culture An organizational culture in which employees are receptive to change, including the ongoing alignment of the organization to its environment and continuous improvement of internal processes. (14)

affective organizational commitment An individual's emotional attachment to, involvement in, and identification with an organization. (4)

anchoring and adjustment heuristic A natural tendency for people to be influenced by an initial anchor point such that they do not sufficiently move away from that point as new information is provided. (7)

appreciative inquiry An organizational change strategy that directs the group's attention away from its own problems and focuses participants on the group's potential and positive elements. (15)

artifacts The observable symbols and signs of an organization's culture. (14)

attitudes The cluster of beliefs, assessed feelings, and behavioural intentions towards a person, object, or event (called an *attitude object*). (4)

attraction-selection-attrition (ASA) theory A theory which states that organizations have a natural tendency to attract, select, and retain people with values and personality characteristics that are consistent with the organization's character, resulting in a more homogeneous organization and a stronger culture. (14)

attribution process The perceptual process of deciding whether an observed behaviour or event is caused largely by internal or external factors. (3)

authentic leadership The view that effective leaders need to be aware of, feel comfortable with, and act consistently with their values, personality, and self-concept. (12)

autonomy The degree to which a job gives employees the freedom, independence, and discretion to schedule their work and to determine the procedures used in completing it. (6)

availability heuristic A natural tendency to assign higher probabilities to objects or events that are easier to recall from memory, even though ease of recall is also affected by nonprobability factors (e.g., emotional response, recent events). (7)

B

balanced scorecard (BSC) A goal-setting and reward system that translates the organization's vision and mission into specific, measurable performance goals related to financial, customer, internal, and learning/growth (i.e., human capital) processes. (5)

best alternative to a negotiated agreement (BATNA) The best outcome you might achieve through some other course of action if you abandon the current negotiation. (11)

bicultural audit A process of diagnosing cultural relations between the companies and determining the extent to which cultural clashes will likely occur. (14)

bounded rationality The view that people are bounded in their decision-making capabilities, including access to limited information, limited information processing, and tendency towards satisficing rather than maximizing when making choices. (7)

brainstorming A freewheeling, face-to-face meeting where team members aren't allowed to criticize, but are encouraged to speak freely, generate as many ideas as possible, and build on the ideas of others. (8)

brainwriting A variation of brainstorming whereby participants write (rather than speak about) and share their ideas. (8)

Brooks's law The principle that adding more people to a late software project only makes it later. (8)

C

categorical thinking Organizing people and objects into preconceived categories that are stored in our long-term memory. (3)

centrality A contingency of power pertaining to the degree and nature of interdependence between the powerholder and others. (10)

centralization The degree to which formal decision-making authority is held by a small group of people, typically those at the top of the organizational hierarchy. (13)

ceremonies Planned displays of organizational culture, conducted specifically for the benefit of an audience. (14)

charisma A personal characteristic or special "gift" that serves as a form of interpersonal attraction and referent power over others. (10)

coalition A group that attempts to influence people outside the group by pooling the resources and power of its members. (10)

cognitive dissonance An emotional experience caused by a perception that our beliefs, feelings, and behaviour are incongruent with each other. (4)

collectivism A cross-cultural value describing the degree to which people in a culture emphasize duty to groups to which they belong, and to group harmony. (2)

communication The process by which information is transmitted and *understood* between two or more people. (9)

confirmation bias The process of screening out information that is contrary to our values and assumptions and to more readily accept confirming information. (3)

conflict The process in which one party perceives that its interests are being opposed or negatively affected by another party. (11)

conscientiousness A personality dimension describing people who are organized, dependable, goal-focused, thorough, disciplined, methodical, and industrious. (2)

constructs Abstract ideas constructed by researchers that can be linked to observable information. (Appendix A)

contact hypothesis A theory stating that the more we interact with someone, the less prejudiced or perceptually biased we will be against that person (3)

continuance commitment An individual's calculative attachment to an organization. (4)

corporate social responsibility (CSR) Organizational activities intended to benefit society and the environment beyond the firm's immediate financial interests or legal obligations. (1)

counterproductive work behaviours (CWBs) Voluntary behaviours that have the potential to directly or indirectly harm the organization. (2)

countervailing power The capacity of a person, team, or organization to keep a more powerful person or group in the exchange relationship. (10)

creativity The development of original ideas that make a socially recognized contribution. (7)

D

decision making The conscious process of making choices among alternatives with the intention of moving towards some desired state of affairs. (7)

deep-level diversity Differences in the psychological characteristics of employees, including personalities, beliefs, values, and attitudes. (1)

distributive justice Perceived fairness in the individual's ratio of outcomes to contributions to contributions relative to a comparison of other's ratio of outcomes to contributions. (5)

distributive situation When the goals of two or more people are zero-sum so that one can gain only at the other's expense. (11)

divergent thinking Reframing a problem in a unique way and generating different approaches to the issue. (7)

divisional structure An organizational structure in which employees are organized around geographic areas, outputs (products or services), or clients. (13)

drives Hardwired characteristics of the brain that correct deficiencies or maintain an internal equilibrium by producing emotions to energize individuals. (5)

E

electronic brainstorming A form of brainstorming that relies on networked computers for submitting and sharing creative ideas. (8)

emotional contagion The nonconscious process of "catching" or sharing another person's emotions by mimicking that person's facial expressions and other nonverbal behaviour. (9)

emotional dissonance The psychological tension experienced when the emotions people are required to display are quite different from the emotions they actually experience at that moment. (4)

emotional intelligence (EI) A set of abilities to perceive and express emotion, assimilate emotion in thought, understand and reason with emotion, and regulate emotion in oneself and others. (4)

emotional labour The effort, planning, and control needed to express organizationally desired emotions during interpersonal transactions. (4)

emotions Physiological, behavioural, and psychological episodes experienced towards an object, person, or event that create a state of readiness. (4)

empathy A person's understanding of and sensitivity to the feelings, thoughts, and situations of others. (3)

employee engagement Individual's emotional and cognitive motivation, particularly a focused, intense, persistent, and purposive effort towards work-related goals. (5)

employee involvement The degree to which employees influence how their work is organized and carried out. (7)

employee share ownership plans (ESOPs) A reward system that encourages employees to buy company shares. (6)

empowerment A psychological concept in which people experience more self-determination, meaning, competence, and impact regarding their role in the organization. (6)

equity theory A theory explaining how people develop perceptions of fairness in the distribution and exchange of resources. (5)

escalation of commitment The tendency to repeat an apparently bad decision or allocate more resources to a failing course of action. (7)

ethics The study of moral principles or values that determine whether actions are right or wrong and outcomes are good or bad. (1)

evaluation apprehension A decision-making problem that occurs when individuals are reluctant to mention ideas that seem silly because they believe (often correctly) that other team members are silently evaluating them. (8)

evidence-based management The practice of making decisions and taking actions based on research evidence. (1)

exit-voice-loyalty-neglect (EVLN) model The four ways, as indicated in the name, that employees respond to job dissatisfaction. (4)

expectancy theory A motivation theory based on the idea that work effort is directed towards behaviours that people believe will lead to desired outcomes. (5)

extraversion A personality dimension describing people who are outgoing, talkative, sociable, and assertive. (2)

F

false-consensus effect A perceptual error in which we overestimate the extent to which others have beliefs and characteristics similar to our own. (3)

Fiedler's contingency model A leadership model stating that leader effectiveness depends on whether the person's natural leadership style is appropriately matched to the situation (the level of situational control). (12)

field surveys Research design strategies that involve collecting and analyzing information in a natural environment, such as an office, a factory, or other existing location. (Appendix A)

five-factor model (FFM) The five broad dimensions representing most personality traits: conscientiousness, emotional stability, openness to experience, agreeableness, and extraversion. (2)

force field analysis Kurt Lewin's model of system-wide change that helps change agents diagnose the forces that drive and restrain proposed organizational change. (15)

formalization The degree to which organizations standardize behaviour through rules, procedures, formal training, and related mechanisms. (13)

four-drive theory A motivation theory based on the innate drives to acquire, bond, learn, and defend, and that incorporates both emotions and rationality. (5)

functional structure An organizational structure in which employees are organized around specific knowledge or other resources. (13)

fundamental attribution error The tendency to see the person rather than the situation as the main cause of that person's behaviour. (3)

G

gain-sharing plans A team-based reward that calculates bonuses from the work unit's cost savings and productivity improvement (6)

general adaptation syndrome A model of the stress experience, consisting of three stages: alarm reaction, resistance, and exhaustion. (4)

global mindset An individual's ability to perceive, appreciate, and empathize with people from other cultures, and to process complex cross-cultural information. (3)

globalization Economic, social, and cultural connectivity with people in other parts of the world. (1)

globally integrated enterprise An organizational structure in which work processes and executive functions are distributed around the world through global centres, rather than developed in a home country and replicated in satellite countries or regions. (13)

goal setting The process of motivating employees and clarifying their role perceptions by establishing performance objectives. (5)

grapevine An unstructured and informal network founded on social relationships rather than organizational charts or job descriptions. (9)

grounded theory A process of developing knowledge through the constant interplay of data collection, analysis, and theory development. (Appendix A)

H

halo effect A perceptual error whereby our general impression of a person, usually based on one prominent characteristic, colours our perception of other characteristics of that person. (3)

high-performance work practices (HPWP) A perspective which holds that effective organizations incorporate several workplace practices that leverage the potential of human capital. (1)

human capital The stock of knowledge, skills, and abilities among employees that provides economic value to the organization. (1)

hypotheses Statements making empirically testable declarations that certain variables and their corresponding measures are related in a specific way proposed by the theory. (Appendix A)

I

implicit favourite A preferred alternative that the decision maker uses repeatedly as a comparison with other choices. (7)

implicit leadership theory A theory stating that people evaluate a leader's effectiveness in terms of how well that person fits preconceived beliefs about the features and behaviours of effective leaders (leadership prototypes), and that people tend to inflate the influence of leaders on organizational events. (12)

impression management Actively shaping through self-presentation and other means the perceptions and attitudes that others have of us. (10)

individualism A cross-cultural value describing the degree to which people in a culture emphasize independence and personal uniqueness. (2)

influence Any behaviour that attempts to alter someone's attitudes or behaviour. (10)

information overload A condition in which the volume of information received exceeds the person's capacity to process it. (9)

inoculation effect A persuasive communication strategy of warning listeners that others will try to influence them in the future and that they should be wary about the opponent's arguments. (10)

integrative situation When parties' goals are linked, but not zero-sum, so that one person's goal achievement does not block the goal achievement of another. (11)

intellectual capital A company's stock of knowledge, including human capital, structural capital, and relationship capital. (1)

interpretivism The view held in many qualitative studies that reality comes from shared meaning among people in a particular environment. (Appendix A)

intuition The ability to know when a problem or opportunity exists and to select the best course of action without conscious reasoning. (7)

J

job characteristics model A job design model that relates the motivational properties of jobs to specific personal and organizational consequences of those properties. (6)

job design The process of assigning tasks to a job, including the interdependency of those tasks with other jobs. (6)

job enlargement The practice of adding more tasks to an existing job. (6)

job enrichment The practice of giving employees more responsibility for scheduling, coordinating, and planning their own work. (6)

job evaluation Systematically rating the worth of jobs within an organization by measuring their required skill, effort, responsibility, and working conditions. (6)

job satisfaction A person's evaluation of his or her job and work context. (4)

job specialization The result of division of labour in which work is subdivided into separate jobs assigned to different people. (6)

Johari Window A model of mutual understanding that encourages disclosure and feedback to increase our own open area and reduce the blind, hidden, and unknown areas. (3)

L

laboratory experiment Any research study in which independent variables and variables outside the researcher's main focus of inquiry can be controlled to some extent. (Appendix A)

large group interventions Highly participative events that view organizations as open systems (i.e. involve as many employees and other stakeholders as possible) and adopt a future and positive focus of change. (15)

leadership Influencing, motivating, and enabling others to contribute towards the effectiveness and success of the organizations of which they are members. (12)

leadership substitutes A theory identifying conditions that either limit a leader's ability to influence subordinates or make a particular leadership style unnecessary. (12)

legitimate power An agreement among organizational members that people in certain roles can request certain behaviours of others. (10)

locus of control A person's general belief about the amount of control he or she has over personal life events. (3)

M

Machiavellian values The belief that deceit is a natural and acceptable way to influence others and that getting more than one deserves is acceptable. (10)

management by walking around (MBWA) A ommunication practice in which executives get out of their offices and learn from others in the organization through face-to-face dialogue. (9)

managerial leadership A leadership perspective stating that effective leaders help employees improve their performance and wellbeing towards current objectives and practices. (12)

Maslow's needs hierarchy theory A motivation theory of needs arranged in a hierarchy, whereby people are motivated to fulfill a higher need as a lower one becomes gratified. (5)

matrix structure An organizational structure that overlays two structures (such as a geographic divisional and a product structure) in order to leverage the benefits of both. (13)

mechanistic structure An organizational structure with a narrow span of control and a high degree of formalization and centralization. (13)

media richness A medium's data-carrying capacity, that is, the volume and variety of information that can be transmitted during a specific time. (9)

mental imagery The process of mentally practising a task and visualizing its successful completion. (6)

mental models Knowledge structures that we develop to describe, explain, and predict the world around us. (3)

mindfulness A person's receptive and impartial attention to and awareness of the present situation as well as to one's own thoughts and emotions in that moment. (2)

moral intensity The degree to which an issue demands the application of ethical principles. (2)

moral sensitivity A person's ability to recognize the presence of an ethical issue and determine its relative importance. (2)

motivation The forces within a person that affect his or her direction, intensity, and persistence of voluntary behaviour. (2)

motivator-hygiene theory Herzberg's theory stating that employees are primarily motivated by growth and esteem needs, not by lower-level needs. (6)

multisource (360-degree) feedback Information about an employee's performance collected from a full circle of people, including subordinates, peers, supervisors, and customers. (5)

Myers-Briggs Type Indicator (MBTI) An instrument designed to measure the elements of Jungian personality theory, particularly preferences regarding perceiving and judging information. (2)

N

need for achievement (nAch) A learned need in which people want to accomplish reasonably challenging goals, and desire unambiguous feedback and recognition for their success. (5)

need for affiliation (nAff) A learned need in which people seek approval from others, conform to their wishes and expectations, and avoid conflict and confrontation. (5)

need for power (nPow) A learned need in which people want to control their environment, including people and material resources, to benefit either themselves (personalized power) or others (socialized power). (5)

needs Goal-directed forces that people experience. (5)

negotiation Decision-making situations in which two or more interdependent parties attempt to reach agreement. (11)

network structure An alliance of several organizations for the purpose of creating a product or serving a client. (13)

neuroticism A personality dimension describing people with high levels of anxiety, hostility, depression, and self-consciousness. (2)

nominal group technique A variation of brainstorming consisting of three stages: participants (1) silently and independently document their ideas, (2) collectively describe these ideas to the other team members without critique, and (3) silently and independently evaluate the ideas presented. (8)

norm of reciprocity A felt obligation and social expectation of helping or otherwise giving something of value to someone who has already helped or given something to you. (10)

norms The informal rules and shared expectations that groups establish to regulate the behaviour of their members. (8)

O

open systems A perspective which holds that organizations depend on the external environment for resources, affect that environment through their output, and consist of internal subsystems that transform inputs into outputs. (1)

organic structure An organizational structure with a wide span of control, little formalization, and decentralized decision making. (13)

organizational behaviour (OB) The study of what people think, feel, and do in and around organizations. (1)

organizational behaviour modification (OB Mod) A theory that explains employee behaviour in terms of the antecedent conditions and consequences of that behaviour. (5)

organizational citizenship behaviours (OCBs) Various forms of cooperation and helpfulness to others that support the organization's social and psychological context. (2)

organizational culture The values and assumptions shared within an organization. (14)

organizational effectiveness A broad concept represented by several perspectives, including the organization's fit with the external environment, internal subsystems configuration for high performance, emphasis on organizational learning, and ability to satisfy the needs of key stakeholders. (1)

organizational efficiency The amount of outputs relative to inputs in the organization's transformation process. (1)

organizational learning A perspective which holds that organizational effectiveness depends on the organization's capacity to acquire, share, use, and store valuable knowledge. (1)

organizational politics Behaviours that others perceive as self-serving tactics for personal gain at the expense of other people and possibly the organization. (10)

organizational socialization The process by which individuals learn the values, expected behaviours, and social knowledge necessary to assume their roles in the organization. (14)

organizational strategy The way the organization positions itself in its setting in relation to its stakeholders, given the organization's resources, capabilities, and mission. (13)

organizational structure The division of labour as well as the patterns of coordination, communication, workflow, and formal power that direct organizational activities. (13)

organizations Groups of people who work interdependently toward some purpose. (1)

P

parallel learning structures Highly participative arrangements composed of people from most levels of the organization who follow the action research model to produce meaningful organizational change. (15)

path-goal leadership theory A leadership theory stating that effective leaders choose the most appropriate leadership style(s), depending on the employee and situation, to influence employee expectations about desired results and their positive outcomes. (12)

perception The process of receiving information about and making sense of the world around us. (3)

personality The relatively enduring pattern of thoughts, emotions, and behaviours that characterize a person, along with the psychological processes behind those characteristics. (2)

persuasion The use of facts, logical arguments, and emotional appeals to change another person's beliefs and attitudes, usually for the purpose of changing the person's behaviour. (9)

positive organizational behaviour A perspective of organizational behaviour that focuses on building positive qualities and traits within individuals or institutions as opposed to focusing on what is wrong with them. (3)

positivism A view held in quantitative research in which reality exists independent of the perceptions and interpretations of people. (Appendix A)

power The capacity of a person, team, or organization to influence others. (10)

power distance A cross-cultural value describing the degree to which people in a culture accept unequal distribution of power in a society. (2)

presenteeism Attending scheduled work when one's capacity to perform is significantly diminished by illness or other factors. (2)

primacy effect A perceptual error in which we quickly form an opinion of people based on the first information we receive about them. (3)

procedural justice Perceived fairness of the procedures used to decide the distribution of resources. (5)

process losses Resources (including time and energy) expended towards team development and maintenance rather than the task. (8)

production blocking A time constraint in team decision making due to the procedural requirement that only one person may speak at a time. (8)

profit-sharing plans A reward system that pays bonuses to employees on the basis of the previous year's level of corporate profits. (6)

prospect theory effect A natural tendency to feel more dissatisfaction from losing a particular amount than satisfaction from gaining an equal amount. (7)

psychological contract The individual's beliefs about the terms and conditions of a reciprocal exchange agreement between that person and another party (typically an employer). (14)

psychological harassment Repeated and hostile or unwanted conduct, verbal comments, actions, or gestures that affect an employee's dignity or psychological or physical integrity and that result in a harmful work environment for the employee. (4)

R

rational choice paradigm The view in decision making that people should–and typically do–use logic and all available information to choose the alternative with the highest value. (7)

realistic job preview (RJP) A method of improving organizational socialization in which job applicants are provided with a balance of positive and negative information about the job and work context. (14)

reality shock The stress that results when employees perceive discrepancies between their pre-employment expectations and on-the-job reality. (14)

recency effect A perceptual error in which the most recent information dominates our perception of others. (3)

referent power The capacity to influence others on the basis of an identification with and respect for the powerholder. (10)

refreezing The latter part of the organizational change process, in which systems and conditions are introduced that reinforce and maintain the desired behaviours. (15)

relationship capital The value derived from an organization's relationships with customers, suppliers, and others. (1)

relationship conflict Type of conflict in which people focus on the characteristics of other individuals, rather than on the issues, as the source of conflict. (11)

representativeness heuristic A natural tendency to evaluate probabilities of events or objects by the degree to which they resemble (are representative of) other events or objects rather than on objective probability information. (7)

representative sampling The process of sampling a population in such a way that one can extrapolate the results of that sample to the larger population. (Appendix A)

rituals The programmed routines of daily organizational life that dramatize the organization's culture. (14)

role A set of behaviours that people are expected to perform because of the positions they hold in a team and organization. (8)

role perceptions The degree to which a person understands the job duties assigned to or expected of him or her. (2)

S

satisficing Selecting an alternative that is satisfactory or "good enough" rather than the alternative with the higher value (maximization). (7)

scenario planning A systematic process of thinking about alternative futures and what the organization should do to anticipate and react to those environments. (7)

scientific management The practice of systematically partitioning work into its smallest elements and standardizing tasks to achieve maximum efficiency. (6)

scientific method A set of principles and procedures that help researchers to systematically understand previously unexplained events and conditions. (Appendix A)

selective attention The process of attending to some information received by our senses and ignoring other information. (3)

self-concept An individual's self-beliefs and self-evaluations. (3)

self-directed teams (SDTs) Cross-functional work groups that are organized around work processes, that complete an entire piece of work requiring several interdependent tasks, and that have substantial autonomy over the execution of those tasks. (8)

self-efficacy A person's belief that he or she has the ability, motivation, correct role perceptions, and favourable situation to complete a task successfully. (3)

self-enhancement A person's inherent motivation to have a positive self-concept (and to have others perceive him/her favourably), such as being competent, attractive, lucky, ethical, and important. (3)

self-fulfilling prophecy The perceptual process in which our expectations about another person cause that person to act more consistently with those expectations. (3)

self-leadership The process of influencing oneself to establish the self-direction and self-motivation needed to perform a task. (6)

self-reinforcement Reinforcement that occurs when an employee has control over a reinforcer but doesn't 'take' it until completing a self-set goal. (5)

self-serving bias The tendency to attribute our favourable outcomes to internal factors and our failures to external factors. (3)

self-talk The process of talking to ourselves about our own thoughts or actions. (6)

self-verification A person's inherent motivation to confirm and maintain his/her existing self-concept. (3)

servant leadership The view that leaders serve followers, rather than vice versa; leaders help employees fulfill their needs and are coaches, stewards, and facilitators of employee performance. (12)

service profit chain model A theory explaining how employees' job satisfaction influences company profitability indirectly through service quality, customer loyalty, and related factors. (4)

share options A reward system that give employees the right to purchase company shares at a future date at a predetermined price. (6)

shared leadership The view that leadership is a role, not a position assigned to one person; consequently, people within the team and organization lead each other. (12)

situational leadership theory (SLT) A commercially popular but poorly supported leadership model stating that effective leaders vary their style (telling, selling, participating, delegating) with the motivation and ability of followers. (12)

skill variety The extent to which employees must use different skills and talents to perform tasks within their jobs. (6)

social capital The knowledge and other resources available to people or social units (teams, organizations) from a durable network that connects them to others. (10)

social cognitive theory A theory that explains how learning and motivation occur by observing and modelling others as well as by anticipating the consequences of our behaviour. (5)

social identity theory A theory that explains that people define themselves by the groups to which they belong or have an emotional attachment. (3)

social loafing The problem that occurs when people exert less effort (and usually perform at a lower level) when working in teams than when working alone. (8)

social networks Social structures of individuals or social units that are connected to each other through one or more forms of interdependence. (10)

span of control The number of people directly reporting to the next level in the hierarchy. (13)

stakeholders Individuals, groups, and other entities that affect, or are affected by, the organization's objectives and actions. (1)

stereotyping The process of assigning traits to people based on their membership in a social category. (3)

strengths-based coaching A positive organizational behaviour approach to coaching and feedback that focuses on building and leveraging the employee's strengths rather than trying to correct his or her weaknesses. (5)

stress An adaptive response to a situation that is perceived as challenging or threatening to the person's well-being. (4)

stressors Environmental conditions that place a physical or emotional demand on a person. (4)

structural capital Knowledge embedded in an organization's systems and structures. (1)

structural hole An area between two or more dense social network areas that lacks network ties. (10)

subjective expected utility The probability (expectation) of satisfaction (utility) resulting from choosing a specific alternative in a decision. (7)

substitutability A contingency of power referring to the availability of alternatives. (10)

superordinate goals Goals that the conflicting parties value and whose attainment requires the joint resources and effort of those parties. (11)

surface-level diversity The observable demographic or physiological differences in people, such as their race, ethnicity, gender, age, and physical disabilities. (1)

T

task conflict A type of conflict in which people focus their discussion around the issue while showing respect for people with other points of view. (11)

task identity The degree to which a job requires completion of a whole or an identifiable piece of work. (6)

task interdependence The extent to which team members must share materials, information, or expertise in order to perform their jobs. (8)

task significance The degree to which a job has a substantial impact on the organization and/or larger society. (6)

taskwork behaviour Efforts devoted to understanding the task requirements, discovering the "rules" by which the tasks are to be performed, establishing the patterns of interaction with equipment, exchanging task-related information, developing team solutions to problems, and so forth. (8)

team-based structure An organizational structure built around self-directed teams that complete an entire piece of work. (13)

team boundary spanning Team actions that establish or enhance linkages and manage interactions with parties in the external environment. (8)

team building A process that consists of formal activities intended to improve the development and functioning of a work team. (8)

team cohesion The degree of attraction people feel towards the team and their motivation to remain members. (8)

team efficacy The collective belief among team members of the team's capability to successfully complete a task. (8)

teams Groups of two or more people who interact and influence each other, are mutually accountable for achieving common goals associated with organizational objectives, and perceive themselves as a social entity within an organization. (8)

teamwork behaviour Activities that are devoted to enhancing the quality of the interactions, interdependencies, cooperation, and coordination of teams. (8)

theory A general set of propositions that describes interrelationships among several concepts. (Appendix A)

third-party conflict resolution Any attempt by a relatively neutral person to help conflicting parties resolve their differences. (11)

transformational leadership A leadership perspective that explains how leaders change teams or organizations by creating, communicating, and modelling a shared vision for the team or organization, and inspiring employees to strive for that vision. (12)

trust Positive expectations one person has towards another person in situations involving risk. (4)

U

uncertainty avoidance A cross-cultural value describing the degree to which people in a culture tolerate ambiguity (low uncertainty avoidance) or feel threatened by ambiguity and uncertainty (high uncertainty avoidance). (2)

unfreezing The first part of the organizational change process, in which the change agent produces disequilibrium between the driving and restraining forces. (15)

upward appeal A type of influence in which someone with higher authority or expertise is called on (in reality or symbolically) to support the influencer's position. (10)

V

values Relatively stable, evaluative beliefs that guide a person's preferences for outcomes or courses of action in a variety of situations. (1)

virtual teams Teams whose members operate across space, time, and organizational boundaries, and are linked through information technologies to achieve organizational tasks. (8)

virtual work Work performed away from the traditional physical workplace by means of information technology. (1)

W

wikis Collaborative web spaces where anyone in a group can write, edit, or remove material from the website. (9)

win–lose orientation The belief that conflicting parties are drawing from a fixed pie, so the more one party receives, the less the other party will receive. (11)

win–win orientation The belief that conflicting parties will find a mutually beneficial solution to their disagreement. (11)

work–life balance The degree to which a person minimizes conflict between work and nonwork demands. (1)

workaholic A person who is highly involved in work, feels compelled to work, and has a low enjoyment of work. (4)

Endnotes

CHAPTER 1

1. R. Holmes, "2 Ways to Keep Company Culture Alive During Rapid Expansion," *LinkedIn Blog*, 18 October 2012; M. Rodgers, "Culture Club: Ambrosia Humphrey – Hootsuite," *Perch Communications Blog*, 9 September 2013, http://perch.co/blog/culture-club-ambrosia-humphrey-hootsuite/; P. Moreira, "Hootsuite Has Eye on Wise Growth," *USA Today*, 9 December 2013; R. Holmes, "Innovate or Die: 3 Ways to Stay Ahead of the Curve," *HootSuite Blog*, 13 September 2013, http://blog.hootsuite.com/innovate-or-die-hackathon/; T. Melanson, "Is Hootsuite Canada's Next Billion-Dollar Tech Titan?," *Canadian Business*, 9 January 2013; E. LePage, "Startup Insight from Our First 5 Employees," *HootSuite Blog*, 25 November 2013, http://blog.hootsuite.com/startup-insight-first-5-employees/.

2. M. Warner, "Organizational Behavior Revisited," *Human Relations* 47 (October 1994): 1151–1166; R. Westwood and S. Clegg, "The Discourse of Organization Studies: Dissensus, Politics, and Paradigms," in *Debating Organization: Point-Counterpoint in Organization Studies*, ed. R. Westwood and S. Clegg (Malden, MA: Blackwood, 2003), 1–42.

3. R.N. Stern and S.R. Barley, "Organizations as Social Systems: Organization Theory's Neglected Mandate," *Administrative Science Quarterly* 41 (1996): 146–62; D. Katz and R.L. Kahn, *The Social Psychology of Organizations* (New York: Wiley, 1966), Chap. 2.

4. L.E. Greiner, "A Recent History of Organizational Behavior," in *Organizational Behaviour*, ed. S. Kerr (Columbus, Ohio: Grid, 1979), 3–14; P.C. Newman, *Company of Adventurers* (Toronto, ON: Viking, 1985); J. Micklethwait and A. Wooldridge, *The Company: A Short History of a Revolutionary Idea* (New York: Random House, 2003).

5. B. Schlender, "The Three Faces of Steve," *Fortune*, 9 November 1998, 96–101.

6. J.A. Conger, "Max Weber's Conceptualization of Charismatic Authority: Its Influence on Organizational Research," *The Leadership Quarterly* 4, no. 3–4 (1993): 277–288; R. Kanigel, *The One Best Way: Frederick Winslow Taylor and the Enigma of Efficiency* (New York: Viking, 1997); T. Takala, "Plato on Leadership," *Journal of Business Ethics* 17 (May 1998): 785–798; J.A. Fernandez, "The Gentleman's Code of Confucius: Leadership by Values," *Organizational Dynamics* 33, no. 1 (February 2004): 21–31.

7. W.L.M. King, *Industry and Humanity: A Study in the Principles Underlying Industrial Reconstruction* (Toronto, ON: Thomas Allen, 1918); H.C. Metcalf and L. Urwick, *Dynamic Administration: The Collected Papers of Mary Parker Follett* (New York: Harper & Brothers, 1940); J. Smith, "The Enduring Legacy of Elton Mayo," *Human Relations* 51, no. 3 (1998): 221–249; E. O'Connor, "Minding the Workers: The Meaning of, 'Human' and 'Human Relations' in Elton Mayo," *Organization* 6, no. 2 (May 1999): 223–246; K. Hallahan, "W.L. Mackenzie King: Rockefeller's 'Other' Public Relations Counselor in Colorado," *Public Relations Review* 29, no. 4 (2003): 401–414.

8. S.L. Rynes et al., "Behavioral Coursework in Business Education: Growing Evidence of a Legitimacy Crisis," *Academy of Management Learning & Education* 2, no. 3 (2003): 269–83; R.P. Singh and A.G. Schick, "Organizational Behavior: Where Does It Fit in Today's Management Curriculum?," *Journal of Education for Business* 82, no. 6 (2007): 349.

9. P.R. Lawrence and N. Nohria, *Driven: How Human Nature Shapes Our Choices* (San Francisco, CA Jossey-Bass, 2002), Chap. 6.

10. OB scholars are currently in a heated debate regarding the field's relevance to practitioners. See, for example: P.R. Lawrence "Historical Development of Organizational Behavior," in *Handbook of Organizational Behavior*, ed. L.W. Lorsch (Englewood Cliffs, NJ: Prentice Hall, 1987), 1–9; S.A. Mohrman, C.B. Gibson, and A.M. Mohrman Jr., "Doing Research That Is Useful to Practice: A Model and Empirical Exploration," *Academy of Management Journal* 44 (April 2001): 357–375; R. Gulati, "Tent Poles, Tribalism, and Boundary Spanning: The Rigor-Relevance Debate in Management Research," *Academy of Management Journal* 50, no. 4 (Aug 2007): 775–782; F. Vermeulen, "'I Shall Not Remain Insignificant': Adding a Second Loop to Matter More," *Academy of Management Journal* 50, no. 4 (2007): 754–761; J.P. Walsh et al., "On the Relationship between Research and Practice: Debate and Reflections," *Journal of Management Inquiry* 16, no. 2 (June 2007): 128–154; D. Palmer, B. Dick, and N. Freiburger, "Rigor and Relevance in Organization Studies," *Journal of Management Inquiry* 18, no. 4 (December 2009): 265–272; A. Nicolai and D. Seidl, "That's Relevant! Different Forms of Practical Relevance in Management Science," *Organization Studies* 31, no. 9–10 (Sept. 2010): 1257–1285. At least one source argues that organizational scholarship does not need to be relevant to practitioners: M.W. Peng and G.G. Dess, "In the Spirit of Scholarship," *Academy of Management Learning & Education* 9, no. 2 (June 2010): 282–298.

11. J.A. Sonnenfeld, "Shedding Light on the Hawthorne Studies," *Journal of Occupational Behaviour* 6, no. 2 (1985): 111–30; C.D. Wrege, "Solving Mayo's Mystery: The First Complete Account of the Origin of the Hawthorne Studies-the Forgotten Contributions of C.E. Snow and H. Hibarger" (paper presented at the Academy of Management Proceedings, August 1976), 12–16; O'Connor, "Minding the Workers: The Meaning of 'Human' and 'Human Relations' in Elton Mayo; "A Field Is Born," *Harvard Business Review* 86, no. 7/8 (2008): 164.

12. M.S. Myers, *Every Employee a Manager* (New York: McGraw Hill, 1970).

13. B.N. Pfau and I.T. Kay, *The Human Capital Edge* (New York: McGraw-Hill, 2002); I.S. Fulmer, B. Gerhart, and K.S. Scott, "Are the 100 Best Better? An Empirical Investigation of the Relationship between Being a 'Great Place to Work' and Firm Performance," *Personnel Psychology* 56, no. 4 (Winter 2003): 965–993; Y.H. Ling and B.-S. Jaw, "The Influence of International Human Capital on Global Initiatives and Financial Performance," *The International Journal of Human Resource Management* 17, no. 3 (2006): 379–398; M.A. West et al., "Reducing Patient Mortality in Hospitals: The Role of Human Resource Management," *Journal of Organizational Behavior* 27, no. 7 (2006): 983–1002. However, one study warns that firm performance seems to predict the presence of OB practices as much as vice versa. See P.M. Wright et al., "The Relationship between HR Practices and Firm Performance: Examining Causal Order," *Personnel Psychology* 58, no. 2 (2005): 409–446.

14. Deloitte & Touche, *Human Capital Roi Study: Creating Shareholder Value through People*, Deloitte & Touche (Toronto, ON: 2002); D. Wheeler and J. Thomson, *Human Capital Based Investment Criteria for Total Shareholder Returns: A Canadian and International Perspective*, Schulich School of Business, York University (Toronto, ON: June 2004); L. Bassi and D. McMurrer, "Maximizing Your Return on People," *Harvard business Review* 85, no. 3 (2007): 115–23, 44; A. Mackey, "The Effect of CEOs on Firm Performance," *Strategic Management Journal* 29, no. 12 (2008): 1357–67; C.A. O'Reilly et al., "How Leadership Matters: The Effects of Leaders' Alignment on Strategy Implementation," *The Leadership Quarterly* 21, no. 1 (2010): 104–13; P. Hodson, "5 Qualities to Look for in Stocks," *National Post*, 15 November 2013.

15. Mohrman, Gibson, and Mohrman Jr., "Doing Research That Is Useful to Practice: A Model and Empirical Exploration" Walsh et al., "On the Relationship between Research and Practice: Debate and Reflections." Similarly, in 1961, Harvard business professor Fritz Roethlisberger proposed that the field of OB is concerned with human behaviour "from the points of view of both (a) its determination . . . and (b) its improvement." See P.B. Vaill, "F.J. Roethlisberger and the Elusive Phenomena of Organizational Behavior," *Journal of Management Education* 31, no. 3 (June 2007): 321–338.

16. R.H. Hall, "Effectiveness Theory and Organizational Effectiveness," *Journal of Applied Behavioral Science* 16, no. 4 (Oct. 1980): 536–545; K. Cameron, "Organizational Effectiveness: Its Demise and Re-Emergence through Positive Organizational Scholarship," in *Great Minds in Management*, ed. K.G. Smith and M.A. Hitt (New York: Oxford University Press, 2005), 304–330.

17. S. Selden and J.E. Sowa, "Testing a Multi-Dimensional Model of Organizational Performance: Prospects and Problems," *Journal of Public*

Administration Research and Theory 14, no. 3 (July 2004): 395–416.

18. Chester Barnard gives one of the earliest descriptions of organizations as systems interacting with external environments and that are composed of subsystems. See: C. Barnard, *The Functions of the Executive* (Cambridge, MA: Harvard University Press, 1938), esp. Chap. 6. Also see: F.E. Kast and J.E. Rosenzweig, "General Systems Theory: Applications for Organization and Management," *Academy of Management Journal* 15, no. 4 (1972): 447–465; P.M. Senge, *The Fifth Discipline: The Art and Practice of the Learning Organization* (New York: Doubleday Currency, 1990); G. Morgan, *Images of Organization*, 2nd ed. (Newbury Park: Sage, 1996); A. De Geus, *The Living Company* (Boston, MA: Harvard Business School Press, 1997).

19. D.P. Ashmos and G.P. Huber, "The Systems Paradigm in Organization Theory: Correcting the Record and Suggesting the Future," *The Academy of Management Review* 12, no. 4 (1987): 607–621.

20. Katz and Kahn, *The Social Psychology of Organizations;* J. McCann, "Organizational Effectiveness: Changing Concepts for Changing Environments," *Human Resource Planning* 27, no. 1 (2004): 42–50; A.H. Van de Ven, M. Ganco, and C.R. Hinings, "Returning to the Frontier of Contingency Theory of Organizational and Institutional Designs," *Academy of Management Annals* 7, no. 1 (2013): 391–438.

21. N. Tokatli, "Global Sourcing: Insights from the Global Clothing Industry–the Case of Zara, a Fast Fashion Retailer," *Journal of Economic Geography* 8, no. 1 (2008): 21–38; L. Osborne, "High Street Fashion Chain Zara Is Hit by 'Slave Labour' Outcry," *Daily Mail (London, UK)*, 2013, 25; S.R. Levine, "How Zara Took Customer Focus to New Heights," *Credit Union Times* (2013): 10; C. Nogueir, "How Inditex Rules the Weaves, and Plans to Carry on Doing So," *El Pais (Madrid, Spain)*, 24 April 2013, 4; G. Ruddick, "Spain's Leader in Fast Fashion Has Much to Teach British Store Rivals," *Daily Telegraph (London)*, 15 March 2013, 2; "The Cult of Zara," *Sunday Independent (Dublin, Ireland)*, 10 February 2013, 24.

22. C. Ostroff and N. Schmitt, "Configurations of Organizational Effectiveness and Efficiency," *Academy of Management Journal* 36, no. 6 (1993): 1345–1361.

23. P.S. Adler et al., "Performance Improvement Capability: Keys to Accelerating Performance Improvement in Hospitals," *California Management Review* 45, no. 2 (2003): 12–33; J. Jamrog, M. Vickers, and D. Bear, "Building and Sustaining a Culture That Supports Innovation," *Human Resource Planning* 29, no. 3 (2006): 9–19.

24. K.E. Weick, *The Social Psychology of Organizing* (Reading, MA: Addison-Wesley, 1979); S. Brusoni and A. Prencipe, "Managing Knowledge in Loosely Coupled Networks: Exploring the Links between Product and Knowledge Dynamics," *Journal of Management Studies* 38, no. 7 (Nov. 2001): 1019–1035.

25. W.C. Bogner and P. Bansal, "Knowledge Management as the Basis of Sustained High Performance," *Journal of Management Studies* 44, no. 1 (2007): 165–88; L. Argote and E. Miron-Spektor, "Organizational Learning: From Experience to Knowledge," *Organization Science* 22, no. 5 (2011): 1123–37.

26. T.A. Stewart, *Intellectual Capital: The New Wealth of Organizations* (New York: Currency/ Doubleday, 1997); H. Saint-Onge and D. Wallace, *Leveraging Communities of Practice for Strategic Advantage* (Boston, MA: Butterworth-Heinemann, 2003), 9–10; J.-A. Johannessen, B. Olsen, and J. Olaisen, "Intellectual Capital as a Holistic Management Philosophy: A Theoretical Perspective," *International Journal of Information Management* 25, no. 2 (2005): 151–171; L. Striukova, J. Unerman, and J. Guthrie, "Corporate Reporting of Intellectual Capital: Evidence from UK Companies," *British Accounting Review* 40, no. 4 (2008): 297–313.

27. J. Barney, "Firm Resources and Sustained Competitive Advantage," *Journal of Management* 17, no. 1 (1991): 99–120.

28. J.P. Hausknecht and J.A. Holwerda, "When Does Employee Turnover Matter? Dynamic Member Configurations, Productive Capacity, and Collective Performance," *Organization Science* 24, no. 1 (2013): 210–25.

29. "Jim Goodnight, Chief Executive Officer, SAS," (Cary, NC: 2011), http://www.sas.com/company/about/bios/jgoodnight.html (accessed 13 June 2011).

30. S.-C. Kang and S.A. Snell, "Intellectual Capital Architectures and Ambidextrous Learning: A Framework for Human Resource Management," *Journal of Management Studies* 46, no. 1 (2009): 65–92; L.-C. Hsu and C.-H. Wang, "Clarifying the Effect of Intellectual Capital on Performance: The Mediating Role of Dynamic Capability," *British Journal of Management* (2011): 179–205.

31. Some organizational learning researchers use the label "social capital" instead of relationship capital. Social capital is discussed later in this book as the goodwill and resulting resources shared among members in a social network. The two concepts may be identical (as those writers suggest). However, we continue to use "relationship capital" for intellectual capital because social capital typically refers to individual relationships whereas relationship capital also includes value not explicit in social capital, such as the organization's goodwill and brand value.

32. G. Huber, "Organizational Learning: The Contributing Processes and Literature," *Organizational Science* 2 (1991): 88–115; D.A. Garvin, *Learning in Action: A Guide to Putting the Learning Organization to Work* (Boston, MA: Harvard Business School Press, 2000); H. Shipton, "Cohesion or Confusion? Towards a Typology for Organizational Learning Research," *International Journal of Management Reviews* 8, no. 4 (2006): 233–52; D. Jiménez-Jiménez and J.G. Cegarra-Navarro, "The Performance Effect of Organizational Learning and Market Orientation," *Industrial Marketing Management* 36, no. 6 (2007): 694–708. One recent study suggests that these organizational learning processes aren't always beneficial because they may be more costly or burdensome than the value they create. see: S.S. Levine and M.J. Prietula, "How Knowledge Transfer Impacts Performance: A Multilevel Model of Benefits and Liabilities," *Organization Science* 23, no. 6 (2012): 1748–66.

33. B. van den Hooff and M. Huysman, "Managing Knowledge Sharing: Emergent and Engineering Approaches," *Information & Management* 46, no. 1 (2009): 1–8.

34. M.N. Wexler, "Organizational Memory and Intellectual Capital," *Journal of Intellectual Capital* 3, no. 4 (2002): 393–414; M. Fiedler and I. Welpe, "How Do Organizations Remember? The Influence of Organizational Structure on Organizational Memory," *Organization Studies* 31, no. 4 (2010): 381–407.

35. C. Hawkins, *Duha Color Group*, Weslat Case Studies, Centre for Education and Work (Winnipeg, MB: 2009); Centre for Education and Work, *The Learning Organization Video*, Centre for Education and Work (Winnipeg, MB: 2009); Salesforce, "Duha Group Invites Their Customers into Their Manufacturing Process Using Salesforce," (2013).

36. "A Cornerstone for Learning," *T&D*, October 2008, 66–89.

37. M.E. McGill and J.W. Slocum Jr., "Unlearn the Organization," *Organizational Dynamics* 22, no. 2 (1993): 67–79; A.E. Akgün, G.S. Lynn, and J.C. Byrne, "Antecedents and Consequences of Unlearning in New Product Development Teams," *Journal of Product Innovation Management* 23 (2006): 73–88.

38. L. Sels et al., "Unravelling the HRM-Performance Link: Value-Creating and Cost-Increasing Effects of Small Business HRM," *Journal of Management Studies* 43, no. 2 (2006): 319–42; G.S. Benson, S.M. Young, and E.E. Lawler III, "High-Involvement Work Practices and Analysts' Forecasts of Corporate Earnings," *Human Resource Management* 45, no. 4 (2006): 519–37.

39. M.A. Huselid, "The Impact of Human Resource Management Practices on Turnover, Productivity, and Corporate Financial Performance," *Academy of Management Journal* 38, no. 3 (1995): 635–70; B.E. Becker and M.A. Huselid, "Strategic Human Resources Management: Where Do We Go from Here?," *Journal of Management* 32, no. 6 (2006): 898–925; J. Combs et al., "How Much Do High-Performance Work Practices Matter? A Meta-Analysis of Their Effects on Organizational Performance," *Personnel Psychology* 59, no. 3 (2006): 501–28.

40. E.E. Lawler III, S.A. Mohrman, and G.E. Ledford Jr., *Strategies for High Performance Organizations* (San Francisco, CA: Jossey-Bass, 1998); S.H. Wagner, C.P. Parker, and D. Neil, "Employees That Think and Act Like Owners: Effects of Ownership Beliefs and Behaviors on Organizational Effectiveness," *Personnel Psychology* 56, no. 4 (Winter 2003): 847–871; P.J. Gollan, "High Involvement Management and Human Resource Sustainability: The Challenges and Opportunities," *Asia Pacific Journal of Human Resources* 43, no. 1 (April 2005): 18–33; Y. Liu et al., "The Value of Human Resource Management for Organizational Performance," *Business Horizons* 50 (2007): 503–511; P. Tharenou, A.M. Saks, and C. Moore, "A Review and Critique of Research on Training and Organizational-Level Outcomes," *Human Resource Management Review* 17, no. 3 (2007): 251–273.

41. M. Subramony, "A Meta-Analytic Investigation of the Relationship between HRM Bundles and Firm Performance," *Human Resource Management* 48, no. 5 (2009): 745-768.

42. L.-Q. Wei and C.-M. Lau, "High Performance Work Systems and Performance: The Role of Adaptive Capability," *Human Relations* 63, no. 10 (2010): 1487-511; J. Camps and R. Luna-Arocas, "A Matter of Learning: How Human Resources Affect Organizational Performance," *British Journal of Management* 23, no. 1 (2012): 1-21; R.R. Kehoe and P.M. Wright, "The Impact of High-Performance Human Resource Practices on Employees' Attitudes and Behaviors," *Journal of Management* 39, no. 2 (2013): 366-91.

43. G. Murray et al., eds., *Work and Employment Relations in the High-Performance Workplace* (London, UK: Continuum, 2002); B. Harley, "Hope or Hype? High Performance Work Systems," in *Participation and Democracy at Work: Essays in Honour of Harvie Ramsay*, ed. B. Harley, J. Hyman, and P. Thompson (Houndsmills, UK: Palgrave Macmillan, 2005), 38-54.

44. J. Tullberg, "Stakeholder Theory: Some Revisionist Suggestions," *The Journal of Socio-Economics* 42 (2013): 127-35.

45. C. Eden and F. Ackerman, *Making Strategy: The Journey of Strategic Management* (London, UK: Sage, 1998).

46. A.L. Friedman and S. Miles, *Stakeholders: Theory and Practice* (New York: Oxford University Press, 2006); M.L. Barnett, "Stakeholder Influence Capacity and the Variability of Financial Returns to Corporate Social Responsibility," *Academy of Management Review* 32, no. 3 (2007): 794-816; R.E. Freeman, J.S. Harrison, and A.C. Wicks, *Managing for Stakeholders: Survival, Reputation, and Success* (New Haven, CT: Yale University Press, 2007).

47. G.R. Salancik and J. Pfeffer, *The External Control of Organizations: A Resource Dependence Perspective* (New York: Harper & Row, 1978); N. Roome and F. Wijen, "Stakeholder Power and Organizational Learning in Corporate Environmental Management," *Organization Studies* 27, no. 2 (2005): 235-263; R.B. Adams, A.N. Licht, and L. Sagiv, "Shareholders and Stakeholders: How Do Directors Decide?," *Strategic Management Journal* 32, no. 12 (2011): 1331-1355; A. Santana, "Three Elements of Stakeholder Legitimacy," *Journal of Business Ethics* 105, no. 2 (2012): 257-265.

48. R.E. Freeman, A.C. Wicks, and B. Parmar, "Stakeholder Theory and 'the Corporate Objective Revisited'," *Organization Science* 15, no. 3 (May-June 2004): 364-369; Friedman and Miles, *Stakeholders: Theory and Practice*, Chap. 3; B.L. Parmar et al., "Stakeholder Theory: The State of the Art," *Academy of Management Annals* 4, no. 1 (2010): 403-445.

49. B.M. Meglino and E.C. Ravlin, "Individual Values in Organizations: Concepts, Controversies, and Research," *Journal of Management* 24, no. 3 (1998): 351-389; B.R. Agle and C.B. Caldwell, "Understanding Research on Values in Business," *Business and Society* 38, no. 3 (September 1999): 326-387; A. Bardi and S.H. Schwartz, "Values and Behavior: Strength and Structure of Relations," *Personality and Social Psychology Bulletin* 29, no. 10 (October 2003): 1207-1220; S. Hitlin and J.A. Pilavin, "Values: Reviving a Dormant Concept," *Annual Review of Sociology* 30 (2004): 359-393.

50. Some popular books that emphasize the importance of personal and organizational values include: J.C. Collins and J.I. Porras, *Built to Last: Successful Habits of Visionary Companies* (London, UK: Century, 1995); C.A. O'Reilly III and J. Pfeffer, *Hidden Value* (Cambridge, MA: Harvard Business School Press, 2000); R. Barrett, *Building a Values-Driven Organization: A Whole System Approach to Cultural Transformation* (Burlington, MA: Butterworth-Heinemann, 2006); R. Tocquigny and A. Butcher, *When Core Values Are Strategic* (Upper Saddle River, NJ: FT Press, 2012).

51. "Vancity Savings Named Best Corporate Citizen in Canada," *Vancouver Sun*, 8 June 2013; "Values-Based Banking," (Vancouver, BC: Vancity, 2014) (accessed 10 February 2014).

52. Aspen Institute, *Where Will They Lead? MBA Student Attitudes About Business & Society* (Washington, DC: Aspen Institute, April 2008).

53. M. van Marrewijk, "Concepts and Definitions of CSR and Corporate Sustainability: Between Agency and Communion," *Journal of Business Ethics* 44 (May 2003): 95-105; Barnett, "Stakeholder Influence Capacity and the Variability of Financial Returns to Corporate Social Responsibility."

54. L.S. Paine, *Value Shift* (New York: McGraw-Hill, 2003); A. Mackey, T.B. Mackey, and J.B. Barney, "Corporate Social Responsibility and Firm Performance: Investor Preferences and Corporate Strategies," *Academy of Management Review* 32, no. 3 (2007): 817-835.

55. "MTN Plants 5,800 Trees in 21 Days of Y'ello Care," *Spy Ghana*, 10 June 2011; "MTN Begins 21 Days of Yellow Care Campaign to Support Children," *All Africa*, 13 June 2012; MTN Group Limited, *Welcome to the New World: MTN Group Limited Sustainability Report for the Year Ended 31 December 2012*, MTN Group (Fairlands, South Africa: 24 April 2013).

56. S. Zadek, *The Civil Corporation: The New Economy of Corporate Citizenship* (London, UK: Earthscan, 2001); S. Hart and M. Milstein, "Creating Sustainable Value," *Academy of Management Executive* 17, no. 2 (2003): 56-69.

57. M. Friedman, *Capitalism and Freedom*, 40th Anniversary ed. (Chicago, IL: University of Chicago Press, 2002), Chap. 8; N. Vorster, "An Ethical Critique of Milton Friedman's Doctrine on Economics and Freedom," *Journal for the Study of Religions and Ideologies* 9, no. 26 (2010): 163-88.

58. M. Johne, "Show Us the Green, Workers Say," *The Globe and Mail*, 10 October 2007, C1.

59. A.B. Carroll and K.M. Shabana, "The Business Case for Corporate Social Responsibility: A Review of Concepts, Research and Practice," *International Journal of Management Reviews* 12, no. 1 (2010): 85-105; H. Aguinis and A. Glavas, "What We Know and Don't Know About Corporate Social Responsibility: A Review and Research Agenda," *Journal of Management* 38, no. 4 (2012): 932-68.

60. W. Immen, "On the Move for Work," *The Globe and Mail*, 15 May 2010, B16.

61. S. Fischer, "Globalization and Its Challenges," *American Economic Review* (May 2003): 1-29. For discussion of the diverse meanings of *globalization*, see M.F. Guillén, "Is Globalization Civilizing, Destructive or Feeble? A Critique of Five Key Debates in the Social Science Literature," *Annual Review of Sociology* 27 (2001): 235-260.

62. The ongoing debate regarding the advantages and disadvantages of globalization are discussed in Guillén, "Is Globalization Civilizing, Destructive or Feeble?"; D. Doane, "Can Globalization Be Fixed?," *Business Strategy Review* 13, no. 2 (2002): 51-58; J. Bhagwati, *In Defense of Globalization* (New York: Oxford University Press, 2004); M. Wolf, *Why Globalization Works* (New Haven, CT: Yale University Press, 2004).

63. K. Ohmae, *The Next Global Stage* (Philadelphia: Wharton School Publishing, 2005).

64. "Japan Real Time: Dear Successful Female Foreign CEO, Hitachi," *Dow Jones International News*, 27 April 2012.

65. D.A. Harrison et al., "Time, Teams, and Task Performance: Changing Effects of Surface- and Deep-Level Diversity on Group Functioning," *Academy of Management Journal* 45, no. 5 (2002): 1029-46; W.J. Casper, J.H. Wayne, and J.G. Manegold, "Who Will We Recruit? Targeting Deep- and Surface-Level Diversity with Human Resource Policy Advertising," *Human Resource Management* 52, no. 3 (2013): 311-32; J.E. Mathieu et al., "A Review and Integration of Team Composition Models: Moving toward a Dynamic and Temporal Framework," *Journal of Management* 40, no. 1 (2014): 130-60.

66. A. Hofschneider, "Bosses Say 'Pick up the Phone'," *Wall Street Journal*, 27 August 2013; M.J. Copps, "Making Connections," *thephonelady blog*, 7 April 2013, http://www.thephonelady.ca/making-connections/.

67. Statistics Canada, "Immigration and Ethnocultural Diversity in Canada," National Household Survey, 2011 (Ottawa, ON: Government of Canada, 2013).

68. R. Zemke, C. Raines, and B. Filipczak, *Generations at Work: Managing the Clash of Veterans, Boomers, Xers, and Nexters in Your Workplace* (New York: Amacom, 2000); S.H. Applebaum, M. Serena, and B.T. Shapiro, "Generation X and the Boomers: Organizational Myths and Literary Realities," *Management Research News* 27, no. 11/12 (2004): 1-28; N. Howe and W. Strauss, "The Next 20 Years: How Customer and Workforce Attitudes Will Evolve," *Harvard Business Review* (July-August 2007): 41-52.

69. Statistics Canada, "Labour Force Characteristics by Age and Sex (Estimates) (2013)," (Ottawa, ON: Statistics Canada, 10 January 2014), http://www.statcan.gc.ca/tables-tableaux/sum-som/l01/cst01/labor20a-eng.htm (accessed 9 February 2014).

70. E. Parry and P. Urwin, "Generational Differences in Work Values: A Review of Theory and Evidence," *International Journal of Management Reviews* 13 (2011): 79-96.

71. E. Ng, L. Schweitzer, and S. Lyons, "New Generation, Great Expectations: A Field Study of the Millennial Generation," *Journal of Business and Psychology* 25, no. 2 (2010): 281-292.

72. M. Wong et al., "Generational Differences in Personality and Motivation," *Journal of Managerial Psychology* 23, no. 8 (2008): 878-90;

J.M. Twenge and S.M. Campbell, "Generational Differences in Psychological Traits and Their Impact on the Workplace," *Journal of Managerial Psychology* 23, no. 8 (2008): 862-77; J. Twenge, "A Review of the Empirical Evidence on Generational Differences in Work Attitudes," *Journal of Business and Psychology* 25, no. 2 (2010): 201-10; B. Kowske, R. Rasch, and J. Wiley, "Millennials' (Lack of) Attitude Problem: An Empirical Examination of Generational Effects on Work Attitudes," *Journal of Business and Psychology* 25, no. 2 (2010): 265-79; J. Deal, D. Altman, and S. Rogelberg, "Millennials at Work: What We Know and What We Need to Do (If Anything)," *Journal of Business and Psychology* 25, no. 2 (2010): 191-99.

73. T. Kochan et al., "The Effects of Diversity on Business Performance: Report of the Diversity Research Network," *Human Resource Management* 42 (2003): 3-21; R.J. Burke and E. Ng, "The Changing Nature of Work and Organizations: Implications for Human Resource Management," *Human Resource Management Review* 16 (2006): 86-94; M.-E. Roberge and R. van Dick, "Recognizing the Benefits of Diversity: When and How Does Diversity Increase Group Performance?," *Human Resource Management Review* 20, no. 4 (2010): 295-308.

74. D. Porras, D. Psihountas, and M. Griswold, "The Long-Term Performance of Diverse Firms," *International Journal of Diversity* 6, no. 1 (2006): 25-34; R.A. Weigand, "Organizational Diversity, Profits and Returns in U.S. Firms," *Problems & Perspectives in Management*, no. 3 (2007): 69-83.

75. "The Business Case for Diversity," *USBanker* 120, no. 5 (2010): 10-11.

76. Kochan et al., "The Effects of Diversity on Business Performance: Report of the Diversity Research Network; G.K. Stahl et al., "A Look at the Bright Side of Multicultural Team Diversity," *Scandinavian Journal of Management* 26, no. 4 (2010): 439-47; L.M. Shore et al., "Inclusion and Diversity in Work Groups: A Review and Model for Future Research," *Journal of Management* 37, no. 4 (2011): 1262-89; S.T. Bell et al., "Getting Specific About Demographic Diversity Variable and Team Performance Relationships: A Meta-Analysis," *Journal of Management* 37, no. 3 (2011): 709-43; S.M.B. Thatcher and P.C. Patel, "Group Faultlines: A Review, Integration, and Guide to Future Research," *Journal of Management* 38, no. 4 (2012): 969-1009.

77. E.D.Y. Greenblatt, "Work/Life Balance: Wisdom or Whining," *Organizational Dynamics* 31, no. 2 (2002): 177-93; W.G. Bennis and R.J. Thomas, *Geeks and Geezers* (Boston, MA: Harvard Business School Press, 2002), 74-79.

78. T.L. Johns, "The Third Wave of Virtual Work," *Harvard Business Review* 91, no. 1 (2013): 66-73.

79. Regus, *A Better Balance*, Regus (Luxembourg: May 2012).

80. Ipsos, "Global Study of Online Employees Shows One in Five (17%) Work from Elsewhere," News release for Ipsos (New York: Ipsos, 23 January 2012); BMO Bank of Montreal, "BMO Poll: Canadian Businesses Report Significant Divide on the Benefits of Telecommuting," News release for Bank of Montreal (Toronto, ON: Bank of Montreal, 26 April 2013).

81. E.J. Hill et al., "Workplace Flexibility, Work Hours, and Work-Life Conflict: Finding an Extra Day or Two," *Journal of Family Psychology* 24, no. 3 (2010): 349-58; A. Bourhis and R. Mekkaoui, "Beyond Work-Family Balance: Are Family-Friendly Organizations More Attractive?," *Relations Industrielles/Industrial Relations* 65, no. 1 (2010): 98-117.

82. "Increased Productivity Due to Telecommuting Generates an Estimated $277 Million in Annual Savings for Company," News release (San Jose, CA: Cisco systems, 25 June 2009); D. Meinert, "Make Telecommuting Pay Off," *HRMagazine*, June 2011, 33; M. McQuigge, "A Panacea for Some, Working from Home Still a Tough Sell for Some Employers," *Canadian Press (Toronto)*, 26 June 2013.

83. Meinert, "Make Telecommuting Pay Off."

84. G.W. Marshall, C.E. Michaels, and J.P. Mulki, "Workplace Isolation: Exploring the Construct and Its Measurement," *Psychology and Marketing* 24, no. 3 (2007): 195-223; V.J. Morganson et al., "Comparing Telework Locations and Traditional Work Arrangements," *Journal of Managerial Psychology* 25, no. 6 (2010): 578-95; S.M.B. Thatcher and J. Bagger, "Working in Pajamas: Telecommuting, Unfairness Sources, and Unfairness Perceptions," *Negotiation and Conflict Management Research* 4, no. 3 (2011): 248-76; J. Mahler, "The Telework Divide: Managerial and Personnel Challenges of Telework," *Review of Public Personnel Administration* 32, no. 4 (2012): 407-18.

85. D.E. Bailey and N.B. Kurland, "A Review of Telework Research: Findings, New Directions, and Lessons for the Study of Modern Work," *Journal of Organizational Behavior* 23 (2002): 383-400; D.W. McCloskey and M. Igbaria, "Does 'out of Sight' Mean 'out of Mind'? An Empirical Investigation of the Career Advancement Prospects of Telecommuters," *Information Resources Management Journal* 16 (2003): 19-34.

86. Most of these anchors are mentioned in: J.D. Thompson, "On Building an Administrative Science," *Administrative Science Quarterly* 1, no. 1 (1956): 102-11.

87. This anchor has a colourful history dating back to critiques of business schools in the 1950s. Soon after, systematic research became a mantra by many respected scholars. See, for example: Thompson, "On Building an Administrative Science."

88. J. Pfeffer and R.I. Sutton, *Hard Facts, Dangerous Half-Truths, and Total Nonsense* (Boston, MA: Harvard Business School Press, 2006); D.M. Rousseau and S. McCarthy, "Educating Managers from an Evidence-Based Perspective," *Academy of Management Learning & Education* 6, no. 1 (2007): 84-101; R.B. Briner and D.M. Rousseau, "Evidence-Based I-O Psychology: Not There Yet," *Industrial and Organizational Psychology* 4, no. 1 (2011): 3-22.

89. J.M. Bartunek, "Evidence-Based Approaches in I-O Psychology Should Address Worse Grumbles," *Industrial and Organizational Psychology* 4, no. 1 (2011): 72-75; M.J. Burke, "Is There a Fly in the "Systematic Review" Ointment?," *Industrial and Organizational Psychology* 4, no. 1 (2011): 36-39; M.A. Cronin and R. Klimoski, "Broadening the View of What Constitutes "Evidence"," *Industrial and Organizational Psychology* 4, no. 1 (2011): 57-61.

90. S.L. Rynes, T.L. Giluk, and K.G. Brown, "The Very Separate Worlds of Academic and Practitioner Periodicals in Human Resource Management: Implications for Evidence-Based Management," *Academy of Management Journal* 50, no. 5 (2007): 987-1008; D.J. Cohen, "The Very Separate Worlds of Academic and Practitioner Publications in Human Resource Management: Reasons for the Divide and Concrete Solutions for Bridging the Gap," *Academy of Management Journal* 50, no. 5 (2007): 1013-19; E.E. Lawler, "Why HR Practices Are Not Evidence-Based," *Academy of Management Journal* 50, no. 5 (2007): 1033-36.

91. J. Greenberg and E.C. Tomlinson, "Situated Experiments in Organizations: Transplanting the Lab to the Field," *Journal of Management* 30, no. 5 (2004): 703-24.

92. Pfeffer and Sutton, *Hard Facts, Dangerous Half-Truths, and Total Nonsense.*

93. M.N. Zald, "More Fragmentation? Unfinished Business in Linking the Social Sciences and the Humanities," *Administrative Science Quarterly* 41 (1996): 251-61; C. Heath and S.B. Sitkin, "Big-B Versus Big-O: What Is Organizational About Organizational Behavior?," *Journal of Organizational Behavior* 22 (2001): 43-58; C. Oswick, P. Fleming, and G. Hanlon, "From Borrowing to Blending: Rethinking the Processes of Organizational Theory Building," *Academy of Management Review* 36, no. 2 (2011): 318-37.

94. D.M. Rousseau and Y. Fried, "Location, Location, Location: Contextualizing Organizational Research"," *Journal of Organizational Behavior* 22, no. 1 (2001): 1-13; C.M. Christensen and M.E. Raynor, "Why Hard-Nosed Executives Should Care About Management Theory," *Harvard Business Review* (2003): 66-74. For excellent critique of the "one best way" approach in early management scholarship, see P.F. Drucker, "Management's New Paradigms," *Forbes* (1998): 152-77.

95. H.L. Tosi and J.W. Slocum Jr., "Contingency Theory: Some Suggested Directions," *Journal of Management* 10 (1984): 9-26.

96. D.M.H. Rousseau, R.J. House, "Meso Organizational Behavior: Avoiding Three Fundamental Biases," in *Trends in Organizational Behavior*, ed. C.L. Cooper and D.M. Rousseau (Chichester, UK: John Wiley & Sons, Inc., 1994), 13-30.

CHAPTER 2

1. T. McMahon and C. Sorensen, "Boardroom Blunders at SNC-Lavalin," *Maclean's*, 5 December 2012, 24; A. Posadzki, "Former SNC-Lavalin Employee Sues Company, Blames Boss for Alleged Bribery," *Canadian Press*, 8 September 2013; D. Seglins, "SNC-Lavalin International Used Secret Code for 'Bribery' Payments," *CBC News*, 15 May 2013; T. Watson, "Former SNC-Lavalin CEO Jacques Lamarre Once Promised an Algerian Contact He'd Send Him a Polar Bear," *National Post (Financial Post)*, 5 February 2013; "SNC-Lavalin Says Former Executive's Illegal Actions Justify Firing," *Maclean's*, 17 May 2013; "Full Text of Wb Panel's Letter to Acc," *Daily Star (Dhaka, Bangladesh)*, 15 January 2013, 1;

G. McArthur, "Two Former SNC-Lavalin Executives Charged with Bribery, Other Criminal Offences," *The Globe and Mail*, 31 January 2014.

2. L.L. Thurstone, "Ability, Motivation, and Speed," *Psychometrika* 2, no. 4 (1937): 249–254; N.R.F. Maier, *Psychology in Industry*, 2nd ed. (Boston, MA: Houghton Mifflin Company, 1955); V.H. Vroom, *Work and Motivation* (New York: John Wiley & Sons, Inc., 1964); J.P. Campbell et al., *Managerial Behavior, Performance, and Effectiveness* (New York: McGraw-Hill, 1970).

3. U.-C. Klehe and N. Anderson, "Working Hard and Working Smart: Motivation and Ability During Typical and Maximum Performance," *Journal of Applied Psychology* 92, no. 4 (2007): 978–992; J.S. Gould-Williams and M. Gatenby, "The Effects of Organizational Context and Teamworking Activities on Performance Outcomes–A Study Conducted in England Local Government," *Public Management Review* 12, no. 6 (2010): 759–787.

4. E.E.I. Lawler and L.W. Porter, "Antecedent Attitudes of Effective Managerial Performance," *Organizational Behavior and Human Performance* 2 (1967): 122–142; M.A. Griffin, A. Neal, and S.K. Parker, "A New Model of Work Role Performance: Positive Behavior in Uncertain and Interdependent Contexts," *Academy of Management Journal* 50, no. 2 (April 2007): 327–347.

5. Only a few sources have included all four factors. These include J.P. Campbell and R.D. Pritchard, "Motivation Theory in Industrial and Organizational Psychology," in *Handbook of Industrial and Organizational Psychology*, ed. M.D. Dunnette (Chicago, IL: Rand McNally, 1976), 62–130; T.R. Mitchell, "Motivation: New Directions for Theory, Research, and Practice," *Academy of Management Review* 7, no. 1 (1982): 80–88; G.A.J. Churchill et al., "The Determinants of Salesperson Performance: A Meta-Analysis," *Journal of Marketing Research (JMR)* 22, no. 2 (1985): 103–118; R.E. Plank and D.A. Reid, "The Mediating Role of Sales Behaviors: An Alternative Perspective of Sales Performance and Effectiveness," *Journal of Personal Selling & Sales Management* 14, no. 3 (1994): 43–56. The *MARS* acronym was coined by senior officers in the Singapore armed forces. Chris Perryer at the University of Western Australia suggests the full model should be called the "MARS BAR" because the outcomes might be labelled "behaviour and results"!

6. Technically, the model proposes that situation factors moderate the effects of the three within-person factors. For instance, the effect of employee motivation on behaviour and performance depends on (is moderated by) the situation.

7. C.C. Pinder, *Work Motivation in Organizational Behavior* (Upper Saddle River, NJ: Prentice-Hall, 1998); G.P. Latham and C.C. Pinder, "Work Motivation Theory and Research at the Dawn of the Twenty-First Century," *Annual Review of Psychology* 56 (2005): 485–516.

8. M. Fletcher, "Iceland Banks on Disney Magic to Rub Off," *Conference and Incentive Travel* (2009): 20–21; A. Duff, "Cool Operator," *Director* 2010, 44–48; "An 'on Fire' Iceland Moves up to Become a New Hot Favourite," *Sunday Times (London)*, 4 March 2012, 11; J. Halliwell, "Iceland CEO Malcolm Walker: Walking Back to Happiness," *The Grocer*, 4 August 2012, 43–44; A. Lawson, "Iceland: Success in a Cold Climate," *Retail Week*, 24 February 2012; "A Winning Warmth," *Sunday Times (London)*, 4 March 2012, 1; C. Kelsey, "Iceland Moves Back into the Internet Shopping Market," *Western Mail (Cardiff, Wales)*, 8 May 2013, 12; "A Great Place to Work," (Deeside, UK: Iceland Foods Group, 2013) (accessed 22 May 2013).

9. L.M. Spencer and S.M. Spencer, *Competence at Work: Models for Superior Performance* (New York: Wiley, 1993); R. Kurz and D. Bartram, "Competency and Individual Performance: Modelling the World of Work," in *Organizational Effectiveness: The Role of Psychology*, ed. I.T. Robertson, M. Callinan, and D. Bartram (Chichester, UK: John Wiley & Sons, Inc., 2002), 227–258; D. Bartram, "The Great Eight Competencies: A Criterion-Centric Approach to Validation," *Journal of Applied Psychology* 90, no. 6 (2005): 1185–1203; H. Heinsman et al., "Competencies through the Eyes of Psychologists: A Closer Look at Assessing Competencies," *International Journal of Selection and Assessment* 15, no. 4 (Dec. 2007): 412–427.

10. P. Tharenou, A.M. Saks, and C. Moore, "A Review and Critique of Research on Training and Organizational-Level Outcomes," *Human Resource Management Review* 17, no. 3 (2007): 251–273; T.W.H. Ng and D.C. Feldman, "How Broadly Does Education Contribute to Job Performance?," *Personnel Psychology* 62, no. 1 (Spring 2009): 89–134.

11. Randstad Canada, "Survey Says: Canadians Expect Employers to Foot the Bill for Skills Training," News release (Toronto, ON: Randstad Canada, 27 November 2013); Randstad, *Employee Expectations 2014*, Randstad Workmonitor, (Amsterdam, the Netherlands: R.h. nv, December 2013); Environics Research Group, *Career Development in the Canadian Workplace: National Business Survey*, Canadian Education and Research Institute for Counselling (Toronto, ON: Environics Research Group, January 2014).

12. "Canadian Organizations Must Work Harder to Productively Engage Employees," Watson Wyatt Canada news release for Watson Wyatt Canada (Toronto, ON: 25 January 2005); BlessingWhite, *Employee Engagement Report 2011*, BlessingWhite (Princeton, NJ: January 2011).

13. W.H. Cooper and M.J. Withey, "The Strong Situation Hypothesis," *Personality and Social Psychology Review* 13, no. 1 (February 2009): 62–72; D.C. Funder, "Persons, Behaviors and Situations: An Agenda for Personality Psychology in the Postwar Era," *Journal of Research in Personality* 43, no. 2 (2009): 120–126; R.D. Meyer, R.S. Dalal, and R. Hermida, "A Review and Synthesis of Situational Strength in the Organizational Sciences," *Journal of Management* 36, no. 1 (2010): 121–140; R.A. Sherman, C.S. Nave, and D.C. Funder, "Situational Similarity and Personality Predict Behavioral Consistency," *Journal of Personality and Social Psychology* 99, no. 2 (2010): 330–343.

14. K.F. Kane, "Special Issue: Situational Constraints and Work Performance," *Human Resource Management Review* 3 (Summer 1993): 83–175; S.B. Bacharach and P. Bamberger, "Beyond Situational Constraints: Job Resources Inadequacy and Individual Performance at Work," *Human Resource Management Review* 5, no. 2 (1995): 79–102; G. Johns, "Commentary: In Praise of Context," *Journal of Organizational Behavior* 22 (2001): 31–42.

15. Meyer, Dalal, and Hermida, "A Review and Synthesis of Situational Strength in the Organizational Sciences."

16. J.P. Campbell, "The Definition and Measurement of Performance in the New Age," in *The Changing Nature of Performance: Implications for Staffing, Motivation, and Development* ed. D.R. Ilgen and E.D. Pulakos (San Francisco, CA: Jossey-Bass, 1999), 399–429; R.D. Hackett, "Understanding and Predicting Work Performance in the Canadian Military," *Canadian Journal of Behavioural Science* 34, no. 2 (2002): 131–140.

17. L. Tay, R. Su, and J. Rounds, "People-Things and Data-Ideas: Bipolar Dimensions?," *Journal of Counseling Psychology* 58, no. 3 (2011): 424–40.

18. Griffin, Neal, and Parker, "A New Model of Work Role Performance; A. Charbonnier-Voirin and P. Roussel, "Adaptive Performance: A New Scale to Measure Individual Performance in Organizations," *Canadian Journal of Administrative Sciences* 29, no. 3 (2012): 280–93.

19. D.W. Organ, "Organizational Citizenship Behavior: It's Construct Clean-up Time," *Human Performance* 10 (1997): 85–97; J.A. LePine, A. Erez, and D.E. Johnson, "The Nature and Dimensionality of Organizational Citizenship Behavior: A Critical Review and Meta-Analysis," *Journal of Applied Psychology* 87 (February 2002): 52–65; M.C. Bolino, J. Harvey, and D.G. Bachrach, "A Self-Regulation Approach to Understanding Citizenship Behavior in Organizations," *Organizational Behavior and Human Decision Processes* 119, no. 1 (2012): 126–39.

20. K. Lee and N.J. Allen, "Organizational Citizenship Behavior and Workplace Deviance: The Role of Affect and Cognitions," *Journal of Applied Psychology* 87, no. 1 (2002): 131–142.

21. E.W. Morrison, "Role Definitions and Organizational Citizenship Behavior: The Importance of the Employee's Perspective," *The Academy of Management Journal* 37, no. 6 (1994): 1543–67; E. Vigoda-Gadot, "Compulsory Citizenship Behavior: Theorizing Some Dark Sides of the Good Soldier Syndrome in Organizations," *Journal for the Theory of Social Behaviour* 36, no. 1 (2006): 77–93; M.C. Bolino et al., "Exploring the Dark Side of Organizational Citizenship Behavior," *Journal of Organizational Behavior* 34, no. 4 (2013): 542–59.

22. M. Ozer, "A Moderated Mediation Model of the Relationship between Organizational Citizenship Behaviors and Job Performance," *Journal of Applied Psychology* 96, no. 6 (2011): 1328–36; T.M. Nielsen et al., "Utility of OCB: Organizational Citizenship Behavior and Group Performance in a Resource Allocation Framework," *Journal of Management* 38, no. 2 (2012): 668–94.

23. A.C. Klotz and M.C. Bolino, "Citizenship and Counterproductive Work Behavior: A Moral Licensing View," *Academy of Management*

Review 38, no. 2 (2013): 292–306; Bolino et al., "Exploring the Dark Side of Organizational Citizenship Behavior."

24. M. Rotundo and P. Sackett, "The Relative Importance of Task, Citizenship, and Counterproductive Performance to Global Ratings of Job Performance: A Policy-Capturing Approach," *Journal of Applied Psychology* 87 (February 2002): 66–80; P.D. Dunlop and K. Lee, "Workplace Deviance, Organizational Citizenship Behaviour, and Business Unit Performance: The Bad Apples Do Spoil the Whole Barrel," *Journal of Organizational Behavior* 25 (2004): 67–80; R.S. Dalal, "A Meta-Analysis of the Relationship between Organizational Citizenship Behavior and Counterproductive Work Behavior," *Journal of Applied Psychology* 90, no. 6 (2005): 1241–1255; N.A. Bowling and M.L. Gruys, "Overlooked Issues in the Conceptualization and Measurement of Counterproductive Work Behavior," *Human Resource Management Review* 20, no. 1 (2010): 54–61.

25. The relationship between employee turnover and firm performance is actually very low, but this is due to moderators and is stronger for some forms of firm performance. See: J.I. Hancock et al., "Meta-Analytic Review of Employee Turnover as a Predictor of Firm Performance," *Journal of Management* 39, no. 3 (2013): 573–603.

26. W. Chabun, "People Key to Brandt's Success," *Regina Leader-Post*, 12 December 2011, D1; "Brandt Named One of Canada Fastest-Growing Private Companies," *Regina Leader-Post*, 6 December 2013.

27. D. Oysey, "Motivating Alberta's 'Entitled' Workers," *National Post (Financial Post)*, 19 March 2013; Environics Research Group, *Career Development in the Canadian Workplace: National Business Survey*.

28. N. Chaudhury et al., "Missing in Action: Teacher and Health Worker Absence in Developing Countries," *The Journal of Economic Perspectives* 20, no. 1 (2006): 91–116; L. Yssaad, "Work Absences in 2009," *Perspectives on Labour and Income* 22, no. 3 (June 2010): 14–23.

29. A. Väänänen et al., "The Role of Work Group in Individual Sickness Absence Behavior," *Journal of Health and Social Behavior* 49, no. 4 (2008): 452–67; W. Beemsterboer et al., "A Literature Review on Sick Leave Determinants (1984–2004)," *International Journal of Occupational Medicine and Environmental Health* 22, no. 2 (2009): 169–79; C.M. Berry, A.M. Lelchook, and M.A. Clark, "A Meta-Analysis of the Interrelationships between Employee Lateness, Absenteeism, and Turnover: Implications for Models of Withdrawal Behavior," *Journal of Organizational Behavior* 33, no. 5 (2012): 678–99; S. Störmer and R. Fahr, "Individual Determinants of Work Attendance: Evidence on the Role of Personality," *Applied Economics* 45, no. 19 (2012): 2863–75; M. Sliter, K. Sliter, and S. Jex, "The Employee as a Punching Bag: The Effect of Multiple Sources of Incivility on Employee Withdrawal Behavior and Sales Performance," *Journal of Organizational Behavior* 33, no. 1 (2012): 121–39; M. Biron and P. Bamberger, "Aversive Workplace Conditions and Absenteeism: Taking Referent Group Norms and Supervisor Support into Account," *Journal of Applied Psychology* 97, no. 4 (2012): 901–12.

30. G. Johns, "Presenteeism in the Workplace: A Review and Research Agenda," *Journal of Organizational Behavior* 31, no. 4 (2010): 519–42; E. Gosselin, L. Lemyre, and W. Corneil, "Presenteeism and Absenteeism: Differentiated Understanding of Related Phenomena," *Journal of Occupational Health Psychology* 18, no. 1 (2013): 75–86.

31. G. Johns, "Attendance Dynamics at Work: The Antecedents and Correlates of Presenteeism, Absenteeism, and Productivity Loss," *Journal of Occupational Health Psychology* 16, no. 4 (2011): 483–500; D. Baker-McClearn et al., "Absence Management and Presenteeism: The Pressures on Employees to Attend Work and the Impact of Attendance on Performance," *Human Resource Management Journal* 20, no. 3 (2010): 311–28.

32. C. Crawshaw, "Personality Testing Can Be a Sticky Subject," *Edmonton Journal*, 29 March 2008, D14.

33. Personality researchers agree on one point about the definition of personality: It is difficult to pin down. A definition necessarily captures one perspective of the topic more than others, and the concept of personality is itself very broad. The definition presented here is based on C.S. Carver and M.F. Scheier, *Perspectives on Personality*, 6th ed. (Boston, MA: Allyn & Bacon, 2007); D.C. Funder, *The Personality Puzzle*, 4th ed. (New York: W.W. Norton & Company, 2007).

34. D.P. McAdams and J.L. Pals, "A New Big Five: Fundamental Principles for an Integrative Science of Personality," *American Psychologist* 61, no. 3 (2006): 204–217.

35. B.W. Roberts and A. Caspi, "Personality Development and the Person-Situation Debate: It's Déjà Vu All over Again," *Psychological Inquiry* 12, no. 2 (2001): 104–109.

36. B. Reynolds and K. Karraker, "A Big Five Model of Disposition and Situation Interaction: Why a 'Helpful' Person May Not Always Behave Helpfully," *New Ideas in Psychology* 21 (April 2003): 1–13; W. Mischel, "Toward an Integrative Science of the Person," *Annual Review of Psychology* 55 (2004): 1–22.

37. K.L. Jang, W.J. Livesley, and P.A. Vernon, "Heritability of the Big Five Personality Dimensions and Their Facets: A Twin Study," *Journal of Personality* 64, no. 3 (1996): 577–591; N.L. Segal, *Entwined Lives: Twins and What They Tell Us About Human Behavior* (New York: Plume, 2000); G. Lensvelt-Mulders and J. Hettema, "Analysis of Genetic Influences on the Consistency and Variability of the Big Five across Different Stressful Situations," *European Journal of Personality* 15, no. 5 (2001): 355–371; T. Bouchard and J. Loehlin, "Genes, Evolution, and Personality," *Behavior Genetics* 31, no. 3 (May 2001): 243–273; P. Borkenau et al., "Genetic and Environmental Influences on Person X Situation Profiles," *Journal of Personality* 74, no. 5 (2006): 1451–1480.

38. B.W. Roberts and W.F. DelVecchio, "The Rank-Order Consistency of Personality Traits from Childhood to Old Age: A Quantitative Review of Longitudinal Studies," *Psychological Bulletin* 126, no. 1 (2000): 3–25; A. Terracciano, P.T. Costa, and R.R. McCrae, "Personality Plasticity after Age 30," *Personality and Social Psychology Bulletin* 32, no. 8 (Aug. 2006): 999–1009.

39. M. Jurado and M. Rosselli, "The Elusive Nature of Executive Functions: A Review of Our Current Understanding," *Neuropsychology Review* 17, no. 3 (2007): 213–233.

40. J.M. Digman, "Personality Structure: Emergence of the Five-Factor Model," *Annual Review of Psychology* 41 (1990): 417–440; O.P. John and S. Srivastava, "The Big Five Trait Taxonomy: History, Measurement, and Theoretical Perspectives," in *Handbook of Personality: Theory and Research*, ed. L.A. Pervin and O.P. John (New York: Guildford Press, 1999), 102–138; R.R. McCrae, J.F. Gaines, and M.A. Wellington, "The Five-Factor Model in Fact and Fiction," in *Handbook of Psychology*, ed. I.B. Weiner (2012), 65–91.

41. J. Hogan and B. Holland, "Using Theory to Evaluate Personality and Job-Performance Relations: A Socioanalytic Perspective," *Journal of Applied Psychology* 88, no. 1 (2003): 100–112; D.S. Ones, C. Viswesvaran, and S. Dilchert, "Personality at Work: Raising Awareness and Correcting Misconceptions," *Human Performance* 18, no. 4 (2005): 389–404; I.-S. Oh and C.M. Berry, "The Five-Factor Model of Personality and Managerial Performance: Validity Gains through the Use of 360 Degree Performance Ratings," *Journal of Applied Psychology* 94, no. 6 (2009): 1498–1513; D.S. Chiaburu and N.C. Carpenter, "Employees' Motivation for Personal Initiative," *Journal of Personnel Psychology* 12, no. 2 (2013): 97–103.

42. M.R. Barrick and M.K. Mount, "Yes, Personality Matters: Moving on to More Important Matters," *Human Performance* 18, no. 4 (2005): 359–372; S.J. Perry et al., "P = *F* (Conscientiousness × Ability): Examining the Facets of Conscientiousness," *Human Performance* 23, no. 4 (2010): 343–360; A. Neal et al., "Predicting the Form and Direction of Work Role Performance from the Big 5 Model of Personality Traits," *Journal of Organizational Behavior* 33, no. 2 (2012): 175–92.

43. M.R. Barrick, M.K. Mount, and T.A. Judge, "Personality and Performance at the Beginning of the New Millennium: What Do We Know and Where Do We Go Next?," *International Journal of Selection and Assessment* 9, no. 1&2 (2001): 9–30; T.A. Judge and R. Ilies, "Relationship of Personality to Performance Motivation: A Meta-Analytic Review," *Journal of Applied Psychology* 87, no. 4 (2002): 797–807; A. Witt, L.A. Burke, and M.R. Barrick, "The Interactive Effects of Conscientiousness and Agreeableness on Job Performance," *Journal of Applied Psychology* 87 (February 2002): 164–169; J. Moutafi, A. Furnham, and J. Crump, "Is Managerial Level Related to Personality?," *British Journal of Management* 18, no. 3 (2007): 272–280.

44. R. Ilies, M.W. Gerhardt, and H. Le, "Individual Differences in Leadership Emergence: Integrating Meta-Analytic Findings and Behavioral Genetics Estimates," *International Journal of Selection and Assessment* 12, no. 3 (September 2004): 207–219; Oh and Berry, "The Five-Factor Model of Personality and Managerial Performance: Validity Gains through the Use of 360 Degree Performance Ratings;" A. Minbashian, J.E.H. Bright, and K.D. Bird, "Complexity in the Relationships among the Subdimensions of Extraversion and Job Performance in Managerial Occupations," *Journal of Occupational and*

Organizational Psychology 82, no. 3 (2009): 537–49.

45. K.M. DeNeve and H. Cooper, "The Happy Personality: A Meta-Analysis of 137 Personality Traits and Subjective Well-Being," *Psychological Bulletin* 124 (September 1998): 197–229; M.L. Kern and H.S. Friedman, "Do Conscientious Individuals Live Longer? A Quantitative Review," *Health Psychology* 27, no. 5 (2008): 505–512; P.S. Fry and D.L. Debats, "Perfectionism and the Five-Factor Personality Traits as Predictors of Mortality in Older Adults," *Journal of Health Psychology* 14, no. 4 (May 1, 2009): 513–524; H.S. Friedman, M.L. Kern, and C.A. Reynolds, "Personality and Health, Subjective Well-Being, and Longevity," *Journal of Personality* 78, no. 1 (2010): 179–216.

46. H. Le et al., "Too Much of a Good Thing: Curvilinear Relationships between Personality Traits and Job Performance," *Journal of Applied Psychology* 96, no. 1 (2011): 113–33.

47. C.G. Jung, *Psychological Types* trans. H.G. Baynes (Princeton, NJ: Princeton University Press, 1971); I.B. Myers, *The Myers-Briggs Type Indicator* (Palo Alto, CA: Consulting Psychologists Press, 1987).

48. Adapted from an exhibit found at http://www.16-personality-types.com.

49. L. Cunningham, "Does It Pay to Know Your Type?," *Washington Post*, 18 December 2012.

50. M. Gladwell, "Personality Plus," *New Yorker*, 20 September 2004, 42–48; R.B. Kennedy and D.A. Kennedy, "Using the Myers-Briggs Type Indicator in Career Counseling," *Journal of Employment Counseling* 41, no. 1 (March 2004): 38–44.

51. K.M. Butler, "Using Positive Four-Letter Words," *Employee Benefit News*, April 2007; M. Weinstein, "Personality Assessment Soars at Southwest," *Training*, 3 January 2008.

52. R.R. McCrae and P.T. Costa, "Reinterpreting the Myers-Briggs Type Indicator from the Perspective of the Five-Factor Model of Personality," *Journal of Personality* 57 (1989): 17–40; A. Furnham, "The Big Five Versus the Big Four: The Relationship between the Myers-Briggs Type Indicator (MBTI) and NEO-PI Five Factor Model of Personality," *Personality and Individual Differences* 21, no. 2 (1996): 303–307.

53. R.E. Guadagno, B.M. Okdie, and C.A. Eno, "Who Blogs? Personality Predictors of Blogging," *Computers in Human Behavior* 24, no. 5 (2008): 1993–2004; D.H. Kluemper and P.A. Rosen, "Future Employment Selection Methods: Evaluating Social Networking Web Sites," *Journal of Managerial Psychology* 24, no. 6 (2009): 567–80; M.D. Back et al., "Facebook Profiles Reflect Actual Personality, Not Self-Idealization," *Psychological Science* (2010); T. Yarkoni, "Personality in 100,000 Words: A Large-Scale Analysis of Personality and Word Use among Bloggers," *Journal of Research in Personality* 44, no. 3 (2010): 363–73.

54. R.J. Lopez, D. Weikel, and R. Connell, "NTSB Blames Engineer for 2008 Metrolink Crash," *Los Angeles Times*, 22 January 2010; "Metrolink Train Crews in Southern California Threaten Boycott over New Personality Tests," *Associated Press*, 1 April 2010.

55. R. Hogan, "In Defense of Personality Measurement: New Wine for Old Whiners," *Human Performance* 18, no. 4 (2005): 331–341; K. Murphy and J.L. Dzieweczynski, "Why Don't Measures of Broad Dimensions of Personality Perform Better as Predictors of Job Performance?," *Human Performance* 18, no. 4 (2005): 343–357; F.P. Morgeson et al., "Reconsidering the Use of Personality Tests in Personnel Selection Contexts," *Personnel Psychology* 60, no. 3 (2007): 683–729; R.P. Tett and N.D. Christiansen, "Personality Tests at the Crossroads: A Response to Morgeson, Campion, Dipboye, Hollenbeck, Murphy, and Schmitt (2007)," *Personnel Psychology* 60, no. 4 (2007): 967–993.

56. D.L. Whetzel et al., "Linearity of Personality-Performance Relationships: A Large-Scale Examination," *International Journal of Selection and Assessment* 18, no. 3 (2010): 310–20; Le et al., "Too Much of a Good Thing."

57. L.A. Witt, M.C. Andrews, and D.S. Carlson, "When Conscientiousness Isn't Enough: Emotional Exhaustion and Performance Among Call Center Customer Service Representatives," *Journal of Management* 30, no. 1 (2004): 149–160; J. Stoeber, K. Otto, and C. Dalbert, "Perfectionism and the Big Five: Conscientiousness Predicts Longitudinal Increases in Self-Oriented Perfectionism," *Personality and Individual Differences* 47, no. 4 (2009): 363–368; C.J. Boyce, A.M. Wood, and G.D.A. Brown, "The Dark Side of Conscientiousness: Conscientious People Experience Greater Drops in Life Satisfaction Following Unemployment," *Journal of Research in Personality* 44, no. 4 (2010): 535–539.

58. S.D. Risavy and P.A. Hausdorf, "Personality Testing in Personnel Selection: Adverse Impact and Differential Hiring Rates," *International Journal of Selection and Assessment* 19, no. 1 (2011): 18–30.

59. N.S. Hartman and W.L. Grubb, "Deliberate Faking on Personality and Emotional Intelligence Measures," *Psychological Reports* 108, no. 1 (2011): 120–38.

60. B.S. Connelly and D.S. Ones, "An Other Perspective on Personality: Meta-Analytic Integration of Observers' Accuracy and Predictive Validity," *Psychological Bulletin* 136, no. 6 (2010): 1092–122.

61. V. Baker, "Why Men Can't Manage Women," *The Guardian*, 14 April 2007, 1.

62. K.C. Neel, "Abdoulah Sets Wow Apart," *Multichannel News*, 29 January 2007, 2; D. Graham, "She Walks the Talk," *Denver Woman*, April 2009; "Wow! Management Team," (Denver, CO: 2010), http://www.wowway.com/internet-cable-phone-company/wow-management-executive-bios/ (accessed 6 December 2010).

63. B.M. Meglino and E.C. Ravlin, "Individual Values in Organizations: Concepts, Controversies, and Research," *Journal of Management* 24, no. 3 (1998): 351–389; B.R. Agle and C.B. Caldwell, "Understanding Research on Values in Business," *Business and Society* 38, no. 3 (September 1999): 326–387; S. Hitlin and J.A. Pilavin, "Values: Reviving a Dormant Concept," *Annual Review of Sociology* 30 (2004): 359–393.

64. D. Lubinski, D.B. Schmidt, and C.P. Benbow, "A 20-Year Stability Analysis of the Study of Values for Intellectually Gifted Individuals from Adolescence to Adulthood," *Journal of Applied Psychology* 81 (1996): 443–451.

65. L. Parks and R.P. Guay, "Personality, Values, and Motivation," *Personality and Individual Differences* 47, no. 7 (2009): 675–684.

66. S.H. Schwartz, "Universals in the Content and Structure of Values: Theoretical Advances and Empirical Tests in 20 Countries," *Advances in Experimental Social Psychology* 25 (1992): 1–65; D. Spini, "Measurement Equivalence of 10 Value Types from the Schwartz Value Survey across 21 Countries," *Journal of Cross-Cultural Psychology* 34, no. 1 (2003): 3–23; S.H. Schwartz and K. Boehnke, "Evaluating the Structure of Human Values with Confirmatory Factor Analysis," *Journal of Research in Personality* 38, no. 3 (2004): 230–55; S.H. Schwartz, "Studying Values: Personal Adventure, Future Directions," *Journal of Cross-Cultural Psychology* 42, no. 2 (2011): 307–19. Schwartz's model is currently being revised, but the new model is similar in overall design and still requires refinement. See: S.H. Schwartz et al., "Refining the Theory of Basic Individual Values," *Journal of Personality and Social Psychology* 103, no. 4 (2012): 663–88.

67. L. Parks and R.P. Guay, "Can Personal Values Predict Performance? Evidence in an Academic Setting," *Applied Psychology* 61, no. 1 (2012): 149–73; M.L. Arthaud-Day, J.C. Rode, and W.H. Turnley, "Direct and Contextual Effects of Individual Values on Organizational Citizenship Behavior in Teams," *Journal of Applied Psychology* 97, no. 4 (2012): 792–807.

68. G.R. Maio et al., "Addressing Discrepancies between Values and Behavior: The Motivating Effect of Reasons," *Journal of Experimental Social Psychology* 37, no. 2 (2001): 104–17; B. Verplanken and R.W. Holland, "Motivated Decision Making: Effects of Activation and Self-Centrality of Values on Choices and Behavior," *Journal of Personality and Social Psychology* 82, no. 3 (2002): 434–47; A. Bardi and S.H. Schwartz, "Values and Behavior: Strength and Structure of Relations," *Personality and Social Psychology Bulletin* 29, no. 10 (2003): 1207–20; G.R. Maio et al., "Changing, Priming, and Acting on Values: Effects Via Motivational Relations in a Circular Model," *Journal of Personality and Social Psychology* 97, no. 4 (2009): 699–715; L. Sagiv, N. Sverdlik, and N. Schwarz, "To Compete or to Cooperate? Values' Impact on Perception and Action in Social Dilemma Games," *European Journal of Social Psychology* 41, no. 1 (2011): 64–77.

69. E. Dreezens et al., "The Missing Link: On Strengthening the Relationship between Values and Attitudes," *Basic and Applied Social Psychology* 30, no. 2 (2008): 142–52.

70. N. Mazar, O. Amir, and D. Ariely, "The Dishonesty of Honest People: A Theory of Self-Concept Maintenance," *Journal of Marketing Research* 45 (December 2008): 633–644.

71. G. Scott, "Vancity's Staff Buy into Changing the World," *Vancouver Sun*, 27 October 2012, C4; E. Weinreb, "Motivating Employees, with or without Money," *GreenBiz*, GreenBiz Group, 21 August 2013, http://www.greenbiz.com/blog/2013/08/21/motivating-employees-and-without-money.

72. M.L. Verquer, T.A. Beehr, and S.H. Wagner, "A Meta-Analysis of Relations between Person-Organization Fit and Work Attitudes," *Journal of Vocational Behavior* 63 (2003): 473–89; J.W. Westerman and L.A. Cyr, "An Integrative Analysis of Person-Organization Fit Theories," *International Journal of Selection and Assessment* 12, no. 3 (2004): 252–61; J.R. Edwards and D.M. Cable, "The Value of Value Congruence," *Journal of Applied Psychology* 94, no. 3 (2009): 654–77; B.J. Hoffman et al., "Person-Organization Value Congruence: How Transformational Leaders Influence Work Group Effectiveness," *Academy of Management Journal* 54, no. 4 (2011): 779–96.

73. K. Hornyak, "Upward Move: Cynthia Schwalm," *Medical Marketing & Media*, June 2008, 69. For research on the consequences on value congruence, see A.L. Kristof, "Person-Organization Fit: An Integrative Review of Its Conceptualizations, Measurement, and Implications," *Personnel Psychology* 49, no. 1 (1996): 1–49; M.L. Verquer, T.A. Beehr, and S.H. Wagner, "A Meta-Analysis of Relations between Person-Organization Fit and Work Attitudes," *Journal of Vocational Behavior* 63 (2003): 473–489; J.W. Westerman and L.A. Cyr, "An Integrative Analysis of Person-Organization Fit Theories," *International Journal of Selection and Assessment* 12, no. 3 (September 2004): 252–261; D. Bouckenooghe et al., "The Prediction of Stress by Values and Value Conflict," *Journal of Psychology* 139, no. 4 (2005): 369–382.

74. T. Simons, "Behavioral Integrity: The Perceived Alignment between Managers' Words and Deeds as a Research Focus," *Organization Science* 13, no. 1 (Jan–Feb 2002): 18–35; Watson Wyatt, "Employee Ratings of Senior Management Dip, Watson Wyatt Survey Finds," Watson Wyatt News release (New York: 4 January 2007).

75. Z. Aycan, R.N. Kanungo, and J.B.P. Sinha, "Organizational Culture and Human Resource Management Practices: The Model of Culture Fit," *Journal of Cross-Cultural Psychology* 30 (July 1999): 501–526; M. Naor, K. Linderman, and R. Schroeder, "The Globalization of Operations in Eastern and Western Countries: Unpacking the Relationship between National and Organizational Culture and Its Impact on Manufacturing Performance," *Journal of Operations Management* 28, no. 3 (2010): 194–205. This type of values incongruence can occur even when the company is founded in that country, that is, when a local company tries to introduce a culture incompatible with the national culture. See for example: A. Danisman, "Good Intentions and Failed Implementations: Understanding Culture-Based Resistance to Organizational Change," *European Journal of Work and Organizational Psychology* 19, no. 2 (2010): 200–220.

76. C. Savoye, "Workers Say Honesty Is Best Company Policy," *Christian Science Monitor*, June 15 2000; Ekos Politics, *Women See It Differently*, Ekos Politics (Ottawa, ON: 6 May 2010); J.M. Kouzes and B.Z. Posner, *The Leadership Challenge*, 4thrd ed. (San Francisco, CA: Jossey-Bass, 2010), pp. 32–33.

77. P.L. Schumann, "A Moral Principles Framework for Human Resource Management Ethics," *Human Resource Management Review* 11 (Spring–Summer 2001): 93–111; J. Boss, *Analyzing Moral Issues*, 3rd ed. (New York: McGraw-Hill, 2005), Chap. 1; M.G. Velasquez, *Business Ethics: Concepts and Cases*, 6th ed. (Upper Saddle River, NJ: Prentice-Hall, 2006), Chap. 2.

78. For analysis of these predictors of ethical conduct, see: J.J. Kish-Gephart, D.A. Harrison, and L.K. Treviño, "Bad Apples, Bad Cases, and Bad Barrels: Meta-Analytic Evidence About Sources of Unethical Decisions at Work," *Journal of Applied Psychology* 95, no. 1 (2010): 1–31.

79. T.J. Jones, "Ethical Decision Making by Individuals in Organizations: An Issue Contingent Model," *Academy of Management Review* 16 (1991): 366–95; T. Barnett, "Dimensions of Moral Intensity and Ethical Decision Making: An Empirical Study," *Journal of Applied Social Psychology* 31, no. 5 (2001): 1038–57; J. Tsalikis, B. Seaton, and P. Shepherd, "Relative Importance Measurement of the Moral Intensity Dimensions," *Journal of Business Ethics* 80, no. 3 (2008): 613–26; S. Valentine and D. Hollingworth, "Moral Intensity, Issue Importance, and Ethical Reasoning in Operations Situations," *Journal of Business Ethics* 108, no. 4 (2012): 509–23.

80. K. Weaver, J. Morse, and C. Mitcham, "Ethical Sensitivity in Professional Practice: Concept Analysis," *Journal of Advanced Nursing* 62, no. 5 (2008): 607–18; L.J.T. Pedersen, "See No Evil: Moral Sensitivity in the Formulation of Business Problems," *Business Ethics: A European Review* 18, no. 4 (2009): 335–48. According to one recent neuroscience study, the emotional aspect of moral sensitivity declines and the cognitive aspect increases between early childhood and young adulthood. See: J. Decety, K.J. Michalska, and K.D. Kinzler, "The Contribution of Emotion and Cognition to Moral Sensitivity: A Neurodevelopmental Study," *Cerebral Cortex* 22, no. 1 (2012): 209–20.

81. N. Van Praet, "SNC Halts Payments to Ousted Former CEO," *National Post*, 14 December 2012, FP1.

82. D. You, Y. Maeda, and M.J. Bebeau, "Gender Differences in Moral Sensitivity: A Meta-Analysis," *Ethics & Behavior* 21, no. 4 (2011): 263–82; A.H. Chan and H. Cheung, "Cultural Dimensions, Ethical Sensitivity, and Corporate Governance," *Journal of Business Ethics* 110, no. 1 (2012): 45–59; G. Desautels and S. Jacob, "The Ethical Sensitivity of Evaluators: A Qualitative Study Using a Vignette Design," *Evaluation* 18, no. 4 (2012): 437–50.

83. N. Ruedy and M. Schweitzer, "In the Moment: The Effect of Mindfulness on Ethical Decision Making," *Journal of Business Ethics* 95, no. 1 (2010): 73–87.

84. S.J. Reynolds, K. Leavitt, and K.A. DeCelles, "Automatic Ethics: The Effects of Implicit Assumptions and Contextual Cues on Moral Behavior," *Journal of Applied Psychology* 95, no. 4 (2010): 752–760.

85. D.R. Beresford, N.D. Katzenbach, and C.B. Rogers Jr., *Report of Investigation by the Special Investigative Committee of the Board of Directors of Worldcom, Inc.* (31 March 2003).

86. Ipsos Reid, "Four in Ten (42%) Employed Canadians Have Observed Some Form of Workplace Misconduct," News release (Toronto, ON: Ipsos Reid, 3 July 2013).

87. H. Donker, D. Poff, and S. Zahir, "Corporate Values, Codes of Ethics, and Firm Performance: A Look at the Canadian Context," *Journal of Business Ethics* 82, no. 3 (2008): 527–537; L. Preuss, "Codes of Conduct in Organisational Context: From Cascade to Lattice-Work of Codes," *Journal of Business Ethics* 94, no. 4 (2010): 471–487.

88. J.T. Kennedy, "Alcoa's William O'Rourke: Ethical Business Practices, from Russia to Sustainability," *Carnegie Council*, 27 April 2011; A. Graham, "The Thought Leader Interview: William J. O'Rourke," *strategy + business*, Winter 2012, 1–7.

89. SNC-Lavalin's ethics initiatives are described in: SNC-Lavalin, "Our Latest Measures Towards Ethics and Compliance," News release (Montreal, QC: SNC-Lavalin, 1 October 2013); "Canada's SNC Lavalin Offers Amnesty to Staff for Corruption Information," *Reuters News (Toronto)*, 27 May 2013; SNC-Lavalin, *Code of Ethics and Business Conduct*, (Montreal, QC: SNC-Lavalin, 17 January 2014); "SNC-Lavalin Hires Chief Compliance Officer," *Compliance Week*, 24 February 2014.

90. S.L. Grover, T. Nadisic, and D.L. Patient, "Bringing Together Different Perspectives on Ethical Leadership," *Journal of Change Management* 12, no. 4 (2012): 377–81; J. Jordan et al., "Someone to Look up To: Executive–Follower Ethical Reasoning and Perceptions of Ethical Leadership," *Journal of Management* 39, no. 3 (2013): 660–83; J. Jaeger, "Compliance Culture Depends on Middle Management," *Compliance Week*, February 2014, 47–61. The ethical culture quotation is from: Canadian Centre for Ethics and Corporate Policy, "Business Ethics Faqs," (Toronto, ON: Canadian Centre for Ethics and Corporate Policy, 2014), http://www.ethicscentre.ca/EN/resources/faq.cfm (accessed 26 February 2014).

91. L. Gettler, "The New Global Manager Needs to Understand Different Work Cultures," *The Age*, 6 February 2008.

92. Individual and collectivism information are from the meta-analysis by Oyserman et al., not the earlier findings by Hofstede. See: D. Oyserman, H.M. Coon, and M. Kemmelmeier, "Rethinking Individualism and Collectivism: Evaluation of Theoretical Assumptions and Meta-Analyses," *Psychological Bulletin* 128 (2002): 3–72. Consistent with Oyserman et al., a recent study found high rather than low individualism among Chileans. See: A. Kolstad and S. Horpestad, "Self-Construal in Chile and Norway," *Journal of Cross-Cultural Psychology* 40, no. 2 (March 2009): 275–281.

93. F.S. Niles, "Individualism-Collectivism Revisited," *Cross-Cultural Research* 32 (1998): 315–41; C.P. Earley and C.B. Gibson, "Taking Stock in Our Progress on Individualism-Collectivism: 100 Years of Solidarity and Community," *Journal of Management* 24 (1998): 265–304; C.L. Jackson et al., "Psychological Collectivism: A Measurement Validation and Linkage to Group Member Performance," *Journal of Applied Psychology* 91, no. 4 (2006): 884–99.

94. Oyserman, Coon, and Kemmelmeier, "Rethinking Individualism and Collectivism," Also see F. Li and L. Aksoy, "Dimensionality of Individualism–Collectivism and Measurement

Equivalence of Triandis and Gelfand's Scale," *Journal of Business and Psychology* 21, no. 3 (2007): 313–329. The vertical-horizontal distinction does not account for the lack of correlation between individualism and collectivism. See: J.H. Vargas and M. Kemmelmeier, "Ethnicity and Contemporary American Culture: A Meta-Analytic Investigation of Horizontal-Vertical Individualism-Collectivism," *Journal of Cross-Cultural Psychology* 44, no. 2 (2013): 195–222.

95. M. Voronov and J.A. Singer, "The Myth of Individualism-Collectivism: A Critical Review," *Journal of Social Psychology* 142 (August 2002): 461–480; Y. Takano and S. Sogon, "Are Japanese More Collectivistic Than Americans?," *Journal of Cross-Cultural Psychology* 39, no. 3 (May 1, 2008 2008): 237–250; D. Dalsky, "Individuality in Japan and the United States: A Cross-Cultural Priming Experiment," *International Journal of Intercultural Relations* 34, no. 5 (2010): 429–435. Japan scored 46 on individualism in Hofstede's original study, placing it a little below the middle of the range and around the 60th percentile among the countries studied.

96. G. Hofstede, *Culture's Consequences: Comparing Values, Behaviors, Institutions, and Organizations across Nations*, 2nd ed. (Thousand Oaks, CA: Sage, 2001).

97. "Rolling up the Sleeves," *Shanghai Daily*, 3 September 2012.

98. Hofstede, *Culture's Consequences: Comparing Values, Behaviors, Institutions, and Organizations across Nations*. Hofstede used the terms *masculinity* and *femininity* for *achievement* and *nurturing orientation*, respectively. We (along with other writers) have adopted the latter two terms to minimize the sexist perspective of these concepts. Also, readers need to be aware that achievement orientation is assumed to be opposite of nurturing orientation, but this opposing relationship might be questioned.

99. V. Taras, J. Rowney, and P. Steel, "Half a Century of Measuring Culture: Review of Approaches, Challenges, and Limitations Based on the Analysis of 121 Instruments for Quantifying Culture," *Journal of International Management* 15, no. 4 (2009): 357–373.

100. R.L. Tung and A. Verbeke, "Beyond Hofstede and GLOBE: Improving the Quality of Cross-Cultural Research," *Journal of International Business Studies* 41, no. 8 (2010): 1259–1274.

101. W.K.W. Choy, A.B.E. Lee, and P. Ramburuth, "Multinationalism in the Workplace: A Myriad of Values in a Singaporean Firm," *Singapore Management Review* 31, no. 1 (January 2009).

102. N. Jacob, "Cross-Cultural Investigations: Emerging Concepts," *Journal of Organizational Change Management* 18, no. 5 (2005): 514–528; V. Taras, B.L. Kirkman, and P. Steel, "Examining the Impact of Culture's Consequences: A Three-Decade, Multilevel, Meta-Analytic Review of Hofstede's Cultural Value Dimensions," *Journal of Applied Psychology* 95, no. 3 (2010): 405–439.

103. M. Adams, "New Canadians, Old Values?," *The Globe and Mail*, 2 March 2005, A17.

104. Z. Wu and D. Baer, "Attitudes toward Family and Gender Roles: A Comparison of English and French Canadian Women," *Journal of Comparative Family Studies* 27 (Autumn 1996): 437–452. The reference to "two solitudes" comes from: H. McLennan, *Two Solitudes* (Toronto, ON: MacMillan of Canada, 1945).

105. M. Laroche et al., "The Influence of Culture on Pro-Environmental Knowledge, Attitudes, and Behavior: A Canadian Perspective," *Advances In Consumer Research* 23 (1996): 196–202; M. Major et al., "Meanings of Work and Personal Values of Canadian Anglophone and Francophone Middle Managers," *Canadian Journal of Administrative Sciences* 11 (1994): 251–63.

106. I. Chapman, D. McCaskill, and D. Newhouse, "Management in Contemporary Aboriginal Organizations," *Canadian Journal of Native Studies* 11, no. 2 (1991): 333–349; L. Redpath and M.O. Nielsen, "A Comparison of Native Culture, Non-Native Culture and New Management Ideology," *Canadian Journal of Administrative Sciences* 14, no. 3 (September 1997): 327–339; M. Julien, B. Wright, and D.M. Zinni, "Stories from the Circle: Leadership Lessons Learned from Aboriginal Leaders," *The Leadership Quarterly* 21, no. 1 (2010): 114–126.

107. M. Adams, *Fire and Ice: The United States, Canada, and the Myth of Converging Values* (Toronto, ON: Penguin Canada, 2004), 142.

108. J. Laxer, *The Border: Canada, the U.S. And Dispatches from the 49th Parallel* (Toronto, ON: Anchor Canada, 2004).

109. C. Cobb, "Canadians Want a Diverse Society: Poll," *Ottawa Citizen*, 18 February 2002, A5; K. May, "Canadian Nationalism Growing: Study," *Ottawa Citizen*, 5 June 2002, A8; C. Boucher, "Canada-Us Values: Distinct, Inevitably Carbon Copy, or Narcissism of Small Differences?," *Horizons: Policy Research Initiative* 7, no. 1 (June 2004): 42–49.

110. Adams, *Fire and Ice*. For earlier research, see; M. Adams, "What Makes Us Different," *The Globe and Mail*, 4 July 2001, A11; M. Adams, *Better Happy Than Rich?* (Toronto, ON: Viking, 2001); M. Adams, *Sex in the Snow* (Toronto, ON: Penguin Canada, 1998).

111. E. Grabb and J. Curtis, *Regions Apart: The Four Societies of Canada and the United States* (New York: Oxford University Press, 2005); D. Baer, E. Grabb, and W. Johnston, "National Character, Regional Culture, and the Values of Canadians and Americans," *Canadian Review of Sociology and anthropology* 30, no. 1 (1993): 13–36. Evidence of small differences in Canadian-American culture are also reported in: Boucher, "Canada-US Values."

CHAPTER 3

1. *City of Calgary and Calgary Fire Fighters Association, International Association of Fire Fighters, Local255, with Respect to a Grievance by Charles Hendricks*, 47218 Canadian Legal Information Institute(2012); J. Perron-Clow, "Young Women Urged to Pursue a Career in Firefighting," *Orleans Star (Orleans, Ontario)*, 11 May 2011; K. Chen, "Camp Ffit Lets Teenage Girls Experience the Life of a Firefighter," *Ottawa Citizen*, 15 August 2012, C5; V.M. Cruz, "Camp Fury Gives Girl Scouts a Look at What It Takes to Be a Firefighter," *Arizona Daily Star*, 8 June 2012; S. Ptashkin, "Camp Fury Gives Girl Scouts inside Look at Fire and Police Training," *NBC News*, 31 May 2013; K. Garvey, "As Fire Department Looks to Recruit Women, Sexist Tweets Suggest Some Firefighters May Not Be So Welcoming," *National Post (Toronto)*, 9 August 2013.

2. K. Morgan, "Camp Houston Fire," *Houston Chronicle*, 7 March 2010, 1.

3. D. Cooper and S.M.B. Thatcher, "Identification in Organizations: The Role of Self-Concept Orientations and Identification Motives," *Academy of Management Review* 35, no. 4 (2010): 516–38; J. Schaubroeck, Y.J. Kim, and A.C. Peng, "The Self-Concept in Organizational Psychology: Clarifying and Differentiating the Constructs," in *International Review of Industrial and Organizational Psychology* (John Wiley & Sons, Inc., 2012), 1–38.

4. L. Gaertner et al., "A Motivational Hierarchy Within: Primacy of the Individual Self, Relational Self, or Collective Self?," *Journal of Experimental Social Psychology* 48, no. 5 (2012): 997–1013; R.E. Johnson et al., "Leader Identity as an Antecedent of the Frequency and Consistency of Transformational, Consideration, and Abusive Leadership Behaviors," *Journal of Applied Psychology* 97, no. 6 (2012): 1262–72.

5. E. Rafaeli-Mor and J. Steinberg, "Self-Complexity and Well-Being: A Review and Research Synthesis," *Personality and Social Psychology Review* 6, no. 1 (2002): 31–58; E.J. Koch and J.A. Shepperd, "Is Self-Complexity Linked to Better Coping? A Review of the Literature," *Journal of Personality* 72, no. 4 (2004): 727–60; A.R. McConnell, R.J. Rydell, and C.M. Brown, "On the Experience of Self-Relevant Feedback: How Self-Concept Organization Influences Affective Responses and Self-Evaluations," *Journal of Experimental Social Psychology* 45, no. 4 (2009): 695–707.

6. J.D. Campbell et al., "Self-Concept Clarity: Measurement, Personality Correlates, and Cultural Boundaries," *Journal of Personality and Social Psychology* 70, no. 1 (1996): 141–56.

7. J. Lodi-Smith and B.W. Roberts, "Getting to Know Me: Social Role Experiences and Age Differences in Self-Concept Clarity During Adulthood," *Journal of Personality* 78, no. 5 (2010): 1383–410.

8. G. Quill, "HeLeNe Joy : Successful – and Ignored," *Toronto Star*, 10 January 2009; "Canada Wins Aussie Joy," *West Australian*, 29 June 2011, 5.

9. Koch and Shepperd, "Is Self-Complexity Linked to Better Coping? A Review of the Literature; T.D. Ritchie et al., "Self-Concept Clarity Mediates the Relation between Stress and Subjective Well-Being," *Self and Identity* 10, no. 4 (2010): 493–508.

10. A.T. Brook, J. Garcia, and M.A. Fleming, "The Effects of Multiple Identities on Psychological Well-Being," *Personality and Social Psychology Bulletin* 34, no. 12 (2008): 1588–600.

11. J.D. Campbell, "Self-Esteem and Clarity of the Self-Concept," *Journal of Personality and Social Psychology* 59, no. 3 (1990).

12. T.W.H. Ng, K.L. Sorensen, and D.C. Feldman, "Dimensions, Antecedents, and Consequences

of Workaholism: A Conceptual Integration and Extension," *Journal of Organizational Behavior* 28 (2007): 111-36; S. Pachulicz, N. Schmitt, and G. Kuljanin, "A Model of Career Success: A Longitudinal Study of Emergency Physicians," *Journal of Vocational Behavior* 73, no. 2 (2008): 242-53; M.N. Bechtoldt et al., "Self-Concept Clarity and the Management of Social Conflict," *Journal of Personality* 78, no. 2 (2010): 539-74.

13. B. George, *Authentic Leadership* (San Francisco, CA: Jossey-Bass, 2004); S.T. Hannah and B.J. Avolio, "Ready or Not: How Do We Accelerate the Developmental Readiness of Leaders?," *Journal of Organizational Behavior* 31, no. 8 (2010): 1181-87.

14. This quotation has been cited since the 1930s, yet we were unable to find it in any of Dewey's writing. The earliest known reference to this quotation is Dale Carnegie's famous self-help book, where the statement is attributed to Dewey. See: D. Carnegie, *How to Win Friends and Influence People*, 1st ed. (New York: Simon & Schuster, 1936), pp. 43-44 (p. 19 in later editions).

15. C.L. Guenther and M.D. Alicke, "Deconstructing the Better-Than-Average Effect," *Journal of Personality and Social Psychology* 99, no. 5 (2010): 755-70; S. Loughnan et al., "Universal Biases in Self-Perception: Better and More Human Than Average," *British Journal of Social Psychology* 49 (2010): 627-36; H.C. Boucher, "Understanding Western-East Asian Differences and Similarities in Self-Enhancement," *Social and Personality Psychology Compass* 4, no. 5 (2010): 304-17; A. Gregg, C. Sedikides, and J. Gebauer, "Dynamics of Identity: Between Self-Enhancement and Self-Assessment," in *Handbook of Identity Theory and Research*, ed. S.J. Schwartz, K. Luyckx, and V.L. Vignoles (Springer New York, 2011), 305-27.

16. D. Dunning, C. Heath, and J.M. Suls, "Flawed Self-Assessment: Implications for Health, Education, and the Workplace," *Psychological Science in the Public Interest* 5, no. 3 (2004): 69-106; D.A. Moore, "Not So above Average after All: When People Believe They Are Worse Than Average and Its Implications for Theories of Bias in Social Comparison," *Organizational Behavior and Human Decision Processes* 102, no. 1 (2007): 42-58.

17. J.A. Doukas and D. Petmezas, "Acquisitions, Overconfident Managers and Self-Attribution Bias," *European Financial Management* 13, no. 3 (2007): 531-77; N. Harrè and C.G. Sibley, "Explicit and Implicit Self-Enhancement Biases in Drivers and Their Relationship to Driving Violations and Crash-Risk Optimism," *Accident Analysis & Prevention* 39, no. 6 (2007): 1155-61; D.A. Moore and P.J. Healy, "The Trouble with Overconfidence," *Psychological Review* 115, no. 2 (2008): 502-17; F. Jiang et al., "Managerial Hubris, Firm Expansion and Firm Performance: Evidence from China," *The Social Science Journal* 48, no. 3 (2011): 489-99; A.S. Ahmed and S. Duellman, "Managerial Overconfidence and Accounting Conservatism," *Journal of Accounting Research* 51, no. 1 (2013): 1-30.

18. K.P. Cross, "Not Can, but *Will* College Teaching Be Improved?," *New Directions for Higher Education*, no. 17 (1977): 1-15; U.S. Merit Systems Protection Board, *Accomplishing Our Mission: Results of the 2005 Merit Principles Survey*, U.S. Merit Systems Protection Board (Washington, DC: 6 December 2007); J. Montier, *Behavioral Investing* (Chicester, UK: John Wiley & Sons, Inc., 2007), pp. 82-83; V.G. Perry, "Is Ignorance Bliss? Consumer Accuracy in Judgments About Credit Ratings," *Journal of Consumer Affairs* 42, no. 2 (2008): 189-205; J.M. Twenge, W.K. Campbell, and B. Gentile, "Generational Increases in Agentic Self-Evaluations among American College Students, 1966-2009," *Self and Identity* 11, no. 4 (2011): 409-27; A. Sundström, "The Validity of Self-Reported Driver Competence: Relations between Measures of Perceived Driver Competence and Actual Driving Skill," *Transportation Research Part F: Traffic Psychology and Behaviour* 14, no. 2 (2011): 155-63; Heart & Stroke Foundation (Canada), *Denial Is Putting Canadians at High Risk of Cutting Their Lives Short*, Heart & Stroke Foundation (Ottawa, ON: 2011).

19. W.B. Swann Jr, "To Be Adored or to Be Known? The Interplay of Self-Enhancement and Self-Verification," in *Foundations of Social Behavior*, ed. R.M. Sorrentino and E.T. Higgins (New York: Guildford, 1990), 408-48; W.B. Swann Jr, P.J. Rentfrow, and J.S. Guinn, "Self-Verification: The Search for Coherence," in *Handbook of Self and Identity*, ed. M.R. Leary and J. Tagney (New York: Guildford, 2002), 367-83; D.M. Cable and V.S. Kay, "Striving for Self-Verification During Organizational Entry," *Academy of Management Journal* 55, no. 2 (2012): 360-80.

20. F. Anseel and F. Lievens, "Certainty as a Moderator of Feedback Reactions? A Test of the Strength of the Self-Verification Motive," *Journal of Occupational & Organizational Psychology* 79, no. 4 (2006): 533-51; T. Kwang and W.B. Swann, "Do People Embrace Praise Even When They Feel Unworthy? A Review of Critical Tests of Self-Enhancement Versus Self-Verification," *Personality and social psychology review* 14, no. 3 (2010): 263-80.

21. M.R. Leary, "Motivational and Emotional Aspects of the Self," *Annual Review of Psychology* 58, no. 1 (2007): 317-44.

22. D.M. Cable, F. Gino, and B. Staats, "Breaking Them in or Eliciting Their Best? Reframing Socialization around Newcomers' Authentic Self-Expression," *Administrative Science Quarterly* 58, no. 1 (2013): 1-36.

23. T.A. Judge and J.E. Bono, "Relationship of Core Self-Evaluations Traits-Self-Esteem, Generalized Self-Efficacy, Locus of Control, and Emotional Stability-with Job Satisfaction and Job Performance: A Meta-Analysis," *Journal of Applied Psychology* 86, no. 1 (2001): 80-92; T.A. Judge and C. Hurst, "Capitalizing on One's Advantages: Role of Core Self-Evaluations," *Journal of Applied Psychology* 92, no. 5 (2007): 1212-27. We have described the three most commonly identified components of self-evaluation. The full model also includes emotional stability (low neuroticism), but it is a behaviour tendency (personality dimension), whereas the other three components are self-evaluations. Generally, the core self-evaluation model has received limited research and its dimensions continue to be debated. For example, see T.W. Self, "Evaluating Core Self-Evaluations: Application of a Multidimensional, Latent-Construct, Evaluative Framework to Core Self-Evaluations Research" (Ph.D., University of Houston, 2007); R.E. Johnson, C.C. Rosen, and P.E. Levy, "Getting to the Core of Core Self-Evaluation: A Review and Recommendations," *Journal of Organizational Behavior* 29 (2008): 391-413.

24. R.F. Baumeister and J.M. Twenge, *The Social Self*, Handbook of Psychology (New York: John Wiley & Sons, Inc., 2003); W.B. Swann Jr, C. Chang-Schneider, and K.L. McClarty, "Do People's Self-Views Matter?: Self-Concept and Self-Esteem in Everyday Life," *American Psychologist* 62, no. 2 (2007): 84-94.

25. A. Bandura, *Self-Efficacy: The Exercise of Control* (New York: W.H. Freeman, 1997). However, one review found that self-efficacy's effect on task and job performance is much lower when also including the effects of personality traits on performance. See: T.A. Judge et al., "Self-Efficacy and Work-Related Performance: The Integral Role of Individual Differences," *Journal of Applied Psychology* 92, no. 1 (2007): 107-27.

26. G. Chen, S.M. Gully, and D. Eden, "Validation of a New General Self-Efficacy Scale," *Organizational Research Methods* 4, no. 1 (2001): 62-83.

27. J.B. Rotter, "Generalized Expectancies for Internal Versus External Control of Reinforcement," *Psychological Monographs* 80, no. 1 (1966): 1-28.

28. P.E. Spector, "Behavior in Organizations as a Function of Employee's Locus of Control," *Psychological Bulletin* 91 (1982): 482-97; K. Hattrup, M.S. O'Connell, and J.R. Labrador, "Incremental Validity of Locus of Control after Controlling for Cognitive Ability and Conscientiousness," *Journal of Business and Psychology* 19, no. 4 (2005): 461-81; T.W.H. Ng, K.L. Sorensen, and L.T. Eby, "Locus of Control at Work: A Meta-Analysis," *Journal of Organizational Behavior* 27 (2006): 1057-87; Q. Wang, N.A. Bowling, and K.J. Eschleman, "A Meta-Analytic Examination of Work and General Locus of Control," *Journal of Applied Psychology* 95, no. 4 (2010): 761-68.

29. J.M. Twenge, L. Zhang, and C. Im, "It's Beyond My Control: A Cross-Temporal Meta-Analysis of Increasing Externality in Locus of Control, 1960-2002," *Personality and Social Psychology Review* 8, no. 3 (2004): 308-19.

30. M.A. Hogg and D.J. Terry, "Social Identity and Self-Categorization Processes in Organizational Contexts," *Academy of Management Review* 25 (2000): 121-40; L.L. Gaertner et al., "The "I," the "We," and the "When": A Meta-Analysis of Motivational Primacy in Self-Definition," *Journal of Personality and Social Psychology* 83, no. 3 (2002): 574; S.A. Haslam, R.A. Eggins, and K.J. Reynolds, "The Aspire Model: Actualizing Social and Personal Identity Resources to Enhance Organizational Outcomes," *Journal of Occupational and Organizational Psychology* 76 (2003): 83-113; S.A. Haslam, S.D. Reicher, and M.J. Platow, *The New Psychology of Leadership* (Hove, UK: Psychology Press, 2011).

31. C. Sedikides and A.P. Gregg, "Portraits of the Self," in *The Sage Handbook of Social Psychology*, ed. M.A. Hogg and J. Cooper (London, UK: Sage

Publications, 2003), 110-38. The history of the social self in human beings is described in M.R. Leary and N.R. Buttermore, "The Evolution of the Human Self: Tracing the Natural History of Self-Awareness," *Journal for the Theory of Social Behaviour* 33, no. 4 (2003): 365-404.

32. M.R. Edwards, "Organizational Identification: A Conceptual and Operational Review," *International Journal of Management Reviews* 7, no. 4 (2005): 207-30; D.A. Whetten, "Albert and Whetten Revisited: Strengthening the Concept of Organizational Identity," *Journal of Management Inquiry* 15, no. 3 (2006): 219-34.

33. M.B. Brewer, "The Social Self: On Being the Same and Different at the Same Time," *Personality and Social Psychology Bulletin* 17, no. 5 (1991): 475-82; R. Imhoff and H.-P. Erb, "What Motivates Nonconformity? Uniqueness Seeking Blocks Majority Influence," *Personality and Social Psychology Bulletin* 35, no. 3 (2009): 309-20; K.R. Morrison and S.C. Wheeler, "Nonconformity Defines the Self: The Role of Minority Opinion Status in Self-Concept Clarity," *Personality and Social Psychology Bulletin* 36, no. 3 (2010): 297-308; M.G. Mayhew, J. Gardner, and N.M. Ashkanasy, "Measuring Individuals' Need for Identification: Scale Development and Validation," *Personality and Individual Differences* 49, no. 5 (2010): 356-61.

34. See, for example: W.B. Swann Jr., R.E. Johnson, and J.K. Bosson, "Identity Negotiation at Work," *Research in Organizational Behavior* 29 (2009): 81-109; H.-L. Yang and C.-Y. Lai, "Motivations of Wikipedia Content Contributors," *Computers in Human Behavior* 26, no. 6 (2010): 1377-83; Bechtoldt et al., "Self-Concept Clarity and the Management of Social Conflict; Hannah and Avolio, "Ready or Not: How Do We Accelerate the Developmental Readiness of Leaders?"

35. E.I. Knudsen, "Fundamental Components of Attention," *Annual Review of Neuroscience* 30, no. 1 (2007): 57-78. For an evolutionary psychology perspective of selective attention and organization, see: L. Cosmides and J. Tooby, "Evolutionary Psychology: New Perspectives on Cognition and Motivation," *Annual Review of Psychology* 64, no. 1 (2013): 201-29.

36. A. Bechara and A.R. Damasio, "The Somatic Marker Hypothesis: A Neural Theory of Economic Decision," *Games and Economic Behavior* 52, no. 2 (2005): 336-72; T.S. Saunders and M.J. Buehner, "The Gut Chooses Faster Than the Mind: A Latency Advantage of Affective over Cognitive Decisions," *The Quarterly Journal of Experimental Psychology* 66, no. 2 (2012): 381-88; A. Aite et al., "Impact of Emotional Context Congruency on Decision Making under Ambiguity," *Emotion* 13, no. 2 (2013): 177-82.

37. Plato, *The Republic*, trans. D. Lee (Harmondsworth, England: Penguin, 1955).

38. D.J. Simons and C.F. Chabris, "Gorillas in Our Midst : Sustained Inattentional Blindness for Dynamic Events," *Perception* 28 (1999): 1059-74.

39. R.S. Nickerson, "Confirmation Bias: A Ubiquitous Phenomenon in Many Guises," *Review of General Psychology* 2, no. 2 (1998): 175-220; A. Gilbey and S. Hill, "Confirmation Bias in General Aviation Lost Procedures," *Applied Cognitive Psychology* 26, no. 5 (2012): 785-95; A.M. Scherer, P.D. Windschitl, and A.R. Smith, "Hope to Be Right: Biased Information Seeking Following Arbitrary and Informed Predictions," *Journal of Experimental Social Psychology* 49, no. 1 (2013): 106-12.

40. E. Rassin, A. Eerland, and I. Kuijpers, "Let's Find the Evidence: An Analogue Study of Confirmation Bias in Criminal Investigations," *Journal of Investigative Psychology and Offender Profiling* 7, no. 3 (2010): 231-46; C. Wastell et al., "Identifying Hypothesis Confirmation Behaviors in a Simulated Murder Investigation: Implications for Practice," *Journal of Investigative Psychology and Offender Profiling* 9, no. 2 (2012): 184-98.

41. The Sherlock Holmes quotation is from S.A. Conan Doyle, "A Study in Scarlet," in *The Complete Sherlock Holmes* (New York: Fine Creative Media, 2003), 3-96. Sherlock Holmes offers similar advice in "A Scandal in Bohemia", p. 189. The Ottawa case is described in: A. Seymour, "Charges in Museum Graffiti Case Dropped," *Ottawa Citizen*, 16 May 2013, C3.

42. C.N. Macrae and G.V. Bodenhausen, "Social Cognition: Thinking Categorically About Others," *Annual Review of Psychology* 51 (2000): 93-120. For literature on the automaticity of the perceptual organization and interpretation process, see J.A. Bargh, "The Cognitive Monster: The Case against the Controllability of Automatic Stereotype Effects," in *Dual Process Theories in Social Psychology*, ed. S. Chaiken and Y. Trope (New York: Guilford, 1999), 361-82; J.A. Bargh and M.J. Ferguson, "Beyond Behaviorism: On the Automaticity of Higher Mental Processes," *Psychological Bulletin* 126, no. 6 (2000): 925-45; M. Gladwell, *Blink: The Power of Thinking without Thinking* (New York: Little, Brown, 2005).

43. E.M. Altmann and B.D. Burns, "Streak Biases in Decision Making: Data and a Memory Model," *Cognitive Systems Research* 6, no. 1 (2005): 5-16. For a discussion of cognitive closure and perception, see A.W. Kruglanski, *The Psychology of Closed Mindedness* (New York: Psychology Press, 2004).

44. J. Willis and A. Todorov, "First Impressions: Making up Your Mind after a 100-Ms Exposure to a Face," *Psychological Science* 17, no. 7 (2006): 592-98; A. Todorov, M. Pakrashi, and N.N. Oosterhof, "Evaluating Faces on Trustworthiness after Minimal Time Exposure," *Social Cognition* 27, no. 6 (2009): 813-33; C. Olivola and A. Todorov, "Elected in 100 Milliseconds: Appearance-Based Trait Inferences and Voting," *Journal of Nonverbal Behavior* 34, no. 2 (2010): 83-110. For related research on thin slices, see: N. Ambady et al., "Surgeons' Tone of Voice: A Clue to Malpractice History," *Surgery* 132, no. 1 (2002): 5-9; D.J. Benjamin and J.M. Shapiro, "Thin-Slice Forecasts of Gubernatorial Elections," *Review of Economics and Statistics* 91, no. 3 (2009): 523-36.

45. P.M. Senge, *The Fifth Discipline: The Art and Practice of the Learning Organization* (New York: Doubleday Currency, 1990), Chap. 10; T.J. Chermack, "Mental Models in Decision Making and Implications for Human Resource Development," *Advances in Developing Human Resources* 5, no. 4 (2003): 408-22; P.N. Johnson-Laird, *Mental Models and Deductive Reasoning*, ed. J.E. Adler and L.J. Rips, Reasoning: Studies of Human Inference and Its Foundations (Cambridge: Cambridge Univ Press, 2008); S. Ross and N. Allen, "Examining the Convergent Validity of Shared Mental Model Measures," *Behavior Research Methods* 44, no. 4 (2012): 1052-62.

46. G.W. Allport, *The Nature of Prejudice* (Reading, MA: Addison-Wesley, 1954); J.C. Brigham, "Ethnic Stereotypes," *Psychological Bulletin* 76, no. 1 (1971): 15-38; D.J. Schneider, *The Psychology of Stereotyping* (New York: Guilford, 2004); S. Kanahara, "A Review of the Definitions of Stereotype and a Proposal for a Progressional Model," *Individual Differences Research* 4, no. 5 (2006): 306-21.

47. V. Christidou, V. Hatzinikita, and G. Samaras, "The Image of Scientific Researchers and Their Activity in Greek Adolescents' Drawings," *Public Understanding of Science* 21, no. 5 (2012): 626-47; S. Cheryan et al., "The Stereotypical Computer Scientist: Gendered Media Representations as a Barrier to Inclusion for Women," *Sex Roles* 69, no. 1-2 (2013): 58-71.

48. I.M. O'Bannon, "The 'Certifiable' Public Accountant," *CPA Technology Advisor* 20, no. 7 (2010): 28-29. Blumer's comment can be found in a response to Joey Brannon's blog. See: J. Brannon, "10 Ways You Know You Were Born to Be an Accountant (or Not)," (Bradenton, FL: Axiom CPA, 2010) (accessed 12 May 2011).

49. C.N. Macrae, A.B. Milne, and G.V. Bodenhausen, "Stereotypes as Energy-Saving Devices: A Peek inside the Cognitive Toolbox," *Journal of Personality and Social Psychology* 66 (1994): 37-47; J.W. Sherman et al., "Stereotype Efficiency Reconsidered: Encoding Flexibility under Cognitive Load," *Journal of Personality and Social Psychology* 75 (1998): 589-606; Macrae and Bodenhausen, "Social Cognition: Thinking Categorically About Others."

50. J.C. Turner and S.A. Haslam, "Social Identity, Organizations, and Leadership," in *Groups at Work: Theory and Research*, ed. M.E. Turner (Mahwah, NJ: Lawrence Erlbaum Associates, 2001), 25-65; J. Jetten, R. Spears, and T. Postmes, "Intergroup Distinctiveness and Differentiation: A Meta-Analytic Integration," *Journal of Personality and Social Psychology* 86, no. 6 (2004): 862-79; M.A. Hogg et al., "The Social Identity Perspective: Intergroup Relations, Self-Conception, and Small Groups," *Small Group Research* 35, no. 3 (2004): 246-76; K. Hugenberg and D.F. Sacco, "Social Categorization and Stereotyping: How Social Categorization Biases Person Perception and Face Memory," *Social and Personality Psychology Compass* 2, no. 2 (2008): 1052-72.

51. N. Halevy, G. Bornstein, and L. Sagiv, "`In-Group Love" and "out-Group Hate" as Motives for Individual Participation in Intergroup Conflict: A New Game Paradigm," *Psychological Science* 19, no. 4 (2008): 405-11; T. Yamagishi and N. Mifune, "Social Exchange and Solidarity: In-Group Love or out-Group Hate?," *Evolution and Human Behavior* 30, no. 4 (2009): 229-37; N. Halevy, O. Weisel, and G. Bornstein, "In-Group Love" and "out-Group Hate" in Repeated Interaction between Groups," *Journal of Behavioral*

Decision Making 25, no. 2 (2012): 188–95; M. Parker and R. Janoff-Bulman, "Lessons from Morality-Based Social Identity: The Power of Outgroup "Hate," Not Just Ingroup "Love"," *Social Justice Research* 26, no. 1 (2013): 81–96.

52. K. Gladman and M. Lamb, *Gmi Ratings' 2012 Women on Boards Survey*, Governance Metrics International (New York: 2012); Catalyst, *Quick Takes: Women on Boards*, Catalyst (New York: 9 April 2012).

53. S.N. Cory, "Quality and Quantity of Accounting Students and the Stereotypical Accountant: Is There a Relationship?," *Journal of Accounting Education* 10, no. 1 (1992): 1–24; P.D. Bougen, "Joking Apart: The Serious Side to the Accountant Stereotype," *Accounting, Organizations and Society* 19, no. 3 (1994): 319–35; A.L. Friedman and S.R. Lyne, "The Beancounter Stereotype: Towards a General Model of Stereotype Generation," *Critical Perspectives on Accounting* 12, no. 4 (2001): 423–51; A. Hoffjan, "The Image of the Accountant in a German Context," *Accounting and the Public Interest* 4 (2004): 62–89; T. Dimnik and S. Felton, "Accountant Stereotypes in Movies Distributed in North America in the Twentieth Century," *Accounting, Organizations and Society* 31, no. 2 (2006): 129–55.

54. S.O. Gaines and E.S. Reed, "Prejudice: From Allport to Dubois," *American Psychologist* 50 (1995): 96–103; S.T. Fiske, "Stereotyping, Prejudice, and Discrimination," in *Handbook of Social Psychology*, ed. D.T. Gilbert, S.T. Fiske, and G. Lindzey (New York: McGraw-Hill, 1998), 357–411; M. Hewstone, M. Rubin, and H. Willis, "Intergroup Bias," *Annual Review of Psychology* 53 (2002): 575–604.

55. E. Cediey and F. Foroni, *Discrimination in Access to Employment on Grounds of Foreign Origin in France*, International Labour Organization (Geneva: I.L. Organization, 2008); P. Gumbel, "The French Exodus," *Time International*, 16 April 2007, 18; "Study Finds Major Discrimination against Turkish Job Applicants," *The Local (Germany) (Berlin)*, 9 February 2010.

56. J.A. Bargh and T.L. Chartrand, "The Unbearable Automaticity of Being," *American Psychologist* 54, no. 7 (1999): 462–79; S.T. Fiske, "What We Know Now About Bias and Intergroup Conflict, the Problem of the Century," *Current Directions in Psychological Science* 11, no. 4 (2002): 123–28; R. Krieglmeyer and J.W. Sherman, "Disentangling Stereotype Activation and Stereotype Application in the Stereotype Misperception Task," *Journal of Personality and Social Psychology* 103, no. 2 (2012): 205–24. On the limitations of some stereotype training, see: B. Gawronski et al., "When 'Just Say No' Is Not Enough: Affirmation Versus Negation Training and the Reduction of Automatic Stereotype Activation," *Journal of Experimental Social Psychology* 44 (2008): 370–77.

57. H.H. Kelley, *Attribution in Social Interaction* (Morristown, NJ: General Learning Press, 1971); B.F. Malle, "Attribution Theories: How People Make Sense of Behavior," in *Theories of Social Psychology*, ed. D. Chadee (Chicester, UK: Blackwell Publishing, 2011), 72–95. This "internal-external" or "person-situation" perspective of the attribution process differs somewhat from the original "intentional-unintentional" perspective, which says that we try to understand the deliberate or accidental/involuntary reasons why people engage in behaviours, as well as the reasons for behaviour. Some writers suggest the original perspective is more useful. See: B.F. Malle, "Time to Give up the Dogmas of Attribution: An Alternative Theory of Behavior Explanation," in *Advances in Experimental Social Psychology, Vol 44*, ed. K.M. Olson and M.P. Zanna, *Advances in Experimental Social Psychology* (San Diego: Elsevier Academic Press Inc., 2011), 297–352.

58. H.H. Kelley, "The Processes of Causal Attribution," *American Psychologist* 28 (1973): 107–28.

59. J.M. Schaubroeck and P. Shao, "The Role of Attribution in How Followers Respond to the Emotional Expression of Male and Female Leaders," *The Leadership Quarterly* 23, no. 1 (2012): 27–42; D. Lange and N.T. Washburn, "Understanding Attributions of Corporate Social Irresponsibility," *Academy of Management Review* 37, no. 2 (2012): 300–26.

60. J.M. Crant and T.S. Bateman, "Assignment of Credit and Blame for Performance Outcomes," *Academy of Management Journal* 36 (1993): 7–27; B. Weiner, "Intrapersonal and Interpersonal Theories of Motivation from an Attributional Perspective," *Educational Psychology Review* 12 (2000): 1–14; N. Bacon and P. Blyton, "Worker Responses to Teamworking: Exploring Employee Attributions of Managerial Motives," *International Journal of Human Resource Management* 16, no. 2 (2005): 238–55.

61. D.T. Miller and M. Ross, "Self-Serving Biases in the Attribution of Causality: Fact or Fiction?," *Psychological Bulletin* 82, no. 2 (1975): 213–25; J. Shepperd, W. Malone, and K. Sweeny, "Exploring Causes of the Self-Serving Bias," *Social and Personality Psychology Compass* 2, no. 2 (2008): 895–908.

62. E.W.K. Tsang, "Self-Serving Attributions in Corporate Annual Reports: A Replicated Study," *Journal of Management Studies* 39, no. 1 (2002): 51–65; N.J. Roese and J.M. Olson, "Better, Stronger, Faster: Self-Serving Judgment, Affect Regulation, and the Optimal Vigilance Hypothesis," *Perspectives on Psychological Science* 2, no. 2 (2007): 124–41; R. Hooghiemstra, "East-West Differences in Attributions for Company Performance: A Content Analysis of Japanese and U.S. Corporate Annual Reports," *Journal of Cross-Cultural Psychology* 39, no. 5 (2008): 618–29; M. Franco and H. Haase, "Failure Factors in Small and Medium-Sized Enterprises: Qualitative Study from an Attributional Perspective," *International Entrepreneurship and Management Journal* 6, no. 4 (2010): 503–21.

63. S.S. Van Dine (Willard Huntington Wright), *The Benson Murder Mystery* (New York: Charles Scribner's Sons, 1926), Chap. 6.

64. D.T. Gilbert and P.S. Malone, "The Correspondence Bias," *Psychological Bulletin* 117, no. 1 (1995): 21–38.

65. I. Choi, R.E. Nisbett, and A. Norenzayan, "Causal Attribution across Cultures: Variation and Universality," *Psychological Bulletin* 125, no. 1 (1999): 47–63; R.E. Nisbett, *The Geography of Thought: How Asians and Westerners Think Differently – and Why* (New York: Free Press, 2003), Chap. 5; S.G. Goto et al., "Cultural Differences in Sensitivity to Social Context: Detecting Affective Incongruity Using the N400," *Social Neuroscience* 8, no. 1 (2012): 63–74.

66. B.F. Malle, "The Actor-Observer Asymmetry in Attribution: A (Surprising) Meta-Analysis," *Psychological Bulletin* 132, no. 6 (2006): 895–919; C.W. Bauman and L.J. Skitka, "Making Attributions for Behaviors: The Prevalence of Correspondence Bias in the General Population," *Basic and Applied Social Psychology* 32, no. 3 (2010): 269–77.

67. Similar models are presented in D. Eden, "Self-Fulfilling Prophecy as a Management Tool: Harnessing Pygmalion," *Academy of Management Review* 9 (1984): 64–73; R.H.G. Field and D.A. Van Seters, "Management by Expectations (Mbe): The Power of Positive Prophecy," *Journal of General Management* 14 (1988): 19–33; D.O. Trouilloud et al., "The Influence of Teacher Expectations on Student Achievement in Physical Education Classes: Pygmalion Revisited," *European Journal of Social Psychology* 32 (2002): 591–607.

68. D. Eden, "Interpersonal Expectations in Organizations," in *Interpersonal Expectations: Theory, Research, and Applications* (Cambridge, UK: Cambridge University Press, 1993), 154–78.

69. K.S. Crawford, E.D. Thomas, and J.J.A. Fink, "Pygmalion at Sea: Improving the Work Effectiveness of Low Performers," *Journal of Applied Behavioral Science* 16 (1980): 482–505; D. Eden, "Pygmalion Goes to Boot Camp: Expectancy, Leadership, and Trainee Performance," *Journal of Applied Psychology* 67 (1982): 194–99; C.M. Rubie-Davies, "Teacher Expectations and Student Self-Perceptions: Exploring Relationships," *Psychology in the Schools* 43, no. 5 (2006): 537–52; P. Whiteley, T. Sy, and S.K. Johnson, "Leaders' Conceptions of Followers: Implications for Naturally Occurring Pygmalion Effects," *Leadership Quarterly* 23, no. 5 (2012): 822–34.

70. S. Madon, L. Jussim, and J. Eccles, "In Search of the Powerful Self-Fulfilling Prophecy," *Journal of Personality and Social Psychology* 72, no. 4 (1997): 791–809; A.E. Smith, L. Jussim, and J. Eccles, "Do Self-Fulfilling Prophecies Accumulate, Dissipate, or Remain Stable over Time?," *Journal of Personality and Social Psychology* 77, no. 3 (1999): 548–65; S. Madon et al., "Self-Fulfilling Prophecies: The Synergistic Accumulative Effect of Parents' Beliefs on Children's Drinking Behavior," *Psychological Science* 15, no. 12 (2005): 837–45.

71. W.H. Cooper, "Ubiquitous Halo," *Psychological Bulletin* 90 (1981): 218–44; P. Rosenzweig, *The Halo Effect. . .And the Eight Other Business Delusions That Deceive Managers* (New York: Free Press, 2007); J.W. Keeley et al., "Investigating Halo and Ceiling Effects in Student Evaluations of Instruction," *Educational and Psychological Measurement* 73, no. 3 (2013): 440–57.

72. B. Mullen et al., "The False Consensus Effect: A Meta-Analysis of 115 Hypothesis Tests," *Journal of Experimental Social Psychology* 21, no. 3 (1985): 262–83; G. Marks and N. Miller, "Ten Years of Research on the False-Consensus Effect: An Empirical and Theoretical Review,"

Psychological Bulletin 102, no. 1 (1987): 72–90; F.J. Flynn and S.S. Wiltermuth, "Who's with Me? False Consensus, Brokerage, and Ethical Decision Making in Organizations," *Academy of Management Journal* 53, no. 5 (2010): 1074–89.

73. C.L. Kleinke, *First Impressions: The Psychology of Encountering Others* (Englewood Cliffs, NJ: Prentice Hall, 1975); E.A. Lind, L. Kray, and L. Thompson, "Primacy Effects in Justice Judgments: Testing Predictions from Fairness Heuristic Theory," *Organizational Behavior and Human Decision Processes* 85 (2001): 189–210; O. Ybarra, "When First Impressions Don't Last: The Role of Isolation and Adaptation Processes in the Revision of Evaluative Impressions," *Social Cognition* 19 (2001): 491–520.

74. D.D. Steiner and J.S. Rain, "Immediate and Delayed Primacy and Recency Effects in Performance Evaluation," *Journal of Applied Psychology* 74 (1989): 136–42; K.T. Trotman, "Order Effects and Recency: Where Do We Go from Here?," *Accounting & Finance* 40 (2000): 169–82; W. Green, "Impact of the Timing of an Inherited Explanation on Auditors' Analytical Procedures Judgements," *Accounting and Finance* 44 (2004): 369–92.

75. L. Roberson, C.T. Kulik, and M.B. Pepper, "Using Needs Assessment to Resolve Controversies in Diversity Training Design," *Group & Organization Management* 28, no. 1 (2003): 148–74; D.E. Hogan and M. Mallott, "Changing Racial Prejudice through Diversity Education," *Journal of College Student Development* 46, no. 2 (2005): 115–25; Gawronski et al., "When 'Just Say No' Is Not Enough."

76. Eden, "Self-Fulfilling Prophecy as a Management Tool: Harnessing Pygmalion; S.S. White and E.A. Locke, "Problems with the Pygmalion Effect and Some Proposed Solutions," *Leadership Quarterly* 11 (2000): 389–415.

77. T.W. Costello and S.S. Zalkind, *Psychology in Administration: A Research Orientation* (Englewood Cliffs, NJ: Prentice Hall, 1963), pp. 45–46; J.M. Kouzes and B.Z. Posner, *The Leadership Challenge*, 4th ed. (San Francisco, CA: Jossey-Bass, 2007), Chap. 3.

78. George, *Authentic Leadership;* W.L. Gardner et al., "'Can You See the Real Me?' A Self-Based Model of Authentic Leader and Follower Development," *Leadership Quarterly* 16 (2005): 343–72; B. George, *True North* (San Francisco, CA: Jossey-Bass, 2007).

79. W. Hofmann et al., "Implicit and Explicit Attitudes and Interracial Interaction: The Moderating Role of Situationally Available Control Resources," *Group Processes Intergroup Relations* 11, no. 1 (2008): 69–87; A.G. Greenwald et al., "Understanding and Using the Implicit Association Test: III. Meta-Analysis of Predictive Validity," *Journal of Personality and Social Psychology* 97, no. 1 (2009): 17–41; J.D. Vorauer, "Completing the Implicit Association Test Reduces Positive Intergroup Interaction Behavior," *Psychological Science* 23, no. 10 (2012): 1168–75.

80. Hofmann et al., "Implicit and Explicit Attitudes and Interracial Interaction: The Moderating Role of Situationally Available Control Resources; J.T. Jost et al., "The Existence of Implicit Bias Is Beyond Reasonable Doubt: A Refutation of Ideological and Methodological Objections and Executive Summary of Ten Studies That No Manager Should Ignore," *Research in Organizational Behavior* 29 (2009): 39–69.

81. A. Kalev, F. Dobbin, and E. Kelly, "Best Practices or Best Guesses? Assessing the Efficacy of Corporate Affirmative Action and Diversity Policies," *American Sociological Review* 71 (2006): 589–617; J. Watson, "When Diversity Training Goes Awry," *Black Issues In Higher Education*, 24 January 2008, 11; A. Nancherla, "Why Diversity Training Doesn't Work. . .Right Now," *T&D*, Nov. 2008, 52–61; E.L. Paluck and D.P. Green, "Prejudice Reduction: What Works? A Review and Assessment of Research and Practice," *Annual Review of Psychology* 60, no. 1 (2009): 339–67; A. Carrns, "Training in Trouble," *Boston Globe*, 5 December 2010, 8.

82. J. Luft, *Of Human Interaction* (Palo Alto, CA: National Press, 1969). For a variation of this model, see J. Hall, "Communication Revisited," *California Management Review* 15 (1973): 56–67.

83. S. Vazire and M.R. Mehl, "Knowing Me, Knowing You: The Accuracy and Unique Predictive Validity of Self-Ratings and Other-Ratings of Daily Behavior," *Journal of Personality and Social Psychology* 95, no. 5 (2008): 1202–16; S. Vazire, "Who Knows What About a Person? The Self-Other Knowledge Asymmetry (Soka) Model," *Journal of Personality and Social Psychology* 98, no. 2 (2010): 281–300.

84. P.J. Henry and C.D. Hardin, "The Contact Hypothesis Revisited: Status Bias in the Reduction of Implicit Prejudice in the United States and Lebanon," *Psychological Science* 17, no. 10 (2006): 862–68; T.F. Pettigrew and L.R. Tropp, "A Meta-Analytic Test of Intergroup Contact Theory," *Journal of Personality and Social Psychology* 90, no. 5 (2006): 751–83; T.F. Pettigrew, "Future Directions for Intergroup Contact Theory and Research," *International Journal of Intercultural Relations* 32, no. 3 (2008): 187–99; F.K. Barlow et al., "The Contact Caveat: Negative Contact Predicts Increased Prejudice More Than Positive Contact Predicts Reduced Prejudice," *Personality and Social Psychology Bulletin* 38, no. 12 (2012): 1629–43.

85. The contact hypothesis was first introduced in: Allport, *The Nature of Prejudice*, Chap. 16.

86. K. Grimmelt, "People Behind Success of Pulp and Paper Mill," *Peace River Record-Gazette*, 14 September 2010.

87. G. Avery, "Colleen Abdoulah Sees Wow! As Different Type of Cable Company," *Denver Business Journal*, 19 October 2012; M. MacLeod, "House Found a Home in Tim Hortons," *Hamilton Spectator*, 16 June 2012; S. Long, "The Change-Makers: Save, Give, Value All," *Straits Times (Singapore)*, 26 April 2013; R. Myles, "Driven to Distraction," *Calgary Herald*, 31 October 2013; L. White, "Born to Be Wild," *24 Hours Vancouver*, 21 January 2013.

88. C. Duan and C.E. Hill, "The Current State of Empathy Research," *Journal of Counseling Psychology* 43 (1996): 261–74; W.G. Stephen and K.A. Finlay, "The Role of Empathy in Improving Intergroup Relations," *Journal of Social Issues* 55 (1999): 729–43; S.K. Parker and C.M. Axtell, "Seeing Another Viewpoint: Antecedents and Outcomes of Employee Perspective Taking," *Academy of Management Journal* 44 (2001): 1085–100; G.J. Vreeke and I.L. van der Mark, "Empathy, an Integrative Model," *New Ideas in Psychology* 21, no. 3 (2003): 177–207.

89. M. Tarrant, R. Calitri, and D. Weston, "Social Identification Structures the Effects of Perspective Taking," *Psychological Science* 23, no. 9 (2012): 973–78; J.L. Skorinko and S.A. Sinclair, "Perspective Taking Can Increase Stereotyping: The Role of Apparent Stereotype Confirmation," *Journal of Experimental Social Psychology* 49, no. 1 (2013): 10–18.

90. A. Sugimoto, "English Is Vital, Rakuten Boss Says – but It Isn't Everything," *Nikkei Weekly (Tokyo)*, 22 April 2013.

91. There is no consensus on the meaning of global mindset. The elements identified in this book are common among most of the recent writing on this subject. See, for example: S.J. Black, W.H. Mobley, and E. Weldon, "The Mindset of Global Leaders: Inquisitiveness and Duality," in *Advances in Global Leadership* (JAI, 2006), 181–200; O. Levy et al., "What We Talk About When We Talk About 'Global Mindset': Managerial Cognition in Multinational Corporations," *Journal of International Business Studies* 38, no. 2 (2007): 231–58; S. Beechler and D. Baltzley, "Creating a Global Mindset," *Chief Learning Officer* 7, no. 6 (2008): 40–45; M. Javidan and D. Bowen, "The 'Global Mindset' of Managers: What It Is, Why It Matters, and How to Develop It," *Organizational Dynamics* 42, no. 2 (2013): 145–55.

92. "Sharing Experiences," *Offshore Marine*, March 2008, 26–27; J. Kwok, "Values Weld Keppel's Global Force," *Sunday Times (Singapore)*, 28 May 2013.

93. A.K. Gupta and V. Govindarajan, "Cultivating a Global Mindset," *Academy of Management Executive* 16, no. 1 (2002): 116–26.

94. M. Jackson, "Corporate Volunteers Reaching Worldwide," *Boston Globe*, 4 May 2008, 3.

95. IBM, *Sam Palmisano Discusses IBM's New Corporate Service Corps*, (Armonk, NY: IBM, 2007); "IBM's Corporate Service Corps Heading to Six Emerging Countries to Spark Socio-Economic Growth While Developing Global Leaders," (Armonk, NY: IBM, 2008); C. Hymowitz, "IBM Combines Volunteer Service, Teamwork to Cultivate Emerging Markets," *Wall Street Journal*, 4 August 2008, B6.

CHAPTER 4

1. V. Lu, "Life among the Worker Bees," *Toronto Star*, 26 May 2012, B1; S. Deveau, "WestJet Expansion Worth a Few Ruffled Feathers," *National Post*, 14 December 2013, FP3; "WestJet Head Talks Effective Employee Engagement," (Vancouver, BC: Simon Fraser University, 25 April 2013), http://beedie.sfu.ca/blog/2013/04/westjet-head-talks-effective-employee-engagement-ceo-series/ (accessed 3 March 2014); WestJet, "WestJet Christmas Miracle: Real-Time Giving," (Calgary, AB: YouTube, 8 December 2013), https://www.youtube.com/watch?v=zIElvi2MuEk, Video 5:25 (accessed 4 March 2014); "WestJet Named Value Airline of the Year," *Canada Newswire (Calgary)*, 14 January 2014.

2. Emotions are also cognitive processes. However, we use the narrow definition of cognition as a well-used label referring only to reasoning processes. Also, this and other chapters emphasize that emotional and cognitive processes are intertwined.
3. For discussion of emotions in marketing, economics, and sociology, see: M. Hubert, "Does Neuroeconomics Give New Impetus to Economic and Consumer Research?," *Journal of Economic Psychology* 31, no. 5 (2010): 812–17; D.D. Franks, *Neurosociology: The Nexus between Neuroscience and Social Psychology Introduction,* Neurosociology: The Nexus between Neuroscience and Social Psychology (New York: Springer, 2010); N. Martins, "Can Neuroscience Inform Economics? Rationality, Emotions and Preference Formation," *Cambridge Journal of Economics* 35, no. 2 (2011): 251–67; H. Plassmann, T.Z. Ramsøy, and M. Milosavljevic, "Branding the Brain: A Critical Review and Outlook," *Journal of Consumer Psychology* 22, no. 1 (2012): 18–36.
4. The definition presented here is constructed from the following sources: N.M. Ashkanasy, W.J. Zerbe, and C.E.J. Hartel, "Introduction: Managing Emotions in a Changing Workplace," in *Managing Emotions in the Workplace* ed. N.M. Ashkanasy, W.J. Zerbe, and C.E.J. Hartel (Armonk, NY: M.E. Sharpe, 2002), 3–18; H.M. Weiss, "Conceptual and Empirical Foundations for the Study of Affect at Work," in *Emotions in the Workplace* ed. R.G. Lord, R.J. Klimoski, and R. Kanfer (San Francisco, CA: Jossey-Bass, 2002), 20–63. However, the meaning of emotions is still being debated. See, for example, M. Cabanac, "What Is Emotion?," *Behavioral Processes* 60 (2002): 69–83; B. Russell and J. Eisenberg, "The Role of Cognition and Attitude in Driving Behavior: Elaborating on Affective Events Theory," in *Experiencing and Managing Emotions in the Workplace,* ed. N.M. Ashkanasy, C.E.J. Hartel, and W.J. Zerbe, *Research on Emotion in Organizations* (Bingley, UK: Emerald Group, 2012), 203–24.
5. R. Kanfer and R.J. Klimoski, "Affect and Work: Looking Back to the Future," in *Emotions in the Workplace* ed. R.G. Lord, R.J. Klimoski, and R. Kanfer (San Francisco, CA: Jossey-Bass, 2002), 473–90; J.A. Russell, "Core Affect and the Psychological Construction of Emotion," *Psychological Review* 110, no. 1 (2003): 145–72.
6. R. Reisenzein, M. Studtmann, and G. Horstmann, "Coherence between Emotion and Facial Expression: Evidence from Laboratory Experiments," *Emotion Review* 5, no. 1 (2013): 16–23.
7. R.B. Zajonc, "Emotions," in *Handbook of Social Psychology,* ed. D.T. Gilbert, S.T. Fiske, and L. Gardner (New York: Oxford University press, 1998), 591–634; P. Winkielman, "Bob Zajonc and the Unconscious Emotion," *Emotion Review* 2, no. 4 (2010): 353–62.
8. R.J. Larson, E. Diener, and R.E. Lucas, "Emotion: Models, Measures, and Differences," in *Emotions in the Workplace* ed. R.G. Lord, R.J. Klimoski, and R. Kanfer (San Francisco, CA: Jossey-Bass, 2002), 64–113; L.F. Barrett et al., "The Experience of Emotion," *Annual Review of Psychology* 58, no. 1 (2007): 373–403; M. Yik, J.A. Russell, and J.H. Steiger, "A 12-Point Circumplex Structure of Core Affect," *Emotion* 11, no. 4 (2011): 705–31.
9. R.F. Baumeister, E. Bratslavsky, and C. Finkenauer, "Bad Is Stronger Than Good," *Review of General Psychology* 5, no. 4 (2001): 323–70; A. Vaish, T. Grossmann, and A. Woodward, "Not All Emotions Are Created Equal: The Negativity Bias in Social-Emotional Development," *Psychological Bulletin* 134, no. 3 (2008): 383–403; B.E. Hilbig, "Good Things Don't Come Easy (to Mind): Explaining Framing Effects in Judgments of Truth," *Experimental Psychology* 59, no. 1 (2012): 38–46.
10. A.P. Brief, *Attitudes in and around Organizations* (Thousand Oaks, CA: Sage, 1998); A.H. Eagly and S. Chaiken, "The Advantages of an Inclusive Definition of Attitude," *Social Cognition* 25, no. 5 (2007): 582–602; G. Bohner and N. Dickel, "Attitudes and Attitude Change," *Annual Review of Psychology* 62, no. 1 (2011): 391–417. The definition of attitudes is still being debated. First, it is unclear whether an attitude includes emotions (affect), or whether emotions influence an attitude. We take the latter view. Although emotions influence and are closely connected to attitudes, an attitude is best defined as an evaluation of an attitude object. That evaluation is not always conscious, however. Second, a few writers argue that attitudes are formed each time they think about the attitude object, which is contrary to the traditional view that attitudes are fairly stable predispositions toward the attitude object. Third, although less of an issue now, some attitude models refer only to the "feelings" component, whereas we view attitude as a three-component construct (beliefs, feelings, behavioural intentions). For various definitions of attitude and discussion of these variations, see I. Ajzen, "Nature and Operation of Attitudes," *Annual Review of Psychology* 52 (2001): 27–58; D. Albarracín et al., "Attitudes: Introduction and Scope," in *The Handbook of Attitudes,* ed. D. Albarracín, B.T. Johnson, and M.P. Zanna (Mahwah, NJ: Lawrence Erlbaum Associates, 2005), 3–20; W.A. Cunningham and P.D. Zelazo, "Attitudes and Evaluations: A Social Cognitive Neuroscience Perspective," *TRENDS in Cognitive Sciences* 11, no. 3 (2007): 97–104; B. Gawronski, "Editorial: Attitudes Can Be Measured! But What Is an Attitude?," *Social Cognition* 25, no. 5 (2007): 573–81; R.S. Dalal, "Job Attitudes: Cognition and Affect," in *Handbook of Psychology, Second Edition* (John Wiley & Sons, Inc., 2012).
11. Neuroscience has a slightly more complicated distinction in that conscious awareness is "feeling a feeling" whereas "feeling" is a nonconscious sensing of the body state created by emotion, which itself is a nonconscious neural reaction to a stimulus. However, this distinction is not significant for scholars focused on human behaviour rather than brain activity, and the labels collide with popular understanding of "feeling." See: A.R. Damasio, *The Feeling of What Happens: Body and Emotion in the Making of Consciousness* (New York, NY: Harcourt Brace and Company, 1999); F. Hansen, "Distinguishing between Feelings and Emotions in Understanding Communication Effects," *Journal of Business Research* 58, no. 10 (2005): 1426–36; T. Bosse, C.M. Jonker, and J. Treur, "Formalisation of Damasio's Theory of Emotion, Feeling and Core Consciousness," *Consciousness and Cognition* 17, no. 1 (2008): 94–113.
12. Cunningham and Zelazo, "Attitudes and Evaluations; M.D. Lieberman, "Social Cognitive Neuroscience: A Review of Core Processes," *Annual Review of Psychology* 58, no. 1 (2007): 259–89; M. Fenton-O'Creevy et al., "Thinking, Feeling and Deciding: The Influence of Emotions on the Decision Making and Performance of Traders," *Journal of Organizational Behavior* 32 (2011): 1044–61. The dual emotion-cognition processes are likely the same as the implicit-explicit attitude processes reported by several scholars, as well as tacit knowledge structures. See: B. Gawronski and G.V. Bodenhausen, "Unraveling the Processes Underlying Evaluation: Attitudes from the Perspective of the Ape Model," *Social Cognition* 25, no. 5 (2007): 687–717; W.J. Becker and R. Cropanzano, "Organizational Neuroscience: The Promise and Prospects of an Emerging Discipline," *Journal of Organizational Behavior* 31, no. 7 (2010): 1055–59.
13. D. Trafimow et al., "It Is Irrelevant, but It Matters: Using Confluence Theory to Predict the Influence of Beliefs on Evaluations, Attitudes, and Intentions," *European Journal of Social Psychology* 42, no. 4 (2012): 509–20.
14. S. Orbell, "Intention-Behavior Relations: A Self-Regulation Perspective," in *Contemporary Perspectives on the Psychology of Attitudes,* ed. G. Haddock and G.R. Maio (East Sussex, UK: Psychology Press, 2004), 145–68.
15. H.M. Weiss and R. Cropanzano, "Affective Events Theory: A Theoretical Discussion of the Structure, Causes and Consequences of Affective Experiences at Work," *Research in Organizational Behavior* 18 (1996): 1–74; A. Bechara et al., "Deciding Advantageously before Knowing the Advantageous Strategy," *Science* 275, no. 5304 (1997): 1293–95; H.A. Elfenbein, "Chapter 7: Emotion in Organizations," *The Academy of Management Annals.* 1 (2007): 315–86.
16. J.A. Bargh and M.J. Ferguson, "Beyond Behaviorism: On the Automaticity of Higher Mental Processes," *Psychological Bulletin* 126, no. 6 (2000): 925–45; J.M. George, "The Illusion of Will in Organizational Behavior Research: Nonconscious Processes and Job Design," *Journal of Management* 35, no. 6 (2009): 1318–39; K.I. Ruys and D.A. Stapel, "The Unconscious Unfolding of Emotions," *European Review of Social Psychology* 20 (2009): 232–71; P. Winkielman and K.C. Berridge, "Unconscious Emotion," *Current Directions in Psychological Science* 13, no. 3 (2004): 120–23.
17. A.R. Damasio, *Descartes' Error: Emotion, Reason, and the Human Brain* (New York: Putnam Sons, 1994); P. Ekman, "Basic Emotions," in *Handbook of Cognition and Emotion,* ed. T. Dalgleish and M. Power (San Francisco, CA: Jossey-Bass, 1999), 45–60; J.E. LeDoux, "Emotion Circuits in the Brain," *Annual Review of Neuroscience* 23 (2000): 155–84; Damasio, *The Feeling of What Happens: Body and Emotion in the Making of Consciousness;* R.J. Dolan, "Emotion, Cognition, and Behavior," *Science* 298, no. 5596 (2002): 1191–94.
18. N. Schwarz, "Emotion, Cognition, and Decision Making," *Cognition and Emotion* 14, no. 4 (2000): 433–40; M.T. Pham, "The Logic of Feeling," *Journal of Consumer Psychology* 14, no. 4 (2004): 360–69. One recent proposition is that a person's confidence in their beliefs is also influenced by their emotional experiences regarding

those beliefs. See: Z. Memon and J. Treur, "On the Reciprocal Interaction between Believing and Feeling: An Adaptive Agent Modelling Perspective," *Cognitive Neurodynamics* 4, no. 4 (2010): 377–94.

19. G.R. Maio, V.M. Esses, and D.W. Bell, "Examining Conflict between Components of Attitudes: Ambivalence and Inconsistency Are Distinct Constructs," *Canadian Journal of Behavioural Science* 32, no. 2 (2000): 71–83.

20. P.C. Nutt, *Why Decisions Fail* (San Francisco, CA: Berrett-Koehler, 2002); S. Finkelstein, *Why Smart Executives Fail* (New York: Viking, 2003); P.C. Nutt, "Search During Decision Making," *European Journal of Operational Research* 160 (2005): 851–76.

21. S. Bolton, C. and M. Houlihan, "Are We Having Fun Yet? A Consideration of Workplace Fun and Engagement," *Employee Relations* 31, no. 6 (2009): 556–68.

22. J. Dehaas, "All Work and Some Play," *Maclean's*, 2012 May 28 2012, 74; G. Puliatti, "Coolest Offices in Canada – 5 Awesome Workplaces in Toronto," *adzuna*, adzuna, 4 September 2013, http://www.adzuna.ca/blog/2013/09/04/coolest-offices-in-canada-5-awesome-workplaces-in-toronto/.

23. M. McLaughlin, "Bosses Blind to Horrors of 'Fun Days'," *Scotland on Sunday*, 3 January 2010, 10; E. Lamm and M.D. Meeks, "Workplace Fun: The Moderating Effects of Generational Differences," *Employee Relations* 31, no. 6 (2009): 613–31; "Schumpeter: Down with Fun," *Economist Intelligence Unit – Executive Briefing (London)*, 22 September 2010; E.J. Romero and L.A. Arendt, "Variable Effects of Humor Styles on Organizational Outcomes," *Psychological Reports* 108, no. 2 (2011): 649–59.

24. S. Davies, "Razer Employees Wear Shorts, T-Shirts and Flip-Flops to Work," *Straits Times (Singapore)*, 10 May 2008; S. Long, "Meet the Chief Gamer," *Straits Times (Singapore)*, 8 February 2013; F. McInnis, "Great Offices: An Ad Agency's Quirky John Street Headquarters, Complete with Slide," *Toronto Life*, 4 April 2013; ClearlyContacts, "Play Hard-How We Have Fun," (Vancouver, BC: 2014), http://career.clearlycontacts.ca/playHard.html#ad-image-0 (accessed 3 March 2014).

25. Weiss and Cropanzano, "Affective Events Theory."

26. L. Festinger, *A Theory of Cognitive Dissonance* (Evanston, IL: Row, Peterson, 1957); A.D. Galinsky, J. Stone, and J. Cooper, "The Reinstatement of Dissonance and Psychological Discomfort Following Failed Affirmation," *European Journal of Social Psychology* 30, no. 1 (2000): 123–47; J. Cooper, *Cognitive Dissonance: Fifth Years of a Classic Theory* (London, UK: Sage, 2007).

27. N. Wijewardena, C.E.J. Hartel, and R. Samaratunge, "A Laugh a Day Is Sure to Keep the Blues Away: Managers' Use of Humor and the Construction and Destruction of Employees' Resilience," in *Emotions and Organizational Dynamism*, ed. W.J. Zerbe, C.E.J. Hartel, and N.M. Ashkanasy, *Research on Emotion in Organizations* (Bradford: Emerald Group Publishing Limited, 2010), 259–78; C. Robert and J.E. Wilbanks, "The Wheel Model of Humor: Humor Events and Affect in Organizations," *Human Relations* 65, no. 9 (2012): 1071–99; J. Mesmer-Magnus, D.J. Glew, and C. Viswesvaran, "A Meta-Analysis of Positive Humor in the Workplace," *Journal of Managerial Psychology* 27, no. 2 (2012): 155–90.

28. D.L. Collinson, "Managing Humour," *Journal of Management Studies* 39, no. 3 (2002): 269–88; K. Owler, R. Morrison, and B. Plester, "Does Fun Work? The Complexity of Promoting Fun at Work," *Journal of Management and Organization* 16, no. 3 (2010): 338–52.

29. G.R. Salancik, "Commitment and the Control of Organizational Behavior and Belief," in *New Directions in Organizational Behavior*, ed. B.M. Staw and G.R. Salancik (Chicago, IL: St. Clair, 1977), 1–54; J.M. Jarcho, E.T. Berkman, and M.D. Lieberman, "The Neural Basis of Rationalization: Cognitive Dissonance Reduction During Decision-Making," *Social Cognitive and Affective Neuroscience* 6, no. 4 (2011): 460–67.

30. T.A. Judge, E.A. Locke, and C.C. Durham, "The Dispositional Causes of Job Satisfaction: A Core Evaluations Approach," *Research in Organizational Behavior* 19 (1997): 151–88; T.W.H. Ng and K.L. Sorensen, "Dispositional Affectivity and Work-Related Outcomes: A Meta-Analysis," *Journal of Applied Social Psychology* 39, no. 6 (2009): 1255–87.

31. C.M. Brotheridge and A.A. Grandey, "Emotional Labor and Burnout: Comparing Two Perspectives of 'People Work,'' *Journal of Vocational Behavior* 60 (2002): 17–39; P.G. Irving, D.F. Coleman, and D.R. Bobocel, "The Moderating Effect of Negative Affectivity in the Procedural Justice-Job Satisfaction Relation," *Canadian Journal of Behavioural Science* 37, no. 1 (2005): 20–32.

32. J. Schaubroeck, D.C. Ganster, and B. Kemmerer, "Does Trait Affect Promote Job Attitude Stability?," *Journal of Organizational Behavior* 17 (1996): 191–96; C. Dormann and D. Zapf, "Job Satisfaction: A Meta-Analysis of Stabilities," *Journal of Organizational Behavior* 22 (2001): 483–504.

33. J.A. Morris and D.C. Feldman, "The Dimensions, Antecedents, and Consequences of Emotional Labor," *Academy of Management Review* 21 (1996): 986–1010. This is a person-centred definition, which is supplemented by other approaches to the topic. For recent reviews, see A.S. Wharton, "The Sociology of Emotional Labor," *Annual Review of Sociology* 35, no. 1 (2009): 147–65; F.M. Peart, A.M. Roan, and N.M. Ashkanasy, "Trading in Emotions: A Closer Examination of Emotional Labor," in *Experiencing and Managing Emotions in the Workplace*, ed. N.M. Ashkanasy, C.E.J. Hartel, and W.J. Zerbe, *Research on Emotion in Organizations* (Bingley, UK: Emerald Group, 2012), 279–304; A.A. Grandey, J.M. Diefendorff, and D.E. Rupp, "Bringing Emotional Labor in Focus: A Review and Integration of Three Research Issues," in *Emotional Labor in the 21st Century: Diverse Perspectives on Emotion Regulation at Work* ed. A.A. Grandey, J.M. Diefendorff, and D.E. Rupp, *Series in Organization and Management* (Hove, UK: Routledge, 2013), 3–28.

34. Morris and Feldman, "The Dimensions, Antecedents, and Consequences of Emotional Labor; D. Zapf, "Emotion Work and Psychological Well-Being: A Review of the Literature and Some Conceptual Considerations," *Human Resource Management Review* 12 (2002): 237–68.

35. P. O'Neil, "Canada a Top Draw for French Seeking Jobs," *Montreal Gazette*, 18 November 2010, B2; L. Pivot, "Objectif Canada: A Vos Marques, Prêts. . . Partez!," *L'Express*, 4 June 2008.

36. A.E. Raz and A. Rafaeli, "Emotion Management in Cross-Cultural Perspective: 'Smile Training' in Japanese and North American Service Organizations," *Research on Emotion in Organizations* 3 (2007): 199–220; D. Matsumoto, Seung Hee Yoo, and J. Fontaine, "Mapping Expressive Differences around the World," *Journal of Cross-Cultural Psychology* 39, no. 1 (2008): 55–74; S. Ravid, A. Rafaeli, and A. Grandey, "Expressions of Anger in Israeli Workplaces: The Special Place of Customer Interactions," *Human Resource Management Review* 20, no. 3 (2010): 224–34. Emotional display norms might also explain differences in aggression across cultures. See: N. Bergeron and B.H. Schneider, "Explaining Cross-National Differences in Peer-Directed Aggression: A Quantitative Synthesis," *Aggressive Behavior* 31, no. 2 (2005): 116–37.

37. A.E. Kramer, "Russian Service, and with Please and Thank You," *New York Times*, 2 November 2013, 1.

38. F. Trompenaars and C. Hampden-Turner, *Riding the Waves of Culture*, 2nd ed. (New York: McGraw-Hill, 1998), Chap. 6. Also see: S. Safdar et al., "Variations of Emotional Display Rules within and across Cultures: A Comparison between Canada, USA, and Japan," *Canadian Journal of Behavioural Science* 41, no. 1 (2009): 1–10.

39. W.J. Zerbe, "Emotional Dissonance and Employee Well-Being," in *Managing Emotions in the Workplace* ed. N.M. Ashkanasy, W.J. Zerbe, and C.E.J. Hartel (Armonk, NY: M.E. Sharpe, 2002), 189–214; F. Cheung and C. Tang, "The Influence of Emotional Dissonance on Subjective Health and Job Satisfaction: Testing the Stress-Strain-Outcome Model," *Journal of Applied Social Psychology* 40, no. 12 (2010): 3192–217; Grandey, Diefendorff, and Rupp, "Bringing Emotional Labor in Focus."

40. N.-W. Chi et al., "Want a Tip? Service Performance as a Function of Emotion Regulation and Extraversion," *Journal of Applied Psychology* 96, no. 6 (2011): 1337–46; S. Côté, I. Hideg, and G.A. van Kleef, "The Consequences of Faking Anger in Negotiations," *Journal of Experimental Social Psychology* 49, no. 3 (2013): 453–63.

41. S.D. Pugh, M. Groth, and T. Hennig-Thurau, "Willing and Able to Fake Emotions: A Closer Examination of the Link between Emotional Dissonance and Employee Well-Being," *Journal of Applied Psychology* 96, no. 2 (2011): 377–90; R.S. Rubin et al., "A Reconceptualization of the Emotional Labor Construct: On the Development of an Integrated Theory of Perceived Emotional Dissonance and Emotional Labor," in *Emotions in Organizational Behavior*, ed. C. Hartel, N.M. Ashkanasy, and W. Zerbe (Hoboken, NJ: Taylor and Francis, 2012), 189–211.

42. Zapf, "Emotion Work and Psychological Well-Being; J.D. Kammeyer-Mueller et al., "A Meta-Analytic Structural Model of Dispositional Affectivity and Emotional Labor," *Personnel Psychology* 66, no. 1 (2013): 47–90; H. Ozcelik, "An Empirical Analysis of Surface Acting in Intra-Organizational Relationships," *Journal of Organizational Behavior* 34, no. 3 (2013): 291–309.

Deep acting is considered an adaptation of method acting used by professional actors.

43. L. Peterson, "USF Seeking Medical Students Nicer Than 'House'," *Tampa Tribune*, 20 June 2011.

44. This model is very similar to Goleman's revised emotional intelligence model. See D. Goleman, R. Boyatzis, and A. McKee, *Primal Leadership* (Boston, MA: Harvard Business School Press, 2002), Chap. 3. Recent studies indicate that this model (when framed as abilities) provides the best fit to data. See: R.P. Tett and K.E. Fox, "Confirmatory Factor Structure of Trait Emotional Intelligence in Student and Worker Samples," *Personality and Individual Differences* 41 (2006): 1155–68; P.J. Jordan and S.A. Lawrence, "Emotional Intelligence in Teams: Development and Initial Validation of the Short Version of the Workgroup Emotional Intelligence Profile (Weip-S)," *Journal of Management & Organization* 15 (2009): 452–69; D.L. Joseph and D.A. Newman, "Emotional Intelligence: An Integrative Meta-Analysis and Cascading Model," *Journal of Applied Psychology* 95, no. 1 (2010): 54–78.

45. H.A. Elfenbein and N. Ambady, "Predicting Workplace Outcomes from the Ability to Eavesdrop on Feelings," *Journal of Applied Psychology* 87, no. 5 (2002): 963–71.

46. The hierarchical nature of the four EI dimensions is discussed by Goleman, but it is more explicit in the Salovey and Mayer model. See D.R. Caruso and P. Salovey, *The Emotionally Intelligent Manager* (San Francisco, CA: Jossey-Bass, 2004). This hierarchy is also identified (without the self-other distinction) as a sequence in: Joseph and Newman, "Emotional Intelligence."

47. E.A. Locke, "Why Emotional Intelligence Is an Invalid Concept," *Journal of Organizational Behavior* 26 (2005): 425–31; J. Antonakis, "Emotional Intelligence": What Does It Measure and Does It Matter for Leadership?," in *Lmx Leadership-Game-Changing Designs: Research-Based Tools*, ed. G.B. Graen (Greenwich, CT: Information Age Publishing, 2009), 163–92; J. Antonakis, N.M. Ashkanasy, and M.T. Dasborough, "Does Leadership Need Emotional Intelligence?," *Leadership Quarterly* 20 (2009): 247–61; M. Fiori and J. Antonakis, "The Ability Model of Emotional Intelligence: Searching for Valid Measures," *Personality and Individual Differences* 50, no. 3 (2011): 329–34.

48. D.L. Reis et al., "Emotional Intelligence Predicts Individual Differences in Social Exchange Reasoning," *NeuroImage* 35, no. 3 (2007): 1385–91; C. Cherniss, "Emotional Intelligence: Toward Clarification of a Concept," *Industrial and Organizational Psychology* 3, no. 2 (2010): 110–26; F. Walter, M.S. Cole, and R.H. Humphrey, "Emotional Intelligence: Sine Qua Non of Leadership or Folderol?," *Academy of Management Perspectives* 25, no. 1 (2011): 45–59.

49. Some studies have reported situations where EI has a limited effect on individual performance. For example, see A.L. Day and S.A. Carroll, "Using an Ability-Based Measure of Emotional Intelligence to Predict Individual Performance, Group Performance, and Group Citizenship Behaviors," *Personality and Individual Differences* 36 (2004): 1443–58; Z. Ivcevic, M.A. Brackett, and J.D. Mayer, "Emotional Intelligence and Emotional Creativity," *Journal of Personality* 75, no. 2 (2007): 199–236; J.C. Rode et al., "Emotional Intelligence and Individual Performance: Evidence of Direct and Moderated Effects," *Journal of Organizational Behavior* 28, no. 4 (2007): 399–421.

50. R. Bar-On, *Preliminary Report: A New Us Air Force Study Explores the Cost-Effectiveness of Applying the Bar-on EQ-I*, eiconsortium (August 2010); W. Gordon, "Climbing High for EI," *T + D* 64, no. 8 (2010): 72–73; "Occupational Analysts Influence Air Force Decision Makers," *US Fed News*, 3 November 2010.

51. H.A. Elfenbein, "Learning in Emotion Judgments: Training and the Cross-Cultural Understanding of Facial Expressions," *Journal of Nonverbal Behavior* 30, no. 1 (2006): 21–36; D. Nelis et al., "Increasing Emotional Intelligence: (How) Is It Possible?," *Personality and Individual Differences* 47, no. 1 (2009): 36–41; L.J.M. Zijlmans et al., "Training Emotional Intelligence Related to Treatment Skills of Staff Working with Clients with Intellectual Disabilities and Challenging Behaviour," *Journal of Intellectual Disability Research* 55, no. 2 (2011): 219–30; D. Blanch-Hartigan, "An Effective Training to Increase Accurate Recognition of Patient Emotion Cues," *Patient Education and Counseling* 89, no. 2 (2012): 274–80; J. Shaw, S. Porter, and L. ten Brinke, "Catching Liars: Training Mental Health and Legal Professionals to Detect High-Stakes Lies," *Journal of Forensic Psychiatry & Psychology* 24, no. 2 (2013): 145–59.

52. D.A. Harrison, D.A. Newman, and P.L. Roth, "How Important Are Job Attitudes? Meta-Analytic Comparisons of Integrative Behavioral Outcomes and Time Sequences," *Academy of Management Journal* 49, no. 2 (2006): 305–25. Another recent study concluded that job satisfaction and organizational commitment are so highly correlated that they represent the same construct. See: H. Le et al., "The Problem of Empirical Redundancy of Constructs in Organizational Research: An Empirical Investigation," *Organizational Behavior and Human Decision Processes* 112, no. 2 (2010): 112–25. They are also considered the two central work-related variables in the broader concept of happiness at work. See: C.D. Fisher, "Happiness at Work," *International Journal of Management Reviews* 12, no. 4 (2010): 384–412.

53. Ipsos-Reid, "Ipsos-Reid Global Poll Finds Major Differences in Employee Satisfaction around the World," in *Ipsos-Reid News Release* (Toronto, ON: 2001); International Survey Research, *Employee Satisfaction in the World's 10 Largest Economies: Globalization or Diversity?*, International Survey Research (Chicago, IL: 2002); Watson Wyatt Worldwide, "Malaysian Workers More Satisfied with Their Jobs Than Their Companies' Leadership and Supervision Practices," (Kuala Lumpur: Watson Wyatt Worldwide, 2004); Kelly Global Workforce Index, *American Workers Are Happy with Their Jobs and Their Bosses*, Kelly Services (Troy, MI: November 2006).

54. Randstad, *Women in Leadership: Still a Tough Battle*, Randstad Workmonitor, Global Press Report, Wave 1, 2013, Randstad holding nv (Amsterdam: March 2013). Survey data were collected from a minimum of 400 interviews per country of adults working 24 hours or more per week. Respondents were asked: "How satisfied are you in general working for your current employer?"

55. E.A. Locke, "The Nature and Causes of Job Satisfaction," in *Handbook of Industrial and Organizational Psychology*, ed. M. Dunnette (Chicago, IL: Rand McNally, 1976), 1297–350; H.M. Weiss, "Deconstructing Job Satisfaction: Separating Evaluations, Beliefs and Affective Experiences," *Human Resource Management Review*, no. 12 (2002): 173–94. Some definitions still include emotion as an element of job satisfaction, whereas the definition presented in this book views emotion as a cause of job satisfaction. Also, this definition views job satisfaction as a "collection of attitudes," not several "facets" of job satisfaction.

56. Treasury Board of Canada, "2011 Public Service Employee Survey: Focus on Employee Engagement," (Ottawa, ON: Treasury Board of Canada, 29 April 2013), http://www.tbs-sct.gc.ca/pses-saff/2011/engage-mobil-eng.asp (accessed 4 March 2014).

57. L. Saad, *Job Security Slips in U.S. Worker Satisfaction Rankings*, Gallup, Inc. (Princeton, NJ: I. Gallup, 27 August 2009); *Employee Engagement Report 2011*, BlessingWhite (Princeton, NJ: 2011). A recent Kelly Services Workforce Index survey reported that 66 percent of the 170,000 respondents in 30 countries plan to look for a job with another organization within the next year. See: Kelly Services, *Acquisition and Retention in the War for Talent*, Kelly Global Workforce Index, Kelly Services (Troy, MI: April 2012).

58. The problems with measuring attitudes and values across cultures is discussed in: L. Saari and T.A. Judge, "Employee Attitudes and Job Satisfaction "*Human Resource Management* 43, no. 4 (2004): 395–407; A.K. Uskul et al., "How Successful You Have Been in Life Depends on the Response Scale Used: The Role of Cultural Mindsets in Pragmatic Inferences Drawn from Question Format," *Social Cognition* 31, no. 2 (2013): 222–36.

59. H. Rao and R.I. Sutton, "Innovation Lessons from Pixar: An Interview with Oscar-Winning Director Brad Bird," *McKinsey Quarterly* (2008): 1–9.

60. For a review of the various job satisfaction outcome theories, see: Dalal, "Job Attitudes: Cognition and Affect."

61. M.J. Withey and W.H. Cooper, "Predicting Exit, Voice, Loyalty, and Neglect," *Administrative Science Quarterly*, no. 34 (1989): 521–39; W.H. Turnley and D.C. Feldman, "The Impact of Psychological Contract Violations on Exit, Voice, Loyalty, and Neglect," *Human Relations*, no. 52 (1999): 895–922. Subdimensions of silence and voice also exist. See L. van Dyne, S. Ang, and I.C. Botero, "Conceptualizing Employee Silence and Employee Voice as Multidimensional Constructs*," *Journal of Management Studies* 40, no. 6 (2003): 1359–92.

62. T.R. Mitchell, B.C. Holtom, and T.W. Lee, "How to Keep Your Best Employees: Developing an Effective Retention Policy," *Academy of*

Management Executive 15 (2001): 96–108; C.P. Maertz and M.A. Campion, "Profiles of Quitting: Integrating Process and Content Turnover Theory," *Academy of Management Journal* 47, no. 4 (2004): 566–82; K. Morrell, J. Loan-Clarke, and A. Wilkinson, "The Role of Shocks in Employee Turnover," *British Journal of Management* 15 (2004): 335–49; B.C. Holtom, T.R. Mitchell, and T.W. Lee, "Increasing Human and Social Capital by Applying Job Embeddedness Theory," *Organizational Dynamics* 35, no. 4 (2006): 316–31.

63. B.S. Klaas, J.B. Olson-Buchanan, and A.-K. Ward, "The Determinants of Alternative Forms of Workplace Voice: An Integrative Perspective," *Journal of Management* 38, no. 1 (2012): 314–45. For a critique and explanation for historical errors in the EVLN model's development, see: S.L. McShane, "Reconstructing the Meaning and Dimensionality of Voice in the Exit-Voice-Loyalty-Neglect Model (Paper Presented in the Voice and Loyalty" Symposium)," in *Annual Conference of the Administrative Sciences Association of Canada, Organizational Behaviour Division* (Halifax, 2008).

64. A.O. Hirschman, *Exit, Voice, and Loyalty: Responses to Decline in Firms, Organizations, and States* (Cambridge, MA: Harvard University Press, 1970); E.A. Hoffmann, "Exit and Voice: Organizational Loyalty and Dispute Resolution Strategies," *Social Forces* 84, no. 4 (2006): 2313–30.

65. J.D. Hibbard, N. Kumar, and L.W. Stern, "Examining the Impact of Destructive Acts in Marketing Channel Relationships," *Journal of Marketing Research* 38 (2001): 45–61; J. Zhou and J.M. George, "When Job Dissatisfaction Leads to Creativity: Encouraging the Expression of Voice," *Academy of Management Journal* 44 (2001): 682–96.

66. M.J. Withey and I.R. Gellatly, "Situational and Dispositional Determinants of Exit, Voice, Loyalty and Neglect," *Proceedings of the Administrative Sciences Association of Canada, Organizational Behaviour Division* (1998); D.C. Thomas and K. Au, "The Effect of Cultural Differences on Behavioral Responses to Low Job Satisfaction," *Journal of International Business Studies* 33, no. 2 (2002): 309–26; S.F. Premeaux and A.G. Bedeian, "Breaking the Silence: The Moderating Effects of Self-Monitoring in Predicting Speaking up in the Workplace," *Journal of Management Studies* 40, no. 6 (2003): 1537–62; D.J. Travis, R.J. Gomez, and M.E. Mor Barak, "Speaking up and Stepping Back: Examining the Link between Employee Voice and Job Neglect," *Children and Youth Services Review* 33, no. 10 (2011): 1831–41.

67. V. Venkataramani and S. Tangirala, "When and Why Do Central Employees Speak Up? An Examination of Mediating and Moderating Variables," *Journal of Applied Psychology* 95, no. 3 (2010): 582–91.

68. T.A. Judge et al., "The Job Satisfaction-Job Performance Relationship: A Qualitative and Quantitative Review," *Psychological Bulletin* 127, no. 3 (2001): 376–407; C.D. Fisher, "Why Do Lay People Believe That Satisfaction and Performance Are Correlated? Possible Sources of a Common Sense Theory," *Journal of Organizational Behavior* 24, no. 6 (2003): 753–77; Saari and Judge, "Employee Attitudes and Job Satisfaction". Other studies report stronger correlations with job performance when both the belief and feeling components of job satisfaction are consistent with each other and when overall job attitude (satisfaction and commitment combined) is being measured. See D.J. Schleicher, J.D. Watt, and G.J. Greguras, "Reexamining the Job Satisfaction-Performance Relationship: The Complexity of Attitudes," *Journal of Applied Psychology* 89, no. 1 (2004): 165–77; Harrison, Newman, and Roth, "How Important Are Job Attitudes?" The positive relationship between job satisfaction and employee performance is also consistent with emerging research on the outcomes of positive organizational behaviour. For example, see: J.R. Sunil, "Enhancing Employee Performance through Positive Organizational Behavior," *Journal of Applied Social Psychology* 38, no. 6 (2008): 1580–600.

69. R. Evans, "'Our Success at Admiral Is All Thanks to Brilliant Staff'," *Western Mail (Cardiff, Wales)*, 2 January 2013, 1; S. Leonard, "Tuned in to the People Who Matter," *Sunday Times (London)*, 26 February 2014; "It's Plain Sailing at Admiral," *South Wales Evening Post*, 1 March 2014, 5.

70. However, panel studies suggest that satisfaction has a stronger effect on performance than the other way around. For a summary, see: Fisher, "Happiness at Work."

71. L. Wirthman, "Container Store Moves Ahead with Superb Communications among Employees," *Denver Post*, 21 April 2013; J. Mossman, "Employee-Friendly Workplace Culture a Key to Company Success," *Denver Post*, 21 April 2013.

72. J.I. Heskett, W.E. Sasser, and L.A. Schlesinger, *The Service Profit Chain* (New York: Free Press, 1997); S.P. Brown and S.K. Lam, "A Meta-Analysis of Relationships Linking Employee Satisfaction to Customer Responses," *Journal of Retailing* 84, no. 3 (2008): 243–55; T.J. Gerpott and M. Paukert, "The Relationship between Employee Satisfaction and Customer Satisfaction: A Meta-Analysis (Der Zusammenhang Zwischen Mitarbeiter- Und Kundenzufriedenheit: Eine Metaanalyse)," *Zeitschrift für Personalforschung* 25, no. 1 (2011): 28–54; R.W.Y. Yee, A.C.L. Yeung, and T.C.E. Cheng, "The Service-Profit Chain: An Empirical Analysis in High-Contact Service Industries," *International Journal of Production Economics* 130, no. 2 (2011): 236–45; H. Evanschitzky, F.v. Wangenheim, and N.V. Wünderlich, "Perils of Managing the Service Profit Chain: The Role of Time Lags and Feedback Loops," *Journal of Retailing* 88, no. 3 (2012): 356–66; Y. Hong et al., "Missing Link in the Service Profit Chain: A Meta-Analytic Review of the Antecedents, Consequences, and Moderators of Service Climate," *Journal of Applied Psychology* 98, no. 2 (2013): 237–67.

73. W.-C. Tsai and Y.-M. Huang, "Mechanisms Linking Employee Affective Delivery and Customer Behavioral Intentions," *Journal of Applied Psychology* 87, no. 5 (2002): 1001–08; P. Guenzi and O. Pelloni, "The Impact of Interpersonal Relationships on Customer Satisfaction and Loyalty to the Service Provider," *International Journal Of Service Industry Management* 15, no. 3-4 (2004): 365–84; S.J. Bell, S. Auh, and K. Smalley, "Customer Relationship Dynamics: Service Quality and Customer Loyalty in the Context of Varying Levels of Customer Expertise and Switching Costs," *Journal of the Academy of Marketing Science* 33, no. 2 (2005): 169–83; P.B. Barger and A.A. Grandey, "Service with a Smile and Encounter Satisfaction: Emotional Contagion and Appraisal Mechanisms," *Academy of Management Journal* 49, no. 6 (2006): 1229–38. On the reciprocal effect, see: E. Kim and D.J. Yoon, "Why Does Service with a Smile Make Employees Happy? A Social Interaction Model," *Journal of Applied Psychology* 97, no. 5 (2012): 1059–67.

74. Data provided in several country-specific news releases from Kelly Services. For a white paper summary of the survey, see: Kelly Services, *Employee Loyalty Rises During Global Economic Recession, Kelly International Workforce Survey Finds*, Kelly Services (Troy, MI: 8 March 2010).

75. R.T. Mowday, L.W. Porter, and R.M. Steers, *Employee Organization Linkages: The Psychology of Commitment, Absenteeism, and Turnover* (New York: Academic Press, 1982); J.P. Meyer, "Organizational Commitment," *International Review of Industrial and Organizational Psychology* 12 (1997): 175–228. The definition and dimensions of organizational commitment continue to be debated. Some writers even propose that "affective commitment" refers only to one's psychological attachment to and involvement in the organization, whereas "identification" with the organization is a distinct concept further along a continuum of bonds. See: O.N. Solinger, W. van Olffen, and R.A. Roe, "Beyond the Three-Component Model of Organizational Commitment," *Journal of Applied Psychology* 93, no. 1 (2008): 70–83; H.J. Klein, J.C. Molloy, and C.T. Brinsfield, "Reconceptualizing Workplace Commitment to Redress a Stretched Construct: Revisiting Assumptions and Removing Confounds," *Academy of Management Review* 37, no. 1 (2012): 130–51.

76. M. Taing et al., "The Multidimensional Nature of Continuance Commitment: Commitment Owing to Economic Exchanges Versus Lack of Employment Alternatives," *Journal of Business and Psychology* 26, no. 3 (2011): 269–84; C. Vandenberghe and A. Panaccio, "Perceived Sacrifice and Few Alternatives Commitments: The Motivational Underpinnings of Continuance Commitment's Subdimensions," *Journal of Vocational Behavior* 81, no. 1 (2012): 59–72.

77. J.P. Meyer et al., "Affective, Continuance, and Normative Commitment to the Organization: A Meta-Analysis of Antecedents, Correlates, and Consequences," *Journal of Vocational Behavior* 61 (2002): 20–52; M. Riketta, "Attitudinal Organizational Commitment and Job Performance: A Meta-Analysis," *Journal of Organizational Behavior* 23 (2002): 257–66; J.P. Meyer and E.R. Maltin, "Employee Commitment and Well-Being: A Critical Review, Theoretical Framework and Research Agenda," *Journal of Vocational Behavior* 77, no. 2 (2010): 323–37.

78. J.P. Meyer et al., "Organizational Commitment and Job Performance: It's the Nature of the Commitment That Counts," *Journal of Applied Psychology* 74 (1989): 152–56; A.A. Luchak and

I.R. Gellatly, "What Kind of Commitment Does a Final-Earnings Pension Plan Elicit?," *Relations Industrielles* 56 (2001): 394–417; Z.X. Chen and A.M. Francesco, "The Relationship between the Three Components of Commitment and Employee Performance in China," *Journal of Vocational Behavior* 62, no. 3 (2003): 490–510; H. Gill et al., "Affective and Continuance Commitment and Their Relations with Deviant Workplace Behaviors in Korea," *Asia Pacific Journal of Management* 28, no. 3 (2011): 595–607. The negative effect on performance might depend on the type of continuance commitment. See: Taing et al., "The Multidimensional Nature of Continuance Commitment."

79. J.E. Finegan, "The Impact of Person and Organizational Values on Organizational Commitment," *Journal of Occupational and Organizational Psychology* 73 (2000): 149–69; A. Panaccio and C. Vandenberghe, "Perceived Organizational Support, Organizational Commitment and Psychological Well-Being: A Longitudinal Study," *Journal of Vocational Behavior* 75, no. 2 (2009): 224–36.

80. A.L. Kristof-Brown, R.D. Zimmerman, and E.C. Johnson, "Consequences of Individuals' Fit at Work: A Meta-Analysis of Person-Job, Person-Organization, Person-Group, and Person-Supervisor Fit," *Personnel Psychology* 58, no. 2 (2005): 281–342; J.R. Edwards, "Chapter 4: Person-Environment Fit in Organizations: An Assessment of Theoretical Progress," *The Academy of Management Annals* 2 (2008): 167–230; M.E. Bergman et al., "An Event-Based Perspective on the Development of Commitment," *Human Resource Management Review* 23, no. 2 (2013): 148–60.

81. D.M. Rousseau et al., "Not So Different after All: A Cross-Discipline View of Trust," *Academy of Management Review* 23 (1998): 393–404.

82. D.K. Datta et al., "Causes and Effects of Employee Downsizing: A Review and Synthesis," *Journal of Management* 36, no. 1 (2010): 281–348.

83. Similar concepts on information acquisition are found in socialization and organizational change research. See, for example: P. Bordia et al., "Uncertainty During Organizational Change: Types, Consequences, and Management Strategies," *Journal of Business and Psychology* 18, no. 4 (2004): 507–32; H.D. Cooper-Thomas and N. Anderson, "Organizational Socialization: A Field Study into Socialization Success and Rate," *International Journal of Selection and Assessment* 13, no. 2 (2005): 116–28; T.N. Bauer, "Newcomer Adjustment During Organizational Socialization: A Meta-Analytic Review of Antecedents, Outcomes, and Methods," *Journal of Applied Psychology* 92, no. 3 (2007): 707–21.

84. T.S. Heffner and J.R. Rentsch, "Organizational Commitment and Social Interaction: A Multiple Constituencies Approach," *Journal of Vocational Behavior* 59 (2001): 471–90.

85. J. Pierce, L. , T. Kostova, and K.T. Dirks, "Toward a Theory of Psychological Ownership in Organizations," *Academy of Management Review* 26, no. 2 (2001): 298–310; M. Mayhew et al., "A Study of the Antecedents and Consequences of Psychological Ownership in Organizational Settings," *The Journal of Social Psychology* 147, no. 5 (2007): 477–500; T.-S. Han, H.-H. Chiang, and A. Chang, "Employee Participation in Decision Making, Psychological Ownership and Knowledge Sharing: Mediating Role of Organizational Commitment in Taiwanese High-Tech Organizations," *The International Journal of Human Resource Management* 21, no. 12 (2010): 2218–33.

86. J.C. Quick et al., *Preventive Stress Management in Organizations* (Washington, DC: American Psychological Association, 1997), pp. 3–4; R.S. DeFrank and J.M. Ivancevich, "Stress on the Job: An Executive Update," *Academy of Management Executive* 12 (1998): 55–66; A.L. Dougall and A. Baum, "Stress, Coping, and Immune Function," in *Handbook of Psychology*, ed. M. Gallagher and R.J. Nelson (Hoboken, NJ: John Wiley & Sons, Inc., 2003), 441–55. There are at least three schools of thought regarding the meaning of stress, and some reviews of the stress literature describe these schools without pointing to any one as the preferred definition. One reviewer concluded that the stress concept is so broad that it should be considered an umbrella concept, capturing a broad array of phenomena and providing a simple term for the public to use. See T.A. Day, "Defining Stress as a Prelude to Mapping Its Neurocircuitry: No Help from Allostasis," *Progress in Neuro-Psychopharmacology and Biological Psychiatry* 29, no. 8 (2005): 1195–200; R. Cropanzano and A. Li, "Organizational Politics and Workplace Stress," in *Handbook of Organizational Politics*, ed. E. Vigoda-Gadot and A. Drory (Cheltenham, UK: Edward Elgar, 2006), 139–60; R.L. Woolfolk, P.M. Lehrer, and L.A. Allen, "Conceptual Issues Underlying Stress Management," in *Principles and Practice of Stress Management*, ed. P.M. Lehrer, R.L. Woolfolk, and W.E. Sime (New York: Guilford Press, 2007), 3–15.

87. Finegan, "The Impact of Person and Organizational Values on Organizational Commitment; Dougall and Baum, "Stress, Coping, and Immune Function; R.S. Lazarus, *Stress and Emotion: A New Synthesis* (New York: Springer Publishing, 2006); L.W. Hunter and S.M.B. Thatcher, "Feeling the Heat: Effects of Stress, Commitment, and Job Experience on Job Performance," *Academy of Management Journal* 50, no. 4 (2007): 953–68.

88. Sun Life Financial, "National Survey Reveals 90 Per Cent of Young Canadians Are Stressed out in Today's Economy," News release (Toronto, ON: Sun Life Financial, 5 November 2012); "Tis the Season for Work-Life Balance According to Canadian SBOs," *Canada Newswire*, 9 December 2013.

89. Quick et al., *Preventive Stress Management in Organizations* pp. 5–6; B.L. Simmons and D.L. Nelson, "Eustress at Work: The Relationship between Hope and Health in Hospital Nurses," *Health Care Management Review* 26, no. 4 (2001): 7ff. The eustress survey is reported in: Towers Watson, "Debunking Workforce Myths," (Towers Watson, 2008).

90. H. Selye, "A Syndrome Produced by Diverse Nocuous Agents," *Nature* 138, no. 1 (1936): 32; H. Selye, *Stress without Distress* (Philadelphia: J.B. Lippincott, 1974). For the history of the word stress, see: R.M.K. Keil, "Coping and Stress: A Conceptual Analysis," *Journal of Advanced Nursing* 45, no. 6 (2004): 659–65.

91. S.E. Taylor, R.L. Repetti, and T. Seeman, "Health Psychology: What Is an Unhealthy Environment and How Does It Get under the Skin?," *Annual Review of Psychology* 48 (1997): 411–47.

92. D. Ganster, M. Fox, and D. Dwyer, "Explaining Employees' Health Care Costs: A Prospective Examination of Stressful Job Demands, Personal Control, and Physiological Reactivity," *Journal of Applied Psychology* 86 (2001): 954–64; M. Kivimaki et al., "Work Stress and Risk of Cardiovascular Mortality: Prospective Cohort Study of Industrial Employees," *British Medical Journal* 325 (2002): 857–60; A. Rosengren et al., "Association of Psychosocial Risk Factors with Risk of Acute Myocardial Infarction in 11 119 Cases and 13 648 Controls from 52 Countries (the Interheart Study): Case-Control Study," *The Lancet* 364, no. 9438 (2004): 953–62; S. Andrew and S. Ayers, "Stress, Health, and Illness," in *The Sage Handbook of Health Psychology*, ed. S. Sutton, A. Baum, and M. Johnston (London, UK: Sage, 2004), 169–96.

93. C. Maslach, W.B. Schaufeli, and M.P. Leiter, "Job Burnout," *Annual Review of Psychology* 52 (2001): 397–422; J.R.B. Halbesleben and M.R. Buckley, "Burnout in Organizational Life," *Journal of Management* 30, no. 6 (2004): 859–79; G.M. Alarcon, "A Meta-Analysis of Burnout with Job Demands, Resources, and Attitudes," *Journal of Vocational Behavior* 79, no. 2 (2011): 549–62.

94. R.C. Kessler, "The Effects of Stressful Life Events on Depression," *Annual Review of Psychology* 48 (1997): 191–214; M.S. Hershcovis et al., "Predicting Workplace Aggression: A Meta-Analysis," *Journal of Applied Psychology* 92, no. 1 (2007): 228–38.

95. K. Danna and R.W. Griffin, "Health and Well-Being in the Workplace: A Review and Synthesis of the Literature," *Journal of Management* (1999): 357–84.

96. This is a slight variation of the definition in the Quebec antiharassment legislation. See http://www.cnt.gouv.qc.ca/en/in-case-of/psychological-harassment-at-work/index.html. For related definitions and discussion of workplace incivility, see H. Cowiea and e. al., "Measuring Workplace Bullying," *Aggression and Violent Behavior* 7 (2002): 33–51; C.M. Pearson and C.L. Porath, "On the Nature, Consequences and Remedies of Workplace Incivility: No Time for 'Nice'? Think Again," *Academy of Management Executive* 19, no. 1 (2005): 7–18. For recent discussion of workplace harassment legislation in the United States, see: D.C. Yamada, "Workplace Bully and American Employment Law: A Ten-Year Progress Report and Assessment," *Comparative Labor Law and Policy Journal* 32, no. 1 (2010): 251–84.

97. "Power Harassment Cases Rising," *Daily Yomiuri (Tokyo)*, 10 June 2009, 2; H. Mulholland, "Bullied Teachers Fear Culture of 'Macho Managers'," *The Observer (London)*, 8 April 2012, 4; "Monster Global Poll Reveals Workplace Bullying Is Endemic," (London, UK: OnRec, 2011), www.onrec.com (accessed 26 June 2012).

98. P. McDonald, "Workplace Sexual Harassment 30 Years On: A Review of the Literature," *International Journal of Management Reviews* 14, no. 1 (2012): 1–17.

99. "Let's Slow Down!," *The Royal Bank of Canada Monthly Letter*, September 1949.

100. L. Duxbury and C. Higgins, *Revisiting Work-Life Issues in Canada: The 2012 National Study on Balancing Work and Caregiving in Canada*, Carleton University (Ottawa, ON: October 2012).

101. P. Elmer-DeWitt, "Foxconn's 11th: Death by Exhaustion," *CNN Money*, 4 June 2010; M. Liang, "Young Woman's Death Raises Concern of Overwork," *Beijing Today*, 22 April 2011; L. Xu, "A Hard Day's Night," *China Daily*, 12 July 2012, 20; "Poll Triggers Work Pressure Concern in China," *Xinhua News Agency (Beijing)*, 19 October 2012; Regus, *A Better Balance*, Regus (Luxembourg: May 2012); Y. Yuan, "White Collars Overworked," *Beijing Review*, 20 June 2013.

102. R. Drago, D. Black, and M. Wooden, *The Persistence of Long Work Hours*, Melbourne Institute Working Paper Series, Melbourne Institute of Applied Economic and Social Research, University of Melbourne (Melbourne: August 2005); L. Golden, "A Brief History of Long Work Time and the Contemporary Sources of Overwork," *Journal of Business Ethics* 84, no. 0 (2009): 217–27.

103. R. Karasek and T. Theorell, *Healthy Work: Stress, Productivity, and the Reconstruction of Working Life* (New York: Basic Books, 1990); N. Turner, N. Chmiel, and M. Walls, "Railing for Safety: Job Demands, Job Control, and Safety Citizenship Role Definition," *Journal of Occupational Health Psychology* 10, no. 4 (2005): 504–12.

104. Lazarus, *Stress and Emotion: A New Synthesis*, Chap. 5.

105. M. Zuckerman and M. Gagne, "The Cope Revised: Proposing a 5-Factor Model of Coping Strategies," *Journal of Research in Personality* 37 (2003): 169–204; S. Folkman and J.T. Moskowitz, "Coping: Pitfalls and Promise," *Annual Review of Psychology* 55 (2004): 745–74; C.A. Thompson et al., "On the Importance of Coping: A Model and New Directions for Research on Work and Family," *Research in Occupational Stress and Well-Being* 6 (2007): 73–113.

106. S.E. Taylor et al., "Psychological Resources, Positive Illusions, and Health," *American Psychologist* 55, no. 1 (2000): 99–109; F. Luthans and C.M. Youssef, "Emerging Positive Organizational Behavior," *Journal of Management* 33, no. 3 (2007): 321–49; P. Steel, J. Schmidt, and J. Shultz, "Refining the Relationship between Personality and Subjective Well-Being," *Psychological Bulletin* 134, no. 1 (2008): 138–61; G. Alarcon, K.J. Eschleman, and N.A. Bowling, "Relationships between Personality Variables and Burnout: A Meta-Analysis," *Work & Stress* 23, no. 3 (2009): 244–63; R. Kotov et al., "Linking "Big" Personality Traits to Anxiety, Depressive, and Substance Use Disorders: A Meta-Analysis," *Psychological Bulletin* 136, no. 5 (2010): 768–821.

107. G.A. Bonanno, "Loss, Trauma, and Human Resilience: Have We Underestimated the Human Capacity to Thrive after Extremely Aversive Events?," *American Psychologist* 59, no. 1 (2004): 20–28; F. Luthans, C.M. Youssef, and B.J. Avolio, *Psychological Capital: Developing the Human Competitive Edge* (New York: Oxford University Press, 2007).

108. J.T. Spence and A.S. Robbins, "Workaholism: Definition, Measurement and Preliminary Results," *Journal of Personality Assessment* 58 (1992): 160–78; R.J. Burke, "Workaholism in Organizations: Psychological and Physical Well-Being Consequences," *Stress Medicine* 16, no. 1 (2000): 11–16; I. Harpaz and R. Snir, "Workaholism: Its Definition and Nature," *Human Relations* 56 (2003): 291–319; R.J. Burke, A.M. Richardson, and M. Martinussen, "Workaholism among Norwegian Senior Managers: New Research Directions," *International Journal of Management* 21, no. 4 (2004): 415–26; T.W.H. Ng, K.L. Sorensen, and D.C. Feldman, "Dimensions, Antecedents, and Consequences of Workaholism: A Conceptual Integration and Extension," *Journal of Organizational Behavior* 28 (2007): 111–36.

109. M. Siegall and L.L. Cummings, "Stress and Organizational Role Conflict," *Genetic, Social, and General Psychology Monographs* 12 (1995): 65–95.

110. L.T. Eby et al., "Work and Family Research in IO/OB: Content Analysis and Review of the Literature (1980–2002)," *Journal of Vocational Behavior* 66, no. 1 (2005): 124–97.

111. N. Davidson, "Vancouver Developer Looks to Make Video Games without Burning out Staff," *Canadian Press*, 21 February 2006; F. Jossi, "Clocking Out," *HRMagazine*, June 2007, 46–50; American Psychological Association, "San Jorge Children's Hospital: A Culture of Collaboration and Care," News release for A.P. Association (Washington, DC: 2011).

112. S.R. Madsen, "The Effects of Home-Based Teleworking on Work-Family Conflict," *Human Resource Development Quarterly* 14, no. 1 (2003): 35–58; S. Raghuram and B. Wiesenfeld, "Work-Nonwork Conflict and Job Stress among Virtual Workers," *Human Resource Management* 43, no. 2/3 (2004): 259–77.

113. Organization for Economic Co-operation and Development, *Babies and Bosses: Reconciling Work and Family Life*, vol. 4 (Canada, Finland, Sweden and the United Kingdom) (Paris: OECD Publishing, 2005); J. Heymann et al., *The Work, Family, and Equity Index: How Does the United States Measure Up?*, Project on Global Working Families, Institute for Health and Social Policy (Montreal, QC: June 2007).

114. M. Secret, "Parenting in the Workplace: Child Care Options for Consideration," *The Journal of Applied Behavioral Science* 41, no. 3 (2005): 326–47.

115. A.E. Carr and T.L.-P. Tang, "Sabbaticals and Employee Motivation: Benefits, Concerns, and Implications," *Journal of Education for Business* 80, no. 3 (2005): 160–64; S. Overman, "Sabbaticals Benefit Companies as Well as Employees," *Employee Benefit News*, 15 April 2006; O.B. Davidson et al., "Sabbatical Leave: Who Gains and How Much?," *Journal of Applied Psychology* 95, no. 5 (2010): 953–64. For discussion of psychological detachment and stress management, see: C. Fritz et al., "Happy, Healthy, and Productive: The Role of Detachment from Work During Nonwork Time," *Journal of Applied Psychology* 95, no. 5 (2010): 977–83.

116. "Vigilant Staff Appreciates Tight-Knit, Family Environment," *Montreal's Top Employers 2013 (Montreal Gazette insert)*, 6 February, 15; "Vigilant Global Keeps Staff Energized with Free Meals," *Montreal's Top Employers 2014 (Montreal Gazette insert)*, 20 February 2014, 18.

117. M.H. Abel, "Humor, Stress, and Coping Strategies," *Humor: International Journal of Humor Research* 15, no. 4 (2002): 365–81; N.A. Kuiper et al., "Humor Is Not Always the Best Medicine: Specific Components of Sense of Humor and Psychological Well-Being," *Humor: International Journal of Humor Research* 17, no. 1/2 (2004): 135–68; E.J. Romero and K.W. Cruthirds, "The Use of Humor in the Workplace," *Academy of Management Perspectives* 20, no. 2 (2006): 58–69; M. McCreaddie and S. Wiggins, "The Purpose and Function of Humor in Health, Health Care and Nursing: A Narrative Review," *Journal of Advanced Nursing* 61, no. 6 (2008): 584–95.

118. W.M. Ensel and N. Lin, "Physical Fitness and the Stress Process," *Journal of Community Psychology* 32, no. 1 (2004): 81–101.

119. S. Armour, "Rising Job Stress Could Affect Bottom Line," *USA Today*, 29 July 2003; V.A. Barnes, F.A. Treiber, and M.H. Johnson, "Impact of Transcendental Meditation on Ambulatory Blood Pressure in African-American Adolescents," *American Journal of Hypertension* 17, no. 4 (2004): 366–69; P. Manikonda et al., "Influence of Non-Pharmacological Treatment (Contemplative Meditation and Breathing Technique) on Stress Induced Hypertension - A Randomized Controlled Study," *American Journal of Hypertension* 18, no. 5, Supplement 1 (2005): A89–A90.

120. C. Viswesvaran, J.I. Sanchez, and J. Fisher, "The Role of Social Support in the Process of Work Stress: A Meta-Analysis," *Journal of Vocational Behavior* 54, no. 2 (1999): 314–34; S.E. Taylor et al., "Biobehavioral Responses to Stress in Females: Tend-and-Befriend, Not Fight-or-Flight," *Psychological Review* 107, no. 3 (2000): 411–29; R. Eisler and D.S. Levine, "Nurture, Nature, and Caring: We Are Not Prisoners of Our Genes," *Brain and Mind* 3 (2002): 9–52; T.A. Beehr, N.A. Bowling, and M.M. Bennett, "Occupational Stress and Failures of Social Support: When Helping Hurts," *Journal of Occupational Health Psychology* 15, no. 1 (2010): 45–59; B.A. Scott et al., "A Daily Investigation of the Role of Manager Empathy on Employee Well-Being," *Organizational Behavior and Human Decision Processes* 113, no. 2 (2010): 127–40.

CHAPTER 5

1. T.P. Bingham, "Telus Reveals Its Secret to Success," (American Society for Training & Development, 2012); D. Pontefract, "As a Competitive Advantage," *T + D* 66, no. 9 (2012): 40; D. Pontefract, "The Social C-Suite," *Chief Learning Officer* 12, no. 3 (2013): 38–41; "Putting Customers First Is Critical to Success: Telus," *National Post*, 4 February 2013; N.M. Crawford and J. Blair, "Unlocking Your Organization's Potential," *Vancouver Sun*, 21 January 2014, C4.

2. C.C. Pinder, *Work Motivation in Organizational Behavior* (Upper Saddle River, NJ: Prentice-Hall, 1998); R.M. Steers, R.T. Mowday, and D.L. Shapiro, "The Future of Work Motivation Theory," *Academy of Management Review* 29 (2004): 379–87.

3. W.H. Macey and B. Schneider, "The Meaning of Employee Engagement," *Industrial and Organizational Psychology* 1 (2008): 3–30; A.B. Bakker and W.B. Schaufeli, "Positive Organizational Behavior: Engaged Employees in Flourishing Organizations," *Journal of Organizational Behavior* 29, no. 2 (2008): 147–54.

4. J. Engen, "Are Your Employees Truly Engaged?," *Chief Executive*, March 2008, 42; S. Flander, "Terms of Engagement," *Human Resource Executive Online*, January 2008; D. Macleod and N. Clarke, *Engaging for Success: Enhancing Performance through Employee Engagement*, (London, UK: UK Government. Department for Business Innovation and Skills, July 2009).

5. K. Allen, "The Art of Engagement," (Bonn, Germany: Deutsche Post DHL, 12 August 2013), http://www.dpdhl.com/en/logistics_around_us/from_our_divisions/ken_allen_the_art_of_engagement.html (accessed 21 August 2013); "Rewards to Spur on Latent Talent," *Cape Argus (South Africa)*, 13 February 2013, E1; "DHL Africa Puts Employee Recognition at the Centre of Its Business," *African Press Association*, 19 June 2013.

6. BlessingWhite, *Employee Engagement Report 2011*, BlessingWhite (Princeton, NJ: January 2011); Towers Watson, *Engagement at Risk: Driving Strong Performance in a Volatile Global Environment*, 2012 Global workforce study, Towers Watson (New York City: September 2012); S. Crabtree, "Worldwide, 13% of Employees Are Engaged at Work," News release (Washington, DC: Gallup, Inc., 8 October 2013).

7. Several sources attempt to identify and organize the drivers of employee engagement. See, for example: D. Robinson, S. Perryman, and S. Hayday, *The Drivers of Employee Engagement*, Institute for Employment Studies. (Brighton, UK: 2004); W.H. Macey et al., *Employee Engagement: Tools for Analysis, Practice, and Competitive Advantage* (Malden, MA: Wiley-Blackwell, 2009); Macleod and Clarke, *Engaging for Success: Enhancing Performance through Employee Engagement;* M. Stairs and M. Galpin, "Positive Engagement: From Employee Engagement to Workplace Happiness," in *Oxford Handbook of Positive Psychology of Work*, ed. P.A. Linley, S. Harrington, and N. Garcea (New York: Oxford University Press, 2010), 155–72.

8. The confusing array of definitions about drives and needs has been the subject of criticism for a half century. See, for example, R.S. Peters, "Motives and Motivation," *Philosophy* 31 (1956): 117–30; H. Cantril, "Sentio, Ergo Sum: 'Motivation' Reconsidered," *Journal of Psychology* 65, no. 1 (1967): 91–107; G.R. Salancik and J. Pfeffer, "An Examination of Need-Satisfaction Models of Job Attitudes," *Administrative Science Quarterly* 22, no. 3 (1977): 427–56.

9. D.W. Pfaff, *Drive: Neurobiological and Molecular Mechanisms of Sexual Motivation* (Cambridge, MA: MIT Press, 1999); A. Blasi, "Emotions and Moral Motivation," *Journal for the Theory of Social Behaviour* 29, no. 1 (1999): 1–19; T.V. Sewards and M.A. Sewards, "Fear and Power-Dominance Drive Motivation: Neural Representations and Pathways Mediating Sensory and Mnemonic Inputs, and Outputs to Premotor Structures," *Neuroscience and Biobehavioral Reviews* 26 (2002): 553–79; K.C. Berridge, "Motivation Concepts in Behavioral Neuroscience," *Physiology & Behavior* 81, no. 2 (2004): 179–209. We distinguish drives from emotions, but future research may find that the two concepts are not so different as is stated here. Woodworth is credited with either coining or popularizing the term "drives" in the context of human motivation. His classic book is certainly the first source to discuss the concept in detail. See: R.S. Woodworth, *Dynamic Psychology* (New York: Columbia University Press, 1918).

10. G. Loewenstein, "The Psychology of Curiosity: A Review and Reinterpretation," *Psychological Bulletin* 116, no. 1 (1994): 75–98; A.E. Kelley, "Neurochemical Networks Encoding Emotion and Motivation: An Evolutionary Perspective," in *Who Needs Emotions? The Brain Meets the Robot*, ed. J.-M. Fellous and M.A. Arbib (New York: Oxford University Press, 2005), 29–78; M.R. Leary, "Motivational and Emotional Aspects of the Self," *Annual Review of Psychology* 58, no. 1 (2007): 317–44; L.A. Leotti, S.S. Iyengar, and K.N. Ochsner, "Born to Choose: The Origins and Value of the Need for Control," *Trends in Cognitive Sciences* 14, no. 10 (2010): 457–63.

11. K. Passyn and M. Sujan, "Self-Accountability Emotions and Fear Appeals: Motivating Behavior," *Journal of Consumer Research* 32, no. 4 (2006): 583–89; S.G. Barsade and D.E. Gibson, "Why Does Affect Matter in Organizations?," *Academy of Management Perspectives* 21, no. 2 (2007): 36–59.

12. A.R. Damasio, *The Feeling of What Happens: Body and Emotion in the Making of Consciousness* (New York: Harcourt Brace & Company, 1999), p. 286.

13. S. Hitlin, "Values as the Core of Personal Identity: Drawing Links between Two Theories of Self," *Social Psychology Quarterly* 66, no. 2 (2003): 118–37; B. Monin, D.A. Pizarro, and J.S. Beer, "Deciding Versus Reacting: Conceptions of Moral Judgment and the Reason-Affect Debate," *Review of General Psychology* 11, no. 2 (2007): 99–111; D.D. Knoch and E.E. Fehr, "Resisting the Power of Temptations. The Right Prefrontal Cortex and Self-Control," *Annals of the New York Academy of Sciences* 1104, no. 1 (2007): 123.

14. A.H. Maslow, "A Theory of Human Motivation," *Psychological Review* 50 (1943): 370–96; A.H. Maslow, *Motivation and Personality* (New York Harper & Row, 1954).

15. D.T. Hall and K.E. Nougaim, "An Examination of Maslow's Need Hierarchy in an Organizational Setting," *Organizational Behavior and Human Performance* 3, no. 1 (1968): 12; M.A. Wahba and L.G. Bridwell, "Maslow Reconsidered: A Review of Research on the Need Hierarchy Theory," *Organizational Behavior and Human Performance* 15 (1976): 212–40; E.L. Betz, "Two Tests of Maslow's Theory of Need Fulfillment," *Journal of Vocational Behavior* 24, no. 2 (1984): 204–20; P.A. Corning, "Biological Adaptation in Human Societies: A 'Basic Needs' Approach," *Journal of Bioeconomics* 2, no. 1 (2000): 41–86. For a recent proposed revision of the model, see: D.T. Kenrick et al., "Renovating the Pyramid of Needs: Contemporary Extensions Built Upon Ancient Foundations," *Perspectives on Psychological Science* 5, no. 3 (2010): 292–314.

16. L. Parks and R.P. Guay, "Personality, Values, and Motivation," *Personality and Individual Differences* 47, no. 7 (2009): 675–84.

17. B.A. Agle and C.B. Caldwell, "Understanding Research on Values in Business," *Business and Society* 38 (1999): 326–87; B. Verplanken and R.W. Holland, "Motivated Decision Making: Effects of Activation and Self-Centrality of Values on Choices and Behavior," *Journal of Personality and Social Psychology* 82, no. 3 (2002): 434–47; S. Hitlin and J.A. Pilavin, "Values: Reviving a Dormant Concept," *Annual Review of Sociology* 30 (2004): 359–93.

18. K. Dye, A.J. Mills, and T.G. Weatherbee, "Maslow: Man Interrupted – Reading Management Theory in Context," *Management Decision* 43, no. 10 (2005): 1375–95.

19. A.H. Maslow, "A Preface to Motivation Theory," *Psychsomatic Medicine* 5 (1943): 85–92.

20. S. Kesebir, J. Graham, and S. Oishi, "A Theory of Human Needs Should Be Human-Centered, Not Animal-Centered," *Perspectives on Psychological Science* 5, no. 3 (2010): 315–19.

21. A.H. Maslow, *Maslow on Management* (New York: John Wiley & Sons, Inc., 1998).

22. F.F. Luthans, "Positive Organizational Behavior: Developing and Managing Psychological Strengths," *The Academy of Management Executive* 16, no. 1 (2002): 57–72; S.L. Gable and J. Haidt, "What (and Why) Is Positive Psychology?," *Review of General Psychology* 9, no. 2 (2005): 103–10; M.E.P. Seligman et al., "Positive Psychology Progress: Empirical Validation of Interventions," *American Psychologist* 60, no. 5 (2005): 410–21.

23. D.C. McClelland, *The Achieving Society* (New York: Van Nostrand Reinhold, 1961); D.C. McClelland and D.H. Burnham, "Power Is the Great Motivator," *Harvard Business Review* 73 (1995): 126–39; D. Vredenburgh and Y. Brender, "The Hierarchical Abuse of Power in Work Organizations," *Journal of Business Ethics* 17 (1998): 1337–47; S. Shane, E.A. Locke, and C.J. Collins, "Entrepreneurial Motivation," *Human Resource Management Review* 13, no. 2 (2003): 257–79.

24. McClelland, *The Achieving Society*

25. Shane, Locke, and Collins, "Entrepreneurial Motivation."

26. C. Fletcher, "Heineken Revival in U.S. Starts with Multicultural Beer," *Bloomberg Businessweek*, 3 December 2012; D. Meinert, "Wings of Change," *HRMagazine* 57, no. 11 (2012): 30-36; J. Cirillo, "Heart of Green," *Beverage World*, 10 January 2012; J. Golden, "Young CEO Taps Millennials for Heineken USA," *Westchester County Business Journal*, 29 April 2013, 2.

27. McClelland and Burnham, "Power Is the Great Motivator; J.L. Thomas, M.W. Dickson, and P.D. Bliese, "Values Predicting Leader Performance in the U.S. Army Reserve Officer Training Corps Assessment Center: Evidence for a Personality-Mediated Model," *The Leadership Quarterly* 12, no. 2 (2001): 181–96.

28. Vredenburgh and Brender, "The Hierarchical Abuse of Power in Work Organizations."

29. D. Miron and D.C. McClelland, "The Impact of Achievement Motivation Training on Small Business," *California Management Review* 21 (1979): 13–28.

30. P.R. Lawrence and N. Nohria, *Driven: How Human Nature Shapes Our Choices* (San Francisco, CA: Jossey-Bass, 2002); N. Nohria, B. Groysberg, and L.-E. Lee, "Employee Motivation: A Powerful New Model," *Harvard Business Review*

(2008): 78-84. On the application of four-drive theory to leadership, See: P.R. Lawrence, *Driven to Lead* (San Francisco, CA: Jossey-Bass, 2010).

31. The drive to acquire is likely associated with research on getting ahead, desire for competence, the selfish gene, and desire for social distinction. See R.H. Frank, *Choosing the Right Pond: Human Behavior and the Quest for Status* (New York: Oxford University Press, 1985); L. Gaertner et al., "The "I," the "We," and the "When": A Meta-Analysis of Motivational Primacy in Self-Definition," *Journal of Personality and Social Psychology* 83, no. 3 (2002): 574-91; J. Hogan and B. Holland, "Using Theory to Evaluate Personality and Job-Performance Relations: A Socioanalytic Perspective," *Journal of Applied Psychology* 88, no. 1 (2003): 100-12; R. Dawkins, *The Selfish Gene*, 30th Anniversary Edition ed. (Oxford, UK: Oxford University Press, 2006); Leary, "Motivational and Emotional Aspects of the Self; B.S. Frey, "Awards as Compensation," *European Management Journal* 4 (2007): 6-14.

32. R.E. Baumeister and M.R. Leary, "The Need to Belong: Desire for Interpersonal Attachments as a Fundamental Human Motivation," *Psychological Bulletin* 117 (1995): 497-529.

33. J. Litman, "Curiosity and the Pleasures of Learning: Wanting and Liking New Information," *Cognition and Emotion* 19, no. 6 (2005): 793-814; T.G. Reio Jr et al., "The Measurement and Conceptualization of Curiosity," *Journal of Genetic Psychology* 167, no. 2 (2006): 117-35.

34. W.H. Bexton, W. Heron, and T.H. Scott, "Effects of Decreased Variation in the Sensory Environment," *Canadian Journal of Psychology* 8 (1954): 70-76; Loewenstein, "The Psychology of Curiosity."

35. A.R. Damasio, *Descartes' Error: Emotion, Reason, and the Human Brain* (New York: Putnam Sons, 1994); A. Bechara et al., "Deciding Advantageously before Knowing the Advantageous Strategy," *Science* 275, no. 5304 (1997): 1293-95; J.E. LeDoux, "Emotion Circuits in the Brain," *Annual Review of Neuroscience* 23 (2000): 155-84; P. Winkielman and K.C. Berridge, "Unconscious Emotion," *Current Directions in Psychological Science* 13, no. 3 (2004): 120-23; M. Reimann and A. Bechara, "The Somatic Marker Framework as a Neurological Theory of Decision-Making: Review, Conceptual Comparisons, and Future Neuroeconomics Research," *Journal of Economic Psychology* 31, no. 5 (2010): 767-76.

36. Lawrence and Nohria, *Driven*, pp. 145-47; R.F. Baumeister, E.J. Masicampo, and K.D. Vohs, "Do Conscious Thoughts Cause Behavior?," *Annual Review of Psychology* 62, no. 1 (2011): 331-61.

37. S.H. Schwartz, B.a. Hammer, and M. Wach, "Les Valeurs De Base De La Personne: TheOrie, Mesures Et Applications," [Basic Human Values: Theory, Measurement, and Applications.] *Revue française de sociologie* 47, no. 4 (2006): 929-68.

38. Lawrence and Nohria, *Driven*, , Chap. 11.

39. M.T. Bitti, "Rewards of Hard Work," *National Post (Canada)*, 17 October 2007, WK2; G. Joseph, "Man of the People," *Business Times Singapore*, 13 November 2010; Randstad Canada, *Women Shaping Business: Challenges and Opportunities in 2013*, Randstad Canada (Toronto, ON: October 2013).

40. Expectancy theory of motivation in work settings originated in V.H. Vroom, *Work and Motivation* (New York: Wiley, 1964). The version of expectancy theory presented here was developed by Edward Lawler. Lawler's model provides a clearer presentation of the model's three components. P-to-O expectancy is similar to "instrumentality" in Vroom's original expectancy theory model. The difference is that instrumentality is a correlation whereas P-to-O expectancy is a probability. See J.P. Campbell et al., *Managerial Behavior, Performance, and Effectiveness* (New York: McGraw-Hill, 1970); E.E. Lawler III, *Motivation in Work Organizations* (Monterey, CA: Brooks-Cole, 1973); D.A. Nadler and E.E. Lawler, "Motivation: A Diagnostic Approach," in *Perspectives on Behavior in Organizations*, ed. J.R. Hackman, E.E. Lawler III, and L.W. Porter (New York: McGraw-Hill, 1983), 67-78.

41. M. Zeelenberg et al., "Emotional Reactions to the Outcomes of Decisions: The Role of Counterfactual Thought in the Experience of Regret and Disappointment," *Organizational Behavior and Human Decision Processes* 75, no. 2 (1998): 117-41; B.A. Mellers, "Choice and the Relative Pleasure of Consequences," *Psychological Bulletin* 126, no. 6 (2000): 910-24; R.P. Bagozzi, U.M. Dholakia, and S. Basuroy, "How Effortful Decisions Get Enacted: The Motivating Role of Decision Processes, Desires, and Anticipated Emotions," *Journal of Behavioral Decision Making* 16, no. 4 (2003): 273-95. The neuropsychology of valences and its associated "expected utility" is discussed in: A. Bechara and A.R. Damasio, "The Somatic Marker Hypothesis: A Neural Theory of Economic Decision," *Games and Economic Behavior* 52, no. 2 (2005): 336-72.

42. Nadler and Lawler, "Motivation: A Diagnostic Approach,", pp. 70-73.

43. B. Moses, "Time to Get Serious About Rewarding Employees," *The Globe and Mail*, 28 April 2010, B16.

44. T. Matsui and T. Terai, "A Cross-Cultural Study of the Validity of the Expectancy Theory of Motivation," *Journal of Applied Psychology* 60 (1975): 263-65; D.H.B. Welsh, F. Luthans, and S.M. Sommer, "Managing Russion Factory Workers: The Impact of U.S.-Based Behavioral and Participative Techniques," *Academy of Management Journal* 36 (1993): 58-79.

45. This limitation was recently acknowledged by Victor Vroom, who had introduced expectancy theory in his 1964 book. See G.P. Latham, *Work Motivation: History, Theory, Research, and Practice* (Thousand Oaks, CA: Sage, 2007), 47-48.

46. J.B. Watson, *Behavior: An Introduction to Comparative Psychology* (New York: Henry Holt & Co., 1914).

47. B.F. Skinner, *About Behaviorism* (New York: Alfred A. Knopf, 1974); J. Komaki, T. Coombs, and S. Schepman, "Motivational Implications of Reinforcement Theory," in *Motivation and Leadership at Work*, ed. R.M. Steers, L.W. Porter, and G.A. Bigley (New York: McGraw-Hill, 1996), 34-52; R.G. Miltenberger, *Behavior Modification: Principles and Procedures* (Pacific Grove, CA: Brooks/Cole, 1997).

48. T.K. Connellan, *How to Improve Human Performance* (New York: Harper & Row, 1978), pp. 48-57; F. Luthans and R. Kreitner, *Organizational Behavior Modification and Beyond* (Glenview, IL: Scott, Foresman, 1985), pp. 85-88.

49. B.F. Skinner, *Science and Human Behavior* (New york: The Free Press, 1965); Miltenberger, *Behavior Modification: Principles and Procedures* Chap. 4-6.

50. T.R. Hinkin and C.A. Schriesheim, "If You Don't Hear from Me You Know You Are Doing Fine," *Cornell Hotel & Restaurant Administration Quarterly* 45, no. 4 (2004): 362-72.

51. L.K. Trevino, "The Social Effects of Punishment in Organizations: A Justice Perspective," *Academy of Management Review* 17 (1992): 647-76; L.E. Atwater et al., "Recipient and Observer Reactions to Discipline: Are Managers Experiencing Wishful Thinking?," *Journal of Organizational Behavior* 22, no. 3 (2001): 249-70.

52. G.P. Latham and V.L. Huber, "Schedules of Reinforcement: Lessons from the Past and Issues for the Future," *Journal of Organizational Behavior Management* 13 (1992): 125-49; B.A. Williams, "Challenges to Timing-Based Theories of Operant Behavior," *Behavioural Processes* 62 (2003): 115-23.

53. D. Zielinski, "Giving Praise," *HRMagazine*, October 2012, 77; "Cineplex Succeeds in Fostering Winning Corporate Culture after Mergers," *National Post (Financial Post)*, 4 February 2013.

54. "The Games Business Play," *Economist Intelligence Unit - Executive Briefing*, 28 June 2012, 1; D. Robb, "Let the Games Begin," *HRMagazine*, September 2012, 93; L. Brousell, "Gamification Boosts Class Participation," *CIO*, 5 February 2013; J.C. Meister, "How Deloitte Made Learning a Game," *HBR Blog Network*, 2 January 2013, http://blogs.hbr.org/cs/2013/01/how_deloitte_made_learning_a_g.html; "Ford of Canada Success Story," (Redwood City, CA: Bunchball, 2014), http://www.bunchball.com/customers/ford (accessed 20 February 2014).

55. J.A. Bargh and M.J. Ferguson, "Beyond Behaviorism: On the Automaticity of Higher Mental Processes," *Psychological Bulletin* 126, no. 6 (2000): 925-45. Some writers argue that behaviourists long ago accepted the relevance of cognitive processes in behaviour modification. See I. Kirsch et al., "The Role of Cognition in Classical and Operant Conditioning," *Journal of Clinical Psychology* 60, no. 4 (2004): 369-92.

56. A. Bandura, *Social Foundations of Thought and Action: A Social Cognitive Theory* (Englewood Cliffs, N.J: Prentice Hall, 1986); A. Bandura, "Social Cognitive Theory of Self-Regulation," *Organizational Behavior and Human Decision Processes* 50, no. 2 (1991): 248-87; A. Bandura, "Social Cognitive Theory: An Agentic Perspective," *Annual Review of Psychology* 52, no. 1 (2001): 1-26.

57. M.E. Schnake, "Vicarious Punishment in a Work Setting," *Journal of Applied Psychology* 71 (1986): 343-45; Trevino, "The Social Effects of Punishment in Organizations: A Justice Perspective; J. Malouff et al., "Effects of Vicarious Punishment: A Meta-Analysis," *Journal of General Psychology* 136, no. 3 (2009): 271-86.

58. A. Pescuric and W.C. Byham, "The New Look of Behavior Modeling," *Training & Development* 50 (1996): 24–30.

59. A. Bandura, "Self-Reinforcement: Theoretical and Methodological Considerations," *Behaviorism* 4 (1976): 135–55; C.A. Frayne and J.M. Geringer, "Self-Management Training for Improving Job Performance: A Field Experiment Involving Salespeople," *Journal of Applied Psychology* 85, no. 3 (2000): 361–72; J.B. Vancouver and D.V. Day, "Industrial and Organisation Research on Self-Regulation: From Constructs to Applications," *Applied Psychology: an International Journal* 54, no. 2 (2005): 155–85.

60. City of Toronto. Office of the Treasurer, *2014 Operating Budget Overview*, Toronto 2014 budget, City of Toronto (Toronto, ON: 25 November 2013).

61. E.A. Locke and G.P. Latham, *A Theory of Goal Setting and Task Performance* (Englewood Cliffs, N.J: Prentice Hall, 1990); G.P. Latham, "Goal Setting: A Five-Step Approach to Behavior Change," *Organizational Dynamics* 32, no. 3 (2003): 309–18.

62. There are several variations of the SMARTER goal setting model; "achievable" is sometimes "acceptable," "reviewed" is sometimes "recorded," and "exciting" is sometimes "ethical." Based on the earlier SMART model, the SMARTER goal setting model seems to originate in British sports psychology writing around the mid-1990s. For early examples, see: P. Butler, *Performance Profiling* (Leeds, UK: The National Coaching Foundation, 1996), p. 36; R.C. Thelwell and I.A. Greenlees, "The Effects of a Mental Skills Training Program Package on Gymnasium Triathlon Performance," *The Sports Psychologist* 15, no. 2 (2001): 127–41.

63. For debate on the value and limitations of measurement, see: J.M. Henshaw, *Does Measurement Measure Up? How Numbers Reveal and Conceal the Truth* (Baltimore, Maryland: Johns Hopkins Press, 2006).

64. A. Li and A.B. Butler, "The Effects of Participation in Goal Setting and Goal Rationales on Goal Commitment: An Exploration of Justice Mediators," *Journal of Business and Psychology* 19, no. 1 (2004): 37–51.

65. Locke and Latham, *A Theory of Goal Setting and Task Performance* Chap. 6 and 7; J. Wegge, "Participation in Group Goal Setting: Some Novel Findings and a Comprehensive Model as a New Ending to an Old Story," *Applied Psychology: An International Review* 49 (2000): 498–516.

66. M. London, E.M. Mone, and J.C. Scott, "Performance Management and Assessment: Methods for Improved Rater Accuracy and Employee Goal Setting," *Human Resource Management* 43, no. 4 (2004): 319–36; G.P. Latham and C.C. Pinder, "Work Motivation Theory and Research at the Dawn of the Twenty-First Century," *Annual Review of Psychology* 56 (2005): 485–516.

67. E. Weir et al., "Applying the Balanced Scorecard to Local Public Health Performance Measurement: Deliberations and Decisions," *BMC Public Health* 9, no. 1 (2009): 127; R. Mostray, "The RCMP's Experience with the Balanced Scorecard: 8 Years + ," in *Centre of Excellence on Performance Management & Accountability* (Ottawa, ON: 2010); Canadian Tourism Commission, *2012 Annual Report: Delivering Value for Canada's Tourism Businesses through Innovation and Efficiency*, Canadian Tourism Commission (Vancouver, BC: May 2013); Edmonton Airports, *Villeneuve Airport Strategic Plan: 2013-2017*, Edmonton Airports (Edmonton, AB: January 2014).

68. Mostray, "The RCMP's Experience with the Balanced Scorecard: 8 Years + ."

69. S.P. Brown, S. Ganesan, and G. Challagalla, "Self-Efficacy as a Moderator of Information-Seeking Effectiveness," *Journal of Applied Psychology* 86, no. 5 (2001): 1043–51; D. Van-Dijk and A.N. Kluger, "Feedback Sign Effect on Motivation: Is It Moderated by Regulatory Focus?," *Applied Psychology: An International Review* 53, no. 1 (2004): 113–35; P.A. Heslin and G.P. Latham, "The Effect of Upward Feedback on Managerial Behaviour," *Applied Psychology: An International Review* 53, no. 1 (2004): 23–37; J.E. Bono and A.E. Colbert, "Understanding Responses to Multi-Source Feedback: The Role of Core Self-Evaluations," *Personnel Psychology* 58, no. 1 (2005): 171–203.

70. R. Bostelaar, "Fast Feedback," *Ottawa Citizen*, 26 October 2013, D1; N. Wuttunee, "A&W Canada Tool Closes 'Loop' on Guest Feedback," *QSR*, 26 November 2013.

71. P. Drucker, *The Effective Executive* (Oxford, UK: Butterworth-Heinemann, 2007), p.22. Drucker's emphasis on strengths was also noted in D.K. Whitney and A. Trosten-Bloom, *The Power of Appreciative Inquiry: A Practical Guide to Positive Change*, 2nd ed. (San Francisco, CA: Berrett-Koehler Publishers, 2010), p. xii.

72. "Management People: Getting to Know You," *Retail Jeweller*, 27 March 2012.

73. M. Buckingham, *Go Put Your Strengths to Work* (New York: Free Press, 2007); S.L. Orem, J. Binkert, and A.L. Clancy, *Appreciative Coaching: A Positive Process for Change* (San Francisco, CA: Jossey-Bass, 2007); S. Gordon, "Appreciative Inquiry Coaching," *International Coaching Psychology Review* 3, no. 2 (2008): 19–31.

74. A. Terracciano, P.T. Costa, and R.R. McCrae, "Personality Plasticity after Age 30," *Personality and Social Psychology Bulletin* 32, no. 8 (2006): 999–1009; Leary, "Motivational and Emotional Aspects of the Self."

75. A.N. Kluger and D. Nir, "The Feedforward Interview," *Human Resource Management Review* 20, no. 3 (2010): 235–46; H. Aguinis, R.K. Gottfredson, and H. Joo, "Delivering Effective Performance Feedback: The Strengths-Based Approach," *Business Horizons* 55, no. 2 (2012): 105–11.

76. D. Hendry, "Game-Playing: The Latest Business Tool," *The Globe and Mail*, 17 November 2006, C11.

77. F.P. Morgeson, T.V. Mumford, and M.A. Campion, "Coming Full Circle: Using Research and Practice to Address 27 Questions About 360-Degree Feedback Programs," *Consulting Psychology Journal* 57, no. 3 (2005): 196–209; J.W. Smither, M. London, and R.R. Reilly, "Does Performance Improve Following Multisource Feedback? A Theoretical Model, Meta-Analysis, and Review of Empirical Findings " *Personnel Psychology* 58, no. 1 (2005): 33–66; L.E. Atwater, J.F. Brett, and A.C. Charles, "Multisource Feedback: Lessons Learned and Implications for Practice," *Human Resource Management* 46, no. 2 (2007): 285–307.

78. A.S. DeNisi and A.N. Kluger, "Feedback Effectiveness: Can 360-Degree Appraisals Be Improved?," *Academy of Management Executive* 14 (2000): 129–39; M.A. Peiperl, "Getting 360 Degree Feedback Right," *Harvard Business Review* 79 (2001): 142–47; M.-G. Seo, L.F. Barrett, and J.M. Bartunek, "The Role of Affective Experience in Work Motivation," *Academy of Management Review* 29 (2004): 423–49.

79. S.J. Ashford and G.B. Northcraft, "Conveying More (or Less) Than We Realize: The Role of Impression Management in Feedback Seeking," *Organizational Behavior and Human Decision Processes* 53 (1992): 310–34; J.R. Williams et al., "Increasing Feedback Seeking in Public Contexts: It Takes Two (or More) to Tango," *Journal of Applied Psychology* 84 (1999): 969–76.

80. J.B. Miner, "The Rated Importance, Scientific Validity, and Practical Usefulness of Organizational Behavior Theories: A Quantitative Review," *Academy of Management Learning and Education* 2, no. 3 (2003): 250–68. Also see Pinder, *Work Motivation in Organizational Behavior*, p. 384.

81. P.M. Wright, "Goal Setting and Monetary Incentives: Motivational Tools That Can Work Too Well," *Compensation and Benefits Review* 26 (1994): 41–49; E.A. Locke and G.P. Latham, "Building a Practically Useful Theory of Goal Setting and Task Motivation: A 35-Year Odyssey," *American Psychologist* 57, no. 9 (2002): 705–17.

82. Latham, *Work Motivation*, 188.

83. R. Colman, "Packing the Perfect HR Punch," *CMA Management*, March 2007, 40–43.

84. J. Greenberg and E.A. Lind, "The Pursuit of Organizational Justice: From Conceptualization to Implication to Application," in *Industrial and Organizational Psychology: Linking Theory with Practice* ed. C.L. Cooper and E.A. Locke (London, UK: Blackwell, 2000), 72–108; D.T. Miller, "Disrespect and the Experience of Injustice," *Annual Review of Psychology* 52 (2001): 527–53; R. Cropanzano and M. Schminke, "Using Social Justice to Build Effective Work Groups," in *Groups at Work: Theory and Research* ed. M.E. Turner (Mahwah, NJ: Lawrence Erlbaum Associates, 2001), 143–71.

85. M. Bloom, "The Performance Effects of Pay Dispersion on Individuals and Organizations," *Academy of Management Journal* 42, no. 1 (1999): 25–40; P.A. Siegel and D.C. Hambrick, "Pay Disparities within Top Management Groups: Evidence of Harmful Effects on Performance of High-Technology Firms," *Organization Science* 16, no. 3 (2005): 259–74; C. Grund and N. Westergaard-Nielsen, "The Dispersion of Employees' Wage Increases and Firm Performance," *Industrial & Labor Relations Review* 61, no. 4 (2008): 485–501; M. Mondello and J. Maxcy, "The Impact of Salary Dispersion and Performance Bonuses in Nfl Organizations," *Management Decision* 47, no. 1 (2009): 110–23; H. Katayama and H. Nuch, "A Game-Level Analysis of Salary Dispersion and Team Performance in the National

Basketball Association," *Applied Economics* 43, no. 10 (2011): 1193–207.

86. J.S. Adams, "Toward an Understanding of Inequity," *Journal of Abnormal and Social Psychology* 67 (1963): 422–36; R.T. Mowday, "Equity Theory Predictions of Behavior in Organizations," in *Motivation and Work Behavior*, ed. L.W. Porter and R.M. Steers (New York: McGraw-Hill, 1991), 111–31; R.G. Cropanzano, J., "Progress in Organizational Justice: Tunneling through the Maze," in *International Review of Industrial and Organizational Psychology* ed. C.L. Cooper and I.T. Robertson (New York: Wiley, 1997), 317–72; L.A. Powell, "Justice Judgments as Complex Psychocultural Constructions: An Equity-Based Heuristic for Mapping Two- and Three-Dimensional Fairness Representations in Perceptual Space " *Journal of Cross-Cultural Psychology* 36, no. 1 (2005): 48–73.

87. C.T. Kulik and M.L. Ambrose, "Personal and Situational Determinants of Referent Choice," *Academy of Management Review* 17 (1992): 212–37; G. Blau, "Testing the Effect of Level and Importance of Pay Referents on Pay Level Satisfaction," *Human Relations* 47 (1994): 1251–68.

88. T.P. Summers and A.S. DeNisi, "In Search of Adams' Other: Reexamination of Referents Used in the Evaluation of Pay," *Human Relations* 43 (1990): 497–511.

89. Y. Cohen-Charash and P.E. Spector, "The Role of Justice in Organizations: A Meta-Analysis," *Organizational Behavior and Human Decision Processes* 86 (2001): 278–321.

90. K. Hille, "Fresh Labour Disputes Hit Foxconn," *Financial Times (London)*, 15 January 2012.

91. Canadian Press, "Pierre Berton, Canadian Cultural Icon, Enjoyed Long and Colourful Career," *Times Colonist (Victoria, B.C.)*, 30 November 2004.

92. K.S. Sauleya and A.G. Bedeian, "Equity Sensitivity: Construction of a Measure and Examination of Its Psychometric Properties," *Journal of Management* 26 (2000): 885–910; G. Blakely, M. Andrews, and R. Moorman, "The Moderating Effects of Equity Sensitivity on the Relationship between Organizational Justice and Organizational Citizenship Behaviors," *Journal of Business and Psychology* 20, no. 2 (2005): 259–73.

93. J. Fizel, A.C. Krautman, and L. Hadley, "Equity and Arbitration in Major League Baseball," *Managerial and Decision Economics* 23, no. 7 (2002): 427–35; M. Ezzamel and R. Watson, "Pay Comparability across and within UK Boards: An Empirical Analysis of the Cash Pay Awards to CEOs and Other Board Members," *Journal of Management Studies* 39, no. 2 (2002): 207–32.

94. R. Boswell, "Nearly Half of Canadians Think They're Underpaid: Poll," *Canada.com*, 7 September 2010; L. Saad, "More Workers Ok with Their Pay in 2010," *Gallup Daily News*, 19 August 2010; Randstad Canada, *Women Shaping Business: Challenges and Opportunities in 2013*.

95. Greenberg and Lind, "The Pursuit of Organizational Justice; K. Roberts and K.S. Markel, "Claiming in the Name of Fairness: Organizational Justice and the Decision to File for Workplace Injury Compensation," *Journal of Occupational Health Psychology* 6 (2001): 332–47; J.B. Olson-Buchanan and W.R. Boswell, "The Role of Employee Loyalty and Formality in Voicing Discontent," *Journal of Applied Psychology* 87, no. 6 (2002): 1167–74.

96. R. Hagey et al., "Immigrant Nurses' Experience of Racism," *Journal of Nursing Scholarship* 33 (2001): 389–95; Roberts and Markel, "Claiming in the Name of Fairness: Organizational Justice and the Decision to File for Workplace Injury Compensation; D.A. Jones and D.P. Skarlicki, "The Effects of Overhearing Peers Discuss an Authority's Fairness Reputation on Reactions to Subsequent Treatment," *Journal of Applied Psychology* 90, no. 2 (2005): 363–72.

97. Miller, "Disrespect and the Experience of Injustice."

98. M.L. Ambrose, M.A. Seabright, and M. Schminke, "Sabotage in the Workplace: The Role of Organizational Injustice," *Organizational Behavior and Human Decision Processes* 89, no. 1 (2002): 947–65.

CHAPTER 6

1. Shopify Inc., "Life at Shopify," (Ottawa, ON: YouTube, 31 May 2012), https://www.youtube.com/watch?v=XMRufdqpFnM, Video 1:57 (accessed 13 December 2013); M. Anderson, "Canada's Smartest Company: Shopify," *Profit*, December 2012, 34-38; S. Silcoff, "A Rare Startup Success Story: Shopify Hits $1-Billion Milestone," *The Globe and Mail*, 12 December 2013, B1; "Shopify: Doing Human Relations Right," *Qwalify Blog*, 1 October 2013, http://qwalify.org/blog/shopify-human-relations-right/; T. Beale, "Why Turnover Is Unimaginable at Shopify," *Achievers Blog*, 5 March 2014, http://blog.achievers.com/2014/03/voluntary-turnover-unimaginable-shopify/.

2. M.C. Bloom and G.T. Milkovich, "Issues in Managerial Compensation Research," in *Trends in Organizational Behavior*, ed. C.L. Cooper and D.M. Rousseau (Chicester, UK: John Wiley & Sons, Inc., 1996), 23–47. For an excellent review of the history of money, see: N. Ferguson, *The Ascent of Money: A Financial History of the World* (New York: Penguin, 2008).

3. S.E.G. Lea and P. Webley, "Money as Tool, Money as Drug: The Biological Psychology of a Strong Incentive," *Behavioral and Brain Sciences* 29 (2006): 161–209; G.M. Rose and L.M. Orr, "Measuring and Exploring Symbolic Money Meanings," *Psychology and Marketing* 24, no. 9 (2007): 743–61; S. Jia et al., "Attitude toward Money Modulates Outcome Processing: An Erp Study," *Social Neuroscience* 8, no. 1 (2012): 43–51; M. Kouchaki et al., "Seeing Green: Mere Exposure to Money Triggers a Business Decision Frame and Unethical Outcomes," *Organizational Behavior and Human Decision Processes* 121, no. 1 (2013): 53–61.

4. D.W. Krueger, "Money, Success, and Success Phobia," in *The Last Taboo: Money as Symbol and Reality in Psychotherapy and Psychoanalysis*, ed. D.W. Krueger (New York: Brunner/Mazel, 1986), 3–16.

5. P.F. Wernimont and S. Fitzpatrick, "The Meaning of Money," *Journal of Applied Psychology* 56, no. 3 (1972): 218–26; T.R. Mitchell and A.E. Mickel, "The Meaning of Money: An Individual-Difference Perspective," *Academy of Management Review* (1999): 568-78; R. Trachtman, "The Money Taboo: Its Effects in Everyday Life and in the Practice of Psychotherapy," *Clinical Social Work Journal* 27, no. 3 (1999): 275–88; S. Lea, "Money: Motivation, Metaphors, and Mores," *Behavioral and Brain Sciences* 29, no. 2 (2006): 196–209; Lea and Webley, "Money as Tool, Money as Drug; T.L.-P. Tang et al., "The Love of Money and Pay Level Satisfaction: Measurement and Functional Equivalence in 29 Geopolitical Entities around the World," *Management and Organization Review* 2, no. 3 (2006): 423–52.

6. A. Furnham and R. Okamura, "Your Money or Your Life: Behavioral and Emotional Predictors of Money Pathology," *Human Relations* 52 (1999): 1157–77.

7. Tang et al., "The Love of Money and Pay Level Satisfaction: Measurement and Functional Equivalence in 29 Geopolitical Entities around the World; T. Tang et al., "To Help or Not to Help? The Good Samaritan Effect and the Love of Money on Helping Behavior," *Journal of Business Ethics* 82, no. 4 (2007): 865–87; T. Tang and Y.-J. Chen, "Intelligence Vs. Wisdom: The Love of Money, Machiavellianism, and Unethical Behavior across College Major and Gender," *Journal of Business Ethics* 82, no. 1 (2008): 1–26.

8. R. Lynn, *The Secret of the Miracle Economy* (London, UK: SAE, 1991); A. Furnham, E. Wilson, and K. Telford, "The Meaning of Money: The Validation of a Short Money-Types Measure," *Personality and Individual Differences* 52, no. 6 (2012): 707–11.

9. A. Furnham, B.D. Kirkcaldy, and R. Lynn, "National Attitudes to Competitiveness, Money, and Work among Young People: First, Second, and Third World Differences," *Human Relations* 47 (1994): 119–32; K.O. Doyle, "Introduction: Ethnicity and Money," *American Behavioral Scientist* 45, no. 2 (2001): 181–90; G. Dell'Orto and K.O. Doyle, "Poveri Ma Belli: Meanings of Money in Italy and in Switzerland," *American Behavioral Scientist* 45, no. 2 (2001): 257–71; V.K.G. Lim, "Money Matters: An Empirical Investigation of Money, Face and Confucian Work Ethic," *Personality and Individual Differences* 35 (2003): 953–70; T.L.-P. Tang, A. Furnham, and G.M.-T. Davis, "A Cross-Cultural Comparison of the Money Ethic, the Protestant Work Ethic, and Job Satisfaction: Taiwan, the USA, and the UK," *International Journal of Organization Theory and Behavior* 6, no. 2 (2003): 175–94; R. Tung and C. Baumann, "Comparing the Attitudes toward Money, Material Possessions and Savings of Overseas Chinese Vis-À-Vis Chinese in China: Convergence, Divergence or Cross-Vergence, Vis-À-Vis 'One Size Fits All' Human Resource Management Policies and Practices," *International Journal of Human Resource Management* 20, no. 11 (2009): 2382–401.

10. S.L. Rynes, B. Gerhart, and K.A. Minette, "The Importance of Pay in Employee Motivation: Discrepancies between What People Say and What They Do," *Human Resource Management* 43, no. 4 (2004): 381–94; D.G.Gardner, V.D. Linn, and J.L. Pierce, "The Effects of Pay Level on Organization-Based Self-Esteem and Performance: A Field Study," *Journal of Occupational and Organizational Psychology* 77 (2004): 307–22;

B.S. Frey, "Awards as Compensation," *European Management Journal* 4 (2007): 6-14; A.E. Mickel and L.A. Barron, "Getting "More Bang for the Buck": Symbolic Value of Monetary Rewards in Organizations," *Journal of Management Inquiry* 17, no. 4 (2008): 329-38.

11. J.S. Mill, *Utilitarianism*, Seventh ed. (London, UK: Longmans, Green, and Co., 1879; repr., Project Gutenberg EBook), Chap. 4.

12. "Conditions of Employment," (Villigen, Switzerland: Paul Sherrer Institut, 2011) (accessed 30 May 2011).

13. A. Wright, ""Modernising" Away Gender Pay Inequality? Some Evidence from the Local Government Sector on Using Job Evaluation," *Employee Relations* 33, no. 2 (2011): 159-78; K. Gilbert, "Promises and Practices: Job Evaluation and Equal Pay Forty Years On!," *Industrial Relations Journal* 43, no. 2 (2012): 137-51.

14. E.E. Lawler III, *Rewarding Excellence: Pay Strategies for the New Economy* (San Francisco, CA: Jossey-Bass, 2000), pp. 30-35, 109-19; R. McNabb and K. Whitfield, "Job Evaluation and High Performance Work Practices: Compatible or Conflictual?," *Journal of Management Studies* 38 (2001): 293-312.

15. P.K. Zingheim and J.R. Schuster, "Competencies and Rewards: Substance or Just Style?," *Compensation Benefits Review* 35, no. 5 (2003): 40-44.

16. A. Mitra, N. Gupta, and J.D. Shaw, "A Comparative Examination of Traditional and Skill-Based Pay Plans," *Journal of Managerial Psychology* 26, no. 4 (2011): 278-96. The High Liner Foods example is cited in: M. Mayer, "Maintaining a Seafood Savviness Like No Other," *Refrigerated & Frozen Foods* 23, no. 12 (2013): 30, 34, 36, 38.

17. J.D. Shaw et al., "Success and Survival of Skill-Based Pay Plans," *Journal of Management* 31, no. 1 (2005): 28-49; R.J. Long, "Paying for Knowledge: Does It Pay?," *Canadian HR Reporter*, 28 March 2005, 12-13; E.C. Dierdorff and E.A. Surface, "If You Pay for Skills, Will They Learn? Skill Change and Maintenance under a Skill-Based Pay System," *Journal of Management* 34, no. 4 (2008): 721-43; A.H.Y. Hon, "When Competency-Based Pay Relates to Creative Performance: The Moderating Role of Employee Psychological Need," *International Journal of Hospitality Management* 31, no. 1 (2012): 130-38.

18. Zingheim and Schuster, "Competencies and Rewards; F. Giancola, "Skill-Based Pay–Issues for Consideration," *Benefits & Compensation Digest* 44, no. 5 (2007): 1-15.

19. Kelly Services, *Workplace Performance*, Kelly global workforce index, Kelly Services (Troy, MI: 26 June 2013).

20. N. Byrnes and M. Arndt, "The Art of Motivation," *BusinessWeek*, 1 May 2006, 56; M. Bolch, "Rewarding the Team," *HRMagazine*, February 2007, 91-93; J. McGregor, "Nucor's CEO Is Stepping Aside, but Its Culture Likely Won't," *Washington Post*, 20 November 2012.

21. G. Hamel, *The Future of Management* (Boston, MA: Harvard Business School Press, 2007), pp. 73-75.

22. J.D. Ketcham and M.F. Furukawa, "Hospital-Physician Gainsharing in Cardiology," *Health Affairs* 27, no. 3 (2008): 803-12; J. Ferenc, "Gainsharing Poised for a Comeback," *Hospitals & Health Networks*, June 2010, 12-14; I.M. Leitman et al., "Quality and Financial Outcomes from Gainsharing for Inpatient Admissions: A Three-Year Experience," *Journal of Hospital Medicine* 5, no. 9 (2010): 501-07.

23. L.R. Gomez-Mejia, T.M. Welbourne, and R.M. Wiseman, "The Role of Risk Sharing and Risk Taking under Gainsharing," *Academy of Management Review* 25 (2000): 492-507; K.M. Bartol and A. Srivastava, "Encouraging Knowledge Sharing: The Role of Organizational Reward System," *Journal of Leadership & Organizational Studies* 9 (2002): 64-76.

24. P. Patel, "Midsize-Company Winner Hilcorp Is an Open Book," *Houston Chronicle*, 29 October 2010; S. Sebastian, "All Share in Fruits of Hilcorp's Success," *Houston Chronicle*, 5 November 2011; L. Leyne, "Province, BCGEU Ink Novel Deal for 5 Years," *Victoria Times-Colonist*, 4 December 2013, A1.

25. O. Hammarström, *Handelsbanken, Sweden: Make Work Pay - Make Work Attractive*, Attractive workplace for all: company cases, Eurofound (Dublin, Ireland: October 2007).

26. D. Jacobs, "The Right Tools for the Job," *Ottawa Citizen*, 1 August 2005, A2; T. Grant, "How One Company Levels the Pay Slope of Executives and Workers," *The Globe and Mail*, 16 November 2013, B6.

27. J. Chelius and R.S. Smith, "Profit Sharing and Employment Stability," *Industrial and Labor Relations Review* 43 (1990): 256s-73s; S.H. Wagner, C.P. Parkers, and N.D. Christiansen, "Employees That Think and Act Like Owners: Effects of Ownership Beliefs and Behaviors on Organizational Effectiveness," *Personnel Psychology* 56, no. 4 (2003): 847-71; G. Ledford, M. Lucy, and P. Leblanc, "The Effects of Stock Ownership on Employee Attitudes and Behavior: Evidence from the Rewards at Work Studies," *Perspectives (Sibson)*, January 2004; C. Rosen, J. Case, and M. Staubus, "Every Employee an Owner [Really]," *Harvard Business Review* 83, no. 6 (2005): 122-30.

28. A.J. Maggs, "Enron, Esops, and Fiduciary Duty," *Benefits Law Journal* 16, no. 3 (2003): 42-52; C. Brodzinski, "ESOP's Fables Can Make Coverage Risky," *National Underwriter. P & C*, 13 June 2005, 16-17.

29. D. Ariely et al., "Large Stakes and Big Mistakes," *Review of Economic Studies* 76, no. 2 (2009): 451-69.

30. J. Pfeffer, *The Human Equation* (Boston, MA: Harvard Business School Press, 1998); B.N. Pfau and I.T. Kay, *The Human Capital Edge* (New York: McGraw-Hill, 2002); D. Guest, N. Conway, and P. Dewe, "Using Sequential Tree Analysis to Search for 'Bundles' of HR Practices," *Human Resource Management Journal* 14, no. 1 (2004): 79-96. The problems with performance-based pay are discussed in W.C. Hammer, "How to Ruin Motivation with Pay," *Compensation Review* 7, no. 3 (1975): 17-27; A. Kohn, *Punished by Rewards* (Boston, MA: Houghton Mifflin, 1993); M. Beer and M.D. Cannon, "Promise and Peril of Implementing Pay-for-Performance," *Human Resource Management* 43, no. 1 (2004): 3-48.

31. Watson Wyatt, *WorkCanada 2004/2005–Pursuing Productive Engagement*, Watson Wyatt (Toronto, ON: January 2005); J.M. Jones, *Talent Town Hall: A Presentation to Oesa*, Towers Watson (New York: 25 October 2012); Towers Watson, *Highlights from the Emea Region*, Global Workforce Study, Towers Watson (London, UK: 26 April 2013).

32. S. Kerr, "Organization Rewards: Practical, Cost-Neutral Alternatives That You May Know, but Don't Practice," *Organizational Dynamics* 28 (1999): 61-70.

33. S.A. Culbert and L. Rout, *Get Rid of the Performance Review!* (New York: Business Plus, 2010); "Should Performance Reviews Be Fired?," *Knowledge@Wharton* (2011); R. Pyrillis, "The Reviews Are In," *Workforce Management*, May 2011, 20. Along with expert critiques, surveys indicate that most employees view performance reviews as more harmful than helpful.

34. C. Atchison, "How to Build a Super Staff," *Profit*, May 2010, 30-34.

35. M. Buckingham and D.O. Clifton, *Now, Discover Your Strengths* (New York: Free Press, 2001), p. 226; M. Rotundo and P. Sackett, "The Relative Importance of Task, Citizenship, and Counterproductive Performance to Global Ratings of Job Performance: A Policy-Capturing Approach," *Journal of Applied Psychology* 87 (2002): 66-80.

36. M. Goldsmith, "Try Feedforward Instead of Feedback," *Leader to Leader* (2002): 11-14; Culbert and Rout, *Get Rid of the Performance Review!*, Chap. 7.

37. J.S. DeMatteo, L.T. Eby, and E. Sundstrom, "Team-Based Rewards: Current Empirical Evidence and Directions for Future Research," *Research in Organizational Behavior* 20 (1998): 141-83; S. Rynes, B. Gerhart, and L. Parks, "Personnel Psychology: Performance Evaluation and Pay for Performance," *Annual Review of Psychology* 56 (2005): 571-600.

38. B. Moses, "Time to Get Serious About Rewarding Employees," *The Globe and Mail*, 28 April 2010, B16.

39. "Dream Teams," *Human Resources Professional* (1994): 17-19.

40. S. Kerr, "On the Folly of Rewarding a, While Hoping for B," *Academy of Management Journal* 18 (1975): 769-83; B. Gerhart, S.L. Rynes, and I.S. Fulmer, "Pay and Performance: Individuals, Groups, and Executives," *Academy of Management Annals* 3 (2009): 251-315.

41. D.R. Spitzer, "Power Rewards: Rewards That Really Motivate," *Management Review* (1996): 45-50.

42. R.M. Johnson, D. Lucking-Reiley, and J.C. Munos, *'The War for the Fare': How Driver Compensation Affects Bus System Performance* (SSRN, 2005); M. Munger, "Planning Order, Causing Chaos: Transantiago," *Library of Economics and Liberty* (2008); R. Banick, *Bus Rapid Transit and the Latin American City: Successes to Date, but Miles to Go*, Council on Hemispheric Affairs (Washington, DC: December 2009).

43. T. Gubler, I. Larkin, and L. Pierce, *The Dirty Laundry of Employee Award Programs: Evidence from the Field*, Harvard Business School Working

Paper, Harvard Business School (Cambridge, MA: 11 February 2013).

44. G.T. Milkovich, J.M. Newman, and C. Milkovich, *Compensation*, 5th ed. (Homewood, IL: Irwin, 1996), p. 315.

45. A. Holecek, "Griffith, Ind., Native Takes over as Steel Plant Manager," *Northwest Indiana Times (Munster, Ind.)*, 25 May 2003.

46. D. MacDonald, "Good Managers Key to Buffett's Acquisitions," *The Gazette (Montreal)*, 16 November 2001. The survey is reported in "Survey Shows What Matters Most to Canadian Workers When Deciding on the Right Choice of Job," News release for Kelly Services (Toronto, ON: 25 February 2009).

47. J.R. Edwards, J.A. Scully, and M.D. Brtek, "The Nature and Outcomes of Work: A Replication and Extension of Interdisciplinary Work-Design Research," *Journal of Applied Psychology* 85, no. 6 (2000): 860–68; F.P. Morgeson and M.A. Campion, "Minimizing Tradeoffs When Redesigning Work: Evidence from a Longitudinal Quasi-Experiment," *Personnel Psychology* 55, no. 3 (2002): 589–612.

48. E. Clark, "The Cost of Fun," *The Telegraph (London)*, 26 March 2007.

49. S. Leroy, "Why Is It So Hard to Do My Work? The Challenge of Attention Residue When Switching between Work Tasks," *Organizational Behavior and Human Decision Processes* 109, no. 2 (2009): 168–81.

50. H. Fayol, *General and Industrial Management*, trans. C. Storrs (London, UK: Pitman, 1949); E.E. Lawler III, *Motivation in Work Organizations* (Monterey, CA: Brooks/Cole, 1973), Chap. 7; M.A. Campion, "Ability Requirement Implications of Job Design: An Interdisciplinary Perspective," *Personnel Psychology* 42 (1989): 1–24.

51. A. Smith, *An Inquiry into the Nature and Causes of the Wealth of Nations* ed. E. Cannan, 5th ed., (London, UK: Methuen and Co., 1904), pp. 8–9.

52. F.W. Taylor, *The Principles of Scientific Management* (New York: Harper & Row, 1911); R. Kanigel, *The One Best Way: Frederick Winslow Taylor and the Enigma of Efficiency* (NY: Viking, 1997).

53. F.C. Lane, *Venice: A Maritime Republic* (Baltimore: Johns Hopkins University Press, 1973), pp. 361–64; R.C. Davis, "Arsenal and *Arsenalotti:* Workplace and Community in Seventeenth-Century Venice," in *The Workplace before the Factory*, ed. T.M. Safley and L.N. Rosenband (Ithaca, NY: Cornell University Press, 1993), 180–203.

54. C.R. Walker and R.H. Guest, *The Man on the Assembly Line* (Cambridge, MA: Harvard University Press, 1952); W.F. Dowling, "Job Redesign on the Assembly Line: Farewell to Blue-Collar Blues?," *Organizational Dynamics* (1973): 51–67; E.E. Lawler III, *High-Involvement Management* (San Francisco, CA: Jossey-Bass, 1986).

55. R. Moorhead, "Lawyer Specialization–Managing the Professional Paradox," *Law & Policy* 32, no. 2 (2010): 226–59.

56. M. Keller, *Rude Awakening* (New York: Harper Perennial, 1989), p. 128.

57. F. Herzberg, B. Mausner, and B.B. Snyderman, *The Motivation to Work* (New York: Wiley, 1959).

58. S.K. Parker, T.D. Wall, and J.L. Cordery, "Future Work Design Research and Practice: Towards an Elaborated Model of Work Design," *Journal of Occupational and Organizational Psychology* 74 (2001): 413–40. For a decisive critique of motivator-hygiene theory, see N. King, "Clarification and Evaluation of the Two Factor Theory of Job Satisfaction," *Psychological Bulletin* 74 (1970): 18–31.

59. J.R. Hackman and G. Oldham, *Work Redesign* (Reading, MA: Addison-Wesley, 1980).

60. M. Gagné and D. Bhave, "Autonomy in the Workplace: An Essential Ingredient to Employee Engagement and Well-Being in Every Culture," in *Human Autonomy in Cross-Cultural Context*, ed. V.I. Chirkov, R.M. Ryan, and K.M. Sheldon, *Cross-Cultural Advancements in Positive Psychology* (Springer Netherlands, 2011), 163–87.

61. C.E. Shalley, L.L. Gilson, and T.C. Blum, "Interactive Effects of Growth Need Strength, Work Context, and Job Complexity on Self-Reported Creative Performance," *Academy of Management Journal* 52, no. 3 (2009): 489–505.

62. R.B. Tiegs, L.E. Tetrick, and Y. Fried, "Growth Need Strength and Context Satisfactions as Moderators of the Relations of the Job Characteristics Model," *Journal of Management* 18, no. 3 (1992): 575–93; J.E. Champoux, "A Multivariate Test of the Job Characteristics Theory of Work Motivation," *Journal of Organizational Behavior* 12, no. 5 (1991): 431–46.

63. G.R. Oldham and J.R. Hackman, "Not What It Was and Not What It Will Be: The Future of Job Design Research," *Journal of Organizational Behavior* 31, no. 2-3 (2010): 463–79; A.M. Grant, Y. Fried, and T. Juillerat, "Work Matters: Job Design in Classic and Contemporary Perspectives," in *APA Handbook of Industrial and Organizational Psychology*, ed. S. Zedeck (Washington, DC: American Psychological Association, 2011), 417–53.

64. C. Perrow, "A Framework for the Comparative Analysis of Organizations," *American Sociological Review* 32, no. 2 (1967): 194–208; R.L. Daft and N.B. Macintosh, "A Tentative Exploration into the Amount and Equivocality of Information Processing in Organizational Work Units," *Administrative science quarterly* 26, no. 2 (1981): 207–24. This job characteristics category is part of "job complexity," the latter of which has too many dimensions and interpretations. See: P. Liu and Z. Li, "Task Complexity: A Review and Conceptualization Framework," *International Journal of Industrial Ergonomics* 42, no. 6 (2012): 553–68.

65. Bang & Olufsen, "Manufacturing Environment," (Denmark, 2011), http://www.bang-olufsen.com/occupational-health-and-safety (accessed 2 June 2011).

66. G. Jones, "Anything but Burnt Out," *Smart Business Cleveland*, March 2013, 24.

67. M.A. Campion and C.L. McClelland, "Follow-up and Extension of the Interdisciplinary Costs and Benefits of Enlarged Jobs," *Journal of Applied Psychology* 78 (1993): 339–51; N.G. Dodd and D.C. Ganster, "The Interactive Effects of Variety, Autonomy, and Feedback on Attitudes and Performance," *Journal of Organizational Behavior* 17 (1996): 329–47.

68. J.R. Hackman et al., "A New Strategy for Job Enrichment," *California Management Review* 17, no. 4 (1975): 57–71; R.W. Griffin, *Task Design: An Integrative Approach* (Glenview, IL: Scott Foresman, 1982).

69. E. Frauenheim, "Making the Call for Themselves," *Workforce Management*, August 2010, 16.

70. P.E. Spector and S.M. Jex, "Relations of Job Characteristics from Multiple Data Sources with Employee Affect, Absence, Turnover Intentions, and Health," *Journal of Applied Psychology* 76 (1991): 46–53; P. Osterman, "How Common Is Workplace Transformation and Who Adopts It?," *Industrial and Labor Relations Review* 47 (1994): 173–88; R. Saavedra and S.K. Kwun, "Affective States in Job Characteristics Theory," *Journal of Organizational Behavior* 21 (2000): 131–46.

71. Hackman and Oldham, *Work Redesign*, pp. 137–38.

72. This definition is based mostly on G.M. Spreitzer and R.E. Quinn, *A Company of Leaders: Five Disciplines for Unleashing the Power in Your Workforce* (San Francisco, CA: Jossey-Bass, 2001). However, most elements of this definition appear in other discussions of empowerment. See, for example, R. Forrester, "Empowerment: Rejuvenating a Potent Idea," *Academy of Management Executive* 14 (2000): 67–80; W.A. Randolph, "Re-Thinking Empowerment: Why Is It So Hard to Achieve?," *Organizational Dynamics* 29 (2000): 94–107; S.T. Menon, "Employee Empowerment: An Integrative Psychological Approach," *Applied Psychology: An International Review* 50 (2001): 153–80.

73. The positive relationship between these structural empowerment conditions and psychological empowerment is reported in H.K.S. Laschinger et al., "A Longitudinal Analysis of the Impact of Workplace Empowerment on Work Satisfaction," *Journal of Organizational Behavior* 25, no. 4 (2004): 527–45.

74. Y. Melhem, "The Antecedents of Customer-Contact Employees' Empowerment," *Employee Relations* 26, no. 1/2 (2004): 72–93; M.T. Maynard, L.L. Gilson, and J.E. Mathieu, "Empowerment–Fad or Fab? A Multilevel Review of the Past Two Decades of Research," *Journal of Management* 38, no. 4 (2012): 1231–81.

75. X. Zhang and K.M. Bartol, "Linking Empowering Leadership and Employee Creativity: The Influence of Psychological Empowerment, Intrinsic Motivation, and Creative Process Engagement," *Academy of Management Journal* 53, no. 1 (2010): 107–28; Maynard, Gilson, and Mathieu, "Empowerment–Fad or Fab?"

76. P. Gallant, "Cisco's Transparency Works for Its Staff," *Toronto Star*, 24 November 2011, X4; A. Seale, "Empowered Workforce Key to Success," *Toronto Star*, 29 November 2012, L6.

77. J.-C. Chebat and P. Kollias, "The Impact of Empowerment on Customer Contact Employees' Role in Service Organizations," *Journal of Service Research* 3 (2000): 66–81; H.K.S. Laschinger, J. Finegan, and J. Shamian, "The Impact of Workplace Empowerment, Organizational Trust on Staff Nurses' Work Satisfaction and Organizational Commitment," *Health Care Management Review* 26 (2001): 7–23.

78. "Bosses Love Team Workers," *Lancashire Evening Post (U.K.)*, 25 May 2006; A. Kravcova, "The

Man Behind the Curtain," *Baltic Times (Riga, Latvia)*, 4 August 2010.

79. C.P. Neck and C.C. Manz, "Thought Self-Leadership: The Impact of Mental Strategies Training on Employee Cognition, Behavior, and Affect," *Journal of Organizational Behavior* 17 (1996): 445–67.

80. C.C. Manz, "Self-Leadership: Toward an Expanded Theory of Self-Influence Processes in Organizations," *Academy of Management Review* 11 (1986): 585–600; C.C. Manz and C. Neck, *Mastering Self-Leadership*, 3rd ed. (Upper Saddle River, NJ: Prentice Hall, 2004); C.P. Neck and J.D. Houghton, "Two Decades of Self-Leadership Theory and Research," *Journal of Managerial Psychology* 21, no. 4 (2006): 270–95.

81. O.J. Strickland and M. Galimba, "Managing Time: The Effects of Personal Goal Setting on Resource Allocation Strategy and Task Performance," *Journal of Psychology* 135 (2001): 357–67.

82. R.M. Duncan and J.A. Cheyne, "Incidence and Functions of Self-Reported Private Speech in Young Adults: A Self-Verbalization Questionnaire," *Canadian Journal of Behavioral Science* 31 (1999): 133–36.

83. A. Hatzigeorgiadis et al., "Mechanisms Underlying the Self-Talk–Performance Relationship: The Effects of Motivational Self-Talk on Self-Confidence and Anxiety," *Psychology of Sport and Exercise* 10 (2009): 186–92; S.G. Rogelberg et al., "The Executive Mind: Leader Self-Talk, Effectiveness and Strain," *Journal of Managerial Psychology* 28, no. 1-2 (2013): 183-201.

84. J.E. Driscoll, C. Copper, and A. Moran, "Does Mental Practice Enhance Performance?," *Journal of Applied Psychology* 79 (1994): 481–92; C.P. Neck, G.L. Stewart, and C.C. Manz, "Thought Self-Leadership as a Framework for Enhancing the Performance of Performance Appraisers," *Journal of Applied Behavioral Science* 31 (1995): 278–302. Some research separates mental imagery from mental practice, whereas most studies combine both into one concept.

85. A. Joyce, "Office Parks: Re-Energize to Get through the Blahs," *Washington Post*, 28 August 2005, F05.

86. A. Wrzesniewski and J.E. Dutton, "Crafting a Job: Revisioning Employees as Active Crafters of Their Work," *Academy of Management Review* 26 (2001): 179–201.

87. M.I. Bopp, S.J. Glynn, and R.A. Henning, *Self-Management of Performance Feedback During Computer-Based Work by Individuals and Two-Person Work Teams*, Paper presented at the APA-NIOSH conference, (March 1999).

88. A.W. Logue, *Self-Control: Waiting until Tomorrow for What You Want Today* (Englewood Cliffs, NJ: Prentice-Hall, 1995).

89. Neck and Manz, "Thought Self-Leadership: The Impact of Mental Strategies Training on Employee Cognition, Behavior, and Affect; A.M. Saks and B.E. Ashforth, "Proactive Socialization and Behavioral Self-Management," *Journal of Vocational Behavior* 48 (1996): 301–23; L. Morin and G. Latham, "The Effect of Mental Practice and Goal Setting as a Transfer of Training Intervention on Supervisors' Self-Efficacy and Communication Skills: An Exploratory Study," *Applied Psychology: An International Review* 49 (2000): 566–78; J.S. Hickman and E.S. Geller, "A Safety Self-Management Intervention for Mining Operations," *Journal of Safety Research* 34 (2003): 299–308.

90. S. Ming and G.L. Martin, "Single-Subject Evaluation of a Self-Talk Package for Improving Figure Skating Performance," *Sport Psychologist* 10 (1996): 227–38; J. Bauman, "The Gold Medal Mind," *Psychology Today* 33 (2000): 62–69; L.J. Rogerson and D.W. Hrycaiko, "Enhancing Competitive Performance of Ice Hockey Goaltenders Using Centering and Self-Talk," *Journal of Applied Sport Psychology* 14, no. 1 (2002): 14–26; A. Papaioannou et al., "Combined Effect of Goal Setting and Self-Talk in Performance of a Soccer-Shooting Task," *Perceptual and Motor Skills* 98, no. 1 (2004): 89–99; R.A. Hamilton, D. Scott, and M.P. MacDougall, "Assessing the Effectiveness of Self-Talk Interventions on Endurance Performance," *Journal of Applied Sport Psychology* 19, no. 2 (2007): 226–39. For a review of the self-talk research, including limitations of this self-leadership strategy, see J. Hardy, "Speaking Clearly: A Critical Review of the Self-Talk Literature," *Psychology of Sport and Exercise* 7 (2006): 81–97.

91. S. Williams, "Personality and Self-Leadership," *Human Resource Management Review* 7, no. 2 (1997): 139–55; J. Houghton, D. et al., "The Relationship between Self-Leadership and Personality: A Comparison of Hierarchical Factor Structures," *Journal of Managerial Psychology* 19, no. 4 (2004): 427–41; R.W. Renn et al., "The Roles of Personality and Self-Defeating Behaviors in Self-Management Failure," *Journal of Management* 31, no. 5 (2005): 659–79.

92. J.D. Houghton and S.K. Yoho, "Toward a Contingency Model of Leadership and Psychological Empowerment: When Should Self-Leadership Be Encouraged?," *Journal of Leadership & Organizational Studies* 11, no. 4 (2005): 65–83; J.D. Houghton and D.L. Jinkerson, "Constructive Thought Strategies and Job Satisfaction: A Preliminary Examination," *Journal of Business and Psychology* 22 (2007): 45–53.

CHAPTER 7

1. Transportation Safety Board of Canada, Rail Safety Advisory Letter 09/13, retrieved from: http://www.tsb.gc.ca/eng/medias-media/sur-safe/letter/rail/2013/r13d0054/r13d0054-617-09-13.asp (accessed: 11 Feb 2014); "Insight: how a train ran away and devastated a canadian town," Reuters (2014), retrieved from: http://www.reuters.com/article/2013/07/09/us-train-narrative-insight-idUSBRE96801Q20130709 (accessed: 11 Feb 2014); "The equation of a disaster: what went wrong in lac-mégantic," *The Globe and Mail* (2013), retrieved from: http://www.theglobeandmail.com/news/national/the-equation-of-a-disaster-what-went-wrong-in-lac-megantic/article13214911/#dashboard/follows/ (accessed: 11 Feb 2014); "MM&A regularly left loaded trains unsupervised, using siding track for storage," *The Globe and Mail* (2013), retrieved from: http://www.theglobeandmail.com/news/national/mma-regularly-left-loaded-trains-unsupervised-on-main-track/article13411395/#dashboard/follows/ (accessed: 11 Feb 2014); S. Hamm and W.C. Symonds, "Mistakes made on the road to innovation," *Businessweek* (2006), retrieved from: http://www.businessweek.com/stories/2006-11-26/mistakes-made-on-the-road-to-innovation (accessed: 11 Feb 2014).

2. F.A. Shull Jr., A.L. Delbecq, and L.L. Cummings, *Organizational Decision Making* (New York: McGraw-Hill, 1970), p. 31.

3. M.V. White, "Jevons in Australia: A Reassessment," *The Economic Record* 58 (1982): 32-45; R.E. Nisbett, *The Geography of Thought: How Asians and Westerners Think Differently–and Why* (New York: Free Press, 2003); R. Hanna, "Kant's Theory of Judgment," (Stanford Encyclopedia of Philosophy, 2004), http://plato.stanford.edu/entries/kant-judgment/ (accessed 31 March 2008); D. Baltzly, "Stoicism," (Stanford Encyclopedia of Philosophy, 2008), http://plato.stanford.edu/entries/stoicism/ (accessed 30 March 2008).

4. J.G. March and H.A. Simon, *Organizations* (New York: John Wiley & Sons, Inc., 1958); K. Manktelow, *Thinking and Reasoning : An Introduction to the Psychology of Reason, Judgment and Decision Making* (Hoboken: Taylor and Francis, 2012), Chap. 8. In economics, SEU is usually presented in the context of correlated choices (such as probability of a result when rolling dice), such that the probability of all choices must add up to 1.0. In organizational behavior, subjective expected utility is applied to independent choices (e.g. five job applicants), not correlated choices, so probabilities can be scaled independently rather than add up to 1.0.

5. This model is adapted from several sources, including H.A. Simon, *The New Science of Management Decision* (New York: Harper & Row, 1960); H. Mintzberg, D. Raisinghani, and A. Théorêt, "The Structure of 'Unstructured' Decision Processes," *Administrative Science Quarterly* 21 (1976): 246–75; W.C. Wedley and R.H.G. Field, "A Predecision Support System," *Academy of Management Review* 9 (1984): 696–703.

6. P.F. Drucker, *The Practice of Management* (New York: Harper & Brothers, 1954), 353–57; B.M. Bass, *Organizational Decision Making* (Homewood, IL: Irwin, 1983), Chap. 3.

7. L.R. Beach and T.R. Mitchell, "A Contingency Model for the Selection of Decision Strategies," *Academy of Management Review* 3 (1978): 439–49; I.L. Janis, *Crucial Decisions* (New York: The Free Press, 1989), pp. 35–37; W. Zhongtuo, "Meta-Decision Making: Concepts and Paradigm," *Systematic Practice and Action Research* 13, no. 1 (2000): 111–15.

8. J. de Jonge, *Rethinking Rational Choice Theory : A Companion on Rational and Moral Action* (Basingstoke: Palgrave Macmillan, 2011).

9. A. Howard, "Opinion," *Computing* (1999): 18.

10. For a recent discussion on problem finding in organizations, see: M.A. Roberto, *Know What You Don't Know: How Great Leaders Prevent Problems before They Happen* (Saddle River, NJ: Wharton School Publishing, 2009).

11. T.K. Das and B.S. Teng, "Cognitive Biases and Strategic Decision Processes: An Integrative Perspective," *Journal Of Management Studies* 36,

no. 6 (1999): 757–78; P. Bijttebier, H. Vertommen, and G.V. Steene, "Assessment of Cognitive Coping Styles: A Closer Look at Situation-Response Inventories," *Clinical Psychology Review* 21, no. 1 (2001): 85–104; P.C. Nutt, "Expanding the Search for Alternatives During Strategic Decision-Making," *Academy of Management Executive* 18, no. 4 (2004): 13–28.

12. O. Moore, "Go Train Drama Illustrates the Risks of Don Valley Transit Corridor," *The Globe and Mail (Toronto)*, 9 July 2013; J. Edmiston and P. Kuitenbrouwer, "Right Call to Send Go Train," *National Post (Toronto)*, 10 July 2013, A8.

13. P.C. Nutt, *Why Decisions Fail* (San Francisco, CA: Berrett-Koehler, 2002); S. Finkelstein, *Why Smart Executives Fail* (New York: Viking, 2003).

14. E. Witte, "Field Research on Complex Decision-Making Processes – the Phase Theorum," *International Studies of Management and Organization*, no. 56 (1972): 156–82; J.A. Bargh and T.L. Chartrand, "The Unbearable Automaticity of Being," *American Psychologist* 54, no. 7 (1999): 462–79.

15. M. Hock and H.W. Krohne, "Coping with Threat and Memory for Ambiguous Information: Testing the Repressive Discontinuity Hypothesis," *Emotion* 4, no. 1 (2004): 65-86; J. Brandtstadter, A. Voss, and K. Rothermund, "Perception of Danger Signals: The Role of Control," *Experimental Psychology* 51, no. 1 (2004): 24–32.

16. R. Rothenberg, "Ram Charan: The Thought Leader Interview," *strategy + business* (2004).

17. D. O'Brien, "The Fine Art of Googling," *Sunday Times (London)*, 20 July 2000; K.J. Delaney and A. Grimes, "For Some Who Passed on Google Long Ago, Wistful Thinking " *Wall Street Journal*, 23 August 2004, A1; "Google Wanted to Sell for $1 Million and Got Rejected," (30 September 2010), http://news.softpedia.com/news/Google-Wanted-to-Sell-for-1-Million-and-Got-Rejected-158828.shtml (accessed 27 August 2013).

18. M. McCarthy, "Top 20 in 20 Years: Apple Computer–1984," (2003), www.adweek.com/adweek/creative/top20_20years/index.jsp (accessed 16 January 2003); O.W. Linzmayer, *Apple Confidential 2.0: The Definitive Story of the World's Most Colorful Company* (San Francisco, CA: No Starch Press, 2004), pp. 109–14.

19. R. Collison, "How Bata Rules Its World," *Canadian Business*, September 1990, 28; J. Portman, "Harry Potter Was Almost a Yankee," *Vancouver Sun*, 5 July 2007.

20. "Kodak's last days," (editorial), *New Straits Times* (2014), retrieved from: http://www.nst.com.my/opinion/editorial/kodak-s-last-days-1.42251 [Accessed: 11 Feb 2014].

21. H.A. Simon, *Administrative Behavior*, Second ed. (New York: The Free Press, 1957); H.A. Simon, "Rational Decision Making in Business Organizations," *American Economic Review* 69, no. 4 (1979): 493–513.

22. Simon, *Administrative Behavior*, pp. xxv, 80-84.

23. S. Sacchi and M. Burigo, "Strategies in the Information Search Process: Interaction among Task Structure, Knowledge, and Source," *Journal of General Psychology* 135, no. 3 (2008): 252–70.

24. P.O. Soelberg, "Unprogrammed Decision Making," *Industrial Management Review* 8 (1967): 19–29; J.E. Russo, V.H. Medvec, and M.G. Meloy, "The Distortion of Information During Decisions," *Organizational Behavior & Human Decision Processes* 66 (1996): 102–10; K.H. Ehrhart and J.C. Ziegert, "Why Are Individuals Attracted to Organizations?," *Journal of Management* 31, no. 6 (2005): 901–19. This is consistent with the observations by Milton Rokeach, who famously stated, "Life is ipsative, because decisions in everyday life are inherently and phenomenologically ipsative decisions." M. Rokeach, "Inducing Changes and Stability in Belief Systems and Personality Structures," *Journal of Social Issues* 41, no. 1 (1985): 153–71.

25. A.L. Brownstein, "Biased Predecision Processing," *Psychological Bulletin* 129, no. 4 (2003): 545–68.

26. T. Gilovich, D. Griffin, and D. Kahneman, *Heuristics and Biases: The Psychology of Intuitive Judgment* (Cambridge: Cambridge University Press, 2002); D. Kahneman, "Maps of Bounded Rationality: Psychology for Behavioral Economics," *American Economic Review* 93, no. 5 (2003): 1449–75; F.L. Smith et al., "Decision-Making Biases and Affective States: Their Potential Impact on Best Practice Innovations," *Canadian Journal of Administrative Sciences* 27, no. 4 (2010): 277–91.

27. A. Tversky and D. Kahneman, "Judgment under Uncertainty: Heuristics and Biases," *Science* 185, no. 4157 (1974): 1124–31; I. Ritov, "Anchoring in Simulated Competitive Market Negotiation," *Organizational Behavior and Human Decision Processes* 67, no. 1 (1996): 16; D. Ariely, G. Loewenstein, and a. Prelec, "Coherent Arbitrariness": Stable Demand Curves without Stable Preferences," *The Quarterly Journal of Economics* 118 (2003): 73; N. Epley and T. Gilovich, "Are Adjustments Insufficient?," *Personality and Social Psychology Bulletin* 30, no. 4 (2004): 447–60; J.D. Jasper and S.D. Christman, "A Neuropsychological Dimension for Anchoring Effects," *Journal of Behavioral Decision Making* 18 (2005): 343–69; S.D. Bond et al., "Information Distortion in the Evaluation of a Single Option," *Organizational Behavior & Human Decision Processes* 102 (2007): 240–54.

28. A. Tversky and D. Kahneman, "Availability: A Heuristic for Judging Frequency and Probability," *Cognitive Psychology* 5 (1973): 207-32.

29. D. Kahneman and A. Tversky, "Subjective Probability: A Judgment of Representativeness," *Cognitive Psychology* 3, no. 3 (1972): 430; T. Gilovich, *How We Know What Isn't So: The Fallibility of Human Reason in Everyday Life* (New York: Free Press, 1991); B.D. Burns, "Heuristics as Beliefs and as Behaviors: The Adaptiveness of the 'Hot Hand'," *Cognitive Psychology* 48 (2004): 295–331; E.M. Altmann and B.D. Burns, "Streak Biases in Decision Making: Data and a Memory Model," *Cognitive Systems Research* 6, no. 1 (2005): 5–16.

30. H.A. Simon, "Rational Choice and the Structure of Environments," *Psychological Review* 63 (1956): 129–38.

31. S. Botti and S.S. Iyengar, "The Dark Side of Choice: When Choice Impairs Social Welfare," *Journal of Public Policy and Marketing* 25, no. 1 (2006): 24–38; K.D. Vohs et al., "Making Choices Impairs Subsequent Self-Control: A Limited-Resource Account of Decision Making, Self-Regulation, and Active Initiative," *Journal of Personality and Social Psychology* 94, no. 5 (2008): 883–98.

32. J. Choi, D. Laibson, and B. Madrian, *Reducing the Complexity Costs of 401 (K) Participation through Quick Enrollment™*, National Bureau of Economic Research, Inc. (Jan 2006); J. Beshears et al., "Simplification and Saving," (SSRN, 2006); S. Iyengar, *The Art of Choosing* (New York: Hachette, 2010), pp. 194–200.

33. P.C. Nutt, "Search During Decision Making," *European Journal of Operational Research* 160 (2005): 851–76.

34. S.S. Iyengar and M.R. Lepper, "When Choice Is Demotivating: Can One Desire Too Much of a Good Thing?," *Journal of Personality and Social Psychology* 79, no. 6 (2000): 995–1006; Iyengar, *The Art of Choosing*, pp. 177–95.

35. P. Winkielman et al., "Affective Influence on Judgments and Decisions: Moving Towards Core Mechanisms," *Review of General Psychology* 11, no. 2 (2007): 179–92.

36. A.R. Damasio, *Descartes' Error: Emotion, Reason, and the Human Brain* (New York: Putnam Sons, 1994); P. Winkielman and K.C. Berridge, "Unconscious Emotion," *Current Directions in Psychological Science* 13, no. 3 (2004): 120–23; A. Bechara and A.R. Damasio, "The Somatic Marker Hypothesis: A Neural Theory of Economic Decision," *Games and Economic Behavior* 52, no. 2 (2005): 336–72.

37. J.P. Forgas and J.M. George, "Affective Influences on Judgments and Behavior in Organizations: An Information Processing Perspective," *Organizational Behavior and Human Decision Processes* 86 (2001): 3–34; G. Loewenstein and J.S. Lerner, "The Role of Affect in Decision Making," in *Handbook of Affective Sciences*, ed. R.J. Davidson, K.R. Scherer, and H.H. Goldsmith (New York: Oxford University Press, 2003), 619–42; M.T. Pham, "Emotion and Rationality: A Critical Review and Interpretation of Empirical Evidence," *Review of General Psychology* 11, no. 2 (2007): 155–78; H.J.M. Kooij-de Bode, D. Van Knippenberg, and W.P. Van Ginkel, "Good Effects of Bad Feelings: Negative Affectivity and Group Decision-Making," *British Journal of Management* 21, no. 2 (2010): 375-92; J.P. Forgas and A.S. Koch, "Mood Effects on Cognition," in *Handbook of Cognition and Emotion*, ed. M.D. Robinson, E.R. Watkins, and E. Harmon-Jones (New York: Guilford, 2013), 231-51.

38. D. Miller, *The Icarus Paradox* (New York: HarperBusiness, 1990); D. Miller, "What Happens after Success: The Perils of Excellence," *Journal of Management Studies* 31, no. 3 (1994): 325–68; A.C. Amason and A.C. Mooney, "The Icarus Paradox Revisited: How Strong Performance Sows the Seeds of Dysfunction in Future Strategic Decision-Making," *Strategic Organization* 6, no. 4 (2008): 407–34.

39. M.T. Pham, "The Logic of Feeling," *Journal of Consumer Psychology* 14 (2004): 360–69; N. Schwarz, "Feelings-as-Information Theory," in *Handbook of Theories of Social Psychology*, ed. P. Van Lange, A. Kruglanski, and E.T. Higgins (London, UK: Sage, 2012), 289–308.

40. L. Sjöberg, "Intuitive vs. Analytical Decision Making: Which Is Preferred?," *Scandinavian Journal of Management* 19 (2003): 17-29.

41. W.H. Agor, "The Logic of Intuition," *Organizational Dynamics* (1986): 5-18; H.A. Simon, "Making Management Decisions: The Role of Intuition and Emotion," *Academy of Management Executive* (1987): 57-64; O. Behling and N.L. Eckel, "Making Sense out of Intuition," *Academy of Management Executive* 5 (1991): 46-54. This process is also known as naturalistic decision making. For a discussion of research on naturalistic decision making, see the special issue in Organization Studies: R. Lipshitz, G. Klein, and J.S. Carroll, "Introduction to the Special Issue: Naturalistic Decision Making and Organizational Decision Making: Exploring the Intersections," *Organization Studies* 27, no. 7 (2006): 917-23.

42. M.D. Lieberman, "Intuition: A Social Cognitive Neuroscience Approach," *Psychological Bulletin* 126 (2000): 109-37; G. Klein, *Intuition at Work* (New York: Currency/Doubleday, 2003); E. Dane and M.G. Pratt, "Exploring Intuition and Its Role in Managerial Decision Making," *Academy of Management Review* 32, no. 1 (2007): 33-54.

43. Klein, *Intuition at Work*, pp. 12-13, 16-17.

44. Y. Ganzach, A.H. Kluger, and N. Klayman, "Making Decisions from an Interview: Expert Measurement and Mechanical Combination," *Personnel Psychology* 53 (2000): 1-20; A.M. Hayashi, "When to Trust Your Gut," *Harvard Business Review* 79 (2001): 59-65. Evidence of high failure rates from quick decisions is reported in Nutt, *Why Decisions Fail;* Nutt, "Search During Decision Making; P.C. Nutt, "Investigating the Success of Decision Making Processes," *Journal of Management Studies* 45, no. 2 (2008): 425-55.

45. R. Bradfield et al., "The Origins and Evolution of Scenario Techniques in Long Range Business Planning," *Futures* 37, no. 8 (2005): 795-812; G. Wright, G. Cairns, and P. Goodwin, "Teaching Scenario Planning: Lessons from Practice in Academe and Business," *European Journal of Operational Research* 194, no. 1 (2009): 323-35; T.J. Chermack, *Scenario Planning in Organizations* (San Francisco, CA: Berrett-Koehler, 2011).

46. *Whatif. . . Edition: Shipping,* Dreyer Kompetense (Harstad, Norway: 16 July 2009); Z.A. Wahab, "Norwegian Firm Offers Board Game as Training Tool," *Bernama Daily Malaysian News (Kuala Lumpur)*, 25 March 2010.

47. J. Pfeffer and R.I. Sutton, "Knowing 'What' to Do Is Not Enough: Turning Knowledge into Action," *California Management Review* 42, no. 1 (1999): 83-108; R. Charan, C. Burke, and L. Bossidy, *Execution: The Discipline of Getting Things Done* (New York: Crown Business, 2002).

48. R.F. Bruner, "In Defense of Reorganizations," *Washington Post*, 13 May 2013, A22.

49. R.S. Nickerson, "Confirmation Bias: A Ubiquitous Phenomenon in Many Guises," *Review of General Psychology* 2, no. 2 (1998): 175-220; O. Svenson, I. Salo, and T. Lindholm, "Post-Decision Consolidation and Distortion of Facts," *Judgment and Decision Making* 4, no. 5 (2009): 397-407.

50. B.M. Staw and J. Ross, "Behavior in Escalation Situations: Antecedents, Prototypes, and Solutions.," in *Research in Organizational Behavior*, ed. L.L. Cummings and B.M. Staw (Greenwixh, CT: JAI, 1987), 39-78; J. Brockner, "The Escalation of Commitment to a Failing Course of Action: Toward Theoretical Progress," *Academy of Management Review* 17, no. 1 (1992): 39-61; D.J. Sleesman et al., "Cleaning up the Big Muddy: A Meta-Analytic Review of the Determinants of Escalation of Commitment," *Academy of Management Journal* 55, no. 3 (2012): 541-62.

51. F.D. Schoorman and P.J. Holahan, "Psychological Antecedents of Escalation Behavior: Effects of Choice, Responsibility, and Decision Consequences," *Journal of Applied Psychology* 81 (1996): 786-93; N. Sivanathan et al., "The Promise and Peril of Self-Affirmation in De-Escalation of Commitment," *Organizational Behavior and Human Decision Processes* 107, no. 1 (2008): 1-14.

52. N.J. Roese and J.M. Olson, "Better, Stronger, Faster: Self-Serving Judgment, Affect Regulation, and the Optimal Vigilance Hypothesis," *Perspectives on Psychological Science* 2, no. 2 (2007): 124-41; C.L. Guenther and M.D. Alicke, "Deconstructing the Better-Than-Average Effect," *Journal of Personality and Social Psychology* 99, no. 5 (2010): 755-70; S. Loughnan et al., "Universal Biases in Self-Perception: Better and More Human Than Average," *British Journal of Social Psychology* 49 (2010): 627-36.

53. M. Keil, G. Depledge, and A. Rai, "Escalation: The Role of Problem Recognition and Cognitive Bias," *Decision Sciences* 38, no. 3 (2007): 391-421.

54. G. Whyte, "Escalating Commitment in Individual and Group Decision Making: A Prospect Theory Approach," *Organizational Behavior and Human Decision Processes* 54 (1993): 430-55; D. Kahneman and J. Renshon, "Hawkish Biases," in *American Foreign Policy and the Politics of Fear: Threat Inflation since 9/11*, ed. T. Thrall and J. Cramer (New York: Routledge, 2009), 79-96.

55. Sleesman et al., "Cleaning up the Big Muddy."

56. J.D. Bragger et al., "When Success Breeds Failure: History, Hysteresis, and Delayed Exit Decisions " *Journal of Applied Psychology* 88, no. 1 (2003): 6-14. A second logical reason for escalation, called the Martingale strategy, is described in J.A. Aloysius, "Rational Escalation of Costs by Playing a Sequence of Unfavorable Gambles: The Martingale," *Journal of Economic Behavior & Organization* 51 (2003): 111-29.

57. I. Simonson and B.M. Staw, "De-Escalation Strategies: A Comparison of Techniques for Reducing Commitment to Losing Courses of Action," *Journal of Applied Psychology* 77 (1992): 419-26; W. Boulding, R. Morgan, and R. Staelin, "Pulling the Plug to Stop the New Product Drain," *Journal of Marketing Research*, no. 34 (1997): 164-76; B.M. Staw, K.W. Koput, and S.G. Barsade, "Escalation at the Credit Window: A Longitudinal Study of Bank Executives' Recognition and Write-Off of Problem Loans," *Journal of Applied Psychology*, no. 82 (1997): 130-42; M. Keil and D. Robey, "Turning around Troubled Software Projects: An Exploratory Study of the Deescalation of Commitment to Failing Courses of Action," *Journal of Management Information Systems* 15 (1999): 63-87; B.C. Gunia, N. Sivanathan, and A.D. Galinsky, "Vicarious Entrapment: Your Sunk Costs, My Escalation of Commitment," *Journal of Experimental Social Psychology* 45, no. 6 (2009): 1238-44.

58. D. Ghosh, "De-Escalation Strategies: Some Experimental Evidence," *Behavioral Research in Accounting*, no. 9 (1997): 88-112.

59. M.I. Stein, "Creativity and Culture," *Journal of Psychology* 36 (1953): 311-22; M.A. Runco and G.J. Jaeger, "The Standard Definition of Creativity," *Creativity Research Journal* 24, no. 1 (2012): 92-96.

60. V. Khanna, "The Voice of Google," *Business Times Singapore*, 12 January 2008.

61. G. Wallas, *The Art of Thought* (London, UK: Jonathan Cape, 1926). For recent applications of Wallas's classic model, see T. Kristensen, "The Physical Context of Creativity," *Creativity and Innovation Management* 13, no. 2 (2004): 89-96; U.-E. Haner, "Spaces for Creativity and Innovation in Two Established Organizations," *Creativity and Innovation Management* 14, no. 3 (2005): 288-98.

62. R.S. Nickerson, "Enhancing Creativity," in *Handbook of Creativity* ed. R.J. Sternberg (New York: Cambridge University Press, 1999), 392-430.

63. E. Oakes, *Notable Scientists: A to Z of STS Scientists* (New York: Facts on File, 2002), pp. 207-09.

64. For a thorough discussion of illumination or insight, see R.J. Sternberg and J.E. Davidson, *The Nature of Insight* (Cambridge, MA: MIT Press, 1995).

65. R.J. Sternberg and L.A. O' Hara, "Creativity and Intelligence," in *Handbook of Creativity* ed. R.J. Sternberg (New York: Cambridge University Press, 1999), 251-72; S. Taggar, "Individual Creativity and Group Ability to Utilize Individual Creative Resources: A Multilevel Model," *Academy of Management Journal* 45 (2002): 315-30.

66. G.J. Feist, "The Influence of Personality on Artistic and Scientific Creativity," in *Handbook of Creativity*, ed. R.J. Sternberg (New York: Cambridge University Press, 1999), 273-96; T. Åstebro, S.A. Jeffrey, and G.K. Adomdza, "Inventor Perseverance after Being Told to Quit: The Role of Cognitive Biases," *Journal of Behavioral Decision Making* 20 (2007): 253-72; J.S. Mueller, S. Melwani, and J.A. Goncalo, "The Bias against Creativity: Why People Desire but Reject Creative Ideas," *Psychological Science* 23, no. 1 (2012): 13-17.

67. R.W. Weisberg, "Creativity and Knowledge: A Challenge to Theories," in *Handbook of Creativity*, ed. R.J. Sternberg (New York: Cambridge University Press, 1999), 226-50.

68. E. Dane, "Reconsidering the Trade-Off between Expertise and Flexibility: A Cognitive Entrenchment Perspective," *Academy of Management Review* 35, no. 4 (2010): 579-603; R.I. Sutton, *Weird Ideas That Work* (New York: Free Press, 2002), pp. 121, 53-54.

69. T. Koppell, *Powering the Future* (New York: Wiley, 1999), p. 15.

70. Feist, "The Influence of Personality on Artistic and Scientific Creativity; C.E. Shalley, J. Zhou, and G.R. Oldham, "The Effects of Personal and Contextual Characteristics on Creativity: Where Should We Go from Here?," *Journal of Management* 30, no. 6 (2004): 933-58; S.J. Dollinger, K.K. Urban, and T.A. James, "Creativity and Openness to Experience: Validation of Two Creative Product Measures," *Creativity Research Journal* 16, no. 1 (2004): 35-47; T.S. Schweizer, "The Psychology of Novelty-Seeking, Creativity

and Innovation: Neurocognitive Aspects within a Work-Psychological Perspective," *Creativity and Innovation Management* 15, no. 2 (2006): 164–72; S. Acar and M.A. Runco, "Creative Abilities: Divergent Thinking," in *Handbook of Organizational Creativity*, ed. M. Mumford (Waltham, MA: Academic Press, 2012), 115–39.

71. Innovation Tools, *2009 Creativity Survey*, InnovationTools.com (Milwaukee: July 2009); *Working Beyond Borders*, IBM Institute for Business Value (Somers, NY: September 2010); "Though 57% Say Innovation Is Key in 2011, Few Have Applied It to Drive Personal Growth," News release for FPC (New York: 25 May 2011); *2010 Federal Employee Viewpoint Survey Results*, (Washington, DC: 2011).

72. Shalley, Zhou, and Oldham, "The Effects of Personal and Contextual Characteristics on Creativity; T.M. Amabile et al., "Leader Behaviors and the Work Environment for Creativity: Perceived Leader Support," *The Leadership Quarterly* 15, no. 1 (2004): 5–32; S.T. Hunter, K.E. Bedell, and M.D. Mumford, "Climate for Creativity: A Quantitative Review," *Creativity Research Journal* 19, no. 1 (2007): 69–90; T.C. DiLiello and J.D. Houghton, "Creative Potential and Practised Creativity: Identifying Untapped Creativity in Organizations," *Creativity and Innovation Management* 17, no. 1 (2008): 37–46.

73. R. Westwood and D.R. Low, "The Multicultural Muse: Culture, Creativity and Innovation," *International Journal of Cross Cultural Management* 3, no. 2 (2003): 235–59.

74. "Samsung CEO Yun Picks Google as New Role Model," *Korea Times*, 1 October 2007.

75. T.M. Amabile, "Motivating Creativity in Organizations: On Doing What You Love and Loving What You Do," *California Management Review* 40 (1997): 39–58; A. Cummings and G.R. Oldham, "Enhancing Creativity: Managing Work Contexts for the High Potential Employee," *California Management Review*, no. 40 (1997): 22–38; F. Coelho and M. Augusto, "Job Characteristics and the Creativity of Frontline Service Employees," *Journal of Service Research* 13, no. 4 (2010): 426–38.

76. T.M. Amabile, "Changes in the Work Environment for Creativity During Downsizing," *Academy of Management Journal* 42 (1999): 630–40.

77. J. Moultrie et al., "Innovation Spaces: Towards a Framework for Understanding the Role of the Physical Environment in Innovation," *Creativity & Innovation Management* 16, no. 1 (2007): 53–65.

78. J.M. Howell and K. Boies, "Champions of Technological Innovation: The Influence of Contextual Knowledge, Role Orientation, Idea Generation, and Idea Promotion on Champion Emergence," *The Leadership Quarterly* 15, no. 1 (2004): 123–43; Shalley, Zhou, and Oldham, "The Effects of Personal and Contextual Characteristics on Creativity; S. Powell, "The Management and Consumption of Organisational Creativity," *Journal of Consumer Marketing* 25, no. 3 (2008): 158–66.

79. L. Sin, "Ideas, Passion Drive Inspired Designer," *Vancouver Province*, 19 October 2010; J. Ross, "Interactive Design," *North Shore Outlook (North Vancouver)*, 1 December 2010.

80. A. Hiam, "Obstacles to Creativity - and How You Can Remove Them," *Futurist* 32 (1998): 30–34.

81. M.A. West, *Developing Creativity in Organizations* (Leicester, UK: BPS Books, 1997), pp. 33–35.

82. For discussion of how play affects creativity, see: S. Brown, *Play: How It Shapes the Brain, Opens the Imagination, and Invigorates the Soul* (New York: Avery, 2009).

83. S. Hemsley, "Seeking the Source of Innovation," *Media Week*, 16 August 2005, 22.

84. A. Hargadon and R.I. Sutton, "Building an Innovation Factory," *Harvard Business Review* 78 (2000): 157–66; T. Kelley, *The Art of Innovation* (New York: Currency Doubleday, 2001), pp. 158–62; P.F. Skilton and K.J. Dooley, "The Effects of Repeat Collaboration on Creative Abrasion," *Academy of Management Review* 35, no. 1 (2010): 118–34.

85. M. Burton, "Open Plan, Open Mind," *Director* (2005): 68–72; A. Benady, "Mothers of Invention," *The Independent (London)*, 27 November 2006; B. Murray, "Agency Profile: Mother London," *Ihaveanidea*, 28 January 2007.

86. "John Collee-Biography," (IMDB (Internet Movie Database), 2009), http://www.imdb.com/name/nm0171722/bio (accessed 27 April 2009).

87. N. Desai, "Management by Trust in a Democratic Enterprise: A Law Firm Shapes Organizational Behavior to Create Competitive Advantage," *Global Business and Organizational Excellence* 28, no. 6 (2009): 7–21.

88. M. Fenton-O'Creevy, "Employee Involvement and the Middle Manager: Saboteur or Scapegoat?," *Human Resource Management Journal*, no. 11 (2001): 24–40. Also see V.H. Vroom and A.G. Jago, *The New Leadership: Managing Participation in Organizations* (Englewood Cliffs, NJ: Prentice Hill, 1988).

89. Vroom and Jago, *The New Leadership*.

90. J.R. Foley and M. Polanyi, "Workplace Democracy: Why Bother?," *Economic and Industrial Democracy* 27, no. 1 (2006): 173–91; P.A. Woods and P. Gronn, "Nurturing Democracy," *Educational Management Administration & Leadership* 37, no. 4 (2009): 430–51.

91. R. Semler, *The Seven-Day Weekend* (London, UK: Century, 2003); G. de Jong and A. van Witteloostuijn, "Successful Corporate Democracy: Sustainable Cooperation of Capital and Labor in the Dutch Breman Group," *Academy of Management Executive* 18, no. 3 (2004): 54–66.

92. K. Cloke and J. Goldsmith, *The End of Management and the Rise of Organizational Democracy* (San Francisco, CA: Jossey-Bass, 2003); L. Gratton, *The Democratic Enterprise: Liberating Your Enterprise with Freedom, Flexibility, and Commitment* (London, UK: FT Prentice-Hall, 2004).

93. P.E. Slater and W.G. Bennis, "Democracy Is Inevitable," *Harvard Business Review* (1964): 51–59; D. Collins, "The Ethical Superiority and Inevitability of Participatory Management as an Organizational System," *Organization Science* 8, no. 5 (1997): 489–507; W.G. Weber, C. Unterrainer, and B.E. Schmid, "The Influence of Organizational Democracy on Employees' Socio-Moral Climate and Prosocial Behavioral Orientations," *Journal of Organizational Behavior* 30, no. 8 (2009): 1127–49.

94. Collins, "The Ethical Superiority and Inevitability of Participatory Management as an Organizational System; R. Bussel, "Business without a Boss": The Columbia Conserve Company and Workers' Control, 1917–1943," *The Business History Review* 71, no. 3 (1997): 417–43; J.D. Russell, M. Dirsmith, and S. Samuel, "Stained Steel: ESOPs, Meta-Power, and the Ironies of Corporate Democracy," *Symbolic Interaction* 27, no. 3 (2004): 383–403.

95. J.C. Barbieri and A.C.T. Álvares, "Innovation in Mature Industries: The Case of Brasilata S. A Metallic Packaging," in *International conference on technology policy and innovation* (Curitiba, Brazil2000); "ParticipaçãO É Desafio Nas Empresas (Participation Is a Challenge in Business)," *Gazeta do Povo*, 16 November 2008; "Brasilata Internal Suggestion System Is a Benchmark in Innovation in the Brazilian Market," (São Paulo, Brazil: Brazilata, 2010), http://brasilata.jp/en/noticias_detalhada.php?cd_noticia=219 (accessed 10 June 2011); C. Heath and D. Heath, *Switch: How to Change Things When Change Is Hard* (New York: Broadway Books, 2010); "Brasilata Inventors Turned in 205,536 Innovative Suggestions in 2010," (São Paulo, Brazil: Brasilata, 2011), http://brasilata.jp/en/noticias_detalhada.php?cd_noticia=264 (accessed 10 June 2011); "Simplification Project," (São Paulo, Brazil: Brasilata, 2011), http://brasilata.jp/en/projeto_cronologia.php (accessed 10 June 2011); "Business Management," (São Paulo, Brazil: Brasilata, 2011), http://brasilata.jp/en/pessoal_negocios.php (accessed 14 June 2011).

96. Some of the early OB writing on employee involvement includes C. Argyris, *Personality and Organization* (New York: Harper & Row, 1957); D. McGregor, *The Human Side of Enterprise* (New York: McGraw-Hill, 1960); R. Likert, *New Patterns of Management* (New York: McGraw-Hill, 1961).

97. Towers Watson, *Engagement at Risk: Driving Strong Performance in a Volatile Global Environment*, Global Workforce Study, (New York: Towers Watson, September 2012).

98. A.G. Robinson and D.M. Schroeder, *Ideas Are Free* (San Francisco, CA: Berrett-Koehler, 2004).

99. R.J. Ely and D.A. Thomas, "Cultural Diversity at Work: The Effects of Diversity Perspectives on Work Group Processes and Outcomes," *Administrative Science Quarterly* 46 (2001): 229–73; E. Mannix and M.A. Neale, "What Differences Make a Difference?: The Promise and Reality of Diverse Teams in Organizations," *Psychological Science in the Public Interest* 6, no. 2 (2005): 31–55.

100. D. Berend and J. Paroush, "When Is Condorcet's Jury Theorem Valid?," *Social Choice and Welfare* 15, no. 4 (1998): 481–88.

101. K.T. Dirks, L.L. Cummings, and J.L. Pierce, "Psychological Ownership in Organizations: Conditions under Which Individuals Promote and Resist Change," *Research in Organizational Change and Development*, no. 9 (1996): 1–23; J.P. Walsh and S.-F. Tseng, "The Effects of Job Characteristics on Active Effort at Work," *Work & Occupations*, no. 25 (1998): 74–96; B. Scott-Ladd and V. Marshall, "Participation in Decision Making: A Matter of Context?," *Leadership & Organization Development Journal* 25, no. 8 (2004): 646–62.

102. Vroom and Jago, *The New Leadership*.

CHAPTER 8

1. http://www.theglobeandmail.com/sports/olympics/canadas-mens-olympic-hockey-team-to-be-unveiled-in-toronto/article16228127/?page=all; http://sports.nationalpost.com/2014/02/23/canada-vs-sweden-sochi-olympics-mens-hockey-gold-medal-game-live/; http://bleacherreport.com/articles/1969476-breaking-down-the-canadian-olympic-hockey-teams-stellar-defense-in-sochi.

2. "Go Teams! Firms Can't Do without Them," (American Management Association, 2008), http://amalearning.com (accessed 21 April 2010); "Trends: Are Many Meetings a Waste of Time? Study Says So," News release (MeetingsNet, 1 November 1998); "Teamwork and Collaboration Major Workplace Trends," *Ottawa Business Journal*, 18 April 2006.

3. S. Wuchty, B.F. Jones, and B. Uzzi, "The Increasing Dominance of Teams in Production of Knowledge," *Science* 316 (2007): 1036–39.

4. E. Sundstrom, "The Challenges of Supporting Work Team Effectiveness," in *Supporting Work Team Effectiveness* ed. E. Sundstrom and Associates (San Francisco, CA: Jossey-Bass, 1999), 6–9; S.A. Mohrman, S.G. Cohen, and A.M. Mohrman Jr., *Designing Team-Based Organizations: New Forms for Knowledge Work* (San Francisco, CA: Jossey-Bass, 1995), 39–40; M.E. Shaw, *Group Dynamics*, 3rd ed. (New York: McGraw-Hill, 1981), 8.

5. J.R. Hollenbeck, B. Beersma, and M.E. Schouten, "Beyond Team Types and Taxonomies: A Dimensional Scaling Conceptualization for Team Description," *Academy of Management Review* 37, no. 1 (2012): 82–106.

6. S.I. Tannenbaum et al., "Teams Are Changing: Are Research and Practice Evolving Fast Enough?," *Industrial and Organizational Psychology* 5, no. 1 (2012): 2–24; R. Wageman, H. Gardner, and M. Mortensen, "The Changing Ecology of Teams: New Directions for Teams Research," *Journal of Organizational Behavior* 33, no. 3 (2012): 301–15.

7. http://www.rottentomatoes.com/m/toy_story_3/.

8. R.A. Guzzo and M.W. Dickson, "Teams in Organizations: Recent Research on Performance and Effectiveness," *Annual Review of Psychology* 47 (1996): 307–38; L.R. Offerman and R.K. Spiros, "The Science and Practice of Team Development: Improving the Link," *Academy of Management Journal* 44 (2001): 376–92.

9. P.R. Lawrence and N. Nohria, *Driven: How Human Nature Shapes Our Choices* (San Francisco, CA: Jossey-Bass, 2002); J.R. Spoor and J.R. Kelly, "The Evolutionary Significance of Affect in Groups: Communication and Group Bonding," *Group Processes & Intergroup Relations* 7, no. 4 (2004): 398–412.

10. M.A. Hogg et al., "The Social Identity Perspective: Intergroup Relations, Self-Conception, and Small Groups," *Small Group Research* 35, no. 3 (2004): 246–76; M. Van Vugt and C.M. Hart, "Social Identity as Social Glue: The Origins of Group Loyalty," *Journal of Personality and Social Psychology* 86, no. 4 (2004): 585–98; N. Michinov, E. Michinov, and M.-C. Toczek-Capelle, "Social Identity, Group Processes, and Performance in Synchronous Computer-Mediated Communication," *Group Dynamics: Theory, Research, and Practice* 8, no. 1 (2004): 27–39.

11. S. Schacter, *The Psychology of Affiliation* (Stanford, CA: Stanford University Press, 1959), 12–19; A.C. DeVries, E.R. Glasper, and C.E. Detillion, "Social Modulation of Stress Responses," *Physiology & Behavior* 79, no. 3 (2003): 399–407; S. Cohen, "The Pittsburgh Common Cold Studies: Psychosocial Predictors of Susceptibility to Respiratory Infectious Illness," *International Journal of Behavioral Medicine* 12, no. 3 (2005): 123–31.

12. R. Cross and R.J. Thomas, *Driving Results through Social Networks: How Top Organizations Leverage Networks for Performance and Growth* (San Francisco, CA: Jossey-Bass, 2009); R. McDermott and D. Archibald, "Harnessing Your Staff's Informal Networks," *Harvard Business Review* 88, no. 3 (2010): 82–89; J. Nieves and J. Osorio, "The Role of Social Networks in Knowledge Creation," *Knowledge Management Research & Practice* 11, no. 1 (2013): 62–77.

13. M. Moldaschl and W. Weber, "The 'Three Waves' of Industrial Group Work: Historical Reflections on Current Research on Group Work," *Human Relations* 51 (1998): 347–88. Several popular books in the 1980s encouraged teamwork, based on the Japanese economic miracle. These books include W. Ouchi, *Theory Z: How American Management Can Meet the Japanese Challenge* (Reading, MA: Addison-Wesley, 1981); R.T. Pascale and A.G. Athos, *Art of Japanese Management* (New York: Simon and Schuster, 1982).

14. C.R. Emery and L.D. Fredenhall, "The Effect of Teams on Firm Profitability and Customer Satisfaction," *Journal of Service Research* 4 (2002): 217–29; G.S. Van der Vegt and O. Janssen, "Joint Impact of Interdependence and Group Diversity on Innovation," *Journal of Management* 29 (2003): 729–51.

15. R.E. Baumeister and M.R. Leary, "The Need to Belong: Desire for Interpersonal Attachments as a Fundamental Human Motivation," *Psychological Bulletin* 117 (1995): 497–529; S. Chen, H.C. Boucher, and M.P. Tapias, "The Relational Self Revealed: Integrative Conceptualization and Implications for Interpersonal Life," *Psychological Bulletin* 132, no. 2 (2006): 151–79; J.M. Feinberg and J.R. Aiello, "Social Facilitation: A Test of Competing Theories," *Journal of Applied Social Psychology* 36, no. 5 (2006): 1087–109; N.L. Kerr et al., "Psychological Mechanisms Underlying the Kohler Motivation Gain," *Personality & Social Psychology Bulletin* 33, no. 6 (2007): 828–41; A.M. Grant, "Relational Job Design and the Motivation to Make a Prosocial Difference," *Academy of Management Review* 32, no. 2 (2007): 393–417.

16. E.A. Locke et al, "The Importance of the Individual in an Age of Groupism," in *Groups at Work: Theory and Research* ed. M.E. Turner (Mahwah, NJ: Lawrence Erbaum Associates, 2001), 501–28; N.J. Allen and T.D. Hecht, "The 'Romance of Teams': Toward an Understanding of Its Psychological Underpinnings and Implications," *Journal of Occupational and Organizational Psychology* 77 (2004): 439–61.

17. I.D. Steiner, *Group Process and Productivity* (New York: Academic Press, 1972); N.L. Kerr and S.R. Tindale, "Group Performance and Decision Making," *Annual Review of Psychology* 55 (2004): 623–55.

18. M.W. McCarter and R.M. Sheremeta, "You Can't Put Old Wine in New Bottles: The Effect of Newcomers on Coordination in Groups," *PLoS ONE* 8, no. 1 (2013): e55058.

19. B.R. Staats, K.L. Milkman, and C.R. Fox, "The Team Scaling Fallacy: Underestimating the Declining Efficiency of Larger Teams," *Organizational Behavior and Human Decision Processes* 118, no. 2 (2012): 132–42. Brooks's Law is discussed in: F.P. Brooks, ed. *The Mythical Man-Month: Essays on Software Engineering*, Second ed. (Reading, MA: Addison-Wesley, 1995).

20. S.J. Karau and K.D. Williams, "Social Loafing: A Meta-Analytic Review and Theoretical Integration," *Journal of Personality and Social Psychology* 65 (1993): 681–706; R.C. Liden et al., "Social Loafing: A Field Investigation," *Journal of Management* 30 (2004): 285–304; L.L. Chidambaram, "Is out of Sight, out of Mind? An Empirical Study of Social Loafing in Technology-Supported Groups," *Information Systems Research* 16, no. 2 (2005): 149 –68; U.-C. Klehe and N. Anderson, "The Moderating Influence of Personality and Culture on Social Loafing in Typical Versus Maximum Performance Situations," *International Journal of Selection and Assessment* 15, no. 2 (2007): 250–62.

21. J.R. Engen, "Tough as Nails," *Bank Director*, July 2009, 24.

22. M. Erez and A. Somech, "Is Group Productivity Loss the Rule or the Exception? Effects of Culture and Group-Based Motivation," *Academy of Management Journal* 39 (1996): 1513–37; Kerr and Tindale, "Group Performance and Decision Making; A. Jassawalla, H. Sashittal, and A. Malshe, "Students' Perceptions of Social Loafing: Its Antecedents and Consequences in Undergraduate Business Classroom Teams," *Academy of Management Learning and Education* 8, no. 1 (2009): 42 –54.

23. G.P. Shea and R.A. Guzzo, "Group Effectiveness: What Really Matters?," *Sloan Management Review* 27 (1987): 33–46; J.R. Hackman et al., "Team Effectiveness in Theory and in Practice," in *Industrial and Organizational Psychology: Linking Theory with Practice*, ed. C.L. Cooper and E.A. Locke (Oxford, UK: Blackwell, 2000), 109–29.

24. M.A. West, C.S. Borrill, and K.L. Unsworth, "Team Effectiveness in Organizations," *International Review of Industrial and Organizational Psychology* 13 (1998): 1–48; M.A. Marks, J.E. Mathieu, and S.J. Zaccaro, "A Temporally Based Framework and Taxonomy of Team Processes," *Academy of Management Review* 26, no. 3 (2001): 356–76; J.E. McGrath, H. Arrow, and J.L. Berdahl, "The Study of Groups: Past, Present, and Future," *Personality & Social Psychology Review* 4, no. 1 (2000): 95–105.

25. M. Kouchaki et al., "The Treatment of the Relationship between Groups and Their Environments: A Review and Critical Examination of Common Assumptions in Research," *Group & Organization Management* 37, no. 2 (2012): 171–203.

26. Sundstrom, "The Challenges of Supporting Work Team Effectiveness; J.N. Choi, "External Activities and Team Effectiveness: Review and Theoretical Development," *Small Group Research* 33 (2002): 181–208; G. Hertel, S. Geister, and U. Konradt, "Managing Virtual Teams: A Review of

Current Empirical Research," *Human Resource Management Review* 15 (2005): 69–95; G.L. Stewart, "A Meta-Analytic Review of Relationships between Team Design Features and Team Performance," *Journal of Management* 32, no. 1 (2006): 29–54; J.B. Stryker and M.D. Santoro, "Facilitating Face-to-Face Communication in High-Tech Teams," *Research Technology Management* 55, no. 1 (2012): 51–56.

27. M.A. Campion, E.M. Papper, and G.J. Medsker, "Relations between Work Team Characteristics and Effectiveness: A Replication and Extension," *Personnel Psychology* 49 (1996): 429–52; D.C. Man and S.S.K. Lam, "The Effects of Job Complexity and Autonomy on Cohesiveness in Collectivistic and Individualistic Work Groups: A Cross-Cultural Analysis," *Journal of Organizational Behavior* 24 (2003): 979–1001; N. Sivasubramaniam, S.J. Liebowitz, and C.L. Lackman, "Determinants of New Product Development Team Performance: A Meta-Analytic Review," *Journal of Product Innovation Management* 29, no. 5 (2012): 803–20; M. Valentine and A.C. Edmondson, *Team Scaffolds: How Minimal Team Structures Enable Role-Based Coordination*, Harvard Business School working paper (Boston, MA: 15 April 2013).

28. M.-P. Gröndahl, "Le Plan RéUssite Du Patron De Psa," *Paris Match*, 27 September 2010; PSA Peugeot Citroën, *2010 Sustainable Development and Annual Report*, (Paris: 2011); M. Assayas, "Les Médias Sont Ennuyés," *Enjeux Les Echos*, 1 February 2011, 46.

29. G. Van der Vegt and E. Van de Vliert, "Intragroup Interdependence and Effectiveness: Review and Proposed Directions for Theory and Practice," *Journal of Managerial Psychology* 17, no. 1/2 (2002): 50–67; R. Wageman, "The Meaning of Interdependence," in *Groups at Work: Theory and Research* ed. M.E. Turner (Mahwah, NJ: Lawrence Erlbaum Associates, 2001), 197–217; M.R. Barrick et al., "The Moderating Role of Top Management Team Interdependence: Implications for Real Teams and Working Groups," *Academy of Management Journal* 50, no. 3 (2007): 544–57.

30. S.W.J. Kozlowski, and B.S.Bell, "Work groups and teams in organizations," in W.C. Borman, D.R. Ilgen, and R.J. Klimoski (Eds.), *Handbook of psychology: Vol. 12. Industrial and organizational psychology* (London, UK: Wiley, 2003): 333–375.

31. J.R. Katzenbach and D.K. Smith, *The Wisdom of Teams: Creating the High-Performance Organization* (Boston, MA: Harvard University Press, 1993), 45–47; S.J. Guastello, "Nonlinear Dynamics of Team Performance and Adaptability in Emergency Response," *Human Factors: The Journal of the Human Factors and Ergonomics Society* 52, no. 2 (2010): 162–72; C. Aube, V. Rousseau, and S. Tremblay, "Team Size and Quality of Group Experience: The More the Merrier?," *Group Dynamics-Theory Research and Practice* 15, no. 4 (2011): 357–75.

32. J. O'Toole, "The Power of Many: Building a High-Performance Management Team," *ceoforum.com.au* (2003).

33. J.S. Mueller, "Why Individuals in Larger Teams Perform Worse," *Organizational Behavior and Human Decision Processes* 117, no. 1 (2012): 111–24.

34. F.P. Morgenson, M.H. Reider, and M.A. Campion, "Selecting Individuals in Team Setting: The Importance of Social Skills, Personality Characteristics, and Teamwork Knowledge," *Personnel Psychology* 58, no. 3 (2005): 583–611; V. Rousseau, C. Aubé, and A. Savoie, "Teamwork Behaviors: A Review and an Integration of Frameworks," *Small Group Research* 37, no. 5 (2006): 540–70. For a detailed examination of the characteristics of effective team members, see M.L. Loughry, M.W. Ohland, and D.D. Moore, "Development of a Theory-Based Assessment of Team Member Effectiveness," *Educational and Psychological Measurement* 67, no. 3 (2007): 505–24.

35. S. McComb et al., "The Five Ws of Team Communication," *Industrial Management* 54, no. 5 (2012): 10–13.

36. C.E. Hårtel and D. Panipucci, "How 'Bad Apples' Spoil the Bunch: Faultlines, Emotional Levers, and Exclusion in the Workplace," *Research on Emotion in Organizations* 3 (2007): 287–310; C.O.L.H. Porter et al., "Backing up Behaviors in Teams: The Role of Personality and Legitimacy of Need," *Journal of Applied Psychology* 88, no. 3 (2003): 391–403. The bad apple phenomenon is also identified in executive team "derailers". See: R. Wageman et al., *Senior Leadership Teams* (Boston, MA: Harvard Business School Press, 2008), pp. 97–102.

37. D. van Knippenberg, C.K.W. De Dreu, and A.C. Homan, "Work Group Diversity and Group Performance: An Integrative Model and Research Agenda," *Journal of Applied Psychology* 89, no. 6 (2004): 1008–22; E. Mannix and M.A. Neale, "What Differences Make a Difference?: The Promise and Reality of Diverse Teams in Organizations," *Psychological Science in the Public Interest* 6, no. 2 (2005): 31–55; G.K. Stahl et al., "A Look at the Bright Side of Multicultural Team Diversity," *Scandinavian Journal of Management* 26, no. 4 (2010): 439–47; H. Haas, "How Can We Explain Mixed Effects of Diversity on Team Performance? A Review with Emphasis on Context," *Equality, Diversity and Inclusion: An International Journal* 29, no. 5 (2010): 458–90; L.M. Shore et al., "Inclusion and Diversity in Work Groups: A Review and Model for Future Research," *Journal of Management* 37, no. 4 (2011): 1262–89.

38. D.C. Lau and J.K. Murnighan, "Interactions within Groups and Subgroups: The Effects of Demographic Faultlines," *Academy of Management Journal* 48, no. 4 (2005): 645–59; S.M.B. Thatcher and P.C. Patel, "Group Faultlines: A Review, Integration, and Guide to Future Research," *Journal of Management* 38, no. 4 (2012): 969–1009.

39. A.P. Hare, "Types of Roles in Small Groups: A Bit of History and a Current Perspective," *Small Group Research* 25 (1994): 443–48; A. Aritzeta, S. Swailes, and B. Senior, "Belbin's Team Role Model: Development, Validity and Applications for Team Building," *Journal of Management Studies* 44, no. 1 (2007): 96–118.

40. S.H.N. Leung, J.W.K. Chan, and W.B. Lee, "The Dynamic Team Role Behavior: The Approaches of Investigation," *Team Performance Management* 9 (2003): 84–90; G.L. Stewart, I.S. Fulmer, and M.R. Barrick, "An Exploration of Member Roles as a Multilevel Linking Mechanism for Individual Traits and Team Outcomes," *Personnel Psychology* 58, no. 2 (2005): 343–65.

41. K. Lewis, "Measuring transactive memory systems in the field: Scale development and validation," *Journal of Applied Psychology*, 88, (2003): 587–604.

42. D.C. Feldman, "The Development and Enforcement of Group Norms," *Academy of Management Review* 9 (1984): 47–53; E. Fehr and U. Fischbacher, "Social Norms and Human Cooperation," *Trends in Cognitive Sciences* 8, no. 4 (2004): 185–90.

43. N. Ellemers and F. Rink, "Identity in Work Groups: The Beneficial and Detrimental Consequences of Multiple Identities and Group Norms for Collaboration and Group Performance," *Advances in Group Processes* 22 (2005): 1–41.

44. K.-D. Opp, "How Do Norms Emerge? An Outline of a Theory," *Mind & Society* 2, no. 1 (2001): 101–28.

45. J.J. Dose and R.J. Klimoski, "The Diversity of Diversity: Work Values Effects on Formative Team Processes," *Human Resource Management Review* 9, no. 1 (1999): 83–108.

46. S. Taggar and R. Ellis, "The Role of Leaders in Shaping Formal Team Norms," *Leadership Quarterly* 18, no. 2 (2007): 105–20.

47. D.J. Beal et al., "Cohesion and Performance in Groups: A Meta-Analytic Clarification of Construct Relations," *Journal of Applied Psychology* 88, no. 6 (2003): 989–1004; Kozlowski and Ilgen, "Enhancing the Effectiveness of Work Groups and Teams."

48. R.M. Montoya, R.S. Horton, and J. Kirchner, "Is Actual Similarity Necessary for Attraction? A Meta-Analysis of Actual and Perceived Similarity," *Journal of Social and Personal Relationships* 25, no. 6 (2008): 889–922; M.T. Rivera, s.B. Soderstrom, and B. Uzzi, "Dynamics of Dyads in Social Networks: Assortative, Relational, and Proximity Mechanisms," *Annual Review of Sociology* 36 (2010): 91–115.

49. van Knippenberg, De Dreu, and Homan, "Work Group Diversity and Group Performance; K.A. Jehn, G.B. Northcraft, and M.A. Neale, "Why Differences Make a Difference: A Field Study of Diversity, Conflict, and Performance in Workgroups," *Administrative Science Quarterly* 44, no. 4 (1999): 741–63. For evidence that diversity/similarity does not always influence cohesion, see S.S. Webber and L.M. Donahue, "Impact of Highly and Less Job-Related Diversity on Work Group Cohesion and Performance: A Meta-Analysis," *Journal of Management* 27, no. 2 (2001): 141–62.

50. E. Aronson and J. Mills, "The Effects of Severity of Initiation on Liking for a Group," *Journal of Abnormal and Social Psychology* 59 (1959): 177–81; J.E. Hautaluoma and R.S. Enge, "Early Socialization into a Work Group: Severity of Initiations Revisited," *Journal of Social Behavior & Personality* 6 (1991): 725–48.

51. B. Mullen and C. Copper, "The Relation between Group Cohesiveness and Performance: An Integration," *Psychological Bulletin* 115 (1994): 210–27; C.J. Fullagar and D.O. Egleston, "Norming and Performing: Using Microworlds to Understand the Relationship between

Team Cohesiveness and Performance," *Journal of Applied Social Psychology* 38, no. 10 (2008): 2574–93.

52. Wageman et al., *Senior Leadership Teams*, pp.69–70.

53. M. Rempel and R.J. Fisher, "Perceived Threat, Cohesion, and Group Problem Solving in Intergroup Conflict," *International Journal of Conflict Management* 8 (1997): 216–34; M.E. Turner and T. Horvitz, "The Dilemma of Threat: Group Effectiveness and Ineffectiveness under Adversity," in *Groups at Work: Theory and Research* ed. M.E. Turner (Mahwah, NJ: Lawrence Erlbaum Associates, 2001), 445–70.

54. A.V. Carron et al., "Cohesion and Performance in Sport: A Meta-Analysis," *Journal of Sport and Exercise Psychology* 24 (2002): 168–88; Beal et al., "Cohesion and Performance in Groups; Fullagar and Egleston, "Norming and Performing; DeChurch and Mesmer-Magnus, "The Cognitive Underpinnings of Effective Teamwork: A Meta-Analysis."

55. W. Piper et al., "Cohesion as a Basic Bond in Groups," *Human Relations* 36 (1983): 93–108; C.A. O'Reilly, D.E. Caldwell, and W.P. Barnett, "Work Group Demography, Social Integration, and Turnover," *Administrative Science Quarterly* 34 (1989): 21–37.

56. S.M. Gully, D.J. Devine, and D.J. Whitney, "A Meta-Analysis of Cohesion and Performance: Effects of Level of Analysis and Task Interdependence," *Small Group Research* 43, no. 6 (2012): 702–25.

57. F. Piccolo, "Brownie Points," Atlantic Business, Oct/Nov 2004, 22; http://www.southshorenow.ca/about/lighthouse/index.php Retrieved January 14, 2010.

58. K.L. Gammage, A.V. Carron, and P.A. Estabrooks, "Team Cohesion and Individual Productivity: The Influence of the Norm for Productivity and the Identifiablity of Individual Effort," *Small Group Research* 32 (2001): 3–18; C. Langfred, "Is Group Cohesiveness a Double-Edged Sword? An Investigation of the Effects of Cohesiveness on Performance," *Small Group Research* 29 (1998): 124–43; N.L. Jimmieson, M. Peach, and K.M. White, "Utilizing the Theory of Planned Behavior to Inform Change Management," *Journal of Applied Behavioral Science* 44, no. 2 (2008): 237–62. Concerns about existing research on cohesion-performance are discussed in: M. Casey-Campbell and M.L. Martens, "Sticking It All Together: A Critical Assessment of the Group Cohesion-Performance Literature," *International Journal of Management Reviews* 11, no. 2 (2009): 223–46.

59. Fullagar and Egleston, "Norming and Performing."

60. S.M. Gully, K.A. Incalcaterra, A. Joshi, and J.M. Beaubien, "A meta-analysis of team-efficacy, potency, and performance: Interdependence and level of analysis as moderators of observed relationships," *Journal of Applied Psychology* 87 (2002): 819–832; A.D. Stajkovic, D. Lee, and A.J. Nyberg, "Collective efficacy, group potency, and group performance: Meta-analyses of their relationships, and test of a mediation model," *Journal of Applied Psychology* 94 (2009): 814–828.

61. A. Bandura, Self-efficacy: The exercise of control. (New York: W.H. Freeman, 2002); C.B. Gibson and P.C. Earley, "Collective cognition in action: Accumulation, interaction, examination, and accommodation in the development and operation of group efficacy beliefs in the workplace," *Academy of Management Review*, 32, (2007): 438–458.

62. P.W. Mulvey, and H.J. Klein, "The impact of perceived loafing and collective efficacy on group goal processes and group performance," *Organizational Behavior and Human Decision Processes*, 74, (1998): 62–87.

63. K. Tasa and G. Whyte, "Collective efficacy and vigilant problem solving in group decision making: A non-linear model," *Organizational Behavior and Human Decision Processes*, 92, (2005): 119–129.

64. K. Tasa, G.J. Sears, and A.C.H. Schat, "Personality and teamwork behavior in context: The cross-level moderating role of collective efficacy," *Journal of Organizational Behavior*, 32, (2011): 65–85.

65. K. Tasa, S. Taggar, and G.H. Seijts, "The development of collective efficacy in teams: A multilevel and longitudinal perspective," *Journal of Applied Psychology*, 92, (2007): 17–27.

66. S.W. Lester, B.M. Meglino, and M.A. Korsgaard, "The antecedents and consequences of group potency: A longitudinal investigation of newly formed work groups," *Academy of Management Journal*, 45, (2002): 352–368.

67. D.M. Rousseau et al., "Not So Different after All: A Cross-Discipline View of Trust," *Academy of Management Review* 23 (1998): 393–404; R. Searle, A. Weibel, and D.N. Den Hartog, "Employee Trust in Organizational Contexts," in *International Review of Industrial and Organizational Psychology 2011* (John Wiley & Sons, Inc., 2011), 143–91.

68. D.J. McAllister, "Affect- and Cognition-Based Trust as Foundations for Interpersonal Cooperation in Organizations," *Academy of Management Journal* 38, no. 1 (1995): 24–59; M. Williams, "In Whom We Trust: Group Membership as an Affective Context for Trust Development," *Academy of Management Review* 26, no. 3 (2001): 377–96; M. Pirson and D. Malhotra, "Foundations of Organizational Trust: What Matters to Different Stakeholders?," *Organization Science* 22, no. 4 (2011): 1087–104.

69. R.J. Lewicki, E.C. Tomlinson, and N. Gillespie, "Models of Interpersonal Trust Development: Theoretical Approaches, Empirical Evidence, and Future Directions," *Journal of Management* 32, no. 6 (2006): 991–1022.

70. Lewicki, Tomlinson, and Gillespie, "Models of Interpersonal Trust Development: Theoretical Approaches, Empirical Evidence, and Future Directions; F.-Y. Kuo and C.-P. Yu, "An Exploratory Study of Trust Dynamics in Work-Oriented Virtual Teams," *Journal of Computer-Mediated Communication* 14, no. 4 (2009): 823–54.

71. E.M. Whitener et al., "Managers as Initiators of Trust: An Exchange Relationship Framework for Understanding Managerial Trustworthy Behavior," *Academy of Management Review* 23 (1998): 513–30; J.M. Kouzes and B.Z. Posner, *The Leadership Challenge*, 3rd ed. (San Francisco, CA: Jossey-Bass, 2002), Chap. 2; T. Simons, "Behavioral Integrity: The Perceived Alignment between Managers' Words and Deeds as a Research Focus," *Organization Science* 13, no. 1 (2002): 18–35.

72. S.L. Jarvenpaa and D.E. Leidner, "Communication and Trust in Global Virtual Teams," *Organization Science* 10 (1999): 791–815; L.P. Robert, A.R. Dennis, and Y.-T.C. Hung, "Individual Swift Trust and Knowledge-Based Trust in Face-to-Face and Virtual Team Members," *Journal of Management Information Systems* 26, no. 2 (2009): 241–79; C.B. Crisp and S.L. Jarvenpaa, "Swift Trust in Global Virtual Teams Trusting Beliefs and Normative Actions," *Journal of Personnel Psychology* 12, no. 1 (2013): 45–56.

73. K.T. Dirks and D.L. Ferrin, "The Role of Trust in Organizations," *Organization Science* 12, no. 4 (2004): 450–67.

74. B.B. Morgan, E. Salas, and A.S. Glickman, "An analysis of team evolution and maturation. *The Journal of General Psychology*, 120, (1993): 277–291.

75. V. Rousseau, C. Aube, and A. Savoie, (2006): 540–570.

76. M.A. Marks, J.E. Mathieu, and S.J. Zaccaro, (2001): 356–376.

77. D.G. Ancona, "Outward bound: Strategies for team survival in an organization," *Academy of Management Journal*, 33, (1990): 334–365; D.G. Ancona, and D.F. Caldwell, "Bridging the boundary: External activity and performance in organizational teams," *Administrative Science Quarterly*, 37, (1992): 634–665.

78. A. Joshi, N. Pandey, and G.H. Han, "Bracketing team boundary spanning: An examination of task-based, team-level, and contextual antecedents," *Journal of Organizational Behavior*, 30, (2009): 731–759.

79. D.G. Ancona and D.F. Caldwell, (1992): 634–665.

80. K. Tasa, S. Taggar, and G.H. Seijts, "The development of collective efficacy in teams: A multilevel and longitudinal perspective," *Journal of Applied Psychology*, 92, (2007): 17–27.

81. B.W. Tuckman and M.A.C. Jensen, "Stages of Small-Group Development Revisited," *Group and Organization Studies* 2 (1977): 419–42; B.W. Tuckman, "Developmental Sequence in Small Groups," *Group Facilitation* (2001): 66–81.

82. C.J. Gersick, "Time and transition in work teams: Toward a new model of group development," *Academy of Management journal, 31* (1), (1988): 9–41.

83. M.J. Waller, M.E. Zellmer-Bruhn, and R.C. Giambatista, "Watching the clock: Group pacing behavior under dynamic deadlines," *Academy of Management Journal, 45* (5), (2002): 1046–1055.

84. G.R. Bushe and G.H. Coetzer, "Group Development and Team Effectiveness: Using Cognitive Representations to Measure Group Development and Predict Task Performance and Group Viability," *Journal of Applied Behavioral Science* 43, no. 2 (2007): 184–212.

85. C. Lee, J.-L. Farh, and Z.-J. Chen, "Promoting Group Potency in Project Teams: The Importance of Group Identification," *Journal of Organizational Behavior* 32, no. 8 (2011): 1147–62.

86. B.-C. Lim and K.J. Klein, "Team Mental Models and Team Performance: A Field Study of the Effects of Team Mental Model Similarity and Accuracy," *Journal of Organizational Behavior* 27 (2006): 403–18; S.W.J. Kozlowski and D.R. Ilgen, "Enhancing the Effectiveness of Work Groups and Teams," *Psychological Science in the Public Interest* 7, no. 3 (2006): 77–124; R. Rico, M. Sánchez-Manzanares, and C. Gibson, "Team Implicit Coordination Processes: A Team Knowledge-Based Approach," *Academy of Management Review* 33, no. 1 (2008): 163–84; S. McComb et al., "Temporal Patterns of Mental Model Convergence: Implications for Distributed Teams Interacting in Electronic Collaboration Spaces," *Human Factors: The Journal of the Human Factors and Ergonomics Society* 52, no. 2 (2010): 264–81.

87. L.A. DeChurch and J.R. Mesmer-Magnus, "The Cognitive Underpinnings of Effective Teamwork: A Meta-Analysis," *Journal of Applied Psychology* 95, no. 1 (2010): 32–53.

88. W.G. Dyer, *Team Building: Current Issues and New Alternatives*, 3rd ed. (Reading, MA: Addison-Wesley, 1995); C.A. Beatty and B.A. Barker, *Building Smart Teams: Roadmap to High Performance* (Thousand Oaks, CA: Sage Publications, 2004).

89. J.E. Mathieu et al., "Scaling the Quality of Teammates' Mental Models: Equifinality and Normative Comparisons," *Journal of Organizational Behavior* 26 (2005): 37–56; J. Langan-Fox and J. Anglim, "Mental Models, Team Mental Models, and Performance: Process, Development, and Future Directions," *Human Factors and Ergonomics in Manufacturing* 14, no. 4 (2004): 331–52.

90. I. Nadler, P.M. Sanderson, and H.G. Liley, "The Accuracy of Clinical Assessments as a Measure for Teamwork Effectiveness," *Simulation in Healthcare* 6, no. 5 (2011): 260–68.

91. R.W. Woodman and J.J. Sherwood, "The Role of Team Development in Organizational Effectiveness: A Critical Review," *Psychological Bulletin* 88 (1980): 166–86.

92. L. Mealiea and R. Baltazar, "A Strategic Guide for Building Effective Teams," *Personnel Management* 34, no. 2 (2005): 141–60.

93. G.E. Huszczo, "Training for Team Building," *Training and Development Journal* 44 (1990): 37–43; P. McGraw, "Back from the Mountain: Outdoor Management Development Programs and How to Ensure the Transfer of Skills to the Workplace," *Asia Pacific Journal of Human Resources* 31 (1993): 52–61.

94. Two of the most important changes in teams are empowerment (evident in self-directed teams) and technology and distance (evident in virtual teams). See: Tannenbaum et al., "Teams Are Changing."

95. Mohrman, Cohen, and Mohrman Jr., *Designing Team-Based Organizations: New Forms for Knowledge Work;* D.E. Yeatts and C. Hyten, *High-Performing Self-Managed Work Teams: A Comparison of Theory and Practice* (Thousand Oaks, CA: Sage, 1998); E.E. Lawler, *Organizing for High Performance* (San Francisco, CA: Jossey-Bass, 2001); R.J. Torraco, "Work Design Theory: A Review and Critique with Implications for Human Resource Development," *Human Resource Development Quarterly* 16, no. 1 (2005): 85–109.

96. "The Amazing Chase," http://www.calgaryteambuilding.com/teambuilding_chase.php Retrieved January, 15, 2011; "Recent Client Feedback," http://www.calgaryteambuilding.com/teambuilding_chase.php Retrieved January 15, 2011.

97. "Absence Makes the Team Uneasy," News release (Menlo Park, NJ: OfficeTeam, 6 March 2008); "Go Teams! Firms Can't Do without Them"; N. Weil, "Global Team Management: Continental Divides," *CIO*, 23 January 2008.

98. P. Panchak, "Production Workers Can Be Your Competitive Edge," *Industry Week*, October 2004, 11; S.K. Muthusamy, J.V. Wheeler, and B.L. Simmons, "Self-Managing Work Teams: Enhancing Organizational Innovativeness," *Organization Development Journal* 23, no. 3 (2005): 53–66.

99. Emery and Fredenhall, "The Effect of Teams on Firm Profitability and Customer Satisfaction; A. Krause and H. Dunckel, "Work Design and Customer Satisfaction: Effects of the Implementation of Semi-Autonomous Group Work on Customer Satisfaction Considering Employee Satisfaction and Group Performance (Translated Abstract)," *Zeitschrift Fur Arbeits-Und Organisationspsychologie* 47, no. 4 (2003): 182–93; H. van Mierlo et al., "Self-Managing Teamwork and Psychological Well-Being: Review of a Multilevel Research Domain," *Group & Organization Management* 30, no. 2 (2005): 211–35; G.L. Stewart, S.H. Courtright, and M.R. Barrick, "Peer-Based Control in Self-Managing Teams: Linking Rational and Normative Influence with Individual and Group Performance," *Journal of Applied Psychology* 97, no. 2 (2012): 435–47.

100. Moldaschl and Weber, "The 'Three Waves' of Industrial Group Work; W. Niepce and E. Molleman, "Work Design Issues in Lean Production from Sociotechnical System Perspective: Neo-Taylorism or the Next Step in Sociotechnical Design?," *Human Relations* 51, no. 3 (1998): 259–87; J.L. Cordery et al., "The Impact of Autonomy and Task Uncertainty on Team Performance: A Longitudinal Field Study," *Journal of Organizational Behavior* 31 (2010): 240–58.

101. E. Ulich and W.G. Weber, "Dimensions, Criteria, and Evaluation of Work Group Autonomy," in *Handbook of Work Group Psychology* ed. M.A. West (Chichester, UK: John Wiley & Sons, Inc., 1996), 247–82.

102. K.P. Carson and G.L. Stewart, "Job Analysis and the Sociotechnical Approach to Quality: A Critical Examination," *Journal of Quality Management* 1 (1996): 49–65; C.C. Manz and G.L. Stewart, "Attaining Flexible Stability by Integrating Total Quality Management and Socio-Technical Systems Theory," *Organization Science* 8 (1997): 59–70.

103. J. Lipnack and J. Stamps, *Virtual Teams: People Working across Boundaries with Technology* (New York: John Wiley & Sons, Inc., 2001); Hertel, Geister, and Konradt, "Managing Virtual Teams; L. Schweitzer and L. Duxbury, "Conceptualizing and Measuring the Virtuality of Teams," *Information Systems Journal* 20, no. 3 (2010): 267–95.

104. Weil, "Global Team Management: Continental Divides."

105. S. Kiesler and J.N. Cummings, "What Do We Know About Proximity and Distance in Work Groups? A Legacy of Research," in *Distributed Work*,, ed. P. Hinds and S. Kiesler (Cambridge, MA: MIT Press, 2002), 57–80; Rivera, Soderstrom, and Uzzi, "Dynamics of Dyads in Social Networks."

106. M. O'Brien, "Long-Distance Relationship Troubles," *Human Resource Executive Online*, 7 July 2009.

107. *Long-Distance Loathing (Summary and Data)*, VitalSmarts (Provo, Utah: March 2009).

108. "Virtual Teams Now a Reality," News release for Institute for Corporate Productivity (Seattle, WA: Institute for Corporate Productivity, 4 September 2008).

109. L.L. Martins, L.L. Gilson, and M.T. Maynard, "Virtual Teams: What Do We Know and Where Do We Go from Here?," *Journal of Management* 30, no. 6 (2004): 805–35.

110. J.L. Cordery and C. Soo, "Overcoming Impediments to Virtual Team Effectiveness," *Human Factors and Ergonomics in Manufacturing & Service Industries* 18, no. 5 (2008): 487–500; A. Ortiz de Guinea, J. Webster, and D.S. Staples, "A Meta-Analysis of the Consequences of Virtualness on Team Functioning," *Information & Management* 49, no. 6 (2012): 301–08.

111. G. Hertel, U. Konradt, and K. Voss, "Competencies for Virtual Teamwork: Development and Validation of a Web-Based Selection Tool for Members of Distributed Teams," *European Journal of Work and Organizational Psychology* 15, no. 4 (2006): 477–504; J.M. Wilson et al., "Perceived Proximity in Virtual Work: Explaining the Paradox of Far-but-Close," *Organization Studies* 29, no. 7 (2008): 979–1002; L.L. Martins and M.C. Schilpzand, "Global Virtual Teams: Key Developments, Research Gaps, and Future Directions," in *Research in Personnel and Human Resources Management*, ed. A. Joshi, J.J. Martocchio, and H. Liao, *Research in Personnel and Human Resources Management* (2011), 1–72.

112. G.G. Harwood, "Design Principles for Successful Virtual Teams," in *The Handbook of High-Performance Virtual Teams: A Toolkit for Collaborating across Boundaries*, ed. J. Nemiro and M.M. Beyerlein (San Francisco, CA: Jossey-Bass, 2008), 59–84. Also see: H. Duckworth, "How TRW Automotive Helps Global Virtual Teams Perform at the Top of Their Game," *Global Business and Organizational Excellence* 28, no. 1 (2008): 6–16; L. Dubé and D. Robey, "Surviving the Paradoxes of Virtual Teamwork," *Information Systems Journal* 19, no. 1 (2009): 3–30.

113. Dubé and Robey, "Surviving the Paradoxes of Virtual Teamwork."

114. V.H. Vroom and A.G. Jago, *The New Leadership* (Englewood Cliffs, NJ: Prentice-Hall, 1988), 28–29.

115. M. Diehl and W. Stroebe, "Productivity Loss in Idea-Generating Groups: Tracking Down the Blocking Effects," *Journal of Personality and Social Psychology* 61 (1991): 392–403; B.A. Nijstad, W. Stroebe, and H.F.M. Lodewijkx, "Production Blocking and Idea Generation: Does Blocking Interfere with Cognitive Processes?," *Journal of Experimental Social Psychology* 39, no. 6 (2003): 531–48; B.A. Nijstad and W. Stroebe, "How the Group Affects the Mind: A Cognitive Model of Idea Generation in Groups," *Personality & Social Psychology Review* 10, no. 3 (2006):

186–213; W. Stroebe, B.A. Nijstad, and E.F. Rietzschel, "Beyond Productivity Loss in Brainstorming Groups: The Evolution of a Question," in *Advances in Experimental Social Psychology*, ed. P.Z. Mark and M.O. James (Academic Press, 2010), 157–203.

116. B.E. Irmer, P. Bordia, and D. Abusah, "Evaluation Apprehension and Perceived Benefits in Interpersonal and Database Knowledge Sharing," *Academy of Management Proceedings* (2002): B1–B6.

117. D. Miller, *The Icarus Paradox: How Exceptional Companies Bring About Their Own Downfall* (New York: HarperBusiness, 1990); G. Whyte, "Recasting Janis's Groupthink Model: The Key Role of Collective Efficacy in Decision Fiascoes," *Organizational Behavior and Human Decision Processes* 73, no. 2–3 (1998): 185–209; K. Tasa and G. Whyte, "Collective Efficacy and Vigilant Problem Solving in Group Decision Making: A Non-Linear Model," *Organizational Behavior and Human Decision Processes* 96, no. 2 (2005): 119–29; H.J.M. Kooij-de Bode, D. Van Knippenberg, and W.P. Van Ginkel, "Good Effects of Bad Feelings: Negative Affectivity and Group Decision-Making," *British Journal of Management* 21, no. 2 (2010): 375–92; S.K. Lam and J. Schaubroeck, "Information Sharing and Group Efficacy Influences on Communication and Decision Quality," *Asia Pacific Journal of Management* 28, no. 3 (2011): 509–28; J.A. Minson and J.S. Mueller, "The Cost of Collaboration: Why Joint Decision Making Exacerbates Rejection of Outside Information," *Psychological Science* 23, no. 3 (2012): 219–24; K.D. Clark and P.G. Maggitti, "TMT Potency and Strategic Decision-Making in High Technology Firms," *Journal of Management Studies* 49, no. 7 (2012): 1168–93.

118. The term "brainstorm" dates back to a New York murder case in 1909 as one expert's reference to temporary insanity. By the early 1930s, a brainstorm was associated with creative thinking. Advertising executive Alex Osborn (the "O" in BBDO, the largest creative agency owned by Omnicom) first described the brainstorming process in the little-known 1942 booklet How to Think Up (p. 29). Osborn gave a fuller description of the brainstorming process in his popular 1948 (Your Creative Power) and 1953 (Applied Imagination) books. See: A.F. Osborn, *How to Think Up* (New York: McGraw-Hill, 1942), Chap. 4; A.F. Osborn, *Your Creative Power* (New York: Charles Scribner's Sons, 1948); A.F. Osborn, *Applied Imagination* (New York: Charles Scribner's Sons, 1953).

119. B. Mullen, C. Johnson, and E. Salas, "Productivity Loss in Brainstorming Groups: A Meta-Analytic Integration," *Basic and Applied Psychology* 12 (1991): 2–23. The 1957 business article critiquing brainstorming is: B.S. Benson, "Let's Toss This Idea Up," *Fortune*, October 1957, 145–46.

120. R.I. Sutton and A. Hargadon, "Brainstorming Groups in Context: Effectiveness in a Product Design Firm," *Administrative Science Quarterly* 41 (1996): 685–718; T. Kelley, *The Art of Innovation* (New York: Currency Doubleday, 2001); V.R. Brown and P.B. Paulus, "Making Group Brainstorming More Effective: Recommendations from an Associative Memory Perspective," *Current Directions in Psychological Science* 11, no. 6 (2002): 208–12; K. Leggett Dugosh and P.B. Paulus, "Cognitive and Social Comparison Processes in Brainstorming," *Journal of Experimental Social Psychology* 41, no. 3 (2005): 313–20.

121. J. Baruah and P.B. Paulus, "Effects of Training on Idea Generation in Groups," *Small Group Research* 39, no. 5 (2008): 523–41; N.W. Kohn, P.B. Paulus, and Y.H. Choi, "Building on the Ideas of Others: An Examination of the Idea Combination Process," *Journal of Experimental Social Psychology* 47 (2011): 554–61.

122. N.W. Kohn and S.M. Smith, "Collaborative Fixation: Effects of Others' Ideas on Brainstorming," *Applied Cognitive Psychology* 25, no. 3 (2011): 359–71; A. Fink et al., "Stimulating Creativity Via the Exposure to Other People's Ideas," *Human Brain Mapping* 33, no. 11 (2012): 2603–10.

123. P.A. Heslin, "Better Than Brainstorming? Potential Contextual Boundary Conditions to Brainwriting for Idea Generation in Organizations," *Journal of Occupational and Organizational Psychology* 82, no. 1 (2009): 129–45; J.S. Linsey and B. Becker, "Effectiveness of Brainwriting Techniques: Comparing Nominal Groups to Real Teams," in *Design Creativity 2010*, ed. T. Taura and Y. Nagai (London, UK: Springer, 2011), 165–71; N. Michinov, "Is Electronic Brainstorming or Brainwriting the Best Way to Improve Creative Performance in Groups? An Overlooked Comparison of Two Idea-Generation Techniques," *Journal of Applied Social Psychology* 42 (2012): E222–E243.

124. R.B. Gallupe, L.M. Bastianutti, and W.H. Cooper, "Unblocking Brainstorms," *Journal of Applied Psychology* 76 (1991): 137–42; W.H. Cooper et al., "Some Liberating Effects of Anonymous Electronic Brainstorming," *Small Group Research* 29, no. 2 (1998): 147–78; A.R. Dennis, B.H. Wixom, and R.J. Vandenberg, "Understanding Fit and Appropriation Effects in Group Support Systems Via Meta-Analysis," *MIS Quarterly* 25, no. 2 (2001): 167–93; D.M. DeRosa, C.L. Smith, and D.A. Hantula, "The Medium Matters: Mining the Long-Promised Merit of Group Interaction in Creative Idea Generation Tasks in a Meta-Analysis of the Electronic Group Brainstorming Literature," *Computers in Human Behavior* 23, no. 3 (2007): 1549–81.

125. A.L. Delbecq, A.H. Van de Ven, and D.H. Gustafson, *Group Techniques for Program Planning: A Guide to Nominal Group and Delphi Processes* (Middleton, Wis: Green Briar Press, 1986).

126. D.M. Spencer, "Facilitating Public Participation in Tourism Planning on American Indian Reservations: A Case Study Involving the Nominal Group Technique," *Tourism Management* 31, no. 5 (2011): 684–90.

127. S. Frankel, "NGT + MDS: An Adaptation of the Nominal Group Technique for Ill-Structured Problems," *Journal of Applied Behavioral Science* 23 (1987): 543–51; H. Barki and A. Pinsonneault, "Small Group Brainstorming and Idea Quality: Is Electronic Brainstorming the Most Effective Approach?," *Small Group Research* 32, no. 2 (2001): 158–205.

128. P.P. Lago et al., "Structuring Group Decision Making in a Web-Based Environment by Using the Nominal Group Technique," *Computers & Industrial Engineering* 52, no. 2 (2007): 277–95.

CHAPTER 9

1. http://www.microsoft.com/Canada/casestudies/Case_Study_Detail.aspx?casestudyid=4000007261, Microsoft Canada | BC Hydro gets Connected with SharePoint 2010–Microsoft Canada | Videos–YouTube.

2. A.H. Van de Ven, A.L. Delbecq, and R. Koenig, Jr., "Determinants of Coordination Modes within Organizations," *American Sociological Review* 41, no. 2 (1976): 322–38; J.H. Gittell, R. Seidner, and J. Wimbush, "A Relational Model of How High-Performance Work Systems Work," *Organization Science* 21, no. 2 (2010): 490–506; R. Foy et al., "Meta-Analysis: Effect of Interactive Communication between Collaborating Primary Care Physicians and Specialists," *Annals of Internal Medicine* 152, no. 4 (2010): 247–58.

3. C. Barnard, *The Functions of the Executive* (Cambridge, MA: Harvard University Press, 1938), pg. 82. Barnard's entire statement also refers to the other features of organizations that we describe in Chapter 1, namely that (a) people are willing to contribute their effort to the organization and (b) they have a common purpose.

4. M.T. Hansen, M.L. Mors, and B. Løvås, "Knowledge Sharing in Organizations: Multiple Networks, Multiple Phases," *Academy of Management Journal* 48, no. 5 (2005): 776–93; S.R. Murray and J. Peyrefitte, "Knowledge Type and Communication Media Choice in the Knowledge Transfer Process," *Journal of Managerial Issues* 19, no. 1 (2007): 111–33; S.L. Hoe and S.L. McShane, "Structural and Informal Knowledge Acquisition and Dissemination in Organizational Learning: An Exploratory Analysis," *Learning Organization* 17, no. 4 (2010): 364–86.

5. J. O'Toole and W. Bennis, "What's Needed Next: A Culture of Candor," *Harvard Business Review* 87, no. 6 (2009): 54–61.

6. W.J.L. Elving, "The Role of Communication in Organisational Change," *Corporate Communications* 10, no. 2 (2005): 129–38; P.M. Leonardi, T.B. Neeley, and E.M. Gerber, "How Managers Use Multiple Media: Discrepant Events, Power, and Timing in Redundant Communication," *Organization Science* 23, no. 1 (2012): 98–117; D.A. Tucker, P. Yeow, and G.T. Viki, "Communicating During Organizational Change Using Social Accounts: The Importance of Ideological Accounts," *Management Communication Quarterly* 27, no. 2 (2013): 184–209.

7. N. Ellemers, R. Spears, and B. Doosje, "Self and Social Identity," *Annual Review of Psychology* 53 (2002): 161–86; S.A. Haslam and S. Reicher, "Stressing the Group: Social Identity and the Unfolding Dynamics of Responses to Stress," *Journal of Applied Psychology* 91, no. 5 (2006): 1037–52; M.T. Gailliot and R.F. Baumeister, "Self-Esteem, Belongingness, and Worldview Validation: Does Belongingness Exert a Unique Influence Upon Self-Esteem?," *Journal of Research in Personality* 41, no. 2 (2007): 327–45.

8. A.M. Saks, K.L. Uggerslev, and N.E. Fassina, "Socialization Tactics and Newcomer Adjustment: A Meta-Analytic Review and Test of a

Model," *Journal of Vocational Behavior* 70, no. 3 (2007): 413–46.

9. S. Cohen, "The Pittsburgh Common Cold Studies: Psychosocial Predictors of Susceptibility to Respiratory Infectious Illness," *International Journal of Behavioral Medicine* 12, no. 3 (2005): 123–31; B.N. Uchino, "Social Support and Health: A Review of Physiological Processes Potentially Underlying Links to Disease Outcomes," *Journal of Behavioral Medicine* 29, no. 4 (2006): 377–87.

10. A.R. Fragale, "The power of powerless speech: The effects of speech style and task interdependence on status conferral," *Organizational Behavior and Human Decision Processes,* 101 (2006), 243–61.

11. C.E. Shannon and W. Weaver, *The Mathematical Theory of Communication* (Urbana, Il: University of Illinois Press, 1949); R.M. Krauss and S.R. Fussell, "Social Psychological Models of Interpersonal Communication," in *Social Psychology: Handbook of Basic Principles,* ed. E.T. Higgins and A. Kruglanski (New York: Guilford Press, 1996), 655–701.

12. J.R. Carlson and R.W. Zmud, "Channel Expansion Theory and the Experiential Nature of Media Richness Perceptions," *Academy of Management Journal* 42 (1999): 153–70.

13. P. Shachaf and N. Hara, "Behavioral Complexity Theory of Media Selection: A Proposed Theory for Global Virtual Teams," *Journal of Information Science* 33 (2007): 63–75.

14. M. Hauben and R. Hauben, "Netizens: On the History and Impact of Usenet and the Internet," *First Monday* 3, no. 8 (1998); J. Abbate, *Inventing the Internet* (Cambridge, MA: MIT Press, 1999).

15. One recent study found that email was the first or second choice for almost every situation (urgency, confidentiality, accountability, integrity, and social interaction). See: P. Palvia et al., "Contextual Constraints in Media Choice: Beyond Information Richness," *Decision Support Systems* 51, no. 3 (2011): 657–70.

16. N.B. Ducheneaut and L.A. Watts, "In Search of Coherence: A Review of E-Mail Research," *Human–Computer Interaction* 20, no. 1–2 (2005): 11–48; R.S. Mano and G.S. Mesch, "E-Mail Characteristics, Work Performance and Distress," *Computers in Human Behavior* 26, no. 1 (2010): 61–69.

17. W. Lucas, "Effects of E-Mail on the Organization," *European Management Journal* 16, no. 1 (1998): 18–30; D.A. Owens, M.A. Neale, and R.I. Sutton, "Technologies of Status Management Status Dynamics in E-Mail Communications," *Research on Managing Groups and Teams* 3 (2000): 205–30; N.B. Ducheneaut, "Ceci n'est pas un Objet? Talking About Objects in E-Mail," *Human–Computer Interaction* 18, no. 1–2 (2003): 85–110.

18. N. Panteli, "Richness, Power Cues and Email Text," *Information & Management* 40, no. 2 (2002): 75–86; N.B. Ducheneaut, "The Social Impacts of Electronic Mail in Organizations: A Case Study of Electronic Power Games Using Communication Genres," *Information, Communication, & Society* 5, no. 2 (2002): 153–88.

19. N. Epley and J. Kruger, "When What You Type Isn't What They Read: The Perseverance of Stereotypes and Expectancies over E-Mail," *Journal of Experimental Social Psychology* 41, no. 4 (2005): 414–22.

20. J. Kruger et al., "Egocentrism over E-Mail: Can We Communicate as Well as We Think?," *Journal of Personality and Social Psychology* 89, no. 6 (2005): 925–36.

21. J.B. Walther, "Language and Communication Technology: Introduction to the Special Issue," *Journal of Language and Social Psychology* 23, no. 4 (2004): 384–96; J.B. Walther, T. Loh, and L. Granka, "Let Me Count the Ways: The Interchange of Verbal and Nonverbal Cues in Computer-Mediated and Face-to-Face Affinity," *Journal of Language and Social Psychology* 24, no. 1 (2005): 36–65; K. Byron, "Carrying Too Heavy a Load? The Communication and Miscommunication of Emotion by Email," *Academy of Management Review* 33, no. 2 (2008): 309–27; J.M. Whalen, P.M. Pexman, and A.J. Gill, "'Should Be Fun–Not!': Incidence and Marking of Nonliteral Language in E-Mail," *Journal of Language and Social Psychology* 28, no. 3 (2009): 263–80.

22. R. Dube, "No e-mails, please. I'm trying to work", *The Globe and Mail,* Feb. 18 2008.

23. https://communities.intel.com/community/itpeernetwork/blog/2008/06/14/-quiet-time-and-no-email-day-pilot-data-is-in.

24. http://www.itbusinessedge.com/cm/blogs/all/no-e-mail-fridays-a-band-aid-approach-to-bigger-problem/?cs=45381 Comment posted by NZ on Feb 3, 2011 2:46 AM.

25. http://iorgforum.org/.

26. http://www.youtube.com/watch?v=oGBZW5odAYc "No Email Friday" at PBD Worldwide Jun 20, 2012.

27. http://www.itbusinessedge.com/cm/blogs/all/no-e-mail-fridays-a-band-aid-approach-to-bigger-problem/?cs=45381 Comment posted by SD on Feb 4, 2011 11:50 AM.

28. Byron, "Carrying Too Heavy a Load?"

29. G. Hertel, S. Geister, and U. Konradt, "Managing Virtual Teams: A Review of Current Empirical Research," *Human Resource Management Review* 15 (2005): 69–95; H. Lee, "Behavioral Strategies for Dealing with Flaming in an Online Forum," *The Sociological Quarterly* 46, no. 2 (2005): 385–403.

30. G.F. Thomas and C.L. King, "Reconceptualizing E-Mail Overload," *Journal of Business and Technical Communication* 20, no. 3 (2006): 252–87; S.R. Barley, D.E. Meyerson, and S. Grodal, "E-Mail as a Source and Symbol of Stress," *Organization Science* 22, no. 4 (2011): 887–906.

31. R.D. Waters et al., "Engaging Stakeholders through Social Networking: How Nonprofit Organizations Are Using Facebook," *Public Relations Review* 35, no. 2 (2009): 102–06; J. Cunningham, "New Workers, New Workplace? Getting the Balance Right," *Strategic Direction* 26, no. 1 (2010): 5; A.M. Kaplan and M. Haenlein, "Users of the World, Unite! The Challenges and Opportunities of Social Media," *Business Horizons* 53, no. 1 (2010): 59–68.

32. J.H. Kietzmann et al., "Social Media? Get Serious! Understanding the Functional Building Blocks of Social Media," *Business Horizons* 54, no. 3 (2011): 241–51.

33. S. Holtz, "Open the Door," *Communication World,* September 2010, 26.

34. Towers Watson, *Capitalizing on Effective Communication,* Towers Watson (New York: Towers Watson, 4 February 2010).

35. http://habaneroconsulting.com/employee-portals/servus.

36. L.Z. Tiedens and A.R. Fragale, "Power Moves: Complementarity in Dominant and Submissive Nonverbal Behavior," *Journal of Personality and Social Psychology* 84, no. 3 (2003): 558–68.

37. P. Ekman and E. Rosenberg, *What the Face Reveals: Basic and Applied Studies of Spontaneous Expression Using the Facial Action Coding System* (Oxford, England: Oxford University Press, 1997); P. Winkielman and K.C. Berridge, "Unconscious Emotion," *Current Directions in Psychological Science* 13, no. 3 (2004): 120–23.

38. W.J. Becker and R. Cropanzano, "Organizational Neuroscience: The Promise and Prospects of an Emerging Discipline," *Journal of Organizational Behavior* 31, no. 7 (2010): 1055–59.

39. "Body Language in the Job Interview," News release for CareerBuilder (London, UK: CareerBuilder, 23 August 2011). The sample size of this survey was not stated, but is likely quite large. The same survey the previous year in the United States had a sample size of 2,500 employers. Results of the US survey were similar to the more recent UK results reported here.

40. M. Sonnby-Borgstrom, P. Jonsson, and O. Svensson, "Emotional Empathy as Related to Mimicry Reactions at Different Levels of Information Processing," *Journal of Nonverbal Behavior* 27 (2003): 3–23; S.K. Johnson, "I Second That Emotion: Effects of Emotional Contagion and Affect at Work on Leader and Follower Outcomes," *Leadership Quarterly* 19, no. 1 (2008): 1–19; V. Vijayalakshmi and S. Bhattacharyya, "Emotional Contagion and Its Relevance to Individual Behavior and Organizational Processes: A Position Paper," *Journal of Business and Psychology* 27, no. 3 (2012): 363–74.

41. J.R. Kelly and S.G. Barsade, "Mood and Emotions in Small Groups and Work Teams," *Organizational Behavior and Human Decision Processes* 86 (2001): 99–130; T.L. Chartrand and J.L. Lakin, "The Antecedents and Consequences of Human Behavioral Mimicry," *Annual Review of Psychology* 64, no. 1 (2013): 285–308.

42. J. Fulk, "Social Construction of Communication Technology," *Academy of Management Journal* 36, no. 5 (1993): 921–50; L.K. Treviño, J. Webster, and E.W. Stein, "Making Connections: Complementary Influences on Communication Media Choices, Attitudes, and Use," *Organization Science* 11, no. 2 (2000): 163–82; B. van den Hooff, J. Groot, and S. de Jonge, "Situational Influences on the Use of Communication Technologies," *Journal of Business Communication* 42, no. 1 (2005): 4–27; J.W. Turner et al., "Exploring the Dominant Media: How Does Media Use Reflect Organizational Norms and Affect Performance?," *Journal of Business Communication* 43, no. 3 (2006): 220–50; M.B. Watson-Manheim and F. Bélanger, "Communication Media Repertoires: Dealing with the Multiplicity of Media Choices," *MIS Quarterly* 31, no. 2 (2007): 267–93.

43. Z. Lee and Y. Lee, "Emailing the Boss: Cultural Implications of Media Choice," *IEEE Transactions on Professional Communication* 52, no. 1 (2009): 61–74; D. Holtbrügge, A. Weldon, and H. Rogers, "Cultural Determinants of Email Communication Styles," *International Journal of Cross Cultural Management* 13, no. 1 (2013): 89–110.

44. R.C. King, "Media Appropriateness: Effects of Experience on Communication Media Choice," *Decision Sciences* 28, no. 4 (1997): 877–910.

45. A.K.C. Au and D.K.S. Chan, "Organizational Media Choice in Performance Feedback: A Multifaceted Approach," *Journal of Applied Social Psychology* 43, no. 2 (2013): 397–407; K.K. Stephens, A.K. Barrett, and M.J. Mahometa, "Organizational Communication in Emergencies: Using Multiple Channels and Sources to Combat Noise and Capture Attention," *Human Communication Research* 39, no. 2 (2013): 230–51.

46. K. Griffiths, "KPMG Sacks 670 Employees by E-Mail," *The Independent (London)*, 5 November 2002, 19; "Shop Worker Sacked by Text Message," *The Post (Claremont/Nedlands, Western Australia)*, 28 July 2007, 1, 78.

47. R.L. Daft and R.H. Lengel, "Information Richness: A New Approach to Managerial Behavior and Organization Design," *Research in Organizational Behavior* 6 (1984): 191–233; R.H. Lengel and R.L. Daft, "The Selection of Communication Media as an Executive Skill," *Academy of Management Executive* 2 (1988): 225–32.

48. R.E. Rice, "Task Analyzability, Use of New Media, and Effectiveness: A Multi-Site Exploration of Media Richness," *Organization Science* 3 (1992): 475–500.

49. R.F. Otondo et al., "The Complexity of Richness: Media, Message, and Communication Outcomes," *Information & Management* 45, no. 1 (2008): 21–30.

50. N.L. Reinsch Jr., J.W. Turner, and C.H. Tinsley, "Multicommunicating: A Practice Whose Time Has Come?," *Academy of Management Review* 33, no. 2 (2008): 391–403; A.-F. Cameron and J. Webster, "Multicommunicating: Juggling Multiple Conversations in the Workplace," *Information Systems Research* 24, no. 2 (2013): 352–71.

51. Carlson and Zmud, "Channel Expansion Theory and the Experiential Nature of Media Richness Perceptions; N. Kock, "Media Richness or Media Naturalness? The Evolution of Our Biological Communication Apparatus and Its Influence on Our Behavior toward E-Communication Tools," *IEEE Transactions on Professional Communication* 48, no. 2 (2005): 117–30.

52. V.W. Kupritz and E. Cowell, "Productive Management Communication: Online and Face-to-Face," *Journal of Business Communication* 48, no. 1 (2011): 54–82.

53. D. Muller, T. Atzeni, and F. Butera, "Coaction and Upward Social Comparison Reduce the Illusory Conjunction Effect: Support for Distraction-Conflict Theory," *Journal of Experimental Social Psychology* 40, no. 5 (2004): 659–65; L.P. Robert and A.R. Dennis, "Paradox of Richness: A Cognitive Model of Media Choice," *IEEE Transactions on Professional Communication* 48, no. 1 (2005): 10–21.

54. E.V. Wilson, "Perceived Effectiveness of Interpersonal Persuasion Strategies in Computer-Mediated Communication," *Computers in Human Behavior* 19, no. 5 (2003): 537–52; K. Sassenberg, M. Boos, and S. Rabung, "Attitude Change in Face-to-Face and Computer-Mediated Communication: Private Self-Awareness Ad Mediator and Moderator," *European Journal of Social Psychology* 35 (2005): 361–74; P. Di Blasio and L. Milani, "Computer-Mediated Communication and Persuasion: Peripheral vs. Central Route to Opinion Shift," *Computers in Human Behavior* 24, no. 3 (2008): 798–815.

55. Kruger et al., "Egocentrism over E-Mail: Can We Communicate as Well as We Think?"

56. R.M. Krauss, "The Psychology of Verbal Communication," in *International Encyclopedia of the Social and Behavioral Sciences*, ed. N. Smelser and P. Baltes (London, CA: Elsevier, 2002), 16161–16165.

57. H. Tsoukas, "The Missing Link: A Transformational View of Metaphors in Organizational Science," *The Academy of Management review* 16, no. 3 (1991): 566–85; G. Morgan, *Images of Organization*, Second ed. (Thousand Oaks, CA: Sage, 1997); J. Amernic, R. Craig, and D. Tourish, "The Transformational Leader as Pedagogue, Physician, Architect, Commander, and Saint: Five Root Metaphors in Jack Welch's Letters to Stockholders of General Electric," *Human Relations* 60, no. 12 (2007): 1839–72.

58. M. Rubini and H. Sigall, "Taking the Edge Off of Disagreement: Linguistic Abstractness and Self-Presentation to a Heterogeneous Audience," *European Journal of Social Psychology* 32 (2002): 343–51.

59. T. Walsh, "Nardelli Brags on Vip Recruits, Game Plan," *Detroit Free Press*, 8 September 2007.

60. D. Goleman, R. Boyatzis, and A. McKee, *Primal Leaders*, (Boston, MA: Harvard Business School Press, 2002), pp. 92–95.

61. O'Toole and Bennis, "What's Needed Next: A Culture of Candor."

62. T.W. Jackson and P. Farzaneh, "Theory-Based Model of Factors Affecting Information Overload," *International Journal of Information Management* 32, no. 6 (2012): 523–32.

63. A.G. Schick, L.A. Gordon, and S. Haka, "Information Overload: A Temporal Approach," *Accounting, Organizations & Society* 15 (1990): 199–220; A. Edmunds and A. Morris, "The Problem of Information Overload in Business Organisations: A Review of the Literature," *International Journal of Information Management* 20 (2000): 17–28; R. Pennington, "The Effects of Information Overload on Software Project Risk Assessment," *Decision Sciences* 38, no. 3 (2007): 489–526.

64. D.C. Thomas and K. Inkson, *Cultural Intelligence: People Skills for Global Business* (San Francisco, CA: Berrett-Koehler, 2004), Chap. 6; D. Welch, L. Welch, and R. Piekkari, "Speaking in Tongues," *International Studies of Management & Organization* 35, no. 1 (2005): 10–27.

65. D. Woodruff, "Crossing Culture Divide Early Clears Merger Paths," *Asian Wall Street Journal*, 28 May 2001, 9; "Differentstrokes," *Personnel Today*, 25 November 2008, 190.

66. S. Ohtaki, T. Ohtaki, and M.D. Fetters, "Doctor-Patient Communication: A Comparison of the USA and Japan," *Family Practice* 20 (2003): 276–82; M. Fujio, "Silence During Intercultural Communication: A Case Study," *Corporate Communications* 9, no. 4 (2004): 331–39.

67. T. Hasegawa and W.B. Gudykunst, "Silence in Japan and the United States," *Journal of Cross-Cultural Psychology* 29, no. 5 (1998): 668–84.

68. D.C. Barnlund, *Communication Styles of Japanese and Americans: Images and Realities* (Belmont, CA: Wadsworth, 1988); H. Yamada, *American and Japanese Business Discourse: A Comparison of Interaction Styles* (Norwood, NJ: Ablex, 1992), Chap. 2.

69. Adapted from: M. Nakamoto, "Cross-Cultural Conversations," *Financial Times (London)*, 12 January 2012, 16.

70. P. Harris and R. Moran, *Managing Cultural Differences* (Houston: Gulf, 1987); H. Blagg, "A Just Measure of Shame?," *British Journal of Criminology* 37 (1997): 481–501; R.E. Axtell, *Gestures: The Do's and Taboos of Body Language around the World*, Revised ed. (New York: Wiley, 1998).

71. D. Tannen, *You Just Don't Understand: Men and Women in Conversation* (New York: Ballentine Books, 1990); L.L. Namy, L.C. Nygaard, and D. Sauerteig, "Gender Differences in Vocal Accommodation: The Role of Perception," *Journal of Language and Social Psychology* 21, no. 4 (2002): 422–32; J.L. Locke, *Duels and Duets: Why Men and Women Talk So Differently* (Cambridge, UK: Cambridge University Press, 2011); M.R. Atai and F. Chahkandi, "Democracy in Computer-Mediated Communication: Gender, Communicative Style, and Amount of Participation in Professional Listservs," *Computers in Human Behavior* 28, no. 3 (2012): 881–88; N.S. Baron and E.M. Campbell, "Gender and Mobile Phones in Cross-National Context," *Language Sciences* 34, no. 1 (2012): 13–27.

72. A. Mulac et al., "Uh-Huh. What's That All About?' Differing Interpretations of Conversational Backchannels and Questions as Sources of Miscommunication across Gender Boundaries," *Communication Research* 25 (1998): 641–68; N.M. Sussman and D.H. Tyson, "Sex and Power: Gender Differences in Computer-Mediated Interactions," *Computers in Human Behavior* 16 (2000): 381–94; D.R. Caruso and P. Salovey, *The Emotionally Intelligent Manager* (San Francisco, CA: Jossey-Bass, 2004), p. 23; D. Fallows, *How Women and Men Use the Internet*, Pew Internet and American Life Project (Washington, DC: 28 December 2005).

73. Amernic, Craig, and Tourish, "The Transformational Leader as Pedagogue, Physician, Architect, Commander, and Saint: Five Root Metaphors in Jack Welch's Letters to Stockholders of General Electric."

74. A. Hill, "Ge's Bright Sparks Take the Lead," *Financial Times (London)*, 13 October 2011, 12.

75. This quotation is varied slightly from the original translations by: E. Carter, *All the Works of Epictetus, Which Are Now Extant*, Third ed., 2 vols., vol. 2 (London, UK: J. and F. Rivington, 1768), pg. 333; T.W. Higginson, *The Works of Epictetus* (Boston, MA: Little, Brown, and Company, 1866), pg. 428.

76. L.B. Comer and T. Drollinger, "Active Empathetic Listening and Selling Success: A Conceptual Framework," *Journal of Personal Selling*

& Sales Management 19 (1999): 15–29; T. Drollinger, L.B. Comer, and P.T. Warrington, "Development and Validation of the Active Empathetic Listening Scale," *Psychology and Marketing* 23, no. 2 (2006): 161–80.

77. K. Shevory, "Office Work Space Is Shrinking, but That's Not All Bad," *New York Times*, 19 January 2011, 8; "The Shrinking Cubicle," *Chicago Tribune*, 9 February 2011.

78. A. Leaman and B. Bordass, "Productivity in Buildings: The Killer Variables," *Building Research & Information* 27, no. 1 (1999): 4–19; T.J. Allen, "Architecture and Communication among Product Development Engineers," *California Management Review* 49, no. 2 (2007): 23–41; F. Becker, "Organizational Ecology and Knowledge Networks," *California Management Review* 49, no. 2 (2007): 42–61.

79. G. Evans and D. Johnson, "Stress and Open-Office Noise," *Journal of Applied Psychology* 85 (2000): 779–83; F. Russo, "My Kingdom for a Door," TIME magazine, 23 October 2000, B1.

80. S.P. Means, "Playing at Pixar," *Salt Lake Tribune (Utah)*, 30 May 2003, D1; G. Whipp, "Swimming against the Tide," *Daily News of Los Angeles*, 30 May 2003, U6.

81. C. Wagner and A. Majchrzak, "Enabling Customer-Centricity Using Wikis and the Wiki Way," *Journal of Management Information Systems* 23, no. 3 (2006): 17–43; C. Karena, "Working the Wiki Way," *Sydney Morning Herald*, 6 March 2007; R.B. Ferguson, "Build a Web 2.0 Platform and Employees Will Use It," *eWeek*, 20 June 2007.

82. D. Waisberg, "Quiet Please! We're Working," *National Post*, 30 May 2007.

83. T. Hsieh, "How Twitter Can Make You a Better (and Happier) Person," (Las Vegas, 2009), http://blogs.zappos.com/blogs/ceo-and-coo-blog (accessed 17 March 2011); J. Vijayan, "Staying on Message," *Computerworld*, 19 October 2009; "Social Media Training Programs: Different Approaches, Common Goals," *PR News*, 4 January 2010; A. Bryant, "On a Scale of 1 to 10, How Weird Are You?," *New York Times*, 10 January 2010.

84. T. Fenton, "Inside the Worldblu List: 1-800-Got-Junk's CEO on Why "Being Democratic Is Extremely Important to Maintaining Our Competitive Advantage"," (Atlanta: WorldBlu, 3 January 2008). The original term is "management by wandering around", but this has been replaced with "walking around" over the years. See: W. Ouchi, *Theory Z* (New York: Avon Books, 1981), pp. 176–77; T. Peters and R. Waterman, *In Search of Excellence* (New York: Harper and Row, 1982), p. 122.

85. R. Rousos, "Trust in Leaders Lacking at Utility," *The Ledger (Lakeland, Fl)*, 29 July 2003, B1; B. Whitworth and B. Riccomini, "Management Communication: Unlocking Higher Employee Performance," *Communication World*, Mar-Apr 2005, 18–21.

86. A. De Bruyn and G.L. Lilien, "A Multi-Stage Model of Word-of-Mouth Influence through Viral Marketing," *International Journal of Research in Marketing* 25, no. 3 (2008): 151–63; J.Y.C. Ho and M. Dempsey, "Viral Marketing: Motivations to Forward Online Content," *Journal of Business Research* 63, no. 9-10 (2010): 1000–06; M. Williams and F. Buttle, "The Eight Pillars of WOM Management: Lessons from a Multiple Case Study," *Australasian Marketing Journal (AMJ)* 19, no. 2 (2011): 85–92.

87. K. Dyer, "Changing Perceptions Virally at Novo Nordisk," *Strategic Communication Management* 13, no. 2 (2009): 24–27.

88. K. Davis, "Management Communication and the Grapevine," *Harvard Business Review* 31 (1953): 43–49; W.L. Davis and J.R. O'Connor, "Serial Transmission of Information: A Study of the Grapevine," *Journal of Applied Communication Research* 5 (1977): 61–72.

89. S.R. Clegg and A. van Iterson, "Dishing the Dirt: Gossiping in Organizations," *Culture and Organization* 15, no. 3-4 (2009): 275–89; C. Mills, "Experiencing Gossip: The Foundations for a Theory of Embedded Organizational Gossip," *Group & Organization Management* 35, no. 2 (2010): 213–40.

90. R.L. Rosnow, "Inside Rumor: A Personal Journey," *American Psychologist* 46 (1991): 484–96; C.J. Walker and C.A. Beckerle, "The Effect of State Anxiety on Rumor Transmission," *Journal of Social Behaviour & Personality* 2 (1987): 353–60; M. Noon and R. Delbridge, "News from Behind My Hand: Gossip in Organizations," *Organization Studies* 14 (1993): 23–36.

91. N. Nicholson, "Evolutionary Psychology: Toward a New View of Human Nature and Organizational Society," *Human Relations* 50 (1997): 1053–78; E.K. Foster, "Research on Gossip: Taxonomy, Methods, and Future Directions," *Review of General Psychology* 8, no. 2 (2004): 78–99; B. Beersma and G.A. Van Kleef, "Why People Gossip: An Empirical Analysis of Social Motives, Antecedents, and Consequences," *Journal of Applied Social Psychology* 42, no. 11 (2012): 2640–70.

CHAPTER 10

1. R. Doolittle, *Crazy Town: The Rob Ford Story* (Toronto, ON: Viking Canada, 2014) pp. 110, 185.

2. J.R.P. French and B. Raven, "The Bases of Social Power," in *Studies in Social Power*, ed. D. Cartwright (Ann Arbor, Mich: University of Michigan Press, 1959), 150–67; A.D. Galinsky et al., "Power and Perspectives Not Taken," *Psychological Science* 17, no. 12 (2006): 1068–74. Also see: H. Mintzberg, *Power in and around Organizations* (Englewood Cliffs, NJ: Prentice Hall, 1983), Chap. 1; J. Pfeffer, *Managing with Power* (Boston, MA: Harvard Business University Press, 1992), pp. 17, 30; A. Guinote and T.K. Vescio, "Introduction: Power in Social Psychology," in *The Social Psychology of Power*, ed. A. Guinote and T.K. Vescio (New York: Guilford Press, 2010), 1–18.

3. R.A. Dahl, "The Concept of Power," *Behavioral Science* 2 (1957): 201–18; R.M. Emerson, "Power-Dependence Relations," *American Sociological Review* 27 (1962): 31–41; A.M. Pettigrew, *The Politics of Organizational Decision-Making* (London, UK: Tavistock, 1973).

4. G.A. Van Kleef et al., "Breaking the Rules to Rise to Power: How Norm Violators Gain Power in the Eyes of Others," *Social Psychological and Personality Science* 2, no. 5 (2011): 500–07.

5. J. Pfeffer and G.R. Salancik, *The External Control of Organizations* (New York: Harper & Row, 1978), pp. 52–54; R. Gulati and M. Sytch, "Dependence Asymmetry and Joint Dependence in Interorganizational Relationships: Effects of Embeddedness on a Manufacturer's Performance in Procurement Relationships," *Administrative Science Quarterly* 52, no. 1 (2007): 32–69.

6. French and Raven, "The Bases of Social Power; P. Podsakoff and C. Schreisheim, "Field Studies of French and Raven's Bases of Power: Critique, Analysis, and Suggestions for Future Research," *Psychological Bulletin* 97 (1985): 387–411; P.P. Carson and K.D. Carson, "Social Power Bases: A Meta-Analytic Examination of Interrelationships and Outcomes," *Journal of Applied Social Psychology* 23 (1993): 1150–69. The alternative models of power bases are reviewed in a recent dissertation by Heinemann, who points out that most of them parallel French and Raven's list. See: P. Heinemann, *Power Bases and Informational Influence Strategies: A Behavioral Study on the Use of Management Accounting Information* (Wiesbaden, Germany: Deutscher Universitäts-Verlag, 2008). Raven subsequently proposed information power as a sixth source of power. We present information power as forms of legitimate and expert power rather than as a distinct sixth power base.

7. C. Barnard, *The Function of the Executive* (Cambridge, MA: Harvard University Press, 1938), pp. 167–70; C. Hardy and S.R. Clegg, "Some Dare Call It Power," in *Handbook of Organization Studies* ed. S.R. Clegg, C. Hardy, and W.R. Nord (London, UK: Sage, 1996), 622–41.

8. A.I. Shahin and P.L. Wright, "Leadership in the Context of Culture: An Egyptian Perspective," *Leadership & Organization Development Journal* 25, no. 5/6 (2004): 499–511; Y.J. Huo et al., "Leadership and the Management of Conflicts in Diverse Groups: Why Acknowledging Versus Neglecting Subgroup Identity Matters," *European Journal of Social Psychology* 35, no. 2 (2005): 237–54.

9. B.H. Raven, "Kurt Lewin Address: Influence, Power, Religion, and the Mechanisms of Social Control," *Journal of Social Issues* 55 (1999): 161–86.

10. A.W. Gouldner, "The Norm of Reciprocity: A Preliminary Statement," *American Sociological Review* 25 (1960): 161–78.

11. G. Yukl and C.M. Falbe, "Importance of Different Power Sources in Downward and Lateral Relations," *Journal of Applied Psychology* 76 (1991): 416–23; Raven, "Kurt Lewin Address: Influence, Power, Religion, and the Mechanisms of Social Control."

12. P.L. Dawes, D.Y. Lee, and G.R. Dowling, "Information Control and Influence in Emergent Buying Centers," *Journal Of Marketing* 62, no. 3 (1998): 55–68; D. Willer, "Power-at-a-Distance," *Social Forces* 81, no. 4 (2003): 1295–334; D.J. Brass et al., "Taking Stock of Networks and Organizations: A Multilevel Perspective," *Academy of Management Journal* 47, no. 6 (2004): 795–817.

13. B. Crumley, "Game of Death: France's Shocking Tv Experiment," *Time*, 17 March 2010; R.L. Parry, "Contestants Turn Torturers in French Tv Experiment," *Yahoo! News*, 16 March 2010.

14. S.L. Robinson, J. O'Reilly, and W. Wang, "Invisible at Work: An Integrated Model of

Workplace Ostracism," *Journal of Management* 39, no. 1 (2013): 203-31.

15. J.M. Peiro and J.L. Melia, "Formal and Informal Interpersonal Power in Organisations: Testing a Bifactorial Model of Power in Role-Sets," *Applied Psychology* 52, no. 1 (2003): 14-35.

16. C.R. Hinings et al., "Structural Conditions of Intraorganizational Power," *Administrative Science Quarterly* 19 (1974): 22-44. Also see: C.S. Saunders, "The Strategic Contingency Theory of Power: Multiple Perspectives," *The Journal of Management Studies* 27 (1990): 1-21.

17. R.B. Cialdini and N.J. Goldstein, "Social Influence: Compliance and Conformity," *Annual Review of Psychology* 55 (2004): 591-621.

18. C.K. Hofling et al., "An Experimental Study in Nurse-Physician Relationships," *Journal of Nervous and Mental Disease* 143, no. 2 (1966): 171-77.

19. C. Perkel, "It's Not CSI," *Canadian Press,* 10 November 2007; "Dr. Charles Smith: The Man Behind the Public Inquiry," *CBC News (Toronto),* 10 August 2010. Evidence-based management writers also warn against blindly following the advice of management gurus. See: J. Pfeffer and R.I. Sutton, *Hard Facts, Dangerous Half-Truths, and Total Nonsense* (Boston, MA: Harvard Business School Press, 2006), pp.45-46.

20. K. Miyahara, "Charisma: From Weber to Contemporary Sociology," *Sociological Inquiry* 53, no. 4 (1983): 368-88; J.D. Kudisch and M.L. Poteet, "Expert Power, Referent Power, and Charisma: Toward the Resolution of a Theoretical Debate," *Journal of Business & Psychology* 10 (1995): 177-95; D. Ladkin, "The Enchantment of the Charismatic Leader: Charisma Reconsidered as Aesthetic Encounter," *Leadership* 2, no. 2 (2006): 165-79.

21. M.T. Bitti, "Why Dr. Joey's Skinnychews found the perfect partner in Arlene Dickinson" *Financial Post,* October 28, 2013.

22. D.J. Hickson et al., "A Strategic Contingencies' Theory of Intraorganizational Power," *Administrative Science Quarterly* 16 (1971): 216-27; Hinings et al., "Structural Conditions of Intraorganizational Power; R.M. Kanter, "Power Failure in Management Circuits," *Harvard Business Review* (1979): 65-75.

23. Hickson et al., "A Strategic Contingencies' Theory of Intraorganizational Power," pp. 219-21; J.D. Hackman, "Power and Centrality in the Allocation of Resources in Colleges and Universities," *Administrative Science Quarterly* 30 (1985): 61-77; D.J. Brass and M.E. Burkhardt, "Potential Power and Power Use: An Investigation of Structure and Behavior," *Academy of Management Journal* 36 (1993): 441-70.

24. S.D. Harrington and B. Ivry, "For Commuters, a Day to Adapt," *The Record (Bergen, NJ),* 21 December 2005, A1; S. McCarthy, "Transit Strike Cripples New York," *The Globe and Mail (Toronto),* 21 December 2005, A17.

25. M. Kennett, "Remote Control," *Management Today,* 1 March 2011, 46.

26. R. Madell, "Ground Floor," *Pharmaceutical Executive (Women in Pharma Supplement),* June 2000, 24-31.

27. A. Chatterjee and D.C. Hambrick, "It's All About Me: Narcissistic Chief Executive Officers and Their Effects on Company Strategy and Performance," *Administrative Science Quarterly* 52, no. 3 (2007): 351-86.

28. M.E. Porter, J.W. Lorsch, and N. Nohria, "Seven Surprises for New CEOs," *Harvard Business Review* 82, no. 10 (2004): 62-72.

29. G. Owen and T. Kirchmaier, "The Changing Role of the Chairman: Impact of Corporate Governance Reform in the United Kingdom 1995-2005," *European Business Organization Law Review (EBOR)* 9, no. 02 (2008): 187-213; M.A. Bliss, "Does CEO Duality Constrain Board Independence? Some Evidence from Audit Pricing," *Accounting & Finance* 51, no. 2 (2011): 361-80.

30. J.G. Combs et al., "The Moderating Effect of CEO Power on the Board Composition-Firm Performance Relationship*," *Journal of Management Studies* 44, no. 8 (2007): 1299-323.

31. C. Crossland and D.C. Hambrick, "Differences in Managerial Discretion across Countries: How Nation-Level Institutions Affect the Degree to Which CEOs Matter," *Strategic Management Journal* 32, no. 8 (2011): 797-819.

32. D. Pressey, "Urbana, Ill.-Area Hospitals Chief Extends Personal Touch," *News-Gazette (Champaign-Urbana, Ill.),* 18 April 2011.

33. A. Caza, "Typology of the Eight Domains of Discretion in Organizations," *Journal of Management Studies* 49, no. 1 (2012): 144-77.

34. Kanter, "Power Failure in Management Circuits; B.E. Ashforth, "The Experience of Powerlessness in Organizations," *Organizational Behavior and Human Decision Processes* 43 (1989): 207-42.

35. "Tim Hortons fires single mom over free Timbit" *Toronto Star,* May 08 2008.

36. D. Hambrick, C. and E. Abrahamson, "Assessing Managerial Discretion across Industries: A Multimethod Approach," *Academy of Management journal* 38, no. 5 (1995): 1427-41; M.A. Carpenter and B.R. Golden, "Perceived Managerial Discretion: A Study of Cause and Effect," *Strategic Management Journal* 18, no. 3 (1997): 187-206.

37. S. Wasserman and K. Faust, *Social Network Analysis: Methods and Applications,* Structural Analysis in the Social Sciences (Cambridge, UK: Cambridge University Press, 1994), Chap. 1; Brass et al., "Taking Stock of Networks and Organizations: A Multilevel Perspective."

38. M. Grossetti, "Where Do Social Relations Come From?: A Study of Personal Networks in the Toulouse Area of France," *Social Networks* 27, no. 4 (2005): 289-300.

39. Y. Fan, "Questioning Guanxi: Definition, Classification, and Implications," *International Business Review* 11 (2002): 543-61; W.R. Vanhonacker, "When Good Guanxi Turns Bad," *Harvard Business Review* 82, no. 4 (2004): 18-19; R.J. Taormina and J.H. Gao, "A Research Model for Guanxi Behavior: Antecedents, Measures, and Outcomes of Chinese Social Networking," *Social Science Research* 39, no. 6 (2010): 1195-212.

40. D. Krackhardt and J.R. Hanson, "Informal Networks: The Company Behind the Chart," *Harvard Business Review* 71 (1993): 104-11; A. Portes, "Social Capital: Its Origins and Applications in Modern Society," *Annual Review of Sociology* 24 (1998): 1-24.

41. P.S. Adler and S.-W. Kwon, "Social Capital: Prospects for a New Concept," *Academy of Management Review* 27, no. 1 (2002): 17-40.

42. R.F. Chisholm, *Developing Network Organizations: Learning from Practice and Theory* (Reading MA: Addison Wesley Longman, 1998); W.S. Chow and L.S. Chan, "Social Network, Social Trust and Shared Goals in Organizational Knowledge Sharing," *Information & Management* 45, no. 7 (2008): 458-65.

43. R.S. Burt, *Structural Holes: The Social Structure of Competition* (Cambridge, MA: Harvard University Press, 1992).

44. M.T. Rivera, S.B. Soderstrom, and B. IUzzi, "Dynamics of Dyads in Social Networks: Assortative, Relational, and Proximity Mechanisms," *Annual Review of Sociology* 36 (2010): 91-115.

45. M.L. Seidel, J.T. Polzer and K.J. Stewart, "Friends in high places: The effects of social networks on discrimination in salary negotiations," *Administrative Science Quarterly,* 45 (2000), 1-24.

46. R. Cross and R.J. Thomas, *Driving Results through Social Networks: How Top Organizations Leverage Networks for Performance and Growth* (San Francisco, CA: Jossey-Bass, 2009); R. McDermott and D. Archibald, "Harnessing Your Staff's Informal Networks," *Harvard Business Review* 88, no. 3 (2010): 82-89.

47. M. Kilduff and D. Krackhardt, *Interpersonal Networks in Organizations: Cognition, Personality, Dynamics, and Culture* (New York: Cambridge University Press, 2008).

48. S. Humphries, "Companies Warm up to Social Networks," *Christian Science Monitor,* 8 September 2008, 13.

49. T. Gibbs, S. Heywood, and L. Weiss, "Organizing for an Emerging World," *McKinsey Quarterly* (2012): 1-11.

50. N.B. Ellison, C. Steinfield, and C. Lampe, "The Benefits of Facebook "Friends:" Social Capital and College Students' Use of Online Social Network Sites," *Journal of Computer-Mediated Communication* 12, no. 4 (2007): 1143-68.

51. M.S. Granovetter, "The Strength of Weak Ties," *American Journal of Sociology* 78 (1973): 1360-80; B. Erickson, "Social Networks," in *The Blackwell Companion to Sociology,* ed. J.R. Blau (Malden, MA: Blackwell Publishing, 2004), 314-26.

52. B. Uzzi and S. Dunlap, "How to Build Your Network," *Harvard Business Review* 83, no. 12 (2005): 53-60.

53. S.C. de Janasz and M.L. Forret, "Learning the Art of Networking: A Critical Skill for Enhancing Social Capital and Career Success," *Journal of Management Education* 32, no. 5 (2008): 629-50.

54. A. Mehra, M. Kilduff, and D.J. Brass, "The Social Networks of High and Low Self-Monitors: Implications for Workplace Performance," *Administrative Science Quarterly* 46 (2001): 121-46.

55. Burt, *Structural Holes: The Social Structure of Competition.*

56. B.R. Ragins and E. Sundstrom, "Gender and Power in Organizations: A Longitudinal Perspective," *Psychological Bulletin* 105 (1989): 51-88; M. Linehan, "Barriers to Women's Participation in International Management," *European Business Review* 13 (2001).

57. A. DeFelice, "Climbing to the Top," *Accounting Technology* 24, no. 1 (2008): 12-18.

58. D.M. McCracken, "Winning the Talent War for Women: Sometimes It Takes a Revolution," *Harvard Business Review* (2000): 159-67.

59. J. Lammers, J.I. Stoker, and D.A. Stapel, "Differentiating Social and Personal Power: Opposite Effects on Stereotyping, but Parallel Effects on Behavioral Approach Tendencies," *Psychological Science* 20, no. 12 (2009): 1543-49.

60. R. Hodigere, D. Bilimoria, "Women on Public-Company Boards: Factors That Affect their Odds of Board Membership Relative to Those of Men," ASONAM, pp. 960-965, 2012 International Conference on Advances in Social Networks Analysis and Mining (ASONAM 2012), 2012.

61. D. Keltner, D.H. Gruenfeld, and C. Anderson, "Power, Approach, and Inhibition," *Psychological Review* 110, no. 2 (2003): 265-84; B. Simpson and C. Borch, "Does Power Affect Perception in Social Networks? Two Arguments and an Experimental Test," *Social Psychology Quarterly* 68, no. 3 (2005): 278-87; Galinsky et al., "Power and Perspectives Not Taken."

62. K. Atuahene-Gima and H. Li, "Marketing's Influence Tactics in New Product Development: A Study of High Technology Firms in China," *Journal of Product Innovation Management* 17 (2000): 451-70; A. Somech and A. Drach-Zahavy, "Relative Power and Influence Strategy: The Effects of Agent/Target Organizational Power on Superiors' Choices of Influence Strategies," *Journal of Organizational Behavior* 23 (2002): 167-79.

63. J. Shetcliffe, "Questions Brokers Ask - How to Manage the Boss," *Insurance Brokers Monthly & Insurance Advisor*, 4 February 2009, 32; C. Chynoweth, "Subtle Art of Managing the Boss," *Sunday Times (London)*, 17 May 2009, 1; P. Lencioni, "How to Manage Your Boss," *Wall Street Journal*, 3 January 2009; J. Espinoza, "Culture Change Is the Final Frontier," *Wall Street Journal*, 23 February 2010; W. Immen, "How to Get What You Need from Your Boss," *The Globe and Mail*, 3 November 2010, B24; J. Weed, "The Perks and Pitfalls of Travel with a Boss," *International Herald Tribune*, 23 February 2011, 2; R.C. Matuson, *Suddenly in Charge: Managing up, Managing Down, Succeeding All Around* (Boston, MA: Nicholas Brealey, 2011).

64. D. Kipnis, S.M. Schmidt, and I. Wilkinson, "Intraorganizational Influence Tactics: Explorations in Getting One's Way," *Journal of Applied Psychology* 65 (1980): 440-52; A. Rao and K. Hashimoto, "Universal and Culturally Specific Aspects of Managerial Influence: A Study of Japanese Managers," *Leadership Quarterly* 8 (1997): 295-312; L.A. McFarland, A.M. Ryan, and S.D. Kriska, "Field Study Investigation of Applicant Use of Influence Tactics in a Selection Interview," *Journal of Psychology* 136 (2002): 383-98.

65. Cialdini and Goldstein, "Social Influence: Compliance and Conformity."

66. Rao and Hashimoto, "Universal and Culturally Specific Aspects of Managerial Influence." Silent authority as an influence tactic in non-Western cultures is also discussed in: S.F. Pasa, "Leadership Influence in a High Power Distance and Collectivist Culture," *Leadership & Organization Development Journal* 21 (2000): 414-26.

67. "One-in-Four Workers Have Felt Bullied in the Workplace, Careerbuilder Study Finds," News release for CareerBuilder (Chicago, IL: PR Newswire, 20 April 2011); "Monster Global Poll Reveals Workplace Bullying Is Endemic," *OnRec: Online Recruitment Magazine*, 10 June 2011; E. Weinbren, "Pharmacists Facing Employer Intimidation," *Chemist & Druggist*, 19 May 2012, 12; "UK's Bully Bosses," *Daily Mirror (London)*, 9 January 2012, 2.

68. "Be Part of the Team If You Want to Catch the Eye," *Birmingham Post (UK)*, 31 August 2000, 14; S. Maitlis, "Taking It from the Top: How CEOs Influence (and Fail to Influence) Their Boards," *Organization Studies* 25, no. 8 (2004): 1275-311.

69. A.T. Cobb, "Toward the Study of Organizational Coalitions: Participant Concerns and Activities in a Simulated Organizational Setting," *Human relations* 44 (1991): 1057-79; E.A. Mannix, "Organizations as Resource Dilemmas: The Effects of Power Balance on Coalition Formation in Small Groups," *Organizational Behavior and Human Decision Processes* 55 (1993): 1-22; D.J. Terry, M.A. Hogg, and K.M. White, "The Theory of Planned Behavior: Self-Identity, Social Identity and Group Norms," *British Journal of Social Psychology* 38 (1999): 225-44.

70. A.P. Brief, *Attitudes in and around Organizations* (Thousand Oaks, CA: Sage, 1998), pp. 69-84; D.J. O'Keefe, *Persuasion: Theory and Research* (Thousand Oaks, CA: Sage Publications, 2002).

71. These and other features of message content in persuasion are detailed in: R. Petty and J. Cacioppo, *Attitudes and Persuasion: Classic and Contemporary Approaches* (Dubuque, Iowa: W.C. Brown, 1981); M. Pfau, E.A. Szabo, and J. Anderson, "The Role and Impact of Affect in the Process of Resistance to Persuasion," *Human Communication Research* 27 (2001): 216-52; O'Keefe, *Persuasion: Theory and Research*, Chap. 9; R. Buck et al., "Emotion and Reason in Persuasion: Applying the Ari Model and the CASC Scale," *Journal of Business Research* 57, no. 6 (2004): 647-56; W.D. Crano and R. Prislin, "Attitudes and Persuasion," *Annual Review of Psychology* 57 (2006): 345-74.

72. N. Rhodes and W. Wood, "Self-Esteem and Intelligence Affect Influenceability: The Mediating Role of Message Reception," *Psychological Bulletin* 111, no. 1 (1992): 156-71.

73. M.C. Bolino and W.H. Tunley, "More Than One Way to Make an Impression: Exploring Profiles of Impression Management," *Journal of Management* 29 (2003): 141-60.

74. T. Peters, "The Brand Called You," *Fast Company*, August 1997; J. Sills, "Becoming Your Own Brand," *Psychology Today* 41, no. 1 (2008): 62-63.

75. J.S. Wilson, "Personal Branding in Today's Economy," *Atlanta Journal - Constitution*, 29 May 2011, D1.

76. D. Strutton and L.E. Pelton, "Effects of Ingratiation on Lateral Relationship Quality within Sales Team Settings," *Journal of Business Research* 43 (1998): 1-12; R. Vonk, "Self-Serving Interpretations of Flattery: Why Ingratiation Works," *Journal of Personality and Social Psychology* 82 (2002): 515-26.

77. C.A. Higgins, T.A. Judge, and G.R. Ferris, "Influence Tactics and Work Outcomes: A Meta-Analysis," *Journal of Organizational Behavior* 24 (2003): 90-106.

78. D. Strutton, L.E. Pelton, and J. Tanner, J. F., "Shall We Gather in the Garden: The Effect of Ingratiatory Behaviors on Buyer Trust in Salespeople," *Industrial Marketing Management* 25 (1996): 151-62; J. O'Neil, "An Investigation of the Sources of Influence of Corporate Public Relations Practitioners," *Public Relations Review* 29 (2003): 159-69.

79. C.M. Falbe and G. Yukl, "Consequences for Managers of Using Single Influence Tactics and Combinations of Tactics," *Academy of Management Journal* 35 (1992): 638-52.

80. R.C. Ringer and R.W. Boss, "Hospital Professionals' Use of Upward Influence Tactics," *Journal of Managerial Issues* 12 (2000): 92-108.

81. G. Blickle, "Do Work Values Predict the Use of Intraorganizational Influence Strategies?," *Journal of Applied Social Psychology* 30, no. 1 (2000): 196-205; P.P. Fu et al., "The Impact of Societal Cultural Values and Individual Social Beliefs on the Perceived Effectiveness of Managerial Influence Strategies: A Meso Approach," *Journal Of International Business Studies* 35, no. 4 (2004): 284-305.

82. This has become the generally-agreed definition of organizational politics over the past two decades. See: G.R. Ferris and K.M. Kacmar, "Perceptions of Organizational Politics," *Journal of Management* 18 (1992): 93-116; R. Cropanzano et al., "The Relationship of Organizational Politics and Support to Work Behaviors, Attitudes, and Stress," *Journal of Organizational Behavior* 18 (1997): 159-80; E. Vigoda, "Stress-Related Aftermaths to Workplace Politics: The Relationships among Politics, Job Distress, and Aggressive Behavior in Organizations," *Journal of Organizational Behavior* 23 (2002): 571-91. However, organizational politics was previously viewed as influence tactics outside the formal role that could be either selfish or altruistic. This older definition is less common today, possibly because it is incongruent with popular views of politics and because it's meaning is too ambiguous. For the older perspective of organizational politics, see: J. Pfeffer, *Power in Organizations* (Boston, MA: Pitman, 1981); Mintzberg, *Power in and around Organizations*

83. L. Hull, "Covert War in the Workplace...over the Holiday Rota," *Mail Online*, 7 August 2013; "Office Wars: Tis the Season to Be Spiteful," *Officebroker Blog*, 2013, http://www.officebroker.com/blog/.

84. K.M. Kacmar and R.A. Baron, "Organizational Politics: The State of the Field, Links to Related Processes, and an Agenda for Future Research," in *Research in Personnel and Human Resources Management*, ed. G.R. Ferris (Greenwich, CT: JAI Press, 1999), 1-39; Vigoda, "Stress-Related Aftermaths to Workplace Politics: The Relationships among Politics, Job Distress, and Aggressive Behavior in Organizations; C.-H. Chang, C.C. Rosen, and P.E. Levy, "The Relationship between Perceptions of Organizational Politics and Employee Attitudes, Strain, and Behavior: A Meta-Analytic Examination," *Academy of Management Journal* 52, no. 4 (2009): 779-801. The

quotation is from: M. Landry, "Navigating the Political Minefield," *PM Network*, March 2013, 38–43.

85. C. Hardy, *Strategies for Retrenchment and Turnaround: The Politics of Survival* (Berlin: Walter de Gruyter, 1990), Chap. 14; G.R. Ferris et al., "Perceptions of Organizational Politics: Prediction, Stress-Related Implications, and Outcomes," *Human Relations* 49 (1996): 233–63; M.C. Andrews and K.M. Kacmar, "Discriminating among Organizational Politics, Justice, and Support," *Journal of Organizational Behavior* 22 (2001): 347–66.

86. S. Blazejewski and W. Dorow, "Managing Organizational Politics for Radical Change: The Case of Beiersdorf-Lechia S.A., Poznan," *Journal of World Business* 38 (2003): 204–23.

87. L.W. Porter, R.W. Allen, and H.L. Angle, "The Politics of Upward Influence in Organizations," *Research in Organizational Behavior* 3 (1981): 120–22; R.J. House, "Power and Personality in Complex Organizations," *Research in Organizational Behavior* 10 (1988): 305–57.

88. R. Christie and F. Geis, *Studies in Machiavellianism* (New York: Academic Press, 1970); S.M. Farmer et al., "Putting Upward Influence Strategies in Context," *Journal of Organizational Behavior* 18 (1997): 17–42; K.S. Sauleya and A.G. Bedeian, "Equity Sensitivity: Construction of a Measure and Examination of Its Psychometric Properties," *Journal of Management* 26 (2000): 885–910.

CHAPTER 11

1. D. Nebenzahl, "Managing the Generation Gap," *Montreal Gazette*, 28 February 2009, G1; D. Deveau, "L'Oréal Canada Discovers the Beauty of Motivation," *Postmedia News (Toronto)*, 24 January 2011; "L'Oréal Canada Considers Inter-Generational Teams a Strength," *National Post*, 13 May 2013; "Embracing the New Demographic," *National Post*, 13 May 2013.

2. J.A. Wall and R.R. Callister, "Conflict and Its Management," *Journal of Management*, 21 (1995): 515–55; M.A. Rahim, *Managing Conflict in Organizations*, 4th ed. (New Brunswick, NJ: Transaction Publishers, 2011), pp. 15–1; D. Tjosvold, *Working Together to Get Things Done* (Lexington, MA: Lexington, 1986), 114–11; D. Tjosvold, "Defining Conflict and Making Choices About Its Management," *International Journal of Conflict Management* 17, no. 2 (2006): 87–95.

3. For example, see: R.R. Blake, H.A. Shepard, and J.S. Mouton, *Managing Intergroup Conflict in Industry* (Houston: Gulf Publishing, 1964; K.E. Boulding, "Organization and Conflict," *Conflict Resolution* 1, no. 2 (June 1957): 122–13; C. Argyris, "The Individual and Organization: Some Problems of Mutual Adjustment," *Administrative Science Quarterly* 2, no. 1 (1957): 1–2; L. Urwick, *The Elements of Administration*, 2nd ed. (London, UK: Pitman, 1947).

4. Rahim, *Managing Conflict in Organizations*.

5. K.A. Jehn and C. Bendersky, "Intragroup Conflict in Organizations: A Contingency Perspective on the Conflict-Outcome Relationship," *Research In Organizational Behavior* 25 (2003): 187–24; C.K.W. De Dreu and L.R. Weingart, "A Contingency Theory of Task Conflict and Performance in Groups and Organizational Teams," in *International Handbook of Organizational Teamwork and Cooperative Working*, ed. M.A. West, D. Tjosvold, and K.G. Smith (Chicester, UK: John Wiley & Sons, Inc., 2003), 151–16; L. Troyer and R. Youngreen, "Conflict and Creativity in Groups," *Journal of Social Issues* 65, no. 2 (2009): 409–427.

6. *Workplace Conflict and How Businesses Can Harness It to Thrive*, CPP Global Human Capital Report (Mountain View, CA: CPP, Inc., July 2008).

7. F.R.C. de Wit, L.L. Greer, and K.A. Jehn, "The Paradox of Intragroup Conflict: A Meta-Analysis," *Journal of Applied Psychology* 97, no. 2 (Mar 2012): 360–39; L.L. Meier et al., "Relationship and Task Conflict at Work: Interactive Short-Term Effects on Angry Mood and Somatic Complaints," *Journal of Occupational Health Psychology* 18, no. 2 (Apr 2013): 144–156.

8. S. Farberov, "American Airlines Flight Delayed Four Hours after Two Female Flight Attendants Start a Fight over Cell Phone," *Mail Online (London)*, 20 September 201; M. O'Sullivan, "Fighting Kangaroo," *Canberra Times*, 21 August 2012, ; "American Eagle Flight Attendants' Argument Causes 4-Hour Delay at JFK," *NBC News*, 20 September 201; S. Grossman, "Fight or Flight?," *Time*, 21 September 2012.

9. J. Dewey, *Human Nature and Conduct: An Introduction to Social Psychology* (New York: Holt, 1922), pg. 300.

10. M.P. Follett, "Constructive Conflict," in *Dynamic Administration: The Collected Papers of Mary Parker Follett*, ed. H.C. Metcalf and L. Urwick (Bath, UK: Management Publications Trust, 1941), 30–49.

11. M. Duarte and G. Davies, "Testing the Conflict-Performance Assumption in Business-to-Business Relationships," *Industrial Marketing Management* 32 (2003): 91–9; M.A. Rahim, "Toward a Theory of Managing Organizational Conflict," *International Journal of Conflict Management* 13, no. 3 (2002): 206–235. Although the 1970s marked a point when the benefits conflict became widely acknowledged, this view was expressed earlier by some writers. See: H. Assael, "Constructive Role of Interorganizational Conflict," *Administrative Science Quarterly* 14, no. 4 (1969): 573–58; L.A. Coser, *The Functions of Social Conflict* (New York: Free Press, 1956; J.A. Litterer, "Conflict in Organization: A Re-Examination," *Academy of Management Journal* 9 (1966): 178–186.

12. J.L. Farh, C. Lee, and C.I.C. Farh, "Task Conflict and Team Creativity: A Question of How Much and When," *Journal of Applied Psychology* 95, no. 6 (Nov 2010): 1173–118; J.D. Shaw et al., "A Contingency Model of Conflict and Team Effectiveness," *Journal of Applied Psychology* 96, no. 2 (Mar 2011): 391–400.

13. P.J. Carnevale, "Creativity in the Outcomes of Conflict," in *The Handbook of Conflict Resolution: Theory and Practice*, ed. M. Deutsch, P.T. Coleman, and E.C. Marcus, 2nd ed. (San Francisco, CA: Jossey-Bass, 2006), 414–43; P.J. Boyle, D. Hanlon, and J.E. Russo, "The Value of Task Conflict to Group Decisions," *Journal of Behavioral Decision Making* 25, no. 3 (2012): 217–227.

14. K.M. Eisenhardt, J.L. Kahwajy, and L.J. Bourgeois III, "How Management Teams Can Have a Good Fight," *Harvard Business Review* (July-August 1997): 77–8; T. Greitemeyer et al., "Information Sampling and Group Decision Making: The Effects of an Advocacy Decision Procedure and Task Experience," *Journal of Experimental Psychology-Applied* 12, no. 1 (Mar 2006): 31–4; U. Klocke, "How to Improve Decision Making in Small Groups: Effects of Dissent and Training Interventions," *Small Group Research* 38, no. 3 (June 2007): 437–46; K.M. Eisenhardt, J.L. Kahwajy, and L.J. Bourgeois III, "Conflict and Strategic Choice: How Top Management Teams Disagree," *California Management Review* 39 (Winter 1997): 42–62.

15. K.A. Jehn & C. Bendersky, Intragroup conflict in organizations: A contingency perspective on the conflict-outcome relationship, *Research in Organizational Behavior, 25* (2003): 187–242. L.H. Pelled, K.M. Eisenhardt, and K.R. Xin, "Exploring the Black Box: An Analysis of Work Group Diversity, Conflict, and Performance," *Administrative Science Quarterly* 44 (March 1999): 1–2; H. Guetzkow and J. Gyr, "An Analysis of Conflict in Decision-Making Groups," *Human Relations* 7, no. 3 (Aug. 1954): 367–382. The notion of two types of conflict dates back to Georg Simmel, who described two types of conflict: one with a personal and subjective goal, the other which has an impersonal and objective quality. See: Coser, *The Functions of Social Conflict*, pg. 112. Contemporary scholars use various labels for task and relationship conflict. We have avoided the "cognitive" and "affective" conflict labels because cognitions and emotions are interconnected processes in all human activity. A third type of conflict, process conflict, is exclude due to limited research and some questions about its distinction from task conflict.

16. C.K.W. De Dreu, "When Too Little or Too Much Hurts: Evidence for a Curvilinear Relationship between Task Conflict and Innovation in Teams," *Journal of Management* 32, no. 1 (Feb. 2006): 83–10; F.R. de Wit, L.L. Greer, & K.A. Jehn, The paradox of intragroup conflict: a meta-analysis, *Journal of Applied Psychology, 97* (2), (2012): 360.

17. R.S. Lau and A.T. Cobb, "Understanding the Connections between Relationship Conflict and Performance: The Intervening Roles of Trust and Exchange," *Journal of Organizational Behavior* 31, no. 6 (2010): 898–917.

18. C.K.W. De Dreu and L.R. Weingart, "Task Versus Relationship Conflict, Team Performance, and Team Member Satisfaction: A Meta-Analysis," *Journal of Applied Psychology* 88 (August 2003): 587–60; A.C. Mooney, P.J. Holahan, and A.C. Amason, "Don't Take It Personally: Exploring Cognitive Conflict as a Mediator of Affective Conflict," *Journal of Management Studies* 44, no. 5 (2007): 733–75; K. Choi and B. Cho, "Competing Hypotheses Analyses of the Associations between Group Task Conflict and Group Relationship Conflict," *Journal of Organizational Behavior* 32, no. 8 (2011): 1106–1126.

19. J.X. Yang and K.W. Mossholder, "Decoupling Task and Relationship Conflict: The Role of Intergroup Emotional Processing," *Journal of Organizational Behavior* 25 (2004): 589–60; B.H. Bradley et al., "Ready to Rumble: How Team Personality Composition and Task Conflict Interact to Improve Performance," *Journal of Applied Psychology* 98, no. 2 (2013): 385–39; B.H. Bradley et al., "Reaping the Benefits of Task Conflict in Teams: The Critical Role of Team

Psychological Safety Climate," *Journal of Applied Psychology* 97, no. 1 (2012): 151–158.

20. P.L. Curseu, S. Boros, and L.A.G. Oerlemans, "Task and Relationship Conflict in Short-Term and Long-Term Groups the Critical Role of Emotion Regulation," *International Journal of Conflict Management* 23, no. 1 (2012): 97–10; A. Schlaerth, N. Ensari, and J. Christian, "A Meta-Analytical Review of the Relationship between Emotional Intelligence and Leaders' Constructive Conflict Management," *Group Processes & Intergroup Relations* 16, no. 1 (January 1, 2013 2013): 126–136.

21. de Wit, Greer, and Jehn, "The Paradox of Intragroup Conflict: A Meta-Analysis."

22. D. Senor and S. Singer, *Start-up Nation: The Story of Israel's Economic Miracle* (New York: Hachette Book Group, 2009; J. Detar, "Andy Grove, Intel's inside Man," *Investor's Business Daily*, 24 July 200; A. Grove, "How to Make Confrontation Work for You," in *The Book of Management Wisdom*, ed. P. Krass (New York: John Wiley & Sons, Inc., 2000), 83–89.

23. A.C. Amason and H.J. Sapienza, "The Effects of Top Management Team Size and Interaction Norms on Cognitive and Affective Conflict," *Journal of Management* 23, no. 4 (1997): 495–516.

24. L. Pondy, "Organizational Conflict: Concepts and Models," *Administrative Science Quarterly* 2 (1967): 296–32; K.W. Thomas, "Conflict and Negotiation Processes in Organizations," in *Handbook of Industrial and Organizational Psychology*, ed. M.D. Dunnette and L.M. Hough, 2nd ed. (Palo Alto, CA: Consulting Psychologists Press, 1992), 651–718.

25. H. Barki and J. Hartwick, "Conceptualizing the Construct of Interpersonal Conflict," *International Journal of Conflict Management* 15, no. 3 (2004): 216–244.

26. M.A. Von Glinow, D.L. Shapiro, and J.M. Brett, "Can We Talk, and Should We? Managing Emotional Conflict in Multicultural Teams," *Academy of Management Review* 29, no. 4 (2004): 578–592.

27. J.M. Brett, D.L. Shapiro, and A.L. Lytle, "Breaking the Bonds of Reciprocity in Negotiations," *Academy of Management Journal* 41 (August 1998): 410–42; G.E. Martin and T.J. Bergman, "The Dynamics of Behavioral Response to Conflict in the Workplace," *Journal of Occupational & Organizational Psychology* 69 (December 1996): 377–387.

28. R.E. Walton and J.M. Dutton, "The Management of Conflict: A Model and Review," *Administrative Science Quarterly* 14 (1969): 73–8; S.M. Schmidt and T.A. Kochan, "Conflict: Toward Conceptual Clarity," *Administrative Science Quarterly* 17, no. 3 (Sept. 1972): 359–370.

29. J.A. McMullin, T. Duerden Comeau, and E. Jovic, "Generational Affinities and Discourses of Difference: A Case Study of Highly Skilled Information Technology Workers," *British Journal of Sociology* 58, no. 2 (2007): 297–316.

30. Data are from the 2009 Kelly Global Workforce Index, based on information published in news releases in each country by Kelly Services in September 2009.

31. R.M. Sarala, "The Impact of Cultural Differences and Acculturation Factors on Post-Acquisition Conflict," *Scandinavian Journal of Management* 26, no. 1 (3// 2010): 38–56.

32. T. Taylor, "Change Is an Inevitable Part of Life," *Denver Business Journal Online*, 8 October 2012.

33. G.S. van der Vegt, B.J.M. Emans, and E. van der Vliert, "Patterns of Interdependence in Work Teams: A Two-Level Investigation of the Relations with Job and Team Satisfaction," *Personnel Psychology* 54, no. 1 (2001): 51–6; R. Wageman and G. Baker, "Incentives and Cooperation: The Joint Effects of Task and Reward Interdependence on Group Performance," *Journal of Organizational Behavior* 18, no. 2 (1997): 139–158.

34. P.C. Earley and G.B. Northcraft, "Goal Setting, Resource Interdependence, and Conflict Management," in *Managing Conflict: An Interdisciplinary Approach*, ed. M.A. Rahim (New York: Praeger, 1989), 161–17; K. Jehn, "A Multimethod Examination of the Benefits and Detriments of Intragroup Conflict," *Administrative Science Quarterly* 40 (1995): 245–282.

35. A. Risberg, "Employee Experiences of Acquisition Processes," *Journal of World Business* 36 (March 2001): 58–84.

36. Jehn and Bendersky, "Intragroup Conflict in Organizations."

37. M. Hewstone, M. Rubin, and H. Willis, "Intergroup Bias," *Annual Review of Psychology* 53 (2002): 575–60; J. Jetten, R. Spears, and T. Postmes, "Intergroup Distinctiveness and Differentiation: A Meta-Analytic Integration," *Journal of Personality and Social Psychology* 86, no. 6 (2004): 862–879.

38. Follett, "Constructive Conflict,"; Blake, Shepard, and Mouton, *Managing Intergroup Conflict in Industry;* T. Ruble and K. Thomas, "Support for a Two-Dimensional Model of Conflict Behavior," *Organizational Behavior and Human Performance* 16 (1976): 143–15; C.K.W. De Dreu et al., "A Theory-Based Measure of Conflict Management Strategies in the Workplace," *Journal of Organizational Behavior* 22 (2001): 645–66; Rahim, "Toward a Theory of Managing Organizational Conflict."

39. *Workplace Conflict and How Businesses Can Harness It to Thrive*, CPP Global Human Capital Report (Mountain View, CA: CPP, Inc., July 2008).

40. Q. Wang, E.L. Fink, and D.A. Cai, "The Effect of Conflict Goals on Avoidance Strategies: What Does Not Communicating Communicate?," *Human Communication Research* 38, no. 2 (2012): 222–252.

41. Several studies identify the antecedents of preferred conflict style. For example, see: P.J. Moberg, "Linking Conflict Strategy to the Five-Factor Model: Theoretical and Empirical Foundations," *International Journal of Conflict Management* 12, no. 1 (2001): 47–6; H.-A. Shih and E. Susanto, "Conflict Management Styles, Emotional Intelligence, and Job Performance in Public Organizations," *International Journal of Conflict Management* 21, no. 2 (2010): 147–16; J.E. Barbuto, Jr., K.A. Phipps, and Y. Xu, "Testing Relationships between Personality, Conflict Styles and Effectiveness," *International Journal of Conflict Management* 21, no. 4 (2010): 434–447

42. D.W. Johnson et al., "Effects of Cooperative, Competitive, and Individualistic Goal Structures on Achievement: A Meta-Analysis," *Psychological Bulletin* 89 (1981): 47–6; G.A. Callanan, C.D. Benzing, and D.F. Perri, "Choice of Conflict-Handling Strategy: A Matter of Context," *Journal of Psychology* 140, no. 3 (2006): 269–28; Z. Ma et al., "The Impact of Group-Oriented Values on Choice of Conflict Management Styles and Outcomes: An Empirical Study in Turkey," *The International Journal of Human Resource Management* 23, no. 18 (2012/10/01 2012): 3776–3793.

43. X.M. Song, J. Xile, and B. Dyer, "Antecedents and Consequences of Marketing Managers' Conflict-Handling Behaviors," *Journal of Marketing* 64 (January 2000): 50–6; R.A. Friedman et al., "What Goes around Comes Around: The Impact of Personal Conflict Style on Work Conflict and Stress," *International Journal of Conflict Management* 11, no. 1 (2000): 32–5; M. Song, B. Dyer, and R.J. Thieme, "Conflict Management and Innovation Performance: An Integrated Contingency Perspective," *Academy of Marketing Science* 34, no. 3 (2006): 341–35; L.A. DeChurch, K.L. Hamilton, and C. Haas, "Effects of Conflict Management Strategies on Perceptions of Intragroup Conflict," *Group Dynamics* 11, no. 1 (2007): 66–78.

44. G.A. Chung-Yan and C. Moeller, "The Psychosocial Costs of Conflict Management Styles," *International Journal of Conflict Management* 21, no. 4 (2010): 382–399.

45. C.K.W. De Dreu and A.E.M. Van Vianen, "Managing Relationship Conflict and the Effectiveness of Organizational Teams," *Journal of Organizational Behavior* 22 (2001): 309–32; Wang, Fink, and Cai, "The Effect of Conflict Goals on Avoidance Strategies: What Does Not Communicating Communicate?"

46. A. Ergeneli, S.M. Camgoz, and P.B. Karapinar, "The Relationship between Self-Efficacy and Conflict-Handling Styles in Terms of Relative Authority Positions of the Two Parties," *Social Behavior & Personality: An International Journal* 38, no. 1 (2010): 13–28.

47. J. Simms, "Blood in the Boardroom," *Director* 2009, 48.

48. C.H. Tinsley, "How Negotiators Get to Yes: Predicting the Constellation of Strategies Used across Cultures to Negotiate Conflict," *Journal of Applied Psychology* 86, no. 4 (2001): 583–59; J.L. Holt and C.J. DeVore, "Culture, Gender, Organizational Role, and Styles of Conflict Resolution: A Meta-Analysis," *International Journal of Intercultural Relations* 29, no. 2 (2005): 165–19; Z.Z. Ma, "Conflict Management Styles as Indicators of Behavioral Pattern in Business Negotiation," *International Journal of Conflict Management* 18, no. 3–4 (2007): 260–279.

49. D.A. Cai and E.L. Fink, "Conflict Style Differences between Individualists and Collectivists," *Communication Monographs* 69 (March 2002): 67–8; F.P. Brew and D.R. Cairns, "Styles of Managing Interpersonal Workplace Conflict in Relation to Status and Face Concern: A Study with Anglos and Chinese," *International Journal of Conflict Management* 15, no. 1 (2004): 27–5; C.H. Tinsley and E. Weldon, "Responses to a Normative Conflict among American and Chinese

Managers," *International Journal of Conflict Management* 3, no. 2 (2003): 183-194.

50. Holt and DeVore, "Culture, Gender, Organizational Role, and Styles of Conflict Resolution,"; M. Davis, S. Capobianco, and L. Kraus, "Gender Differences in Responding to Conflict in the Workplace: Evidence from a Large Sample of Working Adults," *Sex Roles* 63, no. 7 (2010): 500-514.

51. K. Lewin, *Resolving Social Conflicts* (New York: Harper, 1948).

52. J.D. Hunger and L.W. Stern, "An Assessment of the Functionality of the Superordinate Goal in Reducing Conflict," *Academy of Management Journal* 19, no. 4 (1976): 591-605 M. Sherif, "Superordinate Goals in the Reduction of Intergroup Conflict," *The American Journal of Sociology* 63, no. 4 (1958): 349-356.

53. Sherif, "Superordinate Goals in the Reduction of Intergroup Conflict,"; Eisenhardt, Kahwajy, and Bourgeois III, "How Management Teams Can Have a Good Fight,"; Song, Xile, and Dyer, "Antecedents and Consequences of Marketing Managers' Conflict-Handling Behaviors,"; O. Doucet, J. Poitras, and D. Chenevert, "The Impacts of Leadership on Workplace Conflicts," *International Journal of Conflict Management* 20, no. 4 (2009): 340-354.

54. R.S. Lau and A.T. Cobb, Understanding the connections between relationship conflict and performance: The intervening roles of trust and exchange. *Journal of Organizational Behavior* 31, no. 6 (2010): 898-917.

55. H.C. Triandis, "The Future of Workforce Diversity in International Organisations: A Commentary," *Applied Psychology: An International Journal* 52, no. 3 (2003): 486-495.

56. M. Cash, "CN Chief Builds Bridges with Prairie Clientele," *Winnipeg Free Press*, 18 February 2011, B4; E. White, "Railways Improved, but Regulation Needed, Says CWB," *Western Producer*, 24 February 2011.

57. "Can the New CEO End a Culture Clash after a Merger?," *Financial Times*, 10 September 2008, 16.

58. T. Rutledge, "No. 4 Small Company: Brookstone," *Houston Chronicle*, 10 November 2012

59. T.F. Pettigrew, "Intergroup Contact Theory," *Annual Review of Psychology* 49 (1998): 65-8; S. Brickson, "The Impact of Identity Orientation on Individual and Organizational Outcomes in Demographically Diverse Settings," *Academy of Management Review* 25 (January 2000): 82-10; J. Dixon and K. Durrheim, "Contact and the Ecology of Racial Division: Some Varieties of Informal Segregation," *British Journal of Social Psychology* 42 (March 2003): 1-23.

60. N. Yemchenko, "I'm a Corporate Volunteer," *System Capital Management: Corporate Blog*26 April 201; "About 18,000 Employees of SCM Group Clean Up 73 Ukrainian Cities." news release for S. C. Management (Donetsk: 22 April 2013).

61. H.C. Triandis, The future of workforce diversity in international organisations: A commentary, *Applied Psychology* 52, no. 3 (2003): 486-495.

62. M.A. Von Glinow, D.L. Shapiro, and J.M. Brett, Can we talk, and should we? Managing emotional conflict in multicultural teams, *Academy of Management Review* 29, no. 4 (2004): 578-592.

63. L.L. Putnam, "Beyond Third Party Role: Disputes and Managerial Intervention," *Employee Responsibilities and Rights Journal* 7 (1994): 23-3; A.R. Elangovan, "The Manager as the Third Party: Deciding How to Intervene in Employee Disputes," in *Negotiation: Readings, Exercises, and Cases*, ed. R.J. Lewicki, J.A. Litterer, and D. Saunders, 3rd ed. (New York: McGraw-Hill, 1999), 458-469. For a somewhat different taxonomy of managerial conflict intervention, see: P.G. Irving and J.P. Meyer, "A Multidimensional Scaling Analysis of Managerial Third-Party Conflict Intervention Strategies," *Canadian Journal Of Behavioural Science* 29, no. 1 (January 1997): 7-18. A recent review describes 10 species of third-party intervention, but these consist of variations of the three types described here. See: D.E. Conlon et al., "Third Party Interventions across Cultures: No 'One Best Choice'," in *Research in Personnel and Human Resources Management* (JAI, 2007), 309-349.

64. K. Bollen, H. Ittner, and M.C. Euwema, "Mediating Hierarchical Labor Conflicts: Procedural Justice Makes a Difference–for Subordinates," *Group Decision and Negotiation* 21, no. 5 (2012/09/01 2012): 621-63; J.A. Wall and T.C. Dunne, "Mediation Research: A Current Review," *Negotiation Journal* 28, no. 2 (2012): 217-244.

65. B.H. Sheppard, "Managers as Inquisitors: Lessons from the Law," in *Bargaining inside Organizations*, ed. M.H. Bazerman and R.J. Lewicki (Beverly Hills, CA: Sage, 1983; N.H. Kim, D.W. Sohn, and J.A. Wall, "Korean Leaders' (and Subordinates') Conflict Management," *International Journal Of Conflict Management* 10, no. 2 (April 1999): 130-15; D.J. Moberg, "Managers as Judges in Employee Disputes: An Occasion for Moral Imagination," *Business Ethics Quarterly* 13, no. 4 (2003): 453-477.

66. R. Karambayya and J.M. Brett, "Managers Handling Disputes: Third Party Roles and Perceptions of Fairness," *Academy of Management Journal* 32 (1989): 687-70; R. Cropanzano et al., "Disputant Reactions to Managerial Conflict Resolution Tactics," *Group & Organization Management* 24 (June 1999): 124-153.

67. A.R. Elangovan, "Managerial Intervention in Organizational Disputes: Testing a Prescriptive Model of Strategy Selection," *International Journal of Conflict Management* 4 (1998): 301-33; P.S. Nugent, "Managing Conflict: Third-Party Interventions for Managers," *Academy Of Management Executive* 16, no. 1 (February 2002): 139-154.

68. Bollen, Ittner, and Euwema, "Mediating Hierarchical Labor Conflicts: Procedural Justice Makes a Difference–for Subordinates,"; R. Nesbit, T. Nabatchi, and L.B. Bingham, "Employees, Supervisors, and Workplace Mediation: Experiences of Justice and Settlement," *Review of Public Personnel Administration* 32, no. 3 (September 1, 2012 2012): 260-287.

69. J.P. Meyer, J.M. Gemmell, and P.G. Irving, "Evaluating the Management of Interpersonal Conflict in Organizations: A Factor-Analytic Study of Outcome Criteria," *Canadian Journal of Administrative Sciences* 14 (1997): 1-13; L.B. Bingham, "Employment Dispute Resolution: The Case for Mediation," *Conflict Resolution Quarterly* 22, no. 1-2 (2004): 145-17; M. Hyde et al., "Workplace Conflict Resolution and the Health of Employees in the Swedish and Finnish Units of an Industrial Company," *Social Science & Medicine* 63, no. 8 (2006): 2218-2227.

70. W.H. Ross and D.E. Conlon, "Hybrid Forms of Third-Party Dispute Resolution: Theoretical Implications of Combining Mediation and Arbitration," *Academy of Management Review* 25, no. 2 (2000): 416-42; W.H. Ross, C. Brantmeier, and T. Ciriacks, "The Impact of Hybrid Dispute-Resolution Procedures on Constituent Fairness Judgments," *Journal of Applied Social Psychology* 32, no. 6 (Jun 2002): 1151-1188.

71. L.L. Thompson, J. Wang, B.C. Gunia, Negotiation. *Annual Review of Psychology*, 61 (2010): 491-515.

72. R.J. Lewicki, et al., *Essentials of Negotiation*, 2nd Canadian Edition. February 2014.

73. Lax and Sebenius, 1986.

74. B.J. Dietmeyer, *Strategic Negotiation*, (Chicago, IL: Dearborn Trade Publishing, 2004); J.M. Brett, "Managing Organizational Conflict," *Professional Psychology: Research and Practice* 15 (1984): 664-678.

75. R. Stagner and H. Rosen, *Psychology of Union–Management Relations* (Belmont, CA: Wadsworth, 1965), pp. 95-96, 108-11; R.E. Walton and R.B. McKersie, *A Behavioral Theory of Labor Negotiations: An Analysis of a Social Interaction System* (New York: McGraw-Hill, 1965), pp. 41-4; L. Thompson, *The Mind and Heart of the Negotiator* (Upper Saddle River, NJ: Prentice-Hall, 1998), Chap. 2.

76. A. Tversky and D. Kahneman, "Judgment under Uncertainty: Heuristics and Biases," *Science* 185, no. 4157 (27 September 1974): 1124-113; J.D. Jasper and S.D. Christman, "A Neuropsychological Dimension for Anchoring Effects," *Journal of Behavioral Decision Making* 18 (2005): 343-369.

77. S. Kwon and L.R. Weingart, "Unilateral Concessions from the Other Party: Concession Behavior, Attributions, and Negotiation Judgments," *Journal of Applied Psychology* 89, no. 2 (2004): 263-27; R. Fells, *Effective Negotiation* (Cambridge, UK: Cambridge University Press, 2012), Chap. 8.

78. D. Malhotra, "The Fine Art of Making Concessions," *Negotiation* (January 2006): 3-5.

79. J.Z. Rubin and B.R. Brown, *The Social Psychology of Bargaining and Negotiation* (New York: Academic Press, 1976), Chap. 9.

80. A.F. Stuhlmacher, T.L. Gillespie, and M.V. Champagne, "The Impact of Time Pressure in Negotiation: A Meta-Analysis," *International Journal of Conflict Management* 9, no. 2 (April 1998): 97-11; C.K.W. De Dreu, "Time Pressure and Closing of the Mind in Negotiation," *Organizational Behavior and Human Decision Processes* 91 (July 2003): 280-295. However, one recent study reported that speeding up these concessions leads to better negotiated outcomes. See: D.A. Moore, "Myopic Prediction, Self-Destructive Secrecy, and the Unexpected Benefits of Revealing Final Deadlines in Negotiation," *Organizational Behavior and Human Decision Processes* 94, no. 2 (2004): 125-139.

81. R.J. Robertson, "Defusing the Exploding Offer: The Farpoint Gambit," *Negotiation Journal* 11, no. 3 (1995): 277-285.

82. L.L. Thompson, "Information Exchange in Negotiation," *Journal of Experimental Social Psychology* 27 (1991): 161-179.

83. S.R. Covey, *The 7 Habits of Highly Effective People* (New York: Free Press, 1989), pp. 235-260.

84. R.J. Lewicki et al., *Negotiation*, 4th ed. (New York: McGraw-Hill/Irwin, 2003), p. 9; M. Olekalns and P.L. Smith, "Testing the Relationships among Negotiators' Motivational Orientations, Strategy Choices, and Outcomes," *Journal of Experimental Social Psychology* 39, no. 2 (Mar 2003): 101-117.

85. M. Olekalns and P.L. Smith, "Moments in Time: Metacognition, Trust, and Outcomes in Dyadic Negotiations," *Personality and Social Psychology Bulletin* 31, no. 12 (Dec 2005): 1696-1707.

86. D.W. Choi, "Shared Metacognition in Integrative Negotiation," *International Journal of Conflict Management* 21, no. 3 (2010): 309-333.

87. J.M. Brett et al., "Sticks and Stones: Language, Face, and Online Dispute Resolution," *Academy of Management Journal* 50, no. 1 (Feb 2007): 85-9; D. Pietroni et al., "Emotions as Strategic Information: Effects of Other's Emotional Expressions on Fixed-Pie Perception, Demands, and Integrative Behavior in Negotiation," *Journal of Experimental Social Psychology* 44, no. 6 (2008): 1444-145; D. Druckman and M. Olekalns, "Emotions in Negotiation," *Group Decision and Negotiation* 17, no. 1 (2008): 1-1; M.J. Boland and W.H. Ross, "Emotional Intelligence and Dispute Mediation in Escalating and De-Escalating Situations," *Journal of Applied Social Psychology* 40, no. 12 (2010): 3059-3105.

88. P.J. Carnevale and A.M. Isen, "The Influence of Positive Affect and Visual Access on the Discovery of Integrative Solutions in Bilateral Negotiation," *Organizational Behavior and Human Decision Processes* 37 (1986): 1-1; Thompson, *The Mind and Heart of the Negotiator.*

89. N. Rackham and J. Carlisle, "The effective negotiator–Part I: The behaviour of successful negotiators," *Journal of European Industrial Training*, 2-6 (1978): 6-11.

CHAPTER 12

1. V. McTavish, "Turnaround Winner: Amiee Chan," *BC Business*, October 2008, 93; "Dr. Amiee Chan, 2012 Corporate Executives, President & CEO, Norsat International," *Conversations with Top 100 Winner:* (Toronto, ON: Women's Executive Network, 23 September 2012), https://www.wxnetwork.com (accessed 23 March 2014); "Woman in Orbit," *Taste of Life Magazine*, December 2012, 46-49; "How Norsat Is Building a Stable Platform," *HSBC Global Connections* (Toronto, ON: HSBC, 17 June 2013), https://globalconnections.hsbc.com/canada/en/articles/how-norsat-building-stable-platform (accessed 23 March 2014); C. Suttles, "Keeping Us Connected," *Business in Focus*, October 2013, 112-17; "3 Steps to Getting Your Company Back on Track," *Profit*, 15 October 2013; "Executive Spotlight: Amiee Chan," *Sat-Magazine*, March 2013.

2. Most of these statistics were collected in September 2013. Library of Congress data were collected in 2010.

3. Many of these perspectives are summarized in R.N. Kanungo, "Leadership in Organizations: Looking Ahead to the 21st Century," *Canadian Psychology* 39 (1998): 71-82; G.A. Yukl, *Leadership in Organizations*, 8th ed. (Upper Saddle River, NJ: Pearson Education, 2013).

4. R. House, M. Javidan, and P. Dorfman, "Project GLOBE: An Introduction," *Applied Psychology: An International Review* 50 (2001): 489-505; R. House et al., "Understanding Cultures and Implicit Leadership Theories across the Globe: An Introduction to Project GLOBE," *Journal of World Business* 37 (2002): 3-10.

5. C. Hosford, "Flying High," *Incentive* 181, no. 12 (2007): 14-20; "Powered by Frontline People," *Employee Engagement Today*, September 2007.

6. J.A. Raelin, "We the Leaders: In Order to Form a Leaderful Organization," *Journal of Leadership & Organizational Studies* 12, no. 2 (2005): 18-30; C.L. Pearce, J.A. Conger, and E.A. Locke, "Shared Leadership Theory," *Leadership Quarterly* 19, no. 5 (2008): 622-28; E. Engel Small and J.R. Rentsch, "Shared Leadership in Teams: A Matter of Distribution," *Journal of Personnel Psychology* 9, no. 4 (2010): 203-11.

7. C. McMorrow, *Entrepreneurs Turn Us On: 20 Years of Recognizing Bright Ideas*, EY Entrepreneur of the year–Ontario 2013, Ernst & Young (October 2013); D. Ovsey, "'Get out of the Way'," *National Post*, 18 February 2014.

8. C.A. Beatty, "Implementing Advanced Manufacturing Technologies: Rules of the Road," *Sloan Management Review* (1992): 49-60; J.M. Howell, "The Right Stuff: Identifying and Developing Effective Champions of Innovation," *The Academy of Management Executive* 19, no. 2 (2005): 108-19; J.M. Howell and C.M. Shea, "Effects of Champion Behavior, Team Potency, and External Communication Activities on Predicting Team Performance," *Group & Organization Management* 31, no. 2 (2006): 180-211.

9. J.A. Raelin, *Creating Leaderful Organizations: How to Bring out Leadership in Everyone* (San Francisco, CA: Berret-Koehler, 2003).

10. S. Marchionne, "Fiat's Extreme Makeover," *Harvard Business Review* (2008): 45-48.

11. J.W. Gardner, *On Leadership* (New York: Free Press, 1990), pp.138-55.

12. Most or all of these elements are included in: W. Bennis and B. Nanus, *Leaders: The Strategies for Taking Charge* (New York: Harper & Row, 1985); N.M. Tichy and M.A. Devanna, *The Transformational Leader* (New York: Wiley, 1986); B.M. Bass and R.E. Riggio, *Transformational Leadership*, 2nd ed. (Mahwah, NJ: Lawrence Erlbaum Associates, 2006); J.M. Kouzes and B.Z. Posner, *The Leadership Challenge*, 5th ed. (San Francisco, CA: Jossey-Bass, 2012).

13. Strategic collective vision has been identified as a key factor in leadership since Chester Barnard's seminal book in organizational behaviour. see: C. Barnard, *The Functions of the Executive* (Cambridge, MA: Harvard University Press, 1938), pp. 86-89.

14. Bennis and Nanus, *Leaders*, pp. 27-33, 89; R.E. Quinn, *Building the Bridge as You Walk on It: A Guide for Leading Change* (San Francisco, CA: Jossey-Bass, 2004), Chap. 11; R. Gill, *Theory and Practice of Leadership* (London, UK: Sage, 2011), Chap. 4; D. O'Connell, K. Hickerson, and A. Pillutla, "Organizational Visioning: An Integrative Review," *Group & Organization Management* 36, no. 1 (2011): 103-25.

15. J. Faragher, "Employee Engagement: The Secret of UKRD's Success," *Personnel Today*, 3 May 2013; S. Waite, "Warm Hearts Bring Cheer and Rewards," *Sunday Times (London)*, 3 March 2013.

16. J.M. Strange and M.D. Mumford, "The Origins of Vision: Effects of Reflection, Models, and Analysis," *Leadership Quarterly* 16, no. 1 (2005): 121-48; S. Kantabutra, "Toward a Behavioral Theory of Vision in Organizational Settings," *Leadership & Organization Development Journal* 30, no. 4 (2009): 319-37; S.A. Kirkpatrick, "Lead through Vision and Values," in *Handbook of Principles of Organizational Behavior*, ed. E.A. Locke (Chichester, UK: Wiley, 2010), 367-87; Gill, *Theory and Practice of Leadership*, Chap. 4.

17. W.G. Hardwick, "Responding to the 1960s: Designing Adaptable Communities in Vancouver," *Environment and Behavior* 26, no. 3 (1994): 338-62; R. Mickleburgh, "Visionary Mayor Art Phillips Remade Vancouver," *The Globe and Mail*, 25 April 2013, S8; J. Lee, "Art Phillips Was "the Best Mayor Vancouver Ever Had": Gordon Campbell," *Vancouver Sun*, 30 March 2013; S. Ip, "Phillips Remembered as 'Visionary Leader'," *Vancouver Province*, 31 March 2013, A12.

18. J.A. Conger and R.N. Kanungo, *Charismatic Leadership in Organizations* (Thousand Oaks, CA: Sage, 1998), 173-83; M. Venus, D. Stam, and D. van Knippenberg, "Leader Emotion as a Catalyst of Effective Leader Communication of Visions, Value-Laden Messages, and Goals," *Organizational Behavior and Human Decision Processes* 122, no. 1 (2013): 53-68.

19. R. Shook, *Heart & Soul: Five American Companies That Are Making the World a Better Place* (Dallas: BenBella Books, 2010), pp. 155-222; Kouzes and Posner, *The Leadership Challenge*, pp. 79-81.

20. K.W. Parry and H. Hansen, "The Organizational Story as Leadership," *Leadership* 3, no. 3 (2007): 281-300; D.A. Waldman, P.A. Balthazard, and S.J. Peterson, "Leadership and Neuroscience: Can We Revolutionize the Way That Inspirational Leaders Are Identified and Developed?," *Academy of Management Perspectives* 25, no. 1 (2011): 60-74; S. Denning, *The Leader's Guide to Storytelling: Mastering the Art and Discipline of Business Narrative*, Revised ed. (San Francisco, CA: Jossey-Bass, 2011).

21. S. Franklin, *The Heroes: A Saga of Canadian Inspiration* (Toronto, ON: McClelland and Stewart, 1967); L. Black, "Hamburger Diplomacy," *Report on Business Magazine* August 1988, 30-36.

22. D.E. Berlew, "Leadership and Organizational Excitement," *California Management Review* 17, no. 2 (1974): 21-30; Bennis and Nanus, *Leaders*, pp. 43-55; T. Simons, "Behavioral Integrity: The Perceived Alignment between Managers' Words and Deeds as a Research Focus," *Organization Science* 13, no. 1 (2002): 18-35.

23. M. Webb, "Executive Profile: Peter C. Farrell," *San Diego Business Journal*, 24 March 2003, 32; P. Benesh, "He Likes Them Breathing Easy," *Investor's Business Daily*, 13 September 2005,

A04. For a discussion of trust in leadership, see C.S. Burke et al., "Trust in Leadership: A Multi-Level Review and Integration," *Leadership Quarterly* 18, no. 6 (2007): 606–32. The survey on leading by example is reported in J.C. Maxwell, "People Do What People See," *BusinessWeek*, 19 November 2007, 32.

24. K. Tyler, "Evaluating Values," *HRMagazine*, April 2011, 57.

25. Bass and Riggio, *Transformational Leadership*, pg. 7; Kouzes and Posner, *The Leadership Challenge*, Chaps. 6 and 7.

26. W.E. Baker and J.M. Sinkula, "The Synergistic Effect of Market Orientation and Learning Orientation on Organizational Performance," *Academy of Marketing Science Journal* 27, no. 4 (1999): 411–27; Z. Emden, A. Yaprak, and S.T. Cavusgil, "Learning from Experience in International Alliances: Antecedents and Firm Performance Implications," *Journal of Business Research* 58, no. 7 (2005): 883–92.

27. Kouzes and Posner, *The Leadership Challenge*.

28. X. Wang, "A Mysterious Message Millionaire," *China Daily*, 12 January 2009; R. Kapadia, "China's King of All Social Media," *Barron's*, 18 May 2013; W. Wee, "Tencent CEO Pony Ma Talks Wechat, Competition, Going Mobile and Global," *Techinasia*, 7 May 2013.

29. R.J. House, "A 1976 Theory of Charismatic Leadership," in *Leadership: The Cutting Edge*, ed. J.G. Hunt and L.L. Larson (Carbondale, IL.: Southern Illinois University Press, 1977), 189–207; J.A. Conger, "Charismatic Leadership," in *The Sage Handbook of Leadership*, ed. A. Bryman, et al. (London, UK: Sage, 2011), 86–102.

30. J.E. Barbuto Jr., "Taking the Charisma out of Transformational Leadership," *Journal of Social Behavior & Personality* 12 (1997): 689–97; Y.A. Nur, "Charisma and Managerial Leadership: The Gift That Never Was," *Business Horizons* 41 (1998): 19–26; M.D. Mumford and J.R. Van Doorn, "The Leadership of Pragmatism– Reconsidering Franklin in the Age of Charisma," *Leadership Quarterly* 12, no. 3 (2001): 279–309; A. Fanelli, "Bringing out Charisma: CEO Charisma and External Stakeholders," *The Academy of Management Review* 31, no. 4 (2006): 1049–61; M.J. Platow et al., "A Special Gift We Bestow on You for Being Representative of Us: Considering Leader Charisma from a Self-Categorization Perspective," *British Journal of Social Psychology* 45, no. 2 (2006): 303–20.

31. B. Shamir et al., "Correlates of Charismatic Leader Behavior in Military Units: Subordinates' Attitudes, Unit Characteristics, and Superiors' Appraisals of Leader Performance," *Academy of Management Journal* 41, no. 4 (1998): 387–409; R.E. De Vries, R.A. Roe, and T.C.B. Taillieu, "On Charisma and Need for Leadership," *European Journal of Work and Organizational Psychology* 8 (1999): 109–33; R. Khurana, *Searching for a Corporate Savior: The Irrational Quest for Charismatic CEOs* (Princeton, NJ: Princeton University Press, 2002); R.E. de Vries, R.D. Pathak, and A.R. Paquin, "The Paradox of Power Sharing: Participative Charismatic Leaders Have Subordinates with More Instead of Less Need for Leadership," *European Journal of Work and Organizational Psychology* 20, no. 6 (2010): 779–804. The effect of charismatic leadership on follower dependence was also noted earlier by noted U.S. government leader John Gardner. See: Gardner, *On Leadership*, pp. 34–36.

32. J. Lipman-Blumen, "A Pox on Charisma: Why Connective Leadership and Character Count," in *The Drucker Difference: What the World's Greatest Management Thinker Means to Today's Business Leaders*, ed. C.L. Pearce, J.A. Maciariello, and H. Yamawaki (New York: McGraw-Hill, 2010), 149–74.

33. A. Mackey, "The Effect of CEOs on Firm Performance," *Strategic Management Journal* 29, no. 12 (2008): 1357–67.

34. J. Barling, T. Weber, and E.K. Kelloway, "Effects of Transformational Leadership Training on Attitudinal and Financial Outcomes: A Field Experiment," *Journal of Applied Psychology* 81 (1996): 827–32.

35. A. Bryman, "Leadership in Organizations," in *Handbook of Organization Studies*, ed. S.R. Clegg, C. Hardy, and W.R. Nord (Thousand Oaks, CA: Sage, 1996), 276–92; D. van Knippenberg and S.B. Sitkin, "A Critical Assessment of Charismatic–Transformational Leadership Research: Back to the Drawing Board?," *Academy of Management Annals* 7, no. 1 (2013): 1–60.

36. B.S. Pawar and K.K. Eastman, "The Nature and Implications of Contextual Influences on Transformational Leadership: A Conceptual Examination," *Academy of Management Review* 22 (1997): 80–109; C.P. Egri and S. Herman, "Leadership in the North American Environmental Sector: Values, Leadership Styles, and Contexts of Environmental Leaders and Their Organizations," *Academy of Management Journal* 43, no. 4 (2000): 571–604.

37. A. Zaleznik, "Managers and Leaders: Are They Different?," *Harvard Business Review* 55, no. 3 (1977): 67–78; J.P. Kotter, *A Force for Change: How Leadership Differs from Management* (New York: Free Press, 1990); E.A. Locke, *The Essence of Leadership* (New York: Lexington Books, 1991); G. Yukl and R. Lepsinger, "Why Integrating the Leading and Managing Roles Is Essential for Organizational Effectiveness," *Organizational Dynamics* 34, no. 4 (2005): 361–75.

38. R.J. House and R.N. Aditya, "The Social Scientific Study of Leadership: Quo Vadis?," *Journal of Management* 23, no. 3 (1997): 409–73.

39. Bennis and Nanus, *Leaders*, pg. 20. Peter Drucker is also widely cited as the source of this quotation. The closest passage we could find, however, is in the first two pages of *The Effective Executive* (1966) where Drucker states that effective executives "get the right things done." On the next page, he states that manual workers only need efficiency, "that is, the ability to do things right rather than the ability to get the right things done." See: P.F. Drucker, *The Effective Executive* (New York: Harper Business, 1966), pp. 1–2.

40. Yukl and Lepsinger, "Why Integrating the Leading and Managing Roles Is Essential for Organizational Effectiveness."

41. S.R. Satterwhite, "Dell's Poisonous Culture Is Sinking Its Ship–and Raises Questions for Potential Buyers," *Forbes*, 1 April 2013.

42. C. Riley, "At the Table with...Karen Forrester," *Eat Out Magazine*, 12 January 2010; "The Arena Lunch with Karen Forrester, UK Managing Director, T.G.I. Friday's," (UK: Arena: The hospitality network, 11 July 2011), http://www.arena.org.uk/event/198 (accessed 11 September 2013); P. Martin, "Forrester Leads Friday's out of the Woods," *Peach Report*, 20 February 2013, www.peach-report.com.

43. E.A. Fleishman, "The Description of Supervisory Behavior," *Journal of Applied Psychology* 37, no. 1 (1953): 1–6. For discussion on methodological problems with the development of these people vs task-oriented leadership constructs, see: C.A. Schriesheim, R.J. House, and S. Kerr, "Leader Initiating Structure: A Reconciliation of Discrepant Research Results and Some Empirical Tests," *Organizational Behavior and Human Performance* 15, no. 2 (1976): 297–321; L. Tracy, "Consideration and Initiating Structure: Are They Basic Dimensions of Leader Behavior?," *Social Behavior and Personality* 15, no. 1 (1987): 21–33.

44. A.K. Korman, "Consideration, Initiating Structure, and Organizational Criteria–a Review," *Personnel Psychology* 19 (1966): 349–62; E.A. Fleishman, "Twenty Years of Consideration and Structure," in *Current Developments in the Study of Leadership*, ed. E.A. Fleishman and J.C. Hunt (Carbondale, IL: Southern Illinois University Press, 1973), 1–40; T.A. Judge, R.F. Piccolo, and R. Ilies, "The Forgotten Ones?: The Validity of Consideration and Initiating Structure in Leadership Research," *Journal of Applied Psychology* 89, no. 1 (2004): 36–51; D.S. Derue et al., "Trait and Behavioral Theories of Leadership: An Integration and Meta-Analytic Test of Their Relative Validity," *Personnel Psychology* 64, no. 1 (2011): 7–52; Yukl, *Leadership in Organizations*, pp. 62–75.

45. B.A. Scott et al., "A Daily Investigation of the Role of Manager Empathy on Employee Well-Being," *Organizational Behavior and Human Decision Processes* 113, no. 2 (2010): 127–40.

46. V.V. Baba, "Serendipity in Leadership: Initiating Structure and Consideration in the Classroom," *Human Relations* 42 (1989): 509–25.

47. R.K. Greenleaf, *Servant Leadership: A Journey into the Nature of Lergitimate Power & Greatness* (Mahwah, NJ: Paulist Press, 1977; repr., 2002); D. van Dierendonck and K. Patterson, "Servant Leadership: An Introduction," in *Servant Leadership: Developments in Theory and Research*, ed. D. van Dierendonck and K. Patterson (Houndmills UK: Palgrave Macmillan, 2010), 3–11.

48. Greenleaf, *Servant Leadership*, pg. 27.

49. S. Sendjaya, J.C. Sarros, and J.C. Santora, "Defining and Measuring Servant Leadership Behaviour in Organizations," *Journal of Management Studies* 45, no. 2 (2008): 402–24; R.C. Liden et al., "Servant Leadership: Development of a Multidimensional Measure and Multi-Level Assessment," *Leadership Quarterly* 19, no. 2 (2008): 161–77; K.-Y. Ng and C.S.-K. Koh, "Motivation to Serve: Understanding the Heart of the Servant-Leader and Servant Leadership Behaviours," in *Servant Leadership: Developments in Theory and Research*, ed. D. van Dierendonck and K. Patterson (Houndmills, UK: Palgrave Macmillan, 2010), 90–104; D. van Dierendonck, "Servant

Leadership: A Review and Synthesis," *Journal of Management* 37, no. 4 (2011): 1228–61.

50. S.J. Peterson, B.M. Galvin, and D. Lange, "CEO Servant Leadership: Exploring Executive Characteristics and Firm Performance," *Personnel Psychology* 65, no. 3 (2012): 565–96.

51. S. Kerr et al., "Towards a Contingency Theory of Leadership Based Upon the Consideration and Initiating Structure Literature," *Organizational Behavior and Human Performance* 12 (1974): 62–82; L.L. Larson, J.G. Hunt, and R.N. Osbom, "The Great Hi–Hi Leader Behavior Myth: A Lesson from Occam's Razor," *Academy of Management Journal* 19 (1976): 628–41.

52. "Soldier to Run for Councillor in Caledon," *Share News (Toronto)*, 7 April 2010; "Kevin Junor New Deputy Superintendent at Maplehust," *Share News (Toronto)*, 10 April 2013; B. Powell, "Don Jailhouse Led by 'Servant Leader'," *Toronto Star*, 2 January 2013, GT6.

53. For a thorough study of how expectancy theory of motivation relates to leadership, see R.G. Isaac, W.J. Zerbe, and D.C. Pitt, "Leadership and Motivation: The Effective Application of Expectancy Theory," *Journal of Managerial Issues* 13 (2001): 212–26.

54. R.J. House, "A Path Goal Theory of Leader Effectiveness," *Administrative Science Quarterly* 16, no. 3 (1971): 321–39; M.G. Evans, "Extensions of a Path-Goal Theory of Motivation," *Journal of Applied Psychology* 59 (1974): 172–78; R.J. House and T.R. Mitchell, "Path-Goal Theory of Leadership," *Journal of Contemporary Business* (1974): 81–97; M.G. Evans, "Path Goal Theory of Leadership," in *Leadership*, ed. L.L. Neider and C.A. Schriesheim (Greenwich, CT: Information Age Publishing, 2002), 115–38.

55. R.J. House, "Path-Goal Theory of Leadership: Lessons, Legacy, and a Reformulated Theory," *The Leadership Quarterly* 7, no. 3 (1996): 323–52.

56. J. Indvik, "Path-Goal Theory of Leadership: A Meta-Analysis," *Academy of Management Proceedings* (1986): 189–92; J.C. Wofford and L.Z. Liska, "Path-Goal Theories of Leadership: A Meta-Analysis," *Journal of Management* 19 (1993): 857–76.

57. J.D. Houghton and S.K. Yoho, "Toward a Contingency Model of Leadership and Psychological Empowerment: When Should Self-Leadership Be Encouraged?," *Journal of Leadership & Organizational Studies* 11, no. 4 (2005): 65–83.

58. R.T. Keller, "A Test of the Path-Goal Theory of Leadership with Need for Clarity as a Moderator in Research and Development Organizations," *Journal of Applied Psychology* 74 (1989): 208–12.

59. R.P. Vecchio, J.E. Justin, and C.L. Pearce, "The Utility of Transactional and Transformational Leadership for Predicting Performance and Satisfaction within a Path-Goal Theory Framework," *Journal of Occupational and Organizational Psychology* 81 (2008): 71–82.

60. B. Carroll and L. Levy, "Defaulting to Management: Leadership Defined by What It Is Not," *Organization* 15, no. 1 (2008): 75–96; I. Holmberg and M. Tyrstrup, "Well Then– What Now? An Everyday Approach to Managerial Leadership," *Leadership* 6, no. 4 (2010): 353–72.

61. C.A. Schriesheim and L.L. Neider, "Path-Goal Leadership Theory: The Long and Winding Road," *Leadership Quarterly* 7 (1996): 317–21.

62. P. Hersey and K.H. Blanchard, *Management of Organizational Behavior: Utilizing Human Resources*, 5th ed. (Englewood Cliffs, NJ: Prentice Hall, 1988).

63. R.P. Vecchio, "Situational Leadership Theory: An Examination of a Prescriptive Theory," *Journal of Applied Psychology* 72 (1987): 444–51; W. Blank, J.R. Weitzel, and S.G. Green, "A Test of the Situational Leadership Theory," *Personnel Psychology* 43 (1990): 579–97; C.L. Graeff, "Evolution of Situational Leadership Theory: A Critical Review," *Leadership Quarterly* 8 (1997): 153–70; G. Thompson and R.P. Vecchio, "Situational Leadership Theory: A Test of Three Versions," *Leadership Quarterly* 20, no. 5 (2009): 837–48.

64. F.E. Fiedler, *A Theory of Leadership Effectiveness* (New York: McGraw-Hill, 1967); F.E. Fiedler and M.M. Chemers, *Leadership and Effective Management* (Glenview, IL: Scott, Foresman, 1974).

65. Kelly Services, *The Leadership Disconnect*, (Troy, MI: Kelly Services, August 2012).

66. F.E. Fiedler, "Engineer the Job to Fit the Manager," *Harvard Business Review* 43, no. 5 (1965): 115–22.

67. For a summary of criticisms, see Yukl, *Leadership in Organizations*, pp. 217–18.

68. Judge, Piccolo, and Ilies, "The Forgotten Ones?: The Validity of Consideration and Initiating Structure in Leadership Research; T.A. Judge, R.F. Piccolo, and T. Kosalka, "The Bright and Dark Sides of Leader Traits: A Review and Theoretical Extension of the Leader Trait Paradigm," *Leadership Quarterly* 20 (2009): 855–75.

69. N. Nicholson, *Executive Instinct* (New York: Crown, 2000).

70. This observation has also been made by C.A. Schriesheim, "Substitutes-for-Leadership Theory: Development and Basic Concepts," *Leadership Quarterly* 8 (1997): 103–08.

71. D.F. Elloy and A. Randolph, "The Effect of Superleader Behavior on Autonomous Work Groups in a Government Operated Railway Service," *Public Personnel Management* 26 (1997): 257–72; C.C. Manz and H. Sims Jr., *The New SuperLeadership: Leading Others to Lead Themselves* (San Francisco, CA: Berrett-Koehler, 2001).

72. M.L. Loughry, "Coworkers Are Watching: Performance Implications of Peer Monitoring," *Academy of Management Proceedings* (2002): O1–O6.

73. P.M. Podsakoff and S.B. MacKenzie, "Kerr and Jermier's Substitutes for Leadership Model: Background, Empirical Assessment, and Suggestions for Future Research," *Leadership Quarterly* 8 (1997): 117–32; S.D. Dionne et al., "Neutralizing Substitutes for Leadership Theory: Leadership Effects and Common-Source Bias," *Journal Of Applied Psychology* 87, no. 3 (2002): 454–64; J.R. Villa et al., "Problems with Detecting Moderators in Leadership Research Using Moderated Multiple Regression," *Leadership Quarterly* 14, no. 1 (2003): 3–23; S.D. Dionne et al., "Substitutes for Leadership, or Not," *Leadership Quarterly* 16, no. 1 (2005): 169–93.

74. J.R. Meindl, "On Leadership: An Alternative to the Conventional Wisdom," *Research in Organizational Behavior* 12 (1990): 159–203; L.R. Offermann, J.J.K. Kennedy, and P.W. Wirtz, "Implicit Leadership Theories: Content, Structure, and Generalizability," *Leadership Quarterly* 5, no. 1 (1994): 43–58; R.J. Hall and R.G. Lord, "Multi-Level Information Processing Explanations of Followers' Leadership Perceptions," *Leadership Quarterly* 6 (1995): 265–87; O. Epitropaki and R. Martin, "Implicit Leadership Theories in Applied Settings: Factor Structure, Generalizability, and Stability over Time," *Journal of Applied Psychology* 89, no. 2 (2004): 293–310. For a broader discussion of the social construction of leadership, see: G.T. Fairhurst and D. Grant, "The Social Construction of Leadership: A Sailing Guide," *Management Communication Quarterly* 24, no. 2 (2010): 171–210.

75. R.G. Lord et al., "Contextual Constraints on Prototype Generation and Their Multilevel Consequences for Leadership Perceptions," *Leadership Quarterly* 12, no. 3 (2001): 311–38; K.A. Scott and D.J. Brown, "Female First, Leader Second? Gender Bias in the Encoding of Leadership Behavior," *Organizational Behavior and Human Decision Processes* 101 (2006): 230–42; S.J. Shondrick, J.E. Dinh, and R.G. Lord, "Developments in Implicit Leadership Theory and Cognitive Science: Applications to Improving Measurement and Understanding Alternatives to Hierarchical Leadership," *Leadership Quarterly* 21, no. 6 (2010): 959–78.

76. S.F. Cronshaw and R.G. Lord, "Effects of Categorization, Attribution, and Encoding Processes on Leadership Perceptions," *Journal of Applied Psychology* 72 (1987): 97–106; J.L. Nye and D.R. Forsyth, "The Effects of Prototype-Based Biases on Leadership Appraisals: A Test of Leadership Categorization Theory," *Small Group Research* 22 (1991): 360–79.

77. L.M. Fisher, "Ricardo Semler Won't Take Control," *strategy + business*, no. 41 (2005): 1–11.

78. Meindl, "On Leadership: An Alternative to the Conventional Wisdom," 163; B. Schyns, J.R. Meindl, and M.A. Croon, "The Romance of Leadership Scale: Cross-Cultural Testing and Refinement," *Leadership* 3, no. 1 (2007): 29–46; J. Felfe and L.E. Petersen, "Romance of Leadership and Management Decision Making," *European Journal of Work and Organizational Psychology* 16, no. 1 (2007): 1–24.

79. J. Pfeffer, "The Ambiguity of Leadership," *Academy of Management Review* 2 (1977): 102–12.

80. R. Weber et al., "The Illusion of Leadership: Misattribution of Cause in Coordination Games," *Organization Science* 12, no. 5 (2001): 582–98; N. Ensari and S.E. Murphy, "Cross-Cultural Variations in Leadership Perceptions and Attribution of Charisma to the Leader," *Organizational Behavior and Human Decision Processes* 92 (2003): 52–66; M.L.A. Hayward, V.P. Rindova, and T.G. Pollock, "Believing One's Own Press: The Causes and Consequences of CEO Celebrity," *Strategic Management Journal* 25, no. 7 (2004): 637–53.

81. The history of the trait perspective of leadership, as well as current research on this topic, is nicely summarized in S.J. Zaccaro, C. Kemp, and P. Bader, "Leader Traits and Attributes," in *The Nature of Leadership*, ed. J. Antonakis, A.T. Cianciolo, and R.J. Sternberg (Thousand Oaks, CA: Sage, 2004), 101–24.

82. R.M. Stogdill, *Handbook of Leadership* (New York: The Free Press, 1974), Chap. 5.

83. J. Intagliata, D. Ulrich, and N. Smallwood, "Leveraging Leadership Competencies to Produce Leadership Brand: Creating Distinctiveness by Focusing on Strategy and Results," *Human Resources Planning* 23, no. 4 (2000): 12-23; J.A. Conger and D.A. Ready, "Rethinking Leadership Competencies," *Leader to Leader* (2004): 41-47; Zaccaro, Kemp, and Bader, "Leader Traits and Attributes." For a recent discussion on leadership traits and evolutionary psychology, see: Judge, Piccolo, and Kosalka, "The Bright and Dark Sides of Leader Traits: A Review and Theoretical Extension of the Leader Trait Paradigm."

84. This list is based on S.A. Kirkpatrick and E.A. Locke, "Leadership: Do Traits Matter?," *Academy of Management Executive* 5 (1991): 48-60; R.M. Aditya, R.J. House, and S. Kerr, "Theory and Practice of Leadership: Into the New Millennium," in *Industrial and Organizational Psychology: Linking Theory with Practice*, ed. C.L. Cooper and E.A. Locke (Oxford, UK: Blackwell, 2000), 130-65; D. Goleman, R. Boyatzis, and A. McKee, *Primal Leaders* (Boston, MA: Harvard Business School Press, 2002); T.A. Judge et al., "Personality and Leadership: A Qualitative and Quantitative Review," *Journal Of Applied Psychology* 87, no. 4 (2002): 765-80; T.A. Judge, A.E. Colbert, and R. Ilies, "Intelligence and Leadership: A Quantitative Review and Test of Theoretical Propositions," *Journal Of Applied Psychology* 89, no. 3 (2004): 542-52; Zaccaro, Kemp, and Bader, "Leader Traits and Attributes."

85. M. Popper et al., "The Capacity to Lead: Major Psychological Differences between Leaders and Nonleaders," *Military Psychology* 16, no. 4 (2004): 245 - 63; R.G. Lord and R.J. Hall, "Identity, Deep Structure and the Development of Leadership Skill," *Leadership Quarterly* 16, no. 4 (2005): 591-615; D.V. Day, M.M. Harrison, and S.M. Halpin, *An Integrative Approach to Leader Development: Connecting Adult Development, Identity, and Expertise* (New York: Routledge, 2009); D.S. DeRue and S.J. Ashford, "Who Will Lead and Who Will Follow? A Social Process of Leadership Identity Construction in Organizations," *Academy of Management Review* 35, no. 4 (2010): 627-47.

86. Carroll and Levy, "Defaulting to Management: Leadership Defined by What It Is Not."

87. R. Davidovitz et al., "Leaders as Attachment Figures: Leaders' Attachment Orientations Predict Leadership-Related Mental Representations and Followers' Performance and Mental Health," *Journal of Personality and Social Psychology* 93, no. 4 (2007): 632-50.

88. J.B. Miner, "Twenty Years of Research on Role Motivation Theory of Managerial Effectiveness," *Personnel Psychology* 31 (1978): 739-60; R.J. House and R.N. Aditya, "The Social Scientific Study of Leadership: Quo Vadis?," *Journal of Management* 23 (1997): 409-73.

89. The large-scale studies are reported in C. Savoye, "Workers Say Honesty Is Best Company Policy," *Christian Science Monitor*, June 15 2000; J. Schettler, "Leadership in Corporate America," *Training & Development*, September 2002, 66-73; Kouzes and Posner, *The Leadership Challenge*, Chap. 2.

90. J. Hedlund et al., "Identifying and Assessing Tacit Knowledge: Understanding the Practical Intelligence of Military Leaders," *Leadership Quarterly* 14, no. 2 (2003): 117-40; R.J. Sternberg, "A Systems Model of Leadership: WICS," *American Psychologist* 62, no. 1 (2007): 34-42.

91. J. George, "Emotions and Leadership: The Role of Emotional Intelligence," *Human Relations* 53 (2000): 1027-55; Goleman, Boyatzis, and McKee, *Primal Leaders;* Lord and Hall, "Identity, Deep Structure and the Development of Leadership Skill; C. Skinner and P. Spurgeon, "Valuing Empathy and Emotional Intelligence in Health Leadership: A Study of Empathy, Leadership Behaviour and Outcome Effectiveness," *Health Services Management Research* 18, no. 1 (2005): 1-12.

92. B. George, *Authentic Leadership* (San Francisco, CA: Jossey-Bass, 2004); W.L. Gardner et al., "'Can You See the Real Me?' A Self-Based Model of Authentic Leader and Follower Development," *Leadership Quarterly* 16 (2005): 343-72; B. George, *True North* (San Francisco, CA: Jossey-Bass, 2007), Chap. 4; M.E. Palanski and F.J. Yammarino, "Integrity and Leadership: Clearing the Conceptual Confusion," *European Management Journal* 25, no. 3 (2007): 171-84; F.O. Walumbwa et al., "Authentic Leadership: Development and Validation of a Theory-Based Measure," *Journal of Management* 34, no. 1 (2008): 89-126.

93. W.G. Bennis and R.J. Thomas, "Crucibles of Leadership," *Harvard Business Review* 80, no. 9 (2002): 39-45; R.J. Thomas, *Crucibles of Leadership : How to Learn from Experience to Become a Great Leader* (Boston, MA: Harvard Business Press, 2008).

94. "Woman in Orbit; "Executive Spotlight: Amiee Chan."

95. Liza Minnelli makes this statement to explain why she doesn't perform the songs made famous by her mother, Judy Garland. The earliest versions of this quotation are found in *New Woman* magazine, Vol 8, 1978 and Vincente Minnelli's 1975 autobiography. The version cited here is from: E. Santosuosso, "Minnelli Brings a Real-Life Concert to Town," *Boston Globe*, 24 September 1992, 61.

96. B.J. Avolio et al., "Unlocking the Mask: A Look at the Process by Which Authentic Leaders Impact Follower Attitudes and Behaviors," *Leadership Quarterly* 15 (2004): 801-23.

97. R.J. Ellis, "Self-Monitoring and Leadership Emergence in Groups," *Personality and Social Psychology Bulletin* 14, no. 4 (1988): 681-93; D.V. Day et al., "Self-Monitoring Personality at Work: A Meta-Analytic Investigation of Construct Validity," *Journal of Applied Psychology* 87, no. 2 (2002): 390-401; I.O. Tueretgen, P. Unsal, and I. Erdem, "The Effects of Sex, Gender Role, and Personality Traits on Leader Emergence–Does Culture Make a Difference?," *Small Group Research* 39, no. 5 (2008): 588-615; D.U. Bryant et al., "The Interaction of Self-Monitoring and Organizational Position on Perceived Effort," *Journal of Managerial Psychology* 26, no. 2 (2011): 138-54.

98. A.G. Bedeian and D.V. Day, "Can Chameleons Lead?," *The Leadership Quarterly* 15, no. 5 (2004): 687-718.

99. W. Bennis, "We Need Leaders," *Executive Excellence* 27, no. 12 (2010): 4.

100. Bedeian and Day, "Can Chameleons Lead?."

101. D. Gruenfeld and L. Zander, "Authentic Leadership Can Be Bad Leadership," *Harvard Business Review Blog*, Harvard Business School, 2011, http://blogs.hbr.org.

102. R. Jacobs, "Using Human Resource Functions to Enhance Emotional Intelligence," in *The Emotionally Intelligent Workplace* ed. C. Cherniss and D. Goleman (San Francisco, CA: Jossey-Bass, 2001), 161-63; Conger and Ready, "Rethinking Leadership Competencies."

103. R.G. Lord and D.J. Brown, *Leadership Processes and Self-Identity: A Follower-Centered Approach to Leadership* (Mahwah, NJ: Lawrence Erlbaum Associates, 2004); R. Bolden and J. Gosling, "Leadership Competencies: Time to Change the Tune?," *Leadership* 2, no. 2 (2006): 147-63.

104. Six of the Project GLOBE clusters are described in a special issue of the *Journal of World Business*, 37 (2000). For an overview of Project GLOBE, see House, Javidan, and Dorfman, "Project GLOBE: An Introduction; House et al., "Understanding Cultures and Implicit Leadership Theories across the Globe: An Introduction to Project GLOBE."

105. J.C. Jesiuno, "Latin Europe Cluster: From South to North," *Journal of World Business* 37 (2002): 88. Another GLOBE study, of Iranian managers, also reported that "charismatic visionary" stands out as a primary leadership dimension. See A. Dastmalchian, M. Javidan, and K. Alam, "Effective Leadership and Culture in Iran: An Empirical Study," *Applied Psychology: An International Review* 50 (2001): 532-58.

106. D.N. Den Hartog et al., "Culture Specific and Cross-Cultural Generalizable Implicit Leadership Theories: Are Attributes of Charismatic/Transformational Leadership Universally Endorsed?," *Leadership Quarterly* 10 (1999): 219-56; F.C. Brodbeck and e. al., "Cultural Variation of Leadership Prototypes across 22 European Countries," *Journal of Occupational and Organizational Psychology* 73 (2000): 1-29; E. Szabo and e. al., "The Europe Cluster: Where Employees Have a Voice," *Journal of World Business* 37 (2002): 55-68. The Mexican study is reported in C.E. Nicholls, H.W. Lane, and M.B. Brechu, "Taking Self-Managed Teams to Mexico," *Academy of Management Executive* 13 (1999): 15-25.

107. G.N. Powell, "One More Time: Do Female and Male Managers Differ?," *Academy of Management Executive* 4 (1990): 68-75; M.L. van Engen and T.M. Willemsen, "Sex and Leadership Styles: A Meta-Analysis of Research Published in the 1990s," *Psychological Reports* 94, no. 1 (2004): 3-18.

108. R. Sharpe, "As Leaders, Women Rule," *BusinessWeek*, 20 November 2000, 74; M. Sappenfield, "Women, It Seems, Are Better Bosses," *Christian Science Monitor*, 16 January 2001; A.H. Eagly and L.L. Carli, "The Female Leadership Advantage: An Evaluation of the Evidence," *The Leadership Quarterly* 14, no. 6 (2003): 807-34; A.H. Eagly, M.C. Johannesen-Schmidt, and M.L. van Engen, "Transformational, Transactional, and Laissez-Faire Leadership Styles: A Meta-Analysis Comparing Women and Men," *Psychological Bulletin* 129 (2003): 569-91.

109. A.H. Eagly, S.J. Karau, and M.G. Makhijani, "Gender and the Effectiveness of Leaders: A

Meta-Analysis," *Psychological Bulletin* 117 (1995): 125–45; J.G. Oakley, "Gender-Based Barriers to Senior Management Positions: Understanding the Scarcity of Female CEOs," *Journal of Business Ethics* 27 (2000): 821–34; N.Z. Stelter, "Gender Differences in Leadership: Current Social Issues and Future Organizational Implications," *Journal of Leadership Studies* 8 (2002): 88–99; M.E. Heilman et al., "Penalties for Success: Reactions to Women Who Succeed at Male Gender-Typed Tasks," *Journal of Applied Psychology* 89, no. 3 (2004): 416–27; A.H. Eagly, "Achieving Relational Authenticity in Leadership: Does Gender Matter?," *The Leadership Quarterly* 16, no. 3 (2005): 459–74.

CHAPTER 13

1. Valve Corporation, *Valve Handbook for Employees* (Bellevue, WA: Valve Press, 2012); M. Abrash, "Valve: How I Got Here, What It's Like, and What I'm Doing," *Ramblings in Valve Time*, 13 April 2012, http://blogs.valvesoftware.com/abrash; J. Cook, "Valve Designer Greg Coomer: How Getting Rid of Bosses Makes for Better Games," *GeekWire*, 29 October 2012; N. Wingfield, "Game Maker without a Rule Book," *New York Times*, 9 September 2012.

2. S. Ranson, R. Hinings, and R. Greenwood, "The Structuring of Organizational Structure," *Administrative Science Quarterly* 25 (1980): 1–14; J.-E. Johanson, "Intraorganizational Influence," *Management Communication Quarterly* 13 (2000): 393–435; K. Walsh, "Interpreting the Impact of Culture on Structure," *Journal of Applied Behavioral Science* 40, no. 3 (2004): 302–22.

3. N. Alcoba, "TTC Told How to Improve Customer Service 78 Different Ways," *National Post*, 23 August 2010; "Listening Is Job One," *Toronto Star*, 23 March 2011.

4. H. Mintzberg, *The Structuring of Organizations* (Englewood Cliffs, NJ: Prentice Hall, 1979), 2-3.

5. E.E. Lawler III, *Motivation in Work Organizations* (Monterey, CA: Brooks/Cole, 1973); M.A. Campion, "Ability Requirement Implications of Job Design: An Interdisciplinary Perspective," *Personnel Psychology* 42 (1989): 1–24.

6. G.S. Becker and K.M. Murphy, "The Division-of-Labor, Coordination Costs and Knowledge," *Quarterly Journal of Economics* 107, no. 4 (1992): 1137–60; L. Borghans and B. Weel, "The Division of Labour, Worker Organisation, and Technological Change," *The Economic Journal* 116, no. 509 (2006): F45–F72.

7. Mintzberg, *The Structuring of Organizations* Chap. 1; D.A. Nadler and M.L. Tushman, *Competing by Design: The Power of Organizational Architecture* (New York: Oxford University Press, 1997), Chap. 6; J.R. Galbraith, *Designing Organizations: An Executive Guide to Strategy, Structure, and Process* (San Francisco, CA: Jossey-Bass, 2002), Chap. 4.

8. J. Stephenson, Jr., "Making Humanitarian Relief Networks More Effective: Operational Coordination, Trust and Sense Making," *Disasters* 29, no. 4 (2005): 337.

9. A. Willem, M. Buelens, and H. Scarbrough, "The Role of Inter-Unit Coordination Mechanisms in Knowledge Sharing: A Case Study of a British MNC," *Journal of Information Science* 32, no. 6 (2006): 539–61; R.R. Gulati, "Silo Busting," *Harvard Business Review* 85, no. 5 (2007): 98–108.

10. Borghans and Weel, "The Division of Labour, Worker Organisation, and Technological Change."

11. T. Van Alphen, "Magna in Overdrive," *Toronto Star*, 24 July 2006.

12. Galbraith, *Designing Organizations*, pp. 66–72; D. Aaker, *Spanning Silos: The New CMO Imperative* (Cambridge, MA: Harvard Business Press, 2008), pp.95–96; A. Pike, *Brands and Branding Geographies* (Cheltenham, UK: Edward Elgar, 2011), pg. 133.

13. S.M. Sapuan, M.R. Osman, and Y. Nukman, "State of the Art of the Concurrent Engineering Technique in the Automotive Industry," *Journal of Engineering Design* 17, no. 2 (2006): 143–57; D.M. Anderson, *Design for Manufacturing: How to Use Concurrent Engineering to Rapidly Develop Low-Cost, High-Quality Products for Lean Management* (Boca Raton, FL: CRC Press/Taylor & Francis, 2014), Chap. 2.

14. A.H. Van De Ven, A.L. Delbecq, and R.J. Koenig Jr., "Determinants of Coordination Modes within Organizations," *American Sociological Review* 41, no. 2 (1976): 322–38.

15. M. Villano, "The Control Freak in the Corner Office," *New York Times*, 28 May 2006, 10; "One-Third of Employees Feel Micromanaged by Boss," News release (Skillman, NJ: BlessingWhite, 27 October 2008); T. Gould, "How Employees Really Feel About Their Bosses," *HR Morning*, 7 July 2011; Kelly Services, *Effective Employers: The Evolving Workforce*, Kelly Global Workforce Index, Kelly Services (Troy, MI: November 2011); "Something to Talk About," News release (Toronto, ON: Accountemps, 22 October 2013).

16. Y.-M. Hsieh and A. Tien-Hsieh, "Enhancement of Service Quality with Job Standardisation," *Service Industries Journal* 21 (2001): 147–66.

17. M. Guadalupe, J. Wulf, and H. Li, "The Rise of the Functional Manager: Changes Afoot in the C-Suite," *European Business Review* (2012); G.L. Neilson and J. Wulf, "How Many Direct Reports?," *Harvard Business Review* 90, no. 4 (2012): 112–19.

18. B. Davison, "Management Span of Control: How Wide Is Too Wide?," *Journal of Business Strategy* 24, no. 4 (2003): 22–29; N.A. Theobald and S. Nicholson-Crotty, "The Many Faces of Span of Control: Organizational Structure across Multiple Goals," *Administration Society* 36, no. 6 (2005): 648–60; R.M. Meyer, "Span of Management: Concept Analysis," *Journal of Advanced Nursing* 63, no. 1 (2008): 104–12.

19. D.D. Van Fleet and A.G. Bedeian, "A History of the Span of Management," *Academy of Management Review* 2 (1977): 356–72; H. Fayol, *General and Industrial Management*, trans. C. Storrs (London, UK: Pitman, 1949); D.A. Wren, A.G. Bedeian, and J.D. Breeze, "The Foundations of Henri Fayol's Administrative Theory " *Management Decision* 40, no. 9 (2002): 906–18.

20. D. Drickhamer, "Lessons from the Leading Edge," *Industry Week*, 21 February 2000, 23–26.

21. S. Nix et al., *Span of Control in City Government Increases Overall*, Office of City Auditor, City of Seattle (Seattle, WA: 19 September 2005); "Fedex 2008 Shareowners Meeting," (Memphis, TN: Fedex, 29 September 2008); J. McLellan, *Administrative Review: An Agenda for Business Improvement*, Multnomah County (Portland, OR: 19 May 2009); D. Thompson, "More on the Span of Control Issue," *Statesman Journal Blog (Oregon)*, 16 May 2011; Iowa State. Legislative Services Agency, *Span of Control*, Fiscal Note, Iowa State (Des Moines: Iowa Legislature, 10 March 2011); Western Management Consultants, *Service Efficiency Study Program Management Span of Control Review Report to the City Manager*, City of Toronto (Toronto, ON: 31 October 2012); United States Postal Service, *Supervisor Workhours and Span of Control: Management Advisory*, (Washington, DC: United States Postal Service, 4 April 2013).

22. G. Anders, "Overseeing More Employees–with Fewer Managers–Consultants Are Urging Companies to Loosen Their Supervising Views," *Wall Street Journal*, 24 March 2008, B6.

23. J. Greenwald, "Ward Compares the Best with the Rest," *Business Insurance*, 26 August 2002, 16.

24. J.H. Gittell, "Supervisory Span, Relational Coordination and Flight Departure Performance: A Reassessment of Postbureaucracy Theory," *Organization Science* 12, no. 4 (2001): 468–83.

25. S. Marchionne, "Navigating the New Automotive Epoch," *Vital Speeches of the Day* (2010): 134–37.

26. T.D. Wall, J.L. Cordery, and C.W. Clegg, "Empowerment, Performance, and Operational Uncertainty: A Theoretical Integration," *Applied Psychology: An International Review* 51 (2002): 146–69.

27. J. Morris, J. Hassard, and L. McCann, "New Organizational Forms, Human Resource Management and Structural Convergence? A Study of Japanese Organizations," *Organization Studies* 27, no. 10 (2006): 1485–511.

28. Q.N. Huy, "In Praise of Middle Managers," *Harvard Business Review* 79 (2001): 72–79; C.R. Littler, R. Wiesner, and R. Dunford, "The Dynamics of Delayering: Changing Management Structures in Three Countries," *Journal of Management Studies* 40, no. 2 (2003): 225–56; H.J. Leavitt, *Top Down: Why Hierarchies Are Here to Stay and How to Manage Them More Effectively* (Cambridge: Harvard Business School Press, 2005); L. McCann, J. Morris, and J. Hassard, "Normalized Intensity: The New Labour Process of Middle Management," *Journal of Management Studies* 45, no. 2 (2008): 343–71; "Why Middle Managers May Be the Most Important People in Your Company," *Knowledge @ Wharton*, 25 May 2011.

29. K. Tyler, "The Strongest Link," *HRMagazine* 2011, 51–53.

30. Littler, Wiesner, and Dunford, "The Dynamics of Delayering: Changing Management Structures in Three Countries," 244.

31. J. Denby, "Leaders in African Electricity," *African Business Review*, 11 May 2010; "Q1 2012 Sandvik Ab Earnings Conference Call," News release for Sandvik AB (Stockholm, Sweden: CQ FD Disclosure, 27 April 2012).

32. R.M. Lindsay and T. Libby, "Svenska Handelsbanken: Controlling a Radically Decentralized Organization without Budgets," *Issues in*

Accounting Education 22, no. 4 (2007): 625–40; P. Aldrick, "'Old' Is the New Thing in Banking," *Daily Telegraph (London),* 28 February 2011, 4; A. Saunders, "Slay the Bank Monster," *Management Today* 2012, 36–39; J. Coney, "A New High Street Bank That Cares Only About Good Service?," *Mail Online (London),* 17 July 2013.

33. The variations of decentralization within a company are discussed in: G. Masada, "To Centralize or Decentralize?," *Optimize,* May 2005, 58–61. The 7-Eleven example is described in: J.G. Kelley, "Slurpees and Sausages: 7-Eleven Holds School," *Richmond (Va.) Times-Dispatch,* 12 March 2004, C1; S. Marling, "The 24-Hour Supply Chain," *InformationWeek,* 26 January 2004, 43.

34. Mintzberg, *The Structuring of Organizations* Chap. 5.

35. W. Dessein and T. Santos, "Adaptive Organizations," *Journal of Political Economy* 114, no. 5 (2006): 956–95; A.A.M. Nasurdin et al., "Organizational Structure and Organizational Climate as Potential Predictors of Job Stress: Evidence from Malaysia," *International Journal of Commerce and Management* 16, no. 2 (2006): 116–29; C.-J. Chen and J.-W. Huang, "How Organizational Climate and Structure Affect Knowledge Management—the Social Interaction Perspective," *International Journal of Information Management* 27, no. 2 (2007): 104–18.

36. T. Burns and G. Stalker, *The Management of Innovation* (London, UK: Tavistock, 1961).

37. Cook, "Valve Designer Greg Coomer."

38. J. Tata, S. Prasad, and r. Thom, "The Influence of Organizational Structure on the Effectiveness of TQM Programs," *Journal of Managerial Issues* 11, no. 4 (1999): 440–53; A. Lam, "Tacit Knowledge, Organizational Learning and Societal Institutions: An Integrated Framework," *Organization Studies* 21 (2000): 487–513.

39. W.D. Sine, H. Mitsuhashi, and D.A. Kirsch, "Revisiting Burns and Stalker: Formal Structure and New Venture Performance in Emerging Economic Sectors," *Academy of Management Journal* 49, no. 1 (2006): 121–32.

40. Mintzberg, *The Structuring of Organizations* 106.

41. Mintzberg, *The Structuring of Organizations* Chap. 17; R.M. Burton, B. Obel, and G. DeSanctis, *Organizational Design: A Step-by-Step Approach,* 2nd ed. (Cambridge, UK: Cambridge University Press, 2011), 61–63.

42. A. Joseph, "The Cream Always Rises," *Canadian Packaging,* April 2012, 18–22; D. Crosby, "Chapman's Mixes in Some Fun," *Owen Sound Sun Times,* 26 February 2014, C11.

43. Galbraith, *Designing Organizations,* 23–25; Burton, Obel, and DeSanctis, *Organizational Design,* 63–65.

44. E.E. Lawler III, *Rewarding Excellence: Pay Strategies for the New Economy* (San Francisco, CA: Jossey-Bass, 2000), 31–34.

45. The evolutionary development of the divisional structure is described in: J.R. Galbraith, "The Evolution of Enterprise Organization Designs," *Journal of Organization Design* 1, no. 2 (2012): 1–13.

46. These structures were identified from corporate Web sites and annual reports. These organizations typically rely on a mixture of other structures, so the charts shown have been adapted for learning purposes.

47. M. Goold and A. Campbell, "Do You Have a Well-Designed Organization," *Harvard Business Review* 80 (2002): 117–24. Others have added factors such as economies of scale and what resources need to be controlled to most. See: G. Kesler and A. Kates, *Leading Organization Design: How to Make Organization Design Decisions to Drive the Results You Want* (San Francisco, CA: Jossey-Bass, 2011), Chap. 3.

48. J.R. Galbraith, "Structuring Global Organizations," in *Tomorrow's Organization* ed. S.A. Mohrman, et al. (San Francisco, CA: Jossey-Bass, 1998), 103–29; C. Homburg, J.P. Workman Jr., and O. Jensen, "Fundamental Changes in Marketing Organization: The Movement toward a Customer-Focused Organizational Structure," *Academy of Marketing Science. Journal* 28 (2000): 459–78; T.H. Davenport, J.G. Harris, and A.K. Kohli, "How Do They Know Their Customers So Well?," *Sloan Management Review* 42 (2001): 63–73; J.R. Galbraith, "Organizing to Deliver Solutions," *Organizational Dynamics* 31 (2002): 194–207.

49. S.J. Palmisano, "The Globally Integrated Enterprise," *Foreign Affairs* 85, no. 3 (2006): 127–36; S. Palmisano, "The Globally Integrated Enterprise," *Vital Speeches of the Day* 73, no. 10 (2007): 449–53.

50. M. Dewhurst, "An Interview with Michael Cannon-Brookes, Vice-President, Business Development, China and India, IBM Corporation," *Perspectives on Global Organizations,* May 2012, 35–40.

51. Burton, Obel, and DeSanctis, *Organizational Design,* 65–68.

52. J.R. Galbraith, E.E. Lawler III, and Associates, *Organizing for the Future: The New Logic for Managing Complex Organizations* (San Francisco, CA: Jossey-Bass, 1993); R. Bettis and M. Hitt, "The New Competitive Landscape," *Strategic Management Journal* 16 (1995): 7–19.

53. P.C. Ensign, "Interdependence, Coordination, and Structure in Complex Organizations: Implications for Organization Design," *Mid-Atlantic Journal of Business* 34 (1998): 5–22.

54. M.M. Fanning, "A Circular Organization Chart Promotes a Hospital-Wide Focus on Teams," *Hospital & Health Services Administration* 42 (1997): 243–54; L.Y. Chan and B.E. Lynn, "Operating in Turbulent Times: How Ontario's Hospitals Are Meeting the Current Funding Crisis," *Health Care Management Review* 23 (1998): 7–18.

55. P. Lavoie, "TAXI," *Campaign,* 12 October 2007, 15; L. Sylvain, "Taxi Deconstructed," *Strategy,* June 2007, 50; E. Wexler, "There's No Stopping TAXI," *Strategy,* January 2011, 40–42; M. Chung, "Aoy Silver: Taxi's Customized Ride," *Strategy,* November 2013, 35.

56. R. Cross, "Looking before You Leap: Assessing the Jump to Teams in Knowledge-Based Work," *Business Horizons* 43, no. 5 (2000): 29–36; M. Fenton-O'Creevy, "Employee Involvement and the Middle Manager: Saboteur or Scapegoat?," *Human Resource Management Journal* 11 (2001): 24–40; C. Douglas and W.L. Gardner, "Transition to Self-Directed Work Teams: Implications of Transition Time and Self-Monitoring for Managers' Use of Influence Tactics," *Journal of Organizational Behavior* 25 (2004): 47–65; G. Garda, K. Lindstrom, and M. Dallnera, "Towards a Learning Organization: The Introduction of a Client-Centered Team-Based Organization in Administrative Surveying Work," *Applied Ergonomics* 34 (2003): 97–105.

57. S.M. Davis and P.R. Lawrence, *Matrix* (Reading, Mass: Addison-Wesley, 1977); J.R. Galbraith, *Designing Matrix Organizations That Actually Work* (San Francisco, CA: Jossey-Bass, 2009).

58. "Organizational Structure and Business Activities," (Melbourne, Australia: MacQuarie Group, 2013), http://www.macquarie.com.au/mgl/au/about-macquarie-group/profile/organisation-structure (accessed 7 June 2013). Other global matrix structures are also discussed in: Kesler and Kates, *Leading Organization Design,* Chap. 7.

59. Deloitte U.S. Chinese Services Group, *Balancing Flexibility and Control: Optimizing Your Organizational Structure in China,* Board Brief China, (New York: Deloitte, 2008).

60. R.C. Ford and W.A. Randolph, "Cross-Functional Structures: A Review and Integration of Matrix Organization and Project Management," *Journal of Management* 18 (1992): 267–94.

61. R. Muzyka and G. Zeschuk, "Managing Multiple Projects," *Game Developer,* March 2003, 34–42.

62. J.X.J. Qiu and L. Donaldson, "Stopford and Wells Were Right! MNC Matrix Structures Do Fit a 'High-High' Strategy," *Management International Review (MIR)* 52, no. 5 (2012): 671–89; D. Ganguly and M. Mitra, "Survive the Matrix," *Economic Times (Mumbai, India),* 29 March 2013.

63. G. Calabrese, "Communication and Co-Operation in Product Development: A Case Study of a European Car Producer," *R & D Management* 27 (1997): 239–52; T. Sy and L.S. D'Annunzio, "Challenges and Strategies of Matrix Organizations: Top-Level and Mid-Level Managers' Perspectives," *Human Resource Planning* 28, no. 1 (2005): 39–48; J. Wolf and W.G. Egelhoff, "An Empirical Evaluation of Conflict in MNC Matrix Structure Firms," *International Business Review* 22, no. 3 (2013): 591–601.

64. D. Ganguly, "Matrix Evolutions," *Economic Times (Mumbai, India),* 18 February 2012.

65. Nadler and Tushman, *Competing by Design,* Chap. 6; M. Goold and A. Campbell, "Structured Networks: Towards the Well-Designed Matrix," *Long Range Planning* 36, no. 5 (2003): 427–39.

66. J.-Y. Lee, "Matrix Structure No Easy Fit for Local Financial Groups," *Joins,* 3 February 2012.

67. D. Ciampa and M. Watkins, "Rx for New CEOs," *Chief Executive,* January 2008.

68. P. Siekman, "This Is Not a BMW Plant," *Fortune,* 18 April 2005, 208; "Magna's Austria Plant to Lose Production of BMW X3," *Reuters,* 16 May 2007.

69. R.F. Miles and C.C. Snow, "The New Network Firm: A Spherical Structure Built on a Human Investment Philosophy," *Organizational Dynamics* 23, no. 4 (1995): 5–18; C. Baldwin and K. Clark, "Managing in an Age of Modularity," *Harvard Business Review* 75 (1997): 84–93.

70. J. Hagel III and M. Singer, "Unbundling the Corporation," *Harvard Business Review* 77

(1999): 133–41; R. Hacki and J. Lighton, "The Future of the Networked Company," *McKinsey Quarterly* 3 (2001): 26–39.

71. J. Dwyer, "Mind How You Go," *Facilities Management*, May 2008, 22–25.

72. M.A. Schilling and H.K. Steensma, "The Use of Modular Organizational Forms: An Industry-Level Analysis," *Academy of Management Journal* 44 (2001): 1149–68.

73. G. Morgan, *Images of Organization*, Second ed. (Newbury Park: Sage, 1996); G. Morgan, *Imagin-I-Zation: New Mindsets for Seeing, Organizing and Managing* (Thousand Oaks, CA: Sage, 1997).

74. H. Chesbrough and D.J. Teece, "When Is Virtual Virtuous? Organizing for Innovation," *Harvard Business Review* 74, no. 1 (1996): 65–73; P.M.J. Christie and R. Levary, "Virtual Corporations: Recipe for Success," *Industrial Management* 40 (1998): 7–11.

75. L. Donaldson, *The Contingency Theory of Organizations* (Thousand Oaks, CA: Sage, 2001); J. Birkenshaw, R. Nobel, and J. Ridderstråle, "Knowledge as a Contingency Variable: Do the Characteristics of Knowledge Predict Organizational Structure?," *Organization Science* 13, no. 3 (2002): 274–89.

76. P.R. Lawrence and J.W. Lorsch, *Organization and Environment* (Homewood, IL: Irwin, 1967); Mintzberg, *The Structuring of Organizations* Chap. 15.

77. Burns and Stalker, *The Management of Innovation;* Lawrence and Lorsch, *Organization and Environment*

78. J. Kersnar, "Forget What You Think You Know," *CFO Magazine*, Jan/Feb 2011, 29–33.

79. Mintzberg, *The Structuring of Organizations* p. 282.

80. D.S. Pugh and C.R. Hinings, *Organizational Structure: Extensions and Replications* (Farnborough, England: Lexington Books, 1976); Mintzberg, *The Structuring of Organizations* Chap. 13.

81. Galbraith, *Designing Organizations*, 52–55; G. Hertel, S. Geister, and U. Konradt, "Managing Virtual Teams: A Review of Current Empirical Research," *Human Resource Management Review* 15 (2005): 69–95.

82. C. Perrow, "A Framework for the Comparative Analysis of Organizations," *American Sociological Review* 32 (1967): 194–208; D. Gerwin, "The Comparative Analysis of Structure and Technology: A Critical Appraisal," *Academy of Management Review* 4, no. 1 (1979): 41–51; C.C. Miller et al., "Understanding Technology-Structure Relationships: Theory Development and Meta-Analytic Theory Testing," *Academy of Management Journal* 34, no. 2 (1991): 370–99.

83. R.H. Kilmann, *Beyond the Quick Fix* (San Francisco, CA: Jossey-Bass, 1984), p. 38.

84. A.D. Chandler, *Strategy and Structure* (Cambridge, MA: MIT Press, 1962).

85. D. Miller, "Configurations of Strategy and Structure," *Strategic Management Journal* 7 (1986): 233–49.

CHAPTER 14

1. J. Pachner, "The Gospel According to Bruce," *Profit*, 7 October 2011; "A Travel Guru's Guide to Good Leadership," *National Post (Toronto)*, 17 June 2013, FP6; J. Whittock, "Get Ahead: Tap into the G-Factor," *Travel Trade Gazette UK (London)*, 21 February 2013, 29; M.E. May, "Looptail: How Bruce Poon Tip Created an Entirely New Way of Doing Business," *American Express OPEN Forum*, American Express, 17 September 2013, https://www.americanexpress.com/us/small-business/openforum; Travel Trade Gazette UK, "Michael Edwards, Managing Director for the UK, G Adventures," (YouTube, 2013); B. Poon Tip, *Looptail: How One Company Changed the World by Reinventing Business* (New York, NY: Business Plus, 2013).

2. A. Williams, P. Dobson, and M. Walters, *Changing Culture: New Organizational Approaches* (London, UK: Institute of Personnel Management, 1989); E.H. Schein, "What Is Culture?," in *Reframing Organizational Culture*, ed. P.J. Frost, et al. (Newbury Park, CA: Sage, 1991), 243–53.

3. B.M. Meglino and E.C. Ravlin, "Individual Values in Organizations: Concepts, Controversies, and Research," *Journal of Management* 24, no. 3 (1998): 351–89; B.R. Agle and C.B. Caldwell, "Understanding Research on Values in Business," *Business and Society* 38, no. 3 (1999): 326–87; S. Hitlin and J.A. Pilavin, "Values: Reviving a Dormant Concept," *Annual Review of Sociology* 30 (2004): 359–93.

4. N.M. Ashkanasy, "The Case for Culture," in *Debating Organization*, ed. R. Westwood and S. Clegg (Malden, MA: Blackwell, 2003), 300–10.

5. K. Ladendorf, "For Facebook Workers, It's Not Just a Job," *Austin American-Statesman*, 1 May 2011, E1; "CEO Zuckerberg: Facebook's 5 Core Values," *CBS News*, 17 May 2012.

6. B. Kabanoff and J. Daly, "Espoused Values in Organisations," *Australian Journal of Management* 27, no. Special issue (2002): 89–104.

7. "Norway Criticizes BP, Smedvig over Safety," *Energy Compass*, 3 January 2003; "Norway Criticizes BP, Smedvig over Safety; J.A. Lozano, "BP Refinery Had History of Dangerous Releases, Report Finds," *Associated Press*, 28 October 2005; S. McNulty, "A Corroded Culture? ," *Financial Times (London)*, 18 December 2006, 17; U.S. Chemical Safety and Hazard Investigation Board, *Investigation Report: Refinery Explosion and Fire (BP, Texas City, Texas, March 23, 2005)*, U.S. Chemical Safety Board (Washington, DC: March 2007); S. Greenhouse, "BP Faces Record Fine for '05 Refinery Explosion," *New York Times*, 30 October 2009; L.C. Steffy, *Drowning in Oil: BP and the Reckless Pursuit of Profit* (New York, NY: McGraw-Hill, 2011).

8. C. Ostroff, A.J. Kinicki, and R.S. Muhammad, "Organizational Culture and Climate," in *Handbook of Psychology*, 2nd ed. (John Wiley & Sons, Inc., 2012), 643–76.

9. R. Hastings, *Netflix Culture: Freedom and Responsibility*, (Los Gatos, CA: Netflix, August 2009).

10. C.A. O'Reilly III, J. Chatman, and D.F. Caldwell, "People and Organizational Culture: A Profile Comparison Approach to Assessing Person-Organization Fit," *Academy of Management Journal* 34 (1991): 487–516; J.J. van Muijen, "Organizational Culture," in *A Handbook of Work and Organizational Psychology: Organizational Psychology*, ed. P.J.D. Drenth, H. Thierry, and C.J. de Wolff (East Sussex, UK: Psychology Press, 1998), 113–32; P.A. Balthazard, R.A. Cooke, and R.E. Potter, "Dysfunctional Culture, Dysfunctional Organization: Capturing the Behavioral Norms That Form Organizational Culture and Drive Performance," *Journal of Managerial Psychology* 21, no. 8 (2006): 709–32; C. Helfrich et al., "Assessing an Organizational Culture Instrument Based on the Competing Values Framework: Exploratory and Confirmatory Factor Analyses," *Implementation Science* 2, no. 1 (2007): 13. For reviews of organizational culture survey instruments, see T. Scott et al., "The Quantitative Measurement of Organizational Culture in Health Care: A Review of the Available Instruments," *Health Services Research* 38, no. 3 (2003): 923–45; D.E. Leidner and T. Kayworth, "A Review of Culture in Information Systems Research: Toward a Theory of Information Technology Culture Conflict," *MIS Quarterly* 30, no. 2 (2006): 357–99; S. Scott-Findlay and C.A. Estabrooks, "Mapping the Organizational Culture Research in Nursing: A Literature Review," *Journal of Advanced Nursing* 56, no. 5 (2006): 498–513.

11. J. Martin, P.J. Frost, and O.A. O'Neill, "Organizational Culture: Beyond Struggles for Intellectual Dominance," in *Handbook of Organization Studies*, ed. S. Clegg, et al. (London, UK: Sage, 2006), 725–53; N.E. Fenton and S. Inglis, "A Critical Perspective on Organizational Values," *Nonprofit Management and Leadership* 17, no. 3 (2007): 335–47; K. Haukelid, "Theories of (Safety) Culture Revisited–an Anthropological Approach," *Safety Science* 46, no. 3 (2008): 413–26.

12. G. Hofstede, "Identifying Organizational Subcultures: An Empirical Approach," *Journal of Management Studies* 35, no. 1 (1990): 1–12; J. Martin and C. Siehl, "Organizational Culture and Counterculture: An Uneasy Symbiosis," *Organizational Dynamics* (1983): 52–64; E. Ogbonna and L.C. Harris, "Organisational Culture in the Age of the Internet: An Exploratory Study," *New Technology, Work and Employment* 21, no. 2 (2006): 162–75.

13. H. Silver, "Does a University Have a Culture?," *Studies in Higher Education* 28, no. 2 (2003): 157–69.

14. A. Sinclair, "Approaches to Organizational Culture and Ethics," *Journal of Business Ethics* 12 (1993); T.E. Deal and A.A. Kennedy, *The New Corporate Cultures* (Cambridge, MA: Perseus Books, 1999), Chap. 10; A. Boisnier and J. Chatman, "The Role of Subcultures in Agile Organizations," in *Leading and Managing People in Dynamic Organizations*, ed. R. Petersen and E. Mannix (Mahwah, NJ: Lawrence Erlbaum Associates, 2003), 87–112; C. Morrill, M.N. Zald, and H. Rao, "Covert Political Conflict in Organizations: Challenges from Below," *Annual Review of Sociology* 29, no. 1 (2003): 391–415.

15. J.S. Ott, *The Organizational Culture Perspective* (Pacific Grove, CA: Brooks/Cole, 1989), Chap. 2; J.S. Pederson and J.S. Sorensen, *Organizational Cultures in Theory and Practice* (Aldershot, England: Gower, 1989), pp. 27–29; M.O. Jones, *Studying Organizational Symbolism: What, How, Why?* (Thousand Oaks, CA: Sage, 1996).

16. A. Furnham and B. Gunter, "Corporate Culture: Definition, Diagnosis, and Change," *International Review of Industrial and Organizational*

Psychology 8 (1993): 233–61; E.H. Schein, "Organizational Culture," *American Psychologist* (1990): 109–19; E.H. Schein, *The Corporate Culture Survival Guide* (San Francisco, CA: Jossey-Bass, 1999), Chap. 4.

17. M. Doehrman, "Anthropologists–Deep in the Corporate Bush," *Daily Record (Kansas City, MO)*, 19 July 2005, 1.

18. R. Ouzounian, "Cirque's Dream Factory," *Toronto Star*, 1 August 2004; M. Miller, "The Acrobat," *Forbes*, 15 March 2004, 100–03.

19. T.E. Deal and A.A. Kennedy, *Corporate Cultures* (Reading, MA: Addison-Wesley, 1982), chap. 5; C.J. Boudens, "The Story of Work: A Narrative Analysis of Workplace Emotion," *Organization Studies* 26, no. 9 (2005): 1285–306; S. Denning, *The Leader's Guide to Storytelling* (San Francisco, CA: Jossey-Bass, 2005).

20. A.L. Wilkins, "Organizational Stories as Symbols Which Control the Organization," in *Organizational Symbolism*, ed. L.R. Pondy, et al. (Greenwich, CT: JAI Press, 1984), 81–92; R. Zemke, "Storytelling: Back to a Basic," *Training* 27 (1990): 44–50; J.C. Meyer, "Tell Me a Story: Eliciting Organizational Values from Narratives," *Communication Quarterly* 43 (1995): 210–24; W. Swap et al., "Using Mentoring and Storytelling to Transfer Knowledge in the Workplace," *Journal of Management Information Systems* 18 (2001): 95–114.

21. D. Roth, "My Job at the Container Store," *Fortune* (2000): 74–78.

22. R.E. Quinn and N.T. Snyder, "Advance Change Theory: Culture Change at Whirlpool Corporation," in *The Leader's Change Handbook* ed. J.A. Conger, G.M. Spreitzer, and E.E. Lawler III (San Francisco, CA: Jossey-Bass, 1999), 162–93.

23. G. Smith, *Why I Left Goldman Sachs: A Wall Street Story* (New York: Grand Central Publishing, 2012).

24. A.C.T. Smith and B. Stewart, "Organizational Rituals: Features, Functions and Mechanisms," *International Journal of Management Reviews* 13 (2011): 113–33.

25. "The Ultimate Chairman," *Business Times Singapore*, 3 September 2005.

26. Churchill apparently made this statement on October 28, 1943 in the British House of Commons, when London, damaged by bombings in World War II, was about to be rebuilt.

27. G. Turner and J. Myerson, *New Workspace New Culture: Office Design as a Catalyst for Change* (Aldershot, UK: Gower, 1998).

28. A. Clark, "Life in Mars," *The Guardian (London)*, 3 May 2008; D.A. Kaplan, "Mars Incorporated: A Pretty Sweet Place to Work," *Fortune*, 17 January 2013. Also based on a virtual Google street view tour of Mars' head offices in Maclean Virginia, Slough UK, and Bolton, Ontario in Canada.

29. K.D. Elsbach and B.A. Bechky, "It's More Than a Desk: Working Smarter through Leveraged Office Design," *California Management Review* 49, no. 2 (2007): 80–101.

30. M. Burton, "Open Plan, Open Mind," *Director* (2005): 68–72; B. Murray, "Agency Profile: Mother London," *Ihaveanidea*, 28 January 2007.

31. B. O'Connor, "CEO Credits Quicken Loans' Culture for Firm's Success," *Detroit News*, 1 May 2013, C2; "First West Credit Union CEO Places Focus on Leadership Brand," *CEO Series* (Vancouver, BC: Simon Fraser University, 29 October 2013), http://beedie.sfu.ca/blog/2013/10/7405/ (accessed 30 March 2014).

32. J.C. Collins and J.I. Porras, *Built to Last: Successful Habits of Visionary Companies* (London, UK: Century, 1994); Deal and Kennedy, *The New Corporate Cultures;* R. Barrett, *Building a Values-Driven Organization: A Whole System Approach to Cultural Transformation* (Burlington, MA: Butterworth-Heinemann, 2006); J.M. Kouzes and B.Z. Posner, *The Leadership Challenge*, Fourth ed. (San Francisco, CA: Jossey-Bass, 2007), Chap. 3.

33. C. Siehl and J. Martin, "Organizational Culture: A Key to Financial Performance?," in *Organizational Climate and Culture*, ed. B. Schneider (San Francisco, CA: Jossey-Bass, 1990), 241–81; G.G. Gordon and N. DiTomasco, "Predicting Corporate Performance from Organizational Culture," *Journal of Management Studies* 29 (1992): 783–98; J.P. Kotter and J.L. Heskett, *Corporate Culture and Performance* (New York: Free Press, 1992); C.P.M. Wilderom, U. Glunk, and R. Maslowski, "Organizational Culture as a Predictor of Organizational Performance," in *Handbook of Organizational Culture and Climate*, ed. N.M. Ashkanasy, C.P.M. Wilderom, and M.F. Peterson (Thousand Oaks, CA: Sage, 2000), 193–210; A. Carmeli and A. Tishler, "The Relationships between Intangible Organizational Elements and Organizational Performance," *Strategic Management Journal* 25 (2004): 1257–78; S. Teerikangas and P. Very, "The Culture-Performance Relationship in M&A: From Yes/No to How," *British Journal of Management* 17, no. S1 (2006): S31–S48.

34. "Define Core Values First," *National Post*, 7 February 2011, JV1; "Sharing a Vision with Clearly Contacts CEO Roger Hardy," *PeopleTalk*, Spring 2013, 50.

35. Y. Wiener, "Forms of Value Systems: A Focus on Organizational Effectiveness and Cultural Change and Maintenance," *Academy of Management Review* 13, no. 4 (1988): 534–45; J.A. Chatman and S.E. Cha, "Leading by Leveraging Culture," *California Management Review* 45 (2003): 20–34; M. Alvesson, *Understanding Organizational Culture*, 2nd ed. (London, UK: Sage, 2013).

36. B. Ashforth and F. Mael, "Social Identity Theory and the Organization," *Academy of Management Review* 14 (1989): 20–39.

37. Heidrick and Struggles, *Leadership Challenges Emerge as Asia Pacific Companies Go Global*, Heidrick and Struggles (Melbourne: August 2008).

38. M.R. Louis, "Surprise and Sensemaking: What Newcomers Experience in Entering Unfamiliar Organizational Settings," *Administrative Science Quarterly* 25 (1980): 226–51; S.G. Harris, "Organizational Culture and Individual Sensemaking: A Schema-Based Perspective," *Organization Science* 5 (1994): 309–21.

39. J.W. Barnes et al., "The Role of Culture Strength in Shaping Sales Force Outcomes," *Journal of Personal Selling & Sales Management* 26, no. 3 (2006): 255–70.

40. D. Frith, "Follow the Leader," *BRW*, 19 April 2012, 18.

41. C.A. O'Reilly III and J.A. Chatman, "Culture as Social Control: Corporations, Cults, and Commitment," *Research in Organizational Behavior* 18 (1996): 157–200; B. Spector and H. Lane, "Exploring the Distinctions between a High Performance Culture and a Cult," *Strategy & Leadership* 35, no. 3 (2007): 18–24.

42. Kotter and Heskett, *Corporate Culture and Performance;* J.P. Kotter, "Cultures and Coalitions," *Executive Excellence* 15 (1998): 14–15; B.M. Bass and R.E. Riggio, *Transformational Leadership*, Second ed. (New York: Routledge, 2006), Chap. 7. The term adaptive culture has a different meaning in organizational behaviour than it has in cultural anthropology, where it refers to nonmaterial cultural conditions (such as ways of thinking) that lag the material culture (physical artifacts). For the anthropological perspective, see W. Griswold, *Cultures and Societies in a Changing World*, Third ed. (Thousand Oaks, CA: Pine Forge Press (Sage), 2008), p. 66.

43. The terms "organizational culture" and "corporate culture" were popularized in 1982 in: Deal and Kennedy, *Corporate Cultures;* T.J. Peters and R.H. Waternam, *In Search of Excellence: Lessons from America's Best-Run Companies* (New York: Warner, 1982). However, there are a few early references to an organization's culture, including: N. Margulies, "Organizational Culture and Psychological Growth," *The Journal of Applied Behavioral Science* 5, no. 4 (1969): 491–508; S. Silverzweig and R.F. Allen, "Changing the Corporate Culture," *Sloan Management Review* 17, no. 3 (1976): 33.

44. P.F. Hewlin, "And the Award for Best Actor Goes To . . .: Facades of Conformity in Organizational Settings," *Academy of Management Review* 28, no. 4 (2003): 633–42.

45. G.R. Maio and J.M. Olson, "Values as Truisms: Evidence and Implications," *Journal of Personality and Social Psychology* 74, no. 2 (1998): 294–311; G.R. Maio et al., "Addressing Discrepancies between Values and Behavior: The Motivating Effect of Reasons," *Journal of Experimental Social Psychology* 37, no. 2 (2001): 104–17.

46. T. Krisher and D.-A. Durbin, "General Motors CEO Akerson Leads Comeback from Bankruptcy by Ruffling Company's Bureaucracy," *Associated Press Newswires*, 17 December 2011.

47. W.E. Baker and J.M. Sinkula, "The Synergistic Effect of Market Orientation and Learning Orientation on Organizational Performance," *Academy of Marketing Science Journal* 27, no. 4 (1999): 411–27; Z. Emden, A. Yaprak, and S.T. Cavusgil, "Learning from Experience in International Alliances: Antecedents and Firm Performance Implications," *Journal of Business Research* 58, no. 7 (2005): 883–92.

48. "Antony Jenkins to Staff: Adopt New Values or Leave Barclays," *The Telegraph (London)*, 17 January 2013. Also, original email to Barclays employees distributed in January 2013.

49. M. Pascoe, "Worst is Yet to Come for Murdoch," *Sydney Morning Herald*, 18 July 2011; "News International and Phone-Hacking," ed. UK House of Commons: Culture Media and Sport Committee (London, UK: The Stationery Office Limited, 2012).

50. A. Lopez-Pacheco, "Building Bridges to Better Business," *National Post (Toronto)*, 28 October 2011.

51. M.L. Marks, "Adding Cultural Fit to Your Diligence Checklist," *Mergers & Acquisitions* 34, no. 3 (1999): 14–20; Schein, *The Corporate Culture Survival Guide* Chap. 8; Teerikangas and Very, "The Culture-Performance Relationship in M&A: From Yes/No to How; G.K. Stahl and A. Voigt, "Do Cultural Differences Matter in Mergers and Acquisitions? A Tentative Model and Examination," *Organization Science* 19, no. 1 (2008): 160–76.

52. J.P. Daly et al., "The Effects of Initial Differences in Firms' Espoused Values on Their Postmerger Performance," *Journal of Applied Behavioral Science* 40, no. 3 (2004): 323–43; C. Cook and D. Spitzer, *World Class Transactions*, KPMG (London, UK: 2001); J. Krug, *Mergers and Acquisitions: Turmoil in Top Management Teams* (Williston, VT: Business Expert Press, 2009).

53. C.A. Schorg, C.A. Raiborn, and M.F. Massoud, "Using a 'Cultural Audit' to Pick M&A Winners," *Journal of Corporate Accounting & Finance* (2004): 47–55; W. Locke, "Higher Education Mergers: Integrating Organisational Cultures and Developing Appropriate Management Styles," *Higher Education Quarterly* 61, no. 1 (2007): 83–102.

54. A.R. Malekazedeh and A. Nahavandi, "Making Mergers Work by Managing Cultures," *Journal of Business Strategy* (1990): 55–57; K.W. Smith, "A Brand-New Culture for the Merged Firm," *Mergers and Acquisitions* 35 (2000): 45–50.

55. Hewitt Associates, "Mergers and Acquisitions May Be Driven by Business Strategy– but Often Stumble over People and Culture Issues," (Lincolnshire, IL: PR Newswire, 1998).

56. J. Martin, "Can Organizational Culture Be Managed?," in *Organizational Culture*, ed. P.J. Frost, et al. (Beverly Hills, CA: Sage, 1985), 95–98.

57. A.S. Tsui et al., "Unpacking the Relationship between CEO Leadership Behavior and Organizational Culture," *Leadership Quarterly* 17 (2006): 113–37; Y. Berson, S. Oreg, and T. Dvir, "CEO Values, Organizational Culture and Firm Outcomes," *Journal of Organizational Behavior* 29, no. 5 (2008): 615–33; B. Schneider, M.G. Ehrhart, and W.H. Macey, "Organizational Climate and Culture," *Annual Review of Psychology* 64, no. 1 (2013): 361–88.

58. Pachner, "The Gospel According to Bruce; "A Travel Guru's Guide to Good Leadership," FP6.

59. E.H. Schein, "The Role of the Founder in Creating Organizational Culture," *Organizational Dynamics* 12, no. 1 (1983): 13–28; R. House, M. Javidan, and P. Dorfman, "Project GLOBE: An Introduction," *Applied Psychology: An International Review* 50 (2001): 489–505; R. House et al., "Understanding Cultures and Implicit Leadership Theories across the Globe: An Introduction to Project GLOBE," *Journal of World Business* 37 (2002): 3–10.

60. O'Connor, "CEO Credits Quicken Loans' Culture for Firm's Success," C2.

61. M. De Pree, *Leadership Is an Art* (East Lansing, MI: Michigan State University Press, 1987).

62. J. Kerr and J.W. Slocum Jr., "Managing Corporate Culture through Reward Systems," *Academy of Management Executive* 1 (1987): 99–107; J.M. Higgins et al., "Using Cultural Artifacts to Change and Perpetuate Strategy," *Journal of Change Management* 6, no. 4 (2006): 397–415; H. Hofstetter and I. Harpaz, "Declared Versus Actual Organizational Culture as Indicated by an Organization's Performance Appraisal," *International Journal of Human Resource Management* (2011): 1–22.

63. R. Charan, "Home Depot's Blueprint for Culture Change," *Harvard Business Review* (2006): 61–70.

64. D. Ovsey, "Authenticity Key Ingredient in Recipe to Produce Employee Evangelists," *Financial Post (Toronto)*, 31 July 2012.

65. B. Schneider, "The People Make the Place," *Personnel Psychology* 40, no. 3 (1987): 437–53; B. Schneider et al., "Personality and Organizations: A Test of the Homogeneity of Personality Hypothesis," *Journal of Applied Psychology* 83, no. 3 (1998): 462–70; T.R. Giberson, C.J. Resick, and M.W. Dickson, "Embedding Leader Characteristics: An Examination of Homogeneity of Personality and Values in Organizations," *Journal of Applied Psychology* 90, no. 5 (2005): 1002–10.

66. T.A. Judge and D.M. Cable, "Applicant Personality, Organizational Culture, and Organization Attraction," *Personnel Psychology* 50, no. 2 (1997): 359–94; D.S. Chapman et al., "Applicant Attraction to Organizations and Job Choice: A Meta-Analytic Review of the Correlates of Recruiting Outcomes," *Journal of Applied Psychology* 90, no. 5 (2005): 928–44; A.L. Kristof-Brown, R.D. Zimmerman, and E.C. Johnson, "Consequences of Individuals' Fit at Work: A Meta-Analysis of Person-Job, Person-Organization, Person-Group, and Person-Supervisor Fit," *Personnel Psychology* 58, no. 2 (2005): 281–342; C. Hu, H.-C. Su, and C.-I.B. Chen, "The Effect of Person-Organization Fit Feedback Via Recruitment Web Sites on Applicant Attraction," *Computers in Human Behavior* 23, no. 5 (2007): 2509–23.

67. P. Nunes and T. Breene, "Reinvent Your Business before It's Too Late," *Harvard Business Review* 89, no. 1/2 (2011): 80–87.

68. A. Kristof-Brown, "Perceived Applicant Fit: Distinguishing between Recruiters' Perceptions of Person-Job and Person-Organization Fit," *Personnel Psychology* 53, no. 3 (2000): 643–71; A.E.M. Van Vianen, "Person-Organization Fit: The Match between Newcomers' and Recruiters' Preferences for Organizational Cultures," *Personnel Psychology* 53 (2000): 113–49.

69. T. Hsieh, *Delivering Happiness: A Path to Profits, Passion, and Purpose* (New York: Business Plus, 2010); K. McGee, "Education for Life: Companies Offer Different Corporate Culture," *Las Vegas Business Press*, 30 July 2012, S22.

70. D.M. Cable and J.R. Edwards, "Complementary and Supplementary Fit: A Theoretical and Empirical Integration," *Journal of Applied Psychology* 89, no. 5 (2004): 822–34.

71. "WestJet, Tim Hortons and RBC Financial Group," News release for Waterstone Human Capital and National Post (Toronto, ON: CNW, 13 October 2005); Y. Lermusi, "The No. 1 Frustration of Your Job Candidates," (15 August 2006), www.ere.net (accessed 2 June 2010); S. Singleton, "Starbucks, Goodlife Fitness among Most Admired Companies," *Money.Canoe.ca (Toronto)*, 12 November 2009; Taleo Research, "Talent Management Processes," (Dublin, CA: Taleo, 2010), www.taleo.com (accessed 2 June 2010); "Survey: 37% Use Social Media to Check Candidates," *Workforce*, 18 April 2012; Kelly Services, *Acquisition and Retention in the War for Talent*, Kelly Global Workforce Index, Kelly Services (Troy, MI: April 2012).

72. J. Van Maanen, "Breaking In: Socialization to Work," in *Handbook of Work, Organization, and Society*, ed. R. Dubin (Chicago, IL: Rand McNally, 1976).

73. S.L. McShane, G. O'Neill, and T. Travaglione, "Managing Employee Values in Values-Driven Organizations: Contradiction, Façade, and Illusions" (paper presented at the 21st Annual ANZAM Conference, Sydney, Australia, December 2007); S.L. McShane, G. O'Neill, and T. Travaglione, "Rethinking the Values-Driven Organization Process: From Values Engineering to Behavioral Domain Training," in *Academy of Management 2008 Annual Meeting* (Anaheim, CA: 2008).

74. D.G. Allen, "Do Organizational Socialization Tactics Influence Newcomer Embeddedness and Turnover?," *Journal of Management* 32, no. 2 (2006): 237–56; A.M. Saks, K.L. Uggerslev, and N.E. Fassina, "Socialization Tactics and Newcomer Adjustment: A Meta-Analytic Review and Test of a Model," *Journal of Vocational Behavior* 70, no. 3 (2007): 413–46.

75. G.T. Chao et al., "Organizational Socialization: Its Content and Consequences," *Journal of Applied Psychology* 79 (1994): 450–63; H.D. Cooper-Thomas and N. Anderson, "Organizational Socialization: A Field Study into Socialization Success and Rate," *International Journal of Selection and Assessment* 13, no. 2 (2005): 116–28.

76. N. Nicholson, "A Theory of Work Role Transitions," *Administrative Science Quarterly* 29 (1984): 172–91; A. Elfering et al., "First Years in Job: A Three-Wave Analysis of Work Experiences," *Journal of Vocational Behavior* 70, no. 1 (2007): 97–115; B.E. Ashforth, D.M. Sluss, and A.M. Saks, "Socialization Tactics, Proactive Behavior, and Newcomer Learning: Integrating Socialization Models," *Journal of Vocational Behavior* 70, no. 3 (2007): 447–62; T.N. Bauer, "Newcomer Adjustment During Organizational Socialization: A Meta-Analytic Review of Antecedents, Outcomes, and Methods," *Journal of Applied Psychology* 92, no. 3 (2007): 707–21.

77. J.M. Beyer and D.R. Hannah, "Building on the Past: Enacting Established Personal Identities in a New Work Setting," *Organization Science* 13 (2002): 636–52; H.D.C. Thomas and N. Anderson, "Newcomer Adjustment: The Relationship between Organizational Socialization Tactics, Information Acquisition and Attitudes," *Journal of Occupational and Organizational Psychology* 75 (2002): 423–37.

78. M. Johne, "Workplace Loyalty a Two-Way Street," *The Globe and Mail*, 5 August 2009, B13.

79. S.L. Robinson and E. Wolfe Morrison, "The Development of Psychological Contract Breach and Violation: A Longitudinal Study," *Journal of Organizational Behavior* 21, no. 5 (2000): 525–46; K.J. McInnis, J.P. Meyer, and S. Feldman, "Psychological Contracts and Their Implications for Commitment: A Feature-Based Approach," *Journal of Vocational Behavior* 74, no. 2 (2009): 165–80; M.-È. Lapalme, G. Simard, and M. Tremblay, "The Influence of Psychological Contract Breach on Temporary Workers' Commitment

and Behaviors: A Multiple Agency Perspective," *Journal of Business and Psychology* 26, no. 3 (2011): 311-24.

80. S.L. Robinson and D.M. Rousseau, "Violating the Psychological Contract: Not the Exception but the Norm," *Journal of Organizational Behavior* 15 (1994): 245-59; E.W. Morrison and S.L. Robinson, "When Employees Feel Betrayed: A Model of How Psychological Contract Violation Develops," *Academy of Management Review* 22 (1997): 226-56; S.D. Montes and P.G. Irving, "Disentangling the Effects of Promised and Delivered Inducements: Relational and Transactional Contract Elements and the Mediating Role of Trust," *Journal of Applied Psychology* 93, no. 6 (2008): 1367-81.

81. L.W. Porter, E.E. Lawler III, and J.R. Hackman, *Behavior in Organizations* (New York: McGraw-Hill, 1975), pp. 163-67; Van Maanen, "Breaking In: Socialization to Work," pp. 67-130; D.C. Feldman, "The Multiple Socialization of Organization Members," *Academy of Management Review* 6 (1981): 309-18.

82. B.E. Ashforth and A.M. Saks, "Socialization Tactics: Longitudinal Effects on Newcomer Adjustment," *Academy of Management Journal* 39 (1996): 149-78; J.D. Kammeyer-Mueller and C.R. Wanberg, "Unwrapping the Organizational Entry Process: Disentangling Multiple Antecedents and Their Pathways to Adjustment," *Journal of Applied Psychology* 88, no. 5 (2003): 779-94.

83. Porter, Lawler III, and Hackman, *Behavior in Organizations* Chap. 5.

84. Louis, "Surprise and Sensemaking."

85. Robinson and Rousseau, "Violating the Psychological Contract."

86. D.L. Nelson, "Organizational Socialization: A Stress Perspective," *Journal of Occupational Behavior* 8 (1987): 311-24; Elfering et al., "First Years in Job."

87. J.P. Wanous, *Organizational Entry* (Reading, MA: Addison-Wesley, 1992); J.A. Breaugh and M. Starke, "Research on Employee Recruitment: So Many Studies, So Many Remaining Questions," *Journal of Management* 26, no. 3 (2000): 405-34.

88. J.M. Phillips, "Effects of Realistic Job Previews on Multiple Organizational Outcomes: A Meta-Analysis," *Academy of Management Journal* 41 (1998): 673-90.

89. Y. Ganzach et al., "Social Exchange and Organizational Commitment: Decision-Making Training for Job Choice as an Alternative to the Realistic Job Preview," *Personnel Psychology* 55 (2002): 613-37.

90. H. Blodget, "Mark Zuckerberg, Moving Fast and Breaking Things," *Business Insider*, 14 October 2010; Ladendorf, "For Facebook Workers, It's Not Just a Job," E1; M. Swift, "Facebook Landing Team Transports Company Culture," *San Jose Mercury News (Calif.)*, 25 March 2011; K. Raghav, "'We Paint the Walls'," *LiveMint*, 10 June 2011.

91. C. Ostroff and S.W.J. Koslowski, "Organizational Socialization as a Learning Process: The Role of Information Acquisition," *Personnel Psychology* 45 (1992): 849-74; Cooper-Thomas and Anderson, "Organizational Socialization: A Field Study into Socialization Success and Rate; A. Baber and L. Waymon, "Uncovering the Unconnected Employee," *T&D* (2008): 60-66.

92. S. Nifadkar, A.S. Tsui, and B.E. Ashforth, "The Way You Make Me Feel and Behave: Supervisor-Triggered Newcomer Affect and Approach-Avoidance Behavior," *Academy of Management Journal* 55, no. 5 (2012): 1146-68.

93. N. Singh, "Buddies Build Bonds, Leadership Skills at Companies," *Times of India*, 5 March 2013; M. Smith, "Australia's 50 Best Places to Work," *BRW*, 27 June 2013; R.E. Silverman, "First Day on Job: Not Just Paperwork," *Wall Street Journal*, 29 May 2013, B10.

CHAPTER 15

1. The Mitel Networks case relied on information in a series of twelve monthly "diaries" by Martyn Etherington in DMNews. However, the main specific sources for the case study content are: J. Bagnall, "Mitel's Secret of Survival," *Ottawa Citizen*, 1 August 2013, B10; B. Pleasant, "Mitel Invigorated," (St. Helena, CA: UCStrategies, 1 July 2013), http://www.ucstrategies.com/unified-communications-strategies-views/mitel-reinvigorated.aspx (accessed 13 April 2014); M. Etherington and E. Krell, "As Marketing Strategy Evolves, So Must People and Processes," *DMNews*, February 2013, 14-15; M. Etherington and E. Krell, "An Inside View of a Year in the Life of a CMO," *DMNews*, January 2013, 14-15; M. Etherington and E. Krell, "Look Back and Learn," *DMNews*, October 2013, 18-19; J. O'Kane, "Into the Cloud: Mitel's Life as a 'Powerhouse'," *The Globe and Mail (Toronto)*, 12 March 2014, B5.

2. D. Howes, "Future Hinges on Global Teams," *Detroit News*, 21 December 1998.

3. J. Welch, *Jack: Straight from the Heart* (New York: Warner Business books, 2001), pg. 432.

4. K. Lewin, *Field Theory in Social Science* (New York: Harper & Row, 1951).

5. D. Coghlan and T. Brannick, "Kurt Lewin: The 'Practical Theorist' for the 21st Century," *Irish Journal of Management* 24, no. 2 (2003): 31-37; B. Burnes, "Kurt Lewin and the Planned Approach to Change: A Re-Appraisal," *Journal of Management Studies* 41, no. 6 (2004): 977-1002.

6. "Ogilvy & Mather Corporate Culture," (New York, 2011), http://www.ogilvy.com/About/Our-History/Corporate-Culture.aspx (accessed 17 May 2011).

7. D. Howell, "Nardelli Nears Five-Year Mark with Riveting Record," *DSN Retailing Today*, 9 May 2005, 1, 38; R. Charan, "Home Depot's Blueprint for Culture Change," *Harvard Business Review* (2006): 61-70; D. Grosse Kathoefer and J. Leker, "Knowledge Transfer in Academia: An Exploratory Study on the Not-Invented-Here Syndrome," *Journal of Technology Transfer* 37, no. 5 (2012): 658-75; R. DeGross, "Five Years of Change: Home Depot's Results Mixed under Nardelli," *Atlanta Journal-Constitution*, 1 January 2006, F1.

8. D. Miller, "Building Commitment to Major Change – What 1700 Change Agents Told Us Really Works," *Developing HR Strategy*, no. 22 (2008): 5-8; W. Immen, "When Leaders Become Glory Hounds," *The Globe and Mail (Toronto)*, 5 March 2010, B15; J. Wright, "How Well Do Leaders Communicate Change?," *PeopleTalk (BC-HRMA)*, Summer 2013, 34-35.

9. Some experts suggest that resistance to change should be restated in a more positive way by its opposite: readiness for change. See: M. Choi and W.E.A. Ruona, "Individual Readiness for Organizational Change and Its Implications for Human Resource and Organization Development," *Human Resource Development Review* 10, no. 1 (2011): 46-73.

10. M. Haid et al., *Ready, Get Set. . .Change!: The Impact of Change on Workforce Productivity and Engagement*, Leadership Insights, (Philadelphia, PA: Right Management, 2009).

11. S. Chreim, "Postscript to Change: Survivors' Retrospective Views of Organizational Changes," *Personnel Review* 35, no. 3 (2006): 315-35.

12. E.B. Dent and S.G. Goldberg, "Challenging 'Resistance to Change'," *Journal of Applied Behavioral Science* 35 (1999): 25-41; D.B. Fedor, S. Caldwell, and D.M. Herold, "The Effects of Organizational Changes on Employee Commitment: A Multilevel Investigation," *Personnel Psychology* 59, no. 1 (2006): 1-29.

13. B.J. Tepper et al., "Subordinates' Resistance and Managers' Evaluations of Subordinates' Performance," *Journal of Management* 32, no. 2 (2006): 185-209; J.D. Ford, L.W. Ford, and A. D'Amelio, "Resistance to Change: The Rest of the Story," *Academy of Management Review* 33, no. 2 (2008): 362-77.

14. D.A. Nadler, "The Effective Management of Organizational Change," in *Handbook of Organizational Behavior*, ed. J.W. Lorsch (Englewood Cliffs, NJ: Prentice Hall, 1987), 358-69; R. Maurer, *Beyond the Wall of Resistance: Unconventional Strategies to Build Support for Change* (Austin, TX: Bard Books, 1996); P. Strebel, "Why Do Employees Resist Change?," *Harvard Business Review* (1996): 86-92; D.A. Nadler, *Champions of Change* (San Francisco, CA: Jossey-Bass, 1998).

15. J. Mouawad, "Largest Airline Has Bigger Troubles," *International Herald Tribune*, 30 November 2012, 14; M. Mecham, "Not yet United," *Overhaul & Maintenance*, April 2012, 46; M. Brownell, "Here's Why United Was Just Named America's Worst Airline," *Daily Finance*, 18 June 2013.

16. J.K. Galbraith, *Economics, Peace, and Laughter* (Boston, MA: Houghton Mifflin, 1971), pg. 50.

17. S. Oreg et al., "Dispositional Resistance to Change: Measurement Equivalence and the Link to Personal Values across 17 Nations," *Journal of Applied Psychology* 93, no. 4 (2008): 935-44.

18. R.R. Sharma, *Change Management: Concepts and Applications* (New Delhi: Tata McGraw-Hill, 2007), Chap. 4; I. Cinite, L.E. Duxbury, and C. Higgins, "Measurement of Perceived Organizational Readiness for Change in the Public Sector," *British Journal of Management* 20, no. 2 (2009): 265-77; A.A. Armenakis and S.G. Harris, "Reflections: Our Journey in Organizational Change Research and Practice," *Journal of Change Management* 9, no. 2 (2009): 127-42; S. Jaros, "Commitment to Organizational Change: A Critical Review," *Journal of Change Management* 10, no. 1 (2010): 79-108.

19. D.T. Holt et al., "Readiness for Organizational Change: The Systematic Development

of a Scale," *Journal of Applied Behavioral Science* 43, no. 2 (2007): 232–55; G. Bohner and N. Dickel, "Attitudes and Attitude Change," *Annual Review of Psychology* 62, no. 1 (2011): 391–417; S. Oreg, M. Vakola, and A. Armenakis, "Change Recipients' Reactions to Organizational Change: A 60-Year Review of Quantitative Studies," *The Journal of Applied Behavioral Science* 47, no. 4 (2011): 461–524.

20. R. de la Sablonnière et al., "Profound Organizational Change, Psychological Distress and Burnout Symptoms: The Mediator Role of Collective Relative Deprivation," *Group Processes & Intergroup Relations* 15, no. 6 (2012): 776–90.

21. Oreg, Vakola, and Armenakis, "Change Recipients' Reactions to Organizational Change."

22. R. Davis, *Leading for Growth: How Umpqua Bank Got Cool and Created a Culture of Greatness* (San Francisco, CA: Jossey-Bass, 2007), pg. 40.

23. Grosse Kathoefer and Leker, "Knowledge Transfer in Academia: An Exploratory Study on the Not-Invented-Here Syndrome; A.L.D.A. Burcharth, M.P. Knudsen, and H.A. Søndergaard, "Neither Invented nor Shared Here: The Impact and Management of Attitudes for the Adoption of Open Innovation Practices," *Technovation* 34, no. 3 (2014): 149–61.

24. V. Newman, "The Psychology of Managing for Innovation," *KM Review* 9, no. 6 (2007): 10–15.

25. L. Brody and D. Raffa, *Everything I Need to Know About Business. . .I Learned from a Canadian*, 2nd ed. (Mississauga, ON: John Wiley & Sons Canada, 2009), pp. 201–02.

26. *Bosses Want Change but Workers Want More of the Same!*, Talent2 (Sydney: 29 June 2005).

27. C. Lawton and J. Lublin, "Nokia Names Microsoft's Stephen Elop as New CEO, Kallasvuo Ousted," *Wall Street Journal*, 11 September 2010; C. Ziegler, "Nokia CEO Stephen Elop Rallies Troops in Brutally Honest 'Burning Platform' Memo? (Update: It's Real!)," *Engadget*, 8 February 2011.

28. J.P. Kotter, *A Sense of Urgency* (Boston, MA: Harvard Business School Press, 2008); S.H. Appelbaum et al., "Back to the Future: Revisiting Kotter's 1996 Change Model," *Journal of Management Development* 31, no. 8 (2012): 764–82.

29. L.D. Goodstein and H.R. Butz, "Customer Value: The Linchpin of Organizational Change," *Organizational Dynamics* 27 (1998): 21–35.

30. I.J. Bozon and P.N. Child, "Refining Shell's Position in Europe," *McKinsey Quarterly*, no. 2 (2003): 42–51.

31. W.C. Vantuono, "2013 Freight Rail Outlook: The Challenge of Change," *Railway Age*, December 2012, 28; V. Lu, "CP Rail Speeds up Its Delivery Times," *Toronto Star*, 18 September 2012, B1; B. Yauch, "CP Rail CEO Harrison Fixing 'Permissive' Culture," *Business News Network*, 27 May 2013; H. Brilliant, *Putting Railroads on the Right Track, Video Reports* (Toronto, ON: Morningstar, 2014), Online video.

32. D. Miller, *The Icarus Paradox: How Exceptional Companies Bring About Their Own Downfall* (New York: HarperBusiness, 1990); S. Finkelstein, *Why Smart Executives Fail* (New York: Viking, 2003); A.C. Amason and A.C. Mooney, "The Icarus Paradox Revisited: How Strong Performance Sows the Seeds of Dysfunction in Future Strategic Decision-Making," *Strategic Organization* 6, no. 4 (2008): 407–34. Richard Goyder's quotation is from: "Sustaining High Performance (Richard Goyder: Wesfarmers)," *CEOForum*, September 2006.

33. D. Darlin, "Growing Tomorrow," *Business 2.0*, May 2005, 126.

34. T.F. Cawsey and G. Deszca, *Toolkit for Organizational Change* (Los Angeles, CA: Sage, 2007), p. 104.

35. J.P. Kotter and L.A. Schlesinger, "Choosing Strategies for Change," *Harvard Business Review* (1979): 106–14.

36. M. Meaney and C. Pung, "Creating Organizational Transformations: Mckinsey Global Survey Results," *McKinsey Quarterly*, July 2008, 1–7; A.E. Rafferty, N.L. Jimmieson, and A.A. Armenakis, "Change Readiness: A Multilevel Review," *Journal of Management* 39, no. 1 (2013): 110–35.

37. J.P. Kotter and D.S. Cohen, *The Heart of Change* (Boston, MA: Harvard Business School Press, 2002), pp. 83–98; J. Allen et al., "Uncertainty During Organizational Change: Managing Perceptions through Communication," *Journal of Change Management* 7, no. 2 (2007): 187–210; T.L. Russ, "Communicating Change: A Review and Critical Analysis of Programmatic and Participatory Implementation Approaches," *Journal of Change Management* 8, no. 3 (2008): 199 - 211; M. van den Heuvel et al., "Adapting to Change: The Value of Change Information and Meaning-Making," *Journal of Vocational Behavior* 83, no. 1 (2013): 11–21.

38. G. Jones, "Chemical Reaction," *Smart Business Pittsburgh*, February 2011, 10.

39. D.M. Herold and S.D. Caldwell, "Beyond Change Management: A Multilevel Investigation of Contextual and Personal Influences on Employees' Commitment to Change," *Journal of Applied Psychology* 92, no. 4 (2007): 942–51; D.T. Holt and J.M. Vardaman, "Toward a Comprehensive Understanding of Readiness for Change: The Case for an Expanded Conceptualization," *Journal of Change Management* 13, no. 1 (2013): 9–18.

40. K.T. Dirks, L.L. Cummings, and J.L. Pierce, "Psychological Ownership in Organizations: Conditions under Which Individuals Promote and Resist Change," *Research in Organizational Change and Development* 9 (1996): 1–23; E.A. Lofquist, "Doomed to Fail: A Case Study of Change Implementation Collapse in the Norwegian Civil Aviation Industry," *Journal of Change Management* 11, no. 2 (2011): 223–43; L.K. Lewis and T.L. Russ, "Soliciting and Using Input During Organizational Change Initiatives: What Are Practitioners Doing," *Management Communication Quarterly* 26, no. 2 (2012): 267–94.

41. S.G. Bamberger et al., "Impact of Organisational Change on Mental Health: A Systematic Review," *Occupational and Environmental Medicine* 69, no. 8 (2012): 592–98.

42. N.T. Tan, "Maximising Human Resource Potential in the Midst of Organisational Change," *Singapore Management Review* 27, no. 2 (2005): 25–35; A.E. Rafferty and S.L.D. Restubog, "The Impact of Change Process and Context on Change Reactions and Turnover During a Merger," *Journal of Management* 36, no. 5 (2010): 1309–38.

43. M. McHugh, "The Stress Factor: Another Item for the Change Management Agenda?," *Journal of Organizational Change Management* 10 (1997): 345–62; D. Buchanan, T. Claydon, and M. Doyle, "Organisation Development and Change: The Legacy of the Nineties," *Human Resource Management Journal* 9 (1999): 20–37.

44. T. Wakefield, "No Pain, No Gain," *Canadian Business*, January 1993, 50–54; M. Cash, "Standardaero Back on the Sale Block," *Winnipeg Free Press*, 14 December 2010.

45. K. Dobinson, "Turning around London's 'Worst' Council," *The Guardian (London)*, 21 November 2012, 42; "Soliciting and Using Input During Organizational Change Initiatives: What Are Practitioners Doing; "'Resistance Lets Our Residents Down'," *Local Government Chronicle*, 28 February 2013.

46. D. Nicolini and M.B. Meznar, "The Social Construction of Organizational Learning: Conceptual and Practical Issues in the Field," *Human Relations* 48 (1995): 727–46.

47. E.E. Lawler III, "Pay Can Be a Change Agent," *Compensation & Benefits Management* 16 (2000): 23–26; Kotter and Cohen, *The Heart of Change* pp. 161–77; M.A. Roberto and L.C. Levesque, "The Art of Making Change Initiatives Stick," *MIT Sloan Management Review* 46, no. 4 (2005): 53–60.

48. Lawler III, "Pay Can Be a Change Agent."

49. Goodstein and Butz, "Customer Value: The Linchpin of Organizational Change; R.H. Miles, "Leading Corporate Transformation: Are You up to the Task?," in *The Leader's Change Handbook* ed. J.A. Conger, G.M. Spreitzer, and E.E. Lawler III (San Francisco, CA: Jossey-Bass, 1999), 221–67.

50. R.E. Quinn, *Building the Bridge as You Walk on It: A Guide for Leading Change* (San Francisco, CA: Jossey-Bass, 2004), Chap. 11; D.M. Herold et al., "The Effects of Transformational and Change Leadership on Employees' Commitment to a Change: A Multilevel Study," *Journal of Applied Psychology* 93, no. 2 (2008): 346–57.

51. M.S. Cole, S.G. Harris, and J.B. Bernerth, "Exploring the Implications of Vision, Appropriateness, and Execution of Organizational Change," *Leadership & Organization Development Journal* 27, no. 5 (2006): 352–67; S. Kirkpatrick, "Leading through Vision and Values," in *Handbook of Principles of Organizational Behavior : Indispensable Knowledge for Evidence-Based Management*, ed. E. Locke (Hoboken: Wiley, 2010), 367–87; V. Lundy and P.-P. Morin, "Project Leadership Influences Resistance to Change: The Case of the Canadian Public Service," *Project Management Journal* 44, no. 4 (2013): 45–64.

52. Kotter and Cohen, *The Heart of Change* pp.61–82; D.S. Cohen and J.P. Kotter, *The Heart of Change Field Guide* (Boston, MA: Harvard Business School Press, 2005).

53. J.P. Kotter, "Leading Change: Why Transformation Efforts Fail," *Harvard Business Review* (1995): 59–67.

54. J.B. Cunningham and S.K. James, "Implementing Change in Public Sector Organizations," *Management Decision* 47, no. 2 (2009): 330.

55. S. Keller and C. Aiken, *The Inconvenient Truth About Change: Why It Isn't Working and What to Do About It*, McKinsey & Company (New York: 2008).

56. N. Edwards, *Using a Viral Communication Approach for Engaging Pfizer's Field Workforce in Realising Its Vision*, Pfizer (London, UK: 19 May 2008); K. Dyer, "Changing Perceptions Virally at Novo Nordisk," *Strategic Communication Management* 13, no. 2 (2009): 24-27; L. Herrero, *Homo Imitans* (Beaconsfield Bucks, UK: meetingminds, 2011).

57. A. De Bruyn and G.L. Lilien, "A Multi-Stage Model of Word-of-Mouth Influence through Viral Marketing," *International Journal of Research in Marketing* 25, no. 3 (2008): 151-63; J.Y.C. Ho and M. Dempsey, "Viral Marketing: Motivations to Forward Online Content," *Journal of Business Research* 63, no. 9-10 (2010): 1000-06; M. Williams and F. Buttle, "The Eight Pillars of Wom Management: Lessons from a Multiple Case Study," *Australasian Marketing Journal (AMJ)* 19, no. 2 (2011): 85-92.

58. Herrero, *Homo Imitans*.

59. M. Beer, R.A. Eisenstat, and B. Spector, *The Critical Path to Corporate Renewal* (Boston, MA: Harvard Business School Press, 1990).

60. J. Riel, "Building a Design Thinking Organization from Within," in *Design of Business: Why Design Thinking Is the Next Competitive Advantage*, ed. R. Martin (Boston, MA: Harvard Business Press, 2009), 166-86.

61. Beer, Eisenstat, and Spector, *The Critical Path to Corporate Renewal* Chap. 5; R.E. Walton, "Successful Strategies for Diffusing Work Innovations," *Journal of Contemporary Business* (1977): 1-22; R.E. Walton, *Innovating to Compete: Lessons for Diffusing and Managing Change in the Workplace* (San Francisco, CA: Jossey-Bass, 1987).

62. E.M. Rogers, *Diffusion of Innovations*, Fourth ed. (New York, NY: Free Press, 1995).

63. P. Reason and H. Bradbury, *Handbook of Action Research*, (London, UK: Sage, 2001); Coghlan and Brannick, "Kurt Lewin: The 'Practical Theorist' for the 21st Century; C. Huxham and S. Vangen, "Researching Organizational Practice through Action Research: Case Studies and Design Choices," *Organizational Research Methods* 6 (2003): 383-403.

64. V.J. Marsick and M.A. Gephart, "Action Research: Building the Capacity for Learning and Change," *Human Resource Planning* 26 (2003): 14-18.

65. L. Dickens and K. Watkins, "Action Research: Rethinking Lewin," *Management Learning* 30 (1999): 127-40; J. Heron and P. Reason, "The Practice of Co-Operative Inquiry: Research 'with' Rather Than 'on' People," in *Handbook of Action Research*, ed. P. Reason and H. Bradbury (Thousand Oaks, CA: Sage, 2001), 179-88.

66. P.K. Sweeney, "Corporate Compliance without Burdening the End User: Change Management Lessons from Ergon Energy," *iQ* (2006): 24-26.

67. D. Miller and P.H. Friesen, "Momentum and Revolution in Organizational Adaptation," *Academy of Management Journal* 23, no. 4 (1980): 591-614; D. Miller and M.-J. Chen, "Sources and Consequences of Competitive Inertia: A Study of the U.S. Airline Industry," *Administrative Science Quarterly* 39, no. 1 (1994): 1-23.

68. J. Isern and C. Pung, "Driving Radical Change," *McKinsey Quarterly*, no. 4 (2007): 24-35.

69. D.A. Nadler, "Organizational Frame Bending: Types of Change in the Complex Organization," in *Corporate Transformation: Revitalizing Organizations for a Competitive World*, ed. R.H. Kilmann, T.J. Covin, and a. Associates (San Francisco, CA: Jossey-Bass, 1988), 66-83; K.E. Weick and R.E. Quinn, "Organizational Change and Development," *Annual Review of Psychology* 50 (1999): 361-86.

70. T.M. Egan and C.M. Lancaster, "Comparing Appreciative Inquiry to Action Research: OD Practitioner Perspectives," *Organization Development Journal* 23, no. 2 (2005): 29-49.

71. N. Turner, J. Barling, and A. Zacharatos, "Positive Psychology at Work," in *Handbook of Positive Psychology*, ed. C.R. Snyder and S. Lopez (Oxford, UK: Oxford University Press, 2002), 715-30; K. Cameron, J.E. Dutton, and R.E. Quinn, eds., *Positive Organizational Scholarship: Foundation of a New Discipline* (San Francisco, CA: Berrett Koehler Publishers, 2003); S.L. Gable and J. Haidt, "What (and Why) Is Positive Psychology?," *Review of General Psychology* 9, no. 2 (2005): 103-10; M.E.P. Seligman et al., "Positive Psychology Progress: Empirical Validation of Interventions," *American Psychologist* 60, no. 5 (2005): 410-21.

72. D.K. Whitney and D.L. Cooperrider, "The Appreciative Inquiry Summit: Overview and Applications," *Employment Relations Today* 25 (1998): 17-28; J.M. Watkins and B.J. Mohr, *Appreciative Inquiry: Change at the Speed of Imagination* (San Francisco, CA: Jossey-Bass, 2001).

73. D. Meinert, "Positive Momentum," *HRMagazine* 58, no. 6 (2013): 68-74.

74. D.L. Cooperrider and D.K. Whitney, *Appreciative Inquiry: A Positive Revolution in Change* (San Francisco, CA: Berrett-Koehler, 2005). Recent writing has extended this list to eight principles. see: D.K. Whitney and A. Trosten-Bloom, *The Power of Appreciative Inquiry: A Practical Guide to Positive Change*, 2nd ed. (San Francisco, CA: Berrett-Koehler Publishers, 2010).

75. F.J. Barrett and D.L. Cooperrider, "Generative Metaphor Intervention: A New Approach for Working with Systems Divided by Conflict and Caught in Defensive Perception," *Journal of Applied Behavioral Science* 26 (1990): 219-39; Whitney and Cooperrider, "The Appreciative Inquiry Summit: Overview and Applications; Watkins and Mohr, *Appreciative Inquiry: Change at the Speed of Imagination*, pp. 15-21.

76. Z. Pedersen, "Using Appreciative Inquiry to Focus on Positives, Transform Workplace Culture," *Canadian HR Reporter*, 13 August 2012, 10-12; Z. Pedersen, *Appreciative Inquiry and Changing Workplace Culture*, (Toronto, ON: YouTube, 2012), Online video; M.K. McCarthy, M.J. McNally, and K. Sabo, "Toronto Western Hospital Positive Leadership Program: Creating a Culture of Excellence," in *National Health Leadership Conference* (Niagara Falls, ON: Canadian College of Health Leaders, 2013).

77. M. Schiller, "Case Study: Avon Mexico," in *Appreciative Inquiry: Change at the Speed of Imagination* ed. J.M. Watkins and B.J. Mohr (San Francisco, CA: Jossey-Bass, 2001), 123-26; P. Babcock, "Seeing a Brighter Future," *HRMagazine* 50, no. 9 (2005): 48; D.S. Bright, D.L. Cooperrider, and W.B. Galloway, "Appreciative Inquiry in the Office of Research and Development: Improving the Collaborative Capacity of Organization," *Public Performance & Management Review* 29, no. 3 (2006): 285; D. Gilmour and A. Radford, "Using OD to Enhance Shareholder Value: Delivering Business Results in BP Castrol Marine," *Organization Development Journal* 25, no. 3 (2007): P97-P102; Whitney and Trosten-Bloom, *The Power of Appreciative Inquiry*.

78. T.F. Yaeger, P.F. Sorensen, and U. Bengtsson, "Assessment of the State of Appreciative Inquiry: Past, Present, and Future," *Research in Organizational Change and Development* 15 (2004): 297-319; G.R. Bushe and A.F. Kassam, "When Is Appreciative Inquiry Transformational? A Meta-Case Analysis," *Journal of Applied Behavioral Science* 41, no. 2 (2005): 161-81.

79. G.R. Bushe, "Five Theories of Change Embedded in Appreciative Inquiry" (paper presented at the 18th Annual World Congress of Organization Development, Dublin, Ireland, July 14-18, 1998).

80. J.M. Bartunek, J. Balogun, and B. Do, "Considering Planned Change Anew: Stretching Large Group Interventions Strategically, Emotionally, and Meaningfully," *Academy of Management Annals* 5, no. 1 (2011): 1-52.

81. M. Weisbord and S. Janoff, *Future Search: An Action Guide to Finding Common Ground in Organizations and Communities* (San Francisco, CA: Berrett-Koehler, 2000); R.M. Lent, M.T. McCormick, and D.S. Pearce, "Combining Future Search and Open Space to Address Special Situations," *Journal of Applied Behavioral Science* 41, no. 1 (2005): 61-69; S. Janoff and M. Weisbord, "Future Search as 'Real-Time' Action Research," *Futures* 38, no. 6 (2006): 716-22.

82. J. Pratt, "Naturalists Deserve More Credit," *St. John's Telegram*, 22 June 2002, B3; C. Chowaniec, R. Gordezky, and J. Grieve, "Supporting the Merger of Two School Boards in Ottawa, Ontario, Canada: The Ottawa-Carleton Community and Public Education to 2015," in *Future Search in School District Change*, ed. R. Schweitz, K. Martens, and N. Aronson (Lanham, Maryland: Scarecrow Education, 2005), 56-70; P. Deans, K. Martens, and R. Gordezky, "Success and System Readiness: Lester B. Pearson School Board and Its Commitment to Educational Excellence, Montreal, Quebec," in *Future Search in School District Change*, ed. R. Schweitz, K. Martens, and N. Aronson (Lanham, Maryland: ScarecrowEducation, 2005), 192-208; R. Lent, J. Van Patten, and T. Phair, "Creating a World-Class Manufacturer in Record Time," in *The Handbook of Large Group Methods*, ed. B.B. Bunker and B.T. Alban (New York: Wiley, 2006), 112-24.

83. For a critique of future search conferences and similar whole-system events, see A. Oels, "Investigating the Emotional Roller-Coaster Ride: A Case Study-Based Assessment of the Future Search Conference Design," *Systems Research and Behavioral Science* 19 (2002): 347-55; M.F.D. Polanyi, "Communicative Action in Practice: Future Search and the Pursuit of an Open, Critical and Non-Coercive Large-Group Process," *Systems Research and Behavioral Science* 19 (2002): 357-66; A. De Grassi, "Envisioning

Futures of African Agriculture: Representation, Power, and Socially Constituted Time," *Progress in Development Studies* 7, no. 2 (2007): 79–98.

84. G.R. Bushe and A.B. Shani, *Parallel Learning Structures* (Reading, MA: Addison-Wesley, 1991); E.M. Van Aken, D.J. Monetta, and D.S. Sink, "Affinity Groups: The Missing Link in Employee Involvement," *Organization Dynamics* 22 (1994): 38–54.

85. D.J. Knight, "Strategy in Practice: Making It Happen," *Strategy & Leadership* 26 (1998): 29–33; R.T. Pascale, "Grassroots Leadership – Royal Dutch/Shell," *Fast Company*, no. 14 (1998): 110–20; R.T. Pascale, "Leading from a Different Place," in *The Leader's Change Handbook* ed. J.A. Conger, G.M. Spreitzer, and E.E. Lawler III (San Francisco, CA: Jossey-Bass, 1999), 301–20; R. Pascale, M. Millemann, and L. Gioja, *Surfing on the Edge of Chaos* (London, UK: Texere, 2000).

86. T.C. Head and P.F. Sorenson, "Cultural Values and Organizational Development: A Seven-Country Study," *Leadership and Organization Development Journal* 14 (1993): 3–7; R.J. Marshak, "Lewin Meets Confucius: A Review of the OD Model of Change," *Journal of Applied Behavioral Science* 29 (1993): 395–415; C.-M. Lau, "A Culture-Based Perspective of Organization Development Implementation," *Research in Organizational Change and Development* 9 (1996): 49–79; C.M. Lau and H.Y. Ngo, "Organization Development and Firm Performance: A Comparison of Multinational and Local Firms," *Journal Of International Business Studies* 32, no. 1 (2001): 95–114.

87. M. McKendall, "The Tyranny of Change: Organizational Development Revisited," *Journal of Business Ethics* 12 (1993): 93–104; C.M.D. Deaner, "A Model of Organization Development Ethics," *Public Administration Quarterly* 17 (1994): 435–46.

88. G.A. Walter, "Organization Development and Individual Rights," *Journal of Applied Behavioral Science* 20 (1984): 423–39.

89. The source of this often-cited quotation was not found. It does not appear, even in other variations, in the books that Andrew Carnegie wrote (such as Gospel of Wealth, 1900; Empire of Business, 1902; and Autobiography, 1920). However, Carnegie may have stated these words (or similar ones) elsewhere. He gave many speeches and wrote numerous articles, parts of which have been reported by other authors.

APPENDIX A

1. F.N. Kerlinger, *Foundations of Behavioral Research* (New York: Holt, Rinehart, & Winston, 1964), 11.

2. J.B. Miner, *Theories of Organizational Behavior* (Hinsdale, IL.: Dryden, 1980), 7–9.

3. Ibid., 6–7.

4. J. Mason, *Qualitative Researching* (London, UK: Sage, 1996).

5. A. Strauss and J. Corbin (eds.), *Grounded Theory in Practice* (London, UK: Sage Publications, 1997); B.G. Glaser and A. Strauss. *The Discovery of Grounded Theory: Strategies for Qualitative Research* (Chicago, IL: Aldine Publishing Co, 1967).

6. Kerlinger, *Foundations of Behavioral Research*, 13.

7. A. Strauss and J. Corbin (eds.), *Grounded Theory in Practice* (London, UK: Sage Publications, 1997); B.G. Glaser and A. Strauss. *The Discovery of Grounded Theory: Strategies for Qualitative Research* (Chicago, IL: Aldine Publishing Co, 1967).

8. W.A. Hall and P. Callery, "Enhancing the Rigor of Grounded Theory: Incorporating Reflexivity and Relationality," *Qualitative Health Research*, 11 (March 2001), 257–72.

9. P. Lazarsfeld, *Survey Design and Analysis* (New York: The Free Press, 1955).

10. This example is cited in D.W. Organ and T.S. Bateman, *Organizational Behavior*, 4th ed. (Homewood, IL.: Irwin, 1991), 42.

11. Ibid., p. 45.

12. R.I. Sutton and A. Hargadon, "Brainstorming Groups in Context: Effectiveness in a Product Design Firm," *Administrative Science Quarterly* 41 (1996), 685–718.

Name and Organization Index

A

ABB Group, 336, 336n, 337
Abdoulah, Colleen, 38, 39, 75
Abrash, Michael, 321
Accenture, 233
Adams, Michael, 49
Adconion Media Group, 366
Admiral Group, 94
Aeroflot, 88
Air Canada, 5
AirTran Airways, 358
Aizu, Miho, 233
Akerson, Dan, 356
Alcoa Russia, 45
Allen, Ken, 111
Amazon, 298
American Airlines, 271
American Express, 390
Amtrak, 38, 39
Ancona, 204
Anderson, Derrick, 381, 382
Andrews, Tracey, 258
Antal International, 48
Apple Inc., 3, 145, 167, 378
Ashton, M.C., 54n, 136n
Atwater, John, 218
Aubé, C., 198n
Audi, 291, 292
Autodesk, 128
AVON Mexico, 390
A&W Canada, 126

B

Baiocco, Maja, 15
Ballard, Geoffrey, 177
Ballard Power Systems, 177
Bancroft, Ashley, 269, 270
Banduram Albert, 124
Bang & Olufsen, 151
Bank of Montreal, 333, 333n
Barbalas, Michael, 337
Barber, Chris, 258
Barclays Bank PLC, 357
Barnard, Charles, 3
Barnard, Chester, 219
Barrett, F.J., 389n
Barrick Gold Corporation, 333, 333n
Bartrem, Richard, 81
Bavelas, Alex, CA-12
Baxter, Patty, 16, 241
BC Hydro, 218, 219
Beersma, B., 277n, 296n
Beim, Alex, 178
Bennett, Steve, 379
Bennis, Warren, 315
Bentall Capital, 207
Bentley, 291
BHP-Billiton, 145, 373
Bigler, Nathan, 302
Bird, Brad, 92
Black, Willa, 154
BlackBerry, 10
Blake, R.R., 277n, 296n
Blanchard, Ken, 309
Blossom, D., 344n
Blumer, Jason, 66
BMW AG, 338, 339, 353
Bogyo, Terrance J., 395
Bombardier Inc., 3
Bonaparte, Napoleon, 326, 326n
Borough of Lambeth, 382
Bouchard, Christian, 269, 270
Bourgois, Emilie, 48
Bouvin, Anders, 329
BP, 349
Brandt Group of Companies, 32
Brasilata, 181
Brenner, Joanna, 241n
Bridgewater Bulletin, 201
Brin, Sergey, 167
British Broadcasting Corporation, 390
British Columbia Ferry Services, 173
British Gas New Energy, 251
Broadcast Australia, 197
Brookstone Construction, 281
Brown, Alexandra, 236
Brown, Mike, 252
Brown, Rachael, 362
Brown, S.P., 95n
Bryant, Adam, 292
Budner, S., 396n
Budweiser, 138
Bugatti, 291
Burton, Pierre, 131
Business Objects, 280, 281

C

The Cake Box, 344
Calcraft, Stef, 179
Caldwell, 204
Caldwell, D.F., 350n
Calgary Airport, 81
Calgon Carbon Corporation, 380
Callanan, G.A., 295n
Camp FFit, 56
Campbell, Gordon, 301
Campbell Soup, 146
Canadian Centre for Ethics and Corporate Policy, 46
Canadian Federal Government, 92, 178
Canadian Forces, 307
Canadian Institute of Chartered Accountants, 26, 45–46
Canadian International Development Agency, 26
Canadian National Railway (CN), 281
Canadian Nature Federation, 391
Canadian Outback Adventures & Events, 207
Canadian Pacific Railway Limited (CP), 379
Canadian Tire, 6, 324, 335, 390
Canadian Tourism Commission (CTC), 125, 126
Canadian War Museum, 64
Canadian Wheat Board (CWB), 281
Cannon-Brookes, Michael, 334
Carnegie, Andrew, 392
Castrol Marine, 390
CBC, 250
Celestica, 339
Center of Automotive Research (CAR), 292
CenturyLink, 275
Chan, Amiee, 297, 298, 300, 302, 314
Chapman, David, 332
Chapman, Penny, 332
Chapman's Ice Cream Limited, 332
Chatman, J., 350n
Cherniss, C., 90n
Cherrington, David J., CA-16, CA-17
Cherry, S., 344n
Chilton, David, 250
Christianson, Art, 141
Chrysler Corp., 231, 299, 327
Churchill, Winston, 353
Cineplex Inc., 123
Cirque du Soleil, 30, 352
Cisco Canada, 154
Cisco Systems, 18
City of Toronto, 244
City of Toronto's Customer Service Call Centre, 124
City of Toronto's Revenue Services, 124
Clark, Carolyn, 118
Clark, Christy, 301
Clarkson, David, 154
Clear Channel Communications, 366
ClearlyContacts, 85, 354
Cloninger, C.R., 54n, 136n
Coastal.com, 354
Coca-Cola Co., 260, 333, 334
Cohen, George, 302
Coles, 355
Collee, John, 179
Concordia University, 134
Confucius, 3
Connellan, T.K., 122n
Container Store, 94, 352
Continental Airlines, 376
Converse Shoes, 178
Cook Medical Asia-Pacific, 241
Coomer, Greg, 321, 330
Coon, H.M., 47n
Cooperrider, D.L., 389n
Copps, Mary Jane, 16, 241
Cornerstone Research, 326
Corus Entertainment, 86
Covey, Stephen, 288
CPP, Inc., 37n
CPR, 162
Croon, M.A., 320n
Cummins Inc., 337
Cunard, Samuel, 302
Cunard Steamship Lines, 302
Currie, Richard, 146

D

Daft, R.L., 229n
Daimler AG, 338
Daimler Benz, 338
Daishowa-Marubeni, 74
Damp, Stephen, 357
Davis, Ray, 377
DaVita Inc., 94, 301
de Condorcet, Marquis, 181
de Dreu, C.K.W, 277n, 296n

de Mestral, Georges, 176
De Pree, Max, 360
Dearth, Randall, 380
Dell Inc., 304
Deloitte LLC, 18
Deloitte Touche Tohmatsu, 123, 256
Descartes, 163
Deutsche Post, 111
Dewey, John, 59, 271, 272
DHL Express, 111
Dickinson, Arlene, 250
Dittrich, J.E., CA-3
Diuggan, Maeve, 241n
Dockter, Scott, 224
Donnelly, Paul, 2
Doolittle, Robyn, 244
Dougherty, C., 292
Dragons' Den, 250
Dreyer Kompetense, 173
Drucker, Peter, 127, 303
Dudenhoeffer, Ferdinand, 292
Duggan, Maeve, 241n
Duha Group, 10
Duha, Rick, 10
Duke University, 222
DuPont, Karen, 57

E

Eastern Idaho Regional Medical Center, 302
Eastman Kodak Company, 167
eBay Canada, 236
Eber, H.W., 54n, 136n
Edmonton/Villeneuve Airports, 125
Einstein, Albert, 20, 165
EllisDon, 299, 357, 358
Elop, Stephen, 378
Emerson & Cuming, 391
Emerson, Bill, 353, 359
Engelhardt, Henry, 94
Entwistle, Darren, 109
Epictetus, 234
Ergon Energy, 387
Ernst & Young, 77
Etherington, Martyn, 372, 373, 381, 383, 386
Evers, A., 277n, 296n
Excite. Inc., 167
L'Express, 88
EYE Lighting International, 151

F

Facebook, 38, 110, 122, 193, 218, 219, 224, 225, 233, 238, 240, 241, 255, 348, 366
Fairmont Hotels & Resorts, 118
FairPrice, 75
Farrall, Frank, 123
Faxander, Olof, 327-328
Fayol, Henri, 270, 326, 326n
Fedex Corporation, 326, 326n
Fiat, 299, 327
Fiedler, Fred, 309, 310
Finkelstein, Harley, 139
First West Credit Union, 353
Follett, Mary Parker, 3, 271, 277
Ford, 286
Ford Canada, 123, 128
Ford, Rob, 244, 245
Forrester, Karen, 305
Fortune 500, 145
Foxconn, 100, 131
French, John, 247
Freshbooks, 361
FRHI Hotels & Resorts, 118
Friedman, Milton, 13
Frost, Harriet, 179

G

G Adventures, 347, 348, 350, 357, 359, 361, 362
Galbraith, J., 324n
Galbraith, John Kenneth, 375
Galloro, Jaimie, 86
Gardner, John, 299
Gatorade, 138
Gaudes, Alexandra, 56
GE Aircraft Engines, 335
Gendreau, Kyle, 341
General Electric Company (GE), 234, 373, 374
General Motors, 356
Giga Omni Media, 222n
GO Transit, 165
Goldberg, L.R., 54n, 136n
Goldcorp, 377
Goldman Sachs, 352
Goleman, D., 90n
Goodnight, Jim, 8
Goodrich Corporation, 337
Google, 13, 62, 138, 167, 175, 178, 298, 378
Google Scholar, 298
Gough, H.C., 54n, 136n
Gough, H.G., 188n
Government of British Columbia, 143
Goyder, Richard, 355, 379
Gray, M., CA-2n
Great Little Box Company, 128
Great Western Brewing Company, 143
Green Mountain Coffee Roasters, 390
Grip Ltd., 85
Gronvold, Frode, 154
Grove, Andy, 273
The Guardian, 382
Gushin, Vadim, CA-1, CA-2

H

Habanero Consulting, 225
Hackman, J.R., 150n, 159n
Hamaberg, Bob, 381
Hammer, Allen L., 37n
Hana Financial Group, 337, 338
Hanks, Tom, 174
Hardwick, Walter, 301
Hardy, Roger, 354
Harrison, Hunter, 379
Harvard University, 3, 4, 270
Harvey, C., 345n
Hassell, Jim, 197
Hawranek, D., 292
Heidelberg Druckmaschinen AG, 388
Heidelberg USA, 388, 390
Heilbrun, A.B. Jr., 188n
Heineken Canada, 115
Heineken USA, 115
Helm, Matt, 138
Hennigar, Lynn, 201
Herman Miller Inc., 360
Hermkens, K., 225n
Hersey, Paul, 309
Herzberg, Frederick, 149
Heskett, J.I., 95n
Hewlett-Packard, 237, 337
High Liner Foods, 141
Hilcorp Energy Company, 143
Hillier, Rick, 307
Hitachi, 15
Ho, Elizabeth, CA-11
Hodo, Chikamoto, 233
Hofschneider, Anita, 241n
Hofstede, G., 47n
Hogan, R., 54n, 136n
Holmes, Ryan, 1
Home Depot, 231, 360, 374
Hood Group, 145
HooteSuite Media Inc., 1, 2, 3, 5, 8, 9
Horvath, Cheryl, 56
House, Paul, 75
Houston Fire Department, 57
HP Enterprise Business, 339
Hsieh, Tony, 237, 362
Huateng, "Pony" Ma, 303
Hudson's Bay Company, 3, 363
Hughes, Mark, 241n
Humphrey, Ambrosia, 1
Hunter Douglas, 390
Hurd, Mark, 337, 338
Hutton, R., 292

I

IBM, 7, 18, 49, 77, 197, 209, 236, 334, 337, 339
Iceland Foods Group Limited, 28, 29
Iksil, Bruno, 245
Information Overload Research Group (IORG), 223
Infoseek, 167
Infosys, 354
Ingram, Harry, 73
Institute for Biomedical Problems (IBMP), CA-1, CA-2
Intel, 223, 236, 273
Intercontinental Hotels Group, 118
International Fitness Holdings, 122
International Space Station, CA-1
International Space University, CA-1
Intuit, 379
Israeli Defence Force, 70
Iwasaki Electric of Japan, 151

J

Jago, A.G., 186n
Jenkins, Antony, 357
Jijang, Wang, 100
Jobs, Steve, 3, 192
John Shetcliffe Marketing, 258
Johnson, J.A., 54n, 136n
Jones, Glyn, CA-4
Jones, T.J., 44n
Jordan, Peter J., 90n, 107n
Joy, Hélène, 59
JP Morgan, 245
Jung, Carl, 36, 37, 38
Junor, Kevin, 307

K

Kahneman, Daniel, 169
Kanungo, R.N., 80n
Kawamura, Takashi, 15
Kaza, Divakar, 366
KBR, 173
Keehn, Chris, 18
Kelly Services, 96n, 142n, 310n
Kemmelmeier, M., 47n
KenGen, 327
Keogh, Kyron, 127
Keppel Offshore & Marine, 76
Kietzmann, J.H., 225n
King, William Lyon MacKenzie, 3
Kirn, S.P., 95n
Kluwer, E.S., 277n, 296n
Kolliopoulos, John, 363, 364

Kotter, J.P., 380n
KPMG, 232
Kraft, Norbert, CA-2
Kraus, Joe, 167
Kreitner, R., 122n

L

Laliberté, Guy, 352
Lam, S.K., 95n
Lamborgini, 291
Lamothe, Marie-Josée, 269
Landler, M., 292
Langlois, Ryan, 138
Lapierre, Judith, CA-1, CA-2
Larcher, Laura, 138
Lavoie, Paul, 335
Law, K.S., 107n
Lawrence, P.R., 117n, 380n
Lawrence, Sandra A., 90n, 107n
LeasePlan USA, 87
Lebeter, David, 214, 215
Lee, Leonard, 144
Lee Valley Tools, 144
Lengel, R.H., 229n
Lester B. Pearson School Board, 391
Levie, A., 222n
Levy, Carmi, 1
Lewin, Kurt, 373, 374, 378, 383, 386, 392
Lewis, John, 258
Lighthouse Media Group, 201
LinkedIn, 123, 193, 224, 240, 255
Linstow Management Centre, 154
Loblaw Companies Limited, 5, 146, 223
London School of Economics, 175
Looby Construction, 357, 358
L'Oréal Canada, 269, 270, 281
Lotia, Nuzhat, CA-16
Loughry, M.L., 198n
Luchans, F., 122n
Luechauer, D.L., 370n
Luft, Joseph, 73, 73n
Lupin Limited, 366

M

MacDonald, Emily, 56
Machiavelli, Niccolò, 264
Macquarie Group, 337
Magna International, 324, 339
Magna Steyr, 338
Malekzedeh, A.R., 358n
Maplehurst Correctional Complex, 307
Marchionne, Sergio, 299, 327
Margles, Liz, 223
Mars, Inc., 353
Martin, H.J., 136n
Martin, S., CA-2n
Maslow, Abraham, 110, 113, 113n, 114, 118
Maurer, Rick, 209
Mayo Clinic, 351
Mayo, Elton, 3, 4, 270
McBee, Richard, 372, 373, 383
McCarthy, I.P., 225n
McClelland, David, 110, 114, 115, 116
McDerment, Mike, 361
McDonald's Canada, 302
McDonald's Restaurants, 329, 333, 334
McEwan, Rob, 377
Mclain, D.L., 396n
McMath, Iain, 258
McShane, Steven L., 23, 106, 107n, 158, 186n, 214, 216n, 240, 241n, 243n, 266, 268n, 291, 292, 296n, 318, 319, 345n, 369n, 370n, 395, CA-1, CA-2, CA-3, CA-8, CA-11, CA-17
Medicare, 299
Meggy, Robert, 128
Mei, Li, 147, 148, 149
Meindl, J.R., 320n
Mencius, 148
Mercedes, 338
Merritt, Bobbie, 344
Merritt, Christian, 344
Merritt, Larry, 344
Merritt's Bakery, 344
Metro Guide Publishing, 16, 241
Metrolink, 38, 39
The Metropolitan Transit Authority, 251
Microsoft, Inc., 241, 352, 362, 378
Mikitani, Hiroshi, 75
Milgram, Stanley, 248
Mill, John Stuart, 140
Minnelli, Lisa, 315
Mintzberg, H., 324n
Mitel Networks, 372, 373, 381, 383, 386
Mongeau, Claude, 281
Montreal, Maine and Atlantic Railway (MMA), 162, 163
Moore, D.D., 198n
Morgan, Doug, 75
Morouney, K., 345n
Mother, 179, 353
Mount Sinai Hospital, 249
Mouton, J.S., 277n, 296n
MTN Group, 13
Muldoon, Gary, 75
Murdoch Mysteries, 59

N

Nadler, D.A., 324n
Nahvandi, A., 358n
Nardelli, Robert, 231, 360, 374
Nasser, Jacques, 373
National Transportation Safety Board (U.S.), 162
Nauta, A., 277n, 296n
NBN Corp., 197
Neale, Tim, CA-2
Nestlé, 333, 336, 353
Netflix, 350
Newell, Gabe, 321
News Corp, 357
NHL, 189
Nilekani, Nandan, 354
Niller, E., CA-2n
Nishith Desai Associates (NDA), 179
Nohria, N., 117n
Nokia Corp., 378
Nolen, S., CA-2n
Norsat International Inc., 297, 298, 300, 302, 314
Nova Chemicals, 127
Novo Nordisk, 238, 384
Nucor Inc., 143, 146

O

Obama, 298
O'Hagan, Jane, 379
Ohland, M.W., 198n
Oldham, G., 150n, 159n
OMD, 179
OMERS Ventures, 1
1-800-Got-Junk?, 237, 353
17173.com, 100
Oppenheimer, Robert J., 134
Oracle, 337
O'Reilly III, C.A., 350n
Orkin Canada, 75
O'Rourke, William, 45
Osborn, Alex, 212
Ottawa-Carleton School Board, 391
Oyserman, D, 47n

P

Page, Larry, 167
Paquette, Sid, 1
Paul Sherrer Institut, 140
PBD Worldwide Fulfilment Services (PBD), 223, 224
PCL, 348
Peace River Pulp Division, 74
Pekeles, Ellen, 42n
Peking University, 100
Peng, Sean Kian, 75
Perri, D.F., 295n
Peters, Susan, 234
Peters, Tom, 326, 326n
Pfizer, 384
Philips, 333, 333n, 334
Phillips, Art, 300, 301
Piëch, Ferdinand, 292
Pitcher, Mike, 87
Pivot, Laurence, 88
Pixar Animation Studios, 3, 92, 138, 192, 236
Plato, 3, 63, 148, 163
Pontefract, Dan, 109
Poon Tip, Bruce, 347, 348, 359
Porsche AG, 292
Porsche, Wolfgang, 292
Price, Gordon, 301
PricewaterhouseCoopers LLP, 15, 39, 100
Procter & Gamble, 77, 336, 384, 385
Project GLOBE, 316
Provena United Samaritans Medical Center, 252
PSA Peugeot Citroën, 196, 209
Putre, Laura, 241n

Q

Qantas, 271
Quicken Loans, 353, 359
Quinn, R.T., 95n
Quist, Don, 145
Qwest, 275–276
Qzone, 303

R

Rahim, M.A., 277n, 296n
Rakuten Inc., 75
Randstad Holdings NV, 92n
Ranran, Kong, 100
Raven, Bertrand, 247
Razer, 85
RBC Capital Markets, 31
Reckitt Benckiser, 361
Regus, 17
Reliance Industries, 9
Research in Motion, 10
Reynolds, M., 344n
Roberts, J.A., 160n
Robison, Wesley, 241n
Roethlisberger, Fritz, 4
Rogers, William, 300
Rokeach, Milton, 40
Rolls-Royce Engine Services, 298
Rompré, Marjolaine, 269
Rotten Tomatoes, 192
Rousseau, V., 198n

Rox Ltd., 127
Royal Bank of Canada, 16, 100, 283
Royal Canadian Mounted Police (RCMP), 26, 27, 125, 126
Royal Dutch/Shell, 391
Ruble, T.L., 277n
Rucci, A.J., 95n
Russell, J.A., 83n

S

Sabo, Kathy, 390
Sage Software, 256
Sagie, G., 40n
Salpietra, Tom, 151
Samsonite, 341
Samsung Electronics, 178
San Jorge Children's Hospital, 102
Sanders, James, 123
Sanvik, 327
SAP, 280, 281
Saretsky, Gregg, 81, 82, 90
SAS Institute, Inc., 8
Sasser, W.E., 95n
Savoie, A., 198n
Schau, C., 389n
Schlesinger, L.A., 95n
Schutte, N.S., 107n
Schwartz, N.D., 292
Schwartz, Shalom, 40, 40n, 41, 117
Schwarz, John, 281
Schyns, B., 320n
Scudamore, Brian, 237
SEAT, 291
Seaton, B., 44n
Seeger, John A., 266
Seidl, Peter, CA-9
Selye, Hans, 98, 99n
Semco SA, 180, 299, 312, 335
Semler, Ricardo, 312
Semple, Gavin, 32
Sepulveda, C.J., 160n
Serasa Experian, 263
Servus Credit Union, 225, 226
7-Eleven, 328, 329
Shadbolt, Lucy, 251, 252, 253
Shaw, George Bernard, 230
Shell, 336
Shell Canada, 283
Shell Europe, 378
Shepard, H.A., 277n, 296n
Shepherd, P., 44n
Sherwin-Williams, 181
Shetcliffe, John, 258
Shopify, 138, 139, 143
Shulman, G.M., 370n
Shulman, Joey, 250
Siemens AG, 232, 337
Silva, Renan, 263
Silvestre, B.S., 225n
Simon, Herbert, 128, 171
Sinclair, A., 222n
Sinclair, G. Jr., CA-2n
Skinner, Launi, 353
SkinnyChews, 250
Skoda, 291
Skype, 66, 222n, 228
Smisek, Jeffrey, 376
Smith, Aaron, 241n
Smith, Adam, 3, 148
Smith, Geoff, 299, 357
Smith, Greg, 352
Smith, K.W., 358n
Smith, Nina, 256
Smith, Ross, 241
Smollan, Roy, CA-6
SNC-Lavalin (SNCL), 26, 27, 41, 43, 44, 45, 46
Sodexo Motivation Solutions Ltd., 258
Southwest Airlines, 358
Sripada, Chandrasekhar, 337
St. Luke's Medical Center, 241
Standard Chartered Bank, 110
StandardAero, 381
Stanford University, 167
Starbuck, William, CA-12
Starbucks U.S., 353
Stathopolous, Melina, 361
Statistics Canada, 33
Steiger, J.H., 83n
Stewart, Wendy, 269, 270
Strategic Investments, 194
Stuermer, Christoph, 292
Sûreté du Québec, 162
Svenska Handelsbanken AB, 143, 328, 329
Sweeney, Petá, 387
System Capital Management, 281

T

Tamarack Industries, CA-16–CA-17
Tanaka, Satoshi, 233
Tangible Interaction Design, 178
TAXI, 335
Taylor, Carole, 301
Taylor, Frederick Winslow, 3, 148, 149
TD Canada Trust, 283
TEAM, 301
Team Canada, 189, 190
Teixeira, Antonio Carlos Alvares, 181
Telus Corp., 18, 109, 110, 111, 119
Templer, D., 160n
Tencent, 303
Tencent Weibo, 303
TenPay, 303
Tesla Motors, 138
T.G.I. Friday, 305
Thomas, Barry, 241
Thomas, K., 277n
Thomas, K.W., 296n
Thomson Reuters, 254
3M, 248
Tim Hortons, 75, 253
Timoney. Maggie, 115
Tindell, Kip, 94
Toews, Jonathan, 190
Toor, Sukh, 110
Toronto City Council, 244, 245
Toronto City Hall, 244, 245
Toronto District School Board, 391
Toronto Fire Services, 56
Toronto Transit Commission (TTC), 322
Toronto Western Hospital (TWH), 390
Toyota, 209
Tracy, J., CA-2n
Transportation Safety Board of Canada (TSB), 162
Trosten-Bloomm A., 389n
Tsalikis, J., 44n
Tunmore, Neil, 236
Tushman, M.L., 324n
Tversky, Amos, 169
Twillman, Brian, 37
Twitter, 66, 110, 221, 222, 224, 228, 233, 234, 237, 238, 240, 255
Typepad, 224

U

UKRD, 300
Umpqua Bank, 377
Undercover Boss, 75
United Airlines, 271, 376
United States Air Force (USAF), 91
University of Delaware, 73
University of South Florida (USF) College of Medicine, 89–90
Urwick, Lindall, 326, 326n
U.S. Department of Defense, 222
U.S. Federal Government, 178
U.S. Library of Congress, 298
U.S. Postal Service, 326, 326n
Utt, Bill, 173

V

Valve Corporation, 299, 321, 322, 323, 324, 325, 330, 335
van den Brink, Dolf, 115
Vancouver City Savings Credit Union (Vancity), 12, 42, 362
Varin, Philippe, 196
Venture Communications, 250
Vigilant Global, 103
Volkswagen Group (VW), 291, 292
von Helmholtz, Hermann, 175
Vroom, V.H., 186n

W

Walker, Malcolm, 29
Wallas, Graham, 175, 176n
Walt Disney Studios, 92
Wang, Tony, 155
Warren, M., CA-2n
Weber, Max, 3, 270
WeChat, 303
Weisensel, Ward, 281
Welch, Jack, 373
Wesfarmers, 355, 379
WestJet Airlines, 81, 82, 85, 88, 90
Whirlpool, 352
Whitney, D.K., 389n
Whole Foods Market, 143
Wide Open West (WOW), 39, 75
Wiedeking, Wendelin, 292
Wikipedia, 138, 224, 236
Wilson, Jerry, 260
W.L. Gore & Associates, 180, 299, 335
Wolf, M., 222n
Wolter, Jakob, 238
Wong, C-S, 107n
World Bank, 26, 43, 46
Wuttunee, Nancy, 126

Y

Yahoo!, 167
Yamauchi, K., 160n
York, G., CA-2n
YouInc.com, 250
YouTube, 81
Yun Jong-yong, 178
Yzerman, Steve, 189

Z

Zaid, Tariq, 138
Zappos, 145, 237, 361, 362, 632
Zara, 6, 7, 8
Zawacki, R.A., CA-3
Zebro, David, 194
Zeldes, Nathan, 223
Zollinger, Cindy, 326, 327

Subject Index

A

ability, 27, 28-29, 385
absenteeism, 33, 58, 122, 152
absorption, 249
achievable goals, 125
achievement, need for, 115
achievement-nurturing orientation, 47, 48
achievement-oriented leadership, 308
acquisition (drive), 116
action research, 386-388, 392
action scripts, 172
action teams, 191
actions of founders and leaders, 359
active listening, 234-235, 241-243
adaptability, 31
adaptive culture, 355-356
adjourning stage, 205
advisory teams, 191
affective organizational commitment, 95-97
affiliation, need for, 115
agreeableness, 35, 36, 40
alarm reaction stage, 98
alternatives, 168-170
ambassador activities, 204
ambiguous accountability, 337
ambiguous rules, 276
ambiguous situations, 224
American values, 49-50
analyzability, 342
anchoring and adjustment heuristic, 169
anchors of organizational behaviour
knowledge, 19-21
Anglophones, 49
anonymous reporting, 46
antecedents, 121-122
anticipatory principle, 388-389
applied performance practices
  competency-based rewards, 141-142
  empowerment practices, 153
  financial reward practices, 140-144
  improvement of reward effectiveness, 144-146
  job design, 146-153
  job status-based rewards, 140-141
  linking rewards to performance, 144-145
  membership-based rewards, 140, 141
  money in the workplace, 139-140
  performance-based rewards, 141, 142-146
  relevance of rewards, 145-146
  seniority-based rewards, 140, 141
  unintended consequences, 146, 147
appreciative coaching, 127
appreciative inquiry, 388-390
aptitudes, 28-29
arbitration, 282-283
ARPANET, 222
artifacts, 351-353, 360
assertiveness, 257, 258-259
assimilation, 358
associative play, 179
attitude object, 83
attitudes, 83-85
attraction-selection-attrition (ASA) theory,
361-362
attribution errors, 69
attribution process, 68
attribution theory, 68-69
authentic leadership, 314-316
autonomy, 150
availability heuristic, 169
average negotiators, 289-290
avoiding, 278-279, 280

B

Baby Boomers, 16
balanced scorecard (BSC), 125-126
bargaining zone model, 287
BATNA, 285
behaviour modelling, 124
behavioural intentions, 84-85
behaviourism, 121
beliefs, 84-85
belongingness needs, 113
best alternative to a negotiated agreement
(BATNA), 285
bias
  awareness of perceptual biases, 72
  confirmation bias, 63, 173
  correspondence bias, 69
  decision heuristics, 169
  fundamental attribution error, 69, 74
  halo effect, 71
  and performance reviews, 145
  primacy effect, 71
  recency effect, 71
  self-serving bias, 69
  stereotyping, 65-68, 79
bicultural audit, 358
Big Five personality dimension, 177
blind area (Johari Window), 73
board of directors, 67
body language, 227
bonding (drive), 116
bottom line, 5
boundary spanning, 204-205
bounded rationality, 168
brainstorming, 212
brainwriting, 212
breaking routines, 377
bribery, 26
Brooks's law, 194
buffers, 282
bullying bosses, 259
burnout. *See* job burnout
business ethics. *See* ethics

C

calculus-based trust, 203
can-do belief system, 36
Canada
  absenteeism, 33
  Canadian *vs.* American values, 49-50
  cultural diversity, 49
  diversity of Canadian cultural values, 49-50
  employee engagement, 111
  workforce diversity, 16
case studies
  Ancol Ltd., 23-24
  Arbrecorp Ltée, 214-215
  Arctic Mining Consultants, CA-2-CA-3
  Barrie Super Subs, CA-3-CA-4
  car wars at Wolfsburg, 291-292
  communicating with the
  Millennials, 240-241
  employee involvement cases, 184-186
  ethics dilemma vignettes, 52
  Fran Hayden joins Dairy
  Engineering, CA-4-CA-6
  going to the X-Stream, CA-6-CA-8
  Hillton's transformation, 368-369
  Hy Dairies Ltd., 79
  keeping Suzanne Chalmers, CA-8-CA-9
  Merritt's Bakery, 344
  A Mir kiss, CA-1-CA-2
  Northwest Canadian Forest Products Limited
  (revised), CA-9-CA-10
  the Outstanding Faculty Award, CA-17
  predicting Harry's work effort, 134-135
  the Regency Grand Hotel, CA-11-CA-12
  Resonus Corporation, 266
  rough seas on the LINK650, 105-106
  Simmons Laboratories, CA-12-CA-15
  Star Enterprises–Rita's issues at
  work, CA-15-CA-16
  Tamarack Industries, CA-16-CA-17
  Transact Insurance Corporation, 394-395
  a window on life, 316-317
  Yakkatech Ltd., 158
categorical thinking, 64, 68
categorization, 66
cause-effect relationships, 69
centrality, 251, 255-256
centralization, 328-329
CEOs, and power, 252
ceremonies, 353
challenge, 41
change. *See* organizational change
change agents, 375-376
change self-efficacy, 381
channels of communication, 221-230
charisma, 250, 303
charismatic visionary, 316
child care support, 102
China, 48, 100
circumplex model of emotions, 83
clarity of self-concept, 58, 59
client-consultant relationship, 386
client divisional structure, 333
client relationships, 153
closed systems, 6
closeness, 255
clustering illusion, 169
coalition, 259, 383-384
coalition formation, 257, 259
coalitions, 192-193
code of ethical conduct, 45-46
codebooks, 221, 230
coercion, 380, 381-382
coercive power, 249
cognition, 82
cognitive dissonance, 86-87

cognitive intelligence, 177, 313, 314
cognitive reasoning, 85
cohesion. *See* team cohesion
collective expertise, 20
collective self, 57
collectivism, 46-47, 47, 280
comfort, 198
communication, 198, 219
  active listening, 234-235
  communication barriers, 230-232
  communication channels, 221-230
  communication process model, 220-221
  conflict, and communication problems, 276-277
  and conflict management, 281-282
  cross-cultural communication, 232-233
  decoding, 221
  e-mail, 222, 223-224
  electronic communication channels, 223-225, 229-230
  encoding, 221
  face-to-face communication, 228, 230
  functions of, 219-220
  gender differences, 233-234
  getting your message across, 234
  grapevine, 237-239
  importance of, 219-220
  improvement of interpersonal communication, 234-235
  improvement through the hierarchy, 235-237
  informal communication, 323-324
  information overload, 231-232
  Internet-based communication, 222, 236
  lean media, 228
  media richness, 228-230
  multi-communicate, 229
  noise, 220, 230-232
  nonverbal communication, 225-227
  and organizational change, 379-380
  persuasion, 230
  proficiency, 229
  social acceptance, 228
  social media, 224-225
  social presence effects, 229-230
  top management, direct communication with, 237
  workspace design, 236
communication barriers, 230-232
communication process model, 220-221
communities of practice, 191
competence, 153
competency-based rewards, 141-142
competency development, 10-11
complex environments, 340
complex situations, 224
complexity of self-concept, 57
compliance, 261-262
comprehension (drive), 116-117
compromising, 278, 279, 280
concentration of effort, 44
concessions, 287, 288
confirmation bias, 63, 173
conflict, 182, 270
  in airline industry, 271
  ambiguous rules, 276
  benefits of conflict, 271-272
  communication problems, 276-277
  conflict process model, 274
  constructive conflict, 272-274
  differentiation, 275-276
  good *vs.* bad, 270-272
  incompatible goals, 275
  interdependence, 276
  interpersonal conflict handling styles, 277-280
  meaning and consequences of, 270-272
  optimal conflict perspective, 272
  relationship conflict, 272-274
  resistance to change, 375
  resolution of. *See* conflict management
  scarce resources, 276
  and stress, 270
  structural sources, 274-277
  task conflict, 272-274
conflict avoidance, 278-279, 280
conflict episodes, 274
conflict handling styles, 277-280, 292-296
conflict management, 198
  clarification of rules and procedures, 282
  conflict handling styles, 277-280, 292-296
  differentiation, reducing, 280-281
  improvement of communication, 281-282
  interdependence, reducing, 282
  mutual understanding, 281-282
  negotiation, 284-290
  resources, increase in, 282
  structural approaches, 280-282
  superordinate goals, 280
  third-party conflict resolution, 282-284
conformity, 41, 211
conscientiousness, 35, 36, 312
consensus, 68-69
consequences, 121-122, 124
conservation, 41
consistency of self-concept, 58, 68-69
conspiracy, 26
constructionist principle, 388, 389
constructive conflict, 272-274
constructive thought patterns, 155
contact hypothesis, 74
contemporary challenges for organizations, 15-19
contingencies of reinforcement, 122
contingency anchor, 21
continuance commitment, 96-97
continuous reinforcement, 122
control system, 354
convergent thinking, 176
cooperation, 197-198
coordination, 8, 198, 219, 323-325
  standardization, 323, 325
  through formal hierarchy, 323, 324-325
  through informal communication, 323-324
  through micromanagement, 324
coping strategy, 101
core affect, 83
core competencies, 338-339
core job characteristics, 150
corporate cult, 42
corporate culture. *See* organizational culture
corporate social responsibility (CSR), 12-13
correspondence bias, 69
counterculture, 351
counterproductive work behaviours (CWBs), 32
countervailing power, 246
coworkers, 366
creativity, 41, 175, 188
  activities encouraging creativity, 179
  brainstorming, 212
  brainwriting, 212
  characteristics of creative people, 177
  creative decision making in teams, 211-213
  creative process, 175-176
  the creativity advantage, 178
  electronic brainstorming, 212
  nominal group technique, 213
  organizational conditions supporting creativity, 178
  self-assessment, 188
credible feedback, 126
critical psychological states, 150
cross-cultural knowledge, 49
cross-cultural organizational research, 49
cross-cultural values, 46-50
cross-pollination, 179
cultlike companies, 353
cults, 355
cultural diversity, 49, 232
  see also workforce diversity
cultural norms, 280
cultural values, 39, 46-50, 92, 280, 316
culture
  communication, 232-233
  conflict handling styles, 279-280
  conversational overlaps, 232
  cultural norms, 280
  cultural values, 39, 46-50, 92, 280, 316
  emotional display norms, 88-89
  and leadership, 316
  and money, 140
  nonverbal differences, 232-233
  and organizational change, 391-392
  organizational culture. *See* organizational culture
customer-driven change, 378
customer satisfaction, 94-95
cycle time, 148
cynicism, 99

D

decentralization, 328-329, 340
decision commitment, 182
decision heuristics, 169
decision knowledge, 182
decision making, 163
  alternatives, 168-170
  biased decision heuristics, 169
  bounded rationality, 168
  effective choices, 172
  emotions, role of, 171
  employee involvement, 179-182
  evaluation of decision outcomes, 173-175
  goals, problems with, 168
  implementation, 173
  information processing, problems with, 168-169
  intuition, role of, 172
  maximization, problems with, 170
  opportunity evaluation, 170
  opportunity identification, 165-168
  problem identification, 165-168
  rational choice paradigm, 163-165, 168-170, 174
  team decision making, 210-213
decision outcomes, 173-175
decision structure, 182
decisive leadership, 166
decoding, 221
deculturation, 358-359
deep acting, 89
deep-level diversity, 16
defending (drive), 117

degree centrality, 255
delivering, 390
democracy in organizations, 180
democratic enterprise model, 180
departmental teams, 191
departmentalization, 331
divisional structure, 333-334
forms of, 331-340
functional structure, 331-332
M-form structure, 333-334
matrix structure, 336-338
multidivisional structure, 333-334
network structure, 338-340
simple structure, 331
team-based structure, 335-336
depersonalization, 99
design thinking, 384
designing, 389-390
destiny, 390
developing countries, 77
differentiation, 66, 275-276, 280-281
direction, 28
directive leadership, 307, 310
disclosure, 74
discovery, 389
discretion, 252
discretionary behaviours, 32
discrimination, 67
distinctiveness, 68-69
distress, 98, 99
distributive justice, 43, 128
distributive negotiation, 285, 286-287
distributive situation, 285
divergent thinking, 176
diverse environments, 340
diversity
cultural diversity, 49, 232
in teams, 198-199
workforce diversity. *See* workforce diversity
diversity training programs, 73
divine discontent, 373-374
division of labour, 322-323
divisional structure, 333-334
dominant culture, 351
dreaming, 389
drive to acquire, 116
drive to bond, 116
drive to comprehend, 116-117
drive to defend, 117
drives, 111-112
behaviour, influence on, 117
four-drive theory, 116-119
and leadership, 313
motivation, influence on, 117
needs and drives theories, 113-119
driving forces, 373
dynamic environments, 340

E

e-mail, 222, 223-224
E-to-P expectancy, 119, 120
economic sphere of sustainability, 13
effective communication. *See* communication
efficiency, 147-149
electronic brainstorming, 212
electronic communication channels, 223-225, 229-230
emerging employment relationships, 17-19, 19
emoticons, 223
emotional contagion, 226-227
emotional display norms, 88-89
emotional dissonance, 89
emotional exhaustion, 99
emotional intelligence (EI), 89-91, 107, 273, 313, 314
emotional labour, 88, 106
emotional markers, 63
emotional stability, 36, 273
emotions, 82, 83
and attitudes, 83-85
awareness of others' emotions, 90
awareness of our own emotions, 90
and behaviour, 83-85
circumplex model of, 83
cognitive dissonance, 86-87
and decision evaluation process, 171
and decision making, 171
and e-mail, 223-224
and early preferences, 171
and evaluation of alternatives, 171
as experiences, 82-83
management of, 88-89, 90
management of others' emotions, 90
model of emotions, attitudes, and behaviour, 84
and personality, 87
positive emotions at work, 85-86
types of emotions, 83
in the workplace, 82-87
empathy, 36, 44, 74
employee drives and needs, 111-119
employee engagement, 110-111
employee involvement, 10-11, 97, 179
benefits of, 181-182
cases, 184-186
contingencies of, 182
and organizational change, 380, 381
employee motivation. *See* motivation
employee share ownership plan (ESOP), 143, 144
employee training. *See* training
employee well-being, 11
employment relationships, 17-19, 19
employment selection, and discrimination, 67
empowerment, 153
enacted values, 349
encoding, 221
encounter, 365
environment, and personality, 34
environmental conditions, 194-195
environmental sphere of sustainability, 13
equality principle, 129
equity principle, 129
equity sensitivity, 131-132
equity theory, 129-132
escalation of commitment, 173-174
espoused-enacted value congruence, 42
espoused values, 348-349
establishment of client relationships, 153
esteem needs, 113
ethical principles, 43
ethical sensitivity, 44-45
ethics, 12, 43
anonymous reporting, 46
audits, 46
and behaviour, 43-46
code of ethical conduct, 45-46
distributive justice, 43
employee training, 46
ethical principles, 43
ethics dilemma vignettes (case studies), 52
individual rights, 43
and job satisfaction, 95
moral intensity, 43-44
moral sensitivity, 44-45
and organizational change, 391-392
and organizational culture, 357
situational influences, 45
supporting ethical behaviour, 45-46
utilitarianism, 43
eustress, 98
evaluation, 235
evaluation apprehension, 211
evaluation of decision outcomes, 173-175
evidence-based management, 19-20
EVLN model. *See* exit-voice-loyalty-neglect (EVLN) model
exchange, 257, 261
excitement, 41
exciting goals, 125
exhaustion stage, 98
exit, 93
exit-voice-loyalty-neglect (EVLN) model, 92, 94
expectancy theory, 119-121
expectations, 41, 203
experience, 177, 308
experienced meaningfulness, 150
experienced responsibility, 150
experimentation, 302
expert negotiators, 289-290
expert power, 249-250
exploding offer, 287
expressive language, 223
external competition, 195
external environment, 340-341, 355
external locus of control, 61
external self-concept, 61-62
external team processes, 204-205
extinction, 122
extraversion, 35, 36, 54, 312

F

face-to-face communication, 228, 230
false-consensus effect, 71
famous missed opportunities, 167
fear of the unknown, 376
feedback
and blind area, 74
choosing feedback sources, 128
in communication, 220
decision outcomes, evaluation of, 175
effective feedback, 126-127
evaluation of, 128
and goal setting, 125
job feedback, 150
and motivation, 126-128
multisource (360-degree) feedback, 127-128, 211
performance review, use of, 145
sources of, 127-128
through strengths-based coaching, 127
feedforward events, 145
feeling (F) orientation, 37
feelings, 84-85
Fiedler's contingency model, 309-310
fight or flight, 99, 103, 117
financial reward practices, 140-144
individual rewards, 142-143
job status-based rewards, 140-141
membership-based rewards, 140, 141
organizational rewards, 143-144
performance-based rewards, 141

reward objectives, advantages and disadvantages, 141
seniority-based rewards, 140, 141
team rewards, 143, 146
first offers, 286-287
Five C's model, 197-198
five-factor model (FFM), 34-36, 38
flaming, 224
flat structures, 327-328
flexible work time, 102
force field analysis, 373-374
forcing, 278, 279
forecasting, 249
foreign exchange, 31
forgery, 26
formal hierarchy, 323, 324-325
formalization, 329-330
forming stage, 205
founders's actions, 359
four-D model of appreciative inquiry, 389-390
four-drive theory, 116-119
Francophones, 49
fraud, 26
frequent feedback, 126-127
frontline staff, 75
fun at work, 87
functional structure, 331-332
fundamental attribution error, 69, 74
future search conferences, 391

G

gainsharing plan, 143
gamification, 123
gender differences
see also women
in communication, 233-234
conflict handling styles, 279-280
leadership, 316-317
social media, 233-234
general adaptation syndrome, 98, 99
Generation X, 16
Generation Y, 16
genetic code, 34
geographic divisional structure, 333
"getting ahead," 36
"getting along," 36
global mindset, 75-77
global organizations, 337
global work-life balance index, 17
globalization, 15, 19, 49, 209-210, 232, 392
globally integrated enterprise (GIE), 334
goal setting, 124-126, 128, 154-155
goals, 168, 285
see also goal setting; specific types of goals
golden handcuffs, 140
good guy-bad-guy contrast, 68
grapevine, 237-239
groups, 192-193
see also teams
growth need strength, 151
guiding coalition, 383
gut feelings, 172

H

halo effect, 71
happy worker hypothesis, 93
harassment, 99-100
hard influence tactics, 261, 262
hazards, 30
health, and stress, 101
hedonism, 41
hidden area (Johari Window), 73
hierarchy of needs, 113-114
high collectivism, 47
high-performance work practices (HPWP), 10-11
hiring process, 363
historical foundations of organizational behaviour, 3
holidays, 102
holistic perspective of motivation, 114, 118
homogenization, 66
honour system, 41
horizontal boundary spanning, 205
hostile environment, 340-341
hostile work environment harassment, 100
human capital, 8
humanistic perspective of motivation, 114, 118
hygienes, 149
hype, 20

I

ideal self, 57
identical twins, 34
identification-based trust, 203, 204
illumination stage, 176
imagination, 177
immersion, 77
impact, 153
imperfect rationality, 165
implementation of decisions, 173
Implicit Association Test (IAT), 72
implicit favourite, 169
implicit leadership theory, 311-312
impression management, 257, 260-261
incivility, 99-100
incompatible goals, 275
incongruent organizational systems, 377
incongruent team dynamics, 377
incremental change, 387
incubation stage, 176
independent imagination, 177
independent thought, 41
individual behaviour
counterproductive work behaviours (CWBs), 32
drives, influence of, 117
and emotions, 83-85
and ethical values, 43-46
joining the organization, 32-33
MARS model, 27-30
organizational citizenship behaviours (OCBs), 31-32
presenteeism, 33
self-concept, effect of, 58-59
staying with the organization, 32-33
task performance, 31
types of, 31-33
values, 41
work attendance, 33
individual differences
equity sensitivity, 131-132
job design and motivation, 151
in needs, 112-113
in stress, 101
individual rewards, 142-143
individual rights, 43
individual self, 57
individualism, 46-47
inequity, 130-131
inflated team efficacy, 211
influence, 257
assertiveness, 257, 258-259
coalition formation, 257, 259
consequences of influence tactics, 261-262
contingencies of influence tactics, 261-262
exchange, 257, 261
hard tactics, 261, 262
impression management, 257, 260-261
information control, 257, 259
ingratiation, 257, 261
leaders, 320
managing your boss, 258
persuasion, 257, 259-260
self-assessment, 267-268
silent authority, 257, 258
soft tactics, 261, 262
types of influence tactics, 257, 258-261
upward appeal, 257, 259
informal communication, 323-324
informal groups, 192-193
information control, 248-249, 257, 259
information gathering, 288
information load, 232
information overload, 224, 231-232
information processing, 168-169
information processing capacity, 232
information processing job characteristics, 151
ingratiation, 257, 261
initial offer point, 286
innovation. *See* creativity
inoculation effect, 260
inquisition, 283
insight, 176
integrated environments, 340
integration, 358, 359
integrative model of organizational behaviour, 13-15
integrative negotiations, 285, 287-289
integrative situation, 285
integrator roles, 324
integrators, 282
integrity, 313
intellectual capital, 8
intensity, 28
intentional discrimination, 67
interdependence, 196, 197, 276, 282, 327
interdependent jobs, 146
intergenerational differences, 275
internal locus of control, 61, 101, 156, 308
internal self-concept, 61
internal subsystems effectiveness, 7-8
internal team processes, 204
Internet-based communication, 222, 236
interpersonal conflict handling styles, 277-280
introversion, 35, 40, 54
intuition, 172

J

jargon, 231
job, 146, 282
job autonomy, 10-11
job burnout, 89, 99
job characteristics model, 149-151
job design, 146
job redesign, 29
motivational practices, 151-153
self-leadership practices, 154-156
and work efficiency, 147-149
and work motivation, 149-153
job dissatisfaction, 93, 329
job enlargement, 152
job enrichment, 152-153, 159-160
job evaluation, 140

job feedback, 150
job interviews, 227
job rotation, 151-152
job satisfaction, 91
  and business ethics, 95
  and customer satisfaction, 94-95
  job dissatisfaction, employee responses to, 93
  and performance, 93-94
  selected countries, 92
  and work behaviour, 92-93
job sharing, 102
job specialization, 148-149, 323
job status-based rewards, 140-141
Johari Window, 73
joining the organization, 32-33
judging orientation, 37
judgments, 83
Jungian personality theory, 36-38
justice, 97, 128-132

K

key performance indicators (KPIs), 125
knowledge acquisition, 9, 177, 314
knowledge-based trust, 203, 204
knowledge of results, 150
knowledge of the business, 313
knowledge sharing, 9
knowledge storage, 8-9
knowledge use, 9

L

labour unions, 251
language issues, 230-231
language of culture, 352
large group interventions, 390-391
lateness, 33
leader-member relations, 310
leadership, 298
  achievement-oriented leadership, 308
  actions of leaders, 359
  authentic leadership, 314-316
  cross-cultural issues, 316
  decisive leadership, 166
  directive leadership, 307, 310
  employee satisfaction with leadership style, 310
  gender and leadership, 316-317
  influence of, 320
  interdependent perspectives, 304
  leadership styles, 307-308
  managerial leadership, 304-306
  participative leadership, 307
  people-oriented leadership, 305, 306
  personal attributes perspective, 312-316
  prototypes of effective leaders, 311
  romance of leadership, 311-312
  self-leadership, 154-156
  servant leadership, 306
  shared leadership, 298-299
  supportive leadership, 307, 310
  task-oriented leadership, 305, 306
  theories of. *See* leadership theories
  transformational leadership, 299-304
leadership motivation, 313
leadership substitutes, 311
leadership teams, 191
leadership theories
  Fiedler's contingency model, 309-310
  implicit leadership theory, 311-312
  path-goal leadership theory, 306-309, 319-320
  situational leadership theory (SLT), 309
lean media, 228
learned capabilities, 28-29
learned needs theory, 114-116
learning, and organizational change, 380-381
learning needs, 116
learning orientation, 178, 356
legends, 352
legitimate power, 247-249
Lewin's force field analysis model, 373-374
liaison roles, 324
life experiences, 34
limited work time, 102
limits, 285-286
local councils in United Kingdom, 382
locus of control, 61, 308
logical thinking, 82
love needs, 113
low collectivism, 47
low task control, 101
loyalty, 93

M

M-form structure, 333-334
Machiavellian values, 264
magnitude of consequences, 44
management
  direct communication with top management, 237
  grapevine, use of, 238
  middle management, 328
management by walking around (MBWA), 237
managerial leadership, 304-306
many ties, 255
MARS model, 27-30, 61
  ability, 28-29
  motivation, 28
  resistance to change, 376-377
  role perceptions, 30
  situational factors, 30
Maslow's needs hierarchy theory, 113-114
matching strategy, 29
matrix structure, 336-338
maximization, 170
McClelland's learned needs theory, 114-116
meaning, 153
meaningful interaction, 74-75, 281
measurable goals, 125
mechanistic structure, 330-331
media richness, 228-230
mediation, 283
mediation-arbitration, 283
membership-based rewards, 140, 141
mental imagery, 155
mental models, 65, 166, 206, 221
merging organizational cultures, 357-359
micromanagement, 324
middle management, 328
Millennials, 16, 240-241
mindfulness, 44
mindless behaviour, 177
minimization of effort, 45
moderation, 41
money, 139-140, 160
  see also financial reward practices
money laundering, 26
moods, 82
moral intensity, 43-44
moral sensitivity, 44-45
morphological analysis, 179
motivation, 27, 28
  communication channel motivation, 221
  diffusion of change from pilot project, 385
  employee drives and needs, 111-119
  employee engagement, 110-111
  equity theory, 129-132
  expectancy theory, 119-121
  feedback, 125-128
  goal setting, 124-126, 128
  holistic perspective, 114, 118
  humanistic perspective, 114, 118
  and inequity, 130-131
  job characteristics model, 149-151
  and job design, 149-153
  leadership motivation, 313
  Maslow's contributions to, 114
  and money, 140
  motivator-hygiene theory, 149
  needs and drives theories, 113-119
  organizational behaviour modification, 121-123
  organizational justice, 128-132
  positive perspective, 114
  social cognitive theory, 124
  teams, 192
motivator-hygiene theory, 149
motivators, 149
multiculturalism, 49
multidisciplinary anchor, 20-21
multidivisional structure, 333-334
multiple levels of analysis anchor, 21
multisource (360-degree) feedback, 127-128, 211
munificent environment, 340-341
mutual understanding, 281-282
Myers-Briggs Type Indicator (MBTI), 36-38, 171

N

natural grouping approach, 152
natural rewards, 155
nature, 34
need for achievement (nAch), 115
need for affiliation (nAff), 115
need for power (nPow), 115-116
need principle, 129
needs, 112, 135-136
  individual differences, 112-113
  Maslow's needs hierarchy theory, 113-114
  McClelland's learned needs theory, 114-116
  needs and drives theories, 113-119
  needs-strength questionnaire, 136
needs and drives theories
  four-drive theory, 116-119
  Maslow's needs hierarchy theory, 113-114
  McClelland's learned needs theory, 114-116
negative reinforcement, 122
negative self-talk, 155
negative valence of change, 376
neglect, 93
negotiation, 284
  bargaining zone model, 287
  best alternative to a negotiated agreement (BATNA), 285
  distributive negotiations, 285, 286-287
  expert *vs.* average negotiators, 289-290
  goals, 285
  integrative negotiations, 285, 287-289
  limits, 285-286
  and organizational change, 380, 381
  preparing to negotiate, 285-286
  time-limited offers, 287
  value creation, 286, 287-288

network structure, 338-340
neuroticism, 35, 36
noise, 220, 230-232
nominal group technique, 213
nonprogrammed decisions, 164
nonsubstitutability, 251
nonverbal communication, 225-227
norm of reciprocity, 248
norming stage, 205
norms, 199
  cultural norms, 280
  social norms, 41, 112
  team norms, 199-200, 273-274
not-invented-here syndrome, 376-377
novel situations, 224
nurture, 34

O

offers, 286-287, 288
open area (Johari Window), 73
open systems, 5-8, 390-391
openness to change, 40-41
openness to experience, 35, 36
opportunities
  evaluation of, 170
  identification, 165-168
organic structure, 330-331
organization-community values congruence, 42
organization-environment fit, 6-7
organizational behaviour (OB), 2
  anchors of organizational behaviour knowledge, 19-21
  and bottom line, 5
  field of organizational behaviour, 2-5
  historical foundations, 3
  integrative model of organizational behaviour, 13-15
  organizational effectiveness, 5-15
  positive organizational behaviour, 71, 114, 388
  and self-concept, 62
  study of, 3-5
  ultimate dependent variable, 2
  value for everyone, 4
organizational behaviour modification (OB Mod), 121-123
organizational change
  action research approach, 386-388, 392
  appreciative inquiry approach, 388-390
  approaches to, 386-391
  change agents, 375-376
  coalitions, 383-384
  cross-cultural issues, 391-392
  customer-driven change, 378
  diffusion of change, 384-385
  ethical issues, 391-392
  handling change, globally, 375
  incremental change, 387
  large group interventions, 390-391
  Lewin's force field analysis model, 373-374
  parallel learning structures, 391
  pilot projects, 384-385
  rapid change, 387
  refreezing, 374, 382-383
  resistance to change, 374-377, 379-382
  restraining forces, 374, 379-382
  self-assessment, 396
  social networks, 383-384
  speed of, 387
  transformational leadership, 383
  unfreezing, 374, 378-383
  urgency for change, creation of, 378-379
  viral change, 383-384
organizational citizenship behaviours (OCBs), 31-32
organizational commitment
  affective organizational commitment, 95-97
  building organizational commitment, 97
  consequences of affective and continuance commitment, 96-97
  continuance commitment, 96-97
organizational comprehension, 97
organizational culture, 348
  actions of founders and leaders, 359
  adaptive culture, 355-356
  artifacts, 349, 351-353, 360
  assimilation, 358
  assumptions, 348, 349
  attraction-selection-attrition (ASA) theory, 361-362
  bicultural audit, 358
  and business ethics, 357
  ceremonies, 353
  changing organizational culture, 359-362
  content of, 350-351
  contingencies, 354-356
  corporate culture, as overused phrase, 356
  counterculture, 351
  cults, 355
  culturally consistent rewards and recognition, 360
  deculturation, 358-359
  dominant culture, 351
  during hiring process, 363
  elements of, 348-351
  external environment, 355
  importance of, 353-357
  integration, 358, 359
  merging organizational cultures, 357-359
  metaphors, 369-370
  organizational language, 352
  organizational socialization, 362-366
  physical structures and symbols, 353
  profile dimensions and characteristics, 350
  rituals, 353
  self-assessment, 370
  separation, 358, 359
  stories and legends, 352
  strengthening organizational culture, 359-362
  subcultures, 351
  values, 348-349
  workforce stability and communication, 360-361
organizational design, 340-342
  see also organizational structure
organizational effectiveness, 5
  high-performance work practices (HPWP), 10-11
  integrative model of organizational behaviour, 13-15
  open systems, 5-8
  organizational learning, 8-10
  stakeholders, 11-13
organizational efficiency, 8
organizational environment, 194-195, 340-341
organizational justice, 128-132
organizational learning, 8-10
organizational memory, 8-9
organizational politics, 262-264
organizational rewards, 143-144
organizational socialization, 362, 363
  encounter, 365
  improvement of process, 365-366
  as learning and adjustment process, 363
  pre-employment socialization, 364-365
  and psychological contracts, 363-364
  role management, 365
  socialization agents, 365-366
  stages of, 364-365
organizational strategy, 342
organizational structure, 322
  centralization, 328-329
  contingencies of organizational design, 340-342
  coordination, 323-325
  decentralization, 328-329
  departmentalization, 331-340
  division of labour, 322-323
  divisional structure, 333-334
  elements of, 325-331
  external environment, 340-341
  flat structures, 327-328
  formalization, 329-330
  functional structure, 331-332
  M-form structure, 333-334
  matrix structure, 336-338
  mechanistic structure, 330-331
  multidivisional structure, 333-334
  network structure, 338-340
  organic structure, 330-331
  organizational size, 341
  organizational strategy, 342
  self-assessment, 345
  simple structure, 331
  span of control, 325-328
  structure follows strategy, 342
  tall structures, 327-328
  team-based structure, 335-336
  technology, 341-342
organizational values, 39
organizations, 2
  bottom line, 5
  common objectives, 3
  contemporary challenges, 15-19
  and democracy, 180
  joining, 32-33
  people working together, 4
  personality in organizations, 33-38
  size of, 341
  staying with the organization, 32-33
outcome/input ratio, 129
outcome valences, 119-121
overconfidence, 59, 211

P

P-to-O expectancy, 119, 120
parallel learning structures, 391
participative leadership, 307
participative management, 179
  see also employee involvement
past experience, 112
path-goal leadership theory, 306-309, 319-320
pauses, 232
pay differential, 129
pay for pulse, 140
people-oriented leadership, 305, 306
perceived self, 57
perceiving orientation, 37
perception, 62
  attribution theory, 68-69
  awareness of perceptual biases, 72
  false-consensus effect, 71

global perceptions, 75-77
halo effect, 71
improving perceptions, 72-75
meaningful interaction, 74-75
model of perceptual process, 63
perceptual organization and interpretation, 64-65
primacy effect, 71
recency effect, 71
role perceptions, 30, 385
selective attention, 63
self-awareness, improvement of, 72-74
self-fulfilling prophecy, 69-71
similar-to-me effect, 71
specific perceptual processes and problems, 65-71
stereotyping, 65-68
stress perceptions, change of, 102-103
perceptual defence, 166
perfectly rational, 165
performance, 27
see also applied performance practices
cohesion-performance relationship, 201-202
and job satisfaction, 93-94
performance-based rewards, 141, 142-146
performance review, 145
performing stage, 205
persistence, 28, 177
person, 27
person-job matching strategy, 29
person-organization values congruence, 41-42
personal attributes perspective of leadership, 312-316
personal goal setting, 154-155
personal identity, 61
personal leave, 102
personality, 34, 53-54
determinants of, 34
and emotions, 87
five-factor model (FFM), 34-36, 38
Jungian personality theory, 36-38
and leadership, 312, 313
Myers-Briggs Type Indicator (MBTI), 36-38
nature *vs.* nurture, 34
in organizations, 33-38
personality testing, 38, 39
personality traits, 34, 40
and stress, 101
personality clashes, 272
personality testing, 38, 39
personality traits, 34, 40
personalized power, 116
persuasion, 230, 257, 259-260
physical structures and symbols, 353
physiological needs, 113
pilot projects, 384-385
poetic principle, 388, 389
politeness, 224
political tactics, 263
pooled interdependence, 196, 276
position power, 310
positive (can-do) belief system, 36
positive emotions at work, 85-86
positive expectations, 203
positive organizational behaviour, 71, 114, 388
positive perspective of motivation, 114
positive principle, 388, 389
positive reinforcement, 122
positive self-talk, 155
post-decisional justification, 173
power, 245
centrality, 251
and CEOs, 252
coercive power, 249
consequences of power, 256-257
contingencies of power, 247, 251-253
countervailing power, 246
discretion, 252
expert power, 249-250
legitimate power, 247-249
meaning of power, 245-247
need for power (nPow), 115-116
personalized power, 116
power dependence model, 245-246
referent power, 250, 254
reward power, 249
of social networks, 253-256
source of power, 247-250
substitutability, 251
visibility, 251-253, 254
power distance, 47-48, 140, 284
practical intelligence, 177, 313, 314
pre-employment socialization, 364-365
prejudice, 67
preparation stage, 176
presenteeism, 33
prevention, 249
primacy effect, 71
primary needs, 111
see also drives
priorities, 288
privacy rights, 392
proactivity, 31
probability of effect, 44
problem, 164
problem identification, 165-168
problem redefinition, 179
problem solving, 278, 279, 280
procedural justice, 128, 132
process losses, 193-194
product/service divisional structure, 333
production blocking, 211
production teams, 191
productivity, 8, 275
proficiency, 31
profit-sharing plan, 143
programmed decisions, 164
project teams, 191, 337
prospect theory effect, 174
proximity, 44
psychological contract, 363-364
psychological harassment, 99
punctuated-equilibrium model, 205
punishment, 122

Q

quid pro quo harassment, 100

R

rapid change, 387
rapport talk, 233
rational choice paradigm, 163-165, 168-170, 174
realistic job preview (RJP), 365
reality shock, 365
recency effect, 71
reciprocal interdependence, 196, 276
reduced personal accomplishment, 99
referent power, 250, 254
refreezing, 374, 382-383
Regus work-life balance index, 17
reinforcement, 122-123
relational contracts, 364
relational self, 57
relationship building, 288-289
relationship capital, 8
relationship conflict, 272-274
relevant feedback, 126
relevant goals, 125
report talk, 233
representativeness heuristic, 169
resistance point, 286
resistance stage, 98, 261
resistance to change, 374-377, 379-382
resource scarcity, 276, 282
respect, 224
responding, 235
restraining forces, 374, 379-382
reverse engineering, 8
reward power, 249
rewards, 10-11
see also financial reward practices
risk, 97
rituals, 353
Rokeach's lists of values, 40
role, 199, 216, 324
role ambiguity, 30
role clarity, 30
role management, 365
role perceptions, 30, 385
role-specific self-esteem, 61
routine tasks, 327
Russian culture, 88

S

safety, 41
safety needs, 113
satisficing, 170
scarce resources, 276, 282
scenario planning, 172, 173
schedules of reinforcement, 122
Schwartz's values circumplex, 40-41
scientific management, 148-149
scouting activity, 205
security, 41
selection, 361-362
selective attention, 63
self-actualization, 114
self-actualization needs, 113
self-assessment
active listening, 242-243
change, tolerance for, 396
conflict handling style, 295-296
creative personality, 188
emotional intelligence, 107
extraversion *vs.* introversion, 54
influence, 267-268
influence of leaders, 320
money, 160
needs-strength questionnaire, 136
organizational culture, 370
personal theories, 24
self-concept, 80
team roles, 216
self-awareness, 72-74
self-beliefs, 57
self-concept, 57, 80
behaviour, effect on, 58-59
characteristics and processes, 58
clarity, 58, 59
complexity, 57
consistency, 58
drives, needs and behaviour, 112

external self-concept, 61-62
internal self-concept, 61
and leadership, 313
and organizational behaviour, 62
self-assessment, 80
self-enhancement, 59, 60
self-evaluation, 60-61
self-verification, 59-60
social self, 61-62
and stress, 101
well-being, effects on, 58-59
self-determination, 153
self-directed teams (SDTs), 191, 207-208
self-direction, 41, 177
self-efficacy, 61, 101, 126, 156
self-enhancement, 59, 60, 66
self-enhancement effect, 174
self-esteem, 60-61, 101, 156
self-evaluation, 57, 60-61
self-fulfilling prophecy, 69-71
self-justification effect, 174
self-leadership, 154
effectiveness of, 156
personal predictors, 156
self-leadership strategies, 154-156
situational predictors, 156
self-monitoring, 155
self-presentation, 260
self-regulation, 124
self-reinforcement, 124, 156
self-serving bias, 69
self-talk, 155
self-verification, 59-60
seniority-based rewards, 140, 141
sense making, 354
sensing, 235
separation, 358, 359
sequential interdependence, 196, 276
servant leadership, 306
service profit chain model, 94-95
service teams, 191
share options, 143
shared assumptions, 348
shared leadership, 298-299
shared values, 39, 97, 348
shock events, 93
silence, 232, 233
silent authority, 257, 258
similar-to-me effect, 71
similarity-attraction effect, 200-201
simple environments, 340
simple structure, 331
simultaneity principle, 388, 389
situation, 27
situation favourableness, 310
situational control, 310
situational factors, 30, 385
situational leadership theory (SLT), 309
skill, 308, 325
skill-and-will model, 27
skill variety, 150
skills gap, 30
skunkworks, 191
SMARTER, 125
smileys, 223
social acceptance, 228
social capital, 253-254
social cognitive theory, 124
social consensus, 44
social glue, 354
social harassment, 100
social identity, 61-62, 66
social identity theory, 61-62
social inclusion, 60
social interaction, 91
social job characteristics, 151
social loafing, 194
social media, 224-225, 233-234
social networks, 253-256, 266-267, 383-384
social norms, 41, 112
social responsibility missions, 77
social self, 61-62
social sphere of sustainability, 13
social support, 103
socialization, 34, 60, 361-362
see also organizational socialization
socialization agents, 365-366
soft influence tactics, 261, 262
solution-focused problems, 166
span of control, 325-328
span of management, 326
specific feedback, 126
specific goals, 125
stability, 41
see also emotional stability
stable environments, 340
stakeholder framing, 166
stakeholders, 11-13, 24
standardization, 323, 325
standardized outputs, 325
standardized processes, 325
standardized skills, 325
status quo, 41
staying with the organization, 32-33
stereotyping, 65-68, 79, 276
stimulation, 41
stories, 20, 352
storming stage, 205
strategic vision, 300-302, 383
strengths-based coaching, 127
stress, 98
causes of stress, 99
change of stress perceptions, 102-103
cognitive appraisal perspective, 98
and conflict, 270
control of stress consequences, 103
distress, 98, 99
eustress, 98
and formalization, 329
general adaptation syndrome, 98, 99
harassment, 99-100
incivility, 99-100
individual differences, 101
low task control, 101
management of work-related stress, 101-103
removal of stressor, 102
social support, 103
stress management, 101-103, 380, 381
stressors, 99, 102
surface acting, 89
withdrawal from stressor, 102
work overload, 100-101
stress management, 101-103, 380, 381
stressors, 99
strong ties, 255
structural capital, 8
structural hole, 256
study of organizational behaviour, 3-5
subcultures, 351
subjective expected utility (SEU), 163-164
substitutability, 251
subsystems, 6, 7-8
sunk costs effect, 174
superordinate goals, 280
support, 97
supportive leadership, 307, 310
surface acting, 89
surface-level diversity, 15-16
swift trust, 203-204
systemic discrimination, 67
systemic research anchor, 19-20

T

tall structures, 327-328
target point, 286
task analyzability, 151
task characteristics, 195-196
task conflict, 272-274
task coordination, 205
task force teams, 191
task identity, 150
task interdependence, 196, 197, 276
task-oriented leadership, 305, 306
task performance, 31
task significance, 150
task structure, 308-309, 310
task variability, 151
taskwork behaviour, 204
team-based structure, 335-336
team boundary spanning, 204
team building, 206-207
team cohesion, 200-202, 273
team decision making, 210-213
team development, 205-207
team dynamics, 309
team effectiveness model, 194-195
team efficacy, 202-203
team norms, 199-200, 273-274
team states, 199-204
team trust, 203-204
teams, 190
advantages of, 193
authority differentiation, 190-192
composition of team, 197-199
creative decision making, 211-213
decision making, 210-213
disadvantages of, 193-194
distinguishing characteristics, 190-192
diversity, 198-199
exercises, 215-216
external team processes, 204-205
Five C's model, 197-198
incongruent team dynamics, 377
internal team processes, 204
mental models, 206
model of team effectiveness, 194-195
motivation, 192
norms, 199-200, 273-274
organizational environment, 194-195
permanence, 190
process losses, 193-194
roles, 199, 216
self-directed teams, 191, 207-208
size of team, 197, 201
skill differentiation, 190
social loafing, 194
task characteristics, 195-196
team building, 206-207
team cohesion, 200-202, 273
team design elements, 195-199
team development, 205-207
team efficacy, 202-203
team environment, 194-195

team identities, 206
team processes, 204-207
team rewards, 143, 146
team states, 199-204
team trust, 203-204
transactive memory, 199
types of teams, 191
virtual teams, 191, 208-210
teamwork behaviour, 204
technology, 341-342
telecommuting, 18-19, 102
telework, 18-19, 102
temporal immediacy, 44
tend and befriend response, 103
thinking (T) orientation, 37
third-party conflict resolution, 282-284
thought patterns, 155
360-degree feedback, 127-128, 211
time constraints, 211
time-framed goals, 125
time-limited offers, 287
timely feedback, 126
tradition, 41
training, 29, 30
diversity training programs, 73
emotional intelligence outcomes, 91
in ethics, 46
self-fulfilling-prophecy awareness training, 72
and stereotyping, 68
traits, 34
transactional contracts, 364
transactive memory, 199
transformational leadership, 299-304
and change, 383
charisma, 303
commitment toward vision, 302
elements of, 300
evaluation, 303-304
experimentation, 302
strategic vision, 300-302, 383
trust, 97, 203-204, 246, 262, 288
tunnel vision, 64
turnover, 58, 152

U

uncertainty avoidance, 47, 48
unfreezing, 374, 378-383
unintentional (systemic) discrimination, 67
United Kingdom, 382
United States, 49-50
upward appeal, 257, 259
urgency for change, 378-379
utilitarianism, 43
utility, 163-164, 170

V

vacations, 102, 263
value creation, 286, 287-288
value-expressive function, 132
value system, 39
values, 11-12, 39, 348
across cultures, 46-50
cultural values, 39, 46-50, 92, 280, 316
enacted values, 349
espoused values, 348-349
hierarchy of values, 41
and individual behaviour, 41
instrumental-terminal values distinction, 40
Machiavellian values, 264
organizational values, 39
and personality traits, 40
Rokeach's lists of values, 40
Schwartz's values circumplex, 40-41
shared values, 39, 97, 348
types of values, 40-41
value system, 39
values congruence, 41-42
in the workplace, 38-42
values-based vision, 300
values congruence, 41-42
values-driven organization model, 12
Vancouver, 301
variability, 342
variable ratio schedule, 122
verification stage, 176
vertical boundary spanning, 205
viral change, 383-384
virtual teams, 191, 208-210
virtual work, 17-18
visibility, 251-253, 254
vision, 300-302
vocal authority, 258-259
voice, 93, 132

W

wage dispersion, 129
weak ties, 255
well-being
employee well-being, 11
self-concept, effect of, 58-59
wellness programs, 103
whole systems, 390
wikis, 236
win-lose orientation, 278
win-win orientation, 278
women
see also gender differences
communication, 233-234
as corporate board members, 67
and empathy, 44
money, meaning of, 140
and moral sensitivity, 44
tend and befriend response, 103
work addict, 101
work attendance, 33
work efficiency, 147-149
work-life balance, 17
work-life balance index, 17
work overload, 100-101
workaholic, 101
workforce diversity, 19, 79
consequences of diversity, 16-17
deep-level diversity, 16
globally, 49
increasing workforce diversity, 15-17
as sound business proposition, 16-17
surface-level diversity, 15-16
workplace anti-harassment legislation, 99
workspace design, 236

Y

yielding, 278, 279

Z

zone of indifference, 247-248